Travellers
Survival
Kit

South America

EMILY HATCHWELL &
SIMON CALDER

with additional research by Oliver Tickell,
John Forrest and Charles Seville

Published by
VACATION WORK, 9 PARK END STREET, OXFORD

TRAVELLERS SURVIVAL KIT: SOUTH AMERICA
by Emily Hatchwell and Simon Calder

Copyright © Vacation Work 1992

ISBN 1 85458 069 8 (softback)
ISBN 1 85458 070 1 (hardback)

Cover Design:
Mel Calman
Miller Craig and Cocking Design Partnership

Illustrations by William Swan

Maps by Lovell Johns Ltd

Town plans by Marcia Cea and Emily Hatchwell

Printed by William Gibbons & Sons, Wolverhampton, England

Contents

SOUTH AMERICA AND ITS PEOPLE   **11**
Geography.. 11
Climate.. 12
History.. 12
The People — Religion.. 17
Language.. 19
Further Reading... 22

SOUTH AMERICA — PRACTICAL INFORMATION

GETTING THERE   **24**
Air — Air Passes — Courier Flights...................................... 24
By Sea.. 29

RED TAPE   **29**
Passports — Visas — Crossing Borders — Customs — Health
Requirements.. 29

MONEY   **32**
Living Costs — Changing Money — The Black Market — Emergency
Cash — Work... 32

COMMUNICATIONS   **36**
Mail.. 36
Telephone... 37
Fax, Telegrams and Telex.. 39
Newspapers — Radio — Television... 39

GETTING AROUND   **40**
Maps.. 41
Air — Train — Bus — Collective Taxis — Hitching — Boat.................. 41
Cycling... 45
City Transport — Finding Your Way....................................... 46
Driving... 47

ACCOMMODATION   **49**
Youth Hostels — Camping... 50

EATING AND DRINKING   **51**

EXPLORING   **55**
Museums and Churches — Archaeological Sites — The Great
Outdoors — Beaches.. 55

ENTERTAINMENT   **58**
Cinema and Theatre — Music and Dance — Festivals........................ 58

SPORT 60
Soccer — Baseball — Cricket... 60

SHOPPING 61

CRIME AND SAFETY 62
How to Avoid Robbery — Drugs — Photography — Dealing with the
Military... 62

HEALTH AND HYGIENE 66
Sources of Information... 66
Natural Hazards — Altitude — Frostbite — Heat — Sun — Water........ 67
Creatures to Avoid — Leeches — Mosquitoes — Sharks — Snakes and
Scorpions — Ticks.. 69
Diseases and How to Avoid Them — Chagas' Disease — Dengue Fever
— Gastric Problems — Cholera — Hepatitis — Malaria — Rabies —
Yellow Fever.. 70
Aids — Travellers with HIV and Aids... 74
Medical Treatment... 75
Insurance... 76

WOMEN TRAVELLERS 77
Women's Health... 77
Travelling with Babies... 77

HELP AND INFORMATION 78
Gay Travellers... 78
Travellers with Disabilities... 78
Business Travellers... 78
Electrical Equipment... 78
Sources of Information... 79
Time... 81
Public Holidays... 81

THE COUNTRIES OF SOUTH AMERICA

*The first part of each country chapter follows the same order as the introduction
to the book, i.e.* Geography — Climate — History — The People — Language —
Getting There — Red Tape — Money — Communications — Getting Around —
Accommodation — Eating and Drinking — Exploring — Entertainment — Sport
— Shopping — Crime and Safety — Health and Hygiene — Help and Information.
    Sections dealing with large cities are dealt with as follows: City Layout — Arrival
and Departure — City Transport — Accommodation — Eating and Drinking —
Exploring — Entertainment — Shopping — Crime and Safety — Help and
Information.

VENEZUELA 82
Caracas...91
The Coast near Caracas — Catia La Mar — La Guaira — Macuto...........100
Northeast Venezuela — Barcelona — Puerto La Cruz — Cumaná.............100
Margarita Island 103
Ciudad Bolívar — Ciudad Guayana/Puerto Ordaz.............................104
Angel Falls and Canaima..105

Western Venezuela — Valencia — Maracaibo — Coro............ 106
Mérida............ 108
Los Llanos............ 110

COLOMBIA 111

Bogotá............ 130
North of Bogotá — Zipaquirá — El Dorado lake and Guatavita — Tunja — Villa de Leyva — Bucaramanga — Valledupar — La Guajira............ 138
Caribbean Colombia — Santa Marta — Tayrona National Park — La Ciudad Perdida (The Lost City) — Barranquilla — Cartagena — Mompós — Montería — Turbo............ 143
San Andrés — Providencia............ 156
Chocó and the Darién Gap — Quibdó............ 160
Medellín and the Northwest — Marinilla — El Peñol............ 164
Southwest Colombia — Cali — Popayán — Tierradentro — San Agustín — Pasto — Ipiales — Las Lajas............ 168
Eastern Colombia — Leticia — Los Llanos............ 173

ECUADOR 175

Quito............ 191
Around Quito — Guapulo — San Antonio — Volcán Pichincha............ 198
Northern Ecuador — Otavalo — Ibarra — Tulcán............ 198
The Northwest — Santo Domingo de Los Colorados — Esmeraldas — Atacames — San Lorenzo............ 203
The West Coast — Manta and Tarqui — Montecristi............ 206
The South Coast — Guayaquil — Puerto López — Machala............ 207
The Sierra — Cotopaxi National Park — Latacunga — Ambato — Baños — Riobamba — Alausí — Achupallas to Ingapirca............ 212
The Southern Sierra — Cañar — Ingapirca — Cuenca — Loja............ 218
The Oriente — Puyo — Tena — Misahuallí — Coca — Lago Agrio — Baeza............ 224
The Galapagos Islands............ 228

PERU 234

Lima............ 256
Around Lima — Pachacámac — Marcahuasi............ 268
North of Lima — Huaráz — Chavín de Huantar — Yungay — Caráz............ 268
Northern Peru — Trujillo — Chan-Chan — Cajamarca — Chiclayo — Sipán — Piura — Tumbes —............ 273
The Central Andes — Huancayo............ 280
The Coast South of Lima — Pisco — Ica — Nazca — Arequipa — Tacna............ 281
The Southern Andes — Puno — Lake Titicaca — Juliaca............ 291
Qosqo (Cusco)............ 297
The Sacred Valley — Pisac — Ollantaytambo — Machu Picchu — The Inca Trail............ 305
La Selva (Amazonia) — Iquitos — Manú — Puerto Maldonado............ 311

BOLIVIA 318

La Paz............ 337
Around La Paz — La Muela del Diablo — Valle de la Luna — Chacaltaya — Zongo Valley — Tiahuanaco — Sorata............ 346
Lake Titicaca — Copacabana — Isla del Sol — Suriqui............ 349
Los Yungas — Coroico — Choro Trail............ 351
Amazonia............ 353
Río Beni Route — Guanay — Rurrenbaque — Riberalta............ 354
Río Mamoré Route — Puerto Villarroel — Trinidad — Guayaramerín............ 355

Santa Cruz — Samaipata......... 356
Cochabamba — Pairumani — Inka-Rakay — The Tarata, Cliza and
Punata Circuit — Inkallajta — Totora......... 361
Sucre — Tarabuco......... 367
Potosí — Cerro Rico — Laguna de Tarapaya......... 372
Oruro — Lago Uru Uru — Cala Cala — Siglo Veinte — Chipaya......... 377
The Southwest — Uyuni — Salar de Uyuni — Laguna Colorada —
Tupiza — Tarija — Crossing into Argentina......... 380

CHILE **384**
Santiago......... 400
Around Santiago — Pomaire — Callejón del Maipo — Farellones —
Valparaíso — Viña del Mar......... 409
The Atacama Desert — Arica — Iquique — Calama — San Pedro de
Atacama — Antofagasta — Copiapó......... 413
South to the Heartland — La Serena — Valle de Elquí......... 422
Santiago to Temuco — Rancagua — Curicó — Talca — Concepción —
Los Angeles — Curacautín......... 424
The Lake District — Temuco — Valdivia — Osorno — Puerto Montt —
Chiloé Island......... 427
The Camino Austral — Chaitén — Coihaique — Puerto Aisén/Puerto
Chacabuco — Laguna San Rafael — Lago General Carrera —
Cochrane......... 443
Magallanes — Puerto Natales — Torres del Paine National Park —
Punta Arenas......... 449
Chilean Antarctica......... 455
Tierra del Fuego (Chile and Argentina) — Porvenir — Río Grande —
Ushuaia — Puerto Williams......... 455

ARGENTINA **461**
Buenos Aires......... 481
Buenos Aires Province — La Plata — Mar del Plata — Bahía Blanca.. 492
Santa Fé Province — Santa Fé — Rosario......... 496
Northeast Argentina......... 497
Entre Ríos Province — Paraná — North along the Río Uruguay —
Concordia......... 498
Corrientes Province — Corrientes — Along the Río Uruguay......... 500
Misiones Province — Posadas — San Ignacio Miní — Iguazú Falls..... 502
The Chaco — Santiago del Estero — Resistencia — Formosa —
Clorinda......... 505
Northwest Argentina — Salta — Jujuy — Tilcara — Humahuaca —
Cafayate......... 506
Tucumán Province — San Miguel de Tucumán — Tafí del Valle —
Quilmes......... 513
Catamarca Province — San Fernando del Valle de Catamarca —
Andalgalá — Belén — Antofagasta de la Sierra — Tinogasta —
Santa María......... 516
La Rioja Province — La Rioja — Chilecito......... 519
The Cuyo — San Juan — Mendoza — San Luís — Merlo......... 521
Central Argentina — Córdoba — Santa Rosa......... 527
The South: Patagonia......... 531
Neuquén Province — Neuquén — Zapala — Aluminé — Junín de los
Andes — San Martín de los Andes......... 531
Río Negro Province — Bariloche — El Bolsón — Viedma......... 534
Chubut Province — Esquel — Puerto Madryn — Peninsula Valdés —
Trelew — Comodoro Rivadavia......... 537

Santa Cruz Province — Perito Moreno — Río Gallegos — El Calafate — Parque Nacional Los Glaciares — Río Turbio.............................. 543

URUGUAY 547
Montevideo 554
East of Montevideo — Maldonado — Punta del Este.................... 559
The Interior — Minas — Treinta y Tres — Florida — Rivera.................. 560
Ríos Plata and Uruguay — Colonia del Sacramento — Carmelo — Mercedes — Fray Bentos — Salto........................ 562

PARAGUAY 564
Asunción........................ 578
Around Asunción — Yaguarón — Ybicuy National Park....................... 585
Ciudad del Este........................ 587
Los Misiones — San Ignacio — Santa María de Fé.......................... 587
Encarnación — Trinidad — Jesús.................... 589
Northern Paraguay — Concepción — Pedro Juan Cabellero................. 592
The Chaco — Filadelfia.................... 593

BRAZIL 595
Rio de Janeiro.................... 619
Rio de Janeiro State — Ilha Grande — Parati — Búzios — Petrópolis — Teresopolis — Itatiaia National Park.................... 632
Espírito Santo — Vitória — Caparão National Park.......................... 636
Minas Gerais — Belo Horizonte — Ouro Prêto — Congonhas — São João del Rei — Tiradentes — Diamantina — The Spa Towns........... 637

The Northeast........................ 649
Bahia — Salvador — Cachoeira — Valença — Ilheus — Porto Seguro — The Sertão.................... 650
Sergipe and Alagoas — Aracajú — Maceió.................... 664
Pernambuco — Recife — Olinda — Fernando de Noronha Islands — Caruarú — Nova Jerusalem — The Sertão.................... 665
Paraíba and Rio Grande do Norte — João Pessoa — Campina Grande — Natal.................... 675
Ceará — Fortaleza — Canoa Quebrada — Jericoacoara — Ubajara....... 679
Piauí and Maranhão — Teresina — São Luís — Alcântara.................... 685

The Amazon.................... 688
Pará — Belém — Ilha do Marajó — Santarém.................... 691
Amapá.................... 698
Amazonas — Manaus.................... 698
Roraima — Boa Vista.................... 705
Rondônia — Porto Velho — Guajara-Mirim.................... 707
Acre.................... 708

The Centre West.................... 709
The Mato Grosso States — Cuiabá — Campo Grande — Corumbá — The Pantanal.................... 709
Goiás — Goiânia — Goiás Velho.................... 714
Brasília 714
Tocantins — Ilha do Bananal.................... 717

São Paulo.................... 717
São Paulo State — Paranapiacaba — Ilha de São Sebastiao — Ubatuba — Iguape.................... 722

Southern Brazil.. 724
Paraná — Curitiba — Paranaguá — Ilha do Mel — Foz do
   Iguaçu — The Iguaçu Falls.. 725
Santa Catarina — Florianópolis — Ilha de Santa Catarina —
   Joinville — Blumenau and Pomerode — Porto Belo................... 735
Rio Grande do Sul — Porto Alegre — Litoral Gaúcho — Serra
   Gaúcha — São Miguel.. 738

THE GUIANAS   742
Guyana.. 746
Surinam... 758
Guyane (French Guiana).. 764

MAPS

South America.....inside front cover
Malaria and Yellow Fever Zones..72

Venezuela..............................85
Caracas................................93
Caracas — centre.......................96

Colombia..............................117
Bogotá................................133
Bogotá — area.........................138
Santa Marta...........................144
Cartagena.............................151
San Andrés............................160
Medellín..............................165

Ecuador...............................177
Quito.................................193
Guayaquil.............................208
Cuenca................................219

Peru..................................237
Lima — area...........................257
Lima..................................259
Arequipa..............................287
Puno..................................292
Lake Titicaca.........................295
Qosqo (Cusco).........................299

Bolivia (and northern Chile)......320
La Paz................................339
La Paz — centre.......................340
Santa Cruz............................357
Cochabamba............................363
Sucre.................................369
Potosí................................374

Chile.................................460
Santiago..............................401

Santiago — metro......................403
Valparaíso............................410
Arica.................................414
Antofagasta...........................421
Puerto Montt..........................438

Argentina.............................460
Buenos Aires..........................483
Buenos Aires — metro..................485
Salta.................................508
Tucumán...............................513
Mendoza...............................524
Córdoba...............................528

Uruguay...............................548
Montevideo............................555

Paraguay..............................566
Asunción..............................580
Encarnación...........................588

Brazil................................597
Rio de Janeiro — area.................620
Rio de Janeiro........................623
Rio de Janeiro — metro................624
Belo Horizonte........................638
São João del Rei......................646
Salvador..............................651
Recife................................667
Fortaleza.............................680
Belém.................................691
Manaus................................701
Curitiba..............................726
Foz do Iguaçu.........................732

The Guianas...........................743
Georgetown............................755

Acknowledgements

A book of this scale could be realised only with a committed team of researchers. The following people have travelled widely in South America, providing information on a number of countries (none of them are related): Barbara Evans, Matthew Evans, Orwyn Evans, Tony Grant, Steve Lodge, Katie Reeves and Pat Yale.

Substantial contributions on individual countries have been made by Oliver Tickell and Neil Bamford (Chile), John Forrest (Ecuador and Peru) and Charles Seville (Argentina).

Other people who have helped in the production of this book include: Hernán Arriaga, Tim Ashburner, Eustace Barnes, Leanne Beard, Andrea and Ralph Bullivant, Caroline Caulfield, Marcia Cea, Leon Ford, Amy Goldfarb, Sarah Goodwin, Susan Griffith, Belinda Hacking, Simon Hall, Jane Hatfield, David Horwell, Elizabeth Huangal, Paul Huertas, Edward James, Debbie Kelly, Sid Lothian, Matt MacDougall, Val McEwan, John McGee, André Mendonça, George Monbiot, Hugh O'Donnell, Simon Opit, Frank Partridge, the late Alex Robertson, Jackie Skeer, Barry Walker, Carole Walker and Catherine Watt. Special thanks to all the Hatchwells and, most valuable of all, Lesley Totten.

Every effort has been made to ensure that the information in this book was accurate at the time of going to press in February 1992. Nevertheless some information is bound to change during the lifetime of this book. If you encounter errors or omissions, please write to Emily Hatchwell and Simon Calder at Vacation Work Publications, 9 Park End Street, Oxford OX1 1HJ. Those whose contributions are used will receive a complimentary copy of the next edition.

SOUTH AMERICA AND ITS PEOPLE

In no other continent is reality so different from image. South America is not run by gun-toting military dictatorships — in the Spring of 1992 all but the smallest countries were governed by democracies. And despite the alarming number of beggars on city streets, reflecting deep inequalities of wealth, the continent is struggling more than ever before against its crippling poverty.

Graham Greene called South America 'a continent of exiles', a reference to the disparate roots and cultures which populate the region. Direct descendants of the Inca people share the region with pure-blooded Iberians, and Mennonites from Germany mend tractors for the grandchildren of Japanese immigrants. The pervading air of perseverance is gradually giving way to one of optimism, tempered with memories of all-too-recent atrocities and the continuing despair in the shanty towns, where the spread of cholera has compounded the misery of the continent's poor.

As the Old World and the New reassess their relationship, South America is in social, political and economic flux. Its physical characteristics are more tangible, and thoroughly superlative. Starting with a brief resumé of the geographical characteristics of South America, this section comprises a wide-ranging briefing on this extraordinarily diverse region and its people.

GEOGRAPHY

The distance from the driest desert of northern Chile to the wettest place in the world, Chocó in Colombia, is 2,500 miles/4,000km. This is less than the distance from London to Istanbul or New York to San Francisco. Yet the journey takes you along the world's longest mountain range, supporting the world's highest cities, passing the point furthest from the centre of the earth; continue a little further and you reach the impenetrable rainforest of the Darién Gap, the only interruption along the course of the world's longest road, the Pan-American Highway. Go east to find the world's biggest jungle, and continue further to South America's smallest country, Guyane — though even this is the size of Portugal. The continent is huge in all dimensions.

The great mountain range of the Andes dominates the west side of South America, stretching from southern Patagonia through to Colombia and Venezuela in the north. North of Chile, it splits into several *cordilleras* (spines), which run in parallel, creating high valleys and plateaux. The tablelands (*altiplano*) of southern Peru and Bolivia are bounded east and west by branches of the Andes, and are two miles/3.3km above sea level.

East of the northern Andean ranges is Amazonia, a huge lowland area watered by the river Amazon and its many tributaries: the basin is mainly in Brazil, but extends also into Venezuela, Colombia, Ecuador, Peru and Bolivia. These lowlands are still covered in jungle, though large tracts have been destroyed by logging and colonization. North of Amazonia and the Guiana Highlands is the much smaller Orinoco Basin.

The River Plate basin dominates the southern part of the continent. It is washed by the Uruguay, Paraguay and Paraná rivers and tributaries, which flow eventually into the Río Plata and thence into the Atlantic. Beyond the fertile plains of the Argentinian pampas lies Patagonia, spanning both Argentina and Chile. It is a region of arid and featureless plain extending southwards to wild areas of lakes, glaciers and mountains and, ultimately, to Tierra del Fuego.

CLIMATE

The bulk of South America is in the tropics. Lowland areas — Amazonia, parts of the northeast coast of Brazil and the west coast of Colombia — are hot and humid throughout the year. Torrential rain falls during the summer wet season, but it can rain at any time. Further south, seasons are more clearly identifiable, though they are the reverse of those in the northern hemisphere. Thus winter falls in June, July and August. Temperatures can reach greater heights than further north: this zone includes the Atacama desert of northern Chile, where some areas have had no rain since records began; the coastal region of Peru also consists largely of desert.

The areas south of the Tropic of Capricorn, i.e. a small chunk of Brazil, southern Paraguay, Argentina and central Chile, fall into a temperate zone. In this region, seasons are well defined. Summers are warm and winters generally mild. Rain falls mostly in winter. In southern Patagonia, temperatures are low for most of the year, and the climate is characterized by rain and fierce winds.

South America boasts more than its fair share of high-altitude capitals: Bogotá, Quito and La Paz are all above 8,500ft/2,590m. Throughout the Andes it can be bitterly cold at night. During the day the sun can warm you thoroughly, though temperatures drop dramatically when the skies are cloudy. Most rain in the Andes falls between December and April.

More specific details of climate are given in the country chapters.

When to go. Most people like to avoid rain as much as possible. The odd tropical downpour does no harm, but since rain can affect transport by road, rail or air, steering clear of the peak wet season is generally a good idea. So to avoid the summer rains of Amazonia, for example, you can head down to Patagonia, where conditions are best from December to March. The extremes of disruption are less in other regions, though March to May and September to November are generally the best months to travel in most Andean countries. Also bear in mind that the main domestic holiday period is December to March, the peak being in January and February.

Clothing. Anyone not planning to travel in the Andes or into the most southerly regions of Patagonia, can take fairly normal clothes — plenty of t-shirts, lightweight trousers or skirts, a sweatshirt, etc. In the mountains and in the extreme south, however, a warm jacket or a couple of jumpers are essential. Don't bother bringing the latter from home: alpaca and sheep's wool jumpers can be bought for a song in the Andes, particularly in Peru and Bolivia. Lightweight thermals are a great investment, however, since they give excellent insulation but take up next to no room.

HISTORY

South America was one of the last places on earth to be settled. The first humans reached the American continent from northeast Asia, across the Bering Strait. They gradually penetrated southwards, and Stone Age groups are estimated to have reached South America 20,000 years ago. These people were nomadic hunter-gatherers. The earliest evidence of agriculture is in the Andes, and dates from around 3000BC.

The Incas created the most celebrated civilization, but did so relatively late. Organized village communities appear to have evolved first in Peru. A sophisticated people known as the Tiahuanaco built a city on the altiplano of Bolivia, near Lake Titicaca, but they had mysteriously disappeared by the 11th century — about the time the Incas were emerging.

Little is known about other indigenous groups in South America, though the most developed cultures were in northern Colombia. One legendary figure was El Dorado, the ruler of a Colombian tribe who ritually bathed in gold. Only recently did fortune-hunters cease the search for his riches.

The Incas. Like the Aztecs, the Incas were at the height of their power during the 15th century. At its peak, their empire stretched from Ecuador, through Peru and Bolivia, and south into central Chile and northern Argentina. Its heart was Qosqo (Cusco), in Peru, and its population has been estimated to have reached somewhere between eight and twelve million.

The Incas were imperialists. They took advantage of what they found, often seeking to preserve any features of conquered territories they considered useful — even allowing their new subjects to retain their own religion. But by uprooting entire tribes or villages in order to colonize new areas (and to reduce the chance of rebellion), the Incas managed to organize a ready-made and highly efficient labour force.

The Incas built many roads, including one that stretched 3,000 miles/5,000km from Quito to Santiago; parts of it survive. They also erected great cities and defensive fortresses (*pucara*). These structures are solid rather than elegant, but remarkable for the fact that the builders had no wheels or beasts of burden to aid them. The Incas also created sophisticated agricultural techniques that were more productive than the methods used today.

The Conquest. Nobody was looking for the Americas; European sea-farers were searching for sea routes to the spice-rich Orient. The Portuguese explored eastwards while the Spanish sailed west. A Genoese mariner, Christopher Columbus, persuaded the court of Spain to invest heavily in a mission across the uncharted Atlantic. In 1492 Columbus landed in Hispaniola in the Caribbean, thinking that he had discovered India. Due to this misapprehension, the indigenous people of the island — and later of the entire continent — were called Indians. This error has been handed down through the centuries.

Initially Spain concentrated on pillaging Central America and the Caribbean. The real conquest of South America didn't start until the 1530s, when Francisco Pizarro explored the west coast south from Panama. He landed in Peru in 1531 with the aim of finding the kingdom of gold, which was said to rival that already discovered in Mexico. Fortunately for Pizarro, the Inca empire was in the throes of civil war, with a prince named Atahualpa gaining the upper hand. The conquistador was able to exploit this conflict. The Spanish won a fierce battle at Cajamarca in 1532, during which Atahualpa was taken prisoner. Pizarro held the Inca to ransom for a legendary room of gold, but then had him strangled anyway.

This ruthless act brought Inca rule to an end, and the empire rapidly fell apart. The Spanish set about looting the territory, while destroying anything associated with the Incas.

Lima, founded in 1535, became the capital of the Viceroyalty of Peru, and the base for some of the subsequent exploration and exploitation of the continent. To say that South America was colonized, is an understatement. The Spanish conquistadores did not make the long and arduous voyage across the Atlantic with noble intentions. The thirst for gold and silver meant that Spain wished to establish control as quickly as possible, killing any indigenous people that stood in the way. Although there were Indian communities all over the continent, they were so scattered that there was little scope for anything more than token opposition. One of the few pockets of resistance was in southern Chile, where the Araucanian Indians were never subjugated by the Spanish.

The Portuguese had already become a thorn in the Spanish side. In response to claims by Portugal that Spain had infringed its rights in the Atlantic, the extraordinary Treaty of Tordesillas was signed in 1494. This drew an imaginary north-south line through the Atlantic: all that lay east of that line belonged to Portugal, and everything to the west was Spanish. At the time it was thought that this gave Portugal Africa and Asia, and the Spanish the New World. But when Brazil was first encountered in 1500, it was discovered that the line actually cut through the eastern portion of South America. The treaty thereby provided the basis for Portugal to claim sovereignty over the new territory.

By the mid-16th century, Spain had established virtually full control over the rest of South America. Benalcázar had pushed into the highlands of Colombia via Quito in 1538; and from Chile, which had been claimed by Valdivia in 1540, parties crossed the Andes into Argentina. Mendoza founded Buenos Aires in 1535 and later sailed up the River Plate to Paraguay. The area that is now Uruguay was largely ignored until the early 18th century, as was the northeastern coast: settlements were established in Venezuela, but only slowly. The Spanish positively turned their noses up at the land further east, with the result that the British, Dutch and French each managed to claim a chunk for themselves: the three Guianas became the only non-Iberian colonies on the continent, geographically and culturally isolated from the rest of South America.

Colonization. The Spanish Crown was represented in the New World by a Viceroy. Beneath him was a hierarchy of officials, but government remained so centralized that for many years the whole of the territory was administered by the Viceroy of Peru. In the end, however, it was divided up into a number of viceroyalties: Granada (Colombia, Venezuela and Ecuador), Perú (Peru and Bolivia), La Plata (Argentina) and Chile. Perú remained the richest and most valued region, and goods bound for Spain from all the colonies were obliged to pass through Lima. From here most of it was sent north to Panama, where it was hauled across from the Pacific to the Atlantic. The remainder was despatched to Cartagena in Colombia.

Colonization took place largely thanks to the *encomienda* system, whereby individuals who had served the Crown in the Conquest (*encomenderos*) were given land and a labour force of Indians. The native people living in the most accessible regions were forced off their land and into a life of serfdom; the most unfortunate were sent down the mines. In some areas the indigenous population was all but obliterated. Those who weren't killed by ill-treatment, either died from diseases against which they had no immunity or else married Spaniards. Many others were converted to Christianity by the hordes of priests and missionaries that came rushing over from Europe. Portuguese colonization was slow and disorganized by Spanish standards. There were no Indian empires requiring immediate or vicious subjugation, nor, initially, any riches on the scale discovered by Spain. So Brazil was largely left to its own devices.

Independence. The history of the Spanish colonies up to independence was peaceful, simply because of the strict and racist nature of government. Authority was given only to people born in Spain, a group known as the *peninsulares*. This policy aroused the greatest resentment among the creoles, or *criollos*, who had Spanish parents but were born in South America. There was also widespread anger among merchants concerning the restrictive laws which prevented trade direct with South American provinces or with European countries other than Spain. (This was not the case with Brazil, which had greater freedom.)

Talk of independence among urban intellectuals was encouraged by news of the American War of Independence and the French Revolution, and by Spain's own domestic problems. The first significant move came in 1810, the year which saw the defeat of the Spanish king by Napoleon. Creoles in South America refused to accept the authority of Napoleon's brother, who had been installed as the new king. They demanded that power be handed over to the Creole-controlled local councils. By the time Napoleon had been defeated and Ferdinand VII installed as King of Spain in 1814, the Creoles had no intention of giving up their newly-acquired influence. There followed one of the most astounding military campaigns in history, and one that the Spanish found themselves in no position to resist.

The first serious rebellions were in Venezuela. They were led by Colonel Simón Bolívar, known later as El Gran Libertador. A democrat and an intellectual, Bolívar was also one of the world's greatest military men: with the aid of just a small army he managed to win over a territory far greater than that ever conquered by Napoleon.

Following a series of difficult but brilliant victories from 1819-21, Bolívar pushed through Venezuela and Colombia, and eventually reached Quito in Ecuador. Meanwhile, General José de San Martín had secured Argentina and Chile, and by 1821 had occupied Lima. The next year, the two men met to discuss a final campaign against the Royalists, who had taken refuge in the mountains. But San Martín, very much the monarchist, couldn't agree with Bolívar, and he retired to France. Bolívar proceeded to defeat the Royalists at Ayachucho in 1824.

The colonies were independent but shattered by the heavy fighting. With the collapse of the Spanish apparatus of government, and with nothing to replace it, Bolívar's dream of a South American union came to a halt: Bolivia seceded from Peru, and Bolívar's own Gran Colombia split into the three separate republics of Venezuela, Colombia and Ecuador. In a letter Bolívar wrote before his death he said: 'If it were possible for any part of the world to revert to primordial chaos, that would be America's final state ... the only thing we can do is emigrate'. He died, a disillusioned man, at a farmhouse outside Santa Marta, in Colombia. His last, melancholy days are chronicled by Gabriel García Márquez in *The General in His Labyrinth*.

Although also the result of the Napoleonic Wars, independence in Brazil was won more peacefully. In 1822 the country became an independent monarchy under an Emperor, but declared itself a republic in 1889. British Guyana and Dutch Guiana were granted independence only in 1966 and 1975 respectively; French Guiana remains an Overseas Department of France.

Post-Independence Period. The creoles dominated the new independent states, and life for the majority of people barely changed. But divisions in the top ranks were quick to reveal themselves. Conservative and Liberal camps emerged and were highly antagonistic — setting the stage for a long-standing resentment which persists to this day. The Liberals were primarily the urban intellectuals, and the Conservatives the rural landowners, who tended to be pro-church and pro-centralization.

Violence and rapid changes in government became part of every day life. Power was concentrated in the hands of the *caudillos*, the traditional strongmen of Latin American society. These men usually commanded private armies, which they used to advance their personal interests. The strongest among them used their armies to seize political power. This was often encouraged by the middle classes, which were increasingly powerful and keen to keep the rabble under control. More than anything else, however, *caudillismo* was a cult of personality. As such, it prevented continuity on the political scene, and countries were subjected to rule by a succession of dictators. Much of the instability in South America today is a result of caudillismo.

Recent History. The heyday of dictatorship — in the traditional sense of the word — may be over, but the countries of South America still have much in common. They share similar social and economic problems, not least the gap between the rich and the poor; and they are bound by a common history, the same national language, and Catholicism.

More modern phenomena binding the countries together are a large foreign debt and, linked with that, the need to create a workable relationship with the West. Foreign debts are South America's greatest shared burden. Rampant borrowing during the 1970s was followed by debt crises that have dogged the region since the early 80s. In an effort to tackle the situation, South American financiers have abandoned the highly-protected home markets, and are embracing more open economies. This involves fiscal reform, liberalization of trade and capital, deregulation and privatization, i.e. the right-wing free market policies beloved by politicians from Thatcher to Yeltsin. Economics have meant that the traditional love-hate relationship between North and South America has undergone fundamental change; as have relations with the West as a whole.

The world craze for regional cooperation and the reduction of trade barriers is catching on in South America too. In 1991, Paraguay, Uruguay, Brazil and Argentina signed a pact creating the new Mercosur ('market south'): when fully operational it will affect 60% of Latin America. And in 1992 the Andean countries — from Venezuela down to Bolivia — began their own free trade zone. While such agreements are designed to boost the countries' economies, they also symbolize a willingness to cooperate with each other on other fronts: particularly concerning drug-trafficking and, to a lesser extent, the protection of the environment.

South American economics no longer deserve a reputation for instability and hyperinflation, but no country has been able to reduce price rises to below 10% annually. And despite the signs of new growth and stability, the mass of South Americans have yet to benefit. Indeed the cost in human terms has been great: austerity measures have worsened social inequality, unemployment is rising, and shortages have sparked food riots from Venezuela down to Argentina. The situation remains fragile and potentially volatile.

Politically, however, tensions within the region are less than ever before. Democratic elections have placed new demands on governments and parties. Old political loyalties are changing. The Left, battered almost to death by right-wing regimes and by the debt crisis, is adapting to new conditions and attitudes. Indigenous peoples — traditionally looked down upon by most of society — are becoming increasingly vocal in their demands for rights and respect. A new confidence on all sides can only help liven up political debate and promote badly needed reform throughout the region.

THE PEOPLE

'Being a Latin American, like being a European, is a state of mind. It is never a recipe for uniformity'.   *Hugh O'Shaughnessy*

Indigenous Peoples: the total number of indigenous people in South America is about 22 million, compared with the continent's total population of 250 million. The largest groups are in Ecuador, Peru and Bolivia, where Indians make up about half of the population. They live mainly in the Andes, often in the most basic conditions. The Quechua, descendants of the Incas, are the principal group, followed by the Aymará. Many continue to wear their traditional clothes.

The other main concentration of indigenous tribes is in Amazonia, and in scattered pockets elsewhere. They and their lands are under threat through mining, logging and colonization, and tribes are forced to retreat further and further into the hinterland.

While we refer to the native people as Indians, *indio* in Spanish is considered a derogatory term. In South America the word *campesino* (peasant, farmer) is the accepted term, particularly in the mountains.

Mestizos: these are people of mixed indigenous and European origins, though the term is also used to describe pure-blooded Indians who have abandoned their traditions. In many South American countries the mestizos represent a sizeable proportion of the population. One interesting sub-group are the *gauchos* or cattle-herders of the grasslands of southern Brazil, Argentina and Uruguay.

Creoles: known as *criollos* in Spanish, these are people born in South America, but of European (white) descent. They often form a surprisingly large community, and traditionally control most political and economic power.

Blacks: African slaves were brought to South America to work primarily on the plantations and in the mines. The largest numbers arrived in Brazil — where an estimated 8,000 a year were shipped in during most of the 17th century. In that country over 15% of the population are black. The other largest groups are in Colombia and Venezuela where, in each case, they make up about 10% of the population. Smaller groups exist in the other South American countries; even these retain a strong and very particular culture.

While overt racism as seen in the West is comparatively rare, the blacks occupy the lowest position in society — lower even than the Indians.

Immigrant Communities: waves of immigrants came to South America following independence, but particularly during the late 19th and early 20th century. They came mainly from Europe, and the vast majority settled in southern Brazil and in Argentina, with significant numbers of Germans also making their homes in southern Chile. More disparate groups include a large Japanese community in Brazil, Welsh farmers in Patagonia, and East Indians in Guyana and Surinam. There are several Mennonite towns in Paraguay and Bolivia, which are home to a German religious sect.

Religion. In Brazil, where people die every day through deprivation of some kind, millions of dollars were spent in preparation for a visit by the Pope in 1991. This demonstrates the importance of the Catholic church in the region. Both the Spanish and Portuguese spread Catholicism efficiently in their colonies, sending missionaries into the hinterland of many countries. Most of South America has been officially Catholic since the Conquest.

The church was traditionally a highly paternalistic, conservative force, but in some cases priests and missionaries were important defenders of the indigenous people. The Jesuits were an especially strong influence in parts of southern Brazil, Paraguay and northeastern Argentina. The relics of some of their highly-organized missions, known as *reducciones* still survive; these are testimony to the skill of the Indian craftsmen. The Jesuits eventually became too self-sufficient and autocratic for their own good: they were expelled by the Spanish in 1767. The story of the Jesuits in the area is described in the film *The Mission*.

On paper, 90% of South Americans are Catholic. However, this doesn't reflect the important role played by native religions, both pre-Columbian and African. In the most remote regions, people have adopted few or no Christian beliefs or rituals. Tribes in the depths of the Amazonian jungle practise animist religions, in which shamans (spiritual leaders) and the use of hallucinogenic drugs play an essential part. In the Andes, the Quechua and Aymará Indians also practise ancient rituals, which have been handed down from their Inca and pre-Inca forebears. People often attend both Christian and non-Christian ceremonies, and find no difficulty reconciling the two different beliefs. The blend of Catholic and non-Catholic beliefs is most remarkable among the black community: during the colonial era slaves had no freedom of worship, so they disguised their own rituals and gods behind the trappings of the Catholic church. Afro-Christian sects have a particularly strong following in Brazil.

Reflecting the worldwide trend, the latest thing to hit Latin America is evangelism. Hundreds of Protestant sects are currently challenging the supremacy of Catholicism. It has been estimated that they have a combined following of around 40 million in the region. Disillusionment with the established Church has aided the spread, with evangelicals finding the greatest support among the rural poor — largely thanks to their involvement in development projects.

Meeting the People. Europeans stick out a mile. You will be instantly identified as a person of uncertain morals, imperfect language and almost infinite wealth; and probably also as *norte americano*. These categorizations are made not through xenophobia but through experience. It does not automatically mean that you will be ripped off, treated rudely, etc. The term *gringo* or *gringa* — used universally to describe someone of Western appearance — is sometimes spoken with a smile, but is rarely used pejoratively. *Yanqui*, however, is less complimentary. A new term to have made inroads recently is *mochilero*, or backpacker.

The majority of South Americans are friendly, and they are almost always curious. In countries where there is a high proportion of Spanish blood, the people tend to be extrovert and quick to start a conversation. Indians, particularly those in the Andes, often seem dour and monosyllabic by comparison. These are a traditional people, many of whom have chosen to shun Western culture. Most are diffident or shy rather than unfriendly, and it is up to you to make the overtures. See Indians at festival time, however, and all your assumptions will be shattered.

In areas unused to travellers, the response to you may depend very much on the contact they have had with foreigners in the past: in some areas white people are often taken to be missionaries. The idea that you could be one usually arouses curiosity rather than hostility, but it is useful to bear in mind the possibility of such a misapprehension.

Wherever you are, it is a courtesy to ask permission to take photographs. (It is a sure sign that you have hit a well-trodden path when the subject asks for money in return.) And when travelling in extremely remote areas, take small gifts to give anyone who offers you hospitality or assistance, or to give to children you meet.

LANGUAGE

English is the national language in Guyana. French is spoken in Guyane, Dutch in Surinam, and Portuguese in Brazil. Elsewhere, Spanish is the *lingua franca* even among Indian groups. Many indigenous people are bilingual, though in the most isolated communities they may have some difficulty with Spanish. They may not speak it at all, preferring to speak their own dialect. South Americans often refer to Spanish as *castellano* (Castilian) as well as *español*.

Do not assume that people outside the tourist traps can speak English. Although it is surprising how much two people can communicate without knowing the other's language, you would do well to learn some Spanish. Travellers without at least a modicum of the language will find life in South America difficult, and certainly less rewarding. Since in some countries you may have brushes with dodgy policemen or with obstructive immigration officials, the ability to argue your case is invaluable. Although English is rarely spoken, most professionals, for example doctors and dentists, have a good understanding of the language.

Learning Spanish. Most local authorities in Britain run evening classes in the subject. If you have neither the time nor the dedication to turn out on the same night each week, then try to learn some Spanish at home. The BBC produces an excellent course for beginners in Latin American Spanish, called *Mexico Vivo*, which includes a book and cassette. If time is short, try the BBC *Get By In Spanish* course — intended mainly for holidaymakers bound for Spain — which consists of a book and two cassettes. An alternative, available worldwide, is the Berlitz *Latin American Spanish for Travellers* book and cassette.

The best plan is to do a Spanish course after you arrive. Quito is the most popular place in which to do this: see page 180. You will learn Latin American Spanish, the pronunciation of which is far removed from the pure Castilian which is more often taught in England. In particular, the soft 'th' sound — corresponding to the letters *ce, ci* or *z*— is rendered as 's'; the use of 'th' will cause great amusement and lead locals to assume that you have a lisp. Furthermore, pronunciation varies between countries, and is particularly distinctive in Argentina and Chile.

Pronunciation. Unless an accent indicates otherwise, Spanish words which end in a vowel or n or s are always stressed on the last-but-one syllable: Argen*ti*na. Words ending in any other consonant are always stressed on the last syllable: Ecuad*or*. If the stress is to be placed on any other syllable, an acute accent is written over the vowel which needs to be stressed: Bogotá. Unlike in some languages (e.g. French), an acute accent on a letter does not affect the sound of that letter; it merely indicates where the stress falls on a multi-syllable word if it does not comply with the rules outlined above.

The letter h is never pronounced, i.e. *hijo* (son) is pronounced *ee*-jo. J is pronounced as an aspirated h, as is g when followed by e or i: so José should be spoken as Ho-say. The diphthong ll is usually pronounced y, as in *allá* — aya, but sometimes as ly or even zh. The letter v is almost indistinguishable from the letter b, so *veinte* (20) sounds like *beinte*. The wave above an n (ñ), known as a tilde, changes the letter n to ny. Thus *mañana* is pronounced man-yana. Accents other than the tilde are rarely used on capital letters, and are not used in this book.

In dictionaries, indexes and telephone directories, listings beginning with the diphthong ch (pronounced as in chair) are listed after c, ll follows l, and ñ follows n.

See the chapter on Brazil for an outline of the Portuguese language.

Useful Words and Phrases

hello	*hola*	I would like ...	*quisiero ...*
goodbye	*adiós*	I need ...	*me necesita ...*
yes	*sí*	to go	*ir*
no	*no*	help me	*ayúdeme*
please	*por favor*	quickly	*rapidamente*
thank you	*gracias*	slowly	*despacio*
excuse me	*perdón*	stop	*párese*
how much	*cuánto*	here	*aquí*
where is	*dónde está*	there	*allí*
good	*bueno*	is there any	*hay*
bad	*malo*	no there isn't	*no hay*
good morning	*buenas días/hola*	river	*río*
good afternoon	*buenas tardes*	hill	*cerro, colina*
good evening	*buenas tardes*	mountain	*montaña*
goodnight	*buenas noches*	valley	*valle, quebrada*
till we meet again	*hasta la vista*	church	*iglesia*
don't mention it	*de nada*	school	*escuela*
	(or just *nada*)	garden	*jardín*
how are you	*qué tal*	house	*casa*
I am well	*estoy bien*	apartment	*apartamiento*
I am hungry	*tengo hambre*	town	*ciudad*
I don't understand	*no entiendo*	estate	*finca, hacienda*
I don't speak Spanish	*no hablo español*	village	*pueblo*
do you speak English	*habla inglés usted*	big	*grande*
a little	*un poquito*	small	*pequeño*
more	*más*	hot	*caliente*
less	*menos*	cold	*frío*
can I photograph you	*puedo tomar su*	don't touch	*no tocar*
	fotografía	no smoking	*no fumar*
I am ... years old	*tengo ... años*	no entry	*no pase*

Time

time *or* weather	*tiempo*	year	*año*
what time is it?	*qué hora es?*	yesterday	*ayer*
minute	*minuto*	today	*hoy*
hour	*hora*	tomorrow	*mañana*
day	*día*	morning	*mañana*
week	*semana*	afternoon	*tarde*
month	*mes*	evening	*tarde* (early); *noche* (late)

Sunday	*domingo*	April	*abril*
Monday	*lunes*	May	*mayo*
Tuesday	*martes*	June	*junio*
Wednesday	*miércoles*	July	*julio*
Thursday	*jueves*	August	*agosto*
Friday	*viernes*	September	*septiembre*
Saturday	*sábado*	October	*octubre*
January	*enero*	November	*noviembre*
February	*febrero*	December	*diciembre*
March	*marzo*		

Numbers

1	uno or *una*	20	*veinte*
2	*dos*	21	*veintiuno*
3	*tres*	22	*veintidós*
4	*cuatro*	23	*veintitrés*
5	*cinco*	24	*veinticuatro*
6	*seis*	25	*veinticinco*
7	*siete*	26	*veintiséis*
8	*ocho*	27	*veintisiete*
9	*nueve*	28	*veintiocho*
10	*diez*	29	*veintinueve*
11	*once*	30	*treinta*
12	*doce*	31	*treinta y uno*
13	*trece*	32	*treinta y dos*
14	*catorce*	40	*cuarenta*
15	*quince*	50	*cincuenta*
16	*dieciséis*	60	*sesenta*
17	*diecisiete*	70	*setenta*
18	*dieciocho*	80	*ochenta*
19	*diecinueve*	90	*noventa*
100	*cien* (before nouns) or *ciento*	1000	*mil*
200	*doscientos* or *doscientas* (before feminine nouns)	10,000	*diez mil*
500	*quinientos* or *quinientas*	1,000,000	*un millón*

Nationality and Status

English	*inglés*	divorced	*divorciado/a*
England	*Inglaterra*	widowed	*viudo, a*
Scotland	*Escocia*	mother	*madre*
Wales	*País de Gales*	father	*padre*
Great Britain	*Gran Bretaña*	sister	*hermana*
Ireland	*Irlanda*	brother	*hermano*
Canada	*Canadá*	wife, woman	*mujer*
Australia	*Australia*	husband	*esposo*
New Zealand	*Nueva Zelanda*	daughter	*hija*
United States	*Estados Unidos* (written *EE.UU.*)	son	*hijo*
		man	*hombre*
married	*casado*	child	*niño*
single	*soltero, a*		

FURTHER READING

A brief overview of some of the many books on or by South Americans is given here. Other titles are described in the relevant chapters.

South American Literature. Books written by South American authors mirror the agonies and complexities of life in the continent. War, dictatorship, the military, poverty and religion are common threads, all tempered with a pervading sense of the family and community. The three most famous South American writers in the West are Gabriel García Márquez, Mario Vargas Llosa and Isabel Allende. All of their books convey the unique atmosphere of the region. While some are set in a specific country, the exact location is rarely important. Most of their works have been translated into English.

Gabriel García Márquez, a Colombian, was awarded the Nobel Prize for Literature for *One Hundred Years of Solitude* (Picador, 1978), a truly remarkable book that describes a family struggle spanning one century. This and his other classics, such as *Love in the Time of Cholera* (Penguin, 1978), each provide a glimpse of the despair of South America and a glimmer of hope for the future.

Mario Vargas Llosa, who recently failed in his attempt to become President of Peru, is a most inspiring writer. He is staunchly right-wing, but his novels are real works of art: from the *Real Life of Alejandro Majta* (Faber, 1987), about the futility of revolution, to his wacky comic novel *Aunt Julia and the Scriptwriter* (Picador, 1984), about a radio station in 1950s Lima.

Isabelle Allende is a Peruvian-born niece of the late President Salvador Allende of Chile. Her books have a dream-like quality while remaining humorous and always poignant. Most celebrated is the hugely entertaining *House of the Spirits* (Corgi, 1986), but her more recent novel, *Eva Luna* (Penguin, 1990), is also highly recommended.

Politics and History. There are two excellent accounts of Spain's conquest of the Inca Empire: *The Conquest of the Incas* by John Hemming (Penguin, 1983) is a narrative masterpiece, being both well-researched and highly readable. *The Spanish Conquistadores* by F. Kirkpatrick (Cresset, 1988) was first published in the 1930s and covers the Spanish campaign in both Central and South America. See the Peru chapter for details of other books about the Incas.

Open Veins of Latin America: Five Centuries of the Pillage of a Continent by Eduardo Galeano (Monthly Review Press, 1973), should be read by anyone who is seriously interested in penetrating the complexities of the region. It deals with political, social and cultural issues and is extremely well written. His *Memory of Fire*, a trilogy, handles the region in an even more imaginative style and is also highly recommended. George Pendle's *A History of Latin America* (Penguin, 1971) is less innovative, but is a reasonable potted history.

Latin Americans by Hugh O'Shaughnessy (BBC Books, 1988) is an excellent and concise read that gives a lively overview of the region. He homes in on the military, the church and guerrillas, which he sees as the three important forces in South America. It also has a good bibliography.

The Latin America Bureau (see page 80) published books that offer some of the most up-to-date analysis on events in the region, spanning politics, economics and social matters.

Travelogues. So many books have been written about journeys to South America, that it would be easy to become simply an armchair traveller. The best travelogues, however, will spur you on to arrange your own trip.

Some of the best accounts of trips to the region are, sadly out of print. One such is *Tschiffely's Ride*, which chronicles an epic journey on horseback from Washingon to Tierra del Fuego in the 1930s. One of the earliest and most widely read books on Amazonia is *Exploration Fawcett*, which describes the trip by Lieutenant Colonel Fawcett, who demarcated the Peru/Bolivia border early this century. It is still in print, published by Century. Another classic work is *A Naturalist's Voyage*, written by Charles Darwin in 1839. This is a highly readable book in which Darwin gives an often amusing insight into the people and animals he encounters. For another account of this trip, read Alan Moorhead's illustrated *Darwin and the Beagle* (Penguin, 1971).

Modern travelogues tend to be disappointing by comparison. One such is *The Old Patagonian Express* by Paul Theroux (Penguin, 1980), which records a journey from Boston to the tip of Chile by rail. A potentially fascinating book is ruined by the self-obsessed and negative attitude of its author. *Coups and Cocaine: Two Journeys in South America* by Anthony Daniels (Century, 1986) is a more sympathetic book.

The two main areas to attract writers are Patagonia and the Andes. The most widely read book on South America's southern region is *In Patagonia* (Picador, 1979) by the late Bruce Chatwin. The choice is harder for anyone interested in penetrating the Andean countries. The best include *The Incredible Voyage* by Tristan Jones, in which the author spent eight months cruising Lake Titicaca (Futura) and *Eight Feet in the Andes: Travels with a mule from Ecuador to Cusco* by Dervla Murphy (Century, 1989). Try also to get hold of a copy of the out-of-print *Traveller's Guide to El Dorado and the Inca Empire* by Lynn Meisch (Penguin). This gives an excellent background to culture in Bolivia, Peru, Ecuador and Colombia, particularly concerning festivals, music, traditional costume and crafts.

Thurston Clarke's *Equator* (Arrow, 1988), in which he travels around the girdle of the Earth, is an interesting idea. It falls short of being a great work, but anyone visiting the equatorial regions may find it a worthwhile read.

Bookshops. Those living in London or other capital cities will have the greatest choice as far as travel bookshops are concerned. Many shops produce their own catalogue, however, and ordering a book by phone or post should present no problem.

Daunt Books (83 Marylebone High Street, London W1M 4DE; tel: 071-224 2295; fax 071-224 6893) has taken the concept of a travel bookshop to its logical conclusion: as well as a good collection of guides and travelogues, related literature is also included — from novels to cookery books. A similar approach can be found at the Travel Bookshop (13 Blenheim Crescent, London W11 2EE; tel 071-229 5260; fax 071-243 1552), which also sells secondhand guidebooks and literature. Another specialized shop is Stanfords at 12-14 Long Acre WC2E 9LP; tel: 071-836 1321. It has some of the more obscure guidebooks published in South America, as well as US publications.

A good mail order service in the USA is the Travellers Bookstore (113 Corporation Road, Hyannis, MA 02601); in Canada, try Travel Bug (2667 W Broadway, Vancouver, BC V6K 2G2). By far the best selection of books on the region, however, is available by mail order from the South American Explorers' Club, based in Denver: see page 80.

SOUTH AMERICA —
PRACTICAL INFORMATION

This chapter deals with the information necessary to plan a journey to South America: buying an air ticket, getting the documents you need, etc. It also briefs you on how things work (or fail to work) in South America, from making an international telephone call to taking essential precautions to safeguard your health.

AIR
As recently as ten years ago, air passengers crossing the Equator en route to South America were given a certificate to celebrate the fact. Nowadays, however, travel to the Southern Hemisphere is commonplace. As the number of airlines and routes has increased, competition has kept fares down. In 1982 the cheapest flight from London to Rio and back (on the Venezuelan airline Viasa) cost £460. In 1992, Viasa was still the cheapest, and the fare had increased only £100, far lower than the rate of inflation over the decade.

The best deal for you depends on your exact plans, but for many people the open-jaw arrangement is best. This allows you to fly in to one city and back from another, e.g. out to Lima and back from Buenos Aires. These are particularly cheap on Avianca of Colombia or Viasa.

FROM BRITAIN
Rarely need you pay the full fare for flights from Europe, especially from the UK. Early in 1992 British Airways (081-897 4000) was quoting £1011 as its lowest return fare to Rio, while it was selling seats on the same flight through agents for only £650. Any travel agent can book you a flight to South America, but the best range of options and cheapest fares tend to be available from specialists. The following three agencies were used by researchers for this book, and each is recommended. To find the best fare, call all three:

> *Journey Latin America (JLA):* 16 Devonshire Road, London W4 2HD; tel 081-747 3108; fax 081-742 1312.
> *South American Experience (SAX):* 47 Causton Street, London SW1P 4AT; tel 071-976 5511; fax 071-976 6908.
> *Steamond:* 23 Eccleston Street, London SW1V 9LX; tel 071-730 8646; fax 071-730 3024.

Airlines and Routes. Tickets issued at a discount usually show a higher fare than you actually paid; for instance, a London to Caracas round-trip on KLM may show the official fare of around £800, rather than the £500 it cost through a discount agency such as Steamond. This is merely an administrative convenience designed to circumvent official regulations, as you will discover if you try to cash in the ticket for face value. Many discount tickets are flexible: you can change dates

24

KLM: the Dutch national carrier flies to a variety of interesting places: Paramaribo in Surinam, Curaçao off the coast of Venezuela, plus Rio, São Paulo, Buenos Aires, Montevideo, Santiago, Lima, Guayaquil, Quito and Caracas. Discounted tickets via Amsterdam are easy to find and flights from provincial UK airports cost little more than those from London.

TAP Air Portugal: services to several Brazilian destinations, plus Caracas, via Lisbon.

United: like the other US carriers, United has numerous connecting flights to South American destinations via Miami, Chicago and Los Angeles.

Varig: the largest Brazilian airline links London with Rio and São Paulo, with connections to Uruguay, Argentina, Paraguay, Bolivia and Chile. Fares tend to be higher than on most other airlines, reflecting its quality.

Air Passes. *Condor Air Pass:* if you intend to fly widely around South America, the Avianca air pass is extremely good value. You have to fly the Atlantic on Avianca, but from Colombia you can also fly on Faucett of Peru, LAB of Bolivia and Varig of Brazil. Fares vary depending on your exact itinerary and the season, but in early 1992 a London — Cartagena — Lima — La Paz — Santiago — Buenos Aires — surface to Rio — Caracas — London circuit cost £837. Note you must make your own way from Buenos Aires to Rio, or buy a separate ticket. Even bearing in mind the amount of departure tax you have to pay (at least $100 on the above itinerary) it represents a good deal. Call Avianca direct in London on 071-408 1889.

Air Paraguay Air Pass: the Paraguayan national carrier, LAP, has a much more modest air pass from the USA. For $900 you can fly from Miami to Asunción, where you can connect to a selection of destinations, e.g. Lima, Santiago and Buenos Aires. Bear in mind that LAP is not brilliantly punctual, and that its services run infrequently. To find out more, call 1-800-327-3551.

Flights to Australasia via South America. The only direct link between South America and Australasia connects Buenos Aires with Sydney via New Zealand. This is a joint Aerolíneas Argentinas/Qantas operation, and both carriers offer good fares from London which allow stopovers in South America. Aerolíneas charges around £750 for the one-way fare to Sydney, while a British Airways/Qantas deal for the round trip is excellent: for around £1250-1400 (depending on the season) you can fly around the world via Sydney, Buenos Aires and Rio (or vice versa) and enjoy two additional stops en route. South American Experience (071-976 5511) is the expert on these deals.

The only other bridge between the continents links Sydney with Santiago (Chile) via Tahiti and Easter Island. This route is for well heeled travellers, though, costing around £900 for the one way hop.

Round-the-World Flights. RTW deals can allow you to see something of South America together with other corners of the globe. At 'official' fares, a joint Varig/Singapore Airlines ticket could route you London-Rio-Los Angeles-Tokyo-Singapore-London for under £2,000. Specialist travel agencies can stitch together a deal for less than this which allows a couple of stops within South America, e.g. using Avianca with stopovers in Caracas and Bogotá.

Courier Flights. The cheapest way to reach some parts of South America by air is to act as a courier, which involves carrying documents from one airport to another. The scope of courier flights direct to the region from the UK is usually limited to Rio: a low season return costs £450, up to £525 in high season. One option is to take a courier flight as far as Miami, and make a connection there. It is sometimes possible to book a courier flight on from Miami to Rio, São Paulo or Buenos Aires through Trans Air Systems of Miami: call 010 1-05-592-1771. The main drawback with round-trip courier flights is that the length of stay is limited, usually to between 7 and 28 days. The amount of luggage couriers are entitled to carry may be limited too. It is essential to book in advance, at least three months ahead if you want to get specific dates. Try phoning the first few days of each month since this is when companies begin booking for the following months.

The main agency for booking a courier flight to South America in the UK is Courier Travel Services (CTS, 346 Fulham Road, London SW10 9UH; tel 071-351 0300). Pan Am Express (208 Epsom Square, London Heathrow Airport, Hounslow, Middlesex TW6 2BL) and Shades International (Unit 6, Drumhill Works, Clayton Lane, Clayton, West Yorkshire BD14 6RF; tel 0274-814727) both arrange round-trip courier flights to Miami.

Buying and Selling Tickets. A few years ago it was easy to sell an unwanted half of an air ticket — you simply went to the airport with the buyer, checked in on his or her behalf and handed over the boarding pass. So stringent are security checks nowadays that a passport will be checked several times against the boarding card before reaching the aircraft. Any discrepancy is likely to result in serious consequences.

FROM THE USA
Some of the best newspapers to scour for cheap flights are the *New York Times*, *Los Angeles Times*, *San Francisco Chronicle-Examiner*, *Miami Herald* and the *Chicago Sun-Times*. The best discount travel agents are those based in Miami; try Gables Travel on 305-442-1441. CanoAndes of New York (tel 212-286-9415) is a reputable tour company.

FROM AUSTRALASIA
The only direct flight from Australasia to South America is on Aerolíneas Argentinas from Sydney via Auckland to Buenos Aires. Fares are high, e.g. A$2,500 for the round-trip. The next most direct route involves flying to Tahiti on Qantas or Air New Zealand and transferring to the LanChile flight via Easter Island to Santiago. This route is also expensive. A cheáper access point, and one more suitable for northern South America, is Los Angeles. An agent which specializes in South America is the Elizabeth St Flight Centre, 82 Elizabeth St, Sydney (tel 235-3522; fax 235-2871). Newspapers to scour for cut-price fares include the Travel Review in the Saturday edition of the *Sydney Morning Herald*, where a large selection of Sydney's hundreds of discount travel agencies advertise cheap flights.

GETTING THERE BY SEA

Many cargo ships take a few fare-paying passengers. This provides an interesting alternative to flying, but don't imagine that it is a cheap option — you pay more than the air fare. Furthermore, the schedule is dependent upon the necessities of the cargo rather than the wishes of the passengers; the starting date is often known only a few days in advance, and the course taken may be affected by the commercial considerations. But you get lots of good food, plus a chance to relax and enjoy a form of travel which is disappearing rapidly.

Every two or three weeks, a ship leaves Tilbury in Essex for Brazil via West Africa. The journey takes about 25 days and costs just over £1,000. You can disembark at Paranaguá, Santos or Rio. The same ports are served direct from Genoa every few weeks on the Grimaldi line for around £900. Other destinations are harder to reach, but ports in Colombia and Venezuela are sometimes served from Liverpool. Alternatively, you can sail to one of the Caribbean islands and proceed from there. From the USA, what is claimed to be the world's most luxurious freighter, the *MV Americana*, sails between New Orleans and several South American destinations. For further details of all these services, contact Weider Travel, Charing Cross Shopping Concourse, London WC2N 4HZ (tel 071-836 6363; fax 071-497 0078).

TOURS

Not everyone relishes the thought of venturing unaided into unknown territory, though the following chapters attempt to demystify South America. The advantage of leaving the worrying to someone else must be set against the disadvantages of expense and inflexibility. Latin American Tours (071-499 3675), Passage to South America (071-602 9889), SAX (071-976 5511), The Travel Alternative (0865-791636(, Tucan Travel (0202-827276), Explore (0252-344161), Exodus (081-675 5550) and JLA (tel: 081-747 8315) are among the companies offering tours from Britain.

In addition to the above operators, there is a growing number of 'green' tour companies. Green Flag International (PO Box 396, Linton, Cambridgeshire) produces a directory of companies in the UK which offer conservation-conscious trips. Another source of information is *Holidays that Don't Cost the Earth* by John Elkington and Julia Hailes, published by Gollancz (1992).

GETTING BACK

Price competition between airlines and agents is virtually unknown in South America. Therefore you are most unlikely to find any cheap deals from the continent to North America or Europe. If minimizing costs is crucial, get an agency in London or Miami to send a ticket out to you. The cost of international phone calls and courier delivery will be easily outweighed by the savings.

Passports. All travellers to South America need a full passport. An application form is available from post offices. Send it with the appropriate fee, photographs and supporting documents to your regional passport office. British travellers can choose between a 30-page passport or one with 94 pages costing twice as much. South American entry and exit stamps can swallow up pages at a frightening rate. The larger version may be worthwhile for those who plan to travel widely.

Several South American countries require your passport to be valid for at least six months after your date of entry; get a new one if you think you could be cutting it fine.

Most South American countries insist upon everyone carrying identification at all times. In some places you can get away with using a photocopy of the relevant pages of your passport (including the appropriate entrance stamp), which reduces the risk of losing the document. If your passport is lost or stolen while travelling, contact first the police and then your nearest consulate (in capital cities this is usually part of the embassy). Keep a record of the passport number and its date and place of issue, to make a replacement travel document easier to obtain.

Visas. For many Western travellers intending to make short visits, the only South American country to require a visa is Guyana, though nationals of Australia and New Zealand often need a visa where British and American citizens do not. But if you intend to stay in a country for more than a month (or, in some cases, 90 days), or will be working, then a visa is required. Addresses of consulates abroad where these can be obtained are given under *Red Tape* in each country section.

For an extended stay you may need a visa extension and possibly an exit visa. Either is obtainable from each country's Immigration Department, but in some places the process requires heroic stamina. You may find it quicker to go to an office in a smaller town or city, rather than in the capital, simply because queues will be shorter. A visa can generally only be extended during the last 15 days of its validity. The easiest way to extend your visit is often to leave the country temporarily and re-enter.

Crossing Borders. Government regulations concerning who may or may not enter a country do not necessarily coincide with the views of individual frontier officials. Improved relations within the region have made crossing borders in South America less worrying than a few years ago. Over-zealous immigration officials still exist, but it is extremely rare to be turned away.

Most South American nations have at least a technical requirement for visitors to possess a ticket out of the country, or out of a neighbouring one. A generally acceptable substitute is a Miscellaneous Charges Order (MCO), which any airline can issue. It is effectively an air travel voucher and looks like a ticket; you can cash it in when you return home. Alternatively, you may be asked to demonstrate that you have funds sufficient to buy a ticket home, or to simply sustain you during your stay. A credit card or two may be accepted in lieu of cash and travellers cheques, but this cannot be counted upon.

On entering most South American countries you will be issued with a tourist card; if arriving by air you fill this in during the flight. The length of stay permitted will be decided by an official at Immigration. Check carefully what is stamped in your passport, as mistakes can cause difficulties when you leave. Try not to lose your copy of the tourist card, though it doesn't usually matter if you do; immigration officials seem used to the fanciful sob-stories recounted by travellers, and can rarely be bothered to listen through to the end. They may check your name on their list of *personae non gratae*, or impose a notional 'fine'.

At out-of-the-way border towns you may have to go the local police station to get your passport stamped. If you cross at an unofficial border post — i.e. one without immigration or customs offices — go to the police station or immigration office in the nearest town. This should normally cause no problem, though if you don't have an exit stamp for the country you have just left, you may not be able to return there with the same passport — unless you call in at a consulate first to explain yourself.

Opening Hours: it comes as a shock to some Westerners to discover that an international frontier can close down at night, but most of those in South America do. Borders are generally open all day, or at least 8am-6pm, though a few little-used ones close for an hour or so in the middle of the day.

Bribes and Taxes. It is hard to say where one begins and the other ends. Entry and exit taxes are payable when crossing some frontiers in South America, and you should get a receipt for these. Some border officials supplement their income by demanding an unofficial fee of some kind. Although it is aggravating to pay up, it is wise to do so after negotiating the amount as low as possible. Don't reveal the extent of your wealth if you can help it. Getting angry is unlikely to help your case, and threatening to report them will probably only end in trouble. Notify the tourist office afterwards, to help prevent other people being ripped off.

Stories about the most notorious borders spread fast among travellers. The best way to avoid giving an official the chance to give trouble is by travelling on an international bus: going through immigration with a string of other passengers makes it hard for officials to step out of line. Unfortunately, only the main routes are served by cross-border bus services, and procedures are usually slow.

Health Requirements. Recommended medical precautions are dealt with in detail from page 66 onwards. Individual countries have health regulations which are intended to protect their people. The most common official requirement is for a yellow fever certificate when travelling from areas in which the disease is endemic, i.e. all but the southernmost one-third of South America. In practice the possession of one is not always checked.

The spread of cholera in South America saw the tightening of medical regulations. While these have been relaxed in some areas, when entering the worst affected countries, be prepared for a variety of measures: from filling in a form affirming you have no gastric problems to a compulsory and thorough medical examination.

CUSTOMS

Most border officials are used to travellers, and as such you should encounter few problems. They expect all 'gringos' to be carrying around a motley collection of unwashed socks, well-thumbed novels, etc. Personal effects in reasonable quantities can be imported free of duty. A certain amount of liquor and tobacco is allowed, but this is worth doing only if you crave a particular brand of cigarettes or malt whisky. Most foods are frowned upon, since each country seeks to protect its agriculture from foreign bugs. Meat, animal products and fruit may be confiscated (and will probably be eaten by officials when you have gone).

Books of any kind attract attention, and some authorities are still sensitive about left-wing literature. Note that you may be searched twice, by customs officals looking for contraband and again by army officers seeking weapons or literature, and that this happens on the way out of countries as well as on the way in.

Drugs. Illegal drugs are a big problem (as well as industry) in South America, so you can expect a lot of attention to be paid to any medicines in your luggage. Keep them in their original containers, and bring along copies of the relevant prescriptions. Be warned that any opiate derivatives — such as kaolin and morphine

— are strictly prohibited, even though they are sold openly in the the West. Anyone caught taking illegal narcotics across frontiers can expect to be locked up for a long time.

Export Regulations. Numerous traders in South America will try to sell you products made from endangered species. These include tortoiseshell, butterflies and items made from animal skins. Quite apart from moral considerations, you may offend the Convention on International Trade in Endangered Species (CITES), an international agreement covering all animals at risk.

In Peru and Colombia the looting of pre-Columbian sites is big business, and artefacts are sold for huge sums on the black market. Do not get involved in this illegal and destructive trade.

Returning Home. Apart from the culture shock engendered by returning from Copacabana beach to a wet Monday morning at Heathrow airport, you could be in for a surprise when passing through Customs. You can bring in, free of duty, one litre of spirits, two litres of wine, 200 cigarettes and just £32 worth of other goods: try to obtain receipts to prove that the dozen alpaca sweaters in your luggage cost less than £3 each. If you go through the red channel and present a list of what you have bought, a full search is unlikely — unless, of course, officials don't like the look of you.

Prohibited imports include goods made from endangered species (see above) and many drugs. Arrivals from South America are checked carefully. A glance at your passport will reveal evidence of a visit to Bolivia, Colombia or Peru, for example, and you should not be surprised to be searched thoroughly. Note that substances freely sold in South America may be illegal elsewhere; even though the psychotropic value of coca leaves is nil, these substances are banned in Britain. Importing them could land you in serious trouble. Travellers have been prosecuted for importing coca leaf teabags.

Prices in this book are quoted in US dollars, the currency to which all South American economies are tied. At the start of 1992, £1 was equal to US$1.80.

Living Costs. Inflation is high in much of Latin America. For the local people this is a serious problem, but visitors are insulated from the effect of rising prices by continuing devaluation of South American currencies against those of the West. Since the exchange rate depreciates frequently, you should never change more than you need for a few days. Most visitors find life cheap in Paraguay and the Andean countries, where it is possible to live on $15 a day (less in Ecuador or Bolivia). Costs increase considerably in Argentina, Brazil, Chile and Uruguay, where you should make allowances to spend upwards of $25-30 a day.

Changing Money. In Guyana (and the Falklands), pounds sterling are accepted; in Surinam, Dutch guilders are common, and in French Guyana, French francs are the currency. Elsewhere, the US dollar is the only universal hard currency. It is rarely worth taking any other Western currency, though you may be able to change it at smart hotels catering for foreigners. Most places accept dollars in payment, though you can expect a poor exchange rate. Take low denomination dollar bills ($1, $2, $5 and $10) to avoid making too heavy a loss; change will almost certainly be given in local currency.

You can change money in banks and exchange houses, known as *casas de cambio* or simply *cambios*. The latter usually offer the best rates for cash. Ask for low denomination bills whenever possible, to avoid the recurring problem of a shortage of change. Reject badly torn notes. Cambios open longer hours than banks, often operating a schedule similar to that of a normal business; some even open at weekends. Street moneychangers are found at all land frontiers and often in larger cities.

Travellers Cheques. These represent the safest way to carry funds, but using them is increasingly difficult. Because of widespread fraud, not all banks accept travellers cheques, and cambios are even less likely to; those that do insist more and more on seeing your purchase receipt as well as your passport. American Express is the leading brand, though not all banks accept them; it may be a good idea to take some Thomas Cook cheques too. Rates are almost always poorer than for cash.

American Express has representatives throughout South America, and if your travellers cheques are stolen, replacements are usually issued quickly. Note that the American Express offices in South America cannot always be relied upon to offer the services that are available elsewhere. For example, not all of them cash travellers cheques. Some offices simply check on their computer to ensure that the cheques are yours, and then direct you to the nearest bank or exchange office. Some branches, mainly in Argentina and Chile, change cheques into dollars cash.

For a list of American Express offices worldwide call 071-930 4411. If you lose your American Express travellers cheques, call the company's European headquarters on 0800-521313. Thomas Cook cheques should be reported on the company's Princeton, New Jersey number: 1-609-987-7300. Note that the USA Direct facility from most South American countries allows you to call collect easily.

Cash Machines. Holders of Automatic Teller Machine cards issued by a British building society or North American bank may be pleased to discover that the card works with cash machines in South America. Every country (except the Guianas) has an expanding network of ATMs, many of which belong to the Plus or Cirrus systems. You should be able to withdraw cash from these machines, but do not absolutely count upon it.

Credit and Charge Cards. Access/MasterCard, Visa, American Express and Diners Club cards are useful for buying air tickets, paying for expensive restaurants and settling the bill in top-class hotels. Be warned, however, that you may also be charged a hefty commission. In countries with especially weak currencies, credit card transactions which go through the official banking system are converted at the official rate. When paying by credit card, you must show your passport — a space is left on the voucher for a passport number. Check carefully that the amount charged is correct.

Some banks issue cash advances to holders of Visa and Access cards, and details are given in each country chapter under the heading *Money*. Note that the cash will almost always be given in local currency.

The Black Market. For those arriving from abroad by air, the first chance you will have to change money will be at a bank in the terminal. Anyone crossing by land will probably have to deal with a moneychanger.

Large men in dark glasses, clutching wads of notes and waving pocket calculators, still exist, though this image is gradually fading. The business is more relaxed these days, and a growing number of women are involved in the trade, particularly in Bolivia and Peru. Street moneychangers are found in many large towns and cities and at all border crossings and international airports. The main function is to assist the locals to fight inflation; money keeps its value more effectively in US dollars than in the local currency.

Moneychangers deal quite openly: in most countries it is either legal or condoned. It used to be the case that you could make good profits changing money on the black market, but the recent economic policies of many South American governments mean that you can usually get only a small premium on the official rate for US dollars. But the advantages of black market dealings are the speed (no form-filling) and convenience (much longer hours than banks). Note, however, that rates offered by black marketeers are lower when official exchange houses are closed. They are generally reliable; ask to count the cash before handing over your dollars, a practice which any honest dealer will agree to.

Some black marketeers at borders offer less than the bank rate, hoping to cash in on new arrivals unaware of what the rates are. Ask travellers crossing the frontier the other way or a reliable-looking immigration official. Don't rely upon other dealers to quote a more competitive rate since they are usually all in cahoots. At the more isolated frontiers you'll be a captive market, since you need to change money with the dealers in order to get the local currency you need to buy a bus ticket.

Some traders accept travellers cheques, at a poorer rate than for cash. Those at borders also handle other South American currencies, so if you leave Argentina for Paraguay with no plans to return, you can exchange your pesos for guaranís. Elsewhere, you will normally be given an astonishingly poor rate, and may not be able to change them at all. In some countries you can change a limited amount of local currency back into dollars at the airport before you leave, but you must show exchange receipts from a bank.

Tipping. The only circumstances in which you should ever need to tip in South America is in a posh hotel or restaurant. Add 10% to the bill, unless a service charge is already included, in which case just give some small change. Taxi drivers are not usually tipped unless you hire one for the day.

Emergency Cash. Many travellers end up hanging around waiting anxiously for bank transfers from home. Having money sent to you in South America can be a harrowing business. Bank clerks have an appalling habit of pretending that a transfer has not arrived — often it seems they do not want to bother dealing with the paperwork. You can have money sent from your own bank to a nominated branch of a South American bank — ask your bank which one they deal with before you leave home. If possible get the sender to fax written confirmation with reference numbers, so you have something to wave under the nose of the recalcitrant teller. Money sent out is almost always paid out in local currency.

One of the most efficient methods of getting funds sent out is to use American Express offices, both for the transfer and the receipt of funds. Call 071-930 4411 for more details.

If you have neither resources nor friends who can bail you out, the absolute last resort is to persuade your Embassy to repatriate you. This they will do, though you can expect a large bill when you return home.

South American nations have too many workers chasing too few jobs. Therefore unskilled work in agriculture and tourism — the two staple industries which provide casual employment for travellers elsewhere — is not a possibility. The only sphere of employment in which foreign travellers have prospects is the teaching of English.

From dusty towns in Colombia to Punta Arenas at the southern extremity of the continent, the ability to speak English is regarded as a valuable asset, and many locals pay highly — in terms of their income — to learn the language. Wages for English teachers are low by Western standards (seldom more than US$3 an hour) so teaching is a way of extending a stay rather than saving money to fund further travels. Santiago, São Paulo and Buenos Aires offer the most opportunities, though there are language schools dotted all over the continent which are willing to hire English-speakers on an *ad hoc* basis. These institutions range from prestigious bilingual colleges to backstreet language schools.

Naturally, anyone with a background in English teaching or a relevant qualification will find it easier to get work. However, experience and certificates are not always necessary for finding a temporary teaching job, as long as you look the part. You will not convince a potential employer in your normal travelling attire. Invest in some decent clothes, and have any relevant diplomas, references, etc, sent from home — even a GCSE in English will help. A good handbook for anyone seriously considering teaching their way around the continent is *Teaching English Abroad* by Susan Griffith (Vacation Work).

British travellers quickly notice the preponderance of North American accents among local people who can already speak English. Because of strong cultural influences, there is a decided preference for US accents and teaching materials. The US equivalent of the British Council (i.e. teaching and cultural institute) is the Bi-National Center. These can be found all over the continent, including over 60 in Brazil. They function as independent operations with individual teacher requirements and are worth investigating. While some want their teachers to make a two-year commitment, others are happy to take on someone for eight weeks. Some may demand an American degree in TESL (Teaching English as a Second Language), but for others a good command of English (whatever the accent) will do. A complete list (under the rather worrying heading of 'American Republics') is available from Room 304, US Information Agency, Washington DC 20547.

Several South American nations have a number of British-style bilingual schools which are mainly for local nationals who want a Spanish-English education, and therefore have a very strong emphasis on English language teaching.

Despite the prestige of these schools, some are willing to consider native speakers with no formal training (though you may need great powers of persuasion).

Finding work often involves simply asking around, making phone calls and knocking on a few doors. A useful contact is a great asset — try to befriend a receptionist, librarian or English-language officer at the British Council or a similar institute devoted to language tuition. Consult the local telephone directory, check the classified pages in the English-language press (see page 39) or place your own advertisement. Foreign language bookshops are good places to ask for leads, as are expatriate bars and restaurants.

Work permit requirements vary from country to country, but the prospects for casual teachers to regularize their status are dim. Working visas are usually granted only to fully qualified and experienced teachers on long-term contracts. Often a whole battery of documents is required, all of which must be authenticated by the relevant Embassy in your home country. As a result, you will almost certainly have to be prepared to work unofficially on a tourist visa.

Voluntary Work. Short-term voluntary work projects are surprisingly scarce for such a vast continent. Most organizations operating in Latin America are based in the USA. They carry out archaeological digs or scientific investigations which may need voluntary input. Some useful addresses:

Amigos de Las Américas: runs one- or two-month community service projects mostly in Brazil, Paraguay and Ecuador (618 Star Lane, Houston, TX 77057; tel 713-782-5290).

The American Friends Service Committee: a Quaker organization operating community service projects in various parts of Latin America (1501 Cherry Street, Philadelphia, PA 19102; tel: 215-241-7295).

The Archaeological Institution of America: publishes the *Archaeological Fieldwork Opportunities Bulletin* which gives details of current projects in Latin America (675 Commonwealth Avenue, Boston, MA 02215; tel 617-353-9361).

Earthwatch: recruits paying volunteers for projects it sponsors in Latin America (680 Mount Auburn Street, Box 403, Watertown, MA 02272; tel 617-926-8200).

Communications

anexo	extension
apartado de correos	post office box
casilla	
buzón	mail box
centro telefónico	telephone exchange
correo	post
larga distancia	long distance
lista de correos	poste restante
llamada por cobrar	collect (reverse-charge) call
oficina de correos	post office
paquete	parcel
periódico	newspaper
por avión	air mail
recogida	(postal) collection
sello, estampilla	stamp
sobre	envelope
telefax	fax
teléfono	telephone
telegrama	telegram
tarifa	rate

MAIL

Air mail letters between the UK and South America take between three days and three weeks to reach their destination. Delivery from Brazil, Argentina and (surprisingly) Bolivia is often the fastest; from Colombia, the Guianas and Peru the slowest. The chances that your postcard from South America will arrive quickly are greatly enhanced if you post it in a capital city or big town. Post offices in such places may be open seven days a week, while in provincial towns most open on weekdays and maybe until noon on Saturdays. Collections from rural offices (few countries have mail boxes) may be made only once or twice a week.

When writing to South America, note that addresses often include a box number (*apartado* or *casilla*); for correspondence this is more common than a street address, and whenever possible you should use it.

Poste Restante. Your friends, relations or creditors can write to you care of the *lista de correos* at a post office in South America. While in theory letters could be sent to any post office, you are advised to use only the main office (*Correo Central*) in the capital, where they are used to handling the poste restante service.

While most offices ask you to prove your identity by producing a passport when you collect mail, others let you look through the pile and even take away letters for a friend. This is a good reason never to have valuables (or anything that looks as if it could be valuable) sent to you. Similarly, while some offices return mail to the sender's address after a month, the majority throw out letters that have been hanging around gathering dust. If you are expecting mail that doesn't appear to have arrived, check under your Christian name too in case your letter has been filed wrongly.

You need not rely on post offices to hold mail. If you are using American Express travellers cheques or have an Amex card you are entitled to use their offices for poste restante; parcels, however, are not always accepted. The company will also forward letters for a small fee. Amex offices in South America are given in the relevant capital city section; in the UK, call 071-930 4411 for a full list.

Alternatively, you can ask people to write to a particular hotel. They should mark the envelope *esperar* ('to await arrival') followed by your name. See also *Fax*, below.

Parcels. On a long trip it can be worthwhile sending some of your possessions or purchases home. The quickest and safest way to do this is to use one of the courier companies that operate in every South American country; the staff will look after the bureaucracy for you. Expect to pay around $50 for a 5kg package. In general it is cheaper to send an ordinary parcel (especially if time is unimportant and you use sea mail), but the procedures involved in sending packages from post offices can be time-consuming. There may also be restrictions concerning weight and dimensions. Do not seal the parcel in advance, since a customs official may wish to inspect it. Every large post office seems to have plenty of freelance packagers who will prepare your despatch.

TELEPHONE

South American telephone systems vary from highly efficient (in Argentina, Brazil and Colombia) to chaotic (Peru, Bolivia and the Guianas).

Tones. South America's telephones use the same selection of signals as North America, i.e. a constant buzz or tone before you begin to dial, long rings with even longer pauses when you connect, or short, frequent beeps if the line is engaged. You will also hear the continuous 'number unobtainable' tone more often than you might care to.

Calling South America. Most calls can be made direct from the UK and North America. To dial a number in South America, use the international access code (010 from the UK, 01 from North America), the country code, the area code if any (without the initial zero) and the number. Country codes are given in the relevant chapters.

British Telecom International's charge for calls which you dial direct from the UK from 8am to 8pm and at weekends is £1.11 per minute; at night it falls to £0.95. Rates are 20% higher to Bolivia, Colombia, Ecuador and French Guiana, and 30% lower to Guyana. To place a call through the international operator dial 155.

Payphones. Call boxes vary widely in efficiency. In some countries they are found in most cities, while in the Andes they are rare outside the capitals. But since most payphones are on busy streets it is practically impossible to make a call anyway, simply because of the noise. Most people prefer to use those in telephone offices: see below. Payphones in most South American countries take *fichas* or tokens rather than coins. You can buy these from street traders and kiosks in the vicinity of the call box. Cardphones which take special pre-paid cards are becoming widespread.

Public Telephone Offices. Private telephones are by no means as common as in the West, so every town of any size has a *centro telefónico*. A typical one looks like a waiting room, with a number of poorly insulated booths where calls are made. You can make long-distance and international calls with relative ease. The operators rarely speak English, but this is not usually a problem since all you need to do is to write down the number and wait. Sometimes you will be required to pay a deposit.

Calling Abroad. International calls can be made from most private telephones; the usual access code is 00, followed by the country code (1 for the USA and Canada, 44 for the UK). In general international calls cannot be made from payphones; use a public telephone office instead. Rates are more expensive if you call from your hotel.

Charges are generally much higher than for calls to South America, typically $12 for three minutes to the USA or $15-20 to Europe. Person-to-person calls cost about one-third more than ordinary station-to-station rates. Collect calls may be made from most countries, though the number of destination countries accessible this way may be limited.

Cardphones are easily the cheapest and most efficient way to call home. These are found in Argentina, Venezuela, Colombia and Chile.

USA Direct. The American telephone company AT&T has an efficient service for those wishing to call numbers in the USA collect, or with an AT&T credit card. From telephones in several South American countries, you can get straight through to an AT&T operator in the USA. The numbers are:

Argentina 001-800-200-1111
Brazil 000-8010
Chile 00 (second dialling tone) 0312
Colombia 980-11-0010 (coin required)
Peru ##0 (coin required)
Uruguay 00-0410

For further enquiries call AT&T collect on 412-553 7458 or toll-free on 1-800-874 4000 x 416 within the USA.

Fax. People in South America have taken to fax machines just as enthusiastically as have bankers on Wall Street and publishers in Oxford. Few documents are more likely to settle a dispute over the availabilty of a hotel room than a fax from the hotel confirming your booking. South America has plenty of public fax facilities. You should be able to send and receive faxes at many town post or telephone offices, travel agencies and at some hotels. Outgoing faxes cost about twice the corresponding telephone rate. A charge is made for receiving faxes, so some less scrupulous travellers have faxes sent to them at one of the upmarket hotels, marked *esperar* ('to await arrival') and then just pick them up without booking a room.

Telegrams and Telex. Within South America telegrams are an excellent alternative to the telephone, being cheap and reasonably rapid. Services to the rest of the world are expensive, and if you send a cable to the UK it will be assigned to the ordinary mail once it arrives in Britain.

Telex is a good way to communicate with airlines, hotels, etc., when the telephone system becomes hopelessly overloaded. You can send telexes from some telephone offices and most big hotels.

THE MEDIA

Political stability and the ending of official censorship in many countries has encouraged the birth of newspapers, and radio and television stations. While journalists are certainly enjoying greater freedom, bomb attacks against media targets are not uncommon: journalists are killed at a rate of one each month in Colombia.

Newspapers. South American journals vary enormously in quality. Most have a right-of-centre bias, particularly when dealing with domestic affairs. Foreign coverage is often taken from the same news agencies and sometimes appears word-for-word in several papers. Nevertheless, it is wise to keep abreast of what's going on — whether to find out the latest inflation figures or to read about the latest atrocity committed by the Shining Path guerrillas of Peru.

The best assessment of events is given in the broadsheets. Tabloids tend to suffer from a preponderance of gory photographs and wedding photographs. Newspapers are mostly regionally based, and while a few are distributed nationally, many people prefer to read their local paper. You may have to pay a slightly higher price for a paper that has been sent across the country; and in out-of-the-way places, where papers are sold by itinerant sellers, beware of being sold yesterday's issue. Provincial papers generally include articles of dubious quality, but they are often good for listings.

Few English-language papers are published within South America (except in Guyana). The main ones are the *Daily Journal* of Caracas, the *Brazil Post* and the *Buenos Aires Herald*. News coverage is usually highly selective and uninspiring. The most common foreign English-language newspapers are *USA Today* and the international edition of the *Miami Herald*. The only British newspaper you are likely to find is the *Financial Times*, though the *Guardian* is sometimes found in Chile or Argentina. Most consulates in big cities have a reading room with a range of papers, although these will probably be at least a week out of date.

British Council offices can usually offer a simiilar facility. Magazines like *Time* and *Newsweek* are probably the best way to catch up on events.

Radio. Every South American country has numerous local radio stations, mostly pumping out music of varying degrees of banality. While the odd one has a decent news service, the best source of news is the BBC World Service: you may even hear about local events that you haven't read about in the paper; and you will certainly get an unbiased account. The World Service is broadcast to South America on various short wave frequencies, but there is also a Caribbean relay station on medium wave (940kHz AM), which means you may be able to pick it up on an ordinary receiver in coastal Colombia and Venezuela. You can get information on World Service reception by calling the Broadcast Coverage Department on 071-257 2685. On short wave the Voice of America is easy to tune into in northern South America because of the proximity to the massive transmitting station in Belize.

The best radio to take is a Sony SW1E (the size of two packs of cigarettes), with FM stereo and eight AM bands. It costs £150.

Television. Transmissions are dominated by sport and abysmal soap operas. If you thought *Dynasty* or *Home and Away* were bad, wait until you see some of the series produced in Latin America. Quality has no correlation with popularity, and many of them have vast followings. Most South American TV is so crass that the material picked up from US satellite stations looks good by comparison. Many enterprises, from bars to hotels, have a satellite dish. The principal purpose seems to be to watch baseball games and mediocre quiz shows, but the news network CNN is also available. The Spanish national service, TVE-Internacional, is also available by satellite.

aeropuerto	airport
barco	boat
barrio, colonia	suburb or district
camión, camioneta	lorry, truck
boleto	ticket
equipajes	luggage
esquina	corner
estación	railway station
horario	timetable
ida	one-way
ida y vuelta	round-trip
llegada	arrival
parada (de buses)	bus stop
pasaje	fare, ticket
pasajero, a	passenger
paso a nivel	level crossing
rumbo	(bus) route

or cancel flights without notice. Standards of security, safety and service on most internal flights are not what you might be used to.

International flights within South America are expensive. A much cheaper way to get from A to B is via C and D, where C is in the same country as A, and D is within the same frontier as B. From Bogotá to Quito, for example, the one-way fare (including taxes) is $190. But by flying from Bogotá to the Colombian border town of Ipiales, taking a taxi across the frontier and flying from Tulcán to Quito, the cost falls to only $80. Internal flights are also much easier to organize. Buy them locally to take advantage of the lowest fares, unless the airline has a deal by which internal flights are cheaper when purchased in conjunction with an international ticket.

A succession of international flights may be worthwhile if you have several destinations in different countries. A journey from São Paulo to Lima costs $650 whether you fly direct or stop off at Foz do Iguaçu, Asuncíon (Paraguay), Santa Cruz and La Paz (Bolivia) — cutting the cost of each sector to $130. All fares are subject to tax: sales tax on the ticket and departure tax, payable at the airport. Heavy departure taxes for international air travellers are imposed on the reasonable grounds that they can probably afford it: fees range from $5 to $25. Sales tax can be avoided by buying the ticket in another country, such as the UK. The agents mentioned on page 24 can obtain reservations and tickets.

Flying is on average ten times faster than travelling by land, and costs about ten times more than the corresponding bus fare. In some countries, however, the cost is much less than that. A $20 flight can save travelling for 12 hours along uncomfortable roads in Bolivia, while a $8 jaunt on the Ecuadoran military airline reduces a five-hour bus journey to just 17 minutes. Some of the bigger airlines, including Avianca, Varig and LanChile, issue air passes allowing a certain number of internal flights within a fixed period, usually three weeks. These can reduce the cost quite dramatically and are ideal if you want to see as much of a country as possible in a short time.

If you can't book beforehand, it is often worth going to the airport on the actual day: you may be given the seat of someone who hasn't confirmed. On internal flights passengers are rarely assigned a specific seat, so board in good time in order to sit by the window.

Journeys to airports range from a short stroll (e.g. Popayán in Colombia, where it is behind the bus station) to a long trek (such as the 20 mile/32km trip between Caracas and its airport). Most are served by local buses, which are cheaper than taxis by a factor of a hundred. Details are shown under *Arrival and Departure* for each city. Not all airports are open 24 hours, so you can't always sleep in the terminal overnight between flights.

The names of airlines in South America look as if they have been taken from a bad science fiction story — Pluna, Viasa, Ladeco — and it is difficult to discern the country of origin of most of them. Airport codes are implausible, too — try the following:

EZE — Buenos Aires (Ezeiza airport)   UIO — Quito
GIG — Rio (Galeão)   VVI — Santa Cruz (Viru Viru)
GRU — São Paulo (Garulhas)

TRAIN

While the bus is universally the most popular means of transport for covering long distances, in some countries, such as Bolivia, trains also play a vital role.

But rail travel in South America is rarely the fast, comfortable experience it can be in Europe. With the possible exception of the top services in Chile and Argentina, it is almost always ponderous, best suited to Sunday outings — for admiring the scenery, glimpsing isolated communities not served by road — or for enjoying the company of the locals. Buses are usually twice as fast as trains, and also more expensive.

As entertainment the railway is ideal. Trains are generally sociable places, and provide good, if shaky, vantage points from which to take photographs. South America boasts some of the world's great rail journeys, including the Curitiba-Paranaguá trip in Brazil, the Riobamba-Guayaquil stretch in Ecuador and the jaunt between Lima and Huancayo in Peru. You will have the chance to go on several jaunts by steam train too, such as the old Paraguayan express from Asunción. In the Andes, particularly in Peru and Bolivia, rail tracks have been laid at some ridiculously high altitudes: the trains using them usually carry oxygen on board in case anyone feels ill effects.

Don't expect buffet cars, although some first class carriages have a food service. While it's worth taking fruit and water, train journeys are an excellent opportunity to sample local food: you can buy snacks at stations or from people with baskets of goodies on board.

BUS

South America benefits from the world's best long-distance bus services. Buses often run from one end of a country to the other, even in a place the size of Brazil. While buses are generally fast and comparatively comfortable, the quality deteriorates rapidly in rural areas: many companies keep their most decrepit buses for precisely the sort of gruelling journey along dirt roads where a bit of comfort would be most welcome.

The highest quality service, often called *ejecutivo/executivo*, should include air-conditioning, reclining seats and drinks on board. Executivo buses travel mostly overnight and cover long-distance and international routes only. These and other long-distance buses usually make meal stops en route.

At the bottom of the scale is the simple local bus, sometimes referred to as *común*. This is the one you are likely to use most frequently when exploring the countryside. The standard conveyance in rural parts of South America is a wreck fitted with hard, narrow seats and woefully little leg-room. Whatever size or shape, local buses are often packed to capacity with short, patient locals; therefore tall, intolerant visitors may not enjoy the experience. Management of this heaving, lurching mass is the responsibility of one or more conductors. They pack on the passengers, load luggage (and children, and animals) onto the roof, collect the fares and orchestrate the whole lumbering affair. To lessen the sometimes cramped conditions in which you will have to sit or stand, take as small a pack as possible. Keep it on the bus with you whenever possible.

While bus services between big cities are frequent, they diminish dramatically once you head into rural areas. Remote towns may only have one or two services a day and minor villages only a couple a week. Many local services start early, e.g. at 5am, and finish early: the last departures may be as early as 4pm. But while timetables exist in theory, they are not necessarily paid much heed. Buses can leave 30 minutes early or an hour late if it suits the driver. If a driver or conductor tells you he is leaving *ahorita* ('right now'), take it with a large pinch of salt; they will say almost anything to get your fare.

Bus terminals in South America are extremely colourful. They epitomize what happens when free enterprise is allowed to run riot. The terminals themselves may be laid out in a fairly orderly fashion, but the endless array of kiosks advertising all sorts of destinations in bright colours is enough to give you a headache. If you can bear it, however, it's always worth doing the rounds in search of the best deal — in terms of price, comfort and time taken. Stations in most towns have snack bars, and telephone, post and left-luggage offices.

On long-distance buses you are often allocated a seat, so if there is plenty of space, you can ask to go by the window. Try to watch your bag until it is secured on the roof or in the boot. You are sometimes expected to tip the person unloading baggage at the other end: watch what other people do.

COLLECTIVE TAXIS

Colectivos are found throughout South America. They offer the speed, convenience and relative comfort of a taxi at a price not greatly higher than the bus fare. Colectivos can take the form of anything from an American saloon to a minibus. They generally operate along fairly short, set routes, e.g. between borders and the nearest main town, or along busy routes where the road is good. Colectivos tend to depart from around the bus station or the main market; anyone should be able to point out exactly where. When a taxi is full it sets off, but it may take a long time to fill.

HITCHING

Hitch-hiking is an extremely useful supplement to the public transport services in most South American countries, particularly when travelling along minor roads. Even if you have never hitched you will find it is an accepted and necessary way to get around. This is particularly true in the Andean countries, above all in Bolivia and Peru. Furthermore, hitching is often more comfortable than travelling by bus: you will frequently end up in the back of a truck with plenty of room to stretch out, a welcome breeze and a fine view. And even if you are huddled in the back of a cement truck in a tropical rainstorm, hitching is never a dull way to travel; and it is always a good way to meet people. The disadvantage is the dearth of private vehicles, which means that you can face long waits. Drivers often expect the equivalent of the bus fare for their trouble. This is often waived for foreigners, but you should always offer money to a driver who picks you up.

A degree of discretion is required when hitching. While taking lifts in most rural areas is recommended, this cannot be said of certain parts of South America. Do not hitch in the vicinity of Bogotá, Rio, Lima and other big cities, where levels of crime are high; most other places should be safe.

BOAT

South America is washed by great oceans and laced with thousands of rivers. Hence it has considerable scope for some spectacular boat journeys. More practically, the terrain in parts of the continent — such as the Amazon basin, Patagonia and the Guianas — makes waterborne travel the only sensible way to get around.

You are most likely to encounter water transport when crossing a river; ferries may come in the shape of a clapped-out cruiser shuttling from Asunción across the Río Paraná to Argentina, or a precarious raft of the type which limps across the Canal del Digue outside Cartagena. These operate more or less on demand.

Much more thought needs to be given to a long voyage, whether on a river boat down the Amazon from Manaus to Belém or a coastal vessel navigating the shores of Patagonia. Some routes are served by regular passenger services, but usually you will have to negotiate for space with the captain of a cargo vessel. Be prepared for your itinerary to be changed completely if a good haulage opportunity presents itself to the crew. On whichever type of boat you travel, you can expect few comforts. Furthermore, the food is likely to be abysmal, and you will be expected to bring your own hammock.

CYCLING

South America is extremely tough on bicycles: road surfaces are bad enough for cars, and puddles may conceal a drop of several feet. Some cyclists have suffered from attacks: on the Caribbean coast of Colombia, for example, dispossessing cyclists seems a favourite sport.

Given all this, riding a bike around South America might be regarded as a sign of madness, but it is in fact a reasonable, rewarding and increasingly popular way to get around — particularly off the beaten track. The local people and wildlife will be overwhelmed with curiosity at both you and your bike.

Choosing a Bicycle. Only in established 'traveller' spots are you likely to find bike hire shops. In most South American countries a mountain bike can be picked up for under $150, though so cheap a bicycle may not last long under the rigours of the terrain. Serious cyclists should bring their own. A good mountain bike enables you to cope with difficult terrain, and the gear systems allow you to pedal up the steepest hill. Bear in mind that aluminium cannot be welded, so avoid aluminium bikes and luggage racks. Look for good clearance between rack and wheel, as a build-up of mud can slow your progress; the same applies to the mudguards themselves.

Transporting your Bicycle. Most airlines allow you to take a bike free of charge providing your total luggage weight is within the allowance of the airline (usually 20kg per person); otherwise they can charge you excess. Always check with the airline about bicycle carriage before you buy a ticket: different airlines have different policies. To take a bike on an aircraft, you might have to pack it up: ideally tape cardboard around the whole thing, or failing that just around the gear and brake levers, and the rear wheel gear assembly; remove the pedals.

To get to the most rewarding places for cycling once in South America, you should be able to load your bike onto a train, a boat, a second-class bus or an aircraft. If you belong to the idle tendency of cyclists, the region has plenty of scope for taking your bike on a bus to the top of a mountain and freewheeling down. On trains, you will usually have to pay for your bike and put it in the freight car. Bikes usually travel free on buses. Try to avoid removing the front wheel when stowing the bike — the front forks become extremely vulnerable to damage without an axle between them. Take plenty of food and a five-litre water container — in Patagonia, water supplies can be three days apart.

Essential Equipment. A good lock is essential, and keep a note of the key number. Make sure you and your travelling companion (if you have one) have a key to each other's lock. Panniers should be made with tough waterproof fabric and have strong fasteners; make sure they are raised high enough for good water clearance.

Repairs are generally an exercise in imagination and improvisation, but take a good supply of tools and spares. Recommended tools are: a Swiss Army knife; a set of Allen keys (Cannondale and Madison both make good sets, which include two screwdrivers); an adjustable spanner; a pair of pliers with a wire-cutting facility; and some lubricating oil such as WD40. Suggested spares include: spokes (these can be taped to the frame of the bike and forgotten about); gear cable (long), which can double as brake cable if necessary; inner tubes; a small selection of nuts and bolts; and, of course, a puncture repair kit.

Clothing. Cycling shorts and longer trousers in a stretch fabric are good, while jeans are uncomfortable. Anywhere outside the Atacama desert, waterproofs are useful; a peaked cap will improve visibility both in rain and bright sun. In general, aim for lightness, durability and compactness. Cyclists should choose their clothing in layers — so you can wear three or four layers if cold, and take one layer off at a time as you warm up.

Further Information. Contact the Cyclists' Touring Club at 69 Meadrow, Godalming, Surrey GU7 3HS (tel 0483-417217; fax 0483-426994). The CTC provides members (£25 per annum) with general information sheets on cycling abroad, as well as specific trip reports by people who have cycled in South America. It also sells books, including *Short Summer in South America* by Nick Sanders, which recounts a 6,000-mile cycling trip along the Pan-American Highway from Ecuador to Chile. *A Gringo's Journey* (Impact Books, 1989), describes a trip by bike from the USA to Chile. The account is brief but worth buying just to read about the author's attempt to cycle across the saltpans of Bolivia.

CITY TRANSPORT

Bus. City buses are invariably cheap and crowded. Once you're on, to stop the bus — whether the going has got too tough, or whether you have simply arrived at your destination — shout *parada* ('stop'), *esquina* (meaning 'stop at the next corner') or give a loud whistle. Make it known — to a fellow passenger, the conductor or driver — where you want to get off, to enhance your chances of alighting at the right place. On a crowded bus, ensure you are somewhere near the door; otherwise, you may find it impossible to get off.

Taxi. Most big towns and cities have a plentiful supply of taxis, and in general it is more of a problem persuading their drivers that you don't need a cab than it is to find one. In small towns, where you are less likely to be tormented by the clamour of taxi drivers offering rides, the main square is the best place to pick up a cab. If you fail to hail one, ask around for the nearest taxi stand or order one over the phone. Capital cities often have air-conditioned taxis too, which are more expensive. These tend to hang out around the smart hotels and at airports, and are the ones most likely to make miscellaneous surcharges, for baggage, etc.

Most journeys cost far less than in the West, but taxi drivers are adept at taking gringos for a ride, in both senses. For this reason you should avoid taxis that gather directly outside hotels, transport terminals and tourist spots, since their drivers will be more accustomed than others at ripping people off. Always agree a price in advance or make sure the driver resets his meter. Some taxis don't have meters at all, in which case you must negotiate. Prices are nearly double at night.

You must get rid of the notion that once you've hired a taxi it becomes your private conveyance; often a driver will seek other passengers heading roughly in the same direction. The main reason to use taxis in small towns is to reach places in the surrounding area: either because there's no public transport, it's too far to walk, or because you aren't keen on hitching. Shared taxis are the norm for this sort of journey.

Finding Your Way. Streets in many South American towns are laid out on a grid pattern, at least in the centre. All streets should have names or numbers, but few locals use them. Most South Americans use buildings or other landmarks as points of reference. They are seldom able either to tell you the name of the street you are in, or to direct you. Ask the advice of several locals before moving too far in any one direction. When arriving in a town for the first time, ask for the *plaza principal* or *parque central*, or main square. This is the focus of every community, and is a good place to get your bearings.

Most roads in a town are prefixed either an Avenida (Avenue) or Calle (Street), though in some countries the title is rarely used. Street numbers are often left off too. Thus an address may be given as, for example, Colón y Bolívar (or Colón esq. Bolívar), meaning that it's on Colón near the corner of Bolívar; esq. stands for *esquina*. The suffixes N, S, E, and O in some addresses indicate the orientation from the main square.

DRIVING

alquilar	to hire
alto	stop
autopista	motorway
camino cerrado	road closed
carretera	highway
carretera panamericana/ interamericana	Pan-American Highway
ceda el paso	give way
carro	car
cuidado	take care
curva peligrosa	dangerous bend
desviación	diversion, detour
desvio	turn-off
dirección única	one way
doble tracción	four-wheel drive
no adelantar	no overtaking
no estacionarse	no parking
no hay paso	road closed
peaje	toll
peatones	pedestrians
preferencia	priority
reduzca velocidad	reduce speed
servicentro	service station
topes, túmulos	sleeping policemen, bumpy road
velocidad permitida	speed limit
zona de derrumbes	landslide zone

The Pan-American Highway, the backbone of the American continents, begins in Alaska and runs almost all the way down to southern Chile. It sounds as though it should be the ultimate in roadbuilding, a multi-lane freeway whisking buses, trucks and cars through the heart of the Americas. For parts of its route, such as Interstate I-5 through California and the stretches of *autopista* around Santiago de Chile, it fits this image perfectly. Be prepared, however, for a more modest highway in most of South America.

Some enterprising travellers have bought a camper van once in the region, and then sold it at the end of their trip. Other travellers simply hire a car or jeep locally now and again. One of the main reasons to drive yourself around is to reach the more remote spots not accessible by public transport. Driving in rural areas is a relief in that traffic levels are low; but roads are often in poor condition and signposts are rare.

Rules of the Road. Driving in most of the continent is only for the fearless. Drivers are not a polite breed in South America: do not expect the niceties typically exchanged between motorists in the West, e.g. indicating, giving way, not changing lanes randomly. When coping with other drivers (as well as with animals, children, etc.) the key is the use of the horn. Drive defensively and be particularly wary after dark, since the few rules and regulations that exist are completely disregarded at night. South Americans take a liberal approach to traffic lights at any time of the day.

Traffic nominally travels on the right, except in Guyana. The frequency of accidents is clearly indicated by the state of the majority of cars on the road — if Western standards of roadworthiness were applied, there would be virtually no traffic. Watch out particularly for non-functioning headlights and indicator lights; few cars seem to indicate when turning corners anyway. Breakdowns are indicated by a few leafy branches placed in the road a short distance behind the vehicle.

Documents. Useful information related specifically to driving through South America is limited. In the UK, contact the Touring Information Department of the Royal Automobile Club (RAC), PO Box 100, 7 Brighton Road, Croydon CR2 6XW; tel 081-686 2525), which gives advice to members.

Both the RAC and AA (Fanum House, Basingstoke, Hampshire RG21 2EA; tel 0256-20123) issue International Driving Permits (IDP). These are not strictly necessary for most South American countries, but they may be useful since they are printed in a number of foreign languages, including Spanish. Stand your ground with officials at the border who claim national licences (or even IDPs) are not acceptable. Allow plenty of time when crossing frontiers, and have lots of money ready. All sorts of fees are levied and many different forms are required to be filled. If the paperwork is not completed by the time the border closes, you may well have to park up and recommence the next morning.

Most countries have road checkpoints along certain roads: this normally involves simply showing your licence to a policeman, but patrols may give your luggage a going-over if they suspect you of smuggling or gunrunning.

Fuel. Finding petrol or diesel is easy in most urban areas, tricky in rural parts; at night and weekends, it may be impossible to get fuel if you're off the beaten track. A good rule is to top up the tank whenever you get the chance. Unleaded petrol is non-existent and most countries have just two grades of petrol, although the octane gradings may vary: premium grades range from 89-98 octane and regular octane from 72-90. The quality of petrol plummets in rural areas.

Petrol is sold by the US gallon (*galón*), which is 80% of the UK equivalent, and oil by the US quart (32 fluid ounces or just under 1 litre). The price of fuel varies from one country to the next, but it is in general about the same as or a little more expensive than in the USA, i.e. cheaper than in Europe.

Car Rental. The multinational car hire companies have erratic representation in South America. So while Argentina and Brazil have agents all over the country, Bolivia and the Guianas have none — reflecting either the difficult terrain or the level of foreign interest. To request directories of the main international firms, call the following numbers in Britain: Avis 081-848 8765; Budget 0800-181181;

Europcar/National 081-950 4080; Hertz 081-679 1777. Once in South America, rental agencies are often most easily contacted at the airport, while local firms are best sought out by looking through the Yellow Pages. Local companies usually charge less than the multinationals, but their vehicles may not be so good. Be sure to check the vehicle over minutely before signing.

The cost of hiring a vehicle is generally more than in the UK or USA. Expect to pay at least $35 per day for a car, $50-60 for a four-wheel drive vehicle (necessary for many dirt roads). This price excludes the distance charge: unlimited mileage deals are rare. Insurance is usually given, but the cover is poor: the hirer must accept a high risk, typically $500 for loss or damage. In addition, a credit card or a massive cash deposit is required. The minimum age for those renting a vehicle is usually 23 or 25. You are rarely permitted to take hired cars out of the country.

Rented vehicles are tempting targets for villains: never leave anything of value inside. Avoid parking in city streets; either stay in a hotel with its own car park, or use a guarded parking lot. For a short period during the day you may be able to pay a local kid to keep an eye on your car. Alternatively, a group of youths may offer to 'look after' your vehicle: you have little choice but to pay up.

agua caliente	hot water
aire condicionado	air conditioning
albergue (juvenil)	youth hostel
ascensor	lift
calefacción	heating
cama	bed
climatizado	air-conditioned
con baño	with bathroom
cucuracha	cockroach
desayuno	breakfast
doble	double
habitación	room
hamaca	hammock
huésped	guest
lavandería	laundry
manta	blanket
mosquitero	mosquito net
piso	floor (storey)
planta baja	ground floor
pulga	flea
rata	rat
saco de dormir	sleeping bag
servicios	toilet
sencillo	single (room)
tienda (de campaña)	tent
ventilador	fan

A room for the night in South America ranges from the luxurious and pristine to the uncomfortable and positively insanitary. Fortunately, plenty of places fall somewhere in between.

As a general rule, the smaller the town the more basic the lodgings. Expect to pay $5-10 for an average room, but you can pay as little as $2. A single room often costs at least two-thirds of the price for a double, although in some places guests are charged per person. Prices rise during the main holiday season, at festival time or at weekends. During the low season, however, you may be able to ask for a discount, especially if you are staying for several days. In small towns hotels also fill up the day before the main weekly market.

Hoteles are at the top of the scale, although there can be a wide range of prices within this category. Most provide a fan (if there is no air conditioning), towels and soap, and toilet paper. *Residenciales* (or *residencias*), *alojamientos*, *hospedajes*, *pensiones* and *hostales* are at the lower end of the scale, but they are often indistinguishable from cheap hotels. These are usually family-run, and consist of a private home with guest rooms: either as part of the house or in an extension. The cheapest hotels are near the bus or train stations. Lone women should be advised, however, that these areas are often red-light districts, and some hotels may double as brothels. This doesn't always make them uninhabitable: use your judgement.

Hotel categories are often blurred and misleading: it is possible to find a residencial charging $25 for a plush room with heating and television, next to a hotel charging $3 for a grotty room with no hot water. *Posada*, in particular, is a term which is used by posh and cheap establishments alike. In beach areas you can often rent bungalows (*cabañas*), usually shared between two or four people.

Tourist offices often have a list of accommodation. In some countries, particularly Argentina and Chile, this may include families that take in travellers on an informal basis.

When looking for somewhere to stay always check the room before signing in: for security against thieves, for blankets, or for protection against mosquitoes (in the form of a net, or screens on the windows). The availability of hot water should never be taken for granted, unless you are staying in an upmarket hotel. Water for showers is usually heated by a dodgy coil at the shower head: with plenty of bare wires around, this can be potentially lethal.

Youth Hostels. Because of the low cost of ordinary accommodation in South America, youth hostels are unlikely to attain the success they enjoy in Europe. Nevertheless, Brazil, Uruguay, Argentina, Peru and Colombia have hostels which are affiliated to the International Youth Hostels Federation. Since accommodation in the first three countries can be comparatively expensive, they are worth using; you rarely pay more than $3-5, though there may be an extra charge for bedding. The hostels tend to be in the cities (or towns in the case of Uruguay), but there is a small number in rural spots frequented by travellers.

Though you need not necessarily be a member to use a youth hostel, you should consider joining before you leave home. Membership for people over 21 costs £8.90 in Britain (1992). For an application form contact the YHA for England and Wales at Trevelyan House, St Stephen's Hill, St Albans AL1 2DY (tel 0727-40211).

Camping. If you plan to go off the beaten track in South America, you have to use your initiative to find somewhere to sleep. In some places you may be able to stay with a local family, or else to rig up a hammock (particularly in Brazil); most national parks have *refugios* or shelters of some kind. The best option if you plan to spend much time in remote areas, however, is to bring your own tent. Brazil, Chile and Argentina have numerous campsites, though these are concentrated in the main tourist areas. Elsewhere you may have to improvise. This is not usually a problem, but it may require a certain amount of diplomacy. Some hotels don't mind travellers pitching camp in their gardens. Pack a mosquito net if heading for a malaria zone.

Laundry. Having your clothes washed is one of the modest luxuries of travel in South America. Most cheap hotels will organize it for you, or there are plenty of laundries in towns. A rucksackful of unsavoury clothes might cost $5 to be thoroughly sanitized. The washing is usually so good that you'll find it hard to believe the launderer hasn't gone out and bought brand-new replicas of all your gear.

arroz	rice
asado	roast, grilled
autoservicio	self-service
azúcar	sugar
cantina	bar
carne	meat
cerdo	pork
cocido	cooked
comedor	restaurant, dining room
cuchara	spoon
cuchillo	knife
cuenta	bill
desayuno	breakfast
frijoles	beans
huevo	egg
jamón	ham
limón, citrón	lemon (sometimes lime)
naranja	orange
pan	bread
panadería	bakery
pastelería	cake shop
pato	duck
pescado	fish
a la plancha	grilled
pollo	chicken
sin carne	without meat
tenedor	fork

Eating out in South America is usually cheap and enjoyable. The gourmet could be disappointed at the lack of variety, but the continent has some fine restaurants: serving succulent steak in Porto Alegre, Brazil; bubbling pizzas in Salta, Argentina; exquisite French cuisine in La Paz, Bolivia; or delicious grills in Medellín, Colombia.

The catering business is a massive industry in South America, where people eat out far more than people in the West. Most common are *comedores*, simple cafés-cum-restaurants which are found almost everywhere. Those in the markets are the cheapest, and these are good places to eat during the day — the food is always traditional, though probably not advisable for anyone without a fairly strong constitution. Most people keep going on a set three-course meal at lunchtime, called variously *colación, merienda, almuerzo económico* or *almuerzo familiar.* Normally you get soup (a lump of unidentifiable meat dunked in a watery stock), a main course and possibly a sweet and a soft drink. It rarely costs more than a couple of dollars.

A standard main course is likely to be a piece of anonymous meat (usually beef or chicken), rice and beans and, increasingly, chips. Potatoes, traditionally the most common source of carbohydrate in the Andean countries, are rarely served in restaurants in any other form; they are seen as the food of the poor. Other accompaniments include fried plantain (*plátano*), which is delicious when fresh. In the Andes *chuño*, freeze-dried potatoes, are common, often served mixed with meat or eggs.

Meat lies at the heart of the traditional South American diet. A brief turn around a local market will give you some idea of the more imaginative parts of an animal that are consumed *con gusto* in the region, particularly in the Andes. Fortunately, few of these end up in the dishes served in restaurants. Nevertheless, if you are at all squeamish, ask the waiter for a detailed description of anything you order. Otherwise, you could find yourself enjoying unawares the joys of testicle and gall bladder. Beef and chicken are the most common meats, though the oddest animals turn up on menus. In Peru and Bolivia, for example, a rodent called *viscacha* is popular; even more common in Peru is guinea pig (*cuy*). In some out-of-the-way places you may get the chance to eat llama or alpaca; it tastes rather like mutton.

Lovers of steak need look no further than Brazil, Argentina or Uruguay, the main cattle-breeding areas of South America. While it is at its most succulent in these southern regions, good beef can be eaten all over the continent. Steaks come in all shapes and sizes. The best place to eat it is in a *churraschería* or *parrillada*, where it is freshly barbecued. Mixed grills, consisting of steak, chop, sausages and unsavoury parts of an animal's anatomy, are daunting to look at but often delicious.

South America also has a fine supply of fish and seafood. When the monotony of meat gets too much, head for the coast and indulge in lobster, shrimp and other pleasures. One of the culinary delights of South America is *ceviche* — raw fish marinated in lime juice, chopped up with tomatoes, onion, chilli and coriander. Costing $1 or less, it is the perfect snack. Sadly ceviche was identified as the prime cause of Peru's cholera epidemic in 1991, and *cevicherías* are going out of business at an alarming rate.

Vegetarians who do not eat fish have a problem. Be wary of waiters who insist there is no meat in a particular dish: instead, ask them to describe exactly what's in it. In the larger cities vegetarian restaurants are becoming more popular — particularly in tourist centres. If all else fails, a fried egg on rice and chips is usually an option.

Vegetarians and anyone fed up of the local diet, can seek refuge in the restaurants specializing in foreign cuisine. Most common and also most reliable are the pizzerias and Chinese restaurants, often known as *chifas*. The most obvious foreign influence, however, is from the USA. This is particularly noticeable in towns and cities: if you get a sudden craving for McDonalds you can satisfy it in any South American capital. However, many foreign snacks have been adapted to local tastes, and you can eat excellent hot dogs and sandwiches. A more traditional South American snack is *humitas* (or *tamales*), corncakes stuffed with meat and vegetables, and steamed in banana leaves. Street traders sell all manner of things, including roast corn cobs, kebabs and juicy sausages. Every region has its own specialities.

For breakfast you can usually order eggs, either fried (*frito*) or scrambled (*revueltos*). Beware of ordering a boiled egg in high-altitude towns: water boils only at 188°F, and unless the egg is boiled for a long time, you will end up with a most unappetizing meal. Only in places accustomed to travellers' tastes will you find fruit salads, muesli and toast. Many people have a hard time finding anywhere open for breakfast; the bus station is often the best place for an early morning snack.

Exotic fruit is one of the joys of travelling in the tropics. Everything from bananas to coconuts is available for a song in the markets. People set themselves up in the street as purveyors of fruit snacks — they peel pineapples, oranges and other fruit, ready to eat on the spot, and costing just a few cents.

DRINKING

agua mineral, soda	bottled mineral water
cerveza	beer
jugo	juice
hielo	ice
hora feliz	happy hour
leche	milk
licuado	liquidized fruit drink
refresco, gaseosa	soft drink
ron	rum
trago	shot

Beer. Depending on your point of view, beer in South America is either uniformly refreshing or a characterless, fizzy lager. It is nevertheless cheap. You will find nothing to match British bitter. The most unusual beers available are the dark beers, such as El Inca in Bolivia, which approximate to sweet stouts like Mackeson.

Wine. Most South American countries make wine, though you might wish that they'd invested the time into producing a characterful beer instead. Venezuelan wine is an aberration which does the nation no credit whatsoever. Colombian varieties are only slightly less offensive. Peruvian wine has some merit, though the best is either exported or extremely expensive. Only further south do wines attain real quality. Surprisingly, the whites produced in southern Bolivia are delicate Chardonnays which are excellent by any standard. Brazil makes a number of interesting wines, but most are of the mass-production genre; Argentina produces far better table wine.

Chile ranks with France, California and Australia as a maker of superlative wines. It also has the most significant collection of pre-phylloxera vines in the world. French and Spanish vines were taken to South America in the 18th century. Within the next hundred years the disease phylloxera devastated European vineyards; grapes throughout Europe are now grown on vines re-imported from the Americas. Some maintain that Chile produces wine of a quality higher than that of any other nation.

In restaurants the wine list is generally limited, with Chilean and Argentinian wines predominant.

Spirits. The most widespread spirit in South America is *pisco*, a rough distillation of grape residue. A second refining process of this liquor produces *aguardiente*, which is sometimes made instead from sugar cane. Rum is smoother and more expensive. Prices for imported liquor are high: a bottle of good whisky costs $50.

Chicha. This drink is widespread in the Andean countries, particularly Bolivia and Peru. It is fermented in a massive home-brew operation, usually from corn; in Chile a widely available fruit like grape or apple is used. It is a cloudy, yellow colour with a slightly bitter but not particularly unpleasant taste. The alcohol content varies enormously, but it is never very high — around 5% by volume; but the alcohol is absorbed very fast. Because chicha is so cheap and so easy to make, abuse is commonplace among indigenous people in rural areas. Entire villages seem populated by men with wide, lifeless eyes, a clear sign of the scourge of chicha.

Drinkers seem inordinately keen to share their supplies with passing Westerners, but after trying a sip or two you will probably want to make your excuses and leave. *Chicherías* often consist of nothing but a dingy front room: outside they advertise themselves by means of a flag or some other simple sign, which varies from region to region. When drinking with local people in the Andes, you will usually be expected to pour a small amount of your drink onto the floor: an offering to Pachamama, Mother Earth.

Coffee. Two of the greatest coffee-producing nations are Brazil and Colombia, but the best beans are exported. Coffee is typically served black, strong and sweet, though *café con leche* is also very common and is an excellent way to start the day.

Tea. Don't expect Typhoo. Specialist import shops in Buenos Aires sell 'real' tea, but elsewhere you will be passed off with a tea bag apparently containing sawdust and a mug of tepid water, and be left to get on with it. More invigorating are the herb teas, or *matés*: most common are those made with camomile (*manzanilla*) and mint (*yerba buena*). Most unusual is *maté de coca*, a brew infused from coca leaves; its mind-altering capacity is negligible, but the drink does have a certain restorative effect.

Soft Drinks. For a region so well-endowed with tropical fruits, there is a distressing tendency towards sweet and fizzy drinks rather than natural fruit juices. In a typical city street there may be dozens of vendors selling Coke and Fanta, but none offering fresh fruit juice. Local concoctions in bottles are usually hideously sweet. Bottled mineral water is sold only rarely by soft drink sellers.

Stick to the fruit juices if you want to quench your thirst. In some countries they are sold in plastic bags at bus stops — bite a hole in one corner and suck. Fruit juice sold in shops is seldom pure, so seek out stalls where juice is served out of a big tub or where you can watch the oranges being squeezed. Fresh coconut milk or sugar cane juice are unbeatable.

Batidos (or *licuados*) are liquidized fruit drinks which can be made either with water (*con agua*) or with milk (*con leche*), and nearly always with sugar unless you ask for it to be left out. They are almost invariably delicious but are not as common as the usual fruit juices. One final soft drink worth trying is *horchata*, made of rice water and flavoured with cinnamon; the quality varies, but it can be delicious and is always thirst-quenching.

Exploring

antes de Cristo (AC)	before Christ (BC)
ave, pájaro	bird
bañarse	to swim
buceo	diving
caminata	hike
después de Cristo (DC)	Anno Domini (AD)
guarde-parque	park warden
iglesia, templo	church
montaña	mountain
museo	museum
piscina	swimming pool
playa	beach
reducción	mission

This heading covers sight-seeing, people-watching, and everything from venturing deep into virgin rainforest to a morning at a city museum.

Museums and Churches. Don't expect the British Museum or the Metropolitan Museum of Modern Art. There are some wonderful and beautifully laid out museums, including the Gold Museum in Bogotá and the Anthropological Museum in Lima. Many, however, are modest affairs. The majority of historical museums include a motley collection of archaeological artefacts, colonial furniture, paintings and miscellaneous memorabilia. Provincial museums are frequently entertaining simply in themselves, whether they contain a dusty array of local minerals or a room full of mannequins dressed up in the local costume. The best feature of others is the building itself: some of the loveliest old colonial palaces are museums.

The greatest preponderance of fine colonial buildings is in former areas of economic importance, where rich Spaniards built themselves fine mansions and lived lives of luxury. Money from mining financed the construction of many remarkable towns, including Ouro Prêto in Brazil and Sucre in Bolivia. The colonizers also paid for the building of churches, and much of South America's finest architecture is of a religious nature. Most of what you see was built by indigenous people, under the supervision of Spanish or Portuguese masters. But while buildings are often undeniably European, the Indians were skilled craftsmen and left their mark, particularly in the decorative motifs taken from the natural world. This so-called *mestizo* work can be seen in many of the churches of South America.

Opening hours of museums and churches are erratic, so be prepared for a certain amount of frustration or disappointment. This is particularly true out of the main holiday season, when visitors are in short supply. Labelling is almost entirely in Spanish. Normally a small admission fee is charged, with reductions for students — holders of ISIC cards should always ask.

Archaeological Sites. The continent's most important sites date from the Inca period. The best, including Machu Picchu, are found in Peru. The country also boasts an unrivalled collection of pre-Inca ruins, among which is the largest adobe city in the world, Chan-Chan. Bolivia has the next best archaeological ruins, including the pre-Inca site of Tiahuanaco. The remains left by the Incas are magnificent for their location more than for their aesthetic value. Ecuador is surprisingly empty of impressive ruins, and the sites left by ancient tribes in the mysterious Atacama desert region of northern Chile are perhaps of greater interest. Facilities at sites are usually minimal, and few can be reached on public transport.

THE GREAT OUTDOORS

Almost any journey through South America reveals dramatic scenery. The continent consists largely of wilderness, but tramping through the highlands or jungle is not as easy as it sounds. Few trails are geared to recreation purposes. Nevertheless, since in rural areas many people get around on foot, there are tracks linking small villages. These are ideally suited for walks, because the communities en route provide added interest, ready-made refreshment posts and, on longer trips, potential campsites. In addition, there are always local people around to ask for directions. (Since people living in rural areas rarely walk for pleasure, expect most of them to think you completely mad.)

Some of the most rewarding walks are along old Inca roads. The best of these are in Peru and Bolivia, where even pre-Inca trails have survived. The so-called Inca Trail to Machu Picchu is well-trodden, but still well worth doing.

The most straightforward hikes are possible in national parks, with trails, *refugios* (shelters), wardens and so on. The level of organization varies enormously, however. The best facilities are found in Ecuador, Brazil, Argentina and Chile, reflecting the levels of tourism. While Bolivia and the Guianas, for example, have a fair amount of protected territory, reaching them sometimes requires expedition-style preparations. Parks in Argentina and Chile have seen the greatest development. The organizations which run them have offices in the main towns and are an invaluable source of maps and of information about lodgings, transport, and so on. In some cases, however, visitors must be completely self-sufficient, and may have to rely on their own topographical maps: see page 41.

In certain areas there may be no choice but to go on a tour, simply because of the lack of public transport. This is particularly true, for example, in parts of Patagonia. Other places, including the Amazon and the saltpans of Bolivia, require a guide simply because of the nature of the terrain. In areas with good animals and birds, such as the Galapagos Islands and the Pantanal swamps of Brazil, an experienced guide will greatly enhance your chance of seeing wildlife. If you don't arrange a tour through an agency, it is easy to hire a local guide independently. This is common practice for anyone tackling some of the continent's numerous volcanoes. You can normally arrange this on a fairly informal basis in the nearest town or village. Whether you are going on a tour or arranging your own guide, seek recommendations from other travellers.

People who prefer to experience the local scenery in a more energetic fashion, can go white-water rafting or skiing. Chile is the best country for both these activities, though there is some scope for rafting in Peru, and Argentina has a few ski resorts. Bolivia has just one ski slope, but it is the highest in the world.

Equipment and Books. Depending on what kind of adventures you are planning, you may need anything from a warm sleeping bag to a mosquito net. A large water bottle is always essential, as is a compass for serious trekking. If you plan to do a lot of walking in the jungle, some care should be taken getting footwear. Light

Entertainment

baile	dance
boleto	ticket
boletina	box office
concierto	concert
espectáculo	show
estadio, coliseo	stadium
exposición	exhibition
fiesta	festival
horario	opening hours
partido	match, game
película	film
peña	folklore show

Cinema and Theatre. Films shown in most South American cinemas are violent and sexist. Only in cities are you likely to see popular English-language films. Some may be fairly recent releases, particularly in Argentina, Chile and Brazil. There is also a growing number of arts cinemas. Most movies come from the USA, in the original language but with Spanish subtitles. An average cinema ticket will not cost more than $2-3.

Regular outings to the theatre are unlikely to feature in your schedule unless you spend a good deal of time in the capital cities. Each has its own 'national theatre', which is often an architectural extravaganza and frequently the main attraction. Many theatres were designed as opera houses, though operatic performances are uncommon these days. Touring companies are rare within South America, and relatively few plays are performed. Concerts of traditional or classical music are the most common events.

The staging of shows can be an erratic business. Keep an eye open for programmes published in the newspapers, though you would do better simply to go direct to the theatre box office, preferably in the evening since they are often closed during the day.

Music and Dance. The closest thing some travellers come to live music in some parts of South America is a trio of ageing guitarists doing the rounds of the local restaurants, or a couple of kids banging out a rhythm on an old box. However, those who devote some time and effort to seeking out the local venues or finding out about forthcoming events, should not come away disappointed. You can always find somewhere to dance, whether it's in a flash club in the city or a spartan neon-lit disco in a rural town.

Percussion and wind instruments are the most traditional in South America, and were popular before the Conquest. The Spanish introduced stringed instruments, and these have also become an integral part of South American folk music traditions. Other influences came too, including from Africa with the millions of slaves shipped over the Atlantic.

The music of the Andes is particularly distinctive. The most typical sounds are made by percussion and wind instruments, including the panpipes *(zampoña)*, made with reeds of different lengths. The music is emotional and often haunting: evocative of the mountains and the daily struggles of the campesinos. The music has a considerable following in Europe nowadays, and the Bolivian band *Rumillajta* has won particular renown.

Most of the popular music you hear today is the result of a blending of African and Latin influences. The blacks living in South America have provided the continent with its most exciting music and dance. The strong rhythms are a pleasant change from the soulful sounds of the mountains, and the lighter traditional Hispanic sounds. The central forms are the Brazilian *samba*, closely associated with that country's carnival, and *salsa*, a Cuban form performed widely in Venezuela and Colombia. One of the other most famous styles of music and dance to come out of South America is the *tango*, which originated in Buenos Aires in the late 19th century. It is very much in vogue currently and performances in so-called tango bars are a popular form of entertainment.

For an active evening go to a *salsadromo*, where you can watch live salsa bands perform and usually join in yourselves. You are only likely to find such venues in a capital city, however, and not in all South American countries. Going to a *peña* is normally a more sedate experience: these are clubs specializing in folk music and dance, found mainly in the Andean countries. Most are restaurants that put on shows of traditional music at weekends. Some have become extremely touristy, but out of the capital cities you can find more authentic ones.

Festivals. The indigenous cultures reach their peak of expression during festivals. These also provide the most authentic environment in which to experience music and dance. Most *fiestas* are religious in origin, but they are rarely sombre occasions. And even those which are heavily religious are always colourful. Dancing is often the focus of events, and copious amounts of alcohol are consumed. Evidence that a festival has occurred can persist for some time in the shape of men lying prostrate by the side of the road.

In most South American countries there is barely a day in the year without some kind of festival: you would be extremely unlucky if your visit did not coincide with at least one. It is worth planning your itinerary around the best ones; plan to arrive a couple of days in advance, to enhance your chances of getting a room.

Nationwide religious celebrations include Easter Week, when processions seem to be obligatory, and All Saints' Day, when families flood to their local cemetery to be with their ancestors. In addition, each town, district and village has its own special day, a date usually linked to its patron saint. Other festivals aim to ward off natural disasters such as earthquakes or floods, and big towns often commemorate their founding.

Any festival provides a unique insight into a community and a country. The greatest spectacles (not including Brazil's carnival celebrations) are perhaps in the Andes, where Indians almost invariably dress up in their traditional clothes, or else don costumes representing deities, devils or animals.

Carnival: if there is one festival that people gear their trip around, it is carnival (*carnaval*) in Brazil — and more particularly in Rio. But the festival is also celebrated all over the continent.

Carnival has its origins in the Lent festivities brought across the Atlantic by the Spanish and Portuguese. These heralded the coming of spring and occurred in the last few days before Lent, a period of fasting in the Christian calendar. The tradition was to eat no meat for 40 days: the word carnival itself derives from *carne* and *vale* ('meat' and 'farewell').

The archetypal carnival blends European religious ritual with wild music and dance, most typically African in origin. It is celebrated in February and March, usually from the Saturday before Ash Wednesday; see page 616 for the dates from 1992-1996. Festivities can go on for anything from one to several weeks, not counting the previous months of preparation required for the biggest occasions. The most organized events include parades, shows and firework displays, but the carnival is above all a time of chaos and madness on the streets. People get roaring drunk and large-scale water fights are common: these can involve pickups touring around exchanging fire, or people at windows chucking balloons of water at pedestrians below. Unsuspecting tourists are particularly popular targets.

SPORT

Soccer. Never underestimate the average South American's interest in soccer. Every town and village has its own pitch and the game is played everywhere and with great enthusiasm. South America, as any soccer fan knows, is on a par with Europe in terms of the quality of its *fútbol*. The best club teams compete for the Copa Libertadores de América. The 1991 winners were Colo Colo of Chile, improbably sponsored by the Russian car manufacturer Lada. They beat Olimpia of Paraguay, who were champions in 1990 and runners-up in the very first competition.

The English influence is obvious: in Chile you find Everton, in Uruguay Liverpool, and the big club (and stadium) in Buenos Aires is not Río Plata but River Plate. Even in remote corners of the region, British visitors are closely questioned on Arsenal's prospects for the coming season or the chances of Manchester United winning the Cup.

Baseball. The greatest following for this all-American game is in Colombia and Venezuela. Most large towns have a general-purpose sports stadium, which is used predominantly to stage baseball games. Watching a game is an excellent pastime at weekends or on midweek evenings. Any young local should be able to tell you when the next game is.

Cricket. The world's strangest sport is much more popular than you might imagine. Test matches are staged on South American territory in Georgetown, Guyana — the International Cricket Conference (the game's ruling body) regards Guyana as part of the West Indies. Therefore the Caribbean's best players, plus those from Australia, India or England, can be seen in action each (northern) winter in South America.

Cricket is also popular in Argentina, where it has been played since 1826. The national team has gone on more than 100 tours, mostly within Latin America. Indeed it is largely thanks to Argentina that the game has survived in the region at all. Games are also played among expatriates and Anglophiles in Brazil, Chile and Peru.

Other Sports. Basketball and American football have a significant following, and among some communities, particularly in Ecuador and Peru, bull-fighting draws large crowds.

Shopping

abierto	open
artesanía	crafts
centro comercial	shopping centre
cerrado	closed
cigarillo	cigarette
comprar	to buy
discoteca	record shop
librería	bookshop
mercado	market
película	film (camera)
pilas	batteries
tienda	shop

Safeway and Sainsbury could learn a lot from traders in South America. Everyone seems to be buying or selling something, usually at prices which would put the average Western supermarket out of business. The market is the centre of life in most South American communities. It fulfils a vital social role for rural folk, providing an opportunity to gossip as much as trade. Many towns have a semi-permanent daily market, amplified once or twice a week on the official market days. The best fairs are those held in the Andean countries, where rural markets — like festivals — help break up the monotony of life in the mountains. The sheer human spectacle is the greatest delight: simply seeing hordes of people, often in traditional costume, gathered in one place. The visual feast is enhanced by visions of stalls piled with all manner of extraordinary things; some towns have special animal fairs, which are usually great fun.

The most typical rural markets are dedicated to the selling of food and household goods. Crafts are not traditionally sold, though some markets have become famous for their *artesanía*, such as Otavalo in Ecuador, Tarabuco in Bolivia and Caruarú in Brazil. In such places it is always worth exploring the surrounding villages, where many of the crafts on sale will have been made. The spread of tourism has encouraged the setting up of craft stalls in some traditional markets, though craft fairs have frequently grown up independently of these: in popular tourist centres in the Andes, people simply sit on the pavement surrounded with their wares.

All manner of crafts are available — from soapstone carvings in the Brazilian state of Minas Gerais to dainty lace doilies in Paraguay. The Amazonian Indians make some lovely things, including baskets and woodcarvings, but there are few outlets for these. Anyone seriously into leather should head to Argentina, though rising prices do not make jackets the good value they once were.

The best and easiest buys are frequently the weavings and wool products made by the indigenous people of the Andes. Many wool products are made for the tourist trade, but have traditional indigenous motifs. Jumpers (*chompas*), hats and gloves in natural colours are made from alpaca wool, which is the finest; brightly coloured jumpers are generally made from sheep's wool. Finer even than alpaca is *vicuña*, a relative. However, this animal is an endangered species, and selling its wool violates international law. It is rarely seen on the open market these days: anyone claiming to be selling vicuña is likely to be lying — either way don't buy it. Whether made with alpaca or sheep's wool, winter woollies are always cheap ($5-10), and are life-savers for those who arrive in the mountains without warm clothes. Always try jumpers on because they can come out in extraordinary shapes. You can buy *chullos* — the distinctive Andean hats, pointed at the top and with earflaps — for just a dollar or two.

Weavings, which require greater craftsmanship, make good gifts or souvenirs. Ponchos and shawls (*mantas*) are an especially typical product of the Andes, each community having its own distinctive weave. Large quantities of old weavings have been bought up by traders, who sell them to tourists — as they are, or chopped up and made into bags, moneybelts, etc.

Mundane items, such as soap and toothpaste, are easy to find and cheap. More obscure articles that must be imported are usually both elusive and fearsomely expensive. Camera film, for example, can be twice the price it is in the West. Slide film is extremely hard to come by except in good shops in the capital cities. Beware when buying film in small shops or in markets: one tourist developed a reel when he got home to find half-faded groups of Japanese tourists smiling out at him through his landscapes. Check the film's expiry date, wherever you buy it.

Most cities have a bookshop where you can buy novels in foreign languages. These are often extremely costly, however, and you would do better to track down a secondhand bookshop, many of which allow exchanges.

Crime and Safety

arma	gun
asalto	mugging
bandido	bandit
carcél, prisión	prison
cartera	wallet
contrabandista	smuggler
drogas	drugs
ejército	army
golpe de estado	coup d'état
guerra	war
herido, a	injured
ladrón	thief
multa	fine
narco-traficante	drug-trafficker
policía	police
prohibido entrar	no entry
propiedad privado	private property
(punta de) control	checkpoint
seguridad	security, safety
testimonio	witness
toque de queda	curfew

Most of the South Americans you meet are kind, hospitable and gentle, with a natural generosity which humbles most Westerners. Some people steal because they have no other means of survival. It is impossible to stay for long in South America and not to be affected by the extent of petty crime: either as a victim, or in the precautions that you will undoubtedly be urged to take. The typical visitor carries more in his or her moneybelt than the average person on the street in South America earns in a year.

Avoid stocking up with clothes at your local army surplus store before leaving home: in a region like South America, where the military is still feared by most people, to be taken as one its representatives is unlikely to work in your favour.

How to Avoid Robbery. Dress down. Western visitors displaying ostentatious wealth in darkened backstreets are asking for trouble — as is anyone who leaves anything of value on Copacabana beach while going for a swim, or buys drugs from street dealers.

Leave as much money as possible in your hotel (preferably in a safety deposit box), and conceal what you take with you by using a moneybelt or a leg pouch. Foreigners are required to carry identification, which you can do by photocopying the first six pages of your passport, plus the one bearing your entry stamp; most police patrols will accept this. You can leave the real thing in your hotel. Keep a small amount of change in your pocket, so you don't have to dig into your money belt just to buy an orange. Do not carry around shoulder bags that can be easily swiped. Even a cheap wristwatch or a pair of spectacles can be a target for a thief. If you have a daypack, wear it on your front — where you can see it — rather than on your back: slashing bags is a popular ruse. Cameras symbolize gringo wealth and can be a major worry. In the big cities some people feel more relaxed if they leave their camera behind in the hotel. When in a city with a bad reputation for street crime, such as Lima or Rio, get to know it a little by studying the map before you set out: standing on street corners consulting a map makes you vulnerable, while an air of confidence (however false) is good protection.

The tricks employed by professional thieves are numerous and sometimes ingenious. You may be walking along the street when someone apparently offers to help clean off a bird mess from your shoulder; others may actually spray something — from mustard to shampoo — on your back or in your hair. This is a trick to divert your attention while someone goes through your pockets or slashes your bag. A similar trick is for someone to crouch at your feet in a café, feigning to find a dropped coin. The best remedy is to draw a great deal of attention to yourself. Shout, wave your arms around and hope that you frighten off the would-be thief. Don't worry about what bystanders might think, since they tend to assume that all Westerners are quite mad anyway.

Knowing which areas attract thieves is half the battle. This book warns of particular districts and places to avoid, or where you should take extra care. But every town or city in South America has common danger areas: places particularly notorious for pickpockets are those with lots of people, such as markets and transport terminals. Buses and bus stops are also favourite haunts for pickpockets, bag-slashers and watch-snatchers; keep a firm grip on your valuables and glower at anyone who comes too close. And be careful when coming out of banks or casas de cambio, or when using a cash machine: some tourists have been followed and mugged. Contrary to popular belief, cities such as Medellín in Colombia are less risky than tourist haunts such as Qosqo (Cusco) in Peru. Georgetown, capital of Guyana, has some of South America's most active thieves. Be especially vigilant whenever out after dark, though often more danger comes from falling down a hole or twisting your ankle on an uneven pavement than from a thief. Most South American cities have poor levels of street-lighting.

When driving in cities, conceal your bags and keep the windows tightly closed. One of the reasons attributed to South American drivers' disinclination to stop at red lights is their fear of robbery when halted.

Reporting a Robbery. Armed robbery or physical injury is rare, though this is a risk if you offer resistance. South American pickpockets are very discreet, and the chances are that you will not realise you have been robbed until you reach for your purse or wallet.

In major cities there is usually one police station which handles all robbery reports. The police should be fairly efficient and co-operative, though few speak English. Expect little sympathy, however, if you have been robbed while drunk. (It is illegal in some countries to be drunk in a public place anyway.) Thefts from tourists are sufficiently commonplace that the police usually issue a copy of the report to the victim as a matter of routine. To reclaim losses from your insurers, you need evidence of the incident: the police should issue a duplicate statement (in Spanish), although they may try to palm you off with just a record of the case number. Also make sure that the statement or *denuncio* is stamped.

If you lose air tickets, contact the airline direct. Lost passports should be reported to your Consulate. As well as obtaining new documents you will need to visit the immigration office to get a new tourist card: this is a formality as long as you have the police report of the robbery, and your new passport. If all your money is stolen, the Consul can also arrange for funds to be sent from your home country or, as a last resort, repatriate you.

Other Crimes. Some hotels have a bad reputation for security. Be aware of exactly how much money you have: whether it's in your room or in the safe.

In many countries, villains attempt to separate travellers from their wealth by pretending to be police officers. The standard scam is to stop you in the street, show a fake ID, and ask you to empty your pockets. The robber then makes off with your wealth. To reduce the risks, insist that you go together to the nearest police station; take a witness if possible.

Kidnapping is a threat in some countries (notably Colombia and Peru), where the targets are normally well-dressed business visitors; dressing down can save your skin.

Drugs. People talk about drugs a lot in South America. Consumption, however, is not the main worry — this is a far bigger problem in the West. Illegal drugs are easily obtainable if you look for them, particularly marijuana and cocaine, though most people come away without having had any contact with drugs at all. If someone approaches you trying to sell any, do not even think about being tempted: it could well be a plain clothes policeman, and if you are caught the penalty for possession is severe. Officials do not turn a blind eye where tourists are concerned, and they may well make an example even for possession of small quantities. Some Westerners buy their freedom — the police might offer bail for $10,000, and will not be unduly surprised if you flee the country. Otherwise, when your trial finally comes around, you can expect to be locked up for a long time.

Peru and Bolivia between them produce all the world's coca, from which cocaine is made. Traditionally the leaves have been transported to Colombia for refining, but recently crackdowns on trafficking have encouraged the drug barons to find new territory from which to operate. There is an increasing number of refining laboratories in Peru and particularly Bolivia. Perhaps more significant, however, is the move into Brazil, which shares a border with all three cocaine-producing countries. While there are few laboratories in Brazil, its importance as a transit point reflects the shift in the pattern of drug sales towards Europe, and away from the USA. The Guianas, Ecuador, Argentina, Venezuela and Chile have all become routes for the European markets.

Anti-drug campaigns have been launched all over South America in the last few years. The programmes in Peru and Bolivia are the most controversial, largely because of the involvement of the United States. The USA has sent both money and personnel, and it has actively encouraged the use of the military in the pursuit of traffickers and in the destruction of coca plantations. Worries are expressed increasingly about the possible consequences of the militarization of the anti-drug campaign. Firstly, it could force drug traffickers to become more organized and, in the case of Peru, to rely more heavily on terrorist organizations such as Sendero Luminoso. Secondly, in two countries only recently free of military dictatorships, giving new prominence to the army could spell renewed instability. Thirdly, the campesinos who grow coca simply in order to survive feel threatened.

Photography. In most South American countries, a whole series of rules covers what may and may not be photographed. It is forbidden, for instance, to take photographs of military installations or anything with military connections; this can include railways, ports, radio stations, bridges, factories and even naval museums or post offices. It is probably wise to ask permission if you are in any doubt whatsoever, as it is not unheard of for the militia to wrench a camera off a tourist and confiscate the film. The authorities are also sensitive about photographs that could be seen as harmful or embarrassing to the state, e.g those of strikes or drunken brawls.

Dealing with the Military. South America is heavily militarized. Every country in the region has a highly visible military presence which can be unsettling at first — after a month you become used to the sight of soldiers carrying automatic weapons. The most likely place you will come face to face with either is at military checkpoints. These are a part of everyday life in some countries, even where there is no obvious security risk; they appear to have survived simply as a tradition handed down by past military dictatorships. In Colombia, Peru and Bolivia checkpoints occur mainly in coca-growing or cocaine-processing areas, while in Ecuador and Brazil police are more often looking for smuggled contraband.

Buses are often waved through, but occasionally they are stopped and everyone must have his or her documents checked; you may be asked to get off, so that the bus can be searched. Foreigners are of little concern to the military, who are keener on finding subversives or contrabandistas than weather-beaten travellers.

Health and Hygiene

analgésico	painkiller
brazo	arm
caballeros	gents
consultorio	surgery
culebra	snake
damas	ladies
estómago	stomach
estoy enfermo, a	I am ill
dolor	pain
farmacia (de turno)	pharmacy (on duty)
fiebre	fever
insolación	sunstroke
inyección	injection
llame a un médico	call a doctor
paño higiénico	sanitary towel
picadura	sting, bite
pierna	leg
píldora	pill
preservativo	condom
radiografía	X-ray
sangre	blood
socorro	help
soroche	altitude sickness

Parts of South America are cleaner and safer than anywhere else in the world, but some areas on the continent are indisputably hazardous to your health. The problems of staying well in a region where sanitation is often poor and disease is widespread, are exacerbated by the range of disasters waiting to befall you: from a stomach upset to malaria, and from sunburn to a volcanic eruption. While the threat of disease is much reduced out of the tropics — most of Argentina and Chile, and all of Uruguay lie in a temperate zone — no one should take their good health for granted. Even so, few travellers encounter anything more serious than a bout of diarrhoea as their system adjusts to alien food. The advice below, coupled with sensible precautions and medical assistance, should ensure that distress, disease and disaster do not spoil your visit.

Sources of Information. Once you have decided an itinerary, seek advice about what precautions are necessary. Your doctor may know something about tropical diseases, but you are strongly advised to go to a specialized centre where doctors are experienced in dealing with travellers.

The London School of Hygiene and Tropical Medicine (Keppel Street, London WC1E 7HT) has its own database with the latest information on diseases and health conditions in countries around the world. MASTA (Medical Advisory Service for Travellers Abroad), an independent organization based at the school, provides help to prospective travellers. By phoning 071-631 4408 or 0705-511420 between 9.30am and 5pm (Monday to Friday) you can request information relevant to your trip and personal requirements. This will be sent to you on a print-out, either by first-class post (£5) or by fax (£7), payable for by credit card. Staff do not give out information over the phone. MASTA can also prepare detailed health briefs on demand; these cost £27.50. The £5 print-outs are also available from British Airways Travel Clinics, which have been set up in conjunction with MASTA. They concentrate on administering immunizations and malaria tablets, though they also give out more general advice. The clinics are found all over the UK, from Purley to Manchester; call 071-831 5333 to find out the one nearest you.

An alternative source of information is the International Medical Centre (IMC), which has three clinics in London: 21 Upper Wimpole Street, W1 (tel 071-486 3063), 119 Bishopsgate, EC2 (tel 071-283 0634) and 131-135 Earls Court Road, SW5 (tel 071-259 2180). Staff generally devote more time to you than at the British Airways clinics, and consultations (by appointment only) are free. You can also arrange jabs.

In the USA the Center for Disease Control in Atlanta, Georgia, runs a health hotline: call 404-332-4559.

Books: read *Travellers' Health: How to Stay Healthy Abroad* by Richard Dawood (Oxford University Press). It is the most comprehensive, up-to-date and readable guide for anyone concerned about their health.

NATURAL HAZARDS

Altitude. Much of South America is higher than the tallest mountain in Britain (4,024ft/1,219m). Altitude sickness affects different people at different heights, but about 50% of people feel the effects at about 11,000ft/3,355m — lower than Qosqo in Peru and La Paz in Bolivia. Some people experience a pleasant light-headedness on reaching high altitudes. More common, however, is the shortness of breath, particularly when walking uphill. Always give yourself time to acclimatize: whether you have arrived in one of the high Andean cities for the first time, or whether you are about to tackle one of the Cordillera's many peaks. Being fit is no guarantee of immunity to high altitude. Even if you are fully acclimatized, you may want to take a climb in stages so that your body can adapt gradually to the increasingly reduced level of oxygen. If you experience symptoms ranging from headaches and breathlessness to nausea and palpitations, you should rest and continue at a slower pace. Should there be no improvement, the safest treatment is descent; those attempting to go any higher risk, in severe cases, contracting pulmonary or cerebral oedema (a build-up of fluid in the lungs or brain). Diamox, which you take before you reach high altitudes and continue to do so until you descend, seems to help acclimatization, but it is not a cure.

A more mundane remedy is *maté de coca*, a tea brewed from coca leaves. In Andean countries, mainly in Peru and Bolivia, coca leaves themselves are widely available; a certain amount of coca is grown legally for traditional medicinal purposes. Coca provides a cheap and effective means of desensitizing your body to the rigours of high altitudes, which is why it is so commonly used by Indians living in the highlands. You can buy the stuff easily and legally. Rather like 'salt 'n shake' potato crisps, a bag of leaves should contain a pebble of limestone (calcium carbonate), which acts as a catalyst to release the mind-altering chemicals. Chew a mouthful of leaves with a small corner of the stone.

Other altitude problems include dehydration, sunburn and fluid retention. Drink plenty of water and avoid alcohol. In extremely cold conditions you should be aware of the dangers of frostbite.

Frostbite. This is severe, localized chilling, which is most likely to affect the face, hands and feet. Affected areas become numb and, when frostbite has set in, hard; there may also be swelling and blistering. After several days this could develop into a form of gangrene, which requires either months of careful healing, or even amputation.

Frostbite is preventable by wearing adequate clothes and footwear. When in freezing conditions, being able to move your hands and feet is vital. If you discover numbness in your hands, warm them immediately with gloves, blankets, or by sticking them in your armpits; the traditional way to warm up feet is to stick them on a friend's belly under jumpers and blankets. Important rules include: do not touch bare metal, which can cause instant freezing; do not rub or massage the affected area, or expose it to open fire or hot water; and drink no alcohol. If you cannot warm up, and believe frostbite is a danger, seek medical supervision immediately.

Heat. If you are not accustomed to the heat of the tropics and subtropics, you must allow time to adjust. To avoid collapsing from heat exhaustion in the first week, wear suitable clothing and a hat to keep as much of the sun off as possible. Drink plenty of non-alcoholic fluids, and avoid over-exertion until you acclimatize. If you experience headaches, lethargy or giddiness after a long day outside, you probably have a mild case of heat exhaustion caused by a water deficiency; drink plenty of water and sit in the shade until the symptoms subside. Your body's requirements of salt also rise dramatically in the heat so compensate for this by adding salt to your meals.

Heatstroke is the failure of your body's heat control mechanisms. This causes headaches and delirium, and must be treated immediately; remove all your clothes, cover yourself with a wet sheet (or similar) to stop the body temperature from rising further. Seek medical help if there is no improvement: if the body temperature continues to rise the effects can be fatal. This same condition is often described as sunstroke, but this is misleading since it can occur when you haven't been in direct sunlight.

Prickly heat is the most common heat-related skin problem and can usually be prevented by having frequent showers, keeping your skin clean and dry, and by wearing loose, non-synthetic clothes. The best treatment is calamine lotion. Since the condition is caused by the blockage of sweat ducts avoid any exertion which would induce excessive sweating.

Sun. It is tempting for those escaping a cold European winter (or summer) to head straight for the beach as soon as they arrive. But you should expose yourself to the sun as gradually as you do to the heat. If you get burnt, apply calamine lotion or cold cream liberally, or soak a towel in cold water and place it over the most tender areas. For severe burns use a mild antiseptic and keep the skin clean and dry. Try to be kind to your skin, and do as the natives do, i.e. don't go out in the midday sun.

Natural Disasters. Earthquakes, volcanic eruptions and hurricanes all occur in South America, sometimes with worrying frequency. The Caribbean is a notorious hurricane zone and therefore Colombia and Venezuela are at risk. If caught in a hurricane try to find a ditch to lie in and keep well away from anything which might be blown on top of you.

Earthquakes have left many South American towns permanently scarred, particularly in Colombia, Ecuador and Chile. Minor quakes are fairly frequent, but these are seldom alarming unless there are warnings of more serious activity to follow. If you are in a building during a strong quake, stand in a doorway or shelter under a strong piece of furniture. The volcanoes which punctuate the Andes include some which are active. Many of these have erupted in the past, most recently Mount Hudson in Chile in 1991. The only evidence of seismic activity you are likely to see is a string of smoke coming out of the odd crater. A few, however, spit out molten rock and strong sulphurous fumes, and you should not attempt to climb them.

Water. Supplies are impure in most of South America. Many diseases are waterborne, and water can contain parasites such as worms. Since bottled water is not always easy to find, take some method of water-purification. The most effective sterilizing method is liquid iodine which kills both bacteria and amoebic cysts; chlorine-based purifiers do not. Allow six drops per litre of water and wait at least 20 minutes. Using iodine continuously for more than six months is considered unsafe, so if you are going on a long trip you may want to opt for chlorine-based tablets. Of those currently on the market the most palatable are Puritabs, which take effect in just ten minutes.

Avoid swimming in stagnant or slow-moving water, where the risk of parasites and diseases is highest; bathing in fresh water anywhere is potentially dangerous.

CREATURES TO AVOID

Leeches. Walking through jungle, particularly in wet, swampy areas, makes you a target for these blood-sucking parasites. They are alarming, but they do not carry disease. If you prefer not to wait for the leech to drink its fill of blood, remove it by sprinkling it with salt, alcohol or insect repellent. If no other means are available, apply a hot cigarette or a lighted match — but this is likely to smell horrid and make a mess.

Mosquitoes. These hateful insects can carry anything from malaria to dengue fever. In addition, their bites itch a lot and can make your nights a misery.

Mosquitoes bite primarily at dusk and during the night. At nightfall cover your limbs and apply insect repellent to exposed parts. Sleeping in a room with screened windows is not always possible in budget hotels, in which case you should smother yourself in yet more repellent and sleep with the fan on. If you plan to spend much time in jungle or rural areas, take a mosquito net; you can buy one in Britain for £30-40.

Most insect repellents contain a chemical called Deet. They include Jungle Formula, which comes in an aerosol, lotion or gel; the roll-on applicator is recommended. Eating copious amounts of garlic is also said to act as a repellent to mosquitoes, as well as to other people. Soap, calamine lotion or any of the sting relief creams on the market help to ease itching. Applying ice to the bites can also soothe irritation; this should be made with purified water because otherwise waterborne diseases will have a direct route into the blood stream.

Sharks. These disreputable fish are found off certain stretches of the Atlantic and Pacific. It is most unusual for sharks to attack near the shore, however, and out of the 250 species less than 30 are thought to be potentially dangerous. If you find yourself in shark-infested waters, it is better to do the breast stroke, which creates an impression of calm strength, than the crawl which can make it look as though you are flailing helplessly. As a last resort, a sharp tap on the shark's nose may send it packing.

Snakes and Scorpions. Snakes are the most dangerous creatures you are likely to come across during your travels in South America. But snakes hunt mainly at night and you would have to be extremely unlucky to come face to face with one; and even then you will probably only do so if you start rooting around in the undergrowth. Should you encounter one, remember that the snake is more frightened of you than you are of it, and move away (without treading on any of its pals). If you are bitten try to kill the snake. Not only will this gratify you, it will make identification and subsequent treatment easier. Seek medical advice immediately.

Scorpions are rare. Although they can be dangerously venomous, their bite is not usually fatal. If you are unfortunate enough to find one in your hotel room, the management will probably be better prepared to do battle with it: a heavy saucepan is a suitable weapon whereas a paperback is not. If stung, you should rest, drink lots of water and call a doctor. To avoid the risk, remember to shake out your clothes and shoes before putting them on in the morning.

Ticks. These unpleasant arachnids sit about in the undergrowth and leap onto anything that moves. They burrow their mouths into your skin and stay there sucking your blood until their abdomen is full. At this stage they drop off, but it can take some time. Applying a lighted cigarette to a tick which has implanted itself sometimes works. Nail polish remover or strong liquor is more effective, as is smearing it with vaseline to suffocate the beast. Do not use tweezers as this can leave the tick's jaws in your flesh.

DISEASES AND HOW TO AVOID THEM

Chagas' Disease. This disease is carried in the faeces of beetles: humans are infected when the beetle bites, and then defecates next to the spot. It is a potential danger in much of South America, excluding the Amazon and the southern regions of Chile and Argentina. The disease can be treated in the early stages, but after this first phase it becomes both impossible to detect and incurable. Chagas' can affect various parts of the body, and over a long period. For example, it can lead to heart failure, which may occur ten or more years after infection.

Fortunately, the disease is difficult to catch. Travellers spending a long period in rural areas of Brazil are most at risk. The beetles occur mainly in adobe huts, and venture out only at night. Avoid sleeping in mud houses if possible, even if it means camping outside; alternatively, move the bed into the middle of the room and sleep under a mosquito net. If you develop a serious fever get a blood test, and look out for swelling around a bite.

Dengue Fever. This viral infection is transmitted by daytime-biting mosquitoes. It is found in many tropical regions, and is most prevalent during the wet season, often occurring in urban areas. It is endemic in the northern part of the continent, including Brazil, Venezuela, Colombia and the Guianas, and there are sporadic outbreaks elsewhere, particularly the jungle regions of Peru and Bolivia. Dengue is a nasty illness, but complications are rare. The more serious form, known as dengue haemorrhagic fever, does not occur in South America.

The risk of contracting dengue remains small unless an epidemic occurs. The virus has an incubation period of five to eight days. Symptoms come on fast and include a high fever, severe headaches, photophobia (shrinking from light), loss of appetite, and severe joint and muscle pains (hence the nickname 'breakbone fever'). A skin rash of small spots may appear after a few days. There is no specific treatment, and the best prevention is to avoid being bitten in the first place.

Gastric Problems. The most common ailment among travellers is a stomach upset caused by eating contaminated food. Although cooked food sold by most restaurants and street stalls is safe, you should avoid eating salads or food that appears to have been lying around in a fly-infested environment. Be particularly careful about shellfish, which is a common cause of illness. You are less likely to have problems if you stick to a vegetarian diet. Fruits such as papaya and pineapple are good to eat since they contain protein-digesting enzymes which help digestion and protect against infection from intestinal worms. Strawberries, on the other hand, are notorious carriers of disease.

Diarrhoea is likely to be the first clue that you have eaten something you shouldn't have. If left to its own devices it should clear up in two or three days. Rather than take drugs, drink as much water as possible to avoid dehydration — ideally a mixture of water, sugar and salt. Eat only dry bread, and rest. Lomotil, codeine and immodium, recommended by some doctors, alleviate the effects of the diarrhoea (and will block you up if you are going on a long bus journey), but do nothing about the cause. Antibiotics can have a detrimental effect, and they are best avoided unless fever or serious infection is suspected. In this case you should seek medical advice since you may have amoebic dysentery: this brings violent diarrhoea and painful cramps, and you may pass blood.

If you want to take antibiotics with you, flagyl or tinidazole are recommended for both dysentery and intestinal parasites such as giardia.

Cholera. Many travellers have been deterred from visiting South America by the cholera epidemic which began in Peru in 1991 and has spread to every country on the continent. Ecuador, Colombia and Brazil have been most seriously affected. It has killed around 3,000 people, the vast majority in Peru, which had 300,000 cases. While the epidemic is past its peak on the Pacific coast and in the Andes, the bacteria is now in the waters of the Amazon system. The disease is likely to become endemic in large areas of South America: while it may lie dormant for long periods it will flare up when conditions are favourable.

Cholera is the worst gastric disease you can catch. While easily treated if caught early, severe diarrhoea and dehydration can cause death after only a short time. Some strains are worse than others. Travellers are unlikely to come into contact with cholera because it occurs mainly in slum areas with little or no sanitation, and afflicts those weakened by malnutrition. By avoiding potentially dangerous food (see *Gastric Problems*) you should be safe.

The cholera shot does not give good protection — estimated at just 50% for 2-3 months. Few doctors recommend it, partly because it gives people a false sense of security.

Hepatitis. A viral infection of the liver, hepatitis comes in various types. The one which is most likely to affect travellers is Hepatitis A. It is easy to catch from contaminated food and water where standards of hygiene are poor. Incubation takes two to six weeks, and symptoms include general malaise, loss of appetite, lethargy, fever, pains in the abdomen, followed by nausea and vomiting. The whites of the eyes and the skin turn yellow (this is difficult to detect if you have a suntan), urine turns deep orange and stools become white. Serious infection is comparatively rare, but can lead to liver failure, coma and death.

If you suspect infection, rest and seek medical advice immediately. Do not smoke or drink alcohol, nor eat fat. Some people are only mildly affected, but hepatitis can sometimes take six months to clear up, in which case you are strongly advised to go straight home and recover in comfort.

The gamma globulin vaccine offers good protection against Hepatitis A, and every traveller should have it. The maximum dosage usually administered lasts for six months. If necessary, you can take dried gamma globulin with you as a booster (the normal version must be kept in the fridge). It is also possible to buy the vaccine in the major cities in South America; if you take this or your dried gamma globulin to a medical centre, a doctor or nurse should give you the injection for free.

Since the effect of the vaccine wears off gradually after it is administered, have the injection shortly before departure. The shot in your bottom is not as painful as people say. Even so, it is best to have the injection at least a couple of days in advance of a long journey.

Malaria. This is a parasitic infection of the blood transmitted by mosquitoes. It is the most serious health hazard facing travellers to South America. Every year about 2,000 people return to the UK infected with the disease; of these about a dozen die. Not all strains are malignant, and even malignant malaria is not necessarily fatal if treated quickly. But it can be a thoroughly unpleasant disease;

YELLOW FEVER

Areas of Yellow Fever
Receptive Zones

MALARIA

Other Diseases. The other standard inoculations are typhoid, tetanus and polio. Typhoid, like cholera and Hepatitis A, is caught by consuming contaminated food or water. The typhoid vaccination is more effective than the cholera jab and is administered in two doses. The first should be about six weeks before your departure, with the second just before you leave. The injections can leave you with a sore arm and make you feel lousy for 24 hours. Travellers who have already had a course need only a booster injection. Polio and tetanus require a booster every ten years.

Meningococcal meningitis is a bacterial infection of the brain and spinal cord that can occur anywhere in the world; there have been several epidemics in Brazil. It is spread by droplet infection. Although South America is not a specific risk area, since contamination can occur in crowded areas you may consider being immunized; it gives good protection for three years.

AIDS

The Acquired Immune Deficiency Syndrome (Aids) is caused by a virus called HIV (Human Immunodeficiency Virus). This can damage the body's defence system so that it is unable to fight certain infections and other diseases.

Official figures for most South American countries show the proportion of people infected to be lower than in Western countries. These statistics represent a considerable underestimate, and the disease is spreading alarmingly. Adult HIV infections are estimated at around one million, with Aids cases put at 100,000. Over half the reported cases are in Brazil, which is placed third in the world after Uganda and the USA; the Guianas are also badly affected. Transmission between heterosexuals, which is already common, is increasing, with more and more women being affected.

You cannot become infected with HIV through everyday contact with an infected person. For visitors who take sensible precautions against contracting the virus through unprotected sexual intercourse or intravenous drug abuse, risks are minimal. Take a supply of condoms with you since the quality of those available in South America is poor.

Infection through contaminated blood transfusions, however, is less easy to control due to the state of medical treatment in South America. Although more screening is carried out than ever before, donations are rarely screened effectively. In addition, hypodermic syringes are reused and may not always be adequately sterilized. If you are in an accident and require a blood tranfusion, try to get in touch with your nearest consulate or embassy; the staff there will know the nearest source of 'clean' blood. If a transfusion is not a matter of life and death, decide whether there is more risk involved in having one or going without. Whether or not you are in a possession of an 'Aids Pack' may help you to decide.

Aids Packs. These are a standard feature of many a traveller's backpack nowadays. A normal kit should contain hypodermic needles, suture material (for stitches), intravenous drip needles and alcohol swabs; it is also a good idea to label your pack with your blood group. Doctors can make kits up for you; otherwise buy one pre-packed, from MASTA (see page 66) for example. You should ask whoever gives it to you to supply a letter explaining that the kit is for medical use only — this will save you potential hassle at Customs, especially if you are entering a country with strict anti-drugs laws.

Sources of Information. For up-to-date information on the extent of Aids, contact the Panos Institute at 9 White Lion Street, London N1 9PD (tel 071-278 1111; fax 071-278 0345). It publishes various books, including *Aids and the Third World* (£7.95), which contains the latest worldwide statistics and country-by-country reports. *WorldAIDS* is a bi-monthly magazine which has a section in each issue highlighting Aids in a particular part of the world. If you don't wish to pay for a year's subscription (£12), you can order back copies individually. Panos also has an office at 1717 Massachusetts Avenue, NW, Washington DC 20036, USA (tel 202-483-0044; fax 202-483-3059).

The Terrence Higgins Trust is the UK's leading Aids charity. While it does not produce leaflets aimed specifically at travellers, THT offers good general information and advice on HIV and Aids. Write to the Trust at 52-54 Grays Inn Road, London WC1X 8SU (tel 071-831 0330; fax 071-242 0121), or call its Advice Centre on 071-242 1010. You can also talk to trained advisors by ringing the National Aids Helpline on 0800-567-123: calls are free and confidential.

Travellers with HIV or Aids. Travel can be extremely problematic for known HIV carriers and Aids sufferers: some countries bar entry if they know you are a carrier. Few countries publicize their policies, but Chile, Colombia and Ecuador are known to ask certain people for proof that they are not infected with HIV (i.e. proof of their HIV antibody status). This is most likely to affect anyone staying more than six months and visitors from the USA and Africa.

The other great problem for those who have been diagnosed as HIV positive is that obtaining travel insurance becomes difficult: most policies have an exclusion clause relating to sexually transmitted diseases. For information and advice about this and other HIV and Aids-related subjects consult the centres described above.

MEDICAL TREATMENT

Health care in modern big-city hospitals in South America is as good as any in the world. Elsewhere, the standard of medical treatment is not what most travellers are used to. In rural areas hospitals either don't exist, or else they are poorly equipped and a health risk in themselves. If you fall seriously ill, call your consulate and find out which clinic the expatriate staff use; they can usually direct you to a particular doctor too. This will probably be an expensive private hospital, with English-speaking staff. A consultation is likely to cost $15-20. Charges for treatment are extremely high, but assuming you are insured this will not be your problem. The alternative is to return home or to fly to Miami or another North American city.

Pharmacies. South America seems to have a phenomenal number of drug stores; one reason is that professional health care is beyond the reach of many people, who use commercially available remedies instead. Antibiotics, contraceptive pills, syringes and even valium are available over the counter in most places. Drugs that have been banned or rendered obsolete in the West are often dumped on the Third World, so you are advised to take supplies with you, together with a copy of the prescription: this should avoid problems at Customs.

Pharmacists can be very helpful, and good ones can save you a trip to the doctor if all you have are minor and easily recognizable symptoms. If you require an inoculation, you can sometimes get this done at a pharmacy, though you would do better to go to a hospital: if you don't have your own syringe, make sure a fresh one is used. Most pharmacies keep long hours; newspapers list the late-night rota.

INSURANCE

Given the range of calamities which can befall you in South America, it is essential to have adequate insurance. A good insurance policy will pay for transportation to somewhere with excellent medical facilities. Furthermore, insurance covers you against a range of risks from theft to flight delays. The cover provided by most policies is fairly standard: delay and cancellation insurance of up to £2,000; £1 million for medical expenses; the same amount for personal liability; £20,000 for permanent disability; and lost or stolen baggage up to about £1,000 (sometimes valuable single items are excluded). Most now also offer an emergency repatriation service.

Every enterprise in the travel business is delighted to sell insurance because of the high commission it earns. Shopping around can save money or get you better cover for the same premium. The specialist Travel Insurance Agency Ltd (28 Upper Street, London N1 0PN; tel 071-226 0615) charges about £40 for the first month and slightly less per month thereafter. Endsleigh Insurance (Cheltenham Spa, Gloucestershire GL50 3NR; tel: 0242-223300) offers a similar deal. You should also contact Columbus Travel Insurance (tel: 071-375 0011). In the USA the best rates are available from the Student Travel Network, Suite 507, 2500 Wilshire Boulevard, Los Angeles CA 90057 (tel: 213-380 2184), SOFA, 17 East 45th Street, New York, NY 10017 (tel: 212-986-9470), or campus offices of Council Travel.

If you have to claim on your insurance, amass as much documentation as possible to support your application. Compensation is unlikely to be paid for lost baggage or cash unless your claim is accompanied by a police report of the loss (called a *denuncio*). See *Crime and Safety*, above.

Women Travellers

Any woman who has travelled in southern Europe will be prepared for travel in South America and the macho tendencies of the Latin male. In 1991, a Brazilian court rejected for the first time the traditional and defendable right of a husband to kill or injure his wife in defence of his honour. While the position of women may have improved in certain spheres in certain countries, there is still much to campaign for.

Female travellers undoubtedly attract attention, and not all of it is wanted. However, compared to the persistent and sometimes offensive 'Romeos' you encounter in Italy, most South Americans are positively harmless. In most countries in the region, particularly those where there is only a small tourist trade, people show curiosity more than anything else. Seeing a man and woman tramping around together is unusual enough, but the sight of two women or, in particular, a woman on her own, gives rise to even more speculation.

The attention of the men usually ranges from silent, curious stares to whistles or audible but incomprehensible comments. Neither need be threatening, and outside the bigger towns you are unlikely to be pestered by such overt demonstrations of machismo. To keep the attention down to a minimum, avoid wearing skimpy shorts and T-shirts. Wearing dark glasses can act as a deterrent (or a confidence-giver), although they are seen by some people as a sign of a 'fast' woman. Some single women like to carry a photograph of a partner, real or imaginary, but on the whole you will not have to rely on these props to discourage unwelcome approaches. You should rely instead on your confidently independent and (if necessary) aloof manner to dodgy-looking strangers.

As long as you don't become paranoid about the attentions you will inevitably receive, there is no reason why shouldn't have as good a time or a better time than male travellers. In fact travelling alone can be a real bonus. You are likely to find yourself invited into locals' homes more often than those travelling in groups, and more than single men. On the other hand, sometimes you may have to adopt a more cautious attitud than male travellers. For example, it is probably wise to avoid certain local bars (some of which are traditionally men-only), hitching on your own, etc. But while hiking up a mountain on your own is not advisable, nor is it for male travellers: women need not feel that their freedom is unfairly restricted.

Women's Health. If you are planning to travel while pregnant, check carefully the effects of any vaccinations you might require. It is advisable not to be inoculated with a live vaccine such as polio or yellow fever, especially during the first three months of pregnancy. Malaria tablets present no problem as long as you are prescribed a folate, or vitamin tablet. High altitude can increase the probability of miscarriage. It can also affect menstrual cycles: periods may be delayed, or cramps may be worse than usual.

While tampons (*tampones*) are uncommon in South America, sanitary towels are not difficult to find in big towns and cities. Female embassy staff should be able to tell you the best source of either. As a rule, take a good supply from home.

Travelling with Babies. Most parts of South America are far from ideal for people with babies. Not only is the journey to the region arduous, but once you have arrived there is a host a hazards likely to make life uncomfortable: from the extremes of temperature to the large number of diseases to which babies are particularly susceptible. Another difficulty is the shortage of supplies of essentials such as disposable nappies and baby food.

On the plus side, the locals can be incredibly kind and considerate towards Western children. Offspring with blond hair are likely to become the subject of adoration.

Gay Travellers. Any gay person intending to travel to South America should get hold of a copy of *Spartacus*, a guidebook published in Germany by Bruno Gmunder (and translated into English). It includes a country-by-country directory listing laws on homosexuality, gay bars, etc., and costs £14.95. It is updated annually. You should also phone the Gay Switchboard (tel 071-837 7324) where the staff, if they can't give any advice themselves, will certainly point you in the direction of someone who can.

Travellers with Disabilities. South America is unpromising territory for the less able. Few concessions are made to those with mobility difficulties, and the average urban street presents a tough enough challenge even for the able-bodied. Blind and partially sighted people will find the region particularly hard going. The help of an able-bodied companion is, unfortunately, essential.

There are few sources of information for travellers with disabilities who have a sense of adventure and are keen to go to South America. Mobility International is an organization set up to promote international travel for the disabled. The UK office (228 Borough High Street, London SE1 1JX; tel 071-403 5688; fax 071-378 1292) is unable to be of help to anyone bound for South America. Its associate in Mexico City, however, can be of more help. Contact Fernando Pérez at the Grupo Solidaridad para la Superación y El Trabajo, Congresco Villa Unión 3519, Col. Río Blanco, DF CP0780, Mexico City (tel 11-525 760-4873). The most useful source book is *Nothing Ventured: Disabled People Travel the World*, published by Harrap Columbus.

Business Travellers. The Department of Trade and Industry publishes a series of booklets called *Hints for Exporters*, which include limited useful facts, ranging from hours of business to import licence requirements. All South American countries except Uruguay are covered. The booklets are available by post from DTI Export Publications, PO Box 55, Stratford-upon-Avon, Warwicks CV37 9GE, price £5. For further information phone 0789-296212.

Electrical Equipment. You may wish to take a radio with you, and even a travel iron or hair dryer. Before you pack, make sure that they will work correctly on the South American electricity supply. In northern South America this is the same as in North America, i.e. 110 volts at 60 Hz. In Argentina, Uruguay, Chile and Brazil it corresponds to the European supply of around 240 volts at 50 Hz. Some equipment is switchable between these voltages and frequencies, but other items will not work correctly at the lower voltage, and those with motors will run too fast.

Power cuts, voltage drops and frequency fluctuations are regular occurrences, so think twice before plugging in sensitive equipment such as a portable computer. Most electrical sockets in the region accept plugs with two flat or round pins. Travel adaptors sold abroad should be able to cope with the sockets. Note that there is rarely an earth pin, and that the state of most electrical fittings is dreadful;

an alarming number of hotel rooms have bare live wires showing, even in the shower.

SOURCES OF INFORMATION

Tourist advice available outside South America is variable and usually limited: while the Brazilian tourist office can send large amounts of bumpf, from the Guyanan mission the most you can hope for is a list of hotels, restaurants and nightclubs in the capital. While the material is not geared to the budget traveller, a few pretty pictures might at least whet your appetite.

For information on the advisability of travelling to specific countries you can call the Foreign and Commonwealth Office travel advice department on 071-270 4120, or the State Department's Citizen's Emergency Center in the USA, on 202-647 5225. Both departments tend to be overcautious, but their advice should be noted, especially if you are planning to visit Peru, or if you have heard reports of recent political unrest.

NewsGuide International packs are an excellent source of up-to-date information. These are written for (and usually by) journalists, and include everything from how to get a film crew through customs to the fax numbers of political parties. They also describe in detail the latest political and economic developments, and are updated every year. All the South American countries except the Guianas are covered. The guides come in an A4 format and cost £10 each. Write to Park House, 207-211 The Vale, London W3 7QS or call 081-749 8855 (fax 081-749 7323).

If you get into difficulties, whether caused by theft, ill-health, running out of cash or involvement with crime, your first point of contact should be the consular department of your embassy, or the embassy of the country which represents you; addresses are given under *Help and Information* in each country chapter. The staff understand the way things work in South America, and have better lines of communication with home countries than you are likely to be able to organize. In a real emergency, the Consul will do his or her utmost to help.

Within each country the amount of help you can expect from tourist offices also varies. Most can provide a city map and brochures for the main towns (which sometimes you are expected to pay for), but you may need to pester the staff. Some offices are extraordinarily helpful: at the headquarters of the Peruvian tourist authority in Lima, for example, the staff painstakingly point out areas of danger. Many will book accommodation for you too. There are information desks in transport terminals in most cities. In small towns without tourist offices, travel agencies can usually help, though they may expect business in return. Otherwise go to the *Municipalidad* (town hall) which sometimes has maps. Tourist offices keep erratic opening hours in low season, and may not bother opening at all.

Organizations

Several organizations can provide additional information — from publishers of travel magazines to the promoters of alternative tourism.

Centre for the Advancement of Responsive Travel (CART). This is a Christian organization which aims to raise the standard of international tourism, and is involved in the research and promotion of alternative travel opportunities, particularly in the Third World. For information on CART send a stamped addressed envelope to 70 Dry Hill Park Road, Tonbridge, Kent TN10 3BX (tel: 0732-352757).

Globetrotters Club. A club for independent travellers for the exchange of information and experiences. A year's membership costs £9 for UK and Europe ($18 worldwide). It publishes a club newsletter called *Globe*, with frequently off-beat information on all parts of the world and recent news on border crossings, etc. Write to BCM/Roving, London WC1N 3XX.

Latin American Bureau. LAB is an independent, non-profit making organization, concerned with human rights and related social, political and economic issues in Latin America. Becoming a supporter (which costs £10 per year) entitles you to up-to-date information, discounts on books published by LAB, access to their library, invitations to events, regular mailings, etc. Through LAB you can also subscribe to *NACLA* (£15 per year), which is an English-language magazine on Latin America, published in the USA. Articles cover politics, economics, social affairs, culture, etc. For further information contact LAB at 1 Amwell Street, London EC1R (tel 071-278 2829).

South American Explorers Club. The SAEC is an excellent source of information among travellers to South America. Anyone can visit its offices in the USA, Peru and Ecuador, and consult its books, maps, etc. Staff give good advice about hiking, and have reports from travellers all over the region. You can usually hire camping gear too. By becoming a member ($30 per year) you are eligible to receive a quarterly journal, have access to up-to-date trip reports, and discounts on books. The address of their three offices are given below (postal address in brackets):

USA: 150 York Street, Denver (Box 18327, Denver, CO 80218; tel 303-320-0388).
Peru: Avenida Portugal 146, Breña, Lima (Casilla 3714, Lima 100); tel 31-4480.
Ecuador: Toledo 1254, La Floresta, Quito (Apto 21-431, Eloy Alfaro); tel 566-076.

Survival International. This is a worldwide movement which campaigns on behalf of tribal peoples, supporting their fight to protect their land and their customs. Tribes in Amazonia are the most serious cause for concern, but SI has taken actions in every South American country. Colonization, logging and mining are the main problems, but in some areas tourism plays a part too. For more information about Survival International, write to 310 Edgware Road, London W2 1DY (tel 071-723 5535; fax 071-723 4059) or 212 Decatur Place, NW Washington DC 20008 (tel 202-265-1077; fax 202-265-1297).

Tourism Concern. A network launched in 1989 to promote tourism that is more sensitive to the rights and interests of those living in the world's tourist areas. As well as tapping their sources of information on alternative types of tourism, travellers are encouraged to contact Tourism Concern with their own reports and ideas. For further information write to Froebel College, Roehampton Lane, London SW15 5PU.

TIME

Travelling around South America is fraught with chronological confusion. The continent covers five time zones, from easternmost Brazil (Greenwich Mean Time —2) to the Galapagos Islands (GMT —6). Not only do clocks change as you cross frontiers, they also alter as you move from one province to another in Argentina or Brazil. Some countries have summer and winter time, though in remote areas some communities don't bother changing their clocks. The only way to cope with this confusion is to check with the locals, but the following summary may help.

Argentina is GMT —3 throughout the year except in the provinces of Mendoza and Jujuy, which are GMT —4 in the southern winter (March to early October). In Uruguay and southeast Brazil (including Rio and São Paulo) the clocks are at GMT —2 from late October until late February, GMT —3 for the rest of the year. The Guianas adopt GMT —3 throughout the year. Bolivia and Venezuela adhere to GMT —4. Paraguay and Chile are on GMT —4 in the southern winter and GMT —3 in the southern summer, though in Paraguay this is interpreted as early October until late February and in Chile from mid-October until early March.

Colombia, Ecuador and Peru conveniently stick to GMT —5, except for the Galapagos Islands of Ecuador which are at GMT —6 throughout the year.

The chart below indicates local time in South America and worldwide:

	October-February (approx)				March-September (approx)			
UK	6am	noon	6pm	midn	6am	noon	6pm	midn
East Coast USA	1am	7am	1pm	7pm	1am	7am	1pm	7pm
West Coast USA	10pm	4am	10am	4pm	10pm	4am	10am	4pm
New Zealand	7pm	1am	7am	1pm	5pm	11pm	5am	11pm
Sydney, Australia	5pm	11pm	5am	11am	3pm	9pm	3am	9am
Uruguay, Southeast Brazil	4am	10am	4pm	10pm	2am	8am	2pm	8pm
Guianas, most of Argentina, NE Brazil	3am	9am	3pm	9pm	2am	8am	2pm	8pm
Paraguay, Chile	3am	9am	3pm	9pm	1am	7am	1pm	7pm
Bolivia, Venezuela	2am	8am	2pm	8pm	1am	7am	1pm	7pm
Colombia, Ecuador, Peru	1am	7am	1pm	7pm	midn	6am	noon	6pm
Galapagos	midn	6am	noon	6pm	11pm	5am	11am	5pm

Public Holidays — Moveable Feasts

	Ash Wednesday	Easter Sunday	Ascension	Whit Sunday
1992	March 4	April 19	May 28	June 7
1993	February 24	April 11	May 20	May 30
1994	February 16	April 3	May 12	May 22
1995	March 1	April 16	May 25	June 4
1996	February 21	April 7	May 16	May 26
1997	February 12	March 30	May 8	May 18
1998	February 25	April 12	May 21	May 31
1999	February 17	April 4	May 13	May 23
2000	March 8	April 23	June 1	June 11

Ash Wednesday is the first day of Lent. Holy Week is the seven days leading up to Easter Sunday, and is celebrated with gusto throughout South America. Ascension Day is also known as Holy Thursday. Trinity Sunday is a week after Whit Sunday; Corpus Cristi is the Thursday following Trinity Sunday, i.e. 11 days after Whit Sunday.

Venezuela

Margarita

Population: 20 million   **Capital: Caracas (population 5 million).**

A country with more Caribbean beaches than any other, yet which also has a 2km-high mountain on the edge of its capital, is a candidate for the oldest cliche in travel writing: 'a nation of contrasts'. In Venezuela, these phenomena occur within a few miles of each other, in a land which has the highest waterfall and the highest cable car, plus a Belgium-sized patch of virgin jungle and an arid desert. It also has a certain opulence and political stability. For many Westerners, Venezuela presents a diverse and acceptable face of Latin America.

Venezuela is the fifth-largest country in South America, the size of France and Germany combined, and seven times bigger than Florida. Its Caribbean coastline is 1,800 miles/2,800km long. It is divided into four main regions. The Venezuelan highlands constitute the end of the Andes. The highlands stretch northeast from the Colombian border, enfolding the Maracaibo lowlands. This area is known as the Sierra Nevada de Mérida. The mountain range broadens and flattens to the east. The Maracaibo lowlands are flat, hot and humid. The Llanos del Orinoco are plains spreading out from South America's third-longest river, the Orinoco, which is 1,345 miles/2,150km long. Finally, the Guayana highlands are south and east of the Orinoco. Much of this region is unexplored. Within it is the world's highest waterfall, the Angel Falls. Beyond the existing frontiers of Guayana, the Venezuelan government claims a large chunk of the independent state of Guyana. Although it is shown as a *Zona en reclamación* on maps of the country, there is no immediate prospect of Venezuela gaining control.

CLIMATE

To say that Venezuela is 'a country of eternal sunshine and permanent springtime temperatures', as the tourist literature claims, is pushing it a bit. As elsewhere in South America, temperature is a function of altitude. The hottest and wettest months are July, August and September; the wet season continues to early December. After Christmas the weather becomes significantly drier, and stays fine until early February. Caracas has peak temperatures in the mid-20s C/low 70s F.

HISTORY

Venezuela was one of the last areas in the world to be settled. The Amerindians who populated South America after walking across from Asia reached this part of the continent relatively late, perhaps only 30,000 years ago. Caribs and Arawaks settled but created no great civilizations. Columbus discovered Venezuela — specifically, the island of Margarita — on his third voyage, in 1498. The following year a conquistador named Alonso de Ojeda travelled inland as far as Lake Maracaibo. He saw Indian villages built on stilts and was reminded of Venice. He promptly called the area Venezuela, meaning 'little Venice'.

The country had no obvious resources and links to other parts of South America were poor. It was a backwater ruled more or less directly from Madrid for the next 300 years. Uprisings against the Spanish began, on the heels of the French Revolution, at the start of the 19th century. Simón Bolívar, who was born in Caracas in 1783, fought a brilliant campaign to gain independence for Venezuela and the rest of Spanish South America. At the height of his power he had the glorious title of General Simón José Antonio de la Santísima Trinidad Bolívar y Palacios.

Had the nation of Bolivia not snatched the name of Simón Bolívar, then Venezuela — the country of his birth — would have done. He achieved independence for Venezuela and the rest of northern South America in 1821. El Libertador, as he is affectionately known throughout Spanish-speaking South America, is revered nowhere so strongly as in his country of birth. His image is everywhere, from the coins and notes which bear his name to the statues in the main square of every town. Simón Bolívar is the national hero.

His great dream of a united, independent South America was realized for only a few years. His Gran Colombia took in Colombia, Ecuador, Peru, Panama and Bolivia as well as Venezuela. But it disintegrated just before Simón Bolívar died in Colombia, and Venezuela declared itself independent.

A series of political struggles took place between *caudillos* (leaders) of Venezuela. The names of the strongest rulers are still commemorated in street names: José Antonio Paéz (1830-46 and 1861-63), Antonio Gúzman Blanco (1870-88) and Juan Vicente Gómez (1908-35). Upon Gómez' death, a military regime took over and gradually moved the country towards democracy. The first democratic president was elected in 1945, but a coup three years later installed a harsh and corrupt leader — Marco Pérez Jiménez. A second coup in 1958 removed him and established democracy.

Venezuela has taken great pride in its free elections, but democracy was threatened by an attempted coup in February 1992. The current leader, Carlos Andrés Pérez, was deeply unpopular because of the economic problems besetting the country: a foreign debt of nearly $2,000 per person, falling living standards and rising prices. An army-led coup took place on 4 February 1992. It cost the lives of about 100 people before it was put down. Pérez imposed martial rule, which was not thought likely to increase his standing.

THE PEOPLE

Venezuela's population has rocketed from 5 million in 1960 to 20 million today. Three in five Venezuelans are mestizos; one in five is pure European; one in ten is black; only one in fifty is Indian. These numbers are swelled by thousands if illegal itinerant workers, from Colombia (where the economy is in a worse state), Cuba and elsewhere in the Caribbean.

Making Friends. The film *Gregory's Girl* ends with two love-starved youths attempting to hitch-hike from Scotland to Caracas, in the mistaken belief that women far outnumber men in Venezuela. Not only is the statistic wildly exaggerated, but the capital is not the best place in Venezuela in which to strike up a 'meaningful relationship'. Those hungry for a romantic liaison (either straight or gay) are much more likely to strike lucky at a resort on the Caribbean coast or on Margarita, and success is more probable with other foreigners than with Venezuelans.

British, US and Canadian citizens need no visa for a stay of up to 60 days if arriving by air. You should be given a tourist card (*tarjeta de ingreso*) either when checking in for your flight or on board the aircraft. At the same time you need to complete a customs form (*declaración de aduanas*), plus a health form if you arrive from somewhere heavily infected with cholera. The latter two documents are in Spanish only.

Travellers entering by land from Colombia or Brazil should obtain a visa in advance. In the UK, the Venezuelan consulate is at 56 Grafton Way, London WIP 5LB (tel 071-387 6727). It opens 9.30am-3pm from Monday to Friday. In addition, there are Venezuelan consulates in the main towns near borders. You need two photographs, $10 in cash and proof of your intended departure — a ticket out of somewhere in South America may be allowable, but the authorities may insist upon proof of departure from Venezuela. Travellers may also be asked for evidence of sufficient funds.

To extend your stay, take the tourist card, passport and supporting documents to the National Directory of Foreigners of the Ministry of Foreign Relations — Diex for short. Upon departure by air, tax of $11 is payable by foreigners. Getting out of Venezuela from Caracas airport requires a performance worthy of pre-revolutionary Russia. Get a form for $1 at the departure tax booth. Complete it (the box marked 'V' means Venezuelan, 'E' means foreign). Booth 2 stamps it and charges a further $10. At check-in, the clerk staples the departure form to your boarding card. As you proceed through security and migration, people tear sections from it until you have just a sliver left.

AIR

Venezuela is easy and cheap to reach. If you fly in with the Venezuelan international carrier Viasa or the Colombian airline Avianca, you can treat Caracas as a stopover en route to somewhere else in South America.

From Europe. Numerous European airlines, from KLM of Holland to TAP of Portugal, fly to Caracas. Consequently cheap fares are easy to find. The best deal

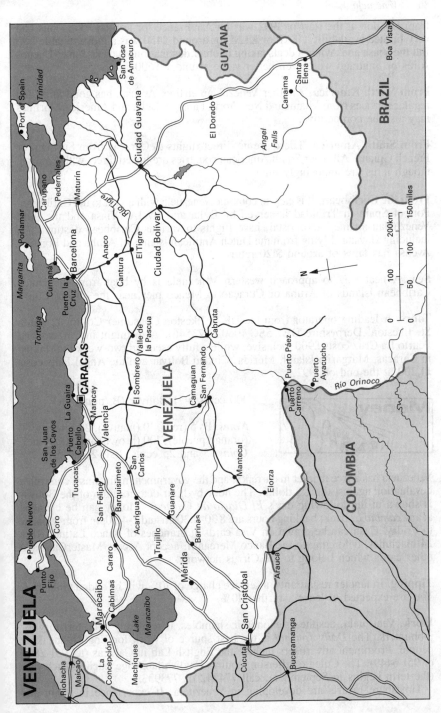

from London at the start of 1992 was on Air France for around £375. This had very limited availability; TAP or KLM for around £450 was a more reliable bet. But the Viasa and Avianca deals taking in other destinations such as Lima, Buenos Aires or Santiago were even better value at under £600.

From North America. Another Venezuelan airline, Avensa, has good fares and regular services from Miami and New York. Fares on Delta and American Airlines may also be competitive.

From South America. There are no direct flights to Caracas from Surinam or French Guiana. All other South American countries are linked direct with Caracas, though fares are annoyingly high.

From the Caribbean. It is easy to combine Venezuela with a visit to the Caribbean. Port of Spain in Trinidad is served by Delta and BWIA. Viasa and the third Venezuelan airline, Aeropostal, have flights to various Caribbean destinations, including Havana. Flying from the Dutch Antillean islands of Aruba and Bonaire, Avensa has fares of around $120 return.

Sea. A neat way to approach western Venezuela is by boat from the Dutch Caribbean islands of Aruba or Curaçao to Muaco pier near the city of Coro.

Tours. A leading operator from the UK is Ilkeston Consumer Co-op, 12 South St, Ilkeston, Derbyshire DE7 5SG (0602 323546). A fortnight in Caracas and Peurto La Cruz costs £900 inclusive, while a fully escorted two-week tour taking in Caracas, Margarita Island, Mérida, Ciudad Bolívar and the Angel Falls costs £1,200 at the end of 1992.

100 cents = 1 Bolívar (B, plural Bs)

Notes: Bs 5 (red), 10 (mauve), 20 (green), 50 (orange/purple), 100 (brown) and 500 (blue). *Coins:* 5 and 25 cents, Bs1, 2 and 5.

Venezuela has a free market in currency, and the government maintains a controlled devaluation against the US dollar. The hour-by-hour deterioration of the Bolívar is shown in the following day's *El Diario de Caracas.* Money can be changed at any *cambio* or bank; banking hours are 8.30-11.30am and 2-4.30pm from Monday to Friday. Cash can be drawn on Visa cards at branches of Banco Latino. Abra 24 machines, belonging to the Banco Mercantil, accept Access/MasterCard and other cards which belong to the Cirrus network.

Tipping. In fancier restaurants, a service charge of 10% will be added to the bill. You are expected to leave a further 10%.

Work. Venezuela, despite its economic shambles, is relatively good territory for jobhunters. The *Daily Journal* is the best source of work for English-speaking people. Prominent advertisers include the English Lab in Caracas (tel 951 2808 or 951 6449). The Colegio Jefferson requires English-language teachers each year (the term begins in September); call 774242 or 773933.

Timeshare resorts are developing in Venezuela. If experience in Spain and

Portugal is anything to go by, this will create opportunities for English-speaking canvassers: you accost passers-by at the beach, and are paid if they agree to visit the resort; you need not actually sell to make money.

Communications

The postal service, run by Ipostel, works more efficiently than most in South America. Aerograms are particularly good value. Every town, however small, has a *correos y telegrafos*. Faxes can be sent from larger post offices.

Telephone. Local time in Venezuela is GMT—4 throughout the year, i.e. an hour ahead of Eastern Standard Time.

Telecommunications are handled by CANTV, which has offices in most towns, as well as at airports. Unfortunately the service is a long way short of perfect. International connections take a long time to arrange and line quality can be poor. The best bet is to use a *Targeta Magnetica* (magnetic card) to call abroad. Plenty of these special telephones have been installed, but unfortunately the cards themselves are in short supply. Offices of CANTV, even though they may have these phones installed, will probably not possess any cards.

If you do track them down, cards are sold in multiples of Bs100. Before making a call you must have at least one minute's worth of credit left on your card. One good trick with phonecards is to dial *0* when you first get it, which allows you to encode a frequently dialled number on it; ** then dials it for you.

The international prefix is 00. Area codes within Venezuela are as follows:

Caracas 02	Coast 031	Barcelona 081	Ciudad Bolívar 085
Coro 068	Cumaná 093	Maracaibo 061	Mérida 074
Porlamar 095	Pto La Cruz 081	Puerto Ordaz 086	Valencia 041

Coin-operated payphones are rare, and can be used only for national calls. They take 0.25, 0.50 and B1 coins. A three-minute call to Europe costs $8. For the USA, the rate is $7, with lower charges for Florida. The USA Direct line is 800-11120.

MEDIA

Press. The two leading newspapers are *El Universal* and *El Nacional*. One of South America's few English-language newspapers is published in Caracas — the *Daily Journal*, mentioned above. It has good foreign coverage and some interesting features on life in Venezuela. Foreign newspapers and magazines are easily available in Caracas.

Radio. It is difficult to avoid loud, badly tuned music stations while travelling on the average *por puesto* minibus. Most adopt the music policy of HITS 1090, an AM station firmly rooted on the Prince — Stevie Wonder — Madonna axis. If you have a decent radio and aerial, you should be able to pick up transmissions from the English-speaking Caribbean.

Television. Venezuela has six main channels, though not all extend to the remotest parts of the country. Most show rubbish, both imported and home-made. Canal 4 has the best news programmes. Satellite TV is watched avidly, and is widely available in hotels. Much of it, including the all-news channel CNN, is in English.

Getting Around

The *Mapa de Carreteras* of Venezuela is widely available and is a good basic guide to the country; it has a street map of Caracas on the reverse.

Air. The two internal carriers are Avensa, whose principal aircraft is the Boeing 727 and Aeropostal, which flies DC9s and M-80s. Both are cheap and efficient. Each sells an air pass which enables the holder to roam Venezuela's flight routes at will. However, as standard domestic air fares are so cheap, buying each individual air ticket locally is probably a better bargain.

Bus. Venezuela has a good network of highways, and long-distance bus services are consequently good. Buses on the nine-hour journey between Caracas and Maracaibo, for example, operate every few minutes around the clock — the fare is around $12, with an extra $5 buying a ride on an ultra-luxurious bus.

Por Puesto. Shorter journeys are covered by a collection of vehicles operating under the general heading of *por puesto* — literally, 'by the place'. These are minibuses which run frequently on popular routes, charging fixed and low fares. It is not immediately apparent where they stop, and it is best to watch the locals. Many of the roads in Venezuela are so fast that there is no chance for them to stop at will. You pay the fare to the driver or his pal as you get off. Some por puestos are more luxurious and travel long distances in competition with the big buses.

DRIVING

In terms of road deaths, Venezuela is the most dangerous country in the world (the runners-up, perhaps surprisingly, are Portugal and New Zealand). This unfortunate record can be explained by the propensity of motorists to drive without lights after dark, to change lane and turn corners without indicating, and generally to drive in a macho and inconsiderate manner. Of course, Venezuela has no monopoly on these characteristics in South America. But the oil boom and subsequent decline means that Venezuela has a large supply of steadily deteriorating vehicles, plus extremely cheap fuel. It follows that you should think twice before renting a car or hitching a ride. Some speculate that the reason you pay the fare when getting off a *por puesto*, rather than at the start of the ride, is because of the high risk of an accident preventing you from completing your journey.

Hitch-hiking is an effective adjunct to the bus and *por puesto* service. Venezuela feels itself to be a cut above other South American countries, argue some, and accordingly its motorists take it upon themselves to help foreigners.

Eating and Drinking

You can eat as finely in Venezuela as in any other South American country. The nation has more than its fair share of fancy restaurants, and a good sprinkling of foreign cuisine — whether you wish to dine on French *nouvelle cuisine* or Peruvian *ceviche*, Caracas has a restaurant to suit you. Other centres, such as Margarita, Maracaibo and Mérida, have almost as good a selection.

The standard Venezuelan cuisine, however, is steak. Cattle are raised by the million on the Llanos, the plains of western Venezuela, and devoured by this nation of carnivores at cafés and restaurants in every town and village. The national dish

Crime and Safety

Venezuela has none of the problems of terrorism from which Colombia suffers, but that does not mean it is a wholly safe country. Violent crime has increased significantly in the 1990s, but it needs to be kept in proportion. Western visitors displaying ostentatious wealth in the backstreets of Caracas are asking for trouble, and accepting a lift in an unmarked taxi can be risky. Government statistics show that 80% of people live in poverty, and theft from Westerners is one way to try to get another square meal. It is essential to be on your guard. About three murders a day take place around the capital.

Carry identification at all times, as the security forces make spot checks. Be wary of supposed police who demand an on-the-spot fine for some imagined irregularity in your papers — insist that you go together to the police station if you suspect that they are tricksters.

Health and Hygiene

Urban areas of Venezuela are free from most nasty diseases, but in the country you should be protected against yellow fever. Precautions against malaria should be taken unless your stay is entirely at high altitude. The water supply in rural areas is probably impure, but in towns it should be safe.

Aids. The number of cases of the disease which have been officially reported in Venezuela is only one-quarter the proportion reported in the UK, and is much lower than the rate in the USA. This undoubtedly represents a considerable underestimate, and given the fearsome spread of the disease through Latin America (particularly in Brazil and French Guiana), it is likely that the rate of cases will increase sharply in the near future.

Help and Information

Tourist information is in the hands of Corpoturismo, whose head office is on the 35th floor of Torre Oeste at Parque Central in Caracas, tel 507 8800 or 507 8611. It produces a lot of high-quality material, but its branch offices are of limited help. Outside Venezuela, contact the airline Viasa for information.

Public Holidays

January 1	New Year
February/March	Carnival (Mardi Gras)
March/April	Holy Thursday, Good Friday
April 19	Declaration of Independence
May 1	Labour Day
June 24	Battle of Carabobo
June 29	Saints Peter and Paul
July 5	Independence Day
July 24	Simón Bolívar's Birthday
October 12	Columbus Day
November 1	All Saints' Day
December 24	Christmas Eve (afternoon only)
December 25	Christmas Day

CARACAS

Several South American capitals are in unusual locations: La Paz, nearly three miles high, or Brasilia, plonked in the middle of the Mato Grosso. But Caracas, sprinkled along a narrow cleft in a northeastern branch of the Andes, defies explanation. It is big, busy and arrogant — the rest of the country is described as 'the interior', even places on the seashore.

Many travellers make their first landfall in South America at Caracas airport. It can be a daunting experience, confirming all sorts of prejudices about the way life in the continent is conducted: the tourist office seems to be acting in league with chosen hotels, taxi drivers are colluding with each other, and hustlers are conspiring to fleece you. The whole atmosphere, particularly at dusk, is threatening and it is easy to imagine that every faintly dubious character — from the customs officials downwards — is sizing up your wallet, your baggage and your chances of fighting back.

Your paranoia may be enhanced by the sight of shacks built precariously from breezeblocks which cling to the roadside and hillsides as you approach the city. The breathless climb up from the airport after dark has skies like a planetarium; you disappear into a tunnel and burst through into the middle of a panorama of a million lights and five million lives. Assuming your failing courage gets you as far as stumbling across the uneven pavements of what was once South America's richest city, you may begin to understand that the vast majority of Venezuelans are friendly and welcoming.

The city is a bewildering mix of sloppy, sleazy, modern and post-modern; nowhere else in the world has so many impediments to movement, more elevated walkways which stop in mid-air, more urban motorways daring you to cross them. On the edges of the capital lie thousands of cardboard and corrugated iron shacks. Many people flock to Caracas in search of a better life, but rarely find anything other than unemployment and insanitation; not suprisingly, a large number turn to crime. Yet the city has all the trimmings associated with any rich western capital: broad boulevards, elegant buildings, chic shopping malls and leafy suburbs. Caracas is a cool, civilized city and a fascinating place to spend a few days. It is well-suited to help travellers adjust to the many challenges of Latin America, or pamper themselves after a journey through difficult terrain.

Caracas is 3,000 feet (920m) above sea level, surrounded by peaks reaching two miles (3,200m) high. The visitor has to adjust to the concept of being in a strictly linear city. Geography, in the form of a branch of the Andes on either side, has squeezed all the usual urban facilities and activities into a ribbon measuring thirteen miles by three (20 x 5km). Travelling to and fro along the ribbon is an easy matter on the city's metro. Most of Caracas is new, and parts of it are still shiny, having been built during the 1970s when oil revenues were high and seemingly unending. Once earnings began to fall, Caracas — like the rest of Venezuela — slumped into some disarray. The shacks and shanties which accompany both economic growth and decline chase up the hillsides, while some of their occupants hustle on the streets. But most Caraqueños are relatively well-to-do and sophisticated, and Caracas needs no more forboding than the usual caution that should be exercised anywhere in South America. Venezuela's capital is a big, bright and exciting city, with some excellent hikes and day-trips.

City Layout. The terrain has forced man's hand in Caracas. The northern edge of the city is delineated by the Avenida Boyaca, an autopista which skirts along the side of Mount Avila. The freeway peters out at the western end, but the trail is soon picked up by the Autopista Caracas-La Guaira, which forms the frontier between the city proper and some straggling suburbs. It exits through a tunnel, and turns smartly right to head down to the airport. To the south, the Autopista Francisco Fajardo runs the length of the city to the east before swinging sharp left and joining the Avenida Boyaca. Most places of interest are contained within these borders; the exceptions are the Armed Forces monument, the Botanic Gardens, the University and some luxury hotels.

While the map in this book puts the city centre in perspective, you are strongly recommended to buy the *Venezuela — Mapa de Carreteras*, which has a plan of Caracas on one side. Though anyone with less-than-perfect eyesight will find the street names impossible to read, it gives a good indication of the shape of the city.

The oldest part of the city can be identified easily by the use of the grid pattern; by the time Caracas' limited number of grand buildings came to be erected, the colonists preferred to build in an orderly fashion, and on flatter ground. The centre is the Plaza Bolívar. It forms the basis of the city's complex street numbering system. The main axes are the Avenidas Norte, Sur, Este and Oeste, running (predictably) north, south, east and west from the square. Using Plaza Bolívar as a starting point, each quadrant has a uniquely numbered set of streets. So the northeast quadrant, bounded by Avenidas Norte and Este, has horizontal streets numbered Este 1, Este 3, Este 5 and so on, plus vertical streets numbered Norte 1, 3, 5 etc. The northwest quadrant has Oeste 1, 3, 5 (continuations of the streets Este 1, 3, 5 etc.) but Norte 2, 4, 6 … The southwest has Oeste 2, 4, 6 and Sur 2, 4, 6 …; while the southeast has Este 2, 4, 6 and Sur 1, 3, 5. Most streets have names as well as numbers, but the name can change several times in the course of a street so it is safest to stick to numbers. Even so, thinking too hard about all this will give you a headache, so instead most Caraqueños use another means of defining addresses which either adds or removes a dimension of complexity, depending on how well you have got on with the explanation so far.

Each street corner in the city centre had a name, so that the intersection of Norte 8 and Oeste 5, for example, is known as Toro. This system allows you to pinpoint places instantly — but only once you have built up a complete mental map of the city

ARRIVAL AND DEPARTURE

Air. International services use La Maquieta airport, ten miles from the city centre in a direct line but 30 miles/50km by road. Built in the 1970s, the airport is showing signs of wear and tear. Arriving passengers are not segregated from departing ones, so something of a melée can develop when the airport is busy — especially late afternoon and early evening. Upon arrival, immigration is conducted in the middle of the arrival/departure hall. The Viasa transfer desk is nearby if you are connecting straight on to another international flight; you do not need to clear immigration, and if you do so mistakenly you have to pay the $10 airport tax.

Assuming you wish to enter Venezuela, procedures are usually cursory. The airport uses the red/green button system whereby you press a large button. It randomly selects red (which subjects you to a thorough search) or green (walk straight through). In practice, however, whether or not you are searched depends upon the mood of the customs official watching over you.

Emerging into the main hall is no exception to the rule that any Westerner arriving at an unfamiliar airport is fair game for every tout and hustler. Change money, then go out of the door and bear right for the bus into Caracas — the blue and white one. It operates to Parque Central, but you are advised to get off at the Gato Negro

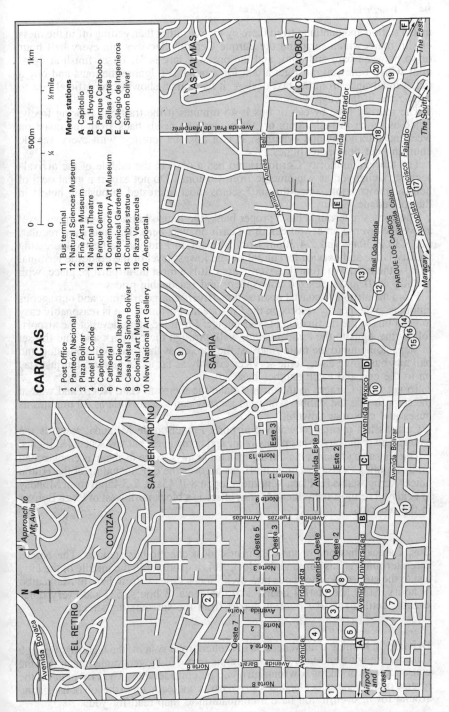

CARACAS

		Metro stations
1 Post Office	11 Bus terminal	A Capitolio
2 Panteón Nacional	12 Natural Sciences Museum	B La Hoyada
3 Plaza Bolívar	13 Fine Arts Museum	C Parque Carabobo
4 Hotel El Conde	14 National Theatre	D Bellas Artes
5 Capitolio	15 Parque Central	E Colegio de Ingenieros
6 Cathedral	16 Contemporary Art Museum	F Simon Bolívar
7 Plaza Diego Ibarra	17 Botanical Gardens	
8 Casa Natal Simon Bolívar	18 Columbus statue	
9 Colonial Art Museum	19 Plaza Venezuela	
10 New National Art Gallery	20 Aeropostal	

metro station and continue from there by metro, rather than getting off in the mess of slip roads which surround the Parque Central. Services run every half-hour or so between 6am and 8pm, and the one-way fare is $1. Buses finish at 8pm, after which time you must get a taxi for around $10. Ignore the touts and buy a ticket in advance from the taxi desk — it has a map showing the official fare to each zone in the city.

The journey time by cab or bus is 45 minutes if the traffic is flowing freely, twice as much in rush hours or when everyone heads back from the coast on weekend afternoons and evenings. It is a noxious journey, with every vehicle churning out poisonous fumes.

The tourism authority Corpoturismo has a desk in the middle of the arrivals section, facing you as you emerge from Customs. Do not expect a great deal of help or information, since the staff seems most interested in pushing hotels in the immediate vicinity.

The domestic terminal has a proper bank, the Banco Latino, on the upper level above the Avensa area; you can draw cash on Visa here. The hours are regular, i.e. 8.30-11.30am and 2-4.30pm from Monday to Friday. The best-value eating facility is the self-service restaurant on the lowest level of the domestic terminal — take the lift down from the Avensa area. It is a most un-airportlike place, with friendly staff and a relaxed atmosphere and reasonable prices.

From the airport to coastal resorts: taxi drivers charge arbitrary and outrageous amounts to the nearby resorts on the Caribbean. Fortunately it is reasonably easy to get a bus to the destination of your choice. From the upper level of the airport, follow the signs to the *estaciamento*, walk through the car park and find the set of steps going up to the main road. At the top, cross the road to the bus stop and hail any bus going east. Some services go only as far as La Guaira, but just stay on to the end and catch another bus.

To get from Caracas to the airport, take the metro to Gato Negro and wait at the stop outside the station. The road journey can take as little as 30 minutes as buses and cars roar downhill.

Caracas has a small downtown airport, Francisco de Miranda, towards the eastern end of the city. It has plenty of air taxi companies, but few scheduled flights.

The Viasa headquarters in the city is hard to miss, since its name is emblazoned on its building. Viasa has branch offices all over the city, including at the Hilton hotel. Aeropostal is on Plaza Venezuela, open 8-11.45am, 2-5.45pm from Monday to Friday. The most convenient Avensa office is a block northwest of Plaza Bolívar in the old city.

Bus. Caracas has one of the continent's most chaotic bus stations. The Nuevo Circo terminal is busy around the clock. It is a quadrant in the middle of the city, just to the east of the enormous new arch. Services leave from here to Maracaibo (9 hours, $12), Mérida (12 hours, $15), Valencia (3 hours, $3) and every other sizeable settlement. *Por puestos* depart from the surrounding streets.

Driving. In keeping with Venezuela's excellent road system, the highways through Caracas are wide and fast. The constraints imposed by geography mean that the consequences of taking a wrong turn can be considerable. The city plan on the reverse of the Venezuela *Mapa de Carreteras* is not really up to the job of navigating around town, even if you have a companion to map-read for you.

CITY TRANSPORT

Metro. Caracas has a good underground railway, with two lines. The first runs the length of the valley, east to west, passing through Capitolio (the station for the centre of the old city), Sabana Grande, for the modern commercial centre, and all points between. The other starts at Capitolio and runs southwest. Most visitors use only the first. Stations are marked with a big, bright M. Trains run every few minutes from 5am to 11pm. The system is clean, safe and fast — in ten minutes you can cover the three miles/5km across to Chacaíto at the eastern end of the city centre.

Fares depend on distance, and range from $0.15 to $0.30. You can buy tickets from machines *(casetas)* if you have the correct change, but the queues for these are almost as long as those for the human ticket sellers. Note that large pieces of luggage are barred from the metro — you would probably get away with a rucksack.

Some bus services connect up with the metro and use through tickets. These Metrobus tickets can only be bought from bus drivers or from manned kiosks in metro stations.

Bus. All other buses are ramshackle and cost about $0.10 per ride. No map of Caracas' maze of routes exists. Most buses run east-west along the main avenues, though some go north-south. The visitor has no chance of comprehending the system of routes, so most people adopt the habit of boarding any bus heading in the right direction and get off when it deviates from the required route.

Taxi. The city has two types: the large, flashy American saloon of the kind that lurks outside the airport, and the smaller Japanese vehicles that clatter around the city. The latter are, unsurprisingly, much cheaper. For any journey you should negotiate the price in advance. Expect to pay $1 for a short journey within the city, $3 for a ride along its length. Fares increase after dark. To summon a cab by telephone, dial Teletaxi on 752 9122 or Monil Enlace on 573 4533.

ACCOMMODATION

Caracas has its fair share of rooms at rock-bottom rates, but it also has some slightly more expensive hotels which are central, comfortable and excellent value. For seeing Caracas' Sights, staying in the old city around El Silencio is the best plan. The Plaza Catedral is optimal in terms of security, comfort and price; it is perfectly situated on the northeast corner of Plaza Bolívar (tel 563 7022). El Conde — on the esquina El Conde, at the corner of Sur 6 and Oeste 6 — is a block west. It describes itself as 'más centrico de Caracas', a title hard to dispute. It is also an excellent mid-range hotel. Cheaper places congregate around Capitalio metro station: the Hotel Junín (tel 418 0031) is the best, costing $20 for two.

If you need to stay in a top-class place, the best is probably the Hilton: Avenida México, west of Parque Los Caobos, visible from everywhere in the city.

EATING AND DRINKING

On Sunday evenings it is sometimes difficult to find the ideal venue, but at virtually any other time you are spoilt for choice. Anywhere within the zone shown on the main city map, you can find good cafés, restaurants and bars charging reasonable prices for tasty food and drink. The following suggestions are popular with locals and are in the Sabana Grande/Chacaíto area:

Parillada Argentina, on Avenida Casanova (just south of the main pedestrian precinct), has a spectacular Parilla Especial — all sorts of grilled innards, plus chops and steaks. Onassis Grill, Avenida Casanova at Calle Baldo — some of the best steaks in town. Cervecería Lindo Mar, at the north end of Avenida Pichincha, close to Chacaíto metro station. It is a bit rough but has live music.

You may be tempted by advertisements for the happy hour at the Anauco Bar Panorama (5.30-7pm, Monday to Friday), but don't expect a terrific view; this bar is actually on the ground floor of the Hilton complex.

EXPLORING

The best panorama of the city is from the peak of Avila. Details of how to reach it are given below. Views which are rather less ambitious but considerably easier to achieve can be had from the top-floor bar of the Caracas Hilton, close to Bellas Artes subway station. The third panorama is from the hill of El Calvario, just west of the old city and close to Plaza Miranda. Whichever viewpoint you choose, you're likely to be startled at how new most of the city seems to be, built within the last forty years of the 20th century.

For the purposes of sightseeing, Caracas falls into three parts. The first, in the west, is the historic core — Simón Bolívar territory. The second is the Parque Central, as unlike the usual Latin American Parque Central as it is possible to get. The third is Sabana Grande, the ultimate in boulevard life.

Old Caracas. Begin the Simón Bolívar trail at the beginning. His Casa Natal, where he was born on 24 July 1783, is most out-of-place amid the office blocks. It is on Plaza San Jacinto, one block east and half a block south of the main square — unsurprisingly, Plaza Bolívar — and two doors down from the huge Banco Industrial Venezuelano. Not only is the Casa Natal interesting because of its connection with the independence hero, it also gives a good impression of how life was 200 years ago in this backwater of the Spanish empire. The Casa Natal opens 10am-noon and 2-4pm daily except Mondays. Next door is the Museo Bolivariano, dedicated to chronicling the deeds of *El Libertador*.

Go south, back past the Casa Natal, and turn right. Continue for two blocks to the church of San Francisco, the loveliest in Caracas. Directly opposite is El Capitolio, which looks far less grand than it once did because of its diminution relative to the other buildings of Caracas. It was built in 1872, and its purpose is mostly ceremonial. You can get in (free) if you show your passport to the guards on the gate. The main place of interest in the complex is the Salon Elliptico, a sumptuous room decorated with paintings showing heroic events in Venezuela's history.

You are now at the Plaza Bolívar, dominated by a statue of the city's favourite son, who presides over it on horseback. Although the square is choked with fumes and prone to lowlife, it is a pleasant enough place at dusk when a certain amount of promenading takes place. On its east side is the cathedral — rather uninspiring — and the idiosyncratic Museo Sacro de Caracas. This old monastery, with gently crumbling cloisters, houses a cartoon history of Caracas and hosts concerts. It opens 10am-6pm daily except Monday.

Go north, passing the cathedral, for six ugly blocks until you reach the Panteón Nacional. It began life as Holy Trinity church, but was destroyed by an earthquake in 1812. It was rebuilt, and in 1874 coverted to the Panteón de los Próceres — Pantheon of the Leaders. Simón Bolívar's remains, having travelled from a farmhouse outside Santa Marta in Colombia via several temporary places of rest, made (probably) their final journey from Caracas cathedral to here in 1876. It is thus a place of reverence for many South Americans, despite its bleak inner-city location. It opens 10am-noon and 3-5pm daily except Mondays.

Parque Central. Passing the dramatic new symbolic arch, which gives Caracas the sort of grand lines that Paris enjoys, you encounter a statue of Simón Bolívar striding off down the avenue named after him. It leads to the Parque Central complex.

Caracas seems to want to put everything in its proper place. Accordingly, a Zona Cultural has been created in the middle of the city to compartmentalize artistic life. Caracas has one of South America's best galleries — the Museo de Arte Contemporaneo Sofia Imber (tel 573 7289) in an imaginative structure in the Parque Central complex. As well as a bold permanent collection, the gallery mounts imaginative exhibitions. The outdoor sculpture merges with the rest of the complex, and even has signs in braille. It also has a rather ritzy restaurant, the Café del Museo, with good coffee and cakes. On the way out you see a spectacular montage of Christ and Caracas. You emerge two levels below the one you entered at; turn right to find two well-stocked shops associated with the museum.

A new national art gallery is under construction. When finished, it should rival the Contemporary Art museum for style.

The Museo de los Niños in the Parque Central complex is open 9am-noon and 2-5pm, but not on Mondays or Tuesdays. It can be difficult to get in at weekends, such are the queues.

The setting of the Science Museum is perhaps more striking than the collection, which is mostly of of local birds and Amazonian animals. The Museo de Bellas Artes is across the circle from the Science Museum, though its entrance is a little further east — look for the big MBA sign. The gallery will not detain you for long, though the Cubist and Egyptian collections are interesting.

Each Sunday, vendors set up stalls selling books, crafts and chicha (rough corn liquor). Sunday is the best day to visit the park, to see the youths clambering all over the fountains and the impromptu musical performances. Sadly the boundaries of the park are tangles of freeways.

Sabana Grande. No-one goes sightseeing here. But the long shopping street/pedestrian precinct is busy and attractive, with plenty of boulevard life. Old men playing chess on oversized chess sets mingle with diligent shoppers and trendy poseurs.

In addition to these places, it is well worth heading south to the Botanical Gardens, close to the university. It involves a treacherous trip across a freeway or two, so take a taxi. The National Military Monument, further south still, is a treat of heroic architecture.

For someting altogether more indulgent, would-be swimmers and sunbathers can find themselves a spot by the pool at the Hilton Hotel, but beware — during the afternoon most of the sun is blotted out by surrounding skyscrapers.

Avila. One of the best day-trips in South America is the ascent of Avila, the mountain that dominates Caracas. In four or five hours a moderately fit person can walk up from the city's level of 3,000ft/920m to the peak of Avila, about 7,000ft/2,000m above sea level. You can walk all the way along a well-worn track, though if you are feeling adventurous you can descend by a different route.

Despite being attainable by most people, the ascent is not a gentle country stroll and some preparation needs to be made. Take plenty of fluid — but *not* alcohol, which is forbidden in the park. Take at least two litres of water or fruit juice per person. Energy-giving snacks, or lots of fruit, is strongly recommended.

Start the climb as early in the day as possible. Six in the morning is ideal, since this is when the park opens. The entrance is just beyond the freeway which skirts the north of Caracas — take a taxi there to conserve your energy. Visitors are required to register and pay a small fee. Luggage is searched to detect alcohol.

The walk itself is not too much of an adventure, since you share a track with motor vehicles — if your legs give out, you can hitch a ride to the top. Water is available at intervals from standpipes, but these should not be relied upon. As you near the summit, the road starts to run along a ridge, presenting splendid views across the city on one side and the Caribbean on the other. This memorable panorama continues to the hotel at the top, which has minimal facilities and the defunct cable car.

You can return the same way, but a network of paths leads directly down from the hotel; the risk of getting lost is not too large, since you can see the city all the way down.

ENTERTAINMENT

Music and Theatre. The Ateneo de Caracas is a fine auditorium at Plaza Morelos in Los Caobos (tel 573 7812). A wide variety of concerts can be heard, ranging from classical to country music, and every couple of weeks a play is staged, often in the original language, which frequently is English — Tennessee Williams or William Shakespeare.

One of the world's most impressive modern theatres is the Teatro Teresa Carreño. It resembles London's Royal National Theatre in terms of its materials — 'the same off-grey concrete that plagued Britain in the 1970s', is one description. But the architect's use of space is far more striking. Sculptures are strewn casually around outside. Other venues include the following:

Teatro Las Palmas — Avenida Las Palmas at Avenida Libertador.

Teatro Chacaíto (two auditoria) — Centro Comercial, Chacaíto.

La Sede — Sótano Caracas level 1, Torre Este, Parque Central.

More experimental work can be seen at the Edificio San Martín in the Parque Central and at the Teatro Alberto de Paz y Mateos.

Tickets for most formal events are sold through Tickexpress on 206 2951. Each November, a Festival Latinamericano de Musica takes place, mostly at the Teatro Teresa Carreño.

Racing. The Hipódromo de La Rinconada is the largest of Caracas' three courses. Completed in 1959, it was modelled on New York's Belmont Park track, and is big and busy on race days.

SHOPPING

Several supermarkets open on Sundays, including the Cada store in the office complex at the Parque Central (8am-6pm on Sundays). El Multitienda, in shop

ICB-44 on the Bolívar Level of the Parque Central complex, has some English-language books and also maps. Steels's Book Store (tel 951 1828) on Calle Baruta in Sabana Grande, next to Banco Venezuela, has English-language books and magazines. To buy and sell secondhand books, go to the German Protestant Church Bookshop, Avenida 4, Altamira. Call 336 504 to check opening times, which at the start of 1992 were 9-11am on Wednesdays, 9am-noon on Saturdays.

HELP AND INFORMATION

Tourist information: the Corpoturismo head office is on the 35th floor of Torre Oeste at Parque Central, tel 507 8800 or 507 8611.

Consulates: UK — 3rd floor, Torre Las Mercedes, Avenida La Estancia tel 751 1022; fax 923 292. The British Council Library (for books and newspapers) is at Torre La Noria, Las Mercedes (tel 915 222). Caracas has numerous expatriate groups, including the Venezuelan Irish Association (77 30 97).

USA — corner of Avenidas Francisco de Miranda and Principal (284 6111), close to La Floresta metro station.

Canada — 7th floor, Torre Europa, Avenida Francisco de Miranda (951 6166).

Australia — 20th floor, Torre C, Centro Plaza, Los Palos Grandes (261 8871).

Argentina — Mezzanine, Torre Capriles, Plaza Venezuela (781 1376).

Bolivia — Avenida Luís Roche, transversal 6 (32 99 74).

Brazil — 6th floor, Centro Gerencial Mohedano, Calle Los Chaguaramos, La Castellana district (261 4481).

Colombia — Quarta 53, Avenida Luís Roche between transversales 6 and 7.

Ecuador — office 130-132, Torre Oeste, Centro Andrés Bello, Avenida Andrés Bello (781 3180).

Guyana — corner of Avenida Libertador and 2 Calle, La Línea, Quarta Roraima, La Florida (284 0846).

Paraguay — office 31, Edificio Siclar, corner of Avenida Libertador and Las Acacias (72 19 87).

Peru — office 71-72, Torre Este, Centro Andrés Bello, Avenida Andrés Bello, Maripérez (781 8013).

Uruguay — Edificio Exa, Avenida Libertador, Urbanación El Rosal (31 31 51).

Post Office: corner of Oeste 1 and Norte 6, two blocks northwest of Plaza Bolívar.

DAY TRIPS FROM CARACAS

El Hatillo. Caracas was the first Venezuelan city to proclaim independence, which it did in 1810. It was followed shortly afterwards by this village, which today narrowly escapes being caught in the Caracas conurbation. El Hatillo was established on 12 June 1784 by Bishop Mariano Martí, and has survived since then remarkably immune from the changes which have affected and afflicted Caracas. Its woodland surroundings isolate it from the noise of the city and have preserved its character. The word 'twee' describes it well. Almost every house lining its steep streets is pastel-painted, and fancy shops and expensive cafés cash in on its extravagant image.

Colonia Tovar. A good one-day round trip can be made into the mountains immediately west of Caracas, taking in this unusual German colony. Board a bus from Calle Sur 9, immediately south of the Nuevo Circo bus station, outside El Mesón del Viajero restaurant. You can go direct to Colonia Tovar, or stop off en route at the pleasant market town of El Junquito — El Junko to the locals; here you can buy high-altitude fruit. It takes 30 minutes by bus to El Junquito, another hour to Colonia Tovar. On the approach not only does the terrain look Alpine, the dwellings do too. A German colony settled here in the 19th century, and imported Alpine building styles. Consequently you could be in Bavaria, an impression reinforced by the *lederhosen* and *bierkellers*. Many of the townsfolk are still pale-skinned, and everything has a Germanic flavour.

You can continue south to La Victoria only by car or hitching, but this journey is a beautiful one through the highlands. The descent to La Victoria is a let-down, as is the town itself, but from here you should be able to pick up a bus back to Caracas or onwards to Valencia.

THE COAST NEAR CARACAS

The international airport on the coast closest to Caracas rather blights the area, but if you can ignore the aircraft noise the coastline is not without its charms: everything from an old port which is graceful in parts to a resort stuffed with luxury hotels and rich visitors. A multi-lane highway runs along the coast, making access easy but being something of an eyesore and a noisy impediment to reaching the beach.

Access from Caracas is easy; por puestos run from Gato Negro metro station to Macuto; note that these stop short of the main resort area of Macuto. You will need to transfer to a por puesto showing 'Caribe', a reference to the Meliá Caribe hotel. The main transport along the coast is a busy por puesto route between Caribe and Catia del Mar. This passes the airport, allowing cheap and easy access. The following survey begins just west of the airport, and runs east to the ritzy surroundings of Macuto.

Catia La Mar. This beach is closest to both Caracas and to the airport, and it shows. It is busy and dirty, and the noise of aircraft from the airport can be deafening. If you have a few hours to spare between flights, you might want to take a taxi here. Alternatively those with an early morning flight may wish to stay at one of the cheap (and grotty) hotels in Catia.

La Guaira. Venezuela's largest port is not as clumsy and commercialized as you might expect. The workings are concealed from the road by high hoardings, but become visible from the hillsides. The houses and shops which are dotted over the hills are pretty in parts; in particular, Calle Bolívar is attractive and colonial.

Macuto. This is the liveliest resort on the coast, full of fast-food joints and poseurs in sunglasses. The Sheraton Macuto has a good beach which foreigners can use. Bands play most evenings at the poolside bar; no admission is charged, but drinks are commensurately expensive. The crowd is a mix of locals and foreigners (many of them flight crew stopping over) and a reasonably good time is had by most.

NORTHEAST VENEZUELA

This section covers the coast east of Caracas as far as the frontier with Guyana, and includes the island of Margarita.

BARCELONA

On New Year's Day 1671 two small settlements agreed to merge and create the city of Barcelona. Almost 150 years later, Simon Bolívar decided to keep his troops supplied using this Caribbean port, and in 1816 he ordered the old Franciscan hospice, Casa Fuerte, to be fortified so that the city could be defended. The work was done in vain and in February 1817 the fort was taken by Royalists who then set about cold-bloodedly killing 1,600 people. The resulting ruins have not been cleared or rebuilt and have been declared a national monument. The site is open daily 8am-noon and 3-6pm.

If you are more fascinated by the remains of saints, then the Catedral San Cristóbal is the place to go — it is the home of the bones of an impressive array: Severino, Eustaquio, Facundo, Pedro Alcatara, Pacifico, Anastasio, Pascual Bailon and Celestino. Competing for your interest is the Museum of Tradition, in the fourth house to be built in Valencia, on Calle Juncal. Among its 400 items is a sign warning you not to lean on lamp posts after the three long whistles have been blown at six o'clock, in case you are electrocuted. The museum is open 8am-noon and 3-6pm daily.

Arrival and Departure. Barcelona airport is 5 miles/8km southwest of the city, a little to the west of Route 9 (tel 77 45 70). There are six connections a day with Caracas, as well as less frequent flights to other Venezuelan cities.

Barcelona's Terminal de Pasajeros is next door to the free market on Avenida San Carlos, one block south of Fuerzas Armadas. The journey to Caracas should take $4\frac{1}{2}$-6 hours, depending on whether you take the *por puesto* or the ordinary bus.

Accommodation. Hotel Barcelona (Avenida 5 de Julio, at the corner of Calle Bolívar; tel 77 10 65), near the cathedral, has clean pleasant and cheap rooms. Less central (best reached by bus) but also recommended is the Hotel Neveri (corner of Avenidas Fuerzas Armadas and Miranda; tel 77 23 76).

Eating and Drinking. The dining room on the sixth floor of the Hotel Barcelona has fine views, providing you don't sit down — when the views will be of your fellow diners. The food is plain but resonably priced. An altogether more interesting place to eat (though some may be put off their food) is the Cockfighting Ring, or Complejo Turístico Los Gallos. It has an open-air restaurant as well as a more formal enclosed one; both serve good meals. The Complejo is between the first and second bridges on Avenida Cajigal (tel 77 10 65). For fast food go to the soda fountain next door to the Pryca supermarket, on the east bank of the Neveri between the second and third bridges.

On the road to Puerto la Cruz you pass the El Morro Tourist Complex. Two hundred and fifty million dollars have been earmarked to develop this area into a marina and resort capable accommodating a horrifying 60,000 tourists.

PUERTO LA CRUZ

Compared with tourist-rich Porlamar on the island of Margarita, with its 'Cheers' bars, four-star hotels and hand-swept beaches, Puerto La Cruz comes as something of a relief: a resort visited and populated mainly by Venezuelans.

The main street is Paseo Colón: two miles of colourful palm-fringed seafront boasting the town's best hotels, shops and restaurants.

Although there is a beach running the length of Paseo Colón, much of it is a little moth-eaten and not much used by the locals. The Lecherias beaches, by the Doral Beach Hotel (Avenida Americo Vespucio), are acceptable however. But better still are the fine Arapito and even finer Colorada beaches twenty minutes' drive from town. These can be reached by bus or by taxi. But you may find it easy and cheap to engage a driver to take you. Once there, he'll doze in the back of the vehicle until you want to drive back. You can also try freshwater swimming by a 100-feet-high waterfall amidst jungle vegetation at La Sirena Park, five miles/8km from town (may be closed Mondays).

If swimming in the pool of a four-star hotel is more to your taste, the Melia (tel 691311), at one end of the Paseo Colón, has a huge pool with views over the Caribbean and a bar alongside. The hotel charges around $110 per night for a double room, plus tax of 10%, excluding breakfast. But even non-residents should find it easy to saunter in, pick up a towel by the pool and enjoy the facilities with no questions asked.

To fix up a game of golf, telephone Morris Fuentes (23816) who lives at Calle 13, Casa 12, Urbanización Guaraguao. He'll arrange for you to enjoy hospitality at the smart Puerto La Cruz Country Club: a package involving caddies, club hire, snacks, cold drinks and a dip in the pool will prove enjoyable if not inexpensive. The Fuentes family can also offer advice on local amenities, drivers, restaurants, nightclubs etc.

Puerto La Cruz has plenty of hotels, but advance booking is recommended particularly during the carnival in mid-February. The Riviera (tel 22268) on Paseo Colón is a medium-grade, three-star establishment where a pleasant room with a view over the sea can be had for around $40. The town has no shortage of nightlife. It ranges from the ubiquitous discotheques to piano bars, hotel facilities and South American-style nightspots like the excellent La Parranda (Calle Carabobo) where you can dance to energetic local salsa bands.

Carnival in mid-February is the liveliest time at Puerto La Cruz, when the town is awash with people, colour, Polar beer and music. Thousands take to the streets to follow a processions of floats. The evening promenade along the Paseo Colón is busier, friendlier, later and more colourful than ever.

CUMANA

At the mouth of the Río Manzanores, Cumaná was one of the first Spanish settlements in South America. It now has a population of around 180,000. Despite numerous earthquakes over the years, many fine buildings survive from the sixteenth century. The Convento de San Francisco is home to another of South America's firsts — the first school. Situated a little behind the city, but dominating it, is the Castillo de San Antonio de la Eminencia: sunset is the best time to enjoy the view that takes in Cumaná, the Caribbean, the Gulf of Cariaco and the Araya Peninsula.

Arrival and Departure. There is a small airport alongside Avenida Universidad, between the Balneario Los Uveros and Plaza del Indio; flights run daily to Caracas and Porlamar.

The bus terminal is on Avenida Las Palomas, just off Avenida Perimetral. Most express buses to Caracas leave late at night. Buy tickets in advance if possible since seats fill quickly.

Accommodation. The hotels cluster around the seafront. Among the smartest places is Hotel Los Bordones (tel 24-736/426), set in the coconut groves of a hacienda. You don't have to stay there in order to take advantage of its large swimming pool. More modest is the Hotel Savoia (Avenida Perimetral; tel 22-206/7), halfway between Plaza del Indio and the Cada supermarket. It doesn't serve breakfast, but it is cheap and there is a handy pizzeria next door. Also recommended is the Gauiqueri (Avenida Bermúdez; tel 24-230), though the places on Calle Sucre (across the river near Plaza Ayacucho) are cheaper, e.g. the Astoria.

Eating and Drinking. Cumaná is not renowned for its restaurants. To sit in the open air and hear the sea lap whilst you eat your fish, try the Bar-Restaurant Los Montones (Avenida Universidad, a ten-minute walk west of the UDO pylon). At El Mar (Avenida Perimetal, near the Route 9 turn-off) you must be content with just good fish.

MARGARITA ISLAND

The Venezuelan tourism authorities curse their misfortune in being unable to lay claim to tropical paradise islands in the Caribbean. Almost every nearby isle from Aruba to Trinidad has been claimed by other countries. All that Venezuela has is Margarita. This twin-peaked haven is ideal for those who suspect that Caribbean islands are way too expensive. It offers the style of other islands at considerably lower cost than elsewhere. Margarita is actually two separate islands, joined by an umbilical of sand. When Columbus landed in 1498, the natives wore bracelets and necklaces dotted with pearls; hence the island's name, Margarita, meaning pearl. Try to visit at Mardi Gras (see page 616 for dates), when the celebrations transcend the routine quest for vacationers' cash.

Any Caribbean island with direct flight links to New York, Paris and London is bound to be a little tainted by tourism. The main town, Porlamar, is barely distinguishable from the high-rise, air-conditioned resorts elsewhere on the Caribbean. To cater with present and future holidaymakers, parts of the island seem to be in a perpetual frenzy of building. If the idea of a shoreline peppered with high-rise development or the tower cranes which presage it appals you, then stay on the mainland.

For those who choose to stay, Margarita has a great deal to offer in a superficial sort of way, notably some splendid beaches. The island has 100 miles/160km of coastline, much of it clean, sandy and inviting. Some of the swimming can be unsafe — check with locals before venturing too far out. The best beaches are in the northeast and on the southern tip of the island.

Most visitors fly into the international airport of Porlamar in the southeast of the island. Its name is misleading, since it is actually 8 miles/13km from the town. The small international building is chaotic when wide-bodied aircraft arrive.

Boats and hydrofoils operate to Punta del Piedra (tel 98148) on Margarita from the mainland at Puerto La Cruz (tel 660389) and Cumaná (tel 661462). Schedules and fares are as follows:

Depart Puerto La Cruz at 4am, 7am, noon, 4pm, 7pm, midnight.
Depart Punta de Piedra at 7am, 10am, noon, 6pm, 10pm, midnight. The fare on this route is $5 first class, $4 second.
Depart Cumaná at 7am and 4pm; depart Punta de Piedra at 11am and 8pm, fare $3.

Watch your bags as you wait to board the vessels — thefts are common.

In Porlamar itself, you can choose from ritzy five-star hotels or more humble dwellings such as El Paraíso — dirt cheap, with standards to match. Eat out is more expensive than on the mainland, and every third enterprise seems to be a pizzeria.

Further Afield. Although Margarita beyond Porlamar might not quite match Corpoturismo's description of 'an abundance of charming villages where dedicated artisans weave', as the tourist literature proclaims, the island is pleasant enough. Hiring a car or four-wheel-drive jeep for a few days will help you to explore the island (and look like a tourist). Driving from the east of the island to the west takes an hour, from north to south half an hour.

Outside Porlamar, accommodation is limited, but some small hotels which lack the upmarket facilities of Porlamar can be remarkably cheap. The town of Juangriego, set on a sandy bay in the north of the island, is worth a visit. It has fine fish restaurants and a castle perched on top of a hill overlooking the bay. The island's capital, Asunción, is a pretty colonial town where life runs at a much slower pace than on the coast. The resort of Pampatar is another good antidote to Porlamar — ask for a room at Antonio's bar on the seafront, and enjoy good food, drink and company.

A must on a trip around the island is La Restinga, a nature reserve where you can hire a boat through the mangrove swamps, see wild birds and enjoy another fine, sandy beach with excellent swimming.

Help and Information. Although each municipality on Margarita has its own post office, most other services are concentrated in Porlamar.
Post Office: corner of Boulevard Guevara and Calle San Nicolas.
Telephone Office (CANTV): Calle Velásquez between Calles Gómez and Fraternidad.

CIUDAD BOLIVAR

Fever was a big problem when Angostura, as this city used to be known, was first settled. A cure was found using the crushed bark of a local tree mixed with honey, known around the world as Angostura Bitters. Historically, the settlement is more famous as the base for Simón Bolívar's troops during the War of Independence. The town's name was changed in his honour in 1846. It was here that the Gran Libertador edited the coutry's first newspaper, *El Correo del Orinoco*. Its offices, on Paseo Orinoco at the corner of Calle Carabobo are now the city museum. It opens 9am-noon and 4-7pm daily (except Sunday afternoons).

Large parts of the centre of Ciudad Bolívar have been restored, making it easy to imagine how the town must have looked at the time of the War of Independence and a lovely place to stroll. Plaza Bolívar is a good place to start meandering around the restored sector, as it is surrounded by many fine buildings including the Cathedral. Good views of the narrows of the Orinoco can be seen from Mirador Angostura.

Arrival and Departure. Logically enough, the airport is on Avenida Aeropuerto, on the road to Puerto Ordaz (Ciudad Guayana). There are flights to most cities in the country. The bus terminal is on the corner of Avenidas República and Sucre.

Accommodation. Hotel rooms are often scarce in Ciudad Bolívar, and certainly during the main holiday periods it is wise to have booked a room before your arrive. Its riverfront location on the Paseo Orinoco near Plaza Bolívar once made the moderately priced Gran Hotel Bolívar (phone 20-100/101/102) the best hotel in town. Its grandeur has now faded, though recent refurbishment has restored some of the former glory. Down a peg or two, but also on the river, are the Caracas and Italia hotels, both recommended. Convenient for the airport is the Hotel Valentina (Avenida Maracay 55; tel 22-145, 23-490/211) which has modern, moderately priced rooms.

of water is considerably less. It is the largest *tepuy*, a local Indian word for a flat-topped outcrop.

The resort of Canaima is devoted to helping people to get a good view of the Angel Falls, though it is 30miles/45km away. The village is on the Carrao river close to its confluence with the broad Caroní. Canaima is accessible only by river or air. The airfield is capable of handling jet aircraft, which is how most visitors arrive. Avensa has services daily from Caracas. Pilots always make a pass of the falls before landing. The usual practice is to book a package tour, since Avensa has a monopoly on both flights and accommodation at Canaima. The camp is a collection of bungalows strung out along pathways from the lagoon.

WESTERN VENEZUELA

The main lines of communication going west from Caracas pass through the industrial city of Maracay, then Valencia. At this stage travellers can choose between the southerly route direct to Bogotá via the beautiful city of Mérida, or the journey due west to Maracaibo and northern Colombia.

VALENCIA

Past glories are the key to Valencia — three times capital of Venezuela and the first city on the continent to have electric street lighting. Being only 100 miles/160km west of the present capital, it was the obvious place to go when the government decided that industry should relocate out of Caracas. Modern Valencia is a fast-growing industrial centre, with little to detain the traveller. (The British Vice-Consulate, c/o Corporación Mercantil Venezolana, Edificio Comersa, Calle Silva 100-70; tel 041-50411, may be useful.) Ten miles/16km east of the city is Lake Valencia, which reached its maximum size sixty years before the Battle of Hastings, and has been shrinking ever since. As it recedes, fossilized mastadons, prehistoric sloths and primitive horses have been found. The historical museum in Valencia is the best place to see these, as the lake is now home to agricultural and industrial waste and a big pollution problem. The museum is in the Casa de Célis, at the junction of Calle Comercio and Avenida Soublette; it opens daily except Monday.

The most significant battle in Venezuelan history was fought nearby. In the battle of Carabobo, the Spanish finally capitulated to the forces of Bolívar and Sucre. The triumphal arch and monuments at the Campo Carabobo commemorate the event.

Arrival and Departure. Valencia is accessible by air in 30 minutes from Caracas, and you can also fly on to Coro or Maracaibo. The city also has good bus connections. The bus station is on Calle 73 between Avenidas 93 and Boca del Río. Caracas-bound buses leave the station every few minutes, taking three hours.

Accommodation and Food. The best place to stay is the Hotel Caracas in the centre of old Valencia (Calle 98 number 100-84, at the corner of Calle 101; tel 84646). It is housed in a traditional town house with rooms built around a central courtyard; a few have a private bathroom. Credit cards are not accepted.

For good seafood at reasonable prices go to El Galeón (at Avenida Miranda and Calle 120). In the colonial centre La Pilarica (Calle Colombia and Avenida 5 de Julio) has Venezuelan food and specializes in paella.

MARACAIBO

When the Spanish sailed into Maracaibo Lake nearly 500 years ago, they had no need for oil. By the middle of the 20th century, however, the lake was producing enough crude to make Venezuela rich beyond its wildest dreams. Maracaibo today reflects the oil industry and has little of interest to the visitor. Most travellers will wish to pass through as rapidly as possible while travelling to Colombia or Mérida. The lake is no longer dotted with houses on stilts, as it was when Alonso de Ojeda first arrived and christened the country little Venice. Instead it is ringed with oil rigs.

Sixty years ago, the area was completely cut off from the rest of the country by Lake Maracaibo. It was known only for its Gaita music and crafts. Then oil was discovered. Maracaibo is now home to 10% of Venezuela's population, making it Venezuela's second city. One in eight of the workforce is unemployed. Many are Colombian; one-third of a million Colombians live in Maracaibo, most illegally. The downturn in oil prices has hit Maracaibo harder than most parts of the country. The city's skyline testifies to the boom years of the 1970s and early 1980s: from the drab plain rises another Chicago, gleaming high-rise apartment blocks and office buildings.

The isolation of the department of Zulia was exploited by the Spanish colonists, who kept it as their last pocket of power during the War of Independence. On 24 July 1823 a battle was fought on the lake, and the Republicans won. Ten days later a Treaty of Capitulation was signed at the Casa de la Capitulación; the building survives and is now home to the Historical Society and Bolivarian Society, open 8am-noon and 2.30-6pm Monday-Friday. If you are ticking off largest and longest things in your *I Spy* book then Maracaibo is the place to go — Lake Maracaibo is the largest lake in South America (although it is connected to the sea and so strictly a lagoon); and spanning the neck of the lake is the Rafael Urdaneta Bridge, which is the longest pre-stressed concrete bridge in the world — over five miles/8km long.

Arrival and Departure. The airport is 12 miles/20km outside Maracaibo and has daily flights to all the major cities in the country.

The Central Bus Terminal is on the east side of Avenida 15, just south of Calle 100. There is a frequent express service between Caracas and Maracaibo. Buses bound for other parts of Zulia and to the Colombian border also depart from here.

Accommodation. As befits its boom-town status Maracaibo has no shortage of hotels catering for the many business visitors. If money is no object, then the lakeside Hotel del Lago is for you; it is on Avenida 2, also known as El Milagro (tel 912022). A more likely choice is the moderately priced Hotel San José at Avenida 3Y (San Martín) and Calle 82, number 82-29 (tel 914647/714); by comparison, it feels like a private house and has a porch where you can sit and watch the world go by.

Eating and Drinking. Maracaibo has many expensive 'international' restaurants to cater for visiting oil executives. There are also less exclusive and more interesting places to eat. *How the North American West Was Won*, complete with saloon-style swing doors, is the theme for Mi Vaquita restaurant (Avenida 3H, number 76-222; tel 911990), off Avenida 5 de Julio. It serves meat Argentinian-style. More typical Venezuelan food can be had at El Tinajero (Avenida 3C number 71-80; tel 915362/919020), more cheaply.

Help and Information. British Consulate, Avenida 9B number 66-146, Maracaibo; tel 061-78642.

CORO

The first substantial Spanish settlement in South America was the city of Coro, now gently decaying but still elegant. It is at the foot of the Paraguaná peninsula, 280 miles/450km west of Caracas. Coro is capital of Falcón and a national monument with fine colonial buildings. In addition, it is a good jumping-off point for the peninsula and the Caribbean. At the port of La Vela de Coro, a few miles northwest, you can take a boat to the Dutch islands of Aruba and Curaçao.

Coro was the first colonial capital of Venezuela. Severe problems with pirates led the architects of the cathedral, Venezuela's oldest, to incorporate heavy fortifications in the design, including gun slits in the tower. The site of the first Mass celebrated in Venezuela is marked by the San Clemente Cross, which stands in the Plaza de San Clemente. Calle Zamora leads out of the square and has many good colonial buildings along its length, including Las Ventanas de Hierro (the House of the Iron Windows), which is usually held up as the finest example of Spanish colonial architecture in the country. Opposite is the Casa del Obispo, another building to be admired.

Despite its population of 100,000, Coro is surprisingly agreeable and at times even sleepy. The tourist office is on Plaza Alameda.

Arrival and Departure. Coro airport is a mile north of the town, on Avenida Josefa Camejo at the corner of Avenida Francisco de Miranda. There are several flights daily to Caracas.

There is no central bus station in Coro, so each company has its own stop. Nor is there a Caracas-Coro express service; simply catch a bus between the capital and Maracaibo (along the coastal route) and get off — check with the driver that he will stop at Coro before you get on. Allow about five hours to travel to or from Caracas.

Accommodation and Food. If you want to stay in one of the old colonial houses, then head for Hotel Caracas (Calle Toledo 17, Avenida Manacure; tel 59-545). It has only cold water, but lots of atmosphere. Slightly more expensive is the Venezia at Avenida Manacura and Urdaneta. Cheaper places are fairly basic: among the best is the Roma at Calle 14 and 20 de Febrero, not far from the main square.

Goat meat is popular in Coro: try it as takari (curry) or served up on a coconut shell dish. El Tizón (Calle 25, Avenida 10) is where the locals head for steak and goat.

Further Afield. The terrain of the Paraguaná Peninsula, which extends north from Coro, defies intuition. Despite protruding into the lush Caribbean, its interior — Los Médanos — is an eerie desert with huge dunes. This is the place to come to recover from the effects of some of Venezuela's less than appealing towns and cities: with its quiet fishing villages, quaint colonial churches, secluded beaches and only the occasional tourist. The main hub of the area (though it hardly deserves such a title) is Punto Fijo. It is served by bus from Coro, and has a few meagre hotels. To explore the peninsula to any great depth, however, you will need a tent; otherwise, try your luck with the locals.

MERIDA

This beautiful city is nearly a travellers' paradise. Set a mile high in dramatic Andean scenery, it is Venezuela's leading university town with culture and entertainment to match. More than anywhere else in South America, Mérida is well-scrubbed, civilised and thoroughly middle-class. As a place to spend a few days it is ideal, but it also constitutes an excellent base for exploring further afield. Mérida and its surroundings — the Sierra Nevada National Park — would be simply perfect, were it not for the predictable irritation of cloud cover. Every afternoon spectacular views are obscured by heavy cloud. The closing in gives everything a greyness which even the city's many parks cannot overcome.

Mérida is where the Andes mountains first make their presence felt — as you can see for yourself as the aircraft begins its descent. Once on the ground, the change in air and temperature is immediately noticeable for anyone travelling from the coast. Mérida is much cooler than the coast, and the air has that fresh, healthy quality associated with the mountains.

Merida was founded in the sixteenth century. It is Venezuela's leading university town. For local noise and colour, carnival time in mid-February is a splendid time to visit Mérida. The highlight of the week is undoubtedly the bullfight, when people dressed in their carnival best stream down from villages in the mountains to watch some of the finest bullfighters from South America and Spain demonstrate their art.

The event could not be more different from those disdainful weekly orgies of violence and ineptitude staged — mainly for the tourists' benefit — in many Spanish cities. Even a non-aficionado can appreciate the levels of skill and excitement on display at this special event, which may culminate with a stunning contest between a bull and a man on horseback. This is no case of an armoured and drugged horse having to withstand charge after charge from an enraged bull. Instead, an unprotected and expertly-ridden thoroughbred animal pits its wits and its mobility against those of a bull determined to avoid humiliation. It's a nail-biting spectacle.

Arrival and Departure. *Air:* flights from Caracas are frequent. The new airport, much safer than the old one, is 30 miles/50km from Mérida at El Vigía.

Bus: the 390 mile/680km journey from Caracas is quick as far as Barinas, but the last hundred miles i˙ considerably slower because of the terrain. The fare for the 12-hour journey is $12. The bus station is a couple of miles west of the city centre.

Accommodation. One of the more expensive hotels is the Pedregosa (630525) set in its own parkland on the outskirts of town. Here, one of the pleasures involves lying on your back in the heated swimming pool looking out at the snow-capped peaks of the Andes beyond. Another good place to splash out is the Belanzante, a quietly spoken resort run by a refugee from the USA (tel 661255). If your budget is more limited, try the Roje (pronounced Rocky) at Avenida 2 and Calle 25, or the Posada La Merideña (corner of Avenida 4 and Calle 16) or Residencias San Pedro on Calle 19 between Avenidas 6 and 7 (tel 522735). A good Italian restaurant is attached to the Hotel Chama at Avenida 4 and Calle 29.

Pico Espejo. The world's highest cable car ascends in four stages to the summit of this three-mile-high mountain. Make the journey to the peak, 4,876 metres above sea level, as early in the day as you can bear, to reduce the risk of your view being hidden by clouds. Assuming the air is clear, you get a fantastic vision of Pico Bolívar, only 420 feet/131m taller than Espejo but looking a lot higher. The cable car operates from Tuesday to Sunday and costs about $5 US return.

The cable car must be enjoyed early in the morning. It starts operating each day at 8am, and you are strongly recommended to join the queues before that. If not, by the time you're halfway through the trip, the clouds are likely to have built up obscuring what could be one of the finest views you'll ever see. In any case, visibility is best in the months between November and June.

A warm sweater is an essential piece of equipment on the cable car. As it heads upwards passing first over tropical vegetation, then over fir trees, barren rock and finally deep snow, the temperature plummets.

The summit provides a spectacular view along the top of the Andes. But the high altitude can make it an uncomfortable experience. Once out of the cable car at the top the advice is: take it very easy as your body only gradually becomes accustomed to the height and feelings of nausea and disorientation are common.

LOS LLANOS

Few visitors stay long in the Llanos, a flat, lazy region — just thousands of square miles of nothing but prairie. Like the Midwest of the USA, it is an area with few obvious stimulations. The life of the cowboys who marshall Venezuela's plentiful supply of beef repays some investigation, and in small-town Llanos you can be sure of a warm welcome. Strangers, as they say, are rare in these parts. The music of the region is particularly rewarding. A typical trio consists of a harp, maracas and a four-stringed guitar known as the cuatro (sounding rather like a ukelele), playing the Venezuelan equivalent of country music.

This dusty, poor rural setting is out of tune with the hydrocarbons below the surface; the Orinoco heavy oil belt is rumoured to contain the world's largest petroleum reserves.

Colombia

Statue of Mother India, Cartagena

Population: 34 million   **Capital: Bogotá (5 million).**

'And did you bring back a false-bottomed suitcase?' is the quip which greets many travellers returning from Colombia. The raw statistics of daily life in South America's northernmost country suggest that its reputation for being the global narcotics centre, a land of abject lawlessness, is deserved. Every 50 minutes, a Colombian is arrested somewhere in the world for smuggling drugs. Every six hours, a guerrilla from the Simón Bolívar movement is killed. Every day, half a ton of illegal narcotics is seized by the authorities, who admit they find only a tiny proportion of the traffic. Colombia is the world's leading processor of cocaine. It has suffered from extreme tension and violence for decades. Initially a bitter civil war was fought between Liberals and Conservatives, but latterly it has become a dirty struggle between drug barons and the forces of law. Colombia's fragile social and economic infrastructure has been shaken by falling commodity prices, and the bloody activities of guerrilla groups. And yet once in Colombia it is hard to find evidence of a nation in chaos.

No other country in the world differs so much from its preconceived image. Everyone who has not been to Colombia regards it as an awful place. Almost everyone who has defied conventional wisdom and been there, rates it as wonderful. Colombia is a nation with terrible physical, social and economic contradictions, yet awesome spirit. Despite its problems, the capital and the countryside are spectacular and the people retain humour and hospitality. In short, Colombia is

111

immensely stimulating, the locals friendly and relaxed, and most visitors are smitten by the beauty and diversity of the country.

Colombia is the third most populous and fourth largest country in South America. Within its considerable size — four times as large as the UK — is a wide range of geography and climate. It is the only South American nation to have coastlines on both the Atlantic and Pacific Oceans. The western half, home to nearly all of Colombia's 30 million people, consists of four ranges of the Andes and the basins and valleys in between. The sparsely populated eastern half comprises plains and vast swathes of lush tropical jungle stretching towards Venezuela and Brazil. This area could be the salvation of Colombia; a huge oil field is being charted, making the long-term economic outlook favourable.

CLIMATE

Colombia has a wide climatic range, but the temperature in each locality varies little around the year. The Chocó, the northernmost portion of the country, is the wettest region on earth — damp, grey and gloomy almost every day. At the other corner of Colombia, the Amazon is hot, wet and humid throughout the year. The rain here is heaviest in June and July, lightest from September through to December. The beaches of the Caribbean bask in sunshine much of the time, punctuated with downpours and days of heavy cloud at times from June to November. *Costeños* (people of the coast) mock the climate in the central highlands; Bogotá is reckoned to be chilly, grey and dismal. And so, sometimes, it is. But the capital and its surroundings have their fair share of blissfully cloudless days. The best climate is found between here and the Chocó, to be precise in the northwestern highlands around Medellín. All the year round, this area enjoys the weather of a good English summer. Further south towards the equator it is either too sultry (Cali), too damp (the Pacific coast) or too cold and clammy (the highland province of Nariño). The coldest temperatures are found at high altitudes in the Sierra Nevada de Santa Marta, where the proximity of the Caribbean is belied by below-freezing temperatures.

HISTORY

Pre-Columbian History. Colombia never had the highly developed and sophisticated societies found further south in Peru and Bolivia, but individual areas had their own civilizations. The most significant of these were in the highlands around Bogotá, near the north coast and in San Agustín in the south. Evidence of their communities is found in the excellent gold museums in Bogotá and Santa Marta, and in the weird relics around San Agustín. No trace remains of El Dorado, 'the gilded one', an Indian prince who washed in gold, but you can marvel at the lake in which he bathed just north of Bogotá.

The Conquest. Christopher Columbus never made it to the country which bears his name. One of his lieutenants, Alonso de Ojeda, landed on the peninsula of La Guajira in 1499, but found it as it is today — dry, drab and inhospitable. Vasco Núñez de Balboa surveyed the Gulf of Uruba, in the northwest corner of the Caribbean coast, while trying to find a way through to the Pacific Ocean. (He eventually succeeded by walking across what is now Panama). The 16th century was a quarter-way through when Rodrigo de Bastidas founded Santa Marta, the first port in South America. The choice was deliberate, since it was close to the gold of the Tayrona people. The Spanish soon heard of gold in the highlands, the tale of El Dorado, and this true story was the impetus that drove them inland.

A desperately ill-provisioned expedition up the Magdalena River to Bogotá was undertaken in the search for El Dorado. A Spanish captain named Jiménez de Quesada took nearly 1,000 men upstream, meeting and terrorizing the Indian people they met. The exhausted expedition found the lake which, by then, had assumed legendary proportions. Distress was considerable when they clambered down to the shore of the lake and found it unrevealing of its treasures (most of which are still submerged beneath the dark waters — see page 140).

Understandably miffed, the treasure-hunters began to press further south, but came upon two other expeditions: a Spanish one which was moving north from Lima and Quito, and a bunch of Germans going east from Venezuela. They formed a coalition and set about exploring and dividing the rest of the country. The New Kingdom of Granada was established, with its capital where it stands today — at Santa Fe de Bogotá (a corruption of the name of the Indian province of Bacatá). Economic development was concentrated upon the areas with gold, i.e the north coast (with Cartagena as commercial hub), around the capital and — later — in the province of Antioquia.

Independence. The astonishing career of Simón Bolívar is chronicled in detail on page 83. *El Libertador* was born in Caracas but moved west to Colombia to pursue his dream of independence from Spain. The triumph of Napoleon over the Spanish monarchy in 1812 loosened the ties with the mother country. Regions of what had been the New Kingdom established a degree of autonomy, but with no great unity — the New Republic was a theoretical concept rather than a reality. Ten thousand men were despatched in 1815 to put down the rebellion across the Atlantic. Despite the cruellest of repressions, Simón Bolívar mustered enough of a force to rise up against these new conquistadores, mounting a brilliant campaign and achieving liberation of the whole country in 1819 after the Battle of Boyacá on August 7. He appointed General Santander as vice-president, and continued his rout of the Spanish through Venezuela, Ecuador and greater Peru (including what is now Bolivia). His prize was Gran Colombia, a federation stretching from the volcanoes on the frontier of Costa Rica in Central America to the Amazon, from Lima and La Paz to the easternmost swamps of Venezuela.

The Fall of Bolívar. El Libertador forgot the first rule of politics — never neglect your home territory. Whilst he was achieving astonishing victories elsewhere in South America, his lieutenants in Bogotá began to manoeuvre for power among themselves. Almost as soon as the last federal knot was tied, Gran Colombia began to unravel. In 1830 Simón Bolívar died a broken man in a farmhouse outside Santa Marta, almost within sight of the shore where the whole colonial adventure had begun 300 years earlier. Gabriel García Márquez' book, *The General in his Labyrinth*, evokes the pain of a hero turned villain. He had, however, established a democracy which has only briefly been overridden by military might. Given the immense misery which was to afflict Colombia, it is a dreadful advertisement for democracy.

The Birth of Colombia. 'Birth' is not the ideal term for a country whose borders were defined by the default of others. In 1830 it became the República de Nueva Granada. As the nation struggled to find an identity, the first evidence of the bloody differences between Conservative and Liberal factions emerged. The anti-clerical Liberals were in favour of a loose federation, so that regions such as the Caribbean would have a certain amount of self-government independent of the other parts of the country. The Conservatives, closely associated with the Catholic church, insisted that tight centralized control was essential to the survival of the nation. These differences were crystalized in the formation of political parties in 1849. Colombia's troubled democracy was reflected in the repeated changes of name: to El Confederación Granadina in 1857, four years later to Los Estados Unidos de Colombia, then finally in 1886 to Colombia. The last change in name was part of a new constitution devised by Rafael Núñez, a poet, politician and one-time Colombian consul in Liverpool. He took a ferry across from the Mersey to Cartagena, set up home by the sea and nurtured the new republic into a state of near-anarchy.

The Turn of the 20th Century. Half a century of political life had seen the two parties grow to be heavy, centralized bureaucracies with hardly a clause of ideological difference between them. By now both were deeply conservative, with power flipping languidly between them. Fifty years had also allowed grievances to grow and bitterness at past injustices to fester. The Liberals rebelled in 1899, triggering the War of 1,000 Days. It lasted until 1902, and 100,000 of the country's 4 million people perished. The USA flexed its regional might in 1903, fomenting a unilateral declaration of independence by Panama. This outlying province of Colombia was separated from the rest of the country by the jungle and swamp of the Darién Gap. The USA applied pressure on the region and provided military 'support' in the shape of warships. Two weeks later the North Americans signed an agreement with the fledgling government which provided for a US-controlled zone to allow the digging of a canal. The intervention was an item of economic policy. After the detachment of Panama, a kind of Cold Civil War took effect.

La Violencia. In April 1948, a populist Liberal politician was shot in Bogotá — assassination is still used to great effect today. The murder punctured the blister of resentment and resulted in a long, vicious war of attrition between two groups which was fuelled by a deepening sense of revenge rather than rhetoric. Over the next ten years about 300,000 died in a futile campaign of vengeance.

A curious coalition between Liberals and Conservatives came into being at national level in 1958, a power-sharing arrangement intended to defuse tensions. The agreement took a long time to filter through to the warring factions, and La Violencia continued well into the 1960s. In the struggle some left-wing guerrilla groups sprang up, seeking to represent the people rather than the political élites. This gave a voice, albeit a lawless one, to the largely unenfranchised Indian community.

The 1970s and 1980s. These two decades saw the decline of internecine political violence but an increase in activity by guerrilla groups and the extreme right wing which opposed them. As in other Latin American countries, terrorist activity was met with harsh repression and the formation of freelance 'death squads' — assassination units often composed of members of the security forces. They targeted moderate left-wing leaders as well as suspected terrorists, robbing the mass of the people of their political representatives.

As support for the left grew, the guerrillas increased strength. To raise funds they began to get involved with the trade in illegal narcotics. Colombia does not produce coca, the raw material of cocaine, but it has the expertise to process, ship and market the drug. Demand for cocaine grew, enriching the *mafiosi* which controlled production and distribution. The guerrillas, though ideologically opposed to such free-marketeers, forged links with the drug barons against the state. Seeking to bring the left wing into mainstream politics, the government negotiated a series of amnesties under which new parties participated peacefully in government. Meanwhile, the power and wealth of the drug smugglers grew. Reflecting the US government's desire to put them on trial, they called themselves the Extraditables. Their immense wealth was matched by their arrogance, to the extent that they offered to pay off the entire National Debt (over $5 billion) in return for immunity from prosecution. Under considerable international pressure, the government refused.

Recent History. The government's pitched battle with the drug traffickers began on 18 August 1989. On that day, charismatic Liberal leader, Luis Carlos Galan, was murdered by gunmen in the pay of the drug barons. They were demanding that extradition of Colombian drug traffickers to the USA should be stopped. It was the start of a period of violence which cost 2,000 lives — including three presidential candidates. One year after it began, the Liberal candidate César Gaviria became Colombia's president. He is a young economist who attained the office by accident. He was campaign manager for Luis Carlos Galan, the murdered leader, whose son suggested at the funeral that Gaviria take up the cause.

Gaviria appears to be doing remarkably well at juggling the forces which hitherto have threatened to tear Colombia apart. At the beginning of 1991 numerous drug barons gave themselves up to Colombian police in a bid to minimize the extent of punishment. Under a recent law (strongly opposed by the USA) anyone surrendering to the Colombian authorities becomes immune from extradition. Even the Ochoa brothers and Pablo Escobar, who between them controlled the Medellín trade, gave themselves up. (Or, at least, someone claiming to be Escobar surrendered; the priest who negotiated the surrender warned that he was not recognizable because of 'the wonders of plastic surgery', and some have suggested that a stand-in has been organized.) In any event, such are the peculiarities of Colombian law that a man who has organized murder on a grand scale may serve only three years in prison.

Whatever the ethics of the government's tactics, the evidence suggests that the tide is beginning to turn against the drugs trade. The authorities are concentrating upon seizing funds obtained through drugs, which provides them with more money to step up the fight. And Gaviría's seemingly magical tightrope exercise is bestowing a degree of unity on Colombia hitherto unknown for a century. Unfortunately, just when everything seemed to be going not-too-badly, it emerged that heroin was becoming the latest diversification in the narcotics industry. Opium poppies, unlike coca plants, can be grown in Colombia — huge numbers are under cultivation in the south central provinces of Huila and Tolima, and it was estimated in February 1992 that opium was grown in ten other departments. The revolutionary group FARC is believed to control much of the industry. Strains in the coalition government have appeared between Gaviria — in favour of using pesticides to destroy the crop — and the Health Minister, a former M-19 guerrilla, citing environmental considerations.

As Gabriel García Márquez said recently, 'We are sinking in the quicksands of ambiguity ... there are promises but no negotiations. There are starts but no conclusions.' Meanwhile, Gaviria is seeking at least a middle. He has set up a Constitutional Assembly, with a brief to reform Colombian law and institutions fundamentally. It will be interesting to see if one of its recommendations is to remove the restriction on a president serving successive terms; if not, Gaviria will be turfed out in 1994.

THE PEOPLE

Colombia is the third most populous country in South America, with 34 million people. Three-fifths are *mestizos*, i.e a mix of Hispanic and Indian. White-skinned Europeans — mostly of Spanish descent — comprise one-fifth of the population, and have a disproportionate share of wealth and power. The next largest ethnic group comprises the *mulattos* — a mix of Spanish and black blood. There is also a sizeable community of pure-blooded blacks. Most of these live close to the Caribbean, especially around Cartagena.

Native Indian people make up just 2% of the present population, and most are concentrated in the Andean highlands; concentrated is an inappropriate term, since the Indians and their villages are thinly spread. They belong to three main tribes, the Chibchas, the Quimbayas and the Agustinians. After centuries of injustice, the latest constitution is beginning to recognize the rights of the native people — four Indian representatives are guaranteed seats in the National Assembly. But evidence of repression continued in 1992, when 20 Indians were massacred outside Popayán, allegedly at the behest of large landowners.

FURTHER READING

Colombia: a Travel Survival Kit (Lonely Planet, 1988, £6.95) is out-of-date but the best single guidebook available. An excellent account of the workings of the cocaine industry appears in *The Fruit Palace* by Charles Nicholl (Picador, £6.99), which is also a jolly good traveller's tale. *Colombia — Inside the Labyrinth* by Jenny Pearce (Latin American Bureau, £8.99) is a useful analysis of the country's chaos.

Gabriel García Márquez, the Nobel Prize-winning author, is Colombian. His novels reflect the tensions of his nation. His birthplace was Aracataca in the north of Colombia. It became the basis for the fictional village of Macondo. Here he described the Buendia family struggles over *One Hundred Years of Solitude*. His other notable works are *Love in the Time of Cholera*, *Chronicle of a Death Foretold* and *No-one Writes to the Colonel* — an early novel, but perhaps his bitterest and wittiest observation of the Colombian psyche.

Getting There

AIR

From Europe. Bogotá is served by numerous European airlines, including Air France, British Airways, Lufthansa and Iberia. The national carrier Avianca and the Venezuelan airline Viasa also offer services from Europe. Fares reflect the degree of competition, and are considerably cheaper than those to Quito in Ecuador. From London fares are as low as £450 return on Air France, with tickets on BA direct flights only £550. High-season fares are cheapest on Viasa.

Avianca flies to Bogotá from Madrid, Paris and Frankfurt, though with numerous stops: passengers on connecting services from London have compulsory stops at Paris, Madrid and Caracas or Cartagena. Avianca is the only airline serving Cartagena direct from Europe, though note that the return service on this route goes via Barranquilla not Cartagena — the runway at the latter airport is too short for fully laden transatlantic aircraft to use.

If your first destination is another Colombian city, you will need to travel via the USA, changing at Miami or New York and connecting as described below.

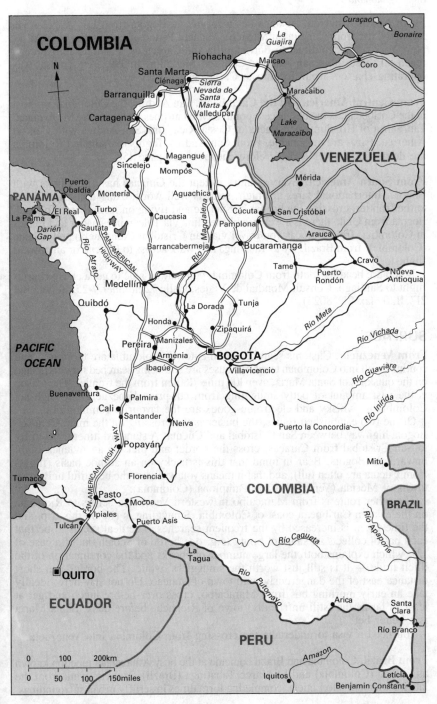

From North America. Avianca has a service to Bogotá from Los Angeles via Mexico City, from Cancún on Mexico's Yucatan Peninisula and from New York. New York flights go direct to Barranquilla and Cartagena. From Miami you can reach all these, plus San Andrés, Cali and Medellín. In 1992 Air Transat was operating charters from Toronto to Cartagena.

From Central America and the Caribbean. San Andrés, the Colombian outpost in the Caribbean, is the best access point. Several airlines, including SAM, Avianca, Tan/Sahsa of Honduras and Lacsa of Costa Rica, link San Andrés with Central America. Fares are reasonable. From San Andrés, flights to mainland Colombia are domestic services and therefore cheap — see page 158.

From South America. Every country except the Guianas has direct links with Bogotá. International fares are high, so it is well worth using domestic flights to the frontier, crossing the border by surface and flying on from there. To reach Bogotá from Quito there is a well established link via Tulcán in Ecuador and Ipiales in Colombia; from Caracas you travel via San Cristóbal (Venezuela) and Cúcuta (Colombia); from Brazil, fly to Tabatinga and walk across to Leticia for an onward flight to Bogotá.

If you are heading south from Colombia, you may be able to get a cheap charter flight to Santiago. Consult Mondial de Viajes, Calle 72 number 9-25, Bogotá (tel 217 1120; fax 212 8023).

SURFACE

From Venezuela. Customs searches upon entering Colombia are thorough, and continue well into Colombian territory; buses are still being searched for contraband on the outskirts of Santa Marta, over 100 miles/160km from the frontier. The reason is the vast amount of petty smuggling from cut-price Venezuela into high-tax Colombia — whisky and electronic goods are the favourite commodities.

Of the two established routes, the busier is the crossing on the main Caracas-Bogotá highway between San Cristóbal and Cúcuta. A standard itinerary is to fly to San Cristóbal from Caracas, cross the border and pick up an Avianca flight onwards to Bogotá. Bear in mind that this is tricky on an ad-hoc basis (flights from Cúcuta are often full), and that it means you will miss the beautiful university towns of Mérida (Venezuela) and Pamplona (Colombia).

The other route is from Maracaibo in western Venezuela across to Riohacha on the eastern Caribbean coast of Colombia. Smuggling is rife on this trip, and the time taken is increased by the frequent searches. The deal seems to be that each patrol collects its share of booty (e.g. one bottle of Scotch out of a case of 12), which explains both the large number of checks and the continuation of the illicit trade — it is still just worth the smugglers' while. The border is a short distance east of the dangerously wild town of Maicao. Do not stay here; ideally take an early morning bus from Maracaibo, cross over before lunch and get at least as far as the (still unfriendly) town of Riohacha before dusk; Santa Marta is a better bet.

You need a visa to undertake the crossing from Colombia into Venezuela.

From Brazil. Colombia and Brazil coincide at the busy Amazonian junction known as Leticia (Colombia) and El Marco/Tabatinga (Brazil). You can walk from the latter settlement into Leticia, completing formalities in scruffy urban surroundings.

The resort of Benjamin Constant (in Brazil, but across the river) is linked to Leticia by riverboat.

From Ecuador. Crossing by land from Colombia's southern neighbour has several advantages. Formalities are smooth and efficient; you save money compared with the cost of international flights from Ecuador; and fascinating sights await you at the towns on each side of the frontier: Tulcán (Ecuador) and Ipiales (Colombia). See pages 202 and 173 respectively for details. In terms of through journeys, you should get a bus or aircraft to Tulcán (TAME flights daily at 11am from Quito, $8). Taxis run to the frontier ($1 per person — any more is a 'special price' for gringos). Check out from Ecuador at the hut by the car park, then walk across the natural bridge; you can expect to be searched on the bridge itself. Once across proceed to the ritzy new immigration complex; it looks like a motorway service station, even down to the burger bar. While you walk, you will be assailed with offers of onward transportation; bear in mind the following advice.

Although Ipiales has an airport, the only flight to Bogotá is early in the morning. Therefore you may want to stay overnight, or get an onward bus; negotiate a collective taxi into Ipiales from the border ($0.50). If your destination is Pasto or beyond, you should find a collective taxi going straight through for $5; another $1.50 takes you to Pasto airport, from where you can fly on to Cali and Bogotá.

From Panama. The Pan-American Highway peters out at Yaviza in Panama, and the jungle prevents vehicles going any further. The trip across the Darién Gap is described on page 162. For those who wish to do the budget version, fly from Panama City to Puerto Obaldía at the extreme east of Panama. Walk for two hours to the village of La Miel, and across the Colombian frontier to Sapzurro. Another hour brings you to Capurgana. From here you can fly to Medellín or continue on foot or by sea to Acandí (and from there by boat or air to Turbo).

Red Tape

IMMIGRATION

British and Irish passport holders need no visa. A tourist visa is required by citizens of Australia, New Zealand, the USA and Canada. To get one, you must apply at a Colombian consulate and allow three working days. Colombia does not have missions in Australia or New Zealand. Addresses in North America are:

USA: 2118 Leroy Place, NW Washington DC 20008 (tel 202-387-8338).
Canada: Suite 605, 150 Kent St, Ottawa, K1P 5P4 (tel 613-230-3760).

All travellers are supposed to have a confirmed ticket out of Colombia, plus at least $30 for each day of the planned stay. These conditions are examined jointly. So if you have a ticket out in ten days' time, you need a minimum of $300. You could circumvent this by having a ticket whose date can be changed. In practice, few visitors are asked to produce evidence of funds. Unless you appear particularly dodgy, the standard length of stay granted upon arrival is 90 days.

Extending Your Stay. By far the easiest way to increase the length of your stay is to leave the country temporarily, e.g. by slipping into Ecuador. This gives another three months in Colombia. Otherwise you can apply for a single one-month extension in Bogotá: at the Foreign Ministry (Calle 49 number 13-57) or the Internal

Security Department (DAS; Carrera 27 number 17-85), but this consumes lots of time and generates huge amounts of anxiety.

Departure Tax. Foreigners must pay $20 in local currency or dollars when leaving Colombia by air. You will need an exemption certificate to pay this lower rate, rather than the higher resident's tax ($30). You can get such an *Exención* either upon arrival or departure by proving your stay is less than 60 days.

CUSTOMS
Upon arrival you must fill out a customs declaration form — tick the box marked Tax Free Luggage unless you have more than six bottles of liquor, two cameras or six copies of the same book. You are unlikely to be much of a target, as thousands of locals bring in millions of contraband bottles of Scotch each year.

Narcotics are taken much more seriously. The contents of your first-aid bag may be closely scrutinized. Although Colombian customs officials are familiar with the hypochondriac Westerner carrying all manner of medication, you can expect anything even vaguely medicinal to be thoroughly examined.

The unit of currency is the Peso Oro (C$), known universally simply as the peso. One hundred pesos is often referred to as one peso. It is normally clear which is meant; if a taxi driver says *ocho pesos* he means 800 pesos, while if another asks for *mil pesos* he certainly expects 1,000.

The Colombian peso does not depreciate as quickly as some other South American currencies, but you would not want to change too much of it at a time. You can convert US dollars to pesos at banks (which usually have a special counter for this purpose) or a *casa de cambio*; the latter keep longer hours.

It is easy to withdraw cash with plastic in Colombia. Most of the country's numerous bank companies accept Visa, among them the banks of Bogotá, Cafetro, Colombia and Popular. Access/Mastercard is less widely accepted, but try the Banco de Occidente. The one drawback is the length of time it takes for authorization to be granted by the credit card company. You might have to wait at a bank for two or three hours, yet still leave penniless, because the shortage of lines to the authorization department is so acute.

A more reliable method is to use a bank card to withdraw cash from automatic teller machines. British bank and building society ATM cards belonging to the Link network can be used to withdraw pesos from cash machines operated by Banco Popular — marked *Telecaja*. It is therefore possible to finance your entire visit using plastic, starting with the cash machine at Bogotá airport (on the departures level of the main terminal).

Only one place in Colombia will convert American Express travellers cheques into US dollars. It is not the Amex office, but a company called Imex. Its office is on the 15th floor at Carrera 7 number 32-29, Bogotá.

Tipping. You should behave as in other South American countries, i.e. nothing in taxis or cheap dives, some loose change to bartenders, but 10-15% in fancy restaurants. Note that some Colombians have a tendency to assume that all westerners mean 'keep the change' when they say 'thank you' — as you might find if you offer a 2,000 peso note to pay a 1,000 peso cab ride.

cartels regard the news media with the same contempt that they do the law, and about ten journalists are assassinated each year. Despite the perils, Colombia has a remarkably free and effective press. The leading newspapers in Bogotá are *El Tiempo* and *El Espectador*. The regional capitals have excellent publications too, such as *El Mundo* in Medellín and *El País* in Cali. Avoid *El Espacio*, a tabloid rag as full of sex and violence as its British counterparts.

Broadcasting. The closest equivalent to BBC Radio 4 is Radio Caracol, a mainly news network. Most other stations carry heavily compressed commercials interspersed with music ranging from schmaltzy to serious, but with an emphasis om Western rock. In 1992 the favourites seemed to be Bryan Adams, REM and Guns'n Roses. For good Colombian music, some of the radio stations on the Caribbean are worth trying. Caribbean, Central American and US radio stations can be picked up in the north of the country.

Television in Colombia is as dismal as elsewhere in South America.

AIR

If you ever wondered what happened to old aircraft worn out after ferrying holidaymakers between Britain and the Mediterranean, you may find the answer in Colombia. At least one clapped-out Boeing 727 which previously belonged to the British charter airline Dan-Air, is flying around Colombia, still in its original colours. But Colombia's air network should not be dismissed. However old the aircraft, the airlines provide a fast and affordable way of getting around a country with forbidding terrain. The 40-minute flight from Medellín to Bogotá saves an overland journey of 12 hours, and costs only $40, about four times the bus fare. Services stretch out to all corners of the country. The two problems are the sheer popularity of air travel — which makes it hard to get a seat on some services — and poor timekeeping. An on-time domestic flight is the exception rather than the rule.

The leading airlines are Avianca and SAM. They are now part of the same company, with interchangeable tickets and common reservations systems (call 9800 11767 free from anywhere in Colombia). The Avianca network is centred on Bogotá, with frequent services to Cali, Medellín, Cartagena, Barranquilla, Santa Marta and San Andrés. Avianca also serves Riohacha, Cúcuta, Bucaramanga, Pereira and Montería, plus the southern towns of Pasto and Leticia. SAM is the airline of Medellín, and operates services from the city to most big destinations.

Four other airlines offer cheaper fares, though usually poorer aircraft and less frequent services. The first is the armed forces airline Satena, which reaches awkward corners of the coutry and runs a 'bus stop' service through the Amazon basin to Leticia. Aces (Aerolineas Centrales de Colombia, pronounced *ass-es*, tel 9800 44747) is the next most popular. It has jet services on the most important routes and an extensive prop-jet network based in Medellín. The world's most inappropriately named airline must be Intercontinental. It fills in a few gaps in the other route networks, such as Bogotá-Popayán-Ipiales. Finally, Aires has a small range of flights, mainly in the Andes.

Inflight service on all these airlines is patchy. You may be offered a drink, but perhaps only rum. Smoking is banned. An airport tax of $2 is levied on all domestic flights. If you buy a ticket in advance, it should include the tax; if you are travelling on an air pass you must pay for it separately and in Colombian pesos.

Air Passes. Avianca/SAM have three passes under the title *Conozca Colombia*:

Ten flights in eight days for $190, if you fly the Atlantic on Avianca.
Ten flights in 30 days for $224, if you fly the Atlantic on Avianca.
Ten flights in 30 days for $325, if you fly the Atlantic on an airline other than Avianca.

These are not quite the bargains they might appear, bearing in mind the low cost of flying within Colombia and the fact that there are some gaps in the Avianca/SAM network. You need to fly frequently to make a 'profit' on the deal; given the problems of booking, this may not be possible. Anyone planning to visit Leticia or the San Andrés islands, however, may find them worthwhile. The saving you get for flying on Avianca is worth bearing in mind when choosing a transatlantic carrier. All passes must be booked in advance outside Colombia. Though you may be told that reservations can be made once you arrive, many travellers find their chosen flights to be full. You should book a rough itinerary in advance and, if necessary, try to modify it once in Colombia.

TRAIN
'There are no timetables, only rumours'. Such a description could apply to many forms of transport in the developing world, but Charles Nicholl uses the phrase most memorably to describe Colombian railways. Services on the two remaining passenger lines are deeply unpredictable. Colombia's main line, the Atlantic Railway, runs twice a week between Santa Marta and Barrancabermeja, a couple of hundred miles north of Bogotá. It uses *ferrobuses*, like bus bodies welded to train chassis, also found in Bolivia and Ecuador. Beware of the propensity of other passengers to place contraband under your seat. The only other passenger service is the steam-hauled excursion train from Bogotá to Nemecón, three hours north of the capital.

BUS
Services are frequent: every 15 minutes, for example, buses operate on the Cartagena-Barranquilla-Santa Marta route along the Caribbean. Bogotá has good links to most destinations from its sparkling new bus station. The great impediment to services, however, is the terrain. The run from the capital to Medellín, as mentioned above, takes 12 hours to cover a distance of 120 miles/200km as the crow flies.

The best companies, with the best buses, are Expreso Brasilia and Expreso Bolivariano. Other operators are cheaper and grottier.

COLLECTIVE TAXIS
Colectivos are big business in Colombia. The locals use them as a fast alternative to buses. Cars are usually well organized on a cooperative basis, and operate from bus terminals; you may need to buy a ticket in advance. You can expect to pay about twice the corresponding bus fare. If you hire a taxi outright for a long journey, you will be responsible for tolls and any other payments to third parties. You will also be expected to pay for fuel upfront.

CAR
All the reasons to avoid driving in South America apply particularly to Colombia: poor roads, imaginative driving techniques, long distances over difficult terrain. If you're still not tempted to leave the driving to someone else, bear in mind some of the nastier crimes committed against foreigners: in 1991 dozens of bodies were

found close to the Bogotá-Caracas highway. Car drivers were stopped, their vehicles were taken and they were killed.

Many motorists, of course, lose neither their lives nor their cars. The main routes are the Bogotá-Caracas highway; the Pan-American Highway, which runs from the Darién Gap on the border with Panama through Medellín and Cali to the Ecuadorean frontier; and the Caribbean Highway through Cartagena, Barranquilla and Santa Marta across to the border with Venezuela.

For further advice, maps, etc, contact the Touring y Automóvil Club de Colombia; its headquarters in Bogotá is a new redbrick building on Carrera 14 (Avenida Caracas) at number 46-72.

Rental cars are predominantly Japanese, though the cheapest is the Renault 4. Fuel comes in two grades: *corriente*, which even a Renault 4 might object to, and *extra*, costing 20% more.

Drivers face a range of impediments to free movement. On the outskirts of most cities are yellow and black booths (charging about $1 for 60 miles/100km) and *puesto de control*, police checkpoints painted green to match the colour of *Policía Vial* (traffic police) cars.

HITCH-HIKING

It might seem reckless to recommend hitching in a country with such lawless tendencies, but in rural areas it is an accepted way to get around. Westerners can get lifts extremely quickly, a consequence of the great hospitality of many Colombians. Offer a few hundred pesos to the driver, but it will probably be refused. Note that hitching should not be tried in the areas mentioned below under *Crime and Safety*.

CYCLING

Carrera 7 in Bogotá, opposite the railway station, is the country's cycle centre — a row of shops selling relatively cheap imports. The cheapest mountain bike is around $100. Try to get out of the capital before putting it through its paces. On the Caribbean coast, some foreign cyclists have been mugged. This involves the driver of a pickup truck dinking you off the bicycle, grabbing the bike and disappearing in a cloud of dust.

CITY TRANSPORT

The usual beaten-up city buses are supplemented by *servicios ejecutivos*, which cost twice as much but guarantee a seat — standing passengers are not allowed, so the bus will drive straight past if it is full. On both types of buses, fares are displayed on the windscreen. Two fares are shown; the higher one applies at night and on Sundays.

Taxis in most cities have a fixed fare per journey. Once you figure out what the going rate is, just proffer this to the driver. But until you find out, you can expect some attempts to overcharge you. These can become aggravating. Always agree a fare in advance. Knock a third off what the driver quotes and when you have agreed a fare, re-state the terms, e.g. 'two people to the airport, $5 total'. Even with this precaution, a driver may try arbitrarily to raise the fare at the end of the journey. The best remedy if this happens is to have the exact change ready to thrust into his hand.

Eating and Drinking

Each region has its own specialities, but the best cuisine is generally held to be from the province of Antioquia, centred on Medellín. Antioquian restaurants can be found throughout Colombia. The country's best dish is a *plato montañero*. The 'mountain plate' is the traditional dish of the Colombian Andes, a mountain of grilled meat and other goodies. Its ingredients read like a menu in a greasy spoon. Sausage, beans, eggs, steak, plus more exotic items: plantain, avocado and *chicharrón*, a Colombian version of pork scratchings far more macho than the British variety.

Most Colombian cuisine is much more mundane. The *comida corriente* is the standard cheap lunch. For $1 you could get soup (lumps of anonymous meat and vegetables floating round in a greasy liquid) followed by fish or meat with some combination of rice, beans, chips and salad.

Street snacks vary from one region to another. Potato crisps (chips) are popular in Bogotá, where vendors deep fry them while you wait. These are guaranteed to be better than the packets of lime-flavoured crisps sold in supermarkets. On the Caribbean coast, beware of the battered sausages on sticks — they taste like the worst kind of frankfurter. *Pan con queso* is worth trying, rings of dough with cheese inside, delicious when warm. But beware of candied mango — like eating a block of marmalade.

The country has lots of good supermarkets if you want to buy the ingredients for a picnic. In fact they usually have good food stalls inside, serving excellent snacks at low prices. If you are desperate for your favourite British breakfast cereal, note that Choco Krispis are Coco Pops and Zucaritas are Frosties.

Colombian fruit is exotic and delicious. Try *tamarillo*, a small, round red fruit which manages somehow to taste both soapy and tart; the effects are strongest nearest the skin. *Feijoa* tastes like bubblegum and is not at all unpleasant. The flesh of the horned melon looks like frog's spawn, but tastes much better. *Zapote* is flesh-coloured, sweet but bland. Look out also for *babaco*, *chirimoya*, *maracuya* and the more familiar mango and papaya.

DRINKING

All these fruits make excellent juices. When selecting a *jugo*, don't be taken in by the most exotic sounding of all — *zanahoria* — which, of course, is plain old carrot. Neither should you be tempted by the *jugo de milo* unless you want a chocolate milkshake; milo is not an exotic fruit but a proprietory powdered drink. *Crema* or *Ballicrema* is a sweet milkshake in various flavours, frequently sold by bus hawkers, and curiously addictive. Mineral water is readily available. The main brands are Bretaña (fizzy) and Agua Cristal (still). Pepsi and Coke are the most popular soft drinks (*gaseosas*). This is not surprising given the quality of the local offerings: Colombiana and Postobón are horribly sweet, with the flavour of food colouring and medicine rather than fruit. Cola Roman is about the least offensive.

Coffee should, you might think, be excellent. But though Colombia is a big producer of coffee, the best is exported. Coffee is served black, in small cups. It is either clear (*claro*) or cloudy (*obscuro*). The difference in taste is not immediately apparent.

One legal mind-altering substance produced by the city of Medellín is rum. Ron Medellín is not the name of a villain from London's East End, but a smooth and warming rum. A full bottle costs around $3. The same price applies to Aguardiente

Antioqueño, made in the same place but tasting a thousand times harsher. The standard beer is Aguila (eagle), though you can also get a stronger, canned brew called Clausen Export. Avoid Costeñita, a beer which is almost indistinguishable from lemonade — in appearance of bottles, taste and strength.

Most wine comes from Argentina and Chile. Grajales is a local attempt at Champagne, and is not at all bad.

Archaeological Sites and National Parks. Colombia takes a good second place to Peru in terms of its pre-Columbian antiquities. The two greatest sites are the Lost City in the Sierra Nevada de Santa Marta, and San Agustín — huge stones carved with outlandish motifs. See pages 146 and 171 respectively for more details of these.

Access to most sites is controlled by Inderena, the national park service. Permits are officially required for most national parks. They cost nothing, but an admission fee is always payable when you arrive at the park. Enquire at an Inderena office for current details of the sites you may wish to visit; the head office in Bogotá is at Diagonal 34 number 5-84.

Colonial Architecture. Cartagena is the city *par excellence* in South America for surviving colonial architecture. The old part of town is, like Havana, thoroughly unspoilt and atmospheric; see page 149. Not far inland, Mompós (page 154) has benefitted from its isolated and protected location to preserve its quaint colonial atmosphere. Just off the highway from Bogotá to Caracas, Villa de Leyva (page 141) is perhaps the most perfectly preserved of all Colombia's colonial towns. Make the most of these places, because the colonial parts of most other towns and cities are either nearly destroyed (Cali, Medellín) or reconstructed (Bogotá and the earthquake-hit town of Popayán).

Hiking. Some say the best place to head for hiking in Colombia is south — across the border in Ecuador. This reflects several factors, not least the dangers to hikers in remote regions of Colombia. Furthermore, the infrastructure for hikers is underdeveloped, with few of the facilities which Ecuador has. And, while large parts of Colombia are undeniably stunningly beautiful, it can be difficult to gain access to areas that are best suited to hiking.

Conversely, of course, Colombia has none of the crowds from which Ecuador suffers. The big trip is in the Sierra Nevada de Santa Marta for which several companies organize tours and can (usually) guarantee safety.

Beaches. Though Colombia is the only South American country washed by both the Pacific and Atlantic oceans, you can virtually write off the entire Pacific coast if you're looking for a decent beach. The best Caribbean beach in Colombia is in Tayrona National Park, easily accessible from Santa Marta. Those closer to Santa Marta are mixed: the country's biggest resort, El Rodadero, is a few miles south and horribly crowded, while Taganga, just north, is beautiful and unspoilt. Cartagena sets itself up as a beach resort, but the best sand is unfortunately directly beneath the flight path into the airport.

Entertainment

Fiestas and Carnivals. Having dreadful social and economic problems does not stop the people of Colombia having a good time. The following festivals, though not the biggest, are especially recommended: March/ April: Popayán — Easter Week parades and festival of religious music; August: Medellín — Flower Fair; December: Cali — La Feria.

Music. The most innovative art is music. Colombia has mixed mountain music with the rhythms of the north coast to produce its own unique sounds. In addition, the influences which produced salsa in Cuba — African and Spanish ingredients — have been developed into a uniquely Colombian form known as *cumbia*. In the Chocó, the African strand predominates, and people who have visited Africa find extraordinary similarities between the two cultures in terms of rhythm and harmony.

SPORT

Colombia has never lived down its humiliation of 1986, when it was due to host the soccer World Cup Finals. Some months before the tournament was due to take place, the country had to admit it could not go ahead with staging a competition of such size and complexity. The only other soccer connection of which British fans are aware is that Bogotá was the scene of the incident which, say some, stopped England from retaining the 1970 World Cup. During a pre-tournament warm-up, England captain Bobby Moore was accused of stealing jewellery, in what was widely believed to be a deliberate frame-up.

Football is still immensely popular, with the country's best teams being the Bogotá sides Santa Fe and Millonarios. Don't show this page to English-speaking supporters of other teams.

Bullfighting is followed with almost as much fervour as soccer. The centre of the 'sport' is Medellín, which stages La Candelaria bullfighting fair for four weeks in January/February.

Shopping

Nobody goes to Colombia specifically to shop, except possibly for those in search of narcotics. If you want to buy a cheap bicycle, good chocolate or dangerously strong rum, then any town should be able to oblige. But don't expect to find any gifts much more exciting than these. The best bet is probably a *ruana*, the lighter version of a poncho. The markets are the best places to find them, as 'artesan' shops increase prices by a factor of three. In Colombia's markets you negotiate over everything from the time of day upwards.

Traditional crafts are harder to find than in other Andean countries. The Cuna Indians occupy the Darién, travelling fairly freely between Colombia and Panama, and their crafts are particularly interesting. The garment known as a *mola* is the most distinctive. Intricate designs are made by combining several layers of brightly coloured fabric, and cutting patterns out. Though women wear them as shirts, Western visitors use them as wall hangings. The town of Pitalito, in the department of Huila near San Agustín, produces a mass of beautifully crafted models. These range from ceramic miniature houses to tiny model *chivas*, brightly coloured buses. Elsewhere, a random selection of *chompas* (jumpers) and other woollen goods is the best you'll find. If you need electronic equipment or a new camera, try to buy it in the tax haven of San Andrés.

As far as record-buying is concerned, the rock clock appears to have stopped when Elton John released his greatest hits and U2 brought out *Rattle and Hum*. Listen to a selection of *cumbia* music if you want something more modern.

Crime and Safety

Colombia has many dangerous places and practices. A country which has to take space in the *Washington Post* to plead its case in full-page advertisements has a serious law and order problem. 'For years they were drug lords. Now, they're dead or in jail' — proclaimed the advertisement above pictures of five rogues. Few people were convinced, and you should not believe for a moment that Colombia is suddenly miraculously safe. But the risks are still relatively small. The first part of this section deals with the everyday problems of theft, while the second part is concerned with the special risks of a country with an active guerrilla movement and a booming narcotics industry.

Theft. Distressingly many travellers are robbed in Colombia, almost always in the big cities; Bogotá and Cartagena are the worst. Usually this is the straightforward economic theft common elsewhere in South America, and the precautions cited on page 63 should help to prevent it. Be especially careful on the streets, on buses, in markets, etc. Colombian pickpockets are among the best in the world. Be careful, too, of con artists.

A nastier risk is of being attacked by someone in what the popular press would call 'a drug-crazed frenzy'. Addicts of *bazuko* (cocaine base) and heroin would do literally anything to get the next fix. Snatching bags or jewellery from the necks of the wearer is routine, and violence is likely to be used if you put up the slightest resistance. Sadly, the perpetrators are often children.

Kidnapping. Abduction for financial gain or political advantage is, literally, an everyday occurence in Colombia. Three or four people are kidnapped each day. Foreigners, especially well-dressed ones, are often targetted as the abductors believe they can claim a large ransom.

Terrorism. Travellers in Colombia must endure an inordinate number of searches. Some years ago over 100 passengers were killed when terrorists planted a bomb on an Avianca flight. So to board a domestic flight you can expect a check upon entering the airport, another as you reach the departure area and a third as you board the airport. All are likely to be cursory, and may be waived if you are in an obvious hurry.

Narco-Violence. Fortunately for the traveller, most violence is directed at Colombians involved in the drugs trade. In response to narco-terrorism and criminal score-settling, community militias have been set up. The authorities claim they are cover organizations for the remaining guerrilla groups. Whatever the truth, having yet another faction roaming around bristling with loaded weapons is not calming for the average visitor. Anyone trespassing upon the drugs trade, whether a field of opium poppies in the Huila province, a bazuko wholesaler's premises in Medellín or a cocaine processing plant in the Amazon basin, is likely to be shot before any questions are asked.

Narco-Tourism. Some people go to Colombia specifically to enjoy cheap drugs. Travellers do not have to dig very deep beneath the skin of legitimate society to procure illegal drugs. Marijuana is fairly widely available. Bazuko is highly dangerous. Cocaine should, of course, be at its purest in Colombia, but street dealers cut (dilute) it with all sorts of other white powders, only some of which are harmless. Buying from a street dealer renders you likely to be swindled, probably poisoned and possibly set up for arrest.

Punishment. Some Westerners, particularly those who dabble in drugs, find themselves on the wrong side of the law. Justice in Colombia is an elastic concept. Gangsters who are known to have killed can find themselves serving paltry sentences. The theory goes like this: criminals who repatriate their ill-gotten gains have their sentences halved. That in turn is cut by two-thirds if the accused confesses. When two years remission for good conduct is sliced off the sentence, someone receiving the maximum sentence of 30 years for drug trafficking could serve just three years. This arrangement is designed to encourage drug barons to give themselves up, and does not apply to the ordinary criminal fraternity nor to Westerners in trouble.

Areas to Avoid. Cynics might suggest the whole country is best avoided. In fact the vast majority of the places you would wish to visit are perfectly safe. Urban areas off-limits are clearly visible — the poorer quarters on the fringes of big cities. It is harder to define dangerous rural regions because, by definition, much of the activity in these areas is clandestine.

Starting in the north, you should not dawdle on the highway between the Venezuelan frontier and Riohacha. Here drug-runners mix with disaffected Indian people on La Guajira peninsula, together with smugglers of cheap stereos and Scotch whisky. The cocktail of criminality is highly volatile.

The city of Barrancabermeja, halfway up the Río Magdalena, does not appear dangerous but it should be avoided because it is the centre of oil refining, which makes it a target for terrorists.

It is difficult for travellers to see much of the Amazon basin, which is probably just as well given the multiplicity of potential dangers. Many of the top cocaine kitchens are deep in the jungle, supply lines bringing in coca from Peru and routing narcotics onwards may be stumbled over, and, of course, rivers are full of carnivorous fish which can devour anyone foolish or unfortunate enough to fall in the river.

Security Forces. The authority which regulates foreigners (e.g. dealing with immigration, extensions, documentation) is DAS — Departmento Administrativo de Seguridad. If you want to be able to leave your passport in your hotel, DAS will authorize a photocopy of its first six pages plus the one with your Colombian immigration stamp. If you have something (or everything) stolen, go to the F-2 branch of the ordinary police.

Health and Hygiene

The water quality in mountain areas of Colombia is generally good. In low-lying regions it should not be trusted unless you purify it. Mosquitoes in the coastal areas, and in the Amazon basin, are voracious and carry malaria. To avoid bites, Autan and Black Flag insect repellent is sold cheaply everywhere.

Cholera is spreading on the Pacific coast and in the Amazon basin. Fish should always be well cooked.

The standard condoms are brand-named Tahiti and cost $0.50 for three.

Tourist Information. Enquiries in the UK should be made to the Colombian Consulate-General, 140 Park Lane, London W1Y 3BF (tel 071-495 4233; open 10am-2pm). In the USA, contact the Colombia Information System, 140 E 57 St, New York City.

Colombia's Corporación Nacional de Turismo is remarkably well-organized and produces a good series of leaflets on all the leading towns and cities. Unfortunately, the reception you get in individual offices is often unwelcoming and unhelpful. You may find commercial travel agents more cooperative.

Embassies and Consulates. The UK Embassy in Bogotá is on the 4th floor, Torre Propaganda Sancho, Calle 98 number 9-03, Bogotá; tel 218 5111; fax 218 2460. There are British consulates in the three next largest cities: Barranquilla, Cali and Medellín. Addresses are: Carrera 44 number 45-57, Barranquilla (tel 326936); Office 407, Edificio Garcés, Calle 1 number 1-07, Cali (tel 832752); Calle 9 number 43B-93, Medellín (tel 246 3114; fax 266 7318).

US Embassy: Calle 38 number 8-61, Bogotá (tel 285 2100; fax 288 5687).

Public Holidays

January 1	New Year's Day
January 6	Epiphany
March 17	St Joseph's Day
March/April	Holy Thursday/Good Friday
May 1	Labour Day
May	Ascension Day
May/June	Corpus Christi
June 29	Saints Peter and Paul
July 20	Independence Day
August 7	Anniversary of the Battle of Boyaca
August 15	Assumption
October 12	Columbus Day
November 1	All Saints' Day
November 11	Independence of Cartagena
December 8	Immaculate Conception
December 25	Christmas Day

BOGOTA

The Colombian capital is one of the most exciting cities in Latin America, and one of the most beautifully situated. Bogotá lies in the centre of Colombia, 8,600 ft/2,630m above sea level, an altitude which makes it cold according to those from the coast, but enlivening to most other people. Only a few of its population of four million are actively engaged in the illegal trafficking of drugs, but they cause enough trouble to create the impression that Bogotá is one of the most dangerous places on earth. That it is not, though it is not the sort of place in which you would wish to relax your guard.

City Layout. The city is hemmed in from the east by an almost impenetrable range of mountains. Therefore it sprawls north, south and west. Within this, Carreras run north-south (i.e. parallel with the mountains), and Calles run east-west.

Bogotá has three centres, all fairly close to each other. The historic centre is the Candelaria district, centred on the church of that name at Calle 11 and Carrera 4. In this hilly area of narrow lanes, street numbers are replaced by names (which nobody uses) — so Calle 13 becomes Calle del Socorro, and Carrera 5 is Calle del Refugio.

The 'political' centre is Plaza de Bolívar to the west, enclosed by Calles 10 and 11 and Carreras 7 and 8. But the main commercial centre, and the city's heart, is the Parque de Santander at Carrera 7 and Calle 16. From here, the most important roads (from the visitor's point of view) head north, with posh hotels, restaurants and embassies strung out along Avenida Caracas (Carrera 13) all the way up to the ring road at Calle 100.

ARRIVAL AND DEPARTURE

Air. So verdant and gentle is the countryside around El Dorado airport that you might imagine you're landing in Sussex rather than South America. The airport is only ten miles/16km west of the city centre. It has two sections: the main terminal, handling most international and domestic flights; and the Puente Aérea terminal, handling Avianca shuttles to Cali and Medellín plus flights to Miami and New York. Free minibuses link the two operations.

Arrival formalities are normally fast and efficient. A green/red push-button system operates for Customs: you press a button which selects a light at random, and you should escape quickly if it comes up green. A *cambio* in the baggage hall sells Colombian pesos at a reasonable rate, and there is a cash dispenser on the Departures level.

If you are connecting to another flight, you need to leave the terminal and re-enter through another door after a body and bag search.

A taxi to the centre costs around $10 for the 20-minute journey. If you cross the first road to the middle island, you can pick up a *micro* to the centre (30 minutes) for $0.25. If you are economizing drastically, one of the buses from the terminus half-concealed by shrubbery costs just $0.10 and takes 45 minutes.

Minibuses from central Bogotá out to the airport leave from the northeastern corner of the junction between Calle 19 and Avenida 10. Larger and cheaper buses tend to travel the course of Avenida Jiménez, e.g. from outside the Banco de la República.

To reach the airport, minibuses start from Calle 19 at Carrera 10. They head north on Carrera 10 as far as San Diego church, then dive down onto the motorway. Under good conditions you can reach the Puente Aérea terminal in 15 minutes, the main airport a couple of minutes later.

Airline Offices: to book domestic flights, head for the Hotel Tequendama. In this complex you can find offices for all the airlines (except the smallest, Aires). You can make all the bookings you need and juggle flights — if Satena has no seats into Leticia, you can check if Avianca has any.

The main offices are as follows:

Aces — Carrera 10 number 26-53 (tel 281 7800; fax 281 6605).
Aires — Avenida 13 number 76-56 (part of Los Héroes shopping complex; tel 286 8711).

Avianca — several offices including Carrera 7 number 16-36; for international flights dial 266 9700; for domestic services, 266 9600.
Intercontinental — Tequendama centre (tel 287 9777).

Train. The only train is the steam-hauled *tren turístico* which leaves each Sunday (and public holidays) to the small town of Nemocón, 45 miles/75km north of the capital. The service departs from the huge railway station in central Bogotá on Avenida Jiménez between Calles 18 and 19. The journey takes three hours (including a ten-minute stop for water), and the return service leaves at 3pm. The return fare is $4. Tickets are sold at the station ticket office at the following times: 8am-noon and 1.20-5.30pm from Monday to Friday, 8-11.50am on Saturday and 6.30-8.30am on the day of travel. Some travel agencies in the city also sell tickets for the trains.

Bus. Bogotá bus station is rather like an out-of-town hypermarket, plonked on a patch of wasteground five miles/8km west of the city centre. Numerous local buses serve it, including number 290 from the corner of Calle 13 and Avenida Caracas. It is a complex of five individual terminals, linked together with shops, restaurants, etc. Unlike the average Colombian bus station it is clean and orderly, though not without its villains — a favourite target is the sleepy and disorientated passenger just off an overnight bus.

The left-luggage facility and the Banco de Bogotá are just on the right as you enter Terminal 1. Expreso Bolivariano services to Cali and Medellín leave from here. The Telecom office is upstairs between Terminals 1 and 2. Both the Post Office and the Tourist Police are in Terminal 2. For services north to Cúcuta and the Venezuelan frontier, and to the Caribbean coast, go to Terminal 3. Long-distance taxis operate from Terminal 4. The tourist information office is in Terminal 5, which is where all the other buses depart from.

City Transport. A metro system, using derelict rail lines, has been planned since 1987, but no action has so far been taken. Therefore public transport consists of a fleet of decrepit ordinary buses (fare $0.10), *ejecutivo* buses which do not take standing passengers (fare $0.20) and smaller, more comfortable *chivas* (fare $0.30). The favourite model is the Chevrolet Luv, looking a little like a hearse. Get in, find a seat and hand the fare to the driver (via another passenger if necessary).

Taxis are even quicker and their drivers are almost all honest — they use the meter and charge what it says, not adding illusory supplements.

ACCOMMODATION

The optimum value is to be found at the Hotel Continental, a slightly jaded place on the east of the city centre at Avenida Jiménez number 4-77 (tel 342 5901). It offers good double rooms for $25 and a decent level of service; there is also a handy laundry next door. If it is full, almost adjacent is the Hotel Zaragoza, not nearly so nice but a fair bit cheaper — $15 double. A good value place in terms of comfort, security, location and price is Hotel La Sabana at Calle 23 number 5-23 (tel 284 4830). A double room costs $15. With a degree of pretension, the Hotel Dann describes its address as Avenida 19 (rather than Calle 19) number 5-72; tel 284 0100, fax 282 3108. A single room costs $24, a double $32.

Moving upmarket, the best-value business class hotel is the comfortable Bacatá, very central at Calle 19 number 5-20 (tel 243 2210), which provides all the features of a luxury hotel for $80 double. The Tequendama (Carrera 10 number 26-21;

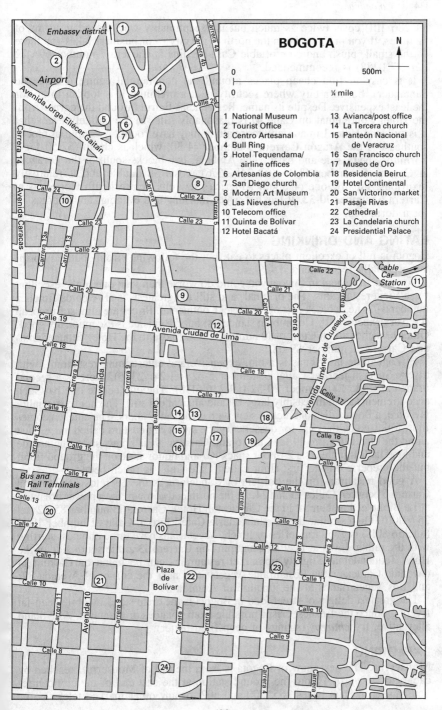

BOGOTA

N

0		500m
0		¼ mile

1 National Museum
2 Tourist Office
3 Centro Artesanal
4 Bull Ring
5 Hotel Tequendama/
   airline offices
6 Artesanías de Colombia
7 San Diego church
8 Modern Art Museum
9 Las Nieves church
10 Telecom office
11 Quinta de Bolívar
12 Hotel Bacatá

13 Avianca/post office
14 La Tercera church
15 Panteón Nacional
   de Veracruz
16 San Francisco church
17 Museo de Oro
18 Residencia Beirut
19 Hotel Continental
20 San Victorino market
21 Pasaje Rivas
22 Cathedral
23 La Candelaria church
24 Presidential Palace

Embassy district

Airport

Avenida Jorge Eliécer Gaitán

Carrera 4a
Carrera 4b
Calle 26

Carrera 14
Avenida Caracas
Carrera 13a
Carrera 13
Carrera 1
Calle 24
Calle 23
Calle 22

Cable Car Station

Calle 22
Calle 21
Calle 20
Avenida Ciudad de Lima
Calle 19
Calle 18
Calle 18
Calle 17
Calle 17

Carrera 4
Carrera 3
Carrera 1
Avenida Jiménez de Quesada

Carrera 12
Avenida 10
Carrera 9
Carrera 8

Calle 16
Calle 15
Calle 16
Calle 15

Carrera 13

Bus and Rail Terminals
Calle 14
Calle 13
Calle 12
Calle 11
Calle 10
Calle 8

Calle 14
Calle 13
Calle 12
Calle 11
Calle 10
Calle 9

Plaza de Bolívar

Carrera 11
Avenida 10
Carrera 9
Carrera 7
Carrera 6
Carrera 5
Carrera 4
Carrera 3
Carrera 2

tel 286 1111) costs twice as much but is exceptionally well placed in terms of facilities. If you prefer to be in the north of the city — or business takes you there — the small, plush and comfortable Casa Medina at Carrera 7 number 69A-22 (tel 217 0288) is recommended.

It is easy to find cheap places around the commercial centre (Parque de Santander), but in a city where security is at a premium it is foolish to go for the least expensive. Despite its name, Residencías Beirut (around the corner from the Hotel Continental on Calle 4) is reasonably safe. In the unlikely event that it is full, the Hotel Lima a few doors along may have room. A couple of blocks southeast is the Aragón Carrera 3 number 14-30, which is cheap ($2.50 for a dormitory bed), safe and basic. The Ambalá, two blocks south of the Zaragoza at Carrera 5 number 13-46 (tel 241 2376), costs $8 double and is relatively luxurious. Finally, one of South America's few city centre Youth Hostels is at Carrera 6 number 10-32. It has hot water morning and evening, and charges $3 for a dorm bed.

EATING AND DRINKING

Bogotá is full of excellent places to eat, but the following (from south to north) are especially recommended.

For your first meal in Bogotá you could do worse than visit one of the excellent Casa Vieja restaurants. The original, and still the greatest, is at Avenida Jiménez number 3-73, i.e. a block east of the Hotel Continental. Prices are almost European (i.e. very expensive by Colombian standards) but the cuisine is exceptionally good. Other branches are at Carrera 10 number 26-50 (close to the Hotel Tequendama) and Carrera 11 number 89-08.

El Zaguan de las Aguas is a big, expensive and entertaining restaurant, with a very Spanish feel, at Calle 19 number 5-62 (tel 241 2336); there is a second branch at Calle 100 number 20-52 (tel 236 6138). The city centre one has such accoutrements as an unfeasibly large till and ancient old still. The house speciality is *ajaico*, a Bogotá dish of chicken stew with cream and capers. The chicken comes first, followed by the egg: for dessert, try the sweet egg custard called *natas*. Just along the street, Centro 19 (at Calle 6 and Carrera 19) is a new shopping arcade and food hall. It includes a 24-hour snack bar and liquor store on the ground floor, but the crêperie on the first floor called Café Café, is much better.

A good restaurant on the borders of Candelaria is the Secretos del Mar, on Carrera 5 between Calles 13 and 14. At the north end of town, try a power breakfast at La Biblioteca restaurant in the Charleston Hotel, Carrera 13 number 85-42 (tel 257 1100). On a similar theme, the Galería Café Libro at Calle 81 number 11-92 (tel 256 8018) is good for coffee or lunch. Vegetarians have three choices, starting with the rather down-at-heel El Champiña on Carrera 13 at the south side of the Hotel Tequendama. Slightly upmarket restaurants can be found on Carrera 14 (Avenida Caracas): the Restaurante Vegetariano near the corner of Avenida 32; and Los Vegetarianos at the junction of Avenida 39.

The greatest delight of street food in Bogotá is the crisp stand. Mobile deep-fat fryers produce the freshest crisps possible from potatoes or plantains. As a bland alternative, try *churros* (strings of deep-fried batter).

EXPLORING

Monserrat. The best view of Bogotá is from the hill of Monserrat, reached by cable car (*teleférico*) from the ground station at the east end of the city centre. You can reach it on buses 265, 500 and 502, or any other marked teleférico or funicular. The cable car costs $2 for the return journey. It runs 7am-midnight from Monday to Saturday, and 5am-6pm on Sundays; at weekends, when queues are long, the cable car is supplemented by a funicular railway. Only the 5am start on Sunday allows you the awesome sight of the sun rising behind you over the sleeping city, but on any other day of the week you can see the sun set beneath you. At the top is a penitential chapel with a bloody figure of Christ. You can buy picture postcards of it at one of the many souvenir shops and cafés. When you descend, a reasonable selection of snack places across the road from the cable car station provides better-value food than that at the top of the hill.

Quinta de Bolívar. From the bottom of Monserrat, go down hill to the Quinta de Bolívar, the *finca* (ranch) where Simón Bolívar enjoyed his greatest glory and the place where his power slipped through his fingers. The Quinta is a beautiful colonial structure set in lovely gardens. You can wander around the rooms in which Simón Bolívar held court and planned manoeuvres. The atmosphere is calm and relaxed except when a party of schoolchildren arrives to pay homage to *El Libertador*. Outside is a monument to Colonel James Moore, who fought in the British Legion during the wars of independence. The Quinta is an ideal place to take refuge from the rigours of Bogotá. It opens 9am-5pm daily except Monday, (although if a Monday is a public holiday then it opens on that day but closes the following Tuesday).

The rest of the itinerary begins in the south of the city and runs northwards through the centre.

The Iglesia de San Ignacio (Calle 10 between Carreras 6 and 7) is big and impressive, the best proportioned church in Bogotá. It is almost adjacent to Plaza Bolívar, disfigured by the new palace of justice, which is being built on the north side. Despite this, the square is thoroughly impressive. To the east is the cathedral of Santa Fe; to the south, the national assembly with stout colonnades and a sandstone veneer. On the west side is the municipal hall, which has a curiously Georgian appearance. Nearby, along Calle 9 close to Carrera 8, the National Police Headquarters building is an impressive century-old structure, a national monument with a modest museum. The area of Candelaria (Calles 8-11, Carreras 3-9) has many other minor gems, and is lovely to stroll around in daylight.

Go north through the semi-restored streets of Candelaria until you reach the commercial heart of Bogotá, the Parque de Santander. Just before you reach it, look up for a visual pun — the office block housing the newspaper *El Tiempo* bears its name right next to a huge digital clock.

The square where Carrera 7 meets Calle 16 is bordered on its western side by three churches. The southernmost of these, San Francisco, has an extraordinary gilt altar, dripping with gold, plus a curious timber ceiling and oriental-looking confession boxes. A bleeding figure of Christ presides over this conglomeration. The church is busy with beggars and worshippers, and is well worth seeing during a service.

The Panteón Nacional de la Veracruz, just north, is much more austere, with a simple silver altar, and elegant ceiling and a smaller congregation. La Tercera — literally, the third church — has some wonderful wood carvings, plus dark timber and white plaster.

On the opposite side of the square from these churches is one of the best museums in South America, the Museo del Oro (Calle 16 number 5-41; tel 281 3065). It is much more than simply an exhibition of pieces of gold. The most priceless exhibit is the exquisite *balsa musica*, a delicate model of the raft on which El Dorado — the golden one — was launched onto the lake at Guatavita. A mechanized three-dimensional model of the scene allows you to see what went on, but you can visit the real site; see page 146. There is also a model of the Lost City. Occasionally live music and poetry are performed here. The Gold Museum opens 9am-4pm from Tuesday to Saturday, 9am-noon on Sundays and holidays. (At the start of 1992 parts of it were closed for refurbishment.) Security is extremely tight.

Continue north along Carrera 7, Bogotá's modest main shopping street — the shops are much better in Medellín. The Parroquia de Nuestra Señora de las Nieves (Carrera 7 between Calles 18 and 20) is the stripiest church in South America, banded with flesh and mauve. Inside, stout marble pillars support an intricate dome. The overall impression is of space and airiness. In the square opposite is a statue of Columbus.

You are now in a rougher part of town, though the main street should be safe. Turn right at Calle 24 — just before the busy underpass — to reach the Museo de Arte Moderno at number 6-55. It has an excellent permanent collection of contemporary South American art, and hosts some good visiting exhibitions. Further north, over the underpass, the beautiful church of San Diego is marooned in a swirl of traffic. Struggle across to it to see the striking interior, and also to browse around the artesans' market which is part of the complex.

Here you are directly opposite the best place in Bogotá to transact travellers' business, the Hotel Tequendama and its associated enterprises — everything from airline offices to a vegetarian restaurant, as well as banks, travel agencies and a Drug Store (selling nothing stronger than aspirin, plus English-language newspapers). In the Tequendama itself, look for the large mural in the foyer by the artist Luis Alberto Acuna, from the colonial town of Villa de Leyva.

Just north, at Carrera 7 number 28-66, is the big, spacious Museo Nacional. It is more interesting as a large piece of colonial architecture than as a museum; the exhibits are a motley collection from banknotes to modern Colombian art. It opens 9.30am-5.30pm from Tuesday to Saturday, 10am-4pm on Sundays.

SHOPPING

Neither the Centro Artesanal next to the Museo Nacional nor the nearby craft stalls at San Diego church are especially good value. For real bargains, head for Carrera 10 below Calle 13. In particular, the Pasaje Rivas (leading from Carrera 10 to Carrera 9, between Calles 10 and 11) is full of cheap crafts. This whole area is like one huge market, which merges with the 'official' market of San Victorino (enclosed by Carreras 11 and 12 and Calles 12 and 13).

Carrera 7 has plenty of bookshops. A good radical one is Libería Nueva Epoca, at Avenida Jiménez 4-88.

ENTERTAINMENT

Most of the nightlife takes place north of the commercial centre. Avenida Caracas is the main drag, with a cluster of restaurants around Calles 40 to 60. Further north, the area around Calles 82 to 85 is positively riotous — chic designer bars such as City Rock Café, Taxi Bar and Charlotte's, elegant restaurants and hotels, and hordes of rich young people on the razzle every night.

This area is relatively safe at night. If you prefer a greater degree of security, and a night out with a difference, join a *chiva* tour. These buses cruise around town, with free-flowing rum and a band playing in the back seat. A recommended agency is Confortur at Calle 68 number 4A-77.

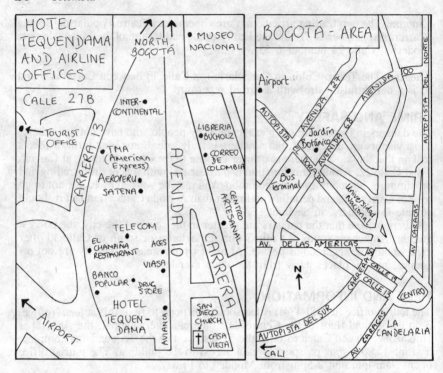

South American consulates:

Argentina — Avenida 40A number 13-09, tel 288 0900.
Brazil — Calle 93 number 14-20, 8th floor, tel 218 0800. Open 9am-noon and 2-4pm.
Chile — Calle 100 number 11B-44, tel 214 7496. Open 9am-2pm.
Ecuador — Calle 100 number 14-63, 6th floor, tel 257 9947.
Paraguay — Calle 57 number 7-11, tel 255 4160.
Peru — Carrera 7bis number 94-43. Open 8.30am-1.30pm.
Venezuela — Avenida 13 number 103-16, tel 256 3015; if you take in two photographs, $10, your passport and a ticket out of South America (it does not have to be out of Venezuela) when it opens at 8.30am, you should get a visa before closing time at 12.30pm.

NORTH OF BOGOTA

This section continues north and northeast from the capital, taking in an excellent day trip from Bogotá then following the route through Tunja, Bucaramanga and Pamplona to Cúcuta on the Venezuelan border. Further north you reach Valledupar, one gateway to the Sierra Nevada de Santa Marta, and the bizarre peninsula of La Guajira, at the northern tip of South America.

Zipaquirá and the Salt Cathedral. The small town of Zipaquirá, about 35 miles/58km north of Bogotá, has one of the most startling sights in South America — a full-sized cathedral, hewn out of salt, deep inside a hill.

Arrival and Departure: Zipaquirá buses run north along Avenida Caracas, marked

Zipa. The fare is $1 for the 90-minute journey. Each Sunday the tourist train from Bogotá (see page 132) sets off at 9am, calling at Zipaquirá about 2½ hours later.

Accommodation: The Hotel Colonial, on Calle 3 between Carreras 7 and 8, is quiet, cheap and friendly, with a pleasant courtyard. The Hosteria El Libertador (tel 3060), on the hill leading up to the Salt Cathedral, is opulent and has splendid views. A double room costs $25.

Exploring: The Salt Cathedral began in 1950, when miners felt they could apply their skills to some spiritual purpose. Thus they removed salt from a hill largely composed of the stuff in such a way as to create a house of God. It is used only once a year for Mass, for the Feast of Santa María del Rosario in October, and then only by miners. The rest of the time, tourists have the cathedral to themselves. Everyone who visits it is astonished.

To reach the cathedral, follow Carrera 7 south from the west side of the square. Bear right at the end of the street, up through a park. The walk from here to the entrance is a stiff 15-minute uphill hike; if you are short of breath or time, you may prefer to get a taxi. On the way up, you pass the luxurious Hosteria El Libertador, a good lunch stop if you're feeling rich. If you're not, the Cafeteria Guasa at the entrance to the cathedral will have to do; the workers' canteen is closed to visitors.

The entrance to the cathedral looks like a rail tunnel. Admission is $1. It opens 10am-noon and 1-4.15pm from Tuesday to Saturday, 10am-4pm on Sundays and holidays. The dramatic effect when you emerge from the dark entrance tunnel to the cavernous space of the cathedral is unforgettable. Inside, lighting is provided by a few flourescent strips. Once your eyes become accustomed to the gloom, you can make out designs such as a nativity scene in sodium chloride, complete with a cow erroneously carved in the sitting position adopted by dogs. The cathedral has eucalyptus fittings to avoid corrosion. The font is empty — water would dissolve the salt. Plans are apparently afoot to dig another church beneath the existing one.

Returning to the centre of town along Carrera 8, you pass the town's museum house at Calle 3. Nearby also is the Funzipa restaurant in a converted 19th century salt-processing works. Old tubs, once used to wash out salt, now boil potatoes. It sells *cuajada*, a soft cheese with syrup. The stone cathedral in the centre of Zipaquirá was consecrated in 1916, and it is worth putting your head around the door.

Help and Information: the Salt Cathedral is owned and operated by Concesión de Salinas, based in Bogotá at Calle 16 number 6-66, floors 3 and 4 (tel 286 0499). Check that the cathedral is open before travelling up to Zipaquirá.

Colectivos from Calle 5/Carrera 10 in Zipaquirá run ten miles/16km north through attractive scenery to the small and sleepy town of Nemocón, a place which comes alive every week for the arrival of the tourist train from Bogotá. The rest of the time it is a quiet, relaxed place where almost all the houses are painted green and white. If your next stop is the lake of El Dorado, you must return to Zipaquirá — a direct route through to the Carretera Central (the Bogotá-Sesquilé highway) is shown on some maps, but it is not passable by vehicles.

To reach Sesquilé from Zipaquirá, first take a colectivo from the railway station (at the foot of Calle 5) to Briceña. This is an unusual place on the main highway, since it has an enormous theme park — the Parque Jaime Duque. You will be at a loss to know how the owners managed to get an old warship and an Avianca DC6 aircraft to the site. Were it not for the park, Briceña would be just a ramshackle collection of roadhouses and a bus stop. Through buses from Bogotá stop here on their way north; board one for the 20-minute hop to Sesquilé.

Sesquilé. This small town is a mile off the main highway, and has been largely bypassed by traffic and the late 20th century. It has an implausibly grand church and a cheerful café/shop on the main square. Buses run through here to Guatavita. To get from Sesquilé back to Bogotá it is worth walking back to the main highway, where far more buses pass.

El Dorado. The original legend concerns an Indian king whose wife was unfaithful to him. Filled with remorse and shame, she drowned herself in the lake of Guatavita, two miles above sea level. The grieving king organized a ceremony whereby his body was covered in gold dust and he boarded a raft which sailed to the middle of the lake. Here he cast gold and jewels into the water, and dived in to wash off the dust. His people, gathered at the water's edge, threw their own gold possessions into the lake. Not surprisingly, this story caught the imagination and greed of the conquistadores. Repeated attempts, all unsuccessful, have been made to drain the lake.

To reach the site, get a bus southeast from Sesquilé. The large lake on the right is a reservoir considerably more modern than El Dorado. The bus driver will drop you at the right place, three miles/5km south of Sequilé. A battered sign points east uphill to Laguna de Guatavita. At a steady yomp the walk takes 75 minutes, but if you want to enjoy it, allow two hours. It is essential to take the correct path. The following times are approximately when you should reach each option if you walk at a good pace. 1 (15 minutes) — right; 2 (25 minutes) — left; 3 (35 minutes, just past the small shop — right; 4 (45 minutes, facing white house) — right; 5 (50 minutes, crossroads) — left; 6 (55 minutes, crossroads) — straight on. You reach the lip of the volcano after 65 minutes, from which it is a ten-minute scramble down to the lake. The journey back is not only much easier, it also gives splendid views of highland country.

If you have time, continue south along the edge of the reservoir to Guatavita, a town which is truly 'colonial-style'. It, like the lake, is an artificial creation. When the valley was flooded to create a reservoir, the old village of Guatavita was destroyed. A slightly Disneyesque replacement was built a few miles away, full of twee but unconvincing mock-colonial houses.

The last bus leaves Guatavita for Bogotá at 5.30pm, and passes the foot of the path to El Dorado lake about 15 minutes later, and leaves Sesquilé at around 6pm. Any later, you must hitch or take a taxi to the Carretera Central, a mile or so beyond Sesquilé. Long-distance buses can be flagged down, but note that most go to the Terminal de Transporte in the western suburbs of Bogotá; get off at Calle 127 (the ring road) if you want to continue straight into the centre of the city.

If, instead, you go northeast from Sesquilé along the Carretera Central, you pass through pleasant countryside and scrubby towns until you reach Tunja, the largest settlement in the department of Boyacá.

Tunja. This pleasant town was founded in 1539. Its altitude of over 9,000 ft/3,000m makes the climate bracing, to say the least. The house of the founder, Suárez Rendón, is the oldest of many lovely colonial houses, and also the location of the tourist office (tel 3272). The staff can provide information on the historic core, though the late 20th century is encroaching unpleasantly. Residencia El Cid (Carrera 10 number 10-66, tel 4111) is probably the most pleasant place to stay.

Villa de Leyva. Twenty miles/32 northwest of Tunja, this is the most perfectly preserved colonial town in Colombia and well worth a visit. The central square — the Plaza Mayor — would not look out of place in Andalucia, and provides a good reference point for just wandering around.

You can reach Villa de Leyva easily by bus from Tunja, an hour and $1 away. Some services go direct to and from Bogotá. Prices for accommodation are high, given the number of people from the capital. The best place to stay is the Duruelo Hospedería, a few minutes walk from the main square. It is beautifully kept, and the rooms are half-timbered. A double room costs $30 without a bath, $45 with. Similar rates apply at the Mesón del Plaza Mayor, on the main square.

An excellent way to enjoy the surrounding countryside is to hire a horse, though don't expect a thoroughbred — old nags are standard. Villa de Leyva has many interesting places to visit around it, including the monastery of La Candelaria, 12 miles/20km by road southwest. Young monks guide you around the monastery, which was founded in 1597. One unhistoric but interesting item here is the copy of the old altarpiece in the sacristry. The original was taken away for restoration after X-ray research showed that it had been overpainted.

Another religious site is the Convento del Santo Ecce Homo, a monastery 20 years younger than La Candelaria. On the way, try to locate Los Infernos, signposted from the road. This is a stone circle of phallic monoliths, which the indignant Spanish tried to destroy but which are now being restored. The site is open 9am-noon and 2-5pm daily except Tuesdays. Nearby is a far more ancient exhibit, El Fosil — a fossil of a massive dinosaur, believed to be over 100 million years old. It is closed on Thursdays.

Due east is the Tota lake, which has good fishing, but it is a long journey (via Paipa and Sogamoso) to reach it. The department of Boyaca stretches northeast right up to the Venezuelan frontier, but the Carretera Central veers north then northeast into the department of Santander. The capital, Bucaramanga, is an important route centre and a pleasant city in which to stop over. Although younger than Tunja (it was founded relatively late, in 1622), Bucaramanga has some pleasant quarters and plenty of parks. It is a busy student centre, with three universities, and wears its political colours on the masthead of its daily newspaper, *Vanguardia Liberal*. The main sight is the house in which Bolívar once lived, at Calle 37 number 12-15.

Barrancabermeja, 125 miles/200 km north of Bogota, is an important centre for oil production: most of Colombia's crude oil is refined here, making the town a frequent target for guerrilla attacks. If you want to risk the train to the coast, you can board the Santa Marta express from here; alternatively, you may find a riverboat heading downstream to Barranquilla or Cartagena. But it is probably better to continue north from Bucaramanga.

The remaining two directions from the huge crossroads of Bucaramanga are east to Pamplona and Cúcuta, close to the border with Venezuela, and north to the Caribbean coast at Santa Marta. These routes are dealt with in this order.

To Venezuela. The road climbs to nearly 4,000 metres as it winds up to Pamplona, under 40 miles/65km as the crow flies, but a journey of two or three hours. The ride beyond Pamplona to Cúcuta is stunning, though this last town is an anticlimax. If you fly in to cross the frontier into Venezuela, you are obliged to travel through Cúcuta; Camilo Daza airport is on the northwest side, while the road out to the border is from the southeast. You must get an exit stamp from DAS at the airport, or from the office at Calle 17 number 2-60. A taxi straight through from the airport to the frontier should cost $2 per person. Unless you have obtained a Venezuelan visa in advance, however, you will need to call in at the consulate at Calle 8 and Avenida 0.

To the Coast. Highway 45 runs north from Bucaramanga through relatively drab scenery, nowhere quite brushing against the Magdalena River. At the dusty road junction of San Rogue, you can choose between turning off on Highway 49 to Valledupar via Codazzi, or continuing on 45 north to Santa Marta. Note that even if your final destination is the Venezuelan frontier near Maicao, the direct highway is not fully surfaced, so a deviation via Santa Marta may actually save time. These two options are dealt with in order. The journey through the drowsy department of César to Valledupar is not without its attractive landscapes, and the villages you pass through seem frozen in time. Valledupar itself is of interest only as a starting or finishing point for Lost City treks — see page 147. Beyond here the road quality deteriorates significantly towards La Guajira peninsula. If you can get beyond Hato Nuevo (where the surfaced road ends) to the old railway, a dirt road parallel to the track goes straight as an arrow to the Caribbean.

Those who choose to head straight up to Santa Marta will have little to report en route. The highlight may be the town of Aracataca, 55 miles/88km before the beaches of Santa Marta. This, as the locals will not hesitate to remind you, is the birthplace of Columbia's greatest writer, Gabriel García Márquez. You will not be surprised that he now chooses to live elsewhere. While Shakespeare had the good fortune to be brought up in the green and pleasant lands of Stratford upon Avon, García Márquez had to make do with a dirty, pointless little town at the junction between the Carretera Central and the road to nowhere. Stay on the bus, and get to the much more pleasing ambience of Santa Marta.

LA GUAJIRA

This peninsula is the northernmost point in South America, but a trip to the continent's Land's End should not be undertaken lightly. It is a flat, bare, dry crust of earth curving around towards Venezuela; the neighbouring country has a sliver of the peninsula, which confers control of the waters of the Coquibacoa gulf leading to Lake Maracaibo. Venezuela claims a larger slice of the peninsula, but like its demand for a portion of Guyana, this is a piece of nationalistic rhetoric rather than a real desire for a patch of inhospitable territory.

The two main towns are Maicao, close to the Venezuelan frontier, and Riohacha on the coast. The Troncal del Caribe links them. Places north of this road are as Charles Nicholl describes them in *The Fruit Palace*: 'There are few reasons for going to the Guajira, and I was going there for the most common one: to do business with a smuggler...The Guajira is one big hideaway, an old-style badlands'.

Columbus' men made landfall at the Cabo de la Vela, but this is not the northernmost point — the honour goes to Punta Gallinas, 20 miles/32km further on. If you insist upon making the journey to either place, take great care. The border is just east of the dodgy town of Maicao. Do not stay here; ideally take an early morning bus from Maracaibo, cross over before lunch and get at least as far as the (still unfriendly) town of Riohacha before dusk; Santa Marta is a better bet. Note that you need a visa to undertake the crossing from Colombia into Venezuela.

CARIBBEAN COLOMBIA

This section covers the most popular region of the country. It begins with the Santa Marta area, including the awesome Sierra Nevada. West along the coast is the dismal port of Barranquilla and the heroic and glorious city of Cartagena. Inland is the equally fine colonial town of Mompós. Continuing west you reach the towns of Sincelejo, Montería and Turbo — the dusty, wild west town on the Gulf of Uraba.

SANTA MARTA

The northernmost city in South America, Santa Marta was also the first point to be settled by Europeans. It has one-third of a million inhabitants. Santa Marta is 430 miles/700km due north of Bogotá, 40 miles/68km northeast of Barranquilla as the crow flies but half as much again by the Carretera Troncal del Caribe. The Venezuelan border is 100 miles/160km east, beyond it the city of Maracaibo.

Physically, the city is similar to San Sebastián in Spain — an embracing bay ringed with hills, with an island planted in the middle. Where the historic old quarter should be, however, is an ugly modern port. A considerable amount of cocaine is exported from here. The coastline is by turns pretty and desecrated. North of the city — at Taganga — it is beautiful. The same distance south, El Rodadero is a fearsome development, highrise hotels wrecking the charm of this gently curving bay.

City Layout. In Santa Marta the coast runs north-south, not east-west as is normal in the Caribbean. Carreras go east-west, Calles north-south. All are numbered. Main thoroughfares are termed Avenidas, and each is named. Therefore Avenida Hernández Pardo is also Carrera 4, and Calle 22 is also Avenida Santa Rita. The main commercial street is Carrera 5, also known as Avenida Campo Serrano.

The railway forms the northern boundary of the city, and the Río Manzanares the southern. The main squares are the Plazas Bolívar and Basílica.

Arrival and Departure. *Air:* Santa Marta has no international flights. Simón Bolívar airport is ten miles/16km south of the city. It is reached on the Carretera Troncal del Caribe, the main highway to Barranquilla and Bogotá. The airport is falling to bits but is beautifully situated, perched between the mountains and the Caribbean (which makes it is an unwise choice for fearful flyers).

The 25-minute ride between the airport and Santa Marta costs $5 by taxi. The bus takes twice as long and makes a couple of disconcerting deviations, but costs only $0.20. The route runs through the beach resort of El Rodadero; if you have no accommodation booked you might choose to stay here, but otherwise get off on the seafront of the town proper. To get a bus to the airport, stand on the seaward side of the street.

Bus: the bus terminal is a chaotic shambles just southeast of the city centre at Calle 22 and Carrera 7. Although it seems to be in the middle of suburban squalor, it is in fact deceptively close to the centre — a walk of eight blocks west takes you to the sea.

Local services leave from the area nearest the street; other companies are based in the shed, rather like a dilapidated aircraft hangar, behind it. The main enterprises and their services are as follows (those marked * are luxury services):

Barranquilla: every 30 minutes from 5am to 8pm on Costeña; 9am, 10am, 11am, noon, 3.30pm, 5.30pm on Expreso Brasilia.

Benco: at 9am on Copetrán.

Bogotá: 11.30am, 3.30pm, 7pm on Copetrán, 2pm and 4.30pm on Expreso Brasilia.

Bucaramanga: 8.30am, 11.30am, 3.30pm on Copetrán; 10.30am, 2pm, 4.30pm on Expreso Brasilia.

Cartagena: 12.30pm and 3.30pm on Copetrán; 3pm on Expreso Brasilia; at other times take the Costeña bus to Barranquilla and change there.

Maicao: every half-hour 6am-4pm on Rapido Ochoa, with luxury services at 6am, 7.30am, 9am and 11am; on Expreso Brasilia at 6.30am, 7.30am*, 9am*, 9.30am, 11.30am, noon*, 12.30pm, 1.30pm, 2pm*, 2.30pm, 4pm.

Medellín: 7am, 8.30am, 12.30pm, 3pm*, 5pm*, 7pm on Rapido Ochoa; 8.15am, 12.15pm, 2.45pm, 4.45pm on Expreso Brasilia.

Plato: 11am on Copetrán.

Valledupar: 10am and 2.30pm on Copetrán.

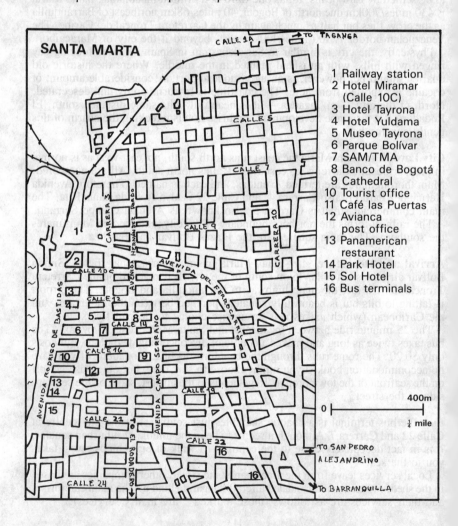

SANTA MARTA

1 Railway station
2 Hotel Miramar (Calle 10C)
3 Hotel Tayrona
4 Hotel Yuldama
5 Museo Tayrona
6 Parque Bolívar
7 SAM/TMA
8 Banco de Bogotá
9 Cathedral
10 Tourist office
11 Café las Puertas
12 Avianca post office
13 Panamerican restaurant
14 Park Hotel
15 Sol Hotel
16 Bus terminals

TO TAGANGA

TO SAN PEDRO ALEJANDRINO

TO BARRANQUILLA

0   400m
¼ mile

The 20-hour journey to Bogotá is most comfortably done with a break at Bucaramanga, halfway in terms of time although a little further than that in distance.

Local services are operated by Caña Verales, whose office is on Calle 20, a block in from the seafront.

Rail: South America's northernmost passenger rail station is at the top end of town, at Carrera 1 and Calle 7. Although Santa Marta is one end of Colombia's railway network, don't expect Grand Central Station or Clapham Junction; trainspotters would get bored silly here. Services are sparse, with just two departures each week. At noon on Sundays, and 8am on Tuesday, a train is scheduled to run south to Barrancabermeja, arriving about 12 hours later. The fare is around $7. If all you want is to say you've been on a Colombian train, take any of these services as far as Ciénaga. To reach Mompós (see page 154) take the train South to Palestinos, a shack in the middle of nowhere, hop on a jeep to El Banco, the cross to Mompós.

Accommodation. The Miramar hotel (Calle 10C number 1C-59) is the gringo hangout in Santa Marta, very popular with travellers taking advantage of dormitory beds at about $2. There have, however, been reports of thefts from here. On the seafront, the Park Hotel (Carrera 1 number 18-67, tel 33166) between Calles 18 and 20 is roomy and comfortable and costs $8 for a good double room. The nearby Miramar (Carrera 1 number 18-23, tel 33351) charges $11 and is no relation to the 'gringo' Miramar further north. The Costa Azul, about the same price, is comfortable and friendly; you can leave bags here.

In El Rodadero, a couple of miles south of the city, four hotels face the beach. From north to south they are La Sierra (tel 27681); El Rodadero (27262); Cañaveral (27002); and Tamaca Inn (27015).

Eating and Drinking. The Panamerican restaurant on the seafront at Calle 18 is an excellent place to eat, drink and listen to music — Sunday afternoons are particularly popular. Of the many other places, the pleasant Café Las Puertas (corner of Carrera 3 and Calle 18) is fine for lunch.

Exploring. Despite Santa Marta being one of the first Spanish settlements in South America, 'sights' as such are thin on the ground. The city's main claim to fame is that Simón Bolívar died here, disillusioned and dispossessed, on 17 December 1830. He lost his final battle, against tuberculosis, at the San Pedro Alejandrino farm, a couple of miles inland, just south of the Río Manzaneres. It is an attractive hacienda which contains some of the Libertador's belongings. He is not buried in Santa Marta, but in the city of his birth, Caracas. The farm opens 9.30am-4.30pm daily except Sundays. A taxi from town should cost $1, from El Rodadero $2; if there is any argument, a sign at the entrance quotes official fares.

The other great treasure of Santa Marta is the Tayrona Gold Museum on the north side of Parque Bolívar. It is in the old Custom House, the oldest surviving building in Santa Marta (the Spanish always saw to it that administration preceded all other activities). The museum is dedicated to the craft of the Tayrona people, and goes into considerable detail about their achievements. The gold work itself is stunning, almost matching that in the Gold Museum in Bogotá, although the whole collection is many times smaller. It opens 8-11.45am and 2-5.45pm from Monday to Friday.

Other sights, such as they are, can be found within a few blocks of the Plaza de Bolívar. If you wish to trace the steps of the writer Charles Nicholl, visit the site of the former Fruit Palace. It is at Calle 10 number 2-49, a couple of blocks inland from the sea between Carreras 2 and 3, and is now known as the Tienda El Progreso.

Help and Information. The tourist office is inside the Convent of Santo Domingo at British 2 number 16-44. A branch office is located at the resort of El Rodadero, on Calle 10. Avianca and its associated post office is on the corner of Calle 17 and Carrera 3.

AROUND SANTA MARTA

Taganga. Pigs and chickens roam the streets of this scrubby resort which oozes charm — if you like the idea of rubbing shoulders with ordinary Colombians taking a break, this is far more likely to be your choice than is El Rodadero. It has an idyllic Caribbean setting, palm trees and a few tolerable cafés and hotels. The background is mountains shrouded in dense green and mist. Taganga is ten minutes by bus from the point marked on the map, and hitching is easy.

Tayrona National Park. If the Sierra Nevada (see below) is too much for you, this stunningly attractive park 30 miles/48km east of Santa Marta is a good day out. Note that the spelling of Tayrona varies; it is sometimes written Tairona, and a hotel on the Santa Marta seafront has two signs, each with a different spelling. Pick up a map of the park from the Santa Marta chamber of commerce, at Carrera 2 number 22-58.

You can reach Tayrona on any eastbound bus from Santa Marta, i.e. those heading for Riohacha and Maicao. It takes about an hour to get there, but allow two for the return journey because of police checks for smugglers. A taxi will do the run for about $10 one way, $25 if you want the driver to wait for some hours before returning.

The park entrance is by a shack in the road. The distance to the park headquarters at Cañaveral is about 3 miles/5km, a difficult walk if the sun is high. Upon arrival you must pay a nominal entrance fee. The beach you stumble on is beautiful and uncrowded, though dangerous — the currents are lethally strong. Playa las Naranjas is safer; to get here, walk 500m into the park from the main road. At the bottom of a long, straight slope, the road curves around to the left and you reach a hut, also on the left. Take the path leading off to the right, and keep walking for three miles/5km.

From the seashore at Cañaveral you can walk for an hour southwest, along marked trails, to Pueblito — an ancient Indian village, with the same stone platforms as the Lost City but on a much smaller scale. From here you must retrace your steps to Cañaveral; it is difficult and dangerous to head south to the highway.

LA CIUDAD PERDIDA

The Lost City, *la ciudad perdida*, is the largest ancient settlement discovered in the Americas this century. It was built by the Tayrona Indians during the equivalent of the European dark and middle ages, in the north of the mountains of what is now the national park of the Sierra Nevada de Santa Marta. It stands on a ridge, surrounded by jungle, at around 4,000 ft/1,250m. When it was occupied it had a population of some 1,500 people.

The wooden buildings of the city were burnt down by the Spanish leaving behind the stone terrace foundations and the network of paved paths you see today. The Conquistadores found little of value and left the site to be overrun by the surrounding jungle. The city was not resettled and apparently remained forgotten until this century.

In 1975 graverobbers — *guaqueros* — rediscovered it. Rumours linked the city to El Dorado (the gilded one), and his legendary city of fabulous wealth. The Spanish discovered little in Indian tombs, and it was said the Indians had spirited the treasure away from the advancing Spanish and had hidden it elsewhere in the mountains. Indian leaders were kidnapped and tortured to reveal the location of the trove. But if the adventurers had any luck they kept quiet about it. Nevertheless, newly discovered tombs became the site of gunbattles between rival gangs of guaqueros. The government intervened, declaring the city a protected archaeological site. A permanent police post was established at the city and permit requirements started.

The lazy and expensive way to get there is by helicopter from Santa Marta. It takes about 20 minutes one way, costs about $300 round trip. You return the same day, having had great views of the jungle from the helicopter.

The alternative is a trek by foot taking up to a week. Opinions as to the best tours vary greatly, and it is essential to ask around as much as possible — a poor guide will ruin the trip and may also place you in danger. So ask other travellers for recommendations. Recent reports suggest that the tourist office in Santa Marta will tell you that you need two permits and that tours not run by the office risk being turned back by the police at the city. The 'official' tours cost about $200 all in. On the other hand the Miramar hotel (Calle 10C number 1C-59) has been running treks for a number of years without problem. All in — guide, porters, food including cooking, hammocks, mosquito nets and truck transport to the start of the trek — the Miramar charges about $120. You can get a cheaper deal if you take your own food, do you own cooking, sort out your own sleeping arrangements and pay for your own transport. Miramar parties do not appear to have a problem with permits — the fact that they take mail and cigarettes to the homesick police at the city may have something to do with it.

It is important to go with a guide. One, the route, which includes crossing the same river about half a dozen times, is not that obvious. Two, the local Kogi indians of the jungle do not like outsiders (nor having their photos taken). Three, marijuana and opium are grown in the jungle and you do not want to be part of the harvest. Guerrillas are less of a problem than they used to be, but it's worth asking the locals.

It should not take longer than a few days to organize a trek at the Miramar. The minimum number of trekkers is four. You carry your personal gear, which should include water bottle, waterproofs, torch, insect repellent (expect to be eaten alive) and a sleeping bag — although you spend the nights under cover, it is still chilly. Also take a book to occupy the hours after finishing the days trekking — you tend to start early and finish early afternoon.

The approach to the city takes $2\frac{1}{2}$ days. Anyone who is reasonably fit and not overburdened should have no problem. The food is surprisingly good and you wash in rivers along the way. The Lost City itself may not be much to look at but the fabulous setting and the sense of discovery both make it one of the most worthwhile and memorable experiences in Colombia.

The journey between Santa Marta and Barranquilla is much faster than it used to be, because of the causeway which has been built across the shore of the Ciénaga swamp. Unfortunately, the view is distressing, since the effect of building the causeway was to deprive the plantlife of the seawater it needed. Most of it has died, leaving grotesque dead branches rotting in the water on the landside of the causeway.

BARRANQUILLA

Just over one million people live in Barranquilla, making it Colombia's fourth largest city. It occupies the south bank of the Río Magdelena, close to the Caribbean coast and midway between Cartagena and Santa Marta. Barranquilla is the least attractive city in Colombia and the sort of place you should pass through as quickly as possible.

Arrival and Departure. The modern airport (tel 470500) is ten miles/16km south of the city centre. A taxi costs $5; look for the despatcher of cabs marked *Servicio Público* to avoid hustlers. To get the bus ($0.20) you need to leave the airport compound and go out to the main road. A peculiarity of Avianca schedules is that you can fly direct to Europe from Barranquilla, but return flights go only as far as Cartagena. You can fly direct to (but not from) Madrid, Paris and Frankfurt on Thursdays and Saturdays. Most domestic destinations are served regularly, and there are direct flights to Miami and Panama City.

All the bus offices are in the area around Calle 34 and Carrera 44. The four leading bus companies are Coolibertador at Calle 34 number 44-40, Expreso Brasilia, Carrera 35 number 44-63, Rapido Ochoa Carrera 45B number 33-01, and Copetrans, Calle 45 number 32-37.

Coastal journeys to Cartagena and Santa Marta leave from the centre of town every 30 minutes during the day, with the the last service at around 4pm. Transportes La Costeña, Calle 34 number 44-14 (tel 322928/411396).

Accommodation. If you want to be close to the bus station (either because you arrive late or want to leave early, or just like buses), stay at the Hotel Canadiense, adjacent to the telephone office at Carrera 38 and Calle 45 (Murillo). The best value place to stay in the centre is the big and friendly Hotel Victoria, at Calle 35 number 43-140 (tel 410055). For $5 you get a comfortable room with bathroom, and the indulgence of the staff. If you've arrived without money, they will even lend you cash until the following morning.

Barranquilla has a good number of more upmarket places, such as the flashy Hotel Majestic at Carrera 53 number 54-41 (tel 320150; fax 413733); despite its accoutrements, it costs only $30 per night for a decent twin room.

Eating and Drinking. Avenida 20 de Julio (also known as Carrera 43) is the restaurant strip, especially around Calle 69/70. In the middle of it is El Merendero, an excellent steak place. The Ostería El Capi, at the corner of Carrera 46 and Calle 72, is a jolly bar which opens until 3am. Nearby is good territory. The fine Mediterraneo is a restaurant/open air bar on Calle 72 at Carrera 47. It is close to two other decent places, Dos Mundos (on Calle 72 between 47 and 48) and La Fondita (Calle 72 between 48 and 49).

Help and Information. Few people hang around long enough to make phone calls, post letters or change money (although if you want to do the latter you should head for the centre of town, lined with casas de cambio). The local newspaper, *La Libertad* gives some indication of what is going on. For Caribbean music tune to 89.2; for rock 96.2; 103.1 for classical. The Barranquilla soccer club Junior is one of the best in Colombia. The British Consulate is at Carrera 44 number 45-57 (tel 326936).

CARTAGENA

'Cartagena de Indias, Colombia, América del Sur. Fundada por Don Pedro de Heredia, el 1º de Junio de 1533'. So reads the municipal seal of South America's most perfect colonial city. A poster in the National Maritime Museum in Greenwich seeks to recruit pirates to rob Spanish galleons at Cartagena. It was one end of the maritime highway, the Spanish Main, which brought treasure back from South America to the country which invested in these expeditions. It therefore became the target of every pirate in the northern hemisphere, and despite an extraordinary system of defensive fortifications it was attacked repeatedly. The only successful defence was against a British admiral called Henry Vernon, who was repulsed in 1740 by one Don Blas, who in the course of his battles lost most of his limbs. Disease among the British crew eventually led to their withdrawal, and Cartagena was pronounced a 'hero city'.

The colonial heart of the old town survived intact. Today — despite being surrounded with the trappings of ugly commercialism, such as an oil refinery — the historic centre of this port of 420,000 is breathtaking.

City Layout. If you look at the layout of Cartagena as a torso with outstretched arms, the airport is at the tip of the right arm and Bocagrande, the new highrise area, at the end of the other arm, slightly crooked. The Old City is at the shoulders, the San Felipe fortress at the waist and the hill of La Popa is at the right thigh. The left armpit is the Muelle de los Pegasos, the main quay. The main commercial area is squeezed between Avenida Venezuela and Avenida Daniel Lemaitre; south of the latter road is the poorer, rougher quarter of Getsemani.

Arrival and Departure. *Air:* Rafael Nuñez airport is three miles/5km north of the walled city. You can arrive from Europe on Avianca, but the return flights go from Barranquilla. From the airport, walk straight out, past the Aeropuerto 78 restaurant and the Soda Clausen sign to Calle 70. Cross the road and wait for a bus outside El Nuevo Almendro; most go to the centre. To reach the airport from the town, take any bus marked Crespo.

Bus: all the companies are strung out along Calle 32, the main road out of the city which begins on the north side of San Felipe fortress. La Costeña, Unitransco and Rapido Ochoa are huddled together just east of the fort, while Expreso Brasilia is further east — almost at the foot of La Popa. Services along the coast, and to Medellín and Bogotá, are frequent. Further east still is the market area, from where local buses leave to Pasacaballos and Palenque.

Accommodation. In the old town, the Hotel Bucaríca could not be more central — at the junction of Calles San Agustín and Porvenir. Unfortunately, the price of convenience is noise almost around the clock. There is a bunch of cheap hotels on Calle de la Media Luna in Getsemani; the Hotel Valle — halfway along — is the best. Avoid the Hotel Montecarlo, a highrise on the fringe of the old town, which is infamous for thefts — most of which seem to be inside jobs. The Del Lago, adjacent, is cheaper ($6 double) and safer; it is the building marked with a Pepsi logo on the illustration at the start of this chapter. Perhaps the best bet, though inconveniently located a mile north of the old town walls, is the Bellavista on Avenida Santander — the seafront — at number 46-50 (tel 654210). A pleasant double room costs $8.

Eating and Drinking. The great local speciality is *peto*, a hot, sweet maize drink sold by street vendors. It tastes rather like liquid rice pudding.

The old city has some fine restaurants, though they are expensive by Colombian standards. Calle Universidad has an excellent place — the Restaurant de la Universidad. Along its continuation, Calle Tejadillo (going north towards the sea) is one of Cartagena's flashiest restaurants, Novedades de Tejadillo, where the high prices are justified. Andrei's, at the corner of Calle Santo Domingo and Calle de las Damas, is elegant, cool and expensive — the menu shows no prices. At the other end of the price scale, the row of huts along the quayside dispenses all manner of snacks. Facing them, just inside the walls, is the Rincón de los Coches, a real dive which is very cheap. Similarly, there are plenty of reasonable comedores and some riotous bars. The centre of the old city is the best place to look.

In Bocagrande, a bunch of steak houses are concentrated at the junction of Avenida 3 and Calle 5: on Avenida 5 is El Chamizo Países, while La Pampa and Dany El Churrasco Argentina are on Calle 5.

For a nightcap, and to plan the next day's exploring, go to the Bodegón de la Candelaria. It is in the exquisite Casa de la Candelaria, an old merchant's house, and is one-third restaurant, two-thirds museum. You can read explanations of why slaves and goods were kept on the ground floor, more valuable goods on the mezzanine, bedrooms on the upper floor. The pinnacle is the Mirador bar, in a lookout tower reached by a creaky staircase. The views over the cathedral and port are excellent, and a wonderfully cooling breeze blows through. You wouldn't want to have too much to drink, partly because of the dangers of descending while inebriated and also because of the high price of drinks. Beer is unavailable, and cocktails are greatly overpriced. The restaurant is wonderful but expensive, so you might just want to go to the Bodegón for a single indulgent drink and a good snoop around the house. It opens 7-11pm (except Sundays), and also for lunch from Monday to Friday. If you want a cheaper late night drink, La Gallería is a fine place, built into the city wall at the west end of Calle Ayos.

Exploring. Cartagena poet Luis Carlos López found his home town only as inspiring as a pair of old shoes. His view is a mystery. The beautiful colonial architecture alone makes Cartagena well worth a visit. To appreciate the town from a spectacular viewpoint make your way to the huge solid-looking fortress of the Castle of San Felipe de Barajas, built between 1536 and 1657. This is the most formidable single structure in South America. It was designed by a Dutchman, Richard Carr, and built in 1657. After a few batterings as the continent's frontline, it was strengthened by an engineer called Antonio de Arevalo, who also added the warren of tunnels which thread through the fortifications.

If you can persuade the unconcerned women at the entrance to sell you a ticket you may stagger up the steep ramparts and gain a superb view of the rusty brown and grey buildings that comprise both the old and new parts of the town. The underground tunnels and barracks are open to wander through and are dimly lit and atmospheric. One of the most startling aspects of the fortress is the enormous owl which, perching on one of the many cannon pointing out over Cartagena towards the sea, gazes sentinel-like across the city.

Walking down the main road from the fortress you reach one end of Avenida Venezuela. Here stands the Monumento a los Indias Catalinas, a modern monument to the indigenous people. A magnificent Indian woman gazes inland into the heart of Colombia, her statue usually flanked by a dissolute gang of Cartagena youths.

Continuing down Avenida Venezuela you will eventually reach the Puerta del

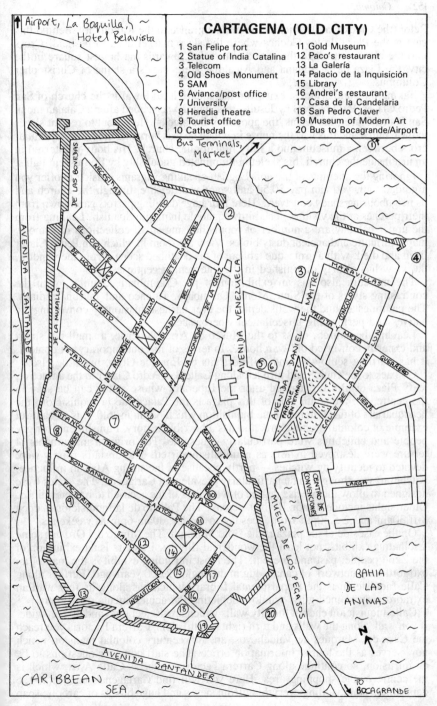

CARTAGENA (OLD CITY)

1 San Felipe fort
2 Statue of India Catalina
3 Telecom
4 Old Shoes Monument
5 SAM
6 Avianca/post office
7 University
8 Heredia theatre
9 Tourist office
10 Cathedral
11 Gold Museum
12 Paco's restaurant
13 La Galería
14 Palacio de la Inquisición
15 Library
16 Andrei's restaurant
17 Casa de la Candelaria
18 San Pedro Claver
19 Museum of Modern Art
20 Bus to Bocagrande/Airport

Airport, La Boquilla, Hotel Belavista

Bus Terminals, Market

AVENIDA SANTANDER

AVENIDA VENEZUELA

DE LAS BOVEDAS

NECESIDAD

SANTO

EL BOQUETE

DE HOYO

DEL SITIAR

DEL CURATO

DE LA MURALLA

SIETE INFANTES

DEL CABO

SANTISIMO

DE LA CRUZ

TABLADA

BADILLO

DE LA MONEDA

TEJADILLO

DE LA MERCED

ESTANCO DEL AGUARDE

UNIVERSIDAD

AGUSTIN

PORVENIR

BADILLO

DANIEL LE MAITRE

TRIPITA

CONCLON

MEJIA

LUNA

MARAVILLAS

SIERPE

GUERRERO

CALLE DE LA NIEVA

PARQUE CENTENARIO

MUELLE DE LOS PEGASOS

CENTRO DE CONVENCIONES

LARGA

ESTANCO DEL TABACO

DON SANCHO

SAN

ARZOBISPADO

FACTORIA

SANTOS DE PIEDRA

SANTO DOMINGO

DE LA INQUISICION

DE LAS DAMAS

BAHIA DE LAS ANIMAS

CARIBBEAN SEA

AVENIDA SANTANDER

TO BOCAGRANDE

N

151

Reloj (the Clock Gate) which is the main entrance to the walled city. Behind this gate is the Plaza de los Coches where the slave market used to be held. Cross into the old city through the gate and turn left towards the largest square in the city, the Plaza de la Aduana and Alcaldia. Here stands a statue of Christopher Columbus.

Taking the southernmost exit from the square head towards the church of San Pedro Claver. Built in 1603 by Jesuits, this church was named after a Catalan monk San Pedro Claver, known as 'the apostle of the blacks'. He set out to recruit slaves to the Church and this was the house in which he was born and died. It is a peculiar cross between a museum and a fully functioning church. His body is interred in an urn inside the church, his skeleton illuminated ghoulishly by flourescent lights.

Ignoring the attempts of the non-English-speaking vagrants outside to offer you a guided tour, you can pay $0.50 and wander at leisure through the church and its neighbouring shady courtyard. Here four huge dazzling parrots gaze down from their perches at the visitors. The birds squabble in pidgin Spanish. Leading from the upper balcony are a number of rooms housing small collections of armour, maps, furniture and ancient dusty bibles. View the room in which San Pedro Claver lived and died, with a grotesque tableau of his deathbed scene. From the window, the view has clearly diminished in the intervening centuries.

The museum also has an exhibition of pre-Columbian ceramics, with the contrasting styles of the Sinu, Monil, Quimbaya, Tumaco and Tayrona Indians. The paintings around the walls depict the ever-earnest missionary converting the natives and performing miscellaneous heroic acts.

Leaving the church, cross to the Museo de Arte Moderno, a small but smart and expertly converted old warehouse. In terms of its contemporary art content, it has startling sculptures and self-portraits by Enrique Grau, but little else.

Go back to the church and turn left along Calle San Pedro Claver to the attractive, leafy Plaza de Bolívar, named after the Liberator whose statue can be seen in the centre. On the south side of this plaza is the Palacio de la Inquisición, the headquarters of the Tribune of the Inquisition which began in 1610. It is a beautiful example of colonial architecture, and has a horrible history. Punishments for gay people and epileptics were particularly gruesome. The original instruments of torture were destroyed in 1811 as nationalism stirred. The upstairs rooms were devoted to identifying witches — partly because of the strong African influence, witchcraft was thought to be particularly prevalent in Cartagena. The scales were designed to allow the precise degree of witchness of the accused to be determined. Other sights include Simón Bolívar's cloak. The Palacio de la Inquisición is open 8-11.30am and 2-5.30pm from Tuesday to Friday, 10am-6pm at weekends.

On the east side of the plaza is the Gold Museum. The Museo del Oro has some fascinating exhibits, not least the wonderful filigree. Upstairs is an exhibition of the Zenú people, past and present. The most intriguing exhibit is the map of an extraordinary network of canals dug in the region 2,000 years ago. Further along Calle Inquisición is the Departmental Library which has along its rear wall an extraordinary stained-glass window depicting the achievements of women.

Calle Inquisición ends at the city walls which are 40 feet high and 50 feet wide. If you walk along the walls and turn right (south) along Carrera Factoria you reach the Casa del Marques de Valdehoyos, an 18th century colonial mansion which now serves as the tourist information office. The staff consider questions to be an intrusion, so continue along Carrera Factoria as far as Calle Ayos, which is the centre of the shopping area. Here you will find Cartagena's answer to the department store, selling everything from sieves and huge blocks of carbolic soap

The Islands. West of Cartagena are some fascinating islands. Launched sail from the town end of the Muelle de los Pegasos, and provide a harbour cruise into the bargain — the ideal way to see Cartagena is at sea; from the water, Bocagrande looks like a Manhattan in the tropics, and only closer inspection reveals its shabbiness.

Tierrabomba is the first island the westbound boat reaches (after 20 minutes), stopping first at a small settlement on the southeastern part of the island, whose chief feature is a derelict church. Ten minutes later you reach the resort of Bocachica; get off at the final stop, the Fuerte San José. The fort, built in conjunction with the San Luis fort across the water, was intended to destroy boats heading through the straights. Vernon flattened the fort in 1741, but it was rebuilt a dozen years later. Now it is a series of empty and uninteresting chambers. None of the amateur guides who offer to show you around is likely to be much help. But the beach life at Bocachica is fun, and it is a good place to meet some Colombians.

A more rewarding day trip is out to the reefs and beaches of the Rosario islands, 25 miles/40km southwest of Cartagena. These coral islands are a delight, and the standard day trip packs in swimming, lunching and hassle from salesmen trying to sell tacky trinkets of black coral. With luck you will also visit the natural aquarium, a cordoned-off inlet on one of the smaller islands where you can see sharks and turtles (segregated) close-up. Most tours set off at 8am from the southwest end of the Muelle in Cartagena, and strenuous efforts are made to get you to buy a ticket in advance. If you just turn up, however, you will be able to play one boatowner off against another and whittle the price down to $15 or so.

Isla Barú is an island only because the Canal del Digue, which links Cartagena with the Río Magdalena, makes it so. It is swampy, steamy and poor. You can reach its nicest spot, Playa Blanca, by launch from Cartagena. Or take the bus out to Pasacaballos, cross the canal on the makeshift ferry and travel on by truck. This takes about three times longer and is not desperately rewarding.

Palenque. San Basilio de Palenque, to give this village its full name, is a fascinating place. It is in the hills south of Cartagena and is an exclusively black settlement, peopled by the descendants of freed and escaped slaves. The social and religious conventions are markedly different from the rest of Colombia, having much more in common with the Caribbean than with Spanish-speaking South America.

The people are engaged mainly in growing produce for Cartagena and the region. Buses to Palenque leave from the main market, mostly in the afternoon since this is when the vendors return. The journey time is around three hours, over poor roads. Formal accommodation does not exist in Palenque, but it should not be difficult to find a family to stay with; the people in the village are overwhelmingly friendly.

To sample something of the life of Palenque without making the long journey out there, visit the *barrio* just northeast of the main city market in Cartagena where a large community of *Palenqueños* live. It is important to be able to speak Spanish, or to go with someone who can, in order to explain your visit and avoid hostility. (On the bus up to Palenque you are sure to arouse interest and to meet people who will look after you.)

MOMPOS

In 1810 Mompós was the first town of the province of New Granada (modern day Panama, Columbia and Venezuela) to declare independence from Spain. Simón

Bolívar once said 'While to Caracas I owe my life, to Mompós I owe my glory'. Mompós is an attractive historical town off the beaten gringo trail. While somewhat isolated, it was once an important commercial centre. All the trade betweeen Cartagena and the interior used to pass along the branch of the River Magdalena on which it is located. Its importance declined in the 19th century but its rich churches and mansions are evidence of more affluent times.

Arrival and Departure. Aces flies daily from Cartagena ($15 one way) and three times a week from both Barranquilla and Montería. The airport is a mile out of Mompós. Jeeps run to and fro according to demand (pay no more than $1). Normally they base themselves in the main plaza in the town.

There is one direct bus daily from Cartagena. Or you can take a bus to Magangue from Cartagena and then a motor launch *(chalupa)* down the river to Mompós. From Magangue you can also go by boat to Bodega and then pick up a jeep for Mompós.

Accommodation and Food. The Hostal Doña Manuela is beautiful and expensive ($12 single, $15 a double). It has a reasonably priced restaurant and the only swimming pool in town. The cheap alternative is the Doña Leyla at about $2.50 a night, overlooking the river and main square (Plaza Real de la Concepción). A family named Urbina Monroy, at Carrera 2A number 20-67, provides cheap lodging and is very friendly. The Manuela is still the place to eat — few other places open in the evening.

Exploring. The original white colonial houses and mansions have been preserved in the centre of the town. Their huge gates open off the streets into pretty courtyards. Among them is the aforementioned Hostal Doña Manuela. Its courtyard has an enormous tree hung with creepers that have reached down to the ground to establish their own roots.

The Casa de Cultura is one block from the Doña Manuela. It contains a few interesting historical artifacts. Take a walk along the river past the 17th century Iglesia de Santa Barbara — unique not only in Mompós but in Colombia. Its Moorish tower with surrounding balcony is different to anything else you will see. For more typical Colombian church architecture see the San Agustín, La Concepción, and San Francisco.

Help and Information. The Doña Manuela serves as something of an unofficial tourist office for Mompós, having a simple map of the town and some basic information. It may also be able to arrange visits to see artisans making filigree gold jewellery — they do not have shops but work and sell from home. Just round the corner from the main square is the airline office — also the only place in town where you can exchange dollars, although at a poor rate.

MONTERIA

The capital of the department of Córdoba has little of interest to travellers. Come here to catch a bus to the mud volcano at Arboletes 50 miles/80km north on the coast, or use the airport. Should you be in Montería for longer than a transit, orientate yourself by finding Carrera 2, the main shopping street lined with market stalls. Most of the bus stations and offices are in the area close to the junction of Carrera 2 and Calle 40. The cheap hotels are close to this main street. Walk down it (decreasing Calle numbers) and you come to the river. The riverbank has plenty of lively bars and restaurants while there are ferries to more secluded drinking holes on the other side of the river.

Arboletes. The mud volcano at Arboletes should not be missed. It is a three-hour ride on a local bus along a poor road from Montería; there are also buses to and from Turbo. Get off in the main plaza and walk down to the beach. Turn right and walk along the sand for ten minutes before cutting inland up an encrusted mud hillock. The 50m-wide pool of natural bubbling mud is at the top. For instant sensory deprivation dive straight in — the mud takes an alarmingly long time to clear from nostrils, eyes and ears. They say it is good for your skin and hair condition. When you've had enough wallowing wash the mud off in the sea.

If you fancy a full course of treatment, Arboletes is a friendly enough place to stay, though the beach is a bit dirty. The bakery-cum-café on the east side of the main plaza serves cheap and delicious pastries.

TURBO

Turbo is a hot and dusty port on the Caribbean, due north of Medellín. It is best considered in terms of its facilities: boats to Cartagena, upstream to Quibdó, across the Gulf of Uraba to Darién; buses direct to Medellín and Cartagena; flights to Medellín and towns in the Chocó. Hang around only long enough to locate your chosen form of transport. If you need to stay overnight, easily the safest and fanciest hotel is the Castillo del Oro.

SAN ANDRES

This name describes three entities. The broadest definition is of the group of islands off the coast of Nicaragua, which for strange historical reasons is Colombian. The largest of these islands is San Andrés itself. And the main town on this island is San Andrés.

San Andrés, the archipelago, changed hands as regularly as most Caribbean islands from the start of the 16th century onwards. After the Spanish abandoned the islands as uninteresting (i.e. devoid of precious metal), the Dutch held them for a time. Then British pirates, with the full collusion of the Crown, saw the potential for using them as bases from which to attack galleons carrying gold from Panama; at this stage all the treasure from western South America was transported from the Panamanian harbour of Portobelo, south of San Andrés, to Cartagena. Captain Henry Morgan, after whom a brand of rum is named, attacked almost anything that moved, on the grounds that any vessel sailing east was guaranteed to be carrying a high-value cargo.

Business with slightly more legitimacy was introduced with the development of agriculture on San Andrés island itself, using black slaves brought in from other British colonies in the Caribbean. Their descendants comprise the dominant ethnic group in San Andrés. British influence waned, and — like the English-speaking communities on the Caribbean coast of the Central American mainland — San Andrés was a real colonial backwater.

Just as the developing nations of Central America took control of these coastal communities, so too did Colombia annex San Andrés. At the time Colombia included what is now Panama, giving a faint legitimacy to the acquisition, although three countries — Costa Rica, Nicaragua and Honduras — are much closer to the islands. The Nicaraguans have the strongest claim, since the Corn Islands, the easternmost part of their territory, are only 50 miles/80km away, and theirs is the nearest piece of mainland. But the paramount wishes of the islanders are to avoid becoming part of Central America's poorest nation, so San Andrés seems set to remain Colombian territory for the foreseeable future.

San Andrés is an excellent junction between Central and South America, as well as a good add-on destination for those visiting Colombia alone. A few days spent on the main island or its northern neighbour, Providencia, is an excellent antidote to the rigours of life on the mainland.

SAN ANDRES ISLAND

Island Layout. The island measures eight miles by two (13 x 3km). The town occupies the top, with the airport runway beginning almost on the northern shore and sticking out southeast. The highest point is El Cliff, an escarpment pinched between the southern reaches of the town and the airport. The central spine of the island is pleasantly hilly.

Arrival and Departure. Boeing 727s operate from early morning to late at night, serving all the large cities in Colombia with the exception of Santa Marta, as everyone within a ten-mile radius is all-too-painfully aware. The airport also has direct links to Central American destinations, including San José (Costa Rica), Tegucigalpa (Honduras), Belize City and Guatemala City.

The cheapest domestic fares are to Cartagena, but those to Cali, Medellín, Barranquilla and Bogotá are not substantially more expensive. If you are heading for Central America and beyond, it is worth asking about the SAM deal whereby you can have stopovers in San José and Guatemala City on the way up to Mexico City. Note that international departure tax of $17 is payable upon leaving San Andrés for Central America, and the standard domestic charge of $2 to Providencia or the mainland.

Queues for check-in are catastrophically long. Colombians do not, in general, visit San Andrés to enjoy the scenery. They go there to buy cut-price electronic goods. Having procured as many washing machines, microwaves and televisions as Colombian law allows, they proceed to fly them out. A good tip to avoid this chaos is to check in at least four hours before your flight, then go off to spend time around the island. You can then breeze up half-an-hour before the flight goes, having avoided all the queues. Even better, travel with hand luggage only. This enables you to bypass the inordinate wait for baggage at your destination, while refrigerators are unloaded in advance of your pack.

The only way to organize a passage to San Andrés by sea is to negotiate at the docks at Cartagena or Barranquilla. You might persuade the captain of a cargo vessel to take you. The government tries to discourage tourists from reaching the island by sea, so don't expect much success.

Red Tape. The tax-haven status of San Andrés means that customs searches apply when you return to the Colombian mainland. They affect only Colombians and foreigners resident in South America, so you need not trouble yourself to fill in the requisite forms unless you intend to buy three or more video recorders.

You can get a Guatemalan visa along with a barbecue set or some new glassware at El Hogar, a shop at Avenida de las Américas number 3-136. The consul, the shop owner, can issue a visa on-the-spot for $10 from 9am-12.30pm and 3-7pm, the longest hours of any consulate in South America. Most travellers need no visa for arriving by air in Panama, Costa Rica or Nicaragua. If necessary, you can get a Panamanian one from Almacén Chebedy on Avenida de las Américas, and an Honduran visa from Lady Vanity, a shop on the seafront at Avenida Colombia number la-50.

Getting Around. The best way to travel around the island is by a combination of buses and hitching. The bus services run through the middle of San Andrés. One goes south to the village of Loma, the other — marked San Luis — runs most of the way down along the east coast. The gap between these services can be filled easily by hitching or, more tiringly, on foot. Taxis are about twice the price of those on the mainland.

Accommodation. Many travellers stay at the Hotel Restrepo, on the west side of the airport and away from the town. It has several advantages: it is (too) convenient for the airport; it has friendly proprietors; and it is cheap, around $5 a night for a comfortable double. Standards are a little higher in the Coliseo ($10 double), just off the seafront. Otherwise there is a excellent choice of higher-class hotels, costing $30 or more for a double.

Eating and Drinking. You must have at least one meal at the Fishermen's Place, basically an open-sided shelter on the seafront just west of the runway. You order a piece of red snapper — *pargo rojo* by weight, and it is cooked in front of you. Wash it down with beer. No other dishes nor drinks are served. It opens 11am-5pm daily.

Two excellent but expensive restaurants can be found on the seafront. La Bahía has one of the best wine lists in Colombia, to accompany its tasty fish dishes. And La Fonda Antioqueño is a good approximation to the best restaurants of Medellín, though prices are higher.

Two decent cheaper places are El Zaguan (at the seafront end of Avenida 20 de Julio), which opens around the clock, and La Pizzeria (where Avenida de las Américas meets Avenida Providencia).

Exploring. San Andrés town is not the sort of place you would wish to spend much time in, unless you are eager to buy a hi-fi system or procure a set of visas. The easiest side trip is to Johnny Cay (often rendered as 'Jhonny Cay'), a sand island facing the town. Boats leave frequently from the shore — buy a ticket in advance from the office opposite the Royal Abacoa restaurant.

To explore the rest of San Andrés could take an afternoon, but you might prefer to spread it over a week. Immediately south of the airport, the path up to El Cliff passes through some very poor areas, but safe ones with interesting people. Along the east side of the island, the Decameron resort is nothing special. The blow-hole, at the far end of the island, is quite an astonishing sight — spurts of foam appearing from an innocent chink in the rocks.

The best sight, however, is just south of Loma. The Big Pond should be approached only by vehicle, since it contains real crocodiles.

Help and Information. The tourist office is a hut on the beach between the runway and the town. It is usually closed. The Telecom office is on Avenida de las Américas, and opens 8am (9am on Sundays) to 9.45pm.

PROVIDENCIA

'She came from Providence — the one in Rhode Island', sang The Eagles. The Providencia in the San Andrés islands is far more impressive. A bus, which constitute's the island's only public transport, is free. 'Welcome to Providencia', grunts the driver as he takes you from the airport.

The most significant sight on the small island is Cabeza de Morgan, a boulder reputedly shaped like the head of Captain Henry Morgan, the British buccaneer who had his headquarters in the vicinity; his store of hidden treasure is allegedly concealed somewhere on the island.

The population is officially nearly 4,000, but you will find yourself wondering where they all are. Providencia is on a human scale, its low houses mingling with the luxuriant vegetation. The deep green extends from the seashores up to the heights of El Pico, over a thousand feet above the western Caribbean. Providencia feels much more like other Caribbean islands than San Andrés, even though it is solidly Colombian territory. You can stay here for just a day (if, for example, you have a couple of coupons on an Avianca/SAM airpass to use up), but a week relaxing in a modest tropical paradise would be more like it.

Physically, Providencia is one of the most beautiful islands in the Caribbean, rocky and lush. But the absence of proper beaches means that development has been limited.

Island Layout. Providencia is shaped rather like a teardrop, with an appendage attached at the top — this is Santa Catalina, an islet attached by a pedestrian bridge. Here you are almost as close to the North Pole as you are to the southern tip of South America.

The bridge links the island to the 'town' of Santa Isabel, a delightful collection of clapboard houses, churches and shops, clustered around the island's main quay.

Going anticlockwise from here, the road is reasonably well surfaced for the three miles/5km to Lazy Hill (also known as San Felipe), but the quality deteriorates temporarily over the next mile to Aguadulce, the island's 'resort'. A less resort-like place is hard to imagine, since the beach is modest and the few buildings hardly encroach upon it; in short, it is a classic example of how tourism does not need to destroy the environment.

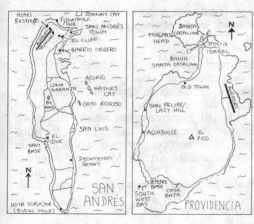

The road follows the sea south to a big defence base (the favourite posting in the Colombian forces), and then swings inland through some pleasant hills. The settlement at the lower end of the island is, fittingly, Casa Baja (Bottom House), but it is not quite such a thriving metropolis as Santa Isabel. Another 90° arc takes you to the airport, the single sign of 20th century life.

Arrival and Departure. About half a dozen flights operate daily, each way between San

Andrés and Providencia; the approximation is used advisedly since weather and other unpredictable factors can affect schedules seriously. The fare for the half-hour flight is $15.

Re-confirm your return flight immediately upon arrival (in the exercise book used for reservations), so at least you have a good claim if the timetable starts to go awry. And try to avoid tight connections at San Andrés for onward flights, since a cancelled service can throw your plans into chaos.

Accommodation. Of the choices at Aguadulce, Cabañas Aguadulce is the best — it has comfortable cabins and extravagant breakfasts on the terrace for $30 a night double. If you enjoyed the Hotel Restrepo in San Andrés town, the proprietor's sister, Sophia Dawkins, has a guest house in Old Town — call 8109.

CHOCO AND THE DARIEN GAP

Just as Colombia is the only country in South America with coastlines on both the Atlantic and Pacific, so Chocó is the only province in Colombia with this distinction. It is quite different from the rest of the country in terms of terrain, climate and culture, and well worth visiting to sample the contrast. Unfortunately, road links to it are poor. On the official Ministry of Public Works map of Colombia, a dotted line is shown to indicate the route of the Pan-American highway, from Acandí on the Gulf of Urabá through the Chocó. It almost touches the Pacific coast before swinging inland to Las Animas south of Quibdó. The plan is that it will eventually join up with the existing Pan-American Highway around Cartago. It has to be said that the plan should not really have got as far as the cartographer's drawing board, since resources considerably greater than the present roads expenditure would be necessary.

QUIBDO

You might feel you've reached the end of the world when you get to this extraordinarily languid town, where every movement is a labour and every day begins with clouds as heavy and grey as lead. But it is well worth making the considerable effort of visiting the place, since you are unlikely to find anything like it, anywhere.

Quibdó is the capital of the Chocó, but is well removed from the far reaches of its control. It is a sloppy sort of town, an air of temporariness lingering like the humidity which washes over it.

Town Layout. Everything is defined in terms of the river which plods past Quibdó on its way to the Caribbean. The most important buildings — the market, the regional administration and the city hall — are alongside it, and all the most useful places like the post office and Telecom office are within a block or two. Quibdó is hard against the Atrato river, a wide and ponderous river which drifts down to the Gulf of Uriba and the Caribbean. A rough grid stretches back from the river. The main government building is at the north end of town, where the main road — Calle 31 — heads east to Medellín (and the airport). Most other important features are south from here, on Carreras 1, 2 or 3 (the riverside streets and the two inland from there). Carrera 3 is also known as Avenida Heliodoro Rodríguez.

Arrival and Departure. Unless you have time to spare and a deep fascination with mud, the best way to arrive is by air. The town's airport is on the road to Medellín, a couple of miles northeast of the town. Aces and Satena have frequent services to Medellín and Cali, plus some into the hinterland of Chocó. All the taxis in Quibdó are Japanese jeeps, with a standard fare of $0.50; they meet all flights. The bus company is Flota Occidental, on Carrera 1 between Calles 22 and 23. It has services to Pereira and Medellín.

To fix up a river trip, ask along the quayside. A boat to Cartagena costs around $50 including meals and takes a week.

Accommodation and Food. The best place to stay is the Hotel Malecón, on Carrera 1 between Calles 26 and 27 (tel 712725). Two cheaper options are nearby: Residencia Costa Azul on Carrera 3 between Calles 25 and 26 and Residencia del Río at Carrera 1 number 27-39. A better option is the Hospedaje El Nogal on Carrera 4 between Calles 23 and 24. The best place to eat, from a modest selection, is La Chaira pizzeria on Carrera 4 between Calles 22 and 23.

Exploring. Quibdó has several beautiful buildings, and some which are plain strange. The cathedral, enclosed by Carreras 1 and 2 and Calles 26 and 27, looks like a concrete Parthenon and dominates the town completely. The new, ugly Banco de la República is opposite. The neo-classical Palacio Municipal is on Carrera 2 between Calles 24 and 25. The most interesting place is the market, which punctuates the town at the foot of Carrera 1, a collection of shacks tumbling down to the river.

Help and Information. The Tourist Office on the ground floor of the three-storey government building at Carrera 1 and Calle 31 gives out maps and a modicum of information. Telecom is at Carrera 2 and Calle 25.

THE DARIEN GAP

Eighty miles/128km of jungle and swamp separating Colombia and Panama, the Darién Gap is the one stretch of land between Alaska and Tierra del Fuego that has prevented the completion of the Pan-American Highway. Unfavourable terrain is not the only obstacle; foot-and-mouth disease is widespread among cattle in Colombia and the rest of South America, and Panamanian farmers fear that a land link could spread it. Even though travel in Darién is possible only by boat, aircraft, or on foot, the jungle is gradually disappearing. Loggers are felling an increasing number of trees, and settlers arriving from exhausted lands elsewhere in the region have begun looking for cultivable land in Darién.

On your trip you will encounter mainly Chocó Indians, who constitute a fascinating ethnic group. Emulating man's earliest activities they are hunter-gatherers. Although guns are now used by most Chocós, those in more isolated areas still use only bows and arrows. Chocó houses, known as *tambos*, are raised off the ground and have distinctive conical, thatched roofs. Most Chocós live along the riverbanks, but they have only recently begun to establish communities in the Western sense.

Many Chocós prefer to live in their traditional isolation, and their customs have changed little: the men still wear loincloths and the women wear the traditional brightly-coloured wrap-around skirts. The Chocó women maintain traditions more effectively than the men. The Chocó language, Embara, is spoken mainly by the women, although many of the younger women are also familiar with Spanish. Western influence has inevitably brought other changes. The introduction of plastic means that there is no need to make pottery, and the number of baskets produced has diminished. Money was previously an unknown concept, but Chocó men now go off to work in towns and traders from further south bring in whisky, cigarettes and clothes, upon which earnings are spent. Yet despite the incursions of the 20th century, the Chocós continue to believe in spirits and the powers of the shaman to cure the sick and cast spells. They are a friendly people, but tend to keep a respectful distance. You should reciprocate this when meeting them.

THROUGH THE DARIEN GAP

The number of travellers going overland between Colombia and Panama is increasing, but the trip across the Darién Gap is still a monumental challenge. As Balboa discovered, the local Indians have numerous trails through the region, and today these are used by Western travellers and Colombian smugglers. Certain stretches, however, can be covered only by boat, so you must rely upon the willingness of the locals for transport. Co-operation is usually forthcoming, but may involve waiting for a day or two.

The trek should be considered only during the dry season between December and March; at other times, rivers become torrents and the terrain is waterlogged. By the end of the dry season the rivers are often too low for boats, so it is best to go mid-season. With so many variables it is impossible to predict how long the journey through the Gap will take. The minimum is one week, though most travellers take at least two weeks. Similarly, it is difficult to predict how much the trip will cost. As more visitors use the route, some of the locals are beginning to exploit their monopoly position to charge travellers high fees for boat journeys. You should expect to pay out $200-300 in addition to any equipment you need. Going overland is certainly not the cheapest way to reach Central America; to save money, go by air.

The prospect of a week or two spent trudging through thick jungle, and travelling by boat along waterways lined with impenetrable vegetation and across swampland, does not appeal to everyone. If you are tempted, choose good company. It is possible to hire a guide for the whole or part of the way, but make sure he is thoroughly trustworthy — the Darién Gap has a reputation for bandits.

Go prepared for a tough jungle trip. You may be able to stay with the locals in some villages, but you need to be prepared to camp or sling up a hammock; whatever option you choose, you must always approach the village chief first. Take plenty of food (canned and dried), though you should be able to arrange meals in most of the villages. Be particularly careful about what you eat since the Darién Gap is not a convenient place in which to fall ill. Take plenty of plastic bags to keep your belongings dry when travelling by boat. A torch is also essential, even though the main villages now have electricity. Finally, don't forget to sort out the necessary visas, return tickets, etc. You are technically required to have a ticket out of Panama before being allowed into the country.

The Route. Fewer people cross the Darién Gap from Colombia to Panama than vice-versa. If you intend to travel west-east, much of the following information still applies but the itinerary is reversed.

The starting point is Turbo, described on page 156. First, you must go to the Policía Distrito Especial office near the harbour for a Colombian exit stamp. Then, you can arrange a boat ride to Cristales on the Río Atrato. This river marks the southern edge of the oppressive swamp of the Darién. You may find you can get a lift in a dugout or a banana boat direct to Cristales. Otherwise, someone from the Katios National Park (see below) who has been to Turbo to pick up supplies, may give you a ride.

Alternatively, the journey must be done in stages. There is a steady flow of boats to Travesía (sometimes called La Loma), near the confluence of the Atrato and Cacarica rivers. Along this last river you can reach Bijao, a cattle and lumber town which is usually full of smugglers. There is a Colombian guard post here where your papers are usually checked. You continue by boat along the Río Cacarica to Cristales. This marks the start of the overland trail through the Darién Gap. Rather than staying in Cristales itself, you can stay overnight at the ranger station of the Katios National Park which you should pass about 30 minutes before you reach the town. The park consists of a huge area of tropical forest containing a magnificent bird population. There are also ranger stations at Travesía and Sautatá (on the Río Atrato, midway between Turbo and Travesía); both have accommodation and are the best places from which to visit the park. It is possible to hire mules.

From Cristales, your next destination is the Palo de las Letras where a cement block at the top of the mountain marks the Panamanian border. This is the hardest stretch of the whole trek, and you are advised to hire a guide in Cristales to take you over the mountains and down to Paya on the other side. A guide from Cristales to Paya, with one night camping out, costs $80-100. The 15-mile/25km stretch up to the Palo de las Letras involves crossing several rivers. It is an easy area in which to get lost — without a guide you must take a machete and a compass. The trail down the mountain to Palo de las Letras is good and well-used.

The first Panamanian border check is in Paya. The officials dip any leather you have into antiseptic, to reduce the spread of foot-and-mouth disease. Searches tend to be thorough.

From Paya, head 11 miles/18km north to Púcuro, a village of Cuna Indians and the next overnight stop. This journey must usually be done on foot, though immediately after the wet season the water levels are sometimes high enough for boats to cover the stretch. Even on foot, the distance can be covered in eight or nine hours. The terrain is not particularly difficult, especially when compared with the stretch before Paya, but you may still consider hiring a guide. If you can afford to take your time, there are good places to camp by some of the rivers. This path is heavily used by the local Indians. Once in Púcuro, the village chief should let you stay in the meeting hall; if not, camp or find somewhere to hang your hammock.

From Púcuro it is possible to go by boat to Boca de Cupe. The boat journey should take six or seven hours, but be prepared to wait a few days to find a boat willing to take you. Boca de Cupe is the first Panamanian settlement of any size — it is here that you must get your entry stamp for Panama. You should be able to stay in someone's house overnight without too much difficulty.

At Boca de Cupe you have a choice of two destinations in Panama: Yaviza and El Real, close together at the southeastern extreme of the country. Yaviza is a jumbled collection of thatched buildings (including one hotel) dotted among open sewers. It marks the southernmost point of the Pan-American Highway and lies 150 miles/240km east of Panama City.

El Real is the commercial centre and the main port of Darién province. Although inaccessible by road, El Real is easier to reach from Boca de Cupe; you can also get a boat upstream from El Real to Yaviza. There are cabins, and it is also possible to camp — stay near the Mercadero, where boats arrive, a couple of miles out of town.

To get to Yaviza from Boca de Cupe you must walk. This takes you through the villages of Capeti, Yape, Unión de Chocó and Pinogana, and involves crossing a couple of rivers. It should take five or six hours, and is an easy and pleasant walk at first, getting tougher the further you go. You may be able to get a boat from Boca de Cupe to Pinogana, but this is the easiest part of the walk. If you are heading for El Real, it is possible to travel from Boca de Cupe by motorized dugout. Boats going direct do not leave frequently, so if you don't want to charter one specially, be prepared either to wait around for a few days or to do the journey in stages. If you do the trip in one go, it should take about four hours.

Both Yaviza and El Real are linked to Panama City by the airline PARSA, or by sea: cargo boats leave from both ports on a fairly regular basis, and take passengers. The sea journey is tough, lasting anything from 15 to 35 hours. From Yaviza you can also reach the Panamanian capital by land. The first 50 miles/80km of the Pan-American Highway is unpaved, running northwest to Santa Fe. You can only cover it by truck, a journey of four hours. During the dry season buses run from Santa Fe four times a day to the Avenida B bus terminal in Panama City; the fare for the five-hour journey is $10. (You may be relieved to learn that US dollars are the currency in Panama.)

At the small settlement of Canazas, where you leave Darién Province, the road turns west and crosses Lake Bayano on the way to Chepo. This is a lively town with a predominantly black population just 37 miles/60km east of the capital. Buses run regularly from Chepo to Panama City. For further details of this fascinating country — and details of covering the route in the opposite direction — see *Travellers Survival Kit: Central America*.

Bahía Málaga. In the middle of Chocó's Pacific coast, this is the largest Colombian naval base. Its coastline is thus ruined by grey, grim ships. Just inland, however, there is some superb territory: unspoilt rainforest, beautiful waterfalls, including Las Tres Marías.

MEDELLIN and Northwest Colombia

Rather tactlessly, a billboard along the road to Medellín from Rionegro airport suggests that you should 'Anticipate Death — Plan for your Family'. The British Foreign Office advises prospective travellers that Medellín is an extremely dangerous place and best avoided. But few cities are so pleasantly situated and have so perfect a climate.

Medellín was founded in the 17th century as a base for Basque gold miners and a refuge for Jews expelled from Spain. It fills the Aburra valley, a fold in the central spine of the Andes a mile above sea level, seven degrees from the Equator and 160 miles/250km northwest of Bogotá. The city has ideal weather, with the serenity of a fine early summer's day in England. Likewise, the setting is faultless, embraced elegantly by the mountains, soft green slopes tempering the brash modernity of a high-rise metropolis. Chicago has been planted in the middle of Colombia, complete with gangsters. Paradise has become the base of Colombia's most powerful cocaine cartel, and one of the world's most violent cities.

Medellín sprawls in the lazily anarchic manner of many South American cities, kept in check by the verdant Andes. The city has two excellent airports and an elaborate new metro lacing through the skyscrapers. How does a city with no natural resources, no visible means of support acquire such accoutrements? 'In addition to being a major center of coffee trade', says the tourist blurb, 'Medellín is an important producer of textiles'. But the rest of the world knows it as the centre of the cocaine business. Medellín follows the standard human geography of any South American city: the higher the hills, the more barren the soil, the less civilized and the smellier it is. Like every city in the continent, Medellín is fringed with shanty towns. Then, as you should be breasting the bare hilltops which ring Medellín, you find yourself passing shiny new barbed wire fences shielding well-watered lawns. The haciendas which are almost hidden from sight, protected by high-security cameras and armed guards, are home to the lieutenants of the drugs trade.

While orchids thrive (the botanical gardens are splendid), coca does not grow here. Leaves are shipped to Colombia from Peru and Bolivia, chemists brought in from Europe and North America, but much of the processing takes place hundreds of miles away in the seclusion of the Amazon basin. Medellín is a huge money-laundering operation, running the business of running drugs. *Dinero caliente* — hot money — gives the city its high-rises and high excitement.

City Layout. The city is funnelled into a long valley, with all the main lines of communication running north-south. At the southern tip of the conurbation is Envigado, location of the drug barons' luxury prison. The highway south to Cali emerges from the southwest of the city. The route to Santa Fe de Antioquia and Turbo winds up into the hill northwest of Medellín. The northern highway runs out past the bus terminal en route to Cartagena, and the main road to Bogotá also starts by going north then swinging round to head southeast. An alternative route

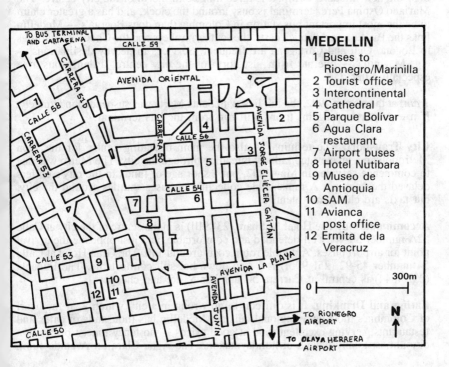

MEDELLIN

1 Buses to Rionegro/Marinilla
2 Tourist office
3 Intercontinental
4 Cathedral
5 Parque Bolívar
6 Agua Clara restaurant
7 Airport buses
8 Hotel Nutibara
9 Museo de Antioquia
10 SAM
11 Avianca post office
12 Ermita de la Veracruz

out of the city is the winding route which climbs out due east and runs to the airport. The city centre is the area shown in the map in this book.

Arrival and Departure. *Air:* the most convenient domestic airport is Olaya Herrera, a couple of miles south of the city centre. When landing you will be convinced you're about to touch down in somebody's garden. Plenty of buses serve the airport, and a cab will cost only a dollar or two. Only propellor aircraft serve Olaya Herrera, but the increase in flight time from Cali or Bogotá is more than offset by the ease of access. Aces has a busy network based at the airport.

The newer international airport is 25 miles/40km east of Medellín at Rionegro; it is often described in timetables or on tickets as Rionegro, rather than Medellín. Confusingly, its official name is José Maria Córdova. By any name it is a big and efficient airport, with international flights to Panama City and Miami, and shuttle (*Puente Aérea*) services to Bogotá. It also has jet links with Cali, San Andrés and many other cities. Every 20 minutes a minibus runs from the airport into the city, costing $2 and taking 30 minutes. The return journey, from the Combuses office indicated on the map, takes ten minutes longer because it is almost all uphill. A taxi between Medellín and the airport costs $10 and shaves a few minutes off these times.

The airports are linked by a helicopter service operated by Helicol (tel 255 9173). It costs about $25 each way. The numbers of other airlines are as follows: Aces — 231 4111; Aires — 255 1522; Avianca — 231 4900; Intercontinental — 245 2312; SAM — 251 5544.

Bus: the new, modern terminal is three miles/5km north of the city centre. The Mariano Ospina Pérez terminal is busy around the clock, and has a greater claim to be the most important bus station in Colombia than does Bogotá's — Medellín links the Pacific and Atlantic coasts, the southern valleys and the Chocó. Departures to Bogotá, Cali and Cartagena are frequent. Services to nearby destinations — e.g. Marinilla — operate from just north of the city centre, a dangerous area especially after dark.

Train: at the start of 1992, the rail link with Santa Marta was suspended indefinitely. If it ever starts up again, trains will run from the bus terminal.

City Transport. The terminal is also the main operating centre for the Tren Metropolitano, an elevated railway threading through the city. The Metro was due to commence services in May 1992, but a shortage of funds in the city's coffers delayed the opening. A ramshackle collection of buses shuttles around the city, but taxis are cheap and plentiful.

Accommodation. The Hotel Nutibara (231 9111) is in the centre of the city at Calle 52A number 50-46, well-defended and comfortable, and just opposite the arrival point for airport buses. A double room costs around $40. The Gran Hotel at Calle 54 number 45-92 (251 9951) is a step down but still comfortable. The Eupacla (231 1844) is central at Carrera 50 number 53-16, and cheaper.

Eating and Drinking. It is difficult to go wrong in a city which is at the heart of Colombia's most tasty regional cuisine. Medellín has thousands of cafés and restaurants, serving excellent food at good prices — no fancy tourist prices in a city almost totally devoid of holidaymakers. The Agua Clara on Avenida Junín is Medellín's best-value restaurant and serves a truly delicious plato montañero, the traditional dish of the Colombian Andes, consisting of a mountain of grilled meat and other goodies.

Exploring. The Plaza de Bolívar, a broad and graceful main square, is the heart of Medellín. Sunlight filters through prim greenery and washes over the shoeshiners and soft-drink sellers. The northern end is dominated by the Catedral Metropolitana, one of the largest churches on the continent — built of 1,200,000 bricks as the locals proudly tell you. Unfortunately, it looks like the gloomy post-war architecture that it is. The inclination of some of the locals to steal its treasures means it is opened only for Mass and confessions. The Basílica de la Candelaria is much smaller and much more impressive. It is in Plaza de Berrío, at Carrera 50 and Calle 50.

On the first Saturday of each month the main square is taken over by a craft fair, with campesinos from all over Colombia selling leather bags and woollen *ruanas* (cloaks) at prices which would put Covent Garden traders out of business. But middle-class locals prefer classier wares. Strolling along Avenida Junín, the main shopping street and an elegant pedestrian precinct, it is hard to believe you are in South America rather than one of the more chic European capitals. The economy of Medellín seems to be on speed. Every day is last-shopping-day-before-Christmas, as frantic buyers rush to convert their rapidly depreciating pesos into consumer goods. Brand names are worn like badges, and Ray-Ban sunglasses are *de rigueur*.

Crime and Safety. Cocaine has brought crime and violence to Medellín. Many people are killed in revenge attacks between gangs, who often work for the drug lords. After nine the city clears in an unofficial curfew. Anyone on the streets thereafter is up to little good, and the drug factions fight their cocaine wars between themselves and against the police. *El Mundo*, the local newspaper, carries a litany of the previous day's murders. The death toll in road accidents is often higher. The traffic in Medellín is terrifying. Life is cheap, the local motorists seem to say, so we'll drive suicidally. As the police have more serious concerns than catching speeding motorists, crossing the street is a nightmare.

Help and Information. The Tourist Office is at Calle 57 number 45-129 (tel 254 0800). Other offices are at Rionegro airport (tel 260 3812) and at Olaya Herrera airport (tel 285 1048); this latter office is particularly helpful. The post office is at Carrera 52 number 51A-1.

The British Consulate is at Calle 9 number 43B-93 (tel 246 3114; fax 266 7318).

FURTHER AFIELD

Exploring the city's surroundings is well worthwhile. A good version of the Wild West is 90 minutes east by bus ($1 — sit on the left for the best views). Marinilla has a town square presided over by an ornate gilt church, but every other building is a bar of some description. All the town needs to become a natural setting for a Western is a posse of horses to replace its noisy, smelly buses. Sipping a *tinto* in Los Remansos saloon, you expect banditos to crash through the swing door at any moment. The men's urinal occupies one wall.

The Hotel Familiar, on the main square, has an unfamiliar selection of insect life but is cheap ($3 double). The only other choice in town is the Hotel California, half a block to the right of the church as you face it. The church itself is incredibly ornate, looking like a toy. Eat at the Fonda del Ayer, a funny little chicken restaurant on the main square.

El Peñol. Medellín's modest lake district is only a little further east. Forty miles/65km from the city, a reservoir has been formed to supply a nearby hydroelectric plant — the power to keep the cocaine cooking, say cynical locals. The lake is dominated by El Peñol, a 600-foot granite outcrop looking like a bad tooth. Take a bus from Marinilla the 12 miles/20km to the village of El Peñol. From there, it is another six miles/10km to the rock, reached by bus from the Cumbre bar in the village; halfway along you pass the Rancho Azul, a pleasant place to pass a few days.

El Peñol pierces the sparkling Colombian sky. It bears the letters GI, a huge but incomplete piece of graffiti which is intended eventually to spell Guatepe, the name of the lake. A staircase to the summit, squeezed into a cleft of the black monolith, takes you to a magnificent view of rugged green hills, steel grey water, sparkling blue skies. At the top is a brand new café and, often, clouds of flying ants.

SOUTHWEST COLOMBIA

This section covers the area towards the Pacific Ocean and the border with Ecuador. It begins with the city of Cali and moves west and south, ending at the extraordinary shrine of Las Lajas.

CALI

Santiago de Cali, Colombia's third city, is not quite so striking as Bogotá and Medellín. It slumps a little, rather than imposing itself firmly upon the landscape. Some say they can sense the mood of the people as also-ran citizens. Even the local soccer team, América de Cali, lost in the final of the Copa Libertadores three years in succession in the late 1980s. The department of Valle, of which Cali is capital, calls itself *el paraíso de Colombia*, but this is done with more hope than reason. Nevertheless, Cali is busy, brash and vibrant, a place where wits are best kept about you.

City Layout. Cali sprawls south from the Río Cali, around which the commercial centre of the city is based. South of the river, Carreras run east-west and Calles go north-south. The south embankment of the river is the Avenida Colombia; it merges into Carrera 1 which in turn heads off north to Bogotá and Medellín. North of the river, Avenidas head off at an angle, of which the most important is Avenida 6 — called, by the locals, Sixth Avenue because of its perceived resemblance to a US city. You can safely ignore everything south of Carrera 10.

Arrival and Departure. *Air:* the old *aeroparque* just east of the city centre is closed to civilian traffic, so everyone has to use Alfonso Bonilla airport, 16 miles/25km northeast of Cali. A constant stream of minibuses operate between the airport and the bus terminal. The bus out to the airport leaves from the upper level of the terminal; buy a ticket in advance. It stops to pick up passengers at the 24-hour Mobil garage on the edge of town, close to the Exstasis motel.

All the airline offices are on Carrera 3 between Calles 13 and 14, or on Avenida 6 around Calle 21. Telephone numbers are as follows: Aces — 670981; Aires — 610078; Avianca — 894011; SAM — 823278; Satena — 836825.

Arrival and Departure. Transport links could hardly be easier. The bus/taxi station is on the western edge of town, at the big roundabout (traffic circle) on the Highway. The walking time to the centre is 20 minutes, and a taxi costs about $0.50.

Buses depart frequently going north to Cali and south to Pasto and Ipiales. Colectivos link the town with Cali frequently from early morning to early evening, costing around $5; services are run by a co-operative, and you buy your ticket from the desk at the bus station. This is easily the fastest (2-3 hours) and most comfortable way to cover the 125 miles/200km; buses cost a couple of dollars less and take an hour longer.

The modest airport is directly behind the bus station. The only scheduled services at present operate in the morning, as part of the Bogotá-Popayán-Ipiales run. An Intercontinental flight departs for Ipiales at around 7.30am, returning from there at about 8.45am for the onward service to the capital. Fares to Ipiales are about $20, to Bogotá $45. The flight to Ipiales gives you an excellent start if you are heading to Ecuador, since it arrives in time for you to take a trip out to Las Lajas (see page 173) and still get across the frontier in time to continue on to Quito.

Hitch-hikers can try their luck on the Pan-American, but since the only sensible place to stand is outside the bus station, drivers may be perplexed as to why a Westerner should want to hitch.

Accommodation and Food. The Panamá, on Carrera 5 between Calles 7 and 8, is cheap but rather grotty and cell-like — natural light is a rare commodity. A double room costs $5. Los Balcones, on Calle 3 between Carreras 6 and 7, costs twice as much but is extremely comfortable for the price. Other good quasi-colonial places include the Hostal Santo Domingo (Calle 4 number 5-14; tel 35676) and the Hotel La Ermita (Calle 5A number 2-77; tel 31936). This is beside the pretty La Ermita church, and charges $15 double. Only the Hotel Monasterio, a beautiful building on Calle 4 at Carrera 10, is better quality, and costs $40 double per night.

The best value restaurant is El Danubio, a cheap and cheerful place on Carrera 8 between Calles 5 and 6. The friendly Lanchería La Viña is open at lunchtimes and in the evenings.

Help and Information. Changing money may seem a real problem in Popayán, since none of the banks seem prepared to convert currency. But track down Salvador Duque, proprietor of Almacén Duque in the main square, who acts as a Casa de Cambio and gives decent rates.

A good day trip from Popayán is out to Silvia, a village 35 miles/58km northeast and $1 each way by bus. Tuesday is the best day to visit, when Indians from the area congregate for the market. Beyond it lies Tierradentro.

TIERRADENTRO

The apex of the Popayán — San Agustín triangle, the Tierradentro district is a curious historic sight. It is also stunningly attractive, in mountainous terrain northeast of Popayán. The town to base yourself in is San Andrés de Pisimbala, reached by direct bus from Popayán. The area is most notable for its pre-Columbian funeral chambers, which come in all shapes and sizes. Only some — the Segovia tombs — are illuminated. The rest require a torch, the candles sold in San Andrés being a poor substitute. You should hire a horse to explore the area, which will cost around $10 for the morning. A $3 ticket covers all the archaeological sights for three days. Rooms are available cheaply in private homes, e.g. El Bosque ($3 per person per night including good meals).

To move on south to San Agustín, the Sotracauca bus to La Plata leaves at around 3pm, providing one of the best (and scariest) rides in Colombia. Sit on the left for spectacular views, or on the right for a sense of security. The bus arrives after 6pm, and you can stay overnight at the Residencias El Terminal.

SAN AGUSTIN

A mystery civilization carved hundreds of free-standing stone statues in the area surrounding this small friendly town sometime before the Spanish conquest. The area was the northernmost limit of the Inca empire, which may explain why the remains bear little resemblance to anything further north in Colombia. Some of the statues are representations of animals — birds, frogs and jaguars, others more monster-like. The biggest is about 13ft/4m high and many decorate tombs or burial mounds. You can view some transplants in the gold museum in Bogotá.

Arrival and Departure. Buses from Bogotá take about 12 hours ($8). From Popayán make sure you take the direct bus via Isnos (6 hours), not the circular route which takes almost double the time. Most journeys are at night.

Your first stop in San Agustín should be the helpful tourist office (Calle 5 number 14-45). It has free maps, leaflets about the statues and the history of the area, and the staff speak English.

Accommodation and Food. San Agustín has plenty of good-value hotels: try the Colonial (Calle 3 number 11-54) or the Familiar next door for a room ($1.50). Alternatively, lots of private accommodation can be found for even less.

The restaurant El Paraiso (Calle 3 at Carrera 11) is good for lunch and dinner.

Exploring. By far the most impressive site is the archaeological park with more than 100 statues. Don't miss those located along a winding forest path (Bosque de las Estatuas). The park also has a museum explaining some of the context and archaeological history of the area. It is just over a mile west of the town, an easy walk up a surfaced road.

The other important site — Alto de los Idolos — is very much second best. The ticket you buy at the archaeological park for about $1.50 covers you for same day entry to both sites, so hang on to it. Alto de los Idolos has the biggest statue in the area (13 feet high, though the staff claim it is 22 feet) but even that is a disappointment because it is not upright. You will be offered jeep and horseback tours to the sites as you walk around the town. Even the tourist office will try to rope you into some expensive deals which include a visit to Los Idolos. If you can get a group together for a day's jeep tour (including some minor sites), it will cost about $6 per person. On your own the jeep ride costs $15 or more.

Alternatively the tourist office can provide a simple local map for the seven-mile/11km walk to Los Idolos. Wear boots and take water and waterproofs. Leave the site by lunchtime if you intend to walk back to the town by nightfall.

Take the northbound minor road out of San Agustín signposted to El Tablón and Obando. Take the second track on the right off this road. It is signposted (if a little rustily) to Alto de los Idolos. The path zigzags down a gorge to cross a river by the only bridge. Follow the steep path on the other side upwards. Do not get distracted by forks off the main path, particularly those off to the left. If you end up heading left along a fence running parallel to the river, behind and below, you are going the wrong way. Otherwise, you should meet a good road from where the site is well signposted. The gorge paths are rough and steep in parts so do not come back this way when the light is failing, even with boots. If you don't want to walk back to San Agustín you should be able to pick up a school party bus or a place on an unfilled jeep to get back. Ask around at the site, especially the staff on the gate.

One other way of seeing Los Idolos on the cheap is to take the Popayán bus to Isnos and walk four miles/7km along a good road to the site. You can leave your gear at the bus office in Isnos, see the site, return and pick up another bus, reaching Popayán from San Agustín the same day.

If you do take a tour, make sure you also get to see the two waterfalls — Salto de Bordones and Salto del Mortino.

PASTO

Amigo Turista, en Nariño Usted es un Nariñense más — 'dear tourist, in Nariño you are one of us'. The province of Nariño, of which Pasto is capital, is pretty and friendly. Pasto itself is unpretentious, with a statue of a steamroller at the northern entrance to the town. Yet Pasto was the capital of the whole of Colombia for six months in 1904. It has since settled back into a fairly quiet life, albeit in beautiful surroundings. The city has 350,000 citizens. It lies in the shadow of Volcán Galeras, a mile and a half (2,500m) above sea level. You get splendid views of the volcano as you approach from the north. The recently spruced-up main square — Parque Antonio Nariño — is a bustling and pleasant place. The best sight is the church of Cristo Rey, a block east of the square, with delightful stained-glass windows.

City Layout. Pasto has a strict grid plan with Calles running north-south and Carreras east-west. The main square is bounded by Carreras 24 and 25 and Calles 18 and 19. The Pan-American Highway arrives at the north of the city from Cali, swinging around to the west to bypass the city centre before heading off to Ipiales.

Arrival and Departure. The airport is 20 miles/32km north of town on the Pan-American Highway to Cali. Collective taxis from the north side of the main square charge $2 per person to the airport. The most useful flights are those to and from Bogotá via Cali. Most buses operate from an area six blocks south of the main square, around Calle 18 and Carrera 20. The main routes are Flota Magdalena (tel 32418) to Popayán, Cali, Buenaventúra and Bogotá; Trasipiales to the Pacific coast; and Super Taxis del Sur to Cali and Ipiales.

Accommodation. If you are obliged to stay out by the airport, the Hotel Imperio de los Incas is the only choice; it is a mile south, tel 32860. Otherwise, try the Zorocan on the southwest corner of the main square (tel 33243) or the Canchalá, a block and a half west at Calle 17 number 20A-38 (tel 33337).

Help and Information. One of Colombia's few fully functioning tourist offices is at Calle 18 number 25-25 (tel 34962).

Casas de Cambio: Internacional de Cambio, Calle 18 number 25-19 (tel 32949); Colombiana de Cambio, Calle 19 number 24-86 (tel 35616).

Telecom: corner of Calle 17 and Carrera 23 (tel 33717).

DAS: Calle 16 number 28-11 (tel 35901).

Ecuadorean Consulate: Calle 17 number 26-55, office 311 (tel 32473).

IPIALES

Fifty miles/80km south of Pasto, Ipiales is not the sort of place in which anyone would want to stay for long. It is a frontier town *par excellence*, with everyone selling something — the most popular product being poor-quality Panama hats. It is nearly two miles (3,000m) above sea level, on a cold and blustery plateau. Its only attributes are its proximity to the Ecuadorean frontier and the extraordinary church a short way from town at Las Lajas.

San Luis airport is five miles/8km west of Ipiales. Rather than pay the $5 demanded by taxi drivers, you might prefer to walk down to the main road and pick up any *colectivo* (usually a jeep) from there. The frontier at Rumichaca is only 2 miles/3km south of the town, accessible by bus number 3 or in a colectivo ($0.50).

Plenty of colectivos go east to Las Lajas, but you might prefer to take bus number 1 to the end of its route and enjoy a breathtaking three mile/5km walk.

Las Lajas. The road east from Ipiales runs along the north side of the Río Guaítara, a beautiful valley reminiscent of Scottish heathland. Five miles/8km from the centre of Ipiales you reach Las Lajas, a shrine which has been described variously as Escheresque and Disneyesque. It is a big church hewn out of — and into — the hillside, perched on a bridge above a spectacular gorge in the Río Guaítara.

The colectivo from Ipiales drops you off in the midsts of plenty of souvenir shops, from where a convenient system of walkways leads down to the church. It is an absurdly beautiful spot, marred only by the abject commercialism. Take care not to rush back to the top, since the air is thin and the hill is steep.

EASTERN COLOMBIA

Few people either live in or visit the eastern half of Colombia. It is as if a line has been drawn from the Venezuelan frontier at Cúcuta down to the meeting of the borders of Colomb. a, Ecuador and Peru, and that everything to the right of it is out-of-bounds. Few travellers visit the region, except those heading for Brazil by way of Leticia, Colombia's port on the Amazon.

LETICIA

The irregular borders of Colombia go into spasm in the southeast corner of the country, where a tongue of Colombian territory sticks out into land which might rightfully belong to Peru or Brazil. It allows Colombia access to the Amazon basin, with river links to Iquitos in Peru, Manaus in Brazil, and the South Atlantic. It is mostly of interest to those who intend to cross to Brazil here, or who are travelling on an airpass and wish to sample another dimension of Colombia.

Three Avianca flights serve Leticia from Bogotá ($80 one-way), plus three Satena ones on other days ($70). These schedules, which applied at the beginning of 1992, are likely to change. You might also get a seat on a cargo flight if you ask around at El Dorado airport in Bogotá; the going rate is around $60, and you should ask at the freight area between the Puente Aérea and the main terminal at Bogotá. The airport in Leticia is a short walk north of town — it is easier to find a suitable cargo plane here, not least because almost all the aircraft are heading for Bogotá. Accommodation in Leticia is concentrated near the waterfront between Carreras 9 to 11 and Calles 7 to 9; try La Manigua on Calle 8 between Carreras 9 and 10, or the Fernando around the corner on Carrera 9 between Calles 8 and 9.

The weather is miserable in comparison with the rest of Colombia: even the Chocó does not get this hot and humid. The mosquitoes are vicious. The fact that you can look across the river at two other countries is small consolation. You can walk into Brazil — the twin towns of Marco-Tabatinga are a short stroll east, and you may not realise you have crossed the border since there are no formal frontier controls. Alternatively there are frequent boats across the river to the Brazilian port of Benjamin Constant. From here or Tabatinga you can get a passage down the Amazon to Manaus and beyond.

If you intend to leave Colombia permanently, you must check out at the office of the immigration police — DAS in Leticia is on Calle 9 between Carreras 8 and 9. This is also the place to go if you're arriving in Colombia for the first time. Colombian, Brazilian and Peruvian currencies circulate freely, as do US dollars.

LOS LLANOS

The plains of eastern Colombia have been forgotten territory for as long as anyone can remember, but in 1992 the Llanos became the focus of a huge oil exploration exercise. Oil companies predict huge reserves may be below the surface. Previously the only thing to disturb the silence of the plains was the fortnightly visits of cowboys to the main towns, where a certain amount of havoc was wrought as they spent their wages in a flurry of drinking and womanizing. But what was a sleepy backwater is now alive with the trappings of foreign oil companies and their entourages. Many hope that the future of Colombia lies beneath the Llanos.

Ecuador

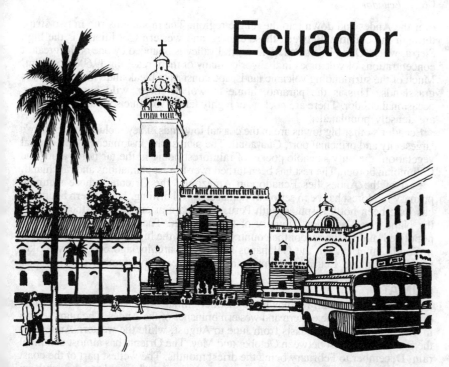

Population: 10 million   **Capital: Quito (1.3 million)**

Ecuador is a pocket of calm and stability sandwiched between Peru and Colombia, both of which have a serious image problem. Ironically, however, those who have become besotted with South America, with all its rough edges, find Ecuador a little bland. Nevertheless, as a gentle introduction to the continent, it is perfect.

While the extraordinary Galapagos Islands have never had difficulty in luring visitors to Ecuador, the rest of the country has struggled to divert people away from Peru. But lately the trend has been reversed, largely because of the continuing guerrilla activity in Peru, and by that country's gradual economic collapse. Yet it is not fair to attribute Ecuador's new appeal solely to the demise of a competitor. For a nation roughly the size of the United Kingdom or the state of Nevada, its geography is remarkably diverse. Furthermore, Ecuador's size makes it one of the easiest countries on the continent to explore. It is also ridiculously cheap.

Quito shares the problems of many other South American capitals, but it is less intimidating than some. From it you can head in all directions with exceptional ease. In a matter of hours you can explore the rich indigenous culture, stroll around delightful colonial towns, hike up spectacular snow-capped volcanoes, take a boat through the Amazon jungle, and even lie prostrate on sandy Pacific beaches. Finally, of course, there are the Galapagos Islands, with their unique natural environment and an astonishing variety of species that provided the basis for Charles Darwin's theories of evolution.

GEOGRAPHY

Ecuador is shaped like a blunted triangle, tapering back from the coastal plain

175

over the Andes and down into the jungle region. The mountains run in two strips through the country. Between these eastern and western Cordilleras is the high Sierra, where Quito is situated. This central valley is bounded by one of the greatest concentrations of volcanoes in the world, many of them reaching 19,600ft/5,800m. Much of the surrounding volcanic landscape consists of bleak and virtually treeless grasslands. This is the paramo, home to wolves, deer, wild horses and the occasional condor. There are pockets of highly fertile volcanic soil, and these areas are densely populated.

Ecuador's other big towns are in the coastal lowlands. They include the country's largest city and principal port, Guayaquil. The plains have lost much of their natural vegetation, the only sizeable pocket of rainforest being in the far north along the Columbian border. The rest has been turned over to vast plantations and ranchland.

East of the Andes lies Ecuadorean Amazonia, the Oriente, whose stunning primary rainforest has been seriously damaged by oil drilling. Its southern boundary has long been hotly disputed with Peru. The main artery through the region is the Napo river, a major tributary of the Amazon. The jungle region is thinly populated, unlike the rest of the country which has the highest population density in South America. On the Galapagos Islands, an archipelago 600 miles/965km west of mainland Ecuador, animals and birds greatly outnumber people.

CLIMATE

Each of the three main regions has a distinct climate. There is also a noticeable difference between the eastern and western branches of the Andes. The rainy season in the eastern Cordillera lasts from June to August, while the western Andes and the Sierra are wettest between October and May. The Oriente has almost continual rain, December to February being the driest months. The wettest part of the coast is in the north, its rainy season running from January to June; along the southern coast the rains have died down by April.

The best time to visit is from June to October, when it is dry in many areas, though September is often wet. In the central Sierra the maximum average temperature is 20°C/68°F, with a minimum of 12°C/54°F. As elsewhere in the Andes, variations in temperature during any single day can be considerable. Quito is the second highest capital in the world after La Paz, and for most of the year it has a pleasant, fresh climate. The warmest months are June, July and August, though it is always cold at night. The average maximum temperature in the jungle and coastal regions is 30°C/86°F, with only slight variation.

Coastal Ecuador is influenced by El Niño ('the child'), a moist warm ocean current that flows down the coast towards Peru. Roughly every ten years, from December to February, El Niño brings very heavy rain to the coast. The last time it struck, in 1982/83, it severely damaged roads and buildings.

The main holiday period is between January and April.

HISTORY

Well before Inca times Ecuador was inhabited by a number of distinct tribes. But their culture was less developed than that of their contemporaries in Peru and populations were small. There was no unifying central authority, so when the Incas moved north the resistance they met was disorganized, albeit fierce.

Topa Inca extended the frontiers of the Inca empire into present day Ecuador in the second half of the 15th century. He met ferocious opposition from the largest tribes in the highlands: principally, the Cañari in the south, the Shyris around present day Quito, and the Caras in the north. They were all subjugated eventually.

A city as superb as Cusco was begun, but never completed, at Tumibamba (Cuenca).

Huayna Capac pushed the boundary of the empire as far north as the Ancasmayo river, which now marks the border with Colombia. Before he died, Huayna Capac divided the territory between two of his sons. Atahualpa was given what is now Ecuador. In the civil war which broke out between him and his stepbrother, Atahualpa won the rest of the Inca empire too.

Francisco Pizarro landed with a handful of adventurers in northern Ecuador in 1529. Three years later he had Atahualpa executed at Cajamarca in Peru. This was not the end of the Inca army, however, since Atahualpa's troops linked up with the Inca General Rumiñaui, who made himself military ruler of Ecuador.

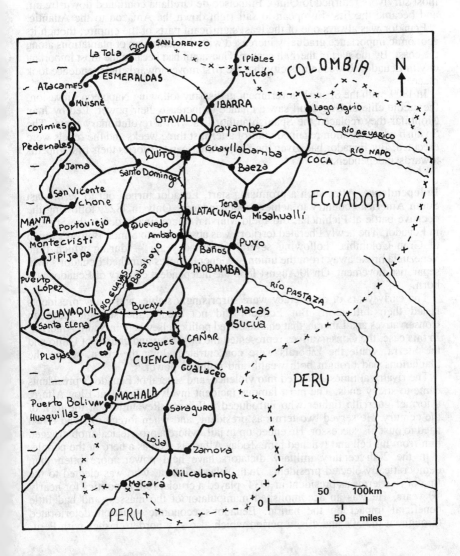

For some time he was left alone, since the Spanish were too busy concentrating on the wealth already discovered further south. In 1534 one of Pizarro's commanders, Sebastián de Benalcázar, marched on Quito, but Rumiñaui and his men had already set fire to the city and fled with all the treasure. Nothing stood in the way of the conquistadores and Benalcázar, joined by Diego de Almagro, set about conquering the rest of the country. After a series of running battles, Rumiñaui was captured and put to death in 1535.

Benalcázar was eventually replaced by Pizarro's own brother, Gonzalo, who was made governor of the new capital of Quito. In 1541 he ordered an expedition to the 'Land of Cinnamon and the Country of El Dorado' in the jungles to the east. Neither gold nor spices materialized and the trip was a disaster. But while most survivors returned to Quito, Francisco de Orellana continued downstream, and became the first European to sail right down the Amazon to the Atlantic.

Ecuador was always one of the least significant parts of the empire, though its economic importance gradually increased with the setting up of plantations along the coast. By the start of the 19th century Guayaquil had became the most important city in Ecuador. It was in this city that the first moves towards independence took place.

In 1809, with the Spanish government in disarray following Napoleon's invasion, the creole elite of Guayaquil saw a chance to increase their power. Led by Juan Montúfar they replaced the Spanish authorities with a revolutionary junta. The Spanish administration regained control after just three weeks and the rebels were executed. But Ecuador had given the South American territories their first impetus towards independence.

Independence. After such a promising start, Ecuador turned out to be the last South American country to achieve independence. Only in 1822, following the decisive battle at Pichincha, did Field Marshal Sucre finally defeat the Spanish in Ecuador. The newly liberated territory was absorbed into Simón Bolívar's union of Gran Colombia. Following several unsettled years — during which time Venezuela broke away from the union — General Flores launched Ecuador's own separatist movement. On 10 August 1830 the independent country of Ecuador was born.

The early years of democracy were surprisingly stable, and many presidents lasted their full term. But Ecuador did not escape the struggle between Conservatives and Liberals that characterized politics elsewhere in South America. In this case, the Conservatives represented the oligarchy and church of Quito and the Sierra, while the Liberals were concentrated along the coast, where the plantations had brought both wealth and political power.

The rivalry at times escalated into violence, and several of Ecuador's presidents came to sticky ends. The most famous incident involved President Eloy Alfaro, a former guerrilla fighter who introduced a 'Liberal Revolution' at the turn of the century. He served two terms as president, and when forced to stand down tried to oust his successor. He ended up in jail, where a pro-clerical mob dragged him from his cell and lynched him. Today Alfaro is seen as a hero of the people.

In the 20th century military dictators have held power more often than democratically elected presidents. Juan Velasco Ibarra, who was elected to the first of five terms as president in 1934, played a crucial role in politics for nearly 40 years. He was an accomplished manipulator of the masses, and had little beneficial impact on the nation. Ecuador's economic situation deteriorated throughout the 30s and 40s, a period which also saw border clashes with Peru.

Territorial disputes with its southern neighbour had erupted sporadically ever since independence: Ecuador had already been forced to concede much land to Peru. Following the defeat of its army in the early 1940s, Ecuador was finally obliged to cede over half its claims to territories in the Upper Amazon. However, the Rio de Janeiro Protocol of 1942 has not buried the issue. In 1961, Ecuador rejected the Accord, and to this day all Ecuadorean maps of the country show an entirely different southern boundary to the one that is internationally accepted. The real border is usually marked with a dotted line. Nevertheless, recent diplomatic moves to resolve the problem once and for all appear to have paved the way for some kind of reconciliation, with Peru possibly giving Ecuador navigation rights on the Amazon.

Recent History. In the 1960s the first big oil discoveries were made in the Oriente. By the mid 70s oil had replaced bananas as Ecuador's most lucrative export. The boom accelerated the political and economic development of the country, and in 1978 Ecuador was given a new democratic constitution.

Fluctuating oil prices have not given Ecuador an easy ride, however, and foreign loans became part of life in the post oil boom era. In the 1980s an ineffective austerity programme was followed by spiralling foreign debt. The 1984 elections saw the victory of a confrontational right-winger called Febres Cordero. The corruption of his regime forced the country deeper into the quagmire. The number of human rights violations also increased dramatically. His presidency ended amid disaster, after several earth tremors in 1987 badly damaged the trans-Andean oil pipeline, cutting sharply the government's revenue.

In 1988 Rodrigo Borja, of the centre-left Izquierda Democrática, was elected. He has proved unable to grapple with one of the highest per capita foreign debts in Latin America, and discontent with his performance is increasing. Crowds demonstrate regularly in Quito, and are often dispersed by tear gas. Borja's reluctance to adopt a market-based system is generally blamed for the country's continued instability. His position is not helped by the fact that the National Congress is controlled by opposition parties. On the right, the main parties are the Social Christian Party (said to have close links with the CIA) and the more extreme Ecuadorean Roldocist Party (PRE). Both are likely to figure significantly in future presidential elections.

THE PEOPLE

Ecuador has a high proportion of indigenous people. Two in five of the population are Indians, many of them pure-blooded. While their influence is considerable in the Sierra and Oriente, it is almost non-existent along the coast. Unlike in Peru, a high proportion of men have maintained their traditional dress. The Otavaleños are the most recognizable group, though the Salasacas, Cañari and Saraguros of the southern Sierra are also distinctive. Their dress is characterized by brightly coloured ponchos or shawls, long trousers cut off just below the knee, and a great variety of weird and wonderful hats; the women wear richly embroidered shawls, skirts and bodices. In the Oriente many tribes have had little contact with the outside world, and now the oil companies are threatening their traditional lands and bringing in diseases to which they have no immunity. Indians, both here and in the Sierra, are becoming increasingly vocal about their discontent.

Mestizos also account for two-fifths of the population. They are the dominant group along the coast which is a world away from the Sierra, culturally as well as topographically. Ten per cent of the population has a well-defined European ancestry and can be described as white. This group lives mostly in urban areas, especially the wealthier suburbs of Quito.

Most of the remaining ten per cent of the population is black, the descendants of African slaves brought to work plantations during the colonial period. There are large concentrations in Guayaquil and in the province of Esmeraldas, in the north. Most live in conditions that are even more appalling than those endured by most Indians — as can be seen in towns such as San Lorenzo.

LANGUAGE

Spanish is the first official language of Ecuador. Quechua (the language of the Incas) is the second, and is spoken widely among the indigenous people of the Sierra. All the various Indian groups have their own distinct dialects. Most indigenous people speak some Spanish.

The highest proportion of English speakers is in Quito, Cuenca and in the prime tourist centres. Several schools in the capital offer one-month Spanish courses, and they can arrange for you to stay with a local family. Recommended academies include the One to One (Amazonas 1001 and Wilson; tel 239030) and Los Andes (Pérez Guerrero 441 and Versalles; tel 565856). The Abraham Lincoln Centre in Cuenca, and individuals in Baños and Otavalo also offer lessons.

FURTHER READING

The most respected travelogue on Ecuador dates back to the 1880s and is, unfortunately, no longer in print. *Travels Amongst the Great Andes of the Equator* by E. Whymper describes the author's climbing and travelling adventures. He was the first man to climb Chimborazo, the highest volcano in the country.

The Panama Hat Trail by Tom Miller (Abacus, 1988) is a highly entertaining book that follows the story of this famous hat, from its place of manufacture on the Ecuadorean coast through to the point of sale in central London. *Living Poor* by the late M. Thomsen (Eland, 1989) is a more serious book, in which the author describes his experiences as a Peace Corps worker in a poor village on the coast.

The only detailed account of the country's early cultures is provided by Betty Meggars in *Ecuador* (Thames and Hudson, 1979), which is out of print. For an account of more recent political and economic developments, read *Ecuador — Fragile Democracy* by David Corkill and David Cubitt (Latin American Bureau, 1987), which concentrates on the oil boom years.

Most literature associated with Ecuador concentrates on the Galapagos. No visitor to the islands should neglect to read Darwin's *A Naturalist's Voyage*. A more recent and also very readable guide is *Galapagos — A Natural History Guide* by M. Jackson (Calgary University Press, 1989). A book about life on the Galapagos is *My Father's Island* by Johanna Angermeyer (Penguin, 1989). *The Galapagos Affair* by John Treherne (Cape, 1983) is much more fun, being a tale of murder, mystery and intrigue, based on events that took place on Floreana Island in the 1930s.

Getting There

AIR

Most South American capitals have at least one flight a week into either Quito or Guayaquil, though there are no direct flights from Bolivia, Paraguay or Uruguay. Ecuatoriana, the national airline, has connections with Argentina, Chile, Colombia,

Peru and Venezuela, but it is notorious for delays. Don't touch this airline with a barge pole if you have an onward connection that depends on a punctual arrival. The main European flights are from Amsterdam, Frankfurt, Paris and Madrid, all stopping off in at least one Caribbean or South American city first. The cheapest fares are offered by Avianca (via Bogotá) and Viasa (via Caracas): about £500 and £550 respectively from London in the low season and £100 higher in the high season.

The cheapest flights from the USA are from Miami and Los Angeles. Ecuatoriana serves these two cities, as well as New York and Chicago. American Airlines offers the most reliable flights from Miami and New York. If you scour the *Miami Herald* you can sometimes find a fare as low as $350.

SURFACE

Both Peru and Colombia have one main border crossing and a second less significant one. There are no international buses with through services to Quito, so you must use local buses.

From Peru. The most common route is along the Pan-American Highway from Piura via Tumbes, the last major town in Peru. Most buses terminate at Tumbes, but there are regular colectivos to Aguas Verdes, the small town on the border 16 miles/25km away. Crossing the frontier is a formality, once you have fought your way through the roadside stalls on either side: both immigration offices are almost hidden amongst the chaos. From Huaquillas, on the Ecuadorean side, buses depart regularly to Cuenca, Guayaquil and Quito and other lesser destinations. The nearest town of any size is Machala, two hours away by bus. There is accommodation at the border if you get stuck.

The alternative route involves leaving the Pan-American Highway at Sullana and heading 125 miles/200km inland to La Tiña on the border. There is nowhere to stay in this small settlement, so arrive in time to cross the frontier, marked by Río Macará. The Ecuadorean town of Macará is over a mile from the border — there are pick-ups if you can't face the walk.

The Amazon frontier between the two countries is closed indefinitely due to the territorial dispute.

From Colombia. Most people cross the border between Ipiales in Colombia, and Tulcán in Ecuador on the Pan-American Highway. Some collective taxis run to the frontier from as far away as Pasto in Colombia, but it is more likely that you'll have to change at Ipiales. From here, collective taxis run the 3 miles/5km to the frontier at Rumichaca. The border is open from 6am until midnight and has good facilities, including a phone office on both sides. (International calls from Colombia are cheaper than those from Ecuador.) Check out of Colombia at the Migración counter in the big new brick building above the car park. Cross the natural bridge to Ecuador and go to the immigration office in the compound. Collective taxis run to the airport (2 miles/3km) or the town of Tulcán, a mile further on, for a fare of about $1 per person.

It is unusual, but possible, to cross from Colombia into the Oriente, though check that the area is safe before you set off. An exit stamp must be obtained in Puerto Asis and not at the border itself. Buses run daily to the border, defined by the Río San Miguel, which is crossed by canoe between Puerto Colón and La Punta. Entry stamps are issued in Lago Agrio, a couple of hours away by bus.

Red Tape

Visas. British passport-holders do not require a visa. Tourist cards are issued on arrival, usually for 60 or 90 days. Citizens of the USA, Canada, New Zealand and Australia may enter under the same terms.

The address of the Ecuadorean mission in the UK is Flat 3B, 3 Hans Crescent, London SW1X 0LS (tel: 071-584 1367); the nearest tube station is Knightsbridge. Opening hours are 10am-4pm, Monday to Friday. In the USA, the Embassy is at 2315 15th Street, NW, Washington DC 20009 (tel 202-234 7200), with a consulate at 1270 Avenue of the Americas, New York, NY 10036 (tel 212-245-5380).

Extending your Stay. Visas and tourist cards can be renewed at the Immigration Office in Guayaquil or Quito (addresses in the text). You can usually obtain at least three 30-day extensions to your tourist card, though officials may try to enforce a rule of a maximum of 90 days in one year.

Border Formalities. Procedures tend to be particularly slow when either entering or leaving Ecuador by plane, often involving you in a seemingly neverending succession of queues. For those travelling by land, the Peruvian border is usually the slowest, particularly if you have to undergo a health check. Crossing from Colombia, formalities are swift and customs searches rare.

Departure Tax. At $25, Ecuador's airport departure tax is the highest in South America.

Money

Notes and Coins. The most common notes in circulation are in denominations of 100 (purple), 500 (blue), 1,000 (green) or 5,000 (red) sucres, though you still see some to the value of 10, 20 and 50 sucres. Coins to the value of 50 and 100 sucres are also used. Some notes are so old that they are in danger of disintegrating in your hands.

Changing Money. The highest rates of exchange are given in Guayaquil, followed by Cuenca and then Quito. Shop around, since either cambios or banks may offer the best rate. The rate is often the same for both travellers cheques and cash. In smaller towns you will usually have to rely on banks, though not all will change cheques; Bancos de Pichincha and Guayaquil are usually reliable. There is no black market to speak of in Ecuador.

Ecuador leads the continent in cash machines. Automatic dispensers operated by the Banco de Guayaquil give out sucres to cardholders whose banks belong to the Plus system; this includes many Australian, US and Canadian banks, and the Abbey National, Co-op and Girobank in Britain. If you have money transferred out to you it is possible to withdraw it in dollars. Changing sucres back into dollars also presents no problem.

In the cities banks open 9am-noon and 4-6pm Monday to Friday, and on Saturday mornings, though exchange desks often close at noon. In smaller towns banks open only in the morning. Cambios tend to operate on a schedule similar to the main town banks, though with a shorter lunch break.

Communications

Mail. Most post offices open 8am-6.30pm Monday to Friday. Large parcels are best sent to Europe from Quito, though you may have difficulty sending packages that weigh over 1kg. In this case the couriers DHL (Reina Victoria and 18 de Septiembre; tel 565059) is a better bet than the post office.

As well as the main post office on Benalcázar in old Quito, members can also use the South American Explorers Club office in the capital for poste restante: see page 197.

Telephone. Ecuador is five hours behind GMT, all year round. The international country code is 593.

The telecommunications network is run by IETEL, which has public phone offices in every town. Making international calls can be difficult outside the big cities, and it is always costly — at about $15 for three minutes to the USA and $18 to Europe. Rates are cheaper after 7pm and on Sundays. Collect calls can be made to the UK but not to the USA. You can also send international faxes from the larger IETEL offices, but these are expensive too.

Internal connections are usually straightforward. The whole country has just three main area codes: 4 for the southern coast (Guayaquil, Machala, Manta and Portoviejo); 7 for the southern Sierra (Cuenca and Loja); and 2 for the north (Quito, Esmeraldas, Ambato and Riobamba).

Street payphones exist in some towns and take *fichas* (tokens). Local calls are extremely cheap.

Useful Numbers: Police — 101; Fire — 102; Directory inquiries — 104; International operator — 116.

THE MEDIA

Newspapers. The main newspapers are published in Quito (*El Comercio* and *Hoy*) and Guayaquil (*El Universo*). There is strong rivalry between them. While distributed nationally, they are available mainly in the Sierra and the coastal lowlands respectively. While *Hoy* is a populist paper, *El Comercio* and *El Universo* are serious broadsheets, and give the best news coverage; the former has particularly good foreign news pages. Official censorship is rare.

Broadcasting. Radio stations on AM have the best news, though you would still probably do better to tune into the World Service. On television, while coverage of international events is bad, the national scene is handled fairly well; the main news programmes are broadcast at around 6pm. Channel 8 has the best range of programmes, from current affairs to sport, as well as the inevitable soaps. On most evenings there is at least one Western film on.

Getting Around

Maps. The best tourist maps are published in book form by Nelson Gómez. One volume, the *Guía Turística del Ecuador*, covers the whole country and is available from good bookshops for $1.20. It contains detailed regional maps as well as city maps of Quito, Guayaquil and Cuenca, and a plan of the Galapagos Islands. Other books in the series cover each of the three largest cities in more detail. The government-run Instituto Geográfico Militar in Quito (see page 197) produces topographical maps. The best place to buy all these maps is the South American Explorers Club, which has a wide range at good prices.

AIR

Internal flights are so reliable and such good value that many travellers hop around by air. The cost of flights ranges from $8 to $25, among the cheapest anywhere in the world. Reserving a seat should be no problem for most of the year, though flights are heavily booked during holiday periods. At this time, over-booking can be a problem, in which case you may have to bribe your way on. Always confirm your flight and don't turn up late.

The principal domestic airline is the military-owned TAME. It has at least one flight each weekday to all the main regional airports. Most flights originate in Quito or Guayaquil; there are five services a day between these two cities. San/Saeta, two private airlines, combine to connect Quito with Guayaquil and Cuenca. Minor delays are not uncommon, but are nothing compared to those experienced on Ecuatoriana. Most flights turn around within 30-60 minutes from the arrival time. Tickets are interchangeable between TAME and San/Saeta flights, though usually only if you have paid in cash.

In the Oriente various small operators fly to strips hacked out of the jungle from Macas, Lago Agrio and Coca. One of the more unorthodox ways to get around the remotest settlements is by hitching on Air Force or Jesuit mission planes. All flights in this region are subject to cancellation at short notice due to poor weather.

TRAIN

Trains provide the best way to enjoy the scenery, but they are invariably slow and uncomfortable. Buses are quicker and only slightly more expensive than the trains, so the railways are used mainly by tourists and local people living close to the line. Ecuadorean trains are famous for their breakdowns and derailments. Landslides are also a major problem, though small ones can usually be dealt with by passengers helping to shift boulders and other obstacles from the line.

Most trains in Ecuador are the so-called *autoferros*, which are similar to the ferrobuses of Bolivia and consist of diesel-engined buses welded to a railway undercarriage. All services are cheap, with just a single class of seat generally available. Most lines have only one departure per day in each direction.

Ecuador boasts more than its fair share of breathtaking train journeys. The trip to San Lorenzo, in northern Ecuador, is rightly famous. But trains have stopped running from Ibarra in the Sierra (they now leave from nearby Carchí or from Lita, in the foothills), and the journey is not quite as good as it once was. As spectacular as ever, however, is the line between Quito and Guayaquil. The railway was completed in 1908 and took nearly thirty years to build. Almost insurmountable engineering problems had to be overcome to bring the line up from the coast to an altitude of nearly 9,840ft/3,000m. The journey through the Avenue of Volcanoes south from Quito is beautiful enough, and if there are several tourists on board, the driver may stop at a couple of places with especially panoramic views: sit on the east-facing side. More stunning, more shaky and more uncomfortable still is the section between Riobamba and Guayaquil.

Riobamba-Guayaquil Railway. The first section of this line has been out of action since it was destroyed by a landslide in 1983. It is due to re-open from Riobamba in 1992, but trains currently run from Alausí, a village 60 miles/96km further south. Until then you must travel that stretch by bus. In whichever direction you

Trucks. You need rely on hitching a lift on trucks only rarely, though drivers are usually happy to take hitch-hikers on board for a small fee.

DRIVING

With such a good, cheap bus service few people feel the need to rent a car — particularly as the cost is high by Ecuadorean standards. You can expect to pay at least $35 a day, though petrol is very cheap at no more than $1 a gallon. And while hiring a car can be done easily in Quito, Guayaquil and Cuenca, where Avis and Hertz — as well as local firms — are represented, elsewhere the scope is limited. Do not expect the latest models; the average motorist regards a Ford Cortina as modern.

Eating and Drinking

Eating out is extremely cheap — you can get a three-course meal for $1-2 — but not always pleasurable. Only in a few restaurants are some of the wonderful ingredients available in Ecuador turned into truly outstanding dishes. In the average restaurant little imagination is displayed in the kitchen, and often the menus are identical across the country. The food is usually bland, and you must use the *ají* (hot chilli sauce), found on most restaurant tables, to spice it up. The traditional South American set lunch or dinner is known in Ecuador as *el menú*.

The standard dishes are fried and involve meat, onions, maize (*choclo*), potato and rice, in various combinations. Sometimes they may be cooked with coconut milk — *encocado*. Banana, which is to the Ecuadorean coast what the potato is to the Sierra, is a welcome addition. It may come fried, boiled or baked, and is often sold at roadside stalls too. Manioc (yucca) is most common as an accompaniment in the tropical regions.

In the Andes guinea-pig (*cuy*) is served in stews and roasted on long poles over charcoal. While not necessarily a gastronomic delight, it is certainly worth trying. Fortunately, there are other choices, including superb steaks. *Churrasco,* consisting of steak and rice with an egg on top, is popular and filling. Stews and soups are also common. One of the most popular offal dishes, *guatita*, is a tripe and potato stew. *Yaguar* is a delicious soup made from potato, onions and cheese. Sometimes it is served with a portion of dried blood and salad, when it is known as *yaguarlocro*: this is not as revolting as it sounds. On the coast you can eat delicious fish and seafood soups: *sancocho* is often prepared with *bagre* (catfish), and *fanesca* is a fish and grain soup.

Ecuador has the usual range of snacks. South of Quito women board buses holding large plastic bags and let out a terrible screech. They are selling *allullas*, a dry uninteresting biscuit.

The increase in the number of tourists has brought with it a growing number of places catering for their tastes. Pizzas and muesli seem to have been deemed the things that gringos like best. Most tourist towns now boast at least one pizzeria and a café serving muesli for breakfast.

DRINKING

The Club brand of beer comes in small bottles and is the most drinkable. It is slightly more expensive than the standard Pilsner. Rum and *aguardiente*, both distilled from sugar cane, are the cheapest spirits. Local wine is best avoided, particularly the extremely sickly type made from bananas. Instead, go for Chilean wine (though it doesn't come cheap) or stick with beer.

Hot drinks, sold in the street and in markets are a good way to get yourself going on a cold morning. Most delicious is the hot maize-based drink called *moroche*, which is similar to *api* found in Bolivia. It is sold mainly in markets, early in the morning. *Anis*, drunk in abundance at fiestas, and *orchata*, a herb drink, are both popular. Coffee almost always consists of liquid essence, in a jug on the table, which you squirt into a tepid mug of milk. As such, it is an inspired experience, though some places have *café puro*.

The collective name for fizzy drinks is *cola*.

Archaeological Sites. Unlike in Peru, there are few remains dating from the pre-Columbian civilizations. Those that have been investigated are generally unimpressive. The main pre-Inca site is Cochasquí, just north of Quito, which consists simply of a series of earth platforms. The only significant Inca ruins in Ecuador are at Ingapirca, north of Cuenca. While unremarkable, it is unusual by Peruvian standards, and the setting is lovely. The best way to get there is by hiking along part of an Inca track from near Alausí, which takes two or three days.

You will often learn more from the excavated artefacts in the museums. Guayaquil has the best pre-Inca and Inca collections, though Quito and Cuenca have good exhibitions too.

Colonial Architecture. Much of Ecuador's colonial architecture has been destroyed by the relentless earthquakes that have troubled the country throughout its history. Nevertheless, old Quito is well preserved, with a large number of churches and streets dating from the early colonial period. Cuenca is Ecuador's other outstanding colonial city. In addition, there are several modest but charming smaller towns, including Ibarra, and Gualacéo near Cuenca.

Hiking and National Parks. Don't leave Ecuador without hiking or riding through the country's stunning scenery, or scaling at least one volcano. The countryside around Otavalo, Riobamba, Baños and Cuenca is excellent for day trips. The national parks and reserves are better for longer hikes. While few of them have organized trail systems, the Podacarpus reserve in the south is a notable exception. In some it is possible to get well off the beaten track, though you will need a tent and good equipment.

For wildlife there is nothing to rival the Galapagos, in terms both of quantity and of the ease with which it can be observed — particularly the birds. By contrast, both animals and birds are extremely difficult to watch in the Amazon, though if you have an experienced guide this will enhance your chances greatly. Unlike in the Galapagos, tours in the rainforest are often disorganized. See page XXX.

Parks are administered by the Ministry of Agriculture (MAG). Most of those along the coast and in the highlands have guard posts which are a useful source of information and sometimes maps. You need permission from MAG in Quito to enter protected areas in the Oriente; the office is at Eloy Alfaro and Amazonas.

Many of Ecuador's volcanoes can be climbed, and this has become increasingly popular among both travellers and young Ecuadoreans. The easiest and most frequently climbed peak is Tungurahua, above Baños, which is perfectly feasible for the inexperienced climber; i.e you need to be fit rather than a mountaineer. Cotopaxi is more of a challenge, but with a guide anyone who is reasonably athletic and fully acclimatized can make the ascent. Chimborazo and Cayambe are both more dangerous, and should be attempted only by people with climbing experience and a local guide.

You can normally arrange guides locally without any difficulty. Otherwise arrange a trip through a company. Recommended for volcano ascents are Gerhard Schutz (Surtrek, Casilla 865, Ambato; tel 827349/821353), Adventure Travels (Juan León Mera 741, new Quito; tel 322331) and Sierra Nevada Expeditions (Avenida 6 de Diciembre and Roca, new Quito; tel 554936). Rafael (tel 432510) and Eduardo Agama (Venezuela 1163 at Manabi, old Quito) are private guides. Prices vary considerably so shop around. Guides charge a flat fee per climb rather than per person, so it is obviously cheaper to get a party together. If you are on your own, register with a number of guides to see which can arrange the most economical party and how quickly.

Beaches. Ecuador has sandy beaches stretching the length of the coast, interrupted only by the Gulf of Guayaquil and the mangrove forests in the far northwest. They are well below the standards of the Caribbean, but considerably more enticing than those in Peru. The northern coast has several small bays to the west of Esmeraldas, where the resort of Atacames is popular. The long sandy beaches between Muisné and Bahía de Caráquez are less developed, and although transport is more erratic, it is well worth making the effort.

Another area frequented by an increasing number of backpackers is south of Manta near Puerto López, where there are some delightful sandy bays with good surf. Simple accommodation is available in small fishing villages, though a tent or hammock would be an asset in certain bays.

For a more energetic beach experience get hold of a copy of a book called *Walking the Beaches of Ecuador*, written and published by J. Cardenas and K. Greiner, available from good bookshops in Quito.

Like all Andean countries, Ecuador is a land of spectacular fiestas. There are distinct variations between those put on in the mountains and in the lowlands. While music in the Andes is dominated by the panpipes (*zampoña*), small guitar (*charango*) and drums, along the coast — especially in areas with a sizeable black population — drum rhythms are the fundamental feature. Otavalo and Latacunga are among the towns most famous for their festivals.

Otherwise, the most likely opportunity you will have to hear traditional music will be at peñas similar to those in Bolivia and Peru. These folkloric shows are easiest to track down in the main cities or tourist centres such as Baños and Otavalo; they usually take place at weekends, beginning at around 10pm.

Nightclubs are rare outside the big towns and cities, though even the tiny jungle town of Misahuallí, where many jungle trips start, has its disco. There are few theatres and concert halls outside the capital. In most towns the cinema is likely to be the main form of entertainment. While cinemas in Guayaquil show some reasonable films, in most places violence or explicit sex is the dominant theme.

SPORT
Soccer, the national game, is played everywhere in Ecuador with great enthusiasm.

The best matches are held in the Atahualpa stadium in Quito. Nearly as popular is volleyball, which is played in the street throughout the day and between people of all ages. Bullfighting and cockfighting have a large following too. Bullfights are not normally to the death, but can still be brutal; the main season is November and December.

The increase in tourism has spawned some unauthentic and poorly finished crafts. But it has also stimulated production of new ones, and a greater variety amongst existing ones. In general the quality has remained high.

The wide range of crafts in Ecuador is largely thanks to the industriousness and ingenuity of the native people, most notably of the Otavalo and Salasaca Indians. Both groups are renowned for their weavings, and the wall-hangings are particularly beautiful. They depict either scenes of Andean life or traditional patterns, and are still coloured with natural dyes and made on rickety looms. The Otavaleños trade their goods throughout the country as well as at their own town's famous market. Other fairs worth visiting are at Saquisilí, near Latacunga, and at Riobamba. This last market is huge, and is particularly good for shawls, blankets and embroidered clothes.

Brightly painted balsa wood animals, especially birds, have flooded foreign markets in recent years. Even so, they are exceptionally light to carry home and make good presents. Other crafts include fine silver jewellery and all kinds of woven and knitted goods. The Otavaleños produce colourful chunky jumpers, using sheep's wool. There are no alpacas or llamas to speak of in Ecuador, bar the odd one brought in for the tourists. You can also buy colourful shawls (*paños*), in cotton and wool, with distinctive traditional patterns.

Few crafts of interest are sold in the markets of the coastal towns. The one exception are Panama hats, which are a bargain if you buy the authentic ones. They need not be awkward to carry around either: it is said that a hat made according to the most traditional method can be rolled up and threaded through a wedding ring. The best Panamas are made in Montecristi, on the coast, though several villages around Cuenca are also involved in the same trade. Elegant trilby hats are worn throughout the Sierra and can be purchased in all the highland towns.

Politically, Ecuador is safe by Latin American standards. No significant military activity has taken place since the 1970s and there are no anti-government terrorist groups. The occasional flare up along the disputed Peruvian frontier may limit access to the far south, but there have been no serious incidents since the early 1980s. The political disturbances most likely to affect visitors are the sporadic demonstrations in Quito, when the hurling of rocks and even molotov cocktails is common — to which the police usually respond with tear gas.

Petty thieves are a growing menace, however, particularly in Quito, Guayaquil and in some tourist centres. Several travellers have been attacked violently in Quito's old city and on Atacames beach, and there have been several robberies on the slopes of the Pichincha and Tungurahua volcanoes.

Passport checks are fairly common, both in the towns and along country roads. Police in Quito sometimes invent regulations to get money out of you, but generally they are a comparatively straight bunch. Be wary of fake plain clothed policemen: see page 64 for information on how to deal with these criminals.

Drugs. Although Ecuador is certainly an important transit point, it is not a significant drug-producer. Drugs are not widely or openly traded, but good quality marijuana and cocaine can certainly be found at very low prices. Penalties for possession are severe, particularly as the fight against trafficking intensifies.

Coca is not grown much in Ecuador, and the leaves are chewed comparatively little by the highland Indians. Nevertheless, coca leaves can still be purchased in small quantities from licensed sellers in markets; they are often used for making tea to soothe altitude sickness. The most unorthodox buzz in Ecuador can be had from the perfectly legal but foul-tasting San Pedro cactus. Its hallucinogenic effects last much of the day, so thrill-seekers take it early in the morning. Vilcabamba, in the far south, has developed a reputation as the place to try it.

While the Sierra is mostly free from malaria, parts of Ecuador, notably the northwestern coast bordering Colombia and the northern Oriente, have a reputation for a virulent form of malaria; the strongest preventative medicines should be taken. The cholera that spread up the coast from Peru in early 1991 affected primarily the poorest districts of the coastal lowlands; the worst of it appears to have passed, though it could well pick up again in hot weather. Tap water is heavily chlorinated but is still best avoided. Bottled water is widely available. The whole of Ecuador lies within a yellow fever zone.

Apart from the usual hazards of unhygienic food, biting insects and poor driving, altitude sickness (*soroche*) in the Sierra is the other major problem: the capital and many other cities in the central valley are at an altitude of nearly 10,000ft/3,000m. A few days acclimatization in the central valley is strongly recommended before setting off on a hiking trip at higher altitudes.

The state tourist board is the Corporación Ecuatoriana de Turismo — CETUR — which has offices in Quito and a few of the major towns. A better, independent source of information is the South American Explorers Club, which has an office at Toledo 1254 and Cordero in Quito. For details of the service offered by the SAEC see page 80.

For advice in the UK, send a large stamped addressed envelope to the Embassy of Ecuador, Flat 3B, 3 Hans Crescent, London, SW1 0LS (tel 071-584 2648). In return you get — eventually — a few brochures and leaflets; personal enquiries after more detailed information are often fruitless.

Public Holidays

January 1	New Year
January 6	Epiphany
March/April	Easter
May 1	Labour Day
May 24	Battle of Pichincha
July 24	Birthday of Simón Bolívar
August 10	Independence Day

October 9	Independence of Guayaquil
October 12	Columbus Day
November 1	All Saints' Day
November 2	All Souls' Day (Day of the Dead)
November 3	Independence of Cuenca
December 6	Foundation of Quito (lasts a week)
December 25	Christmas Day

QUITO

Imagine the average ramshackle South American coastal city taken nearly two miles high and plonked haphazardly on the side of a deep valley. It is ungainly, and in places ugly or positively dangerous. Yet Quito has an atmospheric heart and a most lovely setting. Volcán Pichincha rises to the west, and on clear days Cotopaxi volcano is visible in the distance to the south. Pichincha occasionally showers Quito with ash and dust, but it has so far failed to destroy the city — as others have done to towns elsewhere in the valley.

The Incas built the original city on this site, but they destroyed it when fleeing from Sebastián de Benalcázar and his men in 1534. As if to spite them, the Spanish set about building their own fine city. Quito has an attractive colonial centre, which retains many of its original buildings. It has been declared a World Heritage Site. Admiring the architecture is made frustratingly difficult by the crowds of street traders that block the pavements, and by the menace of pickpockets. But when it all gets too much, you can retreat to the lively pavement cafés in the commercial district.

Because of the bulge around the middle of the globe, Quito's altitude of 9,350ft/2,850m makes it the capital city farthest from the centre of the earth. It is also just eight miles south of the Equator.

CITY LAYOUT

The centre of Quito is divided into two distinct areas: the old colonial city and, to the north, the modern city. Separating them are the La Alameda and El Ejido parks. The old centre's southern boundary is defined by a steep-sided hill, El Panecillo, which is topped by a large statue of the Virgin Mary. While good for views, this hill is extremely dangerous. There have been cases of stabbings and attempted rape as well as robbery. Go up in a taxi and pay for it to wait while you have a look around.

The focus of the colonial district is Plaza Santo Domingo, and most buses serving this part of the city run through it. From the square, buses run along Flores towards the new city, and in the opposite direction along Guayaquil. Maldonado runs south from the opposite side of the square towards the bus and railway stations, and on to southern Ecuador. The other two main squares in this district are Plazas San Francisco and de la Independencia; the latter contains the surprisingly unimpressive presidential palace. The old city has been hit by a massive refurbishment operation, which is aimed above all at relieving the traffic congestion in the steep and narrow streets.

The new city contains the business centre and wealthy suburbs. The streets are broad, the buildings modern. Crossing right through the heart of the district is Avenida Amazonas. The main roads connecting the old and new centres are 10 de Agosto, 6 de Diciembre (which runs through El Ejido park) and 12 de Octubre, also known as Colombia. Avenida América, which runs four blocks to the west of 10 de Agosto, is the main road to the airport and the north of the country.

Maps. Because of the convoluted layout of Quito, a good map is essential. The Nelson Gómez *Guía Turística* is easy to find locally and costs $1.20. Free maps are available from the tourist office.

ARRIVAL AND DEPARTURE

Air. The airport (tel 241580) is surrounded by industrial parks and general urban sprawl in the northern part of the new city; it is 6 miles/10km from the old district. There is a casa de cambio in the terminal, but the tourist information desk is usually closed. Bus 1 takes 40-60 minutes into town, running along Amazonas. Taxis take just 15 minutes to the new city. While these charge $10 from the airport, by going to the main road outside the terminal you can pick up a local cab which will charge just $3 ($4 to the old city). When heading to the airport from the old city in the morning (e.g. for the 9.30am flight to the Galapagos), make allowances for an extremely slow journey caused by traffic jams.

TAME, with services to most of the main towns within Ecuador, is based at Colón and Juan León Mera (tel 547000) in new Quito; the nearest office to the old city is at Avenida 10 de Agosto 239 (tel 523023). San/Saeta, at Colón and 6 de Diciembre (tel 561935), serves mainly Guayaquil and Cuenca. International airline offices are all based along Avenida Amazonas. A recommended agent from which to buy tickets is Turisa at Amazonas 1206 and Foch (tel 552-964).

Bus. The main bus station is just off Maldonado in the old city, five minutes walk from Plaza Santo Domingo. It is well-organized and generally safe. A few companies offering services to towns in northern Ecuador, such as Otavalo and Ibarra, have additional depots close to the junction of Patria and 10 de Agosto, in the new city centre.

Train. The railway station is less than a mile south of the old city. Its impressive façade belies the level of services on offer: there is only one railbus daily to Riobamba, and the line is subject to frequent repairs. The train currently leaves at 3pm, and reaches Riobamba after dark.

Car Rental. As well as the counters in the airport, the main agencies also have offices downtown: Avis — Colón 1541 at 10 de Agosto (tel 550238); Budget — Avenida Colón 1140 at J. L. Mera (tel 237026); Hertz — Santa María 517 at Amazonas (tel 545117).

CITY TRANSPORT

Bus. Quito has a motley collection of buses, including old double-deckers that once graced the streets of London. In the old city a constant stream of these ancient buses struggles up the steep cobbled streets, and pours out an alarming amount of fumes. Fortunately, they do not run along all roads, so the worst affected areas can be avoided. Buses stop at most but not all street corners, and cannot be hailed anywhere. There is a flat fare of $0.10. Being so cheap buses are often crammed full.

Taxi. Cabs are very cheap and most trips, including from the old to the new city, should not cost more than a dollar. Taxis are legally required to have a meter. While most drivers turn it on automatically, in some cases you may have to insist.

QUITO

0   600m

0   ¼ mile

1. Hotel Indoamerica
2. Hotel Grand
3. Plaza Santo Domingo
4. Hotel Gran Casino
5. Hotel Gran Casino II
6. Hotel Yumbo Imperial
7. House of Sucre
8. La Compañía
9. Plaza San Francisco
10. Plaza de la Independencia
11. Cathedral
12. Tourist Office
13. Municipal Museum
14. Post Office
15. San Agustin
16. Hotel Viena
17. El Criollo
18. La Basílica
19. Banco Central
20. Residencial Marsella
21. IGM
22. US Embassy
23. Casa de la Cultura
24. El Patio Restaurant
25. Peña Panchacamac
26. American Express
27. Cambio Rodrigo Paz
28. Tourist Office,
    Reina Victoria Pub
29. San/Saeta
30. TAME
31. Taberna Quiteña
32. Angermeyer Tours
33. Art Forum Café
34. Libri Mundi Bookshop
35. Parcel Office

There are plenty of more taxis to choose from if they refuse. As a rule, however, drivers are friendly and helpful.

ACCOMMODATION

The old city has the greatest choice of hotels, and you can find basic accommodation for as little as $2 single/$3 double.

For many years the main travellers' hotel was the Gran Casino at Moreno and Ambato, but the large building is now run-down. Its annex Gran Casino Internacional (II) nearby is hardly better, and is over-priced at $4. Better are the small hotels around Plaza Santo Domingo. Just off the square at Guayaquil 647 is the Yumbo Imperial (tel 518651), which is clean, friendly and secure. Rates are $3/$4. The Hotel Grand, on Rocafuerte, 100 yards east of the square, is also good.

Moving towards the new city, the Hotel Viena Internacional, on the corner of Flores and Chile, is similar to the Gran Casino Internacional. The original Hotel Viena next door is fairly basic but is clean, friendly and still full of gringos. Further north, near La Alameda park, is the Residencial Marsella (Los Ríos 2035; tel 515884). This has become perhaps the most popular hotel in Quito among low-budget travellers, simply because it is away from the dangers of the old city. It makes up for its small rooms by being extremely helpful and secure and by having a roof-top balcony which overlooks the whole city.

Two modern hotels in the new city are both family-run and highly recommended. La Casona (Andalucía 213; tel 230129) has self-catering facilities, a lounge and garden, but no single rooms. La Casa de la Feliz Eliza (Isabel la Católica 1559; tel 233602) is even more friendly.

EATING AND DRINKING

The busiest restaurants in the old city are those in the most popular hotels — as much as meeting-places as for the food. Other restaurants in the area tend to be simple affairs serving local food. El Criollo, at Flores 825, is one of the best. Cevichería Gala (Guayaquil and Olmedo) and Pizzería Paolo (near Hotel Grand) are also reasonable. For breakfast the Savori, close to the junction of Chile and Guayaquil, and the Cafetería M and S, on Venezuela a block from the main square, are good.

Good restaurants, bars and cafés are the new city's main asset. Prices are generally higher than in the old district, and most menus are dominated by foreign dishes. The main concentration of restaurants is on or off Avenida Amazonas, where you'll also find congenial pavement cafés — good places for watching the world go by and exchanging stories with other travellers. Several good restaurants are on Juan León Mera, including the Café Art Forum, run by the owners of the Libri Mundi bookshop, opposite. The British Council has a café at Amazonas 1534, which offers a good vegetarian lunch. On Sundays a large number of Westerners can be found gorging themselves on the $3 'eat as much as you can' lunch in Hotel Colón (Patria and Amazonas).

To splash out go to the excellent Le Petit restaurant (which has a branch in Baños) at Juan León Mera 1238; or, even better, to El Patio, two blocks north of El Ejido, on Reina Victoria. It serves good food in a delightfully tiled room filled with plants and colonial artefacts.

The English-run El Pub (Reina Victoria at Suárez) is next to the UK embassy and is popular among expats. It has a good atmosphere and serves the nearest thing you'll find to 'pub' food in Ecuador. On the same street, at number 530, is the Reina Victoria bar, where expats also gather.

EXPLORING

The oldest intact street of any length dating from the colonial period is La Ronda, a block south of Plaza Santo Domingo. It is a charming cobbled street, with geraniums and prostitutes lending plenty of colour. The owners of house number 963 are usually prepared to let visitors see inside. La Ronda, however, is also one of Quito's most notorious streets for crime, and many shops have closed down. Local people concerned about your welfare will warn you against going there — even during the day.

The old city boasts a vast number of impressive churches, with spectacular altars covered in gold leaf and splendid decoration. Several have small museums attached, but many of these seem to be permanently closed for repairs. Most churches and museums are closed, more officially, between noon and 3pm.

The church of San Francisco dominates the large square of the same name. It is the oldest in Quito, though it has been rebuilt several times owing to damage done by earthquakes. The adjoining museum contains suberb collections of religious art and handmade wooden bureaux. Even more impressive is the church of La Compañía, on Moreno between Plazas de la Independencia and San Francisco. It is smothered in gold and is one of the most ornate churches in Ecuador. The Cathedral, in Plaza de la Independencia, is not as interesting as many of the other churches, but it contains the graves of General Sucre and several presidents. Also of greater historical than architectural importance is San Agustín, at the intersection of Guayaquil and Chile: Ecuador's first (and failed) declaration of independence was signed here in 1809.

The most bizarre ecclesiastical building in the city is La Basílica, a huge neo-gothic monolith. It dominates the skyline high above both the old and new cities, at Venezuela and Carchi. It was begun in 1926 after a public referendum voted for a new cathedral, but remains unfinished. Three blocks south, on the corner of Venezuela and Esmeraldas, is the Camilio Egas modern art museum, housed in a tiny colonial house.

There are several other museums in old Quito. The Casa de Sucre, at the intersection of Sucre and Venezuela, occupies the former home of the General instrumental in the battle for independence. It has been well restored and contains artefacts from the Independence era, including much of the original furniture of the house. It opens 9am-12.30pm and 3-6pm, Monday to Friday and 9am-1pm on Saturdays. The Municipal Museum, in the pedestrian street running west from Plaza de la Independencia, has exhibits from the colonial era and paintings of the 17th-century Quito school. It was in the basement of this building that the leaders of Ecuador's abortive fight for independence in 1809 were held and then executed. The episode has been reconstructed using life-size models. It opens 9am-noon and 3-6pm daily except Monday. The Museo del Banco Central is housed on the fifth floor in the office block on 10 de Agosto, at the southern end of La Alameda Park. Most of the exhibits are from pre-Inca and Inca times, and they give a good introduction to the early history of the country.

In the new city the focus of interest is the Casa de la Cultura, which comprises a variety of art museums. Only some of them are open at any one time, and there are other rooms for special exhibitions.

To get a feel for modern day Quito and its people, go for a stroll around the La Alameda and El Ejido parks. On Sundays they are positively teeming with people being amused by entertainers ranging from jugglers to magicians, and fed by traders selling hot dogs, corn-on-the-cob and fruit. In the middle of La Alameda is Quito's original astronomical observatory, a filthy boating pond and a huge statue of Bolívar. The northwest corner of the park has a viewing tower reached by a spiral walkway.

ENTERTAINMENT

Quito doesn't have much to offer in terms of classical entertainment. The most likely venues are the Casa de la Cultura, and Teatro Sucre on Calle Flores in the old city. There are several peñas, mostly around Amazonas and Juan León Mera. The Peña Pachacamac, just off Mera on Washington, is fairly tacky although only 40ft/12m high, it provides a good view of the city, but it has varied music and is not too expensive. Also recommended is Taberna Quiteña at Avenida Amazonas 1259, near Colón.

For a lively evening don't miss El Pobre Diablo jazz bar (Santa María and Amazonas), two blocks north of Colón, or the nearby Papillon nightclub. The Blues Bar disco at Amazonas and República is also good, with fairly up-to-date music. For Latin and Salsa music go to the Gatoson Salsateca in Edificio Girón, at 12 de Octubre and Veintimilla.

SPORT

Football matches are held at the Atahualpa stadium (6 de Diciembre and Avenida Naciones Unidas, north of the new city) on Saturday afternoons and Sunday mornings. On Sundays you can also go to the races, which take place near the stadium in Parque La Carolina. The main bull-fighting ring (Plaza de Toros) is on Avenida Amazonas, close to the airport; most fights are held in December. Finally, volleyball fans should attend a match in the brand new stadium at the eastern end of Patria, near the start of Avenida Oriental; admission costs $1.

SHOPPING

Markets are scattered throughout the city, but by Ecuadorean standards they are disappointing. The main market in the old district is around Plaza San Francisco, with food in the blocks south of the square, and clothes and other goods on Cuenca. The best source of crafts at reasonable prices is the stalls and shops within a block or so of Amazonas in the new city. Many of these are run by Otavalo Indians, who offer as good a range of weavings as in their home town (though not the quantity). For camping equipment go to either the shop on Roca, half a block from the CETUR office, or the one on 6 de Diciembre, close to the junction with Roca — both in the new city.

Bookshops. The best bookshop in Quito is Libri Mundi at Juan León Mera 851, eight blocks north of El Ejido. Its stock of books in English is mediocre, but it has a good selection of guidebooks. The smaller branch in Hotel Colón (Amazonas and Patria) usually has at least one buyable novel.

CRIME AND SAFETY

Five years ago crime against visitors was rare. It is now common and many travellers you meet have a story to tell. Even Ecuadoreans have referred to the city as a den of thieves. Be vigilant against pickpockets and bag-slashers in the old city at any time of day. La Ronda and Plaza San Francisco are both notorious. Even when pausing to listen to musicians in Plaza de la Independencia, be sure to hug your bag tightly infront of you. Mugging is a danger after dark, particularly in the old city's more southerly streets: people have been stabbed in the vicinity of the Gran Casino hotel. You would do well to spend your evenings in the new city. To report a theft go to the office at the junction of Cuenca and Mideros in the old city. The police are not particularly helpful.

HELP AND INFORMATION

Tourist Information: the CETUR office is in a large house at Reina Victoria 514 and Roca (tel 239044) in the new city. It is open 8am-3.30pm Monday to Friday. Their printed information is often inaccurate, but the staff are generally helpful. The Ministry of Agriculture, for information on national parks (and permits to enter reserves in Oriente), is at Alfaro and Amazonas.

Much the most accurate and up-to-date advice on the whole of Ecuador (as well as the rest of the continent) is available at the South American Explorers Club at Toledo 1254 and Cordero (tel 566076), three blocks east of 12 de Octubre. As well as dispensing information, the SAEC stores luggage for members (see page 80) and rents out or sells camping gear.

Post Office: the central office in the old city is in an old building at Benalcázar 769, one block from the Plaza de la Independencia. Mail sent to 'Lista de Correos, Quito' arrives here unless marked otherwise. In the new city the main office for letters is at the junction of Juan León Mera and Avenida Colón, on the ground floor of an office block. Parcels should be sent from the office in Calle Ulloa, at the junction with Ramírez Dávalos.

Telephone Office: the main IETEL office is in the new city at Avenida 6 de Diciembre near Colón. It is open 6am-10pm daily. Calls are made from the basement.

Money: there are several cambios in or just off Amazonas, and others in Colón, between Amazonas and 9 de Octubre. The most tried and tested is Rodrigo Paz at Amazonas 659, which also has a branch in the old city and in Hotel Colón (Amazonas and Patria); the latter opens out of hours, including until 1pm on Sundays. In the old city most cambios are on Venezuela, near the junction with Sucre.

The American Express agent is Ecuadorean Tours, Amazonas 399 at Washington (tel 560488/494). It sells international student cards (ISIC) for $16: smile nicely and no proof of status will be needed.

Immigration Department: the visa extensions office is at Amazonas 2639, (tel 451222), near the southwest corner of Parque La Carolina.

Instituto Geográfico Militar: on Paz y Miño, off Avenida Colombia. The office is open 8am-4pm. You will need your passport, even just to browse.

British Council: Amazonas 1615 at Orellana (tel 231686). Its stock of foreign papers in the reading room is more up-to-date than in the Embassy. Hotel Colón also has a reading room.

Medical Care: Dr Hugo Romo of the Centro Médico Quirúrgico de Pichincha (Veintimilla 1259 and Paéz in the new city; tel 562-408), speaks good English and is very helpul. A good dentist is Dr Tugendhat, Edificio Gabriela, Flat 3, República del Salvador (tel 437-752). In emergencies the best place is the American-run Hospital Voz Andes at Juan Villalengua 263 in the new city (tel 241-540).

Embassies and Consulates. All the following are in the new city.
Bolivia: Ramírez Dávalos 258 (tel 231352).
Brazil: Edificio España, Avenida Amazonas 1429, at Colón.
Chile: Juan Pablo Saenz 3617 at Amazonas (tel 249403).
Colombia: Avenida Colón 1133 at Amazonas, 7th floor (tel 524633).
Paraguay: Avenida Gaspar de Villarroel 2013 (tel 245871).
Peru: same building as Brazilian consulate (tel 527568).
UK: Calle González Suárez 111 (Casilla 314); tel 560669/670, fax 560730. The consulate is nearby at number 197.
USA: Avenida 12 de Octubre and Patria (PO Box 538); tel 562890.

AROUND QUITO

Guapulo. Directly east of the new city centre lies a deep wooded ravine. A cobbled street lined with attractive houses runs down it to the beautiful old monastery of Guapulo. It is said that Francisco de Orellana walked passed it at the very start of his journey down the Amazon. A trip to Guapulo is a pleasant half day's walk. Begin by following 12 de Octobre from the new city all the way to Hotel Internacional Quito, from which the street runs down to the monastery. You can go inside 8-11am and 3-6pm, Monday to Saturday.

San Antonio. Eight miles/13km north of Quito is the Mitad del Mundo, the monument marking the equatorial line — a position determined by Charles de la Condamine, a French scientist, in the 1730s. There has been much discussion about its accuracy, and it is now thought to be about twenty yards off. A paved avenue, lined with the stone busts of the scientists who helped to establish the position of the line, leads up to the stone tower marking the spot. The surroundings are hardly impressive, but there's nothing quite like straddling two hemispheres.

Buses leave old Quito regularly from in front of La Merced, at the junction of Cuenca and Chile, and then run along Avenida America through the new city. The trip takes about forty minutes.

Volcán Pichincha. Many travellers use the 15,090ft/4,600m Rucu Pichincha volcano for acclimatization before attempting to climb a higher one. The ascent is relatively easily, but do not attempt it until you have adjusted fully to the altitude of Quito. The round trip is a good day's walk. The traditional route up 24 de Mayo and El Placer from Hotel Gran Casino Internacional is no longer considered safe following a spate of muggings. A better way is up Avenida La Gasca to the viewpoint at Cruz Loma. The climb isn't one of Ecuador's most thrilling and the summit, with its collection of TV aerials and military installations, is hardly scenic. But there are fantastic views of the whole city.

NORTHERN ECUADOR

The Pan-American Highway heads north from Quito, connecting the capital with the Colombian frontier near Tulcán. It alternates between lush high Andean pastures and dry steep-sided valleys. There are spectacular views of mountains including the snow-capped Volcán Cayambe.

The road splits at Guayllabamba, 25 miles/40km north of Quito, and the two branches run on opposite sides of the Pisque valley. Buses running north may use either, so check in advance. A few miles before Tabacundo, on the westerly route,

is the turn-off to the pre-Inca ruins and strange rock formations of Cochasquí; they lie near the village of Tocachi, about an hour's walk off the main road.
The roads meet again in the small market town of Cayambe, where people stop to buy local cheese. From here the highway heads northwest past Lago San Pablo, before dropping down to Otavalo.

OTAVALO

This small market town is set in a broad wooded valley, overshadowed by two extinct volcanoes. Otavalo draws crowds not only because of the beautiful surrounding countryside, but also because of the town's large Indian population and its huge Saturday market. The part of the market devoted to crafts, centred around the Plaza de Ponchos, has become touristy in recent years. One traveller described it as 'Camden Lock in the Andes'. But for a cross-section of crafts from every corner of Ecuador, as well as of the fine weavings from the Otavalo region, this is the place to come.

The large Saturday market is not confined to artesanía, and it is in fact well away from Plaza de Ponchos that you are likely to have the most fun. At dawn on Saturday the animal market starts up in a field northwest of the town centre — across the Pan-American Highway, just beyond the swimming pool. Get there early so you can mingle with the dealers and their animals as they arrive. Interest swings from one type of animal to another in the organized chaos. Make sure that your gestures are not misinterpreted as bids; and do not stray too close to the massive bulls that take pride of place. By about 9am all deals are complete and the animals are loaded up, often with great difficulty, and transported away.

Market day is an undeniable delight, but so is Otavalo at any time. Many of the local people wear traditional clothes, and the streets are a vision of colour on any day of the week. The women are decked out in long dark blue skirts, finely embroidered bodices, dark-coloured shawls, necklaces of gold beads and, frequently, a folded shawl on their heads. The men have long ponytails, trilby hats, white trousers and dark blue ponchos. In addition, there are plenty of stalls selling weavings, hats, etc. during the week, when it is easier to haggle: on Saturdays prices go up as soon as the coach parties begin to arrive.

If you are in the area in the second half of June, keep an ear open for news of Otavalo's stone-throwing festival, which culminates in a drunken exchange of missiles by the Pan-American Highway. Participants stand at least 50 metres apart, so few people are injured. This is above all a light-hearted occasion.

Arrival and Departure. Transportes Otavalo, Expresso Turismo and Los Lagos run a regular bus service throughout the day to and from Quito. The same companies also offer frequent connections to Ibarra, where you can make connections for Tulcán. The offices of the last two companies are opposite the railway station; Transportes Otavalo is a couple of blocks north, on Calderón.

The railway line from Quito has been closed. The connection with Ibarra was re-opened in 1990, but it is still subject to repairs and is closed for lengthy periods.

Accommodation. Otavalo has good hotels, but they fill quickly. One of the most popular places to stay is the friendly Hotel Riviera Sucre, on the corner of Roca and Moreno, one block southeast of the Parque Central (main square). It is a large old house with a courtyard and a small restaurant. Residencial Samar Huasi, in Jaramillo just off Plaza de Ponchos, and El Rocio, a couple of blocks further north up Morales, are both smaller but good. Equally popular is the larger and more expensive Hotel Isabelita, in Quiroga, two blocks south of Plaza de Ponchos.

Other reasonable places that may be options at weekends in July and August, when hotels fill up, include Residenciales Santa Marta and Otavalo, all within a few blocks of each other in the centre of town. More modern and expensive ($10) are Hotels El Indios 1 and 2, next door to each other on Sucre, half a block west of Plaza de Ponchos.

Eating and Drinking. The large number of visitors has produced some uncharacteristically exotic places to eat. Most interesting are the Guacamayo and El Mesón de Arrayan, which offer a mix of French, Italian and Ecuadorean food; they are next door to each other at the intersection of Sucre and Colón, between the Parque Central and Plaza de Ponchos. Ali Micuy, on Plaza de Ponchos itself, is less cosy, but serves many vegetarian dishes. Half a block southwest, on Salinas, is an excellent new Mexican restaurant called Tabasco.

All the gringos in town seem to finish off the evening at the Shanandoa and Galería cafés, on Plaza de Ponchos. The former serves superb fruit pies, the latter good vegetarian food, and both play 60s and 70s music. The Shanandoa also has a book exchange and noticeboard (with guide recommendations, warnings, etc.). Many of the restaurants have live bands at weekends. There are several peñas, the most popular of which is Peña Amauta, opposite Residencial Samar Huasi.

Around Otavalo

A number of small tour companies offer trips to visit workshops in nearby villages. For example, you can watch hat-making in the village of Iluman; wool-dyeing, knitting and weaving in Peguche; reed weaving in San Pablo del Lago; and leather working in Cotacachi.

Lago San Pablo. This large lake lies above Otavalo off the Cayambe road. The village of San Pablo, on the eastern side of the lake, is the starting point for a fine half-day walk around the lake back to Otavalo. Allow a whole day if you decide to walk right around it from Otavalo. Boats can be hired on the lake at the two upmarket hotels close to the Otavalo-Cayambe road; the lake is calmest in the morning. There are regular buses from Otavalo railway station to San Pablo, half an hour away.

Peguche. This small village, 3 miles/5km and a short bus ride northeast of Otavalo, produces some of Ecuador's finest weavings. It also boasts the 50-foot high Peguche waterfall, set in a beautiful wooded ravine. You can walk there from the village (back towards Otavalo) in about 20 minutes. It is also accessible in half an hour on foot along the railway line from Otavalo. Several paths give access to various different points of the cascade which drains from Lago San Pablo.

Lago Cuicocha. This lake lies in the crater of a dormant volcano, in a most spectacular location. The rim of the volcano is almost continuous and you can walk around the crater in about five hours; it is possible to camp in a couple of places. At the small hotel on the shore you may also be able to arrange a short boat trip around one of the islands in the lake.

Lago Cuicocha is accessible along a surprisingly good road from Otavalo via the village of Cotacachi. To get there you either have to hire a taxi or try to hitch a lift from any Ecuadorians heading that way. The lake lies in the southern corner of the Cotacachi/Cayapo National Park, and there is a small fee to enter the area.

and leads up to a dramatic Andean landscape with green pastures spreading out towards rocky volcanic outcrops.

TULCAN

The northernmost town in Ecuador, at an altitude of just under 9,850ft/3,000m, is windswept and chilly. During the day the town centre is lively because of the large number of visiting Colombians; but by 9.30pm the streets are virtually deserted. The most famous site in Tulcán is the cemetery. Over many decades the gardeners have perfected the art of topiary on the cypress bushes in the grounds, to produce an admirable array of animals, people and ornaments.

Arrival and Departure. All buses coming up from the main towns further south terminate at the bus station, which is south of the centre. There are direct daily services to and from Quito. From other destinations you may need to change in Ibarra. Minibuses and taxis connect to Rumichaca on the border.

TAME flies daily from Quito at noon on weekdays, with planes returning to the capital an hour later. The fare is $8. The centre is within walking distance of the airport. At the airport itself, expect to be hassled by a bunch of would-be porters and trainee pickpockets, average age ten.

Accommodation and Food. Residencial Ecuador and Pensión Avenida, opposite the bus station, are basic but cheap. The best value is Hotel Quito, in Ayacucho a block west of the main square, but it is often full. More upmarket are the Quillisinga, in the main square, and Residencial Oasis, on 10 de Agosto, a block to the west. Both are modern and somewhat stark. These and other more expensive hotels fill up with Colombians at weekends.

Near the bus station El Criollo offers very reasonable authentic Ecuadorean food, ranging from substantial soups to large steaks. There is another branch in the town centre. Residencial Oasis has a good bar for breakfast or snacks.

Exploring. Many travellers en route for Colombia bypass Tulcán, but the hedge-trimming in its cemetery deserves close inspection. From the main square, exit at the yellow restaurant with green doors, where taxis congregate. Turn left at the Jehovah's witnesses temple 50 metres on, and you head straight for the graveyard.

THE COAST

Heading west from the high Sierra takes you down into the coastal lowlands and into a different world, where beaches and remote black communities are among the main attractions. Not much remains of the original forest, and the plains are given over mostly to banana, pineapple and palm plantations, ranchlands and, around Guayaquil, rice paddies.

All lines of communication along the coast focus on Guayaquil, Ecuador's largest city, and links with the central Sierra are limited. This does not stop people trooping down in summer to the beaches — particularly to those in the northwest, around the town of Atacames, and to the smarter resorts around Guayaquil. The main centres are heaving with people in summer, but there are plenty of secluded fishing villages that are accessible only by boat or by a truck ride along the beach.

The Northwest

SANTO DOMINGO DE LOS COLORADOS

The town of Santo Domingo lies where the Andes end and the coastal lowlands begin. It is named after the Colorado Indians, who were once a large group in the area but now number under 1,500. Their name derived from their startling appearance, with hair dyed bright red and abundant body paint. You are unlikely to encounter any of them in their traditional dress nowadays. With the virtual extinction of the Colorado culture, the only reason for travellers to stay in Santo Domingo is as an overnight stop en route between the coast and the central valley — unless you are an avid birdwatcher, in which case don't miss the nearby estate of Tinalandia.

Buses run regularly to and from all the main towns, including Quito, Ambato, Esmeraldas, Manta and Guayaquil. All companies operate from the new bus terminal west of the centre. The journey 100 miles/160km east to Quito is spectacular, with the road winding its way up the steep-sided valleys.

Santo Domingo has a surprising number of hotels, and rooms for $2 are not hard to find. Hotel La Perla, which is a short distance west of the centre, close to the market on Avenida 3 de Julio, is the best. Also good and more central is Hotel Las Brisas in Avenida Quito, a block east of the main square. A notch up are Hotel Caleta on Ibarra, and El Ejecutivo on Avenida 29 de Mayo, one and two blocks north of the square respectively.

Few places in the centre serve appetizing food, though the Juan El Marino restaurant, just south of the centre on the Quevedo road, is excellent.

Around Santo Domingo

Tinalandia. Fifteen miles/25km east of Santo Domingo towards Quito, in the semi-tropical foothills of the Andes, Tinalandia is the estate of a former Russian countess. She was forced to flee from France with her husband in the 1930s after he had killed a rival in a duel. The French Government generously awarded them an estate, where she has lived ever since. The former countess turned her home into an expensive but now rundown hotel. But the area is excellent for bird-watching — over 150 species have been recorded. To get to Tinalandia, either take a taxi from Santo Domingo, or try to persuade a Quito bus to take you the short distance.

ESMERALDAS

This dirty, unattractive and expensive town is hard to avoid if you are exploring the northwest coast. Esmeraldas is the principal refinery and export terminal for oil extracted in the Oriente. It is also a provincial capital and the largest town in the northwest, with a population of around 120,000.

The best thing about the town is the salsa music that blares out all day long from the seafront bars in Las Palmas, a couple of miles north of the centre. If you are lured into staying overnight, the Diana and Beatriz hotels, next to each other on Canizares, two blocks south of the main square, are the best value. Otherwise, try the Galeón or Americano, two blocks southwest. For a reasonable meal go to Antojos Caleños, on Piedrahita one block southeast from the square.

Arrival and Departure. Esmeraldas is six to seven hours by bus from Quito. Regular buses, via Santo Domingo, are run by several companies, which have offices within a block or so of the main square. There are services also from most southern towns including Guayaquil (9 hours).

TAME has flights from Quito daily except Sundays. They depart at 10.15am Monday to Saturday and 4.15pm on Friday, returning almost immediately. The airport is 16 miles/25km northeast across the Río Esmeraldas. It is served by taxi and the La Costeñita rancheros to La Tola also pass the entrance.

Help and Information. The tourist office is at Bolívar 517 (2nd floor), just south of the square. The post and IETEL offices are at the eastern end of Montalvo, near the waterfront and opposite the market.

ATACAMES

At Atacames the atmosphere is relaxed, the beach long and sandy, the water warm, and the seafood delicious. Such features have made this resort, 24 miles/32km west of Esmeraldas, the most popular in the country among travellers. During the main holiday periods, it is also full of Ecuadoreans. There is some surf, but beware of the often strong currents.

The beach is actually a sand spit extending across the mouth of a small river; the town centre is a short distance away across a rickety wooden bridge. The seafront is lined with restaurants, bungalow-style hotels and beach bars blaring out 60s and 70s music. The latter open mid-morning and don't normally close until late, though discos tend to operate only in the high season.

Some people have been attacked at knifepoint on Atacames beach, but as long as you leave all your belongings in the hotel, and avoid walking along the beaches after dark, you should be fine.

Arrival and Departure. Transportes La Costeñita and El Pacífico run ancient buses to and from Esmeraldas. Between them they offer a bus every hour. If they are full inside, you can travel on the roof.

Accommodation. At weekends, during the December to March holiday season, and from July to September, the peak period for travellers, accommodation is likely to be full. All the hotels are expensive and few have rooms for single people; in the low season you should be able to negotiate. At any time of year some hotels may let you camp in their grounds. The water supply is erratic and usually only salt water is available in hotels.

Cabañas Chavalitos, at the eastern end of the beach, consists of small cabins and a popular restaurant. More upmarket are the Hotel Jennifer, one block inland, and Cabañas Roger, set amongst pine trees at the western end of the beach. The best of the basic places are Hotel Tahiti, Hostería Los Bohios and Cabañas Costa del Sol, all of which are along the beach.

There are many bars, cafés and restaurants along the beachfront serving excellent seafood.

Around Atacames

West of Atacames are many small bays and beaches. Sharks sometimes come in close to the shore, chasing shoals of fish, but this does not deter Ecuadorean bathers.

Súa. In a beautiful bay an hour or so's walk west of town, Súa is a good alternative to Atacames if you aren't bothered about swimming. Its beach is often dirty, but Súa is at least peaceful. The best places to stay are Cabañas Los Acacias and Oasis, or the hotels Súa and Villa Hermosa. There are a few seafood restaurants along the waterfront. Don't walk along the beach between Atacames and Súa on your own because it is a favourite haunt of muggers.

Muisné. This pretty place lies on a small island further west of Súa. It is the last main resort along this stretch of the coast, and has a fairly good beach and reasonably blue sea. But Muisné is, like Súa, a place in which simply to rent a cabin for a few days, relax and watch the local fishermen. The Cabañas Ipenama offer reasonable and secure accommodation, though water shortages are common. Musiné is reached by bus from Atacames, and then a boat from the end of the road; the trip takes an hour or so.

South to Bahía de Caráquez. By a combination of trucks, rancheros and buses it is possible to travel south along the coast — literally along the beach — to Bahía de Caráquez. The route takes you via Cojimíes, Pedernales and San Vicente and past tiny fishing communities. There are some fine, unspoilt beaches, and in the high season they provide a wonderful refuge from the crowds further north. Those between Cojimíes and Pedernales are the best.

Land transport is at the mercy of the tides and operates to no fixed schedule; the series of small rivers must be crossed by canoe. The alternative is to go by sea: boats from the wharf in Muisné take about three hours to reach Cojimíes. To do the journey on foot would take about a day. Buses run an erratic service from Cojimíes to Pedernales and Bahía de Caráquez. All these places have simple pensiones.

SAN LORENZO

In the depths of the inaccessible region of mangroves and rainforest east of Esmeraldas lies the small decaying town of San Lorenzo. This is one of the most isolated and impoverished towns in Ecuador. It is also among the most fascinating.

The majority of the inhabitants are descendants of black slaves who, in the 18th and 19th centuries, escaped from the coastal plantations and sought refuge in the area. A black 'kingdom' sprang up and, isolated from the rest of Ecuador, remained entirely out of official control for over 100 years, until the early 20th century. A link with the outside world was established with the construction of a single track railway, which is maintained — badly — today. A road is under construction, but for the time being San Lorenzo can be reached only by train or boat. Most houses are built of wood and there is only limited electricity.

Day trips can be made by canoe to communities amongst the mangroves. The latter flower in late summer and are home to pelicans, egrets and many other birds. Their habitat, however, is under threat since large areas of mangrove have been put to the chainsaw in order to create shrimp farms.

All the hotels in San Lorenzo are basic, but always choose one with mosquito nets. The few simple restaurants close early, though at weekends you should be able to enjoy fast and furious *marimba* dancing, which can go on all night in the small bars.

Arrival and Departure. The traditional Ibarra-San Lorenzo train journey takes 10-12 hours. It is crowded but exhilirating, as the line descends rapidly into the Mira valley, which becomes progressively narrower. The track clings to the rocky valleyside above the raging torrent below; but eventually the valley broadens out and a new world is entered. Within a couple of hours the bus is rocking along through verdant jungle which bursts in through the windows when the train slows.

Recently, the daily railbus has left either from Carchí near Ibarra, or from Lita, in the foothills midway between Ibarra and San Lorenzo.

The route southwest to Esmeraldas involves a wonderful two-hour canoe trip through the mangrove swamps to La Tola, and then a four-hour bus or ranchero journey. There are lots of birds along this route, particularly pelicans and egrets.

The West Coast

MANTA and TARQUI

In pre-Inca times the site of modern Manta was known as Jocay. As the capital of the Manteña culture, it was one of the most important early settlements in Ecuador. Things have gone downhill since then. The second largest port in the country, Manta is a chaotic and dirty place.

The adjacent resort of Tarqui is more interesting. Local fishermen land their catches at the far end, and the harbour, nearer the centre, is also lively. If the door of the fish-processing plant is open, you can watch huge tuna being boiled and carried around by forklift trucks. The museum of Manteña culture contains a number of carved stone tablets which are the hallmark of that people. It is between the bus station and Plaza 4 de Noviembre, and well worth a visit.

There is a small tourist information office in the first block of Avenida 3, a block back from Plaza 4 de Noviembre; the post office is in the second block. A casa de cambio is in the first block of Avenida 2.

Arrival and Departure. Manta is over six hours by bus from Santo Domingo, and three hours from Guayaquil along a good road. Both routes are served by regular services throughout the day. All buses terminate at the station just south of the harbour, midway between the town centre and Tarqui.

TAME (on the waterfront, near Calle 3) flies from Quito every day, and from Guayaquil daily except Sunday. The airport is only a short taxi ride from the centre, but the drivers have a reputation for overcharging.

Accommodation. The best hotels are in Tarqui. They include the Pacífico and Boulevard, both close to the creek that divides Tarqui from Manta; and the Playa Brava and Astoria, at the eastern end of the beach and one block inland. In Manta the only hotels worth considering are Pensión Los Mantas, four blocks up the hill from the bus station (not to be confused with the expensive Hotel Manta), and the Hotel Chimborazo, on Plaza 4 de Noviembre.

Tarqui has several good seafood restaurants along the waterfront. In Manta the best places are the Italian joint on Plaza 4 de Noviembre and the nearby restaurant beneath Hotel Chimborazo.

Around Manta

Montecristi. This small crumbling, colonial town gave the world the Panama hat. The misunderstanding about the hats' origins stems from the fact that last century Panama was the main trading outlet for goods from Ecuador. The hat first became fashionable late last century, when they were popular with the workers building the Panama Canal and with US troops in the Caribbean.

Business has suffered recently, because the new craze for the hats has meant that fakes are now being made more cheaply abroad. Though there are still numerous workshops around the town, many have been forced to diversify into other crafts. Visit the workshop of Rosendo Delgado on Rocafuerte, the maker of the highest quality hats, known as *finos*: these can take up to three months to make, but are a snip at under $30; in the West you could expect to pay anything from £200 upwards.

Montecristi is 20 minutes by bus southeast of Manta on the Portoviejo road. A short distance further east a road splits off, heading south to Guayaquil.

Buses heading northeast to Santo Domingo or Quito from Manta take the most direct route via Junín and Chone (the turn-off for Bahía de Caráquez: see page 205). An interesting alternative is to go via Portoviejo and Quevedo, east of Manta. Founded in 1535 by Pedro de Alvarado, a notoriously ruthless conquistador, Portoviejo is one of the oldest towns in Ecuador. But despite its historical significance, the town has few attractions. If you need to stop overnight, stay at Hostal Su Casa, near the bus station, or the Gregório, a friendly hotel in Calle Rocafuerte, near the cathedral.

Portoviejo is just 30 minutes by bus from Manta. From there a ranchero service runs 93 miles/150km — four hours along a poor road — to Quevedo, an important market town with a sizeable Chinese community. From Quevedo buses run to Santo Domingo (55 miles/85km north) and across the Andes to Latacunga. The best hotel is the Flor de los Ríos on Octava.

The South Coast

GUAYAQUIL

There is a long-standing battle between Guayaquil and Quito for the position of Ecuador's most important city. Guayaquileños love to accuse Quiteños of being provincial and backward. But apart from a small area in the centre, much of their own city is rundown, underdeveloped and thoroughly unappealing. The atmosphere of decay is enhanced by the stifling heat. Most of Guayaquil used to be built of wood, and was all but destroyed by fire in 1896 and 1902. There are few sights and the markets are unsafe. Guayaquil is a place that people love to hate.

The city would not seem to have much going for it, but as a centre of economic and political influence it is worth seeing. Guayaquil is capital of Guayas province and a major port, with a population of 1.6 million. It was founded in 1537 as a harbour sheltered from Pacific storms. The surrounding land was swampy and infested with malaria, and it is over this land that the city has expanded in the last few decades. Shanties sprawl endlessly in all directions — built over former mangrove swamps into which most of the city's waste and effluent flow, or perched on low hills overlooking the centre.

Most visitors are happy just to stroll along the Malecón beside the Río Guayas, watching the river traffic and the huge mats of bright green lilies that float back and forth with the tide, many with egrets perched precariously on them — welcome islands of colour in the filthy water.

City Layout. Central Guayaquil is laid out in a grid pattern. It is restricted to the north by a small hill and to the west by one of the many creeks around which the city is built. There are few reasons for the traveller to venture out of the central area which contains all the hotels and most of the places of interest.

Malecón Simón Bolívar is the riverside boulevard. At La Rotonda it intersects with the main street, Avenida 9 de Octubre, which runs west to Parque Centenario. This central square is disappointing as the heart of the city: modern high-rise office buildings stand side by side with semi-derelict houses and kiosks. Nevertheless, on Sundays large crowds gather here to be entertained by performing artists.

The *Guia Turistica* published by Nelson Gómez (see page 183) contains an adequate map of Guayaquil.

Arrival and Departure. *Air:* the airport is a mile or so north of the centre. Buses into town run near the main square. To return to the airport catch the bus along Calle Quito, one block west of Parque Centenario. A taxi between the airport and town costs about $2.

TAME has five flights daily to Quito, and two on Sunday. There are also flights every day except Sundays to Cuenca, Manta, Machala and Loja. San/Saeta has six flights daily to Quito, fewer at weekends. Both TAME and San/Saeta fly daily to the Galapagos: see page 231.

Bus: the bus station is just north of the airport, near the suspension bridge over the river Guayas. There are frequent connections with all the major cities and towns. The bus connecting the centre and the airport also serves the bus station.

GUAYAQUIL

1 Parque Centenario
2 Mercado Central
3 Hotel Ecuatoriano
4 Hotel Reina Victoria
5 Hotel Delicia
6 Hotel Sanders
7 Casa de la Cultura
8 Hotel Colonial

9 Hotel Metropolitano
10 La Pirata
11 Banco Pacífico Museum
12 TAME
13 San/Saeta
14 Post Office & IETEL
15 Government Palace
16 Municipalidad

17 Navy training yacht
18 Parque Bolívar
19 Cathedral
20 Municipal Museum
21 Gran Chifa
22 Tourist Office
23 Banco Central Museum
24 Olympic Pool

Train: see page 184 for an account of the spectacular train ride from the central Andes. The railway station is in Duran, across the river from Guayaquil. A ferry operates from the northern end of the Malecón, by the eastern end of Montalvo, eight blocks from 9 de Octubre. It leaves every 15 minutes from 5am to 11pm. You need to make an early start in order to catch the train, which departs for Bucay at 6.20am. It is easy to miss the jetty for the ferry in the dark, and you should consider taking a taxi since the area is also dangerous. Check the train schedule beforehand, though you can't buy a ticket until your day of departure.

Accommodation. Pleasant hotels are in short supply, and even these fill up quickly and are expensive compared to elsewhere in Ecuador. Hotel Metropolitano, on Icaza just in from the Malecón, is the most popular, despite its unusual location in an office block.

Hotel Colonial (Urdaneta and Rumichaca), just north of the main square, is stark and unfriendly but has reasonable rooms. Better is the Reina Victoria, at Moncayo and Colón close to the market, which is one of the city's friendlier hotels. Further north at Moncayo and Luque, Hotel Sanders is also reasonable. For a cheaper room try Hotel Delicia (Clemente Ballén 1105) or Hotel Ecuatoriano (Sucre and Rumichaca), both in the market area south of the square.

Many of the cheap hotels provide short-let rooms for couples. The real cheapies often consist of little more than rows of wooden cells with inter-connecting ventilation. At the other end of the scale are the luxurious hotels on the Malecón.

Eating and Drinking. Few good restaurants can be found in the heart of the city, although there are numerous Chinese places. The Gran Chifa (Pedro Carbo 1018), seven blocks south of 9 de Octubre, has an elaborate decor but is perfectly affordable. The Cafés La Palma and Cyrano, at Escobedo and Velez, serve good coffee, juice and croissants.

Moored beside the Malecón two blocks north of La Rotonda is El Pirata, a riverboat bar and restaurant. Its a pleasant place to sit in the early evening — away from the smell of rubbish, but not from itinerant traders.

Exploring. There are few better things to do in Guayaquil than wander through the gardens along the Malecón. These draw many vendors, courting couples, beggars and even iguanas. The latter spend most of their time in the trees, but they have an amusing habit of descending suddenly to ground level, surprising people sitting nearby. Iguanas also hang out in Parque Bolívar, which is dominated by the unspectacular Gothic cathedral.

At the northern end of the Malecón, at the base of the bluff, is Barrio Las Peñas, the oldest part of the city. It is a 10-15 minute walk from 9 de Octubre. Calle Pompillo Llona is the most picturesque street, containing the homes of several past presidents and a few art galleries. On the small square at the entrance to the street is a small Fire Service museum. The ancient engines are the most interesting exhibits.

There are other good museums in the centre of Guayaquil, including several with excellent archaeological collections. The Municipal Museum, on Sucre two blocks in from the river, has an interesting array of pre-Inca and colonial exhibits: ranging from portraits of all Ecuador's presidents to examples of head-shrinking, as well as some dreadful modern art. It opens 9am-noon and 3-7pm Monday to Friday, and weekend mornings. The Casa de la Cultura, on the west side of Parque Centenario, contains the best collection of pre-Colombian gold in Ecuador and archaeological artefacts of the early cultures. The latter also form the principal exhibits in the small but good Banco Pacífico Museum (Icaza and Panama) and the Banco Central Museum, four blocks west of Parque Centenario on 9 de Octubre.

For something slightly different, go on a tour around the Navy training yacht which, when it is moored on the Malecón, is open to visitors at weekends. There is an Olympic-sized swimming pool west of Parque Centenario at Hurtado and Moreno.

Help and Information. *Tourist information:* the CETUR office is at Aguirre 104, at the junction with the Malecón (tel 524044). Their knowledge of places outside the city centre is poor.

Communications: the post and IETEL offices occupy a whole block on Pedro Carbo, between Aguirre and Ballén. It is a fine old building with postcards and stamps sold from kiosks outside.

Money: cambios are concentrated along Pichincha, in the two blocks to the south of 9 de Octubre. There is also a large number of banks in the area. American Express is represented by Ecuadorean Tours at 9 de Octubre 1900 (tel 287111/394984).

Consulates: UK — General Córdova 623 at Urdaneta (Casilla 8598); tel 300400. USA — 9 de Octubre and García Moreno (tel 323570).

Around Guayaquil

Salinas. The most upmarket seaside resort in Ecuador, Salinas lines an attractive crescent of golden sand on the Santa Elena peninsula, due west of Guayaquil. The sea is turquoise and the beach reasonably clean. Salinas is popular with wealthy Guayaquileños, who come to waterski and windsurf. You may find it more interesting to visit the large saltpans on the south of the peninsula, where Chilean flamingoes spend the winter. This is a three-hour walk (round trip) along the south side of the peninsula.

Among the town's few affordable hotels are the Yulee and Las Brisas, both about $10, and the more basic Residencial Rachel ($6). Even these three are expensive in the December to February peak season, and may be closed from May to September. The seafood restaurants along the front are expensive but good.

Salinas is 2½ hours by bus from Guayaquil. Buses run regularly from the city to La Libertad, two hours west, from where minibuses run continuously to the resort. La Libertad is an interesting fishing port, where accommodation is much cheaper than in Salinas: the best hotels are the Viña del Mar and Estrella del Mar.

Puerto López. Northwest of Guayaquil, this small town is at the opposite end of the seaside resort spectrum, consisting of just a line of houses along the shore in a small bay. The beach is a hive of activity with fishing boats coming and going throughout the day. As soon as the fish are landed the fishermen's wives gut and salt them, amid swooping vultures and frigate birds.

Primitive accommodation is available in the beachfront restaurants. Five miles/8km south is the French-run Alandaluz Ecology Centre, which has pleasant rooms in thatched cabins for $8-10, and vegetarian food. Nearby, in Salango, is a small museum to the pre-Inca cultures of the area, and the highly recommended Delfin Mágico seafood restaurant.

Machalilla National Park. This park covers some of the most beautiful coastal scenery in the country, including dry and comparatively pristine tropical forest. It contains several beaches, including the lovely Playa Frailes. If you are lucky you may see deer, anteaters and squirrels, but birds like pelicans, frigate birds and parrots are much more conspicuous. There is also an excellent museum at Aguarda Blanca, inside the park, containing pre-Inca artefacts.

The park surrounds the towns of Puerto López, Salango and Machalilla though none of them lies inside it. The main park office is in Puerto López, where you must pay a small entrance fee. From there the park is most easily visited on foot; taxis are few and far between in the area. There are plenty of trails into the park off the main coast road.

MACHALA

Surrounded by vast banana plantations, Machala has been described as the 'banana capital of the world' because of the fruit's complete domination of the local economy. As a town it has little appeal, though a night in Machala is marginally more pleasant than staying at Huaquillas, two hours away on the Peruvian frontier. Even so, its hotels are not marvellous. The best are Residencial Internacional (Guayas and Sucre) and Gran Hotel Machala, one block south of the main square on 9 de Mayo. Eating out isn't much better.

Arrival and Departure. Several companies run frequent buses between Machala and the major cities of the south, including Guayaquil (3 hours), Cuenca (5 hours) and Loja (7 hours). There are no direct buses to Riobamba and Quito (the latter go via Santo Domingo) so your best bet is to take a Guayaquil or Cañar bus and change at El Triunfo or La Troncal, both crossroads towns to the north, where you can wait for connecting buses at the roadside. Most bus company offices are four or five blocks east of the main square along Avenida 9 de Octubre, and in the two streets parallel.

TAME flies from Guayaquil every morning except on Sunday.

Around Machala

Jambelí Island and Puerto Bolívar. The island of Jambelí has a small resort with a long beach fringed by palms. Cabañas del Pescador and María Sol are good places to stay, although Jambelí is easily visited on a day trip. The island is half an hour by motorized canoe from Puerto Bolívar, an important port 3 miles/5km southwest of Machala. There is a regular ferry service through the day, most frequently at weekends; otherwise arrange something privately at the harbour.

The trip through the mangroves is more interesting than the beach itself. Therefore you may prefer simply to hire a canoe in Puerto Bolívar and explore from there what's left of the mangroves — they are fast disappearing to large-scale shrimp farming. The waterfront in Puerto Bolívar is not that pleasant but there are some good seafood restaurants.

Minibuses run to the port every few minutes from the main plaza in Machala.

The route into Peru goes via Huaquillas. Like most frontier towns it is rundown and tatty. There are regular bus connections with Machala; passport checks take place along this road. If you need to stay overnight, the Parador Turístico costs around $10.

THE SIERRA

The volcano-strewn landscape south of Quito is spectacular, and perhaps the biggest attraction for visitors to mainland Ecuador. Commonly known as the 'Avenue of the Volcanoes', the valley is flanked by some of the continent's highest peaks. The most dramatic cones are Cotopaxi, just south of Quito, and Chimborazo, between Ambato and Riobamba. For wonderful views ride along the valley at dawn or dusk, when the glaciers glow pink against the dark sky.

The Pan-American Highway runs through the Sierra, with several major roads leading off it. But no one should travel through the highlands without going for at least part of the way by rail. For a full description of the journey see page 184.

Cotopaxi National Park. This park is characterized by its barren volcanic landscape and bleak paramo where, with luck, you will see condor and wild horses. Cotopaxi, at 19,335ft/5,895m, is the highest active volcano in the world and is an almost perfect cone. The climb is tough, requiring crampons and an ice axe, but you don't have to be an experienced mountaineer to attempt it. All the principal travellers' hotels in Quito, and some in Latacunga (see below) have notes advertising the services of local guides, and the South American Explorers' Club can also advise.

The park entrance is 30 miles/48km along the highway south of Quito, near the village of Lasso. From the village a rough track leads across the paramo and up the lower slopes of the volcano to the José Rivas refugio, just below the snow line. The journey there takes six to eight hours on foot, or an hour by taxi (hired in Lasso for about $20). The refugio officially has room for forty people, but many more than this may be squeezed in during July and August. It has cooking facilities and costs $2 per night.

To make the climb to the top you need to start from the refugio at about 2am — it's hard to sleep at this altitude anyway. The climb to the summit takes seven hours, and the views that reward you at sunrise are out of this world. Even if the sky is thick with clouds you will probably still see peaks rising above them in the distance. You can also look down into the steaming snow-filled volcanic crater beneath.

LATACUNGA

Lying 80 miles/130km from Quito, this is a quiet, traditional Andean town, with a population of 30,000. Latacunga is primarily a staging post for trips around this part of the valley, but it boasts a magnificent setting: on a clear day you can see nine peaks. The town has been destroyed at least twice by Cotopaxi volcano, which dominates Latacunga. Yet it has always been stubbornly rebuilt.

The only sight is an old watermill, backing onto the river in the centre of town, which contains interesting folklore exhibits. There is a large daily outdoor food market, part of which is turned over to volleyball as the day wears on.

Arrival and Departure. The combination of buses plying between Quito and Latacunga and those on longer runs ensures a bus every 10-15 minutes to and from the capital during daylight hours. All buses drop passengers on the Pan-American Highway. The town centre is immediately across the old bridge over the river Cutuchi. The road to Quevedo leads west, in the opposite direction. Transportes Cotopaxi and La Mana run three or four buses a day to Quevedo, leaving from the roadside 50 yards up this road. The journey west over the Andes is uncomfortable but stunning.

The railway station is a couple of blocks northwest of the bus stop. The railbus departs for Quito at 9am and for Riobamba at 6pm.

Accommodation and Food. The best place to stay is Hotel Estambul at Quevedo 7340, one block northwest of the main square. It is set around an attractive courtyard, is clean, safe and friendly, and has a roof balcony. If it is full, try Residencial Los Andes, three blocks back up the Quito road from the bus drop-off point, or the more pricey Hotel Cotopaxi, on the main square.

Good restaurants are in short supply. Pizzería Rodelu, on Quito a block north of the main square, is reasonable. Next door, the large and garish La Carreta has decent food.

Around Latacunga

Saquisilí. This is a small market town 10 miles/16km north of Latacunga, on the western slopes of the valley. Don't fail to visit on a Thursday, when a large traditional market spreads across eight squares. It is much less touristy than the one in Otavalo, though crafts are a recent addition to the usual stalls piled high with everything from fleeces to guns. The animal market is a particular highlight. Buses from Latacunga run non-stop on market day — when they are packed — but are much less frequent at other times.

Lake Quilotoa. This is a beautiful turquoise lake in a volcanic crater surrounded by rocky outcrops; local Indians scrape a living from a patchwork of fields among the crags. The lake is 40 miles/64km west of Latacunga. To get there independently take the Quevedo bus to just before Zumbagua, and walk for three hours north; with luck you may be able to hitch a ride. It is a long trip to undertake in a single day and allows you little time to explore — you could spend several days hiking between remote communities towards the Volcán Iliniza; take a tent.

AMBATO

Ecuador's fourth city (population of 140,000) had to be rebuilt after a devastating earthquake in 1949. Nevertheless, a few pleasant old buildings have survived in the centre, and the backdrop of snow-capped peaks adds appeal to what is otherwise an uninspiring place. Even so, a large number of people get off the bus here solely to make connections east to Baños or Puyo.

The Colegio Bolívar museum on Plaza 10 de Agosto contains an unusual variety of exhibits including animals with terrible deformities pickled in jars and old photos depicting the history of the city. The new municipal museum in the Casa de la Cultura, on Plaza Montalvo, has displays mainly of crafts and modern art.

Much more interesting than Ambato is the village of Salasaca, 7 miles/11km south of the town. The local Salasaca Indians produce fine weavings which they sell by the roadside. They are friendly people and feel they should have received the same level of recognition for their work as the Otavaleños. Consequently, they are keen to encourage visitors, and you have a good chance of being invited into their homes to view weavers at work.

Arrival and Departure. There are frequent bus connections between Ambato and Quito (3 hours), Cuenca (6 hours) and Guayaquil (6½ hours). There is a constant flow of buses southeast to Baños, which take less than an hour. The bus terminal is ten minutes walk northeast of the centre. Next door is the railway station, from where a railbus leaves daily at 8am for Quito (4 hours). TAME flies to Ambato from Guayaquil on Monday, Tuesday and Friday mornings.

Accommodation and Food. Cheap accommodation is plentiful and concentrated in and around the central Plaza 12 de Noviembre. The best of the hotels are the Residencial Orquidea, on 12 de Noviembre southwest of the square, and the Residencial Gran, on Lalama two blocks north of Plaza 10 de Agosto. Both are clean and well-furnished, with reasonably spacious rooms.

Ambato is famous for its hot chocolate, cakes and pastries, and there are several pleasant cafés in the centre. For an above-average meal, El Gran Alamo, La Buena Mesa and El Coyotes restaurants are all recommended, though not particularly cheap. All are within a block of Plazas 10 de Agosto and Montalvo.

BANOS

Over the last decade Baños has acquired a reputation as the best place in Ecuador in which to relax for a few days. There are many reasons for this, not least its pleasant cafés and its fine setting on the floor of the lush Pastaza valley. The sides of the valley rise almost vertically from the town, and to the south culminate in the 16,400ft/5,000m peak of Volcán Tungurahua. On clear days its snow-capped peak is just visible high above from the outskirts of town.

Baños derives its name from the town's thermal baths, though the miraculous statue of the Virgin in the church seems to have greater healing powers than the water. More curative to most travellers is the climate, which is considerably warmer than in the high Sierra, only a short distance away. This warmth is due to the tropical air that blows up the Pastaza valley from the east which, however, also brings much more rain than you will experience in the higher Andean towns.

Many good walks can be made into the side valleys running down from Volcán Tungurahua, or around the waterfalls along the Pastaza valley. Horse-riding can be organized too, as advertised by several tour companies in town. Baños is also a popular launching point for trips into the Oriente.

Arrival and Departure. Roads branch east to Baños from both Riobamba and Ambato, and buses run regularly from both these towns, as well as from Quito and other towns in the central valley. People coming from the southern Sierra will have to change buses in Riobamba. Buses running east to Puyo come mostly from Ambato, and most seats are usually taken by the time they get to Baños. The journey to Puyo is brilliant, and it is well worth waiting for a seat.

The bus station is on the main road, a short distance from the town centre.

Accommodation. Most hotels are reasonably priced and of a good standard. One of the best is the friendly Hotel El Castillo, on Martínez east towards the swimming pools; its rooms are set around a pleasant garden. The Danish-run Casa de la Cultura (tel 740419), at the eastern end of Montalvo near the waterfall, is cosy and hospitable. It has a sitting-room and, at $4, is only slightly more expensive than most of the ordinary hotels in Baños. Le Petit Restaurant (see below) offers similar lodgings.

Two residenciales popular among backpackers are the Patty (Alfaro and Ambato) and the Villa Santa Clara, at the waterfall end of 12 de Noviembre; both have cooking facilities and charge around $2. Both are fairly ramshackle places with erratic water supplies. Tsantsa Expeditions, based at the Patty, runs recommended jungle treks.

More upmarket but good value are the Agoyan and Anita, close to the main square.

Eating and Drinking. As a major tourist centre Baños has generated a good selection of restaurants. A few years ago it was the home of cheap wholefood restaurants, and although such places still exist, they have become much more sophisticated. Recommended are the Casa de la Cultura café, whose pancakes are not to be missed; El Paisano, attached to Hotel El Castillo; the Patto, beside the market; and Café Heluchos, at the intersection of Montalvo and 16 de Diciembre. All serve vegetarian food. Among the more pretentious — but nevertheless good — places is Le Petit Restaurant, set back off the road on Alfaro, which offers superb French cuisine. Pizzería Rincón de Suecia, on Rocafuerte, serves better-than-average pizzas and plays good music.

Opposite Residencial Patty are the Cabaña d'Arthur Bar and Hard Rock Café, both of which are popular meeting-places; informal parties often continue into the small hours. Café Alemán Regine, on Montalvo near 12 de Noviembre, offers excellent pies and hot chocolate, and is open late. Numerous cafés sell tropical fruit mueslis and yoghurt for breakfast; among the best is Café Eden, near the bus station.

Making nougat is a major industry in Baños. All over town you can see long pale strips of it being bashed, stretched and then hung from doorways; almost every shop sells it in small packets. While it looks like traditional nougat, it has the consistency of toffee, tastes disgusting and makes most travellers sick.

At weekends there is usually at least one peña going on. Peña Charanguito is probably the best.

Exploring. The statue of La Virgen de Agua Santa, housed in the Basilica, has attracted pilgrims for many decades. The sick and handicapped come to pray in front of her image, and the crutches and white sticks displayed on the walls nearby are testimony to the Virgin's apparent healing powers. Numerous murals depict weird and wonderful miracles attributed to her: including people being saved from volcanic eruptions and from recent fires in Guayaquil hotels. The museum (within the cloisters, on the first floor) has a bizarre collection of decaying stuffed animals, provincial artesanía and religious memorabilia.

The thermal baths are concentrated near the waterfall behind the town. The municipal pools are often closed; if they are open, go in the morning — the murky water usually reeks of urine and isn't terrifically appealing by the end of the day. Better are the Termas de Salado, a mile west of town, where there are five small pools at different temperatures. Walk up Martínez past the cemetery, and shortly afterwards take the track running down into a small valley. The road on the other side runs up to Salado. Buses also run every half hour or so from behind the market in Baños, via the bus station.

There is a zoo an easy walk east of town, with mostly Amazonian animals. The path continues beyond it, across a suspension bridge and along an attractive route back into town.

Around Baños

Volcán Tungurahua. This is generally considered the easiest volcano over 16,400ft/5,000m to climb in Ecuador. The lower slopes are covered with beautiful cloud forest interrupted by clumps of lilac lupins that attract hummingbirds. The upper part of the cone consists of several hundred metres of unconsolidated volcanic ash, which is not easy to climb. It gives way to snow and ice for the last few hundred metres and an ice axe and crampons are essential for this section. In clear weather there are fantastic views of Chimborazo in the distance as you approach the top. The summit proper is on the far side of the deep crater with fumaroles rising from it.

A few years ago the Refugio Santos Ocaña could be reached only after a long hard ascent via the villages of Salado and Pondua. There is now a road to just above Pondua, and most tour companies in Baños ferry people up the lower slopes to this point, and provide guides to the summit. However, it is still possible to hire pack horses and guides in the village. If you want to hike the whole way, the trail to Pondua runs up the steep bluff that juts out into the valley behind Salado: allow about two hours for this stretch.

The refugio is located at 12,465ft/3,800m, immediately beneath the upper part of the cone and about five hours walk from Pondua. The ascent from the refugio to the summit must begin before dawn to catch the good weather; you can then return to Baños in time for tea. The refugio can sleep only about 20 people and there are sometimes problems with over-crowding in July and August. A new refugio is under construction. The volcano lies within the Sangay National Park and there is a small fee to enter the area, payable at the park office in Pondua.

Manta de la Novia and Río Verde Waterfalls. A short distance down the Pastaza valley, along the spectacular but hair-raising Puyo road, is a spectacular gorge with waterfalls. The Manta de la Novia and Río Verde falls are 7 miles/12km and 10 miles/16km east of town respectively. Take the bus to Agoyán and walk from there, or else try to persuade a Puyo bus to drop you off. Paths to the falls lead down from the main road; reaching Manta de al Novia involves crossing a suspension bridge over the river.

On the way you pass the Agoyán dam, which lies just a few miles east of Baños. A mile or so shortly after the dam the road enters a tunnel, but immediately before it is a viewpoint. From here you can see the raging white water of the Agoyán falls (unless all the water has been channelled into the hydro-electric power plant). Some local buses terminate by the falls.

RIOBAMBA

Situated at 9,840ft/3,000m above sea level, at the southern end of the Avenue of the Volcanoes, Riobamba is the most Andean of the central Sierra's cities. The pace of life is surprisingly slow for a city with a population of 100,000.

Riobamba boasts a fantastic setting that is a good deal more attractive than the city itself. There are several volcanoes nearby: Sangay is one of the most active in the world, and in 1976 a sudden eruption killed several members of a British climbing expedition. Volcán Chimborazo, on the other hand, can be climbed relatively easily in good weather. If you aren't into some serious hiking, you will probably be content to stroll around Riobamba's traditional Saturday market, which extends across a large part of the city and is the largest in Ecuador. Traders sell vast quantities of potatoes, and all kinds of produce from the coast and the jungle, as well as quantities of cheap consumer goods. You won't find the quantity of crafts you do in Otavalo, but there are people selling ponchos, blankets and embroidered shirts. Many of those taking part arrive by horse and cart from the surrounding countryside.

in Sibambe, so if taking a train from here, time your arrival accordingly. In Alausí accommodation is provided by a few simple hotels. The Panamericano is the best of a not outstanding bunch.

ACHUPALLAS TO INGAPIRCA

The small Andean town of Achupallas, 16 miles/25km southeast of Alausí, is the starting point for the two or three day trek along the Inca road to the ruins of Ingapirca (see below). Little of the old road remains, and much of the walk follows a muddy track, but there are some small ruins along the way. Since the track runs through a remote area, it offers an interesting insight into the life of the campesinos of the high Sierra. The terrain varies from lush green valleys to barren plateau, and involves some steep ascents; you may feel the effects of the high altitude. Neither food nor accommodation is available along the trail, so you will need to go fully prepared, with a tent, stove, etc. There are no maps of the route but it is not too difficult to follow.

Trucks and pickups run to Achupallas every so often along the hair-raising road from Alausí; truck-drivers have a reputation for overcharging gringos, so find out beforehand what you should expect to pay.

The Southern Sierra

The southern Sierra deserves much attention. Cuenca is arguably the finest town in Ecuador, and it makes an excellent base for exploring the region with its Inca ruins, thermal baths, Indian markets and wild countryside.

The southern highlands are separated form the rest of the Sierra by mountains. The road from Riobamba drops into the lower foothills of the Andes before climbing again towards Cuenca. Cañar is the first major town along this road.

CANAR

The indigenous Cañari tribe mounted some of the fiercest resistance to the incursions of the Incas, but were eventually defeated and absorbed into the empire. Later they assisted the Spanish in their conquest of the Incas. The Cañari people still live in the surrounding countryside and many of them have retained their traditional dress. They and their town appear to have changed little over the centuries, despite Cañar's position on the main road between Cuenca and Guayaquil. There is a colourful Sunday market, and the Inca ruins of Ingapirca are just a short distance away.

Cañar is served by several buses daily from Quito and Guayaquil and more nearby towns. For most southerly destinations you must change in Cuenca, which is an hour's bus ride south. The basic Residencial Monica provides the only accommodation and the few simple restaurants all close early.

INGAPIRCA

Ecuador's principal Inca site is situated in a most lovely position, at an altitude of about 14,000ft/4,270m. It is dominated by an elliptical platform, the only known example of such a structure amongst Inca remains. It consists of a natural rock outcrop faced with fine close-fitted stonework, as good as that found in Peru. The religious and ceremonial significance of Ingapirca is unknown, but it may have been a Temple of the Sun. The site has various other ruins and a good museum focussing on Cañari culture.

To walk to Ingapirca from Cañar takes about four hours each way. It is tough-going, not least because of the high altitude. Head northwards out of the town along Sucre, which soon turns into a track and climbs to a plateau above the town. It runs through a small village and then along the side of the valley before dropping down towards the river. After 2 miles/3km you cross the railway line and river, and a muddy trail on the other side rises to Ingapirca village; the ruins are just beyond.

Pickups from El Tambo, just north of Cañar on the Guayaquil road, leave for Ingapirca when full. Don't arrive too early because you may have to wait around for other people to make up a quorum. Drivers are notorious for overcharging tourists, but you shouldn't pay more than $0.30-40. There are regular services to El Tambo from Cuenca so day trips are possible; the last bus back leaves at 6.45pm. There is a shelter at the ruins, but it is safer to spend the night in El Tambo, where there is a cheap hotel.

The hike to Ingapira from Achupallas near Alausí is described opposite.

The road from Cañar passes through Azogues (see *Around Cuenca*) and Biblián. The latter has an attractive church built into a steep hillside high above the town, and the local people make Panama hats.

CUENCA

The city of Cuenca lies in a wide valley, with the Río Tomebamba running through the centre. There are fine views upriver from the lower bridges and colonial buildings line the northern bank, with rolling hills for a backdrop. Ecuador's third

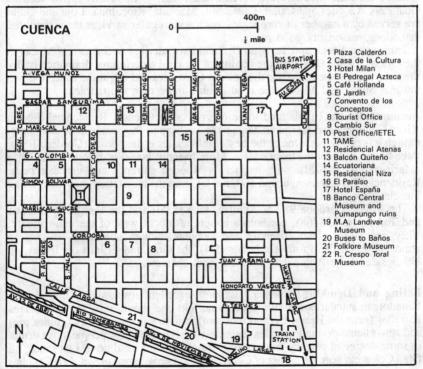

CUENCA   0 —————— 400m
$\frac{1}{4}$ mile

1 Plaza Calderón
2 Casa de la Cultura
3 Hotel Milan
4 El Pedregal Azteca
5 Café Hollanda
6 El Jardín
7 Convento de los Conceptos
8 Tourist Office
9 Cambio Sur
10 Post Office/IETEL
11 TAME
12 Residencial Atenas
13 Balcón Quiteño
14 Ecuatoriana
15 Residencial Niza
16 El Paraíso
17 Hotel España
18 Banco Central Museum and Pumapungo ruins
19 M.A. Landivar Museum
20 Buses to Baños
21 Folklore Museum
22 R. Crespo Toral Museum

city (population 200,000) is relatively prosperous, and it is the country's principal centre of art and culture.

Cuenca was founded in 1557 on the site of Pumapungo, a major Inca town. It is the only city in the country in which Inca stonework is still visible, overlain by impressive colonial buildings of the local pink marble. Cuenca is not only beautiful, but enjoys a spring-like climate for most of the year.

Arrival and Departure. *Air:* TAME (Colombia, near the corner of Borrero) has morning flights between Cuenca and Quito and Guayaquil, daily except Sunday. San/Saeta flies from Quito at 9am on weekdays, returning at 10am; on Fridays and Sundays there is an additional afternoon departure. The airport is east of the centre, and buses run continuously along España.

Train: in addition to the steam train to Azogues (see *Around Cuenca*), a railbus leaves daily at 2pm for Chunchi, on the Guayaquil-Riobamba road. A connection can be made early the next day to Sibambe, on the main line, to catch the Guayaquil train. There are no hotels in Chunchi but lodgings are available with families in the town. The railbus driver will advise you.

The railway station in Cuenca is about twenty minutes walk southeast of the centre.

Bus: nearly all services operate from the main bus terminal, 10-15 minutes walk east of the centre on España; plenty of town buses headed for the centre pass in front of the station. There are several buses hourly for nearby towns such as Gualacéo, Azogues and Cañar. Guayaquil, Machala, Riobamba, Loja and Quito are served by a number of companies, each with regular services throughout the day, along reasonably good roads.

Transportes Sucúa and Turismo Oriental have services to Sucúa and Macas in the Oriente. After Gualacéo the quality of the road deteriorates dramatically. By the time you top the pass over the eastern Cordillera and begin the descent down towards Sucúa and Macas, the road is little more than a dirt track.

Accommodation. Hotels tend to be overpriced in Cuenca. Residencial Siberia (Gran Colombia and Hermano Miguel) is as cheap as they come at $2.50 single, though it is run-down. One of the best residenciales is the Atenas (Cordero 1189), three blocks north of the main square. More friendly, however, is Residencial Niza (Mariscal Lamar 4/51), with its rickety wooden entrance and unstable beds. Residencial España (Sangurima 117), not far from the bus station, has many small but clean rooms.

The Milán (Córdoba 989 at Aguirre; tel 835351) and the Pichincha (Bolívar and Torres; tel 823868), are both a couple of blocks west of the main square. They are large, clean, friendly and popular, though somewhat lacking in atmosphere. Of the up-market hotels ($14), the Gran and El Inca on Torres, on either side of the Pichincha, have the most character.

Eating and Drinking. Cuenca has some excellent restaurants — pricey by Ecuadorean standards but still good value. No one should miss the Salón Tres Estrellas (near the Banco Central museum), where you can eat cuy (guinea pig) and aguardiente in small cubicles seemingly designed to allow people to get drunk in some degree of privacy. For a more straightforward meal go to Los Pibes, on Gran Colombia near the corner of Cordero, which serves great pizzas. Los Capulies and El Jardín, opposite each other on Córdoba near the main square, have extensive menus which include traditional dishes. The food is good but not cheap. A pleasant Mexican bar and restaurant is El Pedregal Azteca, at Gran Colombia 10-29. Further down the scale but still good are the Balcón Quiteño (Sangurima 649) and Fernando's, under Hotel España. Highly recommended is Pizzería Napolitana, at the bottom of B. Malo close to the river; it is clean, friendly and often full. El Paraíso and the Malantial, both within a couple of blocks east of Residencial Niza, cater for vegetarians but are somewhat spartan.

Café Austria on Bolívar serves wonderful cakes and pastries, but it doesn't open until mid-morning. Another possibility for snacks is the more expensive Cafetería Hollanda, on B. Malo just off the main square.

Exploring. The ruined Inca city of Pumapungo, southeast of the centre, consists of just a few stones. It is unspectacular by any (let alone Peruvian) standards, but is worth a visit if only for historical reasons: it was the birthplace of Huayna Capac, the last undisputed ruler of the Inca empire. What remains of the foundations give an idea of the extent of the old city, but not much else. Pumapungo belongs to the Banco Central, which has a museum of pre-Columbian artefacts in one corner of the site. The remains of an Inca flour mill lie three blocks further west, next to the Agustín Landivar Museum which also contains Inca relics.

Cuenca has two cathedrals, which face each other across Plaza Calderón, the main square. The white-painted colonial cathedral sits discreetly on its east side, but is rarely open. The new cathedral opposite is far larger. It is built of the local pink marble, with large domes covered in turquoise mosaics. Of the many other churches, the Convento de los Conceptos, two blocks southeast of the square, is by far the most impressive. It contains a fantastic collection of jewel-encrusted gold and silver pieces.

Works of art dominate the rest of the city's museums. In the Casa de la Cultura in Plaza Calderón is the Museum of Popular Art; it contains mostly works of Ecuadorean artists. The Crespo Toral Museum, at the southern end of Borrero, contains a private collection of religious art which includes a variety of gruesome crucifixes. Nearby, beside the steps running down to the river, is the small but interesting folklore museum. Inside are traditional costumes and musical instruments from the Sierra and Oriente, including Amazonian feather head-dresses and some examples of head-shrinking.

Help and Information. The CETUR office is on Hermano Miguel, near Córdoba, though the staff are not enormously helpful. The post office is on the corner of Borrero and Gran Colombia, with the IETEL phone office adjacent.

The two main cambios are in B.Malo, a block north of the main square, and Cambio Sur in Borrero at the junction with Sucre.

Around Cuenca
Las Cajas Recreational Area. This is a dramatic and bleak but very beautiful upland area, reminiscent of remote parts of Scotland — with weather to match. There are numerous lakes, the land around them being dotted with ancient stunted cloud forest, mosses and coarse grasses; in spring it is carpeted with tiny flowers. The reserve is rich in wildlife, principally birds and particularly on the lower slopes. Conditions are harsh in winter, and the best time to visit is between October to January.

An ancient bus leaves Cuenca at 6am from in front of the church of San Sebastián, six blocks west of Plaza Calderón. It takes three hours to wind its way up a rough road westwards into the heart of the area. The road has been funded by a group of international banks as an alternative and highly controversial route to Guayaquil. Fortunately, the existing road through Cañar is sufficiently good that the new route is unlikely ever to attract much of the Cuenca-Guayaquil traffic.

The best place to get off the bus is near the run-down refugio, which serves as a base for a couple of park guards. There is room for four visitors, and the guards appreciate any extra provisions you can spare: they seem to be expected to survive on the fish they catch in the lakes. Alternatively, you can camp freely within most of the area.

Las Cajas, 25 miles/40km northwest of Cuenca, can be visited as a day trip too: the bus passes the refugio again in mid-afternoon on its way back to Cuenca.

Gualacéo, Chordeleg and Sigsig. These three small towns can be combined to make a very pleasant day trip from Cuenca. There are buses to all three, most frequently on Sunday, when Gualacéo and Chordeleg both have a market (and are full of tourists).

Gualacéo lies in an attractive valley about an hour east of Cuenca. You can spend a few relaxing hours at one of the riverside restaurants (these are usually open only at weekends) or strolling around the market, which is devoted primarily to fresh produce and livestock. The Hotel Gran, two blocks south of the square, is fairly good and phenomenally cheap.

Chordeleg is another small colonial town a couple of miles south of Gualacéo. It is an uphill walk or a short bus ride away. During the week Chordeleg is extremely sleepy, though there is an active community of artisans, who produce mainly straw weavings, including wonderful miniature figurines, and silver jewellery. The latter is displayed in large quantities around the town, including in incongruously smart shops around the main square. Also on the square is a small museum of artesanía run by a local cooperative.

The road continues south through lovely countryside to Sigsig, a charming little place where some of the local people make Panama hats. You should be able to continue in a circuit to return to Cuenca. Otherwise, you must return the way you came.

Azogues. A venerable steam train runs from Cuenca to Azogues, two hours northeast. There is usually a morning and afternoon departure, with extra trains at weekends and holiday times. Although the bus takes half the time, it is worth taking the train for the views of fast-flowing rivers, meadows and eucalyptus woods. Azogues itself is of only minor interest, the huge church of San Francisco that dominates the town being the most interesting sight. Stay in Hotel Charles if you decide to delay your onward or return journey.

LOJA

This 75,000-strong provincial capital is unspectacular to look at. However, Loja is one of the oldest cities in the country, and it has developed a strong identity because of its isolation from the rest of the country.

Alexander von Humboldt, the German scientist and explorer, referred to Loja as the 'Garden of Ecuador' because of the great diversity of plant life in the surrounding area. Some of Ecuador's loveliest scenery lies to the south, around Vilcabamba.

Arrival and Departure. Loja is an important hub between Cuenca to the north and the inland route to Peru (as well as to Vilcabamba). TAME flies between Quito and Loja every morning except Sunday. The same airline runs a similar schedule of flights to and from Guayaquil. The airport at Catamayo, one hour west of Loja, is served by regular buses and colectivos. Transportes Viajero and Loja run several buses daily to Cuenca (5 hours), with various companies also serving Machala (7 hours) regularly. Transportes Viajero and Cajanuma operate daily buses through the desert region of southern Ecuador to Macará (8 hours) on the border with Peru. Most companies have their offices in Calles Kennedy and Guerrero, which run along either side of the river in the town centre.

Accommodation and Food. Hotels in Loja are either cheap or willing to give discounts when business is quiet. Hotel París (10 de Agosto 1637) a block east of the river, and the Acapulco (Sucre 747; tel 960651), a block west of the main square, are modern and pleasant, though not outstanding. Next to the Acapulco are the more basic Cuxibamba, painted a stunning shade of pink, and the Londres. Another possibility is the Hotel Mexico, on 18 de Noviembre near the market.

The Andaluz, in the main square, and the excellent Delfin Dorado, in Imbabura two blocks from the river, are among the best restaurants in town.

Around Loja

Saraguro. This small market town lies in a fertile valley 50 miles/80km north of Loja. It is home to the Saraguro Indians, a tribe moved by the Incas from their homeland further south. The men are easily recognized by their pig-tails and dark knee-length shorts and ponchos. Saraguro is on the Cuenca road, and is easily reached by bus.

Vilcabamba. This small town is set in a lovely valley 19 miles/30km south of Loja, with the almost alpine hills of the Podocarpus National Park to the east. The mild climate is said to be behind the large number of centenarians in Vilcabamba. The sizeable contingent of gringos in the area is more often attributed to the town's reputation as a good place to take the hallucinogenic San Pedro cactus. Anyone into more mundane pastimes, can go horse-riding in the surrounding hills, which are also excellent for camping trips.

Buses run from Loja every hour throughout the day. There are two very good places to stay, both of which rent out horses. The Madre Tierra Cabañas, a short walk north of town, offers full-board for $8, and has the added luxury of a sauna. Cabañas Río Yambala, 3 miles/5km east of town, has a full-board vegetarian package as well as self-catering accommodation. A number of locals and gringos have rooms in town or cabins in the nearby hills, which they rent for as little as $30 a month. La Turista, in the main square, is probably the best of the town's few basic restaurants.

Podocarpus National Park. This park lies in the Cordillera Oriental southeast of Loja. It is a beautiful area of streams, high pastures, lakes and fragments of the formerly widespread Podocarpus Forest. The ecology of the park is under serious threat from small-scale gold mining, especially on the eastern slopes, but this is still a great area for walking and camping.

Eight miles/13km south of Loja a track leads up into the park and after another 10 miles/16km there is a small refugio, with four beds and cooking facilities. Since the cabin is not always open, you may have to be content to sleep beneath the makeshift straw shelters next to it. A number of nature trails have been marked out nearby. There are no buses to the park, so unless you walk you will have to arrange a taxi in Loja.

Anyone travelling south to Peru may have to spend a night in Macará, which lies about a mile north of the border. The town lies in a military zone, so expect several passport checks en route. The Hotels Guayaquil and Amazonas are basic but bearable. The Parador Turístico is probably worth the extra expense and it has the best restaurant in town. There is nowhere to stay on the Peruvian side until Sullana or Piura.

From Loja you can also head northeast into the Amazon. Buses run via Zamora to Macas (see opposite).

THE ORIENTE

Until the early 1970s this area was almost untouched — with rich and diverse wildlife, and widespread groups of Indians living a traditional life in the forest. All this is changing fast due to the inroads made by oil companies, hotly pursued by armies of colonizers and cattle ranchers from the highlands. Many areas covered in dense jungle just a few years ago are now entirely denuded of their trees. The impact on the indigenous people and their cultures has been severe too: the oil companies have been and still are permitted by the government to prospect in recognized indigenous territories and national parks. This has aroused considerable controversy both inside Ecuador and internationally, with the Indians of the area becoming increasingly vocal about their discontent. Do not wander off the beaten track on your own, because tensions in the region have made some Indian groups particularly wary of outsiders.

Coca is the main base for trips into the interior, and even if you arrange your tour elsewhere, such as Misahuallí or Baños, it is likely that this will take you along the Napo river east from Coca anyway. This is because the jungle is more pristine in this area. Wherever you head, however, do not imagine that you are going on some kind of wildlife safari. Your chances of seeing animals are fairly minimal, though birds are easier to spot. Most people find the Peruvian Amazon more rewarding in terms of wildlife.

The Oriente can be approached from various towns in the Sierra, principally Quito, Ambato, Cuenca and Loja. The most popular route is via Baños and Puyo. Indeed Baños, though in the highlands, has become very much a gateway to the jungle. Some people arrange trips from here simply because it's a lovely place to be stuck in if you have to spend a few days trying to arrange the best tour. Note that oil exploration and other developments have affected several of the jungle towns, including Coca and Lago Agrio, with the result that prices for accommodation, etc. are high.

Roads down from the highlands usually deteriorate to dirt tracks in the interior, and in the rainy season they are often subject to landslides and are temporarily impassable. It may be easier to fly in, in which case you should book as far in advance as possible. The southern Oriente, around Macas, is far less developed than further north, and getting around can be even more difficult; facilities for tourists are almost nil.

Jungle Tours. Do not be in a hurry to arrange a trip into the jungle. It is essential to shop around, not only to compare prices. You should verify the calibre of your guide, clarify the route, ascertain whether bedding is provided and so on. Many travellers have returned deeply frustrated at the end of a hastily cobbled-together trip. It is worth paying $10 more per day for a well-organized tour. Your chances of seeing wildlife will also improve markedly if you have a good guide. Some tours may involve building your own raft and, on some days, your shelter for the night.

The cost of a tour is normally $30-40 per person per day for a group of four people, more if there are only two or three of you. Arranging guides locally is not difficult, but recommended tour leaders based in Quito include Wimper Torres (tel 269511) and Hugo Torres at Adventure Travels (Juan León Mera 741; tel 322331). The easiest months for arranging trips are June, July and August.

Permission is required from the Ministry of Agriculture to enter the National Parks in the area, such as Cuyabeno and Yasuní. Guides are not always very efficient at arranging this and the MAG offices in Lago Agrio and Coca are unreliable. It is best to go to one in Quito (see page 197) before you set off.

PUYO

The small capital of Pastaza province is simply a stop-off point for travellers en route to the Oriente by bus. Puyo is also a good place to buy a hammock (which is likely to be your most comfortable bedding in the jungle). The best hotel is the Europa, right in the centre of town. The most upmarket place to stay and eat is Hotel Turinga, which has cabins set in a tropical garden just to the west of the town centre. For good food in town go to the parrillada at Hotel Araucana in Calle Marin.

There are regular bus connections with the main cities in the central Andes, via Baños. These follow a precipitous road which runs high above the Río Pastaza and its waterfalls. The four-hour journey is unforgettable: spectacular but nerve-racking. Make sure you sit on the left-hand side of the bus (unless you suffer from vertigo). Many of the buses continue to Tena in the north, stopping at Puyo's bus station, about a mile west of the centre.

SOUTH OF PUYO

Macas. Lying at the foot of the Andes, and with a population of just 8,000, Macas is still a town very much on the edge of changes in the Oriente. In that lies its appeal. From Puyo, a day's journey north, there are buses as far as the Río Pastaza, which is normally crossed by canoe. Strong currents may render this impossible in the wet season, but a bridge is under construction. After crossing the river there are other buses and trucks to Macas. Cuenca, served by several daily buses, is also a full day's ride away. TAME has flights from Quito on weekdays.

Hotel Orquidea, one block north of the main square, has the most pleasant rooms at a reasonable $1.50. Hotel Peñon Oriente, just behind the market, is also good, but more expensive. Hotel Amazonas, on the main road to Sucúa, and Hotel Upano, near the Peñon Oriente, are better alternatives.

Sucúa. This small town, an hour's bus ride south of Macas, is in the heartland of the Shuar Indians, once famous for their head-shrinking. Most Shuars live in nearby villages, but their culture has been ravaged by the impact of missionaries. There is a Shuar cultural centre south of town, but there is never much going on. The town itself retains its 'frontier' feel, with alternately muddy and dusty streets and the occasional nightime drunken brawl.

Buses between Cuenca and Macas stop in Sucúa. Hotels Rincón Oriental, Alborada and Cumandá in the main street ($1.50) are all fairly new although their plumbing leaves something to be desired.

TENA

This small jungle town is capital of Napo Province — the largest in Ecuador and the source of much of the country's oil. Like Puyo, Tena is above all a pitstop. There is little to draw you here otherwise — except perhaps for the nearby Jumandi caves.

Tena's bus station is ten minutes walk south of the town centre. There are regular connections via Puyo and Baños (7 hours) to the central Andes, and via Baeza to Quito (7 hours). If one of the roads is blocked by landslides, all services will use the other route.

Hotels in Tena tend to be fairly expensive. The cheaper ones include the Napoli, by the bridge on the way into town from the bus station. Nearby are the Alemania and the Hilton, the former set in a pleasant garden. On the north side of town, near the airport and the road to Baeza, is the restaurant Enmita, an ostentatious place serving unusually elaborate food.

Jumandi Caves. These are just outside Archidona, a small, quiet town 10 miles/16km north of Tena. A river runs through the caves, which extend for about 100 metres. It is possible to walk, wade and swim right the way through — bring a torch and wear suitable clothes and shoes if you intend to do so. The caves are best reached on foot from the village; a Frenchman and his family live near the entrance.

MISAHUALLI

This is a tiny and decaying place, but somehow exotic. Lying on the banks of the Río Napo southeast of Tena, Misahuallí used to be the principal place to organize trips into the jungle. But there is now little primary rainforest around and the rivers have been fished out. Your chances of seeing more than a few birds and butterflies are negligible, and going on a one-day tour would be completely pointless. There are still a fair number of tour agencies, but you need to go on a trip of at least four days in order to get into the wilds. As mentioned above, most trips will take you to Coca first anyway.

But even if you don't plan to use Misahuallí as a base, it is the most convenient jumping-off point for Coca: boats up the Napo river to the town leave Misahuallí on most days and take six hours. They normally require a quota of ten passengers to justify running. If there are eight of you, for example, simply split the two missing fares between you. The normal fare is $9. Take plenty of sun cream.

There are few things to occupy your time while waiting for a boat or a tour. You can go on pleasant walks to the village of Pununi, a mile or so north, or along the banks of the river Napo. It is also possible to swim in the Río Misahuallí from a beach just above its confluence with the Napo, close to the dock. A popular and surprisingly good disco is put on in town at weekends.

Arrival and Departure. If approaching from the south, ask to be dropped at Puerto Napo, the turn-off to Misahuallí south of Tena. From here you can hitch a lift, or catch one of the hourly buses from Tena, for the half-hour journey into town.

Accommodation. Hotel El Paisano has clean, comfortable rooms set around a small garden, and rooms fill quickly. Albergue Español is also recommended, and the Hotel Milca Isca, on the main square, is acceptable. The best place to eat is the restaurant in the El Paisano hotel, which prepares excellent vegetarian food and pancakes, served around a couple of long wooden tables.

COCA

This town has grown rapidly over the last two decades — due initially to the establishment of a huge palm plantation nearby, but more recently to a continuous flow of oil exploration and extraction teams. It currently has a population of 16,000. Known officially as Francisco de Orellana, the town is located at the junction of the Napo and Coca rivers — hence it's more user-friendly name. Coca is a base for jungle trips down both the Napo and Tiputini rivers.

Coca is six hours by boat from Misahuallí, and buses connect it with Lago Agrio and Tena. TAME flies from Quito daily except Sunday.

El Auca is the best hotel, but it is often full. It has a lovely big garden with monkeys, which is a great place to while away the hours (and pretend that Coca is a pleasant place really). The Florida is another good bet. Misión Hotel is more expensive but you can change money there (at a poor rate).

Around Coca

Tours along Río Tiputini take you into one of the areas richest in wildlife, though even here animals and birds can be frustratingly elusive. Getting to the river involves travelling by truck for a couple of hours south along an oil exploration road. Once at the river, you can go on trips lasting several days on balsa rafts.

The Tiputini flows through Yasuní National Park, where there should be good opportunities for seeing birds and monkeys. The area is also home to a group of Huoarani Indians known as the Auca. Though they live in a fairly traditional manner, the families settled along the river are likely to be wearing Western-type dress. Their land has been threatened in recent years by oil companies, and some oilmen have been killed. Tourists should only enter Huoarani territory with a local guide.

Pompeya Island and Limoncocha. The island of Pompeya is about four hours by boat east along the Napo river from Coca; boats heading that way can drop you off. There is a Catholic mission and a small museum containing artefacts from the ancient Napo culture. The nuns are unfriendly and do not encourage visitors to camp there.

Limoncocha is two hours walk north of Pompeya. The nature reserve nearby has good wildlife, including at least 12 different types of monkey. There are abundant birds around the lake, which you can explore by canoe.

Limoncocha is a military post. If officials in Coca believe that you are going there, they may insist that you take a guide. This is in fact a good idea if you want to be able to identify plants, butterflies and any wildlife you are lucky enough to spot. If you are determined to head off on your own, it is best to claim that you are going elsewhere. There are a couple of basic hotels in Limoncocha and there is a lodge by the lake, charging about $20 per person a night.

Panacocha. This settlement is some ten hours downriver from Pompeya island. The forest here is fairly rich in birdlife and you can sometimes see a few small mammals too. Visiting Panacocha is a four-day trip out of Coca. On the way you pass La Selva Lodge — it is very expensive, but does have some outstanding wildlife-sighting records.

LAGO AGRIO

Known officially as Nueva Loja, Lago Agrio has boomed as a result of oil exploration and large-scale ranching. It currently has a population of around 30,000. The town is strong on atmosphere, but not much else.

Lago Agrio, which is almost due north of Coca, is the starting point for trips eastwards down the Río Aguarico and to the Cuyabeno National Park. Despite incursions from outside, there are still small groups of Indians within the park and also a good deal of wildlife. You have an even chance of seeing fresh-water dolphins, though you should allow at least three days, preferably more, to make a trip worthwhile.

The best hotels are the Willigram and Putumayo.

Arrival and Departure. TAME flies between Quito and Lago Agrio every morning, except on Sundays. Several bus companies serve Lago Agrio, from Quito (10 hours), Baeza (6 hours) and Coca (2-4 hours, including ferry crossings). The road from the west is often subject to landslides, particularly in around Volcán Reventador, where the land consists of thick deposits of soft volcanic ash.

BAEZA

In a beautiful spot on a hillside surrounded by pastures and forest, the small town of Baeza is 62 miles/100km southeast of Quito, about a mile above the junction of the roads to Lago Agrio and Tena. Buses from Quito to Tena pass through the town, and those going to Lago Agrio and Coca pass nearby: get off at the crossroads below the town and walk, or else hitch a lift up.

The choice of accommodation is limited and facilities are rudimentary, partly due to the town's lack of electricity. The only place to stay in the town itself is the rustic Residencial El Nogal de Jumbandi, a private house with guest rooms attached. Down at the crossroads is the basic Hotel Oro Negro. The local restaurants are simple and close early.

San Rafael Waterfall. With a drop of 475ft/145m this is the highest waterfall in Ecuador. It lies about three hours northeast of Baeza and can be reached by taking a Lago Agrio bus to the tiny community of Reventador. From here, follow the track down to the old oil pipeline workers camp, or else follow the actual pipeline from the shacks by the road; you may well meet children keen to act as guides for a small fee. The falls are about a mile from the camp, along a muddy, overgrown path. The view of the raging water, seen through the sub-tropical vegetation, is superb.

THE GALAPAGOS ISLANDS

The Galapagos Islands, in the Pacific 625 miles/1000km from the mainland, are Ecuador's most highly prized travel destination. This remote archipelago and its unique life forms hold a tremendous fascination, both in their own right and for their role in inspiring Charles Darwin's theory of evolution. *Galapago* means giant tortoise, but the theory evolved from a much more mundane creature, the finch. The islands are incredibly bleak but unimaginably beautiful. Herman Melville, author of *Moby Dick*, wrote in 1856 of 'heaps of cinders' and the islands' 'emphatic uninhabitableness'. Most characteristic are the contorted black lava flows, rugged landscapes covered with tiny volcanic cones and lava tunnels, shady tree-lined roads straight out of West Country England, beautiful sandy bays, and turquoise water full of playful sea-lions.

The islands are essentially volcanoes, and they have never been connected to the continental land mass. Until the early 17th century there was minimal human contact with the islands. Consequently, the wildlife has an almost total lack of fear of people. Humans are, for once, completely ignored, and you are able to pass within a few inches of the animals.

Climate. The islands enjoy a sub-tropical climate, with minor seasonal variations. In general, the small flat islands receive little rain, while the bigger, hillier ones are wetter. Most of this rainfall occurs on the southern side of the islands. This is most obvious on Santa Cruz: while the north is a virtual desert, rich vegetation grows on south-facing hills.

The hottest months are January to May. At this time the uplands are dry with occasional rain, while the lowlands are wetter. The sun can be relentless and there are few trees offering shade, and only a small number of beaches at which to cool off. During the winter season, rainclouds form over the hills and a dense mist, known as *garúa*, appears on the coast — often persisting for weeks at a time. The winds are at times extremely strong and cold: volcanic dust blows up into your eyes, and be prepared for some rough boat journeys. Most people succumb to seasickness at some point.

History. The Galapagos Islands were probably known to the pre-Columbian peoples of Ecuador, though they certainly never lived there for any length of time. The first sighting by a European was made by the Bishop of Panama in 1535, when he was carried seriously off course on his way to Peru. But it was not until 1567 that the Spanish mounted an expedition to the islands. In 1832, shortly after independence, Ecuador claimed the Galapagos and established a base on Floreana island. Three years later Charles Darwin arrived on the *Beagle*.

In the 17th and 18th centuries several of the islands were used by pirates and traders as supply bases. The crews released pigs and goats on the islands to be sure of a supply of food on their return, while carrying away thousands of giant tortoises to eat during their long voyages. The unique ecology of the Galapagos was further damaged by fur sealers and whalers in the 19th century.

All but three percent of the land is now protected, and in 1979 UNESCO declared the Galapagos a World Heritage Site. Besides the menace posed by goats and rats, tourism is the main threat now facing the islands. Though the number of tourists admitted is officially 25,000, the limit is not strictly enforced, and the quantity allowed in rises every year. Some put the figure of visitors to the island at a staggering 80,000. The dilemma is that every tourist pays a large admission fee, which provides vital funds for conservation and research. The Charles Darwin Research Station has turned tourism on the islands into an extremely conservation-conscious business.

Natural History. All the life forms native to the islands are descended from random arrivals from the mainland. They have evolved into unique forms found nowhere else in the world. These endemic species include half of the plants, most of the mammals and reptiles and half the land birds.

Birds: many of the visitors to the Galapagos are bird-watchers. Perhaps the best known birds are the finches, of which there are thirteen different species. Darwin's belief that they were all derived from a single ancestor made them crucial to his theory of evolution. These birds are rarely more exciting to look at than a common sparrow.

A more spectacular bird altogether is the frigatebird, the male with its magnificent red pouch. A rival for attention is the waved albatross, with its broad wingspan and huge black eyes. There are only about 12,000 breeding pairs in the world, and nearly all of them spend part of the year on Española Island. The endemic Galapagos penguin is found on several islands; so too are greater flamingoes, which gather around shallow lagoons. Blue-footed boobies and mockingbirds can be seen on all the islands.

Land birds breed from January to March, and the sea birds from March to September.

Fish: there are some 300 species of fish in the islands' waters. The many tropical species include parrot fish, white-tipped sharks and various types of rays. You can see most of these when snorkelling in the top 50ft/15m of water.

Reptiles: ninety percent of the reptiles are endemic to the islands, including the marine iguanas and giant tortoises. Darwin described the iguanas as 'disgusting, clumsy lizards', and they have a thoroughly prehistoric appearance. The marine iguana is the only sea-going lizard in the world, and is found on nearly all the islands. It can reach up to more than six foot in length and is normally black. You can see these iguanas close to the shore, where they are well camouflaged against the black volcanic rocks; in the early morning they lie in large groups on the rocks, to warm up before entering the sea in search of food.

The land iguana is grey with yellow patches on its head and limbs, and grows up to a metre long. It can live for up to 80 years. Like their marine relatives, land iguanas are most easily spotted on large rocks warming up in the morning sun.

There are fourteen species of giant tortoise on the Galapagos, some of which can live for nearly 200 years. Their numbers have dwindled dramatically, since rats, dogs and pigs eat the eggs and young. Between October and February the East Pacific Green Sea Turtle can be found in quiet shallow mangrove inlets, where they mate for hours at a time; from December to June they go at night to a number of beaches to lay their eggs in the sand. You may see them poking their head up above the surface to breathe.

Sea Mammals: sea lions are found in large numbers on all the islands. They often swim close to people, but be wary of the often aggressive males. The fur seal very nearly became extinct in the 19th century due to extensive hunting. The population has recovered, though the seals are rarely seen since they live in inaccessible rocky areas.

VISITING THE ISLANDS

No one can tour the archipelago without a registered operator and an official guide. Most of the islands can be visited only during the day; camping is not permitted in the protected areas. All the islands have marked paths from which you are not permitted to deviate. Many visitors insist on going beyond the limits, but this is completely unnecessary because the wildlife is everywhere. Touching the animals is strictly forbidden, and there is a ban on smoking and the use of flash guns.

The boats that ferry tourists between the islands may be anything from a floating hotel for 90 people to a much smaller yacht or motorboat with room for 8-12 people. It is worth noting that the best guides tend to be those employed by the tour companies, and this is the main advantage of going on a trip arranged on the mainland. Even so, no one comes away from the Galapagos disappointed.

Organized Tours. A number of companies, both in Ecuador and around the world, offer organized tours to the Galapagos. Most of these are hugely expensive, typically $100 plus per day if booked in the UK/USA. A British company specializing in the islands is Galapagos Adventure Tours, 29 Palace View Road, Bromley, Kent BR1 3EJ (tel 081-460 8107). Tours are also offered by South American specialists, such as those mentioned on page 29.

In general, tours are best booked in Ecuador since foreign operators often use local companies anyway. In the lower range expect to pay anything from $500-600 for eight days, excluding the airfare ($375), though some may include the flight in their quoted price. Some agencies offer a range of classes. Prices are based on a daily rate, currently around $70, even on the days on which you fly to and from the islands. Off-season discounts may be available. The price includes all but drinks on board and the $40 National Park fee. The latter is paid at the airport on arrival and is cheaper if you pay in dollars (cash preferred).

Economic Galapagos, known usually as Galasam, offers tours in the cheaper range. It has offices at Pinto 523 y Amazonas in Quito (tel 550094) and Edificio Gran Pasaje (11th floor), 9 de Octubre 424 in Guayaquil (tel 306289). The Gran Casino hotels in old Quito also charter a no-frills boat for the high season and their prices are among the lowest, but their tours are notoriously bad. More expensive is Angermeyers (Foch y Amazonas, new Quito; tel 569960), which operates a variety of boats.

The busiest time is from the end of June to early September and at the end of the year, so try to book some way ahead if possible.

Independent Travelling. The best and the cheapest place to organize your own tour is in Puerto Ayora on Santa Cruz island. TAME flies daily except Sundays from Quito via Guayaquil to the airport on Baltra island. Flights leave at 9.30am and 10.30am respectively. The fare is $375 return from Quito and $325 from Guayaquil. If you have a student card (available from American Express in Quito) you are eligible for a 20% reduction. Always check the exchange rate to see whether it's cheaper to pay in dollars or sucres. San/Saeta has a daily flight at noon from Guayaquil to San Cristóbal island, and offers student discounts too.

Travel agents block book seats, and if you are flexible you may be able to buy unsold fares at the airport on the day of departure — and for less than the full price.

During the flight and the journey from Baltra to Puerto Ayora, find out if there are any travellers interested in doing the same kind of tour as you. Even if you cannot put a group together immediately, you may find others already in Puerto Ayora trying to fill up a boat. You should be able to arrange something within a couple of days.

Many boat-owners run hotels along Avenida Charles Darwin or have signs outside their homes advertising their boats. These usually have berths for around ten people, available for $40-50 per person per day, including a guide and meals. The *Cormorant* is recommended. The minimum worthwhile length of tour is four days; most people find five or six days sufficient. The islands are not that close together, and you'll need to do several long trips across open water. In order to visit the maximum number of islands in the time available, try to arrange with the captain to motor during the night, so that you can reach a new island by the morning; then, during lunch, motor.to another one.

Details of the agreement you make should be recorded and signed by the owner, the captain and a member of the group. (The South American Explorers Club in Quito has a model agreement in its guide to the islands, price $4.) Make sure it includes the starting and finishing dates and times (an evening departure from Puerto Ayora is recommended), the itinerary, the price of drinks, and the contingency plan in case of mechanical failure. Ask to meet your guide to confirm that he or she speaks reasonable English. Snorkels can be hired from shops for a few dollars a day plus a $20 deposit.

Dollars cash are the preferred means of payment. Avoid paying in full in advance if possible, though some owners insist on it. The captain will want to hold your passport during the voyage in case your boat is stopped by a navy patrol. At the end of the trip it is usual to give the crew and guide a tip of about $5-10 per person, depending on the length of trip, type of boat and friendliness of the crew.

There have been reports that the Government plans to put an end to the so-called 'economical' boats, by enforcing new luxury and safety standards on all launches. The idea appears to be that the owners of these boats will be forced to sell their licences to the companies offering more expensive tours. In addition, the entry tax is set to double to $80. The aim apparently is to limit the number of visitors to the archipelago while increasing expenditure per head. This would obviously be bad news for cost-conscious travellers. It is already virutally impossible to arrange a week's touring in the islands (including flight and spending money) for less than $600.

SANTA CRUZ ISLAND

This is the largest and most populated island in the Galapagos. It is occasionally referred to as Indefatigable, after a British warship. Of all the islands it has the greatest variety of environments. The northern side is dry and barren, while the southern slopes are covered with pasture dotted with farms. As the road drops back down to the coast at Puerto Ayora it returns to desert. Often hidden by clouds in the centre of the island is Cerro Chacras.

Puerto Ayora. With a population of 1,500 people, this is the largest settlement on the islands. It is two hours south of Baltra airport, the journey involving two buses and a ferry and costing about $3. If you want to impress your friends by sending postcards, buy the stamps you need at the first opportunity, since the stock in the small post office soon runs out in high season. You can also buy them from the tourist shop in the town. The bank changes dollars cash and travellers cheques at a rate only marginally lower than on the mainland.

The INGALA (tourist) office gives details of the limited inter-island boat service.

Accommodation: it is important to be among the first off the ferry in the high season so as to have the pick of the cheaper hotels.

There are several delightful places around Pelican Bay and the harbour. The Hotel Sol y Mar is right on the bay, ten minutes walk north along Avenida Darwin from the centre. It has cabins in a well kept garden, for about $10. Further around the bay are a couple of budget hotels, virtually next door to each other. Hostal Angermeyer is run by the formidable Mrs Angermeyer, a descendant of one of the first families to establish themselves on the islands. The accommodation is

Peru

Machu Picchu

Population: 22 million   **Capital: Lima (8 million)**

Peru has a dreadful image. The international news media does not portray it as the home of extraordinary ancient civilizations, nor as a beautiful place with magnificent Andean landscapes and some of the best untouched rainforest in the world. Instead you read of a nation engaged in an apparently all-encompassing civil war and, more recently, of a cholera epidemic contaminating the whole country. Sadly for Peru, and for those who might have visited it, such reporting has deterred many travellers in the last few years.

The violence perpetrated by the ruthless Sendero Luminoso guerrillas, and the government forces that fight them, is frightening. However, it is confined to well-defined areas, and these so-called emergency zones are easily avoided — the tourist organization in the capital, Lima, will brief you fully and frankly on regions to avoid. Similarly, travellers swap tales of the horrors of Lima itself, which is commonly dismissed as a chaotic and filthy place with many dangers. Yet if handled sensibly there is no reason to avoid the city which does, in fact, contain many treasures and some of the best nightlife anywhere in South America. And it is easy to reach other parts of a beautiful and fascinating country. Now, more than any other time in Peru's recent history, you can enjoy some of the continent's most famous sites in virtual solitude.

GEOGRAPHY

Four times the size of the United Kingdom, and almost as big as Alaska, Peru

234

is the third biggest country in South America. It has three distinct geographical regions. Its barren coastal desert strip (*la Costa*) rises dramatically into the western edge of the Andes (*la Sierra*); and the mountains in turn slope eastwards into the lush sub-tropical hinterland of the Amazon basin (*la Selva*).

The narrow coastal desert strip is a continuation of the arid Atacama desert of northern Chile. It is transected intermittently by narrow fertile valleys coming down from the Andes. Lima and most of the big cities lie in this coastal region.

The Andes reach their highest point at Mount Huascarán (22,565ft/6,770m) in the Cordillera Blanca of the northwest. There are other magnificent peaks around Qosqo (Cusco), and several impressive volcanoes — many of them still active — dominate the southern coastal ranges. For much of their length within Peru the Andes split into two *cordilleras* separated by a broad trough. The rolling hills between the two ranges consist mainly of grasslands (paramo). Near Lake Titicaca the valley is known as the Altiplano, a bleak, windswept plain which continues south into Bolivia.

Over half of Peru is taken up by the Amazon. Exploitation of the natural riches of the region has been restricted by the barrier of the Andes. However, the construction of roads, airports and the discovery of oil in the northern jungle have led to many changes in the last three decades. There are only three towns of any size in the jungle, of which Iquitos is by far the largest.

CLIMATE

Peru's climatic variations follow the three geographical zones. On the coast, summer is hot and dry, and temperatures can reach well over 30°C/85°F. Winter conditions are mild but still dry, and in some places there has been no rain since records began in the 19th century. The only reliable moisture comes from the winter mist known as *a garúa*, which sweeps in off the sea. It can extend for a considerable distance inland, often at little more than ground level, creating a positively eerie atmosphere. Temperatures can drop to as low as 6°C/42°F, and it can feel cool for weeks at a stretch.

In the mountains, summer is mild and wet, though temperatures can range from well below freezing on the peaks, to 25°C/76°F at midday on the exposed Altiplano. In winter the weather is cold and dry. This is the best time to go trekking, though temperatures in the high mountains creep to only just above zero at midday.

Summer in the rainforest brings maximum temperatures of about 40°C/104°F and heavy tropical rains. Winter is drier and cooler, and you may even need warm clothes.

Like Ecuador, Peru is subject to the *El Niño* phenomenon, which results from a shifting of currents in the Pacific. It brings warm, wet weather down the coast with devastating effects. When it last struck in 1982-3, the rain did enormous damage to buildings, roads, wildlife, etc. El Niño usually occurs every ten years or so; the 'child' referred to is the infant Jesus, because it has the greatest impact around Christmas.

HISTORY

The Peru region was settled over 10,000 years ago. However, it was not until about 2500BC that the scattered populations in the area began to build permanent settlements in the coastal valleys. The remains of these ancient cultures have been preserved ever since in the dry desert environment.

Contact between the coastal valleys was limited, and the first cohesive culture occurred high in the Andes at Chavín de Huántar. Here a primitive religious cult was established, with ferocious animal deities and a series of complex pyramidal temples. The influence of Chavín can be seen in all the ensuing coastal cultures. Several formidable groups sprang up, including the Moche (AD200-800), the Nazca and the Paracas 'Necropolis' (both AD400-800). Most renowned are the Nazca, mainly because of their extraordinary and extensive drawings in the desert.

The first significant Andean culture, Tiahuanaco, was centred around Lake Titicaca's southern shores, in what is now Bolivia. But the empire extended north to Ayacucho, west of Qosqo, and it had considerable influence over the coast. Around AD1000 there was a split and a secondary culture known as the Huari came to dominate Peru. Many Inca remains, such as those at Ollantaytambo, stand on Huari foundations.

While the Huari strengthened their position in the highlands, the Chimú built up their own empire which at its height claimed the whole of the coast north of Lima. Their highly organized society led to the first urbanizations in Peru, such as the remarkable adobe city of Chan-Chan. But by the 13th century, they and the Huari were in decline.

The Incas. Legend has it that Qosqo was founded in about AD1100 by Manco Capac, the first Inca, and his sister-wife Mama Ocllo, who came north from Lake Titicaca. At first the Incas were simply another minor Andean tribe, but this changed at the turn of the 14th century, when the Inca king Viracocha imposed control over other groups in the Qosqo area. He went on to establish one of the greatest empires ever created. His successor, Pachacutec Inca Yupanqui, expanded Inca territory further to encompass an area that stretched from Lake Titicaca to Quito in Ecuador.

The next king, Topa Inca Yupanqui (1471-93), with his fearless and formidable army, took new territories as far south as Chile. The result was an empire that stretched the same distance as between London and Tehran; but it was not destined to last. Yupanqui's successor, Huayna Capac, split the empire between two of his sons, as he lay dying. Huáscar (1525-32), the rightful but weak heir, was awarded Qosqo and the southern empire, while Atahualpa, his stronger half-brother, got Quito and the northern territories. Civil war erupted immediately, and Atahualpa emerged victorious.

The Conquest. Francisco Pizarro, an illiterate pig farmer from central Spain, landed on the northern coast of Peru in 1532 at a most opportune moment, with the Inca empire weakened by civil war. He marched straight into the mountains and by an amazing coincidence encountered Atahualpa and his victorious army at Cajamarca. The Incas were startled by the white men on horses, whom they believed to be one and the same animal, maybe even gods. Pizarro held Atahualpa to ransom, supposedly for a room of gold, which the Indians supplied with apparent ease. The Spaniard, perhaps only then realizing the riches that were within reach, or simply through malice, had Atahualpa strangled. Pizarro marched on Qosqo, which surrendered without a fight.

A puppet Inca was installed and the Spanish set about looting the empire. The tiny Spanish force met little resistance as their horses and firearms were greatly feared and the Inca army was demoralized and racked with superstition. Although they outnumbered the Spanish by several hundred to one, they could not defeat them.

In 1542 the first Spanish Viceroy arrived in Lima, but he was overthrown by Gonzalo Pizarro, Francisco's brother. He assumed power over all the old Inca

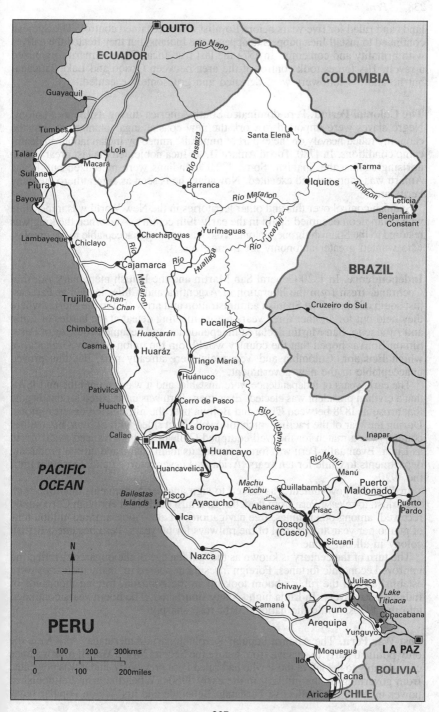

237

lands and ruled for five years before Royalist forces regained control. The Spanish continued to install Inca puppets to appease the Indians, but they treated the natives with brutality and contempt. In 1572 the last true Inca, Tupac Amaru, organized a revolt. His forces took control of the area between Qosqo and Lake Titicaca, but he and his followers were defeated and gruesomely executed.

The Colonial Period. Peru dominated South America during its life as a colony. Negro slaves were imported to work the new coastal sugar plantations, but the economy relied heavily on the export of minerals, mined by Indian labour in death-camp conditions. In 1780, Tupac Amaru II, an Inca noble, led the last great Indian uprising against the Spanish. Some 100,000 Indians were mobilized but Tupac Amaru was captured and executed. Nowadays he is seen as a great hero by many Peruvians.

Spanish control over this and other territories in the New World was impossible when Napoleon occupied Spain in the early 19th century. And when the king was restored to the Spanish throne, colonial rule was no longer acceptable to the creoles, who wanted greater autonomy for themselves.

Independence. In 1820 General San Martín and the British mercenary Admiral Cochrane, fresh from the liberation of Argentina and Chile, landed at Paracas, just south of Lima. The Spanish administration and army fled to the Sierra, where they held out for another three years before meeting defeat at the battles of Junín and Ayacucho. San Martín declared independence and became Protector of Peru. Simon Bolívar hoped that the country would join the union of New Granada, of which Ecuador, Colombia and Venezuela were already part; but this proved unacceptable to the new government.

The early years of independence were unstable, and it was not until the mid-1870s that a civilian president was elected. Even then, Peru was unprepared for the dispute that arose in 1878 between Chile and Bolivia over the nitrate-rich desert regions. During the War of the Pacific which followed, Peru sided with Bolivia; but neither country was a match for the well equipped Chileans, who advanced as far north as Lima. Eventually Peru was forced to cede its main guano and nitrate-producing departments to Chile for ten years. Arica was never returned and Tacna not until the 1920s.

In 1889 the government was forced to sign another agreement, this time with the British to release Peru from its debts. In return the British Peruvian Corporation received, among other things, free navigation on Lake Titicaca, three million tons of guano per year and control of the railways for 66 years. Peru became a British colony in all but name.

The turn of the century is known as the 'golden age of the oligarchy', reflecting improved economic fortunes. Foreign investment poured in, many industries were established and the rubber boom took off in the Amazon, forcing thousands of Indians into slavery. In Lima high society flourished. The boom years continued into the 1920s, while the national debt rose sharply.

Post-War Peru. The Alianza Popular Revolucionaria Americana (APRA) is the only political party to survive from before the Second World War. It took a stance considerably to the left of those who had ruled Peru previously, and it was prevented from governing by the military in the early 1960s. When the army relinquished power in 1963, the ineffective Fernando Belaunde and his Acción Popular party took over. In 1968 the army again seized power rather than let APRA win the forthcoming elections.

The new military president, General Velasco, was a left-wing nationalist. Connections with the Eastern Bloc grew and links with the USA were cut. More importantly, Velasco passed laws which returned land to indigenous communities. But the economy benefitted little, and in 1970 the country had to cope with a severe earthquake in which over 30,000 died. The situation was further exacerbated by a crisis brought on by oil price rises in the mid-1970s. Velasco was ousted by another general.

The 1980s. Belaunde was re-elected in 1980, in the first free elections for nearly twenty years. But the recovery of democracy was overshadowed by a sinister terrorist group called Sendero Luminoso (Shining Path). Belaunde had inherited an economy in ruins, and the poor Andean heartland was the breeding ground for this Maoist-inspired organization whose policies are similar to those of Pol Pot in Cambodia. The night before polling on 18 May 1980, Sendero infiltrated the town of Chuschi and destroyed ballot boxes — the first indication of its contempt for democracy. Its broad aim is the destruction of the apparatus of the state and the elimination of all foreign influence. Following this, Peru will be rebuilt according to pre-Columbian principles of rural self-sufficiency. One consequence is a stated policy of attacking foreigners, which has frightened off many tourists and scared away foreign investors. Operating through a tight cell structure, Sendero outwitted the army, terrorized campesinos and blew up electricity pylons and the central railway. The army responded with its own campaign of terror — abducting and killing anyone suspected of Sendero links — but it had little success.

Against this background the military finally accepted Alan García of APRA, who won the 1985 elections. García began his term as the most popular president in Peruvian history, but his electoral honeymoon was shortlived. Having inherited all the economic and social problems of the Belaunde government, his administration became divided and weak. Strikes were commonplace. García abused his role as President, and efforts are now being made to try him for illegally enriching himself while in office. At the time, rapid economic growth was followed by stagnation, trouble with foreign debt repayments and inflation at an all-time high. Such conditions were ideal for the Sendero Luminoso, which became increasingly confident and broadened its field of activity. At the same time a Marxist terrorist group, the Tupac Amaru Revolutionary Movement (MRTA), appeared in the north.

Recent History. In 1988 a right-wing electoral alliance chose the author Mario Vargas Llosa as its presidential candidate for the 1990 elections. At one stage it looked as though he could win, but instead victory went to a complete unknown of Japanese origin, Alberto Fujimori. This university rector, who claims descent from Samurai warriors, was leader of Cambio 90 (Change 90). This was a loose grouping of centre-right independents, mainly small businessmen and evangelists.

Within days Fujimori introduced his 'El Shock' economic package, involving huge price rises for staple goods and wage freezes. The President is playing all-out to win back support for Peru within the international financial community. But he has so far made little headway, despite his attempts to kick start the Peruvian economy. A wide range of state employees have protested against low wages, and even health workers were driven to strike during their fight against the cholera epidemic. Meanwhile, economic hardship among the indigenous people of th

Andes has increased support for the Sendero. The campaign against the terrorists has, if anything, become more violent under Fujimori; he has, in a fit of bravado, predicted that the guerrillas will be put down by 1995. Fears are being expressed that the President is falling increasingly under the military's influence. A report by Amnesty International, detailing human rights abuses perpetrated by his government, was condemned by the President. Fujimori's reaction caused alarm among Western governments, who may cut vital aid to the country. The immediate future for the already impoverished Peruvians looks grim.

THE PEOPLE

Peru has four distinct peoples. By far the largest group are the Quechua and Aymará Indians of the Andes, who account for about 50% of the population. The Quechua are the most numerous and most widespread, while Aymará-speaking communities are concentrated mainly around Lake Titicaca. The indigenous tribes in the jungle number only about 200,000.

The creoles, descendants of the Spanish or subsequent European immigrants, amount to roughly 10% of the population; the remainder are principally mestizos. These two last groups are concentrated in Lima and the big cities, though in recent years significant numbers of Indians have been driven by poverty down to the coast from the Andes.

The Amazon Indians have the jungle pretty much to themselves apart from the sizeable settlements of Iquitos and Pucallpa. The principal tribal groups are the Jivaro in the north and the Shipibo-Conibo in the central jungle.

Other groups of any size live mainly in Lima and along the northern coast. They include about 50,000 blacks, descendants of slaves, and a similar number of Asians, primarily Japanese and Chinese. The latter have established a niche in Peruvian society as traders and restauranteurs.

LANGUAGE

Spanish and Quechua are the two official languages of Peru. The latter has only recently achieved this status, despite being spoken by the great majority of indigenous people — particularly in the central and southern Andes. The sixty or so tribes in the Peruvian jungle all have their own languages and are unlikely to speak any or much Spanish; most Quechua and Aymará-speakers, on the other hand, usually know some.

You can learn Spanish at institutes in Lima and Qosqo, though the courses in Ecuador offer a far greater choice and are much cheaper. Lima's most reputable school is Centro de Idiomas (Olguín 215, Monterrico; tel 350601).

FURTHER READING

The rich history and culture of Peru has attracted many writers and you should not have difficulty finding books on many aspects of the country.

There is only one detailed study of the early cultures, *The Ancient Civilizations of Peru* by J. Alden Mason (Penguin, 1990). There are, on the other hand, numerous ᵘmes about the Incas. The best insight into their lifestyle is found in *The 'ᵃy Life of the Incas* by Ann Kendall (Dorset Press, USA; 1990). *The Royal ᵗaries of the Incas*, translated into English from the original text of de la Vega, is the most readable of the accounts written by the early roniclers; you can buy it in bookshops in Lima and Qosqo. Books about t Peruvian history are harder to get hold of: *Peru — Paths to Poverty* by Mike Reid (Latin America Bureau, 1985), which concentrates on the 70s and early 80s, is sadly out of print.

Lost City of the Incas (Greenwood Press, 1948) by Hiram Bingham is a dramatic account of the archaeologist's discovery of Machu Picchu, which he insists, quite erroneously, to be the lost city of Vilcabamba. If you don't have £50 to spare, go to your local library, where you may also find the out-of-print books of Gene Savoy, who spent many years exploring the furthest corners of the country in search of the last refuge of the Incas.

The search for modern travelogues is easier. In *Journey along the Spine of the Andes* (Oxford Illustrated Press, 1984), Chris Portway describes his trip along the Inca road between Qosqo and Quito — a journey it is no longer possible to make due to terrorism. In the highly readable *Cut Stones and Crossroads: A Journey in Peru* (Penguin, 1984) Ronald Wright intersperses his travel narrative with quotes from the chroniclers and Quechua sayings. More recent is *Inka-Kola* by the *Times* journalist Matthew Parris (Weidenfeld and Nicolson, 1990), in which he gives a good feel for Peru in the late 80s. *Peregrinations of a Pariah* (Virago, 1986) is a more unusual book written by a French feminist and socialist and first published in 1838. In it Flora Tristan (Paul Gauguin's grandmother) gives a remarkable portrait of Peru, in addition to account of her struggle to save her marriage. One of the few books to deal with the tribes of the Peruvian rainforest is *At Play in the Fields of the Lord* by Peter Matthiessen (Bantam), an outstanding book which has recently been made into a film.

For a good read on your travels take any book by Mario Vargas Llosa, Peru's greatest novelist, whose work is described on page 22.

Getting There

AIR

Lima is one of the cheapest South American destinations to fly to from Europe, and it is a starting point for many travellers to the continent.

From North America. The national carrier, AeroPeru, has flights from Miami, New York and Los Angeles in the USA, and from certain South American capitals. Faucett, Peru's largest private airline, also flies from Miami, and sometimes stops over at Iquitos en route. Both operators have a reputation for delays and poor maintenance. The fare from Miami to Lima is about $450. For only a little extra you can add internal flights; these are usually offered at a third of the normal price. Faucett's office in London is at 27 Cockspur Street, SW1 (tel 071-930 1136).

The most reliable airline from the USA is American Airlines, with daily flights into Lima.

From Europe. At the start of 1992, Aeroflot was offering the lowest fares for its flights via Shannon and Havana to Lima. Unfortunately, the fate of the former Soviet airline is uncertain. Otherwise, the cheapest deals are on Viasa of Venezuela and Avianca of Colombia, with slow journeys and long connections in Caracas and Bogotá. Avianca has a deal with AeroPeru and Faucett so that it can sell cheap flights within Peru when you buy an international ticket — an offer well worth taking up. European carriers (KLM, Iberia, Air France) are more expensive, though Air France sometimes offers special rates for last-minute bookings in the off season.

From South America. Every country (apart from Guyana) has direct links with

Lima, but fares are high. To reach neighbouring countries it is much cheaper to take an internal flight to near the frontier and cross by land, than it is to fly direct. For a journey from the east, e.g. from Rio or Buenos Aires, it may be worth asking small airlines such as Air Paraguay or LAB of Bolivia for cheap fares via their respective capitals. It is also possible to fly to Iquitos from Manaus and Tabatinga in the Brazilian Amazon.

SURFACE

From Chile. The border between Arica in Chile and Tacna in Peru can be crossed by road or rail. The Pan-American Highway hits the frontier at La Concordia, which consists of two border posts in the desert (open 7am-11pm). Colectivos from the central boulevard in Arica take about an hour, compared with 90 minutes by bus. Trains, which run three times a day from Arica (except Sundays), are even slower than the bus. Trains, buses and colectivos go straight through from Arica to Tacna and vice-versa. There is no need to change. Formalities at the border are usually brisk.

From Bolivia. There are two routes into Peru from Bolivia, both of them ending up in Puno; either can be done easily in a day from La Paz.

The most popular route is via Copacabana, on the shores of Lake Titicaca. Colectivos leave from the town's main square and take half an hour to reach the border at the village of Kasani. The two frontier posts are open 7am-8pm. Some colectivos continue into the nearby town of Yunguyo, but there are others hanging around beyond immigration if not. The drop-off point in Yunguyo (a dusty, unappealing place) is the main square — moneychangers, usually women, sit in a row behind small wooden counters, calculators in hand. Minibuses for the three-hour journey to Puno leave from Plaza 2 de Mayo, four blocks away. The entire journey from Copacabana to Yunguyo should take no more than an hour. Make an early start if you plan to travel from La Paz to Puno in a day. For an easier journey from the Bolivian capital take one of the tourist minibuses which run a direct service, with a lunch stop in Copacabana; see page 349.

The alternative route goes via the border at Desaguadero, on Titicaca's southern shore. Buses from La Paz go as far as the border, but are often very crowded. Once in Peru there are colectivos directly to Puno. Get up early and break your journey at Tiahuanaco; see page 347.

From Brazil and Colombia. The only significant border crossing between Peru and Brazil is along the river Amazon. The principal port on the Brazilian side is Benjamin Constant, which is served by boats coming upriver from Manaus; the border post is actually a short distance away in the town of Tabatinga, which has a small airport. Leticia, in Colombia, is served by air from Bogotá.

Boats from Tabatinga to Santa Rosa, one hour away across the border, leave at 8am, 11am and 3pm. Santa Rosa, and not nearby Islandia, is now the main port for boats going upriver to Iquitos. However, you can still travel to Santa Rosa via Islandia, which has more frequent connections with Tabatinga, if you miss one of the direct boats.

Just a few cargo boats a week run upriver from Santa Rosa to Iquitos, so you may have to stay a couple of days in the very basic accommodation there. Most boats are ancient, dirty, noisy and full of smugglers and thieves. The shared cabins cost only a couple of dollars more than a space to sling your hammock on deck. Expect to pay about $20 for the two to four day passage. An alternative is to take a boat from Santa Rosa across to Leticia, from where speedboats go to Iquitos early in the morning on Mondays and Thursdays. The trip takes just nine hours but costs about $50. You should be able to remain in transit while in Leticia.

The Peruvian navy airline TAN usually has a flight from Islandia to Iquitos on Wednesdays or Thursdays, while Cruzeiro airlines flies from Tabatinga to Iquitos daily.

From Ecuador. There are just two main border crossing points between Peru and Ecuador: the entire Amazon frontier region is closed due to an ongoing border dispute. Most traffic uses the coastal Pan-American Highway and crosses at Aguas Verdes, an extension of the Ecuadoran border town of Huaquillas. The frontier posts, almost hidden behind vast piles of consumer goods, are open 7am-9pm. The border is defined by a revolting rubbish-filled creek.

Some buses head south direct from the frontier, but it is better to take a colectivo to Tumbes, the nearest large town and also a more congenial place to stay if it's late in the day. Buses leave Tumbes for all major towns in northern Peru and as far south as Lima. You can also get taxis from the border to Tumbes airport, from where there are several daily flights to the capital.

The alternative crossing is the inland route between Macará, a few miles from the border in southern Ecuador, to Sullana, just north of Piura. The border is open 7am-6pm. There is no regular transport on either side, but pickups and minibuses cope with the demand. Allow five or six hours for the journey to Sullana from Macará.

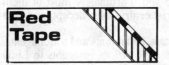

Red Tape

Citizens of the UK and other EC nations, Americans and Canadians do not require a visa, while Australian and New Zealand nationals do. At immigration, officials usually allow a stay of 60 days, but this may go down to 30 or up to 90. The period granted is likely to be more generous at Lima airport than at land borders. For further information contact a Peruvian consulate abroad:

UK: 52 Sloane Street, London SW1X 9SP (tel 071-235 1917); open 10am-noon.
USA: 1700 Massachucetts Avenue NW, Washington DC 20036 (tel 202-833-9860); open 9am-5pm.
Australia: FAI Insurance Building, 197 London Circuit, Canberra ACT 2601 (tel 572953/639). There is no consulate in New Zealand.

Extending your stay. Tourist cards and visas can be extended for up to 90 days at a time at the Dirección de Migración in Lima (Paseo de la República 585; tel 276927). It is an extremely time-consuming business.

Departure tax. Airport tax of $15 is levied when flying out of Peru. There is no such tax at land frontiers.

Customs. The duty-free allowance is 400 cigarettes or 50 grams of tobacco, and two bottles of spirits. Formalities at land borders are surprisngly swift, while anyone arriving by air in Lima can face horrendous queues.

1 Nuevo Sol = 100 centavos.

Hyper-inflation in the 1980s brought a succession of three different currencies in five years. In 1987 Alan García's government replaced the then worthless sol with the inti, which was in turn superseded by the new sol in 1991. Meanwhile, the US dollar is still in common use.

Peru is no longer as cheap for visitors as it once was. Costs are significantly higher than in Bolivia and Ecuador, though the fall-off in tourism has driven local people to offer tourists sometimes embarrassingly cheap deals.

Notes and coins. New sol notes are issued to the value of 10, 20, 50 and 100 new soles, and coins to the value of 1, 5, 10, 20, and 50 centavos, and 1 new sol. Meanwhile, intis are likely to remain in circulation and the mass of different notes leaves ample scope for confusion. Inti banknotes have three to six noughts, from 5,000 to 5,000,000, though the last three zeros were officially dropped in 1991. Where intis are used, primarily in the remoter mountain areas, prices are quoted accordingly. One new sol is worth 1,000,000 intis.

Changing Money. Banco de Crédito, which has branches in all the main towns, is about the only bank to change travellers cheques reliably. Other banks and casas de cambio deal predominantly in cash. Most people — local and foreign — use street moneychangers, who usually offer marginally better rates than the official exchange houses. Every town has at least one area where moneychangers assemble from early morning to late at night. Unlike in some South American countries, they operate perfectly legally — unless they rob you. Fortunately most of them are honest. Moneychangers in big cities and tourist centres even accept travellers cheques, when accompanied by a passport.

Major credit cards can be used in top shops, hotels, restaurants and travel agents, and for cash advances. All the main credit cards have offices or agents in Lima which can arrange limited advances in local currency. Lima Tours is the agent for American Express in Peru, and has offices in the capital, Arequipa, Qosqo and Puno. Amex cheques can be cashed into local currency only.

Banking Hours. Most banks open 8.30-11.30am, Monday to Friday. There is some regional variation, and in larger towns they may also open in the late afternoon, commonly 3.30-5.30pm. In the last few years banks have been affected by strikes, which usually last for several days at a time.

Mail. It is usually impossible to buy stamps because of the rate of inflation. Instead, you must take letters to a post office where they are franked. Postal rates increased dramatically in 1991, so the cost of a postcard and stamp to Europe now comes to $1.

Telephone. Peru is six hours behind GMT. The international country code is 51.

Entel, the state-run telecommunications company, operates a reasonably effective service, though connections with the smaller towns are poor. Payphones (for local calls) can be found on occasional street corners in the major cities. They take a special coin known as a *rin* (plural *rines*), which is worth about $0.10 and allows you to talk for a minute. For long-distance or international calls use Entel offices. These usually open 6am-11pm, with some variation between cities and small towns. A typical inter-city call costs $2-3 for three minutes. The main towns have the following area codes:

Abancay — 84	Chiclayo — 74	Piura — 74
Arequipa — 54	Iquitos — 94	Qosqo — 84
Cajamarca — 44	Lima — 14	Trujillo — 44

An international call costs $7 for three minutes to the USA and $10 to Europe. The easiest way to phone is to buy a special high-value rin (price $4), which you can use in Entel office telephones. Reduced rates operate after 8pm and on Sundays. It is possible to make collect calls.

THE MEDIA

Newspapers. The Peruvian press operates in a difficult climate. While surprisingly free, the press is also very political, with little independent reporting. *El Comercio* is a respected broadsheet, but it is conservative and offers a poor account of domestic news; its coverage of foreign events is much better. *El Expresso*, a right-of-centre tabloid, also gives good coverage of foreign news, and is ideal for a quick and entertaining read. *La República* and *Página Libre* are the principal left-wing dailies. *El Diario* was closed down because of its pro-Sendero stance, and has gone underground. *Cambio*, a weekly paper associated with the MRTA guerrillas, still circulates. The most widely-read magazine is the weekly *Caretas*, which covers topical social and political issues from a centre-right standpoint.

The *Lima Times* is an excellent English-language paper, published on Fridays. It reports on political and other developments in Peru, and also covers cultural events in the capital. It is available mainly in downtown Lima and the wealthier suburbs. American newspapers are found only in the main big city hotels and at Lima airport, but *Newsweek* and *Time* magazine reach the major bookstores. The Peru-British Cultural Association library in Lima (34th block of Avenida Arequipa) has a limited selection of old British newspapers. The British consulate in Lima also has a good choice of papers.

Broadcasting. Vargas Llosa's wonderful novel *Aunt Julia and the Scriptwriter* concerned a scandalous soap opera on a Peruvian radio station. Sadly, no station in Lima or elsewhere has time for such entertaining frivolities today. Much of the airtime on Peruvian radio seems to be dedicated to an extremely popular kind of salsa music called *cumbia chicha*.

There are three national television stations, one of which — Channel 7 — is state-run. The best news coverage is on the other two, Channels 5 and 9. Channel 2 television in Lima offers a reasonable range of programmes, with even the odd one on the environment; but like other stations it is still dominated by American B-movies, appalling Latin American soaps, and sport.

Getting Around

The Andes provide an obvious hindrance to movement around the country but the communication network is not much better on the coast. The Pan-American Highway, which connects the coastal cities, is little more than a track in places. Buses are generally the best means to get around, since there is just a limited rail network. Many destinations in the Amazon, however, can only be reached by air or river. Along minor routes in the rest of the country you may have to rely on lifts in a pickup (*camioneta*).

Rising prices have hit transport virtually more than anything else in Peru, due to a thirty-fold increase in the cost of petrol introduced by President Fujimori when he came to power. Railways and roads suffer from a lack of maintenance and sporadic guerrilla sabotage, bridges being a popular target.

Maps. The best map available is the *Mapa Perú* published by the Librería Internacional del Perú. It has a good road map of the whole country on one side, plus 25 excellent city plans on the reverse. It is sold in some bookshops or can be obtained from the Librería itself, at Jirón Unión 892 in central Lima. Cartografía Nacional produces useful maps in a folded booklet form, among them a tourist road map of the country, a political map and a plan of Lima. These can be bought easily from street vendors for about $3.

The Instituto Geográfico Nacional in Lima produces departmental, topographical and various other maps, which are generally good but not totally accurate. Maps can be consulted or bought at the IGN at Avenida Aramburu 1190 in Lima; most cost $1-3. You may not be able to buy ones of certain areas for security reasons.

Note that in Peru *jirón* is a common term, meaning avenue.

AIR

Services in Peru were chaotic at the start of 1992. AeroPeru, the national carrier, is on the verge of bankruptcy; Faucett, the largest private airline, changed owners in 1991; and business was poor for their four small rivals, Andrea, Aeroexpress, TransAmazon and the new Americana. Neither AeroPeru nor Faucett sticks to its published schedule and the other four have different timetables almost every week. The range of flights has been reduced sharply, both for reasons of security and because of the lack of business.

All airlines except TransAmazon are based in Lima, which has several connections a day with all the big cities. Qosqo, Arequipa, Trujillo and Iquitos are minor hubs, with at least one flight a day to lesser destinations. Smaller regional airports are served infrequently by the major airlines. In remote jungle regions small airstrips are served by light aircraft operators such as AeroCondor; crashes involving these small aircraft are worryingly frequent.

One-way fares from Lima to Qosqo, Iquitos and Arequipa all cost in the region of $70. AeroPeru and Faucett both offer air passes, which are good value but must be purchased outside the country. Faucett can offer an unlimited pass for $200 if you fly with the airline to Lima from Miami.

There is an internal flight tax and a municipal airport tax at some airports, totalling $3-8. It can be paid in dollars or local currency.

TRAIN

Empresa Nacional Ferrocarriles (Enfer) has operated a much reduced service following the destruction of several lines in the great earthquake of 1970. Fujimori is currently opening up the railways to privatization. Just five passenger services operate today: Lima-Huancayo, on the central network; Arequipa-Juliaca-Puno, Puno-Juliaca-Qosqo and Qosqo-Machu Picchu-Quillabamba on the southern network; and Tacna-Arica, a short line across the border into Chile. All bar the last are dramatic trips, and it is worth putting up with the slow and inefficient service for the often spectacular views. Most magnificent is the trip from Lima to Huancayo, along the world's highest railway.

There are four classes of carriage: pullman, tourist, first and second. Pullman is the most comfortable and strongly recommended for night journeys. For a certain amount of comfort during a daytime trip, tourist and first class are more than adequate. Note that pullman and tourist coaches have guards and are kept under lock and key for passenger safety. This does not engender a particularly pleasant feeling, and many travellers prefer to take their chances in the first class carriages, where they can at least be amongst local people. There is a buffet service in all but second class, which is crowded and basic.

Be vigilant against thieves in whichever class you travel. The overnight Arequipa-Puno train is notorious for theft. The Puno-Qosqo train doesn't have a spotless reputation, but at least it runs during the day.

BUS

Peru's roads are in a sorry state. The network of asphalted roads is extremely limited: it consists mainly of the Pan-American Highway and part of the Central Highway, which connects Lima and Pucallpa, in addition to a few branch roads and some around Qosqo and Lake Titicaca. Travel a few miles out of most cities and the road — the Pan-American Highway included — is a pot-holed strip of tarmac barely wide enough for two vehicles to pass.

There is an adequate supply of buses on most routes, but many of them run at night. In the mountains this could feasibly be to keep people unaware of the dangers of the roads, though there are surprisingly few serious accidents. Whenever possible take daytime buses, especially in the Andes where the views are among the most magnificent anywhere in the world. Another reason to avoid travelling at night is to avoid armed hold-ups, which occur occasionally.

The main national bus companies are Ormeño, Sudamericano, Cruz del Sur and TEPSA. The first three offer a particularly good service, and are the best choice for long journeys.

Tacna is the only town in Peru with a central bus terminal; in all other towns bus companies have their separate offices, though they are usually fairly close together. In larger cities they may be split between two sides of town, depending on the destinations they are serving.

Combis. Minibuses, known as *combis*, are often used on busy routes where the road is good. They now connect Juliaca with Puno and the latter with the Bolivian border, and have been used for some time to provide a shuttle from Qosqo along the Urubamba valley. They leave when full and stop only if a seat falls vacant; they charge the same as the buses.

Colectivos. Inter-city *colectivos* are huge American cars, often Cadillacs, with room for six people and lots of luggage. They operate on some of the rougher routes where passengers prefer to pay well above the bus fare in return for speed and comfort. Arequipa to Juliaca/Puno is a good journey to cover by colectivo because the train only runs at night and the road is appalling.

Taxis. In the largest cities, taxis are often private cars, driven by people trying to supplement their income, or simply travelling across town themselves. Since there is no meter, agree the fare in advance.

DRIVING

Motoring around Peru is not recommended because of the bad roads, poor drivers and expensive petrol. Driving in the central Andes is also risky because of guerrilla and counter-insurgency activity. Never drive at night.

Budget, Avid and Hertz all have agents in Lima: see page 260. Expect to pay $35-40 a day for the cheapest car, e.g. a Volkswagen, plus $0.20 per km.

While price increases have affected accommodation as much as anything else, staying in a hotel remains comparatively cheap. In most towns, a reasonably comfortable room in a simple hotel should cost under $6. If you are happy with very basic facilities $2 will be more than enough. In Lima, however, no room costs less than $5, and this is also the case in the northern coastal cities. In Qosqo, Huaráz, and other tourist centres, the surplus of hotels means you may be able to negotiate a discount.

All the main towns have a youth hostel, run by the Asociación Peruana de Albergues Juveniles. The head office is in the Lima hostel at Avenida Casimiro Ulloa 328, Miraflores (tel 465488). You don't have to be a member to use the hostels.

A sleeping bag is essential if you are planning to go trekking, camping in the jungle, or to spend a few days on Taquile island (Lake Titicaca). In the first two cases you'll also need a tent; this can be hired, along with other camping gear, in trekking centres such as Qosqo and Huaráz. For extended expeditions into the jungle a mosquito net and a hammock are essential.

Peru has many distinctive dishes. Restaurants, however, tend to offer a disappointingly small range. The most typical eating places are the *picanterías*, simple restaurants frequented mainly by campesinos. They are amazingly cheap, and invariably serve a range of traditional food and chicha, which they brew in a back room. These are also the places to hear the authentic sound of Peruvian cumbia chicha, with its heavy percussion beat — a far cry from the folksy Andean pan-pipes.

In the Andes the campesinos often breakfast on *caldo*, a broth of the innards or the head of a sheep — not a particularly alluring prospect early in the morning. In remote areas the only alternative may be rice and fried eggs; these are always served with masses of salt so order them *sin sal*. A popular jungle breakfast dish is *juane*, a ball of rice stuffed with chicken, vegetables and olives.

Lomo saltado is one of the most commonly available dishes in Peru. Strips of beef are fried up with chips, onions and tomatoes, and served with rice. It can be excellent if the beef is tender, the onions are still crispy and if it is served hot. For a really solid meal try *sopa a la criolla* or *churrasco*. The soup is a meal in itself with noodles, potato, meat and vegetables, while churrasco consists of a large piece of steak with at least one fried egg on top served with chips, rice and salad. You can rarely go wrong with chicken: throughout the country there are places with birds being grilled in the doorway selling *pollos a la brasa*.

One of the most surprising but also most famous foods in Peru is *cuy*, or guinea-pig. It is usually roasted whole on long poles and sold on street corners, mostly in the highlands. It doesn't look particularly appetizing and the flesh — which

The most traditional Andean brew is *chicha*, a yeasty, alchoholic drink made from maize and also drunk abundantly in Bolivia; see page 54. In rural areas a red or white bunch of flowers, or a plastic bag on a pole, indicates a *chichería*; inside, chicha is often served in daunting one-litre glasses. The best way to drink it is mixed with strawberries, which makes the ridiculously sweet *frutillada*. The non-alcoholic variety known as *chicha morada* is pleasant and often now made up from packets of powder.

Emoliente is a hot herb drink sold by street vendors from dawn to dusk. Other herb teas are available, including *maté de coca*, recommended for those suffering from the effects of the high altitude.

Museums. Peru has many excellent museums, most of which are in Lima and Qosqo, but with some in the coastal towns. They contain some of the finest collections of pre-Columbian objects, ancient weavings and ceramics in South America. The Museo Nacional de Antropología y Arqueología and the Museo Nacional, both in Lima, provide an excellent introduction to Peru's past at the start of a trip. Many museums charge an entrance fee of $3-5.

Archaeological Sites. Peru is the most archaeologically rich country in South America. The greatest density of coastal archaeological remains is in the north of the country. They include some fine pre-Inca sites, including Chan-Chan, the largest adobe city in the world, and several newly discovered and fabulously wealthy tombs deep inside adobe pyramids. The most famous pre-Inca remains in the south are the mysterious lines and drawings in the desert at Nazca.

The most accessible and spectacular Inca ruins are in and around Qosqo, which itself retains close associations with Inca times: from the layout of the city to many of the buildings in the centre. And a train ride or a rewarding trek away is Machu Picchu, one of the world's finest archaeological ruins. The ancient site of Sillustani, near Puno, is unimpressive aesthetically, but its location is positively ethereal.

Most sites are reasonably accessible, though there are some notable exceptions, including Vilcabamba in the jungle beyond Machu Picchu.

Hiking. The most well-trodden route in Peru is the Inca trail from the Urubamba valley to Machu Picchu. But the Peruvian Andes provide a truly fantastic selection of high altitude treks. The best areas are the Cordilleras Vilcanota and Auzengate near Qosqo, and the Cordillera Blanca, to the north of Lima.

The Cordillera Blanca, which includes Huascarán, the country's highest peak, is the most popular trekking area. Huaráz is the main base from which to organize trips into the mountains — to glaciers and hidden emerald lakes, all in the shadow of indescribably beautiful peaks. The Cordillera Huayhuash, further south, has been infiltrated by terrorists in the last few years and is off-limits.

While llamas and alpacas are rare in the north, they are a common sight in the Cordilleras Vilcanota and Auzengate, near Qosqo, where they graze on the high pastures. These areas are also more densely inhabited than around Huaráz, and a trek here gives an excellent insight into rural Andean life. Guides, porters and horses can be hired for about $5 per man or animal per day near the starting point; tour companies can also arrange this for you.

Peru's few protected areas all suffer from a severe lack of funds and they have been unable to develop trail systems or refugios. However, the ancient trail systems used for centuries by local people have been adopted by hikers. Many such treks are perfectly safe.

A recommended handbook for hikers is *Backpacking and Trekking in Peru and Bolivia* by Hilary Bradt (Bradt Publications, 1990), which covers the most popular treks. If you intend to concentrate your efforts in the north, *Trails in the Cordilleras Blanca and Huayhuash* by Jim Bartle (Lima 2000) provides comprehensive coverage with good descriptions, maps and photos. This book is available from Bradt Publications in the UK (41 Nortoft Road, Chalfont St Peter, Bucks SL9 0LA), locally in Huaráz, or from the South American Explorers Club in Lima. The latter also produces its own map of the Inca trail to Machu Picchu. The IGN maps, described on page 246, cover most other trekking areas.

Wildlife. Peru has a great diversity of flora and fauna. The coast is rich in birdlife, particularly the Ballestas Islands near Pisco, where you can see cormorants, boobies and even Humboldt penguins. Sealions are common all along the southern coast. Birds gather in the Andes too, especially around the high mountain lakes, and include flamingoes and the bizarre giant coot. To have a hope of seeing a condor, you must hike to remote areas near bleak and craggy peaks; these magnificent birds are most easily and clearly seen at Cruz del Condor, north of Arequipa.

The main area for wildlife is of course the Amazon, where there is an unimaginable variety of species. On trips into the Puerto Maldonado region and the Manú National Park, you have the chance of seeing such endangered species as giant river otters, macaws, the harpy eagle and, in a few cases, even puma and jaguar. Trips into the rainforest require tremendous patience, but the rewards for the stealthy and the silent are fantastic.

Rafting. The best white-water rafting river is the Urubamba, in the Sacred Valley. Several adventure tour companies in Qosqo can arrange trips, both on the Urubamba and on the more remote rivers of the upper Amazon — though at a far higher cost.

Beaches. Peru does not have a spectacular selection of beaches. The long stretches of almost golden sand are lapped by a cold sea that is only bearable in an El Niño. The best swimming is along the northern coast at Huanchaco, close to Trujillo, and at several small resorts west of Tumbes. There is good surf at all these beaches but the inshore currents are strong. Jellyfish and sea urchins are added dangers.

Festivals. Peru's festivals, along with those of Bolivia, are among the most intriguing in South America. Participants dress up in traditional costumes or as animal deities, such as condors, pumas, llamas and parrots, and perform rites of pre-Columbian origin.

Of the fiestas celebrated throughout the country Holy Week is among the most important, especially in Qosqo where it features the so-called Lord of the Earthquakes procession around the main square. Qosqo also boasts Peru's most spectacular festival, the so-called Inti Raymi, during which hundreds of local people dress up in Inca costumes and enact a vast pageant. The recreation of the arrival of Manco Capac from Lake Titicaca, held in Puno in early November, is also well worth going out of your way to see.

On less religious occasions you will hear plenty of traditional music, accompanied by costumed dancers. In the Andes bands are dominated by the panpipes, flutes, drums and the *charango* (a tiny guitar, often with an armadillo shell back), played also in Bolivia.

Carnival is celebrated in February and March, usually over two or three weeks. Cajamarca claims to offer the best in Peru, but most towns lay on substantial celebrations — with parades, shows, elaborate firework displays and large-scale water fights. Keep a low profile, or else hope the bombs contain water rather than ink or oil.

Nightlife. After dark in the rich Miraflores district of Lima, you feel as if you could be in Manhattan, Rio or Berlin. Bars, restaurants and (especially) discos cater for the bright young things, and plenty of live music can be found. Best are the *peñas* (traditional folklore shows) and the *salsadromos*, discos with a live salsa band. Nowhere else in Peru has anything to touch it; the closest is in Qosqo, though the peñas are strictly for the tourists.

There are few theatres or concert halls outside Lima, though from time to time touring bands play in football or volleyball stadiums. Outside Lima and the main tourist centres, nightlife is usually confined to simple bars and cinemas showing appalling films.

SPORT

The national sport is soccer, but volleyball comes a close second and Peru's women's team is one of the best in the world. The country has fared less well in international soccer in recent years, but no football fan (particularly supporters of Scotland) will forget Quiroga, the mad Peruvian goalkeeper of the early 1980s, who had a penchant for tackling opponents in the opposing half.

The main national stadium for football and athletics is in Lima, where there is also a good race course and even a cricket club; cricket is increasingly popular. However, most large towns have special stadiums (*coliseos*) devoted to volleyball and basketball, and smaller ones for cockfighting. Bullfighting also has a big following: during the main season (December), matadors are attracted from other South American countries, and even Spain.

 The indigenous people of Peru produce a fantastic range of crafts. These originate mostly in the Sierra, especially the southern highlands, but they also find their way to Lima and some other coastal towns. You will find the lowest prices in remoter communities, but often the better quality goods are siphoned off to the tourist centres. Prices in Qosqo, the biggest craft centre, and in the markets of Lima, are still perfectly reasonable.

Qosqo and the surrounding market towns such as Pisac and Chinchero, and Puno and Juliaca further south, are the best places to buy woven and knitted goods. The finest knitwear of all comes from the tiny island of Taquile on Lake Titicaca. The islanders produce beautiful hats, belts and waistcoats, usually in burgundy red, dark blue and white and decorated with traditional symbols. You can buy these in Puno and Qosqo, but the best selection is found on the island itself.

Secondhand shawls (*mantas*), woven from sheep's wool and often colourful, are a fairly common sight in tourist centres nowadays. You also see tapestries (*tapices*), which come in many sizes and styles. Some are woven while others are built up from layers of unspun dyed wool. The latter depict mostly scenes of everyday life and landscapes, while the former tend to consist of geometric designs and animal representations.

Pisac, near Qosqo, is a centre for pottery, hand-painted in stylized designs and extremely cheap. While the complete tea services are not ideally suited to being crammed into a backpack, you can also buy more travelling-friendly plates and beads. An even safer bet are the *retablos*, delightful boxes containing numerous figurines, often depicting the Nativity or a scene from daily life. In recent years this has come to include gruesome encounters between the security forces and Sendero Luminoso. Retablos are made entirely from plaster, and are hand-painted. They originate in Ayacucho but now can be bought in Qosqo and Lima.

It is rare to see a Peruvian without headgear of some kind, and hats are a good buy. Panama hats are best bought in Cajamarca, or along the northern coast. Puno and Juliaca are the principal centres for bowler hats and the Qosqo region for trilbies.

Crime and Safety

Terrorism. Despite almost daily exchanges between the army and terrorist groups for the last decade, there is no end in sight to the conflict. Over 20,000 people have died since 1980, at the hands of both the terrorists and the army. There have been several thousand disappearances, and calls are increasing for the cleaning up of the armed forces. Meanwhile, support for the terrorists has grown since Fujimori took office.

In the central Andes the main terrorist group is Sendero Luminoso, based in the Ayacucho area. The Tupac Amaru Revolutionary Movement (MRTA), the smaller of the two groups, operates out of the northern highlands, and is traditionally more urban-based. However, both groups now operate in rural and urban environments; and they are increasingly active in the outer suburbs of Lima and occasionally in the centre, against specific targets, such as embassies, banks, foreign companies and community leaders. In 1991 there was even a rocket attack against the presidential palace, and in 1992 the US ambassador's residence was bombed. Both Sendero and MRTA have put down roots in the coca-growing area of the upper Huallaga valley. In exchange for protection the drug-traffickers give the terrorists money and arms. This is the most dangerous region in the country.

Tupac Amaru policies follow Marxist doctrines, so most of their actions (often assassination, kidnapping or extortion) are against a specific target and are accompanied by a clear statement. The targets and policies of Sendero are less easily defined, making it the most unpredictable and dangerous group. Violence is an integral part of the philosophy of Sendero. Anyone who wanders into a Sendero-controlled area and who gives reason for their actions to be misinterpreted, is likely to be killed — particularly if they are foreign.

The British government and the US State Department issue stern warnings about travelling to Peru. The information sheets handed out by their missions in South America are succinct and to the point — not the kind of thing you'd want to send home to your parents. However, as long as you obey certain rules and avoid danger zones you should not be put off.

The guerrilla-controlled areas, known officially as emergency zones, currently cover about three-fifths of the country — principally across much of the central Andes, from just south of Cajamarca in the north down to the Abancay area in the south. Lima is included in an emergency zone but the level of security is such that travellers need not regard it as off-limits. The area directly inland is also a risk area, but it is still considered safe to make the fantastic train journey from the capital up to Huancayo. Qosqo, Arequipa, Cajamarca and Iquitos and most of the coast are considered safe.

The most appropriate strategy is one of risk avoidance: keep away from emergency zones, avoid travelling at night, stick to city centres in the evening, avoid wearing military-looking clothing, and always seek advice about an area or a journey, if in any doubt. In addition to foreign missions, the South American Explorers Club (see page 266) is also a good source of information.

Crime. As the fortunes of the urban poor have deteriorated, an increasing number have turned to pick-pocketing, bag-snatching and armed hold-ups. Be vigilant in all the main tourist centres. The trains between Arequipa, Puno and Qosqo have a particularly poor reputation: you are advised to chain you bags to the luggage racks and to be vigilant at stations too. Poorly paid off-duty policemen have also been known to take advantage of their position, especially in Lima.

Incidences of violent crime are also on the increase. In rural areas armed bandits, operating on the edge of their own society, pose a greater threat than terrorists. They hang out in remote regions where the authorities are unlikely to pursue them, and pay special attention to tourist sites. There have been several attacks along the Inca trail, and in the Colca Canyon near Arequipa. Travelling alone in these areas is not recommended; in the main tourist centres it is easy to team up with other travellers.

More traditional highway robbery is a growing danger along the Pan-American Highway and other principal roads. More and more people decide to cover long distances by air. Always avoid travelling at night.

Drugs. Peru vies with Bolivia for second place behind Colombia in its involvement in the international cocaine business. Coca leaves are grown on the steep slopes of the eastern Andes, with up to 60% of world production originating in the upper Huallaga valley. Only a small percentage of the leaves are turned into cocaine in Peru; most are partially processed and then flown to Colombia for final refining. Recently, however, Colombian-owned laboratories have been discovered in the Peruvian Amazon.

The profits are concentrated among the traders and drug barons, who have turned vast areas into no-go zones. The crop substitution schemes of the US government have been a dismal failure, and the semi-covert 'war on drugs', involving all kinds of shady mercenary types, has been similarly ineffective.

Two kinds of cocaine are available in Peru: the white powder, and the 'freebase', which is smoked in cigarettes. Travellers are strongly advised to avoid both types of cocaine, and also marijuana. Most dealers are in league with or else are the police; one way or another they are likely to extract every dollar you've got in bribes, or put you in jail for decades. A cell in a Peruvian prison is not an enticing prospect — if in doubt, visit a few gringos in the Lima or Qosqo jails.

As in Bolivia, Peruvian campesinos chew coca leaves to numb the cold and hunger they cannot afford to satisfy; there are also certain areas where the leaf can be grown legally. See also page 64.

Health and Hygiene

Purify tapwater wherever you are in Peru. Since supplies are by no means regular, even in Lima, you may have to rely sometimes on bottled water — San Luís is much the best. Apart from the usual hazards of poorly cooked food, unfriendly insects and dangerous drivers, altitude sickness or *soroche* is one of the most common complaints: coca leaf tea (*maté de coca*) helps you get over the milder symptoms. Qosqo, Puno, Arequipa, Huancayo, Huaráz and Cajamarca are all at considerable heights, and these are good places to begin acclimatizing if you are planning any high-altitude treks.

The cholera epidemic that hit Peru in early 1991 was confined mainly to Lima and the northern half of the country, particularly the large coastal cities. While the vast majority of the 2,300 deaths were among the urban and rural poor, and while the worst appears to be over (in Peru at least), travellers should remain wary about eating ceviche and other dubious-looking food.

Take malaria pills if you intend visiting the foothills of the eastern Andes or the jungle regions; fortunately the strain is not as virulent in Peru as it is in some other parts of the Amazon. Resistance to chloroquine has been reported, however, so ask your doctor for advice on the alternatives. There are some other nasty diseases in the jungle regions, including dengue fever, of which there are frequent outbreaks around Iquitos. Chiggers, tiny insects that lay eggs in your feet or ankles, and various varieties of biting fly, are not uncommon.

Help and Information

The Peruvian tourist board, Foptur, has offices in most tourist centres and large cities. Each region produces its own brochures (some are better than others) and the staff generally have a reasonable knowledge of the immediate area. They are at their most enthusiastic when directing you to recognized tourist destinations; questions about more obscure places sometimes receive only a blank — and even an annoyed — look. Tourist office opening hours are normally 9am-noon and 2-5pm.

The unrivalled source of information for independent travellers, however, is the South American Explorers Club in Lima (Avenida Portugal 146; tel 314480); see page 80 for details of their services.

For advance information, contact Foptur, 10 Grosvenor Gardens, London SW1W 0BD for some moderately useful information sheets. Individual enquiries will be answered, at leisure. Foptur's main office in the USA is at 1000 Brickell Avenue, Suite 600, Miami, FL 33131 (tel 305-374-0023).

PUBLIC HOLIDAYS (those marked * are half-days from 1pm)

January 1	New Year's Day
March/April	Holy Thursday*/Good Friday
May 1	Labour Day
June 24	Farmer Day*
June 29	Saint Peter and Saint Paul
July 27-29	Independence
August 30	Santa Rosa de Lima
October 8	Anniversary of the Battle of Angamos
November 1	All Saints
December 8	Immaculate Conception
December 25	Christmas Day
December 31	New Year's Eve

LIMA

Once the administrative centre for virtually all of South America, Lima is often dismissed as a squalid place that is rapidly descending into chaos. Superficially this appears to be a fairly accurate assessment. But Lima is also one of the most exciting and interesting capitals in South America, and deserves to be given a fair viewing.

When Francisco Pizarro founded Lima, the 'City of Kings', in 1536, he could hardly have imagined that it would grow into today's sprawling metropolis. He chose a site beside the river Rimac a few miles inland from the coast, thereby hoping to avoid the mists that sweep in off the ocean. Since then, the river has become nothing but a trickle of water — a deficit compensated for with enormous volumes of rubbish; and the desert between the original site and the coast, has now been built over. The rapid growth which has brought Lima's population to eight million, is seen primarily in the shantytowns that sprawl around the city. Slums dominate the area around the airport and many visitors' first impressions.

These early images of human misery will soon be supplemented by visions of fine colonial buildings and museums with unrivalled collections. However, it is as an eye-witness to the daily struggles of a people that must cope with extreme deprivation, regular earth tremors, pollution and ten years of terrorism, that you are likely to be enthralled by the Peruvian capital. Lima appears to be in a permanent state of siege, and heavily-armed military types keep watch in the centre; political demonstrations and riots are commonplace, but these are the least of their worries. Life on the streets is never dull.

The weather plays a significant role in determining the appearance of the city. It rarely rains and the *garúa* does not extend to downtown Lima to clean the dirt and pollutants from the buildings, which as a result look grimy. This is less of a problem in the better residential areas, where fine villas maintain sparkling whitewashed walls.

CITY LAYOUT

The heart of the city lies on the south bank of the Río Rimac, which acts as a natural northern boundary. Just to the north and running parallel to the river is the Pan-American Highway, which runs east before curving off southwards. The other main thoroughfares through the metropolitan area are the Paseo de la República, a six-lane motorway which provides the main north-south connection on the eastern side of the city centre, and Avenida Javier Prado, which runs at right angles to it and heads east-west through the city to the port of Callao.

The colonial heart of Lima is still the centre of government and business. It lies immediately south of the river, in a large area clearly defined by Avenida Tacna, La Colmena (also known as Avenida Nicolás de Piérola) and Avenida Abancay. Most activity is centred around Plaza de Armas and Plaza San Martín, the two main squares; they are linked by Jirón de la Unión, the main shopping street. Plaza San Martín, midway along La Colmena, is a sort of Leicester Square-cum-Speakers' Corner: crowds watch polemicists speechifying on some days, and rioting demonstrators or drunken brawlers on others. In the evening they are joined by

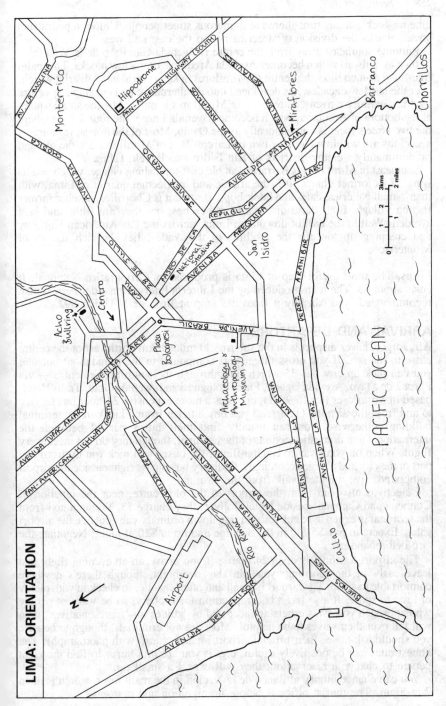

LIMA: ORIENTATION

N

Airport

Río Rímac

Callao

Buenos Aires

PAN-AMERICAN HIGHWAY (NORTH)

AVENIDA TÚPAC AMARU

AVENIDA UGARTE

Acho Bullring

Centro

Plaza Bolognesi

Archaeology & Anthropology Museum

AVENIDA GRAU

AVENIDA BRASIL

AVENIDA LA MARINA

AVENIDA DEL EJÉRCITO

AVENIDA ARGENTINA

AVENIDA BENAVIDES

AVENIDA LA PAZ

AVENIDA PÉREZ ARANÍBAR

PACIFIC OCEAN

28 DE JULIO

National Stadium

PASEO DE LA REPÚBLICA

AVENIDA AREQUIPA

San Isidro

JAVIER PRADO

AV. LARCO

AVENIDA PANAMÁ

AVENIDA ANGAMOS

Miraflores

Barranco

Chorrillos

AVENIDA LA MOLINA

Monterrico

PAN-AMERICAN HIGHWAY (CHOSICA)

FERNANDO BELAÚNDE

AVENIDA CHOSICA

Hippodrome

3kms

2 miles

2

1

1

0

cinema-goers; at any time there are numerous street people. Unión, a pedestrian street, marks the division of street names to the east and west.

Running southeast away from the centre is Avenida Garcilaso de la Vega (also known as Wilson) which becomes Avenida Arequipa after a few blocks. This palm tree-lined avenue links the centre to Miraflores, a smart residential district which, over the last few decades, has developed into an alternative and buzzing city centre for the wealthier citizens. The centre of Miraflores is marked by the small square at the bottom of Arequipa, which becomes Avenida Larco; the roundabout where the two streets meet is known locally as the Ovalo. Most of the hotels, restaurants and clubs are within a block or two of Larco. West of Miraflores are the old and predominantly wealthy districts of San Isidro and Pueblo Libre.

Southeast of Miraflores is Barranco, an old cliff-top fishing village, which retains some of its former charm. It is the artistic and intellectual quarter of Lima, with many small galleries, cafés and bookshops. Beyond it is Chorrillos, another former fishing village. Both these districts have beaches, but they are filthy and best avoided. Well to the east of downtown Lima, across the Pan-American Highway and creeping up towards the foothills of the Andes, lies the rich suburb of Monterrico.

Maps. The most useful map of Lima is produced by Cartográfica Nacional. It costs about $3. The map produced by the Librería Internacional del Perú is also recommended; you can buy it from the shop at Jirón de la Unión 892.

ARRIVAL AND DEPARTURE

Air. Jorge Chávez airport is in the suburbs 10 miles/16km northwest of the centre close to the sea. If you cross the airport compound to the roundabout outside, you can pick up city bus 35 which runs through the south of the centre — via Plaza 2 de Mayo, Avenida Ugarte, Plaza Bolognesi and Avenida Grau. Trans Hotel, based in Miraflores (tel 46-9872), operates a more expensive 24-hour bus service to and from the airport. On arrival you buy a ticket from a kiosk in the terminal building; otherwise, you can usually find their buses parked between the international and domestic sections of the terminal, though they do not meet every flight. When on your way to catch a flight, the buses will pick you up from any part of the city and charge accordingly. Ordinary buses pass right outside the airport compound, five minutes walk from the terminal.

Colectivos also run from the airport to the old centre, near the junction of Colmena and Camaná, beside Hotel Bolívar; they charge $3. Taking a taxi from the terminal is expensive, but you can flag down ordinary cabs outside the airport gates. Expect to pay $5-$10 in the daytime and up to $20 at night. Negotiate the fare beforehand.

The airport terminal is open 24 hours; if you arrive on an evening flight and leave early in the morning, you can stay overnight, though there's nowhere comfortable to sleep. The airport is small and often chaotic, so check in with plenty of time to spare. It also has a bad reputation for robbery, so be wary of people who approach you. Westerners are accosted by 'guides' or 'representatives', who will fall over themselves to be helpful. Most are not criminals, though to be sure you should ask to see their official airport identification (with photograph). The honest ones can be positively useful, e.g. if you are in a hurry to find the right person to change a reservation; they will expect a small tip.

You can change money at Banco de la Nación in the main foyer, which is open 7am-10pm. The tourist office is before immigration and customs.

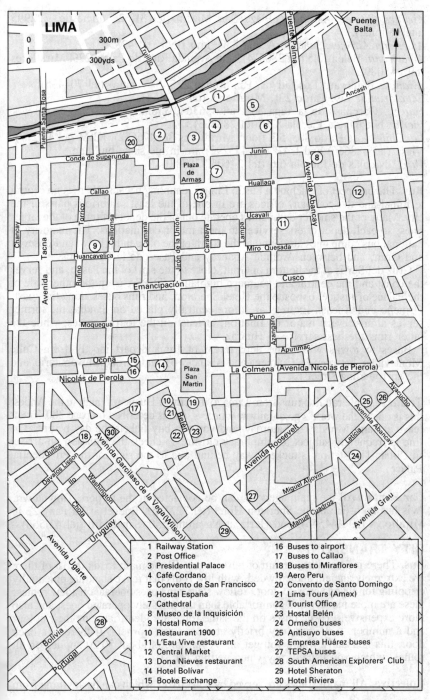

LIMA

1 Railway Station	16 Buses to airport
2 Post Office	17 Buses to Callao
3 Presidential Palace	18 Buses to Miraflores
4 Café Cordano	19 Aero Peru
5 Convento de San Francisco	20 Convento de Santo Domingo
6 Hostal España	21 Lima Tours (Amex)
7 Cathedral	22 Tourist Office
8 Museo de la Inquisición	23 Hostal Belén
9 Hostal Roma	24 Ormeño buses
10 Restaurant 1900	25 Antisuyo buses
11 L'Eau Vive restaurant	26 Empresa Huárez buses
12 Central Market	27 TEPSA buses
13 Dona Nieves restaurant	28 South American Explorers' Club
14 Hotel Bolívar	29 Hotel Sheraton
15 Booke Exchange	30 Hotel Riviera

Airlines Offices: Aeroperu: Plaza San Martín (tel 317626 domestic, 322995 international).
American Airlines: Juan de Arona 830, 14th floor (tel 428555).
Americana: Belén 1015 (tel 280474); and Avenida Ricardo Palma 229, Miraflores (tel 458089).
Avianca: Boulevard Los Olivos, Paz Soldan 225, San Isidro (tel 704435).
Ecuatoriana: José Pardo 231, Miraflores (tel 472454).
Faucett: Garcilaso de la Vega 865 (tel 336364, 338180).
Iberia: Nicolás de Piérola 820 (tel 283833).
LanChile: José Pardo 805, 5th floor, Miraflores (tel 476682). KLM (tel 471277), Viasa (tel 478666) and LAB (tel 473292) are in the same building.
Varig: Nicolás de Piérola 616 (tel 246060/287810).

Bus. The prospect of catching a bus in Lima is daunting because there is no central terminal and the company offices are in one of the least salubrious parts of the city. Many of the smaller companies operate out of the depots of three of the larger ones, so each depot offers services to most major destinations. The majority of national bus companies are found to the south of the old centre, between Roosevelt and Grau, and between Avenida Abancay and Paseo de la República.

Cruz del Sur is at the bottom of Grau, close to the start of the Paseo, and serves the coast and the central and southern highlands. TEPSA is on the other side of the Palace of Justice, opposite the Hotel Sheraton, and runs buses along the coast. Ormeño and Ancash Express are more centrally placed on Sandia; the former serves almost every major destination, at least on the tourist routes, while the latter runs the best service to Huaráz.

Buses to towns within the department of Lima depart mostly from Calle Montevideo, between La Colmena and Abancay beyond Parque Universitario, and the surrounding streets.

Train. A single rail line runs from Lima to the city of Huancayo, high in the Andes; this is one of the world's great railway journeys, and is described on page 280. Trains leave at 8am, Monday to Saturday, and you can buy tickets the day before. The line is frequently subject to temporary closure so check the situation on arrival in Lima. The station is tucked away behind and to the right of the Presidential Palace.

Car Rental. All the main agencies can be contacted at the airport. Downtown, Avis has an office in the Sheraton Hotel (tel 327245), Budget at La Paz 522 in Miraflores (tel 444546), and Hertz at Navarette 550, San Isidro (tel 421566).

CITY TRANSPORT

Bus. There is a constant stream of buses along all the main roads. Most of them are extremely ancient and crowded, with low roofs that make standing potentially crippling for anyone over six foot. Yellow state-run buses operate on a few routes; these are more modern and comfortable than the privately operated ones, and also more expensive. Private buses on the same route are identifiable by their colour and a number; they stop very briefly at most street corners. If there is a back door, this is usually where you get on. A flat fare of about $0.20 applies on all routes, which you usually pay when getting off.

Colectivo. All major routes are served by colectivos, which can be anything from large cars to small minibuses. People are crammed in like sardines, but if you don't object to mild discomfort, this is a good way to get around: colectivos, once they are full, zip pleasingly quickly in and out of the traffic. They can be hailed at most street corners. Expect to pay a flat fare of about $0.25.

Taxi. There are official taxis with meters, but most cabs in Lima are clapped-out wrecks belonging to private individuals making some extra money in their spare time. These sport a small 'Taxi' sign in the top corner of the windscreen, which is replaced at night by a small red light. The free for all results in utter chaos, but it at least gives you plenty of scope to shop around. You must always agree your fare when you get in: expect to pay $1-2 for a short journey, $3-4 for a trip across the city centre. It is an advantage to know exactly where you are going, or at least to have a good map — if you want to go anywhere that is even vaguely obscure, your driver is unlikely to know how to get there.

ACCOMMODATION
With the fall in tourism you are unlikely to have problems finding a room in Lima. Several of the budget hotels that were popular among travellers during the 1980s are now dirty and unsafe. A few in the centre can still be recommended, but an increasing number of people head for the family-run places in San Isidro and Miraflores — these have become popular for their friendliness, security and location away from the chaos and dangers of the centre.

Downtown. Hostal Roma on Ica, three blocks west of Unión (tel 277576) remains popular. It is in an old colonial building, and is safe and reasonably friendly as well as central. Also in a good position is Hostal Wiracocha (Junín 284; tel 271178, 274406), just off Plaza de Armas. It is a zany Art Deco place, and there are good cheap restaurants nearby. Hostal España (Azangaro 105), opposite the San Francisco monastery, is also very popular. It is run by a friendly and trustworthy family, has a roof terrace and cheap rooms, mostly shared; they will look after your luggage while you are out of the city. The San Sebastián (Ica 712, at the junction with Cañete; tel 232740) is more basic than the other two. Hostal Belén (Belén 1049), almost opposite the tourist office in a large old building, is the other good bet in the centre. Expect to pay about $5-6 for a single at all the above places. If you are on your own it's worth seeking out the main travellers' hotels, since downtown Lima is best explored in company.

Miraflores. Casa Escobar (Domingo Elias 230; tel 457565), two blocks east of Arequipa and six blocks north from the centre of Miraflores, is a family home and strongly recommended. Rooms have private bathrooms, and there is a pleasant sitting-room. Also recommended is Casa José Luís (F. de Paula Ugarriza 727; tel 441015), which is several blocks east of the centre of Miraflores across the Paseo. There are English-speakers in both households, and everyone is very helpful. Expect to pay $8-10.
   The Youth Hostel at Avenida Casimiro Ulloa 328 (tel 465488), east of Larco is cheap and a good place to meet travellers. Non-members can stay, and you can pick up a list of Peru's other hostels.

San Isidro. For a more upmarket room stay in the attractive Hostal Señorial (José González 567; tel 459724) in San Isidro, which has rooms arranged around an attractive garden. Similarly priced at $15-20 is the family-run Hostal Mont Blanc

(Emilio Fernández 640; tel 338055), two blocks east of Arequipa and well situated for both downtown Lima and Miraflores. It has a café, and the family can arrange tours of the city. They have a check-in desk at the airport beside the arrival gate.

EATING AND DRINKING

Downtown. There are several cafés and restaurants along Unión, and within a block on either side. Vendors also set up stalls in the street selling churros — the crispy rolled up pancakes are better than the thin piped ones, especially when freshly cooked.

A block east of Unión, next to the Presidential Palace, is Café Cordano. It has changed little since the turn of the century, with its old wall fittings, sawdust on the floor and an interesting clientele consisting primarily of dapper businessmen; it is particularly recommended for breakfast and lunch.

Possibly the most unique restaurant in the whole of Peru is L'Eau Vive (Ucayali 370; tel 275712), near the corner of Lampa. It is run by nuns who serve you at long tables in the refectory. The menu is limited but the food is excellent and good value. At 10pm the nuns put down their trays, and diners are treated to a rendition of Ave Maria. L'Eau Vive is open for lunch and supper. A block west and north takes you to Carabaya between Ucayali and Huallaga; the Doña Nieves restaurant does excellent food from the Arequipa region, while next door the Salon de Té Don Juan is popular and fun.

For more traditional surroundings head for Restaurant 1900 (tel 233590), in the southwest corner of Plaza San Martín. Weavings and musical instruments decorate the walls and there is a pleasant patio where lunches are served. In the evening a band plays Andean music.

Miraflores. Both San Isidro and Miraflores have many expensive restaurants, as well as a range of American fast food joints, including Pizza Hut and Kentucky Fried Chicken. You will search in vain for MacDonald's, but Peru has its own version, known as MacTambo, which has branches dotted all over the place.

For a more tempting and yet affordable meal you will probably have to rely on the pizzerias that spread over the pavement in Pasaje San Ramón, which leads west from Oscar Benavides. This short pedestrian precinct has a higher concentration of pizzerias than any other street in the world: a total of 22 line the street and they compete to offer the cheapest wine and sangria. Choose one of the busiest, such as Don Corleone, at the eastern end. Pasaje San Ramón is a popular hangout for young Peruvians, and it gets very lively in the evenings. More exclusive restaurants are gathered around cobbled courtyards on Avenida La Paz, a couple of blocks east of Larco. At the junction of Arequipa and Larco, bang in the centre of Miraflores, the cafés Liverpool and La Tiendecita Blanca are good places for coffee and cake.

Tucked away on Atahualpa, a block from the bottom of Arequipa, is the Brenchley Arms: This is the nearest thing to an English pub in Lima, though the beer and the high security are distinctly Peruvian: you must ring a bell to be let in. Inside, you could be in an expat pub anywhere — an extraordinarily disorientating experience. A beer costs $2, payable in dollars or local currency.

La Rosa Naútica (tel 470057) is built out over the ocean on a pier below Miraflores. It is Lima's most famous restaurant, boasting politicians and drug-traffickers for customers; armed men stand guard outside. The luxurious décor, wonderful seafood and a glimpse at Lima's rich and famous will cost you $20-25 a head.

Barranco. The Hampstead of Lima can be as lively as Miraflores in the evening. There are cafés and pubs around the main square, and Puente de los Suspiros (The Bridge of Sighs), which overlooks the ocean, is a good place to watch the sun go down. For typical creole cuisine and live music go to El Otro Sitio (Sucre 317; tel 772413), close to the Bridge of Sighs; expect to pay upwards of $15. Barranco is the best place in town to have a few beers. There are lots of *chupodromos*, where beer is sold in a half-litre glass known as a *chopp*. One of the most popular is Curich, on Grau overlooking the municipal park. Virtually next door is the Café Literario, in the back parlour of an old-fashioned pharmacy. La Casona (nearby at Grau 329) is a pub specializing in jazz and contemporary music. There are a number of others in the same street, most of them staying open for much of the night.

EXPLORING
Downtown Lima contains most of the historic sites, all within a few blocks of Plaza de Armas. The museums are spread around the city.

Downtown. Plaza de Armas is the grandest of Lima's squares. It used to have a certain elegance, but it now feels rather bare and forlorn. The square has been the focus for numerous political rallies over the decades, most dramatically in recent years when Alan García attempted to win over the people to his policies in the late 1980s. There are usually large numbers of military personnel and police hanging about, and it's not a place to sit around and relax.

On its north side, backing on to the river, the Presidential Palace is an impressive but not a beautiful building. The best time to visit is 12.30-1pm when you can witness the changing of the guard. The peculiar goose-step style march is a chilling sight. Men armed with automatic weapons stand nearby, keeping a wary eye on spectators.

The exterior of the cathedral, in the southeast corner, was restored in the mid-1980s. The delicate plaster on bamboo construction inside has survived numerous earthquakes and proved more robust than many modern buildings. The first chapel contains what are said to be the mummified remains of Francisco Pizarro, which were discovered beneath the high altar in 1977; the head and body are kept in separate boxes. Adjacent is a small museum of religious art, but more interesting are the workshops of the cathedral's picture restorers, which can also be visited; a tour (obligatory) of both costs $1.

The Convento de San Francisco is one of the oldest and most fascinating places in Lima. It lies on Ancash, two blocks northeast of the Plaza de Armas. The design shows strong Arabic influences (as there are in many of the oldest colonial buildings in the city), and there are numerous decorative tiles imported from Spain. A visit to San Francisco is not complete without a tour to the catacombs, which are piled high with the bones of former worshippers, arranged in extraordinary patterns. The catacombs are open 10am-1pm and 3-6pm, with the last tours running at 12.45pm and 5.45pm respectively.

Two blocks beyond San Francisco is Plaza Bolívar, with a statue of the liberator and the Congress building. Most interesting, however, is the Museo de la Inquisición, which contains many of the instruments of torture used by the officials of the Spanish Inquisition during their time in Peru (1570-1820); these are displayed in the cells where the accused were held. It is open 9am-7pm, Monday to Friday and 9am-4.30pm on Saturdays.

A short walk southwest, on Ucayali, is the Torre Tagle Palace, the attractive early 18th century home of one of independent Peru's first leaders, after whom it is named. It has beautifully carved wooden balconies, further evidence of Moorish influence: the wives of the early colonists were not permitted out onto the streets of the city unaccompanied, and they had to observe the world discreetly from the balconies. The palace now houses part of the Peruvian Foreign Office, but you should still be able to stick your head into the main courtyard during working hours. There are several other houses dating from a similar period in the same area.

The oldest convent in Lima is Santo Domingo, which dates from 1549; it is on Superunda, two blocks northwest of the Plaza de Armas. It has a fine 16th-century wooden cloister, while the tower dates from the 18th century. Inside are the much venerated tombs of Santa Rosa de Lima, the first saint in the New World, and San Martín de Porras, Peru's first black saint. The church is open 7am-1pm and 4-8pm, while the monastery cloisters and tombs are open 9am-noon and 3-5pm.

Pueblo Libre. In this district is the Museo Nacional de Antropología y Arqueología, which presents the history of Peru from pre-historic times to the start of the colonial period. It has a wide variety of exhibits, including scenes of life in pre-Inca times, textiles from the early coastal valley cultures, models of Inca cities and a tall monolith from Chavín de Huántar. Among the most bizarre objects are the distorted skulls and the extraordinary mummies in funeral dress. You need at least half a day to explore the museum thoroughly. The museum is open 9am-6pm Monday to Saturday. The entrance fee is about $4.

Almost adjacent, on Parque Bolívar, is the Museo Nacional de Historia, which was the residence of San Martín and Bolívar in the early days of Independence. The house has been restored to its former glory, with many pieces of colonial furniture and paintings. There is also a very pleasant garden at the rear. It opens 9am-6pm and entrance also costs about $4.

The Museo Rafael Larco Herrera (at Bolívar 1515) contains an excellent archaeological collection, much of it in remarkably good condition. Most exhibits are from the main coastal cultures of the first millenium AD, and there is an interesting display of erotic art. It opens 9am-1pm and 3-6pm.

To get to Pueblo Libre take a bus along Avenida Brasil from Plaza Bolognesi, downtown. Avenida and Parque Bolívar both lie several blocks west of Avenida Brasil.

Other Museums. *Museo de Oro:* this is a truly dazzling spectacle, with the best collection of precious objects in Peru, and probably the best in South America outside Colombia. The pieces date from pre-Inca and Inca times and include huge golden discs, some encrusted with jewels, and fabulous necklaces. Most delicate are the tiny figurines and animals, in both silver and gold. The museum also contains a remarkably extensive and well-preserved collection of weapons and uniforms, mainly dating from the early colonial and immediate post-independence era. The museum, at Avenida Alonso de Molina 1110 in Monterrico district, lies several blocks beyond the Pan-American Highway. Take a taxi or a bus running east along Avenida Angamos from the junction with Arequipa. It opens noon-7pm.

Museo Nacional: this museum opened only in 1990, and is housed in the former headquarters of the Banco de la Nación, a strange-looking office block at Avenida Javier Prado Oeste 2466, in the district of San Borja. Scale and life-size models,

they are rarely advertised, and are small scale, intimate occasions, often taking place in someone's home. The music tends to be based on the sounds and rhythms of the coastal black population, and are a far cry from the stage-managed affairs laid on for tourists. Your hotel should help you to track one down; you usually pay about $5 to get in.

SHOPPING

San Isidro contains some of the most upmarket shops in Lima, including the luxurious Camino Real shopping centre — this is worth a look, whether or not you want to buy anything. Miraflores also has plenty of expensive boutiques, but more interesting is the small fair in the district's central park, where paintings, jewellery and crafts are sold in the afternoon and evening by candlelight. There are other crafts stalls three blocks north, on Avenida Petit Thouars (which runs a block east of Arequipa), open during the day and early evening. Five blocks further north, at Tacna 460, is Antisuyo, a shop specializing in Amazon crafts, with a small selection also from the Sierra; the quality is good throughout.

For many years the main centre for crafts in Lima was Avenida de la Marina, on the way to Callao. A large number of shops and stalls line the road, with products from all over the country. With the recent drop off in tourism, however, traders have found it increasingly hard to make a living, and the quality has declined. If you want to have a look take a bus west along Prado. More central is the small market behind the main post office; prices are fairly reasonable, but the choice small.

Bookshops. The best shop for English-language books is beneath the El Pacífico cinema in Miraflores. In the city centre, the small Booke Exchange shop *(sic)* at Ocoña 211, a block from Plaza San Martín, and the ABC bookstore at La Colmena 689 also keep some English-language books and magazines.

CRIME AND SAFETY

There is occasional terrorist activity in the capital, but this is unlikely to affect you, unless in the form of blackouts and water shortages. The main problem is theft. Foreigners are obvious targets for street children and pickpockets, particularly in the crowded old centre. Be vigilant wherever you are and at any time of day. After dark the centre is the domain of street people, and the lack of good lighting makes the area even more dangerous: do not go out alone. San Isidro and Miraflores are perfectly safe during the day, though even here you should take greater care at night.

HELP AND INFORMATION

Tourist Information: the tourist office is at Belén 1066 (tel 323559), close to Plaza San Martín, in the rear courtyard of a large colonial house. It is open 8am-7pm Monday to Friday. The staff give out city maps and advice on buses, special events, etc., and they are reasonably well informed about places outside the capital. The South American Explorers Club (Avenida Portugal 146, off Avenida Alfonso Ugarte in the centre; tel 314480) provides up-to-date information on all areas of the country, stores luggage, reconfirms flights, sells books and equipment, etc. It opens 9.30am-5pm on weekdays.

Post Office: the main office is a sight in itself, the most spectacular *correo* in South America. This cavernous colonial building is in the first block of Conde de Superunda, west of Plaza de Armas. It is open 8am-6.30pm Monday to Friday, 8.15am-5.30pm on Saturday and 8am-noon on Sunday. The Poste Restante office is on the far side of the building in Calle Camaná. If you need cards, envelopes or wrapping paper, the teeming shopping arcade which runs through the middle of it will provide.

There is a branch office on La Colmena, opposite the luxury Hotel Crillón, which opens 8am-10pm Monday to Saturday, and 8am-noon on Sunday. There are other offices in San Isidro at Libertadores 325 and in Miraflores at Petit Thouars 5201, which open Monday to Friday only.

Telephone Office: the main Entel office is at La Colmena 878, on Plaza San Martín. It opens 7am-11pm Monday to Friday, 8am-10pm on Saturday and 8am-8pm on Sunday.

Money: there are moneychangers virtually everywhere, but their principal hangouts are the bottom of Unión, the southerly blocks of Camaná, and Ocoña; such is the competition that some changers advertise their willingness to buy ripped banknotes. There are several cambios and banks in the same area, but the main banking district is southeast of Plaza de Armas and northeast of Plaza San Martín. If you have problems changing travellers cheques in the street or in a casa de cambio, go to the Banco de Crédito (Lampa 499; tel 275600), which can also give cash advances on a Visa card. Moneychangers also gather in the main shopping streets of Miraflores and San Isidro.

The American Express agent is Lima Tours (Belén 1040; tel 276624/240831), near the tourist office. It opens Monday to Friday, 9.15am-4.45pm.

Immigration Office: Paseo de la República 585, a block before Avenida 28 de Julio (tel 276927).

Instituto Geográfico Nacional: Avenida Aramburu 1190 at Panamá (tel 451939), north of Miraflores. It sells maps and aerial photos, and opens 8am-12.30pm and 1.30-3.30pm, Monday to Friday; take your passport.

Radio: reception isn't good in Lima. For the best news programmes tune into Radio Programas del Perú, on 730AM. You can listen to soul on 94.1FM and soft rock on 88.3FM.

Medical Care: two of the best private clinics, with English-speaking staff, are Clínica Anglo-Americana (Avenida Salazar, San Isidro; tel 403570) and Clínica Internacional (Washington 1475; tel 288060).

Embassies and Consulates. Most are open 9am-1pm Monday to Friday.
Argentina: Avenida Felipe Pardo y Aliaga 640, San Isidro (tel 729920).
Bolivia: Los Castaños 235, San Isidro (tel 223418, 402095).
Brazil: Avenida José Pardo 850, Miraflores (tel 462635).
Chile: Avenida Javier Prado Oeste 790, San Isidro (tel 407965, 403300).
Colombia: Avenida Arequipa 2685 (tel 404140).
Ecuador: Las Palmeras 356, San Isidro (tel 409991, 409941).
Paraguay: Avenida El Rosario 415, San Isidro (tel 418154, 400318).
Uruguay: Avenida Larco 1013, 12th floor, Miraflores (tel 462047).
Venezuela: Avenida Arequipa 298 (tel 314510).

UK: Edificio El Pacífico Washington, 12th floor, Natalio Sánchez 125, Plaza Washington (tel 355032, 334738), off Avenida Arequipa, on the border of downtown Lima and San Isidro. Open 8.45am-5pm Monday to Thursday and 8.45am-1.15pm on Fridays.

USA: Grimaldo del Solar 346-358, Miraflores (tel 443621), a block west of the Paseo; open 8-11am, Monday to Friday. The Embassy is at Garcilaso de la Vega 1400 (tel 338000).

AROUND LIMA

Pachacámac. This site is named after the creator god, who was adopted by the Incas when they subjugated the people of the area. It is 19 miles/30km south of Lima, close to the Pan-American Highway.

The oldest part of the site is on a large hill. The Incas built a Temple of the Sun on its summit, with fine views out to sea and into the adjoining Luren valley. A series of platforms is all that remains of the buildings, but the view at least is still there. Nearer to the entrance are the principal Inca ruins — an *acllahuasi*. This is a 'house of the chosen women' or 'house of the virgins', where girls were educated to serve the Temple of the Sun and fulfil other ceremonial roles. When a new emperor ascended the throne or at times of great hardship a few of them were selected for sacrifice — it was considered a great honour if your daughter was chosen. The adobe walls have been restored and give a clear picture of how the buildings would have looked originally. In comparison, the crumbling remains of the pre-Inca Temple of Pachacámac are disappointing. There is a small museum at the entrance; like the site, it is open 9am-5pm.

Buses leave every half-hour or so from the junction of Montevideo and La Colmena, and run throughout the day; the journey takes about one hour.

Marcahuasi. High in the Andes 50 miles/80km inland from Lima, rises a hillside covered in bizarre rock formations. The strange array of vast rounded boulders and razor sharp rocks are especially dramatic at sunrise and sunset, or under a full moon — at such times it is easy to imagine why the early cultures and the Incas were in awe of them. The ruins of several ceremonial buildings remain.

Marcahuasi lies in a spectacular spot near San Pedro de Casta, a small village high in the mountains at 10,700ft/3,200m. To reach San Pedro begin by taking a bus or colectivo from Parque Universitario to Chosica, 25 miles/40km east. Arrive in Chosica by about 8.30am to be certain of finding transport on to San Pedro. This can be done most easily on Mondays, Wednesdays and Fridays or during major national holidays, when more trucks and pickups head up that way. The journey to San Pedro takes about three hours. Stay the night in one of the village's two cheap hostales.

The rocks lie at 13,300ft/4,000m, a good two-hour walk above San Pedro. Leave at dawn to avoid climbing in the midday heat; you can hire donkeys to carry your pack. To enjoy the spectacular evening and dawn views, camp overnight among the rocks; in the dry season (June-October) you will need to carry water up to the site.

Transport heads down from the village at about 9am most days.

NORTH OF LIMA

The Pan-American Highway heads north out of Lima through progressively more ramshackle suburbs. Eighteen miles/30km north is Ancón, the favoured beach resort of wealthy Limeños. Beyond here the road runs around a series of headlands, with precipitous drops to the ocean below, before crossing the Chancay valley. There are many artefacts from this valley in museums around Peru, but no archaeological sites of note remain in the area.

Huacho is a large market town near the mouth of the river Huaura. Beyond it, not far from the junction of the Pan-American Highway and the Huaráz road, is Barranca. This is a good place to stop overnight en route between the coast and Huaráz; the Hostal Central is the best place to stay.

High on a bluff overlooking the sea, just north of Pativilca and the Huaráz turn-off, are the large adobe ruins of Paramonga. The fortress is of Chimú origin and at one stage marked the southern boundary of the great Chimú empire. It has been reconstructed and consists of several large platforms facing out to sea. It is the size rather than the quality of the construction that impresses.

Callejón de Huaylas

The hidden valley of Callejón de Huaylas lies high in the Andes, 50 miles/80km in from the coast. Carved out by the Santa river, it is lined by the magnificent snow-covered Cordillera Blanca mountains to the east and the lower Cordillera Negra to the west. The Cordillera Blanca is known as the Peruvian Alps — an accurate description apart from the fact that there are no ski resorts — and offers superb trekking and climbing. At the northern end of the valley the Santa river veres down to the coast, cutting through the spectacular Cañon del Pato. To the south are the Huayhuash mountains, which are no less beautiful than the Cordillera Blanca. But the area has been infiltrated by terrorists and it is closed to visitors for the foreseeable future.

The towns of the Callejón are nothing special to look at, but they are all bases for trips up the narrow valleys into the mountains.

HUARAZ

The area around Huaráz, the biggest town in the valley, was severely damaged in the terrible earthquake of 1970. Most of those made homeless moved into the town, which has grown considerably in size as a result; it now has a population of around 80,000. The rebuilding was haphazard and necessarily rapid — even the main square is incomplete. However, the backdrop is breathtaking, dominated by the huge glacial peak of Huascarán, Peru's highest mountain.

Huaráz is the main trekking centre in Callejón de Huaylas, though few hikes begin from the town itself. While trying to arrange a trip, there are various things to see and do. There is a small archaeology museum next to the tourist office in the main square; exhibits include some Chavín obelisks. Fifteen minutes by bus north of town are the thermal baths of Monterrey; though part of Hotel Monterrey, they are open to the public. Buses leave from Avenida Luzuriaga.

The small Huari ruins of Wilkawain make a good half-day walk: they are reached up a signposted track that leads off the main road just north of the town. The stone buildings lie low against the hillside; take a torch so you can see inside. You can continue beyond the ruins towards Lake Llaca or into Quebrada Copjup, but you'll need a tent.

Arrival and Departure. Ancash Express offers the most reliable bus service from Lima (8 hours); competing with it are Norandino, Empresa Transportes 14, Trome and Transportes Rodríguez. Most buses are bound for Caráz, 40 miles/64km north of Huaráz. Chinchaysuyo provides connections via Pativilca to Chimbote, Trujillo and most major northern destinations. Only Transportes Moreno travels through the spectacular Cañon del Pato to Chimbote, a trip that takes 10-12 hours. The road is unpaved and follows the route of the Santa railway, which was wiped out in the 1970 earthquake: it is an extremely dusty ride, especially if you sit at the back. The best bus to get is the 9am departure, and you may need to book a day in advance.

Small buses connecting Huaráz with the other settlements along the main road through the valley run to and from town about every 20 minutes; you can pick them up in Avenida Luzuriaga, between the river and Raimondi in the centre.

Accommodation. There is no shortage of hotels in Huaráz, though few are exceptionally good. Edward's Inn (Avenida Bolognesi 121; tel 722692), three blocks west of Avenida Tarapacá, is the best. It is very friendly, with a cactus garden, a small café, and views of the Cordillera Blanca from the top balcony; it is also a secure place to leave luggage while trekking. Also good, but more cramped, is Alojamiento Galaxia (Romero 638), which overlooks a small square one block east of Tarapacá; try to get a room around the courtyard at the back. The Hostal Alfredo, just over the bridge on Luzuriaga, is also good value. All three officially charge $4-5 per person, but they can be negotiated down if business is poor. The large Hostal Cataluña (Avenida Raimondi 622; tel 72117), a block from Luzuriaga, offers superb views of the mountains, but is overpriced.

Eating and Drinking. Avenida Luzuriaga is lined with restaurants. Close to the bridge are market stalls serving excellent *papas rellenos* and *anticuchos* (kebabs). At the junction with Raimondi are two cafés — the Tabariz and Sandra, which serve good local food. The Chifa Familiar is the best place for semi-oriental food and has good ice-cream. Further along Luzuriaga, beyond the main square, is a collection of pizzerias: Mama Mia's is the best.

If you have some energy left after a trek, the Salsadromo next to Café Sandra in Luzuriaga is an interesting place to finish off an evening.

Help and Information. To find fellow walkers, look at the noticeboard in the tourist information office in the main square. Also visit the Casa de Guías, on a small adjoining square, which is another good source of information. They are keen for you to hire one of their members as a guide, though this is not a prerequisite for them to offer assistance. You can hire equipment here and also from several tour agencies along Avenida Luzuriaga. Stock up on food and other essentials at the market in the blocks either side of Raimondi. Moneychangers congregate at Luzuriaga and Raimondi.

CHAVIN DE HUANTAR

On the opposite side of the Cordillera Blanca to Huaráz, 70 miles/110km east, lies Chavín de Huántar. Near this small town is one of the most significant sites in the early history of Peru. Chavín was the main focus of a state based around a religious cult in the 8th-3rd centuries BC. The temple attracted pilgrims from all over the central Andes.

The main building is a stepped pyramid containing several levels of underground passages, connected by numerous chambers and shafts. At intervals carvings of grotesque heads jut out from the passageway walls. In one high chamber, cutting through several levels, is an extraordinarily tall and thin monolith, which has been sculpted with anthropomorphic figures, reptiles and deities. The precise purpose of the deep, dark chambers is unknown, but they are thought to have provided access to spirit worlds. Outside there are more ferocious figures carved into smooth rock slabs. Only some of the upper levels can now be visited, and take a torch.

There are a couple of basic hotels in the town and all restaurants are simple and close early. Transportes Marino, on Raimondi, and Transportes Huascarán, on San Martín, in Huaráz, both run daily buses to Chavín. It is also possible to arrange a tour, but this makes for a very long day. Check that the area is safe to visit before setting out because a Sendero group was there at one time.

YUNGAY

In 1970 nearly 30,000 people, virtually the entire population of Yungay, died in seconds when a large section of Mount Huascarán slid down into the valley at a fantastic speed. The sheer west face of the mountain is a constant testimony to that terrible day. A statue of Christ on a small hill marks the entrance to the old town from the south; the flat area immediately beyond it is now a monument to those who died. You can see two parts of the old cathedral, which are now 300 yards apart, and the remains of a bus sticks up dramatically out of the ground.

A short distance to the north is new Yungay, which is as unattractive as the rebuilt areas of Huaráz. The only reason to stop here is to visit the Lagos Llanganucos or hike the Santa Cruz Loop, described below.

Yungay is 33 miles/53 km north of Huaráz. Hostal Gledel and La Casa del Señor Blanco are pleasant, friendly places to stay.

CARAZ

This is the last town of any size in the valley. It is also the most picturesque, having survived several recent earthquakes virtually unscathed. On the approach from the south vast fields of flowers line the road, while north of the town groves of orange trees in the shadow of the snow-capped peaks add splashes of colour.

Caráz was once served by a railway from Chimbote which, in a series of tunnels, squeezed dramatically through the narrow Cañon del Pato. A road now runs along the route of the old line, and Transportes Moreño offers a daily departure at 11am; this magnificent journey takes 8-10 hours.

Caráz has a small zoo, which is worth a visit; it is often included on day tours from Huaráz to Lagos Llanganucos (see below).

Accommodation: the best place to stay is in the house of Profesor Bernadino Aguilar Prieto (San Martín 1143), just off the main square. The rooms are cheap and comfortable, and the breakfasts excellent — the professor is an avid beekeeper and serves his own honey. He will take you to his farm, where he also has a swimming pool and horses for hire.

The best hotel is the Chavín, adjoining the professor's house. The once popular Hostal La Suiza Peruana, nearby, is now dirty and neglected; the Hostal Morovi, at the southern entrance to the town, has only a little more to recommend it. There are several basic restaurants around the main square, but they all close early.

Lago Parón. Set high in the mountains and with brilliant turquoise waters fed by glaciers, Lago Parón is the most beautiful lake in the Cordillera Blanca. It is 18 miles/30km east of Caráz and is reached up a steep, rough and winding road. A one-day tour by taxi from Caráz or Huaráz costs $25-30. Alternatively, it is a full day's walk each way from Caráz, through magnificent scenery. There is room to camp below the lake, but it may be possible to stay inside a nearby Electroperú building (if the guard on duty is feeling obliging).

THE SANTA CRUZ LOOP

This is the most spectacular of the easier treks in the Cordillera Blanca. The amount of climbing involved is minimized if you begin in Yungay and proceed via the Lagos Llanganucos and end in Cashapampa, back in the Santa valley, north of Caráz.

The beautiful emerald-coloured Lagos Llanganucos are situated high above Yungay, in a narrow gorge between the peaks of Huascarán and Huandoy. A few trucks usually go up very early in the morning, taking a couple of hours to negotiate the endless hairpin bends. It takes a full day to walk up — an interesting hike up a path through patches of cloud forest. Taxis from Huaráz (but not Yungay) will also take you up there, but expect to pay about $25. The lakes lie within the Huascarán National Park and there is a $2 entrance fee. This can be paid at the entrance or at the Park headquarters in Huaráz (at the top of Raimondi), where you can also arrange to stay in the small lodge by the lower lake. There are possible campsites near the lodge and also beyond the second lake.

In the mid-1980s the road was extended from the lakes over the Portachuelo Pass (15,835ft/4,750m), and down to the tiny communities of Colcabamba and Yanama. This road cuts out what was previously a strenuous and not especially interesting climb from the lakes over the pass: trucks to the lakes continue over the pass to Colcabamba and beyond. Colcabamba, a day's walk from the lakes, is an attractive village of stone houses with wooden balconies and masses of geraniums. You can stay at the Calogne family guest house east of the square, with its incredible assortment of ancient wrought-iron beds, including a four-poster. They provide meals.

From Colcabamba the trail runs northwest up Quebrada Huaripampa, initially through beautiful meadows. Up a side valley to the left you can catch fine glimpses of the sharp-edged Artesonraju (20,085ft/6,025m) — it is over such craggy peaks that you have the best chance of spotting a condor. About three hours further up the valley an interesting detour can be made into the steep-sided Quebrada Paria, where there is a good campsite beyond the waterfall.

The main trail then rises steeply — be sure to stay on the upwards trail on the left side of the valley — before reaching a flatter section with a number of small lakes. It is possible to camp in this area below the pass, in the shadow of Taulliraju, with its impressive glaciers. The climb up to Punta Unión (15,835ft/4,750m), to the west, is steep and traverses some huge rock slabs. The pass itself is a small niche cut into a sharp ridge; on the other side is a fantastic view over Quebrada Santa Cruz.

The initial descent into the valley is also steep, but the path quickly levels out and there is a sizeable lake — known as Jatuncocha or Laguna Grande — with good camping sites around it. The trail crosses from the left to the right side of the valley a couple of times, but is quite distinct. You may well see Andean geese in this area, and the strange giant coot, which resembles the European version except for the fact that it is the size of a large turkey. Up a small side valley to the right, just before the lake, you can see Alpamayo, nominated by climbers in a poll as the 'most beautiful mountain in the world.' The final part of the trek involves a rocky descent into the narrowing valley. It is possible to camp at the end of the trail near the road. The village of Cashapampa lies an hour's walk to the south, and has hourly buses down a hair-raising road to Caráz.

This trek is suitable for anyone with mountain-walking experience and who is well acclimatized. Allow four days if spending the first night at Colcabamba, and an extra day if walking from Yungay to the lakes. As far as Colcabamba the road acts as the trail, though where there are extensive hairpin bends a separate trail shortens the route. Beyond the village, the track is well worn, apart from just above Quebrada Paria, where care is needed. You will need to camp at high altitude at least once, so take appropriate gear.

NORTHERN PERU

Heading north along the coast from Barranca, past Paramonga (see page 269), you reach Casma, in the desert 100 miles/160km further north. Nearby are the ancient ruins of Sechín. They are even more mysterious than those of Chavín, and appear to fit into no known pre-Inca culture. The most fascinating feature are the tall dancers etched onto granite boulders. Several adobe buildings are reasonably well preserved, and they contain further mysterious murals. There are hotels in Casma.

Chimbote is probably Peru's nastiest city. The stench from the combined outpourings of the fishmeal works, steelworks and port is appalling, and on most days a large cloud of pollution turns the sky orange. In the mid-1970s more fish was landed at Chimbote than any other port in the world, but the boom days are long over and the city now has some of the worst shanties in the country. There is every reason to avoid Chimbote, unless you're travelling through the Cañon del Pato to or from the Callejón de Huaylas. The Transportes Moreño bus leaves for Caráz and Huaráz at 7am, so you really have to stay overnight in Chimbote (and hope that it is not fully booked by the time you arrive). Hotel Augusto on Aguirre, at the intersection with de la Torre is a bearable place to stay. Just to add to its charms, Chimbote has a reputation for theft.

TRUJILLO

The city of Trujillo lies near the mouth of the Río Moche, at the heart of an area of great archaeological importance. The valley was one of the first coastal valleys to be settled in Peru and was the homeland of two of the country's great pre-Inca cultures — the Moche or Mochica, and later the Chimú. The Moche are renowned for their beautiful pottery and the huge temples, or *huacas*, which they constructed out of adobe bricks. The Chimú empire, which covered much of northern coastal Peru, was absorbed by the Incas in the 15th century, complete with its customs and buildings. The Chimús' greatest legacy is their capital, the largest adobe city in the world — Chan-Chan.

The Spanish founded Trujillo between the sites of the old Moche and Chimú cities in 1536. Several of the magnificent colonial houses, convents and monasteries remain in the centre, and they have been splendidly restored. The Plaza de Armas is one of the most attractive in Peru, with nearly all the old architecture intact. The good condition of the buildings here and elsewhere in the city is largely a result of the investment that followed the rise to the presidency of Alan García of the APRA party. Haya de la Torre, founder of APRA, was a native of Trujillo, and the city has been the party's base for over 50 years.

With a population of approaching one million, Trujillo is capital of the Department of La Libertad.

City Layout. The busy Avenida España acts as a ring-road, enclosing the city centre; remains of old Spanish fortifications can still be seen along parts of it. Within España, streets are laid out in a grid pattern, with the Plaza de Armas in the centre.

Arrival and Departure. *Air:* the airport is 5 miles/8km north of the city, close to the seaside village of Huanchaco. Faucett and AeroPeru both serve the route from Lima daily, some services continuing beyond Trujillo to other northern cities. The Faucett office is in Pizarro, just east of the square, and the AeroPeru office is at Almagro and Bolívar.

Bus: at least ten bus companies provide frequent connnections with Lima, eight hours south; the most reliable are Sudamericano, TEPSA and Ormeño. Their offices are just south of blocks 22/23 of España, south of the centre close to the intersection with Almagro. The best services to the north are run by Transportes Piura, on Mansiche, close to the main stadium north of the centre; and Expreso Vulkano, on the first turning to the left off Mansiche from España. Both have regular departures to Chiclayo and Piura throughout the day. Vulkano, along with Etecsa (in block 19 of Avenida España, south of the city centre), both run buses to Cajamarca (7 hours), but there are surprisingly few departures; Vulkano is the only company with a daytime bus, leaving at 10.30am.

Accommodation. Most hotels in Trujillo are expensive and there is not a particularly good choice. Hotel Americano (Pizarro 764), three blocks northeast of the main square, is in a huge old colonial building, but it has little else to recommend it. Just around the corner in Colón, is Hotel Colón, which is smaller, brighter and friendlier. Another reasonable place to stay is the new Hotel El Palacio (block 5 of Grau, at Zela), near several bus company offices; with lower prices than some others it is often full. Slightly more expensive is the Hotel Chan-Chan, a block south of España on Huayna Capac, the continuation of Orbegoso.

Eating and Drinking. Calle Pizarro, running east from the square, has the monopoly of good restaurants. El Sol, on block six, serves reasonable vegetarian meals and opens early for breakfast, though it's dim and often crowded. Virtually next door is El Mesón de Cervantes, with tables outside in a large courtyard — a good place to while away an afternoon. One of the most popular places among travellers is the Romano, opposite Hotel Americano.

Exploring. Houses in Trujillo are typically set around courtyards, often with fine wooden, stone or wrought-iron colonnades. Among the finest examples are La Casa del Risco (Junín and Ayacucho) and La Casa de la Emancipación (Pizarro and Gamarra): both have wonderful polished wooden columns and balustrades, and frescoes. Also on Pizarro, near the corner of Junín, is the neo-classical Palacio Iturregui. It was built in the late 18th century, and has superb wrought-iron partitions and window coverings.

The most representative of all the colonial houses in Trujillo, however, is La Casa Ganoza Chopitea, on Independencia. It demonstrates a great variety of architectural styles, with a fine baroque entrance, and a smattering of neo-classical and rococo designs elsewhere in the building. This and most other houses are owned by banks or other institutions, but you can usually step into the courtyards, and in some explore further.

Not far from Casa Chopitea is the convent of Santa Clara, at Independencia and Junín. It dates from 1548, and is the oldest of its kind in the city. Much finer, however, is the high-walled Convento del Carmen, which occupies a whole block near the corner of Bolívar and Colón. Completed in 1759, it is the most beautiful monastery in northern Peru, with particularly fine frescoes. Further down Bolívar, at Orbegoso is the monastery of San Agustín, built in the 16th century; it has a fine altar and pulpit.

The Cathedral, on the main square, dates from 1666, but it was extensively rebuilt in the second half of the 18th century following an earthquake. Attached to it is a small museum of religious art from the Qosqo school. Also on the square is Casa Bracamonte, painted an extraordinarily bright blue.

The best museum in Trujillo is the Museo Cassinelli. It is in a most unlikely position, beneath a petrol station northwest of the centre, near where the road to Huanchaco and the Pan-American meet. The collection belongs to the owner of the petrol station, and contains a large number of very fine examples of Moche and Chimú ceramics. They provide a fascinating insight into the lifestyle, customs and practices of these peoples, depicting their houses, animals and daily activities. More startling are the vessels that portray the punishments administered to criminals and enemies. The museum is within easy walking distance of the centre. If you are short of time, you will have to make do with the archaeology museum at Pizarro 349, which is small and disappointing in comparison.

Help and Information. *Tourist Information:* the Foptur office is in Independencia adjoining Casa Ganoza, two blocks east of the main square. It provides a reasonable city map with the main sites marked on.

Communications: the post office is on the corner of Independencia and Bolognesi, one block west of the main square. Entel adjoins Casa Risco at Ayacucho and Junín.

Money: street changers gather in the first two blocks of Pizarro. There are several banks in the same area and in adjoining streets.

Around Trujillo

Huaca del Sol. These formidable Mochica huacas, the world's largest adobe constructions, lie 4 miles/6km southeast of Trujillo. The Huaca del Sol is by far the largest pyramid, even though part of it was washed away by the Spanish during their vain search for treasure. When complete it was the largest man-made structure in the western hemisphere — reaching a height of 135ft/40m, covering an astonishing 12 acres, and requiring some 140 million bricks. The labour required to construct it must have been colossal. As well as providing enormous ceremonial platforms, it contained the burial chambers of rulers and priests, and would have been enlarged with each burial. No major tomb has ever been discovered: entrances can be seen, but they have long since been searched by *huaqueros*, or grave robbers.

It is possible to scramble up to the summit, and from the top there is an excellent view over the valley. Across a large plaza is the smaller Huaca de la Luna, nestled at the base of Cerro Blanco.

To reach the huacas take the bus to Moche, which departs from Suárez at the junction with Los Incas, two blocks southeast of España. There is a sign on the main road as you enter Moche, from where it is a 40-minute walk through fields to the site. Attacks by robbers have occurred in the area, and if you are alone you are advised to take a taxi from Trujillo.

Chan-Chan. The largest adobe city ever built, Chan-Chan was the capital of the Chimú empire, which flourished during the early stages of the Inca empire. The city covered 28 square kilometres and consisted of nine palaces (one for each ruler), ceremonial sites and the dwellings of the ordinary people. The ruins were damaged when the El Niño of 1982/83 brought rains to the area for the first time in centuries; some of the remains are now protected with a coating of plaster.

A considerable amount of work has been done on one of the palaces to protect the walls, preserve the details and recreate it in part. Most of the internal walls are decorated with wave motifs, pelicans, sea otters and fishing nets. Behind the large plaza lie the quarters of the ruler and his servants; you can see food storage areas and a well, now dry.

The site can be reached on a Huanchaco bus from Trujillo, which you can catch from the junction of España and Mansiche. Entrance to the site costs $5, including entry to the new Chan-Chan museum and Huaca El Dragón, also known as Arco Iris. This is a reconstructed square huaca, in the northeastern suburb of Porvenir, a ten-minute bus ride north of the centre of Trujillo. A heavily decorated building, it was Chan-Chan's principal ceremonial site.

Huanchaco. There has been a fishing village on this site, 6 miles/10km north of Trujillo, for many centuries. As in Moche and Chimú times, the fishermen overcome the strong surf by using long reed boats with turned-up bows; these can be seen lined up vertically along the beach. You may be able to persuade one of the local fishermen to let you take one out, but you are less likely to persuade the surfers to part with their boards. The beach is good and sandy. Away from the fishing boats it is also very clean.

Buses run from Trujillo every 15-20 minutes, and take half an hour. Hotel Bracamonte, on the Trujillo side of the village, and Hotel Huanchaco, in the centre, charge $8; both have large, comfortable rooms and a swimming pool. Cheaper are the Sol y Mar and Estetes. Eat at the seafood restaurants along the beachfront.

CAJAMARCA

This city has a special place in Peruvian history, for it was here that Pizarro had Atahualpa, the last independent Inca ruler, put to death in 1532. Although Cajamarca's historical importance is not a patch on that of Qosqo, the two cities have a certain amount in common: an agreeable climate, fine colonial architecture, and a location in a fertile valley high in the Andes. However, at 9,165ft/2,750m, Cajamarca is quite a bit lower than Qosqo. It is also smaller (population 70,000), quieter, less commercial, and has retained a more traditional Andean feel. Finally, the beautiful countryside that surrounds the town is more accessible.

There is only one Inca building of note in the town; but within a few miles are several interesting sites, mainly pre-Inca, which make good day or half-day trips.

Arrival and Departure. Cajamarca is not well served by any form of transport. There is just one regular flight to and from Lima — on Tuesdays with AeroPeru, whose Cajamarca office is next to Hotel Turistas, on Lima just west of the square. The airport is a short taxi ride east of the centre.

Vulkano has three buses a day from Trujillo (7 hours), but the 10.30am departure is the only daytime service. The Etecsa and Sudamericano buses also leave Trujillo in the late evening; the same goes for the return journeys. El Cumbe runs three buses a day to Chiclayo, six hours northwest; you may also be able to take the daily TEPSA or Sudamericano bus to Tumbes and get off en route.

Empresa Díaz and Atahualpa each has services three days a week east to Celendin (6 hours) but beyond here there is only one weekly bus to Chachapoyas (15-18 hours), which runs on Sundays; trucks and camionetas run on other days. Empresa Díaz's office is in Ayacucho, four blocks southeast of the main square. The offices of all the other bus companies are located within a stone's throw of each other on Casanova, about fifteen minutes walk southeast of the main square.

Accommodation. There are two types of hotel in Cajamarca: those with hot water and those without. Of those in the first category, the clean and friendly Residencial Atahualpa (on Atahualpa, just northwest of the square) is recommended; a single room with private bathroom costs $5. Similarly priced, but with larger rooms, is Residencial San Lorenzo at Amazonas 1078. Big rooms, cold water and lower prices are available at Hotel Amazonas (Amazonas 528, near Arequipa). Of the hotels on the main square, the ramshackle Hotel Plaza has the most charm; it is fairly basic, but at $3 you can't complain.

Eating and Drinking. Opposite Hotel Amazonas is a lively and friendly restaurant of the same name. Between it and the square is the Chifa El Zarco, which is in a spacious but slightly gloomy courtyard; the staff are very friendly and the food plentiful. The restaurant beneath Hotel Plaza is a rather surreal place, with its courtyard lit by neon lights. The food is tasty enough, though a glance through the hatch into the kitchen could put you off.

Exploring. Plaza de Armas, a large and attractive square with well-tended gardens, is said to mark the spot of Atahualpa's execution. The Cathedral, on its north side, is built from volcanic rock (tufo). So too is the church of San Francisco opposite, with its ornate façade. More elaborate still is the exterior of the Convento de Belén, a block southeast of the square near the corner of Lima. The volcanic rock has been carved extremely finely and the interior is also highly decorative.

Behind San Francisco, on Amalia Puga, is the so-called Cuarto del Rescate. This is where Atahualpa was held to ransom by Pizarro for a room of gold. The Incas met their part of the bargain but the conquistadores did not, and the rest is history. The room has some fine Inca stonework, and there is a line around it, well above head height, which is said to be the 'gold' line.

Cajamarca is quiet at night: a lot of young people congregate in the main square, but not a lot seems to go on. Keep an eye out for posters advertising folklore evenings in one of the cinemas or at the university.

Help and Information. The Foptur office is on the small square at the corner of Belén and Sántisteban, near El Belén church.

The post office is hidden away near the corner of Lima and Pisagua, five blocks west of the main square. Entel is on Plaza de Armas itself, which is also the main hang out for moneychangers, particularly in the northeast corner; they can also be found in the first block of Arequipa.

Around Cajamarca

Baños del Inca. A 15-minute bus ride southeast of the city, past the university, brings you to the Baños del Inca. It is said that Atahualpa was bathing his wounds here, after defeating the forces of Huáscar, when Pizarro and his followers arrived in the area. The main reason to come here is to get clean, particularly if your hotel in Cajamarca doesn't have hot water. The individual tourist baths, which can take up to three people, are the best on offer: they are clean, the water is hot, and the entrance fee is less than a dollar per person. Buses leave every ten minutes or so from Amazonas, a block east of Plaza de Armas.

Ventanillas de Otuzco. This is a pre-Inca necropolis carved into a 50ft/15m-high sandstone cliff. Its name stems from the square niches that resemble windows. Otuzco is 5 miles/8km east of Cajamarca. Buses leave from Arequipa, five blocks east of the main square.

Cumbe Mayo. This is an important pre-Inca site possibly dating from the Chavín era. The principal feature is a small irrigation canal, carved out of natural rock and running around a hillside. Along its length are carvings in the rock of deities and mysterious symbols.

Cumbe Mayo is in the mountains, 12 miles/20km west of Cajamarca along a rough road. To get there you must hitch, take a tour or hire a taxi.

The Northern Coast

Pre-Columbian ruins line the Pan-American Highway north of the Cajamarca turn-off at El Cumbe. The Jequetepeque and Lambayeque valleys seem to have been particularly fertile during the Moche era, and each was a small state, with its own ruler. The greatest evidence for this has only recently come to light with the discoveries at Sipán and Tucmane, in the desert near Chiclayo.

CHICLAYO

This town is as unmemorable as the riches of Sipán are memorable. The vultures perched on the Cathedral façade say much about this modern city, with its large (and noticeably young) population of half a million.

If you have to stay overnight, which you may well do if en route to Sipán, there are several hotels on or just off Balta, immediately north of the main square. Hostales Cruz de Chalpón and Adriático are marginally the best of several basic and over-priced hotels; both charge $4. Hotel Monaco, on Pedro Ruíz, and the Venezuela, two blocks north of the main square, are worth the extra couple of dollars. The best choice of restaurants is also along Balta, and on the square.

Transa and Expresso Chiclayo offer good services to Piura (3 hours). Their offices are five blocks south of the main square, on Bolognesi.

SIPAN

At Sipán the tombs of two important dignitaries have been unearthed in a single huaca which, amazingly, the grave robbers missed. The coffins of El Señor de Sipán, a warrior, and El Viejo Señor de Sipán, contained fabulous riches. Each was clad in a variety of finely crafted gold, silver and copper jewellery. Most of the pieces have been incredibly well preserved in the dry desert environment.

In the grave of El Señor de Sipán is a reconstruction of the treasure it contained. Beside the small huaca which contains the tombs is the much larger Huaca Rajada. It is divided into two sections and it is possible to scramble up both — from the top there is a good view over the whole valley. The site is not an amazing spectacle, but the huacas are impressive if only for the significance of the treasures that have been found there.

Sipán is 22 miles/35km east of Chiclayo. Buses leave every hour from Calle Oriente, northeast of the centre. Alternatively, take one of the more regular buses to Pampa Grande from Amazonas. Get off after about half an hour, just beyond the village of Salitre, beside a sign for Sipán. It is then about a mile on foot to the ruins.

Lying just a few miles north of Chiclayo is the old colonial town of Lambayeque. The excellent Bruning museum has well displayed artefacts from all the ancient cultures of the northern coastal valleys. Twenty miles/32km beyond the town, at Tucmane, archaeological excavations are going on under the direction of Thor Heyerdahl. The vast area consists of 28 pyramids, but no great treasures have been discovered as yet.

Further north is the vast expanse of the Sechura desert, the largest in Peru.

PIURA

Situated near the original landing point of the conquistadores at San Miguel, Piura was one of the first Spanish settlements in Peru. It is the most attractive of the northern cities, with pleasant shady squares and a few colonial houses with unusual wooden screens. If you choose to cross into Ecuador by the inland route via La Tiña and Macará, you will need to stay overnight in Piura or Sullana, an hour closer to the border. Piura is much the nicer place to stay, with a better choice of hotels. Hostal California (on Junín, two blocks west of Grau) and Hostal Continental (opposite) are both clean, friendly and central. Hotel Hispano (Ica 650) is spartan but clean and at $2 the cheapest. There are plenty of restaurants within a block of Grau.

If you want to head for La Tiña, transport to the border leaves from near the main square in Sullana.

TUMBES

This is the nearest town of any size to the Ecuadoran border at Aguas Verdes. There is an airport, and many people cross into Peru to take advantage of the cheap internal flights, rather than fly direct from Ecuador. The town itself boasts little else capable of attracting visitors, save for a few pleasant old houses.

The town centre is small, so hotels, restaurants and bus company offices are all within a couple of blocks of each other. The tourist office, on the third floor of the far from regal Edificio Majestad (Ugarte and Bodero), is very helpful and for once has plenty of literature.

Arrival and Departure. Bus companies, serving all coastal destinations, are along Tumbes (formerly Vásquez), the main throughfare. The airport is 5 miles/8km north of the city. Faucett flies out of Lima daily at 11am, and returns from Tumbes at 1pm. AeroPeru has just two or three flights a week on the same route.

Accommodation. The most reasonable hotels, which charge about $2.50, are the Córdoba (Abad Puell 777), the Kikos (on Bolívar) and the Sudamericano (on Bolognesi). The Hotel Amazonas (Tumbes 333) is twice the price. The main concentration of restaurants is along the pedestrian section of Bolívar; among the best is the Samoa at number 235.

Around Tumbes

Some of Peru's best beaches are close to Tumbes, though that's not saying much.

Bocapán and Punta Sal, 20 miles/32km and 52 miles/84km south both have long and usually empty beaches of white sand and, for most the year, clear turquoise water; basic accommodation is available. To get there simply take any bus along the coast south of Tumbes and ask to be set down.

Puerto Pizarro. This small port, 10 miles/16km north of Tumbes, lies in Peru's only area of mangrove forest. You can hire a canoe for a one-hour tour of the swamps, for which you can expect to pay about $20. The best time to go is at high tide, when you can penetrate further up the creeks. The mangroves are home to much birdlife. Buses from Tumbes to Puerto Pizarro leave from the market area, and colectivo taxis go from Tacna, just off Tumbes.

THE CENTRAL ANDES

The Rimac valley is by no means the widest that penetrates the western slopes of the Andes. Nevertheless, in the 1860s Henry Meiggs, an American engineer, succeeded in driving a railway up it to the fertile central plateau. In doing so he built the highest railway in the world — reaching 15,935ft/4,780m inside the tunnel where it crosses the Pacific/Atlantic watershed. It took 59 bridges, 12 switchbacks and 66 tunnels, and the line has the steepest sustained ascent of any passenger railway in the world. The line plays a crucial role in the national economy, bringing mineral ores down from Cerro de Pasco and La Oroya to the coast. It was for these economic reasons that General Velasco nationalized the railways in the late 1960s. For almost 70 years prior to this the line had been managed by a British company.

The Rimac valley is exceptionally dry, with coarse paramo vegetation dominating its upper reaches. Once in the central valley, the line passes through contrasting zones. First, the severely polluted industrial town of La Oroya; then the fertile agricultural lands around Jauja, a small quiet colonial town.

Unfortunately, the central Sierra has been severely disrupted by terrorist activity in recent years. The road south to Ayacucho is subject to attack, and the attractive countryside and towns on the eastern slopes of the Andes, such as Tarma, are now off-limits. Do not venture north of Huancayo either: Cerro de Pasco, Huánuco and Tingo María are under the influence not solely of Sendero but also of the drug barons operating in the upper Huallaga valley. It may be possible to visit Lake Junín, between La Oroya and Cerro de Pasco, to view the prolific birdlife, but check with the South American Explorers Club in Lima first.

HUANCAYO

The attraction of Peru's largest Andean city (population 350,000) lies in the railway journey there rather than in the place itself. Situated at 10,865ft/3,260m, Huancayo is Peru's second highest town after Juliaca. It also vies with that town in a competition for the largest Sunday market in the country. Before dawn trucks crammed with campesinos from the surrounding countryside pour into town. They rapidly set up stalls and by daybreak, with the temperature hovering around zero, the market already extends across many blocks. The range of produce for somewhere so inaccessible and in an area subject to terrorist attacks is staggering. Brightly clothed campesino women sit amongst huge sacks of grain, fruits and vegetables from all over the country, and baskets overflow with ducks, chickens and guinea-pigs. All manner of modern consumer goods are promoted to the campesinos by streetwise salesmen from Lima.

Around Pisco

Ballestas Islands. For those who cannot afford a trip to the Galapagos, these islands are the next best thing. The clifftops are covered in a carpet of cormorants, gulls and boobies. Inca terns, elegant dark grey birds with a yellow and red moustache, are also common; and in the winter months a few Humboldt penguins come up from the south. Hundreds of sealions inhabit the rocky outcrops and the huge caves that riddle the islands; they are very inquisitive and swim right up to boats.

The prolific birdlife on the Ballestas Islands, and on others dotted along the coast, gave rise to an extraordinary economic boom in the middle of the last century. The bird droppings, or guano, which covered the islands to a depth of several metres became in great demand in Europe as a fertilizer. Chinese labourers, enticed with stories of a Utopian new life, became guano-digging slaves and died by the thousand. The survivors went on to build Peru's railways and form the basis of the country's Chinese population today. The old workings of the guano industry can still be seen on the islands.

It is not possible to land on the islands, but going on a boat trip is strongly recommended all the same. Several companies with offices in Pisco's main square take people out for around $5, though some require a minimum number of people. Boats normally leave at 7am and return by lunchtime to avoid the rougher afternoon seas — the waves are bad enough in the mornings. There is a good view of the Candelabra desert drawing (see *Paracas*) on the way and, if you are lucky, sharks and dolphins may follow the boat.

Paracas. This area south of Pisco was once home to the advanced Paracas culture. The early 'Caverna' phase (300BC-AD200) has no great claim to fame, but the later 'Necropolis' phase (AD400-800) is fascinating. Despite living in the most basic of dwellings scraped out of the desert, the people of that period produced some of the finest weavings in the world. The intricate designs depict gods, spirits and demons, and are brightly coloured with dyes from plants, fish and shells. While most of the garments were preserved in the bone dry desert for hundreds of years, no archaeological ruins of note remain.

The Paracas Peninsula, with its wide variety of desert creatures, is protected within a reserve. From the cliffs on the southern side are fine views of sealions, pelicans and cormorants. Chilean flamingoes winter at the bottom of the bay — they are visible as specks from outside the small natural history museum.

The mysterious 'Candelabra' desert marking lies on the northern side of the peninsula; it is best viewed from a boat en route to the Ballestas Islands. There is considerable doubt over the drawing's age, though it is certainly unrelated to the Nazca Lines. Some claim that it is just a few decades old, hence the array of theories as to what the drawing depicts, from a candelabra to a diving booby bird or a trident (three-pronged spear). Decide for yourself.

Access to the reserve is on foot or by taxi from the small settlement of Paracas, which lies half an hour south of Pisco, and can be reached by colectivo or taxi from the main market. The village consists largely of the Hotel Paracas and the summer houses of wealthy Limeños. The hotel, which on occasions is used as a secure and secluded retreat for government meetings, is beautiful but expensive. If you can't afford the $25 odd for a room, the pool and restaurant are at least open to non-residents. Cheaper lodgings are available at Hostal El Mirador ($4-5), close to the San Martín memorial on the approach into Paracas. You can camp in the reserve, but you must take your own water.

ICA

In some promotional literature this town is referred to as the 'sunniest town on Earth', and cloudless skies are definitely the norm. The Ica valley is also fertile, and it is Peru's principal wine-producing region. The best thing in town is the archaeology museum, which has some superb Paracas weavings, fine Nazca ceramics and a number of trepanned and elongated skulls. There are also Inca objects, including several *quipus*, the knotted string 'letters' used by the Incas to communicate with each other. The grounds contain a scale model of the Nazca lines, best viewed from the roof terrace. The bus to Huacachina, from the main square, drops you off within 100 metres of the museum, 3 miles/5km west of town.

Ica is served by both direct and through buses running along the Pan-American Highway. The bus company offices are all close together on Elias, a couple of blocks west of the main square. Buses to Lima (5 hours) leave at least once an hour, and there are several buses a day to Nazca (4 hours) and Arequipa (14 hours); most of those to southerly destinations leave in the evening.

Expensive hotels are concentrated off the Pan-American Highway on the Lima side of town, and the very basic ones near the market in the centre. Hotel Las Dunas ($30) is the pick of the smarter ones, but has the facilities, including a beautiful pool and its own sand dune, to justify the price. The new Hotel Palace (a block southwest of Plaza de Armas) is the best value downtown. Hotel Colón in the square itself has long been used by travellers, but it is now rundown.

The landscape remains exceptionally dry south of Ica, as the road heads inland. After a dramatic descent the road crosses the Pampa de San José, the location of the famous desert drawings, on the way into Nazca.

NAZCA

Lying in a dry valley where the foothills of the Andes reach down into the desert, this small town has a well-deserved end of the road feel. The area is steeped in history, stemming from when the valley was populated by the Nazca people, a pre-Inca civilization. The extraordinary Nazca Lines have brought fame to this sleepy town over the last 25 years, but there is a wealth of other remains too. These include the ancient city of Carhuachi, vast desert cemeteries, and aqueducts and irrigation channels which were created over a thousand years ago and are still in use today. Guides with large and decrepit American cars hang around the gringo hotels and are only too keen to take you out to the desert sites.

Arrival and Departure. Only Transportes Lurén runs buses between Lima and Nazca (9 hours), with regular departures throughout the day, stopping off in Ica. Its office in Nazca is at the junction of Lima and Castillo. All other buses that call in are on the Lima-Arequipa run and this is virtually the only transport available to the south; bus companies serving this route have offices along the Pan-American Highway at the northern entrance to the town. Most services to Arequipa (10 hours) leave in the evening, having left Lima in the morning. However, the journey south is wonderful, and it is worth taking one of the few day buses; Ormeño usually has a departure arriving from Lima between 8 and 9am.

The road to Qosqo is subject to landslides, but more significntly there have been several terrorist attacks along it in recent years. Do not therefore take this route for the foreseeable future.

Accommodation. There are lots of places to stay in Nazca. One of the best is the Youth Hostel (Lima 166; tel 62), close to the Pan-American Highway, which is clean and good value. For a similar price you can stay at the Hostal Nazca (Lima 438), which has been the favourite gringo haunt for over a decade. Alternatives include the spartan but clean Hostal Konfort (Lima 587, at Arica) and Hostales Lima and El Sol, on the main square. The Hotel Turistas on Bolognesi, near the junction with Lima, is expensive, but its swimming pool is open to non-residents.

Eating and Drinking. The Hotel Turistas has a decent restaurant, though the service is notoriously slow. You would do better to explore the options nearer the main square. Most popular are La Fontana and La Taverna, next to each other on Lima, near Hotel Turistas. They are not particularly good value in terms of food, but the atmosphere is pleasant enough, and live music is sometimes laid on.

Exploring. There is a small neglected museum in the main square, with some ceramics and bones; a new one is planned. For now, however, the most interesting place to visit is a workshop where pottery is made according to the original Nazca designs. To reach it head down Arica from the main square towards the river (dry), cross the bridge and follow the road round to the right; take the third turning on the right, and the workshop is the fourth house along, opposite you. The owner is extremely friendly, and he will explain to you the authentic techniques he uses to make the pots, which are fairly cheap and well worth buying.

Help and Information. Moneychangers hang around the small square in front of Hotel Turistas and there are a couple of banks at the intersection of Lima and Arica.

The Nazca Lines

Only in the 1920s, in the early days of Peruvian aviation, did it become apparent that the Pampa de San José was covered in a mass of lines and drawings etched into the desert. They were invisible at ground level but were clearly recognizable even from a small height. Overnight they became one of the great mysteries of Peru — a mystery which remains unresolved.

There are vast trapezoids, and narrow lines which run dead straight for several miles, ignoring any obstacles in their path. Most amazing are the animal outlines, which include a stylized monkey, a whale, a lizard and a hummingbird. Typically they are about 30-50 metres across, much smaller than most of the straight or geometric lines which run through them. This has led archaeologists to believe that the drawings originate from the 5th/6th centuries AD, pre-dating the lines and shapes which were probably created in the 7th-8th centuries.

There is little mystery about how the lines were made: researchers have replicated them by clearing a part of the Pampa of all stones, piling them up at the side and revealing the sand beneath. It is clear that after centuries of exposure to the sun the stones have become oxidized and turned to a dark rusty colour which contrasts with the lightly coloured sand, making clearly visible lines. Though breezes blow across the Pampa, there is a thin buffer of still air immediately above the surface which prevents the exposed sand from being blown away.

Why the lines were ever created is a mystery that few have really got to grips with. Even Maria Reiche, who has worked on the lines for over 50 years, has found no answer. She suggests that the Pampa was an astronomical calendar, with the lines and drawings relating to the positions of stars and constellations. However, recent computer analysis indicates that the correlation with star positions a thousand years ago is poor.

One of the earliest and probably the most infamous theories is the one put forward by Erich von Daniken in his book *Chariots of the Gods*, published in 1969. In it the author claims that the lines are the product of an extraterrestial intelligence. He was later forced to admit that many of his photographs were not to scale and had been misinterpreted to fit his fertile imagination. The book is still in print, published by Souvenir Press, and is well worth reading. *Pathways to the Gods: Mystery of the Nazca Lines* by Tony Morrison (Harper & Row) is a much more serious study of the subject.

The most widely accepted view nowadays is that the lines were constructed by local family groups, known as *ayllus*, which prepared and then maintained the lines and drawings as part of their ceremonial activities. Walking along the lines every so often would have been sufficient to keep them clear.

Maria Reiche used to give lectures about her work every night in the Hotel Turistas. She no longer does, but her sister or another researcher may do so.

Visiting the Lines. All access to the Pampa is prohibited, following the damage done by early investigators who drove straight across the lines in their cars. Even the Pan-American Highway bisects at least two of the drawings. The Maria Reiche viewing tower stands 6 miles/10km north of town along the highway, giving a reasonable view of the Tree/Hand, the Lizard and some of the large shapes. If you don't go on a tour you can hitch to and from it. You can also see several lines and shapes from a small hill a couple of miles east of Nazca, off the Abancay road. The turn-off, on the right, is by a small village and is marked by a signpost; the round trip takes two or three hours.

But the most spectacular view is obtained from the air. Aeroica, Aerocondor and Aero Montecarlo offer 50-minute flights over the lines from a small dirt airport just south of town. The price fluctuates around the $40-50 mark, rising during the peak tourist season. The absolute minimum seems to be about $30 but probably only in the late morning or afternoon when visibility is reduced by hazy skies. Discounts are sometimes available for those staying at the youth hostel and those with student cards. Included in the fare is transport to the airport from the airline offices in Calle Lima, between the Pan-American Highway and the Hotel Turistas.

Around Nazca

The Chauchilla cemetery lies about 8 miles/13km south, off the Pan-American Highway. It has been well picked over by grave robbers and souvenir-hunting tourists. The deformed skulls, two-metre lengths of hair and ceramic fragments have nearly all disappeared, leaving only bleached bones and the remains of burial jars. As a result, the site is no longer as fascinating as it once was. But the size is still impressive, and it is staggering just to observe how thoroughly the cemetery has been ransacked.

Carhuachi, the old Nazca capital, is a far more interesting trip (four to five hours altogether) west along a dirt road. There are small cemeteries in the area, large food storage vessels built into the ground, and the foundations of numerous buildings. The most fascinating construction is La Estaquería, an oval enclosure bounded by vertical stakes, some of them over two metres high. It is believed to have been a mortuary-cum-temple, and investigations suggest that entrails and organs were placed on top of the stakes as offerings to the gods.

Five miles/8km east of town up the Nazca valley, are aqueducts that are impressive as an ancient feat of engineering.

Between Nazca and the small town of Camaná there are no large settlements. The terrain is extremely rugged and in places the Highway is reduced to little more than a single lane dirt track. Terrifying moments as the bus squeezes past huge trucks on the hairpin bends, are offset by the beautiful views of the coast. Immediately after Camaná the road climbs steeply from the coast to a desert plateau, and the snow-capped volcanic peaks of Coropuna and Ampato come into view. It is in such stunning scenery that Arequipa, the second city of Peru, is situated.

AREQUIPA

Like countless places all over the world, Arequipa boasts the accolade of 'city of eternal spring', thanks to its crisp, sunny weather. The bright skies allow fantastic views of the three volcanoes which form the backdrop to the city. Most beautiful is El Misti, with an almost perfect cone, a dusting of snow on the summit, and a wisp of smoke rising from the vent. Enterprising couples occasionally have their weddings at the top. Further north is Chachani (19,900ft/6,075m), the highest and most rugged of the three; and to the south is Pichu Pichu, the lowest and the only one free of snow.

Arequipa's other and only slightly more original name is 'the White City', after its buildings of white granite, known locally as *sillar*. The churches, in particular, have extremely elegant façades carved out of the rock. Many of them, including the Cathedral, have had to be repaired following earthquakes, which have hit Arequipa regularly since it was founded in 1540. The colonial centre remains fairly intact, but the city now sprawls across the lower slopes of the volcanoes.

Arequipa is a centre for the department's substantial mining interests. Due to its isolation from the capital, the city and its population of around one million have developed a strong identity of their own. On several occasions in Peruvian history politicians from Arequipa and Lima have vied with each other in a battle to control the country.

Arequipa lies at a height of 7,700ft/2,350m, so if you are coming up from the coast for the first time, you may be mildly affected by the altitude.

City Layout. The old city centre forms a regular grid running down the gentle lower slopes of El Misti. Most of the hotels, restaurants and places of interest are within three or four blocks of Plaza de Armas, the main square. Four blocks west flows the Río Chili, beyond which and a little further north are the wealthy modern suburbs of Cayma and Yanahuara.

The bus offices and the railway station are at the southern end of San Juan de Dios.

Arrival and Departure. *Air:* the airport is 3 miles/5km northeast and a $5 taxi ride from the centre; it is not served by a regular bus service. Faucett, AeroPeru and Americana all offer daily connections with Lima, most flights leaving in the morning. AeroPeru connects Arequipa with Qosqo on Tuesdays, Thursdays and Saturdays, and with Juliaca daily; all flights depart in the morning. The Faucett and AeroPeru offices are based in the southwest corner of the main square. Americana is at Santa Catalina 118-B (tel 237905).

Bus: most of the roads into Arequipa, including the Pan-American Highway are appalling. Nevertheless, bus services are regular: Ormeño, TEPSA, Cruz del Sur and Angelitos Negros serve Nazca (10 hours) and other towns en route to Lima

(20 hours). Unfortunately, most of their departures are in the evening, depriving passengers of an interesting journey. The southerly road to Moquegua and Tacna is better, and Transportes Moquegua and Cruz del Sur provide regular connections. The roads to Qosqo (18-20 hours) and Puno (8-10 hours) are the worst. On the Juliaca/Puno route there is the worthwhile option of travelling by colectivo: Juliaca Express, on Avenida Salaverry, has daily departures, but expect to pay at least $20. The journey is dramatic, taking you around the southern flank of El Misti, past the desolate Laguna Salinas where campesinos dig salt, around the edge of the lovely Lagunas Lagunillas, and finally up to the bleak Altiplano.

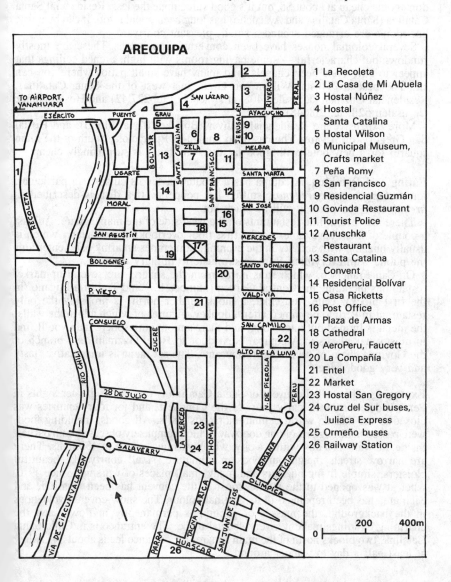

AREQUIPA

1 La Recoleta
2 La Casa de Mi Abuela
3 Hostal Núñez
4 Hostal Santa Catalina
5 Hostal Wilson
6 Municipal Museum, Crafts market
7 Peña Romy
8 San Francisco
9 Residencial Guzmán
10 Govinda Restaurant
11 Tourist Police
12 Anuschka Restaurant
13 Santa Catalina Convent
14 Residencial Bolívar
15 Casa Ricketts
16 Post Office
17 Plaza de Armas
18 Cathedral
19 AeroPeru, Faucett
20 La Compañía
21 Entel
22 Market
23 Hostal San Gregory
24 Cruz del Sur buses, Juliaca Express
25 Ormeño buses
26 Railway Station

Train: the route to Juliaca and Puno is also served by train, though this runs at night, thereby depriving you of the wonderful sights described above; it also has a bad reputation for robbery. The train leaves at 9pm, taking 9-10 hours to reach Juliaca and another hour to Puno, though the last leg is often subject to delays. Tickets ($20) must be bought at the station on the day of departure.

Accommodation. Much the best place to stay is La Casa de Mi Gran Abuela, 'the house of my great grandmother', at Jerusalén 606 (tel 223194) north of the centre. The garden, the safe and comfortable rooms, and the friendly atmosphere don't come cheap at about $8, but it's good value none the less. Residencial Santa Catalina (Santa Catalina and Ayacucho) has long been popular too. It can be noisy, but rooms are arranged around a small, pleasant courtyard.

Several colonial houses have been converted into hotels. These are mostly rundown but characterful — some having rooms with high, arched ceilings that appear to have once been chapels; and many have small patios where you can sit. The best are Hostal Wilson (on Grau, just west of the Santa Catalina), Residencial Guzmán (Jerusalén 408, at Ayacucho; tel 227142) and Hostal Nuñez (Jerusalén 528; tel 218648) nearby.

More expensive are Residencial Bolívar (Bolívar 202, at Moral), and Hostal San Gregory, on Alvarez Thomas (also known as Ejercícios), south of the main square; for a new hotel with good facilities the latter is surprisingly cheap.

Eating and Drinking. Arequipa has a reputation for its cuisine, in particular, for its fiery *rocottos rellenos* (stuffed hot peppers). If a dish is described as *arequipeña*, you know it will be spicy hot.

There are several litle restaurants on the west side of the main square. At least a couple of them have tables on the first floor overlooking the square, which is usually buzzing with activity in the evening. Sometimes an army band entertains the public with everything from salsa music to military marches.

On San Francisco, which runs north from the square, are several upmarket restaurants including the Central Garden (number 127) and Trattoria Lugano (in the first block). Café Anuschka, a block further north, is probably the only restaurant in Peru to be named after a donkey, pictures of which adorn the walls; the menu is limited but interesting, and there's more atmosphere than you'll find in most other places in Arequipa. Next door to Hotel Guzmán, is a branch of the Govinda chain of vegetarian restaurants. The set menu is imaginative, tasty and very good value.

Exploring. The walled convent of Santa Catalina is one of the greater sights in Peru. It dates from the early years of the Conquest, and for four centuries was closed to the outside world behind enormous walls. All goods, including food, were passed in through revolving doorways which completely obscured both parties. Inside the walls is a city within a city, which was once home to 450 nuns. There are narrow streets, neighbourhoods in miniature, small courtyards, beautiful cloisters, simple living quarters and many small places of worship. Since 1970, when it was opened to the public, most of the convent has been restored, and each area has been repainted in its original colour. The snow-covered volcanoes in the background, the masses of geraniums permanently in flower and the charming buildings make it a very special place. The entrance is in Calle Santa Catalina, two blocks north of the main square; the entrance fee is about $4. Allow at least half a day to wander around.

A block northeast of Santa Catalina is the Monastery of San Francisco, with a cool and attractive cloister. Across the delightful little square from the church is the municipal museum, which contains a mix of archaeological, religious and colonial artefacts. Down a pedestrian alley just beyond the museum is Arequipa's largest crafts market, in a pleasant enclosed courtyard.

Nearly all the churches in the centre of Arequipa are a delight, with spectacular interiors and large gilded altarpieces. La Compañía, in the southeast corner of Plaza de Armas, has the most ornate façade. Casas Pozo and Iriberry, on either side of the Cathedral, are also elaborately decorated. These two old merchant houses have been restored by banks, and now contain their administrative offices; you are allowed into the courtyards, and local art exhibitions are sometimes held inside. Casa Ricketts, on San Francisco, is another fine example of colonial architecture.

In the upper part of the city, bounded by Ayacucho and Jerusalén, is the small residential area of San Lázaro, dating from the early days of the city. It is a maze of tiny streets with very little traffic — a good place in which to escape from the bustling city centre.

La Recoleta is a 17th-century Franciscan monastery on the other side of the river from the centre, a short distance down to the left beyond Puente Grau. Like Santa Catalina, it was closed for centuries and was opened to the public only in the 1980s, following heavy restoration work. A small section recreates the spartan lifestyle of the nuns; and there is a museum containing a strange mix of religious art, pre-Columbian ceramics, stuffed Amazonian animals, and the oldest wine jar in Peru, dating from 1550.

On either side of the Río Chili are shady parks where Arequipeños enjoy a stroll at weekends.

Nightlife. Plays and recitals are sometimes put on at the cultural centre, just behind the church of La Compañía. Peñas generally provide the best formal entertainment in town in Arequipa. Most central are Peña Romy, on Plaza San Francisco, which opens only at weekends, and the excellent Peña Sillar, in the cloisters of La Compañía. Los Leños Pub and Pizzería, opposite Hotel Guzmán on Jerusalén, sometimes has live music and stays open late.

Help and Information. *Tourist information:* the tourist office is upstairs in a narrow building on Jerusalén, just before Melgar. It is staffed by the tourist police, a jovial bunch who are helpful and can offer maps and reasonably reliable advice about the city and surrounding area.

Communications: the main post office is on San José, just off San Francisco; Entel is on the corner of Valdivia and A. Thomas, two blocks down from the main square.

Money: there are several banks on Jernsalén, at Mercaderes and Santo Domingo, which is also busy with street moneychangers; the latter also hang around in large numbers in the southeast corner of the main square. Lima Tours (Amex agent) is at Santa Catalina 120 (tel 224210).

UK Consulate: Quesada 107, Yanahuara (tel 213754).

Around Arequipa

Colca Canyon (Cañon Colca). When measured from the top of the mountains flanking the valley, the Colca Canyon is the deepest incision on the surface of the globe. It is an incredible sight and is also probably the best place in Peru to observe condors. In the early morning and late afternoon the birds sweep down across the so-called Cruz del Cóndor viewpoint, sometimes within a few metres of observers.

Cañon Colca is west of Chivay, a small town 95 miles/152km north of Arequipa. There is simple accommodation in Chivay, but to be nearer the viewpoint stay in Cabanaconde, 30 miles/48km west — the Cruz del Cóndor is 5 miles/8km east of the village. Several travellers have been threatened by bandits in recent years, so don't go alone, and ask around in Arequipa about the current situation before setting off.

At least two bus companies have daily departures very early in the morning from Arequipa to both Chivay and Cabanaconde, taking four to five hours. To avoid doubling back, you can return to Arequipa by a southern route via Huambo. Lots of tour companies advertise day trips to the canyon, but the journey is long and your time at the Cruz del Cóndor very short. All the same, it is probably worth it if you have only a day to spare. On the way you pass one of the claimed sources of the Amazon.

El Misti. This volcano can be climbed from the Aguarda Blanca hydroelectric plant, 25 miles/40km north of Arequipa towards Chivay. Buses and trucks run along this route, but it is best to try to get transport to the dam itself. The climb is a strenuous three-day trip, because much of the time is spent walking through soft volcanic sand; you need to be fit and well acclimatized. There is no detailed map of the route, and the path is indistinct on the lower slopes. Seek advice from one of the tour companies or contact Señor Zarate (Tristan 224), a recommended guide. You must take water, food, camping equipment, and plenty of warm clothes — nights on the volcano are very cold.

TACNA

The 'city of heroes' is the last major town in Peru before the Chilean border. It was in the barren desert nearby that Chile defeated Peru at the Battle of Alianza in 1880, to win the War of the Pacific. The victors occupied Tacna after the battle, and retained control until 1929. During this period Chile commissioned the French architect Eiffel to design a new cathedral, to add a suggestion of permanency to their occupation. The result is an elegant building of delicate pink/grey marble, with fine stained glass windows. The continued influence of Peru's southern neighbour is reflected above all in the smart shops and in the pedestrian streets of the centre.

The small Zela museum (on Calle Zela) commemorates the war and its heroes, with numerous weapons and other memorabilia on display. There is also a museum at the train station, consisting of the old railway station building and several old engines, including one that looks like a Model-T Ford with a coach stuck on the back.

Arrival and Departure. The airport is a few minutes by taxi south of town. Faucett flies between Lima and Tacna every morning, a route served daily by AeroPeru in the afternoon. Americana also flies from Lima daily, and from Arequipa on Tuesdays and Thursday mornings.

Ormeño, Cruz del Sur and Sudamericano have daily bus connections with Lima. Cruz del Sur, Moquegua and Flores run regular daily services to and from Arequipa. The bus station is ten minutes walk north of the centre. Moneychangers gather here, and also in the main square.

Buses and colectivos run across the border to Arica in Chile, 38 miles/60km south. The latter are more expensive, charging $3, but they are quicker, taking about an hour. There is also a train service two or three times a day except Sundays, which takes about 90 minutes, marginally slower than the bus; both cost $2. Any food you carry is likely to be confiscated at the border.

Accommodation. There are plenty of reasonable hotels in Tacna, though none of them has any great charm. Among the most decent ones are Hotel Florida (on 2 de Mayo, two blocks north of Plaza de Armas) and the Lima, overlooking the main square. There are several hotels of a similar standard within a block or two. Less luxurious are the friendly Hostal Bon Ami (opposite the Florida) and the Hostal Las Vegas, next door to the Lima.

Eating and Drinking. If you feel like splashing out to mark your arrival or departure from Peru, El Viejo Almacén or the Genova are recommended; both are on San Martín, which runs southeast from Plaza de Armas. For big portions and friendly service go to the Las Vegas, under the hotel of the same name. For an early-morning breakfast try the temporary-looking place under Hotel El Virrey, on Ayacucho opposite Hotel Lima.

THE SOUTHERN ANDES

This section covers the southern part of the high Sierra, and includes two of the main tourist destinations in Peru — Qosqo and Lake Titicaca.

Lake Titicaca, which Peru shares with Bolivia, is the highest navigable lake in the world, at an altitude of 12,700ft/3,865m. Sadly, however, the only passenger service now operating right across it is a luxury tourist catamaran. The Altiplano extends to the north of the lake — a flat bleak region scattered with basic dwellings built from mud bricks and straw. Few crops can be grown in this harsh terrain apart from the hardier varieties of potato and a few vegetables. Most of the Aymará and Quechua Indians who inhabit this region survive from herding sheep, llamas and alpacas.

All roads across the Altiplano are exceedingly rough, and the journey north to Qosqo from the lakeside town of Puno is best made by rail. There are long stretches when the train passes nothing but the odd solitary shepherd in the middle of the vast flatness, with no houses in sight. Then, suddenly, it comes to a halt, and outside the carriage window you are confronted by a mass of women and small girls selling cheeses or stuffed potatoes — or, at the town of Pucara, pottery bulls and figurines. There are glaciers on the peaks of the eastern cordillera, and you can see herds of llamas and alpacas on the lower slopes as the train struggles up the long ascent to La Raya pass (14,400ft/4,321m) which defines the Lake Titicaca/Amazon watershed.

The pass is marked by a llama breeding station at La Raya. The descent into the Urubamba valley is rapid, and the landscape suddenly becomes much more fertile and heavily cultivated; sheep and dairy cattle replace the llamas. Shady eucalyptus groves line the fast-flowing Urubamba river, and high craggy peaks rise above the narrow valley. The market town of Sicuani is the only large settlement in the upper part of the Urubamba valley, and is the last before the railway turns up towards Qosqo.

The train between Puno and Qosqo leaves daily at 7.30am, in both directions, and takes 10-12 hours. Tickets are best bought a day in advance, and cost about $15. If you travel pullman or first class you must pay $20, for the privilege of having a guard. You may consider this a good investment, since trains are worked assiduously by professional thieves, possibly in league with the railway employees. If you balk at the idea of travelling in a padlocked carriage, go for first rather than second class.

PUNO

This is the largest Peruvian town on the shores of Lake Titicaca. It is also capital of the province of José María Mariategui — named after an early 20th-century Peruvian philosopher, from whose writings Sendero Luminoso draws much of its inspiration.

Puno is nestled among hills, with the centre set back some distance from the lake. While few find fault with the location, the town itself generally gets a bad press — for the cold winds blowing off the lake, the burning hot sun, and its complete lack of charm. The word has been spread around so effectively and exaggeratedly among travellers, that most people are pleasantly surprised by the reality.

The streets are dirty but lively, the atmosphere seedy but appealing. Figures lurk in the shadows at night, but these are rarely more threatening than a pack of dogs rooting around in the rubbish around the market, or women trying to sell you ridiculously cheap jumpers and gloves.

PUNO

1 Plaza de Armas	7 Post Office	13 Hotel Ferrocarril
2 Cathedral	8 Restaurante Internacional	14 Peña El Ricoche
3 Museo Colonial, Tourist Police	9 Market	15 Cruz del Sur buses
4 La Hostería	10 Museo de Arte Popular	16 Hotel Posada Real
5 Hotel Monterrey	11 Hotel Los Uros	17 Tourist Office
6 Hotel Nester	12 Rail Station	18 Telephone Office

Arrival and Departure. *Bus:* there are regular combis to Juliaca (one hour), which leave from Tacna, near the corner of Avenida Titicaca. Colectivos leave from in front of Hotel Ferrocarril, by the railway station; these can take you direct to Juliaca airport.

Cruz del Sur and Transportes Jacantaya (Avenida El Sol, opposite the stadium) run several daily overnight buses to Arequipa (10-12 hours) and the former also serves Qosqo (12-14 hours). The roads in either case are appalling and the journeys extremely rough. The more comfortable and safer option if you're heading to Arequipa is to take a colectivo. Juliaca Express (first block of Tacna) runs a car most days, and charges $20; you may need to book at least a day in advance. Buses to Moquegua, on the coast (and also some to Arequipa) leave from Avenida El Sol, about ten minutes walk south of the centre.

Crossing into Bolivia: there are regular combis to Yunguyo (2 hours), near the Bolivian border, which leave as soon as they are full from agencies on Calle Tacna, a block south of the market. From Yunguyo it is just a short ride to the Bolivian frontier, from where colectivos run people to Copacabana: this is the best place to stay if you have the choice, though there are a couple of hotels in Yunguyo. There is a Bolivian consulate in Yunguyo at Calle Grau 339.

If bound for the border post at Desaguadero (3 hours), combis leave only sporadically from Avenida El Sol. An early start is virtually impossible unless you are prepared to pay $20 to charter the entire minibus. If you do so, don't be surprised if the driver stops to pick up other passengers en route, to make a bit of extra cash.

Train: rail is by far the best way to travel between Puno and Qosqo or Arequipa. The train to Qosqo leaves at 7.30am daily except Sunday, and takes 10-12 hours. The fare is $15 ($25 tourist). The service to Arequipa ($20) leaves at 7.45pm, and is meant to take 12 hours, but is invariably late. Tickets for either route must be bought on the day of travel, which means an early start if you're heading for Qosqo. By joining the train at Juliaca, rather than Puno, tickets can be bought with little hassle and you even have time for breakfast. Be vigilant against thieves in Puno station as well as on the train.

Accommodation. Puno has a large number of nasty, overpriced hotels. The lime green Hotel Monterrey (Lima 447A; tel 343), a block north of the main square, is an exception. It is based around a courtyard and charges $2. The Hotel Posada Real (Titicaca 156; tel 738), four blocks from Plaza de Armas towards the lake, is also popular. There are a good many basic hotels in or just off Tacna, a block from the market.

Hotel Los Uros on Valcarcel, a block north of the market, charges about $4 and serves a good breakfast. It is popular with backpackers, but the proprietors are a money-grabbing bunch. The Italia (Valcarcel 122; tel 640), opposite, charges similar rates and is probably a better bet; so too is Hotel Nester (Deústua 268; tel 321), a block down from the main square.

Eating and Drinking. While Puno is not necessarily a town for the gastronome, there are enough places to see you through a few days. There are several pizzerias, including one under Hotel Monterrey; next door is La Hostería, which serves excellent yoghurt and hot chocolate and is invariably full of gringos. The best Peruvian food in town is served at the Internacional, below the Hotel of the same name at the junction of Melgar and Moquegua. Meals are not that cheap, but it's worth splashing out. For a more basic but still nutritious meal, go to El Dorado at Lima 341.

The best way to finish off an evening is with a glass of hot moroche and pasteles by the market. Alternatively, go to El Ricoche, near the railway line on the way to the port — it has modest peñas now and again, and is not a bad place for a beer on other nights.

Exploring. The main square is a pleasant part of town, well away from the chaos around the market. It is dominated by the solid but not unattractive pink granite Cathedral. To its right, the small Museo Colonial has pre-Columbian pottery and colonial paintings and artefacts. Less valuable works of art — in the form of woolly jumpers, socks, etc. — are sold in the square a block west of the central market, and along the railway tracks towards the lake, and on various pavements.

Two ancient British steamers are berthed at the dock. They were built in Hull in the 1930s and were brought over the Andes in pieces and reassembled on the lake. Until the early 1980s they were used to ferry passengers across the lake to Bolivia. There is a plan to restore one of the boats as a tourist cruiser, but progress is slow.

The festival in the first week of November, when the arrival of Manco Capac from the lake is commemorated, is spectacular. A huge reed boat brings Manco Capac and his consort Mama Ocllo to the shore with a flotilla of other boats. There they are greeted by the local chieftains and serenaded by exotically dressed musicians and dancers, before being carried into town.

Help and Information. The Foptur office is on Tacna near the corner of El Puerto. It has maps and brochures, but keeps irregular opening hours. Moneychangers hang around the central market, and most local tour companies on Tacna also oblige, and are open late. Lima Tours (Amex agent) has an office at Lambayeque 175 (tel 351431).

Around Puno

Sillustani. This is an ancient burial ground on a rocky peninsula jutting out into the beautiful Lago Umayo. It is a totally magical place, especially in late afternoon as the dark clouds build up over the wild terrain and deep blue waters of the lake. The site is dotted with burial towers, known as *chullpas*, of which a few are still complete; others are in a state of partial collapse. The rougher ones are Huari, while the finer stone ones are probably the work of the Collas, who lived in the area in pre-Inca times. When the Incas moved in they quickly recognised the Collas' stone-working skills, and used them to construct many of their finer buildings. Indeed classic 'Inca stonework' is really that of the Collas.

It is not easy to reach Sillustani without taking a tour. It is half way between Puno and Juliaca, and about the same distance again off the main road. It makes a three to four hour trip, and you should insist on spending at least an hour at the site; don't miss the small on-site museum. Several companies in Puno offer the tour, mostly the tour agents along Tacna. Expect to pay about $5.

LAKE TITICACA

Uros Islands. A visit to the floating reed islands is the most touristy trip from Puno. The Uros Indians once inhabited a large area stretching from the northern part of Lake Titicaca down to Lake Poopó in central Bolivia. However, they were banished from the land and were forced to live on the lakes and waterways. Nowadays they are found in greatest numbers at the northern end of Lake Titicaca.

Their homes consist of islands made up of a dense matting of *tortora* reeds, with which the people around Lake Titicaca traditionally make their boats. Life on the islands is incredibly hard, with the people exposed to temperatures of up to 30°C/85°F in the daytime and well below zero at night. They live principally from fishing, but they also keep animals and even grow some crops. On the larger islands, which may reach up to 150m square, there are schools, churches and spongy football pitches.

Motorboats leave Puno quay at 7-9am for the three-hour round trip, which includes an hour or so on the islands and costs about $5. On arrival the women and children line up to sell you weavings and other handicrafts, including model reed boats, which are now far more common in miniature than they are in real life. You can't help wondering if they stay put in this damp, squidgy, and altogether miserable environment solely for this income from tourists. For a briefer look at the islands you can ask the captains of the boats to Taquile Island to stop off for five minutes; this is an accepted diversion and is enough to satisfy most people's curiosity.

Taquile Island. Lying far out in the lake, Taquile is a special and powerful place. The silence is disturbed only by cocks crowing, sheep baa-ing, and the faint click of camera shutters. You can easily spend several days walking along the many pathways (there are no roads), climbing the rocky outcrops that dot the island, reading, or simply sitting. There are even small beaches where you can sunbathe

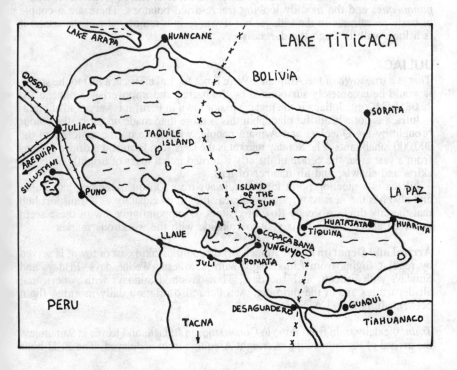

— but certainly not swim. The best views are from the ancient temple on the highest point on the island, which can be unbelievably spectacular at sunrise and sunset.

The inhabitants are extremely friendly. They wear traditional dress and the men in particular are very well turned-out, in their dark-coloured trousers, pristine white shirts, and finely-knitted hats. Most of the islanders' clothes are made on Taquile, and are decorated with traditional designs. The women spin and weave, while the men are responsible for most of the knitting, which they do all the time — even as they walk around the island. You can buy hats, waistcoats, etc. in the shop on the square in the only village on the island. Alternatively, simply barter with any knitters you meet on your travels; most of them have a stash of finished hats in their bag.

Boats to Taquile leave from Puno dock from 7-9am and take about three hours: there is no loo and beware of the strong sun. The first thing to greet you on arrival is a stiff climb up a flight of steps to the top of the hill. Benches are strategically placed for oft-required breathers. The boat back to Puno leaves at 2pm, so day trips are possible. But you are strongly recommended to stay over.

The Taquileans have organized themselves well to receive visitors. Near the entrance to the village, five or ten minutes walk from the top of the cliff, is the Control Recepción de Hospedaje. Here, visitors pay an entrance fee and are allocated to a family. This is organized in rotation so all families benefit — so your family may be a short distance away, or at the far end of the island. You are likely to be provided with your own small house containing little more than an adobe bench to sleep on, so a sleeping bag is essential. It is also a good idea to take plenty of fruit and vegetables, which are lacking on the island — both for yourself and as gifts. The family may provide meals, and be prepared for floury *panqueques* and the mouldy looking freeze-dried potatoes. There are a couple of basic restaurants in the village, but if you're in a remote part of the island it is a long walk through the darkness.

JULIACA

This is a true town of the Altiplano. Were it not for Lake Titicaca just to the south, it would be completely surrounded by the barren and impoverished plateau. At 12,085ft/3,625m, Juliaca is the highest major town in Peru; it is very cold at night.

Juliaca is not a beautiful place, but this is more than made up for by the colour brought by the Quechua and Aymará people, who make up the majority of the 100,000 inhabitants. The Sunday market is the largest in Peru and it draws Indians from a vast area: the centre of the city is turned into a mass of brightly coloured skirts and shawls, and all manner of hats.

Juliaca is a meeting point for the railways from Qosqo, Arequipa and Puno, and also has the nearest airport to Juliaca. It is in its capacity as a transport hub that the city draws a steady flow of visitors. Disappointingly few of these seem bothered about timing their visit to coincide with the wondrous market.

Arrival and Departure. *Air:* Juliaca airport, 3 miles/5km east of town, is served by regular flights from Lima: daily with AeroPeru, Wednesdays, Fridays and Sundays with Faucett, and Tuesdays, Thursdays and Sundays with Americana; all departures are in the morning. AeroPeru also offers a daily morning flight between Juliaca and Arequipa.

Train: the daily train from Puno to Qosqo stops in Juliaca, and leaves at 9am unless the arrival of the connecting overnight Arequipa train is delayed. The 10-12 hour

their city to the Spanish. During the colonial period other cities overshadowed Qosqo, and it was only in the early 1950s — once the railway to Machu Picchu had been built — that tourists started coming to the area in large numbers.

Central Qosqo is a monument to the Incas, with their city layout and many buildings well preserved. There are narrow alleyways between walls of huge stones and the remains of temples and palaces. Mixed in with this are many substantial churches and attractive colonial houses, built on foundations of Inca stonework. The narrowness and steepness of the cobbled streets control the menace of the traffic, at least in the older quarters. Hidden away in these quiet areas are numerous ramshackle crafts shops and delightful cafés and restaurants.

The central area is small and it is possible to visit all the main sights on foot in a couple of days. Half the fascination lies in the streets themselves — where Quechua women bustle up and down the slopes with ragged children or llamas in tow, or else gather on street corners to roast potatoes and anticuchos, the smell of which seems to pervade the city.

City Layout. Qosqo has grown far beyond the original layout. The Incas planned the city after one of their most sacred animals — the puma. Sacsahuamán, the great fortress on a hill above the city to the north, represented the head, and the spine was the Tullumayo stream running down from the fortress, and now beneath the street bearing the same name. The puma's body was formed by Huacaypata, 'the wailing square', a huge area which includes the entire Plaza de Armas and extends southwest to include the small, attractive Plaza Regocijo.

Arrival and Departure. *Air:* Most flights bound for Qosqo leave very early in the morning. This is because aircraft need to be in and out of the airport, which has a very restricted approach, before the skies cloud over and the turbulence increases around midday. The airport is 3 miles/5km southeast of the city centre. Buses run to (and from) the bottom of Avenida Sol, though this is at the opposite side of town to most budget hotels. A taxi costs a couple of dollars.

Faucett, AeroPeru and Andrea all fly at least once daily between Lima and Qosqo. There are also flights between Arequipa and Qosqo on Tuesdays, Thursdays and Saturdays, and LAB flies to and from La Paz on Wednesdays and Saturdays. AeroPeru flights from Lima should normally continue to Puerto Maldonado, though this leg is often cancelled. Much more reliable is the new service offered by TransAmazon, with daily morning flights to Puerto Maldonado. Andrea also sometimes serves this route.

All the airlines have their offices on Avenida Sol, including AeroPeru at number 600 and Faucett at 567. Contact TransAmazon at the airport.

Train: the train between Qosqo and Puno leaves at 7.30am, daily except Sunday, and takes 10-12 hours. Tickets can be bought a day in advance or on the day, if there are any left, and cost $15 ($25 tourist). The Puno train station (as opposed to the one for Machu Picchu) is a block east of the junction of Tullumayo and Avenida Sol, in the southeast corner of the city.

Bus: San Cristóbal/Ormeño offers daily departures direct to Arequipa, an 18-20 hour trip along a rough road. Cruz del Sur does too, and also has daily buses to Juliaca and Puno (12/15 hours). A combination of terrorism and dodgy bridges means that the roads west of Qosqo beyond Abancay to Nazca and Ayacucho should be avoided. Bus companies serving most local destinations are based within a block or two northwest of the Puno station.

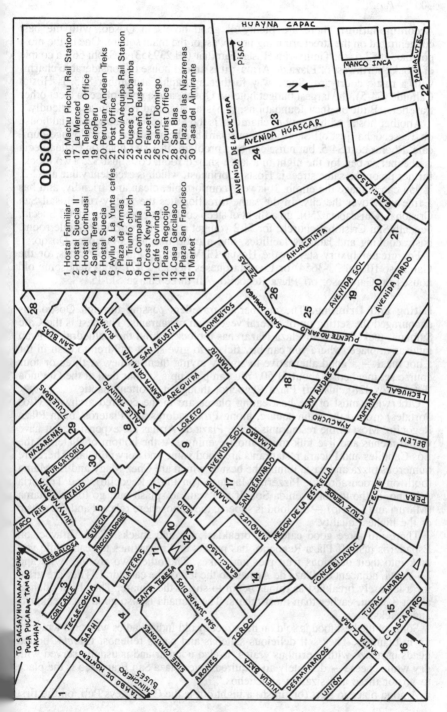

QOSQO

1 Hostal Familiar
2 Hostal Suecia II
3 Hostal Corihuasi
4 Santa Teresa
5 Hostal Suecia
6 Ayllu & La Yunta cafés
7 Plaza de Armas
8 El Triunfo church
9 La Compañia
10 Cross Keys pub
11 Café Govinda
12 Plaza Regocijo
13 Casa Garcilaso
14 Plaza San Francisco
15 Market
16 Machu Picchu Rail Station
17 La Merced
18 Telephone Office
19 AeroPeru
20 Peruvian Andean Treks
21 Post Office
22 Puno/Arequipa Rail Station
23 Buses to Urubamba
24 Ormeño Buses
25 Faucet
26 Santo Domingo
27 Tourist Office
28 San Blas
29 Plaza de las Nazarenas
30 Casa del Almirante

Accommodation. There are plenty of good hotels in Qosqo, with the best concentrated on the streets running northwest of the main square. One of the most popular, at $2, is the family-run Hostal Familiar (tel 239353) at Saphi 661, a couple of blocks northwest of Plaza de Armas; it is an old house of considerable charm, with a rustic courtyard. Some way further up Saphi, at number 845, is Hostal Cahuide ($4-5), the largest budget hotel in Qosqo, and a good place to meet other travellers. Built on Inca foundations, it has a café, and is clean and friendly.

Another hostal with plenty of character is the Suecia II, in a big colonial house on Tecsecocha, just off Saphi; the courtyard has been turned into a lounge-cum-café. Rooms cost $4-5, but noise can be a problem. Its sister hotel on Calle Suecia is cheaper: a bed for the night in a large shared room costs just $2. Two blocks further up on the same street is Hostal Corihuasi, which is excellent value at $2-3, if you can manage the climb. It is very comfortable, clean and friendly, and has a fine view over the city. In the same direction lies the family-run Hostal San Cristóbal (Quiscapata 250), up a flight of steep cobbled steps to the right off Suecia, beneath San Cristóbal church; for $1-2 you get a bed in a dormitory-style room, basic cooking and laundry facilities, and a patio that looks out over Qosqo.

For greater luxury stay in the Hostal El Virrey, on Plaza de Armas, or the Garcilaso III (tel 23-3654) or Los Marqueses (tel 23-2512), both handsome old houses on Garcilaso, off Plaza Regocijo. All three charge $10-15.

Eating and Drinking. The number of travellers passing through Qosqo has encouraged the setting-up of several vegetarian restaurants. The best is the Café Samana, tucked away in Plaza Nazarenas a block behind the Cathedral; it is an innovative place, where you can buy tickets to give street children to cash in for a hot meal — a good alternative to simply giving them money. A three or four course set meal costs about $1.50. You can pick up a similar deal at the Govinda (Espaderos 128), just off Plaza Regocijo, though it is often chaotic.

Otherwise, most of the best eating places are in the covered archways (Los Portales) around the main square, along Procuradores and Plateros, or in Plaza Regocijo. Most of the restaurants in the Plaza de Armas are expensive, but have varied menus and live folk music most evenings. At the bottom of Plateros, the Los Candiles and Pucara restaurants are good value and very popular. There are numerous pizza and pasta joints, the best of which are Chez Magy and La Mama (both on Procuradores), Pizzería Magengo (on Plaza Regocijo), and Trattoria Adriano, at the top of Avenida Sol. If you want to splash out, go to La Retama (Maruri and Loreto) — the food is superb, the atmosphere relaxed and the music of the highest quality.

There are three good cafés for breakfast, tea and snacks. Café Varayoc, on Espaderos just off Plaza Regocijo, has papers and magazines to read while you tuck into their delicious fruit pies and cakes. The other two are the Ayllu and La Yunta, adjacent on Plaza de Armas, to the left of the cathedral. They are great for a leisurely breakfast as things begin to stir in the square. They both open at about 8.30am, earlier than most others. The Samana is also good for breakfasts and snacks.

Some of the best food is sold on the street by old Indian ladies with pots wrapped up in blankets. They sell delicious salteñas and papas rellenos. *Choclo*, boiled heads of maize with enormous grains, is also popular and is usually served with dry white cheese — definitely an acquired taste. Plaza San Francisco is the place to go for these and sizzling anticuchos.

A good place to start (or finish) a night out is the Cross Keys Pub, on the first floor of a fine old building overlooking the Plaza de Armas; it is reached up a narrow flight of stone steps beside the entrance to Hostal Chaski. It is owned and run by British ornithologist Barry Walker. It has a dart board and a lively atmosphere, and is a good meeting place.

Exploring. Qosqo is a fascinating city with many hidden corners and amazing treasures. The walking tour described here takes in all the main sites and many lesser ones en route. A $10 ticket covers entrance to all the churches and museums that charge admission, as well as several sites in the Sacred Valley; you can buy the ticket at any of the sites it covers. Individual tickets are not available. Most churches and museums are open 9am-noon and 3-6pm, though there is some variation.

The tour begins in the Plaza de Armas, where the lower walls of Inca palaces act as the foundations for most of the colonial buildings. On the northeast side of the square stands the pink granite Cathedral, a veteran of many earthquakes. Its shrines and chapels are rich in decoration and artistic works, including fine examples of the Qosqo School, which was renowned throughout the Americas in the 17th and 18th centuries. The most interesting example in the Cathedral is the large painting in the aisle to the right of the altar, in which Christ and the Disciples are about to eat a guinea-pig for their last supper. Outside, traditionally dressed Quechua women with tassled llamas pose for photos — in return for a tip.

Immediately to the right of the Cathedral is the chapel of El Triunfo. Legend has it that an apparition of the Virgin Mary put out the roof fires ignited by burning arrows, when the Spanish force was besieged by the Incas in 1536. The Spanish eventually won the day, and as a sign of gratitude the chapel of El Triunfo was constructed on the site of the apparition. Past the tourist office and a short distance along Arequipa, is the Convento de Santa Catalina, which contains plenty more examples from the Qosqo school. The old decaying house opposite is the unlikely site of the city Police headquarters.

Returning to El Triunfo and heading right down the narrow street of the same name, you reach a tiny s uare, where two small shops sell beautiful ornate candles. More famous, however, is the Religious Art museum, in the wonderfully restored palace of Inca Roca; it contains yet more Qosqo school paintings. Continuing in the same direction, along Hatunrumiyoc, you follow the outer wall of Inca Roca's palace, which is one of the most impressive in Qosqo. Among the massive perfectly fitting stones is the 13-angled stone — with more sides than any other block in an Inca wall.

The extension of Triunfo and Hatunrumiyoc is the steep, cobbled San Blas, which leads up to the old quarter of the same name. Nowadays it is the home of artists, and there are several small galleries selling both new and old works. At the top of the street is the church of San Blas, the main feature of which is its elaborately carved wooden pulpit.

Returning to the square in front of the Religous Art Museum, turn right up San Agustín. After a block this opens out into the delightful Plaza de Los Nazarenas, with its fine, well restored buildings. On the right is the House of the Serpents, named after the wriggling snakes adorning its stone façade; it is now a convent of Carmelite nuns. At the far end of the square is the Casa de Cabrera, which hosts modern art exhibitions.

Following Calle Tucumán back towards the main square you pass the early 17th-century Casa del Almirante Maldonado. Legend has it that the Admiral used to stand in the corner balcony and have any Indian that dared look up at him taken away and beaten. The house is now the Archaeology museum, and contains many fine Huari and Inca objects.

Procuradores runs northwest from Plaza de Armas. In the early 1980s this narrow street was the main travellers' hangout, winning it the epithet of 'gringo alley'. Times have changed and it is not so different from any other street. At the end of the block, turn right and look up Coricalle: with its decaying buildings, it gives you some idea of how the city was before the recent renovations began. Now follow Tecsecocha in the opposite direction and turn left into Tigre. At the bottom, on the other side of Saphi, is the Convento de Santa Teresa, another colonial building with substantial Inca foundations. Saphi, with a fine Inca wall, leads down to the Plaza de Armas. A narrow street connects the main square to Plaza Regocijo, a lovely retreat. In its southwest corner is the restored house of Garcilaso de la Vega, the fabled chronicler of Inca history. It houses the Regional History museum which includes numerous artefacts from the colonial period and, of course, works of the Qosqo school.

Calle Garcilaso runs into Plaza San Fransisco. Overlooking it is the monastery of the same name, with fine exterior stonework and cloisters. The main market and Machu Picchu station are southwest down Santa Clara, while Marquez leads in the opposite direction back to the main square. The latter takes you past the Convento de La Merced, the most ornate and wealthiest of Qosqo's many ecclesiastical buildings. The cloisters are lined with murals depicting the life of San Pedro de Nolasco, the founder of the Order; the ubiquitous paintings of the Qosqo school are the best in the city. The chapels and altars in the church are lavishly decorated in gold.

Back in the main square, La Compañía is an elaborately fronted church, built by the Jesuits on the site of Inca Huayna Capac's palace. Running alongside the church is Loreto, one of the most famous streets in Qosqo. It is lined with nearly a hundred yards of the finest Inca stonework, which once provided an impregnable barrier along one side of the Acllahuasi, the house of the 'chosen women' or 'virgins of the Sun'.

At the bottom of Loreto carry on another block to the Convento de Santo Domingo, built over Koricancha, the most magnificent of Qosqo's Inca temples. It had chapels dedicated to the Sun, Moon, Thunder, Lightening, the Stars and Rainbow, and every wall was covered with gold or silver sheets. It was populated by 4,000 priests and attendants, surrounded by life-size gold and silver images of birds, plants and animals. Koricancha was also the Incas' main observatory, where the calendar which regulated the empire was maintained, taking sightings from towers — huacas — on the skyline around Qosqo. The rather unremarkable Convento de Santo Domingo now stands in the centre of the Koricancha. However, many of the original outer walls of the temple remain, some of the best Inca stonework in existence. The exterior semi-circular wall overlooking Sol is particularly fine.

Nightlife. The most popular club to end the evening at is Kamikaze, which is above Café Varayoc on the northwest corner of Plaza Regocijo. It opens at 9pm and the programme normally starts with an Andean group, changing later to a disco with a mix of western and salsa music.

A more standard disco is Las Quenas (in the basement of the Hotel Savoy at the bottom end of Sol), while the Super Star Disco (Maruri 363, inside a former Inca palace) is popular with the more fashion-conscious Cusqueños. El Mukie, on Arequipa between the main square and Santa Catalina, attracts the local youth and is more down to earth.

Shopping. You can have great fun buying local crafts in Qosqo. There are rundown shops tucked away in narrow back streets, smart boutiques on the main streets, small markets and numerous traders who come out in the evening. Qosqo is famous for its silver jewellery, knitwear and weavings, but almost every type of handicraft produced in Peru is on sale.

The greatest space is given over to woollen and woven goods of every description. The antique mantas and ponchos are increasingly rare as they get snapped up by collectors, but there is an amazing shop full of them a short distance up Saphi from the main plaza; prices are steep. Qosqo is also a good place to buy musical instruments, especially guitars and charangos. One of the best shops is in Cabracancha, an extension of Maruri. The best place to buy jewellery is on the west side of Plaza de Armas, where several shops sell a wide range of silver and gold.

The main crafts market is off Sol near the Faucett office, though there is also an artesanía section in the main city market. Street vendors assemble under the arcades in the main square and Plaza Regocijo as dusk falls: women sit with their infants asleep amidst huge piles of jumpers and other woollens. During the day, women persistently sell colourful hand-woven belts and wristbands in the main square.

Help and Information. *Tourist information:* Foptur is at Portal Belén 11, in Plaza de Armas. It opens 8am-5.30pm Monday to Friday and 8.30am-12.30pm on Saturdays. It has a noticeboard where you can leave messages, which is useful if you are trying to put a trekking group together. The staff are not especially well disposed to answering endless questions from independent travellers, but they give out basic city maps. The tourist police office is upstairs, on the first floor.

Communications: the main post office is on Avenida Sol near Avenida Garcilaso. It opens 8am-6pm Monday to Saturday and 8am-noon on Sundays. The international phone office is three blocks nearer the main square, on the corner of Lechugal.

Money: moneychangers hang out at the top end of Avenida Sol, near the main banks, Banco de Crédito and Banco de la Nación. They are mostly reliable and honest, though you may need to shop around for a good deal. The rate for cheques is often best in the banks or cambios; try those in Mantas, off the main square, some of whom will even change non-dollar currencies.

British Consul: Dr Raoul Delgado de la Flor, Hotel San Agustín, Maruri 390 (tel 23-1000).

Bookshop: the excellent Mini-bookshop under the Portales on the eastern side of Plaza de Armas has a wide selection of books, magazines and tapes, though most of its stock is in Spanish.

Around Qosqo

There is a wealth of Inca sites near Qosqo. Several lone walkers to the more obscure sites have been robbed in recent years, so go in a group of at least three people if possible. Taxis can easily be arranged in Qosqo for a half-day tour; expect to pay $25-30.

Sacsahuamán. The great Inca fort of Sacsahuamán, an integral part of old Qosqo, sits high above the city to the north. It is an incredible construction, with a three-tier zigzag wall running the length of its northern flank. It was built with truly massive stones — the largest is estimated to weigh over 350 tonnes and stands nearly 30ft/9m high. Originally there were three great towers, but they were destroyed in 1536 after Manco Inca's failed rebellion. The stone was used by the Spanish to build much of colonial Qosqo; only the foundations remain.

Nowadays the wide grassy plaza in front of the main defences is used for ceremonies. The most spectacular is Inti Raymi, an ancient Inca celebration marking the winter solstice in the last week of June. Hundreds of Cusqueños dress up in Inca costumes and perform a colourful pageant. On the hill across the plaza are some finely-cut Inca thrones and, beyond, some recent excavations — including natural rock slides where local children play.

Qenko. A mile northeast of Sacsahuamán along the Pisac road is the huaca of Qenko — a large, heavily carved limestone outcrop. A cave runs right through it, with sculpted altars and niches. On the upper surface natural fissures and indentations were adapted to accommodate ceremonial vessels, which contained chicha and possibly blood as well (at least of llamas). There is a fine zigzag channel near the top, and symbols representing the Sun and the Moon. On the far side of the rock is a temple to fertility with a large phallic huaca as its centrepiece. Similar rock outcrops are scattered all over the surrounding hillside, but Qenko is the most ornate and accessible.

Puca Pucara and Tambo Machay. Four miles/6km further north from Qenko on the Pisac road is Puca Pucara. This 'red fort' is a small fortification on the original Inca road to Pisac, little of which remains. Ten minutes walk beyond it is Tambo Machay, with its cascades of spring water pouring down through channels of Inca stonework.

Chinchero. This small village lies 17 miles/28km northwest of Qosqo, halfway to Urubamba. The road passes through beautiful countryside, with its patchwork of fields, Lake Huaypo, and the snow-capped peaks of Veronica and Salkantay in the distance. Chinchero's main square, like the church, is built on Inca foundations. On Sunday, market day, it is a seething, colourful mass of local farmers, traders from Qosqo and crafts stalls. There are vendors with huge glasses of chicha, wicker baskets full of guinea-pigs, mounds of coca leaves, and rows of brightly coloured skirts blowing gently in the wind. Outside the town groups of llamas wait to carry produce back to their villages, each one identifiable from the tassles hanging from its ears.

A variety of trucks, minibuses and pickups leave Qosqo early in the morning from along Arcopata, a couple of blocks southwest of Saphi, for the one-hour journey.

Pikillacta and Rumicolca. These two sites lie east of Qosqo on the road to Urcos. They are best reached on one of the frequent buses to Urcos, which leave from near Puno railway station. Pikillacta is an unrestored sprawling Huari ruin, whose rough stone walls still are over 10ft/3m high.

Less than a mile further along the main road is Rumicolca, the Inca gateway to the Qosqo valley. The valley narrows at this point and the Incas built a huge wall of fine cut stone across it to control access to the city.

Andahuaylillas and Huaro. These small villages, just before Urcos, have peculiarly fine churches containing magnificent 16th-century murals.

Tipón. This little visited site is one of the most phenomenal within easy reach of Qosqo. It lies 15 miles/24km east of Qosqo, off the main road to Urcos. At the small village of Tipón, 12 miles/19km along the main road, there is a large sign directing people up a rough track running northwards. For a small tip, boys in the village offer to accompany you on the one hour walk up the mountain. The stonework of the ceremonial terraces and irrigation channels — still running with clear springwater — is of the highest quality. Further up the mountain is a huge area of unexcavated terraces and buildings.

A full day is needed for the trip. Buses to Urcos can drop you at the roadside sign to the ruins, and can be caught back to Qosqo until dusk.

The Sacred Valley

Running northwest of Qosqo, the Sacred Valley (El Valle Sagrado) was the area of the Incas' earliest expansion. The broad, fertile stretch between Pisac and Ollantaytambo was Qosqo's breadbasket; most of the old Inca terraces are still cultivated today. From the white waters of the Urubamba river to the golden wheat on the terraces, and beyond to the snow-capped peaks towering above, this is a most beautiful place.

Most visitors enter the valley above Pisac, and carry on through Calca and Urubamba down to Ollantaytambo. Combis to Pisac leave from Tacna, near the Puno railway station. Combis direct to Urubamba go via Pisac (though there is another road through Chinchero) and leave from Huáscar, east of the city centre. Once in the valley additional combis and pickups run between Pisac, Urubamba and Ollantaytambo. Vehicles can get very full, mainly on market days, but in general it is easy leap in and out wherever you please.

For a more adventurous trip you can go white-water rafting between Calca and Urubamba. Explorandes (behind the AeroPeru office on Sol; tel 226599), Peruvian Andean Treks (Avenida Pardo 705; tel 225701) and Expediciones Mayoc (Procuradores 354; tel 232666) offer the best deals. They also organize horse-riding, mountain biking and trekking.

PISAC

The Inca ruins at Pisac, precariously positioned on a crag jutting out into the valley, come second only to Machu Picchu. The nucleus of the site, built of pink granite, contains some of the finest Inca stonework in existence.

Even though there are fewer tourists than in the past, during the peak holiday season the small colonial town below (not to mention the ruins) is packed with visitors. At least they are outnumbered by local people at the Sunday market, where old weavings, crafts, fruit, vegetables and coca leaves are sold by the sackful. The market centres on the main square, which is dominated by a splendid tree which in early Spring is covered with brilliant scarlet flowers.

The ruins rise so high and steep above the town that they are barely visible from it. The walk up from town is fairly strenuous but fun. The path leads out of the main square to the left of the church, and it takes about an hour to reach the main site. Across the ravine you can see a necropolis carved into a cliff face — most of the tombs are clearly visible because they have been broken into. The site's principal buildings are the Temples of the Moon and Sun. The latter contains an *intihuatana*, or 'hitching post of the Sun': this large, cleanly cut stone allowed precise astronomical observations and calculations, which would have determined many of the Incas' daily practices. The upper carved section was eventually destroyed by the Spanish.

There is a choice of paths you can follow from here. One continues up to the ruins at the top of the hill, from where there is a fabulous view down over the nucleus, the lower terraces, the town and the valley. Another path to the left of the hill runs down into the ravine beside a small water channel. A third path runs to the right of the hill, through a natural rock tunnel, down an impressive stone staircase and up to the road entrance to the site.

If you are on a tour, the minibus will go directly to the ruins. You are allowed only about an hour to explore the site, which deserves an entire morning or afternoon.

Accommodation and Food. If you stay overnight, sleep at the Hostal Pisac, a pleasant old building overlooking the main square. The hotel restaurant and the Samana Huasi in the opposite corner, with a pleasant garden, are the best places to eat; both close early. On market day there are lots of food stalls, serving anything from tripe stew to chunks of roast pig. Pisac has a good supply of chicherías — watch for a plastic bag on the end of a pole protruding from a doorway.

OLLANTAYTAMBO

Lying 38 miles/60km down the valley from Pisac, Ollantaytambo is the only town in Peru to retain its exact original Inca layout. It lies at 9,300ft/2,800m, at a crucial defensive point where the valley of Urubamba narrows and meets the smaller Patacancha valley. It also marks the division between the high Andes and the eastern foothills. Immediately above the town, to the north, rises an impressive temple-fortress; and there are other inaccessible ruins on the steep valley sides rising high above the town. In 1536 the Incas recorded one of their few victories against the Spanish here — by diverting the Patacancha river Manco Inca flooded the plain below the fortress, thereby immobilizing the Spanish cavalry.

Ollantaytambo is on the Qosqo to Machu Picchu railway line and it is well worth stopping off. There are no buses direct from Qosqo, but once in the Sacred Valley you can pick up local transport.

Accommodation. The Albergue is one of the best hotels of its type in Peru. The entrance is across a footbridge over a small stream near the train station (and about ten minutes walk from the centre). It is extremely friendly and comfortable, and has a beautiful garden. At $15 it costs more than the average hospedaje, but breakfast and dinner are provided. It is also convenient for catching trains.

Only two other places are worth considering: the neglected Hostal Alcázar, on the left just after you have left the main square for the ruins; and Hostal El Tambo, two blocks up the lane immediately on your right as you enter the square from Qosqo. The Café Alcázar, beneath the hotel of the same name, is cosy and the food is appetizing and cheap.

Exploring. The foundations of the fortress date from the Huari period. The Incas built over the old terraces, which are clearly identifiable from the rougher stonework. At the top on the left is the Temple of the Ten Niches. In the centre is the Temple of the Sun, with its huge stone slabs; high up on the opposite side of the valley you can see the place where they were quarried. The Urubamba river was diverted while the stones were transferred across, and then they were dragged to the fortress up a ramp, which is still visible. From the centre of the ruins there is a good view over the town, and the Inca grid layout is clearly visible. A precipitous path leads from the centre of the ruins a short distance around the hillside towards more remains in the lower Patacancha valley.

If you have a half day to spare, hire a boy to take you to the pre-Inca ruins of Patacancha, a couple of hours' walk up the side valley. The ruins are not so extraordinary as the valley itself, which is one of the most intensively terrraced in Peru. In the town, campesinos from the Patacancha valley sometimes gather in the main square, where a few stalls sell food and chicha. The men are especially distinctive in their bright red ponchos and circular white hats.

MACHU PICCHU

From the moment the Spanish conquered Qosqo, rumours began to circulate about a fabulously wealthy lost city. Some confused it with Vilcabamba, the last refuge of the independent Inca royal family, who were finally tracked down and wiped out in 1572. This site, in the jungles north of Machu Picchu, was quickly forgotten. In the first decade of the 20th century Hiram Bingham, an American archaeologist, made several expeditions to Peru in search of Vilcabamba. In 1911 Bingham declared that he had located it, despite obvious discrepancies with the accounts of the Spanish chroniclers.

Regardless of the precise origin of the ruins, the newly discovered site was obviously very important. Despite extensive excavations, the history of Machu Picchu remains a mystery, and there are many unanswered questions about its role in Inca times. It may have been a fort — certainly its position is virtually impregnable — but there is little evidence of a military usage. It was more likely of ceremonial significance: there are substantial royal quarters, evidence of an acllahuasi (house of the chosen women) and several temples.

No one knows why Machu Picchu was abandoned, though it was possibly due to an epidemic or, more likely, to the death of its master — probably Inca Pachacutec — and left as a monument to him. Consequently, by the time the Spanish arrived it would have already been semi-forgotten amongst the turmoil of the preceding years as Atahualpa fought Huáscar.

Whatever the history of Machu Picchu it is the most remarkable Inca site in South America, not just for its completeness but also for its complexity and the quality of the buildings. In recent years much work has been done to clear and renovate the site, so it is now possible to see clearly what the ceremonial centre was like. The setting too is remarkable. Rising high above the site is the dramatic tetrahedral peak of Huayna Picchu. Machu Picchu is the name of the craggy mountain that rises behind the ruins on the south side. You approach the site from this side if you follow the Inca road which runs between Machu Picchu and Qosqo. Hiking along this path is one of the highlights of a trip to the site.

To see Machu Picchu properly, you need to spend a full day there. The ruins are open from 9am to 5pm. The entrance fee is $10 on the first day and $6 on the second.

Arrival and Departure. Machu Picchu is only accessible by train or on foot. The train schedule from Qosqo to Machu Picchu is subject to frequent alteration — confirm it with the tourist office in Qosqo. At the time of writing the Autowagon leaves Qosqo at 6am and arrives at Machu Picchu Ruinas at 9.30am; it returns at 4.30pm. The exclusive service in a comfortable carriage with refreshments costs $55 return. The much cheaper local trains leave Qosqo at 6.15am and 2pm, arriving $2\frac{1}{2}$ hours later in Ollantaytambo and another 90 minutes later at Machu Picchu

Ruinas. The trains continue on to Quillabamba, four hours away. Be careful to distinguish between Machu Picchu station, which is actually at Aguas Calientes (where the cheap hotels are) and Machu Picchu Ruinas, a mile on down the valley.

You are advised to travel tourist or first class on the local train, which costs about $10 return. Tickets can be purchased the morning before you wish to travel in either Qosqo or Ollantaytambo. The local trains return from Quillabamba at 11am and 4.30pm, but by the time they reach Machu Picchu they are usually quite crowded. If there are no seats left you will have to stand. You are advised to take the earlier train since once darkness falls you need to be vigilant for thieves. One option is to stop overnight in Ollantaytambo.

Buses run up to the site from the Ruinas station from 8am, and back down until about 5pm, for $6 return. Alternatively, you can take the path which is a better option down (40 minutes) than up (90 minutes) — just watch out for snakes.

Accommodation and Food. The state-run hotel adjoining the ruins is small and very expensive, so it's better to stay in the small town of Aguas Calientes, a mile or so back up the Urubamba valley. Huge vertical cliffs rise up behind it and the only connection with the outside world is the railway, which runs right through it. Fifteen minutes walk from town are the thermal pools, from which the town takes its name: they are a must after several days on the Inca trail or a full day exploring the ruins.

Gringo Bill's is the most popular place to stay. It has a variety of rooms — while some are excellent, with wooden balconies overlooking the town centre and bizarre murals, others are damp and windowless. If you're offered one of the latter, try the Hostal Machu Picchu, on the river side of the station platform, which is reliably clean and pleasant. Most of the best restaurants, such as El Refugio, are also along the platform; avoid the Samana which is positively unhygienic. Chez Magy, up towards the baths, serves reasonable pizzas. Gringo Bill provides a limited but well cooked menu.

To get from Aguas Calientes to the Ruinas station, walk along the track below the railway. In 1992 a bus service directly from Aguas Calientes up to the ruins was due to commence.

Exploring the Ruins. Once you reach the first buildings, most of the temples and finer quarters are to the left, and the storehouses and lesser quarters to the right. Immediately to the right is the Prison or Temple of the Condor, named after a natural rock formation that resembles the bird. Adjoining it is a semi-circular wall with several niches; it has been suggested that these were used to imprison men by securing them with bars placed across the arms.

Among the buildings immediately to the left is the circular Tower or Temple of the Sun, with extremely fine exterior stonework. It contains niches for sacred objects, and much of the floor space is occupied by a huge rock, which was been carved into natural altar. Beneath the Temple is a cave in which mummies of Inca nobles were kept in niches, ready to be taken out and paraded on ceremonial days. Some of the mummies were still in position when Bingham arrived.

In the centre of the site, there is a long, grassy plaza. To the left a path rises steeply to the Temple of the Three Windows. Just behind it is the principal temple, built from massive slabs, some of which have slipped out of position. Continuing upwards you reach the Intihuatana on top of the rise, one of the few complete hitching posts (see *Pisac*) in Peru. Looking northwest from here you can see snow-capped mountains in the distance, beyond which lies the site of Vilcabamba.

Away from the central ruins are several sites worth visiting. A walk up the Inca Trail towards the Intipunku (Gateway of the Sun), opens up the picture postcard views of the site. It takes an hour to reach Intipunku from the site, but you do not need to go very far to get a good panoramic photo.

The Inca trail arrives at Machu Picchu at the watchkeeper's hut, high up on the left from the main entrance. From behind the hut a much smaller track leads to the Inca Bridge. The path soon becomes precarious, and in some places there is an almost vertical drop down to the river over a thousand feet below. After half an hour the bridge suddenly comes into sight around a curve in the path. A gap, where the path has been built up across an overhanging cliff face, is bridged with a few logs. It is impassable, however, and no one is sure where the trail ends up.

If you are tempted to climb Huayna Picchu, a great deal of care is needed since the slopes are very steep. Even so, it should take less than an hour to reach the top. The view back down to the central ruins from almost directly above is fantastic. The whole site, the Inca trail coming down from Intipunku and the valley far below can be seen clearly. It also provides a quiet retreat when the tourist train arrives mid to late morning — but even then you may find a man selling Coca Cola at the top.

THE INCA TRAIL

The remains of Inca roads and trails exist throughout Peru but it is the one to Machu Picchu which has achieved fame above all others. The current trail covers just the last three or four days walk from Qosqo, incorporating several otherwise inaccessible Inca ruins and crossing some truly spectacular landscapes.

Weather conditions can be tough — wet, cold and windy — and the only accommodation is your tent and sleeping bag. So come well equipped, and carefully examine and test any hired equipment. There is lots of water along the way (though not always near the best camping spots), but you must take all your food. Occasionally robbers have held up trekkers on the Trail so it is best to camp in a group with others; during the day everyone can walk at their own pace.

It is possible to race through and complete the trail on the third day from Qosqo, but this would allow little time to explore the ruins en route. A four-day trek is recommended, with camps made above Huayllabamba, at Runkuracay and Phuyuputamarca. Camping is not permitted at Huinay Huayna or Intipunku. The only detailed map of the trail is produced by the South American Explorers Club, and can be bought in their Lima office.

Setting Off. The trail begins in the Urubamba valley at kilometre 88, on the Qosqo-Machu Picchu railway line; this is where you pay the $15 fee, which includes Machu Picchu entry. After crossing the narrow suspension bridge over the river, you have to double back up the valley for about a mile. The trail then heads west up the Cusichaca valley, at right angles to the Urubamba. At the start of the valley are the ruins of Llactapata, which were renovated a few years ago by British archaeologists. They also restored some terraces and the irrigation system, for the benefit of the local community. You can also join the trail here having walked along the Urubamba valley from Ollantaytambo; allow an extra day to do this.

The climb up the Cusichaca valley is steep but manageable. You pass through small patches of cloud forest, and there are wonderful views back down the valley of the snow-capped Mount Veronica, across the Urubamba valley. After 4 miles/7km you reach the small village of Huallyabamba, where you can sometimes stay in the school building. At Huallyabamba a track from Mollepata, an alternative starting-point for the trek, joins the main trail. This three-day extension involves a 16,400ft/5,000m pass and takes you close to several glaciers. To make the trip less arduous hire horses and a guide in Mollepata, on the Qosqo/Abancay road.

At Huallyabamba the main route turns sharply to the right out of the Cusichaca valley and follows the left flank of the Llullucha valley, through dense woods. The first good camping places are near the stream and also in the woods, though access to water can be a problem. Alternatively, continue an hour or so further and camp above the woods.

The path continues up the left side of the valley across rough pasture towards the highest pass on the trail — the bleak 13,770ft/4,130m Huarmihuanusca (Dead Woman's Pass), which is about two hours walk from the woods. Descending from here, keep to the left above the stream and woods; the trail is rocky and unstable, so tread with care. To the left the river Pacaymayo tumbles in a long waterfall and then bisects the trail, which ascends the far side of the valley up a steep flight of stone steps — the first real sign that you are on a trail built by the Incas. Not far beyond the top of the stairs are the small ruins of Runkuracay, with a fine view back across the Pacaymayo valley.

This is an appropriate campsite for the second night. Just before the ruins, a large cave beneath a huge boulder could provide some additional shelter. The second pass is a short but steep climb up from Runkuracay. On the other side the trail again runs down the left side of the valley above a small lake. The ruins of Sayacmarca sit astride a hill which juts out into the valley; they are reached up a magnificent flight of cut stone steps. Larger than the ruins at Runkuracay, the stonework is unrestored and the buildings heavily overgrown. The trail turns sharply to the right at the foot of the steps and crosses a stream running from the lake, past a small and over-used campsite.

The next stage, leading up to the third pass, is the most beautiful, and has the best sections of the trail, paved with large granite slabs. The bamboo thickets and flowering plants along this stretch attract numerous birds, including spectacular hummingbirds. In crossing the 11,800ft/3,540m pass — a small notch in a ridge, which hardly feels like a pass at all — you return to the Urubamba valley, with the river a trickle far below. Across the valley the majestic white slopes of Mount Veronica are visible again. Just below the pass are the ruins of Phuyuputamarca, and another campsite. The ruins are small but contain six ceremonial stone baths. The trail follows one of the terraces right through the site.

The next couple of miles involve a gentle descent — with some possible campsites — and then a much steeper drop when you reach the first of a line of power pylons (these go to the hydro-electric plant in the Urubamba valley). Down to the left you can just make out some tiny ruins far below — the first sight of Machu Picchu. The path follows the pylons down to a small, very basic hostal. There is also a small camping area, the last on the trail. From here Machu Picchu is three hours away along the lefthand path. First you should make a detour to the right, to visit Huinay Huayna. These ruins are almost vertically below Phuyuputamarca, on a precarious rock spur jutting into a steep ravine. A long flight of steps leads down into the centre of the site, paralleled by a series of ten small stone baths. Though the buildings are of uncut stone they still show some fine workmanship. There is a tiny platform overlooking the river Urubamba, hundreds of feet below — possibly a place for sacrifices.

The final section of the trail runs around the sheer mountainside and is spectacular. Fortunately for the faint-hearted, the 1,000ft/300m drop to the river

is camouflaged by dense woods. Eventually you arrive at a flight of stone steps:
at the top sits Intipunku, the Gateway of the Sun.

LA SELVA — THE RAINFOREST

Peruvian Amazonia accounts for 63% of the land area. Cut off from the rest of
the country by the Andes, this is an incredibly remote region, penetrated by a
single good road — the one to Pucallpa.

The Spanish found it so impenetrable that they largely ignored it once they had
flushed out Manco Inca, who took refuge there. Interest in the region came only
towards the end of the 19th century with the discovery of rubber. Wealthy European
rubber traders gradually spread upriver from Brazil and established themselves
in Peru — principally in Iquitos, where they made vast profits by enslaving the
Indians. All was abandoned when the bottom fell out of the rubber market in the
early 20th century. In the 1960s oil deposits were discovered in the northern jungle.
This region is disputed by Ecuador, though recent diplomatic moves have been
made to resolve the problem once and for all.

Other than Iquitos, the only other town of any size in this vast region is Pucallpa.
For many years the Peru/Brazil Transamazonian Highway was projected to run
through Pucallpa, but following increased terrorist activity in the Andes along
the Pucallpa-Lima road, this plan was shelved. These troubles also spread down
to Pucallpa which led to the closure of several tourist lodges in the area in the
late 1980s, and removed the town from the tourist route. The town can only be
reached by air, or by boat from Iquitos; the latter involves a four-day trip along
the Río Ucayali.

Iquitos has dominated the jungle tour market for many years. But since the nearby
rainforest has been lost to cattle pasture, you must travel for at least a day to reach
unspoilt areas. Iquitos is gradually being superseded by Puerto Maldonado as a
base for jungle trips: good forest can be reached easily from this more southerly
town and, unlike Iquitos, it is accessible by direct flights from Qosqo.

IQUITOS

The largest settlement in La Selva lies on the northern banks of the Amazon which,
even 2,000 miles/3,200km from its mouth, is still over a mile wide. Iquitos is Peru's
most isolated city. In the 19th century the journey there from Lima involved a
three-month trip by boat astonishingly via Cape Horn, London, New York and
finally Manaus. The advent of air travel changed everything, and most visitors
now fly in, including those from Lima.

At the turn of the century Iquitos became a major player in the international
rubber boom. At the height of the boom, the rubber barons lived solely off imported
food, built palatial houses which they filled with the finest European furnishings
and even sent their washing back to Europe. Although it never achieved the social
heights of Manaus, Iquitos is still a reminder of the fabulous wealth of that era.
There are several tree-lined streets containing fine houses with wrought ironwork
and Italian tiles. It remains a major river port, and watching the boats come and
go along the waterfront is one of the greatest charms of the city. Away from the
river, Iquitos is the domain of the motorized rickshaw and motorbike: cross roads
with care.

Arrival and Departure. *Air:* Faucett and Americana both have daily flights between Lima and Iquitos. AeroPeru operates along the same route daily except Saturday. Most flights leave in the morning, both ways, and the trip takes two hours. The military airline flies every Wednesday to Islandia near the Brazilian and Colombian borders; Varig/Cruzeiro do Sul flies on Satudays to and from Tabatinga and Manaus in Brazil. Some Faucett flights from the USA stop at Iquitos en route.

From the airport, 6 miles/10km west of the city, buses run into town along Huallaga and back again along Aguirre. Taxis cost $3-4, and motorcycle rickshaws $2. AeroPeru's office is in the first block and Faucett in the fifth block of Prospero, running west from the main square.

Ferries: there is a constant stream of boats — mostly old, dirty and extremely crowded — to various destinations along the river. The trip to Pucallpa along the Ucayali takes five days ($20), while the journey to Yurimaguas up the Marañon takes four days ($15). Boats usually leave in the early evening from the Malecón. Each boats has a board giving details of destinations and departure times, but these cannot always be trusted; for the most reliable information, seek out the captain. Expect to pay about $4 per day. Some boats have very basic cabins, with one or two bunks; otherwise, you will need a hammock. Also take extra food, drink and plenty of insect repellent.

Accommodation. Hostal La Pascana (Pevas 133, tel 231418), a couple of blocks north of the main square, near the Malecón, is good value; the end of the road has been lost to the river but the hotel is safe, for the near future at least. On Prospero, the Hotels Perú (number 318, two blocks south of the square; tel 234961) and Lima (number 549, four blocks south) are clean and provide air conditioning. Further south still, close to the floating town of Belén, is the brightly painted Hostal Alfert, which is clean and friendly. It sits on top of the river bank at the end of Sáenz, and there are excellent views over the river and part of Belén from the verandah. All these hotels are in the $2-4 price range. Hotel Ambassador (Pevas 260; tel 233110) is the best medium-range hotel.

Eating and Drinking. The smart restaurants along the central part of the Malecón cater mainly for the wealthy package tourist and have prices to match; but they have excellent views across the river. Restaurant Las Crisnejas is the best value, with several types of river fish on the menu, including the enormous *paiche*. There are several chifas around Plaza 28 de Julio, of which El Pacífico is the best.

For snacks, juices, cakes and pies go to Café Ivalu, on Flores, a block southwest of Plaza de Armas. A café preferred by the old timers is Café Expreso, close by on Prospero; it is crowded and friendly, with everyone tucking into rice and chicken balls (*juane*) at 8am.

Exploring. In Iquitos you can't do better than stroll alongside the mighty Río Amazonas, though the main river channel flows at some distance from the centre — revealing extensive mud flats in the low season. The waterfront is divided into three sections: the Malecón, the suburb of Belén and the docks. The houses along the Malecón are attractive but decaying, and the street fails to match the elegant model in the town hall library on the main square. Nevertheless, the view is superb. Interesting architecture is also found in the first couple of blocks inland. Morona, which is lined with palms and many old buildings, is one of the most characteristic streets in Iquitos. The most bizarre building in the city was created by Eiffel for

La Selva Sur — The Southern Jungle

There are good possibilities for getting into the forest and seeing plenty of wildlife in just a few hours from Qosqo. Trips can be organized either independently or through a tour company. The two principal areas for undertaking trips are the Manú National Park, east of Qosqo, and the Tambopata area, close to Puerto Maldonado in the far south. The region resisted the oil and gas companies a few years ago, but colonizers and gold-panners have been moving into the area instead. It is one of the least developed regions in all Amazonia with vast tracts of virtually untouched forest and uncontacted tribes of Indians.

MANU

Manú National Park covers over 1.5 million hectares and takes in a vast range of habitats, from lowland rainforest up to high Andean cloud forest. This diversity gives it exceptionally high wildlife recordings, and it is frequently the location for natural history film footage.

The possibilities for visiting the area are limited — partly because there is only one road into it, but also because the National Park is only open to scientists. The park is home to several small and little contacted groups of Amazonian Indians, and this is another reason for prohibiting tourist access. In the past few years limited contact with outsiders, often missionaries, has brought diseases against which they have no resistance; in some groups up to half their number have perished.

The only lodge lies in the semi-protected buffer zone adjoining the park, and it is extremely expensive. The main alternative is to go on a camping trip into this same area. Several people in Qosqo work as jungle guides — some of them more reliable than others. The part-British owned Expediciones Manú (Procuradores 50; tel 226671) is the principal tour operator in Qosqo. They have a series of permanent shelters along the river Manú and offer an eight-day package costing in the region of $650, covering all transport, food, equipment and the services of an expert guide. For those who cannot afford their full package, Expediciones Manú can also help you set up an independent camping trip.

It takes a day and a half from Qosqo to reach the buffer zone and the first jungle campsite. Independent trips and tour groups both use local trucks to cross the Andes on a long but spectacular drive from Qosqo, through the small town of Paucartambo and the mission station at Shintuya. Soon after Shintuya you switch to a motorized canoe, to descend the Alto Madre de Dios river to the small settlement of Boca Manú. Here you turn up the river Manú. You are likely to see cayman, snakes, flocks of parrots and many other birds, much more if you are extremely quiet and patient.

PUERTO MALDONADO

This small town is the capital of the largely unmapped department of Madre de Dios. It is also the proud owner of the title 'biological capital of the world', awarded by the local town council. If that alone isn't enough to attract you to the place, Puerto Maldonado is also an entry point to vast regions of the Amazon.

The town was founded in 1902, at the height of the rubber boom, by an Irishman called Fitzcarrald. Incredibly, rubber from the area was exported up the Río Manú, over the isthmus of Fitzcarrald, down the Río Ucayali to Iquitos, along the river Amazon to Manaus, and thence to Europe. The tale is commemorated in Herzog's remarkable film, *Fitzcarraldo*. The bottom fell out of the rubber market before the rubber barons could bring the grandeur of Iquitos or Manaus to Puerto Maldonado. The town sank into obscurity. In the last twenty years, Puerto Maldonado has been given a new lease of life by the arrival of tourism, colonists from the Andes, loggers and gold prospectors. However, it remains very much a frontier town, and most of its streets are still unpaved.

The conservation picture for the area was considerably improved in 1990, with the creation of the Tambopata-Candamo Reserve, bounded by the Bolivian border, the road to Qosqo, and the watershed of the Iñambari river. It surrounds the far smaller Río Heath National Sanctuary, an area of unique tropical savannah, and the Tambopata Reserve, which has one of the greatest concentrations of wildlife anywhere in the world.

Arrival and Departure. *Air:* AeroPeru is scheduled to fly from Lima to Puerto Maldonado via Qosqo on Mondays, Wednesdays, Fridays and Sundays, but the last leg is frequently subject to cancellation. The return flight leaves the same morning. If a flight has been cancelled, the next one out is likely to be overbooked, and you may have to fight or bribe your way on board. In 1991 TransAmazon was inaugurated to provide a more reliable link with Qosqo; it currently has two morning flights.

The airport is a couple of miles north of the town and is well served by taxis and motorscooters. If you have organized to go to a jungle lodge, someone will meet you at the airport and handle all arrangements.

Road: the road from Qosqo via Urcos and Ocongate is appalling, especially during the wet season. There are no bus services, but trucks travel throughout the year — carrying rice, beer and consumer goods down, and timber up; many take passengers on board. It is at least a two-day trip in the dry season, and potentially a week in the wet.

Accommodation and Food. There are plenty of hotels catering to itinerant workers. The wood-panelled Hotel Turistas (north of the centre, overlooking the Río Tambopata) is much the best in town, though its rooms cost $10-15. For $3, Hostal El Solar is reasonably clean and comfortable; it is two blocks back from the main street — Avenida Leon Velarde — on 2 de Mayo. More down-market are the Royal Inn, Tambo de Oro, Wilson and Reyport, all on or within a block of Velarde, in the centre of town.

The best food in town is to be had in the Hotel Turistas. There is little to distinguish between the other fairly basic restaurants.

Jungle Trips

There are now six jungle lodges near Puerto Maldonado. Three lie along or near the Río Madre de Dios, and three up the Río Tambopata; all but one are within a few hours journey by motorized canoe. This is a region of enormous bio-diversity and natural wealth, and all lodges specialize in natural history. The local Indians are a reserved people who have to work hard to retain their traditions, customs and lands. It is unlikely that you will meet them during a visit to any of the lodges.

The typical cost of two nights, with one and a half days spent in the jungle, is about $150. Lower prices can be negotiated for longer stays e.g. $30-40 a day for a week, especially if business is quiet. The price covers comfortable accommodation, all food, a guide and transport to and from the airport. Drinks and tips are the only extras. Bring plenty of insect repellent and sun cream.

If you do not want the modest creature comforts of a lodge, you can arrange camping trips almost anywhere into the surrounding region. There are always a few guides waiting at the airport in Puerto Maldonado. Willy Wither may not be the ideal jungle guide but he is as good as they come. Expect to pay about $30 per person per day for a group of at least three people and for a trip of four days or more. The price includes transport, food, a guide and basic camping gear; you will need your own lightweight sleeping bag.

Tambo Lodge. About half an hour downriver on the northern bank of the Madre de Dios, this is the nearest lodge to Puerto Maldonado. It is cheaper than the others but is also fairly basic, and the surrounding jungle is unimpressive. The package includes a trip to Lago Sandoval (see below).

Cuzco Amazónico. This lodge is about an hour down the Madre de Dios from the town, on the edge of a private ecological reserve. The accommodation consists of 36 traditional twin-bed bungalows, with hammocks beneath the porches and private bathrooms. There is reasonable wildlife in the reserve, the birds being particularly good. Most visits include a trip across the river to Lago Sandoval and to the gold-panners a short distance downriver. Guides are native people with limited english, supplemented by any resident naturalists.

Cuzco Amazónico can be contacted at Procuradores 48, Qosqo (tel 232161), and at Andalucía 174, Lima 18 (tel 462775).

Lago Sandoval. Moroche palms, with straight white trunks, fringe one side of the lake. In the water you should be able to see cayman, piranha and paiche, a huge Amazon fish that can grow up to two metres long. Plenty of birds, including hoatzins, are found close by too, but do not expect to see many mammals. There is a good trail system around the lake, and you can hire canoes for paddling silently around the edge. A family living beside the lake has built a couple of basic cabins for visitors, and can also provide food — all for $4-8. To get there independently, hire a canoe ($8) at the dock in Puerto Maldonado, from where it is two hours to the lake — half by canoe and half on foot. Even if the cabins are full (unlikely), the family will usually try to squeeze you in.

Explorers Inn. This is the first of the lodges on the Río Tambopata, four hours upriver from Puerto Maldonado. It lies on the edge of the Tambopata Reserve, and as you approach it the vegetation along the river thickens considerably. The wealth of wildlife includes 587 recorded species of birds, 91 mammals and 127 amphibians and reptiles. In addition, there is a vast range of beautiful plants that are of immense medicinal and spiritual significance to the native people. The reserve has the best trail system in the area, as well as three lakes, which you can explore by canoe and where you can often see giant river otters and the strange hoatzin bird. The latter is a direct descendant of a prehistoric bird; it is rather like an exotic pheasant, with mainly orange and blue feathers and a tufted head.

Explorers Inn consists of several traditional cabins, each with four twin-bedded rooms with private bathrooms. It is the only lodge in the area with mosquito netting in all windows. As at most lodges, the day begins early, so that you are out in the forest for the dawn chorus. If the wildlife is plentiful you may not progress very far during the day: watching for macaws in the canopy, sloths lower down or a puma on the forest floor requires slow, silent movement. The bolder animals may visit the lodge clearing. In the evening you can go searching for cayman along the river.

Guides are either foreign nationals working as resident naturalists or Peruvian scientists; both speak English. The lodge is operated by Peruvian Safaris, who can be contacted in Qosqo and at Avenida Garcilaso de la Vega 1334, Lima (tel 316330).

Tambopata Jungle Lodge. This is a new lodge with simple cabins, an hour upriver from the Explorers Inn. It has a network of trails on both sides of the river and is likely to prove particularly good for birdlife. It is operated by Peruvian Andean Treks, Avenida Pardo 705, Qosqo (tel 225701).

The Colpa. This salt-lick attracts large numbers of parrots, especially macaws, and is one of the most spectacular sights in the region. It can be visited on a camping trip with Tambopata Nature Tours, based in Qosqo. This involves a 10-hour trip up the Rio Tambopata from Puerto Maldonado, into a virtually untouched area with no permanent occupants other than the wildlife. Consequently, there are few trails from the river into the jungle. Petrol is expensive so to visit the *colpa* will cost about $80 per person per day for a group of four people on a four-day trip. Tours are also offered by the other main agencies in Qosqo and Lima.

There are other smaller and less impressive colpas in the region; few are easily accessible.

The Tambopata Reserve Society is a UK registered charity supporting Peruvian scientific research and native peoples' initiatives in the area. For further details write to TReeS, 64 Belsize Park, London NW3 4EH, enclosing a stamped addressed envelope.

Bolivia

From El Alto across to La Paz

Population: 7.3 million

Seat of Government: La Paz (1.5 million)
Legal Capital: Sucre (80,000)

Che Guevara met his death, violently, in Bolivia. So too did Butch Cassidy and the Sundance Kid. Shoot-outs are hardly the traditional image associated with Bolivia — a country that is more commonly evoked by romantic pictures of snow-capped peaks inhabited by llamas and men in ponchoes. But little is romantic about Bolivia: it is one of the poorest countries in South America and, in physical terms, one of the most inhospitable places in the world.

Bolivia is a mysterious, intriguing country in which life is a constant confrontation with nature. The hostility and emptiness of the Andean landscapes provide travellers with some of their most vivid memories of South America. In few countries of the world does the human race seem so insignificant or vulnerable. In Bolivia the ability of the people to eke out a living on a vast, barren and windswept plateau surrounded by peaks rising to more than three miles/5,000m high, is awesome.

Visiting a country in which humans are so much at the mercy of the natural world is an eye-opening and challenging experience, both emotionally and physically; but while travelling through Bolivia can be hard work and at times scary, it is often exhilirating and never boring. And for those who are intimidated by the idea of scaling mountains to track down remote Inca ruins, there is an impressive collection of colonial churches, and a plentiful supply of colourful markets and festivals. At lower altitudes you can go on jungle treks that knock spots off some of the well-trodden paths in Brazil.

The *Guinness Book of Records* gives Bolivia the dubious honour of being the world's least politically stable country. But while the country has had an astonishing number of coups, elected governments are now the norm and economic stability is growing. Nevertheless, many Bolivians wonder whether the army will take control again if the economy weakens.

GEOGRAPHY

Roughly the size of Britain, France and Germany combined, and nearly three times the size of California, Bolivia consists of three geographical areas: the Altiplano, jungle lowlands and fertile valleys.

The Altiplano is (literally) a high plain that is enclosed by the two chains of the Andes that run the length of the country: the Cordillera Real and its continuation, the Cordillera Central, in the east; and the Cordillera Occidental in the west. The plateau lies at an average altitude of about 13,000ft/4,000m above sea level. It occupies only one-tenth of the country's area but is home to 75% of the population — a surprising statistic given the impoverished land that is virtually useless for crops. The southern Altiplano, with its salt deserts and volcanic peaks, is one of the most remote regions in the world.

In stark contrast to the scrubby Altiplano is the sparsely populated tropical lowland which is drained by the Amazon and Plata river systems and takes up 70% of the land area. It consists of jungle and of savannah that is parched in the dry season but turns into swamp during the rains. The blanket of tropical forest, particularly north of Santa Cruz, has been seriously dented by timber-cutting and colonization, to the extent that one-third of it has been lost over the last three decades.

Fertile valleys bridge the gap between the two extremes of the Andes and the jungle: the dramatic and lush Yungas northeast of the Cordillera Real, and the broader highland valleys further south.

CLIMATE

The dry season (winter) lasts roughly from April to October, and the wet season (summer) from November to March. Variations in temperature are determined by altitude. At high altitudes there can be dramatic changes: while temperatures in the highland areas during the dry season reach 21°C/70°F in the sun, at night these drop to around or below freezing. The effect of the sun being obscured behind a cloud is instantly felt. The Altiplano gets chillier the further south you go: Oruro and Uyuni are notoriously cold. In La Paz, Potosí, and the other high-altitude towns, you will need a warm jacket or a couple of alpaca jumpers. In Cochabamba and Sucre, both highland valley cities, a sweatshirt or jumper should be sufficient in the evenings. Wherever you are in the highlands, wrap up warm for overnight journeys.

Rainfall in the tropical lowlands is high, and the climate hot and humid. The heat in the southeastern areas, including Santa Cruz, is tempered between May and August by cool winds, known as *surazos*, blowing off the Argentinian pampas. The Yungas on the northeastern slopes of the Andes have a semi-tropical climate: it rains a fair amount, but temperatures are comparatively mild.

The dry season is the best time to visit Bolivia: the air is cold but beautifully clear and the bright, moonlit nights are unforgettable.

HISTORY

The earliest known inhabitants of Bolivia were the Tiahuanaco people who lived in the Lake Titicaca area, though their history is shrouded in mystery. However, they are known to have lived in the area around the lake between 600BC and AD1200, peaking around AD600, well before the Incas. Some archaeologists believe their empire stretched into Peru and as far south as northern Chile; whatever its boundaries, the civilization exerted great influence throughout ancient Bolivia and Peru. Tiahuanaco, the heart of the empire, had already been abandoned by the time the Incas arrived. The cause of their decline, like their origins, can only be a matter for speculation.

The Quechua-speaking Inca soldiers conquered the area about AD1200, and the Bolivian Altiplano was added to the vast territory of the Incan empire. The Incas themselves were conquered by the Spanish conquistadores more than three centuries later.

The Colonial Period. The first Spanish settlement in what became known as Alto

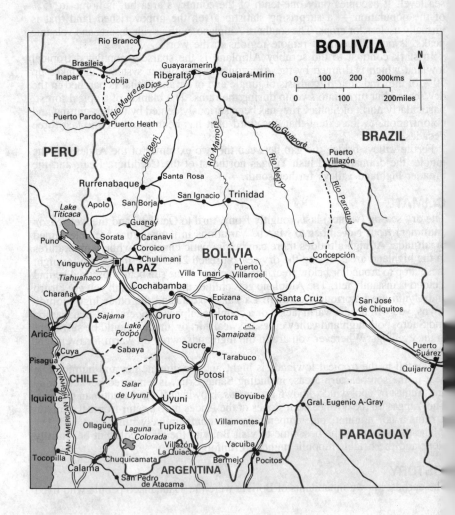

Perú, was established in 1535. Three years later came the foundation of La Plata (later Chuquisaca and now Sucre), which became the administrative centre of the territory.

The most significant date in the early colonial history of Bolivia, however, was 1545, the year in which a mountain seemingly solid with silver was discovered. Local Indians, and later African slaves, were reduced to slavery in the mines which provided the wealth to build the city of Potosí, and fill Spanish coffers. Potosí, at the cost of the death of millions of miners, became one of the largest and richest cities in the New World. For years 'Vale un Potosí' ('worth a Potosí') was the favourite phrase to describe untold riches. Mules and llamas loaded with silver travelled across the Altiplano to the Pacific. La Paz was founded in 1548 as a staging post on this route.

As elsewhere in the Spanish empire, discontent among the creoles and mestizos gave momentum to the independence movement in Bolivia. Dissent was voiced principally in Chuquisaca, a hotbed of liberal thinkers which became the centre of resistance in 1809. But revolts were suppressed with comparative ease, and it wasn't until 1825, when Bolívar and Sucre arrived from the north and San Martín from the south, that Bolivia was able to declare its independence from Spain.

Independence. Bolivia's history since independence has been a rapid succession of military coups and recurrent internal wrangling. Since 1825 there have been around 190 coups, roughly one every ten months, and 70 presidents. As if to divert attention from internal chaos, Bolivia got embroiled in a series of disastrous territorial wars. The result of the War of the Pacific fought with Peru against Chile (1879-83), was that Bolivia lost its part of the mineral-rich Atacama desert and a strip of land that provided its only access to the coast. The issue remains an emotive one. Even today, official maps show the province of Litoral as belonging to the country.

The loss of territory has been the hallmark of Bolivian military history: in 1903 a piece of Bolivia's Acre province, rich in rubber, was ceded to Brazil; and in 1938, following the costly Chaco War with Paraguay, Bolivia lost nearly 100,000 square miles of land in the southeast. Ironically, speculation that the Chaco region contains rich oil deposits has proved to be unfounded.

Recent History. The defeat in the Chaco War had dramatic repercussions in Bolivia. Radicals gathered together to form the Movimiento Nacional Revolucionario (MNR), and then proceeded to turn the political scene on its head. Their leader, Victor Paz Estenssoro, won the presidential elections in 1951, but the military prevented him taking power. There followed in 1952 one of Latin America's most famous and most radical 20th-century revolutions. Organized trade union and peasant movements (in which the miners played a principal role) defeated the army and installed Paz Estenssoro in government.

The new president launched a far-reaching programme of reforms, including the nationalization of the mines, universal suffrage and land reform. The first move was in many ways the most significant, because it was designed to break the power of the tin barons, who dominated political life. The most famous of them was Simón Patiño, a name with which most visitors will be familiar by the end of their trip. The virtual enslavement of the campesinos in his tin mines enabled him to become one of the richest men in the world.

Paz Estenssoro remained in power for 12 years, but he became increasingly autocratic, and discontent brewed. A coup in 1964 heralded a new period of military dictatorship, with the customary instability, and during the 70s drug lords increasingly became the main force in politics. Civilian rule returned in 1982, when Siles Zuazo of the Movimiento de Izquierda Revolucionaria (MIR), the main opposition party, was elected president. Jaime Paz Zamora, a nephew and political opponent of Paz Estenssoro, was his vice-president. The government proved unable to cope with the economy, however, and elections in 1985 returned Paz Estenssoro to power. He formed a coalition with the right-wing Acción Democrática Nacionalista (ADN), led by ex-General Hugo Banzer, who had led a military dictatorship in the 70s. Paz Estenssoro tackled the country's economic problems, one of his most drastic measures being the sacking of more than three-quarters of state mineworkers following the tin crash of October 1985. Bolivia ended up with the lowest inflation rate in the region, but also with incomes that had been reduced in value by 60% and with growing social unrest.

In 1989, although coming third in the elections, Jaime Paz Zamora was elected president when the two other candidates withdrew. The fact that Paz Zamora's MIR is now in a solid political alliance (the so-called Acuerdo Patriótico) with Banzer's ADN is indicative of the way politics have changed in Bolivia.

Paz Zamora's government has carried on Paz Estenssoro's free market polices, opening up the country to foreign investment, introducing privatization, cultivating friendship with the USA, and so on. But while some things have changed, others do not: rumours of government and police corruption (usually involving drugs) abound but are usually suppressed, journalists face intimidation, and demonstrations are dispersed with tear gas and bullets. The slow economic recovery and low inflation continues, but at the cost of no investment in health and education; many Bolivians rely on the cocaine trade, contraband and marginal living to survive. Discontent is expressed increasingly, with strikes and road blocks demonstrating that the Left and labour movements are not a spent force.

THE PEOPLE

Over half of the Bolivian population is of indigenous origin, the rest being split fairly evenly between mestizos and whites, who live mainly in the lowlands. There are also small Asian and black communities. The people of the Altiplano are known locally as *collas*, those from the lowlands as *campas*.

Most Indians live in the barren Altiplano, with only a small number living in Amazonia and southern Bolivia. The biggest group are the Quechua-speakers, who are descendants of the Incas. The Aymará-speakers are said to be descended from the pre-Inca Tiahuanaco civilization, and they live mainly in the department of La Paz, their original homeland. The two groups retain distinct identities, and there is virtually no intermarriage. While there is a great diversity of dress, customs and dialect among the Quechua, the Aymará show more uniformity. The Aymará women are distinctive for the bowler hat (that is said to have been brought to South America by British construction workers at the turn of the century), their hair worn in two long braids, and their layered skirt. *Cholo* is the name given to Indians who have moved into the towns and cities. While this group has abandoned some of its traditional ways, most Indians are strongly resistant to change.

The Amazonian Indians, of which the Chimanes are one of the biggest groups, are having to fight for their rights as much as their counterparts elsewhere in South America. A certain amount of land has been reserved for them, but loggers pay little heed to the boundaries. And the government has postively encouraged colonization of unoccupied areas as a means of dealing with the thousands of unemployed miners. However, the highland Indians are reluctant to leave their traditional homelands, and those that do have great difficulty in coping with life at low altitude. The department of Santa Cruz has seen the most colonization, but ironically it is foreign groups — principally Japanese and German — which have arrived in the greatest numbers. There is a sizeable community of Mennonites, a German religious sect found also in Paraguay; see page 593.

Bolivia's black community, descended from slaves brought to work in the mines, numbers about 17,000. Most blacks live in the Yungas, many of them working on coca plantations. They speak a dialect, based on Spanish, but many speak or understand Aymará, and most women wear the traditional bowler hat and layered skirt.

Religion. The vast majority of Bolivians, including the indigenous peoples, are Catholic. However, ancient cults survive and they have become blended with Christian rituals. Miners, who may well go to church, also sacrifice llamas to give blood to the Devil, their traditional protector. This bizarre belief is most vividly seen in the cities of Oruro and Potosí.

Meeting the People. The Bolivian people have a reputation for being dour, if not positively unfriendly. John Gunther, in his book *Inside Latin America,* makes an extraordinary generalization: 'Most Bolivians vary in character-pattern from extreme apathy, apathy almost to the point of physical numbness, to an intense nervous irritability'. He attributes such characteristics to the high altitude. Gunther's view is extreme, but most visitors do find that the people in the highlands are more reserved than their compatriots in the lowlands, who tend to be fairly relaxed and open. Yet encounters with the rather mysterious Indians of the Altiplano are often the most interesting — whether you're in the back of a crowded truck on a terrifying mountain road or spending an afternoon getting drunk on chicha with a few local campesinos.

LANGUAGE

The official language is Spanish, which is spoken by about two-thirds of the population. The Aymará and Quechua have their own languages and dialects, as do other indigenous groups living in the jungle lowlands. Cholos normally speak Spanish as well as their indigenous tongue. One of the most fascinating languages is Poquina, spoken by the tiny Chipaya community, which lives in the salt desert west of Oruro. The Chipayas are said to be the last of the Urus, the oldest indigenous people of the Altiplano.

FURTHER READING

Books written specifically about Bolivia are scarce, and the country is frequently lumped together with Peru. Matthew Parris ventures briefly into Bolivia in his book *Inca-Kola* (Weidenfeld and Nicolson, 1990), but the country and its people receives more extensive coverage in *Sons of the Moon* by Henry Shukman (Fontana, 1991). This is a quick, easy read but gives interesting insights into life in isolated indigenous villages, including those of the Chipaya. Anyone considering wild trips across the saltpans should read the relevant chapter in *A Gringo's Journey* by Cris Osborn (Impact Books, 1989), who cycles through the region. A more classic work, this time concentrating on the Amazon, is *Exploration Fawcett:* see page 23.

Getting There

AIR

La Paz and Santa Cruz are the international gateways into Bolivia. Direct airfares are high, however, and it is a good deal cheaper to fly to Lima in Peru and travel overland from there. See page 241 for details. A popular route is to fly to Peru and then take an internal flight to Juliaca, on the shores of Lake Titicaca, and then catch a couple of buses across the border from there. The Lima-Juliaca flight costs around $100.

From Europe the cheapest flight to La Paz is with Avianca, but this stops everywhere, can involve two or more changes, and takes over 24 hours. A six-month open return on this route from London costs around £700. The most direct routing is with Varig via Rio, which costs about £870 from London. The other option is to fly via Miami. Lloyd Aéreo Boliviano (LAB), the national airline, for example, flies from Miami to both La Paz and Santa Cruz. American Airlines also flies to La Paz from Miami: London to La Paz via Miami with this airline will cost about £800.

From South America. Bolivia is accessible by air from most South American countries, including from Buenos Aires, Arica and Santiago in Chile, and Rio, São Paulo, Manaus and Belo Horizonte in Brazil. La Paz is well served from Quito in Ecuador, with frequent flights on a number of airlines, including Ecuatoriana, LAB and AeroPeru; the fare is about $200. LAB flies from Qosqo in Peru twice a week, but seats get booked up quickly, and also from Lima — a route served also by AeroPeru.

If you want to fly to La Paz from Asunción in Paraguay, it is cheaper to fly to Santa Cruz and make a connection from there. But there is only one LAB flight a week to Santa Cruz from the Paraguayan capital. LAB and Eastern Airlines have services between Asunción and La Paz.

SURFACE

From Brazil. The principal crossing point from Brazil is near Corumbá, across the border from the Bolivian town of Quijarro. Unless you fly from the nearby town of Puerto Suarez, the only 'sensible' way to travel west from the frontier is by train to Santa Cruz. The journey is notoriously rough, not least because the police have a nasty habit of causing trouble for foreign travellers (see page 358). The most comfortable train is the ferrobus, which currently leaves twice a week and takes about 15 hours.

For a more adventurous trip, cross into northern Bolivia from Amazonia. There are a number of frontier posts, but the main crossing point is from Guajará Mirim (southwest of Porto Velho) to Guayaramerín. The Río Mamoré marks the frontier and must be crossed by boat. From Guayaramerín you can travel upriver south to Trinidad in about five days; otherwise take an internal flight or travel by road to Riberalta and south from there.

From Argentina. The main border crossing from Argentina is at La Quiaca, near the Bolivian town of Villazón. Buses run to the border from Salta and Jujuy, and from Villazón buses depart once or twice a day to Tupiza and Tarija. If you aren't interested in exploring this part of southern Bolivia, you would do better to take the train, which runs north to Uyuni (change here for Potosí), Oruro and La Paz. There is a weekly ferrobus and more frequent ordinary trains.

Another crossing point is at Yacuiba, across the border from the Argentinian town of Pocitos, also accessible by bus from Salta and Jujuy. Yacuiba is 3 miles/5km from the frontier, and you should be able to share a taxi into town. Bus services from Yacuiba are infrequent, with at most one daily service to Tarija. There are two ferrobus services a week to Santa Cruz.

The border crossing at Bermejo east of La Quiaca is rarely used, but is connected by a daily bus to Tarija.

From Chile. The journeys across the Andes from Chile are often bitterly cold — particularly if you travel by rail, which can involve long delays since the engine must be changed (and you may have to switch trains) at the border. A ferrobus runs twice weekly from Arica to La Paz, which takes 20 hours minimum. Buses also run twice a week via Tambo Quemado, taking a similar amount of time and costing $25, less than the train.

A more exciting route is the one via the Chilean town of Ollagüe, across the border from Abaroa, southwest of Potosí. Trains from Calama take about 24 hours to reach Oruro, and 36 to La Paz, often a lot longer. Carriages are usually packed but the views of the saltpans are fantastic. Take no notice of 'reserved' seats, and fight for as much space as you can.

From Peru. There are two overland routes from Puno in southern Peru. Those wanting to explore the Bolivian side of Lake Titicaca should take the northerly route, via Yunguyo, to Copacabana. This is by far the most scenic of the two, and the roads are paved for the most part. From Yunguyo (accessible by minibus from Puno in a couple of hours) there are collective taxis to the border post at Kasani. There is a short walk across the border to Bolivian immigration. From Kasani buses and collective taxis ($0.60 per person) run to Copacabana, from where buses run several times a day to La Paz. Tourist minibuses cover this route direct, leaving Puno in the morning and arriving in La Paz by evening, usually making a lunch stop at Copacabana. This is the best option if you want to get to the Bolivian capital as quickly and as painlessly as possible.

The southern route follows an unpaved road via the border town of Desaguadero. The advantage of taking this route is that it goes via Tiahuanaco (see page 347). The disadvantage is that transport is less frequent than via Yunguyo. There are minibuses from Puno to the border, but these don't leave until full up. The first one is unlikely to leave Puno before 7 or 8am. To charter a minibus will cost about $20, though if you are prepared for the driver to pick up other people en route, you can negotiate a much lower price. Desaguadero is one of the grimmest places in Bolivia, but forgiveably so: four years ago the town was completely washed out when Lake Titicaca flooded. There are several buses a day to La Paz from the border.

From Paraguay. The route into Bolivia across the Chaco region is extremely tough and not served by public transport. See page 593 if you are tempted.

Red Tape

Britons and most other citizens of western Europe (except for the French), Americans and Canadians do not require a visa to enter Bolivia. New Zealanders and Australians do.

For specific enquiries in the UK contact the Consulate at 106 Eaton Square, London SW1 9AD (tel 071-235 4255; fax 071-235 1868), which opens 10am-1pm, Monday to Thursday. Visas cost £6 and are issued on the spot. The Embassy in the USA is at 3014 Massachusetts Avenue, NW, Washington DC, 20008 (tel 202-483 4410). Bolivia does not have a mission in either Australia or New Zealand.

Tourists are normally allowed to stay in Bolivia for 90 days. The stamp obtained when you enter will determine your length of stay, and more often than not this is just for 30 days. If you have plans to stay longer, you can either leave the country briefly, or extend the visa at the Immigration Office in La Paz or at other offices in Bolivia's main towns.

Health Checks. Following the cholera scare, travellers arriving by land from Peru were required to have a compulsory health check. Upon arrival you were directed to the nearest hospital to be prodded around by a doctor, asked about your bowel movements, and required to pay $1 for a health certificate. This procedure was suspended in late 1991, though is likely to be reinstated if there is another outbreak of the disease.

CUSTOMS

You may be subject to lengthy baggage checks when entering or leaving Bolivia. This may be at the hands of either customs officials or narcotics police, and possibly both. Most travellers come out unscathed from these searches, but there is always the odd guard that enjoys flexing his official muscles. This occurs primarily at land borders. A lot of contraband flows across the frontiers and there is always a high police presence looking out for opportunities to seek bribes. The travellers most likely to be picked on are those crossing on foot.

Officials may just try a spot of intimidation (joking about drugs and examining everything in your bag, down to your last pair of dirty knickers), but their ultimate goal is to divest you of as much money as they dare. While some may make some effort to invent a reason for a 'fine' (e.g. your documents are out of order) others are less discreet. The cardinal rule is not to let them see your money in the first place. Show them only a few travellers cheques (which won't interest them) and some loose change.

Those travelling on the Corumbá to Santa Cruz train may be searched by narcotics police actually on the train: they are notorious for demanding bribes and even planting drugs.

Airport Tax. Anyone leaving by air must pay a tax of $15.

Boliviano (B/) = 100 centavos (c).

The boliviano was introduced in 1986. This followed a process of demonetarization in which six zeros were knocked off the value of the old peso. Inflation has been kept under some kind of control since, remaining under 20%. Many people still refer to bolivianos as pesos.

Notes and Coins. In 1991 plans were afoot to issue new notes and coins into circulation, owing to the poor state of those currently in use. At the time of going to press, however, notes were issued to the denominations of 2, 5, 10, 20, 50, 100 and 200 bolivianos. Coins are to the value of 1 boliviano and 5, 10, 20 and 50 centavos.

Changing Money. The best exchange rates are to be had in La Paz, Santa Cruz and Cochabamba, because this is where there is the greatest demand for dollars. Change money whenever possible in casas de cambio, which usually accept travellers cheques as well as cash. The rates for the former, however, are often poor: you will either be charged as much as 3% commission or be offered an appalling rate of exchange. Furthermore, some casas de cambio may change cheques happily during the week, but then show a singular reluctance to do so at weekends.

The government's austerity programmes have reduced to nothing the difference between the official and parallel rates. Nevertheless, you still find unofficial moneychangers, many of them women, all over Bolivia. Deals in the street can be struck at a gratifying speed, and the *cambistas* are generally honest.

Credit Cards. Visa, MasterCard and Diner's Club are the most widely accepted cards, and are of most use in La Paz and Santa Cruz. In addition, there is usually at least one bank in the main towns that deals with cash withdrawals on credit cards e.g. Banco Popular de Perú. Banks open usually 9-11.30am and 2.30-5pm, Monday to Friday.

Communications

Mail. Letters and parcels are best posted in La Paz, since mail sent from elsewhere is likely to take a week to get as far as the capital. To be more certain that your parcel will reach its destination use DHL couriers in La Paz (Alfredo Ascaruz 2518; tel 379422/342965).

Letters can be sent poste restante to any of the main towns with a reasonable chance of success. In most post offices, mail is segregated by gender, but badly, so ask correspondents to write Sr. or Sra. next to your name. Since mistakes can be made regarding the gender of certain names (women called anything from Anna to Zoe have found their letters under *Caballeros*), check both sections.

The address of the central post office in La Paz is Correo Central, Avenida Mariscal Santa Cruz y Oruro. Letters are held for three months.

Telephone. Bolivia is four hours behind GMT. Time remains the same throughout the country, and all year round. To phone Bolivia from abroad, dial 010 591 followed by the required number. Bolivia's telecommunications system is among the worst in South America. Making local calls is easy, however, with plenty of payphones around. These usually take *fichas* (tokens) which you can buy from nearby stalls.

Fichas for long-distance calls are also available, but long-distance and international calls are best done from an office of Entel, the state communications company. To make an internal call you normally just buy fichas from the desk; unused ones are refunded. Normal rates operate between 8am and 8pm Monday to Friday, with reduced rates from 8pm to 8am during the week, and at weekends. The main city codes are Cochabamba — 42; La Paz —2; Oruro — 52; Potosí — 62; Santa Cruz — 33; Sucre — 64; Trinidad — 46.

International calls must be made through the operator, and you may have to pay a deposit of about $5. Collect calls are not possible. Charges are based on call of a minimum of three minutes. Rates (for person to person and station to station calls respectively) are as follows: UK — $10 and $7.50; USA — $8.75 and $6.50 (reduced rate on Sundays); Australia — $12.75 and $10.50.

Useful numbers: Directory: 104; Police: 110; Ambulance: 118; Fire Brigade: 119;

Fax and Telegrams. Both can be sent from Entel offices. Faxes cost about double the telephone rate. The telegram rate for the UK and Australia is $0.50 per word, $0.40 for the USA.

THE MEDIA

Newspapers. Political comment in Bolivian newspapers has improved over recent years. This is most noticeable in the broadsheets, though there is an obvious lack of meaty articles about corruption, particularly when it involves politicians and drug-trafficking. The best coverage of international affairs is usually in *Los Tiempos* (right-wing) and *Opinión*, both of which are published in Cochabamba. These are distributed nationally, as are many of the dailies published in La Paz — including *Presencia*, a Catholic paper which is the best in the capital. *Hoy* and *Ultima Hora* are independent evening papers, also printed in La Paz. The broadsheets generally cost about $0.40. *Notas* is a weekly journal devoted to political and economic commentary.

Getting Around

Travelling around Bolivia requires a certain amount of flexibility and patience. Journeys overland are long and often arduous, and road travel is perhaps worse in Bolivia than anywhere else on the continent: thanks both to the poor condition of the roads and to the country's topography. Only around 400 miles of road are paved, principally in and around the cities. The remainder of the limited network is a pot-holed, crumbling safety risk. Presidente Paz Zamora has made the improvement of the country's roads an important political issue. If the government's promises bear fruit, the result will be much improved communications within the country.

Travel by train is usually a good option for the longer stretches, and internal airfares are surprisingly cheap too. In the Amazon region the road network is even more limited than elsewhere and also more liable to disruption by rain; in this region boat remains the principal means of transport.

Maps. Unless you go to a good specialized map shop, you will be unlikely to find a country map of Bolivia abroad. A good alternative is the map of Northwest South America described on page 41. In Bolivia the best place to look is in branches of the Los Amigos del Libro bookshop, found in most towns.

Country maps can differ disconcertingly when it comes to the category and even the layout of roads. One of the best is that published by the Instituto Geográfico Militar (IGM) in La Paz. You can buy it either from the IGM itself (Avenida 16 de Julio 1471) or from a good bookshop, for about $3. Another reasonable map is the so-called *Bolivia: Red Vial*, printed by the Ministry of Transport. This is a road map superimposed on a satellite photograph, with various city plans on the reverse side.

Topographical maps for serious hiking can also be obtained from the IGM. Since maps (other than city plans) are not easy to buy out of La Paz, you are advised to stock up while in the capital.

The normal train services, going from top to bottom in terms of quality, are the *especial* (or *expreso*), the *rápido* (something of a misnomer) and the *tren mixto* (or *segundo*), which carries both passengers and freight. The tren mixto is best used in extremis, when funds are low, although it will certainly give you the chance to experience rail travel at its most entertaining. The above trains usually have two different classes of carriage, and all take at least several hours longer than the ferrobus.

Buy tickets for the ferrobus the day before whenever possible, especially during the main holiday period. You must always check schedules in advance anyway, since they change constantly: most stations have blackboards displaying both timetables and fares. Be prepared for long-term queueing; some routes require you to queue all night with no guarantee of success. If you fail to get a ticket, you may be able to buy one through a travel agent; alternatively, get on the train anyway and hope for the best. In some cases you can turn up just half an hour before departure and buy a ticket without any problem.

BUS

Long-distance buses are referred to as *flotas*. As many as ten different firms may run services along a single route. But since most buses travel overnight, schedules tend to be bunched so that most departures are between 6pm and 10pm. Beware of buying through tickets, e.g. Cochabamba to Trinidad via Santa Cruz, since this will almost certainly involve a change of bus and a long wait en route. During the busy periods buy your onward or return ticket on arrival. Companies charge similar prices, though a few, such as Mopar, Cosmos and Nobleza, offer a slightly better service and ask about $2 more for an average overnight journey.

Small buses and minibuses serving rural communities are usually referred to as *colectivos* and *micros* respectively, and are often packed to capacity (or beyond). In the case of minibuses, you usually have to sit around until the vehicle is full before the driver will move off.

TRUCKS

Trucks are a vital form of transport for the local people. Not only do they offer an alternative to the buses along the main routes, but frequently are the only way to reach the more remote towns and villages. Journeys by truck may be slower and colder than by bus, but they are not necessarily less comfortable and are certainly more fun: travelling in the back of a truck enables you to enjoy the views and chat more easily with local people. Fares are 10-20% lower than the equivalent fare on the bus.

You need to be flexible since trucks rarely have set departure times, except those created by force of habit. You are in the hands of the driver: if you ask when the truck is due to leave, the response will almost certainly be *ahorita* or *en seguida* (straight away) — to be taken with a large pinch of salt.

Trucks often congregate near a town's main market area or the bus terminal — the locals can point you in the right direction. If all else fails, go to the relevant road leading out of town and wait. As a rule they load up in the early morning or late afternoon.

CAR

Driving in Bolivia is not recommended in most areas because of the dreadful condition and/or the terrifying twists and turns of the roads. Such are the risks and problems that international car rental agencies don't even bother to have agents in the country. There are, however, a small number of local companies, principally in La Paz, Cochabamba and Santa Cruz, and some day trips are perfectly feasible in a hired car.

The best source of information for drivers is the Club Automóvil Boliviano in La Paz, at 6 de Agosto 2993. For the 24-hour rescue service call 342074. The Red Vial map (see page 328) has a breakdown of important roadsigns and distances between towns, etc.

An International Drivers' Permit is required.

CITY TRANSPORT

Buses. City buses are plentiful, cheap and easy to use. They come in all shapes and sizes and get called all sorts of names. However there are basically two types: *colectivos* are the large buses which require payment on entry; while *micros* (minibuses) are faster, and require you either to pay the 'conductor' or driver en route, or to settle up with the driver when you get off. But since a large bus may sometimes be referred to as a micro, and a minibus as a colectivo, it's not worth worrying about the distinction. There are also *trufibuses*, which are minibuses offering a slightly more expensive and faster service than the normal micro.

The large buses normally have fares pasted up on the windscreen, and add a new dimension to the payment of fares: some buses offer discounts for two people: e.g. $0.20 per person or $0.30 for two.

Taxis. British visitors may be shocked to see that the Hillman Avenger — a rather dismal car built in Coventry in the 1970's — is the standard taxi in Bolivia. Since taxis don't have meters, you should discuss the rate before you set off. The fixed price for an average ride within a town is around $0.40, though Westerners may have to pay over the odds. It is common practice to share taxis, and this is done entirely at the discretion of the driver.

Trufis are taxis that operate along fixed routes. They advertise themselves by means of coloured flags attached to the bonnet, and route numbers written on the windscreen. The fare is about twice the corresponding bus fare.

Accommodation

Bolivia has the usual range of hotels, with the categories being as fluid as in any other South American country. Most hotels in the main towns have hot water nowadays, but it isn't always available all day. If you are on a low budget and can afford to stay only in the cheapest hotels, ask around for the *Baños Públicos* — great fun and lots of hot water for less than $1.

A decent double room with bathroom costs anything over $6, up to around $15 in Santa Cruz and Cochabamba, the two most expensive cities. For less comfort and no bathroom, however, you shouldn't need to pay more than $2-3 per person. A middle to top range hotel, with carpets and heating, costs at least $25 for a double. Few places have dormitories, although many hotels can offer rooms with three beds. Some tourist offices keep lists of families that rent out guest rooms privately.

Eating and Drinking

The lack of fertile land might lead you to expect a dull cuisine. The truth is, however, that it is possible to eat extremely well in Bolivia. The food, particularly in the highlands, is often spicy and can be positively hot: beware of the chilli peppers which are capable of burning the roof off an unsuspecting mouth. The worst offenders (owing to the element of surprise) are those which resemble the harmless capiscums found in Europe.

Bolivia, like most South American countries, caters primarily for meat-eaters. You'll encounter the usual gamut of steaks, including *lomo* and *churrasco*, in addition to a whole range of cuts you've never heard of. *Lapping*, for example, is rump steak eaten mainly around Cochabamba. *Silpancho*, one of the most delicious meat dishes, is a piece of beef beaten flat to the size of a plate, fried in breadcrumbs, and served on a bed of rice and chips with an egg on top. Stews are also popular, two of the most common being *picante* and *ají*, both hot dishes that can be made with all kinds of different meats, from chicken to tongue. *Fricasé*, often made with pork, is also recommended, as is *pique macho*, which consists of chopped steak and sausage, served with chips and hot peppers. Intestine sometimes makes an appearance in pique macho, but is more common in stews or the equivalent of a mixed grill: thankfully the pieces are usually large enough to be detected easily. Kebabs (*pacumutu*), make a pleasant change from the normal meat dishes, but only few restaurants serve them. Duck (*pato*) is common in Cochabamba and is highly recommended. Sausages (*chorizo*), which are an integral part of Bolivian cuisine, are a particular speciality around Sucre.

In some areas fish is an alternative to meat. The most common is *pejerrey* (fished in Lake Titicaca) and trout (*trucha*). Unfortunately, due to the cholera scare, many fish restaurants around Lake Titicaca have closed down. In Santa Cruz, in eastern Bolivia, restaurants serve a river fish called *surubí*, also common in Paraguay. Vegetarians who don't eat fish can seek refuge in the growing number of pizzerias or vegetarian restaurants in the big towns. As communications improve within the country vegetables grown in the fertile valleys have a better chance of being more widely distributed. However, the standard accompaniments to most dishes are rice and chips.

The most traditional Bolivian snack is the *salteña*. There is hardly a street that does not have at least one person selling salteñas, and they are almost invariably delicious. They are rather like cornish pasties, containing a mixture of meat (usually chicken), potatoes, hard-boiled egg and usually an olive (with stone). They are best when eaten piping hot, but beware of the gravy that leaks out. *Salteñerías* cater for those who don't want to eat on the hoof.

DRINKING

Most Bolivian lagers are extremely drinkable. The best include Paceña, Cruceña and Pilsener Tropical Extra. Dark beers, such as El Inca, are less common.

Wine is not a drink usually associated with Bolivia, but the country makes significant amounts of it; there is even a suburb of La Paz called Vino Tinto. The Tarija region in the southeast has a sizeable German community which has established some flourishing vineyards. The most popular and cheapest brand is Kohlburg, a bottle of which costs around $2 from the shops and $3 or more in restaurants; the red is the best. More expensive wines, such as the white Santa Ana, can be extremely good; but since these are generally served only in smart restaurants you may have to pay up to $10 for a bottle.

The most common spirit is *singani*, a local liquor made from grapes. Restaurants usually sell it by the bottle, and in towns you often see rowdy groups of men playing dice and getting hideously drunk on the stuff. Carbonated water is the usual accompaniment, although a more tasty mixture is *chuflay*, a combination of Singani, ginger ale and lemon.

In rural Bolivia the most traditional liquor is *chicha*, a cloudy yellow drink fermented from corn and made also in Peru; see page 54. In villages in some rural areas virtually every other house appears to be a *chichería*. They sometimes adveritise themselves using a straightforward sign saying 'chicha', but more common is a white flag at the end of a long pole, or a red or blue star hanging over the doorway. Wandering around any village in Cochabamba Department you cannot fail to encounter groups of heavily intoxicated men eager to offer you a glass of the brew.

The most delicious drink in Bolivia is *api* which is also made from corn, and flavoured with cloves and cinnamon. Unlike chicha it is non-alcoholic and is not a social menace. Api is served hot and can be either *blanco* (white) or *morado* (purple); a mixture of the two is known as *combinado*. Api morado is spicy and the more tasty, being rather like a thick, unalcoholic mulled wine. Api is usually served on the streets, and is accompanied by *pasteles* — large, deep-fried pastries that are ideal for dunking.

A good alternative to the strong coffee, especially as a late evening drink, is *maté de coca*, tea made with coca leaves — either in a sachet, but preferably fresh.

Exploring

Bolivia boasts the usual Andean array of fine colonial buildings and magnificent, hikable mountains, plus a great deal more. One of the country's most off-beat adventures is a visit to the still-functioning mines. Potosí is the favourite place to do this, although a couple of smaller mines around Oruro are also open to the public.

Bolivian culture is a fascinating blend of aboriginal traditions overlaid with Spanish influence. The Quipus Cultural Foundation was established in 1986 'to preserve, maintain and promote Bolivia's rich traditional cultural diversity'. Quipus has its headquarters in La Paz, where it is building a Museum of Popular Arts and Cultures. For further information write to PO Box 1696, La Paz, telephone 390700 or call in at Já regui 2248.

Colonial Heritage. La Paz, Sucre and Potosí are the main centres of colonial art, architecture and history. But they by no means hold the monopoly of fine buildings and museums, and you come across gems in the most unlikely places. Scattered throughout the country, but particularly in the Cochabamba area, are unrestored and crumbling colonial villages that are almost invariably more evocative than all the fine exhibits displayed in the museums.

If you think museum opening times are erratic, you will be even more frustrated by the whimsical hours kept by the country's churches. Many are open for just a couple of hours a day, some only one or two days a week and others are permanently closed. Annoyance is partially offset by the fact that in many cases the façade deserves more attention than the interior — you will lose count of churches with magnificent mestizo stone-carved portals, typical of Alto Perú, and characterized by motifs such as grapes, dwarfs and weird and wonderful creatures.

Archaeological Sites. Bolivia has no archaeological ruins that can rival Machu Picchu in magnificence. Tiahuanaco, the country's most important site not far from La Paz, is important historically but is unimpressive from an aesthetic point of view. Nevertheless there are several Inca sites, such as Inka-Rakay and Inkallajta near Cochabamba, that make excellent trips. The ruins themselves are generally small and neglected, but each is in a beautiful setting that warrants the effort required to get there. None can be reached by bus and most require a hike of some sort.

Hiking. The main hiking area is the Cordillera Real in western Bolivia. This range stretches for about 100 miles/160km, with the peak of Illampú at the northern end and Illimani to the south; it is within easy reach of La Paz. There are a number of well-defined trails through the lush valleys of the Yungas, some of which follow Inca or pre-Inca roads. Most treks require two to four days, and camping equipment is recommended. Several peaks in the Cordillera Real are over 19,700ft/6,000m, and are popular among experienced mountaineers.

The best source of information for both climbers and hikers is Club Andino (Calle Mexico 1638) in La Paz, which can help with the hiring of camping equipment too. It can arrange trips, including to Sajama, one of the country's most remote and highest peaks (21,385ft/6,520m), southwest of La Paz near the Chilean border. Club Andino also organizes trips to Bolivia's one ski slope on Mount Chacaltaya — which also happens to be the highest ski run in the world. The tourist office in La Paz has useful information on the Yungas treks.

Boat and trekking trips are increasingly popular in the Bolivian Amazon, though the scene is less developed than in Brazil; see page 353.

Entertainment

Music. One of the joys of Bolivia is its music. The most traditional sounds are those made by the percussion and wind instruments, particularly the *zampoña* (panpipes) and *quena* (flute). The *charango*, a ukelele-like instrument, traditionally with an armadillo shell for the soundbox, is also an integral part of the Bolivian music scene. The melodies of the southeastern region are heavily influenced by Argentina and Brazil, and are more light-hearted than the more soulful strains produced in the highlands.

While wandering through quiet village streets or travelling along country roads you frequently hear music being played. But to see a proper performance, you will usually have to go to a *peña*, a club specializing in folk music and dance. Most peñas are restaurants that put on shows just at weekends, particularly on Friday nights. Many of those in La Paz cater for the tourist trade and have become over commercialized, with performances on Thursday, Friday and Saturday nights, or even daily. Most highland towns have at least one peña. Performances usually start at around 10pm, and carry on until 1am or 2am; the entrance fee is $3-6.

Festivals. Bolivia has a very rich folk culture, particularly in La Paz and Cochabamba, and some of its festivals are among South America's finest.

As elsewhere in the continent, Carnival is a major celebration, most famously in Oruro. It is almost always a raucous and drunken event. *Alacitas* fairs are held in several Bolivian towns in honour of Ekeko, a pre-Columbian god of prosperity and good fortune. Miniatures are on sale, the idea being that whatever you purchase in miniature will be obtained in real life. The fairs fall at different times of year in different parts of the country: most famously in La Paz (January/February), but also, for example, in Sucre and Tarija (July) and Cochabamba (October). In January, Epiphany (Día de los Reyes Magos) is also celebrated in many places.

The tourist office produces the Calendario Folklórico, which is a booklet listing the festivals around the country. The best place to pick this up is at the office in La Paz; it costs $1.50.

SPORT

The most popular sport in Bolivia is soccer. As with the gallant players and supporters of teams like Crawley Town FC in Britain, football is characterized more by enthusiasm than by skill. Perhaps the most endearing facet of Bolivian soccer is the fashion for curiously Anglicized names. The top teams in the Vladimir Chávez league are: Always Ready, The Strongest, Blooming, and Destroyers. The best quality matches are held at the Hernando Siles stadium in La Paz.

Most Bolivian markets are a marvellous spectacle, and often cover several blocks, filling the surrounding streets. Best of all are the rural fairs, held once a week in many communities. People sit dwarfed by sackfuls of pasta and rice or mountains of oranges, as well as more bizarre products, such as dried llama foetuses that are traditionally buried in the foundations of a new house to bring good luck. Animals are sold at these markets too. You can also pick up a beautifully made trilby or bowler hat for around $5. For a tailor-made version you should go to one of the many hat shops. If you're after textiles, at most markets you are likely to find only the brightly-coloured shawls (*mantas*) that men and women use to carry virtually everything. They are coloured with synthetic dyes, but are at least cheap.

Some of the most spectacular markets are around Cochabamba, although the market at Tarabuco near Sucre is famous nationally. The best source of crafts and traditional-style woven textiles (often secondhand) is La Paz, where prices tend to be lower than elsewhere; the choice is limited at the craft markets in Cochabamba and Potosí. If you want to buy from the villages themselves, ask someone to direct you to the weavers' houses. La Paz is also the best place to look for alpaca or sheep's wool sweaters (*chompas*). For a jumper from an average market stall expect to pay $5-8, a good deal more if you go to a proper shop.

Anyone coming from Peru can relax a little after crossing the border into Bolivia. Depite the extreme poverty, incidences of theft and violence are comparatively rare, and La Paz is one of the safest big cities in South America. Reports in 1991 suggested that the Sendero Luminoso of Peru was expanding its operations into Bolivia, but this appears to be based on speculation rather than hard evidence. Nevertheless, the threat of possible terrorist activity has been taken seriously enough for the Bolivian armed forces to be deployed along the border with Peru.

The main thing travellers should watch out for is corruption among officials, particularly the police. Being asked to pay spurious 'fees' at borders is typical. Within Bolivia, the hassle given to tourists in Santa Cruz is legendary, although in fact only a small number of travellers are unlucky enough to be victimized. If you can't produce your passport when asked, you may face a fine-cum-bribe, with several tedious hours spent in the police station to boot. And such is the nature of the police force, that even if your passport is in order, you may be asked to pay a fine for some other trumped-up charge. You should also watch out for 'police' in plain clothes or with fake ID cards getting up to the same tricks: ask to be taken to the police station if you have any doubts, and try to drag a witness along with you (preferably one you can trust).

Drugs. Bolivia produces 40% of the world's coca — second only to Peru — and is now also the second largest producer after Colombia of the final product. Drug-trafficking is vital to the country's economy, and unemployment would be far worse were it not for the tens of thousands of campesinos employed on coca plantations and in the increasing number of laboratories. Roberto Suárez, Bolivia's 'King of Cocaine' is now languishing in jail, though not without first having offered to pay off the entire Bolivian foreign debt in return for special terms in court.

Stories about drugs fill Bolivia's papers. In 1991, alongside tales of army, police and government involvement in the drug trade, were reports of plans to tackle the growing of coca leaves head on. The armed forces are taking a leading role in the drug war, with the controversial assistance of US money and personnel to train special units. But the campaign is by no means straightforward. The crackdown on coca-growing threatens the lives of the peasantry, who chew coca leaves to help them cope with the altitude, hunger and fatigue. There are an estimated 60,000 coca farmers in the country represented by two powerful unions. While the government has made assurances that the army units will be deployed only against the refiners and traffickers of cocaine, peasant demonstrations have shown the general fear that many small farmers will also be attacked.

Eighty percent of coca is grown in the Chaparé region, north of Cochabamba. The Cochabamba-Santa Cruz road is known as 'cocaine highway' and there are permanent police checkpoints. If in this area don't wander off the beaten track, and don't travel alone at night. The other coca-growing area is in the Yungas, which includes a zone where it is grown legally, for traditional purposes.

Don't drink the water anywhere. If heading into the Yungas, Chaparé or the lowlands, protection against malaria and yellow fever is essential — mosquitoes are a real menace for anyone travelling in the Amazon. Chagas' disease also occurs in rural lowland areas.

Most people will be affected in some way by the high altitudes. Anyone flying direct into La Paz is likely to feel the effects immediately, and there is a doctor on hand to cope with problems among new arrivals by dispensing oxygen. It might be worth visiting cities in order of altitude, finishing up with Potosí or La Paz, thereby giving yourself more chance to acclimatize. The local remedy for *soroche*, as altitude sickness is known, is coca tea (maté de coca); otherwise simply chew the leaves themselves.

Bolivian consulates abroad usually have a tourist department which can send you literature on request. The office in London (106 Eaton Square, London SW1 9AD; te 071-235 4248) is efficient and sends out a moderately useful leaflet on the country. Once in Bolivia, there are branches o the Instituto Boliviano de Turismo (IBT) in all the main towns. These can usually provide you with a city map, and perhaps the odd brochure.

As far as books about the country are concerned, the best one available is A Insider's Guide to Bolivia by Peter McFarren. It costs $19 but includes interesting essays on different aspects of the country, as well as a more straightforward section with lists of museums, hotels, etc. and some good maps. You can usually pic it up in branches of Los Amigos del Libro, a chain of bookshops found in th main towns. These normally have a selection of books about Bolivia, including the odd secondhand and English-language title. Los Amigos also publishes its own series of books about the country, concentrating on historical, cultural and ethnographical subjects; these are good buys if you can read Spanish. Their shops also stock literature in English and other foreign languages. All books are expensive.

Public Holidays

January 1	New Year's Day
February/March	Monday, Shrove Tuesday and Ash Wednesday of Carnival
March/April	Good Friday
May 1	Labour Day
May/June	Corpus Christi
July 16	La Paz Municipal Holiday
August 5-7	Independence Day
October 12	Columbus Day
November 2	All Souls' Day
December 25	Christmas Day

LA PAZ

La Paz is often quoted as being the world's highest capital. While its rival high-altitude cities accept the fact that it is 11,900ft/3,630m above sea level, they may take issue with its status as capital. La Paz is the seat of Bolivian government and to all intents and purposes the capital, but Sucre legally holds the title.

The city lies in a dramatic canyon and is an utterly breathtaking sight as you approach from the Altiplano. A small collection of skyscrapers in the centre is dwarfed by the surrounding cliffs, and crumbling adobe houses tumble down the sheer terraces on either side. The snow-capped Mount Illimani of the Cordillera Real, which rises to the south, is a constant and awesome presence; unexpected views of the mountain reward you as you stagger up and down the city's steep cobbled streets.

La Paz was founded in the 16th century following the discovery of gold in the Choqueyapu valley. The settlement expanded not so much because of the gold, which petered out quickly, but due to the town's position on the trade routes between the silver mines of Potosí and the seaports of Peru. La Paz now has a population of about 1.5 million, swollen by the thousands of rural immigrants. More than half of the inhabitants are Indian, and La Paz is very much an Aymará city: the Indian quarter is one big market that is unlike anything found in other South American cities.

La Paz is manageable, amiable and safe. It is predominantly modern, but a number of fine colonial buildings survive. Many of these are now museums, some of which are excellent. It is easy to spend a couple of weeks here simply enjoying the setting and the colourful streetlife; but La Paz is also ideal as a base from which to explore the Cordillera Real and other sights nearby.

CITY LAYOUT

The main thoroughfare through La Paz follows the line of the unsavoury Coqueyapu river, with cross streets branching up the steep slopes on either side of it. This central artery assumes different names as it progresses through the city. Avenida 16 de Julio, in the heart of the city, is usually referred to as El Prado, a term often used to describe the whole of the main street. The *centro* can be defined roughly as the area along Avenidas Mariscal Santa Cruz and 16 de Julio, with Plaza Murillo, the main square, to the northeast, and the Indian market area to the southwest. The centre is fairly compact. While getting lost is quite an achievement, the chaotic streets of the Indian quarter can be confusing.

The poorest areas are on the higher slopes, and have the best views; the wealthy zone is lower down the canyon where the climate is milder. The poorest district is El Alto, itself a city, on the plateau above La Paz. It is inhabited almost exclusively by Aymará migrants, and has a population of 500,000 and rising.

Maps. A good choice of city maps is available, including the one sold for $1 by the tourist office. The map with the most detail (and an index of street names) is the so-called *Guía Gráfica*, although the *Cicerone* map ($2), which shows street numbers and places of interest, is more user-friendly. You can buy both these at Amigos del Libro at Avenida Mercado 1315, near the corner of Colón, or Libreria Gisbert (Calle Comercio 1270), half a block east of Plaza Murillo.

For topographical maps go to the Instituto Geográfico Militar (IGM) at Avenida 16 de Julio 1471. You may not be able to pick the maps up until the following day, and you need to take your passport. Maps are also available from Club Andino (Calle Mexico 1638; tel 324682) and the Club Automóvil Boliviano (6 de Agosto 2993, where it meets Avenida Arce), which opens 8.30-11.45am and 2-6.30pm from Monday to Friday.

ARRIVAL AND DEPARTURE

Air. El Alto is the highest international airport in the world. Awaiting arrivals is a tourist information desk, but no bank.

The airport is 6 miles/10km from the city, and is connected by motorway to the centre: the run into town takes just 20 minutes. Minibus 212 operates between the airport and Plaza Isabel La Católica (on Avenida Arce) between 7am and 9pm. It follows the main drag through the city, so most places are easy to reach. A shared taxi costs about $1.50, a regular cab about $8 (agreed in advance).

Airline Offices: the main airline offices are on and off Avenida 16 de Julio. For flight information call 810122.

Aerolíneas Argentinas — Avenida 16 de Julio, Banco de la Nación Argentina (tel 351711).

AeroPeru — Edificio Avenida, 16 de Julio 1490, 2nd floor (tel 370002/4).

Avianca — Edificio Petrolera, 16 de Juilo 1616, Mezzanine (tel 350608).

LAB — Avenida Camacho 1456, between Loayza and Bueno (tel 367718/11).

LAP — Edificio Colón, Colón 330 between Potosí and Mercado.

Varig — Edificio Cámara de Comercio, Avenida Mariscal Santa Cruz, near corner of Calle Colombia (tel 358754). Faucett, the Peruvian airline, is in the same building.

TAM — Avenida Montes 738, near the western end of Ingaví.

Bus. The main bus terminal is at Plaza Antofagasta, just off Avenida Montes; phone 367274/5/6 for information. The walk from the station to the centre is downhill; for the return journey, take any micro marked *Terminal*, such as the 2, 130, M or CH.

Services for destinations within La Paz department leave from various locations within the city: from the Cementerio on Avenida Baptista for destinations west

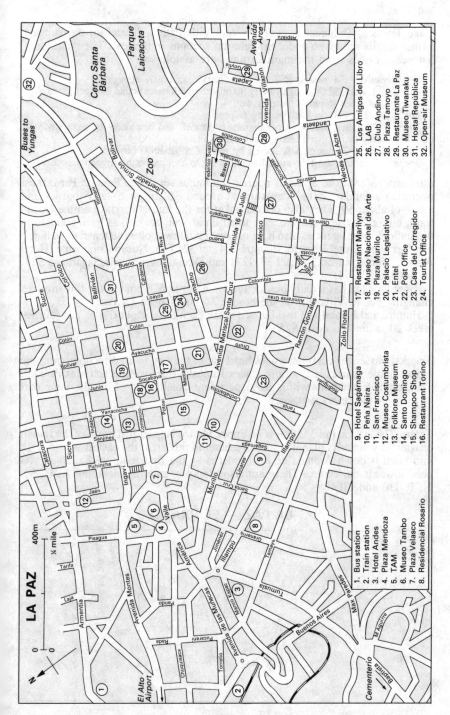

LA PAZ

0 ¼ mile
0 400m

N

Parque Laicacota

Cerro Santa Bárbara

Buses to Yungas

Zoo

1. Bus station
2. Train station
3. Hotel Andes
4. Plaza Mendoza
5. TAM
6. Museo Tambo
7. Plaza Velasco
8. Residencial Rosario
9. Hotel Sagárnaga
10. Peña Naira
11. San Francisco
12. Museo Costumbrista
13. Folklore Museum
14. Santo Domingo
15. Shampoo Shop
16. Restaurant Torino
17. Restaurant Marilyn
18. Museo Nacional de Arte
19. Plaza Murillo
20. Palacio Legislativo
21. Entel
22. Post Office
23. Casa del Corregidor
24. Tourist Office
25. Los Amigos del Libro
26. LAB
27. Club Andino
28. Plaza Tamoyo
29. Restaurante La Paz
30. Museo Tiwanaku
31. Hostal República
32. Open-air Museum

Cementerio
Baptista
M Aguirre

339

(Lake Titicaca, Tiahuanaco, etc.), or from Villa Fátima district for the Yungas; further details are given under the relevant sections in the text. The main long-distance services from the main terminal are as follows:

Cochabamba — 10 hours, $5-7, plenty of services, mostly at night.
Oruro — 3 hours, $2.50, roughly every 30 minutes, with buses bound for Cochabamba or Potosí often stopping there as well.
Potosí — 12 hours, $6-7, all leaving 6-7pm.
Sucre — 18 hours, $12; via Cochabamba or Potosí, and best done in stages since it is likely to involve a change and long wait.
Santa Cruz — 23 hours, $13, served by some Cochabamba buses.
Tarija — 26 hours, most days usually continuing to Yacuiba on the Argentine border.

International: various agencies operate a minibus service to Puno in Peru, most operating a similar deal — departure at around 8.30am, a 10-hour journey and a fare of about $9. They also offer a ticket for the tourist carriage on the Qosqo train, but otherwise arrange one yourself on arrival. As well as having kiosks in the station, these agencies also have offices downtown, often attached to an hotel, e.g. Turisbus (Hotel Rosario, Illampú 704; tel 326531), Nuevo Continente (Hotel Andes, Manco Kapac 366; tel 373423) and Diana Tours (Calle Sagárnaga 328; tel 340356/375374).

Panamericana has a daily bus to Buenos Aires at 6.30pm ($150); this involves changing bus at Villazón, on the border 24 hours from La Paz.

Humire and Litoral run two buses a week each to Arica in Chile. The journey takes 20 hours and costs $25.

Trucks. Passenger-carrying trucks head out of the city in all directions from the Indian quarter, particularly around Calles Tumusla, Buenos Aires and Max Paredes. Trucks for destinations within the department usually leave from the same part of town as the relevant buses.

Train. The station (tel 353510) is on upper Manco Kapac, just north of the Indian quarter. If you aren't planning to find a hotel in this area, the easiest way to walk into town is down Avenida de las Muñecas — the first road on the left as you head towards the centre. There are also plenty of micros, including A, C, M, N, P, 130 and 131.

LA PAZ — EL PRADO

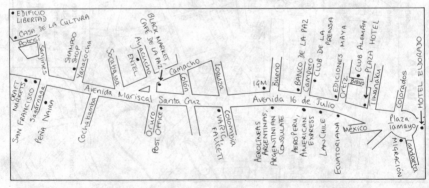

There are currently two ferrobuses to Oruro on Saturday ($7), continuing either to Uyuni and Tupiza, or to Potosí ($13) and Sucre ($19). An expreso runs on Fridays and a tren mixto on Mondays and Thursdays to Oruro, Uyuni and Villazón: the fares are $7, $15 and $24 and $3, $7 and $14 respectively. The ferrobus to Arica in Chile leaves at 7am on Monday, Wednesday and Friday ($49).

Car Rental. The best local company is Imbex (Avenida Arce 2303; tel 379884/322947), which hires out jeeps for $28 per day plus $0.25 per km.

GETTING AROUND

The usual array of micros and colectivos chokes the streets of La Paz; destinations are clearly marked on the windscreens. Most buses travel along the Prado at some point, Plaza San Francisco being a particularly good place to pick them up. Buses run until about midnight, though you see few on the street after 10pm.

A surprising number of taxis are clapped-out Hillman Minxs (a British car popular in the early 1960s). A standard fare of about $0.50 per person applies to most taxi rides within La Paz; shared taxis are the norm. In addition to regular taxis, trufis run on fixed routes along the main streets.

The building a cable-car link (*teleférico*) between La Paz and El Alto is planned. This would have its base at Plaza San Francisco in the centre of town, and would certainly offer marvellous views.

ACCOMMODATION

If you arrive in La Paz towards the end of the day, the most popular cheap hotels may be full; but there is plenty of choice so finding a bed is never a problem. The two main areas for cheap hotels are in and around the market area, and in the vicinity of Plaza Murillo. Addresses, phone numbers and locations are given in the list at the end of this section.

There are several residenciales on Avenida de las Muñecas, virtually within sight of the train station, but most are extremely basic and of dubious reputation. The only decent hotel in this area is the Hotel Bolivia, bang opposite the station; a double room with bathroom costs $7.50. You would do better to look along Manco Kapac. Hotel Andes is friendly and good value, with rooms for $7/$10. On the same street are the Italia, in a lovely building, set back from the road (same rates as the Andes) and the Panamericano (slightly more expensive, takes credit cards).

On Illampú, which runs on from Manco Kapac, is one of the most popular places among travellers and climbers: Residencial Rosario. It is in a lovely building, with a library, good (but expensive) restaurant, and rooms for $9/$16. A few doors along is the Residencial Copacabana, a new hotel which is considerably cheaper at $7/$9. The Alem and Sagárnaga hotels on Calle Sagárnaga are more central but unfriendly. A well-located, quiet and unpretentious hotel is the Oruro in Plaza Mendoza, with rooms for $6/$10.

The other side of El Prado, around Plaza Murillo, tends to be quieter. One of the most popular places among shoestring travellers is Residencial Torino at Socabaya 457. It's cheap, lively and noisy, and has a bar and book exchange. More expensive, but friendly and clean, is the Hostal República, at Comercio and Bueno. It has a courtyard, its own café, and laundry service. Around the corner is the Viena, which charges $9/$12.

Moving down the main drag from Plaza Tamayo (formerly Estudiante), the luxury and cost of hotels increases. The top hotel is the La Paz (formerly the Sheraton), on Avenida Arce at the corner of Guachalla. The best-value business hotel is the 3-star Eldorado, close to Plaza Tamayo. It has good facilities and an excellent view from the top floor. Rates are $27/$35.

Alem: Sagárnaga 334 (tel 367400); between Linares and Illampú.
Andes: Manco Kapac 364 (tel 323461; 378355).
Bolivia: Manco Kapac 287 (tel 375030).
Copacabana: Illampú 734 (tel 367896).
Eldorado: Avenida Villazón (tel 363355; fax 391438)
Italia: Manco Kapac 303 (tel 325101).
Oruro: Plaza Alonso de Mendoza (tel 325893).
Panamericano: Manco Kapac 454 (tel 378370; 340810).
República: Comercio 1455 (tel 357966; 356617); between Loayza and Bueno.
Rosario: Illampú 704 (tel 325348; 326531); Santa Cruz and Graneros.
Sagárnaga: Sagárnaga 326 (tel 350252; 375374).
Torino: Socabaya 457; between Potosí and Comercio.
Viena: Loayza between Potosí and Comercio

EATING AND DRINKING

The centre of town has plenty of cheap but often uninspiring restaurants, offering a limited menu of meat-orientated dishes and set meals. One place to stand out, however, is the Marilyn, at the corner of Socabaya and Potosí. It is lively and particularly popular at lunchtimes when people flock to eat the $1.50 *almuerzo económico*. A good, varied menu is available until 9pm. Vegetarians can try the Manjari (Potosí 1315, at Colón), which also serves hamburgers for carnivorous chums. Another vegetarian place is the Palacio Vegetariano on 16 de Julio at Reyes Ortíz, which opens at 7am for breakfast, noon for lunch and 6pm for dinner, daily except Sundays.

The alternative is to eat in one of the much smarter restaurants, found mainly south of the centre. For a civilized evening in beautiful and quiet surroundings, and excellent food, go to Restaurant La Paz on Calle Goytia (tel 352262) off Avenida Arce. More expensive still is El Refugio, at Avenida 20 de Octubre 2453 (tel 355651). A main dish will set you back about $7, but the atmosphere is unpretentious and the food good and traditional. More central is the Club Alemán, on Calle Carlos Bravo (tel 324397), behind Hotel Plaza, with excellent food and a Central European ambience.

Cheaper are Pizzería El Paso near Plaza Tamayo, and the lively Club de la Prensa on Calle Campero; if you enjoy eating intestine and other dubious parts of animals' bodies, don't miss the *plato periodista*.

Finding cafés open for breakfast before 9am is a problem. One of the best breakfasts in town can be had at Restaurante Torino (Socabaya and Potosí), which opens at 8.15am and has English-language magazines. Its *Desayuno Americano* is highly recommended at under $2. Cheaper and more simple is the café next to the Marilyn, nearby, which also opens early.

The very best salteñas are sold at Super Salteñas on Sánchez Lima at Salinas, but they cost twice the usual price.

Relax over a drink at the most atmospheric bar in town, Café La Paz. It is part of the Club de La Paz, at the foot of Ayacucho between the main drag and Camacho. Prices are twice what you might pay elsewhere, but the classy art deco surroundings make it worthwhile.

EXPLORING

The best view of the city is from the top floor of Hotel Plaza on Avenida Arce, from where you can get your bearings in the city and look eastwards across to snow-clad mountains. Almost as good a view can be had from the Tourist Office, which is on the 18th floor of Edificio Ballivián, on Calle Mercado between Loayza and Colón.

East of El Prado. Plaza Murillo is the centre of old La Paz. It is a gathering place for pigeons and elderly men who while away the day gossiping with friends. It is a deceptively quiet square: it has been the scene of many of Bolivia's coups, and is still a popular rallying point for demonstrations. Facing south, your view is of the modern, gloomy cathedral, and the Presidential Palace (Palacio de Gobierno); the latter is heavily guarded and closed to the public. To your left is the rather rundown National Assembly (Palacio Legislativo), open to the public from Monday to Friday; take your passport.

On the corner of Comercio and Socabaya is the lovely 18th-century Palacio de los Condes de Arana. It houses the Museo Nacional de Arte, whose collection includes some fine colonial works from the various Alto Perú schools and some interesting indigenous sculpture. The top floor is devoted to contemporary art, among which the the works of Cecilio Gúzman de Rojas stand out. The museum is open 9.30am-12.30pm and 3-7pm, Tuesday to Friday, and Saturday mornings.

Heading west along Ingaví, you pass the church of Santo Domingo, which has a fine stone portal. Weddings often take place here on Saturday mornings, and this is a good time to see Aymará cholas in their finest clothes. Further along, at Ingaví 916, is the Museo de Etnografía y Folklore. Housed in another carefully restored mansion, this is one of the city's finest museums, with excellent photographs and displays of weavings, musical instruments, tools, and so on. They give a good background particularly to the Chipaya people, made all the more fascinating by a commentary written by the Indians themselves. The museum opens 8.30-11.30am and 2.30-6.30pm, Monday to Friday, 9am-1pm on Saturday.

A short distance north is Calle Jaén, a narrow cobbled street lined with some of the finest buildings in the city. It has an unreal sense of tranquillity, as well as a greater concentration of tourists than anywhere else in the city. Calle Jaén is a street of museums, four in all. To buy tickets for all of them ($0.75) you must go to the Museo Costumbrista, which overlooks Plaza Riosinho, at the top. The two museums to concentrate on are the Museo de Metales Preciosos, which has a wonderful collection of Tiahuanaco and Inca gold, and the Casa de Murillo, the home of the independence campaigner. The latter contains a rather motley array of exhibits, but it has a particularly fine room devoted to the Callawayas, famous healers of northern Bolivia. All four museums have the same opening hours: 9am-noon and 2.30-6pm Monday to Friday, 10am-12.30pm on Saturday.

The other things worth seeing this side of El Prado are southeast of Plaza Murillo. At the corner of Federico Suaza and Tiwanaku, not far from Plaza Tamayo, is the Museo Nacional de Arqueología, also known as the Museo Tiwanaku. As well as a good selection of pottery and textiles from ancient Tiahuanaco, it has a wonderful collection of Inca *kerus* (wooden pots used for drinking chicha) and smoking apparatus which looks suspiciously like a hookah pipe. There are also maps and photographs of archaeological sites around the country. The museum is open 9.30am-12.30pm and 3-7pm, Tuesday to Saturday. To see larger relics from ancient Tiahuanaco, visit the Templete Semisubterráneo, at the eastern end of Avenida Bolívar in Plaza Sorzana. This bizarre open-air museum is set in the middle of a busy roundabout. Opening hours are erratic, but most of the monoliths can be appreciated from street level. To get there catch any bus going to the stadium (Estadio) which overlooks the square.

Having got this far, it is only a short walk up to Parque Laicacota (off Avenida del Ejército). While offering fairly good views over the southern districts and across to Illimani, the park is nothing special. Visit it at sunset, when it is the last place in La Paz to fall into darkness. The Quipus Foundation is developing the Museo de Arte y Cultura Populares on the opposite Cerro de Santa Bárbara, which will enhance the area considerably. Towards the foot of the park, on the south side of Avenida Bolívar, is the miserable little zoo (open daily 10am-5.30pm).

A mile or so further southeast along the valley, reached from Calle Lucas Jaímes just down from Villalobos, is the Botanical Garden. Don't expect much more than some pleasantly terraced park with plenty of topiary.

West of El Prado. The architectural highlight this side of the Prado is the church of San Francisco, in the buzzing square on the corner of Calle Sagárnaga. It is undoubtedly the city's finest church. Begun around 1550, it took over two centuries to complete. The bell tower, added later, was a hideous mistake, but it detracts only momentarily from the beauty of the façade — an example of mestizo baroque carving at its peak, it reveals fascinating detail, from toucans and monkeys to pineapples and papayas. Saturday is a good day to visit and see a baptism or wedding; these ceremonies usually take place between 10 and 11am.

This area of town is wonderful for markets, which stretch from Plaza San Francisco virtually to the railway station. Almost every street is overflowing with people selling anything from wardrobes to pig trotters. To the right of San Francisco are two small craft markets, the indoor Galería Artesanal and the Mercado Artesanal. The shops in the Galería offer the best quality, but are more expensive; most accept credit cards. Calle Sagárnaga, the narrow cobbled street running alongside San Francisco, is full of crafts shops and people on the pavement selling alpaca jumpers, hats and weavings. Calle Linares has several good shops too, including a number selling musical instruments. But Linares is most famous for the Witchcraft Market, known variously as Mercado de Hechicería or de los Brujos. Here, women sell magic charms, herbal remedies and the extraordinary shrivelled and bird-like dried llama foetuses.

As you penetrate further into the Indian quarter, fewer crafts are on sale; but it is here that the market really takes off. Max Paredes and Buenos Aires are the two main streets, but the whole area is so seething with people and traffic that it is hard to keep your bearings. Simply follow your nose.

The Museo Tambo Quirquincho is on Calle Evaristo Valle between San Francisco church and Plaza Mendoza; there are good views back over the city and across to Illimani from this street. The museum contains mostly modern art, but the highlight is a magnificent collection of silver on the ground floor. The room devoted to the carnival, and the old photographs of the city are also interesting. The museum opens 9.30am-12.30pm and 3-7pm Tuesday to Friday; 10am-12.30pm at weekends.

ENTERTAINMENT

Nightlife. Peñas in La Paz are mostly fairly commercialized, but are at least plentiful. Most have folk music shows on at least Friday and Saturday, usually beginning at 10pm and finishing at around 1am; make a reservation during the holiday season. The entrance fee is $4-5.

The best venue is La Casa del Corregidor (1040 Calle Murillo; tel 363633).

Media: In a poor field 90.1 FM is best for Western rock music. If this doesn't appeal, try 91.1, 92.1 or 98.

Embassies and Consulates. *Argentina:* Avenida 16 de Julio 1486, Edificio Banco de la Nación Argentina, 2nd floor (tel 353089). Open 9am-2pm daily.
Brazil: Avenida 20 de Octubre 2038, Edificio Foncomín, 9-11th floors (tel 350718/352108).
Chile: Avenida Hernando Siles 5843 (corner of Calle 13), Barrio Obrajes (tel 785275). Take any micro bound for Calacoto or Obrajes, e.g. 11.
Colombia: Plaza Abaroa (tel 351199).
Paraguay: Avenida Arce 2105, Edificio Venus, 7th floor, at junction with Calle Montevideo (tel 322018/328734).
Peru: Edificio Alianza, Avenida 6 de Agosto 2190, 1st floor (tel 352031), at corner of Calle Guachalla.
Venezuela: Edificio Illimani, Avenida Arce 2679, corner of Calle Campos, 4th floor. Open 9am-2pm.
UK: Avenida Arce 2732-2754, opposite the huge black and cream Edificio Illimani (tel 351400/329401/391063). Open 9am-noon Monday and Tuesday, 9am-1pm on Wednesday, 1.15-4pm Thursday and Friday.
USA: Embassy in Banco de Perú building at Calle Colón 290 near Mercado. Consulate in Edificio Tobias, 2nd floor, at Avenida Potosí 1285 between Colón and Ayacucho (tel 350120/350251). Open for visa applications 8.30-11am.

AROUND LA PAZ
La Muela del Diablo. The Devil's Tooth is a suitably shaped rock set in staggering scenery. It lies only an hour's walk from the suburbs, southeast of the centre, and it is excellent for a short morning's hike, or a more leisurely day trip.

Begin by taking micro 288 from Calle México to the end of the line in the barrio of Pedregal, which takes about 30 minutes. If you tell the driver that you want to go to Muela del Diablo, he should drive you across the riverbed and up the hill to a dirt football pitch, the start of the walk; otherwise, do this stretch on foot, which takes five minutes.

From the football field, walk up a short slope and turn right on to the road and follow the most obvious track upwards. After ten minutes you reach a small cemetery. From this point on you see a number of different tracks; look for footprints and animal droppings to keep on the right one, and there is usually the odd passer-by to ask too. During the early stages keep an eye on a clump of four eucalyptus trees up on the hill: as long as you head roughly in their direction you should be alright. From the cemetery, take the track leading up and to the right. Take a left turn shortly afterwards, and then bear right and head upwards. Ignore a left fork and some time later you will cross a small 'natural' bridge (about 10 minutes from the cemetery). Beyond here take the second left fork; if you miss it you will hit a black, volcanic slope, in which case you know to turn back.

The track joins another path; go right and up, and at this stage you hit a patch of volcanic terrain; continue up and the path becomes more grassy and easier. The path bends right for a majestic view of the city. As you round the ridge you look down upon pinnacles shaped by the wind and rain, with La Paz silent in the distance. At this point, those who are as terrified of heights as one of the authors will call it a day and just enjoy the stunning panorama. You will have been going for about 30 minutes.

A short distance after the ridge you will have your first sighting of the Devil's

Tooth. In the shadow of this and other bizarre rock formations that should have been the inspiration behind Gaudi's cathedral in Barcelona, is a tiny village. This impossibly idyllic position makes a perfect picnic spot. The path continues through the village (where the children appreciate gifts of sweets), then bends around to skirt the bottom of the Tooth. It ascends sharply and many people turn back at this point: the loose rocks make scaling the Muela del Diablo itself hazardous.

Once back at the bottom, you will probably need to walk down the hill and across the riverbed to catch the bus back into town.

Valle de la Luna. Those who have done the above walk will find 'Moon Valley' a disappointment. Nevertheless, for anyone not keen to tackle the Devil's Tooth, the rock formations in this small valley give an inkling of what you're missing. A few hours is all you need.

Valle de la Luna lies in the outskirts south of the centre, reached by taking Micro 11 from anywhere along the Prado to the end of the line. Cross the nearby bridge and either follow the road (a long way round) or traverse the dried-up riverbed and take the path straight up; after ten minutes the track rejoins the road at a fork. On the left a path leads down into Moon Valley. The trail through the rocks becomes narrow in places, but is well-worn and hence easy to follow. It eventually rejoins the road to the village of Mallasa near a football field. If you don't want to return the way you came, you can follow the road down.

Chacaltaya. Mount Chacaltaya boasts the highest ski slope in the world, at an altitude of 17,716ft/5,400m. Keen or foolhardy skiers may be unable to resist the temptation to ski, but facilities are basic and the safety precautions rudimentary. Furthermore, the ski run is short and the altitude means that even the fittest skier is likely to find it extremely tiring. However, the views on a clear day are staggering. The ski lodge is only 22 miles/35km and 90 minutes north of La Paz. The journey, around hairpin bends with sheer drops, is exhilirating but terrifying. Club Andino in La Paz runs trips at weekends from November to April, for about $30.

Zongo Valley. The peaks of the Cordillera Real attract climbers from all over the world, none more so than Huayna Potosí (19,975ft/6,090m). The closest the casual traveller can come to this magnificent mountain is to take a trip to Zongo Valley. The road to the town of Zongo heads north from La Paz and crosses a spectacular pass between the peaks of Huayna Potosí and Chacaltaya, before its dramatic descent into the tropics. The floor of the valley has some beautiful coloured lakes, as well as several hydroelectric projects. Simply travelling through the valley is a delight, but to explore further you can walk to an ice cave beneath the Chacaltaya glacier.

Buses to Zongo leave from Plaza 16 de Julio in El Alto district; otherwise take a taxi. The start of the walk is about two hours from La Paz, near a guard's house; the driver will know where to drop you. An extremely narrow path leads off to the right beyond the house; the side drops steeply away and can be scary. The path follows an irrigation canal; after a while you pass a plaque in memory of an Israeli who tried to ride a motorbike along it and fell off. When the irrigation canal goes over the track, turn up the slope to the right. Go up the hill beyond some small lakes, and the ice cave is just below you. The return walk takes two hours.

Tiahuanaco. Lying 45 miles/72km west of La Paz, Tiahuanaco is an easy day trip; otherwise, stop off en route to Desaguadero, on the border with Peru.

Tiahuanaco (or Tiwanaku) is Bolivia's most important archaeological site. It was the centre of the empire created by the Tiahuanaco civilization, the history of which is outlined on page 320. The ceremonial complex dates from AD200-700 and was almost certainly built on the shores of Lake Titicaca — now some 12 miles/20km away.

On a bright winter day, when clear blue skies prevail above the rolling, velvetine hills that bound the broad valley, the setting could be called almost picturesque. But even at times like this it is a dusty, shadeless and windswept place. And although the architectural techniques of the Tiahuanaco were more sophisticated than those used by the Incas, it is not a remarkable ruin. The site's archaeological importance outweighs its artistic merit, though it is intriguing that Tiahuanaco should tell us so little about the people that built it. The best time to visit the ruins is on 21 June, when the local Aymará Indians celebrate the winter solstice and the new year (Machaq Mara).

First you must go to the ticket office on the opposite side of the road from the site, before the village if approaching from La Paz. It opens 9am-5pm daily. Your $2 ticket entitles you to visit the various sites, starting at the most important one opposite. This is the Kalasasaya compound, a raised earth plaza whose highlight is the Puerta del Sol, a large carved doorway rather tucked away in one corner. It is thought to be a solar calendar, and the figure is probably Viracocha, the creator-god. Also in the plaza are two impressive monoliths.

Southwest of Kalasasaya, next to the railway line, is what appears to be a run-down 20th century hotel. Indeed it was built as such, but now contains the museum, with its array of textiles, ceramics (some Inca) and skulls; the best relics are abroad or in La Paz. By walking along the railway line away from the main site and taking the first left you reach Puma Punku (the Door of the Puma). Among the jumbled pile of blocks — just south of the largest flat slab — are the remains of a gate thought to have been similar to the Puerta del Sol. Notice the small holes which may have been for nails from which golden streamers were hung.

The journey across the Altiplano from La Paz is interesting but bumpy. Buses to Tiahuanaco from the capital are run by Autolíneas Ingaví (tel 328981) at the corner of J. M. Asín and Eyzaguirre, near the Cemetery. Buses leave at 7.30am, 10.30am, 2pm and 5pm, and take about three hours. The company also has buses to Desaguadero at 7am, 10am, noon and 4pm, which pass the site. You can flag down buses (including local ones from other towns in the area) on the road by the ruins for the return journey; there are no buses after about 6pm.

If stranded you can stay in Alojamiento Tiahuanaco on the main street through the village. Whether you are staying or not, visit the ancient church, with its interesting façade and an almost Norman-looking interior.

Sorata. Local legend has it that Sorata was the site of the Garden of Eden. Whether or not the story is true, this small town lies in an undeniably beautiful setting, nestled at the foot of Mount Illampú at the northern end of the Cordillera Real. The climate is mild and there are good walks in the area, making Sorata an excellent place in which to relax after a few hectic days in La Paz. The San Pedro cave is three or four hours north of town, but for more ambitious treks contact the Sorata Club at Hotel Copacabana, which organizes a range of hikes. Sorata has a good Sunday market, though the one in Achacachi (back towards La Paz) is better.

Sorata is 65 miles/105km northwest of the capital. It is one excursion that cannot be done as a day trip, but there are several simple hotels. Transtur Sorata buses from La Paz (office down a narrow street off Calle J. M. Asín, near the cemetery) leave daily at 7am, returning at 12.30pm; the journey takes four hours and costs $2.

LAKE TITICACA

In a continent of wonders, Lake Titicaca is perhaps the most spectacular, an oasis of colour and beauty in the dry and forbidding Altiplano. Titicaca is the world's highest navigable lake, and is surprisingly large — 40 miles/60km wide and 110 miles/180km long. With its bright, blue waters, thirty islands and border of terraced hills, it is magnificent enough; but the snowy peaks in the distance complete a unique scene.

Lake Titicaca is all that remains of an ancient inland sea called Lago Ballivián, which once covered much of the Altiplano. It has always been of central importance to the people living in the area, from the Tiahuanaco to the Incas, who believed the lake to be the 'womb of mankind', the birthplace of their civilization. The mythical aura surrounding Titicaca remains, and the lake is much revered by both Aymará and Quechua Indians.

More than half of Titicaca lies in Peru, and be sure to explore the lake on both sides of the border. From Copacabana, the main settlement on the Bolivian shores, it is easy to get to Puno, the main base on the Peruvian side. See page 291 for map and information on Peru's Titicaca.

COPACABANA

Close to the Peruvian border, this small town lies in a stunning position on a peninsula jutting into the southern waters of the lake. Historically, Copacabana was a resting place for Indian pilgrims en route to the Inca shrine on the nearby Isla del Sol. Since the colonial era the town has been a place of pilgrimage in its own right. More recently, the slow pace and the relaxed atmosphere of Copacabana has appealed increasingly to travellers.

The magnificent cathedral dominates the town both physically and emotionally. It houses a miracle-working statue of the Black Virgin of the Lake (Virgen Morena), which draws people from miles around. The statue is kept in a chapel reached up some steps to the left of the main altar, and can be seen at any time. But the best time to visit Copacabana is for the Feast Day of the Virgin, on 1-2 February, when people from both Bolivia and Peru come to celebrate with dancing and music.

For the rest of the year Copacabana is an extremely tranquil place — if you prefer somewhere with more bustle, you would be better suited to Puno, across the lake in Peru. Things sometimes liven up at weekends, however, when you may be lucky enough to witness the extraordinary sight of cars decked with flowers and coloured paper being blessed at the church.

Copacabana is primarily a base from which to visit Isla del Sol, but don't neglect to climb El Calvario which provides fine views of the town and lake, particularly at sunset. The hike is short but tiring, taking about 20 minutes; the path begins near the church north of the market.

Be warned that a cold wind often blows off the lake that can make the life of anyone without warm clothing a misery.

Arrival and Departure. Buses from La Paz to Copacabana take the route via Tiquina, where a narrow strait separates the two sides of the lake. At this point, passengers must pile off the bus and pay $0.20 to take the ferry to San Pedro on the other side; the bus follows on behind on a decidedly rickety motorized raft. Bolivia's small marine force oversees activity across the Strait of Tiquina (thereby justifying its existence in a landlocked country), and checks passports. San Pedro has a couple of bars but no hotels. The 75-minute journey from here to Copacabana is breathtaking, and almost Mediterranean.

The main bus services from La Paz, 110 miles/160km southeast, are operated by Manco Kapac (tel 350033) and Transtur 2 de Febrero (tel 377181), both based opposite the cemetery. Manco Kapac offers the most frequent service, with daily buses from La Paz at 6am, 7am, 7.30am, 1pm and 2pm, while 2 de Febrero has just two services a day at 8am and 5pm; the afternoon departure on Sundays leaves at 2pm. The journey takes about four hours and costs $2.25. There are also minibuses to Tiquina, but since you will have to wait for a Copacabana bus in order to continue from the other side of the strait, you would do better to take the conventional bus from the start, and be sure of getting a seat. Tourist minibuses from La Paz to Puno stop off in Copacabana; see page 340.

Those continuing to Puno from Copucabana can take a bus or collective taxi to Kasani, on the border about 20 minutes away. The colectivos are usually marked 'Yunguyo' and hang around the main square. They may continue across the border; otherwise pick up another the other side for the few miles to Yunguyo, from where minibuses run to Puno.

Accommodation. Copacabana's popularity among travellers means it has plenty of cheap alojamientos offering similar rates and standards. One of the best is the Emperador, on Calle Murillo (the road into town from La Paz), not far from the cathedral. Simple, clean rooms cost less than $2, and for $1 you can have breakfast served in your room. Also good are the Imperio (Calle Visconde de Lemos), just south of the main square, and Residencial La Porteñita (Calle General Jáuregui), with doubles with bath for $5. For a more upmarket room try the new Hotel Boston, the Copacabana or the Continental, where a double room with bath and hot water costs $12.

Eating and Drinking. Unlike its choice of lodgings, Copacabana's repertoire of restaurants is disappointing. There is only a handful of establishments (half of them on the main square), all with virtually the same menu. Meals are cheap, however, and you can get a set meal for less than $1. For an even cheaper lunch, go to the market.

Help and Information. The tourist office in the main square should in theory be open daily. You can change money at the bank or in some of the hotels and restaurants, but rates are poor. The post office is on the main square, and Entel is on Calle Murillo (open 7.30am-8pm Monday to Saturday, 7.30am-noon on Sunday).

ISLA DEL SOL

Legend maintains that this island is the site of the Incas' creation, indeed the birthplace of the Sun itself: Inti, the sun god, is said to have created Manco Kapac and his sister-wife Mama Huaca, and commanded them to found an empire. They set off northwards and founded Cusco, and Manco Kapac became the first emperor of the Incas. The local Indians still venerate the myths, and the island is a sacred place.

Inca ruins are dotted all over Isla del Sol, and are connected by a series of paths. At the northwest end is the rock which gave birth to the legend of the Incas' creation. The main site, however, is Pilko Caima, about a mile from the landing stage: though not impressive as a ruin, it offers fine views. You can visit all the main sites in four or five hours, but since there are good walks and fabulous sunsets, it's rewarding to spend at least one night on the island.

The Inca ruins on the small Isla de la Luna (or Coati), further east, have been sadly neglected; the larger Isla del Sol is more fun to explore.

Arrival and Departure. It costs about $40 to hire a motorboat to take you to Isla del Sol from Copacabana; boats hold up to eight people and usually set off between 6 and 8am. If you can't get a big group together or prefer a more leisurely pace, take a sailboat instead. This is cheaper, but the journey takes at least four hours as opposed to two in the motorboat.

The cheapest and arguably the best option, however, is to get a boat from Yampupata, a small village at the top of the headland 10 miles/16km north of Copacabana. It lies across the water from the Isla del Sol and you can arrange a lift with local fishermen. The ride across to Pilko Caima takes 30 minutes and costs around $5. Ask the fisherman to wait, or else arrange to be picked up later. Transport to Yampupata from Copacabana is scarce, but the best way is on foot — the route along the coast follows an old Inca trail and is a beautiful walk; allow four to six hours. If you arrive at Yampupata at dusk, it would be best to stay there until morning, as boatmen may not take you to Pilko Caima, but drop you at a rocky outcrop, leaving you to walk the rest of way (in the dark).

Accommodation. There are a couple of villages on the island, including Challa on the north coast, where you can rent a bed off one of the locals; otherwise camp. You may be able to get a boat back to the mainland from Challa; or else walk to the main landing stage. Bargain hard with boatmen, even if it looks as though you could be stranded, as they will try anything to get as much money as possible out of you; coca leaves go down well as a tip.

SURIQUI

This island lies in Lago Huiñaimarca, on the other side of the Tiquina Strait from Copacabana. The Aymará of Suriqui are the most famous builders of the traditional reed (*tortora*) boats that are still used in a small way on the lake. The islanders were responsible for the creation of the Ra II in which the Norwegian explorer, Thor Heyerdahl, sailed across the Atlantic.

The main gateway for visits to Suriqui is Huatajata, a sleepy town about 90 minutes from La Paz, on the Tiquina road. It is best to make an early start and visit Suriqui en route to Copacabana. To get to Huatajata take any bus along the Tiquina road from the cemetery area of La Paz. Ask to be dropped off at the eastern edge of town, since this is the best place to arrange a boat. Several restaurants, including the Panamerican and Inti Karka (tel 850386), arrange trips. It costs about $20 to hire a boat which can hold up to five people. The journey to the island takes about 45 minutes, and you should be able to stay on the island for a few hours. The last buses to Copacabana pass through Huatajata at about 4.30pm. Inti Karka has rooms if you get stranded.

LOS YUNGAS

The lush subtropical valleys of the Yungas are a world away from the snowy peaks of the nearby Cordillera Real. But they blend into the Andes almost invisibly, and are almost equally awesome. The deep valleys provide travellers with some of their worst memories of hairpin bends and sheer drops, yet few people can resist the draw of the fantastic scenery. The series of trails that cross the mountains and descend into the valleys makes this perfect hiking country — travelling on foot is certainly the best way to enjoy the region.

The road giving access to the Yungas climbs for 40 minutes from La Paz to its maximum altitude at La Cumbre pass (15,500ft/4,725m), from where it descends dramatically for more than 10,000ft/3,000m. It is paved only part of the way, and travelling in the area should not be considered during the rainy season. Buses and trucks to the Yungas leave from Avenida de las Américas in the Villa Fátima district of La Paz; buses 202, 208, 240, 261, 272 and 286 all serve the area from the city centre. Flota Yungueña (Avenida de las Américas 344; tel 312344) runs full-size buses, while Trans Yungas and Transturs use minibuses.

Coroico. The village of Coroico, about 50 miles/80km northeast of La Paz, is perched on a hillside in one of the most spectacular positions imaginable. There is scope for walking and hiring horses, but most people are content just to read, write letters and simply take in the view. It is a popular weekend retreat.

Flota Yungueña runs buses from La Paz to Corioco on Tuesdays, Thursdays and Saturdays at 8.30am ($3), returning at 8am on Monday, Wednesday and Friday, and 1pm on Sunday. Trans Yungas and Trans Tours both have a daily service at 9am and 3pm. Alternatively, take any bus to Caranavi, Guanay or Rurrenabaque and get off at Yolosa, five miles/8km from Coroico; pick-ups run up the hill into town. At busy times of year, especially weekends, book your return or onward ticket on arrival. The journey from La Paz takes about three hours; for the most terrifying views sit on the left.

The most central hotel is Hostal Kory, just off the main square. It has all types of rooms, costing anything from $3 to $7. There is a swimming pool, but best of all is the terrace which provides stunning views. The Hotel Lluvia de Oro has a good pool and costs $5 per person per night. Beneath the town is the Hotel Prefectural, a lavish place with more good views. Rooms at this state-run hotel are fairly expensive, but you can eat or drink there relatively cheaply. About 20 minutes walk above the town is the Hotel Sol y Luna, a cosy place where you can do your own cooking.

On the map it looks easy to take a circular route back to La Paz via Chulumani, a pleasant town just 30 miles/48km southeast of Corioco. But the route is circuitous, the roads dreadful and transport services either erratic or non-existent. If you have the time to rely on trucks, it makes for a rewarding journey. It must be done in stages, probably changing in Arapata and Coripata. From Chulumani there are Flota Yungueña buses to the capital (via Unduavi on the La Paz-Corioco road), with departures just twice a week at noon on Sunday and 7am on Monday; buses from La Paz leave at 8.30am on Friday and Saturday. Services increase during the holiday period. The journey takes six hours. Chulumani has several cheap hotels, and the comfortable Hotel Prefectural, which charges $10-15.

Hiking. Staggering scenery, the odd pre-Columbian ruin and abundant birdlife are the rewards awaiting hikers in the Yungas. There is a choice of routes, often along Inca or pre-Inca roads, and the most used trails are surprisingly easy to follow. The Takesi and Choro trails are both popular, and the latter is particularly recommended since it ends up in Coroico.

Take camping equipment and food since you can't rely on local hospitality. However, there are small Aymará settlements along the way, and you can usually do business with the locals — bartering goods is often more successful than offering money, and presents are always appreciated. In some villages you can rent mules or llamas.

Contact Club Andino in La Paz for further information, and the tourist office produces maps of the main hikes. An agency in the Tiwanaku museum arranges treks and hires out camping equipment.

Choro Trail: this hike goes from the cold, snow-covered La Cumbre pass to Corioco, and follows a pre-Columbian stone road. Allow at least three days. The first part, as you cross the pass, is moderately hard-going, but after that it's downhill virtually all the way. The main villages en route are Chucura, where you can sometimes rent mules, Choro and Chairo, all of which are good camping spots. The start of the trail is near the statue of Christ, which is visible from the La Paz-Coroico road. From here take the path on the left that winds upwards. After half an hour you descend to the beginning of the Choro trail proper. At Easter pilgrims follow the same trail to Coroico, and this is a wonderful time to do the hike.

AMAZONIA

Half of Bolivia lies in the Amazon basin, yet these jungle lowlands are ignored by most travellers and the majority of Bolivians. Beni, the biggest department in the region, is by no means just jungle. Its southern area is taken up by grasslands, where cattle ranching is a major source of income. There are few towns of any size in Bolivian Amazonia, and infrastructure is limited. This has restricted the exploitation of gold and oil deposits in the region, though timber companies have already done serious damage and invaded traditional Indian lands.

There is no central base for trips into the jungle to compare to Manaus in Brazil, nor are there lodges along the lines of those found near Puerto Maldonado in Peru. This means that no single area is ever overrun by visitors; and such is the small interest in the region that even the most popular bases are seldom busy. Some of the jungle towns are delightful. Others are not, but they can all be used as bases for jungle and canoe trips. You can usually swim in the rivers, but beware of piranha-infested waters. Hotels can often help to arrange excursions, otherwise talk directly to the local boatmen.

There are two main routes into the Bolivian Amazon: up the Río Beni via Rurrenabaque, or up the Mamoré via Trinidad. Either one is a possible route north into Brazil. More boats use the Río Mamoré than the Beni, so if time is important then the route via Trinidad is probably the best option. On the other hand, since this is the busiest route, the area is more developed and the jungle more cultivated; but while wildlife is harder to spot, you can still see macaws, storks, cayman and even freshwater dolphins. If, rather than head into Brazil, you would prefer to go on a round trip, this is perfectly feasible since the northern towns of Guayaramerín (on the Mamoré) and Riberalta (on the Beni) are linked by road.

Getting Around. No ferries run along the rivers, but cargo vessels (often full of cattle) ply the main waterways and carry passengers; motorized canoes transport local people along the smaller rivers. To arrange a lift, ask around in the town's port area, or enquire in the port captain's office. Along the most important rivers there is usually a fairly steady flow of vessels, though when water levels are low only small boats can run. Traffic is likely to stop almost completely at the peak of the dry season in August and September. Facilities are basic. You cannot rely upon space to rig a hammock, so take a sleeping bag or a blanket as well. Also bring a plentiful supply of food, though you can buy things en route.

LAB and TAM fly to all the main towns, though few routes are served more than once or twice a week. Roads, which are sadly penetrating deeper and deeper into the jungle, are almost all unusable after heavy rain. During the dry season (March to October), however, the important towns are linked by bus almost daily.

THE RIO BENI ROUTE

The best starting-point for a trip up the Río Beni is Guanay, which is 145 miles/232km north of La Paz and strictly speaking in the Yungas. Allow about a week to travel by boat from Guanay to Riberalta in the far north.

Guanay. The life of this quiet, dirt-street town, changed dramatically following the discovery of gold in 1980. The subsequent gold rush brought panners by the thousand to the area. They continue to come, and during the dry season immigrant prospectors sleep in the main square.

It's worth getting a room in Hotel Ritzy on the main square and staying a few days. You can organize canoe trips to Mapiri and Tipuani, other mining centres on rivers of the same name. Mapiri, to the northwest, is about six hours away by motorized boat, but the rapids can be hazardous.

Flota Yungueña buses from La Paz leave daily at around 10am and take about 12 hours ($6); Transturs services leave at 9.30am and noon.

The trip by motorized canoe from Guanay north to Rurrenabaque can be done in a day if you get an early start. The price depends on how many other people want a ride; expect to pay at least $15.

A road runs northeast from Caranavi (where the road to Guanay branches northwest) to Sapecho, beyond which an extremely rough road continues to Yucumo. Near here the road splits: to the northwest is Rurrenabaque, to the east San Borja. Yucumo is served by sporadic buses from Caranavi (allow 14 hours); otherwise arrange a lift. There are also trucks to San Borja, 30 miles/48km east of Yucumo and about eight hours west of Trinidad on the Río Mamoré. San Borja is a wild-west cattle town that is said to be completely under the control of drug barons; it has an airport and a few basic hotels. Yucumo and Caranavi also have accommodation.

Rurrenabaque. This is a pretty jungle town in a fine setting, with mountains to the south and grasslands to the north. The hotels in town are fairly basic, the Santa Ana near the main square being the best of a poor bunch. Trans Yungas runs daily buses to Rurrenabaque from La Paz, which take 15-20 hours. Travelling by boat from Guanay is much more entertaining. If you plan to head north by river to Riberalta, be prepared to wait since boats leave infrequently.

Riberalta. This town has a population of about 40,000 and lies just south of the confluence of the Beni and Madre de Dios rivers. One of its most memorable features is the number of motorbikes in the streets. But although Riberalta is hot and muggy, the atmosphere is surprisingly relaxed.

The river journey from Rurrenabaque takes about five days. When the roads are clear there are also trucks; otherwise, you may have to fly. Buses run daily from Riberalta to Guayaramerín on the Brazilian border, taking $2\frac{1}{2}$-3 hours; trucks also use this route.

The best of the few hotels are Hotel Noreste (Avenida R. Moreno) and Residencial Los Reyes, near the airport, seven blocks south of the square.

THE RIO MAMORE ROUTE

Puerto Villarroel. This port lies on the banks of Río Ichilo some 150 miles/240km northeast of Cochabamba. It is the main river port to northern Bolivia, and is therefore also the most popular starting place for trips into Amazonia. Puerto Villarroel is a fairly ramshackle place — the streets are covered in an almost permanent layer of mud — but it can be reached comparatively easily from Cochabamba. The best hotel in town is the Hannover.

Puerto Villarroel and Cochabamba are linked by a paved road and daily buses, which usually leave in the morning and take 6-8 hours. The journey across the mountains is spectacular. It takes you through Villa Tunari, which is a good place to visit from Cochabamba if you want a taste of the tropical forest but don't have time to explore further; there are a couple of hotels that can arrange jungle trips. Puerto Villarroel is also accessible by road from Santa Cruz. This whole area is coca-growing territory, so be prepared for police checkpoints and don't go delving off into the jungle on your own.

Both small cargo boats and larger commercial vessels travel up the Río Ichilo to Trinidad. While the smaller boats are family-run and probably more fun to travel on, they are also slower. They take about a week to reach Trinidad, a journey the larger boats can do in four or five days.

Trinidad. The town of Trinidad developed from a 17th-century Jesuit settlement. It is the capital of Beni department, and the centre of Bolivia's cattle industry. The population (45,000 in 1991) rises steadily with the influx of prospective farmers. Yet Trinidad remains a classic colonial town, with a large tree-lined square, pastel-shaded houses and covered walkways. The feel is still very much of a backwater: the people are friendly and horses clatter along dirt streets.

The tourist office is in the Prefectura on Plaza Ballivián, and the travel agencies on 6 de agosto can arrange jungle trips; otherwise ask around at the port. You can also rent motorbikes to explore along the river.

Arrival and Departure: Trinidad's airport is just northwest of the centre, within walking distance of the main square.

The most straightforward overland route is from Santa Cruz, 375 miles/600km southeast; there are direct overnight buses a couple of times a week during the dry season. An alternative route from the west is via San Borja (see above).

Boats leave almost daily for Guayaramerín from Trinidad; the journey takes five to seven days. Note that Trinidad has two ports, and boats dock at either: Puerto Varador is on Río Mamoré (8 miles/13km away) and Puerto Almacén on Río Ibaré (5 miles/8km south); trucks run into town.

Accommodation: unlike the rest of the department, Trinidad is not badly off for accommodation. Hotel Yacuma on the corner of La Paz and Santa Cruz is one of the better cheap places. Or try Residencial Loreto, also on La Paz. Up a notch are the Bajio (Calle Nicolas Suárez 632; tel 21344), and the Ganadero (Avenida 6 de Agosto; tel 21099), the Bolivian Amazonia's answer to a businessman's hotel.

Exploring: one of the most interesting trips is to San Ignacio de Moxos, an old Jesuit settlement about 50 miles/80km west of Trinidad. More than half the population is Indian, and Jesuits still live in the community. San Ignacio is an important folklore centre and is famous for its festivals, when the local people deck themselves out in wonderful feather head-dresses and wooden masks, and play music on rustic, home-made instruments. The best celebrations are at Easter and the Fiesta de San Ignacio (28-31 July). San Ignacio is accessible by road in the dry season: buses and trucks (from the market in Trinidad) take four hours. There are several hotels.

Guayaramerín. The small town of Guayaramerín lies on the Brazilian frontier, which is marked by the Mamoré river. It is a border outpost par excellence, full of gold prospectors and smugglers. Access is primarily by air or river, although a road runs to Riberalta.

The best hotels in town are the Litoral and Santa Ana, both near the main square. Amenities are better in the bustling town of Guajará-Mirim across the border in Brazil. If you are just crossing the frontier for the day you need not get your passport stamped. Guayaramerín has a Brazilian consulate if you need a visa. Money is best changed on the Bolivian side. Ferries run frequently between the two border towns. From Guajará Mirim buses run north to Porto Velho.

COBIJA

The capital of Pando department lies in the remote northwestern corner of Bolivia. It was a buzzing place during the rubber boom around the turn of the century, but has since shrunk and would have disappeared altogether were it not for its proximity to the Brazilian border. There is a bridge across the river to Brasileia, the main traffic consisting of local shoppers. This is certainly an alternative frontier to cross (there is transport from Brasileia to Rio Branco), but note that the only sensible access to Cobija is by air.

SANTA CRUZ

Forty years ago Santa Cruz was a remote, Wild West town, where horses roamed through sleepy and dusty streets — with little to distinguish it from the colonial settlement founded in 1561. Santa Cruz is now the third largest city in Bolivia, with a population of 800,000,

The metamorphosis began in the 1950s, when the completion of the highway from Cochabamba and of the railway to the Brazilian border enabled trade and industry to take off in the region. They did so with a vengeance, and economic migrants have moved in ever since. The resettlement programmes of the 1960s tempted some Indians down from the Altiplano, but more significant was the flood from abroad; Mennonite, Japanese and German colonies have sprung up all over the region. Santa Cruz department is rich in resources, including oil and natural gas, but most of the new immigrants live off the land. There is an increasing amount of timber-felling and cattle-ranching that is adding to the already serious damage done by colonization.

Santa Cruz is a big, noisy and ostentatious place. Its air of confidence is completely alien to the mood of other Bolivian cities. While the suburbs are dominated by petrol stations and agricultural machinery dealers, the centre is the domain of the flash car and expensive restaurant. Santa Cruz is traditionally the city that travellers love to hate, and as a destination it has little going for it. The Cruceños are known for their fun-loving nature, and the city's buzzing nightlife is much vaunted. But the prices for this and almost everything else in the city are high. Santa Cruz is Bolivia's cocaine-trafficking centre, and where there are drugs, high prices and corruption are sure to follow. The reputation its dishonest or fake policemen have for ripping off travellers is notorious.

Nevertheless, while development over the last three decades has virtually obliterated the old town, some of the streets in the centre are still lined with colonial

SANTA CRUZ

1 Los Pozos Market
2 El Arenal
3 Hotel Libertador
4 Plaza 24 de Septiembre
5 Argentinian Consulate
6 Casa de la Cultura
7 Post Office
8 Hotel Bibosi
9 Hotel Viru Viru
10 Posada El Turista
11 Ecuadorean Consulate
12 Cathedral
13 American Express
14 Pizzeria La Capilla
15 LAB
16 Entel
17 Mercado 7 Calles
18 Bus Station
19 Tourist Office
20 Train Station

0   300m

buildings, and retain a more appealing atmosphere. Santa Cruz need not be avoided at all costs, as some would have you believe, but it is as well to be aware of its reputation.

City Layout. The map of Santa Cruz makes it look like a pancake, surrounded as the city is by concentric ring roads; only points within the inner circuit are of much interest. The main north-south axis is 24 de Septiembre north of the central square, René Moreno south of it; east-west, Sucre east of the square, Ayacucho west of it. The numbering system starts at zero from these and spreads outwards. Names of other streets change upon hitting these two axes.

Maps are available from bookshops, including Los Amigos del Libro at Calle Velasco 37.

Arrival and Departure. *Air:* Santa Cruz is served by more flights than any other Bolivian city apart from La Paz. It has several international connections (see page 324) and there are daily flights with LAB from Cochabamba and La Paz, and less frequent services from other towns, including Trinidad, Yacuiba and three heavily booked weekly flights from Puerto Suárez (on the Brazilian border). TAM also serves a number of routes, and is based at El Trompillo airport two miles and a short bus ride south of the centre. Phone 28101 for information.

The Viru-Viru international airport (tel 44411/33473) is 10 miles/16km north of the city. It is Bolivia's most efficient, having an information desk (with maps), and an exchange counter open normal banking hours. At other times, ask around at the check-in desks. Minibuses leave for the bus terminal roughly every 20 minutes between 5.40am and 9pm, fare $1. Rather than continue to the end of the line, get off along Avenida Cañoto (the inner ring road), at the western end of Junín, from where it is an easy walk to the centre. Likewise, to return to the airport you can hail the bus anywhere along Cañoto; services to the airport run from 6am-8pm.

The LAB office is on the corner of Warnes and Chuquisaca (tel 44896). LAP, which has two flights each week to Asunción, is at Junín 249.

Bus: the bus station (tel 340772) is at the junction of Avenidas Cañoto and Irala, southwest of the centre. Ticket offices for long-distance buses are jumbled together at lower ground level. Local buses also leave from here. Long-distance services, with average fares, are as follows:

Cochabamba — 11 hours, $6; buses take the newer road via Villa Tunari. Most leave 7-8pm, though some companies have a morning run too. Some continue to La Paz, but this is likely to involve a change.
Sucre — 18 hours, $12; one bus a day with Comarapa at 8.30am, and on Monday, Wednesday and Saturday at 5pm with Mopar or Cruzazul. Some continue to Potosí.
Trinidad — 10 hours, $10; daily at 6.30pm with Chaco Boreal.
Yacuiba — 18 hours, $9; daily at 6.30pm with Chaco Boreal, via Camiri.

Train: two lines begin in Santa Cruz. One runs 300 miles/480km south to Yacuiba on the Argentinian border, the other to Quijarro on the Brazilian frontier. The struggle and time involved in buying tickets — particularly for Quijarro — is notorious. You must purchase your ticket the day before departure, and although the ticket office doesn't open until 8am, you must arrive at two or three in the morning in order to queue. Once on the Quijarro train, watch out for corrupt narcotics police on the prowl. A few unlucky travellers have been accused of being drug-traffickers (sometimes having had drugs planted on them) and have been forced to pay heavy 'fines'. Whatever the trick, they may threaten to take you back to Santa Cruz, and offering money may be the only way out: if so, do not let them see the extent of your cash supply, and stay cool.

Santa Cruz railway station is on Avenida Argentina, near the eastern end of Avenida Irala and about 20 minutes walk from the centre. The staff at the information desk try to be helpful but are thwarted by the constant bombardment of phone calls; you can yourself phone, on 348488 or 48066.

There are two ferrobuses a week to Yacuiba, currently leaving on Tuesday and Saturday at 8am; the journey takes about 10 hours and the fares are $22 (pullman) and $18 (especial). The tren especial costs $11/$15 and the rápido $8/$11, depending on the class.

Quijarro is also served by two ferrobuses a week, leaving at 6pm on Tuesday and Thursday. The journey, through some of Bolivia's wildest country, takes 12-14 hours. The fare is $25 (pullman) and $20 (especial). The fares on the especial are $12/$18, and on the rápido $9/$12.

Truck: drivers heading out of town congregate on Avenida Grigotá between the second and third *anilo* (ring road); otherwise wait on the other side of the third anilo for passing traffic; to get there take bus 17 from the market. As well as regular trucks, some large long-distance freight lorries offer rides. If you want to go all the way to Cochabamba, check which route the driver plans to use — the old route is the most scenic but far slower.

Accommodation. Santa Cruz has a number of top-notch hotels. The Gran Hotel de Santa Cruz is the fanciest, on Independencia at Pari. A more reasonable but still comparatively classy room can be found in the three-star Hotel Libertador, at the corner of Libertad and Buenos Aires, which charges $25 for a double.

The largest concentration of cheap hotels is west of Plaza 24 de Septiembre, the main square; many are on or near Calle Junín. The best at the bottom of the range is Posada El Turista on Junín between Cordillera and Santa Bárbara; it is cheap and cheerful with simple but clean double rooms for $3.50. In the next block along is the Oriente (Junín 362; tel 21976), with double rooms for $6-8. Next door is the Viru Viru (Junín 338), one step up and good value with doubles for $16 including breakfast. The three hotels clustered alphabetically together between Calles España and 21 de Mayo — the Amazonas, Bibosi and Copacabana — are in a similar price range. Most recommended of these is the Bibosi (Junín 218; tel 348548), which is friendly and has doubles for $15.

There are several cheap places on Cordillera just north of the bus station, such as the España at No. 599, near the corner of Lemoine ($9 double with bath), the Señor de la Sentencia at No. 554 ($6 without bath) and the Virgen de Cotoca ($3 per person).

Eating and Drinking. Restaurants are plentiful but pricey. La Pascana on the main square is a pleasant place with an ample menu including ceviche. This dish is also sold at the Amadeo on Velasco at the main junction with Junín. The Carmina, at Junín 434 between Santa Barbara and Sarah, is cheap and friendly. For pizzas try La Bella Napoli (Independencia between Lemoine and La Riva) or La Capilla on La Paz between Chávez and Warnes.

To economize you might wish to buy the ingredients for a picnic from the huge Extra Supermarket at the top end of 24 de Septiembre.

Exploring. You are unlikely to do much sightseeing in Santa Cruz. The cathedral is uninspiring, but worth having a look at if only to marvel at the busts on the pillars along either side of the nave. Also in the main square are the rest of the city's most important buildings. The Casa de la Cultura, on the west side, has a small archaeological collection, and organizes exhibitions and concerts.

Four blocks north of Plaza 24 de Septiembre, off Chuquisaca, is El Arenal, a park with a lake. Just east of it, on Quijarro, is Los Pozos market, where a few crafts are on sale, including hammocks. The two main city markets, however, are southwest of the centre. Mercado Siete Calles is just south of the junction of Vallegrande and Ingaví and is good for Western clothes (Levi 505s for $40). More interesting is Mercado La Ramada which is off Avenida Grigotá, southwest of the bus station, a real warren full of fascinating stalls.

In the northern barrio of Equipetrol is the zoo, which is one of the few of its kind in South America that is not a wholly distressing affair. Take Micro 8, 11, 16 or 17 from the centre.

If you decide to stay in, try tuning into one of South America's best rock stations, which serves Santa Cruz on 101.5FM.

Crime and Safety. The local police have a reputation for extracting money from unsuspecting travellers. Not carrying a passport is one easy way to be penalized. If approached by a policeman (who may or may not be in uniform), ask to see their identity card, and preferably to be taken to the police station which is adjoining the main square.

Help and Information. *Tourist Information:* the IBT office is well south of the city centre. It is on the first floor of the five-storey building at Irala 563, next to the Toyota showroom. It is between Avenida Velarde (the continuation of Independencia) and Avenida Ejército Nacional. It opens only sporadically and is of little use. The immigration office is in the same building.

Communications: the post office is at Calle Junín 146 (tel 27836), just west of the main square. Entel is at Calle Warnes 83 (between Moreno and Chuquisaca; tel 47418); it opens 7.30am-11pm Monday to Friday, and 8am-10pm at weekends.

Money: the latest rates are given on the front page of the local paper, *El Mundo*. There are several cambios in Plaza 24 de Septiembre, which change both cash and cheques. The Alemán, and Medicambo next door, charge 3% commission on cheques. You get a better deal from the Santa Cruz across the square. Moneychangers loiter both here and along Avenida Libertad. American Express is at Magri Turismo, Ingaví 14 (tel 45663/44559).

Consulates: Argentina — Edificio del Banco de la Nación Argentina (3rd floor), in the main square; open 8am-1pm Monday to Friday.
Brazil — Avenida Busch 330, northwest of the centre (off Avenida Cañoto).
Ecuador — behind Casa de Cambio Alemán, main square.
UK — (Honorary Consul), Calle Parapeti 28, 2nd floor (tel 36415).
Uruguay — Colón 58 (between Ayacucho and Ingaví), Mezzanine, office 5.

AROUND SANTA CRUZ

Samaipata. This small settlement lies in a valley on the edge of the Andes, about 70 miles/112km southwest of Santa Cruz along the old Cochabamba road. A sizeable Japanese community lives here, but the town's main claim to fame is the nearby archaeological site, known as El Fuerte. It is believed to be an Inca ceremonial

an experience which is almost as scary for those on the ground. The terminal is often chaotic, and the information desk has no maps. To get to the centre take Micro B, which follows a circuitous route but does, eventually, pass through the main square.

Bus: a new central bus station has been built in Cochabamba, but at the time of going to press, the bus companies still operated from their own separate offices along Avenida Aroma, five blocks south of the main square. The area between Calle 25 de Mayo and Avenida Ayacucho, where the offices are concentrated, is choked with passengers and buses.

The main long-distance services from Cochabamba are as follows:

La Paz — 8-9 hours, $4.50; most services leave 7-9pm, though there are a few morning departures too.

Oruro — 5 hours, $4; virtually all buses to La Paz stop off in Oruro, and there are additional services too. Avoid evening departures unless you enjoy the prospect of arriving in the bleak Altiplano town in the middle of the night; the journey itself is rough anyway.

Potosí — 12 hours, $7; few services, all via Oruro.

Santa Cruz — 11-12 hours, $6; most companies have one morning and one evening departure. All use the new road via Villa Tunari.

Sucre - 11 hours, $6.50; only a few daily buses, mostly leaving 6-7pm. They follow the old Santa Cruz road, via Totora.

Trinidad — 24 hours, $18; once daily with Korilazo at 7.30pm.

Minibuses to villages on and off the old Santa Cruz road (see *Around Cochabamba*) leave from south of the centre: walk along Avenida San Martín and continue for about a mile beyond the railway station.

Train: at the time of going to press there were no through trains to La Paz, and just one ordinary train to Oruro, leaving at 8.30am on Fridays. It takes ten hours and costs $4 (especial) and $5 (pullman). The station (tel 22402) is about six blocks south of the bus offices.

Car Rental: vehicles, including four-wheel, can be hired from Rent-a-Car International, Colombia 0361 (tel 26635) at the corner of 15 de Mayo.

Accommodation. Hotels are fairly scattered, but several are on or just off Avenida San Martín and Calle 25 de Mayo. The further south you get towards the bus terminals the grottier the hotels become. One which is central, good value and not at all grotty is Gran Hotel Las Vegas, just behind the cathedral at Calle Arce 0352 (tel 29217). It is three-star, and has good double rooms for around $15, including breakfast. For a bit more luxury, go to Hotel Boston on 25 de Mayo, half a block north of Heroínas.

Cheaper than any of these is Residencial Buenos Aires (25 de Mayo 0329 at Ecuador; tel 29518), north of the square. Doubles cost $10 with bath, $6 without. Nearby is Residencial Familiar (25 de Mayo and Colombia; tel 27986), a lovely building with rooms around a courtyard, and a bargain with doubles for just $3. Residencial El Dorado at the corner of Ismael Montes and 25 de Mayo is equally cheap but not so charming.

Eating and Drinking. Cochabamba is a good place to eat out. Lots of cheap and cheerful places are along 25 de Mayo, Bolívar and España, but the best area is

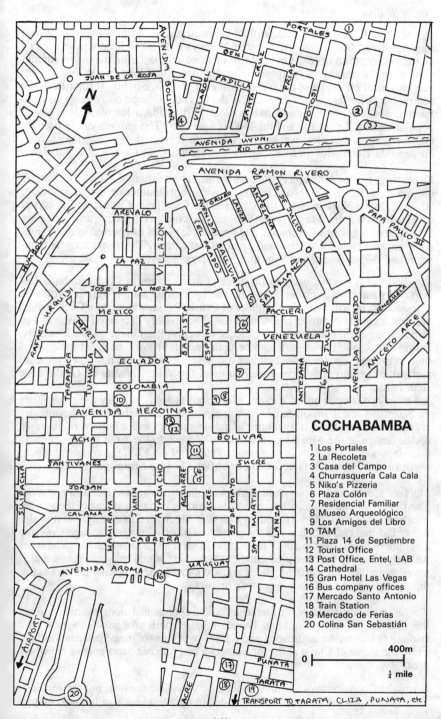

COCHABAMBA

1 Los Portales
2 La Recoleta
3 Casa del Campo
4 Churrasquería Cala Cala
5 Niko's Pizzeria
6 Plaza Colón
7 Residencial Familiar
8 Museo Arqueológico
9 Los Amigos del Libro
10 TAM
11 Plaza 14 de Septiembre
12 Tourist Office
13 Post Office, Entel, LAB
14 Cathedral
15 Gran Hotel Las Vegas
16 Bus company offices
17 Mercado Santo Antonio
18 Train Station
19 Mercado de Ferias
20 Colina San Sebastián

400m

0   ¼ mile

TRANSPORT TO TARATA, CLIZA, PUNATA, etc.

around Plaza Colón, five blocks north of the main square. Avenida Ballivián, which runs northwest from Plaza Colón and is known locally as El Prado, has the city's main concentration of restaurants. Most of these spill out onto the pavement and offer a similar variety of aggressively meaty dishes and loud music. For a more peaceful meal go to one of the pizzerias such as Nico's. Slightly further from the centre, but definitely worth the walk, is the Casa del Campo on Avenida Aniceto Padilla, north of the river and half a block east of Plaza Recoleta. It is lively, popular among the locals, and the food is excellent. The atmosphere is friendly and there are peñas most weekends. A little further west, opposite the stadium on Avenida Libertador Bolívar, the Churrasquería Cala Cala is also popular.

Exploring. Cochabamba has little architecture to be proud of. The cathedral, on the main square, is mildly interesting outside, but its interior is disappointing. At 25 de Mayo Norte number 0145, next to the Casa de la Cultura on the corner of Heroínas, is the Museo Arqueológico. It contains a humdrum collection enhanced by a few pre-Columbian and prehistoric pieces discovered in the region, some unusual pre-Inca textiles, and a marvellous curator. The museum opens 9am-noon and 3-7pm weekdays, 9am-1pm Saturdays.

Los Portales: the most extravagant piece of architecture in Cochabamba is Los Portales palace, the former home of the tin baron, Simón Patiño. Although associated primarily with the tin mines of Oruro, Patiño was born in Cochabamba and had a couple of properties in the area. The lavishly decorated palace of Los Portales, designed by European architects, was completed in the 1920s. Ironically, Patiño never saw it since although he didn't die until 1947, he spent most of his time in Europe. The immense building was never occupied and it is now a museum and cultural centre, and occasionally a hotel for VIPs: General de Gaulle once slept here.

The palace is open only for tours, which start at 5pm, Monday to Friday, 10am on Saturdays and 11am on Sundays. You are guided through some extraordinary creations; among them is a wonderful hall of mirrors and a billiard room based on the design of the Alhambra in Granada — down to the Arab script — and all done in wood. The palace is on Avenida Potosí (tel 42-43137), a couple of blocks north of Río Rocha; it is accessible by Micro G or 10 from the centre.

Markets: Cochabamba's two main markets fill the streets around the railway station. The largest and most interesting is the Mercado de Ferias, just east of the station. Fresh produce from the surrounding valleys is the main commodity, but it is also full of hat-makers, cobblers and the purveyors of delicious fruit juices. Covering a couple of blocks just north of the station is Mercado Santo Antonio. The more westerly block is the so-called handicraft market, which gets going late and is never more than half-hearted. But if you are about to head up into the mountains this is a good place to buy a jumper or two.

San Sebastían hill: west of the market area, and approached along Avenida Aroma, this peak is well worth climbing. The ten-minute uphill hike passes the new town stadium (a blot on the landscape), and is lined with busts of miscellaneous worthies. From the statue of Christ at the top you get a magnificent panorama of the whole area.

Festivals: Cochacamba's Carnival is the city's liveliest festival, but the region is most famous for the feast of the Virgen de Urcupiña, which is celebrated in mid-

August in Quillacollo, a small town ten minutes bus ride away. It is the largest festival in the Cochacamba Department and there is some excellent regional dancing and music.

Help and Information. *Tourist Information:* a kiosk on Bolívar (between the Entel building and the main square), which opens 8am-noon and 2-6pm from Monday to Friday, and 8am-noon on Saturdays.

Money: there are several cambios on and around the main square; the América, opposite the tourist information kiosk, changes travellers cheques free of commission. Moneychangers congregate on the corner of Heroínas and Ayacucho. To draw cash on Visa or MasterCard, go to the Banco de La Paz at the northwest corner of the main square; get approval from the credit card office next to it on Aguirre, before going to the bank itself.

Communications: the post office is on the corner of Heroínas and Ayacucho, and opens 7.30am-8pm from Monday to Friday, 7.30am-7pm on Saturday and 8.30am-noon on Sunday. Entel is next door.

Consulates: Argentina — Avenida Pando 1329, 2nd floor (tel 48268). Brazil — Calle Potosí 1252 (tel 45702), north of the river.

Bookshops: Los Amigos del Libro has a couple of branches in the centre of town. The best is at Heroínas 0311, between España and 25 de Mayo.

Media: the FM waveband is good in Cochabamba: anything from Abba to Tom Waits on 89.10, hip-hop on 102.4, heavy metal on 94.1.

AROUND COCHABAMBA

Pairumani. The hacienda that was at the heart of Simón Patiño's estate lies at the foot of the mountains 15 miles/24km southwest of Cochacamba. Villa Albina is set among lovely gardens and is marvellously incongruous given the surroundings. The house is not as impressive as Los Portales, nor could it be described as beautiful. But it is yet more evidence of Patiño's extraordinary taste: notice the bizarre range of chandeliers.

The ground floor of the house is open to the public for guided tours at 3pm Monday to Friday, 9.30am on Saturdays. At other times you are free to wander around the gardens. You can also visit Patiño's marble mausoleum, which lies at the end of the avenue of palm trees. The mausoleum opens only 3-4pm, and you must get one of the groundsmen to let you in.

Pick up transport for Pairumani along Heroínas near Ayacucho in town. Some micros go direct to Pairumani, but otherwise take one to Quillacollo or Vinto and change there. Quillacollo is 8 miles/13km southwest of Cochacamba, but has been virtually absorbed by the city; micros stop by the dozen on the main road near the square, heading west along the Oruro road.

Inka-Rakay. These mountaintop Inca ruins are one of the highlights of a trip to Bolivia. Inka-Rakay is hard to reach and does not receive much attention. The remains of only a few buildings are distinguishable, but the beauty and tranquillity of the spot is magical. Some might find the place slightly eerie — the local people sometimes burn their dead here, and you can see old funeral pyres.

Begin by taking a micro to Sipe-Sipe, off the Oruro road about 30 minutes from Cochabamba, beyond Quillacollo. You need to reach Sipe-Sipe before 9.30am since this is when the truck that passes Inka-Rakay usually leaves. The vehicle loads up on the road heading southwest off the main square. Make sure you have a good supply of fruit and water before you leave; ideally take a picnic or go prepared to camp.

The journey up to the ruins takes an hour, but the pot-holes and the sheer drops make for an extremely rough ride, in all senses of the word: the views of the mountains and back over the valley are staggering, but you may well end up cursing the Incas for involving you in such a hair-raising ride. A large yellow sign by the roadside signals your arrival. From here it is a short walk down to the ruins themselves.

The best way to return to Sipe-Sipe is on foot. Rather than follow the road, which goes an extremely long way around, head straight downhill. The path is fairly easy to follow — aim more-or-less straight for Sipe-Sipe, which you can see below, and you shouldn't go wrong. The footprints and animal droppings should also help to keep you on the right track. Allow about two hours for the descent, although 30 minutes of this is on flat land from the base of the mountain to the centre of the village. (It is of course possible to walk up too, but the path is hard to follow when approached from the bottom.)

The Tarata, Cliza and Punata Circuit. The Cochabamba valley is scattered with interesting villages and a tour of three of these makes a good day trip. Choose a Sunday if possible, for this is market day in Cliza.

The journey to Tarata, on a branch road south of the old Santa Cruz highway (Route 4), takes about 50 minutes. The bus stops in the main square of one of the most charming colonial villages you could ever hope to see. People stroll along quiet streets lined with buildings that crumble gently. The main square sees the most activity, but it rarely attains a bustle. The church has an interesting old organ and is worth a visit.

Cliza, 7 miles/11km further east (buses leave from Tarata's main square), is the least attractive of the three villages, but its Sunday market is worth making a special trip for. Activity spreads from a huge dusty field near the edge of town to the main square, the livestock drawing some of the biggest crowds. The throngs of people — particularly the women — make a splendid, colourful spectacle; many wear the *chistera* or top hat, characteristic of the region. Blind men mutter religious incantations on behalf of miracle-seeking locals, in exchange for a few coins. Buses and trucks to Cochabamba and Tarata leave from the market, but transport on to Punata departs from one block east of the square, on Calle Santa Cruz.

The 8 miles/12km between Cliza and Punata are, surprisingly for a rural area, built up the whole way. Punata, situated just off Route 4 at km42, rounds off the circuit nicely. It is not as charming as Tarata, but nevertheless fun to wander around. The huge ornate church in the main square is packed for services on Sundays, when worshippers park their bikes in the aisles. It has a pleasant little market, and Restaurante Bolívar, one block from the square, is an excellent place to have lunch. The only pensión is in the market square.

Inkallajta. These Inca ruins, believed to date from the 15th century, form part of one of the country's most important archaeological sites. Inkallajta is 75 miles/120km east of Cochabamba, and requires more effort and time to reach than Inka-Rakay. The easiest way is to hire your own four-wheel drive vehicle; but it is perfectly feasible to get there without. Take any bus or truck along the old Santa Cruz road and get off at Monte Puncu (about $2\frac{1}{2}$ hours from Cochabamba), where a road branches south to Pocona. Catch a truck along this road and ask to be set down at the Inkallajta turn-off. There is a large yellow sign. Do not be persuaded by the locals to get off earlier for a 'shorter' route as this is steeper and badly eroded. The walk up the mountain to the site should take $2\frac{1}{2}$-3 hours. The scenery is lovely and the locals en route very friendly. There is an excellent refugio next to the ruins.

Before setting off visit the archaeological museum in Cochabamba, which has information about the site. The curator can also tell you on what days trucks leave from Monte Puncu for Pocona, and on which they return. Take more food than you need, since transport is unreliable.

Totora. This colonial village lies off the old Santa Cruz road some three hours southeast of Cochabamba. It could be a destination in itself, an extension to the trip around the Tarata circuit or to Inkallajta, or a stopping-off place on the way to Sucre. The journey through the sparsely populated hills beyond Punata is beautiful. The road turns south to Totora (and Sucre) at Epizana, a gloomy collection of restaurants.

At first sight Totora appears to have little to offer, its mud houses blending into the hills behind. But things improve steadily after your first glimpse of the church above the rooftops. Further exploration reveals what must once have been a fine colonial town, though there is a sad air to the place. Every other house has a red star above its door to indicate it is a chichería, and a worryingly large proportion of the male population over-indulges. Artisans in Totora weave wool blankets in bright colours — ask around the houses (or chicherías) if you want to buy any.

Totora's only hotel, the Gran, is on the main street, 50 metres from where the buses stop on the long journey between Cochabamba and Sucre.

SUCRE

The legal capital of Bolivia, and the capital of Chuquisaca department, Sucre is the nation's best preserved and most beautiful city. Yet it is no museum piece, and historical and modern atmospheres complement each other perfectly. While in the centre the streets are buzzing with life, full of chattering students, a few blocks from the main square the pace slackens considerably; here the atmosphere is more colonial, in the traditional sense of the word. The whole city is a feast of architecture: Sucre's churches boast some of the finest stone carving in the country. Its houses are characteristic for their dark wooden balconies and bay windows, beautiful against the sparkling white-washed walls.

The array of fine buildings reflects the wealth and prestige of a town that has played an important role in Bolivia's history ever since its foundation in 1538. During the colonial period Sucre was the administrative centre of an area stretching from Peru to Argentina. It was also one of South America's foremost centres of learning. Sucre was the seat of Bolivia's first university, and Spanish families from all over the territory sent their children to be educated in its schools. Sucre remains Bolivia's most prestigious educational centre: half the buildings seem to be schools of some description.

The university was a breeding ground for the liberals who led the calls for independence in the early nineteenth century. The city's role in the subsequent struggle was recognized when the Declaration of Independence was signed there in 1825 and when the city was renamed Sucre, in honour of the revolutionary general.

The city has 110,000 inhabitants. It lies in the Cordillera Central at an altitude of 9,320ft/2,841m, and has a pleasant climate, although winter nights are cold.

Arrival and Departure. *Air:* LAB has non-stop flights from La Paz several times a week, and three via Cochabamba. It also operates three services a week from Santa Cruz. The LAB city office is at Calle Bustillos 121 (tel 64-21943/25992). TAM offers flights to La Paz, Puerto Suárez (for Brazil) and Santa Cruz; its office is at Calle Ortíz 110. The airport is 3 miles/5km south of the centre. The tourist office sells a fairly useless map for $0.30. To get into town take Micro 1 which runs to the Mercado Central. A taxi costs about $1.

Bus: travelling to Sucre by road is interesting but bumpy and often circuitous. The bus station (tel 22029) is a flashy new building a couple of miles from the centre. Micros A and 3 run into town; to return to the bus station, pick one up by the market. Long-distance services from Sucre are as follows:

Potosí - 5 hours; served by a regular flow of buses and minibuses from the main terminal. Two minibus companies based in central Sucre cater primarily for tourists: Soltrans (Nicolás Ortiz 6; tel 30500/24088), and Transtín (Estudiantes 17; tel 21738).
Cochabamba — 11-12 hours; mostly overnight. The journey via Totora is fun and rough until you join the old Santa Cruz highway.
La Paz — 19 hours; daily via Cochabamba or Potosí, the same buses serving Oruro (16 hours).
Santa Cruz — 15-18 hours; the most direct route is to take a bus bound for Cochabamba, get off at Epizana on the old Santa Cruz road, and hitch a lift on a passing truck. But for comfort and security you must go right to Cochabamba and get a bus along the new road from there.

Train: the train station is behind Parque Bolívar, about ten minutes walk northwest of the city centre. Call 31115/21114 for information.

Ferrobus services to Potosí, Oruro and La Paz leave at 6.50pm on Thursday and Sunday. Tickets go on sale two days in advance of departure, and sell out quickly. Fares (pullman and especial respectively) are as follows: $5.50 and $4.50 to Potosí, $13.50 and $11 to Oruro, and $19 and $15 to La Paz. The journey time to Potosí is about $4\frac{1}{2}$ hours, to La Paz more than 20. Change in Potosí for trains to Uyuni.

Car Rental: Avenida Hernando Siles 945 (tel 24506).

Accommodation. Sucre has plenty of places within a few minutes walk of the main square. For excellent value and a perfect location go to the Gran Hotel on Calle Arce; a large double room with its own bathroom costs $10. Around the corner on Ravelo is the Residencial Bolivia, charging about the same. Cheaper places on Ravelo are nearer the market. The best are Residencial Charcas at 62 (tel 23972), opposite the market ($7-10 double), and Residencial Bustillo at 58 (tel 21560), offering doubles without bathroom for $6. Cheaper still is Alojamiento El Turista at Ravelo 118 (tel 23172) with doubles for $4.

Of the middle-range hotels, which charge about $20, the most recommended are the small and quiet Hostal Cruz de Popayán at Calle Loa 881 (tel 64-25156), and Hostal Sucre, a block from the main square at Calle Bustillos 113 (tel 64-21411). Both are converted colonial mansions with pleasant courtyards. For a few more dollars ($18/$23) you can stay in the comfortable Hostal Colonial (tel 24709) in the main square.

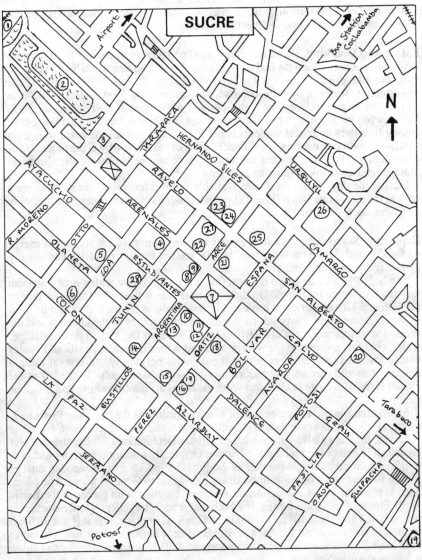

SUCRE

1 Railway Station
2 Parque Bolívar
3 Supreme Court
4 Santa Mónica
5 Los Bajos restaurant
6 Hotel Cruz de Popayán
7 Plaza 25 de Mayo
8 Casa de la Libertad
9 Hostal Colonial

10 Prefectura
11 Cathedral
12 Virgen de Guadalupe chapel
13 Post Office, IGM
14 LAB
15 Felipe Neri church
16 Student tourist office
17 TAM
18 Bibliocafé

19 La Recoleta
20 Tourist Office
21 Gran Hotel & La Taverne
22 Banco Popular de Perú
23 Mercado Central
24 San Francisco
25 Residencial Bolivia
26 Entel
27 Cheap hotels

If you've an early-morning bus to catch, or arrive late in Sucre, stay in the Alojamiento Central opposite the bus terminal.

Eating and Drinking. Sucre has many good restaurants to choose from, though if you are sticking to a tight budget the range is reduced dramatically. One of the most popular gringo haunts is La Taverne, at Arce 35 (tel 23599), just off the main square. It is run by a Frenchman who offers good food — from quiche to coq au vin — and videos. For a cheaper and more typical Bolivian meal, go to El Tropezón on Junín between Estudiante and Olaneta. A favourite drinking-hole among travellers and local students is the Bibliocafé, just off the main square on Ortíz — a good place for an after-dinner coffee or maté. Nearby is the more down-to-earth Snack Paulista bar-cum-restaurant, where anyone hankering after Brazilian indulgence can drink caipirinha cocktails.

During the day, cheap meals are available in the Mercado Central. Also open only in the day is Los Bajos (Loa 761), which is famous for its sausages, a speciality of Chuquisaca department.

Exploring. Sucre's churches have erratic opening hours. Many are closed except on Sunday and 7-9am on weekdays, but the staff at the tourist office can usually give a fairly accurate guideline.

The huge Plaza 25 de Mayo is a beautiful and lively square with a strong Spanish feel and handsome buildings. On the southwest side is the cathedral, built during the 16th and 17th centuries. It has a lovely choir behind the high altar, but its most unusual feature is the tower adorned with ceramic statues of the apostles and the evangelists. Adjacent, on Calle Ortíz, is the Chapel of the Virgen de Guadelupe, which contains a statue of the Virgin, studded with diamonds, pearls and rubies donated by wealthy residents during the colonial period. Worth several million dollars, it should probably be hidden away in some bank vault. To the left of the chapel is the Museo de la Catedral, with the usual array of furniture and religious paintings.

Back at the square, almost next door to the cathedral, is the imposing Prefectura, formerly the Governor's Palace. Continuing around you reach the Casa de la Libertad, the Legislative Palace where Bolivia's Declaration of Independence was signed. It is one of the highlights of Sucre. Originally a Jesuit university and now a museum, it contains all manner of exhibits, including a huge wooden bust of Simón Bolívar and a blood-stained jacket belonging to General Sucre. The plates used to print the act of independence are there, together with pieces of the Berlin Wall. Finest of all is the former Jesuit chapel where the independence document was debated and signed. The original seats are still in place, and it is not difficult to picture the scene. At the back is a magnificent baroque choir loft, coated in gold leaf. The museum is open 9am-noon and 2.30-6pm from Monday to Friday, 9.30am-noon on Saturday.

North up Calle Arenales, past the church of San Miguel, is Igreja Santa Mónica. Its façade is perhaps the best example of mestizo carving in the region. To the right, along Junín to Ravelo, is the Mercado Central. This is primarily a food market, but a few stalls outside sell weavings and crafts. Next door is the 16th-century church of San Francisco, which is open almost all day. Inside are a lovely Moorish ceiling and choir loft.

Going away from the centre to the end of Ravelo, you reach the Supreme Court. This hulk of a building is one of the few reminders of Sucre's status as legal capital. Across the road is Parque Bolívar, a pleasant little park that leads to the railway station. In the centre is a mini Eiffel tower which you can climb — but don't expect much of a view.

A couple of blocks southwest of the main square, on Ortíz, is San Felipe Neri, which has lovely cloisters and good views from the tower. The church is open from 4-6pm during the week, but to arrange a tour you must go to the tourist office run by students in the university opposite. Nearby, on the corner of Dalence and Bolívar, is the university Charcas Museum. It has mainly ethnographical exhibits, and some modern art. It opens 9am-noon and 2.30-6pm, Monday to Friday.

One of the gems of Sucre is the Convento Recoleta, on a hill at the end of Calle Dalence, southeast of the centre; micro 9 goes most of the way up to it. From the square in front of the church you can take in the wonderful views of the town and surrounding hills while also enjoying the tranquillity of life away from the centre. It is an ideal spot to sit and read, or write a few letters. Recoleta itself is a Franciscan monastery, home to just ten monks. Much of it is now part of a museum, a large part of which is taken up with paintings, including some lovely examples from the Cusco school. Other exhibits include interesting indigenous art (note particularly the crucifixes), and Indian tools and artefacts brought back by missionaries. In the oldest of the cloisters you can see the remains of 16th-century frescoes. Finest of all, however, are the 17th-century choir stalls in the church. The crucified figures represent Franciscan martyrs killed in Japan; the figure on the far right is Emperor Charles V.

In the gardens is a cedar tree, which is estimated to be 1,400 years old and has been declared a national monument; it is said that Simón Bolívar wrote letters beneath it. Recoleta is open 9-11am and 3-5pm, Monday to Friday, for guided tours only. Allow 40 minutes, longer if you want to pump the guide with questions.

Entertainment. Peñas are sometimes put on at the Kultor-Café Berlin (Avaroa 326) and Miski Huasi (Calle San Alberto 290; tel 22895). If you prefer to stay at home, tune into 97.1FM, for good Western rock.

Help and Information. The tourist office is some way from the centre, at the corner of San Alberto and Potosí (tel 64-25983). The staff can answer most questions, and sell city maps and a selection of brochures. The tourist police has an office in the same building. Opening hours are 8am-noon and 2-6pm Monday to Friday. If you can't be bothered to walk to the main office, the students run a tourist office on Ortíz (tel 23763). They may not have as wide a knowledge as their professional counterparts, but they have maps and are extremely friendly. They open during term-time, 10am-noon and 2-6pm Monday to Friday, and on Saturday mornings.

Communications: the post office is at Argentina 50, near the main square. Entel is at España 271, between Urquyu and Camargo.

Money: the best exchange rates are given by travel agencies, shops or hotels, and there are also a couple of cambios and street changers near the market. You can withdraw cash on Visa at Banco Popular de Perú, on Arenales between Arce and Junín.

Maps: the IGM (on the corner of Dalence and Argentina, 2nd floor), has a selection of regional and national maps, but nothing too detailed.

AROUND SUCRE

Castillo de la Glorieta. This bizarre building is on the road to Potosí, some 3 miles/5km from the city. It is a huge pink creation whose original owners transported it in pieces from France at the end of last century. The house and lovely gardens are open to the public and are well worth a visit. As it now houses a military school, take your passport. Opening hours are 9am-noon and 2-6pm Monday to Friday. Take micro E from Mercado Central.

Tarabuco. Everyone in Bolivia has heard of Tarabuco, whose market is one of the most colourful in South America. Peasants from all around descend on the village every Sunday. Between July and September so do tourists. The women are renowned for their skill at weaving, examples of which are on sale. Prices are high, however, and the main attraction is the specatacle of seeing so many Indians in traditional dress: the most characteristic feature is the helmet-like hat modelled on that worn by the conquistadores. If you are seriously interested in buying anything go during the week, or avoid the main tourist season. Some things you can buy in Sucre as well, or even further afield — and often at lower prices. Another alternative is to take a truck from Tarabuco to the village of Candelaria (about two hours away), where women also weave.

The local Quechua festival, held in March, is as famous as the market. Thousands flood to take part in the so-called Pujllay, which celebrates a battle in 1816 in which the Indians defeated the Spanish. Tarabuco is a good place to hear traditional music at any time — the men are famous for their charango-playing — but particularly during the Pujllay.

Tarabuco is 40 miles/64km southeast of Sucre, on the Monteagudo road. Buses and trucks leave from the top of Calle Calvo in Sucre on Sunday mornings, until about 9am. The journey takes $2\frac{1}{2}$-3 hours. Trucks return from Tarabuco's main square in the afternoon, until 4pm. Otherwise you can take the train which leaves at 7am, returns at 2pm, and takes 2-$2\frac{1}{2}$ hours. You can buy your seat the same day, but turn up in good time. Few vehicles cover the route on weekdays. Tarabuco has a couple of cheap hotels.

Towards Potosí. The mountain scenery between Sucre and Potosí is bleak, but strangely beautiful, and the roads are extremely dusty. Buses spend a fair part of the 100-mile/160km journey driving along the riverbed; a more reliable surface than the unpaved road. Take plenty of fruit and water to counter the effects of dust on your throat. A stop is usually made at the beautiful village of Millares, which is a good place to experience a slice of sleepy life on the Altiplano. Of the few hotels, the Alonso de Banes is best.

POTOSI

Four kilometres (13,000 feet) above sea level, Potosí is the highest city on earth. At one time it was also one of the largest and best-known places in the world. Potosí has stumbled from glory but Cerro Rico — a mountain once full of minerals, now full of the dead — still casts its ominous shadow. Eight million people have died extracting its riches.

The Spanish founded a small mining settlement here in 1545. The nearby mountain proved to contain the largest deposit of silver the world had ever seen. During the 17th century, the peak of the silver boom, over 150,000 people lived here, compared with the current 110,000. The figure is astonishing given the town's isolation and the harsh conditions that make access difficult even now.

The silver that flowed into the coffers of the Spanish monarchy also financed all manner of extravagances in Potosí. Those who profitted on a local level bought fine clothes, built luxurious mansions and financed the building of churches — with the result that Potosí became one of the continent's finest cities. By the end of the 18th century, however, the silver had diminished dramatically, and Potosí was reduced to little more than a provincial backwater. Its decline was halted in 1905 when more deposits — this time of tin — were discovered in Cerro Rico. Despite 450 years of mining, the mountain is still producing ores. Sadly, conditions in the mines have changed little since colonial times. Furthermore, the drop in tin prices has left thousands of miners without work. Cerro Rico has become a rather macabre tourist trap, where reels of film use up silver as quickly as it is scratched from the rock.

Given its history, it is not surprising that Potosí has a rather grim atmosphere. While its mansions and churches are undeniably impressive, they lack the grandeur of those in Sucre. But the memories of a visit down the mines are likely to remain with you for the rest of your life. So too are the memories of the thin air, the cold night-time temperatures and the dazzling daylight.

Arrival and Departure. *Air:* the US army was involved recently in lengthening Potosí's runway, but access by air is still limited. The only passenger service is operated by Fuerza Aérea Boliviana, the national air force. It has one flight every morning to and from La Paz. The one-way fare is $50. The FAB agent in Potosí is Transamazonas (Edificio Camara de Minera, Calle Quijarro 12; tel 27175); flights depart from Potosí at 10am. The Hotel El Turista (see below) is LAB's agent in Potosí if you want to book onward flights.

Bus: road journeys to Potosí are rough and cold — take sweaters and blankets. The bus station is 2 miles/3km northwest of the centre, beyond the railway station; take a micro. The main long-distance bus services from Potosí are as follows:

Cochabamba — 12 hours, $7; most buses run overnight.
La Paz — 12 hours, $6; most buses leave 6-7pm.
Oruro — 8-9 hours, $4; buses bound for La Paz or Cochabamba often stop off, though there are additional services.
Sucre — 5 hours, $3.50; lots of buses leave at around 8.30am. In addition, there are non-stop minibus services run by Soltrans (Quijarro 34, near main square), Hidalgo (junction of Bolívar and Junín) and Transtín (Linares 89).
Tarija — 11 hours; 8.30am on Tuesday, Friday and Sunday with San Juan del Oro.
Uyuni — 8-9 hours; two buses daily with Villa Imperial.
Villazón — 13 hours; daily, mostly at 6-7pm, or change at Tarija.

Train: the railway is the best way to approach Potosí, particularly from the north. The journey from Oruro and La Paz is along the world's second highest railway track after the Lima-Huancayo line in Peru: Cóndor, a bleak station southwest of Potosí, lies at an altitude of 15,800ft/4,816m. All trains serving Potosí start or end up in Sucre.

The rail station is at the bottom of Avenida Villazón, northwest of the centre. For information call 62-23110/24211. The ferrobus to Oruro (7 hours) and La Paz (10 hours) currently leaves at 11.20pm on Wednesday; there is a tren especial on Thursday. Sucre is $4\frac{1}{2}$ hours away by ferrobus, which leaves at 5am on Sunday;

there is also a weekly tren especial and tren mixto. Uyuni is best reached by bus, though a tren mixto runs on Sunday.

Accommodation. The cheapest places are in the streets between the train station and the main square, particularly on and off Avenidas Oruro and Serrudo. Among the best are Alojamiento La Paz (Oruro 242) and Residencial Copacabana (Avenida Serrudo 319).

For a few dollars more you can stay centrally. You will be besieged by young boys offering to escort you to a good hotel; they speak surprisingly good English and can be persistent. Most of the hotels in the centre cost $7-10 for a double room. One of the best is El Turista (Lanza 19; tel 62-22341/22517), with a helpful owner, hot water in the morning, and comfortable rooms. Another excellent place, but slightly more expensive, is the Hostal Carlos V (Linares 42; tel 25121), with a pleasant sitting area and hot water all day. The Casa de Huéspedes Hispano (Matos

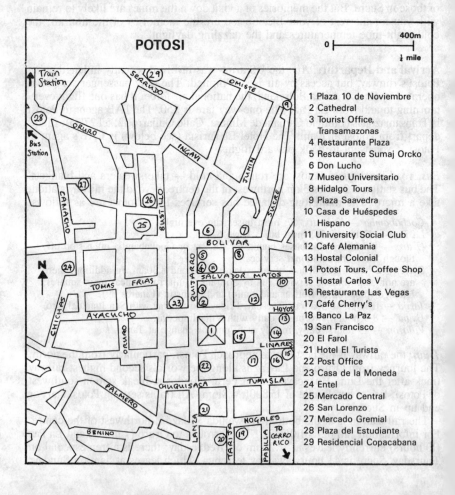

POTOSI

0 —————— 400m
¼ mile

1 Plaza 10 de Noviembre
2 Cathedral
3 Tourist Office,
   Transamazonas
4 Restaurante Plaza
5 Restaurante Sumaj Orcko
6 Don Lucho
7 Museo Universitario
8 Hidalgo Tours
9 Plaza Saavedra
10 Casa de Huéspedes
   Hispano
11 University Social Club
12 Café Alemania
13 Hostal Colonial
14 Potosí Tours, Coffee Shop
15 Hostal Carlos V
16 Restaurante Las Vegas
17 Café Cherry's
18 Banco La Paz
19 San Francisco
20 El Farol
21 Hotel El Turista
22 Post Office
23 Casa de la Moneda
24 Entel
25 Mercado Central
26 San Lorenzo
27 Mercado Gremial
28 Plaza del Estudiante
29 Residencial Copacabana

62; tel 22659) is run by a friendly couple and has a choice of rooms for $5-9.
The best mid-range hotel is the Hostal Colonial, near the square at Calle Hoyos 8 (tel 62-24265). Rooms have heating and cost $18/$22.

Eating and Drinking. Early-risers will have trouble finding breakfast. The Alemania, on the corner of Sucre and Matos, is the first to open, at around 8am. The best food in town is at the Sumaj Orcko on Quijarro, near the corner of Bolívar. It's popular in the evening and you may have to wait for a seat. Dishes include *viscacha*, a South American rodent. Just along the street, the Plaza is alright and less crowded. The Las Vegas (on Padilla near Linares) is a lively, often raucous place, usually full of men knocking back singani by the bottle and playing dice. The food is good, and all the main dishes cost $2.25. On a Friday evening you can go to a peña at Don Lucho (Calle Ingaví).

For coffee, snacks or an after-dinner maté try the Coffee Shop (Padilla, next to Potosí Tours), run by and frequented primarily by women. Café Cherry's, opposite Las Vegas, is expensive, but maté is cheap. A couple of blocks further out, El Farol (on Tarija, opposite San Francisco church) is a jollier place for a drink.

A good place to mingle with the locals is at the University Social Club on Salvador Matos between Quijarro and Junín, which sells cheap beer and canteen-style food. If you need a drink at 4am, the liquor store on the corner of Padilla and Tumulsa is open 24 hours (ring the bell).

Exploring. The opening hours of Potosí's churches are an enigma, and the tourist office does little to help. But since the façades are usually the highlights, don't feel hard done by.

The heart of the old city is Plaza 10 de Noviembre. It has the usual array of public buildings, including the Corte Superior de Justicia (the original royal mint), the Alcaldía and the Prefectura. Dominating the west side is the 19th-century cathedral. Inside, the three naves give it a spacious and grandiose feel. The German organ, above the high altar, was donated by the tin baron Simón Patiño. It should be open 8.30-11am.

Across from the cathedral on Calle Ayacucho, and occupying an entire block, is the Casa de la Moneda. Potosí's pride and joy was designed as the Royal Mint in the mid-18th century by the man also responsible for the mints of Mexico City and Lima. It functioned right up until 1953. The tremendously solid building has been heavily restored, and largely stripped of the atmosphere a place of its age and history should possess. Visitors are taken on fairly intense guided tours (in Spanish), which begin at 9am and 2pm, Monday to Saturday, and last about $2\frac{1}{2}$ hours. The tour begins with the extensive art section: among the highlights are the works of Melchor Pérez Holguín (considered the country's greatest colonial painter) and a picture entitled the Virgen del Cerro, one of the many anonymous paintings showing a fascinating mixture of indigenous and European influences. The most impressive exhibits in the building are the huge wooden presses used to make coins. They were powered by horses or slaves, according to availability. The ubiquitous displays of colonial furniture, ethnographical and archaeological relics all include things worth seeing.

A couple of blocks south of the main square, on Nogales near the corner of Tarija, is the church of San Francisco, the city's oldest. It has an attractive stone portal, beautiful brick domes, and good views from the tower; the attached convent contains a small museum. The other churches most worth visiting are west and north of the main square. North of the centre, on Bustillos, is the church of San

Lorenzo, which boasts a fine mestizo façade in an excellent state of preservation. Opposite it is the central market, a rather lack-lustre affair. More lively is the Mercado Gremial, reached down an alleyway nearby, where traders sell hats, blankets and household goods. Calle Chayanta is an evil-smelling street where skinned animals are displayed proudly on the pavements.

Northeast of the square is the Museo Universitario on Calle Bolívar (between Junín and Sucre), which has a small but excellent historical collection. It opens 8am-noon and 2-6pm Monday to Friday. Further north off Plaza Saavedra (between Sucre and Junín) is a craft market: stock up here on gloves and jumpers if you have arrived unprepared for the cold.

Help and Information. *Tourist Information:* Edificio Cámara de Minería, 2nd floor, Calle Quijarro, near the square (tel 25288/26392). Maps are usually unavailable and the staff are unhelpful. Ask also in one of the many travel agencies, which arrange tours both in the immediate area and further afield, including to the Salar de Uyuni (see page 381).

Communications: the post office is on the corner of Quijarro and Linares, just off the main square. It opens 8am-7.30pm daily except Sunday, when it opens 8.30am-noon. Entel is on Plaza Aniceto Arce, three blocks north and three west of the centre. It opens 8am-10pm daily.

Money: shops, restaurants and travel agencies in the main square and along Sucre and Bolívar change cash; some accept cheques, but at fairly bad rates. There are also street changers, and cash on Visa can be obtained at Banco de la Paz in the main square.

AROUND POTOSI

Cerro Rico. Although 46,000 tonnes of silver have already been extracted from this former volcano, 4,000 miners are still scraping a living from it. Legend claims Simón Bolívar climbed this mountain in 1826 with the flags of five countries to liberate from the Spanish. A statue of him is at the top, together with an antenna for Channel 7.

A visit to the maze of mines in Cerro Rico may be the most memorable point of your journey in South America. Seeing how the miners work, and how they thereby condemn themselves to an early grave, is an extremely shocking and sobering experience. Furthermore, it is not without its dangers and discomforts. Anyone especially prone to claustrophobia should stay away, as should those scared of heights — the mountain has some narrow ledges next to 200-metre drops. Given the thinness of the air and the presence of noxious gases, you are guaranteed to return to the surface physically and mentally frazzled.

Several agencies in Potosí arrange tours down the mines. They all offer roughly the same package — $5 for a morning's trip led by an ex-miner. The best currently on offer is with Potosí Tours (Plaza Alonso de Ibañez 16), whose guide Raúl Braulio (Israel) is excellent and speaks good English. Hidalgo Tours (Bolívar and Junín; tel 25597/22287) has a good reputation but is less daring. If you want to shop around, either visit all the agencies or wait in the main square between 8am and 9am on weekdays, when guides scout around for last-minute business.

A tour lasts three to five hours, depending on the agency and how well members of the group cope with conditions below ground. Wear your worst clothes — the tunnels are so small in places that you have to crawl, and evil fabric-dissolving

Santa Cruz — 15 hours, $7; several daily buses, from 6am to 2.30pm.
Villazón — 24 hours; Universo has a daily service, leaving at 8pm.

Train: Oruro is the Clapham Junction or Chicago of Bolivian railways. It is linked by rail with La Paz, Cochabamba, Potosí and Sucre, and there is also a line south to Uyuni and beyond to the borders with Chile and Argentina. While journeys southwards are best done by train (many are through services from La Paz), it is quicker to reach La Paz or Cochabamba by bus. Phone the train station on 60605 or 60247 for information. Services are currently as follows:

La Paz — 4-5 hours; Wednesday, Friday, Saturday and Sunday.
Potosí and Sucre - 8 hours ($4) and 13 hours ($7) respectively; 10pm on Wednesday and Saturday.
Cochabamba — 5-6 hours, Wednesday, Friday and Sunday 8.15am.
Villazón — 16-18 hours, $8; a tough journey via Tupiza, leaving Wednesday and Sunday.
Abaroa/Ollagüe — 12 hours; Wednesday at 7.45pm. After a change of locomotive or train, you can continue to Calama in Chile ($17). Crowded, freezing journey but wondrous, desolate landscape.

Accommodation. The only time you're likely to have trouble finding a room is during the carnival, though the tourist office can usually fix people up with a bed in a family home. At other times the challenge is to find somewhere that is at all pleasant. To compound matters, Oruro is prone to water shortages: hotels may have supplies only in the morning.

The Residencial Ideal, on Calle Bolívar between Pagador and Potosí, is basic and costs $8 for a double. The Hotel Repostero at Calle Sucre 370, also between Pagador and Potosí is much more comfortable, costing $10/$17. The only thing approaching a luxury hotel is the Terminal (tel 53209) in the bus station itself. Across the road is Residencial El Turista, which is cheap and grotty.

The very cheapest places are the string of alojamientos on Bolívar between the railway and Avenida Brasil. Rates are lowest at the Posada América at 250, costing less than $2 per person.

Eating and Drinking. Starting at the main square, the Restaurant Oruro (next to the Palais Concerts) is adequate. Oruro is the salteña capital of the world; Super Salteñas (which also does pizzas), two blocks east of the square on Galvarro between Ayacucho and Junín, is the best place to eat them. If you'd like something other than salteñas, head around the corner to the Restaurant Rabitos on Ayacucho (between Galvarro and 6 de Octubre).

The Hilton (no relation to the multinational chain), near the main square, is a reasonable breakfast place; the peña here at 9pm each Friday is the biggest fun you're likely to have in Oruro, outside the carnival.

Exploring. Plaza 10 de Febrero, the main square, is the grandest part of town, though that's no great accolade. Notice, however, the fine Palais Concerts — now a cinema — which was built by Simón Patiño, the tin baron. Another building that was owned by Patiño is on Calle Soria Galvarro, just north of Ayacucho: it is now the Casa de la Cultura and contains a motley collection of historical exhibits.

At the western end of Adolfo Mier, about five blocks from the square, is the church of Virgen del Socavón. While the building itself is of no particular interest, beneath it is a 16th-century mine that has been converted into a museum. The entrance to the Museo Minero is at the back of the church, but buy a ticket first from the office outside. A staircase takes you 50 metres underground into an old mining gallery that was rediscovered only in 1989. It contains maps of the mines in the area and a selection of mining paraphernalia, including contraptions used by the miners to smuggle silver out. Look out also for the figure of the Devil (*el Tío de la Mina*), an extraordinary object to have beneath a church. He is surrounded by offerings of money, beer, cigarettes and coca leaves. The guide knows all there is to know about mining around Oruro and will gladly tell you (in Spanish). The museum opens 9-11.30am and 3-5pm Monday to Saturday, and 8am-noon and 4-6pm on Sundays.

Oruro's other main attraction is the excellent Museo Antropológico, south of the town, on Calle Lizarraga. The archaeological section, with ceramics and bizarre pre-Inca stone llama heads, is particularly good. There are also displays relating to the Chipaya Indians, and a fine array of carnival masks. The museum is open 10am-noon and 3-5pm. To get there take any bus marked *Sud*, such as A, C, 1, 101 or 102, all of which pass through the main square and along Galvarro. Just behind the museum is the municipal zoo, full of wretched-looking animals.

The market area is around the Mercado Campero, east of the main square on Pagador and Adolfo Mier. Stalls spreads eastwards, eventually merging into Mercado Bolívar on the other side of the railway line.

Carnival. The main parade, that launches the carnival, takes place on the Saturday before Ash Wednesday. Most famous is the Diablada, which dates from colonial times when it was traditionally performed by Indian miners. Masked dancers, dressed in weird and wonderful costumes, perform a battle between good and evil, usually symbolized as a battle between the Indians and the Spanish. Celebrations are focussed around the main square and the church of the Virgin of Socavón, the patroness of miners.

Ask at the tourist office about buying tickets for special seats, although many of these are booked by tour agencies in La Paz. Dancers rehearse for months prior to the parade, so you may be able to see them practising at other times of the year. If you want to take good, close-up pictures, you may need to arrange a press pass, which you can obtain for about $15 from the mayor's office. This pass also allows you to move in and out of the parades, which otherwise is difficult.

Help and Information. *Tourist Office:* Edificio Prefectural on Plaza 10 de Febrero (tel 52-51764), which has badly printed city maps. The display of photographs of Oruro and environs is interesting, and the staff are helpful when pressed. It opens 9am-noon and 2-6pm Monday to Friday.

Money: exchange rates are bad, but try shops, e.g. on Calle Adolfo Mier, or the moneychangers around the railway station and the Mercado Campero. The Banco de la Paz is on Bolívar between La Plata and Glavarro.

Communications: the post office is a magnificent building at Presidente Montes 1456, half a block from the northeast corner of the square, between Adolfo Mier and Junín. It opens 8am-8pm during the week, 9am-7.30pm on Saturdays and 9am-noon on Sundays.

Telecommunications are run mostly by Coteor, in the big, ugly building just south of the square. Entel is next door.

AROUND ORURO
Lago Uru Uru. This lake lies just south of Oruro and is famous for its birdlife,

particularly the flamingoes. Those approaching Oruro by train from Potosí get a good look at the birds, but for a closer inspection take bus 102 (marked Challacollo) or Micro A from the main square: ask to be dropped at the turn-off, which is a couple of miles from the lake. You can sometimes hire boats, but note that there are few birds during the peak of the dry season. Lago Uru Uru flows into the larger Lago Poopó, which is another popular watering-hole for flamingoes.

Cala Cala. About 15 miles/24km southeast of Oruro is a small cave containing Bolivia's best known rock paintings. Access is via the village of Cala Cala, accessible by bus from Oruro. Ask around for the guardian to the park. He must open up the gate, which is about 30 minutes walk from the village. The coloured paintings of birds, llamas and stylized human figures are remarkable.

Siglo Veinte (XX). Once the largest tin mine in Bolivia and the source of Simón Patiño's greatest wealth, the '20th Century' mine has now been all but abandoned. The collapse of tin prices has reduced nearby Llallagua into a virtual ghost town. A few co-operatives still try to scrape a living, and you can sometimes persuade someone to show you around. Llallagua is 60 miles/96km south of Oruro, served by bus every couple of hours between 7am and 6pm; the fare is $2.50 and the journey takes about three hours.

If disappointed, you may be able to arrange a visit to Mina San José, just a mile or so outside Oruro.

Chipaya. The settlement of Chipaya lies southwest of Oruro in a remote spot near the northern edge of the Coipasa salt desert. It is home to the few remaining Chipaya Indians, a unique and ancient tribe thought to have been one of the earliest to settle on the Altiplano. The Chipaya community is disappearing fast due to contact with the modern world. Until ten years ago virtually all the houses were built according to the traditional circular style, designed to give maximum protection against the cold. Nowadays, houses are built to a rectangular design and offer little shelter from the freezing temperatures of the southern Altiplano.

Chipaya is a fascinating place to visit, but is far from the beaten track. Trucks occasionally leave for Chipaya from Oruro's Plaza Walter Khon, a few blocks down from the anthropological museum. Alternatively, you may be able to get a bus bound for Sabaya, in which case you alight at Escara, where the road to Chipaya branches south. You may be able to get a lift the last 15 miles/24km to the village; otherwise expect a day's walk. Once at Chipaya, you will be directed to the Corregidor, who can arrange a bed for you, and charge you $20 for a 'photography permit'. Make sure you take a selection of presents — the local people don't particularly enjoy receiving visitors.

THE SOUTHWEST

UYUNI

Consisting of a few adobe houses scattered along one dusty and windswept main street, Uyuni shows few signs of life: traffic is virtually non-existent, only a few street traders brave the cold temperatures, and the local men seem to spend most of their time getting drunk.

Uyuni is the main settlement in the sparsely-populated Southern Altiplano, lying vulnerably on the eastern edge of the salt desert. It is one of the coldest places in Bolivia, but there are some compensations: germs cannot survive in this environment and Uyuni's 20,000 inhabitants are said to be the country's healthiest.

The main reason to venture so far south is to explore the saltpans and visit the Laguna Colorada. The best place to stay is the Hotel Avenida, which also arranges tours; there are a few residenciales too. Change sufficient money before you arrive: the only bank doesn't deal in foreign currency, and striking deals with the locals gets only poor rates.

From the north, Uyuni is best reached by train. The town is, astonishingly, a hub of rail transport. The railway line splits here, with one line heading south to Argentina, the other west to Chile. As many as five trains a week depart for Oruro and La Paz. The only road that you might consider taking is that from Potosí, which is served by daily buses when weather permits; the journey takes 8-9 hours. The road between Oruro and Uyuni is appalling.

SALAR DE UYUNI

This is the largest salt desert in southwest Bolivia. The salt beds are thought to be 25 metres deep and contain reserves of over 10 billion tonnes. Salt extraction involves many of the local people living in the villages scattered along the shores. The saltpan is dotted with lakes and a number of islands, some of which support small settlements.

Exploring the Salar de Uyuni is a once-in-a-lifetime experience, one of the greatest adventures in South America. It cannot be undertaken casually. Travellers with plenty of cash may opt for one of the tours that can be arranged in La Paz or Potosí; you can go for a two-day trip from Potosí for around $100. In Uyuni the best person to talk to is the owner of the Hotel Avenida, who has a jeep and has extensive experience of the Salar. You may also be able to hire a jeep and driver independently, but never set out with anyone you don't have full confidence in: it is easy to get lost. For a tour of a few hours expect to pay $30-40.

The cheapest option is to take a truck across the saltpan to Llica, one of the largest settlements in the region, located on the northwest fringe of the Salar; the journey takes about five hours. It has a simple hotel, or you can sleep in the school. You may be able to arrange a lift at the lorry drivers' syndicate (Sindicato de Chóferes) in Uyuni.

May to October is the best season for travelling across the saltpans. Sunglasses are essential to protect your eyes from the glare of the salt.

LAGUNA COLORADA

This lake lies about 250 miles/400km southwest of Uyuni, in one of the most isolated areas of the Bolivian highlands. Algae have turned the waters a startling red colour. With its white salt shores and scattering of flamingoes, the lake is a breathaking sight. The surrounding scenery of hills and volcanic peaks dotted with geysers and steaming pools, is otherwordly.

Organize a trip in Uyuni or Potosí, where you can arrange a four-day tour for around $250. The alternative is to get a lift on a truck going south to one of the mines found in the area. The miners usually give visitors a hospitable reception, and finding somewhere to sleep should not be a problem. However, heading to the area independently requires good preparation and full camping gear.

TUPIZA

This quiet, pleasant little town lies on the west bank of the Río Tupiza, about 120 miles/192km south of Uyuni. It has been an important mining centre ever since the colonial period. While the town is of no great beauty, the surrounding hills and mountains, with their bizarre multi-coloured rock formations, are staggering. The best way to explore is on foot. A topographical map is a real asset; if you don't have one already, ask at the Municipalidad.

There are plenty of cheap hotels, mostly around the train station; the best is the Valle Hermosa, a short distance south on Avenida Pedro Arraya. The main square is a couple of blocks to the west.

Arrival and Departure. A weekly ferrobus links Tupiza with Oruro (9 hours) and La Paz (13 hours), which continues to Villazón, on the border with Argentina. There are several overnight buses daily between Tupiza and Potosí (10 hours along a bad road) and Tarija (8 hours), and many to and from Villazón ($2\frac{1}{2}$-3 hours). The route to Villazón may be closed during the wet season. All buses leave from opposite the railway station.

TARIJA

For anyone who has travelled south through the country, Tarija comes as a shock, both topographically and culturally. Lying at the heart of a fertile valley dotted with orchards and vineyards, and blessed with a mild climate, it is a perfect place to recover from the rigours of the Altiplano. Tarija has a population of around 70,000 and is situated on the banks of the Río Guadalquivir. It is a tranquil place, without being enormously exciting, and is totally different from anywhere else in the country.

The inhabitants of Tarija town and department have always been independent-minded. They declared themselves free of Spain in 1807 — before the rest of South America broke the chains — and founded their own little republic. Tarija was later absorbed into the new republic of Bolivia, but the people have never allowed themselves to be assimilated. Being so far from Bolivia's political centre, it is not surprising that Tarija has a closer relationship with nearby Argentina. The local people are tall Spanish-speakers with light complexions; some even have blond hair.

The *chapacos*, as the local people are known, are famous for their distinctive music and dance, and also for their festivals. The liveliest is the Fiesta de San Roque, held in early September. In honour of San Roque, the patron saint of dogs, the locals adorn their dogs with ribbons, and process, dance and drink copious amounts of alcohol for several days.

Arrival and Departure. LAB and TAM link Tarija with La Paz and Cochabamba three times a week. Services to Santa Cruz, Sucre and Trinidad are less frequent. Micros run near the airport, southeast of the centre.

Daily buses link Tarija with Tupiza and Potosí, and to the Argentinian border post at Villazón. The bus station (tel 22653) is at the southeastern end of Avenida de las Américas, ten blocks from Plaza Luís de Fuentes, the main square.

Accommodation. Most cheap residenciales are north of the main square along Calle Sucre, particularly around the market. The Miraflores (Sucre Norte 920) and the Ochos Hermanos (Sucre Norte 782) are both recommended; the latter has dorms only. Also comfortable are Residenciales Bolívar and América, opposite each other on Bolívar, about four blocks north of Plaza Sucre. For greater comfort stay at the Costanera (Avenida de Las Américas; tel 22851/24817), near the corner of J.M. Saracho.

Exploring. Tarija, founded in 1574, retains traces of its colonial past. One of finest relics is the Casa Dorada on Calle General Trigo, on the corner of Ingaví north of the main square. This old merchant's house now houses the Casa de la Cultura. The finest ecclesiastical building is the 17th-century convent of San Francisco, on the corner of Calles La Madrid and Campos.

The Tarija valley is one of the richest fossil deposits in Latin America. You can see a fine collection in the Museo Universitario, on the corner of Calles Trigo and Lema; it also has displays of pre-Columbian pottery. For more modern examples of craftsmanship go to the market on Calle Sucre; this is also a good place to eat.

Be sure to make the most of the locally-produced wines. Those from the Santa Ana valley are particularly recommended. Local vineyards have offices in town (mostly along 15 de Abril), and you can arrange to go on a tour.

Help and Information. The tourist office is at General Trigo N 662 (tel 25948), the post office in the main square, and Entel a couple of blocks away on Calle Virginio Lema. Cambios and moneychangers are mostly on Sucre and Bolívar. There is an Argentinian consulate on the corner of Ballivián and Bolívar (tel 22661).

CROSSING INTO ARGENTINA

This corner of Bolivia has several crossings into Argentina. All are accessible from Tarija. The roads in this part of the country are rough (especially during the rains), but the scenery is usually ample recompense.

Villazón. The border town of Villazón, about 115 miles/184km southwest of Tarija, is the main crossing point between Bolivia and Argentina. Residencial El Martínez, close to the bus station, is the best choice for accommodation on the Bolivian side, but it is better to cross into Argentina and stay in La Quiaca, which is a slightly more congenial place.

Villazón is accessible by road from Tupiza ($2\frac{1}{2}$-3 hours) and Tarija (7-8 hours); buses run once or twice a day. Potosí buses usually go via Tupiza, and take about 15 hours. Most people opt for the train: three trains a week (including a ferrobus) run to La Paz, via Uyuni and Oruro.

There is an Argentinian consulate in the main square, but to save being stuck in Villazón, get your visa while in Tarija. The casas de cambio on the main street deal in dollars and Argentinian currency.

Bermejo. The border post at Bermejo is 135 miles/216km southeast of Tarija, and is served by daily overnight buses (8 hours). Boats cross the river to Agua Blanca, from where buses run to Pichanal.

Yacuiba. Overnight buses run several times a week to Yacuiba from Tarija. Alternatively, take a bus (infrequent) or truck to Villa Montes and change there. Villa Montes also lies on the railway that connects Santa Cruz and Yacuiba. Rather than take the train right to Salta in Argentina, get a bus from the border to Tartagal and continue from there.

Chile

Torres del Paine National Park

Population: 13 million   **Capital: Santiago de Chile (4.5 million)**

An old Chilean folk story relates that when God lay down to sleep at the end of the sixth day of creation, he pillowed his head in the soft sands of Patagonia, and threw all the natural wonders that he had not yet placed upon the world over the Andes. Thus Chile was formed. This long ribbon of land is an inventory of natural phenomena: the barren salt lakes of the Atacama desert, the waterfalls and volcanoes of the Lake District, the rainforests of the Archipelago, and the Torres del Paine mountains and Laguna San Rafael glacier in the south. And livening up these unique landscapes is abundant wildlife, ranging from the penguin colonies of the far south, to the flamingoes of the northern Altiplano.

This country is tailor-made for people with energy: the scope for walking, riding or cycling is unlimited, and the country's rivers provide the best rafting and canoeing in South America. Chile contains some of the wildest and least explored areas in the world, though you don't have to be a Chris Bonnington or a David Attenborough to enjoy it. The scenery almost everywhere is stunning — whether you are at the top of a mountain or lounging in the back of a bus. If you aren't into hiking, there are lakes to swim in, wineries to visit and rodeos to attend. In comparison with its landscapes, Chilean towns are rather low on interest, both architectural and historical: few have escaped earthquake damage and 20th-century development. Nevertheless, some impressive colonial buildings have survived, and many towns have fine settings and are manageable, unintimidating places.

Chile is the least 'Latin' country in South America. Anyone used to the inescapable chaos that characterizes the Andean nations to the north, will find that the clean and tidy nature of life in Chile comes as a shock. A benefit of its European-ness is that it is a user-friendly country, with a well developed infrastructure. Furthermore, you don't have to venture far from the towns to find less orderly and more atmospheric communities; best of all are the old villages in northern Chile, and the small scattered settlements in the south, where people get around mostly on horseback.

Chileans have been psychologically shaken by the bruising years of repression under Pinochet. The army, still led by the General, continues to flex its muscles. But democracy, however fragile, has given the people a new openness and confidence. Travellers emerge from Chile with tales of the extraordinary hospitality heaped upon them. Chileans have been able to enjoy their beautiful country as never before. For travellers too, this is an ideal time to be there.

GEOGRAPHY

Chile is 2,672 miles/4,926km long. Its entire length is dominated by the backbone of the Andes, or the Cordillera, whose snowcapped peaks are visible from nearly every part of the country. The range is broadest in the north, where it forms the Altiplano, a plateau known in Chile as the *puna*.

Around 80% of the country is mountainous. The rest is plain, bordered by the Andes to the east. To the west is the much lower Cordillera de la Costa. While the far northern area of this central plain contains the forbidding Atacama desert, the land becomes progressively more fertile as you head down to the heavily-populated Valle Central, usually known in English as the Chilean Heartland. Further south still is the forested Lake District, with its startlingly beautiful landscape of lakes and volcanoes.

At Puerto Montt the central plain dips into the sea, the coastal mountains continuing southwards as the hundreds of islands of the Chilean Archipelago. Patagonia, the remote and sparsely populated southerly region, consists of islands and icefields, forests, volcanoes and glaciers. At the southern tip lies Tierra del Fuego, sliced through by the Argentinian frontier. This archipelago of rocky islands — including the large Isla Grande — is separated from the mainland by the Straits of Magellan. Further offshore is the last lonely outpost of the Andes, Cape Horn, from where 2,000 miles/3,220km of unbroken ocean stretch out to Antarctica.

Chile also encompasses a number of islands in the Pacific, including the mysterious Easter Island.

CLIMATE

Chile takes in a number of distinct and extreme climatic zones. At one end of the scale are the desert regions in the north, where some areas are said never to have seen rain. But while generally — and often unremittingly — hot during most of the year, temperatures can drop well below freezing on winter nights.

The Chilean heartland, from just north of Santiago down to the lakes, has a Mediterranean climate. Summers are hot but rarely uncomfortable, though humidity (and smog) levels are high in Santiago. The rains mostly fall during the May to August wet season, but there is also some light rain in April, September and October. Winter lasts from July to September. It can be cold, wet and unpleasant, but snow is unusual.

The Lake District is cooler and damper. During winter, if it's not wet it's probably freezing. Conditions become progressively less clement as you head further south. South of Puerto Montt, summer days can be hot, but there is often a lot of wind and rain. Chilean Patagonia and Tierra del Fuego are cold, wet and windy throughout the year: the winds are among the strongest many people have ever experienced.

When to Go. While you can travel through the desert regions north of Santiago at any time of year, conditions are harder in much of Chile during the winter. This is particularly the case if you plan to head down to the southern tip of the Chilean archipelago, where the best weather for walking is between December and February — the region's short summer. While it is physically possible to travel in the area in winter, certain areas will be inaccessible, and conditions are always difficult: take extra thermals.

The problem with travelling in the December-March summer season is that it coincides with the main Chilean and Argentinian holiday period. These two nations are not the best of neighbours. According to the Chileans, the Argentinians treat the country like a cheap theme park. Both nationalities congregate mainly in the Lake District and at the main beach areas, particularly around Valparaíso. Elsewhere, however, crowds are rare.

HISTORY

The strongest pre-Columbian cultures in Chile were the Diaguita, who lived in the Atacama, and the Mapuche of the Heartland and the Lake District. The latter were made up of a number of different tribes, including the Araucarians. Further north the Altiplano was, and still is, the home of the Aymará — a group which lived also in Bolivia and Peru, and was the first to feel the influence of the Incas.

Arica, near the Peruvian border, came under Inca control in the mid-13th century. The Incas extended their rule down to the Río Maipo, just south of where Santiago now lies. Here a series of bloody conflicts with the Mapuche tribes halted their advance.

The Colonial Period. When Magellan made the first European exploration of the Chilean coast in 1520, it was still in the hands of the Incas. But they withdrew from Chile altogether following the collapse of their empire in the early 1530s. Conquistador Diego de Almagro set off for Chile from Peru in 1535 in search of further Inca riches; but he eventually turned back disappointed, and discouraged by the fierce Indians.

Pedro de Valdivia led the first real colonizing expedition into Chile's fertile heartland. He founded Santiago in 1541. Over the next 12 years Valdivia commanded numerous expeditions to try to break the power of the Mapuche, but he was eventually killed in an ambush. Lautaro, Valdivia's Mapuche guide who had learnt the military secrets of the Spanish, took command of the Indians. He began an insurrection which almost succeeded, and the Mapuche were not far from Santiago when they were forced to withdraw. But apart from the area around the fortified town of Valdivia, control of the lands south of the river Bío-Bío remained with the Mapuche.

The next 200 years of Chile's history remained stormy. Under strong Spanish army protection, settlers began to cultivate the fertile valleys of the north and the heartland. Raids by English pirates, continued attacks by the Mapuche, uprisings of enslaved Indians, and earthquakes all conspired to make life uncomfortable for the beleaguered settlers. In 1811 the smouldering dissatisfaction with life in the colony erupted into full-scale rebellion: so began Chile's War of Independence from the Spanish empire.

Independence. After six years of scattered uprisings, the Spanish were beaten by the rebel Argentinian general, José de San Martín. In an expedition reminiscent of Hannibal's crossing of the Alps, he traversed the Andes to descend on the unsuspecting Spanish forces. Bernardo O'Higgins, the illegitimate son of the Irish-born Viceroy of Lima, joined forces with San Martín. Following the defeat of the Spanish at Chacabuco in 1817, O'Higgins was proclaimed the first president of Chile. The Spanish retreated to the island of Chiloé which they held until 1826, the last outpost of Spanish rule in Latin America.

O'Higgins' presidency was not an easy ride. He was betrayed by the greed of the landowning oligarchy and, in 1823, was forced into exile. Power fell into the hands of the conservatives who brought in a new constitution in 1833, formalizing the supremacy of the property owners.

The most significant developments during the 19th century concerned the rich mineral deposits in the Atacama desert. Chile was so keen to exploit these that it extended mining operations northwards into Bolivia and Peru, and in 1879 launched an all-out invasion. Thus began the War of the Pacific. The most famous engagement of the war was the sea battle off Iquique, in which the Chilean commander, Arturo Prat, was killed and thereby made a national martyr. The war ended in 1883 with the Chilean conquest of La Paz and Lima. When the borders were redrawn, Bolivia lost Antofagasta and its connections to the sea; Peru lost Iquique and Arica.

The new militarization of Chile posed problems. The returning army was not content to return to serfdom. Troops were sent southwards to deal with the Mapuche. In a series of battles of genocidal intensity the regions south of the Bío-Bío river were tamed, and land was given to the soldiers. The opening of this new territory stimulated a further wave of settlers: from the Balkans to Tierra del Fuego and Antofagasta, and from Germany to the rich farmlands of the Lake District.

Recent History. The first decades of the 20th century were a difficult time for Chile. Economic crises and the increasing power of the political left eventually led to the installation by the army of a repressive military government from 1927-32 under Carlos Ibáñez del Campo. There followed a series of coalition governments with well-represented left-wing factions. It was only in 1952 that a resurrected President Ibáñez initiated serious reforms, weakening the power of the landowners and legalizing the communist party. A period of progressive social reform led up to the 1970 elections.

The Marxist candidate, Salvador Allende, won the presidency by a narrow margin. He became the world's first democratically elected communist leader. He initiated a series of radical reforms, introducing free health care and education, and a massive literacy campaign. Lands stolen from the Mapuche were returned, large estates were broken up into smallholdings and nationalization programmes were launched. The capitalist world's reaction was hysterical. The country was soon paralysed by a transport strike organized and funded by the CIA.

Allende's 'Chilean road to socialism' ran into deep economic and political trouble. On 11 Sept 1973 the Commander-in-Chief of the army, General Augusto Pinochet, launched a military coup. No one knows the exact fate of Allende, but the next day he was reported dead by suicide — a story that few ever believed. The next 18 years were a period of terrible repression. Much of the time the cities were under military curfew, several thousand people disappeared, and many tens of thousands were arrested and tortured. Meanwhile Pinochet's so-called 'economic miracle' brought only disaster, with the country facing a horrendous foreign debt, high unemployment and with half the population living in extreme poverty.

In 1980 a new constitution enabled Pinochet, until then leader of the military Junta, to become President. In 1988 the people of Chile were asked in a referendum whether they were for or against his staying on for another eight years. The majority supported a return to an elected government. In the 1989 elections the right vote was split. Patricio Aylwin, leader of the Christian Democratic Party and sole candidate of the United Centre and Socialist alliance, won a clear victory.

Aylwin, who became president in 1990, embarked on a 'Transition to Democracy'. But while political exiles have been free to return, for example, there has been little real reform: such as the setting of a decent minimum wage, the prosecution of those involved in human rights violations under Pinochet, and the loosening of the army's right-wing power block. Although Congress has been elected democratically, military appointees still dominate the Senate, law courts and local municipalities. There is more than a little frustration among those people who had hoped for a new era of justice under Aylwin's government.

The President's position is an unenviable one. On one side are the people clamouring for justice. On the other is the military, still led by General Pinochet. The army is not averse to dishing out threats whenever its power is seen to be tampered with, and it is even trying to increase its influence. Left-wing paramilitary groups formed under the Pinochet regime have not disbanded. While these terrorists are so marginalized as to pose only a minor threat, they are used by the military as an excuse to demand an increased role in the enforcement of law and order. The next few years could prove to be some of the most crucial in Chilean history.

THE PEOPLE

Three out of four Chileans are mestizo. Most of the rest are of pure European descent, mainly Spanish or the descendants of other European immigrants of the 19th and 20th centuries. Several thousand Germans settled in the Lake District, where towns retain a Bavarian architecture and atmosphere, and where many people speak German as well as Spanish. Serbian communities are found both in the Atacama and Tierra del Fuego.

The government ascertains that just 2% of the population are pure-blooded Mapuche Indians, while some people put the number a good deal higher. They lead a marginalized existence having lost most of their traditional lands, though new efforts are being made to re-assert their rights. The Mapuche are concentrated in their old heartland south of the Bío-Bío river, where the sight of indigenous faces gives the area a special appeal. Small numbers of Diaguita Indians remain in the north.

There is a homogeneity about the Chilean people that is rare in South America. This is largely due to their country's physical isolation, blocked off as it is by the Andes. Family ties are very strong, and some visitors find Chilean society closed. The best way to counter this is to stay in private homes as much as possible: see *Accommodation*.

LANGUAGE

Chilean Spanish is spoken rapidly, running words together, and the final *s* often falls off the end of words. One of the most common misunderstandings arises from the similarity between 12.30pm and 2.30pm, sounding like *dos y media* and *do y media* respectively. The word of emphasis, *pues*, is often tacked onto a definitive statement, but it is pronounced simply *po*: hence *si* becomes *sipo*, and *bueno* becomes *buenopo.* In addition, there are many words unique to Chile: *cachai?* means 'do you understand?', and an Argentine is called a *Che.*

Indian languages are not widely spoken, though you may hear the Mapuche language (Mapu-dugun) around Temuco, and Aymará on the Altiplano. Spanish is almost always understood. In southern Chile you may be able to try out your German.

FURTHER READING

Some of the best books about Chile concentrate on the Pinochet regime. *Chile — Death in the South* by Jacobo Timerman (1987, Picador) is a shocking book about the overthrow of Allende and the dark years of dictatorship. On a similar theme is *Storm over Chile* by Samuel Charkin (Lawrence Hill, 1989), a compellingly-told story of the coup, the dictatorship and the popular movement which deposed it. *Chile from Within* (Norton, 1990) is a book of outstanding photographs chronicling the same events through the eyes of Chile's leading photographers.

Of the Chilean writers that provide a guide to the heart of the national character, the most famous is the poet Pablo Neruda, whose works translate well into English. Among his best works are *Twenty Love Poems* and *Ode of Despair.* Another poet of stature is Gabriela Mistral, well-known within Chile.

Getting There

AIR

Chile's main international airports are at Santiago, Chacalluta Airport near Arica and Punta Arenas in the far south. It is significantly more expensive to fly to Santiago from Europe and the USA than to Buenos Aires or Lima, so it is usually better to travel to Chile via an adjacent country. The Chilean airlines Ladeco and LanChile both operate internationally.

From South America. There are services to Santiago from most South American capitals and from Rio de Janeiro, daily in most cases. AeroPeru, as well as some North American airlines, flies between Lima and Santiago daily ($324); LanChile covers the route four times weekly. A cheaper option is to take the daily AeroPeru internal flight from Lima to Tacna, near the border ($120), and then cross by land. Aerolíneas Argentinas, LanChile and Ladeco, among others, fly between Buenos Aires and Santiago; a much cheaper option is to fly from Buenos Aires to Mendoza and cross the Chilean frontier by land — see below.

Flights from Bolivia are less frequent. Lloyd Aéreo Boliviano has just two flights weekly from La Paz to Santiago ($215) and Arica ($150).

From the USA. Many airlines fly from the United States, including most of the principal South American companies. LanChile and Ladeco both fly from New York and Miami; Ladeco also serves Washington.

From Europe. Viasa and Varig fly from Heathrow to Santiago, with changes in Caracas and Rio respectively. There are direct flights with Iberia, KLM, Lufthansa, Swissair and Air France, among others. LanChile flies from Madrid to Santiago via Rio and São Paulo. Most airlines operate at least two flights a week. Prices are similar, at around $1200.

LAND

From Peru. The only road connecting Peru and Chile crosses the border at Concordia. Trains, buses and colectivos ply the 38 miles/60km between Tacna in Peru and Arica, in Chile. There is no need to change at the border, though you must dismount to go through immigration. There are also direct buses to Santiago, both from Tacna and Lima.

From Bolivia. The fastest route from La Paz into Chile is by bus to Arica via Tambo Quemado; the journey takes about 20 hours and costs $25. There should also be a ferrobus twice a week, which is marginally faster but also more expensive; the ordinary train is best avoided.

The best journey to do by train from Bolivia is to Calama from Oruro, via the border town of Ollagüe. This 36-hour long trip across the saltpans is cheap but extremely arduous. Many people catch the train from Oruro, and you need to be very assertive if you want a seat: *contrabandistas* with huge numbers of bags take up all the seats and luggage space. You must change trains at the border, where you may have to wait several hours; this necessitates another rush for seats the other side, when the Chilean train arrives. (If you're lucky, you will have to wait only for the locomotive to be changed.) The journey is extremely cold at night, but the scenery is spectacular and well worth the pushing and shoving.

From Argentina. The many Andean passes along the Chile/Argentina frontier make for easy border-hopping, though winter snows can close some for months at a stretch. Outlined below are just the principal entry points, with fuller details given in the text. Routes into northern Chile are limited: there are bus connections from Salta to Calama when weather permits (which it doesn't in winter); the journey takes 17 hours. Santiago is most easily approached from Mendoza — a stunning journey along a road which is open for most of the year. Through buses run frequently (6 hours, $15), and the driver will guide you through immigration and customs. There is also a shuttle colectivo service between the two cities, which is faster.

There is a choice of entry points in the Lake District, many of them spectacular. There are direct bus services from Bariloche and San Martín de los Andes in Argentina, but the more interesting routes involve local buses and often boats. Bariloche in Argentina is one of the main jumping-off points for the area. From here you can travel to Lago Todos los Santos and Puerto Montt, a great journey involving three boat rides. From San Martín de los Andes you can travel across the border to Lago Pirehueico — an even more magnificent journey, again involving boat rides.

In Patagonia, the easiest borders to cross are near Coihaique or Chile Chico, both accessible by bus. The main entry point in the extreme south is from Río Turbio to Puerto Natales, though the road is generally open only October to March.

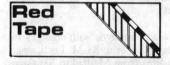

Visas. Nationals of EC countries, with the exception of France, do not require visas for visits of 30 days. Also exempt are citizens of the USA, Canada and Australia, but not New Zealanders. You may have to show an outward ticket or the means to pay for one once in Chile.

Immigration regulations have been changed several times since the fall of

Pinochet. Diplomatic manoeuverings have not yet finished, so be sure to check with the nearest Chilean mission.

UK: 12 Devonshire Street, London WIN 2DS (tel 071-580 1023; fax 071-436 5204). Open 9.30am-noon Monday to Friday.
USA: 1732 Massachusetts Avenue, NW, Washington DC 20036 (tel 202-785-1746).
New Zealand: Robert Jones House, 1-3 Willestone, (PO Box 3861), Wellington.

Extending visas. It is possible to extend your 30-day visa or tourist card twice, i.e. up to a maximum of 90 days in total. Extensions cost $3 from the Extranjero Office at the Departamento de Pasaportes, Moneda 1342 in Santiago (tel 222-2516), or in the provincial capitals. By South American standards, this is usually a quick and easy process.

Departure Tax. A US$12.50 tax is levied on departure from international airports, payable in pesos or dollars.

Border Formalities. Procedures at Chilean border posts are generally courteous and efficient; in-depth searches are uncommon. Fruit may be confiscated, as part of a campaign to stop the spread of fruit flies. For the same reason, there may be roadside checks within Chile.

Peso (C$) = 100 centavos.

Notes are issued in denominations of C$10,000, C$5,000, C$1,000 and C$500, coins in C$100, C$50, C$10, C$5 and C$1.

Changing Money. Banks offer the official rate of exchange. Casas de cambio, which use the parallel (legalized black market) rate, are better. Both the official and parallel rates are published daily in *El Mercurio* and *La Epoca*. There is currently little difference between the two rates, but banks usually impose a higher commission than cambios, occasionally of as much as 10%. Street changers don't really exist; those you meet are probably either crooks or touts for cambios.

Some banks allow you to change dollar travellers cheques for dollars cash, though you must be prepared to trek around. The best bet is American Express in Santiago, though the service is available only to holders of Amex cheques.

Credit Cards. It is possible to pay for many things by credit card. You can withdraw cash on Visa and MasterCard through Fincard, which is also the place to report lost or missing cards. Fincard has branches in every large town. Bancard and Banco de Concepción (Visa only) also allow cash withdrawals. The service is often commission-free.

Mail. An airmail letter from Santiago can reach Europe or the USA in three days, while within Chile it can easily take a week. Sending parcels is generally straightforward. To mail a package weighing 10kg (the maximum allowed) to Europe costs $22 by sea, twice that by air; to send a similar parcel within Chile costs $6. Most post offices open 9am-6pm and 9-1pm Saturdays. As well as the central post office in Santiago, UK passport-holders can also use the British Embassy for poste restante: Avenida El Bosque Norte 0125, 3rd floor, Providencia. Letters are returned after six months.

Telephone. Chile is four hours behind GMT from March until October, when clocks go forward. The international country code is 56.

The Chilean telephone system is fairly efficient, though a shortage of lines means that you may have to wait a while for a call to be put through. International calls can be made from the offices of the various regional telephone companies; the line is usually good. Entel, the state telecommunications company, also handles international communications and charges less than the other companies: around $9 for three minutes to Europe. CTC (Compañía de Teléfonos de Chile) also has telephone offices around the country, but is more expensive.

Payphones: you can make international calls direct from new call boxes, found mainly in cities. These do everything short of singing and dancing, and take any combination of coins, tokens and even credit cards. Local calls are made from the older yellow public boxes, the blue ones being reserved for long-distance calls. You can buy $15 telephone cards.

Codes: the main district codes are as follows: Antofagasta — 02; Arica — 080; Concepción — 041; Iquique — 081; Puerto Montt — 065; Punta Arenas — 061; Temuco — 045; Valparaíso — 032; Santiago — 02.

Fax. Most post offices have a fax machine. You pay about $5 per page.

THE MEDIA

The ending of the blatant censorship of the press, which characterized the Pinochet years, was symbolized in 1990 when one paper published a list of 500 police spies. In reality, journalists and editors are only gradually adapting to the new freedom, and independent coverage is extremely limited.

The most politically digestible paper is probably *La Epoca*, which is sponsored by the Christian Democrats. *El Mercurio* is a long-established right-of-centre paper, and is the most widely available; it is most useful for its daily list of what's on, and a good calendar of events on Friday and Sunday. The best political commentary is found in the magazines *Apsi* and *Análisis*, both of which were very critical of Pinochet, and *Pagina Abierta*.

Essential reading is the comic *Condorito*. It chronicles the life and times of small town Chile through the adventures of an all too human bird.

Broadcasting. Radio has long been the best source of news in Chile: above all Radio Cooperativa (76 AM), which has frequently aroused the wrath of Pinochet and the army. Television news programmes are also good by South American standards, and are improving all the time. The best coverage is given on Channels 7, 9 and 13, particularly the former.

Getting Around

Maps. Finding decent maps of Chile should not be a problem. Basic but useful maps are available free from the tourist board (Sernatur). The best maps, however, are those to be found in good bookshops.

Particularly recommended are the *Turistel* guides published by the CTC telephone

computerized booking system, and you are charged nothing for making a reservation. Bicycles travel free.

BUS

Chile's road network is well maintained, until you hit the extreme south or head off the beaten track. The Pan-American Highway runs through the country down to Puerto Montt, and is well served by buses. From Puerto Montt to Cochrane the highway is known as the Camino Austral; while this is a perfectly passable road, public transport drops dramatically and — like the road — eventually peters out.

On the main paved highways, inter-city buses are mostly reliable, comfortable and uncrowded. Prices and conditions vary enormously between the companies that compete for business on the major routes, so shop around. Nearly all buses provide meals or meal breaks on the long journeys, serve drinks, and show videos. For long journeys it is often worth taking a *salón-cama* sleeper bus, with reclining seats. The Pullman and Tur-Bus companies regulate speed on their coaches, and have an almost unimpeachable safety record. Tickets will usually be refunded if you don't use the return half.

If you are hitching in sparsely populated areas, bus drivers may give you a lift for a reduced, negotiated fare. Generally, however, there are so many pick-up trucks around that hitching is easy and generally safe — even for single women travellers.

CYCLING

You can hire bikes in most tourist centres, especially around the Lake District. They tend to be mountain bikes and cost typically $10 a day to hire.

CAR

Unfortunately, the areas where a car would be most useful are those where the terrain is most difficult: in the south where the roads are bad, and in the Andes where, in winter, snow chains are often needed. A four-wheel drive vehicle is recommended. But for touring around in summer — in the Lake District for example — it is not vital.

Most major international car hire firms (principally Hertz and Avis), as well as local agents, operate in Chile. Although the companies are represented in all main cities and airports, the franchises mostly operate independently. This makes it impossible (or prohibitively expensive) to rent in one place and leave the car in another. However, the Automóvil Club de Chile, which rents out its own cars, can normally arrange this. The ACC (Vitacura 8620, Santiago) is also a good source of information and maps.

Car hire costs a minimum of $15 a day, to which must be added insurance (around $7), $0.15 per km travelled, and the usual 18% IVA (sales) tax. Petrol costs $0.43 per litre.

Both IDPs and national licences are acceptable.

The range of lodgings found in Chile is similar to that elsewhere in the region. The main difference and bonus is that staying with a family is very common and also cheaper than in a normal hotel. *Hospedajes*, *alojamientos* or *pensiones* are all terms used to describe a family home with a couple of spare bedrooms. While some are well organized businesses, many families (especially in the south) simply open up their homes to tourists in the summer. They usually provide the cheapest and most entertaining accommodation. The further you head off the beaten track the more you will be treated as part of the family; guests are often invited to join in family meals. Hospedajes tend to be discreetly advertised, e.g. in shop windows. But it's usually easier simply to ask the local people, your bus conductor or the tourist office for recommendations. Your host will also have an unofficial network of contacts, and will probably pass you the address of a friend at your next destination.

There is no organized network of youth hostels, though in summer makeshift ones are set up in school buildings. There is no need to be a member and rates are cheap. Don't expect great facilities, but hostels are great for meeting young Chileans. Anyone planning to camp their way around the country should buy *Turistel*'s camping guide.

Hot water is standard in the cold south — whether staying in homes or more conventional hotels — but in the north it is considered a luxury.

Eating and Drinking

Chilean food has evolved its distinctive nature by combining traditional dishes with the cooking of subsequent settlers, particularly the Germans. Dishes revel in the climatic diversity of the country and its rich Pacific fishing waters, which are among the most productive in the world.

Food in Chile is generally mildly seasoned, but travellers used to the spicy foods of neighbouring Peru and Bolivia will invariably find chilli sauce on the table which they can add. Many restaurants serve a set-price lunch (*colación* or *almuerzo*), which is the main meal of the day in Chile. *Once*, or tea, is also a standard meal in Chile, consisting of cakes and other goodies. Don't spend too much time looking for breakfast early in the morning. Many places don't get going until 10am, particularly in the rural areas of the south.

There are four principal types of restaurant in Chile:

Picadas. The typical *picada* serves traditional and regional dishes. Freshly barbecued meat (*parrillada*) is common, though not nearly as good as in Argentina. If you like your steak rare ask for it *a l'inglesa*. Most meals are accompanied by a choice of various types of potato, or sometimes rice. Anything served *a la pobre* means heaps of chips, salad or vegetables and an egg: a good, square meal. The best fish to eat is *congrio*, (conger eel and a Chilean speciality), *albacora* (swordfish), *meliza* (hake) and the delicious Pacific salmon, particularly common in southern Chile.

The most universal national dishes are *cazuela*, a soup of meat and vegetables, and *porotos* (beans), which is the staple diet of the poor. In the south, *curanto*, a stew of mussels, chicken, sausage and dumplings is common and very, very filling.

Schoperías. Also known as *sandwicherías*, these bars combine German and Chilean influences. Although many are plastic-upholstered dives, a well-run *schopería* is pure spectacle. The cooks work on a raised central stage, cooking flamboyantly, while beside them is a large ceramic beer pump providing a flow of draught lager (*schop*). Most schoperías serve a wide range of snacks, usually including *completos* (hot dogs) and *Barros Lucos* (meat and cheese sandwiches). Some specialize in *empanadas*, similar to cornish pasties. They come in three types: with meat (*carne*), cheese (*queso*) or shellfish (*marisco*).

Marisco stalls. Seafood stalls, which are common in and around markets in coastal towns, are great places to eat. Given the huge range of seafood available, your best option is simply to point at anything you like the look of. One of the most unusual things to try is *piure*, a very strong tasting shellfish. More mundane, but recommended, is a seafood stew called *paila marina*.

Pastelerías. Also known as *cafés* or *dulcerías*, these are likely to be the downfall of anyone with a penchant for cakes. *Manjar*, a tasty, creamy caramel, crops up in many of them, and is likely to rot your teeth if you treat yourself too frequently. A typical recipe is *torta de mil hojas*, which consists of layers of crisp pastry filled with the stuff. Manjar is sold in bags and it is great to take with you on long hikes.

Chile is also very big on ice cream, which is delicious. The streets of Santiago are littered with people eating it — from businessmen in suits to street sweepers.

DRINKING

Chilean wine has become famous around the world. But it is still dirt cheap at home, where it costs less than milk. You can buy a good table wine for under $1, and a bottle to rival the best French burgundies for under $4. Some to look out for are Don Matias (red), Doña Isadora (white), and Undurraga's excellent red wines. The best buy of all is 'champagne'; good quality sparkling wine, such as Valdivieso, costs under $3.

Beer, has less to distinguish it from the brews available elsewhere in South America. Draught beer is widely available, either *schop blanco*, a straightforward lager, or *schop negro*, a sweeter stout. Bottled lagers are tastier; they include the mild Crystal or the stronger Royal Guard and Escudo.

A more traditional Chilean drink is *chicha*, fermented grape or apple juice, which is famous for its innocuous taste and lethal kick. However, the national drink is *pisco*, a fairly mild (but disgusting) spirit made from grape skins. When served with lemon and egg-white it is known as *pisco sour*. More refined and stronger piscos are drunk neat. *Aguardiente* is much more potent than the standard pisco. It is mixed with milk, coffee and eggs to produce the extremely sweet traditional Christmas drink, *cola de mono* (tail of monkey) — not dissimilar to Bailey's Irish Cream.

Coffee and tea are always served with sugar. Coffee is disappointing anyway: you are frequently given a cup of hot water and a sachet of instant granules and left to get on with it yourself. However, there is usually a range of herbal teas (*yerbas*) to choose from. The best soft drinks are the bottled fruit juices (*nectar de fruta*). *Mote con huesillos* is a sweet peach juice with boiled wheat sold on the streets everywhere — while an acquired taste it is a good way of filling your stomach if peckish or impecunious.

Exploring

Chile's main attraction lies in its splendid landscapes, large areas of which are protected by an excellent network of national parks. Wildlife can be seen in most reserves, though in fact the most easily-spotted animals are the herds of llama and alpaca in the unprotected areas of the desert north; in the same region flamingoes gather by the thousand on the salt lakes.

Also in the north are the well-preserved remains of ancient civilizations, including fortifications and giant designs laid out in stones on the desert. There are also more recent relics, in the form of 19th-century towns built by the British during the nitrate boom. In the north fascinating trips can be made to a number of mines: Chuquicamata near Calama is the world's largest open-cast copper mine. The majority of towns in Chile preserve scant colonial heritage, but pockets of outstanding architecture survive. While many of the most charming churches are the squat structures in the Atacama, Chiloé Island in the south has an unrivalled collection of splendid 17th and 18th century wooden churches, many of them built by the Jesuit and Franciscan missionaries. The architectural interest of some towns stems from the influence of large immigrant communities, such as the Germans in Valdivia in the Lake District, or from the survival of grand mansions built during past economic booms.

Hiking. The national parks provide great hiking opportunities throughout the country. They are managed by the state forestry department, Conaf, which provides wardens, cleared trails, and refuges. The latter are often fairly basic, and are sometimes too far apart for you to walk between them in a day. Therefore a tent is essential if you want to do serious trekking. If you don't have your own, it is possible to hire them in the main southern towns, including Puerto Montt and Puerto Natales. Local Conaf offices are usually the best source of information about a particular park, though the wardens themselves are normally very helpful too. Maps are available both from Conaf or at the park entrance. The central Conaf office at General Bulnes 285, Santiago has a library of conservation and ecology information.

Although in summer the main parks may be crowded with campers and day trippers near the entrance, the parks are invariably empty a day's walk away. *Backpacking in Chile and Argentina*, edited by Hilary Bradt (Bradt Publications, 1989), is recommended for anyone intending to do a lot of hiking. Serious trekkers should also get the detailed 1:50,000 maps, which are available from the Instituto Geográfico Militar at Dieciocho 369 or Santa Isabel 1640 in Santiago; they cost around $9 each. Traucomontt Tours in Puerto Montt holds a limited supply of these maps for parks in the south.

Rafting. White-water rafting is possible on many of the rivers that flow down from the Andes, but it is definitely not for the faint-hearted. Rivers are graded as to difficulty, grade five being the hardest. There are two main centres for rafting. The first is around Santiago, on the Maipo (Grade 3-4), and Clara (3), with trips to the rivers Maule (4) and Bío-Bío (4-5) being the most popular. The second is around Pucón and Villarrica in the Lake District, on the Trancura (3), Liucura (3), Fuy (4-5) and Maychin (4-5), amongst others.

A number of companies offer trips from around $50. In Santiago, Altue Expediciones (Encomenderos 88, tel 232-1103) is recommended. In Pucón there are a number of agencies on the main street, including Trancura (O'Higgins 261, tel 441959) and Altue (O'Higgins 371; tel 441113).

Beaches. With the exception of certain areas in the north, the Pacific Ocean off Chile is unpleasantly cold. The water along the coast of the Atacama is the warmest: the beaches may not be the best in South America (the fishmeal factories do not add to the beauty or the smell of the coast), but travellers fresh from a spell in the desert may welcome the chance to cool off. The most popular resort, however, is Viña del Mar near Santiago, which seethes with domestic and Argentinian holidaymakers in summer. Quieter and more charming village resorts are within easy access along the same stretch of coast. In the south, beachlife is concentrated in the Lake District. The water in the lakes warms up more than the sea, and there is no danger from strong currents and giant Pacific waves. However, most beaches are of black volcanic sand, and anywhere easily accessible fills up with noisy holidaymakers. Even so, only a little extra effort is needed to reach more restful areas.

Skiing. The resorts around Santiago, such as Portillo and Farellones, are the most developed and popular; in this area the sport is no cheaper than in European ski resorts. The standard of facilities and cost is lower in the Lake District: you should be able to stay in a local residencial with ski hire and a lift pass thrown in for around $10 a night.

Few ski resorts are served by bus, though transport of some kind is usually available during the ski season. In some cases you may have no choice but to go on a tour; this may well work out cheaper than going indepedently. The ski season is mid-June to mid-October near Santiago. The more southerly locations support skiing from May to November.

Music and Dance. Andean music is heard most commonly on the street and in clubs. But the most famous bands, such as Inti-Illimani, Queyapayun and Illapu, play open-air concerts periodically; these are always well postered, so keep your eyes open.

Cueca is the traditional music and dancing of the *huasos* (cowboys), which combines immigrant themes from Spain and Germany with Mapuche traditions. It features strongly at festivals in the Chilean Heartland, and particularly at post-rodeo parties. The season of rodeos and farm festivals (*fondas* and *ramadas*) begins in late September. Rodeos take place during the summer in many towns, such as Rancagua. They are a great insight into traditional rural life, and are not to be missed.

Festivals. In comparison with the fiestas held in much of South America, most celebrations are disappointing. Those of the huasos are an exception, however, as are the ones held by the more remote, traditional communities in the north. Here, the religious festivals are particularly interesting. The most famous is the Fiesta de la Tirana, which takes place near Iquique in July. Vast numbers of pilgrims come to enjoy the exotic costumes and dancers.

One of the best time for festivals is around Independence Day on September 18; every community marks the day somehow. During the summer, nearly every town has a local festival, with processions, concerts and cultural events.

SPORT

There is little in Chile to compete with football. Cricket is played, though the Chileans haven't taken to the game as much as in many other South American countries. Interest in the game, which peaked in the 1920s, has waned steadily since World War Two. It is kept going by a small group of enthusiasts at the Prince of Wales Country Club in Santiago. The team's greatest humiliation was in 1929 against Argentina, when their opponents achieved a record 612 for 6.

Shopping

The best and most traditional crafts to look out for are those of the Mapuche Indians. Carpets, carved wood and jewellery are all good buys, though many travellers stick to the ponchos and jumpers, which are warm and carry typical Mapuche motifs. Temuco is famous for its wooden plates, carvings, and distinctive silver jewellery. Puerto Montt and the nearby Chiloé Island are the best places to buy winter woollies. In the extreme North of Chile you can also by knitwear, including alpaca jumpers, to Aymará designs and reminiscent of those sold in Bolivia and Peru. All the above goods are best bought from markets.

Crime and Safety

Chile is largely safe. While there is a certain amount of crime — particularly pickpocketing — in the bigger cities, violent muggings are uncommon.

Terrorist groups, such as the Frente Manuel Rodríguez (FMR), have no effect on the everyday life of the vast majority of Chileans. Most carry out operations against well defined right-wing figures, though a favourite target of the MAPU-Lautaro group is the Mormon church, which is seen as a symbol of US imperialism. This same organization is one of the few guerrilla groups in the world to indulge in gift-giving during its armed operations. An integral part of a Lautaro bank raid is the distribution of condoms and pamphlets that read 'To spread joy, sensuality and dreams now'.

There is no great drug subculture or industry in Chile, but Arica and Iquique are becoming important staging-posts for drug-trafficking. The major dangers lie on the borders with Bolivia and Peru, where drug smuggling does occur; one German tourist died in the area in 1990.

You will probably experience at least one earth tremor while in Chile. Most buildings are earthquake proof but see page 68 for how best to survive a serious earthquake.

Health and Hygiene

You are unlikely to visit many places in Chile without piped drinking water, though it sometimes has a strong taste. The water in the North is often over-rich in minerals and some people get stomach upsets from this alone; bottled water is always available.

Hygiene is good by South American standards, but there is always a risk of contracting diseases through contaminated food and water. Beware of eating unpeeled fruit and vegetables, since the high levels of pesticides used often cause in visitors what has become known as 'Chile tummy'. Generally, however, the health risks of Chile are the same as in Europe. There is no malaria and no yellow fever.

Chile's health service offers medical facilities equal to those of Europe. However, government hospitals and *consultorias*, which are overworked and offer a limited service, are best avoided. Rely either on private clinics or teaching hospitals; the latter are usually equipped with the latest equipment, and are cheap.

The Servicio Nacional de Turismo (Sernatur) has an office in most towns and cities; in smaller centres this may be part of the Intendencia (or Municipalidad). In the south many of the smaller offices are closed in winter. The useful *Turistel* guidebooks to Chile are described on page 393.

Public Holidays

January 1	New Year's Day
March/April	Easter
May 1	Labour Day
May 21	Battle of Iquique
August 15	Assumption Day
September 18	Independence Day
October 12	Columbus Day
November 1	All Saints' Day
December 8	Immaculate Conception
December 25	Christmas

The administrative regions of Chile are referred to both by a name and number, written as a Roman numberal. The regional sections of this chapter are dealth with from north to south, but the first part covers the Heartland and Santiago. This part of the Valle Central is a fertile and most beautiful region. It is a muddle of valleys and rivers between the Andes and the coastal range, which is itself split east to westy by a number of rivers. These include the Mapocho, on which Santiago lies, and the Bío-Bío, which signals the Central Valley's southern limits.

The Heartland contains two-thirds of Chile's population — half of them in Santiago, the capital. In 1985 the area was hit by a severe earthquake, which caused considerable damage — an unwelcome reminder that the mighty snow-capped Andes to the east are still majestically rising.

SANTIAGO

The capital of Chile sits magnificently in a natural amphitheatre formed by the Andes. But Santiago is a modern, noisy, industrialized, smog-laden metropolis. It is an increasingly rare pleasure to have a clear view of the snowy peaks around the city. In summer the mountains are usually invisible by noon, and pollution reaches dangerous levels so frequently that the papers publish a daily smog table. The rich have moved into the Mapocho valley in the mountains.

Santiago experienced a troubled early history. It was destroyed three times in quick succession after its foundation in 1541: twice by hostile Indians, and once by an earthquake. It was not until the late 18th century that Santiago began to develop as a city. Much of it was planned by Chile's own Renaissance man, Vicuña MacKenna — an historian, politician and artist. The city boasts some of the best parks of any South American capital, an array of grandiose buildings and several excellent museums. A fair number of the churches in Old Santiago are dilapidated or have been converted into ugly commercial enterprises; yet they manage to retain some of their original beauty.

Santiago has become so relaxed since the fall of Pinochet that it is at times almost unrecognizable: the streets in the centre are busy at night, where before they were deserted. And if you do not fall for the city itself, you can head into the surrounding

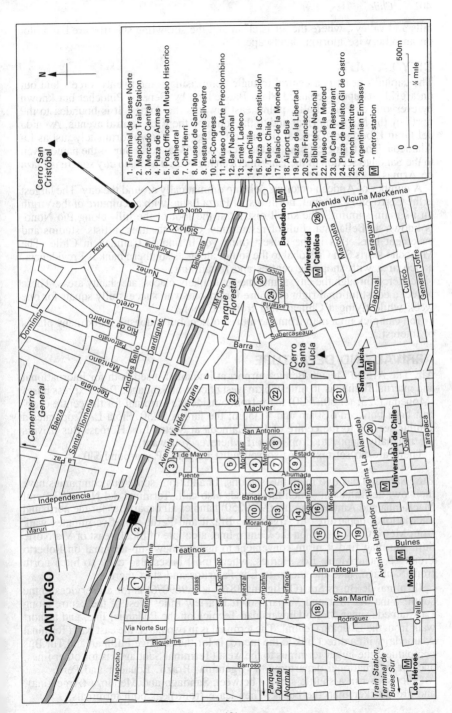

SANTIAGO

Cerro San Cristóbal ▲

1. Terminal de Buses Norte
2. Mapocho Train Station
3. Mercado Central
4. Plaza de Armas
5. Post Office and Museo Historico
6. Cathedral
7. Chez Henri
8. Museo de Santiago
9. Restaurante Silvestre
10. Museo de Arte Precolombino
11. Ex-Congress
12. Bar Nacional
13. Entel, Ladeco
14. LanChile
15. Plaza de la Constitución
16. Telex Chile
17. Palacio de la Moneda
18. Airport Bus
19. Plaza de la Libertad
20. San Francisco
21. Biblioteca Nacional
22. Museo de la Merced
23. Da Carla Restaurant
24. Plaza de Mulato Gil de Castro
25. French Institute
26. Argentinian Embassy

Ⓜ - metro station

0 ____ 500m
0 ____ ¼ mile

401

hills and valleys, where the air is clean and the sprawling suburbs are but a blot on an otherwise glorious landscape.

CITY LAYOUT

The capital's heart is a central triangle comprising some twenty streets laid out on a grid. Its apex, renamed Plaza Baquedano by General Pinochet but known by everyone as Plaza Italia, points east towards the Andes. It is bounded to the north by the Mapocho river and to the south by the wide central avenue, Avenida del Gran Libertador General Bernardo O'Higgins, known fortunately just as La Alameda. The triangle's base, to the west, is the Via Norte Sur — the name given to the Santiago section of the Pan-American highway. The main city square is Plaza de Armas.

A number of Andean outcrops poke up dramatically around the city. The largest is the Cerro San Cristóbal, northwest of Plaza Italia, with a sculpture of the Virgin on its main summit. The small district at the foot of the hill, along Pío Nono, is known as Bellavista. Full of restaurants, clubs, theatres, artists' studios and pavement bars, this is the closest thing you'll find to Camden in Chile. The Mapocho skirts San Cristóbal to the south; along its southern bank is Providencia, a rich area with shopping centres and restaurants.

Scattered through the city, sometimes in unlikely places, are shanty areas. These reflect a constitutional right of tenure for anyone who successfully squats for one week while flying a Chilean flag from the roof.

You can pick up a map from the tourist office, but it doesn't mark many places of interest.

ARRIVAL AND DEPARTURE

Air. The Arturo Merino Benítez airport at Pudahuel, used both for international and internal flights, is 16 miles/26km west of central Santiago. Tour Express buses (Moneda 1523; tel 601-7830) leave from outside the terminal for the centre every half hour between 6.30am and 10.15pm; the fare is $1.50. Flota LAC operates a similar service to the centre of La Alameda at Metro Los Héroes. Bus drivers are normally happy to drop you off wherever you want.

There are no set taxi-fares so you must bargain. Pay around $10.

Bus. Santiago has two main bus stations. In addition, some bus companies have their own terminals at which their buses also call. Terminal del Norte (General MacKenna and Amunátegui; tel 696-9250) handles all departures for the north and international departures to Argentina, Brazil and Peru. It is five minutes walk from Metro Cal y Canto on the Centro line, a couple of blocks east of Via Norte Sur. You may find it more convenient to use the new sub-terminal on Roberto Pretot 25, near Metro Los Héroes, where most buses also call. To hitch north from Santiago, take the metro to Los Pajaritos and start there.

Terminal de Buses Sur (O'Higgins 3878; tel 6969076) is for all services to the south, Viña del Mar and Valparaíso. It is a few miles west of the centre along La Alameda, near Metro Universidad Tecnica on the Pudahuel line, and a short walk from the Estación Central. The terminal is in two parts: the east part (Terminal Alameda) with a direct link to the metro, is for the prestige Pullman and Tur Bus companies; the larger terminus to the west (Terminal Santiago) is for other lines, and for international departures to Argentina, Brazil, Ecuador and Peru.

Colectivos run a shuttle service between Santiago and Mendoza (Argentina), and are quicker than the buses. They leave from near both terminals.

Train. The Estación Central is at Alameda 3322 and Matucana (tel 699-5718/1682), and is served by bus and metro. The central booking office is at La Alameda 853 in the Galeria Hotel Libertador (tel 301818/330746), which opens 8.30am-7pm Monday to Friday, 9am-1pm on Saturday.

CITY TRANSPORT

Metro. Santiago's metro is a modern, efficient underground train system which makes London's rattling old network look like a museum piece. Piped music adds to the calm and orderly atmosphere. So far two lines have been built and a third is under construction. The east-west Las Condes-Pudahuel line (Línea 1) runs along La Alameda and Providencia; the Centro line (Línea 2) runs north to south. The two lines intersect at Los Héroes, the station at Alameda and Via Norte Sur. Trains are crowded but fast — especially when compared with the crawling traffic above ground.

Línea 1 tickets cost $0.30 and can be used to transfer to the other line. Línea 2 tickets cost $0.20 but you must pay a supplement if you change lines. The metro runs 6.30am-10.30pm Monday to Saturday, 8am-10.30pm on Sundays and holidays.

Bus. Santiago's enormous fleet of buses, called *micros*, is a lesson in what can go wrong when public transport is privatized. In all shapes, sizes and states of disrepair, they contribute more than anything to Santiago's pollution and traffic congestion. They are also the scene of a vast travelling fair, as a non-stop stream of hawkers, buskers, clowns and beggars passes through the buses. A flat fare (currently $0.30) is charged for any trip in the city. Route details are plastered confusingly over the front of the bus, and you pay as you get on. Drivers are usually helpful.

A number of routes are served by colectivos, usually minibuses, which have the destination emblazoned on a sign on the roof.

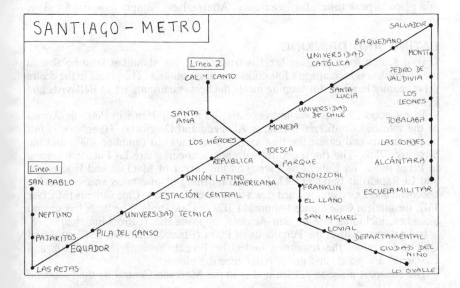

Taxi. Unlike taxi drivers in other Latin American capitals, those in Santiago generally set their meters when you get in, without being prompted, and charge the indicated sum. Not all of them are paragons, however, so check that the meter is set to the right amount. Prices should be displayed on the windscreen in the form of a minimum charge (about $0.50) and the price per 200 metres. Note that not all taxis charge the same rate, so it is worth checking a few before committing yourself.

ACCOMMODATION

The choice for budget travellers is limited, and the better places fill up early. All the hotels listed here are in the central area.

Residencial Santo Domingo (Santo Domingo 735 and MacIver) charges $10, including all meals. The Londres (Londres 54; tel 382215) is a large and grand but faded 19th-century mansion near the church of San Francisco. It is excellent, with cavernous rooms and copious hot water for $10/$18; rooms fill quickly, so get there early. Nearby is the cheaper Residencial Paris (Paris 813), which charges $6; the Alemania (República 220); near Metro República, is similar. Cheapest of all is the Valparaíso (San Pablo and Normandia), which charges just $3-4. Also cheap is the Casa del Estudiante Americano (Huérfanos 1891), which offers dormitory beds for $3.

The red-light district around the northern bus terminal is full of cheap hotels. Most of these are abysmal, but a few are just acceptable. They include the Indiana (Rosas 1334; tel 6714251) with rooms for $5/$7; and the San Felipe (MacKenna 1248) and the Caribe (San Martín 851), both of which charge $4. There are several other places around the southern bus terminal and the railway station: try the Marconi (O'Higgins 2532) if you're not too bothered by noise, or the Antiguo Palace (San Alfonso 24), both with rooms for around $5.

A good alternative is bed and breakfast accommodation in a private house, which usually costs around $10. You can arrange this through the Amigos de Todo El Mundo (Avenida Bulnes 285, near Metro Moneda; fax 698-1474). To be certain of a place at peak times, fax in advance. Alternatively, simply look out for signs in windows.

EATING AND DRINKING

If your search for a pleasant hotel is frustrating, you should at least be able to seek consolation in Santiago's fine collection of restaurants. The places in the centre serve mainly lunches; for evening meals the best restaurants are in Bellavista and Providencia.

To eat good Chilean food in the centre, go to Chez Henri in Plaza de Armas or the splendid Confitería Torres, at Alameda and Dieciocho. Huérfanos is full of restaurants and cafés: the best are the Bar Nacional (number 1087) and the Silvestre (956). The finest and most frantic schoperías are La Fuente Alemana in Plaza Italia, La Cabeza de Ciervo on the corner of MacIver and Huérfanos, and El Rápido at Bandera 347. For mid-morning or afternoon snacks of cake, chocolate and ice cream, washed down by good coffee, go to Café Colonia (MacIver 161), the ancient Café Santos (Ahumada 312) or Café Paula. The latter has several branches, including one on San Antonio, opposite the Teatro Municipal.

In Lastarria district the Pergola de la Plaza (Plaza Mulato Gil de Castro) and Quiche Lorraine, the restaurant under the French Institute (Merced 298 and Lastarria) are good, and are popular meeting places.

The cheapest place to eat seafood is in the Mercado Central by the Mapocho river; for a more formal setting but excellent food go to the gourmet Coco Loco (Rancagua 554). The best vegetarian restaurant downtown is El Naturista (Moneda 846), though it is closed in the evenings. Italian food is also popular and cheap; try Da Carla at MacIver 577.

Good places in Bellavista include the scruffy but famous Venesia (Pío Nono 200) and El Caramano (Purísima 257), both of which serve regional dishes. For cheap and cheerful Italian food try the Tallarín Gordo on Purísima. The main concentration of restaurants in Providencia is in the stretch between Manuel Montt and Pedro de Valdivia. On Las Bellotas try Café Las Palmas at number 182. The branch of El Naturista (vegetarian) at Orrega Luco 52 is highly recommended. Nearby is El Huerto (Orrego Luco 56), expensive but with interesting Aymará and Mapuche dishes; it has live music most weekends. Buses to both Bellavista and Providencia run along La Alameda; Providencia is also accessible by metro.

Show restaurants, which lay on traditional music and dancing while you eat, are not as touristy as they sound since they cater mainly for Chileans. Don't fail to go to Los Adobes de Argomeda (Argomeda 411; tel 2222104), which is seven blocks south of La Alameda, on Lira. Here you can eat good typical Chilean food while being entertained with Cueca and Easter Island dances.

EXPLORING

Much of the central area is dedicated to banking and shopping. The pedestrian-only Paseo Ahumada, that leads south from Plaza de Armas, is foremost among the many overcrowded walkways in the city, full of street vendors, touts for moneychangers, pavement cafés, beggars and buskers.

Plaza de Armas. Begin a tour at the tree-shaded Plaza de Armas, laid out in 1541 by Pedro de Valdivia, founder of the city. Once used for military exercises, the main activity now is on Thursday evenings and Sunday mornings, when musicians play on the stage in the centre.

Historic buildings around the square include the 19th-century Governor's Palace, which is now the post office, and the Museo Histórico Nacional. This is a good museum, with exhibits concentrating on the colonial period and the War of the Pacific. There are also some pre-Columbian Indian textiles and ceramics. The museum opens 10am-5.15pm Tuesday to Saturday, and 10am-1.45pm on Sunday.

On the west side of the square stands the 18th-century cathedral of Santo Domingo; it is the fourth on the site, the earlier ones having been burnt down or destroyed by earthquakes. Behind it is the ornate Edificio del ex-Congreso Nacional, which takes up an entire block. This now houses the Ministry of Justice and the Council of State — Congress has moved to Valparaíso.

A block west of Plaza de Armas is the excellent Museo de Arte Precolombino (Bandera 361). It has a fine collection of pre-hispanic artefacts, from both Peru and Chile. It opens 10am-6pm Tuesday to Saturday, 10am-2pm on Sunday. The Museo de Santiago at Merced 860 is housed in the lovely 18th-century Casa Colorada and follows the colourful history of Santiago from its foundation to the present day, with excellent scale models and other displays. It opens 10am-6pm Tuesday to Saturday, 11am-1.30pm on Sunday. A couple of blocks further east is the Museo Iglesia de la Merced (MacIver 341), which is worth a visit to see archaeological finds from Easter Island. It is closed on Mondays.

Plaza de la Constitución. This is Santiago's second square, lying four diagonal blocks southwest of the Plaza de Armas. It was redesigned by Pinochet to resemble a stage-set for the Nuremburg Rallies. The imposing — indeed forbidding — building on its south side is the Palacio de la Moneda, built by the Spanish in 1799 as the national treasury. Since 1846 it has been the Presidential Palace (Palacio do Gobierno). This is where Allende died in the 1973 coup; the bullet holes and bomb damage have now been repaired. The square is the site of the daily changing of the guard at 10am, and the military displays that mark state occasions.

Plaza de la Libertad, across the broad Alameda, is dedicated to Bernardo O'Higgins. The liberator's remains are kept in a crypt below the so-called Altar de la Patria.

The Alameda. There are some fine buildings on the Alameda. Travelling east from Plaza Constitución, past the university, you reach the church and monastery of San Francisco. Built in 1618, this is the oldest building in Santiago. Next door is the Museo del Arte Colonial, which opens daily except Monday. It has many works of the influential Cusco school, and there is a lovely garden — a veritable haven in the busy city centre. One block east is Calle Santa Rosa: for a good view of old Santiago, take a bus 11 blocks south to Avenida Matta. The streets in this area, particularly to the east, are interesting to explore.

Back on La Alameda, Cerro Santa Lucía is the city's most central park. The hill is elegantly landscaped and winding stairs lead to the top. It provides good views over the city, and is much easier to climb than Cerro San Cristóbal — particularly if you take the lift. Almost opposite, at Santa Lucía 124, is the Instituto Chileño Británico, which has a library with English newspapers.

Palacio Cousiño (Calle Dieciocho 438) is an ornate 19th-century mansion in a run-down part of old Santiago, about five blocks south of La Alameda. It was built by a mining magnate and has original furniture, oriental carpets, and superb gardens. It opens 10am-1pm Tuesday to Sunday.

Lastarria. This district lies between La Alameda, Cerro Santa Lucía and the river. It has Bohemian charm, and is full of antique shops, art galleries and restaurants. In the small Plaza Mulato Gil de Castro is the Museo Arqueológico de Santiago. Also known as the Museo Chileño de Arte Pre-Colombino, it has an alarming collection of skulls that trace the fashions of head compression and binding. It opens 10.30am-2pm and 4-7pm from Tuesday to Saturday, and 11am-2pm on Sunday.

A short distance north, on the banks of the river, is the Parque Forestal. The highlight of this wooded park is the fine baroque Palacio de Bellas Artes, which houses several art museums.

Around Parque Valenzuela. The Mercado Central near the river is an iron building cast in England and erected on site in 1872 for the National Exhibition. It is a good place to eat and has many craft stalls. On the west side of Parque Valenzuela is the Mapocho railway station, which has been converted into a cultural centre. Its earthquake-proof canopy was designed by Eiffel and built, according to the locals, with leftovers from other projects. The prison next door still houses political prisoners awaiting trial, but it is destined also to become a cultural centre.

About ten minutes walk north up Avenida La Paz, across the river, is the Cementerio General, with its fascinating collection of grand family mausoleums. Allende's remains were re-interred here in an official ceremony in 1991. Pablo Neruda's tomb is here also.

Cerro San Cristóbal. This hill is four times higher above the city than Santa

Lucía. It rises about a mile east across the Mapocho from the centre, and forms the city's substantial Parque Metropolitano. A funicular railway runs from Plaza Caupolicán at the north end of Pío Nono. There is a zoo (closed Mondays), which houses some fairly contented-looking animals, including an unrivalled collection of native Chilean species. There are various paths as well as a road leading up to the massive statue at the top. The views across to the Andes are fantastic.

At another entrance to the park, near Metro Pedro de Valdivia, you can pick up a *teleférico* at the Estación Oasis to the summit. The cable car stops en route at Estación Tupahue, near a swimming pool. This is also accessible by minibus from Plaza Caupolicán and opens 10am-3pm during the summer season. It is a great place to cool off, but can get crowded.

Parque Quinta Normal. West of the centre, this park has some interesting sights. On the east side is the old-fashioned Natural History Museum. Its most notable exhibit is the 500-year old body of a child preserved in ice. It also contains a relief model of the country, plus Antarctica; shaped like a shallow arch, it illustrates the curvature of the earth. The exhibits in the Aeronautical Museum are unimpressive, but the building itself is a most bizarre creation — it was built in Paris as the Chilean pavilion in the Paris Exhibition of 1900. Just inside the park is a good collection of steam locomotives. To get there take the metro to Estación Central, then walk or take a bus up Matucana.

Parque O'Higgins. This is a large public park ten blocks south of La Alameda, served by its own Metro station (known simply as Parque). This is a people's park, with amusements, sports facilities and various museums. On Sunday afternoons in the windy months of September and October people fly kites: a wonderful sight. The most interesting museum is the Museo del Huaso, dedicated to the Chilean cowboy; it opens daily except Monday.

For secondhand goods of all descriptions, the market at Bío-Bío not far from the Parque O'Higgins is a bargain hunter's paradise on weekend mornings; it is a short walk from Metro Franklin.

ENTERTAINMENT

The busiest area at night is Bellavista, particularly on weekend nights, with stalls and street performers. Café del Cerro (Lagarrigue 198) is a popular meeting place, as is Penny Lane (S. Filomena 126; tel 375-565), which is dedicated to Beatles music; you need to reserve a table. Salsa is big in Santiago, and it is played in many clubs around Bellavista. The best is El Tucán, on top of the shopping centre at Bilbao and Pedro Valdivia; it charges just $3, and is free on Wednesdays.

Don't miss the chance to see an opera, concert or ballet in the wonderfully ornate Teatro Municipal (San Antonio and Agustinas; tel 879 4948). In summer there is a season of free classical concerts. These rotate around various churches and finish with three nights on top of Santa Lucía. Look out for details of these and other concerts on posters in the metro.

Cinemas in the centre show recent films. Tickets, which are already cheap, are half-price on Wednesdays. In summer it's worth shopping around for a cinema with air-conditioning.

SPORT

Some of the most entertaining sports events are held at the Club Hípico, near Parque O'Higgins. Races are held at weekends, kicking off usually at 1pm, and occasionally during the week. The weekend is also the best time to see a football match at the Estadio Nacional on Avenida Grecia: take a colectivo along La Alameda.

SHOPPING

A wonderful market for crafts is Los Dominicos, in the grounds of an old village church in the fringes of the city. The fact that it is high enough to be above the smog is an added attraction. To get there take the metro to Escuela Militar, and then a micro or colectivo up Avenida Apoquindo — you will see the twin domes of the village church in the distance.

Downtown, you can buy crafts made by disabled artisans at the street market south of the Alameda near Metro Universidad de Chile. In summer there are night-time street markets all over the place. These are great fun, though the food is best avoided.

Bookshops. The Librería Inglesa at Pedro de Valdivia 47 has the best selection of English titles. For secondhand books or exchanges try the numerous bookshops in arcades off the city end of Providencia; or along Merced in the Lastarria district. Kiosks on Ahumada sell US newspapers.

CRIME AND SAFETY

Santiago is one of the safest capital cities in South America, but it still has a fair amount of street crime. The central area all but closes down at night, and becomes a site for open prostitution, street gambling and theft. Lastarria has a poor reputation, so don't wander down dark streets alone at night. Avoid Cerros Santa Lucía and San Cristóbal after dark, and the quiet areas of the latter at any time.

HELP AND INFORMATION

Tourist Information: Sernatur has its main office at Providencia 1550, between Metros Manuel Montt and Pedro de Valdivia (tel 698-2151). It opens 9am-5pm Monday to Friday, 9am-1pm on Saturday. It also has a kiosk on Paseo Ahumada, where you can pick up maps and brochures too. *Santiago Tour* is a monthly brochure in English, available for $3 from most kiosks.

For information on national parks go to Conaf, at General Bulnes 285, 5th floor (tel 696-6749/3664).

Post Offices: Santiago's main post office is on the north side of the Plaza de Armas at Agustinas 1137 (tel 699-4531). It opens 8am-10pm Monday to Friday, 8am-6pm on Saturdy and 9am-2pm on Sunday. There is another office at Moneda 1155.

Telephone Office: though it is possible to make all calls from pay phones, the best place for international calls (and sending faxes) is Entel (Huérfanos 1132), which opens 8.30am-10pm Monday to Friday, 9am-8.30pm on Saturday and 9am-2pm on Sunday.

Money: there are scores of casas de cambio, many of them concentrated along Agustinas. They are usually surrounded by an annoying horde of touts, trying to either change money illicitly or to drag you off to their particular cambio. Marginally less hectic are the cambios upstairs at Ahumada 131. A more interesting place to change money is at the Santiago Stock Exchange (La Bolsa), an ornate building at Nueva York 75 near the Universidad de Chile metro.

One of the most reliable banks to deal with is the Banco Central de Chile, near Plaza Constitución; it changes money only at the official rate.

VALPARAISO

This port, 70 miles/112km west of Santiago, was for a long time the financial and commercial centre of Chile. Some grand mansions remain from its days of glory, but most of Valparaíso's historical buildings have been wiped out in a succession of earthquakes; it still shows the effects of the most recent ones. Nevertheless, Valparaíso's prestige was boosted recently when it was made the official seat of government.

Most of the city's 400,000 people live in a chaos of winding alleys and stairways in the hills that rise up sharply above the coastal plain; charming old funicular lifts carry people up the steep slopes. The narrow streets down below set the scene for the commercial centre, with hotels, bars and shops arranged in bewildering confusion. Buildings come in every conceivable colour and shape, creating an almost magical atmosphere.

Diego de Almagro founded the city in 1536. But the early years of the port were dominated by the attacks of British pirates, including Sir Francis Drake and Richard Hawkins. A more recent British involvement was during the War of Independence, in the course of which Lord Admiral Cochrane assembled a Chilean navy to attack Lima. This period coincided with the arrival of a substantial number of English settlers, who left their mark in the architecture and street names.

Valparaíso attracts a large number of tourists, in addition to those who are merely

VALPARAISO

	3 Market area	7 Post Office
	4 Railway Terminal	8 Plaza Sotomayor
1 National Congress	5 Muelle Prat	9 Museo de Bellas Artes
2 Bus Station	6 Tourist Office	10 Museo del Mar

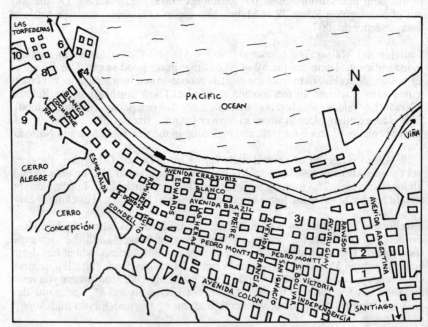

passing through en route to the nearby resort of Viña del Mar. Don't be put off. Valparaíso is wonderful.

Arrival and Departure. Valparaíso is connected by bus to Santiago (2 hours) and other more distant destinations such as La Serena (7 hours north) and Concepción (11 hours south). The Terminal Rodoviário bus station is at the east end of Pedro Montt and Rawson, opposite the new Congress.

Valparaíso is the west terminal of the Porteño railway line, which runs to Viña and then inland to San Felipe and Los Andes. Trains run every day from the terminal by Plaza Sotomayor.

Accommodation. There is a selection of cheap hotels on or near Plaza Sotomayor, most of which charge about $5/$10. On the square itself is the Reina Victoria (tel 212203), which is good but noisy. A couple of blocks away is the quieter Residencial Lily (Blanco Encalada 190; tel 255995), and the Garden Hotel at Serrano 501 is also recommended. On Chacabuco, near the bus station, try the Copihues (number 2883) or María Pizarro (number 2340).

Eating and Drinking. Valparaíso is well off for places to eat. Natur-In (Francia 549) is a good vegetarian restaurant, and La Tentazione (Pedro Montt 2484) serves cheap and hearty meals. Particularly recommended is Bar Inglés (Cochrane 851), an old-fashioned bar and restaurant, full of businessmen. Café Delmónico, off Plaza Sotomayor on Prat, is good too.

You can eat cheap seafood upstairs in the market, and there is also a cluster of seafood restaurants along the coast road towards Torpederas beach; they include the Casino Social de Pescadores, renowned equally for its food as for its erratic service.

Exploring. Plaza Sotomayor is the centre of the city, with the passenger pier to one side and the ornate Intendencia or Government House opposite. The Muelle Prat wharf is packed with craft shops, and is the embarkation point for boat trips around the harbour and to Viña del Mar.

Just behind the Intendencia, up Cerro Cordillera, is the Museo del Mar Almirante Cochrane, which is in the Admiral's house overlooking the harbour. It opens 9.30am-6pm daily except Monday. To get there, take the funicular railway (*ascensor*) from Serrano to Plazuela Ramírez, and walk down Merlet. A further ascensor from Plaza Sotomayor goes up to the Paseo Yugoslavo, with the splendid Palacio Baburizza. It houses the Museo Municipal de Bellas Artes: the hummingbirds in the garden are a source of greater delight than most of the paintings.

Head north from the square along Serrano or Cochrane to Plaza Aduana, with the old customs house. Behind it and accessible by ascensor is Cerro Artillería, which offers fine views over the bay; this is a good place from which to watch the New Year festivities, when there are superb fireworks to an accompaniment of marine foghorns. From here, Avenida Altamirano runs along the Playa Ancha seafront to Las Torpederas beach.

The main market areas are east of the centre: spread over Avenida Argentina and in Plaza O'Higgins, at the east end of Pedro Montt.

Help and Information. The tourist office is on the Muelle Prat wharf near Plaza Sotomayor, where you will also find the post office. There are telephone offices on Pedro Montt at Plaza O'Higgins and at Esmeralda 1054. Banks and cambios are concentrated along Prat and Cochrane, southeast of Plaza Sotomayor.

Around Valparaíso

South from Valparaíso the road heads inland to Casablanca, where there is a turn-off southwest to Algarrobo and other beach resorts. Among the best and quietest is El Quisco, which has fine white sand beaches. Hotel El Quisco and Cabañas Pozo Azul are both good places to stay. Between El Quisco and El Tabo is the village of Isla Negra. It was made famous by the poet Pablo Neruda who built his wonderfully eccentric house on the beach. To visit it you must book in advance through Sernatur in Valparaíso or Santiago. The journey there takes you through lovely rural scenes.

Local buses run along the coast from Valparaíso bus station or along Errázuriz.

VINA DEL MAR

A fresh coat of paint and an air of prosperity distinguishes Viña del Mar from most Chilean towns. Lying 5 miles/8km around the headland north of Valparaíso, it is one of South America's top resorts. This is the place to observe the Chilean and Argentinian elite, who flood here by the thousand — apparently undaunted by the fact that the beaches are occasionally closed due to an overdose of effluent from the town's 250,000 inhabitants.

Viña is modern and fairly characterless. But while you may not be attracted by its beaches or the alarming prices in summer, it's a side of Chile that is certainly worth seeing. Some people prefer to stay in Viña than Valparaíso, simply because it is smaller. Buses run continuously between the two towns. There are also regular connections direct to Santiago (two hours) and most other large towns in the region. The bus terminal is at Avenida Valparaíso and Quillota. The train from Valparaíso to Los Andes also passes through Viña, but you are more likely to get a seat if you start from the central terminal. The tourist office is at Valparaíso 507.

Accommodation and Food. Among the cheapest hotels are the Oxaron (Villanello and Valparaíso) and Blanchait (Valparaíso 82; tel 974949). The Hispano, just across the tracks from the railway station is also good, with rooms for around $15. Private accommodation is available too.

There are scores of restaurants, but for a cheap meal head for the picadas along the coast road heading north. On Wednesdays and Sundays you can eat at the market by the river at Avenida Sporting.

Exploring. The Cultural Centre at Avenida Libertad and 4 Calle Norte contains relics from Easter Island and Mapuche silverware; it is open daily. Less interesting is the Museo Naval, though it is housed in the unusual Castillo Wulff, an out-of-place looking castle built on a small peninsula. Cerro Castillo is the President's summer residence, built in a commanding position above the sea.

Viña's main square is the Plaza Vergara, with its neo-classical Teatro Municipal. It is not to be confused with Quinta Vergara, the beautiful gardens which are a welcome antidote to the beachfront scene. A song festival is held here each February, when Viña is even more packed than usual. Queues for evening performances by Tom Jones lookalikes can last for much of the afternoon.

Beaches Around Viña. The most popular beaches are north of town. Avenida Jorge Montt runs between the rocky shore and the wooded cliffs, and extends along the coast past the resorts of Las Salinas and Reñaca to a number of more peaceful villages. The view is splendid, though marred by rapid development. A good place to stop off is Horcón, a picturesque village set above a small protected bay. The area around Zapallar, a posh resort 22 miles/36km north, has excellent beaches and calm water. More down to earth is Papudo, 6 miles/10km north, where you can stay in the Hotel Moderno.

Buses along the coast leave from the terminal two blocks east of Plaza Vergara, on Valparaiso.

THE ATACAMA DESERT

The idea of a desert 1,240 miles/2,000km long, and stretching right from the Pacific to the Andes, may seem neither plausible nor attractive. Yet this chunk of South America is the driest place on earth. The environment of the Atacama is harsh: the sun is burning hot and nights in the higher regions are often freezing cold. Rain has never been known to fall across most of the northern Atacama. A rare tropical storm in 1991 above Antofagasta caused devastating mudslides, killing many people.

Yet this stark area of scrubby vegetation exerts a strange fascination. Most extraordinary is the number of people living in these inhospitable conditions, drawing their livelihood from the desert's enormous mineral wealth. Indians have occupied these valleys for millenia. They continue to live in a more or less traditional way, especially in the remote highland regions near the Bolivian border. Ancient tribes have left their mark on the land, though their lightness of touch contrasts sharply with the massive mining operations now under way. The Indian legacy is most visible in the geoglyphs — huge designs of gods, men and animals — laid out in stones of different colours. In other places the remains of fortifications can be made out; and the museums of most cities are stocked with artefacts preserved for centuries in the dry salty heat.

The towns are often interesting too. There are several historic settlements, founded during the early days of the Conquest. Reminders of the part the British played in the nitrate business also survive. The end of that particular mineral boom has meant that the great nitrate fields and the nearby settlements have mostly been abandoned, leaving ghost towns in the desert.

The Atacama is not continuous desert. The amount of rainfall increases gradually as you head south, bringing scrub and then pasture to the hills. The final transition into the fertile Chilean Heartland is surprisingly sudden. After travelling through over a thousand miles of desert, the lush greenery of the Central Valley strikes you like a vision of Paradise.

ARICA

Originally a Peruvian town, the word Arica means 'desired land' in Quechua. While this is an obvious over-statement, Arica is important as a port and industrial centre. For many travellers from Peru or Bolivia, it is the first taste of Chile. To most Chileans (and land-locked Bolivians), Arica is significant only as a sea resort: the water is calm and by far the warmest in the country. The town has developed a reputation as a place to have a wild time, and Arica's 140,000 inhabitants are joined by would-be revellers at weekends.

Even if you aren't into seedy clubs or beaches, Arica is not a bad place to stop off — if only to soak up the atmosphere along the seafront.

Arrival and Departure. Arica's position close to Peru and Bolivia has turned it into a major transport hub. There are two railway stations, both near the port — one serving Peru and the other Bolivia. No trains run southwards into Chile.

The bus station is well outside the centre, at Diego Portales and Santa María; from here there are frequent colectivos to the centre ($0.50). Direct buses run to Calama as well as destinations on the Pan-American Highway. Arrive early for buses heading south, as there is often a rigorous baggage search for fruit and vegetables that may have been smuggled in from abroad. Colectivos between Arica and Iquique cost about $9.

LanChile (7 de Julio 148; tel 251641), Ladeco (21 de Mayo 443; tel 252021) and Saba (21 de Mayo 567; tel 253930) all have daily flights to Santiago.

Peru: there are several colectivo services ($3) between Arica and Tacna, 38 miles/60km away in Peru. These leave from Calle Chacabuco between Colón and Baquedano. The train costs just $2 but takes two hours, and runs only twice daily — from the station at Máxima Lira. Allow an extra two hours before departure to obtain an exit stamp. Buses to Tacna are faster and more frequent. Fichtur offers a direct service to Lima for just $30 from the main bus station, and Ormeño has

ARICA

1 Bus Station	6 Residencial Blanquita	11 Post Office/Tourist Office
2 Colectivos to Tacna	7 Residencial Núñez	12 Central Market
3 Railway Station — Peru	8 Bolivian Consulate	13 San Marcos church
4 Argentinian Consulate	9 Entel	14 LanChile
5 Railway Station — Bolivia	10 Customs House	15 Peruvian Consulate

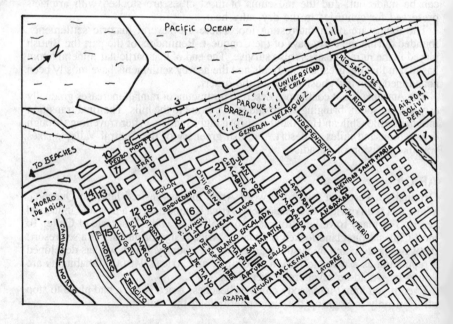

buses to Arequipa ($13, 6 hours). To fly to Lima, go to Tacna and pick up the internal AeroPeru flight for $80.

Bolivia: LAB (Lynch 298; tel 251919) flies three times a week to La Paz. Other routes into Bolivia require more stamina. Humire (Pedro Montt 662) and Litoral (Chacabuco 454) both run twice-weekly buses to La Paz via Tambo Quemado; the journey takes 20 hours and costs around $25. The twice-weekly ferrobus service is expensive at $50, though a little quicker than the bus. You can expect long delays at the freezing cold 13,120ft/4,000m border. All trains to Bolivia leave from the station at Pedro Montt and 21 de Mayo.

Accommodation. Many residenciales are clustered on and around 21 de Mayo, Sotomayor and San Marcos; expect to pay $12 for a double room in summer.
The following are recommended: Residencial La Blanquita (Maipú 472; tel 32064), Las Vegas (120 Baquedano; tel 231355), Las Condes (Vicuña MacKenna 628; tel 251583) and Jardín Del Sol (Sotomayor 848). They are all clean with hot water and private bathrooms. For a more basic room stay at the Residencial Nuñez (Maipú 516 and Lynch), which charges $5.

Eating and Drinking. El Rey del Marisco (upstairs at Colón and Maipú) is good for seafood but is fairly expensive. Govinda's (Bolognesi 367) is recommended for vegetarian meals. There are plenty of cafés in the centre for snacks, including the excellent Bavaria (Colón 611, upstairs). The central bars can get rowdy at weekends. Be vigilant if wandering around late, since there is a lively black market in stolen passports.

Exploring. El Morro is the rocky outcrop above the ocean, whose capture by Chile in 1880 from its Peruvian defenders was decisive in the War of the Pacific. It offers fabulous views over the beaches, ocean and town, particularly at sunset. There is a small military museum at the summit.
Below, in Plaza Cristóbal Colón, is the church of San Marcos, remarkable for its prefabricated iron construction that was designed by Eiffel; only the door is wooden. The attractive series of squares in front of the church lead north to the customs house, another Eiffel creation; and from there to the railway station (for Bolivia) and the entrance to the fishing harbour. This is a good place to watch sealions and pelicans, eat mariscos and watch the busy fishing fleet. Inland, along 21 de Mayo, are attractive alleys with craft stalls; the cheapest place to buy Peruvian and Bolivian goods is the arcade next to the supermarket on 18 de Septiembre, at the corner of Colón.
A road winds south along the waterfront past the city beaches and fishmeal factories to a stretch of unspoilt coastline. Here, the most popular places to swim are El Laucho, the sheltered La Lisera and Playa Brava (good surf). If you're not into sunbathing, you can admire the spectacular congregations of seabirds. Local buses serve the area.

Help and Information. *Tourist Office:* Calle Prat 375, 2nd floor (tel 232101), open 8.30am-1pm, 2.30-6.30pm Monday to Friday. It is worth getting their map of the city, which is also available from the tourist information kiosk on the square. The post office is in the same building.
Telephone Office: Entel is at Baquedano 388 and 21 de Mayo; it opens 9am-10pm.

Money: moneychangers on the corner of 21 de Mayo and Colón trade in dollars as well as the Bolivian, Peruvian and Chilean currencies. There are also a number of cambios on 21 de Mayo. Fincard is at 21 de Mayo 314.

Consulates: Argentina — Manuel Rodríguez 144, near the corner of Prat. Bolivia — Bolognesi 344. Peru — Yungay 304, at Colón. UK — Baquedano 351.

Around Arica

Azapa. The town of Azapa lies in a fruit-growing valley 7 miles/11km southeast of Arica. Its Museo Arqueológico contains pre-Hispanic textiles, ceramics and mummies up to 5,000 years old. It opens daily except Monday. Azapa is especially worth visiting on the first Sunday in October for its festival of the Virgen de Peñas. Colectivos leave from Maipú and Lynch.

Lauca National Park. This spectacular park, 75 miles/120km east of Arica on the Bolivia road, should not be missed. Snow-capped volcanoes reach up to a breathless 20,600ft/6,280m. Near a high pass between two such peaks lies Lago Chungara which, at over 15,000ft/4,573m is the world's highest lake. The park was founded in 1970 as a home for Chile's vicuñas (a cousin of the llama), but if you are lucky you can also see condor, viscachas (rodents found commonly in casseroles) and guanaco (a relative of the vicuña and llama).

In the park is the small Aymará village of Parinacota where llama and alpaca graze freely. The fascinating 17th-century church is cared for by a local man who loves telling visitors about its history and fables.

Anyone without experience of this altitude, and without equipment for the often freezing nights is advised to take one of the tours organized by travel agents in Arica. The 12-hour round trips up the dramatic Lluta valley allow you to see Indian geoglyphs (visible from the road), candelabra cacti, the 17th-century adobe church at Poconchile and the Inca fort at Copaquilla. Two recommended agents are Payachatas (Arturo Prat 163) and Jurasia (Bolognesi 360a), both of which charge around $20.

Anyone wanting to do the trip themselves and stay overnight at the refugios in the park should go to the Conaf office in Arica (Sotomayor 216, 3rd floor), for a basic map. The road to Bolivia runs through the park. You may be able to take a La Paz bus, but not all drivers are willing to stop. Alternatively, take the colectivo to Poconchile, or the 6.30am bus to Putre, and then hitch a lift on the frequent lorries en route to Bolivia. Putre has two hosterías: the San Martín, at Baquedano and O'Higgins, is the cheapest.

IQUIQUE

The capital of Tarapacá (I) Region has the dubious distinction of being the world's largest fishmeal port. More impressive is the approach to Iquique from the elevated coastal plain, which provides dramatic ocean views. The port itself is on a peninsula that juts out to sea near the centre.

Iquique has a population of around 150,000. Its main period of growth came during the 19th-century nitrate and copper booms, though the town had to be virtually rebuilt in the 1920s, following a series of devastating fires. Many interesting brick buildings survive from this period, including imposing mansions, an ornate theatre and the elegantly laid-out Plaza Prat. This main square, like other parts of the city, boasts a resident population of vultures. It also has a clock tower which was a gift from the British in Chile; its chime is hideously noisy.

Iquique is full of enormous shopping emporiums taking advantage of the city's duty-free status. While these are useful if you wish to replace a camera, they hold little other appeal. Concentrate your energies instead on exploring the city or visiting some of the desert's extraordinary geoglyphs.

Arrival and Departure. Iquique lies 47 miles/75km west of the Pan-American Highway, and it is well served by bus; the terminal is at the far north of Patricio Lynch. Numerous companies compete for business to Arica ($5, 4 hours), Santiago ($28, 26 hours), Antofagasta ($11, 9 hours), Calama ($7, 6 hours) and other destinations. Buses and colectivos to Arica and local destinations also leave from around the market at La Torre and Barros Arana.

LanChile (Pinto 641; tel 422526), Ladeco (Pinto 444; tel 420413) and Saba (Plaza Prat 302; tel 428394) have daily flights to Santiago.

There are no passenger rail services from Iquique.

Accommodation. Iquique is full of dirt cheap hotels catering to migrant workers and sailors between boat duties. The cheapest places are around Amunátegui with prices around $3-6: the Viena (729) and the Victoria (770) are at least clean. There is another small cluster of budget hotels near the bus station, including the Esmeralda (Esmeralda and Lynch) or the Aluimar (San Martín 486 at Lynch).

A notch up from these are Residenciales Catedral (253 Obispo Labbe; tel 23395), opposite the cathedral, the José Luis (San Martín 601 and Ramírez) and the Hotel Phoenix (Aníbal Pinto 451; tel 21315), all with rooms at around $15/$20. Also worth trying are the Marclaud (Martínez 753), popular with travellers — a visitors book provides suggestions of things to see; and the Condell (Thompson 684 at Vivar), both around $10 for a double.

Eating and Drinking. To find dinner in Iquique, just stroll along Tarapacá between Plaza Prat and Amunátegui: try the trendy Café Garbo (at Vivar) or La Merienda (at Amunátegui), both with cheap local food. There are several old-fashioned clubs on or near the square, including the Jugoslavenski Club Social (Prat and Tarapacá), the spectacular Club Español (around $10 a head) and the Circolo Italiano (Tarapacá 477).

Seafood is plentiful along the seafront; and the market, which is six blocks southeast of Plaza Prat, has plenty of stalls upstairs.

Exploring. The Regional Museum (Sotomayor 728) illustrates the history both of the nitrate boom and of the long extinct indigenous cultures, featuring a full-size replica of an Indian village. It opens 9am-1pm, 4-8pm Monday to Friday and 10am-1pm at weekends. If you are interested in the escapades of Chile's navy, visit the Museo Naval at Esmeralda and Pinto (closed Mondays). It's worth coming here just to enjoy the dramatic views of the town from the nearby causeway to the harbour.

Despite the fishmeal, there are some popular beaches near Iquique, including Playas Cavancha and Brava. The sea is fairly rough, but there are lifeguards. Alternatively, there is a fresh water swimming pool on the seafront at Riquelme and Aníbal Pinto.

Help and Information. The main tourist office is at Aníbal Pinto 436 (tel 421499), with another small office on Plaza Prat. Also in the square is Banco de Chile; moneychangers sometimes hang around outside. Fincard is at Serrano 430. The post office is near the corner of Obispo Labbe and Lynch, and Entel is at Tarapacá and Ramírez.

Around Iquique

Unlike the better known Nazca lines in Peru, whose designs are on the plain, the geoglyphs around Iquique are laid out on hillsides where they can be seen from the ground. The most accessible ones are at Pintados, above a derelict railway junction off the Iquique-Antofagasta highway. Nearly 400 designs can be made out on the hill. More impressive is the 120m-long Giant of the Atacama, which is laid out on the Sierra Unida, a lone mountain on the desert plain. It lies just off the road leading east to Chuzmisa from the Pan-American highway, some 16 miles/25km north of the Iquique turn-off. Unless you hire a car you you will almost certainly have to go on a tour. Iquitour (Tarapacá 465b) and Viajes Liriama (Baquedano 823) are recommended agencies. Ask also about trips to the Salar de Huesco saltpan.

More easily accessible is Humberstone, one of the many abandoned nitrate-mining settlements scattered across the Atacama. It is next to the Iquique turn-off from the Pan-American Highway, and is accessible by bus.

CALAMA

Lying some way inland, between Iquique and Antofagasta, Calama is a modern mining centre on the high desert plain. The nearby Chuquicamata copper mine employs about half the working population; many of the remainder are engaged in mining salt and other minerals. Calama's 100,000 inhabitants are blessed with the Río Loa, the only river for hundreds of miles around. But the atmosphere remains dry and dusty.

Calama is above all a centre for exploring the surrounding villages. But the archaeological and ethnographical museum, in the park a short walk along the Antofagasta road, is worth a visit.

Arrival and Departure. Ladeco (Ramírez 1937; tel 212970) has daily flights to Antofagasta, Iquique and Santiago ($130). LanChile (La Torre 1499; tel 211394) serves Antofagasta and Santiago six days a week.

Buses do not serve a central bus station. Every company has its own office. The principal firms are: Gemini (Granaderos and Espinoza) to Arica, Iquique, Antofagasta, Santiago, and once a week to Salta in Argentina (weather permitting); Flecha Norte (Ramírez and Balmaceda) to Copiapó, Antofagasta and Santiago; Tramaca (Felix Hoyes and Granaderos) to Arica, Iquique, San Pedro de Atacama and Santiago; Libac (Espinoza and Abaroa) to Antofagasta and Santiago; and Morales Moralito (Balmaceda and Sotomayor) to San Pedro and Toconao.

Trains run direct to Oruro (Bolivia) from the station at Balmaceda and Sotomayor. There is currently one departure a week leaving Wednesday afternoons. It is a fascinating but arduous 36-hour journey involving often long delays at the border. The nearest Bolivian consulate is in Antofagasta.

Accommodation and Food. Residenciales El Tatio (Gallo 1987; tel 212284), the Splendid (Ramírez 1960; tel 212141) and the Internacional (General Velásquez and Vargas) all charge around $5/10.

For ordinary Chilean food go to the Osorno (Granaderos 2013B at Espinoza) or the Bavaria (Sotomayor and Abaroa). For a more stylish atmosphere try the Club Yugoslavia in Plaza 23 de Marzo.

Help and Information. The tourist office is at La Torre 1689 and MacKenna. Banco de Chile is at Vivar and Vargas.

Recommended tour agencies are Viajes Talihue (Gen. Velásquez 1948), Cooper Tour (Sotomayor 2016) and Taxis Azules (La Torre 1250).

Around Calama

Chuquicamata. Usually called simply 'Chuqui', this is the big attraction around Calama — if that is the correct name for a complex of huge open-cast mines, noxious sulphuric acid plants, and smelting furnaces. The main pit, El Yacimiento, is the world's largest open-cast copper mine. It is 600m deep and measures a staggering 4km by 2km. The complex yields half of Chile's copper and a quarter of its export income. Although it was nationalized in 1971, American companies continue to operate the mine.

There are free tours of the mine which start from the Sede Ayuda a Infancia Desvalida (SAID) office, at the top of Avenida J. M. Carrera, in Chuqui town. The three-hour tour begins at 10am, Mondays to Fridays. Bring your passport and ensure that your arms and legs are covered. Colectivos to Chuqui from Calama (10 miles/16km south) leave from the main plaza; they will drop you at the SAID office.

Northeast of Calama. Chiu-Chiu, 20 miles/32km northeast of Calama, was once a stop on the Inca highway; it has an old church. A short distance beyond is the adobe-built Indian village of Lasana, which has the eroded remains of an Inca fort. Both are accessible by bus from Calama, and Lasana also from Chuquicamata, which lies due west.

A road continues northeast from Lasana for 100 miles/160km through a military zone to Ollagüe. This remote border town lies high on a dry saltpan by the Bolivian border, in the shadow of Volcán Ollagüe. Nearby is Aucanquilcha, the highest mine in the world. The easiest way to get to Ollagüe is on a train from Calama. If you have more time, do the journey by road, combining buses and then hitching. If you want to enjoy the scenery in more style, consider hiring a four-wheel vehicle or going on a tour. The scenery is fantastic, and dotted with flamingo lakes, guanaco, llama and alpaca, and traditional Indian villages.

SAN PEDRO DE ATACAMA

This ancient town lies on the edge of the Salar de Atacama, a nearly dry salt lake in a depression surrounded by the Andes. This was once an outstandingly fertile region — an oasis in which the civilizations of the Atacama Indians developed. But sands now cover the remains of forts, villages, tombs and terraces.

The population is a meagre 1,600. Some of the local people work at the nearby sulphur mine, but many are now involved in tourism. A great many visitors are rightly attracted to San Pedro, not only because of its archaeological importance. It is also ideally placed for exploring the geological wonders of the Altiplano. San Pedro is 64 miles/103km southeast of Calama, the town's main contact with the outside world. Direct buses are run by Tramaca daily, and by Morales Moralito on weekdays only; the journey takes two hours.

Accommodation. There are several basic but friendly residenciales charging around $5/$10. The Chiloé, three blocks west of the main square on the Calama road, is recommended; the Juanita on the square itself is more simple. The nearby Porvenir and Takha Takha both charge $10/$20.

Exploring. The main attraction in San Pedro is its archaeological museum, whose collection of 380,000 artefacts is a unique record of millennia of human habitation. It includes mummies and textiles preserved for centuries in the dry salty soil. On the east side of the main square is a large adobe house, said to have been built for conquistador Pedro de Valdivia in 1540; ask next door for admission. The 16th-century church opposite, among the oldest in Chile, is built of cactus wood.

A couple of miles and an easy walk northwest of San Pedro is the ruined fort of Quitor. This was one of the last strongholds of the Indians fighting off Pedro de Valdivia and his followers.

Around San Pedro de Atacama

For tours to the nearby sights in the salt desert and Altiplano enquire at Turismo Ochoa on Toconao, the Residencia Chiloé, or Hostería San Pedro — the town's top hotel, on Solcor. Wherever you go, be prepared for the extreme variations in temperature.

The Valle de La Luna, 12 miles/20km west of San Pedro on the far side of the Salar, is named for its unearthly arid landscape and natural sculptures of eroded salt. The geysers of El Tatio, 44 miles/70km away at a dizzy altitude of 14,100ft/4,300m, are best seen early in the morning. Tours run to the Salar itself, but the flamingoes are frustratingly shy.

Toconao. This small, mostly Indian village lies on the east shore of the Salar de Atacama some 25 miles/40km south of San Pedro. Toconao has a 16th-century church and some old stone buildings. Much of the woollen clothing sold in San Pedro originates here. In the Zapar valley, a short walk along a track leaving the road $2\frac{1}{2}$ miles/4km northwest of Toconao, are the ruins of a pre-hispanic settlement.

Toconao is served by weekly Gemini buses from Calama via San Pedro. The road continues southeast beyond Toconao over remote plains and high passes to Salta, Argentina. International buses to Salta use this route but they are usually direct; and if you are allowed to get off, you will probably have to pay the full fare anyway.

ANTOFAGASTA

The capital of Antofagasta (II) Region is northern Chile's largest city (population 200,000) and its principal port. It is a lively place, with unusually large Balkan and gypsy communities. The disastrous rains of 1991 have leached salt out to crystallize on the surface of the surrounding desert — giving a most unreal impression of snow. But the town itself is almost back to normal. Normality in Antofagasta is not wildly interesting. But since the city lies close to the Pan-American Highway and is a major transport hub, you may find yourself stopping off.

Antofagasta is proud of its 12-mile/19km seafront complete with parks, and beaches. This is well south of the centre, and more interesting is the seafront downtown. The main harbour is open to visitors, but you need to leave your passport at the gate. Many relics of industrial archaeology are preserved here, and it is also a good place to watch sealions and seabirds. More conventional archaeological remains are kept in the museum at 482 Prat (open weekdays). Further north is the fishing harbour and market, which is is fun to wander around. There is a swimming pool (with excellent showers) at Condell and 21 de Mayo.

One trip out of town not to be missed is to La Portada, 10 miles/16km north, with its most fantastic cliff formations. Take bus 20 from Plaza de Armas.

Arrival and Departure. Ladeco (Washington 2589; tel 222860), LanChile (Washington 2552; tel 225151) and Saba (Condell 2448; tel 263908) have daily services to Santiago, Iquique, and Arica. Ladeco also flies weekly to La Paz, Bolivia.

There is a central bus station at Argentina and Díaz Gana, south of the centre. But most bus companies have their own terminals as well, and some seem to ignore the main station altogether. The main companies are: Tramaca (Uribe 936; tel 223624) with buses daily to Calama (3 hours, $4), Iquique (8 hours, $10), Arica (13 hours, $14) and Santiago (20 hours, $24), and weekly to Salta in Argentina (20 hours, $33); Flota Barrios (Condell 2764; 222443) daily to Arica, Valparaíso and Santiago; Gemini (Riquelme 513; 224142) daily to Santiago and weekly to Salta; Flecha Dorada (Latorre 2761; 227102) to Calama, Arica and Santiago. Buses operating out of a terminal at Latorre and Riquelme serve mostly local destinations.

Antofagasta is no longer served by passenger trains.

Accommodation and Food. Residenciales are generally basic but clean, and charge around $5/$8. Try the Rawaya (Sucre 762; tel 225399) the Paola (Prat 766, tel 222208) and the Riojanita (Baquedano 464). For more comfort go to the Pieper (Sucre 509; tel 223433).

The Sociedad Protectora de Empleados (San Martín 2544), near the square, serves huge, cheap meals and is an entertaining place to eat. The Apoquindo (Prat 616) is good for snacks, as are the nearby Express and Haiti cafés. The Club Nautico (Pinto 3051) specializes in seafood.

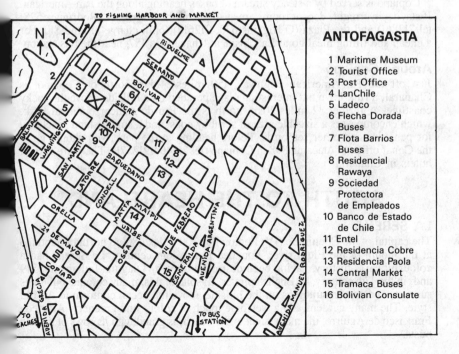

ANTOFAGASTA

1 Maritime Museum
2 Tourist Office
3 Post Office
4 LanChile
5 Ladeco
6 Flecha Dorada Buses
7 Flota Barrios Buses
8 Residencial Rawaya
9 Sociedad Protectora de Empleados
10 Banco de Estado de Chile
11 Entel
12 Residencia Cobre
13 Residencia Paola
14 Central Market
15 Tramaca Buses
16 Bolivian Consulate

Help and Information. *Tourist Office:* Baquedano 360, 2nd floor (tel 264040), and at Balmaceda and Prat (tel 223004).

Communications: the post office is on the square, in a building shared with Telex Chile. Entel is at Prat and Matta.

Money: you can change cash and cheques at the cambios near the post office, and at Banco Estado de Chile (San Martín and Prat). Fincard is at Prat 427.

Consulates: Bolivia — Grecia 563, office 23, near the corner of Matta south of the centre. Argentina — further south still at Manuel Verbal 1632.

COPIAPO

This city is the capital of the Atacama (III) Region, though it actually marks the beginning of the end of the northern desert. The area known as the Norte Chico, which spreads south from the Río Copiapó, sees occasional sprinkles of rain. But conditions are still exceedingly dry, and the oasis that gave rise to the town is surrounded by sand dunes. Copiapó has a population of over 70,000, and is a fairly important regional centre.

While Copiapó is hardly worth crossing the country for, its Museo Mineralógico deserves a visit. This museum is the best of its kind in Chile, with a huge variety of ores from around the Atacama. It is one block east of the delightful Plaza Prat, and opens 10am-1pm and 3.30-8pm Monday to Friday, and 10am-1pm on Saturday. Minerals and mining also receive the most attention at the Regional Museum (Atacama 630), housed in an imposing late 19th-century mansion. Rail buffs should not miss the Railway Museum at the station, where you can see one of South America's first locomotives.

Copiapó is served by a steady stream of buses heading along the Pan-American. If staying overnight, decent rooms are available at the Rodríguez (Rodríguez 528; tel 212861) and the Plaza (O'Higgins 670; 212610); both charge around $10. For a cheap and filling meal go to La Chispa at Chacabuco 157, near the bus station.

Around Copiapó

Just off the Pan-American Highway, 150 miles/240km north of Copiapó, is Chañaral, a run-down but interesting place perched on a hillside above the rocky coastline. A further 12 miles/20km north is the Pan de Azúcar National Park, which encompasses a sizeable area of scrubby coast and a small island sanctuary for penguins and other sea birds. Before heading to the park, you should go to the Conaf office at Atacama 898 in Copiapó (tel 213404/212571). There are several hotels in Chañaral.

SOUTH TO THE HEARTLAND

LA SERENA

The capital of the Coquimbo (IV) Region lies 300 miles/480km north of Santiago at the mouth of the Elquí river. Founded in the 16th century, La Serena had a colourful early history, having been destroyed once by Diaguita Indians in 1549 and, in the 17th century, by English pirates. In spite of this, many colonial buildings survive, and newer buildings on the hillside above the ocean conform to the old style. The many gardens add a welcome touch of colour and greenery. Alameda Francisco de Aguirre, the main street to the beach, is grand with its rows of marble busts.

La Serena is delightful. Good beaches nearby have helped turn the town into a popular resort, but it is remarkably untainted by the attention.

Arrival and Departure. The bus station is south of the centre at El Santo and Amunátegui. Buses run to Arica ($20, 17 hours), Calama ($18, 16 hours), Antofagasta ($12, 13 hours) and Santiago ($10, 8 hours). Buses to Vicuña and the Valle de Elquí (see below) leave from the office at J. Dios Peni, three blocks south of the square.

Accommodation and Food. Residenciales Casa del Turista (Colón 318), El Loa (Bernardo O'Higgins 362) and Alameda (Aguirre 452; tel 213052) all charge around $7/$10. The places along the seafront between La Serena and Coquimbo tend to be expensive. The Club Social (Córdovez 516) and Mi Casa (Aguirre 596) serve a wide range of dishes for low prices.

Exploring. The 16th-century cathedral on the Plaza de Armas is the most important of over thirty religious buildings in La Serena. The best museum is the Museo Arqueológico (Cordóvez and Cienfuegos), which has a collection of Atacama and Diaguita Indian artefacts. It is open 9am-1pm and 4-7pm Tuesday to Saturday, and 9am-1pm on Sundays.

Anyone interested in the monolithic sculptures of Easter Island can see one in La Serena without having to travel half way across the Pacific. The 10-foot sculpture is on top of the hill known as the Colina de Santa Lucía. Down below is the farmers' market, good for local produce such as fruit and cheese.

The best beaches are south of Coquimbo, 7 miles/11km south of La Serena and served by a steady flow of buses. You can't do much better than La Herradura, just a mile or so from the town.

Help and Information. The tourist office is in the Municipalidad at Prat and Matta, in the square. The post office is also in Plaza de Armas. Conaf is at Córdovez 283 (tel 211124).

VALLE DE ELQUI

This valley has a broad appeal, being of potential interest to lovers of beautiful scenery, the local liquor, telescopes, alternative religions and even poetry; but sadly, not to students of indigenous peoples — no pure-blooded descendants of the original Diaguita Indians remain.

The valley becomes steadily more dramatic as you head inland from La Serena, with barren mountainsides closing in ever further. It is astonishing to find so many healthy-looking vineyards in such surroundings; yet grapes thrive along the valley floor, where pre-Columbian irrigation systems have survived. Those grapes which are not exported are used to make *pisco*, the local brandy. To arrange a tour around the largest distillery (in Vicuña) contact Eduardo Calderón at Pisco Capel, Rengifo 318, La Serena (tel 213541).

Valle de Elquí boasts extraordinarily clear air, and this has led to the establishment of some of the world's leading observatories on the mountain tops. The physical characteristics of the area also lie behind the presence of a New Age centre in the Cochiguas valley, which is considered a node of earth energy by modern Taoists; it is also held to be the part of the world most visited by UFOs. Certainly, a night in the valley is an unforgettable experience.

Vicuña, 41 miles/66km east of La Serena, is the main settlement in the valley.

You can use it as a base for pleasant walks to nearby villages. Stay at the Hotel Jasna or Residencial Moderna on Gabriela Mistral; they charge around $5/$10. Vicuña is served by regular buses and colectivos.

The main branch of the river leads to Monte Grande, the birthplace of Gabriela Mistral, Chile's revered, Nobel Prize-winning poet. Her tomb is just outside the town and there is a small museum in her old house. Three buses a day run to Monte Grande from the main square in Vicuña, and there are several basic hospedajes.

The road leads on to Pisco Elquí with its high steepled church and interesting architecture. This is a beautiful centre for walking, but the climate is harsh and local facilities are limited. Stay in Hotel Plaza. Beyond Pisco, Río Cochiguas runs southeast, carving a valley that is the heart of the New Age community.

Travelling south from La Serena the landscape gradually becomes greener, as desert gives way to scrub and range lands. The rocky coastline is dotted with lovely coves and beaches. Guanaqueros and Tongoy are both popular places to swim — particularly the latter, which has a permanent party atmosphere in summer.

Ovalle is 50 miles/80km along the inland route southeast of La Serena. It's not much of a place but it lies in an interesting area. The highlight is the Valle del Encanto (Enchanted Valley), which has many remains of Indian occupation, including petroglyphs, and a dramatic landscape of huge boulders. The park is 13 miles/20km west of Ovalle towards the Pan-American Highway, then a 2-mile/3km walk. The museum in town contains a small but good collection of Diaguita artefacts.

There are a number of cheap hotels along Libertad north of the square, as well as a campsite in the Valle del Encanto.

SANTIAGO TO TEMUCO

The Central Valley — a magnificent landscape of orchards, vineyards, river valleys and the snow-clad Andean mountains — extends for over 300 miles south of Santiago, down to the Bío-Bío river. This great natural boundary enabled the Araucanian heartland, now known as the Lake District, to remain independent until the late 19th century. The remaining Mapuche Indians remain a significant presence there, especially around Temuco. The railway, as well as the Pan-American Highway, cuts through the entire region.

RANCAGUA

This is the capital of the Region del Libertador Bernardo O'Higgins (VI), a splendid rural area with a flourishing huaso culture. The best time to see these cowboys in action is to at the national rodeo championships, hosted by Rancagua towards the end of March. The town itself is not a particularly appealing place at other times. Admirers of O'Higgins, who roundly defeated the Spanish at Rancagua in 1814, may want to track down the museum the Casa del Pilar de Piedra at Estado and Ibieta.

The largest underground copper mine in the world, El Teniente, is 42 miles/67km east of Rancagua. Anyone intending to visit it must get clearance from the head mines office in Santiago (Huérfanos 1270).

Rancagua is easily reached by train (from the north or south), and buses travelling along the highway stop at the Terminal de Buses, seven blocks west of the square.

Continuing south along the Pan-American Highway you reach Chillán. This is another city to have been devastated by earthquakes. It may be a useful pitstop, in which case stay at Residencial Claris (18 de Sieptembre 357; tel 221980) near the square, or at the Real (Libertad 219); both are good value at around $5. If you want to explore, visit the Feria de Chillán, a good crafts market. Termas de Chillán, 51 miles/82km east, is a major ski resort and a popular hiking centre in summer.

CONCEPCION

Devastating earthquakes, wet winters and merciless sea storms are hardly the usual features that lure people to settle. Yet the capital of the Bío-Bío (VIII) Region is Chile's third largest city, with a population of 600,000. The explanation may lie in the fact that many of the people are of hardy Germanic descent. Most of Concepción's history has been obliterated, but it is not an unattractive city. There are a couple of interesting places nearby.

Arrival and Departure. There are three trains daily to and from Santiago (9-10 hours); change at Chillán for services south to Puerto Montt. The station is on Prat, six blocks southeast of Plaza Independencia. The Terminal Rodoviário is well north of the centre, on the Chillán road; local buses to the terminal run along Maipú. There are frequent services to Santiago and Puerto Montt.

Accommodation and Food. There are several hotels along Colo Colo. These include Residencial Colo Colo (number 743), which is central, pleasant, and charges $5. The Youth Hostel (at number 354) closes in winter. The Antuco and San Sebastián hotels are in a block of flats at Barros Arana 741 (near Colo Colo); they are good but in the $15 range. There are many other hotels along Barros Arana towards the railway station.

One of the liveliest places to eat in the evening is the Tagore at Lincoyan 660, which has good seafood and vegetarian dishes, and opens late. The market is two blocks west of the square, for cheap daytime meals.

Exploring. Finca Hualpén, just outside Concepción on the river estuary, is an old farm with a late 19th-century mansion. It is now a museum housing the eclectic collection of adventurer Pedro del Río Zañartu, who bequeathed his estate to the city on his death in 1918. (The municipal museum in Puerto Montt gives more information about him.) Buses run in summer and give views of the extraordinary rock formations along the estuary. The museum opens 9am-12.30pm and 2-6pm Tuesday to Sunday.

Talcahuano, a major port and the Chilean Navy's principal base, lies on a peninsula 9 miles/15km northwest of Concepción. It is home to the Huáscar, the Peruvian vessel on which Arturo Prat met his death during the War of the Pacific. It is open 10.30am-4.30pm. At the entrance to the yard you must surrender your passport and bag, but you can usually hang on to your camera if you ask; the old warship is well away from the navy docks. If staying overnight, try Residencial San Pedro (Manuel Rodríguez 22; tel 542145). There are good seafood restaurants along the waterfront.

Thirty miles/48km south of Concepción is Laraquete, a small resort with long, golden beaches.

Help and Information. The tourist office is in the main square, the post office at O'Higgins and Colo Colo, and CTC has a telephone office at Colo Colo 487. Change money at Cambios Fides, which is on the ground floor of the shopping gallery at Barros Arana 565. Fincard is at O'Higgins 402.

LOS ANGELES

Heading along the inland route south from Concepción, you pass the turn-off to Los Angeles (population 70,000). Although pleasant enough, the town is best used as a pitstop. It is worth stopping off at the Salto del Laja, 20 miles/32km north of town, just off the main road. This is a dramatic waterfall where the Río Laja dives 160ft/49m into a deep gorge. There are delightful walks in the surrounding park at any time, but the falls are best seen during the wet season.

Los Angeles is served by direct buses from Santiago, Concepción, Chillán, Curacautín and Temuco. Residenciales Santa María (on Caupolicán near the bus station) and Winser (Colo Colo 335) are both reasonable places to stay, at about $5.

CURACAUTIN

This small town lies at the heart of a lovely area of forests, mountains and volcanic hot springs. The road to Curacautín turns off the Pan-American Highway at Victoria, which is 44 miles/71km north of Temuco and 71 miles/114km south of Los Angeles. There are direct buses to Curacautín from both towns, some of which carry on into the hinterland. The best hotel is the Turismo (Tarapacá 140; tel 116), which charges just $4 and serves excellent food; if it is full try the Plaza at Yungay 157 (tel 56).

Around Curacautín

Termas de Tolhuaca. These hot springs are 23 miles/36km northeast of Curacautín. Residencial Roja is a cheap but pleasant hotel by the river. The main reason to stay here is to explore the Parque Nacional Tolhuaca, 6 miles/9km from the Termas, which boasts superb scenery of waterfalls and volcanoes, and the Laguna Malleco. Transport is difficult out of the summer, when you will probably have to rely on other local tourists to give you a lift.

Volcán Lonquimay. Fifteen miles/24km east of Curacautín is the village of Malalcahuello. It is a popular base for visiting Volcán Lonquimay (9,480ft/2,890m) in the Reserva Nacional Malalcahuello-Nalcas. The volcano erupted in 1989, doing considerable damage to the surrounding area, and enhancing the already lunar landscape. Stay at the Residencial Los Sauces, where you can arrange for a lift to the volcano. There is a refugio in the park on the lower slopes, some 6 miles/10km from the road. You should enquire at Conaf in Temuco (Caupolicán and Bulnes) for information and bookings.

Lonquimay is a small town 33 miles/57km east of Curacautín, in the headwaters of the Río Bío-Bío. There is a choice of routes from Malalchuello: the southerly route goes through Chile's longest tunnel, while the longer northerly route goes through magnificent mountain scenery. Beyond Lonquimay, the Pino Hachado pass is an unorthodox but perfectly feasible route to Argentina. You must rely on getting a lift as there is no public transport. There is a small hotel in Lonquimay.

THE LAKE DISTRICT

This is one of the most stunning parts of Chile, its landscape of mountains, lakes, volcanoes, waterfalls, primeval rainforest and white water rivers having a wild splendour.

Such heavenly scenes are only one side of the coin, however. Much of the Lake District is preserved in a network of national parks, but large tracts of virgin forest have been converted to plantations of fast-growing pulpwood. The area is also far from paradise for most of its inhabitants. This region was the autonomous homeland of the Mapuche Indians until 1881, since when they have seen their lands taken away, the marginalization of their culture and the undermining of their subsistence. Nevertheless, their numbers make them a force to be reckoned with and the claims of the Mapuche are now being reasserted by an increasingly vocal younger generation.

The other ethnic group most in evidence are the descendants of 19th-century German immigrants. In places like Osorno and Valdivia, where settlement was concentrated, their influence is present not only among the German-speaking people but also in the architecture.

The Lake District attracts thousands of Chilean and Argentinian tourists every summer. Most of them stick to the established resorts, where they swim in the warm waters, sunbathe on the black-sand beaches, and enjoy all manner of diversions, from boat rides to wind-surfing. The fact that few tourists venture far from base, coupled with the remoteness of much of the region, means that it is not hard to escape the crowds. While there are some good beaches, the most fun is to be had by hiking up into the hills. In some areas you can also organize rafting, horse-riding and even mountain-biking.

January and February are the busiest months, when much of the available accommodation fills up. But since many families rent out private rooms, you can usually find somewhere in the end. Otherwise bring a tent, which will also be useful in the national parks, most of which offer no alternative accommodation.

The Lake District is extremely wet, especially in the coastal regions and in the winter months. It can rain at any time of year, and always be prepared for a sudden, unexpected and possibly prolonged downpour.

TEMUCO

This is the capital of the Araucania (IX) Region. Founded in 1881 following the defeat of the Mapuche, it has grown into one of the major cities of the south, with some 220,000 inhabitants. Temuco may not be a place to visit for its architecture, but it is full of atmosphere and has wonderful restaurants. It is also a good place to buy Mapuche crafts. Many Indians live in Temuco, and others come into market from nearby villages. They are very much used to tourists: expect to pay for taking photographs of them.

Arrival and Departure. *Air:* LanChile (Bulnes 667 and Varas; tel 34977) has three flights a week to Santiago and Puerto Montt, and one to Concepción; Ladeco (Prat 535; tel 36414) flies to Santiago, Valdivia and Osorno several times a week.

Bus: the Terminal Rural bus station at Pinto and Balmaceda has buses to local destinations including Curacautín, Chol Chol and Lonquimay, and to San Martín de los Andes and Neuquén in Argentina. Elsewhere, however, the situation is anarchic, with each of about a dozen companies maintaining its own terminal. Thankfully these are clustered near the centre around MacKenna and Claro Solar.

The principal services are as follows: Cruz del Sur (Vicuña MacKenna and Claro Solar) for Santiago, Puerto Montt, Castro (Chiloé Island) and intermediate stops. JAC (MacKenna and Bello) for Santiago, Lican Ray, Coñaripe and buses throughout the day to Villarrica and Pucón. Pangui Sur (Miraflores 871) has many buses to Panguipulli, and summer services to Loncoche, Los Lagos and Mehuín. Other companies are on the 500 and 600 blocks of Claro Solar, including Fenix (Claro Solar 694 at Pedro Lagos), with buses direct to Arica and other Atacama cities, and to Buenos Aires and Mendoza in Argentina. Around the corner on Lagos is Tur-bus, which has the most frequent services to Santiago.

Rail: the railway station is at Barros Arana and Lautaro (tel 226925), with a booking office at Bulnes 590 and Claro Solar (tel 233522). There are daily trains to Santiago, Puerto Montt, Concepción and Valdivia, with the times and number of trains subject to seasonal change.

Car Rental: Hertz has an agent at Hotel de la Frontera, Avenida Bulnes 726 (tel 236190), and Avis at Arturo Prat 800 (tel 231914). Both are represented at the airport.

Accommodation. Cheap accommodation is concentrated in the fairly unsavoury area around the market and railway station: the Omega (Pinto 91) and Rupangue (Barros Arana, near Balmaceda) both charge around $5. In the centre, the Hotel Turismo (Claro Solar 636 at Lagos; tel 232348), the Continental (Varas 708 and Prat; tel 231166) and the Espellete (Claro Solar 492 at Lynch; tel 234255), all charge $10-15. Somewhat cheaper is Casa de Huéspedes Centenario (Aldunate 864).

Private rooms can be easily arranged. While the Gutierrez family (Aldunate 821) offers luxurious and pricey lodgings, a bed in the following houses should set you back no more than $5: Nancy (Lagos, between Solar and Varas), Casa Mirtha Lagos de Concha (Zentano 525) and Casa Veronica Kiekebusch (Alemania 0649; tel 32079).

Eating and Drinking. Calle Manuel Bulnes is lined with restaurants: the Nueva Hostería Allen Clei (at 902), Dino's (at 360), the up-market Julio's Pizza (478) and the pleasant Café Estanbul (563) are all good. Rincón Naturista (Prat 425) is an excellent vegetari. n shop-cum-restaurant.

Exploring. Strolling around Temuco's markets is the best way to see the Mapuche people, some of whom wear traditional dress. The fresh produce market (Feria Libre), northeast of the centre, is best for people-watching. The municipal market northwest of the square, at Aldunate and Diego Portales, has been smartened up for the tourists, but is still a good place to buy local artesanía, including ponchos, blankets, silverware and woodcarving. You can watch the craftsmen at work in the workshops in the Catholic University (Alemania and 18 de Septiembre).

For a good overview of the Mapuche culture visit the Museo Regional de la Araucania at Alemania 84. It opens 9am-1pm and 3-7pm Tuesday to Saturday, and 10am-1pm on Sunday.

Cerro Nielol is a hill park about a mile north of the centre. There are fine views of the city from the top.

Help and Information. *Tourist Information:* Bulnes 586 and Clara Solar. You can pick up maps and information about the surrounding area. Conaf has an office at Caupolicán and Bulnes.

Communications: the central post office is on the main square at Prat and Diego Portales, with another at the railway station. The CTC phone office is on Prat just north of the square; Entel is at Bulnes 307 and Rodríguez.

Money: there are several cambios, including Turismo Money Exchange (Arauco Shopping Centre between Bulnes and Prat), Turcamb (Solar 733) and Christopher (Varas 625). Fincard is at Claro Solar 992.

Around Temuco

Chol-Chol. This small country town lies 19 miles/30km northwest of Temuco, in a strongly Mapuche area. There isn't much to see but there's plenty of atmosphere to be soaked up, and wonderful views en route — look out for the traditional round thatched houses. Chol-Chol is served by buses from Temuco's Terminal Rural.

Los Paraguas and Conguillo National Parks. The snow-capped Llaima Volcano (10,250ft/3,125m) is clearly visible some 60 miles/100km east of Temuco. It marks the division between the Parque Nacional Conguillo to the north, and the Los Paraguas park to the south. The Llaima ski resort nestles on the volcano's lower slopes and there is ample scope for hiking. Los Paraguas preserves a large forest rich in araucaria pine (monkey-puzzle trees). It is at its finest between August and October. The popular Conguillo park also has araucaria woods, and stretches into the high altitude region of the Sierra Nevada. There are several lakes in the park.

The best way to explore the parks is in a hired jeep, though you may have some luck with hitching in the high season. Otherwise access is possible from Curacautín (see page 427) or Melipeuco (to the south), both served by bus from the Terminal Rural in Temuco. In summer some buses travel right through the park between the two villages. The journeys along dusty roads past tiny wooden houses and huge trees are magical. Melipeuco is a wonderful little place; stay at the good value Hotel Central. There is no accommodation in the park, just camping sites. For further information visit Conaf in Temuco.

LAGO VILLARRICA

Set among wooded hills backed by snowy mountains, this lake is one of the loveliest in the region. Volcán Villarrica (9,315ft/2,840m), southeast of the lake, shows sporadic activity: it smokes in the day, glows in the dark, and occasionally burps white hot lava onto the snow at the summit.

Lago Villarrica is reached easily from the Pan-American Highway at Freire or Loncoche, 17 miles/27km and 52 miles/83km south of Temuco respectively.

Villarrica. Paved roads lead from Freire and Loncoche east to Villarrica, the main town on the lake. One of the few notable facts about the place is that Queen Elizabeth II once dropped by and stayed in a lakeside hotel built in her honour. Even so, in summer the town is inundated with visitors, who come mainly to swim and go boating.

In the town the main source of interest is a small museum of Mapuche artefacts, east of the centre at Valdivia and Acevedo. There is also a good craft market, for both Mapuche and run-of-the-mill things. A Mapuche cultural festival is held in the second week in February.

The main bus station at Muñoz and Valdivia serves most destinations, including within the Lake District and across the border in Argentina. JAC, at Reyes and Montt, offers the most frequent service to Pucón and Temuco.

Accommodation: for about $5 you can rent a decent room at the Hotel Fuentes (Vincente Reyes 665 and Henríquez) or the Residencial Victoria (Muñoz 530).

Dormitory-style accommodation is available for around $4 at Residencal San Francisco (Julio Zegers 646) and the Casa San Jorge (Calle Catedral). The hospedaje at San Martín 734 is more comfortable if you don't object to sharing your living space with a hunter's lifetime collection of trophies. Other private houses worth trying are Montt 1027, Letelier 702 and Bilbao 969. For a classier room stay at Residencial Puchi (Valdivia 678 and Henríquez) and pay $8/$11.

Eating and Drinking: there is a fairly good choice of places to eat around Henríquez, its continuation Alderete, and Valdivia. The 2001 at Henríquez 379 is the best bar for light meals and snacks, and is a good place to sit and watch the world go by. Peña La Tranquera (Acevedo 761 and Bilbao) has live folk music most nights.

Help and Information: The tourist office is next to the museum at Valdivia and Acevedo. Banco de Osorno offers reasonable rates of exchange; due to the traffic to and from Argentina, pesos are traded nearly as much as dollars.

Pucón. Unlike Villarrica, which is a town with a life of its own, Pucón is a purpose-built and now over-developed resort. However, it makes a more convenient base from which to travel into the mountains and parks. Tour companies offer all manner of trips, from rafting to mountain biking; otherwise you can simply walk straight into the hills from town. Pucón is quiet and forlorn in winter, but there is enough trade from skiers visiting the nearby slopes to keep most of the facilities open.

Buses serve Pucón from Villarrica (16 miles/26km west) and other local and more distant towns. The main bus company, JAC, has its terminal at 478 O'Higgins. Buses Cordillera, on Miguel Ansorena near O'Higgins, serves local destinations in the mountains including Lago Caburgua. There is a good tourist office at Caupolicán and Brasil (tel 125).

Accommodation: Hospedaje El Fogón (O'Higgins 472; tel 441267) is recommended. It has rooms for around $5 and serves good, filling meals. In a similar price range are Residencial Lincoyan (on Lincoyan, north of O'Higgins), and Hostería Milla Rahue (O'Higgins 460; tel 441179). Hostería El Principito (Urrutia and Fresia) has rooms for $10, and the Bavarian-style Hotel Gudenschwager (Valdivia 12) is even more up-market. It charges $15/$25, but has fine views over the lake. A good many private houses along Lincoyan take in guests; try numbers 815, 565, 485, and 445 (tel 441248). This is also a good street for restaurants, e.g. El Refugio at number 348, catering for vegetarians. Also recommended is El Rinconcito on Colo Colo.

Volcán Villarrica. Pucón is the best place from which to reach the Villarrica Volcano, and the national park which surrounds it. The park entrance is 5 miles/8km south of town, and from there it is eight or nine hours walk to the top and back. While you don't have to be a mountaineer to attempt it, experience, a degree of fitness and proper boots are recommended. The climb must be done in a small group, with a guide offering a complete package of transport and use of equipment, including crampons. This should cost $20-30 per person all in: enquire at the tourist office in Pucón or Villarrica.

Lago Caburgua. North from Pucón lies a lovely area of lakes and volcanic hot springs. Lago Caburgua is in a stunning spot, and boasts unusual white sand beaches which make it popular in summer. The lake is accessible by bus from Pucón.

A road connects Villarrica and Pucón to Junín de los Andes over the border in the Argentinian Lake District. The road uses the Tromen pass, which is snowed up for some four months each winter, causing buses to divert via Panguipulli on Lago Pirehueico (see below) and San Martín de los Andes.

LAGOS PANGUIPULLI, PIREHUEICO and RINIHUE

These lakes are dominated by the impressive Choshuenco volcano. Lake Panguipulli is the most accessible, the resort of the same name and Choshuenco being the main settlements. Pirehueico is smaller, but taking the ferry across it to within travelling distance of Argentina is one of the highlights of this area. Riñihue is not connected to the other two by road from Panguipulli or Pirehueico, but you can reach it on foot.

Panguipulli. Despite being a gateway to the remoter areas towards the Argentinian border, Panguipulli is conspicuously quieter and more peaceful than other lakeside towns. It is a pleasant little place with a good black sand beach, which offers everything the others do except waterskiing.

Panguipulli is well served by bus. The main bus station is on Valdivia two blocks from the square, but Tur-Bus (long-distance services) is based under the Hotel Central, and Buses Rurales Andes (for Villarrica) is outside the centre on Freire.

There is a helpful tourist office on Plaza Prat, with good maps and information about the area. Hotels are mostly fairly simple. Among the best are Residencial Centro (Rozas and Freire) and La Bomba (Rozas 450), which charge around $6. The old wooden Hotel Central (Valdivia at Rozas) is slightly more expensive and tends to be noisy. Private houses and some restaurants, such as the Girasol on Rozas, have rooms to let.

Choshuenco. This tiny village is wedged between a rock and the lake, 25 miles/40km southeast of Panguipulli. The journey there is lovely, with the road skirting deserted beaches and offering stunning views. Bus transport and other facilities are limited, but there are a couple of hotels in the village. The area around Choshuenco is ideal hiking and camping country. You can also walk south to Lagos Pirehueico and Riñihue.

Lago Pirehueico. Most Choshuenco buses continue east to Puerto Fuy on Lago Pirehueico. But the scenery between the two villages is superb, and walking the 14 miles/22 miles is strongly recommended. The entire walk takes about five hours, and you can visit the lovely Huilo Huilo waterfall en route; it is clearly signposted a few hundred yards off the road, about $3\frac{1}{2}$ hours from Choshuenco.

From Puerto Fuy a ferry runs (currently three days a week) to Pirehueico at the far southeast end of the lake, near the Argentinian border. From here buses run direct to San Martín de los Andes, although it is also possible to take a bus over the border to Puerto Hua-Hum on Lake Lacár, and then travel to San Martín de los Andes by ferry. The journey across the lakes is spectacular, and even those who are not on their way to or from Argentina are recommended to travel at least some of the distance. Trippers may have to spend the night at Pirehueico, where food and lodging are available in private houses for a few dollars.

Lago Riñihue. From Choshuenco you can walk the 9 miles/15km south to Enco, near the eastern end of Lago Riñihue. This large lake is little visited, making it a haven of peace and quiet even in the height of summer.

From Enco you can walk to a Club Andino refugio on the slopes of Volcán Choshuenco (off the road to Choshuenco village). It is also possible to follow a rough track the 19 miles/30km west to Riñihue, the lake's principal village. It is 24 miles/39km by road east to Los Lagos on the Pan-American Highway, due east of and accessible by bus from Valdivia.

VALDIVIA

Charles Darwin once visited Valdivia. While he was there he experienced some of the minor earth tremors, to which the city is prone. Yet although a quake in 1960 did serious damage to the oldest and weakest buildings, Valdivia is an interesting, historic place.

The city was founded by Pedro de Valdivia in 1552. It is unique among the settlements south of the Río Bío-Bío: it has a long history of occupation. While one town after another in the region was destroyed by the determined Mapuche Indians, Valdivia held on as a colonial outpost. But even this beleaguered town was finally abandoned after a ferocious Mapuche attack in 1598. It was subsequently occupied by pirates, who used the town as a base for their attacks on Spanish ships. Valdivia was refounded in 1645, and was rebuilt as a military base with 12 forts at the mouth of the estuary. Ruins of these defences survive to this day and are among Valdivia's main attractions.

Following the defeat of the Mapuche last century, the population of Valdivia rapidly swelled as waves of immigrants arrived in the area. Its population has now reached 130,000, and is still rising as rural people are forced off the land. The German immigrants of the 19th century have left their mark on both the people and architecture.

Valdivia is the main port on the coast of the Lake District. It lies near the confluence of the Cruces and Calle Calle rivers, which merge to form the Río Valdivia. Linked to the centre by a bridge across the Valdivia is Teja Island.

Arrival and Departure. Valdivia has a single bus station, near the Río Calle Calle at Muñoz and Prat. Buses run frequently to Osorno, Puerto Montt and Panguipulli, and several times a day to Santiago, Temuco, Villarrica, Riñihue and Puerto Varas. Direct services also run to Bariloche and Neuquén in Argentina, and to Punta Arenas (via Argentina).

Valdivia is on a branch line from Antilhue on the main Santiago to Puerto Montt railway line. There is a direct service daily to and from Santiago (16 hours), but to go south you will usually have to change at Antilhue. The railway station is at the far east of town on Ecuador, near the Río Calle Calle. Tickets are also sold at the booking office on the waterfront at O'Higgins and Arauco.

Accommodation. There are few cheap hotels, but in summer these are supplemented by families renting rooms. Best value are Hospedaje Turismo (General Lagos 874; tel 215946) and the friendly hospedaje opposite at 967. In the centre the Violta Fischen (Valdés 373; tel 213206) is comfortable and warm in the winter. There are lots of places on Picarte, near the bus station, but few can be recommended; the private houses in the same area are a better bet.

Eating and Drinking. The market, one block south of the bridge across to Teja

Island, is a good place to eat during the day. Also try the nearby waterfront and the area east towards Plaza de la República. On the square itself try El Conquistador, which has a good café and upstairs restaurant, and the Club de la Unión, with a reasonable set-menu lunch. La Vie Claire is a vegetarian restaurant at Caupolicán 435.

Exploring. The Museo Austral on Teja Island is an excellent museum. It covers the history of the Mapuche Indians and the German settlers that displaced them. It is housed in the mansion of Karl Andwandter, a German colonist and founder of a local brewery. The museum is a few hundred yards south of the bridge from the centre, and opens 10am-1pm and 3-6pm Tuesday to Friday.

The 17th-century forts that ring the estuary can be reached from the small resort of Niebla, accessible in 15 minutes by bus or colectivo from the square beside the market in Valdivia. From Niebla there is a ferry across to the fort of Corral. Otherwise, go on the three-hour boat trip from the harbour in Valdivia: this takes in the forts (known as *fuerte castillos*) of Mancera Island, Niebla, Amargos and Corral. The boats are extremly crowded and military music is played loudly throughout, but it's a good trip nevertheless. Scores of boats are normally scattered around the estuary, each with a motor-driven air pump and a hose leading into the sea: one man stays on board while another looks for shellfish on the seabed.

If you don't want to return to Valdivia, Niebla has several cheap hosterías and a few places to eat along the seafront. You would do better to go to San Carlos, a lovely little place a couple of miles north of Corral, which has a cheap and friendly hostería.

Help and Information. *Tourist Office:* on the waterfront (Avenida Prat) between Libertad and Maipú, facing the Valdivia river.

Communications: the post office is on the west side of the main square. The phone office is near the Río Valdivia at Yungay and Santa Carlos.

Money: cambios, including Turismo Cochrane (Caupolicán 544), offer surprisingly low rates. Sometimes you can do better at Banco Concepción (Picarte 370, near the square). Fincard is at Picarte 324.

OSORNO

This town was founded soon after Valdivia. But unlike its neighbour, Osorno was quickly abandoned and only resettled by German immigrants in the late 19th century. Osorno is today the most German town in Chile.

Most travellers merely pass through Osorno, perhaps staying one night before heading off towards the lakes. Not much of the old architecture survives, but there are some older wooden buildings in the area between the Plaza de Armas and the railway station. The Museo Histórico Nacional (Matta 809) contains relics of the area's Indian and German past, including old photographs. You can also visit the Fuerte Reina Maria Luisa, an 18th-century fort on the banks of the Río Damas west of the railway station.

Arrival and Departure. The main bus station is well east of the centre at Errázuriz 1400. There are services to most destinations between Santiago and Puerto Montt. Some local destinations are served from the old railway station (Estación Viejo), a few minutes walk west of the current station. There are also international buses to Argentina (Bariloche, Mendoza and Buenos Aires).

Osorno is on the Santiago-Puerto Montt railway line. There is a daily *rápido* service to Santiago (20 hours) throughout the year, with extra trains in summer. Puerto Montt (66 miles/105km south) is just a few hours away, but services south may be suspended in winter.

Accommodation and Food. There is a good selection of hotels geared to the summer trade. Near the bus station, try Residencial Ortega (Colón 602) or the hospedaje at Pinto 1758, both charging around $5. Villa Eduvijes (Eduvijes 856; tel 235023) is good but costs over $10. Otherwise, take your pick from the cheap hotels along Errázuriz.

For good, German-style food go to the Peter Kneipe (Rodríguez 1030). More traditional meals are served at the Bahía (Ramírez 1076) and the Club Social Ramírez (Eduvijes 854). The market is near the bus station.

Help and Information. The tourist office is in the government buildings on O'Higgins near Plaza de Armas. In the square itself you'll find the post and telephone offices. There are a couple of places to change money on MacKenna, and a branch of Fincard at 877.

LAGO PUYEHUE

This large lake is skirted to the south by a main road running east into Argentina via Puyehue Pass (generally impassable in winter). It is therefore served by frequent buses from Osorno, Valdivia, etc. Affordable accommodation in this area is limited, but there are campsites along the shores of the lake.

Aguas Calientes lies just off this road, beyond the lake. It is a jumping-off point for the nearby Parque Nacional Puyehue. The Conaf office in the town has maps of the park, and is also a good source of information about the lovely walks through the rainforest and to the waterfalls along the Río Chanleufú. The main access into the park is along a road running southeast from Agua Calientes through 11 miles/18km of lakes and beech forest to Antillanca. There are dramatic views of the surrounding volcanoes. There is no public transport along this road, but it's a lovely walk and you are unlikely to have much problem hitching in the summer. At the foot of Volcán Casablanca the Hostería Antillanca (tel 235114) has good facilities, including a swimming pool, but charges $25.

Another centre for exploring the park is Anticura, along the main eastbound road from Aguas Calientes. There is an information office here, and signposted walks. This is ideal camping territory too, though Anticura Cabañas (tel 236062) rents out two-person cabins for $34. You may be able to get to Anticura by flagging down a bus bound for Argentina; otherwise hitch.

LAGO LLANQUIHUE

This is the largest lake in the region, and ranks third on the continent. The landscapes are magnificent, with the splendid Volcán Osorno to the northeast, Volcán Calbuco to the southwest, and other peaks in the distance. The Pan-American Highway and the main railway line skirt the west side of the lake, and pass the two lakeside settlements of Frutillar and Puerto Varas. Puerto Octay and Ensenada, on the north and southeast shores respectively, are quieter. There are several buses daily to the main towns from Puerto Montt and Osorno, with extra summer services. A road runs right around the lake. The rough road between Puerto Octay and Ensenada gives access to the most unspoilt and some of the most picturesque areas.

Frutillar is the first town you come to as you approach from the north. The centre, a couple of miles from the highway and bus station, is pretty. But it is touristy, boring and rather kitsch. There's no point in hanging around, though there are plenty of hotels along the lakefront street if you need to stay overnight. The other town on the highway, Puerto Varas, is famous for its casino. It is most useful as a centre for changing money, stocking up on information at the tourist office, and catching buses (including east to Petrohué, on Lago Todos Los Santos). There are plenty of cheap hotels near the bus station, the Residencial Unión (San Francisco 669) being the best of them.

Puerto Octay. This small town lies at the far north of the lake. German influence is felt in the extravagant turn-of-century architecture for which Puerto Octay is famous. It is surrounded by magnificent scenery, making it a good place to spend a few days lazing around. Posada Gubernatis (on Santiago) charges $10, and is good value compared to most lakeside hotels. Hotel Centinela is run-down but cheap and popular. It is on the Centinela Peninsula, 3 miles/5km south around the bay from town, where there is a small holiday park and a campsite. There are good views across the lake.

The best trips are southeast along the Ensenada road, served by sporadic buses. Playa Maitén, 6 miles/10km away, is a lovely, quiet beach with a superb view across the lake to Volcán Osorno. Puerto Fonk, 6 miles/10km beyond, is similar but more secluded, with an excellent beach, good camping (take food) and wonderful sunsets. Las Cascadas is a larger village 19 miles/30km southeast of Puerto Octay, with waterfalls close by.

Ensenada. This rather characterless scattering of houses hardly deserves the title of village. The only reason to stop here is to climb Volcán Osorno. Stay at Hostería Ruedas Viejas, about ten minutes walk from the junction with the Petrohué road, with cabins or rooms for $7. The Toqui grocery shop rents out rooms upstairs for $5.

Volcán Osorno. To climb the volcano you need ropes, crampons, ice axes and a good guide: the glacier is riddled with crevasses and has caused many deaths. However, there are a couple of refuges on the slopes that you can hike up to, even if you don't plan to go the whole way: make sure they are open before leaving, and take your own food.

The approach to the volcano is a few miles north of town along the lake. A signposted track leads up the mountain, and after two or three hours climbing you reach the Hostería Las Pumas. Another hour or so's walk up the mountain, and below the snow line, is the Refugio Teski Ski Club, which is open during the winter ski season, and sometimes at other times. The views are magnificent, and worth the sweat and toil to get there.

A paved road from Ensenada follows the Río Petrohué 19 miles/31km southeast down to Ralún, from where you can hike up to Cayutué on Lake Todos Los Santos.

LAGO TODOS LOS SANTOS

Surrounded by snowy mountains, this is often held up as the most beautiful of the lakes. The steep forested hills around the lake are undisturbed by roads, and are likely to remain so as the entire area is contained within the Vicente Pérez Rosales National Park, which stretches to the Argentinian border. The horseflies, which are dreadful in January and February, are one of the few things to disturb the calm. (For some reason the horseflies bother you less if you lie flat or sit in the shade.)

Petrohué. Situated at the far west of the lake, Petrohué is a resort in its own right. It is also the port for the ferry to Peulla, from where you can continue into Argentina. The three-hour boat trip is lovely. It's quite fun to do even if you aren't crossing the border. You can either return the same day or stay over at Peulla. During the summer a tourist boat runs daily to Isla Margarita, a beautiful little island on the lake. If you want to go hiking into the hills you should be able to get maps from the Conaf office. It is in front of the Hotel Petrohué, the only formal lodgings in town and an excellent hotel; it charges $20 a night. For a cheaper option, ask the Küscher family across the river if they have any spare rooms; they will also let you camp. Meals chez the Küschers often consist of delicious fresh trout.

Petrohué is just 9 miles/14km from Ensenada on Lago Llanquihue. There are buses, and it is also a pleasant walk.

Peulla. There's scope to spend a couple of pleasant days in this tiny village, at the opposite end of the lake from Petrohué. Hotel Peulla is overpriced, and the nearby Residencial Palomita is cheaper; otherwise rent a room from a local family, who will throw in meals for the same money.

One short trip is to the lovely Cascada los Novios waterfalls, a steep walk above Hotel Peulla. A rather longer outing is up the road towards the border, which passes close by the extinct three-peaked Volcán Tronador, offering superb views. The lazy option is to take the bus up as far as you want to go, then walk back down.

For a fun trip across into Argentina take a bus or hitch from Peulla over the border at Pérez Rosales Pass to Puerto Frías, on the small Lago Frías. Ferries cross the lake to Puerto Alegre, from where you can take local transport to Puerto Blest, on Lago Nahuel Huapi. A boat runs from here to Puerto Panuelo, which is about an hour's bus ride from Bariloche. Through tickets can be bought between Puerto Montt or Puerto Varas and Bariloche from Andina del Sur, which runs two buses daily in summer. Note that the route may be blocked by snow in winter.

Cayutué. This village on the southern shore is accessible only by the occasional boat, or by an eight-hour walk from Ralún on the Reloncaví estuary (see below). Just south of the village is the little visited Lago Cayutué, set between steep forested slopes. The local people are usually willing to rent out a room, but bring a tent if you've got one.

PUERTO MONTT

Until the arrival of the railway in 1912, Puerto Montt was just a small fishing village inhabited largely by 19th-century German colonists. It has since grown to become capital of the Los Lagos (X) Region, with a population of over 110,000, and perhaps the liveliest town in southern Chile. Although most of the inhabitants have no German roots, a middle European feeling somehow pervades. The unpainted wooden houses have a jaded look, but retain far more charm than the modern buildings that are replacing them. The oldest structure in the city is the cathedral in the Plaza de Armas; it dates from 1865 and is built entirely of wood. A more sobering sight is the mountain of woodchips in the harbour awaiting exportation — a monument to the environmental rape that is going on behind the scenes.

Puerto Montt is a major transport hub, with many travellers passing through en route to Chiloé island and the remote regions in the deep south. It is also an excellent base for exploring the surrounding coastline and fjord-like tidal inlets. In the town itself, the best thing to do is eat and drink and soak up the atmosphere along the seafront. Puerto Montt is an excellent place for buying Mapuche artesanía, especially jumpers, ponchos, hats and gloves: there are lots of stalls along the seafront as you go west towards Angelmó. The municipal museum, next to the bus station, is excellent. It contains fascinating photos of the area and of the damage done by the last big earthquake, and lots of memorabilia from the Pope's visit.

Arrival and Departure. *Air:* LanChile (San Martín 200; tel 253401), Ladeco (Benavente 350; tel 253002) and Saba (Urmeneta 414; tel 258922) operate daily services to Santiago and Punta Arenas.

Bus: from Puerto Montt buses fan out all over the southern Lake District and to more distant destinations, including Santiago (15 hours, $16) and Bariloche in Argentina. Buses to the deep south, including to Punta Arenas (38 hours; $40) go via Argentina; there is no need to change money as the driver arranges meals. If heading south along the Camino Austral, you must rely on local services.

The bus terminal is on the seafront west of the centre, at Portales and Lota; buses run by Varmontt leave from the east end of Varas.

Train: Puerto Montt is the southern terminus of the line from Santiago. In summer there is at least one train a day heading north to the capital; the expreso takes 23 hours ($12), while the rápido takes 19 hours ($14-70).

PUERTO MONTT

1 Bus Station
2 Museum
3 Residencial Embassy

4 Argentinian Consulate
5 Banco de Chile
6 Post Office
7 Cathedral
8 LanChile
9 Ladeco

10 Tourist Office
11 Hotel Montt
12 Hotel Royal
13 Railway Station
14 Traucomontt Tours
15 Varmontt buses

TO CHILOÉ AND NORTH

Ship: the other way to reach the deep south of Chile is by boat, either from Puerto Montt itself, or from the nearby port of Pargua. The three-day journey to Puerto Natales is absolutely beautiful if the weather is good. Otherwise, you are likely to spend most of the time feeling seasick. To get a cabin you need to book well in advance; this can be done in Santiago. Reclining seats are readily available but uncomfortable. Take extra food.

The main ports of call are Chaitén, Puerto Chacabuco (for Coihaique), Puerto Natales. Several companies offer services, Navimag and Transmarchilay are the principal two. Navimag is at Angelmó 2187 (tel 253754) in Puerto Montt, and at Miraflores 178, 12th floor in Santiago (tel 696-3211). Transmarchilay is at Varas 215 (tel 254654), or at Agustínas 1173, oficina 403 in Santiago (tel 335959). Ferry schedules change at short notice throughout the year, and with the recent bankcruptcy of the Empremar line, the situation is even more confused. Services are currently as follows:

Transmarchilay: Puerto Montt — Chaitén ($9), and Pargua — Chaitén — Chacabuco ($9 and $30 respectively), both on Fridays.
Navimag: Puerto Montt — Chacabuco ($30) on Wednesdays and Saturdays, and Puerto Montt — Puerto Natales ($110) once a week (variable).

Usually once a fortnight the Chacabuco service is extended to include a three-day round trip to the Laguna San Rafael glacier ($210 with reclining seat, $110 for deck space with Transmarchilay). See page 447.

Accommodation. The best place to look is on the hill above the bus station, where nearly every other house has a hospedaje sign in the window. Prices range from $5-10. Particularly recommended is the hospedaje at Freire 123 (María Contreras), which is cheap and friendly, has lots of hot water and serves wonderful breakfasts. Also good are Eliana's (Petorca 121; tel 255353), behind the municipal gym, Gallardo 552 (tel 253334), Vial 754 at Balmaceda (tel 257669), Serrano 286 and Balmaceda 300.

The Residenciales Calypso (Urmeneta 127; tel 254544), Embassy (Valdivia 130), and the Hotel Royal (Quillota and Varas) also charge $5-10. Residencial Raúl (Concepción 136) is gloomy but popular among backpackers; it is at least cheap. Hostal Panorama (San Felipe 192; tel 254049) is also full of gringos, has good views, and charges $15. Hotel Montt (Varas and Quillota, tel 253262) is in a similar price range.

Eating and Drinking. Puerto Montt is seemingly dedicated to eating: everywhere, even by the roadsides, there's a pot of something cooking.

If you arrive by bus, there are two very good restaurants above the station. But you would do better to walk east along the seafront to the fishing harbour at Angelmó, where a busy fleet lands mountains of fresh seafood every day. There are many good places as you approach, including the Asturias; and in the market itself there is a chaotic jumble of cheap and good eating places competing for customers. A local and delicious version of *ceviche* (raw fish with lemon juice) is a speciality, but it has lost favour since the cholera scare.

In the evening the restaurants in the centre come to life. The best place is Nettuno (Illapel 129), which is run by an eccentric Italian woman: excellent food and wine are served at good prices. In the railway station La Llave is recommended, and has a good view over the sea. Near the square the Café Real (Rancagua 119) serves snacks throughout the day. The Club Alemán (Varas 264) is a popular place to down a few beers, and has reasonably good food too. Al Passo, at Varas 625, is another busy place — particularly upstairs.

Help & Information. *Tourist Information:* there is a helpful information kiosk in the square opposite the cathedral. Conaf has an office at Ochagavia 464 (tel 254358), northwest of the centre.

Also visit Traucomontt Tours at Egaña 82 (tel 258555), near the railway station. This is an adventure travel agency-cum-bookshop, which is a focal point for travellers to exchange news, tips and recommendations on the South. It can arrange trips and guides, and rents out camping equipment. IGM topographical maps of the region are usually available.

Communications: the post office is at Rancagua 120, a block west of the square. There are phone offices at Chillán 98 and on Pedro Montt near Varas.

Money: rates in Puerto Montt are better than anywhere else in this region. Exchange in Galería Crystal (Varas 595) changes cheques without commission; also try Turismo Latinoamericano (Urmeneta 351), but there are many others. Of the banks, only Banco de Chile (Urmeneta and Rancagua) takes travellers cheques. Fincard is at Varas 575.

Watch out for gypsies who may try smooth-talking you out of some of your recently acquired money.

Argentinian Consulate: Cauquenes 94 and Varas, 2nd floor. Visas are issued 9am-2pm from Monday to Friday.

Bike Hire: mountain bikes can be hired at Schmuck Bicicletas (Urmaneta 885) and at La Casa de la Ciclista at Pedro Montt 129.

Around Puerto Montt

Calbuco. For a look at the coast take a bus or boat to Calbuco, an important centre of the fishing industry, 35 miles/55km southwest of Puerto Montt. Make sure you take the bus marked Costanera, which takes the coastal road rather than the Pan-American Highway. You can also stop off at the small fishing village of Huelmo on the way. Another interesting old town is Maullín, on the estuary of the same name.

The Reloncaví Estuary. This is a more substantial trip, with more to see and do. The main destination on the estuary is Cochamó, reached by a wonderful nine-hour boat trip from the Angelmó jetty. This direct boat service runs according to demand, and you will probably have to stay at least one night in Cochamó before being able to return. There are several cheap places, including Hotel Cochamó, all for about $5.

More frequent boats run to the small settlement of Río Puelo, a six-hour ride from Puerto Montt. From here it is a few miles to Puelo, from where a bus leaves every morning to Cochamó; families rent out rooms to travellers. The final alternative is to go by bus from Puerto Montt via Ensenada and Ralún, a village further north on the estuary; there are several buses daily, operated by Bohle and Río Frío. Most of the shops and restaurants in Ralún seem to offer lodgings.

From Cochamó you can hike up to Cayutué, 30 miles/48km north on Lago Todos Los Santos — a pleasant two-day trip; from Ralún it can be done in just one day.

On the north side of the estuary is the pristine forest of the Alerce Andino national

tel 2239) and the Miranda family (Errázuriz 350; tel 2261) have private rooms to rent.

The best areas for seafood are around the harbour and along Pudeto: El Jardín at number 263 has a good atmosphere and serves excellent food for both lunch and dinner; its mixed barbecues are recommended too.

Castro. Situated on the east coast due south of Ancud, Castro is a friendly fishing port and the island's capital. Although founded in 1567 the town, with its many wooden buildings, feels old rather than historic. The fishermen's houses built on stilts — known as *palafitos* — are a unique architectural feature: they can be seen just north of the centre, and by the bridge over Río Gamboa to the south. The extraordinary cathedral, built of red corrugated iron, dates from 1906. There is an interesting regional museum on Thompson, near the corner of Blanco.

You can climb up to the Mirador La Virgen, above the cemetery, for a good view over the town. Another pleasant walk is to the headland of Puntilla de Ten Ten, about half an hour away opposite the town. In summer, boats run from the town to beaches around the point and across the estuary.

Buses run from Castro all over the island, mostly from the Municipal Terminal on San Martín north of Aldea, which also handles services south to Coihaique and Punta Arenas. Other long-distance buses use the Cruz del Sur terminal behind the cathedral. Colectivos run to local villages from the square and are almost invariably faster and more frequent.

Accommodation: Castro is busy in summer, with lots of rooms for around $5. Near the bus terminal on San Martín, Hospedaje Angie and Residencial Mirasol are both good. The hospedaje at Las Delicias 287 is also particularly recommended. Rooms in private houses are easily available, for example at O'Higgins 446 and Freire 758. There are several campsites by the shore just south of the town.

The best place to eat is in the market, between Blanco and Serrrano, where palafito restaurants specializing in seafood extend over the sea.

Help and Information: most of what you need is in Plaza de Armas: the tourist office (useful maps and leaflets), the post office, and the Banco del Estado. The Pehuen tour company at Thomson 229 is a good place for finding out about trips and renting mountain bikes.

Dalcahue. Don't miss the chance to go the Sunday morning market at Dalcahue, a delightful village 13 miles/21km north of Castro. Buses also run from Ancud. Pensión San Martín is a good place to stay.

Isla de Quinchao. This island, 16 miles/25km long, is linked to Chiloé by a ferry from Dalcahue. Buses run to Achao, a peaceful fishing village halfway down the island. It has an old wooden church and there are good walks along the coast. You can do a round trip to Achao from Castro in a day, but it's worth staying over; the Delicia and Splendid hotels are both good.

Chonchi. This fishing village, 16 miles/25km south of Castro by paved road, is a pleasant place with typical wooden houses. The main reason to stay is in order to leave on a ferry bound for the mainland — though boats are leaving increasingly from Quellón, further south. During the summer, Transmarchilay car ferries go to Chaitén about three times a week (8 hours, $5) and to Puerto Chacabuco twice a week (18 hours). This last trip costs $15 without a seat, $30 for a reclining seat. Stay in a private house or else the cheap Pensión Turismo on Pedro Andrade ($5). Hospedaje Chonchi (O'Higgins 379, $12) is a notch up.

Quellón. The southernmost town on Chiloé, Quellón is small, remote and friendly. It is about two hours by bus from Castro. There are some good beaches nearby, and traditional boat-building goes on around the harbour. You can also catch boats to the mainland: see *Chonchi*. There are several cheap places to stay on the seafront for around $5, such as the Hotel Playa (Montt 255; tel 298) and the Residencial Quellón, further along; both have good restaurants.

Cucao and the Chiloé National Park. This village and park are on the less populated west coast of the island. The park protects an area of untouched temperate rainforest and adjacent coastline. Access to Cucao, 25 miles/40km west of Castro, is by a rough road. In the summer there is an unreliable daily bus from the Municipal Terminal. If you decide to walk, stay overnight at the lakeside village of Huillinco, halfway there. At Cucao, you can sleep in the Hostal Paraíso ($5 a night); otherwise, camp at the Conaf site across the rope-bridge by a small lake.

Although Cucao is beautiful enough for a visit in its own right, with swimming, walks along the beach and horses for hire, the adventurous should head north into the park. There are two refugios, but take your own bedding and food; your supplies of the latter can usually be supplemented along the way by what you can buy from the Mapuche families that visit the park to gather kelp (seaweed) in the summer. The first day's walk along the beach and across a number of rocky points is gruelling, especially on a hot day when the horseflies are active; but from then on it is extremely beautiful, with many flocks of parrots in the forests. Get details and a basic map from Conaf, who run a reception centre and museum in Cucao.

THE CAMINO AUSTRAL

The district south of Puerto Montt is depicted as a remote region that is perpetually cold, wet, wild and windy. But the summer season, while short, is often dry and sunny. And at any time the landscapes are rarely anything but magnificent. This southerly area takes up a third of the country, but contains just a thirtieth of its population. The northern part is inhabited as far down as Villa O'Higgins. There follows an impenetrable icefield which stretches some 250 miles/400km, down to Puerto Natales. This town can be reached by land only via Argentina.

The northern region is connected to the outside world by the Carretera Austral Presidente Pinochet, officially opened in 1988. *Carretera* means highway, and is a grand name for what is at best a two-lane dirt track. It is more commonly, and more realistically, referred to as the Camino Austral. The unsurfaced road reaches as far as Cochrane, and a further stretch to Puerto Yungay is under construction. Just keeping the road open involves constant work, and stoppages are frequent. The fast-growing vegetation, and other disturbances such as floods, also help to disrupt vehicles. And though the road penetrates ever southwards, public transport doesn't keep up with the progress. Most people get around on horseback. However you choose to travel, be flexible.

Although most settlements are inland, some towns can be reached from the north by boat. The sea route is a most spectacular way to reach Chilean Patagonia and Tierra del Fuego: ships pass through narrow channels between islands of sheer rock, glaciers and Norwegian-style fjords. While travelling by sea helps you avoid some of the uncertainties of going overland, bad weather is not uncommon: this can either make you very sick or simply obscure the views.

PUERTO MONTT TO COIHAIQUE

The first section of the route, from Puerto Montt to Chaitén, involves two ferries. The best option is to take the twice-daily direct bus to Hornopirén, the port for the second ferry.

The first ferry is from Las Arenas on the Reloncaví estuary, about an hour from Puerto Montt, to Puelche; there are five sailings daily in the summer and three in winter, taking about half an hour. The second, from Hornopirén to Caleta Gonzalo, crosses daily in January and February; during the rest of the summer it may run every other day if you're lucky, and in winter may stop altogether. However frequent, the boat leaves Hornopirén at 3pm and returns at 10am; the journey takes five hours. You can check the schedule with Transmarchilay in Puerto Montt (see page 439), but don't rely on the information. If stuck on either side you can at least gorge yourself on wonderful river fish.

There is no accommodation in Caleta Gonzalo, and no onward transport to Chaitén. If you are on foot, try to arrange a lift onwards to Chaitén (54 miles/86km south) before getting on the ferry; hitchhikers travel free. If you need to spend the night at Hornopirén, stay at the excellent Hostería Hornopirén ($7), or at the Hotel Perlas de Reloncaví or Holiday Country nearby; both charge around $10.

Chaitén. While the most important place for several hundred miles in any direction, Chaitén is no great shakes. It boasts a population of just 2,500 people and is the site of a military camp. There is a helpful tourist office in the Centro Comercial on the seafront (O'Higgins). The only bank does not change money, so come well prepared.

The port, the only real reason for Chaitén's existence, is a ten-minute walk north of town. Ferries, which run to Puerto Montt (12 hours) and Chiloé (6 hours), are geared mainly for cars. Foot passengers have to wait until the day of departure to buy a ticket, but people are rarely turned away. The alternative is to hitch a ride from a vehicle going on board and travel free.

If you are northward bound and can't get a lift (traffic is generally thin), it is possible to fly out. The local airline ASA has recently gone bust, but Don Carlos and San Rafael Airlines have daily flights to and from Puerto Montt in high season.

Accommodation: the tourist population varies with the phases of the ferries, so the hotels may all be full, or empty, depending on your luck. The best hotel is Residencial Astoria (O'Higgins 442; tel 263), which charges $6. Most other hotels, several of which are also along the seafront, are in the $10-20 range. You would do better with a family or, even better, to go 6 miles/10km north of Chaitén to Playa Santa Barbara. This is a most beautiful deserted beach backed by temperate rainforest. In summer you sometimes see dolphins. There is a grassy knoll and a river for fresh water, making it perfect for camping.

Tourist buses, operated by Aerobus and Artetur, travel the 272-mile/435km stretch between Chaitén and Coihaique: six times a week in summer, four times in winter. Some winter buses may terminate at La Junta, just 94 miles/150km away. The fare for the 12-hour journey to Coihaique is dear, at about $30, so it is worth checking out the local buses, though these leave infrequently. If you stop off en route you should be able to pick up a passing bus; and the local people are happy to give hitch-hikers a lift, although there isn't much traffic.

There are numerous places where you can stop and camp. Just 20 miles/32km south of Chaitén, for example, is Amarillo, with thermal springs, a hotel and a campsite.

Puerto Cárdenas. This minute village lies on the northern shores of Lago Yelcho, about 30 miles/48km south of Chaitén. It is a good base for some lovely walks around the lake and there are a couple of residenciales. About 10 miles/16km south, off the highway on the west side of the lake, is a Conaf campsite, about two hours walk from a glacier.

Futaleufú. Lying 19 miles/31km south of Puerto Cárdenas, Villa Santa Lucía is a starting-point for travellers heading east to Argentina. Beside the village is a cavalry outpost. It is worth staying overnight in order to see the daily herding of over a hundred horses in the morning.

The road to the border (50 miles/80km) passes through several villages with basic lodgings. Futaleufú, 30 minutes by bus from the frontier, is the best place to stay. There are a few simple places in the village, but for a better chance to enjoy the scenery, rent a cabin by Lake Espolón. This beautiful lake is north of the road, 4 miles/6km before Futaleufú.

The town is served by only a couple of buses a week from Chaitén, and they take the best part of a day. The bus service on to the border (6 miles/10km from Futaleufú) and to Esquel in Chile runs only twice a week too. But hitching is not difficult in summer, or else you can walk to the border. A new bridge over the river makes the crossing easy, and buses from the other side run to Trevelín and Esquel.

La Junta. In winter La Junta, 100 miles/160km south of Chaitén, is the end of the road for some buses. Even if you're not forced to stop, it's worth staying here to walk to the lovely Lago Rosselot, 6 miles/10km east. There are several hosterías in town. Better still, ask the woman who owns the Café Jumblath if her cottage is available for rent: to stay in this gingerbread-style abode you must pay about $6 per person.

Between La Junta and Coihaique you pass through lovely scenery, with several lakes along the road. All have campsites.

Puerto Puyuguapi. Some 74 miles/118km south of Villa Santa Lucía is Puerto Puyuguapi, which lies at the end of a deep sea channel. It is a base from which to explore the Queulat National Park. There are several cheapish hotels, Señora Fuentes' Pensión (Llantureo and Circunvalación) being the best value.

Parque Nacional Quelat contains an impressive glacier called the Ventisquero Colgante. Take advantage of the campsite, from which there are wonderful views on a clear day. The entrance to the park is 15 miles/24km south of Puyuguapi. You have to walk only a short distance east of the highway, past the house of the park ranger (a very helpful man), for your first glimpse of the glacier.

Boats sometimes run south from Puerto Puyuguapi to Puerto Cisnes, a lovely trip along the Cisnes river. There are direct buses more or less daily from Puerto Cisnes to Coihaique; the road from the coast joins the highway 37 miles/59km south of Puyuguapi. Just after this junction is the Piedra del Gato, a narrow gorge of steep cliffs and raging rivers: a truly awesome sight.

COIHAIQUE

Situated in a wide valley, Coihaique is the capital of the Aisén (XI) Region and a military base. It is also a starting-point for hikes into the surrounding mountains, and gives access to the Argentinian border. The resident population of 40,000 grows each summer, when the local people open up their houses to satisfy the demand for lodgings.

Travel agents in town run day trips to the lakes and glaciers around Coihaique, including to the Toro and Bonito lakes, in the Monumento Natural Dos Lagunas, 12 miles/20km east. Scope for independent exploration from Coihaique is limited, but you can walk to a forest reserve, several hours to the north.

Arrival and Departure. *Bus:* the bus station is at Lautaro and Magellanes, with services west to Puerto Aisén and Puerto Chacabuco (the nearest port for boats along the coast); north to Chaitén (in winter you may have to change at La Junta); and south to Puerto Ibañez and Cochrane.

The principal route into Argentina is to Comodoro Rivadavia, via Río Mayo. Buses Giobbi (Bolivar 194 and Barroso; tel 222067) does the 12-hour run three days a week ($25). Details of the route through Chile Chico are given below.

Air: Coihaique is well served by air, through the nearby airport at Balmaceda. Ladeco (General Parra 215, near the square; tel 221188) has daily flights to Santiago, stopping at Puerto Montt, Osorno and Valdivia. LanChile (Gral Parra and 21 de Mayo) also flies daily to Santiago, stopping at Puerto Montt and Concepción. Smaller operators fly to Puerto Montt, Chile Chico and Cochrane; the tourist office has a list of the latest schedules.

Accommodation and Food. The pick of the cheaper ($5/$10) hotels are Hospedaje Gúzman (Baquedano 20; tel 222520), Residencial Puerto Varas (Serrano 168; tel 221212) and Residencial Carrera (12 de Octubre 520). There is also plenty of family accommodation around. Look in the windows along Simpson, a block south of Lautaro: number 647 offers cheap and friendly bed and breakfast, with lots of hot water.

The main concentration of restaurants is along Prat: the Samoa (653) and Kalu (402) are recommended. Steaks are excellent and parrillas are cheap. Locals arrive late in the evening; you will often be treated to some good singing by whoever picks up the guitar.

Help and Information. *Tourist Information:* Cochrane 320, near Bilbao. You can also get good maps from the Dirección de Vialidad on Plaza de Armas. Conaf has an office at Ogana 1060 (tel 21065).

Communications: the post office is at Cochrane 202, near the square. The telephone office is at Barroso 626 and Bolívar.

Money: there is a good cambio at Prat 340 (office 208), or try a travel agent, such as Turismo Prado (21 de Mayo 417). Fincard is also at Prat 340.

PUERTO AISEN (and Puerto Chacabuco)

Once the major port for the region, Puerto Aisén is now silted up and has been superseded by Puerto Chacabuco. Over 13,000 people still live here, however, and it's a pleasant enough place, lying at the confluence of the Palos and Aisén rivers.

Puerto Chacabuco is a drab little port at the bottom of a fjord, and there is no reason to hang around there longer than you have to. The tourist office in Puerto Aisén's Municipalidad (Prat and Aldea) is open only in summer, and the cambio on the square takes only cash.

Arrival and Departure. Puerto Aisén is connected to Puerto Chacabuco (9 miles/15km west) by a paved road served by frequent buses. There is regular transport direct to Coihaique from both towns, including special buses that meet ferries. There are over ten buses a day between Puerto Aisén and Coihaique, 36 miles/57km east. The journey through the Simpson valley is fabulous, with the road running along a narrow, precipitous gorge with numerous waterfalls, before passing through a tunnel into the Coihaique valley.

From Puerto Chacabuco, Transmarchilay (O'Higgins, Puerto Chacabuco; tel 144) runs a boat to Pargua (for Puerto Montt), and to Chonchi/Quellón on Chiloé island (summer only). Navimag (Aldea 398, Puerto Aisen; tel 332699) has a service to Puerto Montt. Boats to the Laguna San Rafael glacier (see below) also call at Puerto Chacabuco.

Accommodation. Most cheap hotels in Puerto Aisén are along Aldea, including the Yaney Ruca (369), El Fogón (355) and the Marina (382); also try Residencial Nene (Serrano 57; tel 332725). The Café Rucuray, on the square, is a useful meeting place, and it displays details of boats.

LAGUNA SAN RAFAEL

This lake is about 100 miles/160km south of Puerto Chacabuco. It is dominated by the San Rafael glacier, which flows right down to the sea where it calves small icebergs. The glacier is 45 miles/70km long, and is a most spectacular sight. It is the star attraction of the huge Laguna San Rafael National Park, where three other glaciers flow down Monte San Valentín. A visit to the park is a once-in-a-lifetime experience, and you may be able to see dolphins, sealions, sea otters, foxes and all kinds of birds. Conaf runs a small hostería in the park, but you need to bring all your own supplies for the week between boats, and plenty of warm clothing.

The glacier can only be reached by air or boat. In summer Transmarchilay and Navimag both run boats from Puerto Montt to the glacier, calling at Puerto Chacabuco; the three-day round trip costs around $100, more if you want a bed.

From Coihaique the Camino Austral runs through magnificent mountainous landscapes south to Cochrane. While the scenery can be appreciated through a bus window, villages with residenciales at strategic points en route make it possible to stop off, particularly around Lago Carrera.

The road to Villa Cerro Castillo, 65 miles/104km south of Coihaique, is particularly dramatic, as you travel from lush, green landscapes to dry, rocky semi-desert. Just before you reach Cerro Castillo, a road spurs off southeast along a fjord-like extension of Lago Carrera to Puerto Ibáñez.

LAGO GENERAL CARRERA

This lake is invisibly split in two by the Chile-Argentina border; on the Argentinian side it is known as Lago Buenos Aires. The main bulk of the Andes is to the west where, in the middle of wild and inaccessible mountainous terrain, Volcán Hudson has become the most active volcano on the continent. Its eruption in 1991 affected the area badly, and many local people were forced from their homes.

The dramatic scenery around the lake is wonderful, but difficult to explore. By taking the route into Argentina via Chile Chico, on the lake's southern shore, you can at least get a taste of it.

Puerto Ibáñez. This is little more than an overnight stopping place. There are several residenciales: the Ibáñez and the Monica, next door to each other on Bertrán Dixon, are the best. Transmarchilay operates a ferry to Chile Chico, two hours away across the lake. It currently leaves early in the morning two or three days a week; check the schedule at a Transmarchilay office before you arrive.

Buses run direct to Puerto Ibáñez several times a week from Coihaique (84 miles/135km away), which arrive the evening before the ferry departs. Colectivos do the journey too, leaving from Prat and Bilbao near Coihaique's main square.

Chile Chico. This town is known as 'Little Chile' since the area's climate resembles that of the Central Valley near Santiago. The region enjoys some 300 sunny days a year, and far higher temperatures than anywhere else in southern Chile. The immigrants who founded Chile Chico in 1928 had grandiose ideas about the future of their colony. But though the climate is ideal for growing fruit, there are few markets for the produce. This has led to a dramatic depopulation — from around 6,000 inhabitants in the 60s to around 2,000 today. Tourism, and catering for people travelling between Chile and Argentina, is increasingly important to the local economy. In August 1991 the town was downwind of the eruption of Volcán Hudson. Large amounts of ash landed on the town, collecting in drifts up to a metre deep.

There are good walks in the mountains south of Chile Chico, but don't set off without a decent map. Enquire at the tourist office at O'Higgins and Gana, both about maps and tours. There is a museum of local Indian remains in the same building. Options for changing money are limited; try the Café Elizabeth y Loly in the square.

Arrival and Departure: in addition to the ferry, Chile Chico is also accessible from Coihaique by light aircraft. A road to link Chile Chico and El Maitén on the Camino Austral, at the southwest end of the lake, is under construction too.

The Argentinian border town of Los Antiguos is just 6 miles/9km east of Chile Chico, on the far side of the wide Río Jeinement. You can usually arrange a lift across the river in a jeep for a few dollars. There are direct buses from Los Antiguos to the nearby town of Perito Moreno, for onward connections.

Accommodation: Residenciales Aguas Azules (Rodríguez 252) and Nacional (Freire and O'Higgins) are recommended. So too is the Casa Quinta, in a smallholding on the road to Argentina. Private rooms for rent are also available: try O'Higgins 332 and 43.

Back on the Camino Austral, Villa Cerro Castillo is a small village in a narrow gorge. If you need to make an overnight stop, you can stay in the Residencial El Viajero, on the main road.

South of here the road makes a spectacular crossing over the Río Ibáñez, and cuts through forest and more superb scenery to Puerto Murta, 40 miles/64km away. This one-horse town by the shores of the lake is delightful. It has a couple of hotels. A further 20 miles/32km south is Puerto Río Tranquilo, also on the lake.

The local attraction is the Catedral de Marmol, a peninsula of marble riddled with caves. You can hire a boat from Tranquilo to visit them, about an hour's rowing each way. There is also a fantastic walk through forests of fuschias and magnificent trees up to Lago Tranquilo, 8 miles/12km west. You can camp by the lake; otherwise stay at the Residencial Los Pinos back in the village.

Another 31 miles/50km almost due south is El Maitén, where a track heads east to Puerto Guadal, and beyond to Chile Chico; it is passable in a four-wheel drive vehicle, but there is no public transport.

COCHRANE

This small town of 1,500 people lies in a sheltered valley 213 miles/341km south of Coihaique. Staying in Cochrane for a few days is strongly recommended, if only to take yourself back in time for a while. The atmosphere is magical, and there are horses everywhere. Check out the rodeo just outside the town.

The Conaf office in the square can give directions for the nearby Reserva Nacional Tamango, which has much interesting wildlife. The reserve encompasses pampa and forest and extends down to Lago Cochrane, 3 miles/5km east of town. It is possible to go on boat trips along the Río Baker, but these must usually be booked in advance, at Sice Travel in Coihaique (tel 223466). Hostería Wellman can arrange horses for trips into the mountains.

The Pudu bus company runs daily buses between Cochrane and Coihaique (11 hours); northbound services leave at around 9am. Cochrane is a centre from which light aircraft fly out to otherwise inaccessible regions. The local airline, Don Carlos, is based in the Residencial Sur Austral (on Prat; tel 150), which is among the cheapest places to stay. Best value of all is La Tranquera (Avenida San Valentín 651), with mediocre beds, but great showers. For $10 or more you can stay at Hostería Wellman (Las Golondrinas 36; tel 171). The tiny Café Sota de Oro on Teniente Merino is a good meeting place — watch for the bar with the most horses outside. Inside, women usually have the choice of sitting in a separate dining room.

MAGALLANES

This remote region at the south tip of the South American continent includes Chilean Patagonia and Tierra del Fuego. It is named after the Portuguese seafaring explorer Fernão de Magalhães (Magallanes in Spanish, Magellan in English). In 1520 he was the first European to enter the region and find a sea-route through the maze of islands and channels. He named the island to the south of his route Tierra del Humo (land of smoke) because of the Indians' smoking fires. The territory was renamed as Tierra del Fuego (land of fire) by the Spanish monarch, Charles V.

All the Indian tribes encountered by Charles Darwin and others, are extinct. The last members of the Yaganes tribe died only recently. One of the few reminders of the area's early inhabitants is the name of the southern mainland regions of Argentina and Chile: Patagonia, which translates as 'big-foot-land', is a reference to the Indians' feet which appeared abnormally large thanks to a thick covering of animal skins.

Patagonia is not a precise geographical term, being neither province nor country. Originally it was applied only to Argentina, but it is now used also in a Chilean context. It normally refers to the area which can only be reached from Argentina — i.e. from Cochrane down to Tierra del Fuego — most of which consists of icefields anyway.

A look at a map of the region shows that Magellan was extremely fortunate not to have got stuck up a frozen fjord in the middle of nowhere. The route he discovered — the Straits of Magellan — soon became a major shipping channel. Several ports, including Punta Arenas, grew up in the 19th and early 20th centuries to service the considerable and diverse shipping that passed through. In 1914 the opening of the Panama Canal reduced sharply this traffic. Sheep raising became an important source of income, but since 1945, oil has been the mainstay of the economy.

The climate is merciless: cold, strong winds are common, especially in the spring months of October and November, summers are wet, and snow is persistent through the winter. The scenery is as wild and magnificent as the climate is harsh. Huge areas are protected within national parks which encompass hundreds of inaccessible islands and thousands of square miles of ice fields and glaciers. The most visited park is Torres del Paine, north of Puerto Natales.

There are several ways of reaching Magallanes: by land via Río Gallegos in Argentina, from where roads fan out to Puerto Natales, Punta Arenas and Tierra del Fuego; by boat from Puerto Montt; and by regular air services to Punta Arenas, Porvenir or Puerto Williams, or to Ushuaia in Argentina.

PUERTO NATALES

This is the northernmost city in the region. It was founded in 1911 as a port for the trade with Puerto Montt. Even now, Puerto Natales' population is only a little over 15,000. The town overlooks the magnificent Seno Ultima Esperanza, or Last Hope Sound. Glaciers and stunning birdlife are visible from the shore. Other treats are in store for anyone who takes the boat to or from Puerto Montt, including whales, sea lion colonies, and remote Patagonian communities.

Arrival and Departure. The bus companies operate from their own stops. The four-hour journey to Punta Arenas is made several times daily by Buses Fernández (Eberhard 555; just east of the square) and Buses Sur (Baquedano 534 and O'Higgins). Three companies around Baquedano and Valdivia have services to Río Turbio, across the border in Argentina, some of which go on to Río Gallegos. Buses Victoria Sur, which serves many destinations in the south, is on the seafront opposite the port at Pedro Montt and Bulnes.

Navimag operates a boat three times a month between Puerto Natales and Puerto Montt, 915 miles/1,460km north; their office is at the port (Pedro Montt 380 and Bulnes; tel 411642, 411287). Seats are booked up well in advance.

There are no scheduled air services from Puerto Natales; the nearest airport is at Punta Arenas.

Accommodation and Food. There are plenty of cheap places along Bulnes, including Residencial Dickson at 307 (tel 411218) and the Grey at 90; the best value is the Temuco (Ramírez 202 and Bulnes; tel 411120) at $4. Señora Teresa at Esmeralda 463 rents out rooms very cheaply, serves great food and is a mine of information on the area and Torres del Paine.

Restaurant Midas on the square is deservedly popular, as is the Café Tranquera (Bulnes 579).

Help and Information. The tourist office is on the waterfront at the bottom of Phillipi. Conaf has an office near the corner of Blanco Encalada and O'Higgins. There are several cambios on Blanco Encalada and on Bulnes; the one at Encalada

226 converts US$ cheques to US$ cash. Cambio Stop at Baquedano 380 doubles as a tour agent.

The post and telephone offices are both in the square.

Around Puerto Natales

Cueva Milodon. This cave is famous for the remains of an extinct giant ground sloth, Milodon, found there in 1895. The cavern is 200m deep and dwarfs the life-size plastic model of the animal. The site is a National Monument and is Puerto Natales' equivalent of the Eiffel Tower: you see miniature models of the sloth all around the town. Other caves nearby contain the remains of 5,000 year-old human habitation.

Lying 13 miles/20km northwest of Puerto Natales, the caves can be reached on the rudimentary bus service operated by Buses Fernández.

Parque Nacional O'Higgins. This enormous national park links up with the Laguna San Rafael park near Cochrane. Tours are available to look at the Balmaceda and Serrano glaciers, which are some 30 miles/50km away by boat from Puerto Natales. The views of the glaciers as they enter the sea are magnificent. The ship 21 de Mayo makes the round-trip daily in summer, leaving at 8.30am. The office is at Ladrilleros 171 (tel 411176); most travel agents sell tickets, currently around $25.

TORRES DEL PAINE NATIONAL PARK

This magnificent park contains vividly coloured lakes, glaciers, and the incomparable Torres del Paine cordillera, whose highest peak, Cerro Paine Grande, reaches over 7,870ft/2,470m. These mountains of granite rise almost vertically from the dry plain, and green valleys nestle amid the peaks, irrigated by the meltwaters. The wildlife is rich and varied: with over 100 species of bird, including condors, black-necked swans, rhea and pink flamingoes, and 25 species of mammal: including puma, skunk, guanaco, foxes and *huemul* (a Chilean deer). The range of spectacular scenery and the chance to creep up on and observe many animals and birds make Torres del Paine one of the highlights of Chile. The hikes rank among the best anywhere in the world, alongside those of Tibet and Nepal.

There are several ways to visit the park: expensively, on a tour; independently, but relying on hotels and refugios; or independently with a tent and everything you will need to disappear into the wilderness for a week or two. The park includes over 150 miles/240km of trails. There is no shortage of dirt roads either, which are little used and perfect for mountain bikes. You can also hire horses from estancias. In summer sunbathing is fun, though not particularly recommended given the depletion of the ozone layer — see below; and watch out for inquisitive condors who are wondering whether you're alive or a legitimate meal.

It is possible to arrange a boat trip to view Glaciar Grey, which regularly calves icebergs into the lake. This last trip requires a group of eight people, though it is also possible to walk to a good vantage point for views of the glacier and lake. Wherever you are, be extremely careful when walking in glacier areas or on high peaks in windy or otherwise dangerous conditions. Accidents are common, and there are fatalities most years.

Don't leave Puerto Natales without visiting Conaf. People both here and in the park are a mine of information. They can give good advice as to the average time required for the various hikes, and also about refugios and campsites. Detailed contoured maps are available and a book called *Conociendo Torres del Paine* is worth getting too.

Arrival and Departure. There are four entrances to the park. The main one is about 80 miles/128km from Puerto Natales, on the best road, which runs along the north side of Lago Sarmiento. The Conaf office is 18 miles/28km beyond the park entrance. From here a road runs 11 miles/18km northwest to Lago Grey. A less-used road runs south of Lago Sarmiento.

Numerous companies run buses in summer to the Conaf office, leaving at 6am and arriving back in Puerto Natales in the afternoon. The journey takes about four hours. Winter services are erratic and cannot be relied upon. A small set-up called Ark Patagonia is recommended: its minibuses are driven by well-informed drivers.

Accommodation. There are two hotels in the park. Posada Río Serrano is a couple of miles south of the Conaf office (tel 223395, $20). Hostería Pehoe (tel 224223, $40) is 6 miles/10km north, off the Puerto Natales road. It is on an island in Lago Pehoe, with superb views to the peaks of Cuernos del Paine. For budget travellers the refugios are a better bet, but don't expect luxury — take your own food, groundsheet and sleeping bag. You may have to pay a few dollars, or nothing at all.

If you take a tent, you must camp only in designated areas. There is a high fire risk in summer — 60,000 hectares were destroyed in 1987 because some overconscientious campers decided to burn their loo paper.

PUNTA ARENAS

The capital of Magallanes (XII) Region, Punta Arenas is the most southerly city in Chile. It was founded in 1848 as a strategic centre for shipping through the straits, and this generated the wealth for the palatial mansions and public buildings. The shipping barons later diversified into sheep grazing, but the discovery of oil in 1945 brought a new industry which rapidly eclipsed the old. Oil money has changed Punta Arenas beyond recognition. But while some of the traditional wooden buildings have been replaced by concrete, the past lives on. There are still fine examples of the old architecture.

There is a large contingent from the Balkans in Punta Arenas, accounting for about a third of the 115,000 population. Lupins and wind are two other features characteristic of Punta Arenas. The wind can be so strong that it blows people over. Much more alarming are the effects of ozone depletion. Punta Arenas lies at the edge of the Antarctic ozone hole — the world's worst. Hunters are finding an increasing number of blind rabbits in the area, and guanacos are giving birth three months later than usual — both results, scientists say, of the lack of protection against harmful ultraviolet rays from the sun. Humans are slower to show the effects, though over-exposure can cause skin cancer and cataracts.

Arrival and Departure. *Bus:* Punta Arenas has no central bus station, with each company operating from its own office. The most common land route to Punta Arenas is via Río Gallegos in Argentina, about six hours away; this route is covered by Río Gallegos (Navarro 971), El Pingüino (Navarro 549) and Viajes Vera (21 de Mayo and Boliviana). Buses Sur (Menéndez 565), Norte (Gamero 1039) and Turibus (Menéndez 647) also run to Río Gallegos, and beyond to Puerto Montt and Santiago. Buses Sur and Fernández (Chiloé 930) also have several buses daily to Puerto Natales, four hours northwest.

Boat: a ferry crosses the Magellan Straits to Porvenir on Tierra del Fuego several times a week, weather permitting. The boats use Puerto Trente, some 3 miles/5km north of Punta Arenas, served by colectivo and the Tres Puentes bus. The three-hour journey is fun, with dolphins often following the boat.

For information about government supply ships to Puerto Williams (Tierra del Fuego) or Antarctica (see page 455) enquire at Navarro 1150 or at the tourist office. The 17-hour journey to Puerto Williams provides a unique opportunity to travel the narrow Beagle Channel, past beech forest, icebergs, glaciers and the peaks of the Darwin mountains.

Air: LanChile (Pedro Montt and Navarro; tel 223338), Ladeco (Roca 924 and Navarro; tel 226100) and Saba (Pedro Montt 957; tel 222381) have flights several times a week to Puerto Montt and Santiago for $150-200. Local airlines Aerovías DAP (Pinto 1022; tel 223958) and Cabo de Hornos (Montt 687; tel 223335) run flights daily to Porvenir and weekly to Puerto Williams. DAP also offers a fortnightly service to Puerto Argentino (Stanley) on the Falklands/Malvinas, as well as sightseeing flights over the mountains and glaciers. The Chilean Navy flies a supply plane once or twice a week to Puerto Williams and sometimes takes passengers. However, you may have to wait around for a couple of weeks.

The airlines all have their own bus service to the airport, 13 miles/20km out of town; otherwise, get a colectivo from Magallanes and Colón.

Accommodation. Punta Arenas is not a cheap place, but there are a few residenciales. Among the best are Nena's (Boliviana 366) and the Internacional (Arauco 1514 and Boliviana; tel 223677). Others include Roca (Roca 1038 and Korner; tel 223803) and Monte Carlo (Colón 605 and Chiloé; tel 223448), which are all good and charge around $15. For private lodgings try Boliviana 375 or Paraguaya 150, or ask at the tourist office.

Eating and Drinking. The seafood in Punta Arenas is so plentiful and delicious that it is easy to gorge yourself on the stuff. The best place for fish is at the docks at the end of Avenida Independencia, where numerous stalls compete for business. The Trovador (Pedro Montt 919 and Navarro) is lively and inexpensive, with music at weekends. The trendiest place in town is El Garage (Pedro Montt 988), which is expensive but serves exquisite fish: try *congrio a lo pobre*. The Monaco (Bories and Menéndez) and Don Quixote (Navarro 1087) cafés serve good snacks and light meals.

Exploring. To step back in time stroll along Bories, the main street, or explore the extravagant cemetery nine blocks north of Plaza de Armas. The greatest relics left by the wealthy shipping families are the Palacio Sara Braun, in the square and now the Club de la Unión, and the Palacio Mauricio Braun, a block north of the square on 21 de Mayo. The latter, built in 1906, is now the Museo Braun Menéndez, which preserves the palace and its opulent contents, which were imported from Europe. It opens 11am-4pm Tuesday to Friday and 11am-1pm on Sunday. Also in the Plaza de Armas is a lovely old cinema with an Art Nouveau style interior.

The Museo Regional Salesiano is by the church at Bories and Sarmiento, six blocks north of the square. Set up by missionaires, this is a completely bizarre place. It contains a fascinating collection of natural history, including stuffed birds that look like *Thunderbirds* puppets and a lamb with two heads. The displays relating to the extinct indigenous peoples are interesting but indicative of the patronizing attitude of the missionaries. The museum opens 10am-1pm and 3-6pm daily except Monday (but on weekday afternoons only in winter).

The Instituto de la Patagonia (Avenida España and Los Flamencos) is well worth a visit. It is a little way north of the centre on the main road out of town. It is full of relics of the early colonists, with a good collection of stereoscopic slides, including early 20th-century pictures of Indian communities. There is also a good selection of antique agricultural machinery. It opens 8.30am-12.30pm, 2.30-6.30pm Monday to Friday, and Saturday mornings only. To get there, take any colectivo heading north along Magallanes.

Help and Information. *Tourist information:* there is a kiosk in the central reservation of Colón near Bories, which is a good source of information about boats to Antarctica, etc. The main Sernatur office is at Waldo Sequel 689 (tel 224435), near the square. Conaf has an office at Menéndez 1147, between Montt and Quillota (tel 227845).

Communications: the post office is at Bories 2, and the telephone office at Nogueira 1116 and Fagnano, in the square. You can send faxes from here.

Money: there are several cambios, including Andino (Roca 886, office 25), Gasic (Navarro 549) and Taurus (21 de Mayo 1502; Navarro 1001). Fincard is at Pedro Montt 849.

Consulates: Argentina — 21 de Mayo 1878. UK Honorary Consul (William Matheson) — Lautaro Navarro 398, Casilla 327 (tel 248001 or 224275).

Around Punta Arenas

To reach most places of interest on the Brunswick Peninsula around Punta Arenas, including a couple of nature reserves, you must either go on an organized tour or rent a car. Hertz has an agent at Lautaro Navarro 1064 (tel 22013), and there are also local rental firms.

Fuerte Bulnes. This fort was built on a rocky promontory in 1843 to check growing British sea power in the Magellan Straits. It lies 36 miles/57km south of Punta Arenas, and has now been restored and accorded the dignity of a national monument. Restaurant Trovador in Puntas Arenas offers daily trips, but there is also a local bus service.

A couple of miles north of Bulnes is Puerto de Hambre, a fishing village, which dates back to 1584 and has a tragic history. After its foundation by conquistador Pedro de Gamboa, the next visitor was the English buccaneer Thomas Cavendish. He found that the entire population, excepting one man who hung from the gallows in the square, had starved to death: hence the village's name, Port of Hunger.

A few miles south along the coast from the fort is the mouth of the Río San Juan, the burial place of Pringles Stokes, captain of the *Beagle*. The road peters out but you can walk along the coast to the tip of the Brunswick Peninsula — the most southerly point of the American mainland; allow a couple of days each way, and go fully prepared to camp.

Penguin Colony. See penguins in their natural state at the colony 38 miles/60km north of Punta Arenas. The birds come ashore between September and March, and live in burrows in the sand, into which they disappear in windy weather. Although generally friendly, penguins can give a nasty nip if provoked (which they are regularly).

CHILEAN ANTARCTICA

The South Pole is a couple of thousand miles away, but you can reach Chilean Antarctica from Punta Arenas. You can get there either with the Chilean Navy or on a private cargo boat. The first option will cost you at least $1800: ask at the Armada office at Navarro 1150, or go to the port and ask the captain directly. You may be able to pay less if you take your own food. The trip on a private tug boat, on the other hand, may set you only back $600: including food, drink and sleeping space in a cargo container (more comfortable than it sounds). Word gets around town if there is a boat about to leave, but also ask at the tourist office.

The journey lasts 14-20 days and is a mind-blowing experience. The scenery, initially of Tierra del Fuego and then of deep blue waters, icebergs and birds, is utterly breathtaking. In between chilly spells on deck, voyagers drink, play cards and games and generally while away a thoroughly pleasant existence. Supply boats stop at a number of stations, but passengers are not usually allowed on shore.

TIERRA DEL FUEGO

For some people Tierra del Fuego symbolizes the end of the world. For most it is at least the end of the road. The archipelago, at the extreme south of the continent, is split between Chile and Argentina. Despite past antagonisms over the division, the border is generally calm — bar the odd bout of bickering.

Isla Grande, the main island, measures some 150 miles/240km across. While most of it belongs to Chile, the Argentinian side is the most developed, with the substantial oil town of Río Grande and the duty-free resort of Ushuaia. The only settlement of any size on the Chilean side is Porvenir, across the Magellan Straits from Punta Arenas. Most of the island, on both sides of the border, consists of vast sheep-rearing estancias. In the south the flat grasslands are replaced by mountains, with the Andes making their final descent beneath the ocean.

Arrival and Departure. You can reach Isla Grande by boat or air. There are two ferries, one between Punta Arenas and Porvenir, the other between Punta Delgada (Argentina) and Puerto Espora on the far north of the island. The latter is mostly used by oil traffic and as the main route between Río Gallegos and Argentinian Tierra del Fuego. Porvenir has only a small airport, but large jets on scheduled services reach the Argentinian side.

The way the island has been split in two means that to get around the island by road, you must cross over the border at least once. The whole of Tierra del Fuego is therefore dealt with in this section. There is an hour's time difference between the two countries.

PORVENIR (Chile)

With barely 6,500 people, this is the biggest town in Chilean Tierra del Fuego. Although founded a century ago, Porvenir has a surprisingly temporary appearance. The Balkan (Yugoslavian) contingent, several hundred strong, retains a strong identity.

Don't expect too much of Porvenir: it is a bleak, cold and windswept place, where the main entertainment is writing cards and getting them stamped with a Tierra del Fuego postmark. But you should visit the Museo Provincial, which has fascinating old pictures of the gold rush, and archaeological remains of the extinct Indians. If it's not raining, take a walk across the bay to El Mirador, with a fine view back to the town.

The country south of Porvenir is magnificent but mostly inaccessible. One worthwhile trip is to take the twice-weekly bus to Camerón, 93 miles/l49km south across the bay. This is the old headquarters of a giant sheep-rearing estate, with a few grand buildings and a guesthouse. Road transport stops here. But if you have the chance to fly or take a boat down to the Cordillera Darwin, in the south, don't turn it down.

Arrival and Departure. Ferries connect Porvenir and Punta Arenas several times a week, weather permitting; the journey takes three hours. The ferry company's headquarters are in the same building as the tourist office, on the seafront. Buses run twice a week to Río Grande, six hours southeast. On other days you must hitch, walk, cycle, or take a taxi. Note that taxis are not allowed to cross into Argentina.

Accommodation and Food. A recommended hotel is Posada Los Cisnes, which serves great food and is a good source of information about the area. Residencial Colón (Riobo and Briceño; tel 580198) is also good. Otherwise, ask about private rooms at the tourist office. The best places to eat are along the seafront, e.g. Club Yugoslavo or Restaurante Puerto Montt.

RIO GRANDE (Argentina)

This is a far more developed town, 150 miles/240km east of Porvenir. It has a population of 40,000, a figure reached largely thanks to the nearby oil wells. It is very much a place to pass through, especially since accommodation is expensive and crowded out with oil workers. Its setting is uninspiring: flat, windswept and arid plains, with little but sheep and oil wells to break the monotony. Don't miss, however, the Salesian mission (founded in 1868), 6 miles/l0km north of town, which contains a great collection of everything from old radios to whale bones.

In your search for an affordable room, try Residenciales Arboles (Rivadavia 637) or Las Lenguitas (Piedrabuena 436), in the $8-16 price range. Exploring the side roads usually reveals the odd cheap hospedaje too. One of the cheapest places to eat is Mary's (Moyano 373), popular among hungry oil workers. The restaurant of the Gran Hotel Villa (San Martín 281) is also surprisingly good value.

There is a tourist office in the Municipalidad, on Sebastián El Cano. Banco del Sud changes travellers cheques.

Arrival and Departure. There are several buses daily to Ushuaia (four hours) in summer, fewer in winter. Buses run twice a week to Porvenir, which take six hours. If you get stuck at San Sebastián, on the frontier, there is a hotel run by the Automóvil Club Argentino, which may or may not let you stay there. The guards at the border occasionally let people sleep in the customs buildings — women should only do this if accompanied by men. Watch out for the tame and extremely playful guanaco, who has a penchant for butting people in the the back.

Aerolíneas Argentinas has frequent flights to Buenos Aires, stopping at Río Gallegos and Comodoro Rivadavia. Lade has just a few flights a week on the same route, but also serves Bariloche. Both airlines fly to Ushuaia.

USHUAIA (Argentina)

This is hardly the town you would expect to find at the end of the world: founded

Around Ushuaia

It is not essential to go on organized trips in order to enjoy the area around Ushuaia. If you aren't well equipped with camping gear, however, tour companies will provide greater scope for exploration. The best companies are El Caminante (Deloqui 368), which specializes in trekking trips and Rumbo Sur (San Martin 512). For more independent information on hiking and climbing in the area, ask Osvaldo Peralta (Invetu XIII — Casa 17), who is a member of the Club Amigos de la Montaña Ushuaia.

If you just want to find a quiet spot from which to enjoy the magnificent surroundings, you can't do much better than stay by Lago Fagnano. The village of Kaikén, near the eastern end of the lake 60 miles/96km from Ushuaia, is strongly recommended. The views are wonderful, the people very friendly, and you can stay in the cheap and welcoming Hostería Kaikén. Thirty-five miles/56km from Ushuaia is the dearer El Petrel Inn. It lies in a most beautiful position on the small Laguna Escondida. If you've got a tent, ask if you can camp in their garden. The Los Carlos bus to or from Río Grande can drop you off at either place.

Martial Glacier. The glacier is $4\frac{1}{2}$ miles/7km north of town. The bus from outside the Rumbo Sur travel agents takes you to a chairlift that runs to the top of the glacier. But the views are much better if you go on foot — this entails a comfortable three to four hour walk along a well-defined trail.

Parque Nacional Tierra del Fuego. The Martial Glacier is just short of this reserve, which contains beautiful lakes and some of the Cordón del Toro mountains. There are few well marked trails within the park; the main one is a seldom-trod track running from Bahía Ensenada (a few miles west of town) to Lago Fagnano, several days walk away. The park is excellent for camping.

A number of companies run buses to Bahía Lapataia, at the mouth of Lago Roca, and back: you can catch passing traffic by walking west along the seafront (Maipú). Bahía Lapataia is fairly developed as a visitor centre for the park, with campsites, wardens and guardposts. There are plenty of scenic walks along the water's edge, with good birdwatching opportunities.

Estancia Harberton. This is the site of an Anglican mission set up in 1887 by Thomas and Mary Bridges. Their son, Stephen Lucas Bridges, wrote an fascinating book called *The Uttermost Part of the Earth* about this lonely outpost; it is still available, published by Century. The estancia lies 23 miles/37km southeast of the Ushuaia-Río Grande road, the turn-off being 26 miles/41km out of town. Visit on a tour, share a taxi with other travellers, or hitch from the turn-off (not difficult in summer). Your reward will be a tour of the estate followed by excellent tea and cakes.

Sea Tours. There is much to explore by boat around the islands and the coastline in the Beagle Channel. In summer there are tours to the Isla los Lobos (fur seal island) and Isla Pájaros (bird island), which offer some of the best views of wildlife. Trips take five or six hours. A longer tour goes on to Isla Gable, Harberton Bay and the penguin colonies on Isla Martello, at the mouth of the Channel.

PUERTO WILLIAMS (Chile)

This Chilean naval base is a solitary outpost on Isla Navarino, the island across the Beagle Channel from Isla Grande. At nearly 55° south, Puerto Williams is the world's most southerly permanently occupied place — as far south as Newcastle-upon-Tyne is north. It has a population of under 2,000. For such a small, remote place Puerto Williams succeeds in being surprisingly lively, as well as friendly. And all around are the awesomely beautiful and untamed wonders of the island.

The indigenous inhabitants of the Isla Navarino, the Yaganes, were first encountered in 1830, during the voyage of the *Beagle*. Four of them were taken back to England to be presented to King William IV. Following on from this, the Yaganes were subjected to three bouts of colonization: first by Anglican missionaries, then by goldminers in the 1890s; finally, the development of sheep-ranching deprived the Yaganes of virtually all their land, and spelt the end of their way of life.

Arrival and Departure. The easy way to get to Puerto Williams from Punta Arenas is by air: the views over Cordillera Darwin and the innumerable small islands are splendid. DAP and Cabo de Hornos both fly weekly, for about $100 return. It is only marginally cheaper to travel with the Chilean navy — on their supply plane or ship — from Punta Arenas. See page 452. For information in Puerto Williams enquire at the Navy office or ask around at the port. Boats run occasionally from Ushuaia: see page 457.

Accommodation. Even if you're not tempted to stay in the stunningly expensive hotel on the way in from the airport, it's worth stopping off for a drink just to have a look. In town, the cheapest places are behind the port. Residencial Onashaga is about the best ($6), and serves good meals. Private accommodation is also easily arranged. The tourist office near the museum is open only in summer.

Exploring. Don't miss the wonderful Museo Martín Gusinde, which has a fascinating collection devoted to local and natural history: about the Yaganes and other tribes of this sub-Antarctic region, the voyage of the *Beagle*, the gold rush and colonization. It is closed on Mondays.

If you want to explore the island you are more or less on your own: on foot, and with no maps. The latter cannot be distributed because the island is a naval base. Those who haven't come prepared for an adventure, should try to negotiate lifts along the coastal road, which runs about 30 miles/50km in both directions: to Puerto Navarino in the west and Puerto Toro in the east.

Some travellers manage to arrive in Puerto Williams just in time to board a boat heading along the Beagle Channel and south to the islands of Cape Horn (Cabo los Hornos). Few are so lucky. Unless you can talk your way on to a private boat (e.g. by offering to help on board), you would do better to go to Ushuaia, and organize some trips from there.

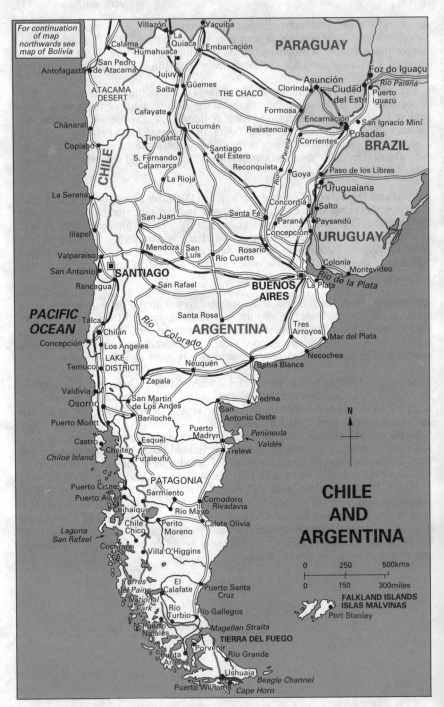

For continuation
of map
northwards see
map of Bolivia

Villazón
Yacuiba
PARAGUAY
Calama
La
Quiaca
Humahuaca
Embarcación
San Pedro
de Atacama
Foz do Iguaçu
Antofagasta
Jujuy
Río Paraná
Asunción
Puerto
Iguazú
**ATACAMA
DESERT**
Salta
Güemes
Clorinda
Ciudad
del Este
THE CHACO
Cafayate
Formosa
Encarnación
San Ignacio Miní
Chañaral
Tucumán
Resistencia
Posadas
Tinogásta
Corrientes
BRAZIL
Copiapo
Santiago
del Estero
S. Fernando
Catamarca
Reconquista
Goya
Paso de los Libres
La Rioja
Uruguaiana
La Serena
Concordia
Salto
San Juan
Santa Fé
Paraná
Paysandú
Illapel
Concepción
URUGUAY
Mendoza
San
Luís
Rosario
Valparaíso
Río Cuarto
Colonia
Montevideo
San Antonio
SANTIAGO
Río de la Plata
Rancagua
San Rafael
**BUENOS
AIRES**
La Plata
**PACIFIC
OCEAN**
Santa Rosa
Talca
Río
ARGENTINA
Tres
Arroyos
Chilán
Concepción
Colorado
Mar del Plata
Los Angeles
**LAKE
DISTRICT**
Neuquén
Necochea
Temuco
Bahía Blanca
Zapala
Valdivia
San Martin
de Los Andes
San
Antonio Oeste
Viedma
Osorno
Bariloche
Puerto Montt
Puerto
Madryn
*Peninsula
Valdés*
Castro
Esquel
Chiloé Island
Chaiten
Trelew
Puerto Cisnes
Futaleufú
PATAGONIA
Puerto Aisén
Sarmiento
Coihaique
Comodoro
Rivadavia
Río Mayo
*Laguna
San Rafael*
Chile
Chico
Perito
Moreno
Caleta Olivia
Cochrane
Villa O'Higgins
**CHILE
AND
ARGENTINA**
Torres
del Paine
National
Park
El
Calafate
Puerto Santa
Cruz
N
Puerto
Natales
Río
Turbio
Río Gallegos
0   250   500kms
0   150   300miles
Magellan Straits
Punta
Arenas
Porvenir
Río Grande
TIERRA DEL FUEGO
**FALKLAND ISLANDS
ISLAS MALVINAS**
Port Stanley
Ushuaia
Beagle Channel
Puerto Williams
Cape Horn

Argentina

Iguazú Falls

Population: 33 million   **Capital: Buenos Aires (12 million)**

Ten years have passed since Argentina emerged from the long dark years of military dictatorship. The country is opening up to the rest of the world with new confidence, and the current economic upturn has brought an optimism unprecedented in Argentina's recent history. Old habits die hard, however, and the people are slow to believe in the durability of the country's newly acquired democratic system. Furthermore, there has been a price to pay for economic stability, with many people facing lower living standards and unemployment. Prices are higher than anywhere else in South America.

There is an air of nostalgia and of paradox in Argentina — it is a nation which craves prosperity, but not at the price of sacrificing the old (and often inefficient) ways of doing things. Many reminders of a more prosperous era survive, including the cafés of Buenos Aires, where musty bottles of spirits lie unopened and gathering dust upon shelves of solid mahogany, and where regular customers are treated like royalty; Coca-Cola still comes strictly in bottles. Argentina is an intriguing place, and this is a fascinating time to be there.

Argentina covers an area not much smaller than India, and it is the largest Spanish-speaking country in the world. The main areas of interest are necessarily scattered within such a large space, but they are as varied as they are numerous. They include the magnificent Iguazú Falls, which Argentina shares with Brazil; the ancient colonial cities and remote Indian villages of the northwest; the ruins of Jesuit missions in the northeast; the lakes of the southern Andes; the unique

461

regions of the deep south, Patagonia and Tierra del Fuego; and, of course, the dynamic, cosmopolitan capital city, Buenos Aires. Many travellers simply fly between these places, but to do so means to miss out on the authentic back-country regions, with their endless, wide open plains and their hospitable people.

There is nothing homogeneous about Argentina. For many years there was open conflict between the capital and the provinces. A fierce spirit of independence survives to this day in the countryside, where the arrogance of the *porteños* — as the inhabitants of Buenos Aires are known — continues to arouse considerable resentment. By contrast, the porteños are convinced that their Plaza de Mayo is the centre of the world, and that their provincial compatriots are dull, boorish peasants. Even the national anthem — taken from a comic opera — seems unintended to promote unity. About the only thing that really holds the country together is the Argentines' fanatical support for the national football team.

GEOGRAPHY

The Andes form a band down Argentina's western side, running practically the entire length of the country — 2,150 miles/3,460km. They include South America's highest mountain, Aconcagua, which at 23,035ft/6,910m is just one of the dozens of peaks over 20,000ft/6,000m. In the north is the Altiplano or *puna*, the bleak and almost uninhabited high plateau which extends through much of Bolivia and down into the west of Jujuy, Salta and Catamarca provinces. Further south, in the so-called Lake District, the mountains become more accessible, and gradually decrease in height as you head deeper into Patagonia.

The Chaco region, in the central north area of Argentina, is a scrubby plain that stretches into parts of Bolivia and Paraguay, and contains forests of *quebracho*, or 'axe-breaker' trees. The usual hot, dusty conditions can be transformed by torrents of heavy rain. The northeast is more lush, with the Iguazú Falls surrounded by subtropical forest. The grasslands to the south form Argentina's most fertile grazing land. This area includes Mesopotamia, between the Uruguay and Paraná rivers, and the Pampa. This is a great grassy plain which extends west from the Río Paraná and Buenos Aires down to the Río Colorado, dominating central Argentina. It is the most populated area in the country, but there are few geographical features to relieve the tedium of the landscape.

Patagonia begins south of the Colorado river. It is a windswept, semi-arid plateau of sandy soil, which in places supports just enough grass to keep flocks of sheep happy. In the west is the country's finest mountain scenery, including icy blue lakes and many glaciers.

CLIMATE

Argentina's climate varies from subtropical in the northeast to subarctic in the deep south. In between, however, much of the country enjoys a temperate climate, with few extremes of temperature. The Andes cast a deep rain shadow in the regions immediately to their east; as a result the eastern half of the country receives the most rain, and this primarily in summer (November to February). In the mountains warm days alternate with cold nights, and unpredictable storms.

Only the small Chaco region lies north of the Tropic of Capricorn. This is one of the driest parts of the country, with a well-defined winter dry season; summer can be unbearably hot and humid. Much of the northeast approaches tropical conditions, with more rainfall than anywhere else in Argentina. Conditions are similar further south in Mesopotamia, while the Pampa has colder winters and temperatures that can drop sharply at night. The Lake District enjoys warm summers and cold winters, when snow blocks roads but attracts skiers.

Patagonia covers a huge area and in the north it is hot and sunny in summer. Further south, however, there is little seasonal variation, being cold throughout the year. Winter and summer temperatures average 7°C/45°F and 11°C/52°F respectively. You can enjoy hot days, even in Tierra del Fuego, but the weather is highly variable. A good quality jacket to give protection against the heavy rain and almost unceasing winds is essential.

Due to its eastern, coastal location, Buenos Aires experiences heavy rainfall, mostly during winter. It can also be surprising cold, though temperatures rarely drop below 6°C/43°F. Buenos Aires in summer is hot and humid; any porteño who can afford to goes off on holiday in January and February, when the city is comparatively empty.

When to go. A trip around Argentina should involve careful planning if you plan to visit the whole country. In winter travelling in Patagonia, for example, can be problematic. Strong winds and poor conditions make flying difficult, and many flights are postponed or cancelled; fares also escalate rapidly, and many tour operators and hotels close down for the season. In the west, mountain roads are often blocked by snow in winter, limiting your horizons and closing most overland routes into Chile. In the rest of the country high summer is worth avoiding, not only because of the heat, but because this is the main domestic holiday period. Between December and March accommodation can get heavily booked in the beach resorts, and also in Patagonia (particularly the Lake District). However, excursions high into the Andes of the northwest are only possible in the summer. To hedge your bets, visit in the spring or autumn.

HISTORY

Argentina's most notable pre-Columbian cultures emerged in the northwest of the country. Chief among them were the Diaguita, who were heavily influenced by the Incas. Though they never developed the architectural skills required to build the likes of Qosqo (Cusco) or Macchu Pichu, they showed a sophistication uncharacteristic of other groups in the region. Other tribes included the forest-dwelling Guaraní, who lived in the northeast. The region south of the Río de la Plata estuary was inhabited by nomadic tribes such as the Querandi, who lived much like their North American counterparts, and survived until the genocidal campaigns of the late 19th century. Further south were the Mapuche, a fearless tribe found also in Chile, where they still live. Last but not least were the incredibly hardy tribes, such as the Yaghan, who inhabited the inhospitable lands of Tierra del Fuego, but who are now extinct.

The Indians were fairly successful at holding back the Incas, who it is believed penetrated only as far south as Tucumán province.

The Colonial Period. Argentina was colonized from different directions. The first European to land in the region was Juan Díaz de Solís, who sailed into the Río de la Plata estuary in 1516, during the search for a route to the spice islands in the Far East. But he and most of his party were massacred by Charrúa Indians in what is now Uruguay. The first settlement was established by Sebastian Cabot ten years later. His reports on returning to Spain gave rise to unfounded tales of an 'enchanted city of the Caesars' piled high with treasure, and this inspired further expeditions from both Spain and Portugal. The country was named after the belief that the country was rich in silver (*argentum* in Latin).

Growing Portuguese power in Brazil prompted the expedition of Pedro de Mendoza, who founded Buenos Aires in 1536. Attacks by the Indians were relentless, and in 1537 Asunción was founded among the much friendlier Guaraní in what is now Paraguay. This became the base for explorations into northern Argentina, and by 1541 Buenos Aires had been abandoned. But colonists from Asunción gradually penetrated south along the Río Paraná, and they eventually re-founded Buenos Aires, in 1580. Meanwhile, conquistadores from Peru and Chile had begun to explore the north and west, founding such towns as Tucumán, Córdoba and Mendoza.

Argentina was settled only slowly, mainly because the land was poor in minerals. The greatest shake-up came when the Spanish crown began to sell huge estates, known as *estancias*, to wealthy creoles. The move ensured the unequal distribution of land, and lay the ground for future struggles between provincial landowners and the powers that be in Buenos Aires.

Argentina was originally ruled from Lima, as part of the Viceroyalty of Peru. But in 1778 Spain created the new Viceroyalty of La Plata. This brought new autonomy and allowed the opening up of direct transatlantic trade for the first time. New markets in Europe brought great prosperity to Buenos Aires whose new prestige was acknowledged in 1806, when British forces attempted to capture the city. They were expelled by the creoles with no help from the Spanish, a fact which served to both fuel a sense of nationalism and to demonstrate the ebb of the power of Spain, then in the thick of civil war back home.

Two rival factions appeared: the pro-Spanish council in Buenos Aires and a republican assembly in Tucumán. The majority of the people gave its support to the latter, which declared independence in 1816. After the end of the Napoleonic wars, Spain tried to reassert its authority by sending an army south from Peru. But this was defeated by José de San Martín, who emerged as the liberator of Argentina and remains a national hero.

Independence. Bernardino Rivadavia became Argentina's first president in 1826, but he could not prevent the internal conflict that arose between Buenos Aires and the provinces — between the mercantile Unitarists, who wanted the country controlled from the centre, and the Federalist caudillos, who preferred to keep power for themselves in the regions. The regional strongmen gained the upper hand, and a Federalist leader, Juan Manuel de Rosas, took over in 1829. He was a typical Latin American caudillo and autocrat, who made it possible for the estancias to grow ever larger. His reign of terror enabled him to retain power until 1851, but he was eventually dislodged by his military chief, General Urquiza.

A new constitution in 1862 settled some differences between Buenos Aires and the provinces, and unprecedented economic growth in the latter half of the 19th century also encouraged unification. Physical communications improved too, with large-scale British investment helping to finance new railways into the interior. The economic boom also brought a flood of immigrants, an astonishing six million arriving between 1860 and 1930. While thousands of them headed south to set up farms in Patagonia, even more people settled in the towns and cities further north. During the same period a campaign was launched against the remaining Indians, obliterating them.

Julio Roca was the major political figure at this time, and his conservative National Autonomist Party controlled the country from 1880 to 1916. In that year he was replaced by Hipólito Irigoyen, the idiosyncratic leader of the Radical Civic Union (UCR). After a break, Irigoyen returned to power in 1928, to the alarm of the conservatives and the army, worried at his close relationship with the unions. In 1930 an army coup removed Irigoyen and installed a military government.

Argentina's phenomenal growth had made it one of the ten richest countries in the world. But it was far from being a modern state. Argentina continued to be riven by squabbling between Buenos Aires and the provinces. Manufacturing was underdeveloped, and largely foreign-owned. By 1930 Argentina could no longer maintain its growth.

Perón. Colonel Juan Perón, one of the great figures of Argentinian politics, began his political career in 1943 by participating in a coup of reformist military officers. He latched onto the discontent of the working classes, whom Perón called the *descamisados* ('shirtless ones'), while also forging an alliance with the military. By 1946 he had been elected President. The importance of his wife Eva, a poor girl made good and glamorous radio actress, cannot be underestimated: she enjoyed genuine popularity and was vital to the Peronist publicity machine. She is remembered with great affection to this day, and was the unlikely star of Andrew Lloyd Webber's musical, *Evita*. However, Perón was inspired by Mussolini, and promoted a highly authoritarian personality cult. Political opponents were exiled and the press censored.

After Eva's death from cancer in 1952, the image of a popular democracy was impossible to maintain. Furthermore, the economy was in tatters. By the time the army took decisive action and removed Perón in 1955, it had much support. Perón was exiled to Spain, while his supporters were purged from government and the unions were placed under military control. The army, however, was split between the *Colorados*, who wanted firm action against Peronists and left-wingers, and the *Azules*, who wanted a constitutional government which included them. Meanwhile, general dissatisfaction with the harsh measures introduced to stabilize the economy brought popular protests, and a number of guerrilla groups, including the Montoneros and the People's Revolutionary Army, also began violent campaigns.

The Peronist candidate who won the 1973 elections later stood down, enabling an aging Perón to return from exile and take office. The economy was still in a mess and campaigns of terror and violence were launched against the left-wing extremists in the provinces. After Perón's death in 1974, his third wife Isabel, a former nightclub dancer, became President. In the same year the world oil crisis brought new economic problems and Isabel announced a severe austerity programme. Ensuing unrest verged on civil war, and in 1976 a military junta, led by Jorge Rafael Videla, took control following a coup.

Recent History. Videla's five-year rule will be remembered above all for the so-called *guerra sucia* or 'dirty war', a ruthless and indiscriminate purge of terrorists, left-wingers and their suspected sympathizers. The tactic of 'disappearance' employed by the security services was used against an estimated 10,000 people, the so-called *desaparecidos*; some say it was double that. People were abducted, tortured and executed, sometimes by being dropped alive from helicopters into the ocean. Even today families campaign for information on those they lost.

By such methods the main guerrilla groups were eradicated. But the army itself had become little short of a terrorist organization, and Videla's authoritarian laws led to serious social unrest and workers' riots. Dissatisfaction with military government persisted after General Leopoldo Galtieri took power in 1981. It was in an attempt to rally public support that the President made an issue out of Argentina's claim to Las Malvinas, or the Falkland Islands, which had been occupied by the British since 1833. Perón had raised the issue some time earlier, and had succeeded in arousing a certain amount of national pride among the Argentinian people. Nevertheless, Galtieri misjudged the British willingness to do battle, and almost 1,000 Argentinians died in war which, though not as one-sided a struggle as the popular British media suggested, was lost comparatively quickly — largely through poor morale. Meanwhile, such was the media censorship at home that until Port Stanley fell the Argentinian people had no idea that they were losing. Indeed reports were so inconsistent that Prince Andrew was captured or killed at least three times.

Following the defeat, the anger felt by the Argentinian people — and by the ill-equipped and ill-informed soldiers — heralded Galtieri's hasty and ignominious departure from government. Even so, the claim to the islands has not been forgotten. The Malvinas are still marked as Argentinian territory on the country's maps, and road signs proclaim *Las Malvinas son Argentinas*.

The 1983 elections were won by by Dr Raúl Alfonsín of the Radical Party (UCR). One of his major tasks was to prosecute the military officers responsible for human rights abuses during the Dirty War, and incompetence during the Falklands conflict. It was the appalling state of the economy, however, that became the most immediate source of grievance. Carlos Menem, elected president in 1989, took over the leadership of a country with a spiralling foreign debt, three-figure inflation and increasingly serious social unrest. A charismatic Peronist from the Partido Justicialista, Menem made a disastrous start, and observers began writing his political obituary within weeks. However, his bacon has been saved (for the moment at least) by his pragmatic economy minister, Domingo Cavallo. Austerity measures introduced in April 1991 — the so-called Cavallo Plan — heralded genuine economic reform, and quelled inflation almost immediately.

One of Menem's main objectives has been to put an end to Argentina's days as an international pariah. His adoption of free market policies has already made him popular among Western governments and has encouraged new foreign investment; and in 1990 diplomatic relations with the UK were restored. However, the President doesn't have such an easy ride at home. His befriending of the USA has not go down well in many circles, unemployment remains high, wages are low, and the army continues to wield a strong arm. On a more personal level, Menem has been beset by corruption scandals, with his son said to be involved in drug-trafficking and his sister-in-law accused of laundering cocaine money.

Menem has tried to renounce his playboy image, even cutting off his world-famous sideburns. But Argentinians continue to regard Menem at best with indifference, at worst as a fraud. It will take more than his well-publicized weekends spent meditating with Trappist monks to dispel the accusations of frivolity, and more than cosmetic surgery to convince Argentinians of his ability to see the country out of its troubles. Nevertheless, Argentina is enjoying greater political stability and more international respect than it has in decades, and the mid-term elections at the end of 1991 gave Menem a clear vote of confidence. Even so, Argentina is a volatile place; the political anarchy and economic chaos that began after the fall of Perón have still not been eradicated.

THE PEOPLE

Argentina has one of the lowest indigenous populations in Latin America — thanks to their almost systematic extermination during the colonial period, and the massacre of large numbers of natives during the 1878-83 Indian Wars. Most of the surviving Indians are concentrated in the northwest, and they are in the majority on the Altiplano. There are also Guaraní in the northeastern province of Misiones, and other small groups in the Chaco and to a lesser extent further south.

Argentina's racial mix has mostly been determined by successive waves of immigrants, principally in the 19th century, when the Italians and Spanish arrived in droves. Italians outnumbered the Spanish by three to one and their descendants are still the largest ethnic group in Argentina, forming over 30% of the population. The British also arrived in considerable numbers during the same period. Particularly famous are the Welsh, who set themselves up as wheat-growers and sheep and cattle farmers in Patagonia; their communities retain a strong identity to this day. Many of the young people in towns such as Gaiman and Trelew speak Spanish almost exclusively; but Celtic names continue to be popular, and you can still get a good cream tea and attend *eisteddfods* (festivals of Welsh culture).

Germans, Central Europeans and Jews also arrived, sizeable contingents settling in Buenos Aires. Germans settled mainly in the northeast and in the Córdoba region, where the town of Villa General Belgrano still holds an Oktoberfest every year. Smaller immigrant groups to arrive included Arabs — Carlos Menem is the son of Syrian immigrants — and Asians.

The famous *gauchos*, the itinerant horsemen of the southern plains, exist primarily in popular memory only, though you still see the genuine article in parts of Patagonia and Tierra del Fuego.

Meeting the People. 'Who is an Argentine? An Italian who speaks Spanish and thinks he's English'. Hugh O'Shaughnessy records this regional joke in his book *Latin Americans*, commenting that Argentinians have a reputation for arrogance. But even though visitors are constantly bombarded by dismissive remarks about Brazilians and Chileans, the Argentinians' reputation is exaggerated. They are arrogant but not haughty, and the porteños are more hospitable than most capital-city dwellers. But the people in the interior are the most open — even the most casual encounter can lead to an invitation into a family home, and conversations lasting into the small hours.

Argentinian girls are often quoted as being among the best-looking in the world, and boys are schooled early in the techniques of eyeing them up and making favourable remarks, known as *piropos*, about their appearance. While educated males go about it in a generally courteous manner, soldiers and policemen in particular are less subtle and can even be threatening. Even so, lone women should feel happy walking around on their own most of the time.

LANGUAGE

Spanish is spoken by the entire population apart from small communities of Indians in the remote northwest, who speak their own tongues. Few people know English or other European languages, though you may be lucky enough to meet the descendants of immigrants who are bilingual.

The main idiosyncrasies of Argentinian Spanish surround pronunciation: 'll' and 'y' — as found in *Llano* or *desayuno* — are pronounced 'zh' as in 'Brezhnev'. The letter 'r' is very heavily rolled, and an initial 'r' can sound almost like the 'zh' sound.

FURTHER READING

The most authoritative history of Argentina is David Rock's *Argentina 1516-1987* (Tauris, 1987). At least look at the introduction, which is excellent. *A State of Terror* by Andrew Graham-Yooll (Eland Books, 1986) gives a disturbing depiction of the violence in Buenos Aires in the 1970s.

Many books on Argentina, including Darwin's *A Naturalist's Voyage* and *Tschiffely's Ride* (see page 23) are concerned mainly with Patagonia. The most interesting book to have been written about the region recently is *In Patagonia* by Bruce Chatwin (Picador, 1979). John Pilkington, in *An Englishman in Patagonia* (Century, 1991), derives great pleasure from taking Bruce Chatwin to task for allegedly misrepresenting the local people. This last book is interesting but at times excruciating. A better and more light-hearted read is *Fat Man in Argentina* by Tom Vernon.

Argentina's most famous novelist is Jorge Luis Borges, whose short stories are renowned internationally. The two classic collections are *A Universal History of Infamy* (1935) and *Labyrinths* (1953).

AIR

There are numerous discounted flights available to Buenos Aires from the UK, Miami and other South American capitals. Aerolíneas Argentinas, the recently privatized national airline, has an extensive network and is generally reliable.

American Airlines has daily flights from Miami and New York to the Argentinian capital. Viasa currently has the cheapest deal to Buenos Aires from Europe, with a return from London via Caracas at around £650. On the return leg you may have to stop overnight in Venezuela, but accommodation is paid for. Varig, KLM and Aerolíneas Argentinas all charge about £700 for the London-Buenos Aires flight.

From South America. The greatest choice of flights to Buenos Aires is from São Paulo in Brazil, from where there are five daily services, costing around $320 one way; flights are marginally cheaper from Rio. Good connections are also available from Bogotá and Caracas; Avianca flies several times a week from the Colombian capital, and also from Santiago in Chile. If approaching from Peru or Bolivia, the one-way fare from La Paz or Lima is over $400. Aerolíneas

Argentinas flies two or three times a week from both capitals, with LAB and AeroPeru offeirng additional services. You may find it cheaper to fly to Santiago first, and continue from there.

If you can't be bothered to take the boat across the estuary from Montevideo (Uruguay), Pluna and Aerolíneas fly several times a day for $50.

SURFACE

Argentina shares frontiers with Uruguay, Paraguay, Bolivia, Brazil and Chile, and there are many points at which to enter the country. The most important ones are summarized below, though further details are given in the text. International bus services connect Buenos Aires to neighbouring capital cities, including Santiago, Montevideo, La Paz and Asunción, together with the Brazilian city of São Paulo. It is also possible to travel by train from Asunción and La Paz.

From Chile. There are passes the length of the Andes between Chile and Argentina, some of which are served by bus. Note that some passes may be snowed up in winter. The most-used border posts are in the southern half of the country. The best trip in the north is from Antofagasta via Calama to Salta, served twice weekly by bus in the summer, weather permitting. The cold, dusty journey takes 20 hours.

The main route from Chile is from Santiago to Mendoza, using the Cristo Redentor tunnel. This is an extremely busy border crossing, so getting a through bus is the best option: the drivers will guide you through the bureaucratic jungle of customs and immigration. Several companies serve the route, but journey times and quality of service vary considerably, so shop around; TAC-Choapa is recommended. The journey should take about ten hours and costs an average of $20. There are various other routes from Chile that are served by daily buses, including from Temuco to Zapala via the Pino Hachado pass (7 hours), and to Bariloche from Osorno (6 hours) and Puerto Montt (9 hours), via the Puyehue pass.

For a more adventurous trip, cross the border at Futaleufú, which is two hours by infrequent bus from the Argentinian town of Esquel. There are several even more southerly entry points, one of the most popular being from Chile Chico to Los Antiguos; there is a rickety bridge across the river, but otherwise you will have to wade across or cadge a lift. Buses from the border run once or twice a day to Perito Moreno; otherwise hitch.

From Bolivia. The major border crossing from Bolivia is across the river between Villazón and La Quiaca. You can walk across the bridge between immigration posts, though if you have copious amounts of baggage you may want to take a taxi — there are no buses. The border is open 8am-6pm. There are hotels in La Quiaca, but also good transport connections southwards, including seven buses a day to Jujuy (7 hours) and three direct to Salta (9 hours). Trains to Jujuy run every other day.

There are two other minor border crossings, the main one being from Yacuiba to Pocitos (also known as Salvador Mazza). Like Villazón, Yacuiba is commonly reached by train. Rather than continuing by train from the border, you would do better to take one of the direct buses to Salta or Jujuy, which run several times daily; otherwise take a local bus to Tartagal, and make onward connections from there. The border post at Aguas Blancas, a ferry ride across the river from Bermejo, is used less frequently. Buses run to Pichanal, on the Jujuy-Yacuiba road, where you can change.

From Paraguay. The main border crossing is the bridge over the Río Paraguay between Asunción and Clorinda. Several buses cross the border daily, some connecting to Formosa. See page 570 for the ins and outs of crossing this border by local bus or boat.

The other busiest border is across the Río Paraná between Encarnación and Posadas: the locals cross the international bridge in large numbers to go shopping, and there is a constant flow of buses to carry them. These leave from the bus station, from where you can also catch buses direct to Buenos Aires; but it is better to make onward connections from Posadas, which is well served by buses from many northern towns as well as the capital. There is a bank in the immigration building on the Argentinian side, but moneychangers are found mainly on the Paraguayan side.

Less used but more adventurous crossing points are across the Río Paraná to Paso de la Patria, west of Posadas, and across the Río Paraguay from Pilar to Puerto Cano. A ferry leaves Pilar daily at 7.30am and 4.30pm. For an even more alternative approach try to negotiate a passage on a boat from Asunción to Buenos Aires, along the Paraguay and Paraná rivers. Anyone crossing from Ciudad del Este in eastern Paraguay, must go via Foz do Iguaçu in Brazil: see below.

From Uruguay. For a comparatively small country, Uruguay has a large number of entry points into Argentina. There are several along the Río Uruguay. Regular buses run from Mercedes to Buenos Aires, which use the bridge near Fray Bentos and Gualeguaychú. There are also good services across the border between Paysandú and Colón. Further north, the town of Salto in Uruguay is linked to Concordia by ferry, though there is also a road across the Salto Grande dam, 13 miles/20km further north.

Unless you have been visiting back-country Uruguay, you are most likely to use one of the ferry services across the Plata estuary: this is also a pleasant, cheap and fairly quick way of travelling between the two capital cities. Ferry services operate to Buenos Aires from both Montevideo (overnight) and Colonia ($3\frac{1}{2}$ hours), and from Carmelo to Tigré ($2\frac{1}{2}$ hours), a short distance northwest of the capital: details of transport into Buenos Aires are given on page 492. Ferrytur and Buquebus, each run three or four ferries a day from Colonia. There are also faster and more expensive hydrofoil services from the same town: through-fares, which include bus and water transport ($30 one way), usually work out cheaper than if you pay for the hydrofoil on its own. Onda sells bus-hydrofoil tickets, the total journey time being roughly five hours; allow about two hours more if you take the ordinary ferry. All tickets should be booked in advance.

From Brazil. Buses run from Foz do Iguaçu to Puerto Iguazú every 30 minutes throughout the day. Even allowing for the time to go through immigration, the journey is a rapid and generally hassle-free one. There are several daily buses from Puerto Iguazú to Posadas, which take six hours.

The most used border is further south, across the bridge between Uruguaiana and Paso de los Libres: buses run to most cities in the northeast, and the Posadas-Buenos Aires train passes through daily.

The border crossing between Porto Mauá and Alba Posse is a convenient place to enter Argentina if you want to head straight for the Jesuit missions. Ferries cross regularly between 8am-5pm, with fewer crossings at weekends. The river between São Borja and Santo Tomé, further south, is crossed by a bridge and is the main route used by buses.

IMMIGRATION

UK citizens no longer require visas to enter Argentina. American, Canadian and EC nationals are also exempt, while New Zealand and Australian nationals are not. But check with the nearest embassy since the list seems to change frequently. On arrival in Argentina you must fill out a tourist card, which allows you to stay in the country for 90 days. This can be extended for up to a total of six months by contacting the immigration office, in Buenos Aires (Antártida Argentina 1365; tel 312-8661) or in any of the main towns.

For further information contact your nearest Argentinian consulate. In the UK this is at 53 Hans Place, London SW1X 0LA (tel 071-589 3104). A visa takes two to three days to process, and costs around £9. You require a letter from your bank and employer. The addresses of other consulates abroad are as follows:

USA: 1600 New Hampshire Avenue, NW, Washington DC 20009 (tel 202-939-6400).
Australia: 1st floor, MLC Tower, Woden, Canberra (tel 2824555).
New Zealand: Harbour View Building, 52 Quay Street, Auckland (tel 391-757).

Departure Tax. Anyone leaving by air must pay a departure tax of $13.

CUSTOMS

You are allowed to take in two litres of alcohol and 400 cigarettes. Border formalities tend to be swift, and searches are either cursory or non-existent. The latter are more in depth if you are crossing from Bolivia or Chile; travellers arriving from Chile are likely to have food and fruit confiscated.

In 1992 the New Peso was brought in to replace the austral, which itself was only introduced in 1985. The new currency is pegged to the dollar, at the rate of US$1 = 1 peso. Meanwhile, the dollar itself is used widely.

Beware of old and worthless notes, which are still in circulation.

Changing Money. Banks and casas de cambio exist in all major cities and towns. The latter deal mostly in cash — and usually offer the best rates. You may have trouble changing travellers cheques, and commission on them ranges from 0.6% (the level of the government tax) to an astonishing 5%. People working in banks and cambios seem perfectly capable of refusing a request to change cheques if they can't be bothered, and some places will only exchange a large minimum amount. In general, however, most sizeable towns have at least one place where you can cash travellers cheques at around 2-3% commission. Unlike in some South American countries, American Express cheques seem to be acceptable virtually everywhere. Surprisingly, hotels only rarely have facilities for changing dollars.

There is no black market and the often shady-looking street moneychangers found in the larger cities deal illegally and are best ignored — they are unlikely to offer anything better than the official rate, and may try to rip you off anyway.

American Express has offices in most of the main towns.

Credit Cards. One of the easiest and most economical ways of obtaining money is by drawing cash on a credit card, particularly Visa or MasterCard. It costs you nothing at the bank, and 1.5% commission is charged to your account at home. Several different banks with branches all over the country work with Visa or MasterCard, notably Banco Río, Banco de Galícia y Buenos Aires, and Banco del Sur in Patagonia. You are allowed to withdraw up to £200 in one transaction. Cash is given in local currency.

MasterCard is affiliated to Argencard, which is accepted by many businesses and hotels; Visa is accepted in marginally fewer places.

Banking Hours. Banks are generally open 8am-1pm, from Monday to Friday, though there are variations within the country. For example, in Buenos Aires they open 10am-3pm, and in the north of the country they may start the day as early as 6am or 7am and then shut at 11am or noon. Visiting the bank can involve a long wait and has become something of an institution in Argentina: people go there to meet their friends or read a good book as much as to carry out financial transactions.

Cambios are usually open 9am-5pm Monday to Friday, though they may close for an hour or so over lunch. In larger cities they sometimes open for longer — perhaps 8am-8pm, and on Saturday mornings.

Argentina is four hours behind GMT from October until March, when the clocks go forward. This can cause some confusion since not all parts of the country change their clocks at the same time.

Mail. Letters posted from Buenos Aires can take just four or five days to reach Europe, though a week to ten days is more typical. To send a postcard to Europe costs a hefty $0.75, only slightly less to the USA. It costs 50% extra to send registered mail, but the ordinary service is reliable enough to make this unnecessary for all but the most important mail and parcels.

Telephone. The international country code is 54. Argentina's telecommunications network was privatized recently. This has brought some improvements, but the inefficiency of Argentina's telephone system is legendary. Lines to some areas can be adversely affected by snow, and in Buenos Aires rain seepage can play havoc with underground cables. All over the capital you see thick bunches of cables strung up illegally over the road by companies bypassing the unreliable official network. Furthermore, telephone numbers — which may have either six or seven digits — change frequently.

When making long-distance or international calls, you will normally be charged afterwards, though sometimes you must buy special tokens to feed into the phone. Some people have perfected the art of jamming the coin slot with a biro after they have inserted one token, enabling them to talk for a long time at low cost.

International calls can in theory be made from any office, though you may have to wait 30 minutes for a line, or else be told to go back later. International charges are expensive at over $4 a minute to Europe. A reduced rate operates from 8pm to 8am and on Sundays, when charges are 30% lower than at other times. Collect calls are possible, but not to Australia.

Payphones: public phones for local calls are found at telephone offices and in small numbers around town centres; many hotels and some restaurants have them too.

an extravaganza such as *La Noche del Domingo con Gerardo Sofovich*, with its array of zany and/or demented guests and performers. News and current affairs programmes are dull by comparison, albeit informative.

Maps. The best road map of the country available in the UK is the standard tourist one prepared by the Automóbil Club Argentino and obtainable free from most Argentinian embassies. It shows all roads and settlements, though it shows few relief markings and no railway lines. This and other regional maps are available from the ACA itself in Buenos Aires (Avenida del Libertador 1850, 1st floor). The International Travel Map of southern South America (see page 41) includes the whole of Argentina, and is better than the Bartholomew equivalent.

The best place for detailed maps is the Instituto Geográfico Militar in Buenos Aires (Cabildo 381), which has a 1:500,000 and 1:100,000 series.

AIR

Argentina is such a large country that taking internal flights makes sense if your time is limited. Buenos Aires is connected to practically every settlement with a civil airstrip, and most northern cities are served at least once or twice daily. Unfortunately, most destinations north of Patagonia are linked only via Buenos Aires or Córdoba, and this can involve some circuitous journeys.

The main internal airlines are Aerolíneas Argentinas, Austral and Lade, which operate all over the country. Several smaller companies, such as Tan and Aerolíneas Federal Argentinas (known as AFA or Federal), operate on a local basis in specific areas only.

Flights are expensive, but there are several ways of cutting costs. Aerolíneas offers an air pass which is valid for a month and varies in price depending on how many journeys you want to make: e.g. four flights for $359, six for $409, and eight for $459. Theoretically, these passes are available only outside the country, though you can sometimes get one in Argentina if you pay extra. You have to plan and specify the itinerary in advance. To help you do this, you can obtain a complete timetable by phoning your nearest Aerolíneas Argentinas office: in London the airline can be contacted at 54 Conduit Street, London W1R 9FD (tel 071-494 1001).

The student travel bureau ASATEJ in Buenos Aires (Florida 833; tel 312-8476; fax 334-2793) is a good agency to talk to, both about passes and discounts. A 50% discount off fares is supposedly restricted to those with residency in Argentina. But anyone with an ISIC card can obtain such a discount through ASATEJ.

Lade (Líneas Aéreas del Estado) is the military airline, which works in conjunction with Aerolíneas Argentinas. It operates solely in Patagonia, apart from connecting flights to Buenos Aires. Small twin-prop planes are used, and flights are frequently cheaper than the equivalent bus journey, and far more exciting. Flights from Buenos Aires are often booked up weeks in advance; wherever you are flying from, you should book your seat as far ahead as possible. It is also worth going to the airport to see if you can get hold of cancelled seats.

TRAIN

In Argentina the railway reached many places before roads did, and the country still has the most extensive network in South America. The trains are poor competition for the fast, modern buses: services are infrequent and often dismally late, and none but a few express trains travel any faster than 40-50 mph. Nevertheless, trains are comfortable and considerably cheaper than the buses, and offer far better views.

Privatization has begun recently and affects all the main lines radiating from Buenos Aires. The Línea General Mitré and Línea General Belgrano, for example, both serve the route northwest from Buenos Aires, and they usually operate from different stations. While some predict that the break-up of Ferrocarriles Argentinos will bring a better service, others foresee a dramatic reduction in the number of passenger trains. Austerity measures have already resulted in cutbacks.

There are four classes of carriage. Most luxurious is the *coche cama* or sleeping car, which has two-person compartments; these are available only on the longest journeys, and are well worth the extra cost. *Pullman* carriages are spacious and have air conditioning. *Primera clase* is only a little less comfortable, though air conditioning is substituted by a row of overhead fans, most of them out of order. The unforgiving, non-reclining seats of *turista clase* seem to be the preserve of the poorest and noisiest passengers, and are usually completely devoid of tourists: but while not recommended for long journeys, a short jaunt in tourist class is good fun.

Prices for a sample journey, from Buenos Aires to Córdoba (12 hours), are: $20 turista, $23 primera, $29 pullman and $45 sleeper. You can obtain up to 30% off fares with an ISIC card. Railpasses, allowing unlimited travel on primera clase for a given period are also available: e.g. 30 days for $150 and 60 for $250. These are available from the railway office in Buenos Aires (Maipú 88), and from some big city stations.

Trains passing through the poorer areas on the outskirts of big cities, especially Buenos Aires, are popular targets for kids throwing stones or shooting air-rifles. Windows are laminated, but injuries to passengers still result when they break, since many of them are cracked already. You may want to follow the example of your fellow passengers and pull the metal shutter over the window in potential trouble spots.

BUS

Buses are the most convenient form of transport for travelling long distances. For the most part they are fast, punctual and comfortable, though the quality deteriorates rapidly in rural areas. Innumerable companies run services within the various regions, though few operate on a nationwide basis. This gives the illusion of competition, but in fact there is often no choice over a given route, and fares are fairly high. Charges are surprisingly unpredictable, ranging from over $3 for every hour of the journey on express routes to about $1.50 an hour on winding country roads. Some companies offer discounts of 20-30% to students with identification.

Some overnight buses get booked up in advance, so buy your ticket the day before whenever possible. On most services this isn't necessary. You can usually get a 75% refund if you redeem the ticket before the stated departure time.

CAR

The terrain doesn't present too many problems outside parts of Patagonia and in the Andes, but many roads are in poor condition and impassable after rain. In winter, or at any time in mountain areas, drivers are required by law to carry wheel-chains. In Patagonia roads may be blocked by snow during the winter.

Whether you have an IDP or simply your national licence, this must be stamped at the offices of the Automóbil Club Argentino. The ACA (see *Maps* for Buenos Aires address) is also a useful source of information and maps.

Car Rental. All the international car hire firms operate in Argentina. Avis and Europcar/National have offices in most of the main towns. Expect to pay about $35 for the cheapest car available, which is likely to be a Fiat. The international companies should allow you to drive in from Brazil.

Room tariffs are regulated by the tourist board and are changed according to inflation and by season. Expect to pay $15 upwards for a single room in a one or two star hotel. A single room with shared bathroom even in a cheap residencial is likely to cost at least $8, and in the northeast and southern Patagonia you may well have to pay $10 for a decent room. The cheapest option is to stay in a private house; this is most easily arranged in the main tourist season. Some addresses are given in the text, and the local tourist office normally has a list of families with rooms to rent.

The official youth hostel network is limited, and is partially supplemented by cheap residenciales which offer 10-20% discounts to holders of ISIC cards. The *Sleep Cheap Guide* lists places offering discounts, and is available from ASATEJ in Buenos Aires for $3; not all the recommendations are particularly sound, however. Argentina has numerous campsites. Those run by the Automóvil Club Argentino tend to have the best facilities.

Argentinian cuisine has soaked up influences from all over the world, though Italian-style cooking predominates. Argentinians eat out whenever possible if they can afford to; they start late, particularly in Buenos Aires, where restaurants may open only at 8pm and then don't fill up until 10pm.

The most common food is beef, which is generally excellent. The extraordinary imposition by law of meat-free days during the recession brought an outcry from all quarters — as any visitor who enjoys his or her meat will be able to appreciate. The cost of steak has shot up over the last year, but it is still good value. *Bife de lomo*, or tenderloin, is the most common type of steak (not to be confused with *lomito*, which is veal), followed by *bife chorizo* or rump steak (not to be confused with *chorizo*, which is sausage). You see huge chunks of beef being char-grilled on barbecues and then sliced into succulent, mouthwatering steaks. *Asado* or *parrilla* is served in many places. It is often brought on a small grill to your table, and consists of various cuts of meat, usually including kidneys and livers. Meat — of different types — is often served *a la milanesa*, which is fried in herbs and breadcrumbs.

Not all Argentinians are totally devoted to beef, but vegetarians can still have a fairly hard time. On the coast fish-eating vegetarians can add to the limited repertoire elsewhere, but fish is comparatively rare inland. A more reliable alternative are the numerous places serving pizza or pasta. The latter is generally good and often very cheap. For the best pizzas go to a pizzeria rather than a restaurant which serves a whole range of dishes.

More exotic and spicy food is hard to find in Argentina, except in the northwest, where you can eat *locro* (maize-based stew), *empanadas* (pasties filled with meat or cheese), or *tamales* (stuffed banana leaves).

Cafés, which serve coffee, alcohol and snacks all day long, are called *confiterías*. These are a central part of life in Argentina, particularly in Buenos Aires. Cakes and pastries are usually excellent and even the smallest towns have places serving large and mouthwatering ice creams. Also delicious is *dulce de leche*, caramelized milk and sugar, sure to appeal to lovers of condensed milk. It is similar to the *manjar* which is eaten by the vatful in Chile.

DRINKING

Coffee is a treat in Argentina, largely thanks to the Italian influence. A typical breakfast consists of a cup of espresso coffee with a *media luna*, a pastry like a croissant only more filling. Milk is cheap and usually fresh, and often sold in plastic bags. Ordinary tea (*té común*) is widely available, but is best drunk without milk.

Yerba maté, a kind of green tea, is Argentina's national drink, and is one feature which clearly distinguishes the provinces from Buenos Aires. The green leaves are infused with hot water in a small gourd, usually with sugar. The tea is left to brew and then the gourd is passed around, as people take it in turns to drink from the straw, or *bombilla*. The traditional strongholds of maté-drinking are the northeast and the pampa. Most people find the drink quite disgusting. Even so, accept yerba maté when it is offered, since this is above all a gesture of friendship.

Beer and wine are the most popular forms of alcohol, though various brands of whisky are popular despite their expense. The hardiest locals even take a drop of gin (*jenever*) with their early morning coffee. Wine is cheap and very good — particularly the red produced in Mendoza province.

The popularity of beer, on the other hand, is more of a mystery. Quilmes, the main brand, not only tastes strange but is also well-known for giving its drinkers sleepless nights and vivid nightmares. The best beer is brewed in the provinces, including Salta Negra of the northwest and Los Andes from Mendoza. *Chopp*, as in Brazil, means draught lager, of a most undistinguished type.

Exploring

Argentina's natural attractions are undoubtedly more interesting than the cities, but to make the most of the country you don't have to stay solely in the wilds. No one should miss Buenos Aires, though if you prefer to immerse yourself in colonial history you would do better to head straight for the northwest, particularly for the city of Salta and the villages of Jujuy province. It is also in this part of Argentina that you can explore the country's best archaeological sites, including Quilmes in Tucumán province, which marked the southern boundary of the Inca empire. In the northeast old relics are mainly in the form of ruined Jesuit missions, primarily that of San Ignacio Miní, east of Posadas.

Museums often close in January and February for the summer holiday, particularly in the capital.

Hiking and Wildlife. The landscape of Argentina offers much scope for hiking, particularly in the Lake District and the Patagonian Andes. The landscapes in the northwest are astounding but inhospitable, and walking is hot work. The Lake District is particularly suited to hiking and camping trips since it has several national parks; and even during the height of the tourist season, you can get away from the crowds surprisingly easily. The most visited national parks, including the magnificent Parque Nacional Los Glaciares in the deep south, are generally well-kept and have campsites with some facilities. Transport into parks can be limited or non-existent, and a fair number of areas are accessible only on a tour or in a hired car.

Two of the best parks for wildlife are the subtropical forest around the Iguazú Falls, in the northeast, and on Peninsula Valdés in Patagonia. The latter, while not technically a national park, is one of the world's most important breeding grounds for various species of marine life; both sealions and whales can be observed at close quarters.

If you plan to do much hiking you should look at *Backpacking in Chile and Argentina* (Bradt Publications), which describes a number of treks in some detail. *South America's National Parks* (The Mountaineers, 1990) by William Leitch, includes an extensive section on Argentina. The National Parks office (Santa Fé 680, Buenos Aires) has maps and general information. National Park offices and branches of Club Andino in the provinces often have maps you can look at, though they are not usually available for purchase. For more general topographical maps, visit the Instituto Geográfico Militar at Cabildo 381, also in the capital. Those interested in wildlife should also contact the main Argentinian naturalists' association, the Fundación de la Vida Silvestre at Defensa 245 in Buenos Aires (tel 331-4864).

Skiing. The same mountains which make good walking country also offer great potential for skiing between June and October. The most popular and expensive resorts are around Bariloche, with several others in Mendoza province. Prices drop the further south you go, where there are numerous minor slopes — these are often under the supervision of the local Club Andino, which hires out equipment.

Beaches. Most Argentinians of sufficient means seem to head off to the beaches east of Montevideo, in Uruguay. Those left behind must make do with Argentina's own beaches. While the muddy Río Plata makes the shores around Buenos Aires unappealing, there is a decent stretch of coastline further south. Strong winds, however, can deter all but the most determined sun-worshippers. The biggest resort is Mar del Plata, which is completely packed in summer. There are also smaller, cheaper and less frenetic places, as well as vast stretches of sandy beach that are still completely untouched.

Entertainment

Nightlife. Though British and American rock has a strong following in Argentina, Latin American dance rhythms are more popular than Western music to dance to. Young Argentinians enjoy a good bop and many confiterías, even in small towns, have a dance hall or disco.

The best theatrical shows are to be seen in Buenos Aires, where satirical revues are especially popular; unfortunately these are inaccessible to those with only a shaky grasp of Spanish. The Argentinian film industry has a good name within Latin America, and Fernando Solanas is one of the country's best directors. Even so, North American films remain the biggest box-office draw. Tickets cost $3-4, not including the tip for the usher for showing you to your seat.

Music and Dance. You are most likely to hear folk music in the northwest. Some bars in the region have *peña* evenings, where you can hear music typical of the Altiplano; this is similar to the Andean melodies of Bolivia and Peru. The gauchos of the pampa have handed down a large repertoire of traditional songs, but performances are not common. The old songs of the lowland valleys have inspired excellent modern performers, such as singer Mercedes Sosa. Tapes are easily available.

Tango: people say that steak and the tango are the two staples of Argentina, or at least of Buenos Aires. Carlos Gardel, the hero of the tango who died in 1935, is still an idol — there are pictures of him all over the capital.

The tango was born in the brothels of Buenos Aires in the 1880s, at a time when there were large numbers of immigrants who had recently arrived from Europe. The strongest influences were Italian and Spanish, though the essential concertina, known as the *bandoneon*, is said to have been brought from Germany. The tango was popular throughout the first half of this century — taking Paris by storm in the 1920s, and reaching its high point in Buenos Aires in the 40s and 50s. It was sent into virtual exile during the dictatorships of the last three decades, often followed by the artists who performed it. Many of those artists have returned to Buenos Aires, and now give concerts in the city's growing number of tango bars: most are live music venues with a tango floor show. These are attended mainly by the older generations and by tourists, though there are few places where you can actually dance yourself.

Festivals. While festivals take place all over Argentina, and throughout the year, the most colourful and fascinating celebrations are those in the Indian communities of the northwest. The festival of Pachamama (Mother Earth) is celebrated in a few places in this region; celebrations sometimes involve the ritual burial and exhumation of the carnival devil, Puljllay. The most traditional occasions last for several days and are thoroughly drunken affairs.

SPORT

Football, introduced by the British in the 19th century, is Argentina's most popular sport and is followed avidly on television or at league matches at the weekend. The country has been blessed with some skilled players and Argentina features in most World Cup tournaments; it won the title in 1978, at home. Top players are showered with praise and criticism, and are thoroughly indulged by the press — none more so than Diego Maradona, one of the world's greatest and most obnoxious players. He was suspended from world soccer for 15 months following his conviction by the Italian authorities for cocaine possession. Back in Buenos Aires, however, elation greeted the news that he was to begin training with the Boca Juniors which, along with River Plate, is the city's most famous team. Any derby match between these two sides brings their loyal supporters out onto the streets in droves, and victory for either one is greeted by the blaring of car horns and general uproar.

Argentina is the world's top polo nation, claiming nine of the world's top ten players. The sport is not followed with any great enthusiasm by the general public, however; racing is a more popular and less exclusive pastime.

Cricket has an enthusiastic following in some parts of Argentina. Introduced to Buenos Aires in the early 19th century, the game spread through Argentina as fast as the British constructed railway lines. Strong clubs were formed at

Tucumán, Córdoba and Jujuy. These three centres got together as 'North' in 1891 and challenged Buenos Aires ('South') to a match. The fixture still survives.

Buenos Aires is one of the world's great shopping capitals, where the main streets cater for the passion of the local rich for expensive clothes and designer labels. Many of the latter, such as Timberland shoes, are manufactured locally. Argentina is less famous for its crafts, though few visitors seem to leave without buying a yerba maté gourd — even if it is destined only to gather dust at home. Nevertheless, in the indigenous strongholds of the northwest you can find woollen jumpers and ponchos and weavings similar to those made in Bolivia. It is also in this area that you will find the most interesting and colourful markets.

Argentina is one of the safest countries in South America, and in most places the threat of danger to you or your possessions is remote. But the big cities, and particularly Buenos Aires, all have their fair share of bagsnatchers; mustard sprayers (see page 63) are unusually common.

Argentinian policemen are suprisingly friendly and fairly uncorrupt by Latin American standards. This doesn't make them efficient when it comes to registering thefts, however.

Drugs. President Menem has spear-headed an anti-drugs campaign: ranging from the deployment of the air force to detect coca plantations to tougher anti-drug laws. He has renewed his call for the death penalty for major offenders.

Hard drugs are not widespread within Argentina (most cocaine is exported), though marijuana and mushrooms (*cacumelos*) are fairly easy to obtain. Penalties for possession are severe. In the northwest you may encounter coca leaves, which are brought in from Bolivia: in cities these are sold discreetly from hot dog stands and other street stalls, and more openly in rural areas. While technically illegal, coca is widely used among the Indians in the Altiplano to combat the effects of altitude.

Such are the relatively high standards of hygiene in restaurants and cafés that it is perfectly possible to travel around Argentina for several months without experiencing even a stomach upset. But do not take these standards for granted, particularly in the more isolated communities in the north. Tap water is safe in Buenos Aires and the cities, but do not rely on it elsewhere.

Since Argentina is largely in a temperate zone, diseases common in other parts of South America are not a risk. Argentina is not in a malarial zone, apart from a very small area along the Bolivian border (in Salta and Jujuy provinces) between October and May. In this area Chagas' disease (see page 70) also occurs occasionally. Yellow fever is endemic in Misiones province, in the northeast, while much of the northern area is a receptive zone: i.e. without yellow fever but with mosquitoes capable of spreading the disease. Argentina has not so far been touched by cholera.

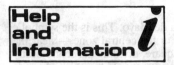

Help and Information *i*

Argentinian embassies abroad can usually answer fairly general questions about the country, and can provide brochures and other information if you send a stamped addressed envelope. In addition, you can contact the Anglo-Argentine Society (Canning House, 2 Belgrave Square, London, SW1X 8PJ; tel 071-235 9505) which holds cultural events throughout the year. Membership is £5 a year for those under 25, otherwise £10.

Enatur is Argentina's national tourist board, while each province also has its own tourist information organization. Most main towns and provincial capitals have information offices, many of which in theory open daily. In smaller towns, offices may well be closed altogether outside the tourist season. Each provincial tourist board has its own information centre in Buenos Aires, and it's worth doing the rounds of these before heading further afield. A full list of the offices is given on page 491.

ASATEJ, the student travel bureau in Buenos Aires, has information on flights and discounted accommodation, a fax facility, books, etc. It is based at Florida 833 (tel 312-8476).

Public Holidays

January 1	New Year's Day
March/April	Easter
May 1	Labour Day
May 25	National Day
June 10	Assertion Day of Argentinian Rights over Malvinas
June 20	Flag Day
July 9	Independence Day
August 17	Death of San Martín
October 12	Discovery of America Day
December 8	Immaculate Conception
December 25	Christmas Day

BUENOS AIRES

Once described by Paul Theroux as 'a most civilized anthill', Buenos Aires is a huge, sprawling megalopolis of over 12 million people. While it is no longer the Paris of the Southern Hemisphere, it remains an historic and elegant city — though a little knocked about by development and re-building. Only by visiting Buenos Aires can you appreciate the full extent of Argentina's European inheritance, and the aspirations that motivated the late 19th-century immigrants. The sheer flamboyance of some of the buildings gives an impression of the confidence of the years of growth, though the confused mix of styles may upset the architectural purist.

Buenos Aires, far from being a forgotten relic, is full of life, with greater economic stability bringing a new buzz to the streets. For those with money it is a lively, hedonistic place where you can party all night. During the day you may be content to sit in old, wood-panelled cafés or stroll along broad boulevards. But Buenos Aires deserves to be explored in depth. While the capital remains very much a European city, it is one torn between the First and Third worlds — where modernity and notoriously high prices are not matched by efficiency.

CITY LAYOUT

At the centre of the capital's urban sprawl is Plaza de Mayo. This is the symbolic heart of the city, though it lies at the eastern end of the central zone — near the docks. Avenida de Mayo runs west from the main square, dividing the centre neatly into northern and southern halves; the real 'downtown' area is to the north. Avenida de Mayo intersects with Avenida 9 de Julio, an extravagantly wide thoroughfare that runs through the city from north to south. At the intersection of Avenida 9 de Julio and Corrientes (the main financial district, with all-night cafés, etc.) is Plaza de la República: with its 67-metre obelisk, commemorating the city's 400th anniverary, this is a useful landmark; it also features in some of the dullest postcards of the city.

The most attractive districts and most coveted residential areas are Recoleta and Palermo, north of the centre, while to the south lie San Telmo and La Boca; the latter is a lively and colourful Italian neighbourhood.

Maps. The map issued by the tourist office is good, but covers the central zone only. For more detailed explorations you should buy the *Lumi* guide, which covers the whole city, and has a street index and details of bus and metro routes; it is available from kiosks, price $7.

ARRIVAL AND DEPARTURE

Air. Ezeiza international airport (tel 620-0217) is 30 miles/48km south of the city. There is a small tourist desk, a casa de cambio and a transport desk, which can advise on how to get into town. The journey to the centre takes about an hour by bus. The number 86 blue bus heads right into town every 30 minutes, running along Irigoyen to Plaza de Mayo; tickets, sold at a kiosk in the airport, cost $2. For some reason people with a lot of luggage are not always allowed on, though persuasion or extra money should normally secure you a place. The bus back to the airport leaves from the main square (and runs along Avenida de Mayo) every half hour from 6am-10.15pm, though the first bus is at 6.30am on Saturdays and 10am on Sundays.

A far more expensive alternative, at $12, is the executive service offered by the Manuel Tienda León (MTL) company, with a counter by the main exit from the arrivals hall. The bus runs to and from the MTL ticket office by Hotel Gran Colón, at Carlos Pellegrini 509 near Lavalle. The service runs roughly every 30 minutes (subject to the airport's programme of flights) from 5.30am to 10pm, daily. Regardless of the expense, the one reason to avoid these buses is because they have been held up several times by armed robbers.

Two kinds of taxi are available: so-called *remise* taxis, an official service for which you buy a ticket at the MTL counter, and ordinary cabs that wait at the rank outside the terminal. Either way, you are unlikely to get much change from $40. Avoid taxis that are not yellow and black, as there are unscrupulous drivers eager to rip off bewildered newcomers.

Aeroparque Jorge Newbery (tel 771-2071), near Palermo district, handles internal flights and some short-haul international flights, including most of those to Uruguay. Bus 33 runs from outside the main building to Retiro train station, from where you can take the subway into the centre. To return to the airport catch the bus from the station, or else take the MTL bus, which serves Jorge Newbery as well as Ezeiza.

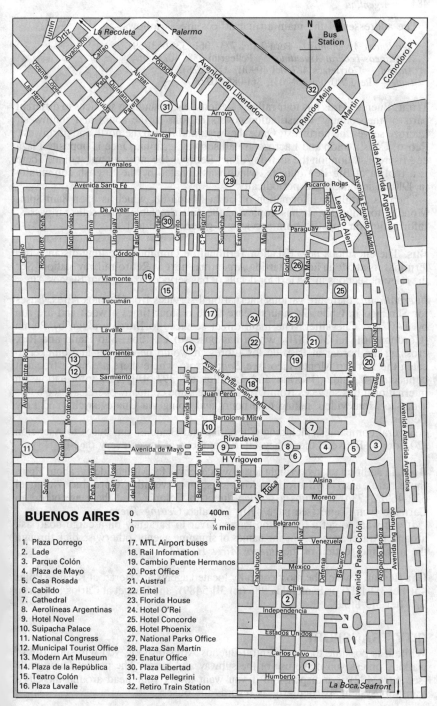

BUENOS AIRES

0   400m

0   ¼ mile

1. Plaza Dorrego
2. Lade
3. Parque Colón
4. Plaza de Mayo
5. Casa Rosada
6. Cabildo
7. Cathedral
8. Aerolíneas Argentinas
9. Hotel Novel
10. Suipacha Palace
11. National Congress
12. Municipal Tourist Office
13. Modern Art Museum
14. Plaza de la República
15. Teatro Colón
16. Plaza Lavalle
17. MTL Airport buses
18. Rail Information
19. Cambio Puente Hermanos
20. Post Office
21. Austral
22. Entel
23. Florida House
24. Hotel O'Rei
25. Hotel Concorde
26. Hotel Phoenix
27. National Parks Office
28. Plaza San Martín
29. Enatur Office
30. Plaza Libertad
31. Plaza Pellegrini
32. Retiro Train Station

The addresses of the main airline offices are as follows:

Aerolíneas Argentinas — Perú 2 (tel 773-2061, 331-6531/39).
Aerolíneas Federal Argentinas — Pellegrini 738, 4th floor.
Austral — Corrientes 487 (tel 499011, 774-2028).
Lade — Perú 710 (tel 331-7031, 361-0853/0278).

Train. Buenos Aires has four railway stations, each handling services to different parts of the country. Constitución covers regions to the south and southwest; Lacroze serves the northeast; Once the west; and Retiro the north and northwest. Retiro, Constitución and Lacroze are all subway termini; Once is opposite Plaza de Miserere station, on the metro's A line. Retiro is the most central station. There is a replica of Big Ben outside, which was donated by the English community in 1910. It is vandalized periodically.

There is a railway information office at Maipú 88, which is open 8am-8pm, Monday to Saturday. It has copies of the full timetable, and sells railpasses. Information on specific train services is given in the text.

Bus. The enormous new Estación Terminal de Omnibus, the long-distance bus terminal, is at Mejía and Antartida Argentina, next to Retiro railway station. See the relevant sections in the text for details of bus services to and from Buenos Aires.

International: there are various international services from Buenos Aires. Buses for Santiago in Chile (24 hours) leave three or four times a week and are run by TAC and Chevallier. The main direct services to Brazil are run by Pluma (Córdoba 461; tel 311-4871), which has buses to Curitiba, São Paulo and Rio, crossing the border at Paso de los Libres. It would be cheaper and quicker to catch the ferry to Montevideo (see *Boat*), from where there are more frequent connections. Onda (Florida and Lavalle; tel 392-5011) has information on international bus services from Uruguay. The same company operates three buses a day to Montevideo, taking nine hours and going via Gualeguaychú and Fray Bentos.

Several companies, including Chevallier and Brújula, run buses to Asunción (20 hours). Between them they offer a number of buses every day.

Boat. In addition to an overnight ferry, which leaves for Montevideo at about 11pm, there are also hydrofoils. Aliscafos at Avenida Córdoba 787 (tel 322-4691/2473/0969) runs a service direct to Colonia, and there are others to Carmelo from Tigré (see page 470). See also *Getting There*.

If you want to get a lift up the Paraná river to Paraguay on a cargo boat, ask around at travel agencies for the names of shipping agents; otherwise flick through the maritime section of the *Buenos Aires Herald*.

Car Rental. Two of the most centrally located agents are Hertz, at Ricardo Rojas 451 (tel 312-1317) or Esmeralda 985 (tel 311-5489), and Budget at Carlos Pellegrini 977 (tel 313-8169).

CITY TRANSPORT
While it is possible to cover central Buenos Aires on foot, you will soon tire of walking unless you make use of the subway and buses. The pocket *Lumi* guide (see page 482) is indispensible if you want to get your head around the city's transport system, particularly as regards the buses.

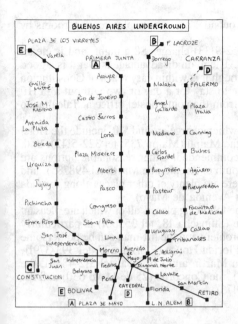

Subte. The capital's subway system was built at the same time as similar networks in Europe, and it is beginning to show its age. Nevertheless, the subte is the quickest and easiest way to get around the city. Travelling on it is made all the more fun by the survival of old wood-panelled carriages with brass lamp fittings. Most stations are livened up by piped music, and some are sights in themselves. The layout of lines is uncomplicated, though some stations are quite far apart. Trains run every five to ten minutes, and are reasonably clean.

There are five lines: A, B, D and E lines run north-south, and are linked at their southern ends by line C. Subte maps (as well as bus timetables) are supposed to be available at stations, but rarely are in practice. The fare system runs on *fichas* (tokens) worth $0.30, which are valid for any journey, including line changes.

The subte is no more dangerous than the London Underground, though it is by turns uncomfortably crowded and unnervingly empty. It shuts at night between 10.30pm and 5am. If you've got a lot of baggage, climb aboard as quickly as possible because the doors don't reopen automatically if you get anything trapped.

Bus. In Buenos Aires buses are called *colectivos*. Most of them are old Mercedes 30-seaters with lots of standing room. The bus network is fearfully complicated, though quick and reliable once mastered. Buses indicate their route with a number, but don't necessarily show their exact destination. Therefore, you need to know the right number first; since one number can cover certain variations of route it's worth checking with the driver too.

Most journeys in the centre cost $0.30. Buses must be hailed at the right stop, though you can usually get on or off when the bus is stationary at a junction. When you want to alight, head to the back and push the buzzer.

Taxi. Cabs in Buenos Aires are more expensive than in other South American capitals. During the day a 20-minute journey should cost around $4-5. Licensed taxis are always yellow and black, and a little red light on the windscreen shows they are free. Meters measure journeys in units, and drivers then use a special chart to calculate the cost.

ACCOMMODATION

Hotels in Buenos Aires are of a generally good standard. You should be able to find a decent room for $10 without too much difficulty if you arrive at a reasonable hour. In the centre the blocks around Florida and Corrientes have a good supply, with cafés, restaurants and cinemas all within easy reach. Hotels marked *Albergue*

Transitório, with a red or green light outside, are for couples renting rooms by the hour.

The Youth Hostel (Brasil 675; tel 362-9133) charges $8 a night, and is clean, safe and frequented by many travellers. The main disadvantage is that it is a good 16 blocks south of Avenida de Mayo, though it is within easy reach of Constitución rail and subte station. You may be able to stay for a day or two without a IYHF card, but otherwise you must get one from the youth hostel office at Talcahuano 214 (tel 451001).

The best of the central cheap hotels, which charge around $10, include the Hotel O'Rei (Lavalle 733; tel 393-7186) and the Maipú (Maipú 735; tel 322-5142), both of which are basic but friendly and recommended. Other reasonable options are the Central (Alsina 1693, two blocks south of Avenida de Mayo; tel 498785), and the Universal (25 de Mayo 740); and there are plenty of other places along Avenida 25 de Mayo (not to be confused with Avenida de Mayo).

For about $15 you can stay at any of the following places, all of which are pleasant and comfortable. The Suipacha Palace (Suipacha 18; tel 355001) is particularly recommended, though noise can be a problem and the lift-man can be bothersome to women. Also good are Hospedaje Florida House (Florida 527; tel 393-3791), the grand, old-fashioned Phoenix (San Martín and Córdoba; tel 312-4845), the Gran Vía (Sarmiento 1450; tel 405763), the Concorde (25 de Mayo 630) and the Novel (Avenida de Mayo 915; tel 389176).

EATING AND DRINKING

Buenos Aires abounds in excellent restaurants of every kind, though they have suffered in the last year because of rising prices: many have either closed or are empty. Lavalle and the nearby streets are full of restaurants patronized by cinema and theatre-goers, and therefore tend to be open late. You should be able to pick up a good meal for about $5.

Few streets in the centre are without their parrilladas. Some of these are huge affairs seating hundreds of people, though there are countless more modest places scattered throughout the city. Two that have become justly famous are La Estancia (Lavalle 941), and La Chacrita (Córdoba 972), both bustling and noisy parrilladas frequented by a varied clientele; but expect to pay around $10 a head.

The city's numerous so-called *tenedor libre* restaurants are the best bet for a cheap meal, though most of them close in the evenings and on Sundays. These restaurants, which are often Chinese-run, usually have a buffet from which you can choose as much as you can eat for $3-4; they are particularly good for vegetarians. Try El Chino (Esmeralda between Lavalle and Tucumán), and La Prima Vera (Maipú 495).

For lunch try the area around the Stock Exchange (La Bolsa), at 25 de Mayo and Sarmiento, where there are many cheap places; these include the Islas Malvinas, at Reconquista 335, with a $3 set menu. Also recommended is Los 8 Balos on the first floor at Corrientes 630, near Hotel Liberty. This is a diner where you can eat lasagne and other baked dishes for $2-3, and go bowling: the music on the jukebox is strictly Seventies.

Buenos Aires has some good vegetarian restaurants, particularly the Evergreen chain of tenedor libres, with branches at Paraná 746 and Tucumán 666. La Verde Esmeralda (Esmeralda 370), which is open daily except Sunday for lunch and dinner, serves all you can eat for $4. La Esquina de las Flores is a combined health shop-cum-restaurant at Montevideo and Córdoba.

On the Italian front, be sure to try Pippo's (Paraná 356), with its excellent value food and no-nonsense service. For some of the best pizzas in town go to the buzzing Broccolino at Esmeralda 776. But the most popular area for Italophiles is La Boca, the primarily Italian district southeast of the centre; to get there take bus 29 from Plaza de Mayo. There are several restaurants on Necochea, including the excellent Napolitano, which has a good, cheap menu, consisting mostly of pasta and chicken dishes.

Confiterías. Nowhere else in Argentina will you find confiterías of such variety and splendour. Café Tortoni (Avenida de Mayo 829-35) is the ultimate Buenos Aires café experience. Housed in an impressive 19th-century palace, it is frequented by elegant city-dwellers, and has a reputation as a haunt of politicians and artists. People play pool, and on Saturday evenings there is a jazz band; poetry readings are staged on other nights. Politicians can also be spotted at Café El Molino (near the Congress building at Rivadavia and Callao), whose décor surpasses even the Tortoni's.

Corrientes and the immediate surrounding area is full of cafés where the stylish and intellectual are also reputed to meet and talk into the small hours: and unlike along the Boulevard Saint Michel in Paris, they actually do. Café La Paz (Corrientes 1599, at Callao) is a popular place, where mime artists and other performers occasionally entertain the punters. Alekhine (Paraguay 860) and Cafetería Richmond (Florida 468) are quieter places with chess-players deliberating in the background. Slightly further afield, Recoleta district has its own collection of buzzing cafés, mostly on or off Quintana; they fill up only after 10pm and are busy until late. One of the best is La Biela (Quintana 598), where it is easy to spend all evening slumped in its old leather chairs.

EXPLORING

Plaza de Mayo. Buenos Aires' main square is a more impressive spectacle than it would have been when the Independence uprising took place there in May 1810. It is surrounded by the city's most important public buildings.

On the west side is the Cabildo, the old town hall, where soldiers wearing the colourful uniforms of the San Martín grenadiers stand to attention; the changing of the guard takes place every day at noon. The building itself is charming, and inside is one of the best historical museums in Buenos Aires: its varied collection includes a British flag captured during the unsuccessful occupation in 1806, and other well-documented items relating to the 1810 revolution.

The imposing Municipal Cathedral nearby was completed in 1827. While of dubious aesthetic merit, it is important to the Argentinian people as the burial place of the Liberator, General San Martín; there are banners and flags hung around the walls to commemorate the successes of the Argentinian army that he created.

On the east side of the square is the Casa Rosada which, like the cathedral, is smothered in a startling pinkish terracotta colour. Also known as the Casa do Gobierno, it contains the offices of the President, and is not open to the public. The palace has been the centre of various coups and it is still the focus of demonstrations. Eva Perón used to make her stirring speeches to the masses from the balcony, from which Galtieri also addressed crowds during the Falklands War. During a naval blockade in 1955 the building was strafed and bombed by aeroplanes. In remembrance of more recent troubles the mothers of those who disappeared during the Dirty War march round the square every Thursday at 3.30pm, as they have been doing since the late 1970s.

A couple of blocks south, at Bolívar and Alsina is the the church of San Ignacio, which was completed in 1722 and is one of the oldest and finest surviving examples of colonial architecture in the capital.

The area immediately north of the square is the main commercial district, with most of the big shops and businesses. The pedestrian precincts of Florida and Lavalle are bustling streets. Florida, like Oxford Street, is increasingly touristy and expensive, and is better for listening to buskers than for shopping; the rows of cinemas showing pornographic films also lend a rather seedy atmosphere. At number 866 is the famous Harrods department store — no relation to the London firm, though rivalling it in grandeur and expense. It is worth going to the gallery on the fourth floor, which is one of the best places in the city to see contemporary Argentinian art.

Corrientes, which runs east-west across Florida, is lined with cafés, theatres, music-halls and bookshops. Near its western end is the small Museum of Modern Art (Corrientes 1530, 9th floor), which contains little of great interest other than minor works by Dali and Renoir. It is open 4-8pm Tuesday to Sunday. Back on Avenida 9 de Julio and heading north for a couple of blocks, you reach Teatro Colón. This is one of the city's most spectacular buildings and one of the world's most famous opera houses, being larger even than La Scala in Milan. In contrast with the surprisingly unpretentious façade is the luxurious interior, smothered in plush and gilt.

At the extreme western end of Avenida de Mayo is Plaza del Congreso. This imposing square is dominated by the Congress building, where you can sit in on a session after 5pm: you must hand in your passport to officials who will give you a pink slip with which to recover it when you've had enough.

Museums. The Museo de Arte Isaac Fernández Blanco (Suipacha 1422), has a good art collection and fine colonial silverware and other crafts. It is open 2-7pm Tuesday to Sunday.

The Museo de Bellas Artes (Libertador 1473, the continuation north of Leandro Alem) houses a superb collection of paintings, including works by Rembrandt, Goya, Pissarro and Manet, and some of Argentina's best artists. Entrance is $1, and a further $3 will take you into the top floor, which hosts major touring international exhibitions. It is open Tuesday to Sunday, 9am-1pm and 3-7pm. Further northwest is the Museo de Motivos Populares Argentinos José Hernández (Libertador 2273), which has an interesting collection of folk art. It is open 2-6pm Tuesday to Sunday.

San Telmo. There are many grand buildings in the streets leading south from the Plaza de Mayo, particularly in San Telmo district, where 'Rosista' buildings have survived from the days of President Rosas (1827-51). Like many inner-city areas, San Telmo was a well-to-do suburb before being turned over to working-class housing. But since the 1960s, gentrification has proceeded apace and the district has become a popular weekend haunt, with cafés, antique emporia and tango bars. San Telmo's focal point is Plaza Dorrego, which is taken over every Sunday by a flea market; tango dancers sometimes give impromptu shows. While it's a lively area, the atmosphere is a little pretentious.

La Boca. This Italian working-class quarter, with its quaint, brightly-painted houses and potted plants, is unlike anywhere else in the city. It is a ramshackle, sleazy district running alongside the port and dotted with warehouses and factories; it

ENTERTAINMENT

The city's numerous cinemas show every kind of film, from obscure art-house offerings to the latest Hollywood smash hits. Cinemas showing the latter are concentrated along the western end of Corrientes. But the glitziest ones — with neon hoardings and video screens to tempt the punters inside — are on Lavalle, mainly around the 700 block. Numerous agencies (*carteleras*) sell tickets during the day (when cinemas aren't open), often at a discount.

It is hard to find authentic tango shows. One of the best is Michelangelo (Balcore 433; tel 30-6542), which is housed in a converted monastery. Also good are San Telmo Tango (Cochabamba 435) and Taconeando (Balcarce 725).

SPORT

If the streets of Buenos Aires seem quiet on Sundays, it is due to the fact that many people are participating in or watching sport, particularly football. Soccer matches at the River Plate stadium kick off at 4pm on Sunday; to get there take bus 130 from Plaza de Mayo.

Other sporting activities centre on the Palermo parks. Polo is played in the summer, the best games being the national finals which are held in November. Horse racing takes place on Sundays all year round. The original Cricket Club pavilion in Palermo park was burnt down by Eva Perón in 1948, apparently in a fit of rage at the Englishmen's refusal to give up the ground for one of her welfare schemes. But the pitch is still there, and games are well attended.

SHOPPING

Shopping is an expensive business in Buenos Aires, and as such is unlikely to take up much of your time. A walk along Florida at almost any time of day illustrates what a popular pastime shopping — or more often window-shopping — is in the city. In this and other streets virtually every other shop seems to sell leather, which is a good buy if you've got upwards of $100 to spare for a top quality jacket, for example.

At the weekends there are several regular street markets, the best of which are the Saturday Recoleta market in Plaza Intendente Alvear, and the Sunday flea market in San Telmo, both described under *Exploring*.

Bookshops. For books in Spanish the greatest concentration of shops is on Corrientes, west of the 1000 block. For books in both Spanish and English go to El Ateneo at Florida 340, which has the city's best selection of English titles, ABC at Córdoba 685, and Rodríguez at Sarmiento 835. Goethe, at San Martín 577, is good for guidebooks to Buenos Aires and Argentina (in Spanish).

CRIME AND SAFETY

Compared with places like Lima, Buenos Aires is safe. In most areas you need not feel nervous walking around alone, though use your common sense. Be careful in the subway at night, and La Boca district has a poor reputation. Some travellers have had bags snatched in the vicinity of the main post office, and you should be extra vigilant in and around the bus and railway stations.

HELP AND INFORMATION

Tourist Information: the main municipal tourist office (Sarmiento 1551, on the 5th floor of the San Martín cultural centre) has little to offer, and you would do as well to use the two information kiosks along Florida: one at the corner with

Diagonal Norte (or Roque Sáenz Peña), and another between Paraguay and Córdoba. They are both open 8.30am-8.30pm, Monday to Friday and 9am-7pm on Saturday.

The National Tourist Office, Enatur, is at Santa Fé 883 (tel 325-2232), open 9am-5pm, Monday to Friday. Nearby, at Santa Fé 680, is the National Parks information office. In addition, every provincial tourist board maintains an office in Buenos Aires, with ample literature in stock and useful town and city plans. Most offices are open 9am-4.30pm. They are located as follows:

Buenos Aires Province: Callao 235 (tel 407045).
Catamarca: Córdoba 2080 (tel 466891).
Córdoba: Callao 332 (tel 456566).
Corrientes: San Martín 333 (tel 394-7432).
Chaco: Callao 322 (tel 450961).
Chubut: Paraguay 876 (tel 312-2340).
Entre Ríos: Pellegrini 547 (tel 394-4010).
Formosa: Yrigoyen 1429 (tel 373699).
Jujuy: Santa Fé 967 (tel 393-1295).
La Pampa: Suipacha 346 (tel 350511).
La Rioja: Callao 745 (tel 441662).
Mendoza: Callao 445 (tel 406683).
Misiones: Santa Fé 989 (tel 393-1615).
Neuquén: Perón, formerly Cangallo, 687 (tel 496385).
Río Negro: Tucumán 1916 (tel 459931).
Salta: Diagonal Norte (or Saenz Peña) 933 (tel 392-8074).
San Juan: Maipú 331 (tel 461698).
San Luís: Azcuenaga 1083 (tel 833641).
Santa Cruz: Córdoba 1345, 14th floor (tel 420381).
Santa Fé: 25 de Mayo 358 (tel 312-4620).
Santiago del Estero: Florida 274 (tel 469398).
Tucumán: Mitré 836 (tel 402214).
Tierra del Fuego: Santa Fé 790.

Post Office: the Correo Central is at Sarmiento and Leandro Alem, and is open 8am-8pm Monday to Friday and 8am-1pm on Saturday. For parcels over 1kg go to the office on Antartida Argentina, near Retiro station, open 9am-3pm.

Telephone Office: the biggest and most central office is at Corrientes and Maipú. It is open 24 hours a day, with a public telex in the basement. To send a fax go to the ASATEJ student travel office at Florida 833/5, 1st floor (tel 312-8476; fax 334-2793), which opens 10am-7pm.

Money: many of the city's numerous banks are on Reconquista. Most have exchange desks which can deal with cheques and credit cards. The best place to cash Amex cheques is at the bank in the basement of the gleaming new American Express block on Plaza San Martín (Arenales 707; tel 312-0900). They charge only 0.6% commission to exchange cheques into cash dollars or the local currency. The office is open 10am-3pm Monday to Friday.

Elsewhere it can be difficult to find places which change cheques at economic rates. Try Puente Hermanos at Corrientes and San Martín, Cambio Unión at Maipú 717, or Casa Piano at San Martín 347. Americantur at Corrientes 787 changes only cash, but is open Saturday mornings.

Lloyds Bank has a branch at Reconquista 101-51 at Mitré (tel 331-3551). For cash advances on Visa cards go to Banco Río, which has central branches at Lavalle

547, Esmeralda 25, Sarmiento 641 and Defensa 113. Cash advances on MasterCard can be obtained from agents at Hipólito Irigoyen 878 (tel 331-2549) or Florida 274. Advances on American Express are given at Avenida Libertador 498 (tel 312-0900).

Immigration Office: Antartida Argentina 1365 (tel 312-8661).

Instituto Geográfico Militar: Cabildo 381, in Palermo. It's a few blocks east of Carranza subte station, the terminus of D line.

Medical Care: recommended is the British Hospital at Perdrieri 74 (tel 231081).

Embassies and Consulates. Opening hours of foreign missions vary, but all are open weekday mornings.
Australia: Santa Fé 846, 7th floor (tel 312-6341/8).
Bolivia: Avenida Belgrano 1670, 1st floor (tel 377038, 375595), west of the centre.
Brazil: Pellegrini 1363 (tel 394-5260/4), open 10am-6pm.
Chile: San Martín 439, 9th floor (tel 394-6582), open 9am-2pm.
Colombia: Santa Fé 782, 1st floor (tel 312-5538/5446).
Ecuador: Quintana 585, 10th floor, La Recoleta (tel 804-6408).
Paraguay: Maipú 464, 3rd floor (tel 392-6536/8865), open 9.30am-1pm.
Peru: San Martín 962, 2nd floor (tel 311-7582/7575).
Uruguay: Las Heras 1907, La Recoleta (tel 803-6030/32/37), open 10am-6pm.
UK: Dr Luís Agote 2412/52, La Recoleta (tel 803-7070/71; fax 803-1731).
USA: Colombia 4300, Palermo (tel 774-8811/9911/8511).

AROUND BUENOS AIRES

Tigré. This is a traditional resort on the Paraná delta 18 miles/29km north of the capital. Subtropical vegetation thrives in the delta's warm, humid microclimate, and barges ply the canals laden with locally-grown fruit. The criss-crossing river channels have created many islands, perfect for exploring by motor boat; you can organize this at the quay by the railway station. For a longer trip you can cross to Carmelo in Uruguay by ferry, which takes three hours one way. Boats leave several times a day and tickets can be booked in Tigré itself or in Buenos Aires.

Tigré is the terminus of the busy Mitré suburban line, and the best way to get there is on one of the frequent trains from Retiro station. Alternatively, take colectivo 60 (marked *Bajo*), which leaves from Leandro Alem. Both the road and the railway line pass through historic coastal suburbs, where cobbled streets and old houses give some idea of the capital's former grandeur.

Tigré's riverside strip has many bars and restaurants, and there is a Youth Hostel at Río Luján and Abra Vieja.

Buenos Aires Province

Several roads head south from Buenos Aires across the vast pampa, the heartland of Argentina's cattle-farming industry. Every so often you pass roadside parrillas, where great sides of beef are being grilled out in the open, or a pair of gauchos on horseback. The Atlantic coast, with its beaches teeming with holidaymakers in summer, is a world away. Most travellers head on swiftly via Bahía Blanca to Patagonia.

SAN ANTONIO DE ARECO

The rural community of San Antonio de Areco, 70 miles/113km northwest of Buenos Aires, has preserved many old buildings since its foundation in 1730. It has also maintained its gaucho traditions, which are best witnessed during the Día de la Tradición festival, on November 10-12. At other times of year, you must be content with a visit to the Museo Gauchesco Ricardo Güiraldes, which is dedicated to a famous gaucho writer. It is in a 19th-century ranch house at Camino Güiraldes and Aurelino,

There are eight buses from Buenos Aires, and you can stay at the Hospedaje Areco at Segundo Sombra and Rivadavia (tel 0326-22166).

LA PLATA

The capital of the province lies 35 miles/56km southeast of Buenos Aires city. It is a large ocean port with a population of around 500,000. Though often touted as a showpiece of urban planning, the wide streets and sweeping diagonals leave the visitor feeling positively agoraphobic. A walk down Avenida 7, which runs between Plazas Italia and San Martín, gives some idea of the intended grandeur. The cathedral on Plaza Moreno, which is a copy of that in Cologne, is one of the few buildings of architectural interest in the city.

The main reason to go to La Plata is to visit the famous Museo de Ciencias Naturales, which is one of the best museums of its kind on the continent. It has a varied collection that includes the skeletons of dinosaurs and other extinct animals. The museum is in a park known as El Bosque, on the northern edge of the city and accessible on bus 202 from the centre; it is open 1-6pm daily, but is closed for the whole of January and on public holidays.

Arrival and Departure. There are frequent trains from Buenos Aires, and buses leave from opposite Retiro station every half hour, taking 90 minutes ($3). Four buses a day connect the port with Mar del Plata (5 hours, $17). La Plata's bus terminal is at Calles 4 and 41. Take your bearings from the big city plan on the wall; otherwise, pick up a map at the tourist office at Calles 12 and 53 (13th floor).

Accommodation and Food. You can stay at the Hospedaje Costa Azul (Calle 46-266; tel 021-218693), or the Roca (Calles 1 and 42) for around $13. Among the best restaurants is Don Quixote on Plaza Passo, and there are good snack places on Calle 60, between Calles 5 and 6.

MAR DEL PLATA

As well as being one of Argentina's main Atlantic ports, Mar del Plata is also the country's grandest, oldest and biggest seaside resort. At the height of the season its 450,000 residents are swamped by over two million visitors from all over South America. People of every size, shape and class crush onto the beaches, and if you can only get to one of the seaside towns, this has to be it.

Mar del Plata first became hugely fashionable during the First World War, when hotels of palatial splendour like the Bristol (which sadly no longer exists) enjoyed their heyday. Little survives from that era, except a certain aura of elegance. Whatever you think of crowds and hiked-up prices, Mar del Plata is best visited in season since at other times many hotels and restaurants close down, and the place is positively forlorn. The bracing sea air will do you good at any time of year.

Arrival and Departure. Trains run five times daily between Mar del Plata and

Buenos Aires (5 hours by express), with less frequent services west to Bahía Blanca. The station is at Luro and Misiones, 16 blocks north of Plaza San Martín; tickets can also be booked in the office at San Martín and Santa Fé.

Mar del Plata is well served by bus, with regular daily services to and from Bahía Blanca, La Plata and Buenos Aires, and good connections with destinations further afield. The bus terminal is at Alberti and Sarmiento, five blocks back from the Hotel Hermitage (on the seafront), which may give you a map of the city if you ask nicely.

Accommodation. The closer you want to be to the sea, the more you have to pay. In the off-season you should be able to bargain your way into any mid-range hotels that are open, such as the Virrey (Alberti 1565; tel 513704). Try to book ahead between December and March. Cheaper places ($7-10) are concentrated around the bus station. They include Hospedaje Litre and the Paraná (both at Lamadrid and Rawson), the Youth Hostel (Tucumán 2728) and Hospedaje Alfa (Garay 1731; tel 023-771125).

Eating and Drinking. Among the many excellent places to eat are Don Pepito (opposite the casino on Ramos), Raviolandia (Colón and Heras), Comedor Naturista (Salta 1571), and the anonymous place at Sarmiento 2648, near the bus station, where a really good meal costs only $3.

Mar del Plata is famous for *alfajores*, scrumptious crumbly biscuits filled with *dulce de leche* and dipped in chocolate. Havanna is the most exclusive variety.

Exploring. Of the 5 miles/8km of beach near Mar del Plata, the strip with the best social cachet is the Playa Grande; it is lined with the private residences of rich porteños. By Bristol beach is the largest casino in the world. It is government-run, and several hundred thousand dollars a night can pour into the coffers of the Welfare Ministry. Admission to the top floor is surprisingly cheap, but only the well-dressed are allowed in. The waterfront has an excellent pier and a promenade, where you can watch the locals playing their own version of bowls.

Make time to visit the Castagnino art museum in the Casa Villa Ortíz Basualdo — an extraordinary building inspired by the chateaux of the Loire and constructed in 1909. The paintings by Castagnino are worth seeing, though the house, with its fabulous furniture and Art Nouveau and Art Deco decoration, is the main attraction. It is at Colón 1189 and Alvear, ten blocks southeast of Plaza Colón, and opens Thursday to Sunday only.

After hours, music and dancing continue right through the night on summer weekends; the clubs along Constitución are the main focus of activity.

Help and Information. *Tourist office:* Ramos 2267 (also known as the Bulevar Marítimo). It opens 8am-8pm Monday to Saturday.

Communications: the post office is at Santiago del Estero and Pedro Luro, open 8am-8pm Monday to Saturday. The telephone office is at Colón 2250, open 7am-2am during the week, and 10am-5.30pm at weekends.

Money: there are various cambios on San Martín and Pedro Luro; Jonestur (San Martín and Córdoba) takes cheques and is recommended. Banco Río (for credit card withdrawals) is at Belgrano and Independencia.

SOUTH OF MAR DEL PLATA

Miramar. This small, unpretentious resort is 28 miles/45km southwest of Mar del Plata. It has some of the best beaches on this coast, and towards the end of the season you can have them practically all to yourself. Furthermore, life in Miramar costs less than in comparable resorts.

Buses run daily from Mar del Plata and Buenos Aires. Good places to stay include the Villa Cruz (Calle 19-864) and the '23' (Calle 23-1728; tel 0291-20937). The tourist office is at Avenida 26-1065.

Necochea. Sixty miles/96km down the coast from Mar del Plata, this is the second biggest resort in the area. The scene is less glamorous than further north, despite the fact that its 16-mile/25km long beach is probably the best in the country.

Buses run daily from Mar del Plata and Buenos Aires, and there are also several trains a week. Budget hotels in Necochea are scarce, though the Gran Splendid (Calle 2-4022; tel 0262-23303) is good value; the Hospedaje Solchaga (Calle 62-2822; tel 25584), near the bus station, is cheaper at $10.

BAHIA BLANCA

For many travellers this is the gateway to Patagonia. With a population of 300,000, it is also the most important town in the south of the province. Bahía Blanca lies slightly inland, but the nearby ports handle a large part of Argentina's agricultural exports, which are the basis of the city's economy. Bahía Blanca is now an oil refining centre too, and you can buy thrilling postcards of the petrochemical complex to send to your friends.

Nevertheless, Bahía Blanca is not a bad place. It is interesting architecturally, and the streets around Plaza Rivadavia (the main square) are full of character; one such is Soler, with its many junkshops. And a short ride away on bus 504 from Calle Moreno is Puerto Ingeniero White, where you can see the harbour at work. Back in town, the best museum is the Museo Histórico y de Ciencias Naturales, in the splendid theatre at Alsina and Coronel Dorrego. The display covering the city's history is enriched by a wide-ranging collection of early 20th-century objects. It is open 4-8pm daily.

East of Bahía Blanca stretch undeveloped sandy beaches almost as far as Monte Hermoso, 66 miles/106km away, where several hotels open in the summer season.

Arrival and Departure. In addition to several daily flights from Buenos Aires, most southern towns are served at least once a week — including Comodoro Rivadavia and Ushuaia. Aerolíneas Argentinas is at San Martín 298 (tel 27030), Austral at Colón 59 (tel 26931) and Lade at Darregueira 21 (tel 21063).

Trains run daily to Buenos Aires (9-10 hours, $21 in primera) and Neuquén, and two or three times a week to Esquel and Bariloche via San Antonio Oeste. The railway station is at Cerri 750, near the centre.

Buses to the main towns in the region run several times a day, including to Buenos Aires (9 hours), with just one a day to more distant destinations such as Comodoro Rivadavia, Mendoza and Bariloche. The bus terminal is at Brown and Estados Unidos, linked to the centre by bus 514 or 517 from the stop on Chiclana block 100.

Accommodation and Food. Hospedaje Brandsen (Brandsen and Soler) and the Roma (Cerri 759, opposite the railway station; tel 091-38500) are good places to stay at around $10 a single. Hogar (Rodríguez 64; tel 23376), near the square, is more basic at $5.

People come from all over town to enjoy the excellent and very cheap parrillada at El Jabalí, beneath the Hotel Roma. Parrilla Los Amigos (Chiclana and Lavalle) is another good place in the centre, though not particularly cheap. Try also Pizzería El Pirata (Lamadrid 360).

Help and Information. The tourist office is in the Municipalidad at Alsina 65, on Plaza Rivadavia, and opens 7am-1pm Monday to Friday. The post office is at Moreno 34, and the phone office at O'Higgins 213, open daily.

The best of the cambios is Pullman, with branches at O'Higgins 23 and San Martín 171. Banco Río (O'Higgins 81) gives cash advances on Visa.

For details of heading from here into Patagonia, leap ahead to page 531. The remainder of this chapter commences north of Buenos Aires and continues anticlockwise down to Tierra del Fuego.

Santa Fé Province

Lying northwest of Buenos Aires, Santa Fé is of scant interest scenically or historically, though the capital city has some appeal. While the rich farmland of the south produces much of Argentina's grain, the north of the province is dry and virtually uninhabited.

SANTA FE

The provincial capital (population 350,000) lies on the west bank of the Río Paraná, 300 miles/480km northwest of Buenos Aires. Founded in 1651, a fair amount of its colonial architecture has survived intact, though industry has taken its toll on the general appearance of the city. The 17th-century Cathedral, at López and San Jerónimo, and the Convento San Francisco, two blocks south, are among the most impressive buildings. The best overview of Santa Fé city and province is given in the Museo Histórico Provincial (San Martín 1490).

Arrival and Departure. In addition to good air links, there are daily trains linking Santa Fé and Buenos Aires (via Rosario), which take $7\frac{1}{2}$ hours and cost $16 in primera. Trains also run to Tucumán and Jujuy in the northwest, and north to Resistencia. The station is at Galvez 1150.

Buses run frequently to Rosario and to Paraná, 19 miles/30km east via a tunnel under the river. There are also daily services to the capital (7 hours), Córdoba (6 hours) and many northern towns, and even to Asunción in Paraguay; buses to Montevideo (Uruguay) run several times a week. The bus station is at Belgrano and Yrigoyen, one block east of the central Plaza España.

Accommodation and Food. There are a number of borderline places around the transport terminals, such as Residencial Claridge (Belgrano 2174) and the Güemes (Galvez 1362); Hotel Niza (Rivadavia 2755; tel 042-22047) is a better though more expensive choice. Nearer the centre, eight blocks south of the bus station, try the comfortable Hotel California (25 de Mayo 2190).

Santa Fé has some good restaurants, including Le Coq au Vin (Santiago del Estero 3299) and the Comedor Tio Carols, which has an excellent value tenedor libre.

Help and Information. The city tourist office is in the bus terminal, and the provincial Dirección de Turismo is at San Martín 1698. The post and telephone offices are both at Mendoza and Rivadavia. Tourfé at San Martín 1609 offers good rates for travellers' cheques; there is a branch of Banco Río at San Martín 2501.

ROSARIO

It is disappointing to discover that Ernesto 'Che' Guevara was born in a big industrial city, where he appears to have been all but forgotten. Not surprisingly, given the political colour of most of the regimes since the early 1960s, there are no museums or memorials in honour of the man who masterminded Cuba's revolution.

With a population of nearly a million, Rosario is an important industrial centre and a major port on the Paraná river; it is also the country's third biggest city. Ugly modern buildings have swamped nearly all the surviving colonial buildings. Nevertheless, the riverfront has not lost its appeal, and there are some impressive early 20th century buildings, particularly along Boulevard Oroño. The mansions and squares mark the height of traditional civic architecture and planning. Examples include the central Parque Independencia and the Parque Nacional a la Bandera. The latter marks the spot where General Belgrano raised the new Argentinian flag following Independence.

The Museo Histórico Provincial concentrates on San Martín's victory at San Lorenzo in 1813, his first in the war of independence; San Lorenzo itself is now an ugly petrochemicals complex 17 miles/27km north. The museum is at the northern end of Parque Independencia and is open 3-6pm Thursday and Saturday, 10am-noon and 3-6pm on Sunday.

Arrival and Departure. Rosario is well served by rail, with trains between Buenos Aires and Santa Fé ($4\frac{1}{2}$ hours and 3 hours respectively) calling in several times a day — either at Rosario Norte-Mitré station (Wheelwright 1520) or at Rosario Oeste-Belgrano (Paraná and 9 de Julio).

Rosario is second only to Buenos Aires and Córdoba as a bus transport hub. There are daily buses to virtually anywhere you could want to go, including Asunción (Paraguay), and several a week to Montevideo (Uruguay), Neuquén and Bariloche. The station is at Cafferata and Santa Fé.

Accommodation and Food. The best central hotels, all under $10, are the Internacional (Entre Ríos 1045; tel 041-211426) and the simpler Crisol (Sarmiento 3038; tel 827683). The Micro (Santa Fé 3650; tel 397192), near the bus terminal, and the Río (Rivadavia 2665; tel 396421) are cheaper.

Among the best places to eat are Restaurant Don Rodrigo (Santa Fé 968), the Elizabeth (Rioja and Mitré) and the Presidente (Corrientes 919).

Help and Information. For tourist information go to the office at Santa Fé 581. The post office is at Córdoba 721, and the 24-hour telephone office at San Luís 936. Cambio Exprinter at Córdoba 960 changes cash and travellers' cheques; Banco Río is at Santa Fé 1260.

NORTHEAST ARGENTINA

Argentina's northeastern region comprises the provinces of Entre Ríos, Corrientes and Misiones. It is also known as Mesopotamia, from its position between the Paraná and Uruguay rivers.

The magnificent Iguazú Falls, the country's biggest tourist attraction, are in the north of Misiones province — most travellers pass through Corrientes and Entre Ríos without giving them a second look. This is understandable in so far as the landscape just looks like a lusher version of the monotonous pampa to the south — populated by herds of contented cattle grazing the meadows or relaxing blissfully up to their hindquarters in flooded ditches. But to ignore this part of the country is to dismiss the special history and atmosphere of the riverside towns, which have survived the architectural ravages of the 20th century better than their counterparts elsewhere. And the influence of the Guaraní Indians and the warmth of the people contribute to the distinctiveness of the region.

This section begins with Entre Ríos province, before heading north to cover Corrientes and Misiones.

Entre Ríos Province

Something of the old Argentina of the estancias seems to linger on in this most untouristy province, which holds the country's most fertile farmland. Apart from Paraná, the capital, most interest lies in the east along the Río Uruguay, though the riverside towns are important primarily as border crossings into Uruguay.

PARANA

Founded in 1588, Paraná was the capital of Argentina for nine years in the mid-19th century, during power struggles between Buenos Aires and the provinces. The grandeur of the city's public spaces reflects its history; the centrepiece is Plaza 1 de Mayo, and Paraná's riverside location adds to its already considerable charm.

Outstanding buildings include the Cathedral, in the main square, the Casa de Gobierno (Plaza Carbo), and the Colegio Nuestra Señora del Huerto (Monte Caseros 51 at Urquiza), which was the seat of government during Urquiza's presidency (1851-1862). The two most interesting museums are the Museo Histórico de Entre Ríos at Laprida and Buenos Aires, and the Museo Ciencias Naturales y Antropología at Rivadavia 462.

Arrival and Departure. Austral (Urquiza 1070; tel 214314) flies to Buenos Aires daily except Sunday. There is also a daily train to the capital (11 hours), from the station at Bulevar Racedo and 9 de Julio.

Paraná's position makes it a good place for catching buses in all directions. There are services daily to virtually everywhere you can think of, though you'll have to make do with buses just several times a week to Montevideo and Asunción. Most frequent of all are the buses running the 30-minute trip west across the river to Santa Fé, which involves going through the 1½-mile long Túnel Subfluvial Hernandarias. The bus station is at Ramírez and Almafuerte.

Accommodation and Food. The railway station area is the best place to look for cheap residenciales. For $10 you can stay at the San Martín (San Martín 832; tel 214901) the Liniers (Santiago del Liniers 400) or the 9 de Julio (9 de Julio 974).

One of the best places to eat fish in Paraná is the Restaurant Club de Pescadores, near the river. Also recommended are the Luisito (9 de Julio 149), and the Cafetería Manabí (Urquiza 1055).

Help and Information. The tourist office is at Corrientes 110. For stamps go to the post office at Monte Caseros and 25 de Mayo. The telephone office (open 24 hours) is at San Martín 735. Cambio Tourfé (San Martín 777) changes cheques, but at a poor rate. Banco Río, for advances on Visa, is at Pellegrini 29.

NORTH ALONG THE RIO URUGUAY

By heading east across the province you hit the Uruguay river and the border with Brazil. If you aren't planning to leave the country, then the route northwards to Concordia is a most pleasant one.

Gualeguaychú. This is a charming town, with a fine promenade along the Río Gualeguaychú. A short distance away is a bridge to the Uruguayan town of Fray Bentos — not to be outdone, the Entrerrianos have christened one of their towns Bovril, which lies northeast of Paraná. There is a good choice of restaurants along the waterfront, and staying overnight is no hardship. Hospedaje Mayo (Bolívar 550; tel 0446-7661) is a decent place.

There are frequent bus connections with Fray Bentos and Mercedes in Uruguay (border formalities are minimal), in addition to daily buses to Paraná and to Buenos Aires, which is just three hours south. The Uruguayan consulate is at Rivadavia 510.

Concepción del Uruguay. Once capital of the province for a century, this is among the most interesting settlements on the Río Uruguay — partly by not being a border post. The main square is pleasant, and the Cabildo (San Martín and Moreno) is worth seeing. The most unusual building in town is the Cathedral, an exceptional Graeco-Roman influenced creation, built in the 19th century. The tourist office (9 de Julio 844) sometimes has maps.

Bus services are good to towns both north and south, with regular departures also west to Paraná. Cheap rooms are available in the Hospedaje Soledad (Gallarza 1034); the Residencial Miguelito (10 del Oeste 190; tel 0442-4848) is more comfortable.

Colón. If you have a particular desire to cross to Paysandú in Uruguay, you must do so via Colón, a short distance north of Concepción. The riverside scene is picturesque, but Colón's status as a frontier town has sapped the town of some of its charm. Buses cross the toll bridge to Paysandú; otherwise take the boat. The Uruguayan consulate is at San Martín 103 (tel 21350).

Buses between Concepción del Uruguay and Concordia pass by several times a day; in addition, there are daily buses to Paraná (5 hours). The Ver-Wei (25 de Mayo 10; tel 21972) is a cheap place to stay, and you can take your pick of the parrilladas along the river promenade.

Parque Nacional El Palmar. This is the most worthwhile stop before you get to Concordia, 30 miles/48km further north. The park is said to contain the most southerly palm trees in the world; it also supports abundant wildlife and conceals pre-Columbian burial sites. You can stay overnight for a few dollars by hiring a tent at the campsite, which is equipped with a cafeteria and an information office.

The park can be visited easily from either Colón or Concordia. Buses between the two towns pass the entrance, though check in advance whether the driver is willing to stop; if not, hitch or take a tour. The Comisión de Turismo in Concordia (La Rioja 622, tel 211551) can arrange the latter.

CONCORDIA

This large town (population 100,000) is 162 miles/260km east of Paraná on the Río Uruguay. The town has a certain old-fashioned charm and is pleasant enough, while not being worth crossing Mesopotamia for. Its main source of interest lies in its position on the Uruguayan border, and its proximity to the Parque Nacional El Palmar, described above.

Most hotels are around the railway station, the cheapest being Residencial Terminal (Yrigoyen and San Lorenzo Este) and the Embajador (San Lorenzo 75). The Imperial at Urquiza 507 (tel 045-212535) is classier. The best choice of restaurants is along Yrigoyen.

Trains stop at Concordia en route between Buenos Aires ($8\frac{1}{2}$ hours) and Posadas (11 hours). The train to Corrientes takes 13 hours. Buses to Salto in Uruguay run from the terminal at J.B. Justo and Yrigoyen. But taking the ferry is more fun: colectivo number 2, marked Puerto, links the municipal bus terminal (Pellegrini and Alberdi) with the port via the railway station. The boat crosses six times between 8am and 6pm on weekdays, and four times on Saturday. The 15-minute journey costs $2.

The best place to change cash or cheques is at Cambio Tourfé (Mitré 43). The Uruguayan consulate at Entre Ríos 661 opens from 7.30am to 3.30pm.

Corrientes Province

Corrientes forms the northern half of Mesopotamia. The environment ranges from subtropical swamp and forest in the north to temperate grazing land in the south. The wide variety of habitats, particularly in the north, is home to many rare species, jaguars and parrots among them. In the east of the province near the Río Uruguay are a couple of old Jesuit missions.

CORRIENTES

Along with its twin city of Resistencia (see page 505), Corrientes owes its existence to the River Paraná. It was founded as a fort and missionary outpost in 1588, and was reportedly saved from capture by 6,000 Indians after a bolt of lightening killed some of them and scattered the rest. This stroke of good fortune was attributed to the divine power of the cross which stood outside the town; this venerable object is now on display at the Iglesia de la Cruz.

Corrientes (population 150,000) is not a bad place once you have got used to the heat and humidity — it's more pleasant than Resistencia at any rate. Wandering around the older parts of the city you can even begin to feel the atmosphere conjured up by Graham Greene in *The Honorary Consul*, which was set in Corrientes. More specifically, there are plenty of colonial buildings to explore. And the city is lively after dark, particularly along Junín with its thronging pavement confiterías.

The carnival in Corrientes is one of the most famous in Argentina, and is a very colourful affair that attracts people from all around.

Arrival and Departure. Flights leave several times a day for Buenos Aires. Other connections are poor, but the proximity of Resistencia facilitates access by air. Buses for the airport leave an hour before each flight from the main Plaza Cabral, and 90 minutes before flights from nearby Resistencia airport. Aerolíneas Argentinas is at Junín 1301 (tel 23850) and Austral at Córdoba 983 (tel 22570).

A crowded train serves Buenos Aires daily, taking 21 hours ($32 in primera). The train station and the bus terminal are combined at Maipú block 2600, a couple of miles south of the centre. Colectivos run between it and the municipal bus terminal at Costanera and Salta, and buses run straight to the main square.

Buses run several times daily to Buenos Aires (12 hours) and Posadas (6 hours), once or twice a day to Puerto Iguazú and neighbouring provincial capitals. Buses to Resistencia, a 30-minute journey, leave from the municipal terminal.

Accommodation and Food. There are few cheap places to stay in Corrientes. Residencial SOS (Irigoyen 1771; tel 60330), which charges $10, is not bad. The Sosa nearby at number 1676 (tel 66747) is more comfortable but double the price.

Junín is the best street in which to look for food and beer, though pacifists may balk at the idea of patronizing Café Exocet. There is an excellent pizzeria at Catamarca and Bolívar, Los Pinos. Also try Cafetería IUS (Salta and Martínez), which is a student hangout.

Exploring. The city retains many of its colonial buildings. Among the best are the Casa del Gobernador (Salta and Moreno), built in 1814, and the early 18th-century Palacio Municipal at 25 de Mayo and San Juan. There are several fine churches too, among them the Iglesia de la Merced (25 de Mayo and Buenos Aires) and the Cathedral, on the main square. The best museums are the Museo de Ciencias Naturales (Buenos Aires and San Martín) and the Museo Colonial e Histórico (9 de Julio and La Rioja).

The waterfront promenade, the Costanera, is good for a stroll; you can continue eastwards as far as the Parque Mitré, of which the Correntinos are justly proud.

Help and Information. *Tourist information:* the tourist office is at Rioja 475 and Quintana (open 7am-9pm), and has details of trains and buses. There is also a helpful municipal office on the square.

Communications: the post office is at San Martín and San Juan, and the telephone office is on Pellegrini near the corner with Mendoza (open 7am-midnight).

Money: scope for changing money is better in Resistencia. In Corrientes, about the only place to exchange travellers' cheques is the Banco de Ibera at 9 de Julio 1002. Banco Río has a branch at Pellegrini 1101.

Paraguayan Consulate: Junín 1052 (tel 20836), open 9am-1pm.

Around Corrientes

Santa Ana de las Guácaras. This Jesuit settlement was founded in 1633, and contains many examples of 18th-century architecture. The chapel of Santa Ana, completed in 1891, is a highly decorated and greatly revered shrine. Buses to Santa Ana, 13 miles/20km east of Corrientes, leave from the municipal terminal and pass through lovely scenery.

Empedrado. This charming colonial town, 32 miles/52km south of Corrientes, has uncrowded beaches on the Río Paraná and restaurants serving the local *dorado* fish. Hotel Rosario (Mitré 1246; tel 30) is a good place to stay. The town is on the Buenos Aires railway and is also linked by bus to both Corrientes and Paraná.

ALONG THE RIO URUGUAY

From Corrientes, one road runs due east to Posadas in Misiones. Another sweeps south and then eastwards across the province to the Uruguay river and to Paso de los Libres. The only reason to stop off here is if you are heading into Brazil, via Uruguaiana. The cheapest place to stay is the Residencial 26 de Febrero (Uruguay 1297, tel 0772-22050), which charges $8.

Buses run several times daily to most of the major cities of the northeast, the main towns in the province, and to Uruguaiana. The town is also on the Buenos Aires-Posadas railway, but the train is usually full by the time it gets here. The two cambios on Colón can change dollars, as well as Brazilian and Argentinian currencies. The Brazilian consulate at Mitré 918 is open on weekday mornings.

Yapeyú is the next town north along the river. It is the site of a once prestigous Jesuit mission, which was founded in the 1620s but burnt to the ground in 1817; no substantial ruins have survived. But Yapeyú is also of interest as the birthplace of the independence figher, General San Martín, whose memorabilia are preserved in a museum. The uncompleted arch in the town centre recalls a more recent conflict: it is a memorial to those from the province who died in the Falklands War. It will not be completed until the islands are given to Argentina. One of the few places to stay is the Hostería del Yapeyú (Matorras and Cabral; tel 93066).

Ninety miles/144km north of Yapeyú, and midway between Paso de los Libres and Posadas, is Santo Tomé. From Puerto Hormiguero, 6 miles/10km south, a ferry crosses to São Borja in Brazil, operating 7.30am-4.30pm on weekdays, slightly shorter hours weekends. There are some Jesuit ruins a short walk south of Santo Tomé, though they are unimpressive in comparison with San Ignacio Miní in Misiones province. Santo Tomé and Yapeyú are connected by daily buses, which take three hours. You can stay at the Residencial Pucará (San Martín 557).

Misiones Province

Misiones takes up most of the wedge which juts out between Paraguay and Brazil in the top northeast corner of Argentina. Subtropical rainforest covers parts of the province, though its extent is fast diminishing.

The area was originally inhabited by Guaraní Indians, who provided a safe haven for the Spanish in the early days of the Conquest. Later came the Jesuits, who set up the missions after which the province is named. Thousands of Indians were settled and converted. Reminders of the Jesuits' once powerful influence are never far away, and there are substantial ruins dotted about the region, of which the most impressive is San Ignacio Miní.

Misiones' rich red soil makes the province an important agricultural producer; much of the country's yerba maté is grown here. The preponderance of fair Anglo-Saxon faces and German names bears witness to the fact that many of those living here are of Central European descent.

POSADAS

The provincial capital, Posadas, is at the western edge of Misiones, on the southern banks of the Paraná river. It is a bustling city of over 150,000 people, but is of interest only as a stopping-off place en route to more interesting destinations, including Paraguay. The bridge, which was built only recently to connect Posadas with Encarnación across the river, has brought the city a new role as an important frontier crossing. Furthermore, a continual stream of buses bring hundreds of Paraguayan shoppers across the border every day.

You can get a good view of the bridge and river from Parque República de Paraguay, at Alberdi and Cabral. However, you may be more interested by the Museo Regional de Posadas, also in the park. It has a small but diverse collection, dating from prehistoric times to the mission era, and also houses a crafts market. Opening hours are 8am-noon and 4-8pm Monday to Friday.

Arrival and Departure. Posadas is connected by air to Buenos Aires, several northern cities and also Puerto Iguazú (for the falls). Aerolíneas is at San Martín 2031 and Austral at Ayacucho and San Martín.

There is a daily train to Buenos Aires (20 hours, $32 primera), via Paso de los Libres (6 hours). The station is nine blocks east of the main square across Roque Saenz Peña, and three blocks south.

Buses run several times a day to Buenos Aires (15 hours), Concordia (9 hours) and Corrientes (4 hours), with fewer connections to lesser cities in the north and to Asunción (Paraguay). Express buses to Puerto Iguazú take six hours and cost around $20, but there are slow buses too, which stop in every small town. The bus terminal is at Mitré and Uruguay, eight blocks south and three blocks west of the main square.

Accommodation and Food. Hotel prices are slightly higher in Misiones than elsewhere in the country, and finding a room can be difficult if you arrive late. The most affordable places, at around $10, are near the bus terminal and include the Horianski (Libano 725; tel 22673) and the Majestic (Santa Fé 485; tel 35740). If everywhere else is full, try the City Hotel (on the Plaza; tel 0752-39401), which charges $20 a night.

You can eat most cheaply in the confiterías near the bus terminal, or try the excellent pollería nearby at Ayacucho and Tucumán. El Tropezón (San Martín 185) is not that cheap but serves wonderful parrilla.

Help and Information. For tourist information go to the municipal office in the main square, open 2-8pm. The post office is at Bolívar and Ayacucho, and the telephone office at Colón and Santa Fé. To change travellers' cheques go to Banco de la Nación (Azara and Bolívar), which gives the best rates.

The RN12 is the main road to Puerto Iguazú, and passes through rich grassland and fast disappearing forest. Ten miles/16km from Posadas is Candelaria, the first capital of the province. Today it is just a small settlement in the hills ten minutes walk north of the highway; there are some minor Jesuit ruins just outside the town. Other old mission sites are found at Santa Ana, 15 miles/24km further on, and also at Loreto, 4 miles/6km beyond and about half an hour's walk from the road. However, by far the best Jesuit ruins are at San Ignacio Miní, 38 miles/61km northeast of Posadas.

SAN IGNACIO MINI

This is the most impressive Jesuit ruin in Argentina, and one of only four well-preserved missions in southern South America. When San Ignacio was founded in 1695, and until the Triple Alliance War of 1865-70, Misiones was part of Paraguay. It was the dictator of that country, Rodríguez de Francia, who ordered San Ignacio to be burnt in 1817 — the Jesuits had already been expelled, in 1767, though the Indians had stayed on. The deserted mission was taken over by thick jungle, and so completely were the ruins concealed that they were not rediscovered until 1896.

Given this history it is surprising that the ruins have survived on such an impressive scale. The centrepiece of the *reducción* was the Plaza de Armas, around which the main public buildings were constructed. All are built from large blocks of red sandstone carved with beautiful bas-relief sculpture. To the west of the plaza are the workshops, schoolrooms and cemetery. The Indians' more crudely-built living quarters are ranged in terraced rows to the north, south and east.

A plan of the mission can be obtained at the site, which is open 7am to 7pm. Further information is available from the San Ignacio Miní museum. To make a proper tour allow two to three hours, and bring insect repellent.

San Ignacio, the small town adjoining the ruins, is served by frequent buses from Posadas (1 hour), and less often from Puerto Iguazú (5 hours). You can stay cheaply at Hospedaje El Descanso (Pellegrini 270), and Padre José Marx (Sarmiento and Rivadavia) offers private accommodation. Otherwise, camp near the site entrance at Rivadavia and Medina, where there are also several simple restaurants.

PUERTO IGUAZU AND THE FALLS

Many thousands of people pass through Puerto Iguazú each year on their way to the waterfalls that the country shares with Brazil. You can stay on either side of the border and cross freely between the two countries, but you would do well to base yourself in Puerto Iguazú, which is far more pleasant than its counterpart in Brazil; but it is also more expensive.

Puerto Iguazú is 11 miles/18km from the Falls, which are described fully on page 733, in the Brazil chapter.

Arrival and Departure. There are several flights daily from Buenos Aires, and weekly from Córdoba and other northern cities. Austral has an office at Aguirre and Bompland, and Aerolíneas at Aguirre and Eppens.

Buses run to most of the major cities in the north, and to Buenos Aires ($55). The bus terminal is at Córdoba and Misiones. Buses to Foz do Iguaçu, Brazil also leave from here, with departures every 15 minutes from 6.30am to 8pm.

Accommodation. Puerto Iguazú's hotels are clean but not cheap, most charging around $15. The most central is Hotel Misiones (Aguirre 389; tel 0757-20991), with friendly staff. Most other residenciales are on or off Aguirre; they include the King (Aguirre 915; tel 20360) and the Paquita (Córdoba 158, at Misiones; tel 20434), opposite the bus station. By far the best deal, however, is the Youth Hostel, which charges $2; it is a couple of miles out of town on the road to Foz do Iguaçu: take any Brazil-bound bus to get there.

Among the considerable number of places to eat out, Pizzería Ser at Victoria Aguirre 483 is reasonable value.

Help and Information. *Tourist information:* the tourist office at Aguirre 396 opens 7am-1pm and 2-8pm daily, but is of no great use.

Communications: the post office is at San Martín and Azara, and the telephone office at Aguirre and Los Cedros.

Money: Cambio Dick, at Aguirre 467, likes to think it has the monopoly of money dealing in town. But although it is open long hours (including weekends) the rate for cheques is poor, so shop around among the other cambios on Aguirre.

Brazilian consulate: Aguirre and Curupy, virtually opposite Entel.

CROSSING INTO BRAZIL

There are several places where you can cross into Brazil from Misiones. Two of them can be reached by bus from Oberá, which is 60 miles/100km east of Posadas and easily accessible from there. From Alba Posse, two hours by bus due east of Oberá, ferries cross the Río Uruguay daily to Puerto Maúa, Brazil. From San Javier, further south and three hours from Oberá, ferries cross to the Brazilian town of Porto Lucena. These leave regularly on weekdays and Saturday mornings.

del Estero, with several services a day to Clorinda and Asunción. Buses run once or twice a day to Salta (15 hours, $35). Ataco Norte runs the buses to Corrientes, which leave every half hour from Santa María de Oro and Santiago del Estero.

Accommodation and Food. The Residencia Alberdi (Alberdi 317, near the bus station), the San José (Rawson 306) and the Santiago del Estero (Santiago del Estero 155) are decent places, all in the $10-15 range. There are plenty of good restaurants, including several on 25 de Mayo, such as El Yate and Pizzería Napoli. Afterwards, stay up all night at the Whiskería Reviens (Yrigoyen and Güemes).

FORMOSA

The capital of Formosa province lies to the north of Resistencia, near the banks of the Río Paraguay and at the eastern extremity of the Chaco. The main reason to get off the bus here is in order to take the train to Embarcación — a long and dusty 19-hour trip west across the Chaco plains. Formosa itself enjoys a wetter and more tropical climate than the rest of the province, and dry spells alternate with violent downpours. The unpredictable weather somehow enhances the frontier town atmosphere, which exists even though Formosa is not a recognised border post for traffic to Paraguay — there is no bridge across the river. Clorinda, 73 miles/115km north, is the main crossing point; see page 569.

NORTHWEST ARGENTINA

This is one of the most popular regions to visit in Argentina, with highly varied and beautiful mountain scenery rising out of the hot, steamy plains. As well as being a challenge for anyone with an adventurous nature, the northwest is also the most historic region in the country — reminders of the past date from before the time of the Incas to the 19th century. Quilmes, in Tucumán province, is Argentina's most important archaeological site, and Salta is one of its most beautiful cities. In the extreme north, the whitewashed adobe villages of Jujuy are enchanting.

The northwest is big enough for tourists to still be fairly thin on the ground outside the main centres. If you venture up to the Indian villages in the high altitude mountain regions, you could well be the first gringo the local people have seen for several weeks or even months. Be wary of wandering completely off the beaten track, however: the Bolivian border is not particularly safe, thanks to the drug trade.

Salta and Jujuy Provinces

These two provinces are the prime tourist destinations of the Northwest. Much colonial heritage has been preserved, and the mountainous countryside is surprisingly remote, with a predominantly indigenous and mestizo population. Although this was the first area to be conquered, in the early 17th century, the Spanish were soon diverted and the Conquest was never quite completed. One of the most fascinating areas lies north and northwest of Jujuy, where there are particularly spectacular landscapes and fascinating Indian villages.

SALTA

This busy provincial capital (population 350,000) comes as a breath of fresh air after some of the more nondescript cities further east. This good impression is enhanced by the sunny, temperate climate. Opinions as to the meaning of the word Salta differ between a choice of 'very beautiful' and 'place of rest'. Both seem appropriate to a place of Salta's history and grandeur, much of which derives from the impressive buildings centred around Plaza 9 de Julio. Founded in 1582, Salta has long been a prosperous city, basing its wealth on agriculture and mining.

Mardi Gras (Shrove Tuesday) is celebrated in Salta in grand style, with a procession of floats, and water-bombing of easy targets. In the second week of September up to 100,000 pilgrims flock to Salta for the festival of the Señor and Señora del Milagro.

Arrival and Departure. There are flights to Santa Cruz (Bolivia) and Antofagasta (Chile) as well as to many important Argentinian cities. For information about flights contact Aerolíneas (Caseros 475; tel 087-214757) and Austral (Buenos Aires 46; tel 224590).

In addition to domestic services, including daily buses direct to Resistencia (15 hours, $35) and less frequent buses to La Quiaca and Pocitos on the border with Bolivia, there are weekly services — usually only in summer, weather permitting — to Antofagasta, an arduous journey of 20 hours. The bus station is in the southeast of town at Irigoyen and Puch, near Parque San Martín.

Salta is not on the main Buenos Aires-La Quiaca railway line, and you must change at Güemes, accessible by bus or train; Buenos Aires is 36 hours away. The railway station is at Ameghino 690.

SALTA

1 Railway Station
2 Residencial Güemes
3 Plaza Güemes
4 Telephone Office
5 Residencial Florida
6 Market
7 Plaza 9 de Julio
8 Cabildo
9 Cathedral
10 Residencial Centro
11 Tourist office
12 Aerolíneas Argentinas
13 San Francisco
14 Residencial España
15 Post Office
16 Bus station
17 San Bernardo
   Cable Car
18 Convento
   San Bernardo
19 Museo Antropológico
20 Peña Gauchos
   de Güemes

Accommodation. Vacant hotel rooms are scarce during the September festival, though you may be able to find space in a private home. The tourist office has a list of families, most of whom charge about $10. Señora Graciela de Toffoli (Mendoza 915; tel 217383) is recommended.

The cheapest hotels are near the railway station on the north side of the city; the Güemes (Necochea 649) is cheap at around $8. The Centro at Belgrano 657 (tel 220132) charges similar rates. A notch up are the Florida (Urquiza 718; tel 212133), on a busy commercial street, and the Balcarce (Balcarce 460; tel 218023). Also recommended is Residencial España (España 319; tel 217898), which costs $13 with private bath.

Eating and Drinking. Specialities include the Salta Negra beer, a strong dark brew, and the local sweets that you can buy at any confitería downtown, including the Río on the main square. There are several restaurants along Balcarce, and the Comedor-Pizzería Carlitos at Belgrano 511 serves excellent food at good prices. Two other Italian places are the Italiano (Buenos Aires and Urquiza, upstairs), and the more lively Sociedad Italiana (Santiago del Estero and Deán Funes). There are also various sandwich stands, including in Parque San Martín and opposite Hotel España.

For nightime drinking head for Cafeteria Mil y Mil, a video bar on España and Balcarce, or the Lions, an English-style pub at Córdoba and Alvarado. In the centre, try the bars at Jujuy 251 and Santa Fé 140.

Several restaurants put on live music, most famously at the Boliche Balderrama (San Martín 1126), though for traditional music Peña Gauchos de Güemes (Uruguay 750) is recommended.

Exploring. One of Salta's main attractions is the cathedral, on the main square, which was built in the late 19th century. The interior is decked out in red and gold, and contains two icons that were sent from Spain in 1592 and are said to have quelled an earthquake in 1862. On the opposite side of the square is the Cabildo, the old town hall, which houses the Museo Histórico del Norte, with a collection of furniture from colonial houses, and some religious art. It opens 10am-2pm and 3.30-7.30pm, daily except Monday.

Other fine buildings in Salta include the Convento San Bernardo and the Iglesia San Francisco, both on Caseros east of the main square, and the Casa de Hernández at Alvarado and Florida. Several colonial mansions are open to the public, including the Casa de Uriburu at Caseros 417.

The Museo Antropológico (Ejército del Norte and Polo Sur) contains finds from nearby Indian sites. It opens 9.30am-1pm and 5-8.30pm daily except Monday. More unusual, however, is the Museo de Arte Popular Ibero Americano at Caseros 476, which has beautiful crafts from all over Spanish America. It is open Thursday to Tuesday 9.30am-12.30pm and 5-8.30pm.

A cablecar connects Parque San Martín to the top of the Cerro San Bernardo, from where there is a fine panoramic view of the city. The cablecar runs 10am-7pm, and costs $4.

Shopping. The Mercado Municipal at San Martín and Florida is a good place to buy artesanía — llamas and alpacas are bred around Salta, so anything woolly is likely to be good value. The market keeps odd hours, closing noon-5pm and all day Sunday. The long boots called *salteños* are good value, and some shops make them to order. The Librería IEI on Belgrano has English books for sale or part exchange.

Help and Information. *Tourist information:* the municipal office at Buenos Aires 75 works in conjunction with the provincial tourist office, Emsatur, at number 95 (tel 310950), which opens every day 7am-1pm and 2-8pm.

Communications: the post office is at Deán Funes near the corner with España. The telephone office at Belgrano 824 is open 24 hours, though for international calls go to the office at Vicente López 124, open 8am-7.30pm.

Money: Banco Roberts (Mitré 43) changes Amex cheques and gives speedy cash advances on Visa cards. Dinar SRL (Mitré and España) changes all brands of travellers cheques, but charges 3% commission.

Consulates: Bolivia — Deán Funes 369 (tel 220954); Chile — Ejército del Norte 312 (tel 210827); Paraguay — Los Almendros 161 (tel 212562).

Around Salta

Tren a las Nubes. This is a tourist train that goes northwest from Salta through magnificent country to San Antonio de Los Cobres and the Polvarillo viaduct, and back again. The track was opened in 1948, having taken almost 30 years to build; the viaduct in particular is a colossal feat of engineering. The railway is lined with the graves of workers who died on the job. One of those who survived was a Yugoslav, Josip Broz, who went on to become Marshal Tito. The train runs through arid, open landscapes, dotted with cacti, llamas and brightly coloured eroded cliffs. The train climbs to 12,000ft/3,660m, so bring some coca leaves (if you can find some) to help mitigate the effects of the altitude.

The tourist train normally runs on Saturdays from April to November, with additional services in July and August. The journey takes 12 hours and the fare is $20. However, the train has been the victim of government cutbacks, and the service was suspended in 1991. The original train is due to be reinstated eventually, but for the moment a passenger carriage is attached to the Monday and Friday freight trains. It is possible to return the next day by train, and there is road transport too. San Antonio is an unattractive and extremely quiet mining town. Most passengers in the crowded carriages are Indians, many returning to work in the mines. You can stay in Hospedaje Los Andes.

Many trains continue to Socompa, on the Chilean border; it takes an impressive 30 hours to cover the 340 miles/544km to the frontier from Salta. Socompa is a small and lonely collection of buildings, in the shadow of huge volcanoes. On the Chilean side trains take freight only, and it's virtually impossible to bribe your way on. You should be able to continue by road north to Calama, but be prepared to wait around for a lift.

The RN51 highway northwest of Salta follows the same, dramatic route as the railway for part of the way (passing San Antonio de los Cobres), before veering northwards to the Chilean border. This is the route taken by buses from Salta to Antofagasta.

SAN SALVADOR DE JUJUY

Though founded in 1593, the capital of Jujuy province looks much like any other Argentinian town — indeed the outskirts are particularly uninspiring. It has retained some of its old architecture and character, but the town loses out in any comparison with Salta. Nevertheless, Jujuy is a pleasant place to use as a base for trips in the province and to conduct business before heading north into Bolivia.

There are bus connections with all nearby towns and cities, operating to and from the station at Dorrego and Iguazú; and three trains a week to Buenos Aires, via Tucumán, a gruelling journey which is likely to end up appreciably longer than its scheduled 36 hours.

The most popular hotel among backpackers is the Lavalle (Lavalle 372; tel 22698). More comfortable is the Belgrano (Belgrano 627; tel 26459). When hungry, head down to the Hotel Chung King catering empire, which now encompasses three restaurants, all next to each other around Alvear 627. None of them is remotely Chinese, and the main restaurant, where fish is cheap, is particularly recommended; add up your bill carefully at the end. The main meeting place is the smart Confitería Royal, on the pedestrian main street, Belgrano.

Help and Information. The tourist office (Belgrano 690) is very helpful and open daily. For stamps go to the post office at Independencia and Lamadrid. The telephone office is at Pérez 141. Tagma, at Belgrano 731, changes travellers' cheques, though travel agencies sometimes offer a better rate. There is a branch of Banco Río at Alvear 802.

The Bolivian consulate is at Güemes 828 (tel 22010), and the Immigration Office at 19 de Abril 105 (tel 22638).

NORTH OF JUJUY

North and northwest of Jujuy the landscape is dry and increasingly barren as the altitude increases and puna vegetation takes over. The RN9 runs north from Jujuy along the valley of the Río Grande, known as the Quebrada de Humahuaca. On each side stand strikingly coloured cliffs of red or green-tinged rock, where cacti grow in abundance. The most impressive view is on the way to the impoverished village of Purmamarca, 3 miles/5km off the road. Some distance south is Tumbaya, which has several beautiful old churches and is typical of the 17th-century Indian villages in the area. With luck you may come across a local festival.

Tilcara. The main attraction in Tilcara, 52 miles/84km and two hours north of Jujuy, is the site of the Pucará fort. Long assumed to be an Inca fortress like the one at Quilmes (see page 516), it is now known to have been constructed by the local Tilcara tribe before the incursions from the north — possibly even to defend themselves against the Incas. The fortress covers a very large area on a hill to the south of the town. You can walk to it by following Calle Padilla out of the town and across the Río Huasamayo. From the hilltop you get a fine view of the Quebrada de Humahuaca. The archaeological museum in the town houses artefacts from this and other pre-Conquest settlements in the region.

The town's major folk festival is held in mid-January, and in the week before Easter Tilcara becomes the focus of the whole region's celebrations, as people pour in from the surrounding villages.

Stay at the friendly Residencia Eden, unless you prefer hot water and greater comfort, in which case try Hotel Antigal. The best place to eat is Restaurant Pucará. Buses between La Quiaca and Jujuy pass through seven times a day.

Humahuaca. This is the largest settlement in the valley, at a height of 9,650ft/2,940m and 78 miles/126km north of Jujuy. It is a beautiful place, with narrow cobbled streets and a delightful atmosphere. There are ancient whitewashed churches both here and in the surrounding villages, many of them panelled in cactus-wood and decorated by Indians. The church in the village of Huacalera (on the main road from Tilcara) is an archetype of simplicity and the finest in the area.

Humahuaca is not an undiscovered gem. Tourist buses arrive every day at lunchtime, and their occupants emerge to have lunch and be entertained by live Andean pipe-music. The tourists are then led to the various craft markets and to the Indian market by the railway station — which has deteriorated but also been made more expensive as a result.

The Museo Folklórico Regional is worth a visit, as is the Instituto de Cultura Indígena, which organizes lectures, tours, concerts, exhibitions and language classes to promote Indian culture. At noon make sure you are in a good position from which to watch the top of the church tower: at this time every day the mechanical statue of St Francis Solano emerges and lifts its hand in a papal gesture.

There are frequent connections by bus to Jujuy, and trains on the Jujuy-La Quiaca line pass through on alternate days. Residencial Humahuaca (Córdoba 401) is a good place to stay, though the Youth Hostel at Buenos Aires 447 is less than half the price at $3. Most restaurants only open during the day for lunchtime peñas, but Del Norte (on Belgrano) is good, cheap, and open in the evenings.

HEADING INTO BOLIVIA

The two main routes north to Bolivia are along the RN9 north from Jujuy to the border at La Quiaca/Villazón, which is the most popular, and along the RN34 to the border crossing at Pocitos/Yacuiba.

Route to La Quiaca. The RN9 north from Humahuaca is largely unpaved; it travels through empty, mountainous terrain and just a few small settlements. These villages are a good antidote if you have had enough of the holiday crowds in Humahuaca. For example from Iturbe, 100 miles/160km north, you should be able to arrange transport to the charming village of Iruya. This journey takes you through fantastic scenery, which alone makes the trip worthwhile.

La Quiaca is a cold, high-altitude and unappealing place, full of Bolivian shoppers. If you need to stay overnight, Residencial Cristal (Sarmiento 539) is reliable, and there are cheaper dormitory-style places too.

The train from Jujuy takes eight hours, while buses take six or seven. Villazón, across the border, is just ten minutes walk away. Immigration is open 8am-6pm, though may be closed at lunchtime. If you need a visa get it in Jujuy or Salta, as the consulate in La Quiaca has been known to charge $10 for one. There are banks in town, which should change excess pesos; cambios at the border may even change travellers' cheques.

Route to Pocitos. The RN34 takes you through a subtropical region that is totally different in character from the area to the west. At Pichanal a road heads northwest through spectacular wilderness to Aguas Blancas, a little-used border crossing into Bolivia.

Pocitos, marked on some maps as Profesor Salvador Mazza, has grim residenciales — stay in Tartagal, further south, if you are running late. The border is open 8am-6pm, and there is a Bolivian consulate at Güemes 446. Buses run to Pocitos direct from Salta.

SOUTH TO CAFAYATE

The main route south to Tucumán runs via Metán and Trancas. But there are more interesting routes further west, which pass through lovely scenery and isolated towns and villages that have changed little over the years; many retain their simple whitewashed houses and narrow streets, and the local people are remarkably hospitable. There is little tourism in this area.

The RN68 runs due south from Salta through Cafayate. This route takes you through the magnificent Quebrada de Cafayate, with its bizarre formations sculpted from the lurid pink rock. Illuminated at dusk the scene could be straight out of *Star Trek*. While Captain Kirk has not been laid on for the tourists, there are signposts along the way identifying the various formations, many of them named after the castles, waterfalls, etc. that they resemble.

The RN40 through the more westerly valley of the Río Calchaquí is a very much longer way round to Cafayate and Tucumán. But it serves some charming villages and is a worthwhile detour.

Cachi. This small community lives in a most fantastic setting, at the head of the Calchaquí valley and beneath the 20,900ft/6,380m Cachi mountain. It is a well-known weaving centre and has a good archaeological museum with carved stones from Indian settlements. For $7 you can stay at the Residencial Nevado de Cachi; the Albergue Juvenil is half the price for a bed in a shared room. Every year brings more tourists, and accommodation is short in the holiday season.

There are daily buses to Salta (5 hours) and Molinos (2½ hours); fewer go on to Cafayate, and you may need to change at Angastaco, south of Molinos. The journey west from Salta involves a breathtaking ascent of over 3,300ft/1,000m through the so-called Valle Encantado.

Molinos. This village is 2¼ hours by bus south of Cachi and 70 miles/112km northwest of Cafayate. It is nestled in the Lurancato valley against a mountainous backdrop which includes the 17,250ft/5,260m Cerro Inca Huasi. There is a Jesuit church, built in 1720, and you can walk to a number of archaeological sites in the neighbouring valleys; the most impressive is El Churcal, where there are remnants of a 15th-century Indian settlement. Molinos' solitary residencial is in the former residence of the last Spanish governor; a bed in a shared room costs $6.

CAFAYATE

This small wine-making centre is popular among Argentinians on holiday. It is an idyllic town where the locals greet each other effusively as they cycle along the wide, sunny streets. Life revolves around the main square, with its golden-coloured church framed by the mountains in the distance. This is also where you'll find several restaurants, the unhelpful tourist office, and crafts shops selling tapestries and cactus-wood boxes. The Rodolfo Bravo museum on Calle Colón is an interesting private collection of pottery and funerary urns; ring the bell to be let in. About a mile north towards the Río Colorado is the Cueva de San Isidro, where there are rock paintings; ask the locals for directions. It is possible to hire a bike in town and this is a good way to explore further afield.

El Indio (on Toscano near the Plaza) runs buses to Salta and south to Santa María, and La Aconquija (Lamadrid 48) serves Tucumán via Santa María twice daily.

A good place to stay is Residencial Arroyo (Quintana de Niño 160), which charges $6. For a little more comfort go to the Gran Real (Güemes Sur 218), where a room costs $10. All prices are higher in the tourist season, when it can be hard to find rooms.

Quilmes, Tafí del Valle and the other important destinations south of Cafayate are in Tucumán province. They are described on page 515-16.

Tucumán Province

Tucumán has a particular sense of history and is one of the most rewarding provinces in Argentina to visit. It possesses numerous archaeological sites, including some relating to the brief presence of the Incas, as well as early colonial settlements founded by the conquistadores as they ventured down from Peru. The mountainous landscape is also magnificent — at times bleak and arid, but always broken by fertile irrigated valleys which have been the focus of human habitation in the area.

SAN MIGUEL DE TUCUMAN

Fans of Kingsley Amis' *Lucky Jim* may remember that in it L. S. Caton, the shadowy academic, absconds from England to take up a chair at the University of Tucumán. A more famous figure locally is General Belgrano, who defeated the royalist forces at the Battle of Tucumán in 1812, an event celebrated on 24 September. The provincial capital is called 'San Miguel' by its 500,000 residents, but is generally known outside as 'Tucumán'.

The provincial capital has a lot more going for it than a fictional literary connection. Founded in 1565, Tucumán is one of Argentina's most historical cities. It is also one of its most attractive, though it has suffered from neglect — many of its old buildings seem to be crumbling their way steadily out of existence. More solid is the massive peak of the Sierra de Aconquija, which rises up to the west.

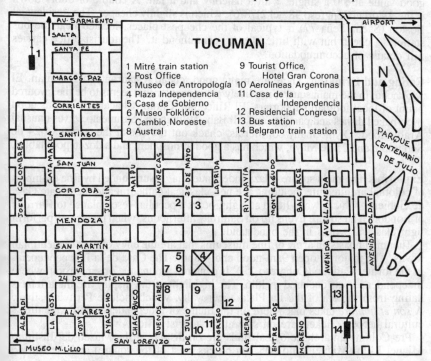

TUCUMAN

1 Mitré train station
2 Post Office
3 Museo de Antropología
4 Plaza Independencia
5 Casa de Gobierno
6 Museo Folklórico
7 Cambio Noroeste
8 Austral
9 Tourist Office,
  Hotel Gran Corona
10 Aerolíneas Argentinas
11 Casa de la
  Independencia
12 Residencial Congreso
13 Bus station
14 Belgrano train station

Tucumán is above all a lively place, with a university and a large young population. Plaza Independencia, at the heart of the city, is busy way into the night.

Arrival and Departure. *Air:* there are several flights a day to Buenos Aires, Córdoba, and Salta, and a few each week to other cities. Aerolíneas Argentinas is at 9 de Julio and San Lorenzo (tel 228747), Austral at 24 de Setiembre 537, and Federal in Hotel de Gran Corona at 24 de Setiembre 498. The airport is 6 miles/9km north of the centre, and is served by bus from outside the Hotel Mayoral (24 de Setiembre 364).

Train: the Tucumán-Buenos Aires express leaves on Wednesdays and Sundays and takes 18 hours; the cheapest seats cost $70. Other trains run once or twice a day and take 28 hours; primera costs $38. Trains also run north to Jujuy and beyond.

The Belgrano station at Sáenz Peña and Charcas, opposite the bus terminal, handles primera and turista clase trains only, while the Mitré station in Plaza Alberdi takes the pullman and coche cama services. The two are linked by bus No. 8, which passes through the city centre.

Bus: buses run several times a day to Córdoba (8 hours), Salta (5 hours) and Catamarca (5 hours), and at least once a day to cities further afield such as Buenos Aires and Mendoza, which are both 16 hours away. The dilapidated bus station is on Sáenz Peña near the end of 24 de Setiembre. The surrounding area is lively but chaotic — watch out for pickpockets among the market stalls.

Accommodation. The Congreso (Congreso 74; tel 222127) is very central and good value at $10 a single, with a balcony and a fan. A couple of doors down is the Astoria (Congreso 98; tel 217876), which is slightly cheaper. The Residencial Boston (Sáenz Peña 77) is typical of the cheapest places, located near the bus station — cheap but with little else to recommend it. The tourist office carries full details of accommodation.

Eating and Drinking. There are many good, cheap restaurants in Tucumán. El Mostacho, in the main square, is a lively pizza counter that seems to be the favoured haunt of local football supporters. El Rincón de Cholo (Chacabuco 31) has good oven-baked dishes and parrilla, and Ali Baba at Junín and Sarmiento serves unusual Arabic food. Of the many confiterías, check out the one at the corner of 24 de Setiembre and 25 de Mayo, which has a good atmosphere and a dozen pool tables.

Exploring. The main square, Plaza Independencia, is surrounded by fine examples of colonial architecture including the neo-classical cathedral and the ornate Casa de Gobierno which, when lit up at night, bears a peculiar resemblance to Harrods of London. The square livens up on Saturday afternoons, when musicians perform light classical works in the bandstand.

Tucumán boasts an array of fine museums that are the envy of most Argentinian towns. The majority open 9am-noon and 4-8pm. The Casa de la Independencia, in the former Cabildo (Congreso 151), is centered around the original room where independence was declared in 1816. The highlight of the display are the artefacts dating from the era of the La Plata Viceroyalty, which include Peruvian silver. A *son et lumiére* takes place here on the theme of Independence and Argentina's cultural heroes. Tickets are on sale at the tourist office.

Pre-Columbian archaeological finds are on display at the Museo del Instituto Miguel Lillo (Miguel Lillo 205, ten blocks west of the square) and the Museo de Antropología (25 de Mayo 265); the latter draws its collection from all over the Americas and Africa. The Museo Folklórico Provincial at 24 de Septiembre 565 is the best of its kind in the region; it is open Wednesday to Sunday only.

When you've had your fill of museums, take a breather in the Parque 9 de Julio, which covers a large area northeast of the bus station, or stroll along 25 de Mayo, one of the main shopping streets.

Help and Information. *Tourist information:* the tourist office is at 24 de Septiembre 484, open daily 7am-10pm. Ask to see the information on Tafí del Valle and Quilmes, as there are no printed handouts. The Mercado Artesanal is in the same building. A recommended travel agent for tours in the area is Delfin Turismo at 24 de Setiembre 370.

Communications: the post office is at 25 de Mayo and Córdoba; the telephone office is at Muñecas and Córdoba.

Money: Cambio Noroeste at 24 de Setiembre 549 changes travellers' cheques at 3% commission. There is a branch of Banco Río at San Martín 586.

TAFI DEL VALLE

This small town lies in a lush valley long inhabited by Diaguita Indians, who farmed on the surrounding hill terraces. Following the Conquest the Jesuits set about converting the natives, and left an adobe chapel. Just outside Tafí is La Banda, which has its own Jesuit chapel and monastery. The main draw to the area, however, are the archaeological sites at El Mollar and Quilmes. At an altitude of 6,600ft/2,000m, Tafí del Valle is exceedingly wet in summer and colder than Tucumán in winter.

There are several buses a day to Tucumán and Santa María, both journeys taking three hours; buses also serve Cafayate, five hours north.

Rooms are hard to find during the December-March season. For $4-5 you can stay at the Hotel Colonial (Belgrano and Faroles; tel 21083) or Hospedaje La Cumbre (Diego de Rojas; tel 21016). The ACA Hostería (San Martín and Campero; tel 21027) is good but twice the price. When looking for food, keep an eye open for the spicy cheese and wine which are local specialities. Las Ruedas and Peñas Azules, both on Critto, are not bad restaurants.

El Mollar. This menhir park contains 129 standing stones (some carved), which were collected from a number of sites. The setting is absolutely magnificent. To attend one of the local festivals staged here is a most unique experience. El Mollar is 6 miles/10km south of Tafí del Valle, easily reached on foot or by bus. You can stay at the Hostería FEIA by the site, which has a restaurant.

Amaichá del Valle. While usually visited merely in passing by people en route to Quilmes, this is an extraordinarily friendly place. It is also one of the few places in Argentina where Pachamama, the earth goddess, is honoured in a festival, which is held in February.

Amaichá is 25 miles/40km northwest of Tafí, and marks the point where the road turns off southwest to Santa María in Catamarca province. It is also the closest place to Quilmes with accommodation. The best value is offered by Hostería Colonial, which charges $8 a night, though the hot water supply is erratic; the Comedor Rancho de Fili is the best restaurant.

Buses between Tucumán and Cafayate or Santa María stop in Amaichá; the journeys take five hours, three hours and one hour respectively.

QUILMES

This fort once marked the southern boundary of the Inca empire and is the most significant archaeological site in Argentina. It is named after the Quilmes tribe who built it, and who held out against the Spanish conquerors until 1667. Following the eventual fall of the fort many of the Quilmes chose to commit suicide rather than be captured. The survivors were resettled elsewhere, mainly in a colony outside Buenos Aires, where they died out within one or two generations.

The fort, which extends up the side of the Cerro Alto del Rey, consists of terracing which the Indians built as they were driven further and further up the mountain. You can climb the ridges on each side of the site: these form excellent vantage points from which to survey the rest of the valley, where there are other fortifications. The present layout gives little clue as to what the fort actually looked like, and some assert that the government has restored the ruins incorrectly. In any case Quilmes is an impressive sight. There is a small museum at the entrance.

Arrival and Departure. Quilmes is 14 miles/22km northwest of Amaichá del Valle along the Cafayate road, and then 3 miles/5km walk down a dirt track. The handful of daily buses running between Cafayate and Tucumán or Santa María pass the turnoff. If approaching from Santa María (see page 519), the best bus to get is the 7am departure with El Indio. From wherever you start, check the timetable so you have a rough idea when to pick up buses for the return journey. Allow two or three hours for a full exploration of the site, not including the hour required to walk there from the road. Take plenty of water.

Catamarca Province

This is a neglected area of the Northwest, even though it has a wealth of picturesque villages and excellent mountain scenery. There are Andean settlements you can explore on horseback and exciting trips to be done north across the puna; and San Fernando is one of the most pleasant northwestern capitals. The province also boasts a rich archaeological legacy, and unexcavated sites are dotted all over the place. Many of these date from the period when Catamarca was an important centre of pre-Columbian civilization: Santa María, in the northeastern corner of the province, spearheaded the resistance to the Spanish conquistadores.

SAN FERNANDO DEL VALLE DE CATAMARCA

Usually referred to simply as Catamarca, the provincial capital is an attractive and atmospheric city set among rolling hills. It boasts entire streets of old buildings, and a fine cathedral. The relaxed pace in summer may be due to the heat, and the siesta is strictly observed among the city's population of 88,000.

Catamarca celebrates two major festivals. The Fiesta del Virgen del Valle falls during Holy Week, but more unusual and colourful is the Fiesta del Poncho, in the winter, which attracts weavers from small villages all over the area.

Arrival and departure. Flights leave daily for Buenos Aires and several times a week for Córdoba and Neuquén. Aerolíneas Argentinas (Sarmiento 589 and República) is the only airline operating out of Catamarca, and runs a bus service to the airport, 17 miles/27km south of town.

There are several buses a day to La Rioja (2 hours), Córdoba (6 hours), Tucumán (5 hours), and at least one daily to Mendoza and Santiago del Estero. The bus station is at Güemes and Tucumán.

Accommodation and Food. One of the cheapest places, with no sign outside, is Hospedaje Jocar (Zurita 740), at $7. The Plaza (Rivadavia 278; tel 26558), and the Familiar (Güemes 841) charge $10, but are recommended.

The only sensible place to eat is at the Club Unión Obrero (Tucumán 830), a working men's club where middle-aged men drink and play billiards and chess well into the night. You are welcome to eat in the hospitable comedor, which has excellent cheap dishes and vies for custom amicably with an equally good Syrian-owned restaurant just across the road.

Exploring. Among the finest examples of colonial architecture are the Cathedral, a beautiful rose-coloured building on the main square, and the Convento de San Francisco, at Esquiú and Rivadavia. The Adan Quiroga archaeological museum in the Esquiú Cultural Institute (Sarmiento 446) contains excellent displays of artefacts from all the major pre-Hispanic cultures, and is well worth a visit.

Three miles/5km west of Catamarca is Ciudad Perdida, a ruined Diaguita Indian settlement. About every half hour colectivo 10 runs along Calle Virgen del Valle, then out of town and past the Balneario Municipal. The site is opposite the pool on top of a hill. Foundations and walls at low level and covering an area the size of a football pitch are all that survive, amid huge cacti and thorn bushes.

Help and Information. *Tourist information:* the provincial tourist office at Urquiza and Maté de la Luna (tel 22999) is open every day 8am-8pm. There is a small craft market in the same building. Ammirati (Sarmiento 524; tel 29464) organizes tours in the region.

Communications: the post office is at San Martín 753, and the telephone office at Rivadavia 758, open 6am-midnight.

Money: Banco de la Provincia de Catamarca (Plaza de 25 de Mayo) charges low commission for changing cheques. Banco de Galícia (Rivadavia 554) gives cash advances on Visa.

ANDALGALA

This small town was founded as a fort by the Spanish in 1658, during the wars against the Indians. Towering in the distance is the Nevado del Candado, a peak over 16,400ft/5,000m high; lower down are fields of fruit trees. There aren't many old buildings left, but you can visit a couple of interesting museums, the Museo Provincial de Arqueología (San Martín Sur 110) and the private Museo Arqueológico Malli. Northeast of the town is Aconquija, an important archaeological site; the ruins are hard to reach, but many finds from the site are displayed in the Adan Quiroga museum in Catamarca.

Andalgalá is northwest of Catamarca, but there is no direct road and the journey by bus takes six hours. Buses run less frequently to Santa María (7 hours) and Tinogasta (5-6 hours), and just three times a week to Córdoba and Tucumán.

The Galileo, on Nuñez del Prado near the corner of López, is a decent place to stay, and there are several restaurants on the same street.

BELEN

Fifty-five miles/85km and $2\frac{1}{2}$ hours by bus west of Andalgalá, Belén lies at the heart of a rich agricultural region. There are numerous archaeological sites in the surrounding area, relics from which are displayed at the Museo Provincial Condor Huasi in town. Among them are finds from the remains of an Indian village near Londres, 10 miles/16km southwest of the town.

Belén is at an altitude of 9,200ft/2,800m, and its fine setting can be admired from Cerro Tiro. The hill is topped by a statue of Our Lady of Belén, who is honoured in a festival held between 20 December and 9 January. Belén is also the centre of the Catamarca weaving industry, examples of which you can buy in the town's main square.

Buses to Catamarca leave daily and take six or nine hours, depending on whether they go via Tinogasta or Andagalá. Services to Córdoba, Salta and Tucumán are weekly. Hotel de Turismo Belén (Belgrano and Cubas), Residencial Doña Pilar (Lavalle 462) and Residencial Gómez (Calchaquí 213) are the best places to stay, in descending order of price.

ANTOFAGASTA DE LA SIERRA

This altiplano settlement of just a few hundred people lies in a remote corner of the province at an altitude of 11,800ft/3,600m. Petrified lava from dormant volcanoes has been eroded into weird shapes and makes an astonishing lunar landscape; the pink flamingoes which gather around the numerous salt lakes add the only splash of colour. The bleak, cold area is inhabited by Indians who speak their own language and retain much of their ancestral culture. There are many archaeological sites near Antofagasta, the most famous being Gruta Salamanca, Pucara de la Alumbrera and Ruinas de Cayparcito. These can only be reached by foot or by mule, but this is not difficult to arrange.

Buses from Belén, 200 miles/320km south, take 12 hours and leave just once or twice a week at 6am. Alternatively, try to hitch a lift on a truck. The road to Antofagasta is a dirt track which may be impassable after rain. Accommodation is basic, and you must rely on family-type hospedajes.

TINOGASTA

This is a predominantly Indian town 50 miles/80km southwest of Belen. It is one of the most picturesque in the province, and has recently been discovered by backpackers. Many of the local people work in nearby copper mines, but others are involved in the cultivation of grapes and olives. The excellent local wine flows freely at the Grape Harvest festival held every February. At other times you'll have to be content drinking it at the local bars. For a more cultural experience visit the Museo Tulio Ribaudi on Constitución, which has a small archaeological collection.

Buses run twice a day to Catamarca ($5\frac{1}{2}$ hours) and La Rioja (5 hours) and weekly to Belén (3 hours), Andalgalá (5 hours) and Tucumán (12 hours). Good and cheap places to stay include the Familiar (Uriburu 231), the Persegoni (Villafañez 415) or the San José (Antonio del Pino 419). The best parrillada is the Rancha Huayra-Puca (Moreno and Copiapó).

Around Tinogasta

Fiambalá. This small town lies 30 miles/48km north up the valley from Tinogasta. Ten miles/16km beyond are hot springs, where you can enjoy the mountain scenery from the comfort of a warm rock pool. You may be able to get a lift on a truck, otherwise hire a horse, or walk; during the week you should have the place to yourself. You can stay in Fiambalá at the Hostería Fiambalá or the Residencial San Francisco. In summer the Club Andino leads expeditions on horseback into the cordillera from Fiambalá.

SANTA MARIA

This small town lies close to Catamarca's eastern boundary. Its main importance is as a base for trips into Tucumán province, including to Quilmes, described on page 516. But there is also a number of small archaeological sites that are within a few hours' walk of Santa María. The small museum in the Municipalidad on the main square is the best place to find out about these. The upmarket Hotel de Turismo Santa María (San Martín and 1 de Mayo) organizes tours to more distant and otherwise inaccessible archaeological sites in the region.

Santa María has daily buses to Tucumán and Salta, and services most days to Catamarca via Tafí del Valle or Belén. You can sleep moderately cheaply at the Hotel Plaza (on the square at San Martín 350; tel 309) or the Alemán (Quintana 146; tel 226); private rooms are also available.

La Rioja Province

The mountain valleys in western Rioja province support abundant orchards and olive groves. In the east, where the conditions are drier and poorer, the landscape is dotted with salt lakes and gnarled 'drunken sticks' — trees known locally as *palos borrachos*. South of the provincial capital the land is particularly arid and there are very few settlements.

LA RIOJA

The provincial capital (population 60,000) was destroyed by a major earthquake in 1894. This dealt a cruel blow to La Rioja's earlier appeal, and compared with Catamarca it seems downtrodden. It is not an unpleasant place and its calendar is peppered with local festivals — most famously the Semana de Rioja, which begins on May 20 and commemorates the founding of the city. Though accommodation is heavily booked, this is the time to see La Rioja at its best. As yet no day is set aside for the celebration of the birth of President Carlos Menem, the town's most famous son.

Arrival and departure. La Rioja is served by comparatively few flights, though there are several services a week from Buenos Aires and Córdoba. Aerolíneas Argentinas (Belgrano 57; tel 26307) is the only airline operating in La Rioja. The airport is 5 miles/8km north of town.

Buses run at least once a day to many of the provincial capitals in this central region, but only several times a week to Buenos Aires. The bus station is south of the centre at España and Artigas.

Accommodation and Food. Residencial Florida (Alberdi near González) is recommended, though at $9 it is more expensive than other reasonable places such as Residencial Sumaj Kanki (Barros and General Lagos) and Hospedaje Margarita (Sarmiento 419). Señor Carreño (Becar Vareza 461; tel 27563) rents out private rooms, and the tourist office has a list of other addresses.

The Spanish Cantina de Juan (Yrigoyen 190), the Facundo (Quiroga 1131) and the Pizzería Centro (Pelagio Luna 441) are the best places to eat. You can also enjoy a good evening's bowling at the Cafetería Kalalo (Luna and 25 de Mayo).

Exploring. Supreme among La Rioja's old buildings is the Dominican church and convent at Luna and Lamadrid, which was built by Diaguita Indians in 1623; the doorway is a beautiful example of their skill at woodcarving. The best museum is the Museo Arqueológico Inca Huasi (Alberdi 650), which has a large and impressive collection of Indian artefacts, mainly ceramics. More recent history is covered by the Museo Histórico de la Provincia (Adolfo Davila 79) and the Museo Folklórico (Luna 811).

For a trip out of town, go to Villa Sanagasta, 19 miles/31km north, which has the old-world charm the capital lacks. It is a popular retreat for the Riojanos, so buses run frequently.

Help and Information. *Tourist information:* at Perón and Urquiza. Yafar Turismo (Lamadrid 172; tel 23053) runs tours to Valle de la Luna and Talampaya (see below).

Communications: the post office is at Perón 764; the telephone office is at Luna and González.

Money: Banco de la Nación Argentina (Belgrano and San Nicolás de Bari) changes travellers' cheques. There is a branch of Banco de Galícia at San Nicolás de Bary 600.

CHILECITO

During a gold boom around the turn of the century, this small town was flooded with Chileans coming over the border in search of work — hence the name 'little Chile'. Initially, the gold ore from the main La Mejicana mine, high up on Cerro Famatina, was brought down by mules. But in 1905 an extraordinary cable car was built, to transport both men to the mine and the ore back to Chilecito. It climbs from 3,530ft/1,075m to 14,440ft/4,400m over a distance of just 21 miles/34km. The mines closed down in 1926, and unfortunately the cable car system no longer works, though there is talk that it may be refurbished in order to carry tourists.

Chilecito is a pleasant place and a good base for exploring this part of the province. The town is northwest of La Rioja, but the road takes a circuitous route: buses, which run daily, take four hours. There are also services daily from Córdoba (8 hours), and two or three times weekly from San Juan (9 hours).

There are few double rooms going for less than $10, which is charged at Residencial Americano (Libertad 68; tel 8104) and the Bellia (Maestro near Marasso). Ask at the tourist office (Libertad and Independencia) about private rooms.

Exploring. At Samay Huasi, a couple of miles north of the centre, is a museum of natural history and archaeology, set in beautiful grounds; it is open 8am-noon and 3-6pm. A few miles beyond is the Jesuit chapel of San Nicolás. Fifteen miles/24km further north still is the village of Famatina, which has changed little since colonial times: panners still look for gold, and the local people make wonderful weavings. All these places are easily reached by bus.

Cañon de Atuel is an extraordinary valley 88 miles/141km north of Chilecito at Talampaya, and now a national park. Wind has eroded rocks into strange shapes and there are also numerous pre-Columbian petroglyphs. The only sensible way

including *locro* (meat and vegetable stew). Tasty hamburgers and hot dogs (*panchos*) are available for $1-2 from the nameless stand-up joint at Mitré 23, on the square.

Help and Information. The tourist office is at Sarmiento and San Martín; in high season it arranges tours to places of interest. The post office is at de la Rosa 259 E and the telephone office at General Acha 29 S.

Cambio Santiago (General Acha 52 S) changes travellers cheques and there is a branch of Banco Río at Mendoza 170 S.

WEST OF SAN JUAN

Calingasta. This pretty village lies 68 miles/109km west of San Juan in a fertile mountain valley. Its orchards produce abundant apples, that are celebrated in the cider festival in April. The local streams attract anglers, but Calingasta's main appeal lies simply in its setting. A couple of days spent soaking in the stunning views of Andean snow-capped peaks, and a night or two in one of the village residenciales is sufficient to rejuvenate any weary traveller.

A bus makes the 4½-hour journey from San Juan daily at 7am on its way to Barreal, and returns a few hours later. There is an additional service on Mondays, Wednesdays and Fridays.

Barreal. This settlement lies on the old Inca highway that linked Argentina to Peru. It is 27 miles/43km south of Calingasta, in the same valley. A private museum near the square contains local Inca artefacts. For tourist information seek out Señor Daniel Muñoz in the Municipalidad, who can arrange mule treks into the Andes. The proprietor of Hotel Jorge is also a mine of information on the area; rooms here cost $5, compared with $10 (including breakfast) at the Hotel Barreal.

Buses run once or twice a day to San Juan, five hours away, and weekly to Uspallata, within reach of Mendoza.

NORTH OF SAN JUAN

San Agustín del Valle Fertil. This is a small, lonely town 153 miles/247km northeast of San Juan, and a centre for weaving and knitting. It is also a base from which to visit the Valle de la Luna, described below. Another interesting destination is the impressive Piedra Pintada petroglyph on a steep hillside outside town; to get there, follow Rivadavia west out of Valle Fertil across the stream for about 40 minutes. Information on this and other sites is available from Señor Americo Cortés, in the office by the Municipalidad, open daily except Sunday. Between December and March he can arrange expeditions on horseback to archaeological sites in the mountains.

Buses run daily to San Juan (4-5 hours) and La Rioja (3 hours). There are several hosterías, including Los Olivos, where $8 buys you a room plus breakfast. One of the most reliable places to eat is the restaurant in the ACA Hostería, which is a short walk west out of town and charges about $6 for a good meal.

Valle de la Luna (Ischigualasto). Before the Andes were formed, 70-80 million years ago, western Argentina enjoyed a wet Pacific climate. Lakes and forests covered the land and dinosaurs thrived. As the mountains began to rise, the area became gradually drier, and the lakes and forests died out, together with the dinosaurs. Valle de la Luna today is a strange and powerful place, a vast arid depression containing the petrified corpses of these dinosaurs. Outcrops of rock, with names like 'Aladdin's Lamp', have been eroded into weird shapes by the wind. The entire area is now a national park. Fossils from the area are on display in the Museo de Ciencias Naturales in San Juan (San Martín and Catamarca).

It takes about two hours to make the 25-mile/40km circular tour of the park. Every vehicle has to be accompanied by a park ranger. The easiest way to see Valle de la Luna is on a coach excursion from La Rioja. From Valle Fertil, 50 miles/80km south along a dirt road, drivers hired privately will take you there for about $60; this is therefore only economic if you can divide the cost among several people. You may be able to arrange a lift with a local tourist (ask around at the ACA Hostería) , though this is hard to arrange outside the tourist season.

You can pitch a tent at the park entrance.

Mendoza Province

The spectacular mountains west of Mendoza, the capital, provide some of Argentina's best skiing and also a most dramatic route west into Chile. There is little else of great interest in the province, though the city of Mendoza is a lively and relaxing place.

Mendoza province is Argentina's biggest producer of olives and grapes, and a famous Wine Festival, with floats and processions, is held in the capital on the first Saturday in March.

MENDOZA

The Spanish expedition that came over the mountains from Chile in 1561, founded Mendoza in a truly magnificent spot: plains stretch away to the east while the Andes rise majestically to the west. The conquistadores could not have known that their chosen site lay on a geological fault line; Mendoza was destroyed by an earthquake in 1861, only to be badly shaken again in 1985. But the provincial capital has evolved into a surprisingly pleasant city, with tree-lined streets and many open spaces. The main drag, San Martín, is invigorating at night, when it is lit up and everyone is out to see and be seen. Many visitors consider Mendoza one of their favourite Argentinian cities, despite its size: with a population of at least 600,000, Mendoza is the largest city in western Argentina.

Arrival and departure. There is a reasonable range of flights to the airport 6 miles/10km from town and accessible by bus number 6 from San Juan and Alem.

The daily El Aconcagua train serves San Luís (4 hours) and Buenos Aires (17 hours), though the El Libertador service on Mondays and Fridays is faster, taking 14 hours to the capital. The station is on Perú and General Paz. Shuttle buses ferry incoming train passengers to the bus station via the centre.

Buses run an almost hourly service to Santiago de Chile (10 hours), and to all nearby provincial capitals. Buses to Santiago vary in quality and fill quickly, so shop around. The terminal is on Costanera, east of the centre, and accessible on buses 71, 72 and 20.

Accommodation. The cheapest place is the Albergue (Tiburcio Benegas 1638; el 270504), where a bed in a shared room costs $4; it is a block west of the railway ine. Closer to the centre and slightly more expensive are the El Descanso (General ²az 463; tel 233474) and the Dardex (Perú 1735; tel 252670). Another notch up s the Líbano (General Paz 227; tel 254973) and the Aragón (Godoy Cruz and ³spaña), both at around $12.

Eating and Drinking. Las Heras and San Martín are both lined with good restaurants. Try Pizzería Un Rincón de la Boca (Las Heras 485), a friendly over-the-counter place, or El Gran Lomo (Rivadavia and San Martín), a noisy 24-hour sandwich and burger bar. Tibagy Café, at San Martín and Godoy Cruz, is worth a mention for its cheapness. Also good value is La Nevada (Chile 1495), where you can get a filling set menu for $4, including beer or wine.

The Sarmiento pedestrian precinct is the best place for pavement cafés and heladerías. To make up a picnic go to La Caruña delicatessen at Mitré and General Paz. Wine is good value in Mendoza. Los Andes, the local beer, is much better than Quilmes, but is still weak and fizzy.

Exploring. Don't fail to go on a tour around a *bodega* (winery), which usually rounds off with complimentary tastings. The Toso bodega is six blocks east of San Martín along Catamarca, and is open 9am-4pm Monday to Friday. Even better, however, is the impressive Giol bodega, which is accessible on colectivo 160 from the stop on Garibaldi between La Rioja and Salta; it is open 8am-1pm and 3-6pm.

Ten blocks west of the centre is the huge Parque San Martín. You can walk along its main avenue, Libertador, to Cerro Gloria, which has an excellent zoo where animals scamper about in semi-wild conditions. From the hilltop you can see the football stadium built for the 1978 World Cup (won by Argentina). A bus runs to Cerro Gloria from the park gates, every hour.

MENDOZA

1 Train Station
2 Telephone Office
3 Plaza Independencia
4 Museo del Pasado Cuyano
5 Post Office
6 Bus Station
7 Austral
8 Tourist office
9 Cambio Santiago
10 Bodega Giol bus stop
11 Aquarium
12 Plaza San Martín
13 Cathedral

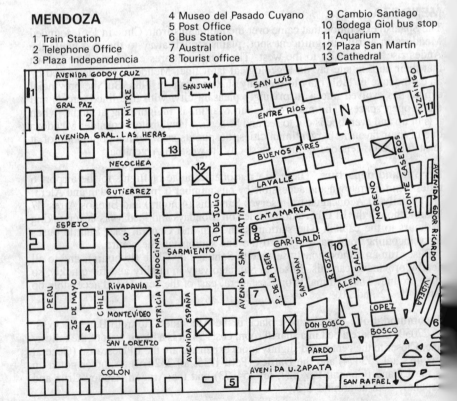

Mendoza's best museum is the Museo del Pasado Cuyano at Montevideo 544. The displays concentrate primarily on the history of the region during the colonial period. The aquarium at Buenos Aires and Ituzaingó is not particularly informative, but the collection of fish, eels, and turtles from all over the world is fascinating; look out for the totally aimless but endearing African albino frogs, *Xenopus Laevis*. It opens 10am-noon and 3.30-9pm.

Help and Information. *Tourist information:* the tourist office at San Martín 1143 (tel 242800) is open 7am-9pm and 8am-1pm Monday to Friday and 5-9pm at weekends. For a less weary attitude try the office in the bus station.

Communications: the telephone office at Chile 1574 is open 24 hours; note that Mendoza is one hour behind the rest of the country. The main post office is at San Martín and Colón.

Money: Cambio Santiago (San Martín 1199) is open 8am-8pm on weekdays and changes a range of currencies and travellers cheques; Galería Tonsa (San Martín 1177) takes cheques and is open until 8pm on Saturdays. Banco Río is at San Martín 898 for cash advances on Visa.

Chilean Consulate: Civit and Rodríguez (tel 255024).

WEST TO CHILE

RN7 runs west to the Andes and Chile, following the Río Mendoza valley for part of the way. The last Argentinian town on this road is Las Cuevas, but you will have to get your passport processed before you arrive here — at Punta de Vacas or in Mendoza. Most people travel straight through on an international bus service to Santiago.

Puente del Inca. This small town near the Chilean border is set among stunning scenery 100 miles/160km west of Mendoza. It is a popular base for Andean mountaineers, including those climbing the 22,800ft/6,960m Mount Aconcagua, the highest in South America. The main attraction is the Puente del Inca itself, a natural 70ft/21m stone bridge formed by sulphurous springs: a most unusual sight. The stone buildings underneath the bridge are the remains of an old spa development. The easiest way to visit is on a day trip from Mendoza — buses run three times a day — though you can stay at the expensive Hostería Puente del Inca.

SOUTH OF MENDOZA

There is little to delay you on a journey south of Mendoza, though the scenery is stunning. The town of San Rafael, 144 miles/232km south, boasts a fine setting, but the place itself has little going for it. If you need to stay overnight, sleep at the Ideal (San Martín 192) or La Esperanza (Avellaneda 263).

Malargüe is a small town nestled in the foothills of the Andes in the south of the province. It is surrounded by archaeological sites, but few of these are accessible by public transport — trips are arranged by the tourist office in high season. You can stay at the Residencial Las Brisas (Fray Inalican 582) or the Scheryl (San Martín 648; tel 71337).

Both towns are served by daily buses from Mendoza, Neuquén and Bariloche.

San Luís Province

Sandwiched between Mendoza and Córdoba, San Luís is the driest of the Cuyo provinces. Its southern part is virtual desert, interspersed with salt lakes. The better watered north is more attractive, and the hills northeast of the capital provide good scope for walking.

SAN LUIS

The provincial capital is a modern city in the hills of the Sierra de San Luís. Its old buildings have practically all been destroyed by earthquakes, though many of the original buildings around Plaza Pringles have survived, making this a reasonably pleasant square. Elsewhere the city is dirty, and many streets are poorly lit at night. There are better places to be.

San Luís is on the Mendoza-Buenos Aires railway, and is also easily reached by bus, with six services a day from Mendoza ($11), and others from Córdoba and San Juan. Of the cheap and grotty hotels near the bus station the best is Residencial 17 (Estado del Israel 1070; tel 0652-23387), which costs $8. In the centre choose the Royal (Colón 878).

The tourist office is in a smart new building off the main square at San Martín and Illia. With little to get excited about, the staff are not particularly helpful.

Around San Luís

A fairly interesting trip can be made by bus along a minor road northeast of San Luís. The first stop is Trapiche, a name that will be familiar to lovers of Chilean wine. It is, in reality, a small resort 25 miles/40km from the capital, set in the arid yet beautiful surroundings of the Sierra de San Luís. From here you can head further north still to the gold-panning village of Carolina. Beyond is San Francisco del Monte del Oro, a pleasant colonial town 71 miles/115km from San Luís. This makes a good overnight stop, and there are pretty walks to local beauty spots, including the Punta del Agua and the Quebrada del López. Stay at the Residencial Ayelén (tel 0651-6223).

Sierra de los Quijadas. This mountain range lies about an hour and a half by bus northeast of San Luís, much of it lying within a national park. Remote, arid and beautiful, it is home to a variety of wildlife, including guanacos. Entry to the park is through the village of Hualtarán, 75 miles/120km from San Luís.

MERLO

This town is popular among tourists at any time of year due to the refreshing and healthy air — a result, apparently, of the high concentration of negative ions. Many local people claim that the climate is so equable that they can't imagine surviving anywhere else.

Merlo is 124 miles/200km northeast of San Luís, at the foot of the rugged Sierra de Comechingones which forms the boundary with Córdoba province. There are good walks to be done in the mountains, and picturesque villages to explore to the south. Turismo Aventuro (Perdenera 24) organizes hikes and other trips. The tourist office is in the main square.

Daily buses run from San Luís to Merlo, the journey taking four hours ($8). Stay in the Residencial Malú (Avenida del Sol 51; tel 0544-75041) which has a friendly owner and a Great Dane called Thatcher; a single including bathroom and breakfast is a bargain at $10. There are other decent places to choose from on the same street, particularly Hospedaje El Castaño. Just up the road from the Malú is an excellent and cheap parrilla, and there are other restaurants on the main square.

CENTRAL ARGENTINA

Vast rolling plains take up most of this region, which encompasses the provinces of Córdoba and La Pampa. The main areas of interest are the hills of Córdoba with their attractive villages.

Córdoba Province

This is one of Argentina's most densely populated regions, and its capital is the country's second city. The green, rolling countryside attracts many Argentinian tourists. Many of them stay in modern resorts in the hills, but for the culture seeker there are pre-Columbian sites and also remains left by Jesuit missionaries.

CORDOBA

Founded in 1573, Córdoba has grown into an industrial centre with a rising population of over one million. Although most of the city is grimy, noisy and indifferent to look at, it has pockets of charm. There are some outstanding churches and other colonial buildings, such as the Cabildo and the University. Like Buenos Aires, the shopping streets and downtown area are attractive and always lively. Cultural life is important for the residents of Córdoba; festivals are frequently staged here and there are theatres and cinemas all over the place.

Arrival and Departure. *Air:* there are flights every day between Córdoba and Buenos Aires and other big cities including Mendoza and Tucumán, with fewer to provincial capitals north of Córdoba. Aerolíneas Argentinas is at Colón 520 (tel 45003), Federal at Terminal de Omnibus, local 1 (tel 38678), Austral at Buenos Aires 59 in Plaza San Martín (tel 34883) and Lade at the airport (tel 814791). The Pajas Blancas airport is 9 miles/15km north of the city; buses leave 30 minutes before the departure of each flight, from the bus stop at Lugones and Perón.

Train: trains to Buenos Aires leave from both the Mitré and Belgrano stations. The daily Rayo de Sol service leaves from the Mitré station (Perón 200, near the bus station), takes 12 hours overnight and costs $23 in primera. The Porteño train, between Buenos Aires and Tucumán (10 hours north) runs three times a week. It serves the Belgrano station, in the suburb of Alto Córdoba north of Río Primero. The two stations are linked by colectivo 71 and 73.

Bus: lying at the heart of Argentina, roads fan out from Córdoba in all directions, and there are a huge number of bus services to and from Córdoba's giant airport-like bus terminal. Long-distance buses run several times a day to Bahía Blanca (15 hours), Buenos Aires (11-13 hours), La Rioja (7 hours), Mendoza (10 hours) and the provincial capitals of the northwest.

The terminal is about eight blocks southeast of the centre on Presidente Perón, between Illia and Entre Ríos.

Getting Around. Colectivos within Córdoba run on tokens, which you buy from white kiosks marked EMIR and some ordinary kiosks. The flat fare for the central zone is about $0.40.

Accommodation. There are lots of budget hotels in the seedy central area near the bus station, and along Balcarce and San Jerónimo. For about $10 you can stay at Mi Valle (Corrientes 586) or the Sportsman (San Jerónimo 590). The Corrientes, a couple of doors down, is friendly and tolerable at $8. More salubrious places in the centre include the Garden (25 de Mayo 35; tel 44729), or the San Francisco (Buenos Aires 272), which charge similar rates.

Eating and Drinking. Most of Córdoba's restaurants are cheap but uninspiring. There is a fairly good choice around the bus station, where a profusion of diners (especially near the eastern end of San Jerónimo) offer simple meals for around $3.

In the centre try Turin Junior's Pizzería (Rosario de Santa Fé and Buenos Aires) and La Bodega (Caseros 79). The branch of the Granix vegetarian chain on the first floor at 9 de Julio 25 is good for lunch; otherwise, grab a sandwich from one of the stands in the shopping streets near the main square. For a quiet drink go to Rigoletto at Entre Ríos 73.

CORDOBA

1 Plaza
  General Paz
2 Aerolíneas
  Argentinas
3 Post Office
4 Tourist Office
5 Telephone
  Office
6 La Compañía
7 Santa Teresa
8 Plaza
  San Martín
9 Cabildo
10 Cathedral
11 Austral
12 Casa Virrey
13 Residencial
  Sportsman
14 Mitré station
15 Bus terminal
16 Sagrado
  Corazón

Exploring. Córdoba contains some fine civic architecture, centred around Plaza San Martín. The Cabildo on the west side was built in 1785 and has recently been restored and turned into a museum. Nearby is the Cathedral, which has an impressive rococo interior. A couple of blocks southwest, at Caseros and Obrero Trejo y Sanabria is La Compañía. Built in the 17th century, this is a simple and beautiful church, with a fine interior of gilt and marble. Next door is the handsome University building and the Colegio Nacional de Monserrat; they overlook a pleasant small square.

The most bizarre creation in Córdoba is the Sagrado Corazón, with an extravagant façade, competing architecutral styles, gargoyles, and multi-coloured stonework. It is at Obispo Oro and Buenos Aires, seven blocks south of Plaza San Martín. Of the many lesser colonial churches the highlight is the Iglesia y Convento de Santa Teresa (Independencia 122), which has a splendid doorway from 1770, and houses a good collection of religious art. Opening hours are 11am-noon on Saturdays only; monks still live there.

The best museum is the Casa de Virrey Sobremonte, a colonial masterpiece containing exhibits relating to the history of the region, including ceramics and musical instruments. It is at Rosario de Santa Fé 218, a couple of blocks east of the square, and opens 8.30am-1pm and 3-7.30pm Tuesday to Friday, 9am-noon at weekends. Also worth a visit is the Centro Cultural General Paz, in an Art Nouveau market building at Catamarca and Pringles, east of the centre across the river.

Help and Information. *Tourist information:* the municipal tourist office is on the square and opens 8am-9pm every day; walking tours of the city leave from here. For information about the region, however, go to the office in the arcade at Tucumán 25, which is open 7am-4.30pm Monday to Friday.

Communications: the main post office is at Colón 201, and the telephone office at General Paz 36, open 24 hours.

Money: of the cambios along Rivadavia, Exprinter at number 39 is the best; it changes cheques into dollars at 2% commission or pesos at 0.6%

Immigration Office: Caseros 680 (tel 22740), for visa extensions.

NORTH OF CORDOBA
Highway RN38 runs into the hills northeast of Córdoba, connecting the city with a number of resorts. The best one to head for is La Cumbre, 60 miles/96km north. There is plenty of scope for walks, including to Ascochinga, a village in the Sierra de Córdoba, 2½ miles/4km west, and to the nearby natural springs of Cristo Redentor. Residencial Peti (General Paz and Rivadavia) is a cheap place to stay. The resort is well served by bus from Córdoba and from towns further north.

SOUTH OF CORDOBA
Alta Gracia. This small town is 24 miles/38km southwest of Córdoba at the confluence of the Punillas and Calamuchita rivers. Before the Conquest it was inhabited by the Comechingones Indians, but they were swept aside by the Spaniards before the town was founded in 1588. About fifty years later the Jesuits took over Alta Gracia, and several of their buildings remain. Most extraordinary among these is the church, which assimilates various European styles. The Museo Histórico Nacional is in Casa del Virrey Liniers, which formed the entrance to

the Jesuits' monastery. Here you can find out more about the area's earlier inhabitants. There is no reference to a more recent inhabitant, Che Guevara, who lived in Alta Gracia for a short time.

In addition to frequent bus connections with Córdoba, there are also services south to Villa General Belgrano, and one bus a day to Buenos Aires. Alta Gracia is a pleasant place to stay overnight. Try the Residencial Reyna (Urquiza 139; tel 21724) or the Flor de Lis (Avellaneda 306; tel 21111), which charge around $8. Restaurant Pizza (Sarmiento and Déan Funes) and Cafetería Lucky (Quintana 295) are recommended for food.

Mina Clavero. Up in the mountains near Cerro Champaquí (9,450ft/2,880m), Mina Clavero has long attracted tourists to its mineral waters and alpine setting. The area has been inhabited since pre-Columbian times, and there are several archaeological sites near the town. They include Panaholma, on the track to Las Maravillas, and Campitos, 2 miles/3km south of town. Best of all is Cañada Larga, 15 minutes walk east of Campitos: a small cave has been decorated with rock paintings, and it is littered with broken pottery and stone tools. Various artefacts from that period can be seen at the Museo Rocsen at Nono, 5 miles/8km south of Mina Clavero.

Córdoba is 87 miles/140km northeast and four hours away by bus. Most of the towns's many hotels open only from December to March. Among the cheaper places open all year round are Residencial España (San Martín and Urquiza; tel 70387) and the Llastaj-Sumaj (Sarmiento 1394; tel 70074); both charge around $10.

Villa General Belgrano. This is a 10,000-strong, mostly German community, 53 miles/85km south of Córdoba in the Calamuchita valley. The beer festival on October 12 is attended by thousands of Argentinians of German extraction — a must for anyone who enjoys an organized alcohol binge. Buses connect the town frequently with Alta Gracia ($1\frac{1}{2}$ hours) and Córdoba (2 hours). You can stay cheaply at the youth hostel, or in Hospedaje Champaquí (tel 0546-6206).

La Pampa Province

To the south of Córdoba, and west of Buenos Aires province, La Pampa is a sparsely populated region of dry plains and woods. It is one of the most arid parts of Argentina, with a harsh climate and low rainfall. La Pampa is ideal for getting away from everything and everyone. Indeed there is little to do except marvel at the emptiness.

SANTA ROSA

The capital of La Pampa is a nondescript city of 65,000 people in the east of the province. The best thing to do there is get a bus to Parque Luro, 20 miles/33km south. This wooded nature reserve, also known as San Huberto, was created as a hunting estate around 1910. Wildlife consists mainly of introduced European species, including a flourishing population of red deer.

Santa Rosa is served by twice-weekly trains from Buenos Aires (13 hours), and there are good connections by bus from the main towns in the region. The cheapest places to stay are the Hospedaje Tredi (Spinetto 35), Residencial Mitré (Mitré 76), near the bus terminal at Corrientes and Luro, and Hostería Santa Rosa (Yrigoyen 696; tel 0954-23868). There is a tourist office at Luro and San Martín (tel 25060).

Lihuel Calel. This park, 150 miles/242km southwest of Santa Rosa, is home to many species of birds and small mammals, and is an exciting area for naturalists. In addition, the caves and rocks of the Sierra de Lihuel Cahel contain interesting rock carvings and paintings. Buses run twice a day from Santa Rosa, and there is a motel at the park entrance.

THE SOUTH AND PATAGONIA

Patagonia begins south of the Río Colorado, encompassing the provinces of Neuquén, Río Negro, Chubut and Santa Cruz. It conjures up images of dusty grassland plains stretching off towards a level horizon, with the occasional lonely flock of sheep to break the monotony. Charles Darwin was typical in his attempts to explain why the wastes of Patagonia had caught his imagination, when he suggested that it was the very absence of any features on the landscape which had struck him so forcefully. Yet Patagonia also contains many of Argentina's most beautiful lakes and mountains, and a coastline inhabited by sealions, penguins and whales. The Lake District spans both Neuquén and Río Negro provinces and draws thousands of visitors in both winter and summer. Another attraction is the anomaly of a 'Wales in Argentina', created by the pockets of Welsh descendants. Isolation has fostered a strong sense of identity, and anyone born and bred in the area regard themselves as Patagonian first, Argentinian second.

The first European accounts of Patagonia come from the journals of Antonio Pigafetta, the chronicler on Magellan's 1520 circumnavigation of the globe; he recalled encounters with a race of giant men, the Tehuelche Indians. The region was long considered as an inhospitable place of little use to anyone. The Welsh were the first Europeans to settle in the region in 1865, mainly in the Chubut Valley. They found the local people cooperative, but President Roca soon began sorting out the 'Indian Problem' by a policy of extermination throughout Patagonia; this opened up the region to further European settlement.

Direct colonization ceased in 1914, by which time 3,000 Welsh had arrived. They were gradually outnumbered by new immigrants from other countries, but for decades they managed to preserve their cultural identity. Nowadays only a minority of the 'Welsh' can actually speak the language, and neither the annual eisteddfods nor the tourists flowing through the tea-rooms are likely to reverse the decreasing relevance of the Welsh heritage. Still, the smaller communities preserve a unique atmosphere which is well worth experiencing.

Neuquén Province

The Andean region of southern Neuquén is one of the most visited in the Lake District, enjoyed by skiers in winter and walkers in summer. There are also many untrammelled areas in the north of the province which have much to offer the more adventurous hiker.

NEUQUEN

The provincial capital is a relatively modern city, with over 100,000 inhabitants. The tree-lined Avenida Argentina and surrounding streets are pleasant, but there is not much reason to hang around — particularly as its easterly position doesn't make it an ideal place from which to explore the mountains. You would do better to move on west to Zapala. Nevertheless, Neuquén is a major air transport hub in the region, and is hard to avoid.

Arrival and Departure. There are daily flights to Buenos Aires, Bahía Blanca and Bariloche, and countless other towns. Most services are run by Lade (Almirante Brown and Rodriguez) and Transportes Aereos Neuquén or TAN (Argentina 377; tel 0943-24834).

Daily trains make the 21-hour trip to Buenos Aires ($34 primera) and to Zapala, a fine four-hour journey ($6 primera). The station is at Mitré and Olascoaga.

Buses run all over the place every day, including to Buenos Aires (19 hours, $24) and Zapala (3 hours; $7) and also weekly to Temuco in Chile. The bus station is on Mitré and Corrientes, near the railway station.

Accommodation and Food. The Premier (Perito Moreno 147) is the best of a rotten bunch of hotels near the bus station, charging $14 a double. You would do better to head north to Residencial Neuquén (Roca 109; tel 22403) or the Justo (J.B. Justo 86); both are off Avenida Argentina and charge $12 a single.

Café Italiano, in the arcade on Alberdi block 100, is a cheap hamburger bar, open during the day only. La Terminal (San Martín 130), opposite the bus station, is cheap, clean, open 24 hours, and shows non-stop Kung-Fu videos.

Help and Information. The tourist office at San Martín 182 sells a city map for $1, and has good handouts on the provincial towns. The post office is at Rivadavia and Santa Fé, and the telephone office at Alberdi and Córdoba. Cambio Pullman (Alcorta 163) changes travellers cheques and there is a branch of Banco Río at Justo 50.

ZAPALA

This is a small, modern Andean town, a sizeable proportion of whose population is of Indian extraction. Though a growing industrial centre, Zapala is a pleasant place, with a sunny, fresh climate. It is also an important crossroads, lying 115 miles/185km west of Neuquén and within easy reach of the mountains. In the town itself the chief point of interest is the Museo Profesor Dr Augusto Olsacher (Olascoaga 421), an internationally famous geological museum with a complete dinosaur's jawbone. If you have come unprepared for the mountain climate, Artesanía Andina on Houssay sells a variety of woven and woolly clothes; it is five blocks east of the YPF service station at San Martín and Trannack.

There are daily trains to Neuquén from the station at Roca and Monti, but the bus service is far more frequent. Other daily buses include services to Bariloche and Temuco in Chile.

The tourist office is in a cabin on the central reservation of San Martín, between Mayor Torres and Almirante Brown.

Accommodation and Food. You can stay for about $10 at the Coliqueo (Etcheluz 165) or Hospedaje Odetto, at Ejército Argentino 455 (tel 21328); Odetto's Grill beneath it is recommended too. The dingy Residencial López, with no sign (Sarmiento 30), is half the price.

For good parrilla try the friendly Don Terencio (Etcheluz and Mitré). The Familiar (Italia 139) is good for cheap food, if you don't mind sharing the room with the local police.

NORTH OF ZAPALA

Copahué. This is an extraordinarily remote community, in the mountains 118 miles/190km northwest of Zapala. It lies in the middle of the Parque Nacional

Copahué, a high-altitude region of boiling mineral springs and geysers. The village is close to the border with Chile, from where people come three times a week to hold a market. Visit Copahué between November and April, when the hotels are open and when buses run from Neuquén and Zapala; but even then it can be very cold. The best hospedajes are the Hualcupén and La Cabañita.

Chos Malal. This small town has changed little since it was founded in 1887, retaining many of its pretty whitewashed buildings. It lies 126 miles/202km north of Zapala and a similar distance from Malargüe in Mendoza; it is accessible by bus from both towns. The old fort has been turned into the Museo Histórico, and the old Casa de Gobierno and the regional museum are also interesting. For $10 you can stay at the Hospedaje Lavalle (Lavalle; tel 0942-21193).

Lago Tromen, with its rich birdlife, forms the centrepiece of a reserve 25 miles/40km north of Chos Malal. Towering above it is the awesome Volcán Tromen (13,000ft/3,980m).

Andacollo. This is a gold-panning town 36 miles/58km northwest of Chos Malal. It lies in the Sierra del Viento, the most rewarding part of Neuquén province, and ideal for hiking and camping. Within walking distance are the weaving village of Huingancó, 3 miles/5km east, and the strange rock formations of Los Bolillos, 9 miles/15km north. There are three buses a week from Zapala. For $17 a double you can stay at the Hostería Andacollo (Varvarco and Nahueve; tel 0948-94055).

ALUMINE

This village lies 96 miles/155km southwest of Zapala along the RP23. It is surrounded by araucania (monkey puzzle) trees, and is a good base for exploring the mountains and nearby lakes. The scenery everywhere is stunning and in whichever direction you head you are unlikely to be disappointed. Lago Rucachoroi is the closest, 19 miles/30km west, where a lakeside Indian community makes exquisite textiles and ponchos. Lagos Aluminé and Moquehue, close to each other 44 miles/70km north, are framed by magnificent mountains; in summer a Unión del Sud bus makes a return trip to Moquehue, allowing a whole day to explore.

Lago Quillén is 27 miles/44km west of Aluminé. Expensive accommodation is available a couple of miles east in the village of Quillén, which forms the northern entrance of the Parque Nacional Lanín. This park stretches along the Chilean border, incorporating Lago Huechulafquén, and is best approached from San Martín de los Andes (see below).

There are several buses a week to Zapala (4 hours), fewer to San Martín de los Andes. About the cheapest hospedaje is the Kengo, on Islas Malvinas (tel 96012). There is a tourist office at Cuatro de Caballería and Carruego.

JUNIN DE LOS ANDES

This small town, 124 miles/199km southwest of Zapala, is a common stopping-off place during forays around the northern lake district. There is little to do in or immediately around Junín itself, but it is the starting-point for a dramatic journey into Chile: Transportes Igi-Laimi runs buses to Puerto Montt, which use the hair-raising Tromen pass and then skirt Lago Villarrica; the road is often closed in winter.

Buses run daily between Junín and Neuquén, San Martín de los Andes and Zapala; the tourist office is near the bus terminal, at Suaréz and Milanesio. Stay at Hospedaje El Cedro (Lamadrid 409; tel 0944-91182) or the Marisa on Rosas (tel 91175).

SAN MARTIN DE LOS ANDES

In a fine setting on Lago Lacar, San Martín is the main centre for exploring the Parque Nacional Lanín. It is also the jumping-off point for another spectacular journey into Chile, through this same park and across Lago Pirehueico. The growth in tourism has made the town expensive, but San Martín is still a delightful place. It is served by several daily buses from Neuquén, Junín de los Andes and Zapala, and several times a week from Bariloche.

In addition to standard hotels, San Martín also has a number of self-catering chalets which can sleep up to six people, at a reasonable cost. Of the cheaper hotels, the best is Residencial Laura (Mascardi 632), but the Marily (Pérez 567) and Hospedaje Mi Ranchito (Rivadavia 341; tel 0944-7421) are also worth trying.

The tourist office is at Rosas 790, on the main square, and there is a national parks office on Frey.

Around San Martín

Boat Trips. A number of different boat trips are operated by Navegación Lago Lacar (at the pier a block west of the bus terminal) and by Hua-Hum Turismo (General Roca 1397; tel 7616). One trip which can be done in an afternoon is a voyage across the lake to Puerto Quina-Quina, where you can see rock paintings. Trips to Puerto Hua-Hum usually include this excursion, but also far more in the way of lake and mountain scenery.

Crossing into Chile: Puerto Hua-Hum is just a mile from the Chilean border. From there you can take a bus across the frontier to Pirehueico, at the southeastern end of the lake of the same name. Boats make the spectacular journey across the lake three times a week, docking at Puerto Fuy, from where you can make onward connections. The journey can be done more quickly by taking a bus direct from San Martín to Pirehueico, which is timed to coincide with the ferry. For anyone who's after an even easier but less impressive journey, there are buses direct to Temuco and Valdivia.

Cerro Chapelcó. This small ski resort 11 miles/18km southwest of San Martín has an Austrian-run ski school, good powder snow and unchallenging slopes; the daily lift pass costs $27. You can stay at the Hotel Los Techos, but it is small and expensive, and you would do better to base yourself in San Martín. In the skiing season tour operators, such as Chapelcó Turismo (San Martín 876; tel 7550) run trips.

Villa la Angostura. This is a resort village near the Chilean border, midway between Bariloche and San Martín de los Andes. It is one of the most attractive places in the region and many people prefer it to Bariloche — particularly for the skiing at Cerro Bayo, 6 miles/9km northeast.

There are buses daily to Bariloche, and several a week to San Martín and Junín de los Andes and Puerto Montt in Chile. You can stay reasonably cheaply at the Hospedaje Río Bonito on Topa Topa (tel 0944-94110).

Río Negro Province

Encompassing scenery from sandy coastline through Patagonian plain to the splendour of snow-capped Andean peaks, Río Negro is one of Argentina's most varied provinces. The largely undeveloped coast is peppered with fairly unappealing towns, and the central area is mostly rugged and sparsely populated tableland. The most beautiful part of Río Negro lies in the west, preserved in the Parque Nacional Nahuel Huapí.

SAN CARLOS DE BARILOCHE

One of the most common questions put to travellers in Argentina is 'When are you going to Bariloche?', such is its fame as a tourist magnet. The town is a mixed blessing. Over the last two decades tourism has spawned both incredible growth (Bariloche now has a population of 70,000) and high prices. But its lakeside location is fabulous, and the beauty of Lago Nahuel Huapí and the surrounding mountains rises above and overpowers the melée down below. The scenery is said to have inspired Paul Simon as he wrote *Sound of Silence*.

In winter the town revolves around skiing at the nearby resort of Cerro Catedral, while in summer hiking and fishing take over. Bariloche is the traditional destination for holidaying groups of high-school graduates and university students, and there's always lots going on. Mitré is the main street, leading to an Alpine-looking square known as the Centro Cívico. Here, the Museo de la Patagonia is a well laid-out museum covering the history and wildlife of the region, with stuffed animals including condors. It opens Tuesday to Friday 10am-12.30pm and 2-7pm, Saturday 10am-1pm.

Arrival and Departure. All the main airlines serve Bariloche. The airport is 4 miles/7km out of town — buses meet incoming flights. Downtown, Aerolíneas (tel 22425) and Lade (tel 22355) are both at Mitré 199, and Austral at Rolando 157 (tel 26126). Catedral Turismo runs buses from Mitré 399, which are scheduled to arrive in time for outgoing flights.

Trains run several times a week to Buenos Aires. The railway station is 3 miles/5km east of the centre, reached by buses 70 and 71; information on trains is available in the centre at San Martín 127.

There is no central bus station, but several companies have their offices along San Martín: TAC (buses to Zapala via San Martín de los Andes) is based with others at San Martín 283 (Visión Turismo), with other companies at Mitré 161 and San Martín 459. A good road runs west into Chile over the Puyehué Pass, and buses run regularly to Osorno and Puerto Montt. The tourist office carries full information on bus services.

Accommodation. Bariloche has an abundance of good hotels, but prices are high in summer (December to March) and winter (June to August), when you may want to book in advance. Good places in the cheap range include the Rosán (Güemes 691; tel 23109), Los Andes (Moreno and O'Connor; tel 22222), the Bariloche (Quaglia 338; tel 26161), and Nikola (Elflein 49; tel 22500), which charge around $10. There are several campsites on the road west to Llao-Llao — the tourist office has a list. Also along this road, 5 miles/8km out of town, is the Alaska Youth Hostel, which is a good base for walks in summer. Bus 20 runs along this road every half hour.

Eating and Drinking. Eating out is generally expensive, though it's not impossible to track down some reasonable places. Among these are Pizza Al Corte (Moreno and Rolando), where a good lunch costs around $3, Pizzería Pizzaiola (Pagano

277), El Oso (Quaglia 217) and the vegetarian La Huerta (Morales 362). For excellent fondue try La Suiza at Quaglia 342. La Alpina (Moreno 98 and Quaglia) and Hola Nicolás (Moreno and Urquiza) are two of Bariloche's most typical confiterías.

El Galpón (downstairs at Moreno 30) has a hippy, late-sixties atmosphere, best enjoyed in the late evening. Many nightclubs and discos compete for visitors' attention along blocks 400 and 500 of de Rosas. Cerebro, at number 466, seems to be the most fashionable and opulent place.

Help and Information. *Tourist Information:* the office in the Centro Cívico (open daily 8am-8pm) is efficient but officious. You can pick up maps and other publications, including the official tourist guide to Patagonia, which costs $7 and comes with a map of the Lake District. The *Guía Busch* contains extensive listings and maps of the surrounding area. There is also a provincial tourist office, at Moreno and Villegas, open every day.

Club Andino: Neumayer 30, two blocks up the hill from the Centro Cívico, open 6-9pm on weekdays, 6-8pm at weekends. This is the best source of information about hiking in the area. They have free maps with the details of walks and the locations of refugios. You can also book refugio accommodation through ASATEJ in Buenos Aires (see page 474).

Communications: the post office is in the same building as the tourist office in the Centro Cívico, and opens 8am-8pm daily except Sunday. For long-distance calls go to the office at Villegas and Mitré; international phones are at Pagano and Moreno, open 7am-8pm.

Money: the best cambio is Biedma (Mitré 25), which changes cheques at low commission. During the winter Kivani's ski boot hire (Mitré 210) changes cheques at higher commission, but is open 9am-9pm daily. Banco Quilmes (Mitré 433) gives advances on Visa.

Around Bariloche

Teleférico Cerro Otto. This is used as a ski lift in winter, but operates all year round. It provides amazing views over the lake, and there is scope for walks from the top — routes are indicated on a notice outside the lift building. The silence, once away from the cable car, is impressive. To get to the base take a bus from the log cabin on Moreno; a $10 ticket includes the chairlift.

Cerro Catedral. Bus number 50 runs from the red bus shelter at Moreno and Rolando to another chairlift at Cerro Catedral, 12 miles/20km west of Bariloche. In winter there are additional ski-lifts; if you are interested in skiing, you would do best to approach a tour operator.

Lago Nahuel Huapí. The best place to arrange boat trips on the Lago Nahuel Huapí is Puerto Pañuelo, an hour west of Bariloche, near Llao-Llao. Several boats a day leave on excursions to Isla Victoria and other places around the lake. The scenery is magnificent, and the reddening leaves of the *arrayanes* trees is a beautiful sight in autumn. From Puerto Blest on the western shores, also accessible by boat from Puerto Pañuelo, you can visit the Laguna Frías and Los Cántaros falls.

Bus number 20 runs to Puerto Pañuelo about every half hour — but it's cheaper to book through a tour operator who will throw in the bus trip for nothing.

the region's Welsh legacy is most apparent. However, there is much to explore in addition to the immigrant communities. Peninsula Valdés is an important nature reserve for marine life; and around Esquel, in the west, there is more fine scenery to explore.

ESQUEL

Although founded by colonists from Wales, this small town somehow lacks the Welsh atmosphere typical of the settlements in the east of the province. Esquel more than makes up for this lack thanks to its postion in the foothills of the Andes, with snowcapped mountains to the west and picturesque valleys to the south — a pleasant change for anyone fresh from the semi-desert further east.

Lying 180 miles/290 km south of Bariloche, Esquel is the gateway to the southern lakes in both Argentina and Chile. There are good trips in the area, particularly to the Parque Nacional Los Alerces.

Arrival and Departure. Esquel marks the southernmost point of the Argentinian — indeed the South American — railway network. Trains from Buenos Aires leave twice a week on the 28-hour journey to Ingeniero Jacobacci, a small railway town 185 miles/300km northeast of Esquel. Here you change onto a rickety old steam train, dubbed the 'Old Patagonian Express' by Paul Theroux — you spend the final 14 hours in Belgian rolling stock dating from the 1920s, clattering along a narrow-gauge line that was only completed with secondhand track in 1945.

Buses run only several times a week to Comodoro Rivadavia, Bariloche and Trelew, and services may be less frequent in winter.

Accommodation and Food. Residencial Zacarias (Roca 636; tel 2270) and Hospedaje Beirut (25 de Mayo 200) are both fairly good; otherwise, experience Welsh hospitality at the residencial at Rivadavia 330.

Don Pipo (Rivadavia 820) is a good pizzeria. Alternatively try Ahla Wasahla (San Martín 1100).

Help and Information. Tourist information is available in the bus terminal. For information on skiing ask at Club Andino Esquel, on Belgrano. You can exchange cash and cheques at the Banco de la Nación, an imposing building at Güemes and San Martín; for cash advances on Visa go to Banco del Sud (25 de Mayo 769).

Around Esquel

The ride from Jacobacci whets many people's appetite for wacky rail journeys. If this is the case, take the tourist train which runs the weekly from Esquel to the 7,020 ft/2,140m Nahuel Pan volcano. The round trip takes three hours.

Parque Nacional Los Alerces. Lying to the west of Esquel, this is one of the wildest national parks in Argentina, though the landscape is similar to that of further north. It is dominated by lakes and forests of arrayanes trees, cedar and larch, from which the park takes its name. Some specimens are comparable to the sequoias of California — huge trees up to 165ft/50m high, whose lifespans are measured in thousands of years.

A daily bus from Esquel (37 miles/60km away) crosses the park, passing most places of interest; at weekends buses run straight to the park entrance. Timetables vary through the year, with restricted winter services. There are several hotels and campsites by the lakes.

Some bus services go directly to Puerto Limanao on the western shores of Lago Futalaufquén, where you can stay cheaply in the Hostería Las Tepúes. There is a regular boat trip during the summer from here to Lago Verde, which takes nine hours and costs around $20. Similar trips can also be arranged on Lago Menéndez by contacting tour operators in Esquel.

Cholila. This small lakeside village lies 75 miles/120km north of Esquel, on the old road to Bariloche. It is remembered chiefly for the Wild Bunch — Butch Cassidy, the Sundance Kid and Etta Place — who sought refuge there at the turn of the century. They settled down to small-time farming, building a cabin which still stands. But before long they grew restless, and bank robberies followed at Río Gallegos in 1905, and as far north as Villa Mercedes in 1907. The three evaded capture by the Argentinian police, but eventually met their deaths in a remote town in Bolivia. Cholila is served by two buses a day during the week. You can stay at Hostería El Treból.

Trevelín. This charming little town, 14 miles/23km south of Esquel, has retained its Welsh identity better than its neighbour — witness all the tea-rooms, two streets named Williams, and the mill (now a museum) from which the village took its name. Bethel chapel is closed and neglected; so too is the nearby rugby field. Stay at the Residencial Trevelín (San Martín 295; tel 0945-8102). There is a tourist information office on Plaza 28 de Julio. Next to it is a monument commemorating the party of settlers who arrived in the 1880s.

Buses run frequently from Esquel, and also direct from Bariloche. Some buses from Bariloche take the road through the Parque Nacional Los Alerces, via Cholila — this is one of the most memorable bus rides in Argentina.

Crossing into Chile. The most convenient entry point from Esquel is via La Balsa 44 miles/70km and two hours by bus west. A new bridge means that you can cross the river on foot; the Chilean town of Futaleufú is 6 miles/10km from the border. Since buses are not that frequent you may have to walk or hitch a lift.

A more spectacular and much longer route starts from Río Mayo, which lies south of the RN40 that connects Esquel to Comodoro Rivadavia on the coast; it is accessible by bus from both towns. Partly due to its inaccessibility, few people bother exploring the bleak and rugged country around Río Mayo. However, taking the bus to the Chilean town of Coihaique is strongly recommended for the excellent views; there are services several times a week.

If you take the RN40 southeast from Esquel to Comodoro Rivadavia, you should consider stopping off at Sarmiento, between lakes Musters and Colhué Huapí. There are two impressive petrified forests to the south, the most accessible of which is the José Ormachea forest, 21 miles/33km away. Even so, it is not served by public transport; and while you should be able to hitch there during the peak summer season, at other times you may have to hire a driver. You can stay in Sarmiento at the Hotel Colón (Moreno 645), or camp at the site outside the town by Lago Musters. There are three buses a day between Sarmiento and Comodoro, and several a week to Río Mayo and Esquel.

PUERTO MADRYN

When the first Welsh colonists dropped anchor in 1865, it was at the site of present-day Puerto Madryn. The town's foundation is celebrated every year on 28 July.

Following rapid growth in the last few decades, Puerto Madryn no longer looks very Welsh to the untrained eye. It even has a couple of high-rises, which come as a shock after the one horse towns further north. The main reason to stop here is to visit the Valdés Peninsula, a barren outcrop of land which is one of world's most important breeding grounds for seals, sealions and sea elephants — it is worth crossing the country in order just to see the awesome Right whales, as they lurch in and out of the water. For a glimpse at what lies in store visit the Museo Provincial de Ciencias Naturales in town, which has displays on the local marine wildlife. It is at García and Menéndez, and opens 4-9pm.

Buses run frequently south to Trelew, and there are daily buses to Río Gallegos (24 hours), Bahía Blanca (12 hours) and other far-off cities.

Accommodation and Food. Though Puerto Madryn has many residenciales, rooms can be hard to find in the summer season. The España (28 de Julio and San Martín) and Hospedaje El Dorado (San Martín 545; tel 71046) are good, clean places charging upwards of $11.

Seafood is the thing to eat, and there are plenty of restaurants that serve it — one of the best and cheapest is the one in the Hotel París (Roque Sáenz Peña 112); La Caleta at San Martín 156 is also good value. There is the usual array of pizzerias and La Goleta (Roca 87) serves good if overpriced Welsh teas.

Help and Information. The tourist office, at Julio Roca 444, is of limited use, and you can usually do better at the local tour operators. These are also likely to be the best places to change dollars, though nowhere in Puerto Madryn offers enticing rates for either cheques or cash. You can get a cash advance on Visa at Banco del Sur (Sáenz Peña and Zar).

PENINSULA VALDES

Exploring the area by land is difficult on your own, since buses are scarce, car hire is expensive, and hitching is often a waste of time. But the best trips are by boat anyway. Several companies organize scuba diving.

Tours normally take place in summer, since this is when you are likely to see most animals, including seals and penguins. On the other hand, the enormous Right whales (*ballena franca*) put in an appearance only in the winter, between May and November; they often circle the boats, allowing you to take wonderful photographs.

On dry land, sheep, guanaco, rheas and armadillos roam the peninsula all year round; watch out for the huge leaping — but harmless — spiders.

Punta Loma. Lying just 11 miles/17km southeast of Puerto Madryn, this is the nearest reserve to the town. Colonies of seals and sealions can be observed at fairly close range; November is the best month for seeing whales. Unlike with the other reserves, hitching to Punta Loma shouldn't present too much of a problem.

Puerto Pirámides. This is a tiny settlement on the stem of Peninsula Valdés, 63 miles/100km northeast of Puerto Madryn. It is a wonderful place to spend a few days, with its extremely friendly people and beautiful beach. It is another good place for wildlife, and excursions to see Right whales can be arranged in winter. You can stay cheaply at the Hospedaje Torino on Julio Roca, and there is also a campsite. Seafood is served along the seafront, and the Paradise Bar is great for a few cold beers.

Buses run several mornings a week to Trelew and Puerto Madryn; tours can also be arranged in both towns. Sur Turismo in Trelew (see below) runs frequent trips to see the whales and charges $20 for one to two hours in the boat.

Punta Norte. On the north end of the Peninsula, this is the best place to see killer whales and sea elephants. Male elephant seals arrive from August onwards to stake out territory and fight with each other in preparation for the arrival of the females, who come ashore to give birth, and then begin the breeding process anew. Not all the baby seals survive: as filmed on David Attenborough's *Trials of Life*, killer whales ride the surf onto the beach and snatch the tiny seals away.

TRELEW

The commercial centre of the region is 39 miles/63km south of Puerto Madryn. Trelew is a prosperous town that has seen much growth in the last two decades — a result of a government policy to encourage the development of the region; it has a population of approaching 100,000. The expansion has taken its toll on the old town, though a few original structures survive around the central square. Trelew has not lost its fascination, and it is also a popular base for tours to the Valdés Peninsula and for visiting the small Welsh settlements of Gaiman and Dolavon.

Arrival and Departure. Aerolíneas Argentinas (25 de Mayo 33; tel 0965-35297), Austral (25 de Mayo 259; tel 234799) and Lade (Fontana 227; tel 35244) all operate flights to Trelew, connecting it with the main southern cities, including Ushuaia. There are frequent buses to Puerto Madryn, an hour away, and further afield to Río Gallegos, etc. Esquel is served by bus about three times a week — a dusty 12-hour trip. The bus station is at Lewis Jones and Urquiza.

Accommodation and Food. Trelew is full of pleasant and reasonable places to stay. Try the Avenida (Lewis Jones and Pasaje Salta) or the Sarmiento (Sarmiento 264), both for around $10. Slightly cheaper is the Plaza (25 de Mayo and Rivadavia), which is good and comfortable.

One of the best restaurants is in the Touring Club Hotel (Fontana 240). For a more standard meal go to Rosselli's pizzas at 25 de Mayo 272. El Sol (Italia and Fontana), is a good place for a late night drink. Roger's, at Moreno 463, serves good Welsh teas. The local edible souvenir is *torta gallesa*, 'Welsh' fruit cake.

Exploring. A must for seekers of Welsh memorabilia is the Museo Regional in the old railway station at 9 de Julio and Fontana. The collection includes books such as *Sermons of the Great Preachers* in Welsh, old posters and some ancient photographs and newspapers. If you want to brush up on the history of Welsh settlement even further, visit the bookshop on 25 de Mayo, which has an interesting selection of titles.

The chapel in the centre of town is Tabernacle; don't miss Sunday school. On the outskirts of town by the bridge across the Chubut stands Capel Moriah and its associated graveyard. The latter is full of the graves of many original settlers, with their traditional Welsh slate headstones; sadly, it is not always open.

When you have had your fill of Welsh culture, retire to the coast, where the sea is good for surfing and windsurfing. You can hire windsurfing boards from Henry González at Moreno 381, though they should also be available on the beach. There are frequent buses 10 miles/16km east to Rawson. (Despite its status as the official capital of Chubut, this quiet little town has little to seize the imagination.) Playa Unión is a short distance beyond it.

Help and Information. There is a tourist information desk in the bus station. The post office is at 25 de Mayo and Mitré; to make a phone call go to the office at Roca and Pasaje Tucumán. The best rates for cheques are offered by Sur Turismo (Belgrano 330), which is run by English-speaking and extremely helpful staff. They also arrange trips to places of interest nearby. For individual tours contact Guías de Turismo de Chubut on 81227.

Around Trelew

Gaiman. People come in ever-increasing numbers to this village 10 miles/16km west of Trelew, in search of the old Chubut atmosphere. Since its foundation the town has managed to preserve many of its original brick houses as well as its beautiful chapel. The cemetery is on the plateau between the town and the main road; note how names were adapted, so that a woman born Rees who married a Jones would become Jones de Rees. There is an historical museum in the old railway station at Sarmiento and 28 de Julio.

For an orgy of Welsh culture, visit at the beginning of August, when Gaiman stages the region's eisteddfod. At other times, few visitors can leave without trying a proper Welsh tea. Three establishments cater to this trade: Plas y Coed (on Michael Jones) is charming and run by a pure-blooded Welsh and English-speaking woman. Casa Té Gaiman on Yrigoyen, near the river, is also recommended.

There are frequent buses to Trelew making day trips easy. Buses go either along the valley floor on gravel roads via Treorcki, or along the main road which runs along the plateau north of the valley. Accommodation in Gaiman is limited, though you can stay at the Draigoch Guest House and there is a municipal campsite by the river.

Punta Tombo. Penguins are the main attraction at this reserve 35 miles/56km south of Trelew. The best time to see them is between September and March, when the population can run into millions, laying eggs and rearing their young. Tours can be arranged at Sur Turismo in Trelew.

COMODORO RIVADAVIA

Oil, discovered here in 1907, has made Comodoro Rivadavia the biggest and most commercially thriving town in Patagonia, with a population of well over 100,000. Along with the oil trucks and pipelines, the military has a sizeable presence in the region, maintained with greater seriousness since the Falklands War.

Comodoro is an unprepossessing place, but most overland travellers end up staying overnight on their way to or from the deep south. If you're heading south buy anything you need here, as prices will only get higher. Diversions are few. The museum of petroleum and paleontology, near the refinery 12 miles/20km north of town, is of limited appeal; but the site itself and the ride out on the workers' bus is interesting.

Arrival and Departure. Comodoro is Patagonia's main transport hub, which is reflected in the huge number of flights available: daily to Buenos Aires, Río Gallegos and Trelew, with a varying number per week to a huge list of other places, including Río Grande in Tierra del Fuego. Aerolíneas is at San Martín 421 (tel

0967-24781), Austral at San Martín 291 (tel 22605) and Lade at Rivadavia 360 (tel 24934).

Comodoro Rivadavia is 241 miles/387km south of Trelew and is served by daily buses (6 hours). Several services a week run to Coihaique (Chile) and Río Gallegos (14 hours). The station is at Pellegrini and Almirante Brown.

Accommodation and Food. Two of the cheapest places to stay are Hospedaje Diana (Belgrano and Rawson) and the Lisboa (San Martín and Francia). For a little more comfort try the Belgrano (Belgrano 546) or the Comercio (Rivadavia 341; tel 22341). Eating out in Comodoro is expensive. If you can't afford to splash out at the Pizzería Giulietta (Belgrano 841), fill up at the municipal market on Rivadavia during the day.

Help and Information. The provincial tourist office is at Rivadavia and Pellegrini. The post office is at San Martín and Moreno, and the telephone office at Urquiza and Rawson.

Most cambios charge at least 5% commission for cheques, and some banks may offer better deals. Travel agents' sometimes give the best rates for cash. Banco del Sud, for advances on Visa, is at San Martín 854.

Santa Cruz Province

South of Comodoro the eastern tableland becomes bleaker and more windswept than ever, and settlements are few and far between. To the west lies the magnificence of the Perito Moreno glacier, and spectacular Andean scenery.

The province was badly affected by the eruption of Mount Hudson in Chile in 1991, which covered the more westerly areas with volcanic dust, wiping out harvests, killing thousands of sheep and destroying buildings. Even now, life is only just returning to normal in the worst affected communities.

PERITO MORENO

The main reason for coming here is not to visit the Perito Moreno glacier — which is in fact reached from El Calafate, further south — but to explore the southern lakes. West of the town is the huge Lago Buenos Aires, which carries on across the border into Chile, where it is called Lago Carrera. It creates its own microclimate, which is a pleasant change from the conditions in most of Patagonia.

Most hotels and other facilities are open only between November and April. Hospedaje Argentino (Buenos Aires 1276) is fairly cheap, and the Hotel Santa Cruz is more comfortable but still good value. The tourist office is at San Martín 1059.

Perito Moreno is reached more easily by air than by bus. Lade (San Martín 1207) has weekly flights from Río Gallegos, Comodoro Rivadavia, Río Grande, Ushuaia and a couple of other southern towns. Buses from the coast leave twice-weekly in the early morning from Caleta Olivia, an uninspiring concrete agglomeration 44 miles/70km south of Comodoro, and 190 miles/305km east of Perito Moreno. You will need to stay overnight in Caleta — Hotel Capri (Hernández 1145) is reasonable.

Las Cuevas de las Manos. You can hire a minibus in Perito Moreno to visit these caves, which are 77 miles/124km south. They contain the best pre-Columbian painting in Argentina, distinguished by the extraordinary hand motif, from which they take their name; there are also pictures of animals, and fascinating geometrical patterns. In summer agencies run tours.

If travelling independently, stay in Bajo Caracoles, southwest along a rough road from the caves. Hotel Los Caracoles is comfortable and extremely hospitable. Even a short stay in this small settlement will give you a taste of life in Patagonia — the village is surrounded by miles and miles of nothing. Undaunted by this fact, Mario Sar has set himself up as an excellent mountain climbing and hiking guide. It is possible to arrange trips on the spot; otherwise write to him in advance (simply 'Mario Sar, Bajo Caracoles, C.P. 9315, Santa Cruz'), and he will probably offer to meet you at Perito Moreno airport.

West into Chile. A bus leaves daily from Perito Moreno for Los Antiguos, 38 miles/60km west, near the Chilean frontier; it was one of the communities worst hit by the eruption of Hudson. You can cross the border to Chile Chico on foot over the rickety bridge or by wading through the river; you may be able to get a lift on a jeep.

RIO GALLEGOS

This is the last town of any real importance on the Argentinian mainland. It is the base for visiting El Calafate, 199 miles/320km northwest, and Tierra del Fuego to the south. Río Gallegos is a bustling, fairly prosperous town, but there's not much to do except browse around the natural history museum at Moreno and Roca. Further afield, you can explore the Reserva Laguna Azul, which contains a large crater lake, 37 miles/60km south. Unless you can arrange a tour, you will have to hitch; this should not be difficult in the summer.

Arrival and Departure. Río Gallego is well served by air within Patagonia, and there are several flights a day to and from Bahía Blanca and Buenos Aires.

There is no central bus terminal in Río Gallegos. The different company offices are: Expreso Pingüino (Zapiola 455; tel 22338), Transportes Patagónicos and Don Otto (Gobernador Lista 330), San Ceferino (Entre Ríos 371) and Transportes Ruta 3 (Entre Ríos 354). Buses run several times a week to and from Comodoro Rivadavia (14 hours), with services also to Río Turbio and El Calafate. Pingüino runs buses weekly to Puerto Natales and daily to Punta Arenas, both in Chile.

Accommodation and Food. Oil workers take up many of the cheap beds in Río Gallegos. In the lower range are the Viejo La Fuente (Sarsfield 64; tel 8304), the Colonial (Urquiza and Rivadavia; tel 22329) and, for more basic conditions, the Esmeralda (Zapiola 636). There's little to choose between the restaurants, though the British Club at Roca and San Martín isn't bad.

Help and Information. The municipal tourist office is on Piedra Buena, and the provincial one at Roca and Córdoba. The best place to cash cheques is Cambio Pingüino (Zapiola 469) — bear in mind that exchange rates are poor in El Calafate. There is a branch of Banco del Sud at Alcorta 57. The Chilean consulate is at Moreno 144.

EL CALAFATE

Lying 200 miles/320km northwest of Río Gallegos, El Calafate is a dusty, one-street town. It is dominated by prefab housing and shops selling junk (though you can find good jumpers). The setting on the shores of Lago Argentino is El Calafate's salvation. It is the jumping-off point for the spectacular Parque Nacional Los Glaciares, and nearby are vantage points from where you can watch flamingoes and other birds; the best way to get to the latter is on horseback — to hire an animal costs about $1.50 per hour.

El Calafate has a resident population of just 3,000, but this swells dramatically in the summer holiday season, when you should consider booking flights and accommodation in advance.

Arrival and Departure. Flights to 'Lago Argentino' actually land at El Calafate. Conditions permitting there are daily flights to Ushuaia and Río Gallegos, fewer to other southern towns.

There are daily buses to Río Gallegos — five hours across an almost featureless landscape — and during the summer to Puerto Natales. The road south to Río Turbio is in poor condition and often impassable. Transport along it is scarce, and even hitching is difficult.

Accommodation and Food. The best place to stay is the Youth Hostel (on Los Pioneros; tel 91423), which has useful information on trips in the area. Most of the other affordable options are friendly family-run places such as Hospedaje Del Norte (Los Gauchos 813), Residencial Borquez (25 de Mayo 345), and Hospedaje Echevarría (Libertador 989). Most hotels are likely to be open only between November and April. There is a campsite with good hot showers. For the best food, stay with a family and eat with them; the Michel Angelo is the most recommended restaurant.

Help and Information. The tourist office is next to the bridge over the river. You would have done well to change money before you arrive, but if you run short, Banco de la Provincia de Santa Cruz changes cash, as do many shops and businesses.

PARQUE NACIONAL LOS GLACIARES

This is one of Argentina's largest national parks, comprising spectacular Andean lakes and mountains. In the northern area, around Lago Viedma, are incredibly steep mountains, of which the most impressive are Cerro Torre and Cerro Fitzroy. The southern region around Lago Argentino is dominated by the Ventisquero (or Glaciar) Perito Moreno, one of the world's few advancing glaciers. The lake itself, with its two fjords extending westwards into the mountains, is also very beautiful. The wildlife frequenting the area includes deer, eagles and even the elusive condor.

The southern entrance of the park is 31 miles/50km west of El Calafate, the Perito Moreno glacier a further 19 miles/30km. All the main points of interest can be reached on tours from town. There are several good tour operators along Libertador, including Interlagos, Calafate Wilderness and Lake Travel Services. For more freedom try to arrange a lift with park rangers. Once in the park some accommodation is available, though the best way to explore is by hiking and camping.

Glaciar Perito Moreno. This ice river is 20 miles/32km long, 3 miles/5km wide and 160ft/50m thick: it is one of the most astonishing sights in the country. The glacier advances steadily across Lago Argentino until, after three or four years, it cuts the lake in two. Meltwater from the mountains builds up behind the glacier until finally it bursts through with a tremendous noise and enormous waves. Even on an average day you can see huge fragments of ice splintering from the face of the glacier, crashing into the lake and drifting as icebergs.

Operators in El Calafate tend to run similar tours, which take a full day. These are available daily between November and April, less often during the rest of the year. Bring your own lunch, and come protected against the constant wind and reflected sunlight. The observation area is on the Magellanes peninsula, directly facing the glacier.

Glaciar Upsala. This glacier is at the western end of Lago Argentino. Though it dwarfs the Perito Moreno glacier it is receding, and thus less exciting; nevertheless, it is still well worth a visit. Tours normally begin early in the morning, with a bus ride from El Calafate to Punta Bandera, 30 miles/48km west, from where you go on a four-hour motorboat trip to view the glacier. The long boat ride pushes up the cost to about $60 per person.

Cerro Fitzroy. At 11,230ft/3,441m, this is the principal peak in the range of mountains around Lago Viedma, in the north of the park. The area is popular among walkers and climbers, and there are breathtaking landscapes to take in. The base for walks in the area is Chaltén, near Lago Viedma and three hours walk from Cerro Fitzroy base camp. There is basic accommodation in the village; nearer the lake, you can stay at the high-class Hostería Lago Viedma, or camp nearby. You can hire horses for treks in the area, and refugios are scattered around the park.

At 7am every day in season a bus leaves El Calafate for Chaltén, which is five hours away; the bus returns at 3pm. Trekkers can get camping permits from the National Parks office, which sometimes has maps too, though these are more reliably obtained from the park office in El Calafate.

RIO TURBIO
This is a shabby place, covered in a permanent layer of dust from Argentina's biggest coal reserves nearby. It has a population of just 6,000. Río Turbio is 149 miles/239km west of Río Gallegos, close to the border with Chile. Most travellers come through here on the way to Puerto Natales across the border in Chile, where there is a better choice of lodgings and more charm all round. However, the nearby Mina Uno Ski resort offers cheap skiing from the June to September season, and the terrain is good for cross-country skiing too. In the summer the area is ideal for riding and hiking.

Lade flies between Río Turbio and Río Gallegos every weekday. The same journey can be done less comfortably by bus, which takes six hours; buses leave early in the morning two or three times a week. The border to Chile is usually only passable between October and March. Argentinian passport control is 2 miles/3km west of Río Turbio; from here a bus goes to the Chilean post, and on to Puerto Natales.

Hotel rooms tend to be taken over by miners, so be prepared to scout around. In the cheaper range Residencial Azteca (Newbery 98; tel 91285) is recommended. The Gato Negro on Peña (tel 91226) is more expensive.

TIERRA DEL FUEGO
Argentinian and Chilean Tierra del Fuego are described together in the Chile chapter, beginning on page 455.

Uruguay

Population: 3.1 million   **Capital: Montevideo (1.8 million)**

The fact that an estimated 20% of Uruguayans live elsewhere is hardly a statistic designed to attract visitors to the country. Large numbers left during the military dictatorship of the 1970s, but more recently and perhaps more surprisingly many have simply gone in search of a better life. The days when Uruguay was known as the Switzerland of South America are long since over, but economically it is still better off than most other countries in the continent.

Rarely do you hear people waxing lyrical about this tiny forgotten corner of South America. Uruguay has no great tourist attractions with the magnetism of the Iguaçu Falls or Macchu Pichu. Yet the unassuming and rather anonymous nature of the country holds a strange appeal. Uruguay has long been on the edge of events in the region, a situation compounded by an apparently nationwide aversion to change. The country is caught in a bizarre time warp, stuck somewhere in the 1950s. The recent move to join the modern world by signing up to Mercosur, South America's first common market, has been the cause of fierce debate at home.

Uruguay is the same size as England and Wales, or the state of South Dakota. It is in some respects merely an appendage of Argentina — or so most Argentinians would like to think. Every year hordes of them flood over the Río Plata to take over the beaches northeast of Montevideo. Although you can find quieter beaches, the best thing to do in Uruguay is to head into the rolling hills and ranchlands of the interior.

Uruguay has a population of just three million, of whom well over half live in Montevideo. Most of the countryside is practically empty of people, supporting instead vast herds of cattle and sheep which outnumber humans by nine to one. There is an overwhelming aura of peace, with animals chewing grass contentedly and gauchos trotting around on horseback. The small, sleepy provincial towns make a pleasant change from the big cities of neighbouring Brazil and Argentina. Uruguay is a safe and hassle-free country that is easy to get around. While there is some street crime in Montevideo, everywhere else is remarkably safe. It is unfortunate that most travellers simply pass through en route between southern Brazil and Buenos Aires, and therefore experience only the developed coast and the rather charmless capital.

CLIMATE

Uruguay is the only country in Latin America that lies entirely in a temperate zone. The climate is generally pleasant, with no extremes of temperature, though there can be wide fluctuations according to whether a cold wind is blowing up from Patagonia, or a hot wind off the Amazon. A strong breeze off the Atlantic can be a cooling factor at any time.

Summer (December to March) is the most popular time to visit Uruguay, at least among Argentinian holidaymakers. If you aren't bothered about swimming, winter, with its bright skies, is a good time to come. Rainfall is possible at any time (though July and August tend to be the wettest) and it varies dramatically from year to year.

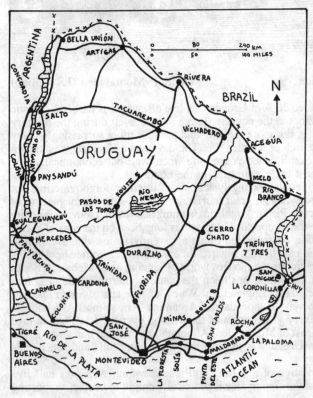

HISTORY

Little is known about the history of Uruguay to the arrival of the Spanish explorer Juan Díaz de Solís in 1516. There was certainly a substantial population of Indians, who were related to the Guaraní — an indigenous group which also dominated what is now Paraguay, and parts of Brazil and Argentina. A group called the Charrúa killed Solís on his second expedition, but did not stop occupation by the Spanish.

The native people of what became known as the Banda Oriental, were left more or less alone for the best part of a century. The only settlers to speak of were the gauchos who came from Argentina and Brazil to take charge of ever-increasing numbers of cattle introduced by the Spanish. Many Indians died at the hands of these cattle-herders, either directly or through disease. A massacre which followed the so-called Guerra Guaranitica in 1752 drastically reduced the indigenous population, and by around 1830 the pure-blooded Indians of Uruguay were completely extinct.

During the colonial period, Uruguay was little more than a buffer zone between Spanish and Portuguese territory. It was only in response to the establishment in 1680 of a Portuguese base at Colonia del Sacramento on the Río de la Plata, that the Spanish founded Montevideo in 1726. The next significant intervention took place in 1806, when an aggressive merchant fleet from Britain occupied Montevideo. The failure of the Spanish to protect them, among other grievances, gave the Uruguayans the idea that they would be better off on their own.

Uruguay declared independence from Buenos Aires in 1808. But there followed a turbulent period during which both Argentina and Brazil sought to crush the infant republic. In 1820 the Portuguese took Montevideo and José Gervasio Artigas, Uruguay's great patriot, and his band of gauchos were forced into exile. Argentina came to the rescue by helping to arm the legendary 'Treinta y Tres', the 33 men under General Lavalleja, who succeeded in defeating the Brazilians in 1827. Concerned at the disruption to trade caused by the fighting, the British also intervened in favour of the patriots. Partly thanks to their pressure both Brazil and Argentina dropped their claims to the country, and a truly independent Uruguay was created in 1828.

Independence took the country into over 70 years of dictatorship and civil war. Political allegiances were divided between the liberal Colorados and the conservative Blancos.

Recent History. The accession of Batlle y Ordóñez to the leadership of the Colorado party in 1903 marked the beginning of a new era. In a series of revolutionary reforms he established Latin America's first welfare state. Batlle (pronounced Bat-ye) dominated politics until he died in 1929, having served two terms as president. But despite his reforming idealism, fundamental social and economic problems remained.

By the early 60s the depth of social discontent had become obvious. A guerrilla group called the Tupamaros began its 'Robin Hood' campaign on behalf of the increasing numbers of poor. They had quite an impact for over a decade, though without achieving their wider revolutionary objectives. (Eventually, in 1985, they became a political party, the Movimiento de Liberación Nacional.)

In 1971 the far-right President Bordaberry took office. He declared a State of Internal War which paved the way for the military to assume widespread political powers in 1973, and close Parliament. There followed one of the continent's bloodiest periods of detentions, torture and disappearances — as the government eliminated first the terrorists, then all political dissenters. During this time, tens of thousands of people fled the country. The turning point came in 1984 when democratic elections were held. They were won by Julio Sanguinetti, of the Colorado party, who had some success in cooling political tempers but not in handling the economy. In 1990 he was replaced by Luis Lacalle of the Partido Nacional (Blancos).

Political debate has livened up considerably. This is thanks to the fact that Lacalle doesn't have a parliamentary majority and that the hegemony of the Blancos and the Colorados has at last been challenged by the left-wing Frente Amplio coalition. Hopefully such a parliament is in a better position than its predecessors to tackle the root causes of unemployment and the country's other problems. Uruguay's signing of the Mercosur agreement with Argentina, Brazil and Paraguay is seen by some as the only hope the nation has of competing on the world market alongside its neighbours. Others see it as the means by which Uruguay will be squeezed out once and for all.

THE PEOPLE

Most Uruguayans are of pure European origin, principally from Spain and Italy. About 10% of the population is mestizo, the only group to recall the former Indian presence. They include the gauchos, who work as cattle-herders on the giant estancias. A fiercely independent group, their traditions and way of life have survived, and you still see many baggy-trousered gauchos around in the provinces.

A black face is a rare sight in Argentina, but several percent of Uruguay's population are descendants of African slaves.

The Uruguayans are courteous and often charming, particularly away from Montevideo and the resorts. But even in the capital the people are noticeably more relaxed than the rather hardened city types across the estuary in Buenos Aires. *West from Montevideo — Uruguay by Bike* by J. D. Holzhauer (Cassell, 1990) gives an excellent feel for the people.

GETTING THERE

Air. For those not already in South America, the most obvious way to get to Uruguay is by flying to Buenos Aires in Argentina, from where it is an easy journey to Montevideo across the estuary. Direct flights from Europe and North America to Montevideo are invariably more expensive than the discounted flights available to Buenos Aires; see page 468. If you can't be bothered to get the ferry, there are several daily flights from Buenos Aires to Montevideo, costing around $50.

The best services from within South America are from Brazil, with frequent flights from São Paulo and Rio de Janeiro with Pluna, Uruguay's national airline. Varig, which is among the other airlines operating on this route, also flies from Porto Alegre. Various airlines offer a total of six flights a week from Santiago de Chile, and there are weekly services from both Paraguay and Peru.

The direct carriers from Europe are KLM, Lufthansa, Air France, Iberia and Pluna; the latter flies from Madrid only. From the USA, LanChile flies from New York and Miami, and Ladeco and United just from New York.

Surface. *From Argentina:* there are various crossing points along the Río Uruguay, which marks the country's western border, all of which are linked to Montevideo by bus. International bridges connect Gualeguaychú and Fray Bentos, and Colón and Paysandú. Further north, a ferry crosses the river from Concordia to Salto, though there is also a road across the Salto Grande dam, 13 miles/20km north.

The best way to travel, however, is by boat across the Plata estuary. Ferry services operate from Buenos Aires to both Montevideo and Colonia del Sacramento, and from Tigré (near Buenos Aires) to Carmelo, further west. Since the ferry direct between the capitals travels overnight, it is more fun to take one of the slightly more expensive hydrofoil services between Buenos Aires and Colonia. If heading straight to Montevideo the cheapest option is to buy a through-fare, which covers both the hydrofoil and the bus and costs around $30.

From Brazil: There are several crossing points from Brazil, stretched along Uruguay's northern frontier. The principal border post is at Chuy, on the coastal highway. Buses run direct from Porto Alegre to Montevideo, though it's cheaper to take local buses to and from Chuy; the bus to Montevideo from the border takes about six hours.

There are four other crossing points from Brazil, the main one being between Santana do Livramento and Rivera. Buses to Montevideo from these borders leave fairly regularly, although you may find it quicker to head to the nearest local town and make an onward connection from there.

As well as buses running direct from neighbouring Argentina and Brazil, there are also long-distance services from Santiago (Chile) and Asunción (Paraguay). Both journeys take more than 24 hours. Buses from Asunción go via both Argentina and Brazil, crossing borders at Uruguaiana and Bella Unión.

RED TAPE

Most western Europeans, and Americans and Canadians do not need visas to visit Uruguay. Australian and New Zealand citizens are not exempt. For information in the UK contact the Embassy at 48 Lennox Gardens, London SW1X 0DL (tel 071-589 8735; fax 071-581 9585). It shouldn't take longer than a day to have your visa processed, but you will be charged the equivalent of around $25 for the privilege. The addresses of other Uruguayan missions abroad are as follows:

USA: 1918 F Street, NW, Washington DC, 20006 (tel 202-331-1313).
Australia: Suite 5, Bonner House, Woden, Canberra (tel 282-4418).
New Zealand: 178 Cashel Street (PO Box 167), Christchurch (tel 650-000).

A tourist card issued on entry permits a stay of up to three months. This period may be extended at the immigration office at Misiones 1513 in Montevideo (tel 951587/989101).

Departure Tax: a $5 tax is levied on departure by air to other Latin American republics; other destinations cost $7.

MONEY

The currency is the New Uruguayan Peso (N$), which currently enjoys levels of inflation similar to those in Argentina. But Uruguay is notably cheaper than its neighbour.

Notes are in denominations of N$10,000, N$5,000, N$1,000, N$500, N$200, N$100 and N$50. Coins are issued to the value of N$10, N$5, N$2 and N$1, but are essentially valueless.

Changing Money. Montevideo and the major beach resorts have both banks and casas de cambio. In smaller towns you must rely on banks, where changing travellers cheques can be difficult. You should consider exchanging dollar cheques for dollars cash, which is no problem in the capital. Visa card holders can get cash advances from branches of Banco Comercial (official Visa agents), both in Montevideo and in many provincial towns. The local MasterCard agent is Argencard.

Banks usually open 1-5pm, but noon-7pm is more common in the summer.

COMMUNICATIONS

Mail. Uruguay's postal system is erratic, and airmail letters can take anything from three days to as many weeks. The cost of sending an airmail letter is about $0.30. Post offices are mostly open 9am-6pm on weekdays and 9am-1pm on Saturday.

Telephone. Uruguay is three hours behind GMT from March to October, when the clocks go forward an hour. The international country code is 598.

The national telephone company is Antel, whose main town offices also offer fax and telex facilities. Making international calls is often time-consuming, and costs around $10 for three minutes. Collect calls can be made to North America and the UK.

THE MEDIA

Newspapers. Uruguay has a surprisingly good choice of papers for such a small country, and it also enjoys one of the freest presses in Latin America. The two main newspapers traditionally associated with the Blancos and Colorados have become increasingly independent: namely, *El País*, the principal daily, and *La Mañana*. The left-wing daily with the widest ciruclation is *La República*. The best political commentary is given in the weeklies, particularly *Busqueda*, which is a respected journal. *Barricada* and *Maté Amargo* are also good reads.

Foreign newspapers are almost impossible to track down. The only one you are likely to find is the English-language *Buenos Aires Herald*, which goes on sale after midday.

Broadcasting. Uruguay has an extraordinary abundance of radio stations, in addition to what can be picked up from Brazil and Argentina. The most accessible news programme is *Telemundo*, broadcast on television's Channel 12.

GETTING AROUND

Maps. The best general purpose maps are published by the Automóvil Club del Uruguay (Avenida del Libertador 1532; tel 984710/915093). Maps are also available from some petrol stations, mainly those of Esso and Ancap, the national oil company. For topographical maps go to the Instituto Geográfico Militar in Montevideo (Abreu and 8 de Octubre; tel 816868).

Air. The military airline Tamu runs the internal network, connecting Montevideo with all the major towns. Flying is good value, with most fares costing $15-25, but the size of the country hardly makes flying necessary.

Train. Since 1988 Uruguay's railway system has been used only for freight.

Bus. Though mostly ancient, buses are generally comfortable, cheap and reliable. Lots of companies operate along the main routes. The biggest firm is Onda, which has long been on the verge of bankruptcy but was still in operation at the time of going to press. Some companies, notably Agencia Central, distribute complimentary Pepsi and *alfajores* (pastries) to passengers.

Car. Uruguay is a treat for lovers of vintage cars. Its collection of 30s, 40s and 50s vehicles, known locally as *cachilas*, turns the streets of Montevideo into a living museum.

SHOPPING

There is no great craft tradition in Uruguay except in leatherwork, though wool products are also popular. You should find a reasonable range in Montevideo and, in smaller quantities, in the provincial markets.

HEALTH AND HYGIENE

Uruguay is without the range of tropical diseases that afflict other South American countries, and lies in neither yellow fever nor malaria zones. Standards of hygiene and health facilities are among the best on the continent. Nevertheless, you should observe the usual precautions, described in the general introduction.

Public Holidays

January 1	New Year's Day
January 6	Epiphany
February/March	Carnival
March/April	Easter (banks may close for a week)
April 19	National Day
May 1	Labour Day
May 18	Battle of Las Piedras
June 19	General Artigas' Birthday
July 18	Constitution Day
August 25	Indpendence Day
October 12	Columbus Day
November 2	All Souls Day
December 25	Christmas Day

MONTEVIDEO

The capital of Uruguay lacks the scenic splendour of Santiago and the cosmopolitan excitement of Buenos Aires. Indeed some travellers come away distinctly bored and unimpressed. Nevertheless, Montevideo is less daunting than many of South America's capitals, and it makes up for some of its shortcomings with its relaxed atmosphere and the absence of serious crime, smog and squalid urban sprawl. Furthermore, the sight of its fine array of vintage cars is enough to soften anyone's heart.

Founded only in the early 18th century, and largely ignored by the Spanish even after that, there are few colonial buildings. You'll see some fine 19th and early 20th century buildings in the centre, but Montevideo is a city in which simply to wander — the sights are mostly incidental.

CITY LAYOUT

The centre of Montevideo is situated on a promontory overlooking the Plata estuary. It is a compact area which, at its western point, is just eight blocks wide. Running through the middle of the downtown district, in a virtually straight line, are six squares. The most westerly is Plaza Zabala, followed by Plaza Constitución (formerly known as Matriz) and Plaza de la Independencia. At the eastern edge of the old city, this last square is the real heart of Montevideo. It also signals the start of the city's main commercial street, Avenida 18 de Julio, which runs east to Plaza Fabini (or del Entrevero), Plaza Cagancha (or Libertad) and, finally, Plaza del Gaucho.

The main residential districts are mostly east of the centre, spread along the coast with its sheltered bays and sandy beaches. They are connected by the Rambla, a busy dual carriageway which adopts various names as it works its way around the tortuous coastline. The city beaches are built-up and polluted, and are no match for those further east.

Many streets in Montevideo are still referred to by both their old and new names: this is confusing for everyone, residents included.

ARRIVAL AND DEPARTURE

Air. Montevideo's airport is in Carrasco, 13 miles/21km east of the centre (tel 602261). The terminal is small but has an exchange and information desk. Buses from outside the arrivals hall run both to downtown Montevideo and Punta del Este. The journey to the centre takes about an hour. A taxi costs about $30.

Buses from Plaza Cagancha heading for Punta del Este often call in at the airport, though check with the driver first. You can also use local route 209, which leaves from Plaza del Entrevero. The major airlines, including Pluna (Avenida Agraciada esq. Colonia 1021; tel 921412-8; fax 921478) and Tamu (Colonia 959 at Río Grande; tel 901938/902667; fax 224302) run their own airport buses for ticket holders. Tamu's service is free and leaves twice daily, coinciding neatly with their flight times. Pluna runs buses usually six times a day, but charges $2.

Bus. Most buses leave from company offices in or around Plaza Cagancha, though the construction of a new terminal is imminent. There is a cambio in Plaza Cagancha which opens at 8am — ideal for those who have arrived on overnight buses from abroad.

MONTEVIDEO

1 Aduana
2 Mercado del Puerto
3 Plaza Zabala
4 Post Office
5 Plaza Constitución
6 Antel
7 Cabildo
8 Teatro Solís

9 Plaza de la Independencia
10 Palacio Salvío
11 Youth Hostel
12 Residencial Claridge
13 Residencial Litoral
14 Bolivian Consulate
15 Plaza del Entrevero
16 Museo del Gaucho

17 Plaza Cagancha
18 Hotel Aramaya
19 Soko's Café
20 Palacio Municipal
21 Plaza del Gaucho
22 Railway Station

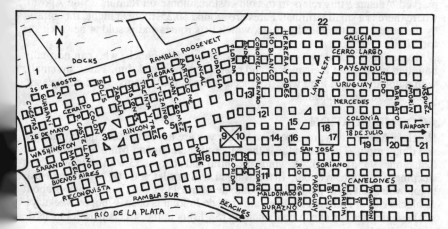

The main companies operating domestic and some foreign services are:

Agencia Central: Rondeau 1475.
CITA: Plaza Cagancha 1149 (tel 910100/419).
COPSA: Uruguay 1313 (tel 905144).
CORA: Avenida Libertador 1440 (tel 917954/908733).
COT: Plaza Cagancha 1126 (tel 921605/6/9).
Onda: Plaza Cagancha 1174 (tel 912333/920324/980514).

Argentina: several companies run services that combine bus and river transport across the estuary to Buenos Aires. A number of these operate from Plaza Cagancha. They include Deltanave, with an eight-hour service via Carmelo and Tigré, and Aliscafos (Plaza Cagancha 1124; tel 905063/904608), which has a four-hour hydrofoil service via Colonia. Buquebus (Río Negro 1400 at Colonia, on Plaza del Entrevero; tel 920670) has three or four departures daily via Colonia, which take six or seven hours and cost $23. Ferry Líneas (Río Branco 1368; tel 906617/900045) has two departures a day, and is slightly more expensive. The bus ride to Colonia takes two hours; note that if you get a through bus/boat ticket it is possible to stop over in Colonia.

Other companies, including Onda, CITA and COT make the entire journey by bus via the bridge at Fray Bentos, which takes ten hours. Going this way costs just $12, but is much less fun than the trip across the estuary.

Brazil: Onda, TTL (Plaza Cagancha 1345; tel 915482) and CYNSA (Paraguay 1311; tel 905321) have services to Porto Alegre (12 hours) and São Paulo (30 hours). Buses leave at night and are often booked up in advance.

Chile: buses to Santiago take about 28 hours; the fare is a hefty $75. Companies serving the route include Empresa Artigas (Avenida del Libertador 1945; tel 985775).

Paraguay: COIT (Paraguay 1473; tel 916619) and Tacuary (Paraguay 1311; tel 982211) both run to Asunción. There is at least one departure every day, and the 25-hour journey costs about $30.

CITY TRANSPORT

Buses to most destinations run along 18 de Julio, and those to the centre are often marked 'Aduana'; this refers to the old customs house on Rambla 25 de Agosto, where there is a small terminal. Fares are around $0.25, more at night. If confused by the buses, buy the *Eureka* guide, which lists routes and is sold at news kiosks for $7.

Montevideo's taxi drivers are a remarkably straight bunch, who can normally be relied upon to set their meters and charge the indicated sum. Fares are small, with a dollar going a long way. You needn't dread traffic jams, since charges are made according to distance.

ACCOMMODATION

Hotels in Montevideo are expensive unless you are happy to make do with a dark and dingy room. The best value is the Albergue Schirrmann-Münker youth hostel (Canelones 935; tel 981324), which is central and charges $3 with your own sheet sleeping bag, more without. If the warden will not let you stay without a card, to join you must go to the office at Pablo de María 1583, 8th floor, which is about 12 blocks east of Plaza del Gaucho, along 18 de Julio; it is open 2-7pm on weekdays.

The main area for cheap residenciales ($8-12) is in the streets parallel to 18 de

Julio. To the north on Colonia, for example, are the Catalunya (1223; tel 915785) and the slightly more expensive Ateneo (1147; tel 912630). On Mercedes, one block north, try the Litoral (887; tel 905812) and the Claridge (942; tel 915746). A block south of 18 de Julio on San José, check out the Itá (1160, near Plaza Cagancha) and the Casablanca (1039; tel 910918). There are some reasonable places on 18 de Julio itself, including the large, comfortable Aramaya (1103 and Paraguay, near Plaza Cagancha; tel 921058) and the Americana (1212).

EATING AND DRINKING

Eating in Montevideo is generally a good if not a strictly gastronomic experience. If you enjoy meat, there is nowhere better than the Mercado del Puerto, the old market on Calle Piedras, three blocks northwest of Plaza Zabala. Steaks are grilled to perfection on smoking charcoal braziers, and are miraculously cheap. You can eat fish at the Rincón del Pescado, but otherwise the market is strictly for carnivores.

The main concentration of restaurants is in the hotel district near Plaza Cagancha and along 18 de Julio east of Plaza de la Independencia. On this last square are Pasaje Sano, good for cheap lunches, and the Cervecería La Pasiva. Further east is Soko's (18 de Julio 1250, at Yí), which is an excellent confitería; the generous helpings make up for the high prices. On San José the Centro Residentes de Artigas (885) and the Viejo Sancho (1229) are both recommended. Oro del Rhin is an old, grand confitería at Colonia and Convención, patronized by some of the richest and most chic members of Montevideo society. One of the best places for vegetarians is Kombi on Plaza Cagancha.

A particularly good restaurant in the old city is La Crêperie (in the crafts market at Mitré and Sarandí), which serves filling pancakes.

EXPLORING

Plaza Independencia marks the boundary between the old city (*la ciudadela*) to the west, and the more modern parts to the east. Unsympathetic modernizations have left Plaza Independencia the grandest if not the most welcoming of the city squares. It is dominated by the gigantic statue of independence hero José Artigas, who sits on horseback above his black marble mausoleum and surrounded by gardens and fountains. The two most important buildings are the Casa del Gobierno (used for ceremonial purposes) and the Palacio Salvío, a much loved but run-down 1920s monstrosity. An archway in what remains of the city wall opens through into the old district. Nearby, on Buenos Aires, is the Teatro Solís, a mid-19th century neo-colonial architectural extravaganza. It is well worth going to see a concert or some other performance just to get a proper look inside.

A few blocks west of Plaza Independencia is Plaza Constitución. While the cathedral is exceedingly plain, it's worth doing a quick turn around the Cabildo (old town hall), which contains a museum illustrating the history of Montevideo. It opens 2-6pm, daily except Saturdays. Continuing west you reach Plaza Zabala, which is at its most lively on Sunday mornings, when there is an antiques and junk market. During the week you would do better to head straight north up Castellano, to the Mercado del Puerto. This is a superb 19th-century creation of cast iron and glass, shipped pre-fabricated from England, and now filled with the smell of grilled beef. Close to the business district and the docks, the market is patronized by a fascinating mix of people. It is bustling six days a week, being closed only on Sundays.

The whole port district is one of the most run-down but also most interesting parts of the city, particularly along Rambla Francia, where dogs and children fight over rubbish. A couple of blocks northwest of the market, on Rambla 25 de Agosto, is the Aduana, the old customs house. Between it and the Admiralty building is a pedestrian entrance to the naval part of the docks. If the sailor at the gate won't let you in, you need only nip across to the captain's office opposite to get a permit.

Four blocks east of Plaza Independencia along 18 de Julio lies Plaza Entrevero, a commercial square full of pizza parlours. It also has the Museo del Gaucho on the south side, which honours Uruguay's famous cattle-herders, and is one of Montevideo's most popular museums. It opens 9.30am-12.30pm and 3.30-7pm, Tuesday to Friday, afternoons only at weekends. Avenida del Libertador heads northeast off the square to the huge Legislative Palace. About seven blocks north of Plaza Entrevero is the railway station, which is adorned with statues of famous railway pioneers. Although the lines are now used only for freight, the station is still full of dusty old passenger coaches.

Heading eastwards beyond Plaza Cagancha you pass the new high-rise Palacio Municipal. There is an excellent view of the city from the 23rd floor, which you reach in an external glass lift — an experience best avoided by sufferers of vertigo. The entrance is at the back, on Soriano. In the same building are several museums, including the Museo del Arte Precolumbino y Colonial, reached from Ejido.

On Sundays the Tristan Narvaja market takes over the area around the junction of Narvaja and 18 de Julio, seven blocks northeast of Plaza El Gaucho. Once past the posters of Che Guevara and John Lennon you reach the more interesting antique and bric-a-brac stalls, where people sell everything from hubcaps to salamanders. There are also many secondhand book and music shops. The market starts packing up in the early afternoon, so arrive in the morning to make the most of it.

The city beaches, such as Playa Pocitos, hold few attractions. A better place to seek solace from the city streets is in Parque del Prado, across the bay about 3 miles/5km north of the centre and reached by bus 125 from Mercedes. The best time to come is during the Semana Criolla during Easter week, for the annual celebration of gaucho culture, or in August, when the park is taken over by the enormous Asociación Rural cattle show.

ENTERTAINMENT

The bars and clubs along Playa Pocitos are busy in the evenings. For a more cultural experience, go to a *boliche*, where you can eat and drink (primarily the latter) to the accompaniment of live music. This is where you are most likely to hear Candombé, the traditional music of Uruguay's black population. One of the best boliches in town is TK, at Bulevar Artigas 1018. For a more typically Uruguayan experience go to a football match in the stadium in Parque Batlle y Ordóñez, at the east end of 18 de Julio. Watch out for matches in the papers or simply ask any local.

HELP AND INFORMATION

Tourist Information: the best source of information is the head tourist office at Avenida del Libertador 1409 (tel 914877), open 12.30-6pm. The kiosks in Plaza Cagancha and at the airport have useful maps, but little else.

Communications: the main post office is at Misiones and Buenos Aires. It opens 8am-6.45pm Monday to Friday, and 8-11.45am at weekends, an hour later in summer. The most convenient phone offices are at San José 1108 (tel 911685), which opens 24 hours, and at Rincón 501 at Treinta y Tres in the old city (tel 951230).

Money: Exprinter, on Plaza Independencia, and the cambio at 18 de Julio 1046 offer the best rates for cash. American Express (Rincón 473; tel 960092) exchanges travellers cheques for dollars or pesos cash without commission. The travel agent Turisport (Mercedes 942) provides a similar service, even giving dollars cash on an Amex card. You can withdraw cash on Visa or MasterCard at many banks and cambios, including at Banco Comercial, which has one of several branches at Convención and Uruguay.

Bookshops: IBANA (Convención 1479) stocks English-language magazines and a small section of secondhand fiction.

Embassies and Consulates. *Argentina:* Avenida Agraciada 3397 (tel 398927). Open 8.30am-1.30pm in summer, 2-7pm in winter.
Bolivia: Río Branco 1320, 4th floor (tel 912394, 985962).
Brazil: Bulevar Artigas 1328 (tel 496201-6).
Canada: Juan Carlos Gómez 1348, 1st floor (tel 958583).
Chile: Andes 1365, 1st floor (tel 982223, 982368).
Colombia: Juncal 1305, 18th floor (tel 961592-4).
Ecuador: Colonia 993 (tel 903745, 906172).
New Zealand: 19 de Abril 3397 (tel 398927).
Paraguay: Bulevar Artigas 1526 (tel 403801/809).
Peru: Soriano 1124 (tel 921046, 912079).
UK: Calle Marco Bruto 1073 (tel 623630/650).
USA: Rambla Wilson 1776 (tel 409051, 409126).

EAST OF MONTEVIDEO

This is the main tourist route in Uruguay, since it takes in the coastal resorts. Even if you aren't tempted by the beaches, the road along the coast, the Interbalnearia, provides the best route to Brazil. There are a few relatively quiet beaches, and beyond Punta del Este the coast is almost completely undeveloped. You pass several lakes and old forts.

One of the best beaches within about an hour of the capital is Las Flores, about 50 miles/80km from Montevideo. This is just a small place, and you may prefer to base yourself at Solís, a few miles west, which has several residenciales and also a campsite; it is very popular among Anglo-Uruguayans. About 10 miles/16km beyond is Piriápolis, which is one of the most popular resorts among Argentinian holidaymakers.

MALDONADO

Lying 90 miles/140km from Montevideo, this is a comparatively large town, with a population of 33,000. If you are fed up with uninspiring resorts Maldonado, which is among Uruguay's most historic towns, brings some relief. It has a colonial parish church and watchtower, and a Regional Museum at Ituzaingo 787. Tourist information is available from the Intendencia.

Maldonado is useful as a cheap place to sleep if you want to have a closer look at Punta del Este. Stay at the Dieciocho on the square, or at the Irish-run Hospedaje Celta (Ituzaingo 839; tel 30139). If you prefer to be away from the coast, head 9 miles/15km inland to San Carlos, another old town, where you can stay at Hotel Reyes (Carlos Reyes and Oliveira).

PUNTA DEL ESTE

On a promontory about 5 miles/8km from Maldonado, Punta del Este is the largest, most expensive and most popular of Uruguay's beach resorts. It is a charmless place, all the more so since the old villas have been torn down to make way for blocks of flats. Buses run to and from towns all along the coast, as well as direct to and from both Brazil and Argentina. The bus station is on Avenida Gorlero, and has a small tourist office. Bus 7 runs into the centre.

Except for the Albergue Puebla Nueva youth hostel (on Terrazas de Manatiales), which is often full in season, there is nowhere to stay unless you've got $30 a night to burn. The cheapest hotels are the Milano (Calle 84, 880) and the Tourbillon (Calle 8 and Calle 12). Out of season most of the hotels, but not the youth hostel, shut down.

The main curiosities in town are near the bus station, including a plaque in memory of Churchill. Not far away, on the Atlantic side of the promontory, are some interesting sculptures in the sands; among them are what appear to be the fingertips of a hand sticking out of the ground. From the harbour you can take a boat to Isla de los Lobos, an island famous for its sealions.

At Rocha, a road heads southeast to La Paloma, an important resort cum yacht marina, whose beaches are popular despite the nearby oil refinery. There is a youth hostel, the Alteña 5000, in the Parque Andresito (tel 6396), which is open November to March. The main reason to stay there is to use it as a base from which to visit La Pedrera, a lovely village 6 miles/10km north, with good, sandy beaches. Development is increasing even here, however, and there are already several resort-type hotels. You can hire bikes in La Paloma to get there.

Continuing northeast, the road passes Laguna Negra. Overlooking the lake is Fortaleza Santa Teresa, built in 1762 by the Portuguese, which can be reached by bus from Rocha and La Coronilla.

Crossing into Brazil. There isn't much to drag you off the bus as you approach the Brazilian border. La Coronilla has vast beaches but the surf is too rough for swimming, and ocean fishing is the main activity.

Chuy is an unappealing frontier town 211 miles/340km northeast of Montevideo. There is a fairly steady stream of buses to and from the border, and you are unlikely to get stranded. If you have an hour or so to kill, catch a bus 6 miles/10km north to Fortaleza San Miguel, an old Spanish fort. It overlooks Laguna Merin, a huge lake split invisibly down the middle by the Uruguay-Brazil frontier.

The best place to stay in Chuy is the Hospedaje Vitória. Change any remaining pesos before you cross the border: Hotel Chuy (Brasil 545) is used to dealing with travellers. From the border buses run to a number of Brazilian towns, including Río Grande (4 hours) and Porto Alegre (7 hours).

THE INTERIOR

Sights are few in the neglected inland areas of Uruguay, and curiosity is likely to be the main thing to sustain a visit. This section covers the main routes running northwards from Montevideo to Brazil: route 8 to Minas, Treinta y Tres and beyond, and route 5 to Durazno and Rivera. For a real back-country experience stick to Routes 6 and 7, which avoid the main towns described below.

MINAS TO TREINTA Y TRES

Minas is an attractive town set in wooded hills 73 miles/117km northeast of the capital; Montevideo and Maldonado are both about two hours away by bus. The Verdun and Residencia Minas are both reasonably cheap hotels on the square. About 7 miles/11km northeast of town, south off the Aiguá road, is the Agua del Penitente waterfall: get any bus along this road, and ask to be set down at the turn-off.

About 100 miles/160km further north is the town of Treinta y Tres, named after the 33 men who liberated the country in 1827. Nearby is the Quebrada de los Cuervos National Park, an area of eroded rocky outcrops and fast-flowng streams. The turn-off to the park is 13 miles/20km north of town, on the Melo road, from where it's another 10 miles/16km. In summer the park is served by bus, but at other times of year access is difficult. Ask at the tourist office in the Intendencia (Lavalleja 280) about the possibility of camping. In Treinta y Tres there are several budget hotels, including the Central; you can also pitch camp in the park by the river.

From Treinta y Tres there are two ways north into Brazil — northeast via Río Branco, or directly north to Melo and Aceguá. Note that the nearest Brazilian consulate to Río Branco is in Melo. If stuck in Río Branco overnight, stay at the youth hostel (Avenida Artigas 279). The route via Aceguá is less used, but passes through more interesting countryside.

FLORIDA TO RIVERA

The countryside along this route consists of rolling hills with fruit orchards and wheatfields leading into more rugged cattle country. It takes you through a number of pleasant provincial towns.

Florida, which lies about 60 miles/96km north of Montevideo, is the first place really worth stopping at. There is a flourishing market of local produce, with a few crafts, and the Museo de Arte y Artesanía at Barreiro 370 is also worth a visit. Florida is positively a destination in its own right on 25 August, when its Independence Day celebrations take the form of a festival of local folklore. For tourist information ask at the Intendencia at Independencia 586. The best places to stay are the Hotel Español (José Rodo 360; tel 2262), or the Giani (Fernández and Rivera; tel 2130). If you want to continue north, Durazno, 52 miles/84km north of Florida, makes a pleasant overnight stop. There are a couple of hotels and a youth hostel at Saravia and Dr Pensa (tel 0362-2835).

Continuing north across the dam at Paso de los Toros, where the Río Negro has formed an enormous lake, you eventually reach Tacuarembo. This is an important town and road junction, some 250 miles/400km north of Montevideo. The Museo del Gaucho y del Indio (Flores and Artigas) gives a fascinating insight into the colourful past of the area. The Residencial Tacuarembo (18 de Julio 133) is cheap and clean. Local information is available at the Intendencia at 18 de Julio 164.

Rivera is an unappealing town 62 miles/100km north of Tacuarembo. A road marks the border between it and the Brazilian town of Santana do Livramento. The only sensible place to stay is at the Casablanca (Sarandi 484; tel 3221), but hotels are cheaper across the border. The only reason to hang around is to visit the Minas de Corrales, a fascinating area of abandoned goldmines about two hours by bus south of town.

The Brazilian consulate in Rivera is at Caballos 1159 and the Argentine consulate at Ituzaingo 524. Get your passport stamped at the Immigration Office at Calle Suárez 516, three blocks from the main square.

THE RIOS PLATA AND URUGUAY

COLONIA DEL SACRAMENTO

Usually known simply as Colonia, this is an important port for boats to Buenos Aires, which lies 31 miles/50km away across the estuary. It is also a thriving town of over 20,000 people, with an unusually historic centre which reflects its origins as Uruguay's oldest city, founded by the Portuguese in 1680.

Many of the buildings around the main square have been turned into museums. An interesting illustration of the town's colonial past can be found in the Museo del Periodo Portugués and the Museo del Periodo Español. The other main things to look out for are the parish church, the Museo Municipal in the Casa del Almirante Guillermo Brown and the lighthouse.

For tourist information ask at the Intendencia at Flores and Rivera.

Arrival and Departure: there are frequent buses east to Montevideo and Punta del Este, and north to Fray Bentos, Paysandú and Salto.

The journey to Buenos Aires by ferry takes four hours and costs $12. The hydrofoil takes two hours, leaves seven times a day and costs $20. Tickets are cheaper when bought at the port than from travel agents. You go through Uruguayan immigration before getting on the boat, while Argentinian immigration is usually on the ferry or hydrofoil itself. Officials in Uruguay won't let you on board if you don't have the correct documents for Argentina.

Accommodation: among the cheapest hotels are the Hotel del Prado youth hostel (Nueva Helvecia; tel 0552-4169), the Italiano (Ituzaingo and de la Peña) and the Posada de la Ciudadela (Barbot 164). Most of the best places to eat are along 18 de Julio and General Flores.

CARMELO

The main reason to get off the bus at Carmelo, which is 46 miles/74km northwest of Colonia, is to get the boat across to Tigré in Argentina. The $2\frac{1}{2}$-hour journey costs just $5 — far cheaper than any other journey across the water. Carmelo is well served by buses from Colonia, Montevideo, Fray Bentos and Salto. The best-value hotels are the Unión (Uruguay 368) and the Centro, next door.

MERCEDES

This is a pleasant town which, founded only in the late 18th-century, has a surprisingly strong colonial stamp. It lies on the banks of the Río Negro, 112 miles/180km north of Colonia, and it is a popular boating and fishing resort. The greatest interest, however, stems from its status as a market town for the large cattle-raising area around. The cheapest places to stay are the Club de Remeros youth hostel (by the river at de la Rivera and Gomensoro; tel 0532-2534), and the hospedajes at Giménez 703 and 848.

FRAY BENTOS

This is not a typographical error, but an extraordinary fact — that a small town in Uruguay should have become a household name in Britain. Sadly, the modern

Fray Bentos meat pie is an imposter, since the meat packing and canning plant has closed down. Much of the local working population was employed in the factory, and Fray Bentos feels downtrodden these days. Nevertheless, it has grown in importance since the building of the bridge across the river 6 miles/9km north, linking Uruguay with Puerto Unzue in Argentina. Several buses a day run across the border to Gualeguaychú. There is an Argentinian consulate in Fray Bentos at Sarandí 3195.

There is a number of hotels on 25 de Mayo, including the Colonial (at the corner with Zorrilla; tel 0535-2260), the more expensive Plaza (corner of 25 de Mayo; tel 2363) and the 25 de Mayo (on the corner with Lavalleja; tel 2586).

SALTO

This is an uncharacteristically large town with a population of about 80,000. Salto suffers from unpleasantly high temperatures, but there are beaches along the river where you can cool off. In the town the main thing to see is the extraordinary Museo de Bellas Artes (Uruguay 1067), housed in an imposing French-style mansion that was built by a wealthy cattle rancher during the 19th century. The building is undoubtedly more interesting than its contents, but alone it is worth a visit. It opens 5-8pm.

Agencia Central runs six buses a day from Montevideo, 310 miles/500km southeast. Express buses go direct and take six hours, while others go via Paysandú and take eight. There are also regular buses to and from Rivera, Paysandú and Colonia, and a ferry service across the river to Concordia in Argentina. The boat make sthe 15-minutes crossing five times a day, daily except Sundays; there is a more limited service on Saturdays and holidays.

The Club de Remeros by the river doubles as the Youth Hostel (Costanera and Belén; tel 0732-3418) and is recommended, as is its restaurant. The Artigas Plaza (Artigas 1146; tel 4824) and the Danaly (Agraciada 2058; tel 4350) charge $8/$12 and are both fairly good. Cheaper are Sabarros (Brasil 1683; tel 3788) and El Hogar (Vareli 961).

The Club de Pesca on the Costanera Sur is one of the best places to eat, since it normally has fresh fish from the river. There are many other places around the centre, among which are the reasonably-priced restaurant at the Gran Hotel Salto (Plaza Artigas) and the Club Bancario (Brasil 765). La Cervecería (Uruguay and Soca) is a cheap and good for a drink.

The tourist office at Uruguay 1052 is very helpful and gives out free maps; it is open 8am-7pm. Also on Uruguay are several cambios, including one at 800. The post office is at Artigas 890, the phone office at Ascensio 50. The Argentinian consulate is at Artigas 1162.

Around Salto

The Salto Dam, 13 miles/20km north, is the big tourist attraction nearby. The best way to get there is on a free two-hour tour organized by the dam's operators — ask at the office in the Gran Hotel Salto. A more peaceful destination is the Meseta de Artigas, in an idyllic spot on the river, 19 miles/30km south towards Paysandú, and then 8 miles/13km west. The 'meseta' or hill, with its precipitous descent to the river, is named after General Artigas, who had his headquarters here.

The Termas de Daymán are 6 miles/9km south of Salto, and combine hot springs and swimming pools. The set up is well-organized, cheap and easily accessible — the number 4 city bus leaves hourly from Calle Artigas, or from Brasil and Chiazzaro. There is a youth hotel (tel 0732-4361), as well as a campsite.

Paraguay

The Old Paraguayan Express

Population: 4.2 million **Capital: Asunción (800,000)**

Elvis Presley, say some, is alive and well and living in Paraguay. So too, claim others, is Adolf Hitler, along with an ageing bunch of Nazi war criminals. Paraguay attracts wild speculation and widespread ignorance. People who know just one or two facts about the country may remember President Stroessner, the dictator whose brutal rule ended only in 1989. The few who have heard of Paraguay's capital, Asunción, probably read about it in Graham Greene's *Travels with my Aunt*. The nearest many travellers get to the country is a visit to the Iguaçu Falls, near where Paraguay converges with Argentina and Brazil.

Paraguay, once relegated by a journalist to 'the etceteras in the list of nations', is isolated from the mainstream of life. Not many travellers make a diversion to visit a country that can be called neither exotic nor beautiful. But it is an outlandish and quirky place that is full of surprises: Paraguay was the first country on the continent to have a railway (its ancient steam locomotives are still in use), and it is the only South American nation in which an indigenous tongue is a fully fledged official language. Furthermore, the people are among the friendliest in South America.

Roughly the size of California, Paraguay is one of the region's smallest nations. Its position — bounded by Brazil, Bolivia and Argentina — would seem to make it a natural crossing-point between these countries. For contraband it certainly is. But while it can be easily included on the itinerary of travellers en route between

Brazil and Argentina, access to Bolivia is impeded by the inhospitable terrain of the country's northern region.

Paraguay offers less scope for travel than most other South American countries, yet there are certainly enough places around which to structure a visit. The most obvious attractions are the Jesuit missions, whose beauty lies not so much in the architecture as in the exquisite woodcarvings that were the work of the indigenous Guaraní Indians. Paraguay also boasts one of the most beautiful churches in the world, which alone makes a trip worthwhile. The remote northern Chaco region is a must for the lovers of off-the-beaten-track adventures.

Since there aren't abundant sights you can enjoy the country and its wonderful people with few distractions, and in this lies the real appeal of Paraguay. Travelling is easy and relaxed, and is a pleasant change from the often tough journeys in the Andean countries. You can witness the struggle to establish a democracy following the overthrow of the last of South America's military dictators.

GEOGRAPHY

The country is divided into two sharply contrasting regions by the Río Paraguay. The western zone, known as the Chaco, is a flat and desolate plain that takes up two-thirds of the country, and spreads over into Argentina and Bolivia. While the northern Chaco consists mostly of forest and grasslands, the southern and eastern areas are permanent swamp. Less than 3% of the country's population lives here.

The eastern zone consists mostly of plain, low hill-country and large areas of primeval forests. The rich red earth of the southeastern provinces is fertile, and new roads have encouraged colonization of the area. The fallen trees and burnt-out stumps that line the Encarnación-Ciudad del Este highway through the region are a depressing sight. Further west the land is used largely as pasture for cattle.

CLIMATE

Most of Paraguay has a sub-tropical climate, with rapid changes in temperature throughout the year. Summer (November to March) can be very hot and wet, with temperatures reaching 40°C/104°F. During this period Asunción can become uncomfortably humid. Winter is generally mild, and is the best time to visit. Since temperatures occasionally drop below freezing during July and August, a jumper wouldn't go amiss. Paraguay has a reputation for being wet, and rain can indeed fall at any time. The northern Chaco is tropical, and is hot throughout the year.

HISTORY

In 1526 and 1529 Sebastian Cabot first explored the area when he sailed up the Paraná and Paraguay rivers from the Atlantic. The main indigenous group in the region were the semi-nomadic Guaraní.

Asunción, founded in 1537, was the first permanent settlement in southern South America, and it was used as a base from which to explore Argentina. However the absence of natural resources and rich cultures to be pillaged meant that Paraguay remained a backwater. It was therefore an easy target for religious groups seeking influence in the region. From the early 17th century until their expulsion from the Spanish dominions in 1767, the Jesuits were active in southern Paraguay. They established over 40 missions, the so-called *reducciones,* which at their peak were home to around 150,000 people.

Paraguay earned self-rule peacefully in 1811. However, its history ever since has been one of turmoil, autocratic rule and senseless war. The first dictator was José Gaspar Rodríguez de Francia, known as 'El Supremo', who ruled from 1814 to

1840. Thanks to his economic policies, by the mid-19th century Paraguay was one of the most advanced countries in South America.

The third president, Marshal Francisco Solano López, was responsible for the greatest physical damage to Paraguay and for ruining its chance of becoming a significant power in the region. This he achieved by involving the country in the Triple Alliance War of 1865-70, which developed as a result of sour relations with Brazil. Every male aged 12 or more was pressganged. The resulting ragbag of an army was ordered to attack, in quick succession, Brazil, Argentina and Uruguay.

Considering that Paraguay faced the combined might of three powerful countries, and that some of its soldiers were forced to use weapons dating from the late 17th century, the Paraguayans did remarkably well. Defeat was inevitable, however, and they were forced to cede a large chunk of their territory. More tragically, 200,000 men were lost in battle and through disease or hunger. This was roughly half the population, leaving just 30,000 men among the remainder. López himself was stabbed in the stomach during the battle of Cerro Corá, and died shortly

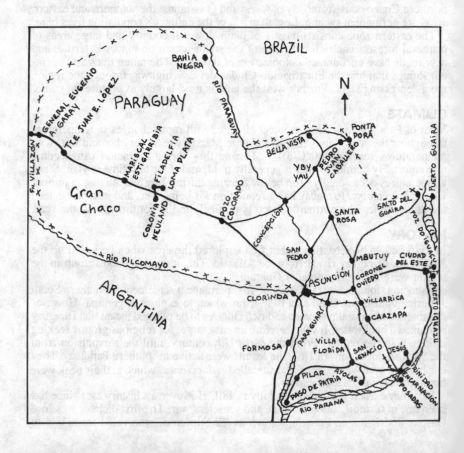

afterwards. Nevertheless, he is very much a hero. Eliza Lynch, his Irish mistress who was with him until he died, is almost as famous.

Following the war, Paraguay sank back into oblivion and the next few decades were characterized by political and economical instability. The early 20th century was a comparatively peaceful period, but during the 1930s the government got Paraguay involved in another bloody conflict. This time it was fought against Bolivia for control of the inhospitable Chaco region. This territory was said to contain oil, and Bolivia was keen to have a slice of it. Paraguay triumphed but lost tens of thousands of men, another cruel blow to the balance of the sexes.

Recent History. Following the human disaster of the Chaco War, continued political chaos culminated in a military coup, led by General Alfredo Stroessner, in 1954. Backed by the armed forces and an extremist faction of the main right-wing group, the Partido Colorado, Stroessner retained power for 34 years. He was one of the world's longest-serving heads of state, and has left a seemingly indelible mark on the country, which struggles to eradicate his memory. Known as 'The General', Stroessner turned Paraguay into a police state in which the people endured gross repression. That he won six presidential elections with massive majorities is unsurprising given the harassment of organized opposition. Stroessner's anti-communist stance brought him support from the USA, though he became one of their more embarrassing allies.

In February 1989, Stroessner was overthrown in a bloody military coup, and escaped to exile in Brazil. The dictator's regime had been increasingly troubled by rapidly decreasing revenue and, more surprisingly, by open protest. The coup was led by General Andres Rodríguez, the President's former deputy and right-hand man. He was another general with a tarnished record, but the fact that he helped rid the country of so unpopular a leader has won him some respect. He won easily the presidential elections of May 1989, though there were accusations of rigging. Apart from the Authentic Radical Liberal Party (PLRA), other parties had surprisingly little support. The ratio was repeated in the congressional elections of December 1991 in which the Colorado party won 55% of the vote and the PLRA 25%.

The democratization process has a long way to go, and some fear that splits in the Partido Colorado have created a potentially explosive tension; it is claimed that this has already led to several deaths. The instability is aggravated by the spectre of Stroessner himself, who retains a strong body of support within the party.

Yet there are glimmers of hope. Newspapers and radio stations that were closed down under Stroessner are functioning again. Congress, which hardly bothered to meet before, has become a forum of debate and Rodríguez has even been known to give the odd speech about the environment. Furthermore, he has promised to stand down in 1993, when the next presidential elections are due, thus clearing the way for a civilian to succeed him.

Greater political stability has increased confidence in other fields. While at one stage it was bracketed with Bolivia in terms of poverty, Paraguay has seen an economic upturn recently. This is thanks partly to neo-liberal trading policies and improved relations with the USA, though the mainstay of the economy is still contraband. Paraguay is a channel through which all manner of goods — from Bolivian cocaine to animal skins from Brazil — are smuggled out of the region.

THE PEOPLE

Paraguayans are more homogenous than most other South Americans. The high proportion of indigenous blood is clearly visible in the noticeable Indian features. The early Spanish settlers mixed freely with the native Guaraní Indians who, it is said, were so friendly that comparatively few of them were killed. Pure-blooded Indians number around 350,000, most of them living a semi-nomadic existence in the Chaco.

About 10,000 Koreans live in Paraguay, and they are particularly noticeable in the capital, where many of them run shops. Japanese immigrants are involved primarily in agriculture, and there are several colonies in the southeast. Of the other foreign groups, the largest is the Mennonite community, a German religious sect which first came to Paraguay in the 1920s. They live mainly in the Chaco and number about 10,000. See page 593 for more information about this group.

The average Paraguayan is puzzled yet delighted that anyone would want to visit his or her country. Many assume that white-skinned people must be missionaries, since religious zealots comprise the largest single group of visitors to Paraguay. In the Chaco, where the Indians have been the prey of the controversial New Tribes Mission, people may be wary of outsiders. Normally, however, people are extremely friendly and always eager to strike up conversations.

LANGUAGE

Though much of the Guaraní culture has been lost, the native language survives: Spanish is the official language, but most people also speak Guaraní — indeed it is the preferred language outside the capital, even among whites. Paraguay is the only country in South America where a native language is in common use by whites. Government officials are required to be bilingual. Wherever you are, expect to find very few English-speakers.

FURTHER READING

Literature on Paraguay is sparse and mostly out of print: including *El Supremo* by Edward White, set in the early days of independence in the 19th century, and *The Woman on Horseback* by William E. Barrett, the background to which is the era of Francisco Solano López and Eliza Lynch. Best of all and still available are two books by Graham Greene: *The Honorary Consul*, about a political kidnapping on the Paraguay/Argentinian border, and *Travels with my Aunt*, which reaches its climax in Asunción.

Getting There

AIR

From South America. *Argentina:* the Paraguayan national airline LAP has flights five times a week from Buenos Aires. Aerolíneas Argentinas (AR) services are less frequent, and call at Puerto Iguazú en route.

Bolivia: LAP and the Bolivian airline LAB have flights once a week from La Paz via Santa Cruz to Asunción. American Airlines flies four times a week non-stop between La Paz and the Paraguayan capital.

Brazil: daily flights from Rio and São Paulo on Varig, LAP and Pluna, and once a week with LAP from Manaus. Another option is to fly to Foz do Iguaçu, across the border in Brazil, and then continue by bus.

Chile: from Santiago with Ladeco and Pluna.

Uruguay: three flights a week from Montevideo on LAP or Pluna.

the last town in Argentina before the Pilcomayo river. Much of the traffic here is local, and formalities for travellers are usually quick and efficient. At the frontier an unidentified man collects passports for processing — make sure the locals are giving in theirs before you part with yours. Travellers on a day-trip from Paraguay leave the tourist card with the Paraguayan migration office and collect it later. No fee is charged. Men with large wallets get on to buses crossing the border, so changing money is not a problem.

There are buses to Clorinda from Buenos Aires, and services direct to Loyola from Resistencia (8am, 1.20pm) and Formosa. The easiest option is to take one of the international services that run daily from Buenos Aires or Córdoba direct to Asunción; the journey takes 20-22 hours. It may be cheaper to travel as far as Clorinda ($60 air-con) and then take a local bus to the frontier, or straight through to Asunción — these leave at 7am, 8am, 9.30am, 11.30am, 4pm, 5pm and 6pm (Argentinian time) and take two hours. Buses from Puerto Falcón leave approximately hourly during the week, but only at 11am and 5pm on Sundays. If you need to stay overnight in Clorinda, the Hotel Embajador, opposite the bus station (tel 21148/21985) is clean, cheap and comfortable.

A quicker and more unusual route into the capital is by boat across the river from Puerto Pilcomayo. A local bus from Clorinda runs here every half hour (30-minute journey, 70c) terminating at the quay, where with luck there will be others waiting to make the crossing; the small wooden hut serves as a waiting room until you reach a quorum. The boat costs $1-2, depending upon what the crew think they can get away with, and takes ten minutes to reach the port of Itá Enramada. The last sailing is around 4pm Argentinian time (5pm Paraguay time) unless you can charter the whole boat. In high winds the service does not operate at all. The vessel is not a handsome one: resembling a converted torpedo boat, it is tied up next to wrecks of a couple of other craft, and takes in small but distressing amounts of water.

Entering Paraguay by this route is sometimes difficult since the Itá Enramada authorities are not used to travellers. Once inside Paraguay, walk a little way up the road and take a local bus (number 9) into Asunción proper. Note that moneychangers are unlikely to be found on this route, so try to obtain Paraguayan currency in Clorinda: the black market operates at the corner of Buenos Aires and San Martín. When travelling from Paraguay into Argentina, take bus 9 direction Lambare to the port.

Puerto Cano/Pilar: a second route across the Paraguay river from Argentina is close to the southwest corner of Paraguay. In 1991 the presidents of the two countries inaugurated a car ferry between Puerto Cano and Pilar. Sailings from Cano are at 7.45am and 4.30pm Argentinian time. Fares are $1 per passenger, $5 for a car.

Posadas/Encarnación: another much used border post is across the Paraná river from Posadas. Buses for Encarnación leave from the bus station every 15 minutes between 6am and midnight; even if you get off at immigration and continue on a different bus, your ticket is valid for the whole journey. Border procedures are straightforward, and plenty of moneychangers patrol the Paraguayan side. It's worth exploring Encarnación, but if you want to continue your journey there are frequent bus services to both Asunción and Ciudad del Este. There are also international bus services from Buenos Aires to Asunción via Posadas, as well as an extremely slow weekly train.

From Bolivia. Crossing overland into Paraguay from Bolivia is the most problematic since it involves travelling through the Chaco region. Getting to the Bolivian border post at Fortín Villazón is difficult enough; and things don't improve once you cross over into Paraguay either since there are no bus services until you reach the town of Mariscal Estigarribia, some 150 miles/240km from the border. Turn to page 593 before deciding to hitch.

From Uruguay. Paraguay and Uruguay do not share a land border, but there are direct bus services from Montevideo to Asunción; these usually go via Brazil and Argentina, crossing borders at Uruguaiana and Posadas.

Red Tape

Visas. These are not required by most EC citizens, including those from Britain, but excluding those from France and the Republic of Ireland. North Americans may also enter the country without a visa, but Australasians cannot. A visa permits a stay of up to 90 days.

The Paraguayan mission in the UK is at Braemar Lodge, Cornwall Gardens, London SW7 4AQ (tel 071-937 1253; fax: 071-937 5687). The consular section (tel 071-937 6629) is open 10am-3pm Monday to Friday. Visas are free and can normally be processed in two or three days. The Paraguayan mission in the USA is at 2400 Massachusetts Avenue NW, Washington DC 20008 (tel 202-483 6960), with consulates in San Francisco and New York. There is no representation in Australia or New Zealand.

Tourist Cards. Those who do not require a visa must obtain a Tourist Card (permiting a stay of three months) at the border. When entering by land, you do this at the desk marked Turismo, having already had your passport stamped at Migración. The fee for the tourist card is US$3, payable in dollars or local currency (including that of the country you've just left if you are entering by land).

Extending Your Stay. The Immigration Office in Asunción is notorious for the length required to process extensions. Nip across the border instead.

Departure Tax. About $6 is payable on all international departures by air. Avoid paying in dollars as the exchange rate used is poor — go to the bureau de change downstairs in the airport and change money into local currency instead.

CUSTOMS

The customs allowance is 200 cigarettes (or half a pound of tobacco) and 'one bottle' of alcohol, interpreted usually as one litre.

Paraguayan border officials are among the most relaxed in South America, and crossing borders is rarely a long-winded or aggravating business. Customs officials are seldom bothered about searching your baggage, and you would have to be very unlucky to encounter one who is out to cause problems for anyone carrying left-wing literature. Travellers with passport stamps from Cuba, China, Albania, etc. used to face difficulties at immigration, but this has been rare since the departure of Stroessner.

Money

The unit of currency is the Guaraní (G)

Notes and Coins. Notes are issued in denominations of 100 (green), 500 (blue), 1,000 (purple), 5,000 (red) and 10,000 (brown/black) guaranís. All are bilingual. The current G10,000 note is worth collecting: it depicts a wonderfully dramatic scene from the time of Paraguay's declaration of independence. But banknotes are often in a terrible state, and it may take time to find one that is legible. Coins are issued to the value of 1, 5, 10, 50 and 100 guaranís.

Changing Money. Staff in banks, in Asunción at least, are more likely to direct you to the nearest cambio than to offer to change your money themselves. Rates are generally better at cambios anyway. And while banks rarely cash cheques into anything other than guaranís, several cambios in Asunción may give dollars cash for cheques: Guaraní Cambios, for example, has many offices including one at Palma 449 in the capital. Note that if you are changing travellers cheques (into dollars or local currency) cambios are likely to insist upon seeing your purchase receipt.

Cambios are found primarily in the capital and at borders. This also where you will find most street moneychangers, though no significant premium is obtained by dealing with private individuals. Most are trustworthy. Rates for foreign currencies are good, particularly for Brazilian cruzeiros. Exchanging guaranís abroad, however, is virtually impossible.

Banks open 7-10.30am Monday to Friday in summer, 7-11am in winter.

Credit Cards. Plastic is of limited use, particularly outside the capital. The only place to issue cash advances to holders of Visa and Access cards is the Banco Unión in Asunción.

Paraguay is four hours behind GMT from October until March, when clocks go forward an hour.

Mail. The postal service is cheap and efficient. Allow about five days for airmail letters to reach Europe. Poste restante letters to Asunción should be sent to the main post office at El Paraguayo Independiente and Alberdi.

Telephone. The international country code is 595. To make international calls from Paraguay, go to any Antelco office, which in the main towns should be open daily until about 10pm. Rates for three minutes are as follows: $8.25 to the UK, $7.80 to the USA, and $10.50 to Australia. There is a reduced rate after 8pm and all day Sunday. It is possible to make collect calls to Britain and the USA, but this is usually a time-consuming business. Telegrams and fax can also be sent through Antelco.

Street payphones are scarce outside Asunción, and you are best off going to the local Antelco office or bus terminal. Tokens (*fichas*) are either *local* or *especiales para larga distancia*, and one should be sufficient for a couple of minutes. The most important area codes are: Asunción 021; Ciudad del Este 061; Concepción 031, Encarnación 071; and Filadelfia 091.

THE MEDIA
Newspapers. Comparatively few people seem to read the newspaper and trying to buy one late in the day can be a challenge. Nevertheless, the level of interest has risen gradually since the lifting of censorship.

The best read is *ABC Color*, which was closed down under Stroessner but has been back on the streets since 1989. The other two main papers are *Hoy*, whose coverage of international news isn't bad, and *Nueva Patria*, which is the official paper of the Colorado party. *La Opinión* is a weekly that contains articles covering anything from current affairs to art and travel.

The German community, which is sizeable in Asunción, has its own papers. They include *Aktuelle Rundschau*, which is full of German news agency reports, and is thus a good way for German speakers to catch up with events in Europe. Foreign papers are hard to find, though you can normally pick up the *Buenos Aires Herald*.

Radio. The best channel is Radio Nandutí which, like *ABC Color*, was closed down under Stroessner. It has a daily chat show that targets government figures. For music, try Radio 1 de Marzo on 780AM or 97.1FM.

Paraguay presents few problems in terms of topography. The network of paved roads is good though limited, and rain renders dirt tracks impassable. Unlike in Bolivia or Peru there is little transport to supplement the buses. Hitching is not common practice and train services are few and extremely slow. There is some boat transport along the Paraná and Paraguay rivers and, more mundanely, cars are easily hired in Asunción.

Maps. Good maps of Paraguay are rare. The best available abroad are in the ITM series (see page 41), though the country is split between the North West and North East maps of South America. The best source once in Paraguay is the Touring y Automóvil Club Paraguayo (25 de Mayo y Brasíl) in Asunción, which has a rough road map of Paraguay for $4.50.

AIR

Given the comparative compactness of the main populated area, domestic flights are likely to be useful only if you head into the wilds.

Most internal services are operated by LATN (Líneas Aereas de Transporte Nacional) and TAM (Transportes Aéreo Militar). Additional flights are operated by Aeronorte and Aerosur. Flights can get booked up in the high season (June to September, and December to March), but usually it is easy to get a seat.

RAIL

While Paraguay cannot boast spectacular train journeys, travelling by rail enables you to see the country at its most rural. Paraguay's railway system has changed little since it was first laid. There is still only one main line, which links Asunción and Encarnación, with a single branch running eastwards from it to Abai; and the trains continue to rely on the original wood-burning steam locomotives.

Trains are used mainly for freight, but they also provide a vital transport service to remote communities. Passenger services are extremely slow and infrequent: just one train a week runs between Asunción and Encarnación, taking 15-16 hours as opposed to 4-5 hours by bus. A journey by train is a must, however. If you can't face the thought of spending an entire day on the tracks, take a ride on the daily train that links Asunción to some of the nearby towns and villages; see page 585. Local trains have only one class, but when travelling long-distance you usually have a choice of first or second class.

BUS

The network of bus services is excellent along the triangle of paved highways that connect Asunción, Encarnación and Ciudad del Este, and fairly good along the lesser roads, e.g. to Filadelfia, Concepción and Juan Pedro Caballero.

Services are operated by various companies. Rysa and Nuestra Señora de la Asunción are usually reliable for long journeys. Executive buses are not that common, with usually just one a day along the main routes. One notch down are the *diferencial* or *especial* services, which usually stop in the main towns. At the bottom of the scale is the *común*: while these local buses are ideal for short hops, travelling between Encarnación and Asunción by stopping bus could add one or two hours to your journey.

Ancient, rickety affairs that are slightly smaller than the standard local buses, and tend to originate in less-important towns, are usually referred to as colectivos. They stop anywhere and everywhere and while uncomfortable are great fun to travel on. They often provide the only means to reach towns and villages off the main highways.

Since many journeys revolve around services along the main highways between Asunción, Ciudad del Este and Encarnación, details of services between these towns are given here. Journeys between any two take four or five hours, though the slow buses can take a good deal longer.

Asunción/Ciudad del Este: services run by Rysa, Nuestra Señora de la Asunción, Sirena del Paraná, Ciudad del Este and Rápido Caaguazú. Buses leave at least every hour between 9am and midnight, with a few services during the night. The fare is around $7.50.

Asunción/Encarnación: departures from early morning until midnight. The most direct services are run by Rysa and Nuestra Señora de la Asunción ($7.50). If you want to stop off en route travel with El Tigre, Flecha de Oro, La Encarnacena, Alborada or Señora de la Encarnación ($5).

Ciudad del Este/Encarnación: Rysa and Yacyreta offer the most direct services ($5). Trans Paraense, El Tigre, Beato R. Gonzalez and Señora de la Encarnación are slower ($3.50). There are departures virtually every 30 minutes from 5am until late.

CAR

The terrain presents few problems for drivers, except during the rainy season, and there is little traffic. A litre of petrol costs $0.50. The main highways require you to pay a toll, usually around $0.40 for a stretch of around 60 miles/100km. The Touring y Automovil Club Paraguayo (TACPy) at the corner of 25 de Mayo and Brasíl in Asunción is generally helpful and reasonably efficient. For roadside assistance, call 24366; for other information, 210550.

Asunción is full of car rental agencies, though they are scarce elsewhere. The cheapest vehicle offered by most companies is a Volkswagen 1300, which costs around $35 per day basic. A smarter car is likely to cost at least $50 per day, a minibus or jeep $80 upwards.

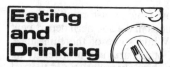

Eating and Drinking

Paraguay is not famous for its cuisine, yet you can eat extremely well. Cattle-breeding is big business in Paraguay, and beef is excellent. If a town has anything other than the standard, unpretentious comedor where everyone goes, it is likely to be a parrillada, where you can eat large quantities of freshly-barbecued meat served with copious amounts of chips. Sausages are also excellent, and are best bought freshly grilled at bus stations and by the roadside. Soups are popular and often meat-based. *So'o-yosopy*, made of cornmeal, beef, garlic and herbs, is almost a national dish, but few restaurants serve it. Another traditional soup is *bori-bori*, made of vegetables, meat, cheese and corn balls.

However, Paraguay has more to offer than meat. Its rivers produce large numbers of fish. One of the most common is *surubí*, which is especially abundant in the Paraná. A common way to serve it, strangely, is in a Gorgonzola sauce.

One of the country's most typical dishes is *sopa paraguaya*. This isn't a soup at all, but a unique creation made from mashed corn, cheese, milk and egg. It is hard to liken sopa paraguaya to anything else, but it has the consistency of an extremely moist and rather heavy cake and tastes like cheese soufflé. It is delicious when served hot and fresh, but is not always easy to find. Sometimes it is served as a starter in restaurants. A much more easily-located food is *chipa*, which is sold in huge baskets mainly in bus stations and markets. This is cassava bread which is shaped into rolls and is usually crusty on the outside and doughy in the middle. In *The Honorary Consul*, Graham Greene claims that chipa 'can only be properly appreciated after semi-starvation'. But however tasteless or stodgy, it is a cheap snack, and people buy it by the bagful before setting off on a long journey. Look out for *chipa soo*, which is similar but with a meat filling.

Copetín is the term used to describe a shop-cum-café where you can eat snacks and drink coffee. Look for a blackboard listing the day's specials.

DRINKING

There are many brands of beer in Paraguay, and Munchen Blanco, Baviera, Bremen and Pilsen are all good. Draught beer is available, and if you agree to it *con spuma* it will have a head which takes up half the glass.

Most of Paraguay's wines, like several of its beers, are made by German immigrants. Local wines are rarely served in restaurants, so you will do better to scout around a few bottle shops. *Caña*, a rough-edged rum made from sugar cane, is sold under brand names such as Aristocrat.

The most popular non-alcoholic drink among the locals is *maté*. Dried *yerba maté* leaves are put into a specially-designed cup (traditionally a gourd) and boiling water poured over them; this rather bitter brew is then drunk through a spout. You see people going about their daily business cup in hand, with a thermos of hot water to keep it topped up. Yerba maté is a drink designed for social gatherings, and it is common to pass the cup around to your friends. It is rarely served in cafés and your best chance to try it is at a bus station or if you are invited into someone's home. If desperate, buy Pajarito — yerba maté in cartons.

Coffee, the most popular breakfast drink, is sold from flasks in bus stations too, usually white with sugar. You can also buy toddy, another hot and even sweeter drink.

Exploring

Paraguay's most famous historical relics are the Jesuit missions in the southern department of Misiones. While some of the ruins have been restored, others are only now receiving attention. The chief characteristic is the red sandstone used to build them, often elaborately sculpted. While the ruins are rarely in a good state — the best-preserved are at Trinidad — the museums are often excellent. The Guaraní Indians were skilled craftsmen, and they created a most attractive mestizo art that is an unusual blend of European baroque and native influences. Their work can also be seen in Franciscan churches, including the remarkable one at Yaguarón. Paraguay's colonial villages are not major destinations, but are interesting as communities.

There is only a small network of national parks, and the scope for hiking is extremely limited. While the richest wildlife is to be found in the remote Chaco region, the lack of infrastructure makes exploration virtually impossible unless you have your own transport or go on a tour organized from Asunción. The best place for walking is in Ybicuy National Park, southeast of the capital.

Entertainment

Jesuit missionaries taught the Indians to play the harp, and this instrument has become an integral part of Paraguayan music. The most traditional songs are still distinctive for their representation of natural sounds. The best-known manifestation of Paraguayan music, however, is the *trío paraguayano*, an ensemble of guitars and harps. The complex musical forms are beautifully weaved, and are popular elsewhere in the Americas and in Europe; a spoof version in Britain was called Alberto y los Tríos Paranoyas.

The most famous dance in Paraguay is the bizarre bottle dance, which involves dancers gyrating to music while balancing bottles on their heads. You are unlikely to have the chance to witness this outside Asunción, where some clubs organize performances.

SPORT

As any knowledgeable soccer fan will tell you, Paraguayan footballers are forces with which to be reckoned. The national team does remarkably well for such a small country, and the club sides are excellent. In the Copa Libertadores de América the 1990 winners were Olimpia of Asunción, who were also runner-up in the very first competition.

Shopping

Paraguay has little to interest the serious shopper. The country is famous for the delicate *ñandutí* lace, associated with the town of Itauguá, and *Aó Po'i*, embroidery work done mainly in Villarrica. These highly distinctive products are sold in good crafts shops around the country, but are certainly not of universal appeal. You can also buy rugs, hammocks, and ceramics, but most interesting is the woodcarving work. Some shops in Asunción sell Guaraní carvings.

You can buy electronic gear cheaply at duty-free shops in Ciudad del Este and Asunción. But if you are good and pay duty when you return, the price is basically the same. In addition, many of the goods are contraband, so don't expect any kind of guarantee.

South Americans often warn travellers to be careful when in Paraguay, suggesting it is a dangerous place. Corruption is part of everyday life but this is unlikely to affect travellers. Similarly, while organized crime is big business, petty crime is minimal. Comparatively few smart mansions in Asunción have the high fences and vicious guard dogs so common in other South American capitals.

It is possible to feel uneasy in Ciudad del Este just because it is patently such an insalubrious place. However the atmosphere elsewhere in Paraguay, even in Asunción, is not at all threatening. There is a fairly heavy police and military presence in the capital, though you won't find men in uniform on every street corner. Officials occasionally board buses and trains to check identification.

Paraguay is in the yellow fever zone, but malaria is only a risk if you plan to travel through the northern Chaco to Bolivia. However, since there are periodic outbreaks of dengue fever, you should still protect yourself against mosquitoes. The cholera epidemic has hardly affected Paraguay, but you should take the usual precautions. Mains water is safe to drink in Asunción, but is risky elsewhere.

The Paraguayan consulate in London will send you a few brochures in return for a stamped addressed envelope. Most of these are fairly useless, though the pages describing the advantages of Paraguay as a place to settle make interesting reading. The same range of brochures is available from tourist offices once you reach Paraguay. Apart from the office in the capital, tourist information desks are found only at busy land frontiers.

The best reference book is the *TAP Guía*, which was printed for the first time in 1991, and is in theory updated annually. It includes maps of the capital and Encarnación, as well as several of the country. There are detailed directories of addresses for the main towns — listing everything from hotels and restaurants to toyshops and political parties. It has text in Spanish, English and German, and costs $5.50.

Public Holidays

January 1	New Year's Day
February 3	Feast of San Blas (patron saint of Paraguay)
March 1	Heroes' Day
March/April	Easter
May 1	Labour Day
May 14-15	Independence Day
June 12	Chaco Armistice
August 15	Founding of Asunción
August 25	Constitution Day
September 29	Victory of Boquerón Day

October 12	Columbus Day
November 1	All Saints' Day
November 8	Feast of the Virgin of Caacupé
December 25	Christmas Day

ASUNCION

One of the streets in the Paraguayan capital is named after Walt Disney, and indeed Asunción is often dismissed as a Mickey Mouse place. Compared with other South American capitals it is a small backwater, but the city is not as provincial as people make out. The pace is undeniably slow, but buses still roar through the streets, and the shanties along the riverbank and in the suburbs are as shabby and depressing as any on the continent. But the old-fashioned atmosphere is positively endearing, and engenders a strange kind of nostalgia. It is a manageable and approachable city, and a safe place too.

Asunción lies on the banks of the Río Paraguay, which marks the country's southwestern border with Argentina. The town was founded in 1537 and was chosen by the Spanish as capital of its southern South American empire. This early importance was shortlived, however, and Asunción was eclipsed by Buenos Aires. Little remains from these colonial days, though Asunción never boasted much fine architecture: Paraguay did not bring great wealth to the colonists, who were therefore disinclined to finance the construction of sumptuous mansions and churches. Central Asunción dates primarily from the late 19th century and is handsome in an unassuming kind of way. There are some pleasant, shady squares and comparatively few modern high-rise blocks. Sights are few, but when you've seen all you want to in the city, it makes a good starting point for trips into the country.

CITY LAYOUT

The centre of the city is fairly small, with the river forming a natural boundary to the north and east. Colón, an important shopping street, runs inland from the port building, marking the northwestern extent of the centre. Roads run southeast from here through the heart of the city, including Palma, another main commercial street. At Independencia Nacional the street names change and the amount of commerce declines. By the time you reach Brasil, the suburbs have just about begun. These fan out in a random sprawl.

On streets parallel with the river, numbers begin at Avenida Independencia Nacional and increase by 100 each block. Perpendicular streets are numbered in 100s starting at El Paraguayo Independiente.

Maps. A large sheet map (Plano Turístico) is available from bookshops. It is useful for trips out of the centre, getting your bearings, and working out the one-way system, but places of interest aren't marked. Supplement it with the free hand-out from the tourist office (at Palma 468), which is tiny but shows all the sights. A better map is available for $2 from the Touring y Automóvil Club Paraguayo at 25 de Mayo and Brasil. It is on the first floor of an unlikely looking building next to a Shell garage, and opens 7.30am-noon daily and 2.30-6pm on weekdays. The *TAP Guía*, sold in some bookshops, has detailed page-by-page maps of the city.

ARRIVAL AND DEPARTURE

Air. Silvio Pettirossi airport (tel 207201/22012) is 10 miles/16km northeast of the centre. A taxi costs $12, but bus 30A runs every half-hour or so to the centre: you can expect to be heckled by taxi-drivers as you make the five-minute walk to the bus stop by the roundabout at the airport gate. Note that bus 30A plies between Asunción and the town of Luque, so half the buses are not going to the capital; make sure you get on one which is. It takes around 40 minutes to reach the city centre, which it enters along Azara and continues to Colón.

The airport has good facilities, including a helpful tourist information desk between immigration and customs. Immigration procedures can be slow, so it is an advantage being first off the flight. The bank, on the right as you leave customs, gives a reasonable rate of exchange, though you can usually do better in Asunción itself.

The most entertaining way to return to the airport is to travel by train from Asunción to Luque at 12.15pm, then walk back down the tracks as far as Pag Peg hamburgers, where you board bus 30A to the airport. Allow a couple of hours for this jaunt. The more conventional method is to board bus 30A along Cerro Corá.

Airline offices: these are clustered around Oliva and Díaz. LAP is at Oliva 467 (tel 491039/46), between 14 de Mayo and Alberdi. LAB and Varig are around the corner on 14 de Mayo at Díaz. Pluna is at Alberdi 513 (tel 490128/9) on the corner of Oliva, and Ladeco on Díaz between Alberdi and Chile. LanChile, Ecuatoriana and Air Canada are on the first floor at the corner of 15 de Agosto at Díaz. Aerolineas Argentina is at Independencia Nacional 365, between 25 de Mayo and Estigarribia (tel 491012).

For internal flights, LATN is at Estigarribia and Brasil (tel 212277/211763) and TAM is on Oliva, near the LAP office.

Rail. As well as the local service to Luque and beyond at 12.15pm daily, trains also run to Encarnación and Buenos Aires: to do the whole journey by rail takes an arduous 45 hours, and most people opt to travel to Encarnación by bus, and then catch one of the more frequent Argentinian trains from across the border. Trains to Encarnación leave on Tuesday and Friday and take 15 hours, the first service only continuing to Buenos Aires; the fare is $36.

The railway station is on Calle Bogado (tel 447316), southeast of the centre near Plaza Uruguaya. Take time to have a look around the 19th-century station and the country's first railway engine, which is on display; those still in use are equally fit to be museum pieces.

Bus. The bus terminal (Terminal Nuevo) is on Avenida República Argentina, southeast of the centre (tel 551730/2, 551668/9). Many city buses pass the station bound for the centre, including number 10 (marked Centro/Azara) which puts you within easy reach of most hotels. Buses 31 and 38 also run to the centre. The street alongside the station is busy and confusing, with many different city buses calling at different stops. People waiting should be able to tell you where to catch a particular bus; otherwise ask at the information desk in the station. A taxi into town costs about $5.

City buses heading to the terminal from the centre run along Oliva or Cerro Corá. Most bus companies have offices in the city centre, from which their buses set off about 30 minutes before reaching the Terminal Nuevo. To find out about the full range of services you should go to the bus station, though some bus companies advertise their services in the newspaper.

Most bus services around Paraguay are described under the relevant sections.

For journeys along the highways to Ciudad del Este and Encarnación see page 574. Listed here are international services:

Argentina: Brújula runs buses to Puerto Falcón across the river hourly on the hour from 5am to 11am, then hourly on the half-hour from 12.30pm to 5.30pm; on Sundays and holidays departures are at 8am and 2pm only. Some services continue across the bridge to Loyola and on to Clorinda; otherwise you can walk across and take another bus from the other side.

Direct buses from Asunción to Buenos Aires take 20-22 hours. Four or five companies run a daily bus, for which the fare is around $47; Brújula and Nuestra Señora de la Asunción also run a daily diferencial service each ($55), and a twice-weekly executivo ($65). Expreso Singer has a daily bus to Posadas leaving at 11.30am. There are also buses to Córdoba (18 hours).

Brazil: Rysa runs two buses a day to Foz de Iguaçu, but Pluma buses are better since they don't stop in Ciudad del Este; the fare is $10. Pluma, Catarinense and Brújula serve São Paulo and southern Brazilian towns.

ASUNCION

1 Port Building
2 Asunción Palace Hotel
3 Palacio de Gobierno
4 UK Embassy
5 Flota Mercantil
6 Bar Restaurant Asunción
7 UnionCard
8 TAP and LAP
9 Le Grand Café
10 Lido Bar
11 Guaraní Hotel
12 Plaza de los Héroes
13 Tourist Office
14 Casa de la Independencia
15 Post Office
16 Plaza Independencia
17 Casa de la Cultura
18 Congress
19 Antelco
20 Museo de Bellas Artes
21 Plaza Uruguay
22 Train station
23 Plaza Hotel
24 Museo Dr Barbero
25 Hotel Azara
26 Hotel Oasis

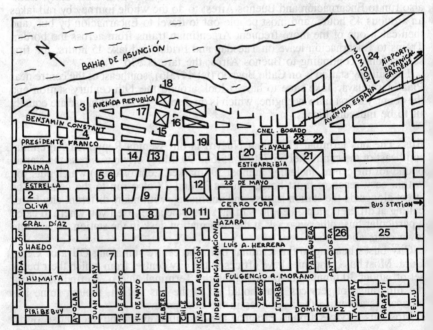

Chile: Brújula has diferencial buses to Santiago de Chile on Monday and Thursday at 1pm; the fare is about $65.

Uruguay: buses to Montevideo take around 20 hours. Brújula has twice-weekly services leaving at 8am on Tuesday and Friday; the fare is $60.

Car Rental. The cheapest rates are offered by Only Rent-a-Car at 15 de Agosto 441 between Estrella and Oliva (tel 492731-3). The more established agents include National (Yegros 501 at Cerro Corá; tel 445890/491379) and Hertz, at the airport (tel 22012-4).

Boat. Flota Mercantil del Estado (FME) at Estrella 672-682 (tel 441100) runs boats weekly to Concepicíon (see page 592) and every two weeks to Corumbá in Brazil.

GETTING AROUND

Bus. Don't be put off by the large number of city buses or the speed at which they move. Once you have mastered the system of one-way streets you should have few problems. Most streets in the centre are one-way in alternate directions: Azara heads northwest, neighbouring Cerro Corá goes southeast, etc. Therefore, while Azara is full of buses heading downtown, Cerro Corá is used by many services leaving the centre. Pay the driver on entry and keep your ticket since inspectors do the rounds sporadically.

Tram. A solitary yellow tram rumbles northwest along Palma, turns around at Colón and heads back along Estrella. Unless you are a tram buff, it's not worth waiting for, especially at weekends when it doesn't run at all.

Taxis. These are not always easy to hail, but there are plenty of ranks, including one in Plaza de los Héroes, at the corner of Nuestra Señora and Oliva (tel 449217). Most journeys cost $2-3, but make sure the driver resets his meter. Normal cabs are yellow; red ones are airport taxis.

ACCOMMODATION

The best area for accommodation is along Cerro Corá and Azara, mostly in the area to the south and west of Plaza Uruguaya. One of the best is the Hotel Azara at Azara 860 (tel 449754), between Tacuary and EE.UU. (Estados Unidos). A comfortable double room with bathroom and hot water costs $12 including breakfast. One block away is the Oasis, at Azara 736 (tel 953398), which is clean and costs $10 for a double. The Plaza, adjacent to the railway station, is reasonably good value at $20 for two.

At the northwest end of the centre is the Asunción Palace Hotel at Colón 415 and Estrella (tel 492151). A double costs $22 with breakfast, and the place is ideal for those who like their hotels rich in faded grandeur.

The Hotel Guaraní, at the southern corner of the Plaza de los Héroes, is the ritziest place in the city centre. But the best place to stay if you feel like splashing out is the Gran Hotel del Paraguay where Graham Greene stayed in 1973 while researching *The Honorary Consul*. Rooms are surprisingly cheap, at $30 for a double, and the restaurant is worth a visit in its own right (see below). The hotel is on Padre Pucheu at de la Residenta, about 20 minutes walk east of the centre (tel 200051/2/3).

EATING AND DRINKING

The choice of good restaurants in Asunción is limited, though street vendors sell all manner of food, including strange sausages and delicious kebabs, so you will not go hungry.

Have at least one meal at the Gran Hotel del Paraguay described above. The house was built in the nineteenth century by Francisco Solano López for his Irish mistress, Eliza Lynch. The dining room was once her private theatre, and it retains the original hand-painted ceiling. Eating a meal in this atmosphere of gone-to-seed elegance is an unbeatable experience; it provides a unique opportunity to observe the local rich. The food is not up to the standard of the surroundings, but nor is it expensive: you can have a plate of pasta for $3.

A good place for lunch or an early evening beer is the Lido bar in Plaza de los Héroes. It is not quite as cosmopolitan as it likes to claim, but the empanadas are delicious. The Grand Café, on Oliva between 14 de Mayo and Alberdi, is just what it says. The Café di Trevi at Palma 573 (near 14 de Mayo) is also good, elegant and colonial, with tables outside in good weather. It is a clean, pleasant refuge, though the food can be disapointing. On Calle Estrella and Alberdi is La Pergola del Bolsi, a good, cheap lunch place, and nearby is the pleasant Cafecito. The closest thing to a British pub is the Art Gallery Pub on Colón between Palma and Estrella. It is closed on Sunday evenings and all day Monday.

EXPLORING

The city's main square is the Plaza de los Héroes which covers four blocks. The square itself is fairly pleasant, with the usual shoeshines, but the architecture enclosing it is nothing special. On Saturday mornings people sell food and crafts, and for a good view go up to the 13th floor of the Guaraní Hotel, on the south side. The building of greatest interest in the square is the Panteón Nacional. It is modelled on Les Invalides of Paris and was completed in 1937. Military heroes are buried inside, and the array of statues and stained glass portraits help you put faces to the men who played important roles in Paraguay's history. Prominent among them are Francisco Solano López, although he is actually buried in the cemetery on Avenida Mariscal López. On the walls are numerous plaques — many of them paying homage to the soldiers who fought in the Chaco War — sent by governments around the world. Most references to Stroessner appear to have been eradicated, although there remains one token plaque in his honour. The pantheon is guarded by two soldiers in the uniform worn during the Triple Alliance War. It is open to the public from 6am-6pm (daily).

Heading southeast along Estigarribia, past street traders and the delightful University, you reach the Museo de Bellas Artes, near the corner of Iturbe. Basically a room staging exhibitions of paintings, even by South American standards the quality and quantity of work is a little thin. One block closer to the river, on Yegros between Ayala and Bogado, is the extraordinary town hall. The size of an aircraft hangar, it is vaguely art deco with ornate staircases — a real palace of bureaucracy. Feel free to wander around.

A couple of blocks northwest of Plaza de los Héroes, on 14 de Mayo, is the Casa de la Independencia, where independence was plotted in 1811. This beautifully restored house is one of Asunción's few colonial buildings. It is a real oasis in a city where the past is largely buried; even the noise of traffic from the streets outside doesn't disturb the peaceful atmosphere. The museum contains a quirky collection of exhibits, from portraits of famous generals to religious relics. It may have rather too many bloodied Christs for your liking. The museum opens 7.30-11.30am and 3-7pm Monday to Friday, 8-11.30am on Saturday.

Further up 14 de Mayo, near the waterfront, is Plaza de la Independencia. This is the city's largest and most handsome square. It is dotted with palm trees and lined with impressive (if not particularly beautiful) 19th-century official buildings. These include the Palacio Legislativo or Congress, the unremarkable cathedral, the main post office and the Casa de la Cultura. The latter is housed in the former military college which contains the Museo Histórico Militar — devoted to Paraguay's war, but with more general historical and anthropological exhibits too. Outside is a tank captured from the Bolivians; it was made in Newcastle-upon-Tyne in 1932 by Vickers Armstrong. Inside are some interesting maps of Paraguay, a petition of gratitude to Eliza Lynch, signed by 80,000 grateful Paraguayans and the shirts and vests belonging to López himself. In the courtyard, the atmosphere is as if from a Western, with an air of waiting for the shooting to start. The museum opens 7.30am-12.30pm and 4-7pm from Monday to Friday, 8am-noon and 3-6pm at weekends.

The Palacio Legislativo is not a beautiful building, but has had an air of activity since something apporoaching real democracy was established. When Congress is in session between April and December you may be able to watch a debate. From the parliament's terrace, overlooking the river, you might expect a beautiful waterside location. In fact all you can see stretching below you are slums. Up on the left is a statue of Francisco López on horseback; the monument used to be on ground level, but was raised because children persisted in daubing it with paint. Continuing northwest along the river you reach the Palacio de Gobierno, a gloomy, grey building, parts of which are open to the public. Beyond it is the port.

Museo Dr Andres Barbero. This museum contains the country's most important archaeological collection as well as interesting ethnographical displays. In addition, there is a good library and archive of photographs. The museum is at España 217 and Mompox, about 15 minutes walk east of the main square.

Botanical Gardens and Zoo. These are about 4 miles/6km northeast of the centre on Avenida Artigas. Both are neglected and the zoo positively depressing, but the main attraction is the former summer residence of the López family. This restored colonial house is now a museum which includes indigenous weaponry and archaeological and natural history collections. Take bus 24 or 35 from Oliva or Cerro Corá or, even better, take the 12.15pm Luque train, which takes about 20 minutes.

SHOPPING

The best market in Asunción is on Pettirossi close to the junction with Perú, south of the centre; but even this lacks the bustle of its South American counterparts. Food is the main commodity, although there are a few stalls selling traditional crafts. To get there, walk southeast from the city centre along Herrera until Pettirossi branches off, or take bus 27.

Shops selling souvenirs and contraband goods are mainly along Colón; between Presidente Franco and Benjamin Constant is the Recova, an old colonnade where you can buy leather and lace, including red, white and blue lace ties for men you don't much like. A good shop from which to buy crafts is Over All (Estigarribia and Caballero), where there is a good general selection. A wonderful, old-fashioned hat shop is on the corner of Cerro Corá and Caballero.

For maps and books (some in English) try the Librería Internacional, which has several branches, including at Oliva and Alberdi.

HELP AND INFORMATION

Tourist Information: Palma 468, between Alberdi and 14 de Mayo (tel 441530/441620). Free maps and useless brochures are available from 7am-noon and 3-6pm Monday to Friday. There are extensive listings in the *TAP Guía* (see page 577).

Post Office: Plaza de la Independencia, on the corner of Paraguayo Independiente and Alberdi (tel 48891). This is one of the best post offices in South America. It has a courtyard where you can sit to read or write letters, and there are even lavatories too. Collect mail from poste restante in room 5, where you must pay $0.15 per letter. For urgent despatches, EMS has a courier office in the same building.

Telephone Office: Antelco is at Nuestra Señora de la Asunción and Presidente Franco. It is open for international calls 24 hours a day. There is another office at Alberdi and Díaz (tel 444001). Both have fax and telex facilities.

Money: there are several cambios on Palma, around the junctions with Chile and Alberdi. Street moneychangers hang around the same area, particularly outside Restaurante Mundo. The only place to get cash advances on Visa and MasterCard is the UnionCard office of the Banco Unión (15 de Agosto between Haedo and Humaitá), which opens 8.45-11.50am Monday to Friday. Cambio Guaraní at Palma 449 (tel 490032/6) is one of several places which will change dollar travellers cheques into dollars cash.

Emergencies: for medical attention go to the Centro Medico Bautista (tel 600171/4) on Avenida República Argentina near the corner of Campos Severa, where there are English-speaking doctors. Take bus 12 or 15 and get off at the junction of Mariscal López and Argentina. You pay $15 in advance for a consultation; Visa and MasterCard are accepted. For specialist medical treatment, consult the newspaper *Ultima hora*, which has a comprehensive list of doctors and their specialities.

To call an ambulance call 204800. The police can be reached on 447316/46105. The police HQ is on Plaza de la Independencia.

Embassies and Consulates. *Argentina:* Banco de la Nación building, at España and Perú (tel 212320/4).
Bolivia: Eligio Ayala 2002 at General Bruguez (tel 22662).
Brazil: 7th floor, Banco do Brasil building, Plaza de los Héroes; the street address is Nuestra Señora de la Asunción 540, by Oliva (tel 441719).
Chile: Guido Spano 1687 (tel 660344/600671).
Colombia: Avenida Mariscal López 2240 (tel 602161/202520/661131).
Ecuador: Herrera 195, 9th floor (tel 446150).
Peru: Estrella 451, 3rd floor, office 27 (tel 441741).
Uruguay: Avenida Uruguay 219 (tel 25022).
UK: 4th floor, Presidente Franco 706, corner of O'Leary — look for the Patria SA sign (tel 449146/444472; fax 446385); open 8am-1pm, weekdays.
USA: the huge building behind railings at Avenida Mariscal López 1776, by Kubitschek (tel 201041/213715). Take bus 12 or 15 from Cerro Corá.
Venezuela: Mariscal Estigarribia 1043 at EE.UU (tel 444242/3).

If you want to stay over, go for the El Uruguayo Hotel (tel 511-222), which is in the centre and famous for its restaurant.

Ten miles/16km east of Caacupé a road branches off to Paraguarí. About 20 minutes south of the turn-off is Piribebuy, which was the scene of a bloody fighting during the Triple Alliance War; the conflict is recalled in a small historical museum. Paraguarí is on the Asunción-Encarnación highway and buses pass through frequently, heading in both directions.

YAGUARON

A gem of a town, Yaguarón lies in an orange-growing region about 30 miles/48km southeast of Asunción, and 15 minutes by bus northwest of Paraguarí. It was founded in 1539 and became the centre from which the Franciscans coordinated their missions in the area. The principal legacy of this period is the church, completed in 1775, which is the country's finest example of colonial architecture. Indeed it is one of the most beautiful and unusual churches in South America and is sufficient reason alone for visiting Paraguay.

The church lies partially hidden behind trees just off the main highway; its size and simple design is striking. The interior is decorated with elaborate paintwork and some exquisite woodcarving. Most of the work was done by indigenous people and all the designs, except for those on the ceiling, are original. The vegetable dyes used by the Indians are still vivid, and the combination of colours and floral designs creates a style not dissimilar to fairground or folk art, with even the odd hint of William Morris. There are also some unusual abstract patterns. The most bizarre creation in the church is the pulpit, an extraordinary affair supported on the head of a woman.

Two blocks from the main road is the Museo Histórico de Doctor Francia, housed in the home of Paraguay's first dictator, El Supremo. The charming little house is rather more interesting than most of the exhibits: notice the hingeless doors, for example. Nevertheless, you will be given a guided tour and an insight into the country's early days of independence. The museum opens 7.30-11.30am, daily except Sunday. At other times Don Lopez, the caretaker (*el sireno*) who lives in the grounds behind the house, should be happy to open up for you. His tour may be less informative than the official one, but it will almost certainly be more entertaining.

A steady stream of southbound and northbound buses runs through Yaguarón; wait at the bus stop opposite the church if you are heading back to Asunción. Nearby is Yaguarón's one hospedaje, where a room will cost you just $2.

YBICUY NATIONAL PARK

This National Park, southeast of Paraguarí, is one of the country's few protected areas; it consists mainly of forest and has several waterfalls. This is one of the few places in Paraguay where you can go for a good, country walk, and it can get fairly busy at weekends. The park is 20 miles/32km from the town of Ybicuy, which is accessible by bus from Asunción. The San Juan bus company runs daily services leaving at 6am, 7am, 12.45pm, 2pm, 3.30pm, 4pm, 5pm and 6pm; the journey takes $3\frac{1}{2}$ hours and costs $1.50. From Ybicuy there are buses to the park, which generally leave in the morning only. There are a few simple hotels in the town, otherwise you can camp in the park.

ASUNCION TO CIUDAD DEL ESTE

Beyond Caacupé there is little of interest between the capital and the Brazilian border. Coronel Oviedo is a ramshackle place, but it marks an important junction, with the road to Concepción and Juan Pedro Caballero turning off north. Another road heads south to Villarrica, which has an interesting cathedral built under the Franciscans. The local women are famous for their Aó Po'i, a special style of embroidery that is only marginally more appealing than ñandutí. Buses run hourly from the capital and take about 3½ hours; in addition, there are buses from Coronel Oviedo and Ciudad del Este, and Villarrica is also on the Asunción-Encarnación railway. Simple accommodation is available.

Ciudad del Este. Lying on the Brazilian border 203 miles/326km east of Asunción, Ciudad del Este is the second largest city in the country, with a population of around 90,000. Known until recently as Ciudad Presidente Stroessner, it is a dirty, chaotic and unappealing place, with an abundance of duty-free shops. People flock over from Brazil and Argentina to stock up on electronic goods and other luxuries, and you have to positively fight your way through the streets near the border. Should you be unfortunate enough to miss the last bus out of town, stay at Mi Abuela Hotel at Adrián Jara 128 (tel 2373) near the corner of García; and there are several cheaper places near the market.

Arrival and Departure: the bus station has been done up and is remarkably more pleasant than much of Ciudad del Este. For details of services to and from Asunción and Encarnación see page 574. Pluma (tel 4097) runs buses direct to Rio, São Paulo and other destinations in southern Brazil. Local buses run a shuttle service between Ciudad del Este to Foz do Iguaçu — you can walk across the bridge between immigration posts and pick up another bus on the other side.

Paraná del Sur has a daily service to the Argentinian capital, leaving at 12.30pm and 8.30pm. The same company runs buses daily to Pedro Juan Caballero (4am and 10pm) and to Concepción at 12.30pm.

LOS MISIONES

The area of greatest interest in southern Paraguay is known as Los Misiones, after the Jesuit missions once based here. There are a number of towns and villages with ruins and/or museums that are well worth visiting. Some lie on the main Asunción-Encarnación road, and can therefore be reached by catching any bus along this route. Those off the highway are served by special services. Yacyreta and Yacyreta Ayolas both run buses to San Miguel, San Ignacio, Santiago and Ayolas, with departures every few hours from early morning until 11pm; La Misionera runs buses along a similar route every hour or so between 7.30am and 4.30pm. San Juan serves San Cosme and Ayolas, but buses are infrequent.

About half way to Encarnación and just north of Los Misiones, is Villa Florida, a small town on the banks of the Tebicuary river. This is a good lunch stop since there are several restaurants that serve fresh fish, including piranha and the so-called *dorado* fish. Just 11 miles/18km further south is the village of San Miguel, where the locals handweave wool: shops along the main street sell blankets, rugs and jumpers. South of here you enter the mission area proper.

SAN IGNACIO

This town straddles the highway 35 miles/56km and an hour by bus south of San Miguel. The mission here was the earliest to be set up by the Jesuits in South America, although theories differ as to the date of its founding. Most researchers hold that it was first built in 1609, but at a site further west, and moved to its present location in 1668.

The Jesuit college has been heavily restored, but you can see some of the original features, including the remains of tree trunks that formed the columns of the old church. The college was closed under President Stroessner, but is functioning again. It contains a wonderful museum, whose collection consists primarily of Guaraní carvings. Many of these are of outstanding beauty and in a remarkable state of preservation; they display many indigenous features, including the distinctive fruit and flower motifs and the child-like faces of the angels. Other designs would not look out of place in a European cathedral and show great refinement: notice the flowing robes with their intricate gold and floral decorations.

In addition, there are excellent maps of the mission areas, making this a good place to start a tour of Paraguay's reducciones. For $0.40 you will be given a tour, usually by a guide who is a mine of information about the history of the area. The museum is on Rua Ignacio Iturbe, a couple of blocks west of the main highway; there is a sign pointing to it opposite the main bus office. It opens 8-11.30am and 2-5.30pm.

There are a couple of hotels in San Ignacio, including the Hotel Unión, on the main street a few blocks north of the main square. It takes a further 2-3 hours

ENCARNACION

1 Railway Station
2 Hotel Repka
3 La Taberna Gordo
4 Restaurante Cuarajhy

5 Main Square
6 Banco Unión
7 Hotel Paraná
8 Hotel Cristal
9 Municipalidad
10 Argentinian Consulate

11 Bus Station
12 Hotel Suizo
13 Antelco
14 Hotel Viena
15 Cambio Asunción
16 Ferry pier

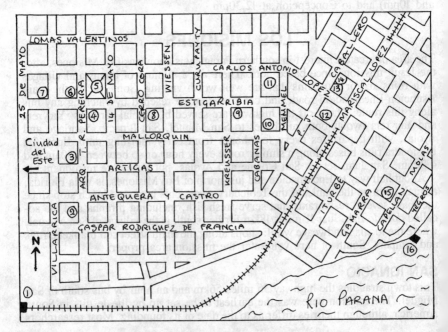

to reach Encarnación (depending on the bus); the fare is about $2.25. A road runs west from San Ignacio to Pilar, from where you can take a boat across to Puerto Cano in Argentina.

Santa María de Fe. About 10 miles/16km from San Ignacio, this is the site of another reducción, built in 1669. There is a museum containing more beautiful sculpture, including an exquisite seated image of the virgin, known as the Virgen del Pesebre. Colectivos run infrequently from San Ignacio, though one usually runs at around 11.30am. There is a small hotel if you get stranded.

A short distance south from San Ignacio is Santa Rosa. Not much remains of the mission, but there is a small museum. Further down the highway from Santa Rosa a road leads south to Ayolas, on the Paraná river near the site of the Yacyreta dam project. Just off this road is the small, colonial town of Santiago, the site of a large mission founded in 1669. Many of the colonial buildings are in a sorry state of repair, although moves are being made to restore them. There is an impressive church and a museum containing yet more fine woodcarving. Buses from Asunción bound for Ayolas stop in Santiago; these can be picked up at the turn-off on the main highway.

Back on the highway to Encarnación, just north of Coronel Bogado a road runs southwest to San Cosme y Damian. This reducción is one of the most important missions in Paraguay. Many buildings were unfinished at the time of the Jesuits' expulsion, and they are currently under restoration.

ENCARNACION

This was the birthplace of General Stroessner — a connection most of the town's 60,000 inhabitants of would probably rather forget. It lies on the banks of the Río Paraná and across the river is Posadas, in Argentina. There is a constant flow of people over the bridge, as shoppers take advantage of the bargains on either side. In Encarnación, most shopping gets done in the oldest part of town near the river, the so-called , ´ona Baja. This is a chaotic area, full of stalls, electronic shops and moneychangers. A world away is the Zona Alta, a tranquil area that is pleasant to wander around and apparently unaffected by all the goings-on near the port. Although more modern than the Zona Baja, there are still virtually no high-rise buildings.

While there is not much to do in Encarnación, it is an interesting place to spend a couple of days and you are well-placed for trips into mission country.

Arrival and Departure. *Bus:* Encarnación lies at the junction of the highways from Asunción and Ciudad del Este, and there are frequent buses to and from both towns. The bus station takes up a block by Estigarribia and Cabañas; walking along Estigarribia, the main street, it is about midway between the main square and the river. If you are overloaded with baggage, there are both horse-drawn and more conventional cabs; pay $2-3.

Finding out about buses can be rather confusing; bear it in mind that tickets for most direct and all international services can be bought on one side, and those for slower, stopping buses on the other.

Argentina — buses (marked Servicio Internacional) leave for Posadas every 15 minutes between 6am and midnight, and stop outside the bus station. Buses returning from Posadas go on a circuitous route, past the bus station and eventually the main square. The journey shouldn't take more than 20-30 minutes, even if you have to go through immigration; and unless you are delayed at either border post you should be able to continue on the same bus. Even so, there is a constant stream of buses, and you can use the same ticket. The fare is $0.75, and may be paid in guaranís or australes. Buses don't stop automatically at both border posts, so get to the front of the bus and ask to be dropped at the Centro de Frontera.

If you plan to cross for only a few hours you should not need to have your passport stamped, but this will depend on your nationality and the disposition of the immigration official on duty. Paraguayan immigration officials are usually relaxed and let everyone through. Argentinian immigration tend to run closer checks and may query your unstamped passport; unless you've got something to hide, this can usually be solved by telling the truth and/or by finding the official who let you through in the first place.

A ferry across the Paraná to Posadas operates every 30 minutes between 6.30am and 4pm, and takes ten minutes; the fare is $0.60. This is not a border crossing point for foreigners.

The Argentine Consulate is at Mallorquín 788 at Cabañas, a block south of the bus station. It opens 8.30am-12.30pm. Visas are issued on the spot.

Buenos Aires — Expreso Río Paraná and La Encarnacena both run buses every afternoon from Encarnación to Buenos Aires. The journey takes about 15 hours and costs $40. La Encarnacena also runs a diferencial bus ($44) on Tuesday and Saturday.

Rail: see page 579 for details of trains from Asunción. For those starting off from Encarnación, the train leaves at 3.30pm on Wednesday. The fare is $3.75 first class, and $3.20 second. There is also a weekly service to Buenos Aires (9.30am on Wednesday; $32), but you would do better to take the daily 5.30pm train from Posadas.

The railway station is at the bottom of Pereira, about six blocks south of the main square. Even if you don't plan to catch a train, it is worth a visit to see the old steam engines.

Accommodation. There are several cheap places near the bus station. Bang opposite for example, at the corner of Cabañas and López, is the Itapuá. Quieter, however, are the places towards the river on Estigarribia, though the road from the station is ill-lit at night. About five minutes walk down the hill, near the corner of Caballero, is Hotel Suizo (Estigarribia 562; tel 3692). This is a big, spacious place with rooms that are good value at $3.60 per person including breakfast. Around the corner at Caballero 568 (tel 3486) is Hotel Viena, near the Antelco office. Rooms cost $7.50/$12 and the restaurant serves good, hearty food. More central and also near the railway station is Hotel Repka, at Arquitecto Pereira 49 (tel 3546). It has simple, but clean rooms around a courtyard, for $6.

There are a few more upmarket places on Estigarribia. Hotel Paraná, at number 1416 (tel 4440/1), half a block west of the square, and Hotel Cristal (between Cerro Corá and Wiessen; tel 2371/2) both have rooms for about $30 (double). The Cristal also has triples for $36.

There is a campsite just outside town on the Ciudad del Este road.

Eating and Drinking. Encarnación's best restaurant is the Cuarajhy in the main square. There is a wide choice of dishes and the food is excellent. The house specials are good, and the surubí (catfish) and sopa paraguaya are both recommended. It is not cheap — main dishes cost $3-6 — but it is lively, popular and open late. There are a few places nearby on Pereira, although these are more geared to the staunch meat-eater. La Taberna Gordo, on the corner of Artigas, serves huge lumps of meat fresh from the barbecue, usually accompanied by a plate of chips. You will find other restaurants along Estigarribia, both east and west of the main square. The bus station is the best place for breakfast: hot coffee and toddy, empanadas and freshly-grilled sausages.

Help and Information. *Tourist Information:* the 'tourist' desk at the border may have the usual collection of useless brochures, but the only place you are likely to get a map is at the Municipalidad, a modern brick building on the corner of Estigarribia and P.J. Kreusser. It is open mornings only.

Money: cambios are mostly in the Zona Baja, including Cambio Asunción on the corner of Mallorquín and Cappellán Molas; but they are unlikely to accept travellers cheques. Moneychangers hang out here and also on either side of the international bridge, and may even get on passing buses touting for business. As a rule, rates are better in Paraguay than in Posadas. Banks are concentrated in the Zona Alta, mainly in and around the main square. In Encarnación, particularly near the port, australes and guaranís are both widely accepted.

Antelco: on the corner of Caballero and Carlos A. López, down the hill from the bus station. It is open 6.30am-10pm daily.

Around Encarnación
Trinidad. About 18 miles/29km northeast of Encarnación is Trinidad, the site of the best preserved Jesuit mission in the country. It dates from the early 18th century, and most of the original walls have survived. The rich, red sandstone has been softened by the effects of wind and rain, but the buildings remain impressively solid. This is a peaceful spot that you're likely to have to yourself during the week.

From the main entrance you come to a large, grassy square, which is ringed by Indians' houses and a lovely arcade. On the other side is the main church. This is the only large structure in the complex and dominates the other, low-slung buildings. It contains some lovely stone carving; note in particular the frieze over the sacristy door, which depicts angels playing musical instruments, including one at an organ and another with a harp. The sacristy has been turned into a small museum, where you can see more fine carving, including rows of angel heads with childish faces and thick curly hair. Beyond is another grassy patio, surrounded by the remains of college buildings and workshops. On the other side is a bell tower which you can climb up for a view over the whole complex. Nearby is another, much smaller church, and the cemetery.

To get to Trinidad take any bus along the Ciudad del Este road; the journey takes about 30 minutes. The mission, on the right-hand side, is open 7am-noon Monday to Friday, 7am-6pm at weekends. If there is no one there to sell you a ticket and open up, ask at the house opposite. A guidebook exists but is not always available. Visitors' facilities are under development, including an information centre and café.

The best place to wait for buses back to Encarnación is at the crossroads, referred to by the locals as 'la cruz', a little way up the road from the entrance. There are no hotels.

Jesús. From Trinidad a dirt road leads 7 miles/11km north to the tiny village of Jesús. This is the largest of all the missions, but restoration work was begun only recently. The church was unfinished when the Jesuits were expelled from Paraguay in 1767. Colectivos runs sporadically from Trinidad (wait at la cruz), but services are disrupted by rain. Your best chance of getting there is at the weekend, though you may have to hitch.

NORTHERN PARAGUAY

CONCEPCION

The town of Concepción is a charming place about 200 miles/320km north of Asunción. Its position on the Río Paraguay has made it the commercial centre of the north, the river being a channel for trade both from the Chaco and Brazil. It is also an important trading centre locally, and there is a good market. Yet Concepción is surprisingly quiet, with a population of 35,000. While only a modest destination in its own right, Concepción is worth a visit if only to enjoy the boat trip from Asunción.

Good hotels are scarce, the Francés (Presidente Franco 1016) and the Victoria (at Franco and Caballero) being the best bets.

Arrival and Departure. Since no direct road links the capital with Concepción, the route up the Río Paraguay is the most obvious one. Boats are scheduled to leave Asunción on Friday mornings, and take around 26 hours. They are surprisingly comfortable. Deck travel in 3rd class costs $8 (you can usually find somewhere to rig a hammock); 2nd class, including a cabin, is $12; 1st class, most often used by Westerners, is $20. The boats are operated by Flota Mercantil del Estado (FME), Calle Estrella 672-682 in Asunción (tel 441100). Other boat lines serve the route on a less regular basis. From Concepción boats back to Asunción leave at noon on Saturday. When the river level is high enough, it's possible to continue north to Bahía Negra, on the Brazilian border, or even to Corumbá in Mato Grosso do Sul.

Flights between Asunción and Concepción are operated by TAM daily except Sunday ($20). Buses from the capital, run by La Ovetense and Amambay, run mainly overnight and take 9-10 hours. There are also buses along a bad road from Pozo Colorado in the Chaco, which take a couple of hours. The bus terminal in Concepción is about nine blocks from the port, but since buses go through the town, you can get off in the centre.

PEDRO JUAN CABALLERO

This town lies on the Brazilian border 130 miles/208km northeast of Concepción. You can travel freely between Pedro Juan Caballero and Ponta Porã in Brazil if you aren't planning to cross the border permanently. However, few people would wish to come here to do anything else. If you need to stay the night, the best cheap hotel in town is the Corina; up a notch is the Eiruzú.

There are several buses a day from Concepción, which take about four hours; the journey is pleasant and takes you past Cerro Corá, where Francisco Solano López died during the Triple Alliance War. At Yby Yaú is the junction with the road south from Coronel Oviedo, which is the route taken by buses from Asunción; these take 8-10 hours, usually overnight.

Rua Internacional is the dividing line between the two border towns. If you need a Brazilian visa go to the consulate at Francia 830, near the corner of Rua Alberdi; once in Ponta Porã, get your passport stamped at the Polícia Federal.

THE CHACO

The hostile environment of the Chaco has attracted little human settlement. The most important towns are the Mennonite colonies of Filadelfia and Loma Plata, which lie at the heart of an important agricultural area. It says much for the Mennonites' industrious and resilient natures that they have managed to prosper in the dusty Chaco plains. Their rather quaint houses and neat gardens are incongruous in such surroundings, and are also a little deceptive. In 1991 a human rights committee revealed that unauthorized prisons had been discovered on Mennonite settlements, and that Indians had been flogged. The priveleged position of these communities (they don't pay taxes) may well come under scrutiny in the future.

Visiting anywhere other than the Mennonite colonies is problematic owing to the lack of roads. Tour operators in Asunción run trips to some of the Mennonite communities, but with difficulty can you explore further afield. The marshes of the Lower Chaco are extremely rich in birdlife, and the area as a whole supports several endangered species, including puma and jaguar. Most of the country's Indians live in the Chaco, but you are unlikely to have contact with any but those who work for the Mennonites.

The main settlements in the area are served by the Trans-Chaco Highway, which is paved as far as Mariscal Estigarribia, north of Filadelfia. Built only comparatively recently, it has brought a trickle of new settlers, but foreign visitors are still a rarity. Buses run only as far as Mariscal Estigarribia, an army base and the last main settlement before you get to Bolivia. Further north is an arid zone of cacti, poisonous snakes and dust storms, that is almost devoid of settlements except for the odd military base. Trucks run sporadically northwards from Mariscal Estigarribia, but there isn't anything that you could call a public service. Soldiers and smugglers seem to be virtually the only people travelling along the road, and for this reason you may think twice about hitching. While hiring a car is certainly one way of covering part of the Chaco, to push further northwards involves careful preparation, determination and a resourceful personality; petrol stations are virtually non-existent north of Mariscal Estigarribia, and the dirt road is a washout after heavy rain.

Filadelfia. This small but flourishing town is the largest and most important Mennonite community in the Chaco. It lies about 25 miles/40km north of the Trans-Chaco highway and about 260 miles/416km northwest of Asunción. Filadelfia's fascination lies simply in being there, though there are a few things to do. The Unger Museum — which traces Mennonite colonization of the Chaco — is interesting, but the opening hours are erratic; you'll probably have to ask around for someone to open up for you. You can also visit some of the well-ordered communities outside Filadelfia, such as Loma Plata, due east. Local people will drive you around (for a fee).

Arrival and Departure: Nasa buses from Asunción serve Filadelfia at 2.30pm and 10pm during the week, with just one daily departure at weekends; book your seat in advance if possible. The same bus also goes to Loma Plata and Colonia Neuland (south across the highway). Allow eight or nine hours for the journey from

Asunción. About midway along the route is Pozo Colorado, where a road branches east to Concepción.

Another option is to go on a tour from the capital. The main agents in Asunción are the Menno Travel Agency (Azara 551; tel 441210/446618) and Rotatour (Piribebuy 513; tel 490596/446005); the latter has a branch in Hotel Boquerón in Colonia Neuland (tel 091-201/2). Both agencies organize visits to Mennonite cooperatives, schools, hospitals, experimental farms, etc., as well as to sites of the 1930s Chaco War.

Accommodation: hotel accommodation in Filadelfia is limited to the moderately expensive Florida hotel, which charges $25 for a double. To be sure of getting a room, write in advance ('Hotel Florida, Filadelfia' is sufficient). The hotel can arrange trips. If no room is available, you should have no difficulty finding a family willing to rent you a bed. Both Loma Plata and Colonia Neuland have hotels as well.

Brazil

Population: 150 million　　　　**Brasília (population 1.5 million)**

Writers twist themselves into knots in an effort to describe the essence of Brazil, but they often seem to fall back on the old cliché 'a land of contrasts'. There is no easy way to convey the complexities and contradictions inherent in the world's fifth largest country.

Brazil both thrills and appals. Awesome, dynamic cities and spectacular natural phemonena make it a wonderfully exciting country. Yet the cruel, grinding poverty of the huge cities is horrific, and the manner in which the rainforest and its Indian population are being destroyed is frightening. Socially, it is the least inhibited nation in the world; the lack of self-consciousness will do any Westerner the world of good. Most Brazilians are exceedingly tolerant, yet brutal death squads murder two homeless children every 24 hours.

These enigmas can be endlessly discussed, but certainly one cause is the anarchic economy. One per cent of the population owns half the nation's wealth. Brazil is the developing world's largest debtor, with a bill of $1,000 billion hanging around its neck. Inflation at ridiculous rates has forced three new currencies on the people in the last decade. Even the traditionally optimistic Latin American politicians can find little hope for changing a system where the rich protect themselves against economic austerity while the financial noose on the poor tightens.

These are long-term concerns for the world as a whole rather than for the individual short-term visitor. You can enjoy wild animals, wild waterfalls, wild beach life and wild street life. Townscapes range from fine colonial architecture with shady squares to nightmare metropoli with appalling pollution, brash high-rises and sprawling shanty towns. Others consider the journey worthwhile just for the football or the food.

In so large and diverse a country, regional differences are naturally intense. Rio, the heart and soul of the nation, is everything you might want it to be and plenty you might not. The spirit of the nation is most visible in the northeast, where the African influence brought by slaves mingles headily with Portuguese tradition. The pace of life in the far south of the country is much slower, but is perhaps a welcome break from the more frenetic pace further north. The economic powerhouse of São Paulo state, based around the world's biggest city, can be terrifying or tremendous fun. Few find fun in the country's soulless new capital, Brasília, but as an urban experiment it deserves to be seen. Furthermore, it gives access to the unspoilt lands of the Pantanal in Mato Grosso, one of the greatest areas on the continent for observing wildlife. Most extravagant of all, there is the Amazon, a river and region of superlatives.

GEOGRAPHY

It is as difficult a task to describe concisely the geography of Brazil as it is of the whole of South America — of which the country takes up almost half. There are five main geographical regions: the Amazon basin, the Guiana Highlands, the Brazilian Highlands or central plateau (known as the Planalto), the River Plate basin and the coastal belt. Brazil is relatively flat topographically, and the highest peak is under 10,000 ft/3,048m.

The Amazon Basin is the largest of these regions, comprising one third of the total area of Brazil. The Rio Amazonas is a massive artery, carving its way through the north of the country for more than 3,900 miles/6,240km. The basin supports what is still the world's largest area of rainforest, despite the rampant destruction that continues unabated. North of the Amazon are the Guiana Highlands, another thinly-populated and largely unexplored region.

The Brazilian Highlands are tablelands

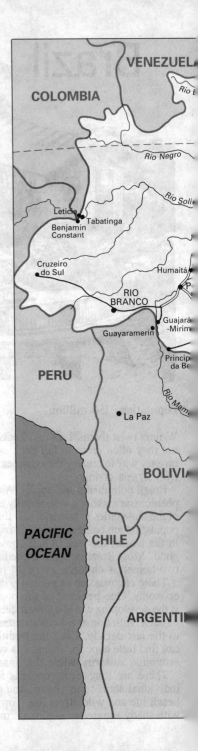

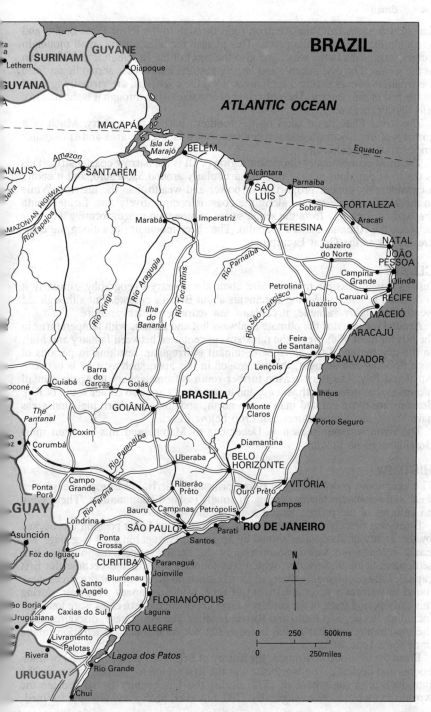

BRAZIL

ATLANTIC OCEAN

Equator

SURINAM
GUYANE
GUYANA
Lethem
Oiapoque

MACAPÁ

Isla de Marajó
BELÉM

Amazon
ANAUS
SANTARÉM
Alcântara
Parnaíba
SÃO LUIS
FORTALEZA
Sobral
Aracati
Marabá
Imperatriz
TERESINA
NATAL
Juazeiro do Norte
JOÃO PESSOA
Campina Grande
Olinda
Petrolina
RECIFE
Caruarú
Juazeiro
MACEIÓ
ARACAJÚ
Feira de Santana
SALVADOR
Lençois
Ilhéus
Monte Claros
Porto Seguro
Diamantina

Rio Parnaíba
Rio Araguaia
Rio Tocantins
Rio Xingu
Rio São Francisco

Ilha do Bananal

Barra do Garças
Goiás
BRASILIA
GOIÂNIA
Cuiabá
coné

The Pantanal
Coxim
Corumbá

BELO HORIZONTE
Uberaba
VITÓRIA
Riberão Prêto
Ouro Prêto
Campos
Campinas
Petrópolis
Campo Grande
Ponta Porã
Bauru
RIO DE JANEIRO
Londrina
SÃO PAULO
Parati
GUAY
Asunción
Ponta Grossa
Santos
Foz do Iguaçu
CURITIBA
Paranaguá
Joinville
Santo Angelo
Blumenau
ão Borja
FLORIANÓPOLIS
Jruguaiana
Caxias do Sul
Laguna
Livramento
PORTO ALEGRE
Rivera
Pelotas
Lagoa dos Patos
Rivera
Rio Grande
URUGUAY
Chui

Rio Paraná
Rio Paranaíba

N

0   250   500kms
0   250miles

that stretch south from the Amazon right through to the River Plate Basin, and touch almost every Brazilian state. This plateau includes several small mountain ranges, savannahs in the west, and also the heart of the Brazilian interior, known as the *sertão*. The dry, infertile and largely pastoral lands of the sertão lie far from the frontiers of concentrated settlement along the coast, and are virtually ignored by the rest of the country. The only river of any size to run through it is the massive Rio São Francisco.

The River Plate basin takes up the southern part of the country. Much of it consists of dry savannah and scrub forest, but it is a fertile area and is of major importance agriculturally.

The most economically important region of all is the narrow coastal strip. This is the most populous area of Brazil, particularly around São Paulo, and it enjoys a considerably greater proportion of power and wealth than the interior. While in the Northeast the terrain along the coast is comparatively flat, further south the land rises steeply from the sea, a series of mountain ranges forming a barrier between the Atlantic and the Planalto. The sheer mountainsides along the coast are known as the Great Escarpment.

CLIMATE

Just as it is impossible to generalize about the country's geography, similarly it is difficult to make sweeping statements about Brazil's climate. But although the weather is highly variable, it contains few extremes of temperature.

Around the equator the climate is always hot and humid, with temperatures in the 80s for most of the year; the rains are concentrated between January and May. In the dry region of the Northeast, rainfall is irregular, resulting in periods of both flooding and drought; the wet season in this area, such as it is, is between April and July. The rainy season further south is from January to April: rainfall increases the further south you go, and temperatures are also cooler south of Rio. Seasons are more defined than in the north, and some southern highland areas have snow, and temperatures can drop below freezing.

The main summer season is December to March, and this is when most Brazilians go on holiday.

HISTORY

The indigenous people living in Brazil prior to the arrival of European explorers were semi-nomadic farmers living in small, isolated communities. There were no cultures of the refined nature found in the Andes.

Brazil was first claimed for the Portuguese in 1500, and their position was backed by the Treaty of Tordesillas signed by Spain and Portugal in 1494 (see page 14). Early colonization was concentrated in the central eastern region, the first settlement being at Salvador, which was founded in 1502 and became the first capital. Other settlements emerged slowly since no great mineral resources were found to warrant a mass investment of time, effort or money. However, during this early period some of the country's most important modern cities were founded, including Recife, São Paulo and Rio de Janeiro. The Portuguese, discouraged by the topography and fear of the Indians, did not contemplate penetration inland until some time later.

From the time of colonization, the history of Brazil has been dominated by trade booms and declines. The Northeast was the first region to prosper, following the introduction of sugar cane in 1532: during the 17th century Brazil became the world's main producer of sugar. By 1700, however, profits had already declined, owing to competition from the Caribbean. The focus shifted to the south, where groups of adventurers known as *bandeirantes* had launched a number of expeditions inland from São Paulo, in search of gold. Initially, they succeeded only in extending Brazil's borders and enslaving large numbers of Indians, but in the early 18th century they eventually struck gold and diamonds. The most important finds were in Minas Gerais, and the subsequent gold rush transformed the state into the country's most prosperous region; the boom towns built during this period are among Brazil's finest colonial relics. At the same time, Rio de Janeiro developed as a port for the shipping of gold to Portugal, and the town's new importance was acknowledged at the end of the 18th century, when it became the country's new capital.

While during the 18th century Brazil produced almost half of the world's gold, the supply had dwindled dramatically by the early 1800s. But just as gold had taken the place of sugar, so in the 19th century coffee became the new basis of the country's prosperity. The principal plantations were inland from São Paulo, which rose greatly in prestige during this period. The boom attracted a flood of European immigrants, and the area still has large foreign communities.

The 19th century also saw the discovery of rubber in the jungles of the Amazon, followed by the rise of Brazil as the only rubber-producing country in the world. But disease and the weight of competition from Malaya led, in the early 1900s, to the collapse of the trade. The economic decline had drastic results on Brazil's political and social life.

Independence. Dissatisfaction with Portugal's control of Brazilian trade was expressed increasingly during the 18th century, and support for independence gained ground as it did in other parts of Latin America. However, the independence campaign was unbloody compared to the struggles waged in other parts of the continent.

The decisive event which was to culminate in Brazil's declaration of independence, was the conquest of Portugal by Napoleon in 1808. The ruler at that time, Dom João, fled to Rio de Janeiro and declared it capital of Portugal and its empire. Thus Brazil became an independent state with a similar status to its former imperial power. This remarkable state of affairs did not last long. In 1821, following the end of the Napoleonic wars, Dom João returned home leaving his son Dom Pedro as regent. When Portugal tried to reduce Brazil to its former status as colony in 1822, Dom Pedro declared Brazil independent and became its first emperor, Pedro I.

This emperor's successor, Pedro II, abolished slavery in 1888. The move emancipated hundreds of thousands of slaves and led directly to independence since it antagonized the all-powerful landowners. A military revolt in 1889 forced Pedro II to abdicate, and Brazil became a republic. In 1891 a federalist constitution was drawn up which followed closely that of the United States. The country was placed under military rule until a revolt some years later sparked off a gradual return to civilian government.

Recent History. The military continued to play an important role in Brazilian politics, and it was behind the country's first revolution in 1930. This came at the end of an uneasy decade characterized by economic instability, and resulted in the installation of Getúlio Vargas as president. Vargas, an admirer of Mussolini, was to dominate politics from 1930 to 1945, thanks largely to repression and alterations to the constitution. He was eventually forced to resign, and a liberal republic was restored. Following a number of unsettled years, a new president was elected in 1956. However, civilian rule was not destined to last long. Juscelino Kubitschek's grand design to encourage the development of the interior — by building the new capital of Brasília — led only to rampant inflation and economic mayhem. Again the military stepped in.

During the 1964-85 dictatorship the people of Brazil endured a regime of suppression and a foreign debt of drastic proportions. Social unrest and pressure for change built up gradually during the early 80s, further encouraged by the end of military rule in Argentina in 1983. Under such pressure, the army was eventually forced to cede power: elections in 1985 gave Brazil its first civilian president for over 20 years, in the shape of Tancredo Neves. To the dismay of many Brazilians, howevere, Neves died before he could take office, and was replaced by his much less popular deputy. José Sarney was corrupt and weak, and proved unable to deal with the country's growing economic problems.

In the presidential elections of 1989, the Conservative Fernando Collor de Mello, leader of the Partido de Reconstrução Nacional, scraped victory over his rival from the Partido dos Trabalhadores, Luis da Silva. Collor was hailed by some as a champion of the poor and the economy's last hope, by others as a playboy with the interests of the rich at heart. He promised to create a First World nation, a 'new Brazil', launching an ambitious plan to reform industry, restore free market capitalism, and bridge the gap between rich and poor. He also made much of his desire to reverse the country's dismal human rights record and halt the destruction of the rainforest. Collor, like Thatcher in Britain, made ecological awareness fashionable.

Yet while at first Collor seemed bold, dashing and energetic, he now appears arrogant, isolated and bedevilled by a series of resignations among his leading ministers. He has been unable to cope with Brazil's economic mess, and the government's quick-fix anti-inflation packages have become a joke in Brazil, if a very painful one. As a result of salary and price freezes, industrial output has plummeted — a disaster for a country where, even though coffee remains the main export, industry generates more wealth than agriculture. Economic unrest has led to a growing number of strikes, shortages are not uncommon, and Brazilians have seen the value of their income drop by 30%. The latest austerity measures forced on the country by the IMF could spell the end of Collor if they fail — the goverment has already failed to keep inflation at the level the IMF has demanded.

Yet much of the mineral, agricultural and industrial potential of this vast country is still untapped. If the government formulates an imaginative long-term development plan — rather than focussing on short-term financing and politically expedient but unviable capital projects — Brazil could yet take its rightful place at the economic helm of the southern hemisphere.

THE PEOPLE

The main races represented in Brazil's extraordinary ethnic mix are Portuguese, black and Indian. Whites — an incredibly generic term — make up just over half the population, *mestiços* or *mamelucos* (people of mixed Portuguese and Indian blood) and *mulattos* (mixed Portuguese and black) about 20%, and blacks 15%. The rest are indigenous/Indian, Japanese and other minorities. However, such raw percentages obscure the true racial mix and homogeneity that exists: most people are descended from more than simply one or two races.

A large proportion of whites, for example, have black or Indian blood. In addition to those of 'pure' Portuguese descent, much white blood came to Brazil with the

LANGUAGE

The national language is Portuguese. It is worthwhile learning at least the basics, since outside the tourist centres few people speak or understand English. Although knowing Spanish is a help, the only way you can hope to communicate in it successfully is if you adopt a Portuguese pronunciation. Brazilian Portuguese is not identical to that spoken in Europe, and there are regional variations, but this is the least of your worries.

The Berlitz *Portuguese for Travellers* is fairly useful, particularly for its excellent section on food and drink.

Pronunciation. There are a large number of vowel sounds in Portuguese. The hardest to get your mouth around are the combinations of vowels that require a nasalized pronunciation: *ão* is pronounced as 'ow', and *oe* as 'oy'. The other most important rules are as follows: *o* at the end of a word (or as the masculine indefinite article) is pronounced 'oo' as in m*oo*n; vowels that precede m or n are nasalized; d before e or i is generally softened to a 'dj' sound; *qu*, as in Spanish, is like 'k' in English; and *il* at the end of word is pronounced 'iu'.

Useful Words and Phrases

hello	*olá*
good morning	*bom dia*
good afternoon, night	*boa tarde, boa noite*
goodbye	*ciao, até logo*
yes	*sim*
no	*não*
please	*por favor*
thank you	*obrigado*
excuse me	*desculpe*
I want	*quero*
how much	*quanto*
where is …?	*onde fica …?*
when	*quando*
Mr, Mrs, Miss	*Senhor, a, ita*
do you speak English?	*você fala inglês?*
I don't speak Portuguese	*no falo português*
today	*hoje*
tomorrow	*amanhã*
yesterday	*ontem*
morning	*manhã*
afternoon	*tarde*

Communications

address	*endereço*
date	*fecha*
newspaper	*jornal*
phone call (collect)	*chamada (a cobrar)*
post office	*correios*
postcard	*cartão postal*
stamp	*selo*
telephone office	*posto telefónico*

Getting Around

arrival	*chegada*
bus	*ônibus*

bus station	*rodoviária*
car rental agent	*locadora*
city	*cidade*
delayed	*atrasado*
departure	*saída*
fare, ticket	*passagem, bilhete*
flight	*vôo*
left	*esquerda*
left-luggage	*guarda-volumes*
railway station	*estação ferroviária*
right	*direita*
road	*estrada*
route	*roteiro*

Accommodation

bath (room)	*banho*
cold	*frio*
double room (one bed)	*casal*
double room (two beds)	*duplo, con duas camas*
hot	*quente*
lavatory	*banheiro, sanitários*
room (with bathroom)	*apartamento*
room (without bathroom)	*cuarto*
safe deposit box	*cofre, caixa*
single room	*cuarto solteiro*

Eating and Drinking

beer	*cerveja*
bottled, fizzy drink	*refrigerante*
bread	*pão*
breakfast	*café de manhã*
cake	*bolo*
cheese	*queijo*
chicken	*frango*
coffee (small black)	*cafezinho*
fish	*peixe*
lunch	*almoço*
milk	*leite*
pasta	*massas*
pudding	*sobremesa*
roast	*assado*
sausage	*lingüiça*
snack	*tira-gosto, petisco*
supper	*jantar*
tea	*cha*
wine	*vinho*

Shopping

open	*aberto*
opening hours	*horario (de atendimento)*
shop	*loja*
shut	*fechado*
weekdays	*dias úteis*

Days of the Week

| Monday | *segunda-feira* |
| Tuesday | *terça-feira* |

Wednesday	*quarta-feira*
Thursday	*quinta-feira*
Friday	*sexta-feira*
Saturday	*sabado*
Sunday	*domingo*

The *feira* of the weekdays is not indispensable: don't be confused if you see weekdays written simply as *2º, 3º*, etc. Numbers in Portuguese are so similar to the Spanish that you can easily get by with those: see page 21.

FURTHER READING

An enormous amount has been written about Brazil. The books described below are the highlights.

Brazilian Adventure, written by Peter Fleming in the 1930s, has to be one of the greatest travelogues ever published. It is also one of the more entertaining books that have been written about the Amazon. Fleming describes his expedition's search for Colonel Fawcett, who disappeared without trace in 1925. Fleming's good humour fills every page, but it is mixed with keen and largely enlightened observations. It is published by Penguin. Read also the Colonel's own book, *Exploration Fawcett:* see page 23. An altogether more serious work is *Amazon Watershed* by George Monbiot (Abacus, 1991). It offers an incisive and highly readable account of the crisis facing the Amazon forest and its people, putting it into the context of the problems facing Brazil as a whole.

Jorge Amado is the country's most famous novelist. His novels, many of which are set in southern Bahia, give a moving — and at times horrifying — insight into life on the plantations. Among his best books are *The Violent Land* (Collins Harvill, 1989), first published in 1943, and *Gabriela, Clove and Cinnamon* (1958; out of print).

The War of the End of the World (Faber, 1986) was written by the renowned Peruvian author, Mario Vargas Llosa. It tells the extraordinary tale of a popular anti-republican movement that took root in the sertão towards the end of the 19th century.

Getting There

AIR

Every large South American airline flies to Rio, as do many European and North American carriers. It is easier to reach Brazil than anywhere else in the region, and as a result of competition fares are low.

From South America. All the capitals (except the Guianas) are linked with Rio and São Paulo by direct flights on one of the three main Brazilian airlines — Varig, Vasp and Transbrasil — and other South American carriers. Other international gateways are Belém, Recife, Salvador and Manaus (for the north), Foz do Iguaçu (to the west) and Porto Alegre (the south).

From North America. From Miami you can fly direct to Belém, Manaus, Recife, Salvador, Rio and São Paulo. Toronto, Chicago, New York and Los Angeles have direct links with Rio and São Paulo. The cheapest flights are with carriers such as LAP of Paraguay and Viasa of Venezuela, which offer low fares requiring a change in Asunción or Caracas.

From Europe. British Airways, Aerolíneas Argentinas and Varig have similar fares for their direct flights from London, typically £650 return to Rio or São Paulo. Slightly cheaper fares may be available on other European carriers (for example Air France or KLM, around £610) or South American airlines (Avianca, £550). Apart from the cost saving, these companies can offer good 'open jaw' deals, flying in to Rio and back from Lima, for example, for no extra cost. Gateways such as Recife are served by only one or two carriers, including Varig which launched a direct flight to that city from London in 1992. Call Journey Latin America (081-747 3108), South American Experience (071-379 0344) and Steamond (071-730 8646) for the best deals.

SURFACE

Brazil borders every South American nation except Ecuador and Chile and, as a result, there are countless places at which to enter the country. In practice, however, access is limited by remoteness, the terrain or lack of transport, and often all three. How to get to and from border posts is dealt with in the text, but below are guidelines as to the main points of entry.

One of the most frequented frontiers is at Foz do Iguaçu, on the border with Argentina and Paraguay and near the famous waterfalls; it is well served by buses from both Buenos Aires and Asunción. The other main crossing point from Argentina is at Uruguaiana in the southwestern corner of Rio Grande do Sul. Anyone travelling from Paraguay with the aim of heading straight for the Pantanal, could cross to Ponta Porã or Bela Vista, both in Mato Grosso do Sul.

The route taken by most buses from Montevideo in Uruguay is via Chuí and north along the coast to Porto Alegre. However, Aceguá or Santana do Livramento, further west, are perfectly feasible alternatives.

From Bolivia, the main entry point is at Corumbá, on the edge of the Pantanal in Mato Grosso do Sul. Once you hit Amazonia further north, easily accessible frontier posts are few and far between, and getting around during the rainy season is problematic unless you fly or go by boat. The main entry point from Bolivia is at Guajará-Mirim, south of Porto Velho from where boats run northeast to Manaus, Benjamin Constant, on the Amazon, is accessible from both Peru (by boat from Iquitos) and Colombia (by air to Leticia); boats run regularly downriver to Manaus.

By comparison, the route from Venezuela via Santa Elena to Boa Vista by bus, is a doddle. There are also buses to Boa Vista from the Guyanan frontier at Bonfim, but to get that far you will probably have to fly to the Guyanan border town of Lethem. It is not possible to enter Brazil from Suriname, and although there is a border post in eastern French Guiana, at St Georges, non-Brazilian passport holders usually have difficulty entering at this point.

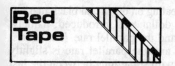
Red Tape

Visas are not required by British or other EC citizens, with the exception of French nationals. North American, Australian and New Zealand nationals also require visas. Anyone may be asked to show an onward or return ticket, although proof of sufficient funds to buy one in Brazil should be enough.

The Brazilian consulate in London is at 6 St Alban's Street, SW1Y 4SG (tel 071-930 9055). It is open 10am-4pm; visa processing takes three days. The visa fee varies according to your nationality; anyone who applies by post must pay £7 extra. You must be able to show your flight ticket.

The Embassy in the USA is at 3006 Massachusetts Avenue NW, Washington, DC 20008 (tel 202-745-2700/2805), and there are consulates in New York and Los Angeles. The Brazilian consulate in Australia is at 19 Forster Crescent, Yarralumla, Canberra 2600 (tel 2732372), to which New Zealand citizens should also apply.

Tourists are eligible to stay in Brazil for up to three months, but the length of stay permitted will be decided on arrival; you may have to exert some pressure to be given the full 90 days.

Visa Extension. You can extend your stay at offices of the Polícia Federal, up to a maximum total of six months. Apply at least a fortnight before your permit is due to expire. Again a return ticket or sufficient funds must be shown. After your six months is up you can, theoretically, leave the country and then re-enter, starting the process all over again.

Departure Tax. On leaving Brazil by air you must pay a tax of $16.

CUSTOMS

You can take in up to two litres of spirits, three litres of wine and 600 cigarettes.

The severity of searches varies between airports and according to your point of departure. So, for example, travellers from Colombia and Bolivia are likely to be searched more thoroughly than those arriving from Lisbon or Heathrow. Buses serving border posts on popular smuggling routes, from Paraguay, for example, may be stopped by police on the look out for people returning home from a big shopping spree. Searches may take place some way from the border, but are unlikely to affect the average traveller.

The troubled state of Brazil's economy has resulted in frequent changes to the currency. The one in circulation at present is the cruzeiro, which replaced the cruzado novo in 1990.

Notes and Coins. Notes are issued in denominations of 100, 500, 1,000, 5,000 and 10,000 cruzeiros, and coins in denominations of 1, 5, 10 and 50 cruzeiros. Most notes are multi-coloured, and en masse are difficult to distinguish from each other. Furthermore, new denominations constantly appear on the scene, many of them simply old notes over-stamped. Beware of old and worthless cruzado notes, some of which are still in circulation.

Changing Money. In response to the amount of dealing on the illegal black market, in 1989 a new system of exchange rates for the dollar was introduced: namely, the commercial or official rate, the tourist rate and the parallel rate. The tourist rate is about 10% higher than the official rate, and the parallel rate is slightly higher still. In reality, you will often have to do with something between the last two. The newspapers normally list all three rates, sometimes on the front page. Note that parallel rates tend to drop during the main holiday seasons and during the Carnival, particularly in the tourist areas.

Money can be changed at the parallel rate in *casas de câmbio*, and also in some hotels, shops and travel agents. You will get the best deals in the cities that see large numbers of foreigners — particularly Rio and São Paulo. Exprinter runs a chain of casas de câmbio, which offer among the best deals for cash. There are still a few street moneychangers about, but they are a disgruntled lot and best avoided.

Travellers cheques are difficult to change at the parallel rate. Some casas de câmbio will oblige, although they have been known to refuse Amex cheques. Exchange houses are thin on the ground out of the state capitals anyway, where you must be prepared to change cash mainly, even at the banks. Bemge, Banespa, Banco Econômico and Banco do Brasil are reliable banks at which to change cheques, and cash if necessary.

Credit Cards. With inflation so high, many shops and restaurants no longer find it profitable to offer credit card facilities. It is relatively easy, however, to withdraw cash on a credit card at a bank: Banco do Brasil is usually willing. MasterCard is most widely accepted, though Visa and Amex are also useful; note that some establishments do not accept non-Brazilian Visa cards. When you pay for goods by credit card, the amount will be exchanged at the tourist rate — and sometimes even at the official rate — so check in advance.

Banking Hours. Banks open 10am-3pm, Monday to Friday. Casas de câmbio work 10am-4.30pm, but may also open on Saturday mornings.

Mail. Sending a letter is not much cheaper than sending a telegram, and you may regret having promised to send postcards to all your friends back home. There is a standard air mail rate — a hefty $0.85 — for all overseas destinations, whether you are sending a letter or postcard. To cope with the constantly-changing cost, stamps simply bear the words *tarifa postal internacional*, with no price.

Telephone. Brazil spans four time zones, so you will have to change your watch a number of times as you flit around the country: the eastern states are GMT —3 (—2 from October to February), the western states (except Acre) GMT —4, and Acre state GMT —5. Some remote areas don't bother changing their clocks in summer. The international country code is 55.

International calls can be made from the offices of Embratel, a government-owned company, or from those of the state telecommunications companies. There are at least one or two *postos telefónicos* in the centre of any town or city, as well as in the bus station and airport. A few are open 24 hours a day, but most from just 8am to 10pm.

Making international phone calls is an expensive business, though lines are generally good. While there is just one standard rate for calls to Australasia, there are cheap rates (8pm-6am) for North America and Europe. The tariff varies according to where you are, rates per minute from Rio usually being the cheapest: $3.60 to the UK ($2.90 off-peak), $3 to the USA ($2.40 off-peak), and $5.50 to Australia. From Manaus, on the other hand, you can expect to pay about a dollar more per minute. It is possible to call collect to most countries.

Payphones: public telephones are plentiful in the main cities but scarce elsewhere. They have distinctive yellow hoods and are known as *orelhãos* or 'big ears', particularly in Rio. Local calls are made from the red phones, and inter-city (DDD) calls from the blue ones. These phones accept tokens *(fichas)* rather than coins, which you can buy from newspaper kiosks or street vendors. You should have little trouble getting hold of a *ficha local*, for a local call: in Rio such is the competition that vendors offer five for the price of four. But the search for *fichas interurbanas* can be more protracted. For this reason it's generally better to make long-distance calls from a posto telefónico. And since public phones are often in a poor state or on a noisy street corner, they are virtually useless anyway. Fichas for local calls cost a few cents, for DDD calls about $0.25; both should let you talk for a couple of minutes.

Telephone Codes: Belém — 091; Belo Horizonte — 031; Brasilia — 061; Curitiba — 041; Manaus — 052; Recife — 081; Rio de Janeiro — 021; Salvador — 071; São Paulo — 011.

Telegrams. The cost per word is $0.75-90 to the UK and $0.50-60 to the USA, depending on where you're sending it from. There is a straight charge of $1.12 for a message of up to twenty words sent inside Brazil.

THE MEDIA
Newspapers. Buying a newspaper in Brazil can be positively daunting, so many are there to choose from. Each state has its own range of papers, usually including several published in the capital and numerous local ones. Only a small number are distributed nationwide, of which the most reputable are those printed in São Paulo and Rio; they generally cost about $0.60. The best reads are the *Folha de São Paulo* and *O Estado de São Paulo*, though Rio would balk at the idea that its *Jornal do Brasil* and *O Globo* are not the best. Financial matters, not surprisingly, take up a lot of space, and the endless array of rather turgid articles on the state of the Brazilian economy are tedious. Interestingly, even the traditionally pro-government papers are more and more outspoken about their opinions of the President and his policies. All the papers (particularly the Sunday editions) have listings of what's on, biased, obviously, towards the paper's city of origin.

Folha de São Paulo is considered Brazil's leading paper, with good and often controversial articles. It has never favoured Collor, and it has been the object of sporadic harassment by government officials. The foreign coverage in its *Mundo* section is good, and it has a so-called *Multimídia* page which is made up of reports from papers around the world, from the *Japan Times* to the *Guardian*. *O Estado* is only marginally inferior, but boasts a Sunday edition that weighs almost as much as the *New York Times*. Of the two Rio papers, the best international news coverage is given in the conservative *O Globo*. A good weekly magazine is *Veja*, which includes incisive articles about current affairs.

There are three English-language newspapers, all of which are weekly. *The Brazil Herald* is published in Rio, its rivals — the *Brazil Post* and *Sunday News* — both being printed in São Paulo. They all lack substance, the standard eight pages providing a thin and unsatisfying selection of stories. The listings can be useful, particularly as they are geared towards the foreign visitor. *Brazil Post* is the easiest to get hold of.

Television. O Globo is the country's biggest television network, and is watched by about three-quarters of Brazilians. The news coverage is disappointing, with most energy apparently going into screening appalling old American movies and locally-made soap operas. The commercials are more interesting than the average programme.

If you are in Brazil for just a short time and wish to visit several different states, you can do nothing better than to get an air pass; but this does mean that a large proportion of your time may be tied to the cities. However, if time is not so pressing and if you don't mind spending the odd night on the move, there is such a good network of long-distance buses that travelling overland is strongly recommended.

Hitching is not that easy or particularly recommended — truck drivers have a bad reputation for hassling hitchers. It is probably best considered only along short distances, and in areas where there are a lot of tourists: near beaches, mountain resorts, etc.

Maps. Don't set out until you have armed yourself with a decent map of the country. The maps of South America published by ITM (see page 41) give a good idea of the topography of the country, but better is the one that comes with the *Quatro Rodas* guide to Brazil, or indeed the special *Quatro Rodas* road map; see *Help and Information*.

AIR

The vast size and impenetrability of parts of Brazil means that air transport is vital; the country has one of the largest internal networks in the world. There are three main airlines — Varig (and its subsidiary Cruzeiro do Sul), Vasp and Transbrasil — and a number of smaller companies. Nordeste, for example, operates in the Northeast, Rio-Sul in the south and TABA in Amazonia. Be prepared for flights, particularly those run by the main airlines, to go all round the houses: a flight from Rio to Manaus, for example, may stop off at all the Northeastern capitals en route, taking the best part of a day.

Fares vary between airlines, and since there are often special deals on offer, it's worth shopping around. If planning to travel at a weekend, book as far in advance as possible, particularly in the holiday season. There is usually a 20-30% discount on tickets booked a month ahead. You can expect to pay about $150 for a one-way flight over the distance from Rio to Salvador, or from Fortaleza to Belém, for example. Flights leaving after 10pm are 30% cheaper than daytime services.

There are a number of shuttle services — known as *ponte aérea* — between the Brazil's main commercial cities: namely, Rio, São Paulo, Curitiba, Brasília and Belo Horizonte. Tickets can usually be bought on the day of departure, and cost $60-90 one way, depending on the route. Air taxi companies do most of their business in the Amazon; this is an expensive way to travel, but may be the only way to reach destinations off the beaten track.

Air Passes. An air pass is an excellent solution for anyone with just two or three weeks in Brazil. It currently costs $440, and entitles you to five flights to be taken within 21 days. Given the fact that a return fare from Rio to Manaus, for example, costs around $400, this is clearly a bargain. In addition, a limited number of flights over and above the standard five can be bought at a cost of $100 each.

Air passes must be purchased abroad, in conjunction with an international ticket, and can be arranged through most travel agencies. Ask them to issue the actual ticket if possible, since otherwise you will be given special coupons (MCOs) which you must then exchange for tickets once in Brazil — providing scope for hours of queuing. All flights must be booked in advance, but you may change them once in the country. All three main Brazilian airlines offer air passes, but Varig is usually the best airline to choose since it covers the largest number of destinations. You can obtain a complete timetable from the Varig office at 16/17 Hanover Street, London W1R 0HG (tel 071-629 9408; fax 071-495 6135), enabling you to prepare a rough itinerary before going to see an agent.

While the domestic air tax — usually $2.50-3.00 — mounts up after several flights, the number of free meals provide some compensation.

TRAIN

Brazil's railway network is in a sorry state. Passenger services have been cut dramatically in recent years — particularly those running between states. RRFSA (Rede Ferroviária Federal), which runs the network, is desperately short of cash, and is closing or actually dismantling thousands of miles of track. The private sector has been invited to take over certain services, but a major revival is unlikely. FEPASA, the state rail company of São Paulo, continues to run trains (including into neighbouring states), but the trains are notoriously slow and unreliable.

The only trains most visitors use are the tourist services between Curitiba and Paranaguá (Paraná) or São João del Rei and Tiradentes (Minas Gerais).

BUS

The vast majority of people in Brazil, except those living in the Amazon, get around by bus. You would do well to join them, since long-distance buses are cheap and comfortable. Most are non-stop, and do not pick up passengers en route. Some pause only at certain designated roadside restaurants, where passengers can eat a meal and stretch their legs, while others call in at intermediate towns en route. Regular buses are known as *comum* or *comercial* and are perfectly adequate for most people's needs, with air-conditioning and loos. A step above are the *executivo* or *leito* buses, which are not that much faster but cost twice as much. Travelling by leito is more like flying Club Class, where every possible luxury is provided. If you want a good night's sleep, this is the way to do it; leito buses almost always run overnight.

The state of the buses reflects the roads on which they travel. The best roads are in the south and along the coast (including the BR-116, the Federal Highway), but the quality deteriorates dramatically as you head into the interior, particularly into the sertão and the Amazon; buses in these areas are often fairly rickety and dirty.

Buses are run by numerous private companies, several of which may operate along the same route. Although it may be worth shopping around to find the best-looking seats or the most convenient schedule, prices are fairly standard. Several big companies (such as Penha, Itapemirim and São Geraldo) specialize in long-haul destinations, between state capitals all over the country.

Every town and city has a central bus station or Rodoviária. Considering the number of people and buses concentrated in one spot, the terminals are surprisingly orderly. They are also well equipped, with loos, restaurants and phone, post and left-luggage offices. Each bus company has its own counter, often with timetables and prices pasted up. It is a good idea to book your seat a day or so in advance if travelling by leito, at weekends or during the holiday season. Bus stations are normally some way from the centre, and if you can't be bothered to trek that far out, you can normally buy tickets from travel agencies in town.

In the capital city sections in the text, long-distance bus services are listed under *Arrival and Departure*; those to local destinations within the state are given with the relevant section.

CAR

Driving in the cities should be avoided. This is mainly because of the volume of traffic, but also because of the danger of theft: in Rio, for example, a car is stolen every 15 minutes. Once on the open road, watch out for the sleeping policemen that greet you at the entrance of virtually every town.

All the main cities have car rental agencies, both international (including Avis, Budget and Hertz) and national, such as Nobre and Belauto. Rates charged by the reputable companies are similar, though they can vary from state to state. The cheapest car is usually a Chevette or a Golf, which cost about $30 per day. A minibus can be hired for just $60. On top of this you must pay roughly $0.15-25 per km. Insurance is compulsory, so check that the cost of it is included in the price.

For general information about driving contact the Touring Clube do Brasil, which has its headquarters at Avenida Presidente Antonio Carlos 130 in Rio (tel 210-2181 ext 43), and branches in all the main cities. For more immediate help on the road, you may want to call on the Polícia Federal Rodoviária, or road police.

Note that petrol stations are often closed at weekends.

CITY TRANSPORT

Buses. Brazilian city streets are overflowing with buses. While at peak hours this is bad news, at other times they offer a frequent and rapid service. Most buses have the route number and destination written at the front, with a board with further details near the door at the back. Drivers stop only at designated stops as a rule. Having hailed the bus, board at the back and pay your fare to the conductor by the turnstile, which is usually at the back or in the middle and a major hurdle for anyone with a lot of baggage. Make your way to the front as soon as possible in a crowded bus, thus enhancing your chances of leaping off when you want: drivers seldom wait for passengers who are stuck at the back.

The layout of Brazil's cities involves a large number of one-way streets, which makes guessing at bus routes a little hazardous; rarely do buses return along the roads they used on the outward journey. Circular routes are also common.

Taxi. Brazilian taxis come in all shapes and sizes, from Volkswagen Beetles to Ford Escorts. Fares are calculated by using the meter in conjunction with a table (*tabela*), which may be pasted up inside the cab; the meter reading is converted into a sensible fare that takes account of inflation. Check the meter is on when you board, and if there is none (not unlikely in small towns), settle the price beforehand.

At airports, cooperatives run fixed-rate taxis, for which you must buy a ticket in advance. Fares are invariably high, so whenever possible take the bus, or look around outside for a regular taxi.

In Brazil you are most likely to stay in a *hotel* or *pousada*. These terms are virtually interchangeable and are equally misleading, as they can incorporate anything from a flea-infested brothel to a luxury mansion.

While in small towns you can pay as little as $2-3 for a room in a simple hotel, in the cities you'll be hard pushed to find many places charging less than $8. A one-star establishment will normally cost at least $10, a two-star place anything from $15 to $25 or more. When visiting the coastal cities, most of which have beach areas, staying by the seafront is usually the safer but also the more expensive option.

The cheapest places to stay are the *dormitórios* or *hospedarias*, which are often found near transport stations. Many of these are little more than flophouses, with basic facilities and minimal security. A more salutary and appealing alternative are the *pensãos*. These are usually on the basic side too, but are mostly family-run and, unlike pousadas, are reliably cheap.

Breakfast will almost always be included in the price of the room: this may consist of just coffee, bread and crackers, but some hotels offer fresh fruit, cakes, eggs and other goodies; indeed some places are worth staying in simply because of the feast in the morning.

During the main holiday periods — January-February and July-August — hotels fill easily and rates go up by at least 10%, often more.

Youth Hostels. There is a well-established network of youth hostels, which are extremely cheap, particularly if you have a IYHF card. The quality varies, but you should rarely have to pay more than $5. The headquarters of the Federação Brasileira do Albergues de Juventude is at Rua Assembleia 10, Rio de Janeiro; it produces a complete list of hostels.

Camping. The Camping Clube do Brasil has 50 or so campsites around the country. These charge about $10 per person, but there are also municipal and private sites which charge half that. As with youth hostels, the standard of sites varies, and they are not that common away from the coast and the main tourist centres. Tents can normally be hired, and all sites provide washing facilities; some have a restaurant. For further information contact the CCB at Rua Senador Dantas 75, 29th floor, Rio (tel 262-7172). Members are charged half rates. The *Quatro Rodas* publishes the *Guia de Areas de Camping* and sites are listed in their other regional guides; see *Help and Information*.

If heading off the beaten track, it is a good idea to take a hammock, which you can buy easily, particularly in the Northeast. At beaches used to visitors you can often hire a hammock as well as the space in which to hang it.

Although it is impossible to talk about Brazilian cuisine as a single entity, there are certain types of food that are found increasingly in many parts of the country. The two most distinguishable cuisines originate in the Northeast and the South.

The food of the Northeast, more specifically Bahia, shows the influence of the large black community. Dishes are spicy and characterized by the use of seafood, coconut, and palm nut oil (*dendê*). A famous dish which, when prepared well, is one of the most delicious things you can eat in Brazil, is *moqueca*, a bright yellow stew of seafood, peppers, tomatoes and coconut milk. Bahian women are also renowned for their snacks, which are sold in the street. The cakes and sweets are often sickly, but *acarajé*, in contrast, is absolutely delicious. This is a deep-fried bean cake-cum-dumpling that is filled with *vatapá* (a dried shrimp and coconut paste), and served with a hot pepper and tomato sauce.

It is in southern Brazil, the main cattle-breeding region and the traditional home of the gaúchos, that committed carnivores will find their true resting place. *Churrasco* — a generic term meaning barbecued meat — reigns supreme. *Churrascarias*, which cater solely for the serious meat-eater, are found all over the country. The best and most authentic ones don't have a menu, and simply give you a choice of whatever's on the barbecue; what comes with the meat (probably beans and chips) is incidental.

Another cuisine which is less widespread through Brazil but no less distinctive, is *comida mineira*, from the central state of Minas Gerais. Many dishes are of colonial origin, and make much use of pork; lovers of crackling will probably make themselves sick on the mineira equivalent, known as *torresmo*. But the most common feature of comida mineira is *tutú*, a thick bean sauce made by cooking ground uncooked beans and manioc flour. It is served most typically as *tutú a mineira*, which comes with *couve* (a spinach-type vegetable), fried eggs, pork and crackling. *Picadinha*, a stew of chopped meat is also popular.

As far as menus in standard restaurants are concerned, these are likely to consist of meat served with rice, beans (*feijão*) and probably chips. Beef and chicken are the most common. A common accompaniment is manioc flour (*mandioca*), which you sprinkle over the food: *farinha* is the raw and rather tasteless version, while *farofa* — which is fried in butter, and may contain bacon or egg — is much more tasty.

The nearest thing there is to the archetypal Brazilian dish is *feijoada* (or *feijoada completa*), which consists of a stew of black beans, cooked with a variety of meats and served with rice, orange and farofa. It is traditionally eaten at weekends, and many restaurants don't prepare it during the week. A feijoada is normally shared between two or more people. Even ordinary meals prepared for just one person are often enough for two people; don't hesitate to ask for a doggy bag that you can give to people going hungry on the street.

If you are feeling less adventurous, there are pizzerias all over the country, and restaurants serving other European and Asian food are common in the south; it's in this area that you are also likely to find the best choice of vegetarian restaurants.

The cheapest places to eat are the *lanchonetes*. These bar-cum-restaurants vary tremendously; in the cities they are busy, stand-up bars, while in smaller towns they are more like a traditional café or restaurant, with a fairly limited menu. In the big towns, lanchonetes invariably offer all manner of things, including hamburgers (*X-burgers*), hot dogs (*cachorro quente*), sandwiches (often rolls served hot, burger-style) and *salgados*, a term that refers to a wide range of savoury snacks, many of them deep-fried. Other good places for snacks are the bakeries and cake shops — *pastelarias*, *confeitarias* or *panificadoras*. These may be simply shops, but some serve coffee and are good places to eat breakfast if the one provided by your hotel is insufficient or inedible.

Don't miss out on the street snacks, ranging from corn on the cob to tapioca cakes, or the fruit, which is best bought in the markets.

DRINKING

Brazilians are keen drinkers and can be seen happily supping beer at any time of day. Lager (*cerveja clara*), such as Antártica and Brahma, is the most common, although there are a few dark (*escura*) brands too. Draught beer, known as *chopp*, often comes with a huge head, and is not such good value as bottled beer, which costs $0.80-$1 for 600ml.

Vineyards were established in southern Brazil by European immigrants, but wine isn't that popular at home. The main alternative to beer is *cachaça* (known in some areas as *pinga*), a potent rum made from sugar cane. It is served most commonly as a *caipirinha*, a cocktail of cachaça, lime, sugar and crushed ice: a glass will set you back about 80c and unless you have a strong head, should be drunk in moderation. *Caipiríssima* is similar, but made with vodka.

After a night on the caipirinhas, you may need something cool and refreshing to ease you back to normality. Mineral water is not hard to find in the main centres, but for a more tasty drink, choose the fruit juices (*sucos de fruta*) or milk-based *vitaminas*. The choice is daunting, particularly in the Amazon, where you can try weird and wonderful fruits, including the untranslatable *açai* and *cupuaçu*. One of the most widespread, cheapest and refreshing juices is cashew fruit or *cajú*. Alternatively, drink fresh coconut milk (*coco verde* or *agua de coco*) or sugar cane juice, which can be bought on the streets, mainly in the Northeast.

Brazilian coffee is wonderful, whether drunk as a *cafezinho* (a tiny cup of strong, sweet espresso), or served with milk (*con leite*); the latter is the preferred breakfast-time drink.

Museums and Churches. Brazil's most magnificent examples of colonial architecture are in Minas Gerais and the Northeastern states of Pernambuco and Bahia. Perhaps the most distinctive mark of the Portuguese influence is the beautiful blue and white painted tilework, known as *azulejos*, that adorns the exterior of many secular buildings and decorate a number of the country's most memorable churches. The influence of Portugal's oriental colony of Macau also found its way to Brazil, brought from the island by missionaries: the eastern features are most visible in the paintwork.

The opening hours of museums and churches are a law unto themselves. As a general rule, however, these places are closed all day Monday, and for a couple of hours in the middle of the day. Opening hours are at their most whimsical out of the main tourist season, and many churches are kept permanently shut for security reasons. If somewhere is closed, it's worth banging on the door, or asking around for the *vigia* (caretaker), who may do you a kindness and let you in.

Beaches. Brazil's huge coastline boasts a plethora of fine beaches. Copacabana apart, most famous are those in the Northeast, particularly in the states of Paraíba and Ceará. Their shores form virtually one continuous beach, peppered with magnificent sand dunes. Further south the best beaches are around Porto Seguro in southern Bahia, in the vicinity of Rio and São Paulo, and in Santa Catarina state. The entire coast north of Rio is dotted with reefs. In some places they form pools near the shore, which are often good for quiet swimming.

Surfing is a favourite sport among the wealthy youth of Brazil. The best beaches for it are along the Costa do Sol east of Rio, and on Ilha de Santa Catarina, where national championships are held every January. Windsurfing has become increasingly popular, but facilities are limited to the most developed resorts.

While the beaches near the big cities are being increasingly developed, usually just a bus ride away are quieter fishing villages that are completely unspoilt. Most beaches, even those which see just a small number of people, have *barracas* which serve food.

Wildlife. The best place to see wildlife is in the Pantanal, a vast area of swamp spanning the two Mato Grosso states. While the Amazon jungle is more famous, animals and birds are far more easily spotted in the Pantanal simply because the terrain is more open. Guided trips in either place are expensive. There is more scope for independent exploration in the Pantanal, but even there it is limited.

One of the most accessible reserves, and one in which you are virtually guaranteed to see a range of birds, is the area surrounding the Iguaçu falls, close to the Argentinian and Paraguayan borders.

Hiking. Brazil is comparatively flat, so scope for the serious hiker is fairly limited. The best areas for walking are mostly in southern Brazil. They include the Serra dos Orgãos and Serra do Mantiqueira in Rio de Janeiro state, Caparão National Park in Minas Gerais, the Marumbi National Park in Paraná, and the Serra Gaúcha in Rio Grande do Sul. An exception is the beautiful national park of Chapada Diamantina in the Northeastern state of Bahia.

Parks are usually administered by the IBDF (national forestry institute) or IBAMA (the national parks organisation). Park facilities vary enormously, but accommodation of some kind is normally available. IBDF or IBAMA may have an office in the nearest big town to the park, where you can pick up maps and other information.

Music and Dance. The Northeast, and particularly Salvador, was the birthplace of Brazilian music. One of the most well-known rhythms is *samba*, which although Northeastern in origin, is now played all over Brazil, and is closely identified with the Rio carnival. More popular in the Northeast, but associated chiefly with the state of Pernambuco, is the faster beat of the *forró*. The basic line-up is an accordian, base drum and a triangle, although it often includes guitars and keyboards nowadays. *Lambada*, which has become so popular abroad, is an all-encompassing term used to describe what are often jazzed up versions of old musical genres. *Carimbó* is another general name, given to the music and dance of the north (including the Amazon).

Most towns and cities, particularly in the Northeast, have venues where the locals go to listen to music and dance; they are often called *danceterias* and get going only at around midnight.

Capoeira, again seen mainly in the Northeast, is a martial art of African origin that has been stylized into a form of dance.

Carnival. The *Carnaval* is the highlight of the year for many Brazilians, and seems to act like a valve, releasing the pent-up energy that has built up over the previous year. The festival has its origins in the country's colonial past, but its main period of development has been since the abolition of slavery in the late 19th century; the celebrations were used by the blacks to poke fun at their ex-slave masters.

Carnival is celebrated all over the country, but most famously in the Northeast (particularly Salvador and Olinda) and in Rio. In the last few decades the carnival has assumed great importance as a tourist attraction. It is now big business, particularly in Rio. Every year there are different themes to the songs (*enredos*) and to the costumes, reflecting national or world events: in 1991 masks of Saddam Hussein were all the rage in Rio. Well-orchestrated parades are the hallmark of this city's festivities, but a more spontaneous type of street carnival — consisting of dancing, singing and drinking — characterizes the celebrations in most places.

The carnaval kicks off on the Saturday before Ash Wednesday, and lasts until the following Wednesday night; it usually falls in mid to late February. The warm-up period beforehand is often the most fun, not only in the days and weeks immediately prior (when there are wild parties known as *bailes*), but also in the months during which rehearsals are held. During the carnival itself, most banks, shops and offices close, and many hotels are full. If you join in the street parties, take nothing with you since crime is one of the more unfortunate trademarks of the carnival, particularly in the big cities. In 1991, for example, around 500 people died — either murdered or in accidents.

Starting dates are as follows: 20 February 1993; 12 February 1994; 25 February 1995; and 17 February 1996.

SPORT

Brazilians are fanatical about soccer. The country produced Pelé, the greatest player of all time, and teams capable of winning three World Cups. The best teams are in Rio and São Paulo, which also boast the finest stadiums. Rio's Maracanã stadium, built for the 1950 World Cup, has become the focal point of soccer in Latin America. Going to a match is strongly recommended, not only for the quality of the football, but also for the wild atmosphere. Matches normally take place on Sundays, and virtually all year round.

A visit to the races should not be missed, the Jockey Club in Rio being particularly famous. Cricket fans may even have the chance to enjoy a match, the main clubs being in Rio, São Paulo, Recife and Santos. A national team meets Argentina regularly, to contest the Norris Trophy which was donated by 'Bing' Norris, a British businessmen, in the 1950s.

As usual, the best shopping can be done in the markets. Comparatively few have the appeal of those of the Andean countries, but there are some excellent markets in the Northeast. Most famous is the huge fair at Caruarú in Pernambuco, but the weekly leather market at Feira de Santana in Bahia also draws thousands of people. Fortaleza, the capital of Ceará state, is an important craft centre, and is a particularly good place to buy hammocks. The markets in the Amazon, including in Manaus and Belém, usually have some Indian crafts for sale, but with their stalls piled high with jungle produce, these places are more interesting as spectacles than as places to go shopping.

FUNAI, the Indian protection agency, runs a series of craft shops called Artindia. These are found in various cities, and although the quality of the products varies, prices are reasonable. These shops are often a good source of last-minute presents.

icate if entering the country from Bolivia, Peru or Colombia; and at the border some states within Brazil, such as Mato Grosso, Goiás and Maranhão, you may be obliged to have an injection on the spot if you don't possess one. Have the jab at home to be on the safe side.

Malaria pills are also essential for anyone travelling in the Amazon and other inland areas, including the Pantanal and around the Iguaçu falls. Dengue fever, also carried by mosquitoes, is endemic in Brazil too.

On the beaches beware of creepy crawlies that penetrate the skin and lay eggs — you would do well to avoid going barefoot as much as possible. Mosquitoes can be a real nuisance by the coast, but the only areas in which they carry malaria are in southern Bahia, Paraná and Santa Catarina.

Aids. Brazil has the biggest Aids problem in South America, and ranks third in the world after Uganda and the USA in the number of reported cases; São Paulo and Rio are particularly badly affected. There are an estimated 19,000 Aids sufferers, a figure that grows by more than 500 per month. It is very common among street children — where drug addiction and homosexuality is common — but the disease affects all classes, and statistics show that 19% are infected through heterosexual contact. Demonstrations in some cities prove that there is an increased awareness of the problem, but people's behaviour, as elsewhere in the world, is slow to change. Blood transfusions are a potential risk, so don't leave home without your Aids kit. See page 74.

The Brazilian Embassy (32 Green Street, London W1Y 4AT; tel 071-499 0877) has a tourist department which, on receipt of a stamped addressed envelope, sends out a large wodge of brochures. These aren't likely to be of any long-term use, but they do contain plenty of pretty pictures. In the USA, the Brazilian tourist office can be contacted at 551 Fifth Avenue, Suite 519, New York, NY 10176 (tel 212-286 9600).

In Brazil, each state and most state capitals have their own tourist board. All the capital cities have tourist offices in the centre, and usually in the main airport and bus station too. The helpfulness of the staff and the information handed out varies in quality, but the staff can normally book hotel accommodation and give you a map. Embratur is the national tourist board, but it is concerned mostly with promoting Brazil overseas.

The *Guia Quatro Rodas: Brazil* costs about $10 but is worth every cent. It is rather like an amalgamation of the red and green French *Michelin* guides, with listings of hotels and restaurants (according to category), museums, airline offices, consulates, local events, and so on. The book also contains excellent town plans and there is a large sheet map of the entire country, marking roads, railways, national parks, etc. You can buy this and other books in the series (including on Rio and São Paulo) from news stands and bookshops.

Calendar of Events

The following list includes official or semi-official public holidays. Local communities may also select their own holidays; details of some of these are given in the text, otherwise ask at the tourist office.

January 1	New Year's Day
February	Carnaval (five days)
March/April	Easter
April 21	Tiradentes Day (Independence hero)
May 1	Labour Day
May 24	Ascension Day
May/June	Corpus Christi
September 7	Independence Day
October 12	Nossa Senhora de Aparecida
November 2	All Souls' Day (Day of the Dead)
November 15	Proclamation of the Republic
December 25/26	Christmas, Boxing Day

RIO DE JANEIRO

'My kind of luck' is how Rio's most famous foreigner signs autographs. Ronnie Biggs, perpetrator of the 1963 Great Train Robbery in England, was an opportunist. So is his adopted home. Rio, one of the world's biggest cities, has cunningly infiltrated into the space between the jungle-covered hills of the escarpment and the sweeping beaches washed by the waters of Guanabara Bay. The setting of Rio de Janeiro is one of the most dramatic and memorable on earth.

Rio was first settled in the mid-16th century. Two hundred years later its port began to be used to ship gold mined in Minas Gerais to Europe. The city's newly acquired prestige was recognized when it became first the capital of the colony and, in 1834, of the new Brazilian republic. Its position at the administrative helm was brought to an end only in 1960, when an experiment in economic geography transferred the seat of government to Brasília. But Rio remains the country's capital in almost every sense of the word.

Tourist brochures get carried away on a stream of hyperbole when describing the virtues of the *cidade maravilhosa*, where the sun always shines and everyone has fun. But Rio is the archetypal city of extremes. While it is impossible to ignore the magnificence of the sweeping beaches that have made the city world famous, nor can you dismiss lightly the blanket of shanties that spreads over the hills. Rio may indeed be the spiritual heart of Brazil, but this is not simply in terms of the exuberance for which the *cariocas*, as the locals are known, are famed; poverty, social tension and crime are more intense here than anywhere else. Tourism in Rio has declined by an astonishing forty percent in the last three years. New efforts are being made to spruce up the city's image, though there is little chance of these being anything but skin deep. Nevertheless, few travellers can or should resist the pull of Rio, undoubtedly one of the world's great cities. Its sights could sustain a visit of many weeks, but it is life on the street that fascinates — especially during its world-famous carnival. Everyone should be aware of the dangers that are part of life in Rio, but only a lively imagination is likely to make you feel threatened.

Temperatures in Rio are warm enough for you to swim all year round. However, it is hot and humid in summer, and winter is a good deal more pleasant. One reason not to overstay in Rio is the appalling pollution: taking a deep breath is like inhaling through an exhaust pipe.

CITY LAYOUT

Rio spreads down the west side of Guanabara bay. The topography can make orientation difficult, but with a basic grasp of the layout of districts and of the bus routes, getting around shouldn't be a problem.

Rio is split into the Centro, Zona Norte and Zona Sul. Centro is the oldest part and the commercial heart of the city. There are two main arteries through the centre, the largest being Avenida Presidente Vargas, which stretches southwest from the waterfront, with the huge Igreja de Candelária sitting rather incongruously at its northern end. Avenida Rio Branco, which runs at right angles to Presidente Vargas, is a more useful reference point for travellers: it is a busy commercial street, with banks, airline offices, etc. You can get around on foot suprisingly easily: even walking from the centre to the northern districts of the Zona Sul, doesn't take much more than half an hour.

The Zona Norte is the industrial area of Rio, and there is little reason to venture there other than to go to the bus station.

If you are into sun, surf and seeing Rio at its most uninhibited, the Zona Sul is where you'll probably spend most of your time. The dividing line between this district and the centre is the Serra da Carioca. These hills are both a physical and social barrier: to the south are Rio's smartest residential areas, including Copacabana and Ipanema, and the beaches from which they take their names.

RIO DE JANEIRO : ORIENTATION

Maps. The only map that has the whole of Rio on one sheet is the *Guia Schaeffer*, which costs about $2 from most street stands. It helps with orientation and has a street index, but landmarks are not highlighted and it isn't much use when exploring individual areas.

Most maps of Rio split the city into districts, usually the Centro and the main beaches. the *Quatro Rodas* guide to Rio (see page 618) has detailed maps, although the ones in the same publishers' guide to the whole of Brazil are sufficient for general purposes. The brochures given out in hotels and travel agents usually include a few maps, but these tend to be of the beach areas only.

ARRIVAL AND DEPARTURE

Air. Rio's Aeroporto Internacional do Galeão is 10 miles/16km north of the centre. For information phone 398-4134/6060/5050. Section A is for domestic flights, B and C for international services. Rio has that rare feature, a duty-free shop for arrivals — if you are visiting friends, buy as much Black Label whisky as you're allowed. Sector C has tourist information, car rental and currency exchange desks, any of which can provide a map of the city. Avoid the privately-run information stand that offers a map and a few useless bits and pieces for $25.

A constant stream of buses leaves for the centre of town from outside Sector B. All go to Santos Dumont Airport in the centre (see below), via the bus station and Avenida Rio Branco, which takes about 30 minutes. While one service terminates there, the other continues to São Conrado in Zona Sul. It takes you within a stone's throw of the principal accommodation areas, and serves all the main beaches. Buses run every 20-30 minutes, from 6am-9.30pm to Santos Dumont, and from 5.20am-11.30pm to São Conrado. When returning to the airport, get the bus from Santos Dumont or flag a bus down on the seafront. The fare of $2.60 can be paid in cruzeiros or dollars. With such a good bus service, there is little point in taking a taxi. Rates are fixed: $14.50 to the centre, and $20 to Copacabana.

Santos Dumont: this airport is downtown near Parque Flamengo. It is used mainly for the shuttle service (*ponte aérea*) to São Paulo, and a few other minor routes. It's only a short walk from Rio Branco, and there are plenty of buses to the Zona Sul. For information phone 210-2457 (or 210-1244 for the shuttle).

Airlines Offices: most airlines are based on or around Avenida Rio Branco. The main Brazilian airlines have their head offices in the centre, around the Cinelândia metro stop, plus branches in Ipanema or Copacabana.

Aerolíneas Argentinas — Rua São José 40a (tel 224-9242).
AeroPeru — Praça M. Gandhi (tel 210-3124, 240-0722), near corner of Dantas.
LAB — Avenida Calógeras 30a (tel 220-9548), between Presidente Wilson and Santa Luzia.
LanChile — Rua São José 70, 8th floor (tel 221-2882).
LAP — Avenida Rio Branco 245, 7th floor (tel 220-4148, 240-9577).
TAP — Rio Branco 311B (tel 210-2414).
Transbrasil — Avenida Calógeras 30 (tel 297-4422/77).
Varig/Cruzeiro — Avenida Rio Branco 277 (tel 292-6600), near Praça M. Gandhi.
Vasp — Rua Santa Luzia 735, off Rio Branco (tel 292-2080).
Viasa — Rua do Carmo 7, 4th floor (tel 224-5345).

Bus. The central bus terminal, known as the Rodoviária Novo Rio, is in the São Cristóvão district of the Zona Norte (tel 291-5151). The station is surprisingly orderly, until you venture outside where scores of city buses fight for space. Many head into the centre, so it's not difficult to escape. Routes 126, 127 and 128, for example, go downtown and continue to the Zona Sul; 170 goes to Catete (a cheap hotel district). Fixed-rate taxis charge $12 to Copacabana.

Below are details of the main long-distance services from Rio:

Asunción — 27 hours, $34; Monday and Friday with Rysa.
Belo Horizonte — 8 hours, $9; ten daily with Cometa and Util; one leito.
Buenos Aires — 38 hours, $70; daily with Pluma via Porto Alegre; less frequently via Foz do Iguaçu.
Campo Grande — 20 hours, $33; four daily with Mato Grosso do Sul, and one leito.
Curitiba - 12 hours, $19; regular daily buses and one leito with Penha or Itapemirim, which also serve Joinville, Florianópolis and Porto Alegre.

Foz do Iguaçu — 24 hours; best served by Pluma, with five morning buses, and several leitos. Most go via Londrina rather than Ponta Grossa.

Ouro Prêto — 8 hours, $11; best with Util, some buses going via Congonhas.

Salvador — 28 hours, $38; two buses daily, leito on Tuesday, with Penha.

São Paulo — 6 hours, $9; a constant flow of regular and leito buses, run by Cometa, Brasileiro and Itapemirim.

Train. At the time of going to press, all interstate services from Rio had been suspended. For the latest news ask at the interstate desk near the Avenida Marechal Floriano entrance to the Centro do Brasil railway terminal. The station (Estação Dom Pedro II; tel 233-1494/296-1244) is just off Presidente Vargas. If you don't feel like walking, grab any bus along Vargas or take the metro: the nearest station is Central.

GETTING AROUND

Bus. At rush hour the streets of Rio are a choking mass of buses, particularly where the topography and road layout create bottle-necks. As for the buses themselves, it is worth quoting one visitor to the city:

'*Bus drivers are paid on a piece rate basis, so understandably they drive like lunatics. The first problem is to flag down one of these monsters as it hurls along, sucking old ladies and small dogs into its slipstream. As you attempt to pay the conductor at the rear of the bus, you are suddenly slammed against the emergency exit as the bus takes off in a flurry of G-forces. At last you manage to flop into the upholstery like a landed fish, and find yourself quivering in a position of uncomfortable intimacy with the person in the window seat'.*

You have been warned. Buses are useful for beach-hopping, although the double set of highways along much of the seafront can be confusing. You can catch virtually any bus heading south when travelling between the centre and the Zona Sul; the buses numbered over the 500s are the best.

Praça 15 de Novembro is a major picking-up point for city buses. A short distance southeast of here, near the corner of Rua da Quitanda and Rua São José, is the Terminal Menezes Cortes (tel 224-7577), also known as Castelo. Air-conditioned buses leave here for Copacabana and the other beaches. If you are worried about pickpockets in crowded buses, paying a little extra to travel in one of these may seem appealing. The station looks like a multi-storey car park, and manages to be more confusing than the Rodoviária Novo Rio. Buses to Petrópolis and Teresopolis (see page 634) also leave from here, from Hall B.

Metro. The subway is an excellent alternative to the bus system. The trains and stations are so clean and quiet that it is hard to believe you're in Rio at all.

The two-line subway links southern Rio with the centre and the Zona Norte. Line 1 is particularly useful: it originates in Botafogo, runs through the main hotel and restaurant areas, virtually follows the line of Avenida Rio Branco and then curves round along Presidente Vargas. It splits at Estácio, from where Line 1 goes west to Tijuca, and Line 2 north to São Cristóvão and beyond.

Services run 6am-11pm daily except Sunday. The standard single fare (*unitário*) is about $0.25; it works out a bit cheaper if you buy two tickets (*duplo*) or, even better, a book of twelve. There is a singular lack of maps of the metro; there aren't even any in the stations. The only map seems to be the one in a booklet produced by the tourist office.

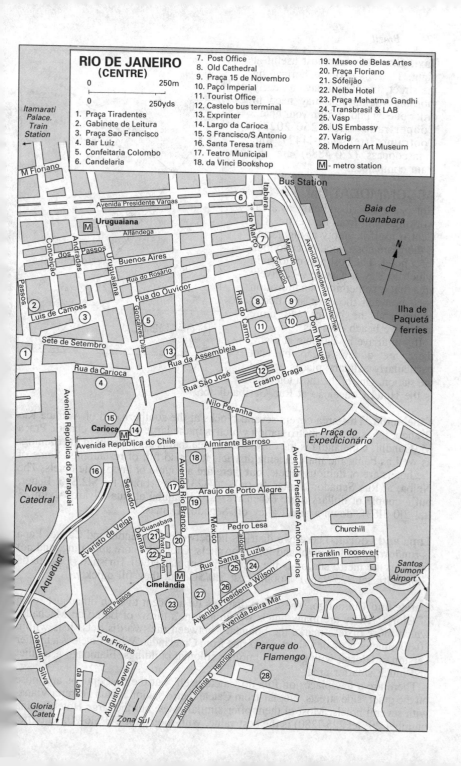

Taxi. City taxis are most useful at night. There is never a shortage on the street, but if you have an early morning flight, you may need to order one by phone from your hotel. Coopertramo (tel 260-2022), Cootramo (tel 270-1442) and Transcoopass (270-4888) are the main companies.

ACCOMMODATION

Hotels are described below by area, working south from the centre. The Centro itself is empty at night, and is therefore not a good place to look for a hotel. The best part of town in which to stay is Catete — a lively area that is something of a transition zone between the dark and dodgy centre and the cooler and more expensive beach districts.

If you arrive by bus late at night, there are a few cheap but not particularly salutary places around the station. One of the most tolerable is the Hotel Conceição at Rua Garibaldi 165.

RIO - METRO

Linha 1
SAENS PEÑA
SAO FRANCISCO
XAVIER
AFONSO PEÑA

Linha 2
IRAJÁ
INHAÚMA
DEL CASTILHO
MO DA GRAÇA
MARACANÃ
SAO CRISTOVÃO

ESTÁCIO
PRAÇA ONZE
CENTRAL
PRESIDENTE VARGAS
URUGUAIANA
CARIOCA
CINELÂNDIA
GLÓRIA
CATETE
LARGO DO MACHADO
FLAMENGO
BOTAFOGO

Cinelândia. This area covers several blocks at the southern end of Avenida Rio Branco; it has its own metro station which is in the large and rather chaotic Praça M. Gandhi. Cinelândia is the only central area that is at all lively in the evening: as well as being the main cinema district, it is also full of restaurants. Some of the hotels are of dubious repute, but there are a couple of good, safe hotels. The Nelba, at Rua Senador Dantas 46 (tel 210-3235) has rooms for $12/$20. Better, but a couple of dollars more expensive, is the Itajubá at Rua Alvaro Alvim 23 (tel 210-3163), down a small alley off Senador Dantas.

Lapa and Glória. These two districts lie between Cinelândia and Catete. Lapa is rundown, ill-lit at night and full of brothels. Glória is more appealing, and not far from the metro station is the extremely popular Hotel Turístico (Ladeira da Glória 30; tel 225-9388). Rooms cost $10/$13, but they fill quickly.

Catete and Flamengo. These two districts lie adjacent to each other just south of Glória. There are many hotels within a stone's throw of Largo do Machado, which more-or-less marks the boundary between the two districts. It is within 20-30 minutes walk or a short metro ride from Cinelândia. While Catete is a livelier version of Glória, with gently crumbling colonial buildings, Flamengo is a quiet and much smarter area.

There are a few places on Rua do Catete itself, but the best options are those on the quiet, side streets. Not far from Catete metro station is Rua Ferreira Viana, with several hotels. Most of them offer similar rates, but the large Hotel Regina (number 29; tel 225-7280) is the best value, with rooms for $13/$16-20; its buffet breakfast is one of the best in town. The Ferriera Viana opposite (number 58; tel 205-7396) has rooms under $10, but the owners are singularly unfriendly. A couple of streets up, at Buarque de Macedo 54 (tel 205-8149/9932) is the Unico. This is a friendly place, but the rooms are over-priced at $12-16. Better value are the family-run places on Rua Arturo Bernardes, on the other side of Rua do Catete: the Monterrey (number 39; tel 265-9899) has rooms for $4-10, and is recommended.

For a better class of room head for Rua Paissandú, a pleasant palm-lined street near Praça de Alençar, in Flamengo proper. The Venezuela (number 34; tel 205-2098) has rooms for $10-14; more welcoming, but also more expensive (over $20) is the Paysandú at number 23 (tel 225-7270).

Copacabana and Ipanema. If you have more money to spend and intend to concentrate your energies on the beaches, head for Copacabana; but expect to pay $20-30 for a room. One of the best places is the friendly Hotel Toledo at Rua Domingos Ferreira 71 (tel 257-1990), between Ruas Figueiredo de Magalhães and Santa Clara; rooms with bathroom cost $22-25. About five blocks further south, near the corner of Xavier da Silveira, is the Hotel Biarritz at Rua Aires Saldanha 54 (tel 521-6542), which charges similar rates. Not far from here, near the corner of Rua Bolívar, is the Copa Linda (Copacabana 956; tel 267-3399). It has recently been done up and is cheaper than the other two. The youth hostel, Albergue de Juventude Copacabana, is at Rua Emilio Berla 41 (tel 236-6472), off the southern end of Barata Ribeiro. Note that buses arriving in Copacabana from the centre go along Barata Ribeiro, returning into town along Avenida Copacabana.

Ipanema and Leblon are Rio's most desirable, upper-class districts, and room prices are therefore higher. However, there are a couple of comparatively reasonable places along Rua Visconde de Pirajá, at the Leblon end of Ipanema. These include the San Marco, at number 524, near Rua Anibal de Mendonça (tel 239-5032), with rooms from $20-26 (double).

EATING AND DRINKING

Cinelândia is one of the best places to eat or spend the evening: it is lively, there is a high concentration of restaurants and bars, and it is easy to get to, both by bus and metro. Open-air restaurants line Praça Floriano, but these offer similar menus and are touristy. Better are the stand-up bars and simpler restaurants in the narrow streets between Rio Branco and Senador Dantas. Among them is the excellent Sófeijão, on the corner of Ruas Alvim and Guanabara. This friendly and bustling restaurant serves good food and is excellent value. The average meal costs $2-3: largely a choice of meats served with feijão and rice.

Largo da Carioca nearby is famous for the grilled meat sold by gaúchos. These men from southern Brazil barbecue some of the most succulent chicken and beef you could ever wish to taste — queues are always long. Largo da Carioca is not a good place to hang around late at night, but there are a few good restaurants on Rua de Carioca nearby. Most famous of these is Bar Luiz at number 39 (tel 262-6900), which has been a meeting-place for Rio's intellectuals for years. It is busy, noisy and moderately expensive, and you may have to wait for a seat. The menu serves predominantly German dishes, and there is a good choice of beer.

If you are staying in Catete or Flamengo, there are plenty of fairly simple places on Rua do Catete and Largo do Machado. Recommended is Café Lamas (Rua

Marquês de Abrantes 18), a meeting place for artists and writers near the corner of Rua Paissandú.

In Copacabana there are a few decent restaurants along Domingos Ferreira and on or near Rua Bolívar. Avoid the overpriced places along the beachfront, except for the Arataca on the corner of Rua Figueiredo Magalhães (tel 255-7448), which serves excellent Brazilian food.

EXPLORING

Centro — A Walking Tour. The tour described below can be done in a day, and includes a couple of side trips which you can defer until a later date.

Praça Marechal Floriano: this square dominates the southern end of Rio Branco and the area known as Cinelândia, and is the city's Speakers' Corner. There is always something going on, whether a debate among a few individuals or a full-scale political rally. The square is full of book stalls, bars and cafés, and is also lined with some of Avenida Rio Branco's finest buildings. These include the Teatro Municipal (a replica of the Paris Opéra), the National Library and the Museu Nacional de Belas Artes (Rio Branco 199). The latter is the city's main fine art museum, and is open 10am-6pm Tuesday to Friday, 3-6pm at weekends. The most interesting section is that devoted to 20th-century Brazilian art.

Largo da Carioca: a short walk from Praça Floriano is the more downtrodden Largo da Carioca. It is another of the city's main areas of activity and inactivity. On a hill overlooking the square are the city's finest churches: the ancient church and convent of Santo Antônio (1606-7) on the left, and the 18th-century church of São Francisco de Penitência.

Near Largo da Carioca is the terminal for the street car to Santa Teresa (see below) and, on Avenida Paraguai, the concrete cone that passes for the cathedral. The Nova Catedral Metropolitana, which was built in the 60s, is unusual, daring and hideous. It is set next to a busy road in a depressing empty space. The austere interior brings little relief, the only colour being provided by the stained glass windows. Plans are afoot to cover the whole thing in vines. With or without them, the building has to be seen.

Running southwest from the Largo da Carioca is Rua da Carioca, a bustling 19th-century street where music blares from loudspeakers in the trees. It ends up in the noisy and polluted Praça Tiradentes. Around it are some of the city's liveliest streets, many of them pedestrian and teeming with shoppers. This is an area in which to follow your nose, but there are a few things to look out for. Just off the square, at the bottom of Luis de Camoes, is the so-called Real Gabinete Portuguez de Leitura, a most remarkable 19th-century library that should not be missed. Further north beyond Largo São Francisco (a pleasant antidote to Tiradentes), is the Confeitaria Colombo, at Rua Gonçalves Dias 32. This perfectly-preserved Art Nouveau building contains a fabulous shop and a tea-room upstairs that is a splendid place to have a break.

If you have time, you should make a small diversion west through more busy streets and across Avenida Vargas to the Itamarati Palace. Alternatively, head northwards up Rua Ouvidor, which takes you across Rio Branco and within a stone's throw of Praça 15 de Novembro.

Itamarati Palace: this large 19th-century building was once the Presidential residence. Part of it now forms the Museu Histórico e Diplomático, which contains among other things some beautiful furniture. At the time of going to press it was shut for restoration, but if open it is certainly worth a visit; normal opening hours are 11am-5pm, Tuesday to Friday. The museum is at Avenida Marechal Floriano 196, not far from the train station.

Praça 15 de Novembro: this is one of Rio's most historic squares, since it was here that King Dom João VI of Portugal stepped ashore in 1808; but it is also one of the city's most unattractive: a chaotic mass of buses, marred by a busy overpass.

The most historically important building in the square is the 18th-century Paço Imperial, a two-storey, white-washed building that was the home of the King of Portugal. Outside, it is dwarfed by the imposing Legislative Assembly on the right. Inside, it is largely empty and charcterless, with an equally uninspiring historical museum. On the next block, on the south side of Rua 1º de Março, are a couple of churches including the old cathedral (Orden Terceira do Carmo), where Emperor Pedro I was crowned in 1822.

On the west side of the square an arch leads beneath the buildings into Travessa do Comércio, a pedestrian street lined with restored 19th-century buildings; several are now chic bars and restaurants. More typical are the streets beyond it, crumbling and full of fascinating little shops and bars.

The only real reason to venture right across to the north side of Praça 15 de Novembro is to reach the dock from where you can take the ferry to Ilha de Paquetá. The island is hardly worth a visit in its own right (the beaches are dirty), but the 60-minute boat ride is a good chance to escape the traffic and enjoy the views from the water; ferries run hourly all day. If you have less time, take the ferry to Niterói, an unpleasant town 15 minutes across the bay. As with Paquetá, you may as well get the next boat back, although Niterói also has buses back to Praça 15 de Novembro.

Santa Teresa. This hilly district, southwest of the centre, contains some of the finest examples of colonial architecture in Rio. There is nothing specific to see, but Santa Teresa is strong on atmosphere and it has great views over the city. Most of the rich have moved out, to be replaced by artists, and there is an increasing number of shanties; avoid visiting the area after dark.

The best way to reach Santa Teresa is by tram from the station opposite the New Cathedral. The tram, which crosses an 18th-century aqueduct and then climbs slowly up the narrow cobbled streets, is in fact one of the main reasons to visit the district in the first place. Go to Dos Irmãos, the end of the line, for the best views; the journey takes about an hour. Don't set off too late in the day: trams going right to the top are not frequent and breakdowns are common, though you can always get a bus back down.

Museu Nacional. The main reason to venture into the Zona Norte (other than to catch a bus), is to go to the Museu Nacional. This is Rio's most important museum and it is housed in the 19th-century Boa Vista Palace, the former residence of the Emperors of Brazil. The old palace houses a sizeable if motley collection, the archaeology and ethnology sections being the most interesting — the majority of Brazilian states are represented. The museum is open 10am-4.45pm, daily except Monday. The easiest way to get there is by metro: São Cristóvão station is just across the road. While being an oasis of greenery in this industrial zone, the grounds of the so-called Quinta da Boa Vista are not particularly safe on quiet days during the week.

Not far from the museum, to the southwest, is Estadio Maracanã, the largest stadium in the world with a capacity of 200,000: see *Sport*. It is open for tours, which begin at Gate 18.

Zona Sul

After a stint around the centre, you may need to cool off at the beach. The scene on Rio's beaches is less flash than some people would have you believe, the roar of traffic from the seafront highways being a constant reminder that you are in a big, dirty city. And the locals don't actually swim much because the surf is strong. Foreigners can expect a certain amount of hassle during the day — mostly from people trying to sell them things. The beaches are also notorious for thieves, so leave as much as possible in your hotel.

The Zona Sul is of interest for more than just its beaches, and sights in the area are also described below.

Catete. One of the best museums in Rio is the Museu do Folclore at Rua do Catete 181. It contains a wonderful collection of folk art, including all sorts of crafts, candomblé costumes and some fabulous wooden ex-votos. It opens 11am-6pm Tuesday to Friday, and 3-6pm at weekends. Next door is the large, 19th-century Palácio do Catete which was the official presidential residence when Rio was federal capital. It is now the Museu da República, and you can see the bedroom in which Presidente Vargas committed suicide in 1954. It opens noon-5pm Tuesday to Sunday. Both museums are right next to Catete metro station.

Flamengo and Botafogo. These districts are long past their prime. Parque do Flamengo is a dull, flat landfill which has little to offer except shade, although there is modern art museum at the northern end; and its sport facilities have made it popular among the locals. To the south, in Botafogo, is the Museu do Indio, which is worth a visit if you can't be bothered to trek to the Museu Nacional. The exhibits are well-displayed and there are some excellent photographs. The FUNAI shop is not a bad place to buy presents. The museum is at Rua das Palmerias 55, off Rua São Clemente, six blocks inland from Botafogo metro station. It is open 10am-5pm Monday to Friday, and 1-5pm on Sunday.

Pão de Açúcar (Sugar Loaf). Jutting out into the bay, between Botafogo and Copacabana, is an enormous granite slab known as the Pão de Açúcar. Even though the views from Corcovado are more spectacular, Sugar Loaf offers a different and equally worthwhile perspective of the city.

Cable cars — made famous by James Bond's fight in *Moonraker* — take visitors to the top. There are departures roughly every half hour between 8am and 10pm. Get there as early as possible or, even better, at sunset, in order to avoid the coachloads of tourists. The trip must be done in two stages, involving a change at the first hill, Morro da Urca.

The departure point is in Praça General Tibúrcio, at the end of Avenida Pasteur, in Urca district. To get there take any bus marked Urca (e.g. 107) from Centro, Flamengo or Botafogo.

Copacabana. Beyond Sugar Loaf and at the heart of Brazil's tourist industry, is Copacabana. The district's prestige has been superseded by the residential areas further west, but the beach remains Rio's most famous — its three-mile sweep of sand and wall of high-rise buildings along the waterfront cannot fail to impress.

In addition, the scene at Copacabana is livelier and more fun than that at Ipanema and Leblon.

To reach Copacabana from Flamengo, take any bus from Praia Flamengo. If coming straight from the centre, catch a bus at the intersection of Rio Branco and Vargas or at Praça M. Gandhi; allow about 30 minutes.

Ipanema and Leblon. Life on and off the beach in Ipanema and Leblon is trendier than elsewhere, but also quieter and in many respects less interesting. However, this does have its advantages: the sand is cleaner and there is less crime and general hassle.

Ipanema's main commercial street, two blocks inland, is Visconde de Pirajá. It is lively at the eastern end, particularly around Praça General Osório, which has a pleasantly down-to-earth food market during the week; on Sundays this is replaced by the so-called Hippy Fair, where crafts are sold at inflated prices.

Ipanema and Leblon are separated by a canal which leads from the sea to Lagoa Rodrigo de Freitas. Nearby is the jockey club (see *Entertainment*) and, beyond it, the Jardim Botânico. These lovely gardens (closed Mondays) contain fine palms and plentiful birds, best seen in the early morning. There have been reports of theft, so be careful if there are few people about. You can catch a bus to the botanic garden from Leblon or Copacabana.

Corcovado. This is one of the peaks in the Serra da Carioca. It is topped by the world-famous Cristo Redentor, a 30m-high statue of Christ. The fresh air matches the excellence of the views.

Most people go up Corcovado on the cog railway, although a road also runs to the top. The railway station is on Rua Cosme Velho, in the district of the same name southwest of Flamengo. If you approach from the south, take bus 583 (circular), which goes via Leblon, Avenida Copacabana and Largo do Machado. From the centre take bus 497 or 498. Trains leave every half hour, and take about 20 minutes; services normally run 8am-8pm, but may stop earlier in the low season. Corcovado lies within the Tijuca National Park and there are good views of the forest, as well as of the nearby shanties; sit on the right-hand side on the way up.

ENTERTAINMENT

Nightlife. The best source of information on events in Rio is the *Programa Riotur* that is put out each month by the tourist office. This lists all the major events, from classical concerts and film shows to football matches. The best classical concerts are generally at the Teatro Municipal in Praça Floriano (tel 210-2463), although the Cecília Meireles Concert Hall at Rua da Lapa (tel 232-9714) is another good venue.

The most famous and outrageous nightclubs are in Copacabana. Help (tel 521-1296) is one of the best known discos in Rio. This salacious paradise, midway along Avenida Atlântica at number 3432, attracts everyone from transvestites to the rich and trendy youth from Ipanema. The dance floor is vast and people dress to kill. To experience this and more will cost just $3. The clubs in Ipanema and Leblon are more reputable but less fun. For a more down to earth evening go to Estudantina in Praça Tiradentes.

For a tamer night altogether go to Lord Jim in Ipanema (Rua Paul Redfern 3), an English pub originally set up by an air stewardess. It has passed into other hands now, but retains its hard core of British customers. You can eat cream teas or shepherd's pie and play darts, but sadly not drink English beer. Lord Jim is just in from the beach, a block east of the canal separating Ipanema and Leblon; it has an old red phone box outside.

Carnival. The carnival in Rio is one of the greatest shows on earth. It is also perhaps the world's most hedonistic, sexually ambivalent and exuberant display of music and dance. It takes over many parts of the city, but the hallmark of Rio's carnival is the samba school parade, involving thousands of people. The main event is the spectacular all-night parade of the top schools on the Sunday and Monday at the so-called Sambódromo. This concrete parade ground-cum-stadium was designed by Oscar Niemeyer (of Brasília fame). It consists of a kilometre-long walkway along Rua Marquês de Sapucaí, leading from Avenida Vargas and ending up at Praça da Apoteose. It is bordered by grandstands where the audience sits. Hundreds of seats are reserved for foreign visitors: tickets are available at hotels and travel agents for around $100. If this seems like a lot, the best seats in the house sell for as much as $25,000. General admission costs around $1, but affords no view. Tickets sell out in a frantic shoving match a few hours after they go on sale.

Living through the carnival is a hot, claustrophobic and exhausting business. For a less frenetic glimpse of the carnival frolics go to the rehearsals that take place every weekend for months beforehand. Among the best schools to visit are the Beija-Flor (Rua Pracinha Wallace Paes Leme 1652, Nilópolis) and Portela (Rua Clara Lunes 81, Madureira). The smaller groups usually try out songs, drink and party all night at weekends too. Ask for information at the tourist office, or read banners in the local neighbourhoods.

SPORT

The late England manager Sir Alf Ramsey claimed that he could pick a team capable of winning the World Cup from the barefooted footballers of Copacabana beach. Don't miss a chance to see a match at the Maracanã stadium in the Zona Norte, for the atmosphere as well as for the football. The stadium is a marvellous spectacle, with the painted faces, coloured flares and huge flags. The samba bands, which continuously beat to the rhythm of the football, contrast strongly with the ''ere we go' heard at most British matches. Rio's best known team is Flamengo.

The Jockey Club is in a marvellous spot beneath Corcovado, behind Ipanema in Gavea district (tel 297-6655). It holds meetings every weekend afternoon and every Monday, Wednesday and Thursday evening.

SHOPPING

There are too many distractions in Rio to make it a good place to shop. The busy streets around Largo da Carioca are best for watching other people shop rather than for buying anything yourself. If you prefer a less distracting ambience, head for one of the massive shopping centres, such as the Rio Sul in Botafogo, or for the more peaceful streets of the Zona Sul.

Rio's markets are disappointing. You cannot fail to stumble across the occasional street food market, but they are rarely worth seeking out. Craft fairs, such as the one in Praça 15 de Novembro on Thursday and Fridays and in Praça Osorio (Ipanema) on Sunday, tend to be low-key and over-priced. The best market is the so-called Feira do Nordeste which takes place every Sunday. Crafts are on sale, but the music and Bahian food are the principal attractions. The market is held in Campo de São Cristóvão, which is northwest of the Museu Nacional, in Zona Norte. To get there take any bus marked São Cristóvão, including the 462 from the Zona Sul.

Bookshops. The best bookshop in Rio is the Nova Livraria Leonardo da Vinci at Avenida Rio Branco 185. It is below ground level in a small arcade, and consists of two shops on either side of the passage. It has an excellent range of travel guides, English literature, and much more. There are many bookstalls in Praça Floriano, plus several bookshops and a couple of secondhand bookstalls on Rua Visconde de Pirajá in Ipanema.

CRIME AND SAFETY

Be extremely vigilant. A robbery takes place in Rio every two minutes. However, most serious crime is confined to the slum areas, and the central areas are generally safe during the day. Avoid walking along the beaches at night, even if you are not alone: muggers and pickpockets often work in highly-organized gangs and comb the beaches looking for victims. Tourist spots, such as Corcovado, inevitably attract trouble-makers, and be careful in any of the parks if they are deserted: Quinta da Boa Vista, Parque Flamengo and the Botanic Garden all have something of a reputation. Santa Teresa and Praça 15 de Novembro after dark are also notorious.

HELP AND INFORMATION

Tourist Information: the main tourist information centre is at Rua Assembléia 10 (tel 297-7117), a tall black building on the left just down from Praça 15 de Novembro. The Riotur information office is on the 9th floor and the staff can answer most questions. The maps have often run out, but you can usually pick up brochures; the most useful of these is a booklet of addresses, opening hours, bus routes, etc. The office opens 9am-6pm on weekdays. Other tourist information kiosks are at the Rodoviária, Sugar Loaf, Corcovado and in the Cinelândia and Carioca metro stations.

Also at Rua de Assembléia 10 is Flumitur (8th floor), for information on Rio state, and the Federação Brasileira de Albergues de Juventude (12th floor; tel 221-8753/252-4829) which runs Brazil's youth hostels.

Post Office: the central post office is on Rua 1º de Março, a couple of blocks west of Praça 15 de Novembro. It is open 8am-5pm on weekdays and 8am-noon on Saturdays. Post offices are also in Praça Tiradentes, the train station, and at Avenida Barroso 63 (off the southern end of Rio Branco).

Telephone Office: international calls can be made from offices in both airports, the Rodoviária (24 hours) and the Castelo bus station. Other offices are at Praça Tiradentes and Avenida Copacabana 462, both open 24 hours, and at Rua Visconde de Pirajá 111 in Ipanema.

Money: Avenida Rio Branco is the heart of Rio's money exchange scene, with the the main concentration of banks and casas de câmbio being towards Avenida Vargas. Even here you may have to scout around to find somewhere willing to accept travellers cheques, and at a reasonable rate. Bemge, on Rio Branco near the corner of Rua de Assembléia, offers among the best deal for Amex cheques. Exprinter, opposite, is good for cash. Agencia Candelária, near the corner of Avenidas Vargas and Rio Branco, does cash withdrawals on Visa at the tourist rate.

There are also casas de câmbio in the Zona Sul. Oito Zero at Rua Bolívar 80 in Copacabana (near Rua Barata Ribeiro) exchanges travellers cheques at a decent rate. Cambitur, which has offices all over Rio, has a couple of branches in Copacabana and on Rua Visconde de Pirajá in Ipanema.

American Express has an agent c/o Kontik-Franstur, Avenida Atlântica 2316A, Copacabana (tel 235-1396, 552-7299).

Policia Federal: Avenida Venezuela 2, near Praça Mauá (tel 203-2142), for visa renewal.

Embassies and Consulates. Many are located in Botafogo and Flamengo, and most open from 8.30am/9am until noon/1pm.

Argentina: Praia de Botafogo 228, 2nd floor (tel 551-5148/5498).
Australia: Rua Voluntários da Patria 45, Botafogo (tel 286-7922).
Bolivia: Avenida Rui Barbosa 664, apt 101, Flamengo (tel 551-2395/1795). Avenida Barbosa runs near the seafront between Flamengo and Botafogo.
Canada: Rua Dom Gerardo 46 (tel 233-9286), off northern end of Rio Branco.
Chile: Praia do Flamengo 344, 7th floor (tel 552-5349/5149).
Colombia: Praia do Flamengo 82, apt 202 (tel 225-5361/7582).
Ecuador: Praia de Botafogo 528, room 1601 (tel 541-0396).
Paraguay: Avenida N.S. de Copacabana 427, room 301 (tel 255-7572/7532).
Peru: Avenida Rui Barbosa 314, 2nd floor, Flamengo (tel 551-4496/6296).
Uruguay: Rua Arturo Bernardes 30, Catete (tel 225-0089).
Venezuela: Praia de Botafogo 242, 5th floor (tel 551-5097/5398/5698).
UK: Praia do Flamengo 284, 2nd floor (tel 552-1422; fax 552-5796).
USA: Avenida Presidente Wilson 147 (tel 292-7117), off Avenida Rio Branco, near the corner of Rua Mexico.

RIO DE JANEIRO STATE

The city is huge and sprawling, but Rio de Janeiro state is decidedly small. However, it contains several mountain resorts that are a good antidote to the heat and pollution of Rio. The Costa Verde is the name given to the lush coast west of the city, which has fine beaches with remarkably few tourists. The coast east of Rio, the Costa do Sol, is less dramatic, with the mountains set further back from the shore, and the beaches are more developed.

COSTA VERDE

Ilha Grande. This island boasts some of the best beaches along the Costa Verde, but the presence of a top-security prison keeps a lot of tourists away. Trails criss-cross the jungle-covered island, giving access to most of the beaches. Ilha Grande is large and mountainous, however, so hiking is not always easy; to reach certain areas, you may need to find somebody to guide you. Many people hire a boat, which can be done very cheaply.

Among the best beaches are Lopes Mendes and Parnaioca, both about three hours walk or a short boat ride from Vila Abraão, a lovely old port which is one of the three villages on the island.

Arrival and Departure: Ilha Grande is accessible from Mangaratiba or Angra dos Reis, 60 miles/96km and 125 miles/200km from Rio respectively. Ferries leave daily at 8.30am from Mangaratiba and at 3.30pm on Mondays, Wednesdays and Fridays from Angra dos Reis. Boats dock at Abraão, and take about 90 minutes.

The best beach within walking distance of Parati is Praia do Jabaquara, about 40 minutes north. Further afield is the lovely Praia Trindade, 22 miles/35km south of Parati; to get there take the bus bound for Laranjeiras and ask to be dropped off. Another fine beach is 17 miles/27km south of Laranjeiras at Parati Mirim, served by two daily buses.

COSTA DO SOL

Arraial do Cabo. This small town lies on a corner of land near the Lagoa de Araruama. It gives access to some stunning beaches, and is far less affected by tourism than Cabo Frio and Búzios further north. The lovely Praia Grande, which stretches for miles westwards, is within walking distance, and has a campsite. Less easily accessible but more beautiful is Praia do Forno, which can be reached only by boat.

Arraial is served by direct buses from Rio ($5 with Util), which take about three hours. There are also frequent services from Cabo Frio, 12 miles/20km north, a popular but rather unattractive resort.

Búzios. If you enjoy lively seaside resorts, Búzios, 15 miles/24km east of Cabo Frio, is ideal. The sandy beaches have made it a popular playground among the rich, with the result that it is crowded, expensive and chic. But Búzios is worth a visit, if only on a day trip from Arraial: it is a charming colonial town, the setting among green hills and rocky promontories is splendid, and virtually all the nearby beaches are magnificent and accessible on foot from town. One of the finest is Praia Azeda, just a mile north.

You'll be lucky to get much change from $20 when paying for a room, but the Pousada do Arco-Iris at Rua Toríbio de Farias 182 (tel 23-1256) is reasonable. There are several campsites, including at Manguinhos beach. Buses to Búzios run hourly along the rough road from Cabo Frio; services from Rio are surprisingly infrequent.

PETROPOLIS

The city of Petrópolis (population 280,000) sits high in the mountains 40 miles/64km north of Rio. It was founded in the 1840s by Emperor Dom Pedro II, who earmarked it as a summer retreat for the royals. The town boasts some fine architecture, though the journey is perhaps more memorable: the road is breathtaking (literally), as it winds up hillsides, through forest and along the edge of sheer cliffs.

Petrópolis' main attraction is the former royal palace, just north of Rua do Imperador, the main street. It now houses the Museu Imperial whose most famous exhibit is the emperor's crown with its 639 diamonds. The museum is open noon-5.30pm, daily except Monday. A short distance further north is the gothic Catedral São Pedro, where both emperors and their wives are buried. Avenida Koeller, which runs west from here, is a handsome boulevard lined with aristocrats' mansions. It ends at Praça Rui Barbosa, beyond which, at Avenida Br. do Amazonas 98, is the tourist office.

Buses leave from the Menezes Cortes/Castelo terminal in central Rio, every 20-30 minutes throughout the day. There are also buses from Belo Horizonte, Cabo Frio and São Paulo. The journey from Rio takes 90 minutes, making a day trip perfectly feasible; in high season buy a ticket back on arrival. Hotels are generally expensive, although the Dom Pedro (tel 43-7170) in the main square, is good value. A cheaper option is the Hotel Comércio opposite the Rodoviária.

TERESOPOLIS

The town itself — a small, modern version of its neighbour — has little going for it. The appeal of Teresópolis lies in its location near the Serra dos Orgãos. This magnificent mountain range, much of which lies within a national park, has become the centre of the trekking and rock climbing scene in Brazil. The chief lure for mountain climbers is the Dedo de Deus (the Finger of God), which is shaped like a closed hand with the index finger pointing skywards. While this is not a peak to be tackled by the uninitiated, most people can climb Pedra do Silo (7,410ft/2,260m), which takes three or four hours. To tackle most other peaks, which have no clear paths to the top, you should hire a guide. Some of the best and easiest views of the Serra are from the Colino dos Mirantes, a steep 30-minute climb above town; approach it from Rua Feliciano Sodré.

If you prefer more leg-friendly terrain, there are plenty of trails through the jungle, and several rivers and waterfalls to swim in: the dos Amores, Fischer and do Imbuí falls are all just a mile or so from town. Maps of the trails are usually available at the Cupelo Banco de Jornais near the Igreja Matriz; for general information go to the tourist office in the Terminal Turístico on Avenida Rotoriana.

Arrival and Departure. The journey from Petrópolis is stunning. Buses run every couple of hours 9am-9pm, and take about 90 minutes; ask for a right-hand seat. There are more frequent services from Rio's Castelo Terminal, but the journey is less spectacular. The trip from Rio takes 100 minutes.

Accommodation. Teresópolis is built along one main street, which assumes a different name every few blocks. The cheap hotels are concentrated around Igreja Matriz, in Praça Baltazar da Silveira. Among these is the best deal in town, the excellent Varzea Palace Hotel, at Rua Sebastião Teixeira 41 (tel 742-0878). There are two campsites inside the park, and the IBDF has hostels where you can rent a bed for a small fee.

ITATIAIA NATIONAL PARK

The Itatiaia National Park lies in the rugged mountains of the Serra do Mantiqueira, close to the borders of São Paulo and Minas Gerais states some 105 miles/168km west of Rio. It consists of alpine meadows and rainforest, criss-crossed by rivers and dotted with lakes and waterfalls. It is also rich in wildlife and while the larger mammals (including monkeys and sloth) are elusive, the birdlife is more easily spotted.

The park provides excellent trekking country, and there is even scope for climbers: the highest mountain is Agulhas Negras (9,170ft/2795m). There are plenty of trails, several of which begin near Hotel Simon. The office at the park entrance has maps, and it can give general advice about possible routes. The best falls are the Moromba and Véu de Noiva.

Even if you are not keen on strenuous hiking, the towns of Itatiaia and nearby Penedo, are good places from which to enjoy the magnificent scenery.

Arrival and Departure. The park is accessible by bus from the town of Itatiaia, which lies just south of the BR-116. To get to Itatiaia, take a bus from Rio to Resende (these run all day and take three hours), from where buses run every 30 minutes between 6am and 11pm. Resende is also accessible from São Paulo.

Accommodation. There are several hotels both inside and outside the park, but these are fairly expensive. The cheapest are the Fazenda do Serra (tel 52-1611) and the Fazenda Saiva (tel 52-1570). In peak season you should book in advance. Alternatively camp, or stay in the Abroucas lodge at the base of Agulhas Negras, which is an eight or nine hour hike from the entrance. You should reserve a bed at the park administration office in Itatiaia. Otherwise stay in the town, or in Penedo, which is another jumping-off point for the park and is even more popular than Itatiaia among weekenders. It has plenty of hotels and is also accessible from Resende.

ESPIRITO SANTO and MINAS GERAIS

The small state of Espírito Santo, north of Rio de Janeiro, is largely untouched by tourism. The beaches are popular among holidaymakers from Minas Gerais, but they are disappointing by Brazilian standards. The main area of interest lies inland, where you find breathtaking scenery of forested mountains and a number of delightful towns that were settled by European immigrants during the 19th century. Heading north from Rio to Vitória, the capital, and then west to Belo Horizonte, is an excellent route into Minas Gerais.

VITORIA

The capital of Espírito Santo (population 280,000) lies on an island connected by several bridges to the mainland. The setting is magnificent, but unfortunately it's downhill from there: Vitória has remarkably little to boast about. Praça Costa Pereira is the main focus of the city, and the most interesting architectural relic is the 16th-century Palácio Anchieta, the governor's palace, in Praça João Climaco. What remains of the old city, Vila Velha, is on the mainland several miles south of the centre. The highlight — above all for the marvellous views — is the hilltop Convento da Penha. Buses to Vila Velha leave from Avenida Monteiro, one of the city's main commercial streets.

There are good bus services from Rio and Belo Horizonte, which are both about 325 miles/520km and eight hours from Vitória. There are also services along the coast from Bahia.

Vitória has a dearth of cheap accommodation, apart from the places around the bus station. There are a few middle range hotels in the centre, including the Cannes Palace at Avenida Monteiro 111 (tel 222-1522), but most hotels are in the beach areas, particularly on Praia Camburi, about 15 minutes north, or Praia da Costa near Vila Velha.

Around Vitória

Domingos Martins. Also known as Campinho, this small town lies up in the mountains 29 miles/46km west of Vitória. Many of its inhabitants are descendants of the original German settlers, and their influence is obvious in the array of bizarre chalet-style houses. The one-hour journey from Vitória is lovely, and once in town there are fabulous views. There is scope for exploring the surrounding hills, and you can stay in the wonderful Hotel Imperador in the main square.

Santa Teresa and São Leopoldina. The town of Santa Teresa is situated in a landscape of mountains, forest and farmland 44 miles/70km northwest of Vitória. It was settled by Italians in 1875, and is a most charming place. Don't miss the Museu de Biologia Mello Leitão, which is a museum-cum-zoo featuring the fauna and flora of the area; it is on Avenida Ruschi, and opens at weekends only. There are a couple of hotels.

The ride to Santa Teresa from Vitória takes two hours. To make a round trip back to the capital take the bus south through more lovely scenery to São Leopoldina. This village was settled by Swiss immigrants, and the Museu da Colônia gives a good insight into its history.

CAPARAO NATIONAL PARK

This huge park spans the border with Minas Gerais, and can be approached with equal ease from Vitória or Belo Horizonte. It contains several peaks, including Pico da Bandeira (9,840ft/3,000m), which is the tallest in southern Brazil. The most beautiful part of the park to explore is the lower area of thick rainforest, where there is a network of trails; these are marked on a map available from the park entrance. If you want to climb Pico da Bandeira you need camping equipment since you must spend at least one night up the mountain; however, the ascent is not difficult.

The park lies near Manhumirim, south of the Vitória-Belo Horizonte road and 30 miles/48km from Manhuaçu in Minas Gerais state. There is a direct bus daily to Manhumirim from Belo Horizonte (5 hours), but if you approach from Vitória you will probably have to change at Manhuaçu. There are a few simple hotels in Manhumirim if you arrive too late to continue immediately. From Manhumirim there is an irregular bus service to Alto do Caparaó, the village near the park. Here you can either rent a room from the locals or pay $30 for a room at the Caparão Parque Hotel, a mile from the park entrance and 15 minutes walk from the town. Campers should contact IBAMA in Belo Horizonte first (Avenida Contorno 8121; tel 275-4266).

MINAS GERAIS

The mountainous state of Minas Gerais is roughly the size of France and is one of the most beautiful parts of Brazil. Virtually every bus journey is a joy, particularly for anyone who's been travelling among the unremittingly flat landscapes that take up so much of the country. In the north the hills give way to the remote and sparsely-populated sertão and the planalto.

Minas Gerais is most famous for the towns which were built during the gold and diamond booms of the 18th century. These so-called *cidades históricas*, with their luxurious mansions and lavishly decorated churches, give a unique insight into life during the colonial period. They are a world away from the realities of modern Brazil and some are in danger of becoming living museum pieces. Nevertheless, the artistry and state of preservation is remarkable. Aleijandinho, Brazil's greatest sculptor and architect (1738-1814), has left works of art in all the main towns.

The climate in Minas Gerais is wet and warm from October to February, dry and cool March to September. Grey skies often hang over the region. Getting around during the rains is not usually a problem since all the main roads are paved; however, in 1992 a month of heavy downpours paralysed traffic in some areas and left 30,00 people homeless; some of Ouro Prêto's churches had to be shored up to keep them from collapsing.

Belo Horizonte

Belo Horizonte is probably best known in the West as the venue for the most extraordinary football result in the history of world soccer. In the 1950 World Cup, the USA (the outsiders) beat England (the favourites) by a goal to nil, and knocked them out of the tournament. This rather characterless city had never seen such excitement, and perhaps never will again.

The gateway to the historic towns of Minas Gerais is a modern, urban sprawl. It was founded as state capital only at the end of last century, but has managed to become the country's third largest city, with a population of well over two million. Few travellers hang around in Belo Horizonte longer than they have to, but the city makes a good base from which to explore the state. Despite its size, the city is an easy place to get around.

CITY LAYOUT

Belo Horizonte was modelled on Washington DC and the heart of the city retains

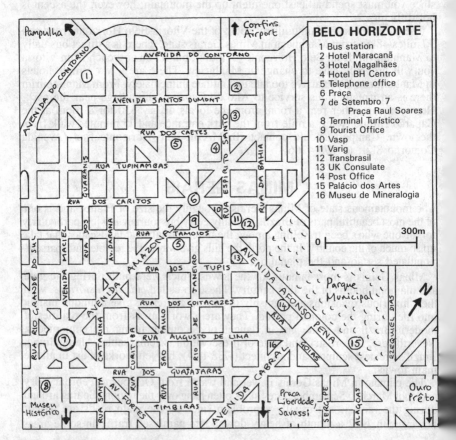

BELO HORIZONTE

1 Bus station
2 Hotel Maracanã
3 Hotel Magalhães
4 Hotel BH Centro
5 Telephone office
6 Praça
7 de Setembro 7
      Praça Raul Soares
8 Terminal Turístico
9 Tourist Office
10 Vasp
11 Varig
12 Transbrasil
13 UK Consulate
14 Post Office
15 Palácio dos Artes
16 Museu de Mineralogia

0   300m

the original design. The centre is enclosed by a ring road, Avenida do Contorno, within which the streets form a regular geometrical pattern: superimposed over the standard grid pattern is another, larger system, running diagonally to the first. While it is difficult to get lost, it is surprisingly easy to lose your bearings, particularly at junctions where perpendicular and diagonal streets meet; the situation is compounded by the fact that most streets in the centre look the same. Since blocks are fairly short, a visitor's life in Belo Horizonte seems to be spent crossing roads.

The main artery, running northwest-southeast through the city, is Avenida Afonso Pena. Praça 7 de Setembro, where this street crosses Avenida Amazonas, is the heart of the city. However, it is not a square in the traditional sense: it's a meeting-place for traffic rather than for people. The atmosphere is hurried and this is not a place to sit and watch the world go by. Nevertheless, there are many hotels, bars, etc. in the vicinity, and most banks and airlines have their main offices nearby.

Maps. A booklet about Belo Horizonte, which contains a map with most landmarks, can be picked up free at the tourist office and at many hotels. The tourist office also gives out a larger map, and the so-called *Mapa Atualizado de Belo Horizonte* is available from some news stands for $3.50. This sheet map tends to cause confusion rather than be of any positive use, but it's useful if you want to explore the area outside the Avenida do Contorno, or require a street-index.

ARRIVAL AND DEPARTURE

Air. Belo Horizonte is well served by domestic flights, with many daily services from Brasília, Rio and São Paulo. Most flights arrive at the international Tancredo Neves airport (tel 689-2700/2274), about 25 miles/40km north of the city. There is a tourist desk and the Banco do Brasil changes cash and cheques, though not at an astoundingly good rate.

Buses run to the Rodoviária every hour or so from 6am to 10.30pm, with an additional departure at 12.30am. These leave from across the car park from the terminal; buy your ticket ($1) at the kiosk. Another company runs executive buses to the Terminal Turístico, a white elephant designed to house a variety of travel agencies, shops and restaurants, but in reality little more than an oversized bus stop. It is near Praça Raul Soares, some way from the cheap hotel area — the regular bus service is both cheaper and more convenient. The first bus from the Rodoviária to the airport leaves at 4.45am (Platform F), and from the Terminal Turístico at 5.15am; the last services leave at 10.30pm and 9.45pm respectively.

Both the above bus services stop at Pampulha airport (tel 441-2000/2857), which is just 5 miles/8km north of the centre. This airport handles flights from smaller centres, including Vitória and Porto Seguro, and the shuttle service from Rio and São Paulo.

The addresses of the main Brazilian airline offices are as follows: Transbrasil, Rua Tamoios 86 (tel 226-3433); Varig, Rua Espírito Santo 643 (tel 273-6566); and Vasp, Rua dos Carijós 279 (tel 226-3282/335-9888).

Bus. The Rodoviária (tel 201-8111/8618/8830) is by Praça Rio Branco northwest of the centre, just inside the ring road. It is only a few blocks and an easy walk from Praça 7 de Setembro and the main hotel area.

Bus departures to the main long-distance destinations are as follows:

Brasília - 12 hours; several overnight buses with Itapemirim and Penha, each with one leito.

Rio — 7 hours; hourly buses 8am-midnight with Util and Cometa.
Salvador — 20 hours; two evening departures with Gontijo and São Geraldo.
Otherwise change at Vitória (8 hours), served by frequent buses.
São Paulo — 10 hours; every hour (morning and evening only) with Impala and Cometa.

Train. At the time of going to press the inter-state train service to Rio had been suspended. For the latest information go the station at Praça Rui Barbosa, a few blocks east of the Rodoviária, or call 273-5033/222-3255.

GETTING AROUND

Belo Horizonte's metro serves the suburbs rather than the centre. However, there is also a well-organized bus system. Yellow buses follow circular routes, and blue buses run up and down diagonal roads (give or take deviations to allow for the fact that most streets are one-way). Red buses serve only the centre, and are express. Destinations are written clearly on the front of buses, but note that only the numbers are written at bus stops. Most buses that you'll need to use can be caught from the streets around Praça 7 de Setembro. The tourist office booklet gives information on bus routes; note that stops are described either as *lado par* or *lado impar*, according to whether the stop is on the even- or odd-numbered side of the road.

Taxis are plentiful and cheap. To order one by phone, call 227-4646.

ACCOMMODATION

Belo Horizonte's cheapest hotels are concentrated in a fairly small area within easy reach of the Rodoviária and Praça 7 de Setembro. There are plenty to choose from, though they fill quickly.

Many hotels are collected around the junction of Avenida Santos Dumont and Rua Espírito Santo. The Hotel Maracanã (Rua Espírito Santo 127; tel 224-1160) is a clean, friendly place with rooms for \$8-10/\$13-15. South across the junction is the popular Magalhães at Espírito Santo 237 (tel 222-9233); rates are similar to those at the Maracanã. More comfortable but excellent value is the large and airy BH Centro, near the corner of Caetés (Rua Espírito Santo 284; tel 222-3390). Its cheapest rooms go for \$11/\$14, while the more standard suite-style rooms cost \$26.

There is a Youth Hostel — Albergue Pousadinha Mineira — at Rua Januária 206 (tel 446-2911), the continuation of Rua da Bahia just north of the ringroad in Floresta district. It's popular, so try to ring in advance.

EATING AND DRINKING

The streets around Praça 7 de Setembro are full of bars, lanchonetes and cake shops, and this area is positively seething with people in the evening; Rua dos Carijós is mostly pedestrian and is particularly busy. There are a couple of good and simple places on Rua Espírito Santo, including the Mineirinho, between Caetés and Tupinambás. The huge lanchonete on the corner of Praça 7 de Setembro is reminiscent of a school dining room, but it's a lively place for an early evening drink, and meals are cheap. For a more classy evening go to the restaurant in Hotel BH Centro. For traditional miniera food eat at Tavares (Rua Santa Catarina; tel 212-6435); you must pay around \$6, but the helpings are huge. Tavares is very popular at weekends, but is closed on Sunday evenings.

Out of the centre, the main area for eating out is the smart residential district of Savassi, where you'll find many mostly upmarket restaurants. One of the best regional places is D. Lucinha (Rua Padre Odorico 38; tel 227-0562), just south of Praça Savassi. If you are counting your pennies, this is an area to have a few beers rather than a meal; possibly followed by a trip to the excellent arts cinema, the Cine Clube, which is at Rua Levindo Lopes 358 (tel 227-6648). To get to Savassi take bus 1001 along Afonso Pena.

EXPLORING

One of the best things to do in Belo Horizonte is to visit the Museu Histórico Abílio Barreto (Rua B. Mascarenhas, Cidade Jardim). The museum is an oasis of history in an otherwise modern city: it is housed in a 19th-century *fazenda* (ranch house), which is one of the few buildings to have survived from the pre-1897 settlement of Curral del Rey. There is a wide range of exhibits, but most fascinating are the photographs illustrating the construction of Belo Horizonte. There are also some understandably nostalgic paintings of the original village. The museum opens 10am-5pm, daily except Tuesdays. To get there take bus 2902 or 8902 from Avenida Amazonas, between Tupinambás and Afonso Pena (lado par). Get off on Rua Conde Linhares, the first stop beyond the ringroad; the museum is a block east of here.

If you want to compare the early photographs with the modern reality, go to Praça da Liberdade. This huge square has one of Brazil's most elegant avenues of palm trees, and some of the city's main public buildings. It is also the site of Belo Horizonte's principal weekly markets. Most important are the craft fairs held on Thursday evening and Sunday morning; there is usually good food to eat and a variety of street entertainment. Regional food is also on sale at the Saturday morning antique market. To get to Praça da Liberdade take bus 1001 (marked Grajaú) from Afonso Pena.

To escape from the downtown traffic go to the Parque Municipal, the large park a few blocks southeast of Praça 7 de Setembro. In its grounds, at Afonso Pena 1537, is the Palácio dos Artes, which has a full programme of concerts, films, exhibitions, etc. On the ground floor is a shop selling good-quality crafts. The centre is open 9am-9pm on weekdays, 9am-1pm on Saturday. If you have more than a passing interest in minerals, while you're in this area you should visit the Museu de Mineralogia south of the park, at Rua da Bahia 1149. It is housed in an extraordinary Gothic building, but those who have already visited the mineral museum in Ouro Prêto will be sorely disappointed by the contents.

Anyone seriously keen on modern Brazilian architecture, should catch a bus to Pampulha, a chic lakeside suburb a few miles northwest of the centre. This district was, like Brasília, the result of a collaboration between Oscar Niemeyer and Burle Marx. Niemeyer's achievements include the staggering 1940s church of São Francisco, the Museu de Arte (an old casino) and the Casa do Baile (now a restaurant). To get to Pampulha take bus 2004 from Afonso Pena, between Amazonas and Tapinambás (lado impar). Once at the lake, catch buses along the shores to reach the various buildngs; otherwise you must be prepared to do a fair amount of legwork.

HELP AND INFORMATION

Tourist Information: for a city without many attractions — probably for that very reason — Belo Horizonte has an impressive tourist information service. The most central Belotur kiosk is in Praça 7 de Setembro, at the top of Rua Rio de Janeiro (tel 212-1400). It opens 8am-8pm Monday to Friday, 8am-4pm on Saturday and

8am-noon on Sunday. The staff are helpful and you can pick up maps and a booklet (in English and Portuguese) packed full of information.

Communications: there is a 24-hour phone office at Rua Tamóios 311 (near Rio de Janeiro), and a smaller office at Rua Caetés 481. The main post office is at Afonso Pena 1270, opposite the Parque Municipal. It opens 8am-6pm Monday to Friday, 8am-noon on Saturday. To send parcels, go around the back to the office on Rua Goias.

Money: there are no casas de câmbio, but plenty of banks around Praça 7 de Setembro change money, including Banco Econômico on Rua Espírito Santo.

Polícia Federal: Rua Nascimento Gurgel 30, Gutierrez (tel 337-9133, ext 144), southwest of the centre. It is about ten blocks beyond the ring road, off Cônego Rocha Franco.

Consulates. *Chile:* Rua Gonçalves Dias 82, Funcionários (tel 221-7230).
UK (Vice-Consulate): Edficio Guimarães, Avenida Afonso Pena 952, Room 500, 5th floor (tel 222-6318), between Tamóios and Tupis.
USA: Avenida Cristóvão Colombo 400, Savassi (tel 224-9339).

OURO PRETO

The state's most famous historic gold-mining town lies in the Serra do Espinhaço, about 60 miles/96km southeast of Belo Horizonte. Once one of the richest cities in the world, its sumptuous mansions and churches survive almost intact as lasting evidence of the staggering wealth enjoyed by the elite during the 18th century. As you stagger up and down the narrow cobbled streets it is difficult not to feel caught up in some kind of time warp. Ouro Prêto would be a museum town par excellence if it weren't for the fact that it has a thriving university whose students fill the bars and lend a lively edge. Furthermore, the bizarre sight of stunning colonial buildings converted into shops overflowing with televisions and hi-fis, helps you keep a grip on reality.

Ouro Prêto is, inevitably, one of Brazil's principal tourist attractions. Do not be put off. The town has to be seen to be believed, and while tourists flood in during the high season and at weekends, you can enjoy relative peace at other times. If the crowds get too much, simply head out to the less visited towns, or seek solace in some of Ouro Prêto's own quieter streets.

The town is famous for its Carnival and Easter celebrations. Even without these added attractions, you should allow at least a couple of days to explore — not least because the streets are steep, even precipitous, and cannot be tackled at speed.

Arrival and Departure. Pássaro Verde runs eleven buses daily from Belo Horizonte, leaving between 6.45am and 8.15pm, and taking about two hours. During the high season and at weekends you are advised to book your seat in advance. There are also buses direct to Rio (9 hours), São Paulo (11 hours) and Vitória (5-6 hours).

The Rodoviária (tel 551-1081) is about ten minutes walk northwest of Praça Tiradentes, the main square. Before heading into town, have a look at the nearby church of São Francisco de Paula; there are excellent views of the town from the steps in front of it.

Accommodation. Ouro Prêto is bursting with hotels, most of which are housed in stunning old buildings and of a high standard. The cheapest deal in town is offered by Pensão Vermelha, in Largo São Francisco, which has dormitory beds for $3.50 per person; it is often full. Down the hill behind Igreja das Mercês is Pousada Ouro Prêto (Largo Musicista José dos Anjos Costa 72; tel 551-3081), a small, homely place with hard beds but lovely views. Rooms cost $7-10. There are a couple of good places west of the main square. The most centrally located, and within easy reach of the main concentration of restaurants and bars, is Pousada Marília de Dirceu at Rua Conde de Bobadela 179). The owners are extremely friendly, and charge $5 for rooms with shared bath. Further out, and involving a hard climb to return to the centre, is Hotel Villa dos Pilares. Housed in a delightful building in Praça Monsenhor Castilho Barbosa, it has good, simple rooms for $10 per person.

If you prefer to be out of the centre, stay at the Pousada Panorama Barroco, a lovely colonial house at Rua Conselheiro Quintiliano 722 (tel 551-3366). It is popular among travellers, and offers the best views in town, a bar, videos, a noticeboard, art gallery, etc. To get there from the bus station or from town, take the bus bound for Mariana.

Of the middle-range hotels in the centre, the best is the Toffolo (Rua São José 76; tel 551-1322). This large, rambling mansion is well-placed and offers fantastic views from the upper floors. Rooms costs $20-30.

The cheapest option is to stay in a student residence, known as a *república*, where visitors are put up for a small fee, usually $3-4. Many close in January and February, but check in the tourist office, which has a full list. The Camping Clube do Brasil has a site about a mile north of the city.

Eating and Drinking. There are numerous restaurants, bars and cafés, particularly along Ruas Conde de Bobadela and São José, west of the main square. One of the cheapest places, that is particularly popular among the locals, is the Pelique (Rua São José 131). The Taverno do Chafariz, nearby at number 167, is good but fairly expensive. Nearby is the trendy Café & Cia, a pleasant place for a break during the day. Much livelier is Bar Alpes, on Bobadela, which is popular among the students, and clearly *the* place to be in the evenings. For snacks go to the Recanto Pão do Queijo, an excellent bakery in Praça Tiradentes.

Exploring. It is difficult to follow a fixed route in a town with so many nooks and crannies, but there are certain churches and museums which should not be missed. Many places close at lunchtime and most charge admission ($0.50-70), so make sure you have a pocketful of change.

Praça Tiradentes is the heart of Ouro Prêto. On the south side is the beautiful Paço Municipal, which now houses the Museu de Inconfidência, named after Brazil's first rebellion against the Portuguese. The 1789 uprising failed and Tiradentes, the dentist who led the revolt, was hung for his efforts. As well as the tomb of Tiradentes and mementoes from the abortive Inconfidência, the museum contains works by Aleijandinho and his collaborator, the painter Manoel Athaíde. Downstairs you can see some of the most beautiful colonial furniture in Brazil. The museum is open noon-5.30pm daily except Monday. Next door is the Igreja do Carmo, whose façade and parts of the interior are the work of Aleijandinho.

Back in Praça Tiradentes, facing the museum, is the old Governor's Palace and present School of Mining or Escola de Minas. This is a fine structure which provides a good vantage point for views over the square. Attached to the school (the entrance is on the left side) is the Museu da Mineralogia. Entering the dark, vault-like room in which the collection is housed is like stepping into another world:

you will see minerals and gems you've never heard of and colours you've not even dreamed of. The museum is open daily noon-5pm.

The church of São Francisco de Assis (1764-1810), a short walk south of Praça Tiradentes, is one of the most important colonial buildings in Brazil. All its exterior carving and much of the interior is by Aleijandinho, and the trompe l'oeil ceilings are by Manoel Athaíde. Notice too, the wonderful paintings in the sacristy. Down the hill, in the church of Conceição is the tomb of Aleijandinho (on the right), and a fascinating museum dedicated to the sculptor. It is open 8-11.45am and 1.30-5pm daily except Monday.

One of the oldest and finest churches in the town is the Igreja do Pilar. Built in the early 18th century, it is a lavish baroque creation, rich in gold and silver. To reach the church from the main square walk down the lovely Rua Brigadiero Mosqueira and the steep Rua do Pilar. Afterwards, heading northwards brings you to Rua São José, a lovely but slightly quaint street. The most important building is the Casa dos Contos, the old treasury: the architecture is more interesting than the museum.

For some of the best views over Ouro Prêto walk up Rua Conselheiro Quintiliano, which heads east towards Mariana. Another good vantage point, giving a different perspective, is the church of Santa Efigênia dos Pretos, east of the centre. This is a lovely church, built by and for slaves. It lacks the gold that adorns other churches in the town, and what gold there is was washed out of slaves' hair or smuggled in under finger nails. The paintings by Athaíde are among the finest in Ouro Prêto.

For a break from colonial architecture, go for a hike up Pico do Itacolomi (5,750ft/1753m), which overlooks the town from the south; it takes three or four hours from the main square.

Help and Information. The tourist office is on the east side of Praça Tiradentes (tel 551-2655/1544), open 8am-6pm. You can pick up a map, list of opening hours, etc. The office is run by the Associação de Guias de Turismo, which can organize guided tours to nearby waterfalls.

The post office is at the bottom of Rua Conde de Bobadela, and the phone office is on Rua Senador Rocha Lagoa, which runs parallel. The Banco do Brasil (Rua São José 195) changes money at a bad rate.

Around Ouro Prêto
Minas de Passagem. This huge mine lies just a few miles east of Ouro Prêto. The mine hasn't functioned since 1986 and it remains open only for tourism. Just a small part can be visited, and the galleries have been cleaned up to such an extent that it is hard to imagine the appalling conditions under which miners used to work. The highlight is probably the ride down in an ancient British-made steam-powered cable car. A tour, usually with an ex-miner for a guide, lasts an hour and costs $6. The mine is open 9am-6pm, daily. To get there, take any Ouro Prêto-Mariana bus and ask to be dropped at the turn-off, which is barely 100 yards from the mine. It is an easy stop en route to Mariana.

Mariana. Given its proximity (just 7 miles/12km) to Ouro Prêto and its own collection of fine 18th-century architecture, Mariana is remarkably unspoilt. The town is only small, but it's worth calling in at the tourist office on Praça Tancredo Neves to get a map. By heading along the lovely Rua Direita and doing a big circle, you will take in the main sights. These include Praça Claudio Manoel, overlooked by the cathedral; the Museu Arquidiocesano (Rua Frei Durão), which contains some fine examples of Aleijandinho's work; and, up the hill, Praça João Pinheiro. This is the town's most handsome square, with its unusually elaborate *pelourinho* (whipping post), the old prison (now the Prefeitura Municipal), and two churches. Athaíde was responsible for the painting in the sacristy of São Francisco de Assis, and is also buried in the church: his tomb is number 94, on the right of the entrance. Up the hill is the Basílica de São Pedro: it's worth the hike for the views rather than the church. At the other end of town, along Rua Antônio Olinto and below the tiny Santo Antônio chapel, you can see *garimpeiros* panning for gold in the river.

There is a steady stream of buses to Mariana from Ouro Prêto, which take about 30 minutes. The most convenient bus stop is to the right of the Escola de Minas. If you want to stay over try Hotel Faisca on Rua Antônio Olinto (tel 557-1765), which charges $5 per person for its cheapest rooms.

CONGONHAS

The predominantly modern town of Congonhas, which lies 50 miles/80km south of Belo Horizonte, is rather surprising as the site of Aleijandinho's most famous piece of work. The Bom Jesus do Matozinho church is the centre of attraction, not because of the building itself, but because of the sculptures outside. Namely, the statues of the twelve apostles, carved in soapstone on the parapet; and the life-size figures beautifully carved in wood by Aleijandinho and his pupils, and painted by Athaíde. The latter represent figures from the Passion and are contained in chapels in the gardens that stretch down the hill from the church.

It is perfectly feasible to visit Congonhas on a day trip from Belo Horizonte, but many people stop off on their way to São João del Rei. Viação Sandra has six buses a day from Belo Horizonte, which take $1\frac{1}{2}$ hours. There are also hourly buses direct from São João del Rei. Access from Ouro Prêto is more complicated. Buses heading southwards along the BR-040 may drop you at Murtinho, the turn-off for Congonhas, but this is not always possible. Otherwise, take a Cristo Rei bus to Conselheiro Lafaite (there are four or five daily), a lovely $2\frac{1}{2}$ hour journey along largely unpaved roads through fascinating rural scenes, and catch a bus to Congonhas from there; this involves doubling back, but getting off earlier and hailing buses on the highway is not always successful. Cristo Rei buses sometimes take the BR-040 rather than the back route, in which case get off at Murtinho. From here there is local transport covering the couple of miles into Congonhas. Get off at the rodoviária, from where there are buses up the hill to the Basilica; there is a tourist desk in the station.

Accommodation is limited, but the Hotel Cova do Daniel (tel 731-1834) and the Colonial, near the church, are both fairly good.

SAO JOAO DEL REI

The town of São João del Rei, 125 miles/200km south of Belo Horizonte, is in some ways the most interesting of the historic towns. As well as having a rich colonial heritage it is also a busy commercial centre with a population of around 80,000. São João del Rei attracts fewer tourists than Ouro Prêto and its colonial heart, which boasts some remarkably grand buildings, has remained largely unspoilt. Furthermore, the spaciousness and the flat terrain are a welcome change.

São João del Rei was the birthplace of the 19th-century rebel, Tiradentes. The efforts of him and his colleagues are celebrated during the Semana da Inconfidência, in the third week of April.

Arrival and Departure. Viação Sandra buses leave Belo Horizonte for São João del Rei every couple of hours from 6.15am to 7pm; the fare is $5. Note that buses may go either via Barbacena or Lagoa Dourada, the latter being the shorter route, taking about 3½ hours. Transur runs three daily buses from Rio ($8) which take about five hours; some stop in Petrópolis.

Anyone trying to get to São João del Rei from Ouro Prêto will be told that it is easier to go back to Belo Horizonte. This isn't necessary, since you can take the bus to Conselheiro Lafaiete (see *Congonhas*), from where buses leave regularly for São João until around 6.30pm; you could also get off at the Lagoa Dourada turn-off, north of Lafaiete, and pick up a passing bus from there; this is common practice.

The bus station is a mile west of the centre, and most passing buses are heading downtown. These usually run along Avenida Tancredo Neves and stop at the Terminal Turístico, within easy reach of most hotels. To get to the terminal from town catch a bus from the stop near the train station.

SAO JOAO DEL REI

1 Railway Station
2 Hotel Brasil
3 Panificação Globo
4 Terminal Turístico
5 Praça Carlos Gomes
6 Igreja do Carmo
7 Catedral do Pilar
8 Museu do Arte Sacra
9 Solar dos Neves
10 Igreja do Rosário
11 Museu Regional
12 Hotel Colonial
13 Igreja de São Francisco
14 Hotel Porto Real
15 Prefeitura
16 Post Office
17 Teatro Municipal
18 Banco do Brasil

0   400m

¼ mile

Accommodation. Most of the cheaper hotels are north of the so-called Córrego do Lenheiro, the small canal running through the centre. The best value in town are the rooms at the Hotel Brasil, at Avenida Tancredo Neves 395 (tel 371-2804). It is housed in a fine old building opposite the train station. Rooms cost a remarkable $3-5 (without breakfast), though anyone who dislikes a hard bed should probably head elsewhere. Further west is the Hotel Colonial (Rua Manoel Anselmo 22; tel 371-1792), which charges $5 per person. For a slightly cheaper and much more basic room try the places on Rua Marechal Deodoro, near the Terminal Turístico.

Eating and Drinking. The best place in town is the Quinto do Ouro in Praça Rezende, next to the Regional Museum. For a more down-to-earth ambience head for Rua Artur Bernardes, where there are a couple of restaurants: the Rex, on the corner of Tancredo Neves, has an average menu of regional food. For breakfast go to Panificação Globo, a couple of blocks west of Hotel Brasil.

Exploring. The Córrego do Lenheiro is a pitiful example of a waterway, and yet the stone bridges that cross it, and the trees and handsome buildings scattered along either side, lend it a remarkable elegance. The largest colonial area lies to the north. West of the Terminal Turístico, and beyond the lovely Igreja do Carmo, is the Catedral do Pilar (1721). This is one of the oldest churches in São João del Rei, and contains lavish gold decoration and beautiful Portuguese azulejos. Behind it are three adjoining squares overlooked by the church of Mercês; it's worth climbing the steps for the view, although the modern block across the river is something of an eyesore.

Continuing west along Getúlio Vargas brings you to Largo do Rosário, with a number of fine buildings. Dominating the square is the church of Rosário, but more famous is the so-called Solar dos Neves, on its right. This was the birthplace of Tancredo Neves, the popular president-elect whose premature death meant Sarney took power in 1985. It is now a private house, but you can at least admire the wrought-iron work.

One of the highlights of the town is the Museu Regional, at the western end of Rua Marechal Deodoro, both for the building and its contents. Most fascinating perhaps are the ex-votos, in the form of small paintings, on the ground floor. There are also carvings by Aleijandinho, a fine collection of beds, and some interesting 19th-century popular sculpture. It is open noon to 5.30pm Tuesday to Sunday.

Across, and a little way up from, the Rosário bridge nearby is Praça Frei Orlando, a handsome square with a row of tall, majestic palms. Reigning supreme over it is the magnificent Igreja de São Francisco de Assis. Aleijandinho worked on both the crowd of angels on the façade and the more sumptuous carving, this time in wood, inside. In the small cemetery behind the church is the grave of Tancredo Neves. Anyone with a surfeit of energy can walk up the hill to the church of Bonfim, from where there are good views.

The street running along the south bank of the Córrego do Lenheiro boasts some of the town's most impressive buildings. Particularly noteworthy are the Prefeitura (1849) and the Teatro Municipal (1891). Last but by no means least, is the 19th-century wrought-iron Railway Station. It is worth a visit in its own right, but it also contains an excellent museum, which follows the history of the railways from their very beginnings. There are a number of old locomotives and carriages, all of which are as lovingly maintained as the train that runs to Tiradentes (see below). The museum is open 9-11.30am and 1-5pm Tuesday to Sunday.

Up the hill behind Praça Carlos Gomes, on the north side, is the small Tancredo Neves gold mine; at the time of going to press it was closed.

Help and Information. The tourist office in the Terminal Turístico (Praça Antônio Viegas; tel 371-2438) opens 8am-6pm daily, and has a good map. The same one can also be picked up at the Hotel Porto Real (Avenida Eduardo Magalhães 254). There is a phone office in the bus station, and the post office is on Avenida Tiradentes, near the corner of Gabriel Passos.

TIRADENTES

The village of Tiradentes, 10 miles/16km east of São João del Rei, is a small version of Ouro Prêto, with its well-preserved 18th-century buildings and and an atmosphere teetering on the quaint. At weekends the place is packed with tourists, and there are a ridiculous number of craft shops, restaurants and hotels for such a small village. Nevertheless, Tiradentes is a light-hearted place which, during the week, reverts to its normal sleepy self.

The architectural highlight of Tiradentes is the hilltop church of Santo Antônio, which has a façade worked on by Aleijandinho and an interior with stunning woodcarvings. One of the main reasons to visit the village, however, is to go on the 19th-century steam train, the so-called Maria Fumaça (Smoking Mary) from São João del Rei. This runs on Fridays, weekends and holidays, leaving at 10am and 2.15pm, and returning at 1pm and 5pm; the fare is $2.50 return. If you sit on the left-hand side you can see people gold-panning along the river, although the over-excited children inside the carriage tend to monopolize attention. There are also buses, which leave every couple of hours between 5.50am and 5.45pm.

Most hotels appear to cater for American package tourists, and charge anything from $15 to $50. Among the cheapest options are Pousada Tiradentes (Rua São Francisco de Paula 44; tel 355-1232) near the bus station, which charges $11 per person; and Pousada dos Inconfidentes (Rua dos Inconfidentes 479; tel 355-1258), which has rooms for $16-20.

DIAMANTINA

The last of the most important mining towns lies in a stunning setting deep in the Serra do Espinhaço, about 180 miles/288km north of Belo Horizonte. Diamantina appears to have changed little since it was founded in the 1720s. Its population of 40,000 still relies on the mining of diamonds and gold, albeit on a small scale, for its main source of income.

Surrounded by an array of awesome peaks, Diamantina feels very much on the edge of the world; beyond lies the sertão and to the west the central plateau. Being more remote than the other historical towns Diamantina is much less worried by tourism. Its churches may be less fine, but it has some impressive mansions; and what it lacks in architecture, the town makes up in atmosphere: Diamantina is truly magical.

There is not much to positively do in town, but don't miss the Diamond Museum. Its collection is fascinating, even though the gems are mostly copies — the real things have been removed to the safety of the local bank. The museum is open noon to 5.30pm, daily except Mondays. It overlooks the main square, which manages to be handsome despite the presence of an ugly modern cathedral.

For tourist information go to the Casa de Cultura in Praça Eulálio. Accommodation is fairly limited, with hotels concentrated around the cathedral

they are also the states in which Afro-Brazilian culture is strongest. However, every Northeastern state has a share of a coastline of spectacular sandy beaches. With the seeringly high temperatures, moderated only slightly by coastal breezes, you will be hard pushed to resist the temptation to join the throngs at the most popular resorts. Nevertheless, only a little extra effort is needed to find some of South America's most secluded tropical beaches.

BAHIA

The quintessence of the Northeast is Bahia. More full of history than any other state, it is the heartland both of traditional Northeastern cuisine and of the most famous Afro-Brazilian cult, candomblé. Salvador is the capital and focus of the state, with Bahia's most famous carnival, the largest colonial complex, and the main concentration of candomblé temples (*terreiros*). It is ironic that religious practices banned by the government for years, are now positively encouraged by the local tourist board as attractions. The ceremonies are more authentic in the smaller towns, which are also safer.

The main area of interest outside the capital lies south of Salvador, and this is also where you'll find the best beaches.

Salvador

The capital of Bahia grabs people by the scruff of the neck: indifference is impossible. Salvador is magnificent and colourful; it is also mysterious and a little unnerving. The city is a melting pot of opposing forces — African and European, old and new, rich and poor. Into this are thrown thousands of tourists, who flood in to gaze admiringly at the churches and lie on the beaches. But these outsiders never play anything but second fiddle to the inhabitants of this powerful city. The best way to enjoy it is to change down a gear or two, while not losing your head completely: Salvador is extremely laid-back, but it also has a serious crime scene.

The city lies on a peninsula at the entrance to the huge Baia de Todos os Santos. Founded in 1549, Salvador later became the country's capital and an important port — it was the centre of the slave trade, which flourished here for three centuries. To this day the majority of Salvador's two million inhabitants is black.

The climate is rainy most of the year, with the heaviest downpours falling between April and September. Temperatures never fall very low, but the beaches provide an easy escape from the heat and humidity.

CITY LAYOUT

Salvador's commercial and historic districts lie on the southwestern corner of the peninsula overlooking the bay. But you are never more than a short bus ride away from the main city beaches on the Atlantic. You are likely to spend most of your time skirting around the coast; heading inland is a confusing business thanks to the topography and to the layout of roads — which on paper resembles a half-eaten plate of spaghetti.

A cliff divides central Salvador into the upper and lower cities, or Cidade Alta and Cidade Baixa respectively. The Cidade Alta is the site of the historic centre, and is also referred to as Centro. The Cidade Baixa is the main commercial area (Comércio) and the port. A series of streets, known as *ladeiras*, link the upper and lower cities, but walking up and down the steep inclines is an exhausting business, as well as being potentially dangerous (see *Crime and Safety*). Travelling between the two districts is most easily done by taking the elegant Elevador Lacerda, a 1930s lift which runs from Praça Cayru up to the Praça Municipal. It operates daily from 5am to 11pm and costs $0.02 a ride. There is also a funicular — the Plano Inclinado Gonçalves — which runs from several blocks north of the

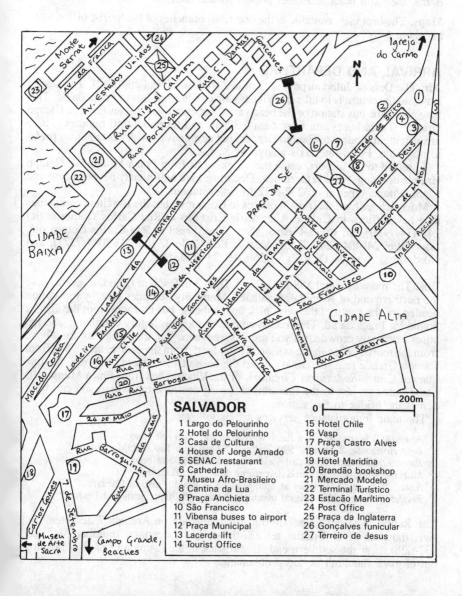

SALVADOR

0 |————————————| 200m

1 Largo do Pelourinho
2 Hotel do Pelourinho
3 Casa de Cultura
4 House of Jorge Amado
5 SENAC restaurant
6 Cathedral
7 Museu Afro-Brasileiro
8 Cantina da Lua
9 Praça Anchieta
10 São Francisco
11 Vibensa buses to airport
12 Praça Municipal
13 Lacerda lift
14 Tourist Office

15 Hotel Chile
16 Vasp
17 Praça Castro Alves
18 Varig
19 Hotel Maridina
20 Brandão bookshop
21 Mercado Modelo
22 Terminal Turístico
23 Estação Marítimo
24 Post Office
25 Praça da Inglaterra
26 Gonçalves funicular
27 Terreiro de Jesus

lift to just behind the cathedral. It is less convenient since it runs less frequently and shuts down completely on Sundays.

The historic centre has little traffic. This cannot be said of Avenida 7 de Setembro, which runs from Praça Castro Alves, at the edge of the old city, right the way down to the Atlantic. It connects a number of districts, and undergoes a metamorphosis about half way along: while the northerly stretch is a bustling commercial zone, beyond Campo Grande it is transformed into a shady avenue running through quiet residential districts. South of Vitória, one such district, is Barra, the main hotel and most popular beach area.

Maps. The best map available is the one from branches of the tourist office, sold for about $0.65.

ARRIVAL AND DEPARTURE

Air. The Dois de Julho airport is 15 miles/24km north (tel 204-1010). The easiest way into the centre is to take the Vibensa air-conditioned bus to Praça da Sé. This may go via the bus station or the beach area, but either way passes through Campo Grande. These buses run from 6am-9.30pm, and take about 40 minutes. There are also regular buses to Campo Grande, but new arrivals with baggage may prefer to play safe. Fixed-rate taxis charge $15.

To return to the airport, catch the Vibensa bus from Praça Municipal, Campo Grande or along Avenida Oceânica. Departures are half-hourly between 5am and 10pm. Phone Vibensa on 237-1022 for information.

Most airlines have their main offices in Comércio, but the Brazilian companies also have offices in Cidade Alta: Varig/Cruzeiro at Rua Carlos Gomes 6 (tel 243-1344/9311), off Praça Castro Alves; Transbrasil at Rua Carlos Gomes 616, Loja 7 (tel 241-1044/242-2743); Vasp at Rua Chile 27 (tel 243-7044/7277); and Nordeste at Avenida D. João VI 259 (tel 244-7533).

Bus. The rodoviária (tel 558-0124/231-5711) is 3 miles/5km from the centre, near the northern end of Avenida Magalhães. Many city bus lines pass by the station headed for the centre, otherwise pick up a Vibensa bus en route from the airport bound for Praça da Sé. The road system in this area is highly confusing, and the buses extremely crowded: if you aren't sure where you are going, ask for advice from the tourist office in the station. To get there from the centre, take a bus from Campo Grande (e.g. the 5004), from the base of the Lacerda lift (e.g. the one marked *Centro-Rodoviária-Circular*), or the Vibensa bus from Praça Municipal. Some buses go just to the Iguatemi shopping centre, from where you can walk across the bridge to the station.

The main long-distance services are as follows:

Aracajú: 5 hours, $8; five daily with Bomfim, with one leito.
Belo Horizonte: 23 hours, $30; daily at 5-6pm with São Geraldo or Gontijo.
Brasília: 23 hours, $34; daily with Paraíso at noon and 8pm.
Maceió: 9 hours, $32; three departures daily with Bomfim.
Natal: 18 hours, $26; daily at 8pm with São Geraldo; also to Caruarú.
Recife: 13 hours, $20; several overnight buses with Itapemirim and Penha.

Car Rental. The most centrally located agents are on Avenida 7 de Setembro: Avis (number 1796, Vitória; tel 237-0154), and Locarauto (number 3145; tel 237-1128), near the southern end. If you stick to the Avenida Oceânica, heading out of town shouldn't be too problematic.

GETTING AROUND

Important points for picking up buses are Praça Cayru, near the base of the Lacerda lift, and Campo Grande. If you are heading for the beach area, both Campo Grande and Avenida 7 de Setembro are the best places to catch buses. There is a bus which runs direct from Praça Municipal to Avenida Oceânica (via Campo Grande), and Vibensa has its own air-conditioned bus along a similar route. The so-called *Jardineira* service is a bus geared for tourists which runs from outside Hotel da Bahia in Campo Grande right along the seafront to Praia do Flamengo beyond Itapuã.

To call a taxi dial 243-4333 or 359-7766.

ACCOMMODATION

Old City. Everyone warns against staying in the historic centre, which is notorious for crime. But as long as you are aware of the dangers (see *Crime and Safety*), there is no need to dismiss the area out of hand.

The cheapest hotels are around Praça da Sé, but the streets around the square are among the area's most disreputable. There are a couple of hotels near the top of Rua Monte Alverne — the Benfica (tel 243-0784) and the America (tel 242-2751) — but don't venture any further down this street after dark; both hotels charge around $7. The Hotel do Pelourinho (Rua Alfredo de Brito 20; tel 321-9022) is in the heart of the colonial district. It has wonderful views and is good value, with standard rooms with bathroom going for $11/$16. Nearby, on Largo do Pelourinho below the church, is the simpler Hotel Solara (tel 321-0202), but it is overpriced.

To be within easy reach of the old city, but nevertheless slightly out of it, consider staying along Rua Chile, which runs south from Praça Municipal. The best along here is the Chile Hotel (number 7; tel 321-0245), which is very near the square and has rooms for $7-15. Otherwise, try one of the places on Rua Rui Barbosa, which charge similar rates.

Avenida 7 de Setembro This extremely long street has lots of hotels. Stay either at the northern or southern end, rather than being stuck in the middle, without the advantage of being close to either the beaches or the centre. The Maridina, overlooking Praça Castro Alves (tel 242-7176), is one of the best options in the centre. It is extremely friendly and clean, with rooms for $12/$16. Several blocks further south, between Largo de São Pedro and Praça de Piedade, are three hotels offering similar facilities for $12-15: the Granada (number 521), the Imperial (751) and the São José (847). This is a lively area, with interesting squares, and lots of shops and snack bars.

You can walk to any of the above hotels from the centre. Those beyond Campo Grande in Vitória district are best reached by bus. The best of the beach-end hotels is the Caramuru (number 2125; tel 247-9951), a short distance south of Campo Grande. It is housed in a lovely building and run by friendly people. Rooms cost $8-11/$10-14. Nearer the square, but less welcoming and more expensive is the Anglo Americano (number 1838; tel 247-7681).

Barra. This is the most popular place to stay if you can afford a middle range hotel. It gives easy access to the sea and a limitless supply of bars and restaurants. Several places are located on or near the seafront between the fort and the Barra lighthouse. One of the cheapest options is the Pousada Malu at Avenida Oceânica 3801. A block inland is the Enseada Praia da Barra (Rua Barão de Itapoã 60; tel

235-9213), with rooms for $24. Further south, at Rua Afonso Celso 439, on the corner of Prof. Brito, is the Hotel Bella Barra (tel 237-8401), in a similar price range.

EATING AND DRINKING

The most entertaining restaurants are in the old city, though many are closed by 8pm. There are a couple on Praca da Sé itself, and several on Largo do Pelourinho and neighbouring streets. One of the liveliest places, with a predominantly young clientele, is the Cantina da Lua, at the top of Alfredo Brito. Live music is put on here, and it is one of the few places in the area to stay open late. The Preto Velho at Rua Gregório de Matos 38, is a small, characterful place with a friendly atmosphere and horrendous pictures on the wall; it's a popular drinking-place among the locals. For a more standard meal try the grill house just down from Cantina da Lua. A better option, however, is Restaurante do SENAC on Largo do Pelourinho. This is a restaurant school that serves buffets of regional food. It's clear that the students still have some way to go, but meals are good value. At the bottom of the square is the Casa do Benin (tel 243-7629), which serves excellent African food.

The restaurant in the Hotel do Pelourinho is not a particularly good place to eat, but it overlooks the bay and offers fine views at sunset: the bar fills up briefly every evening at this time, but otherwise it is quiet.

During the day a good place to eat is in the Mercado Modelo, in Cidade Baixa, where there are a couple of restaurants with tables on the terrace overlooking the bay. If you munch enough snacks from the many street vendors, you won't need supper.

There is an endless choice of restaurants along the Atlantic seafront offering a similar range of food: pizzas, steaks and seafood, for the most part. All these places are packed at weekends.

EXPLORING

Cidade Alta. The old city is not nearly as well-preserved as in Ouro Prêto, for example, but it has more character. And in addition to some fine buildings, the old city's position atop the cliff provides a series of spectacular views across the bay.

The old centre is roughly the area between Praça Municipal and Largo do Santo Antônio. The raised Praça Municipal is a characterless square despite the imposing public buildings that overlook it. The Lacerda lift partially blocks the view over the bay. A short walk northeast is Praça da Sé, which boasts more humble buildings. This is the liveliest and most crumbling of the old city squares; it is full of hawkers, people lounging around and dingy-looking bars playing loud music. Adjacent is the pretty Largo Terreiro de Jesus, a more traditional colonial-style square, with trees, a fountain, and a cathedral. On the corner of Rua Alfredo de Brito is the old Faculty of Medicine. It contains the Museu Afro-Brasiliero, with a small but fascinating collection concerned primarily with Afro-Bahian religion and art. It opens 9am-noon and 2-4pm, Tuesday to Saturday.

Adjoining Terreiro de Jesus is Praça Anchieta, a small and rather self-effacing square but also one of Salvador's most charming. Furthermore, it contains the city's finest churches. The 18th-century Igreja de São Francisco is an exuberant baroque creation, with interesting woodcarving showing African influence. In the cloisters of the attached monastery (closed to the public) are spectacular 18th-century azulejos. Next door, at the top of Rua Ignacio Accioli, is a smaller church with an intricately carved and unusual façade; inside there is a magnificent painted sanctuary.

Rua Alfredo de Brito is a narrow, cobbled street lined with fine but decaying houses, many of which are now craft or souvenir shops. It leads from Terreiro de Jesus to the steeply sloping square of Largo do Pelourinho, also known as Praça José de Alençar. This is the heart of the Pelourinho district and the historic centre. Salvador's oldest and best-restored buildings are found here. The *pelourinho*, the post to which slaves were tied for whipping, has disappeared, but the old slave auction house at the top of the square has survived. It is now the Casa de Cultura, with the attached Museu de Cidade (with some interesting photographs and Candomblé-related displays). The elegant blue house next door is the former home of the writer, Jorge Amado.

By walking north up the hill you reach a much more tranquil part of town and also Largo do Carmo, which is overlooked by two churches. On the left is the Igreja e Convento do Carmo. The church has a beautiful painted wooden ceiling, but it is usually open only for mass from 7-8am. Attached is a museum containing the usual mix of religious art, furniture and manuscripts. Rua do Carmo is one of the loveliest streets in the old city, but Largo do Santo Antônio, to which it eventually leads, is a rather characterless square with an old fort.

Halfway along Rua Carlos Gomes, just south of the old centre, a steep cobbled road on the right leads down to the church of Santa Teresa. The 17th-century convent has been beautifully restored and now houses the Museu de Arte Sacra, one of the finest museums of its kind in Brazil. It is open 10-11.30am and 2-5.30pm Tuesday to Saturday.

Cidade Baixa. This commercial district holds few attractions. The main object of interest is the Mercado Modelo, housed in the former customs building. But this crafts market is orderly, clean and totally lacking in atmosphere. It is also extremely touristy and expensive, although a little hard bargaining usually works. At weekends there are often musicians playing, and *capoeira* groups perform from 11am to 2pm on weekdays.

Near the market is the Terminal Turístico Marítimo and the Estação Marítima from where boats leave for Maragojipe (see page 658).

Monte Serrat. This is a peaceful district on a peninsula several miles north of the centre. The area is most famous for the Igreja do Bonfim, which is an important centre of pilgrimage. The church overlooks a lovely square with its permanent eddy of people. Pilgrims buy ribbons with which to make their wishes, and you will be expected to buy several yourself. Inside, a room to the right of the main altar is full of ex-votos (offerings). They include a bizarre array of rubber limbs, photographs and messages of thanks, together with hundreds of ribbons. There is a museum of ex-votos upstairs (closed on Monday).

Ten minutes walk along Rua São Francisco, southwest from the square, is Forte Monte Serrat. This peaceful spot provides good views back to the city and along the coast. Below is the delightful church of Monte Serrat.

To reach this district, catch the bus marked *Bonfim* from near the base of the Lacerda lift, which goes right to the church. The route passes Mercado Joaquim, which is the busiest and most interesting daily market in Salvador. Food is the main commodity, although you can pick up a few cheap crafts, mainly ceramics and basketry.

Beaches. Salvador's city beaches form one long strip between the Barra and Itapoã lighthouses. As in Rio, a broad highway runs along the seafront, but the atmosphere is totally different. Development here has been far more patchy, and some areas either resemble building sites or are positively seedy.

The long stretch of sand is divided into beaches with different names, but no one really knows where one ends and another begins. The best idea is to get a bus running the length of the seafront (e.g. bound for Itapuã or Flamengo) and get off at whichever point takes your fancy. During the week you may be happy to stick to the small areas of beach in Barra itself (i.e. closest to Salvador). These, however, are rocky and at weekends hopelessly crowded. The best beaches are a fair way east of here towards the Farol de Itapuã, including Piatã, Itapuã (also spelt Itapoã or Itapoan), Flamengo and Stella Maris, and those beyond.

ENTERTAINMENT

Candomblé. It may seem strange to describe a religious ceremony as 'entertainment', but a must for most visitors to Salvador is a trip to a terreiro to watch a candomblé ceremony. Women are the focal point of the rituals: they chant, dance and whirl around to the frenetic beat of drums (played by men), and those receptive to the spirit of candomblé fall into a trance. The costumes are fascinating and the music powerful, yet the authenticity is often questionable. The women whisper and chat among themselves and enter into a trance almost suspiciously fast; but the experience is still extraordinary.

It is not difficult to arrange a visit to a terreiro. Avoid the people who offer to escort you since they will almost certainly rip you off by charging a ludicrous fee of as much as $25-30. Instead, go to the tourist office, where they have a list of terreiros with the days on which visitors can attend ceremonies; there are normally several a month to choose from. Only a few of the thousand-plus terreiros admit tourists, so there's bound to be a crowd, especially in high season.

Many terreiros don't charge an entrance fee, so going independently need cost no more than the taxi fare there and back. The candomblé usually starts some time after 9pm, and lasts several hours; there is no obligation to stay to the end. Note that women and men in the audience must sit separately.

Capoeira. Candomblé is not the only source of evening entertainment in Salvador. One of the most popular performance arts is capoeira, the martial art developed by African slaves in Brazil which, as a dance, forms an integral part of their folkloric tradition. It is usually accompanied by the twang of the *berimbau*, a single-stringed African instrument. Ask at the tourist office for a full list of venues; many capoeira academies admit the public.

Capoeira and other folkloric shows are put on in the smarter restaurants, including at SENAC in Largo do Pelourinho. This same square is also a venue for open-air discos.

CRIME AND SAFETY

Several areas either demand a certain vigilance or should be avoided altogether. Avoid walking through the Cidade Baixa at night. Several people have encountered hassle in the Lacerda lift in the late evening; the ladeiras between the upper and lower cities are dangerous at any time of day. Most notorious, however, are the quiet streets of the historic centre. The favourite technique among thieves is for one person to grab you from behind, while another takes your money. Avoid sightseeing on Sundays, since the old town is deserted and dangerous. Women should be wary of being picked up by men in Pelourinho; several have been drugged and raped.

HELP AND INFORMATION

Tourist Information: the main office of Bahiatursa, the state tourist board, is in Palácio Rio Branco, the former Governor's Palace in the Praça Municipal (tel 241-4333). The staff are extremely helpful and give out maps and all kinds of information about the carnival, festivals, etc. There is a useful noticeboard for leaving messages too. The office opens 8am-6pm.

There are other good information desks in the airport (tel 240-1244), the bus station (ground floor; tel 358-0871), and the Mercado Modelo. Emtursa, the municipal tourist board, has an office in the Casa de Cultura on Largo do Pelourinho (tel 243-6150). It opens 9am-5pm.

Money: there are several casas de câmbio in the centre and in Barra, and hotels sometimes exchange money; rates are not particularly favourable. The banks have their main branches on Avenida Estados Unidos in Cidade Baixa, and most have an exchange desk.

Post Offices: the main office, for poste restante, is on Praça da Inglaterra in Comércio; it opens 8am-6pm Monday to Saturday. There are several other offices dotted around the city, including in the Mercado Modelo and off Praça da Sé (corner of Rua Guedes de Brito).

Telephone Offices: Salvador's phone offices are in surprisingly inconvenient locations. Unless you are at the bus station or airport you may find it easier (but more expensive) to call from your hotel. The main Telebahia office is at Rua Archimedes Gonçalves 37, at Campo da Pólvora near the Otávio Mangabeira stadium south of the centre; it is open 24 hours. More convenient is the one at Avenida 7 de Setembro 533 (open 8am-10pm).

Bookshops: Livraria Graúna is a wonderful bookshop just southwest of Campo Grande, at Avenida 7 de Setembro 1448. It sells and exchanges secondhand books, and has a good selection of English and other foreign language literature. A whole bookcase devoted to the Bahian author, Jorge Amado, and you can buy wonderful postcards of old city scenes. A more central secondhand bookshop is Livraria Brandão at Rua Rui Barbosa 4.

Policia Federal: junction of Ruas da Polonia and Santos Dumont, Cidade Baixa (tel 242-4947); about five blocks northeast of the Mercado Modelo.

Consulates. *Chile:* Avenida Antonio Carlos Magalhães 846, Room 333, Itaigara (tel 258-5431); north of Pituba beach.
UK (Vice-Consulate): Avenida Estados Unidos 4, Edif. Visconde de Cayru, Salas 1109-1113, Comércio (tel 243-9222).
USA: Avenida Magalhães, Edif. Cidadele Centre 1, Room 410, Itaigara (tel 358-9166).

NORTH OF SALVADOR

The coastline north from Salvador consists of almost uninterrupted beach. Choosing where to stop should be approached in a similar fashion to selecting a beach in the state capital: take a northbound bus and follow your instincts. Arembepe, about 30 miles/48km north, used to be a popular hippy hang-out, but is now much more chic. You may prefer to get off at one of the villages en route; there are plenty of places to stay, although they fill up in high season.

The Recôncavo

This is the name given to the lush coastal area around the Baía de Todos os Santos. It has been of great agricultural importance ever since the colonial era, when the prosperity brought by the large sugar and tobacco plantations funded the fine building work done in the Recôncavo itself and in Salvador. The rolling green hills are still dotted with fazendas.

CACHOEIRA

Lying 75 miles/120km around the bay from Salvador, Cachoeira is the highlight of the Recôncavo. Founded in the early 16th century, the town had great prestige at one time, and was even capital of Bahia briefly.

Cachoeira is a most beautiful, peaceful place and one of the finest colonial towns of the Northeast. Some of the buildings have been restored, but many remain in a state of picturesque decay. It is remarkably unspoilt. You can stroll unhurried through silent and virtually traffic-free streets. The sounds that ring in the air are made by people trotting around on horseback, hammering away in sculpture workshops or strumming away at guitars. The clean air and relaxed pace is a welcome change after Salvador. While it is possible to go to Cachoeira on a day trip from the capital, you are strongly advised to stay over.

Across the Rio Paraguaçu, which flows into the bay, is São Felix, Cachoeira's twin town. The only reason to cross the bridge is to get a good view back over the river.

Arrival and Departure. Camurujipe runs buses from Salvador to Cachoeira hourly from 5.30am to 7pm, taking about two hours. Buses may be marked São Felix, because some continue across the river. The last bus back leaves at 7.30pm. There are also regular buses between Cachoiera and Valença to the south. The rodoviária (tel 724-1231) is on Rua Prisco Paraíso, beyond the Camurujipe office.

The best way to travel from Salvador is to take the boat to Maragojipe, about 20 miles/32km south of Cachoeira, and to continue by bus from there. Boats leave from the Estação Marítimo in Salvador, at 2pm Monday to Friday, and at 1pm on Saturday; the journey takes about three hours. The return trip from Maragojipe begins at 5am. Viazul also runs five daily buses to Maragojipe from Salvador, which go via Cachoeira and take about three hours.

Maragojipe is a fascinating place — a blend of old houses, cowboys, fishermen and decay. It is worth delaying your journey to explore. If you want to stay overnight, sleep at the Hotel Oxumaré (Rua Heretiano Jorge de Souza 3; tel 726-1104), which charges $4-5.

Accommodation. The best place to look for a room in Cachoeira is on Rua 25 de Junho, near Praça Teixeira de Freitas, a lovely shady square with a few simple bars. On the corner of Rua 7 de Setembro, is the Hotel Colombo; a fine old building, it has rooms for just $3.50. For a few more creature comforts, try the Pousada Cabana do Pai Thomaz (25 de Junho 12; tel 725-1288), which charges $14. A little further up at number 4 (tel 725-1319/1392) is the Pousada Massapé, in a similar price range. The smart-looking Pousada do Convento, next to the Carmelite church around the corner, is housed in a former convent and is good value at $13/$17.

Eating and Drinking. Rua 25 de Junho, where tables spill out on to the pavements, is the best area for eating out. The trendiest place in town is the Cabana do Pai Thomaz, which has its own restaurant and runs the bar opposite too. For a cheaper meal try one of the simpler restaurants overlooking Praça Teixeira de Freitas, or elsewhere in the centre. There are several places where you can hear live music, particularly at weekends; one such is the Casa da Seresta on Rua 13 de Maio, just near the square.

Exploring. Little guidance is required for a tour around Cachoeira's charming streets, but certain buildings are worth singling out.

The square that recalls more than any other Cachoeira's heyday of the 18th century is Praça da Aclamação, at the top of Rua 25 de Junho. The highlight of the square and of Cachoeira is the church of the Third Order of Carmelites, with its stunning Macau-influenced paintwork. It is open from 8-11.30am and 2-5pm Monday to Friday, 9-11.30am at weekends. On the left of the church is the old prison and prefecture, once the seat of the Bahian government. Across the street is the Regional Museum: the rooms are virtually empty, but it's worth a visit just to see the painted ceilings upstairs.

Northwest along Rua Ana Neri and past the Igreja Matriz do Rosário (with fine azulejos), a steep cobbled alley leads left to Largo da Ajuda. It is dominated by the newer prefecture, a strangely imposing building for this small, delightful square. Next to the tiny 16th-century Ajuda chapel, the oldest church in the town, is a one-room museum. It contains photographs of the Irmandade de Boa Morte, a sisterhood of descendants of women slaves. If you are in Bahia in mid-August, don't miss the opportunity to witness the Boa Morte festival, during which they celebrate their liberation. The sisters in the museum are extremely friendly. By walking down the hill towards the river you join Rua 13 de Maio, another interesting street. In a large building near Praça Teixeira Freitas is the tourist office; ask here about candomblé ceremonies.

Cachoeira is an important centre of candomblé. Ceremonies are usually held on Friday and Saturday evenings. The locals are relatively unused to tourists, so be as unobtrusive as possible. As well as ceremonies, there are important candomblé festivals, of which the Boa Morte is the most famous. The smaller festival of Santa Barbara takes place in in early December. Another oocasion which also attracts a lot of outside interest is the Festa de São João on 22-24 June. You may have difficulty finding a room during any of these celebrations.

South of Salvador

VALENCA

As you head south out of the Recôncavo, the hills gradually give way to swamp. This provides the setting for Valença, a bustling port with a population of around 70,000. It lies at the mouth of the Rio Una, 168 miles/270km southwest of Salvador. Most travellers merely pass through Valença, on their way to the beaches on Tinharé island. It warrants more attention, however, since it is an attractive, friendly and lively town. The harbour, with its handsome seafront, is a hive of activity: fishermen launch their sailboats, bring in their catches — which they do mid-afternoon — and mend their nets; nearby are Valença's famous shipyards (*estaleiros*) where you can see vessels of all shapes and sizes in every stage of construction. Away from the waterfront the most distinctive group of people to fill the streets are the cowboys who work on the cattle ranches in the surrounding country. On certain days they bring their cattle to market — a wonderful sight.

Arrival and Departure. Camurujipe runs buses from Salvador almost hourly between 9am and 11pm. The journey along the BR-101 takes about five hours and costs $6. A quicker route is via Itaparica Island i.e. by taking the ferry from Mercado Joaquim in Salvador (see page 655) to Bom Despacho and picking up a bus from there; the journey from Bom Despacho takes three hours. There are also buses to Valença from Ilhéus, Porto Seguro, Feira de Santana and Cachoeira.

The rodoviária (tel 741-1280) is on Rua Maçônica, near the port. The tourist office is also nearby; ask here for a map and information about the local festivals, of which there are many.

Accommodation. Finding somewhere to stay should not be a problem, although rooms fill quickly at weekends. Hotel Guaibim on Praça da Independência (tel 741-1110) is among the best of the cheaper options. For greater comfort try the Rio Una on Rua Maestro Barrinhão, near the waterfront (tel 741-1614). Don't miss out on the wonderful seafood.

ILHA DO TINHARE

Mangrove swamps cover much of the area between Valença and Tinharé, a beautiful island of lush vegetation. But people come here not so much to admire the palms and birds, as to enjoy the magnificent beaches. Most famous are those around the fishing village of Morro de São Paulo, at the northern end of the island. This is a popular travellers' hang-out and is attracting increasing numbers of young Brazilians too: there are crowds at weekends and prices rise during the high season. Nevertheless, the beaches and the local community have survived all the attention remarkably well: facilities are still basic, and there are no cars. Pousadas and simple restaurants can be found in the village, but elsewhere you will probably have to rent hammock space off the locals.

Rather than swim by Morro de São Paulo itself, head east along the shore to find the finest beaches. If seclusion rather than beaches are the main attraction, take a boat from Morro de São Paulo to one of the other fishing villages on the island, such as Prainha.

Arrival and Departure: boats to Tinharé from Valença leave from by the bridge near the bus station. Departures are at 8am and noon during the high season, just once a day in winter; the schedule may alter at weekends. The trip takes $2\frac{1}{2}$ hours. Since boats serve other settlements on the island, make sure you get on the right one. You can instead pay a local fisherman to take you, though this is of course more expensive.

ILHEUS

This large town lies at the mouth of Rio Cachoeira, 250 miles/400km south of Salvador. It was a backwater until the introduction of cocoa brought an economic upsurge in the 19th century. The area still produces one-sixth of the world's cocoa. The violence and virtual slave labour that accompanied the cocoa boom has been immortalized in the books of Jorge Amado, a native of Ilhéus and Brazil's most famous novelist. He set a number of his books in and around the town. *Terras do sem fim* (*The Violent Land*) gives a real taste for what was in those days little more than an armed camp. Ilhéus may not be as full as assassins as it once was, but life on the plantations has hardly improved: the shanties around Ilhéus shelter thousands of dayworkers who endure appalling conditions for pitiful pay.

Its history is more fascinating than its present, but Ilhéus is well worth a visit.

It is untouristy and likely to stay that way, though there are popular beaches nearby. In *The Violent Land*, Amado describes Ilhéus as the town 'without diversions'. This is not strictly true. The largely modern town has retained part of its colonial centre, and simply wandering through the streets is fun. The main squares are Praça Dom Eduardo, with the huge 1930s cathedral, and Praça Rui Barbosa, near the seafront to the north. This last square contains the 16th-century Igreja de São Jorge, the oldest church in Ilhéus.

The best of the many local festivals take place in January; there is also a cocoa festival in October. While this is a little more exciting than an Ovaltine or Horlicks fiesta might be, it is well short of an Oktoberfest.

Arrival and Departure. There is a small airport (tel 231-3015), served by Nordeste and Varig/Cruzeiro, including from Salvador, Recife and Rio.

Ilhéus lies 20 miles/32km off the BR-101 highway. Most buses from Salvador follow the route via Cachoeira, and take about seven hours; there are several daily services (often overnight) with Sulba and Aguia Branca. Book in advance if possible at weekends or during the high season. There are also services to and from Valença and Porto Seguro, both four hours away. The rodoviária is ten minutes by bus northwest of the centre.

Accommodation and Food. The hotels in Ilhéus are not of outstanding quality, and often seem to be full or expensive, or both. One of the best is Pousada Kazarão on Praça Coronel Pessoa 38 (tel 231-5031), with rooms for around $10. Cheaper is the Lucas at Rua 7 de Setembro 17 (tel 231-3772). You may prefer to base yourself at one of the nearby beaches instead: see below.

The best place to be in the evenings is along the seafront promenade, where you'll find seafood stalls and lots of bars. The best bar is the Vesúvio in Praça Dom Eduardo, which features in *Gabriela, Clove and Cinnamon*, another of Amado's novels; it is pricey but good.

Help and Information. The main Ilheustur office is in Praça Castro Alves; getting hold of a map is a good idea since the layout of Ilhéus can be disorientating. The telephone office is on 7 de Setembro, near the corner of Miguel Calazans; the post office is half way along Marquês de Paranaguá. Banco do Brasil (Rua Marquês de Paranaguá 112) has a foreign exchange desk.

Around Ilhéus

Beaches. Ilhéus has its own beach, but better ones are to the south towards Olivença, some 12 miles/19km away. There are frequent bus services between the two towns, and since the road runs along the coast, you can just get off where you like; Cururupe beach, 6 miles/10km south of Ilhéus, is recommended.

Further afield, but well worth the trip, is Itacaré, about $3\frac{1}{2}$ hours north of Ilhéus. This pleasant colonial town is within reach of some fine beaches. These are becoming increasingly popular, but since there is no road along the coast, if you are prepared to walk further than everyone else, you can get away from the weekend crowds. There are buses to Itacaré from Ilhéus and Salvador, though you may need to change at Ubaitaba on the BR-101.

CEPLAC. For a break away from the coast and an insight into the cocoa industry, visit the plantation run by the Centro de Pesquisa do Cacao (CEPLAC), the government cocoa agency. The demonstration plantation is near Itabuna, 20 miles/32km west of Ilhéus; it is open Monday to Friday. You should arrange your tour in advance through the CEPLAC office near the city bus station in Ilhéus (tel 214-3014) or through the Ilhéus Praia hotel (Praça Dom Eduardo). There is a half-hourly bus service from Ilhéus Rodoviária to Itabuna; since the plantation is about 5 miles/8km out of town, on the Ilhéus road, ask to be dropped off at the entrance.

PORTO SEGURO

Situated on a headland between the Atlantic and the Rio Buranhém, Porto Seguro claims to be the oldest town in Brazil. It was founded in 1526, just over a quarter of a century after Cabral is said to have first set foot in Brazil — supposedly a few miles to the north of the town. Several buildings survive from this early period. However, it is the beaches rather than the small historic centre, which have turned Porto Seguro into Bahia's principal tourist destination after Salvador. The coast is protected by a coral reef, and the sea that washes the beaches north and south of town is clean, shallow and good for swimming.

The Cidade Alta lies on a hilltop about a mile north of the centre, and provides fine views. There is a cluster of ancient churches in this district, mostly dating from the mid-16th century; and also an old fort, a ruined Jesuit college, and a museum in the old Paço Municipal.

Porto Seguro's carnival is one of Bahia's most vibrant.

Arrival and Departure. Porto Seguro's popularity is reflected in the number of direct flights now operating: there are daily flights with Nordeste from São Paulo, Rio and Salvador, and less frequent services from Belo Horizonte. The airport (tel 288-2400) is a mile or so west of Cidade Alta.

There are several buses a day from Ilhéus ($5\frac{1}{2}$ hours), and a couple from Salvador (12 hours) and Vitória (11 hours). In addition, there is one connection a day with Rio (18 hours), more during the peak season when you should book in advance. For more frequent services catch a bus to Eunápolis, where the road to Porto Seguro joins the BR-101. There is a tourist desk in the station, and in Praça Visconde de Porto Seguro, downtown.

Accommodation. You may have to search for an affordable room during the high season, but there is certainly no shortage of hotels. Several reasonable places are on or near Avenidas Getúlio Vargas and Portugal, in the centre. Pousada Aquarias (Rua Cabral 174; tel 288-2738) is recommended.

Bars and restaurants are concentrated along Avenida Portugal, nicknamed Passarela do Alcool, and Avenida 22 de Abril, both in Cidade Baixa near the waterfront. Seafood is, of course, the thing to eat.

Around Porto Seguro

A string of fine beaches extends north of Porto Seguro — Curuípe, Itacimirim, Mundaí, Itaperapuã, and so on — all within a few miles of each other. The most unspoilt beaches are to the south of town, however, simply because they are less accessible.

Just 2 miles/4km south of the Rio Buranhém (crossed by ferry from Porto Seguro) is the village of Arraial da Ajuda. This dusty, hillside settlement is a surprisingly lively and popular seaside haunt. There are lots of pousadas and bars, and you can also rent places on the beach. To get to Ajuda from the ferry landing take a bus or walk along the beach.

Rather than swim at Arraial itself, head a few miles south to Pitinga, or, even better, 5 miles/8km further south to Trancoso. This is a much quieter village, with a few simple pousadas and beach houses for rent. Buses run just twice a day from Ajuda to Trancoso, more frequently during the high season. If not satisfied with life at Trancoso, you can take a boat to Caraiva (a two-hour trip), a tiny settlement with secluded beaches and no facilities to speak of; take a hammock.

Inland — The Sertão

Feira de Santana. This is the main city in the Bahian sertão, with a population of 400,000. It is the centre of a cattle breeding area, and is famous for its leather market — the Feira do Couro — which takes place every Monday and is said to be the largest in Brazil. Don't miss the opportunity to witness this lively and colourful spectacle. It is the best place to buy leather in the Northeast, and stalls sell all manner of other things.

Feira de Santana lies 72 miles/116km northwest of Salvador, not far from the BR-116; it is hard to avoid if you are heading inland. There are buses every 30 minutes from Salvador, but buy your ticket in good time. The most frequent service is operated by Camurujipe, which has buses hourly from 5.40am to 8.40pm. The fare is $3 and the journey takes two hours.

There is no shortage of accommodation, which is to be found mostly around the bus station.

Lençóis. The small town of Lençóis is the main attraction of the Bahian sertão. It lies in the mountainous Chapada Diamantina region, and owes its existence to the discovery of diamonds in the area in the early 19th century. Some of the fine buildings built during the diamond boom still survive. Lençóis is charming, and worth a visit just to get a glimpse of life in the interior. The highlight, however, is the huge Parque Nacional da Chapada Diamantina. This is excellent walking country, with rivers and caves to explore. The park contains a 400m-high waterfall, the Cachoeira de Glass, which is the highest in Brazil. There are numerous trails but no maps, so you need to hire a guide; the best place to ask about this is at the Pousada de Lençóis on Rua Altina Alves.

Lençóis is 250 miles/400km west of Salvador, lying just south of the BR-242 to Brasília. Paraíso runs buses from Salvador, leaving at 7.30am and 10.30pm; the trip takes six hours and costs $8. There are also buses from Feira de Santana and Recife. Of the various cheap hotels Pensão Diamantina (on Rua Miguel Calmon) is one of the best.

Jacobina. If Lençóis gives you a taste for the sertão and the Chapada Diamantina, visit Jacobina, another old mining town. It has a population of 90,000, but it is a friendly place, and you can usually arrange to visit the local gold and emerald mines. São Luiz runs several buses daily from Salvador, mostly leaving in the afternoon and evening; the journey takes six hours. There are a couple of moderately expensive hotels.

SERGIPE AND ALAGOAS

These adjacent states are Brazil's smallest and amongst the poorest. Sergipe is the southern one, Alagoas the northern. Together they separate the much larger states of Bahia and Pernambuco, and they are often merely passed through. Yet both have a scattering of historical towns and beaches. Tourists are rare and the local people are friendly.

ARACAJU

The principle city of Sergipe (population 400,000) deserves the prize for being the least interesting of the Northeastern capitals. The original settlement was given a total facelift in the 19th century, when it became Sergipe's state capital. The result is a clean, orderly place that is uncharacteristic of the region. There is nothing much to detain you, but if you need to stay overnight the grid layout and the compactness of the centre make it an easy place to get around.

Buses take about five hours from Salvador, and $4\frac{1}{2}$ from Maceió in Alagoas. The station is on Avenida 31 de Março, some way south of the centre. Two centrally-located hotels are the Oásis (Rua São Cristóvão 446; tel 224-2125) and the Brasília (Rua Laranjeiras 580; tel 224-8022). For tourist information visit the Centro do Turismo in Praça Olimpio Campos.

Around Aracajú. The state's two finest colonial towns are an easy day trip from town. Laranjeiras, 10 miles/16km northwest, is a pleasant place to wander around, but São Cristóvão, about an hour southwest of Aracajú, is more impressive. It is the former state capital and very unspoilt. Both towns are accessible by bus from the Estação Velha in Praça João XXIII, in the city centre.

About 50 miles/80km north of Aracajú, off the BR-101, is Propriá. The town lies on the Rio São Francisco: for an alternative route into Alagoas, ask along the waterfront about boats headed for Penedo (see below).

MACEIO

The capital of Alagoas, founded in the early 19th century, once boasted some fine architecture but most of this has been pulled down to make way for the modern buildings that now dominate the city. The virtue of Maceió is its proximity to some attractive beaches and interesting towns. It is a relaxing place, however, and it's worth digging out the highlights of the capital's old centre. The best of the museums are the Museu Theo Brandão, a folklore museum in Praça Visconde Sinimbu and the Instituto Histórico at Rua João Pessoa 382. A couple of blocks northwest is Praça dos Martírios, the city's most elegant square.

Buses to Maceió run frequently from Recife and Aracajú, taking four hours. Services from Salvador take about ten hours and run mostly overnight. The rodoviária is 3 miles/5km from the centre, and is served by city buses. The best hotels in town include the Zumbí (Rua Barão de Atalaia 67) and the middle-range Parque in Praça D. Pedro II (tel 221-9099). But most people opt to stay in Pajuçara, a lively beachfront area a short bus ride east of the centre. It has an ample supply of cheap pousadas, most of which are on or off Avenida Antônio Gouveia and

And when you've had enough of the hassles downtown, you can escape to Boa Viagem beach, Recife's equivalent of Copacabana.

The city's saving grace, touristically, is its proximity to Olinda, the old capital. Recife itself was founded in 1627 by a Dutch prince called Maurice of Nassau, whose troops had burned down the original Portuguese capital. The Dutch lost control about 30 years later, and Recife developed rapidly as the main port through which sugar from local plantations was exported. It is now the fourth largest city in the country, with a population of 1.5 million.

CITY LAYOUT

The heart of the city is made up of three interconnecting islands: Recife, Santo Antônio and Boa Vista. Between them flow the Capibaribe and Beberibe rivers. The most historic district is Santo Antônio, which is also the main commercial centre. It is a chaotic area in which ancient churches and buzzing markets lie hidden along narrow alleys that lead off traffic-choked roads lined with office blocks. Avenida Dantas Barreto is the principal thoroughfare. Santo Antônio is not a good place to wander at night, particularly in the area around the fort and the southern end of Dantas Barreto. To the west, across the Rio Capibaribe, is Boa Vista, with both commercial and residential districts. This is also where cheap hotels are concentrated, and where you will probably spend most of your evenings. The principal axis for this part of town is Avenida Conde de Boa Vista; the main square is the huge and rather confusing Parque 13 de Maio. The docks are in Recife, the least appealing of the three districts, and an area you can all but ignore.

Four miles/6km south of the centre is Boa Viagem, a smart residential area with a spectacular beach, and the main restaurant district.

Maps. The map issued free by the tourist office is the best all-round map. You can also buy a bigger map (*Recife — Planta da Cidade*) from news stands: it has no landmarks, but is better for locating particular streets and covers the whole city from Boa Viagem to Olinda.

ARRIVAL AND DEPARTURE

Air. For many visitors Recife is the gateway to both Brazil and South America. The main connections are from London, Paris, Lisbon and Miami.

Guararapes airport (tel 341-1888) is 6 miles/10km south of the city, near Boa Viagem. Banco do Brasil accepts cash and cheques, and also does cash withdrawals on credit cards. Buses for the centre of town leave every ten minutes or so until late; these go along Avenida Ferreira in Boa Viagem and continue on to Avenida Dantas Barreto, from where you can walk to the hotel district in Boa Vista. The fixed-rate taxis charge about $11.

To return to the airport catch the bus (marked Aeroporto) from Rua do Carmo, just east of Avenida Dantas Barreto. Alternatively, take the Setúbal bus from Parque 13 de Maio to Boa Viagem, and pick up the airport bus along the less chaotic Avenida Aguiar.

Airline Offices: Varig — Avenida Guararapes 120 (tel 224-8273/3235).
Transbrasil — Avenida Conde de Boa Vista 1546 (tel 231-0522/221-0068).
Vasp — Manuel Borba 488, west of Praça Pinheiro (tel 421-3611/3088).
TAP (Air Portugal) — Avenida Guararapes 111 (tel 224-2700/2548).
Nordeste — at the airport (tel 341-3187/4222).

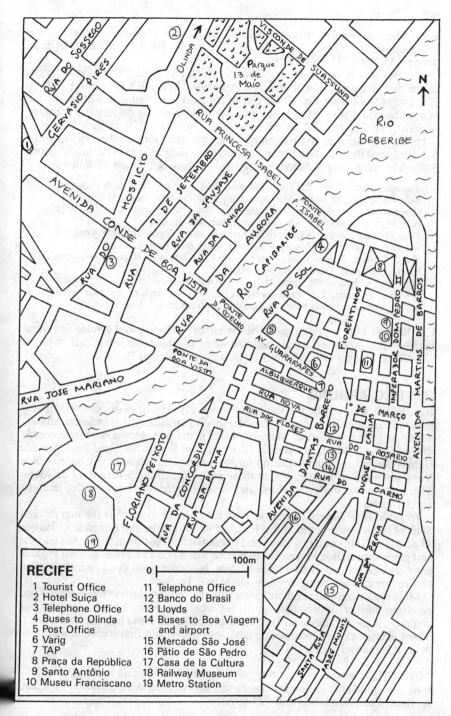

RECIFE

1 Tourist Office
2 Hotel Suiça
3 Telephone Office
4 Buses to Olinda
5 Post Office
6 Varig
7 TAP
8 Praça da República
9 Santo Antônio
10 Museu Franciscano
11 Telephone Office
12 Banco do Brasil
13 Lloyds
14 Buses to Boa Viagem and airport
15 Mercado São José
16 Pátio de São Pedro
17 Casa de la Cultura
18 Railway Museum
19 Metro Station

Bus. The bus station, usually referred to as TIP (Terminal Integrado dos Passageiros), is 7 miles/12km southwest of the centre. For information about buses phone 455-1999, 251-4666/3849.

The easiest way into town is by metro, which takes just 30 minutes. The end of the line is Estação Recife in Santo Antônio, which is nicely central and just 20 minutes walk from Boa Vista. Out of the rush hour, going downtown by bus is not a bad alternative. Several bus routes pass right outside the terminal entrance, including IV Curado/TIP, which runs along Avenida Conde de Boa Vista.

Penha, São Geraldo and Itapemirim offer the usual long-haul services to Rio, São Paulo and Brasília. Boa Esperança runs a bus daily at 8pm to Belém (35 hours; $39). The main long-distance bus departures from Recife are as follows:

Aracajú: 8 hours, $11; daily at noon with Real Alagoas, 11pm with Progresso.
Belo Horizonte: 36 hours, $40; 8pm with Gontijo, daily except Friday.
Campina Grande: $3\frac{1}{2}$ hours, $5; every two hours with Progresso, 7am-7.30pm.
Fortaleza: 12 hours, $18; six daily with Expresso de Luxo.
João Pessoa: 2 hours, $3; every 30 minutes 5am-8.30pm with Boa Vista.
Maceió: $4\frac{1}{2}$ hours, $6; hourly 4.30am-12.45am with Real Alagoas.
Natal: 5 hours, $7; every couple of hours 6.30am-7pm with Napoles, less often on Sundays; there is a daily leito at 11.50pm.
Salvador: 13 hours, $18; three buses a day with Itapemirim.
Teresina: 19 hours, $26; Princesa do Agreste has one daytime and two overnight buses. Some Progresso buses to Teresina continue to São Luis.

Car Rental. This is best arranged at the airport so as to avoid driving in central Recife. Many agencies are represented here; to sound out a few call Avis (tel 326-5730), Budget (tel 325-0110) or Belauto (tel 341-6677).

GETTING AROUND

Bus. Recife seems to be the subject of a sick experiment to discover how many buses it takes to make a city unbearable: this is particularly true in Santo Antônio where congestion is infernal. Many city buses in this part of town leave from outside the main post office (from Avenida Guararapes or Rua do Sol), and from Avenida Dantas Barreto and Rua do Carmo further south. The buses along Conde de Boa Vista are easier to handle, not so those streaming through Parque 13 de Maio. There are several trolleybus lines, and these are generally less crowded than the regular buses.

To get to Boa Viagem from Boa Vista the best bus to catch is the one marked Setúbal, which stops outside the Facultad de Direita on the east side of Parque 13 de Maio. This same bus stops on Dantas Barreto, but from Santo Antônio the best place to catch Boa Viagem buses is from Rua do Carmo. Buses marked Piedade and Candeias both go south. In Boa Viagem, buses run south along Avenida Aguiar, and return to town along Avenida Domingos Ferreira.

Most routes you will need are given with the relevant destination below. If you need any further information, go to the headquarters of EMTU, the city bus company, in the old station building at the end of Rua de Santa Rita (Santo Antônio). There is no organized information desk, but you should find someone willing to help. Alternatively, call 158.

Metro. This elevated railway was not designed with visitors in mind. The only time you are likely to use it is between the bus station and the centre. It runs 5am to 11pm. For information call 224-0922.

ACCOMMODATION

Few cheap hotels in the centre are tolerable. Many people prefer to stay in Olinda, which is a cleaner, safer and more pleasant, or in Boa Viagem.

Centre. The main concentration of cheap hotels is around Parque 13 de Maio in Boa Vista. This is a lively part of town full of bars and restaurants frequented by local students. On the square itself, on Rua do Hospício, is Hotel Suíça. This rambling and decrepit colonial mansion has gloomy and overpriced rooms, and serves an unappetizing breakfast. Nevertheless, it is well-situated and the attached restaurant is a popular watering-hole in the evenings. Most other places are south from here, on or near Rua do Hospício. At Rua do Riachuelo 547, a short way south, is Hotel Lido (tel 221-1467), with rooms for $5-12; it is one of the better places, but the street is ill-lit at night. Further south, at Rua do Hospício 51, is Hotel do Parque (tel 222-5427/4744), an unfriendly place with rooms for $5-9. You would do better to continue to Praça Maciel Pinheiro, a pleasant, tranquil square. Here the Hotel America (number 48; tel 221-1300/1389) is slightly more expensive but also better value, charging $8-13.

Boa Viagem. Staying in Boa Viagem is the more expensive option, but it places you within easy reach of the beach or the city's best restaurants. Hotel Quebramar (Rua dos Navegantes 2930; tel 465-1151), near the northern end of the street, has rooms costing $12-15, and there are several restaurants nearby. About ten blocks further south is a cluster of places on Rua Félix de Brito Melo. Pousada Aconchega (number 382; tel 326-2989) is a two-star hotel with a swimming pool and a good restaurant. It is friendly and clean, with rooms for $16-20. Nearby, at number 372, is the Hotel Alameda Jasmins (tel 325-1591), with similar facilities and prices.

EATING AND DRINKING

Bars and restaurants around Pátio de São Pedro in Santo Antônio cater primarily for the tourist trade and are overpriced. Try instead the Leite in Praça Joaquim Nabuco (near Ponte de Boa Vista), which has a good varied menu. Most people are content with the simple but busy restaurants around Parque 13 de Maio, which offer fairly standard menus and similar quality; the liveliest streets are Ruas do Hospício and 7 de Setembro. This is the best area for evening drinking, though not many places stay open late.

For a better class of meal you must go to Boa Viagem. But be prepared to do a certain amount of leg work, since the restaurants are scattered all along the main thoroughfares. Be warned that the streets are quiet and fairly dark at night, particularly the seafront boulevard. There are many restaurants on or off Avenida Aguiar, including several near the northern end of Rua dos Navegantes. Coisas de Minas is one of the best restaurants in the city, and its moqueca (fish served in a creamy, coconut sauce) is excellent. Prices are high, but most helpings are big enough for two people. Nearby are the Pizzeria Fiorentino (Rua Laete Lemos, around the corner from Hotel Quebramar) and Frutas & Folhas (four blocks south near Rua João Cícero), which serves mainly crêpes and salads. Also try the restaurants in the hotels on Felix de Brito, which serve good food. In Praça de Boa Viagem, about 20 blocks south, is Bar Lapinha (tel 326-1914), a popular bar which also serves good regional food.

EXPLORING

Santo Antônio. Praça da República, at the eastern end of Santo Antônio, is a large and impressive square, with the usual array of public buildings and palm trees. The square lacks the atmosphere of the streets a few blocks south, but it is one of the few spots in the centre where you can enjoy a sense of spaciousness. On the north side is the Palácio do Governo, constructed on the site of a palace built by the Dutch prince, Maurice of Nassau.

A block or so south along Rua do Imperador is the 17th-century church and convent of Santo Antônio, which is one of the highlights of Recife. The blue and white Flemish tilework is some of the finest in South America. Through some railings on the left-hand side of the church is a beautifully gilded chapel, the so-called Capela Dourada. Particularly interesting are the paintings of Jesuit martyrs strung up on crosses; the faces of the guards have been obscured. The chapel is part of the Museu Franciscano de Arte Sacra, next door. The rest of the museum boasts no other great treasures, but don't miss the rather bizarre statues of nuns and monks in the courtyard. The chapel and museum is open 8-11.30am and 2-5pm Monday to Friday, 8-11.30am on Saturday.

Walking south along Rua Duque de Caxias you end up at Mercado São José, a huge ironwork structure built in 1875 and now a National Monument; it resembles a cross between a giant greenhouse and a railway station. The narrow streets west of São José are lined with crumbling early 19th-century buildings. The whole area is simply one big market, seething with people and smells: the fresh meat stalls are enough to make even those with iron constitutions nauseous. Coming across Pátio de São Pedro, further west, is totally unexpected. The square has been beautifully restored, but in terms of the decrepit and chaotic state of the streets in this part of town, it is decidedly incongruous. It is, significantly, virtually empty of people: Pátio de São Pedro is said to be the heart of Recife's intellectual and artistic quarter, but the art galleries and craft shops hold few attractions for the local people. Nevertheless, it is a good place to catch your breath, and you may well wish to seek refuge in one of the quiet bars. The main point of interest is the cathedral of São Pedro dos Clérigos (1782), which contains a fine trompe l'oeil ceiling and several magnificent wooden altars. On the west side is the Fundaçao de Cultura (FCCR), which gives out information on cultural performances and sells books.

On the banks of Rio Capibaribe, off Rua Floriano Peixoto, is the Casa da Cultura — formerly a prison. It has been immaculately transformed, and craft shops now occupy the cells. The centre is open daily 10am-5pm. Opposite is the old train station, a handsome late 19th-century building, with a railway museum.

Museu do Homem do Nordeste. This is the best museum in the city. It lies 4 miles/6km northwest of the centre on Avenida 17 de Agosto, in Casa Forte district. It actually consists of several museums which house displays of anthropology, folklore, Afro-Brazilian rituals, indigenous medicine, and the history of sugar and other Northeastern crops. Don't miss the section devoted to popular art. Guided tours are given in Portuguese, English and French.

The museum is open evrey day except Monday. It opens at 11am on Tuesday, Wednesday and Friday, 8am on Thursday, and 2pm at weekends, and closes daily at 5pm. To get there catch the bus marked Dois Irmãos-Rui Barbosa, from the post office or Parque 13 de Maio (Rua do Hospício), which takes 30 minutes. To make a day trip, continue on the same bus route a little further to the Horto Zoobotânico; while the zoo is distressing, the botanical gardens are a peaceful change from the busy streets of the city.

Museu da Abolição (Museum of Slavery). Sadly, at the time of going to press this museum was closed until further notice, owing to government cutbacks. Don't miss going if it has reopened. It is housed in the home of the abolitionist, João Alfredo, a beautiful early 19th-century mansion covered in remarkably well-preserved azulejos. The museum is at Rua Benefica 150, in Madalena district, about ten minutes by bus west of Boa Vista. To get there you can take one of several buses from Conde de Boa Vista, including the trolleybus marked Varzea-Caxangá; get off at the first stop along Avenida Caxangá.

Boa Viagem. The five-mile long beach is magnificent to look at. However, not everyone enjoys swimming there because of the pools formed by the reef, and the stony seabed. The main square on the seafront is Praça de Boa Viagem, at the southern end of Rua dos Navegantes. It is given over to a fair on Saturday and Sunday afternoons, when people sell regional food.

ENTERTAINMENT

On weekend evenings there are music, poetry and folklore performances in Pátio de São Pedro, though during the low season the entertainment may take the form simply of a forró disco. There are also occasional performances in the Casa de Cultura. For information on any of these events, ask at the Fundaçao de Cultura in Pátio de São Pedro, or at the tourist office. The monthly *Itinerario* brochure, which you can usually pick up in the smarter hotels, has a couple of pages devoted to forthcoming events.

The tourist office also gives out information on the carnival routes. Most characteristic of Recife's carnival are the wild rhythms played by the *frevo* groups, the dances and colourful costumes of the so-called *caboclinhos*, and the distinctive sounds of the *maracatú* groups (local to Pernambuco).

HELP AND INFORMATION

Tourist Information: Empetur, the state tourist board, has its main office at Avenida Conde de Boa Vista 700, 3rd floor (tel 231-7941/4104/7744). It is open 7.30am-1.30pm Monday to Friday. The staff working in the tiny office seem surprised whenever a tourist arrives, but they give out maps and are extremely helpful.

Communications: the central post office is at Avenida Guararapes 250 (Santo Antônio), near Ponte Duarte Coelho. It opens 8am-6pm Monday to Friday, 8am-1pm on Saturday.

There are Telpe (telephone) offices at Rua Diário de Pernambuco 38 (between Avenida Dantas Barreto and Rua Imperador), Rua do Hospício 148 (near the corner of Conde de Boa Vista), and in Pátio de São Pedro.

Money: the banks on Avenida Dantas Barreto are the ones most likely to change money. Banco do Brasil's exchange office is on the 7th floor, reached through a side entrance on Rua do Rosário. It changes cheques and cash, and does credit card withdrawals. Lloyds has a branch on Rua do Rosário, but it doesn't normally change money. If desperate try the shops in Pátio de São Pedro or the Casa de Cultura, but the rates are appalling. You can get a better deal in hotels in Boa Viagem, where banks will also exchange foreign currency.

American Express is at Kontik-Franstur, Rua da Concordia 278, Santo Antônio (tel 224-9888).

Polícia Federal: Cais do Apolo, which runs along the Rio Caparibe on Recife island (tel 231-2041).

Bookshop: the best source of secondhand books is Livraria Brandão (Rua da Matriz 22) near Praça Pinheiro. There is not a huge selection of foreign-language books, but you can find the odd good novel; exchanges are usually possible.

Consulates. *Argentina:* Avenida Aguiar 4887, Edif. Marisol 106, Boa Viagem (tel 326-5378).
Peru: Rua dos Coelhos 300 (tel 222-5713), southern end of Boa Vista.
UK: Avenida Domingos Ferreira 222, Sala 203 (tel 326-3733).
USA: Rua Gonçalves Maia 163, Boa Vista (tel 221-1412/3).

OLINDA

Considering that it was burnt down by the Dutch in the 17th century, Olinda is a truly remarkable sight — largely thanks to early restoration work done by the Portuguese. Scaling the town's steep, cobbled streets is an exhausting business, but the views from the hilltops are magnificent: the skyline of modern Recife is an uncanny but pleasantly remote backdrop to the view of white-washed churches and red-roofed houses that are draped over Olinda's green hills. This is a wonderful, breezy haven so near and yet so far from the busy and polluted streets of Recife.

Olinda is, inevitably, inundated with tourists. The atmosphere has suffered to some extent (you can expect to be pestered by hordes of would-be guides), but this is no reason to miss it. Olinda is the Bohemian side of Recife. Among the ancient buildings are lively artistic, intellectual and gay communities: the colourful graffiti and buzzing cafés are as typical of Olinda as the beautifully carved doors and skilful stucco-work. At weekends it is a vibrant place to be. In addition, Olinda's carnival is famous nationwide.

Arrival and Departure. There is a constant stream of buses from the centre of Recife, marked Jardim Atlántico, Rio Doce and Casa Caiada to give just a selection. All buses pass along Rua do Hospício and through Parque 13 de Maio; some, including the Jardim Atlántico bus, can be picked up from Rua do Sol, outside the post office. The best place to get off is at Praça do Carmo; you can catch buses back into town from anywhere along the seafront.

Accommodation. The standard of accommodation is good, but beware of a ridiculous rise in rates during the Carnival and high season.

There are several excellent places in the old city. Pousada Flor de Manhã (Rua São Francisco 162; tel 429-2266) is in a lovely position just north of Praça do Carmo. Rates vary according to the view, but rooms with shower cost about $12/$15; there is also a dorm with bunk beds for around $6. Pousada do Bonfim (Rua do Bonfim 115; tel 429-1674) is up another hill from the square. This is a youth hostel and charges about $5 per bed ($4 with a IYHF card). Pousada dos Quatros Cantos (Rua Prudente de Morais 441; tel 429-0220/1845) is housed in a most beautiful building. The cheapest rooms cost $12-16 ($14/20 for a triple).

There are also several places along Rua do Sol, a short walk north of Praça do Carmo along the seafront. The best option is the Albergue da Olinda (Rua do Sol 233; tel 429-1592), a friendly place with rooms for $9/$12. A little further along at number 311 is Pousada do Fortim (tel 429-3762), which is extremely good value at $8/$10. The cheapest option in the area is the pousada on Praça Dantas Barreto, a little further north, which charges $5 per person.

Eating and Drinking. Olinda is a good place to eat seafood, particularly crab, and there are several restaurants along the seafront. These are simple places for the most part, a pleasant change from the smart seafood restaurants in Boa Viagem. A popular haunt in the evenings is Alto da Sé, particularly the Coutinho do Sé restaurant, which stays open late; the food is expensive, but it's a good place for a few beers. Also in the square are people selling charcoal-grilled meat and other goodies. The restaurant in the Quatro Cantos hotel is also open to non-residents.

Exploring. Rua do Bonfim, which heads west off Praça do Carmo, is typical of Olinda: low houses, painted different shades. Turn right on to Ladeira da Sé which leads steeply up to Alto da Sé. Dominated by the cathedral (1537), this square provides your first proper views over Olinda and across to Recife. In high season the square is busy with tourists scouring the stalls for souvenirs; at other times of year it livens up only at night.

West of the square past the former Bishop's Palace (now the Museu de Arte Sacra) is the church of Misericordia. Inside is beautiful tiling, outside are the best views of Olinda. The road running down the hill and up the other side takes you through a lovely part of town. Near the dip of the hill, through the green gates at Rua Bernardo Vieira de Melo 322, is the tourist office (it has another entrance on Rua 13 de Maio). You can pick up maps and brochures from 7.30am-1.30pm, daily except Sunday. At the top of the hill is Mercado Ribeiro, where a fairly good selection of crafts is sold at imaginatively high prices. If you continue down to the next junction, you can turn right onto Rua 13 de Maio. Along here is the former jail of the Inquisition, a fine 18th-century building which now houses the Museu de Arte Contemporânea. This is an excellent gallery and contains some interesting local scenes; it opens 8am-5pm on weekdays (except Tuesday) and 2-6pm at weekends.

Rejoining your former route and continuing down the hill, you reach the Mosteiro São Bento, one of the highlights of Olinda: the church has some stunning carving work. It opens 8-11am and 1-5pm daily. Recitals are sometimes put on here: ask the caretaker or at the tourist office for information. Walking down the hill brings you once more to Praça do Carmo. If you have any energy left, climb to the top of Rua São Francisco, to the monastery of the same name. Built in 1585, and with fantastic woodcarving and azulejos, this was Brazil's first Franciscan monastery.

AROUND RECIFE

Beaches. The best beaches are south of Recife, and are good for swimming: the coral reef protects the coast and the sea is calm. Most beaches have at least a couple of hotels and a campsite of sorts. Some are accessible by bus direct from Recife, but otherwise you must change at Cabo, a town just off the BR-101 about 30 minutes from the capital.

Guaibú, about 15 miles/24km south, has a lovely beach and it is within walking distance of the sheltered and often deserted beach at Calhetas. Further south is the splendid Porto de Galinhas, about an hour by bus south of Recife, and with good facilities.

Igarassú. Set among green hills on a ridge by the coast north of Recife, Igarassú is a remarkably unspoilt colonial town, and a welcome contrast to the twee commercialism of Olinda. Founded in 1535, it is one of Brazil's oldest towns: the São Cosme e Damião church, begun in the same year, is held by some to be the oldest of its kind in the country.

Igarassú lies 22 miles/35km north of Recife, just east of the BR-101. Buses are frequent and take about 45 minutes. They leave from Avenida Martins de Barros (Santo Antônio), but can also be picked up along Rua do Hospício. Hotels in Igarassú are scarce and expensive.

Ilha de Itamaracá. Ten miles/16km beyond Igarassú, at Itapissuma, a causeway joins the mainland to the island of Itamaracá. The first thing you see on arrival is a large prison, whose inmates work in the surrounding fields and sell souvenirs by the roadside. Nearby is a fine 18th-century sugar estate. The town of Itamaracá is nothing special, though you can see the ruins of the old port, Vilha Velha. The main attraction is the lovely beaches. While those within easy access of the town have been ruined by development and are swarming with people at weekends, it is possible to find more secluded spots. To get to the best beaches you need to walk for an hour or more from Itamaracá town (e.g. to Janguaribe), or to walk from Forte Oranje, a Dutch fort about 3 miles/5km from town. All hotels are in or around the town, and are moderately expensive. Camping is discouraged because potentially dangerous prisoners escape periodically.

Buses bound for Itamaracá leave Recife hourly, from Martins de Barros and go via Igarassú. Limited public transport is available on the island.

THE FERNANDO DE NORONHA ISLANDS

This archipelago of volcanic islands lies in the Atlantic about 330 miles/528km northeast of Recife. Only one small island — itself called Fernando de Noronha — is inhabited. Having remained largely undisturbed since the colonial days (apart from when it was a US base during the Second World War), Fernando de Noronha is now discovering the joys of tourism. Daily flights from Recife bring an increasing number of visitors to enjoy the beautiful beaches and excellent marine life. Local fishermen down their nets to take people out snorkelling and diving, and families take guests into their homes. There is only one main settlement, Vila dos Remédios, and just one hotel, though a bed in a local home costs $15-20.

Booking a package deal is the standard way to visit the island, but there is nothing to stop you travelling independently: the Nordeste flight costs a reasonable $130 return.

Inland From Recife

CARUARU

The fame of Caruarú stems from its market, which is the biggest in the Northeast and has been designated by UNESCO as the largest centre of folk art in the Americas. The market draws traders from all the surrounding communities and takes over the entire town. Saturday is the main day for it, but there is a fair amount of activity on Wednesday and Friday too. The market is divided up into sections, the most interesting parts being those given over to food, crafts and goods for barter (known as *troca-troca*). The small clay statues (*figurinhas*) made in the nearby village of Alto do Moura, are particularly famous; so too is the *literatura de cordel*, popular poetry performed in the streets.

Caruarú, which lies on the edge of the sertão and has a population of around 200,000, is 84 miles/134km west of Recife. Buses, which take two hours, leave every 30 minutes and are operated by several companies, including Progresso and Caruarense. There are also daily buses from Salvador. Most people visit Caruarú as a day trip, but there is no shortage of hotels. The choice in the lower range is limited, the Centenário (Rua 7 de Setembro 84; tel 721-9011) being among the cheapest.

NOVA JERUSALEM

This is the name given to an extraordinary theatre in the dusty village of Fazenda Nova, some 30 miles/48km northwest of Caruarú. It is a replica of Jerusalem, and is the largest open-air theatre in the world. It was the brainchild of a local landowner, and was built in the 70s by farmers in the region. Every Easter the Passion of Christ is performed by several hundred local people, and attracts people from all over Brazil, and also from abroad. The huge audience moves around the city for each scene, guided by centurions with torches. To attend is a once-in-a-lifetime experience. It is also a good time to try the regional food, as well as a bonanza for pickpockets. The hotels in town are basic, but there is also a campsite. There are buses to Fazenda Nova from Caruarú and Recife.

THE SERTAO

If you are interested in getting a taste of the sertão and its extraordinary landscapes, the best place to aim for is Petrolina on the banks of the Rio São Francisco which marks the border with Bahia. Petrolina is served by buses from Recife (via Caruarú), some 450 miles/720km east, and the journey provides an excellent overview of the interior. If you want to stop off, expect spartan hotels. From Juazeiro, across the river in Bahia, there are occasional boats down to Pirapora in Minas Gerais. Otherwise head southeast to Salvador or northwards into Piauí or Ceará.

PARAIBA and RIO GRANDE DO NORTE

The state of Paraíba is not worth crossing the country for, but the locals, unused to foreigners, are open and friendly. The capital, João Pessoa, is a worthwhile stop for anyone en route to the beaches of Rio Grande do Norte or beyond.

JOAO PESSOA

The capital of Paraíba has a decrepit but not unpleasant feel to it. The setting is lovely and it's a relaxing place to spend a couple of days. The city lies on the banks of the Rio Sanhauá, and has a population of around 450,000. Founded in 1585, it has a number of old churches and other colonial buildings worth visiting. Among the locals, however, João Pessoa is best known for the nearby Tambaú and Cabo Branco beaches.

Arrival and Departure. The airport (tel 229-1009) is 7 miles/11km south of the centre and is served by daily flights from all over the country.

Buses run hourly to João Pessoa from Recife, 75 miles/120km south; the journey takes two hours. Buses serve Natal (115 miles/184km north) every two hours, taking three hours; the daily overnight services to and from Fortaleza take ten hours. The Rodoviária (tel 221-9611) is on Avenida Francisco Londres, ten minutes west of the centre. Buses run to the Parque Sólon de Lucena, the city's greatest landmark commonly known as Lagoa after the circular lake in the middle. Lagoa is a stop on many city bus routes.

Accommodation. One of the best places to stay is Hotel Aurora (tel 221-2238) in Praça João Pessoa, a few blocks west of Lagoa. Cheaper is the Pedro Américo, northwest of the Aurora on the square of the same name.

The hotels on Tambaú beach, a ten-minute bus ride east from Lagoa, are more expensive, but you have the advantage of being in the liveliest part of the city, with bars, good seafood restaurants and several venues where you can hear regional music. The hotel offering the best value is the Gameleira (Avenida João Maurício 157; tel 226-1576), which charges under $10. If it is full, try the Beira-Mar (Avenida Antônio Lira 380; tel 226-6501). There is a campsite near Ponte de Seixas (see below).

Exploring. You should be able to pick up a city map from the information kiosk in the bus station; otherwise, go to the tourist office at Avenida Getúlio Vargas 301, or the Centro Turístico at Avenida Tamandaré 100 in Tambaú.

The main area to explore lies west of Lagoa. Praça João Pessoa is a pleasant square, with an old Jesuit college and the Palácio do Governo. North, beyond a couple of other squares, is Rua Visconde de Pelotas where there are several churches. However, the highlight of João Pessoa is the church of São Francisco, on a hilltop at the northern end of Rua Duque de Caxias. Despite the motley amalgamation of styles, this is one of Brazil's most magnificent churches. The azulejos (tiles) in the courtyard are breathtaking, and the cloisters in the adjacent convent are no less impressive. Ladeira São Francisco leads west down the hill. On it is the Casa de Pólvora, the old arsenal which now houses a museum containing good photographs of the city as it once was.

Rather than swim at Tambaú, head for the secluded beach at Baía da Traição. This is a lovely fishing village with a ruined Dutch fort, about 50 miles/80km north of João Pessoa. Buses run twice daily and take two hours; bring a hammock.

Land's End. Nearer home, just 9 miles/14km south of João Pessoa, is the palm-fringed beach of Cabo Branco. This is a smart residential suburb, but modern developments have left the beach surprisingly unscathed. From Cabo Branco you can walk up the hill to Ponta de Seixas, the easternmost point in the Americas. The views from the clifftop lighthouse are magnificent. Buses to Cabo Branco leave from the Rodoviária or Lagoa.

CAMPINA GRANDE

The BR-230 highway runs west from João Pessoa, into the hills of the sertão. About 75 miles/120km and two hours by bus along this road is Campina Grande, a city with a population of 300,000. It is proud of its claim to be the 'Porta do Sertão', but Campina Grande could never be described as an attractive place. Its interest lies in its position as a distribution point for products of the sertão, which feed its Wednesday and Saturday market. Compared with other great fairs of the Northeast it is small. Nevertheless, it is a fascinating spectacle, with good local crafts on sale. The best time to visit Campina Grande is in June, when its main annual festival lasts all month.

Buses run hourly between João Pessoa and Campina Grande, and there are daily buses from other Northeastern towns, including Caruarú; buses also head west into Ceará. The best place to stay is in the Rique Palace Hotel at Rua Venâncio

Neiva 287 (tel 341-1433), in the town's tallest building; cheaper but noisier is the Belfran at Avenida Floriano Peixoto 258.

RIO GRANDE DO NORTE

The state capital is Natal. North of it, the coast of Rio Grande do Norte is virtually one long beach, with huge sand dunes. Tourist development is only in its infancy away from Natal, and although access can be a problem, there are many unspoilt fishing villages and beaches.

NATAL

This city lies 114 miles/182km north of João Pessoa, on a peninsula flanked by the Potengi estuary and the Atlantic. Natal itself (population 400,000) is of scant interest to the passing visitor. However, it has become popular among local holidaymakers, who come to take advantage of the beaches within reach of the city. Natal is doing all it can to cultivate the interest, but it is unlikely ever to be anything more than a poor man's Fortaleza.

City Layout. The heart of Natal is Cidade Alta, which is what little remains of the old city. The grid layout extends into the residential areas of Petrópolis and Tirol further east. The terrain becomes less user-friendly as dusty streets descend circuitously and steeply to the city beaches on the east side of the headland; travelling between the Cidade Alta and beach area is often best done by bus.

Avenida Rio Branco is the main thoroughfare through the centre and it continues northwards down the hill: the only reason to venture into this rather scruffy part of town is to go to the old bus station (Rodoviária Velha) in Praça Augusto Severo, off Avenida Duque de Caxias. This is the main terminal for city buses and for those heading to nearby beaches.

Arrival and Departure. *Air:* the Augusto Severo airport (tel 272-2811) is 10 miles/16km south of town, off the João Pessoa-bound BR-101. Buses (usually marked Cidade de Esperança) from outside the terminal head downtown, generally terminating at the old bus station; most run along Avenida Rio Branco, and this is the best place to get off. A fixed-rate taxi will set you back $14.

Bus: the bus station (Rodoviária Nova; tel 231-1170) is in Cidade de Esperança district, 4 miles/6km southwest of the centre. Cross the road to catch a bus into the centre: virtually any one will do. Numbers 34 and 41, for example, run to the old bus station via Rio Branco. The best place to pick up the bus to head back to the station is in Praça João Tiburcio, behind Santo Antônio church; allow 20-30 minutes.

The main long-distance bus services from Natal are as follows: Fortaleza (7 hours; $10) — three daytime services with Viação Nordeste; João Pessoa (3 hours; $4) — every two hours (5.30am-7.30pm) with Viação Nordeste; Recife ($4\frac{1}{2}$ hours; $7) — buses every hour or so from 6am-7pm, with Nápoles, and one leito service. São Geraldo has one daily service to Maceió (8pm; $12) and Aracajú (4pm; $17); Viação Progresso has a daily service to Teresina and São Luis at 3pm.

Accommodation. But for a couple of excellent low-budget hotels, Natal has little to offer. Hotel Casa Grande (Rua Princesa Isabel 529; tel 222-1513), a block east of Rio Branco, is exceptionally clean and friendly. Rooms with bathroom are excellent value at $6-10/$10-13, which includes one of the best breakfasts in Brazil.

A short distance down the same street is Pousada Sertaneja. Slightly further out in the Petrópolis suburb, about 15 minutes walk east of the centre, is the Pousada Meu Canto (Rua Manoel Dantas 424; tel 222-8351). This youth hostel is welcoming and sociable, with rooms for $6-8.

If you want to stay by the seafront, within easy reach of the main concentration of restaurants and bars, head for Avenida Presidente Café Filho, which skirts the two main city beaches, Praia do Meio and Praia dos Artistas. Pousadas on and off the main drag include Pousada Maria Bonita (Travessa Café Filho 50; tel 222-3836) which charges $12-14 per room.

Eating and Drinking. Finding somewhere to eat along the seafront is easy. But locating a decent restaurant in the centre requires a certain amount of patience, particularly if you don't want to splash out. The Cidade Alta is like a ghost town in the evening, and few restaurants are open after 8pm. One of the best options is the Casa Grande Hotel, which has its own excellent restaurant, or try the friendly restaurant on the corner of Cascudo and Felipe Camarão. If you are out and about late, you should be able to get a meal along Avenida João Pessoa, one of the few streets that is at all animated at night.

For a better class of restaurant look east of the centre, in Tirol and Petrópolis. (Note that these areas are quiet and ill-lit at night, so it might be a good idea to get a taxi back to your hotel.) Best is Raízes (tel 222-7338), on the corner of Campos Sales and Mossoró, which specializes in regional cooking. There are also several restaurants scattered along Avenida Afonso Pena, two blocks east of Campos Sales.

The best bar in which to have a beer downtown is the *whiskería* upstairs on the corner of Caldas and Felipe Camarão. It is one of the few places in the centre to have any atmosphere, largely thanks to the dim lighting and good music (sometimes live). There is a cover charge of $1.

Exploring. The most interesting part of the Cidade Alta lies west of Rio Branco. Praça João Maria is a pleasant enough square with a few public buildings and an unremarkable church, plus a few stalls selling crafts. Around the corner is a much more interesting church, the 18th-century Igreja de Santo Antônio, which has a fine wooden altar.

The best museum is the Museu da Câmara Cascudo (Hermes da Fonseca 1440), southwest of the centre. It contains a fairly interesting anthropological collection, including displays of regional crafts. It is open 8-11am and 2-4pm, Tuesday to Friday, and on Saturday mornings.

Natal's old prison, off Rua Cordeiro de Farias, has been converted into a tourist centre. This large, solid building is in a magnificent hilltop position, and commands great views both of the city and across to the other side of the estuary. There are various shops, most interesting of which is the gallery-cum-shop upstairs, which sells modern paintings and has a good selection of books and regional crafts. From the windows you can see the Forte dos Reis Magos, which lies off the tip of the headland. This 16th-century Portuguese fort is the oldest structure in the city, but it is best viewed from a distance: to get there from the centre is a not particularly pleasant trek.

From the tourist centre it is easy to head down to the city beaches. By turning left on to Nilo Peçanha, near the top of the hill is a stairway which takes you directly down to the seafront. The city beaches are narrow, and the reef hampers bathing. Nevertheless, this is the liveliest part of town, with lots of barracas.

Help and Information. The information desk in the tourist centre (see above) is often unstaffed during the low season. The post office is on the corner of Rio Branco and Caldas. Natal is a bad place to change money, but the Banco do Brasil on Rio Branco can normally oblige. Varig and Vasp have their offices on Avenida João Pessoa; Transbrasil is at Deodoro 363.

Around Natal

Some would say that the most interesting thing about Natal is the Brazilian Air Force rocket base about 12 miles/20km away. Known as Barreira do Inferno (Hell's Gate), it is open to the public periodically: ask at the tourist office.

South of Natal. The beaches south of Natal are the most heavily developed. Ponte Negra, with its huge sand dune, is spectacular. But being just 9 miles/14km south of the city, it has a mass of smart hotels and is positively teeming at weekends. You would do better to head further south. Pirangi do Norte, 19 miles/30km south of Natal, has a beach but it is more renowned for its cashew nut tree, which is the largest in the world: its canopy measures an incredible 7,000 square metres. South across the river is Pirangi do Sul. The shore from here down to Búzios (3 miles/5km south) is lovely, and deserted during the week. If you hanker for greater seclusion, head for Baia Formosa, near the border with Paraíba, which sees next to no tourists but has a couple of hotels. The two daily buses from Natal take about $2\frac{1}{2}$ hours.

North of Natal. Dunes stretch for miles along this stretch of coast, most famously at Genipabú, 20 miles/32km north of Natal. The beach is busy at weekends and during the high season, but nothing can detract from its magnificent 40m-high dunes, which are dotted with palms and slope steeply into the sea. The craze is to hire beach buggies and career up and down the sand — a reason to avoid weekend visits. There are several hotels, cheapest among which are Pousada Dunas de Genipabú (tel 225-2112), Villa do Sol (better views; tel 225-2132) and Pousada Marazul (tel 225-2065). Buses to Genipabú run from the city bus terminal, but not that regularly.

If you want to head further from the city, go to Maxaranguape or Touros, 40 miles/63km and 80 miles/128km north of Natal respectively. Both these small communities have simple facilities, including a couple of pousadas, and are accessible by bus from Natal.

CEARA

The coastline of Ceará, like that of northern Rio Grande do Norte, forms virtually one long beach. It is the most popular stretch of the Northeastern coast. Fortaleza, the capital, is one of the largest cities in the region, with a population of around 1.8 million. It is also a major craft centre, reflecting the state's rich folkloric tradition.

Fortaleza

The capital of Ceará is a sprawling, uncohesive city. On paper it has little to offer, yet most travellers end up staying in Fortaleza longer than they had intended: not only because the city is a good base from which to go beach-hopping along the coast, but also because its own seafront is extremely lively. But the beachside scene is far removed from the reality of Fortaleza, a poor and troubled city. The number of beggars is alarming, and there is a heavy police presence: while the men in uniform are easily obscured by tourists along the seafront boulevards, they are only too visible in the centre.

CITY LAYOUT

The heart of Fortaleza is small and easy to get around. It takes in roughly the area between Praça da Sé and Praça José de Alençar; the latter is dominated by a fine Art Nouveau theatre which is a useful landmark. The main beach area is a ten-minute bus ride east from the centre along Avenida Tabosa; Avenida Kennedy is the seafront promenade.

Most buses from the centre to the beach leave from Praça Carreira, which is the main city bus terminal, or the nearby Rua 24 de Maio; buses marked Praia do Futuro, Caça e Pesca or Dom Luiz are among those heading for the beach. There is also the so-called Praia Circular, a special bus which does the rounds of all the beaches; you can pick it up on Rua Castro e Silva, just off Praça Carreira. Buses back to the centre are frequent until 10.30-11pm: wait anywhere along Avenidas Abolição or Tabosa.

A taxi from the seafront to the centre costs about $4, but bargain. There is a rank (tel 244-7080) in the square near the junction of Abolição and Tabosa: haggling with these taxi-drivers is easier than with those hanging around the posh hotels.

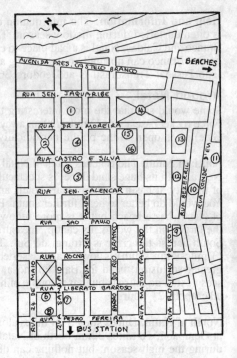

FORTALEZA

1 Tourist Centre
2 Praça Carreira
3 Stop for beach bus
4 Hotel Savoy
5 Hotel Moreira
6 Teatro José Alençar
7 Stop for bus to terminal
8 Stop for airport bus
9 Museu do Ceará
10 Mercado Central
11 Cathedral
12 Post Office
13 Hotel Caxambú
14 Passeio Público
15 Hotel Passeio
16 Restaurante Belas Artes

Maps. A good free map can be picked up at the tourist office. A more detailed map is sold for $3 from some news stands.

ARRIVAL AND DEPARTURE

Air. Pinto Martins airport (tel 227-8066) is 4 miles/6km west of the centre. The

Hotel Caxambú (Rua General Bezerril 22; tel 231-0339), a smart-looking but not overpriced place near the Mercado Central.

Beach. Hotels are scattered along the seafront, but by heading a couple of blocks inland you can find the cheaper and quieter places.

There are two hotels opposite each other on Avenida Tabosa near the corner of Avenida Rui Barbosa, a few blocks before the bottom of the hill. Pousada da Praia (number 1315; tel 224-5935) is friendly and the better of the two. Rooms with bath cost $9/$13, more for hot water. The Pousada Casa Grande opposite is scruffier, but charges just $4-5 per person. Near the bottom of the hill, at Avenida Barão de Studart 157, is the Ladeira Praia Hotel (tel 261-3668/224-3301), a welcoming place with rooms for around $10.

To be nearer the action stay at the Pousada Sol e Mar (Avenida Kennedy 3052; tel 224-5636), on the seafront near the Clube Nautico, which charges $22 for a double room. For a quieter location and better value for money, head a couple of blocks inland to Rua Ana Bilhar. At number 132 is Nossa Pousada (tel 261-4699), on the corner of Joaquim Nabuco, which is clean and has double rooms for $13. Further east, at number 507 (tel 244-2568) is Prata de Casa Pousada, which charges $13/$18.

EATING AND DRINKING

Downtown Fortaleza isn't well off for restaurants, and most close early. The best and certainly the most popular place is Restaurante Belas Artes (Rua Major Facundo 82), a block from Praça dos Mártires. Alternatively, try the Kury Restaurant, at Senador Pompeu 959. In the early evening, the best place to be is in Praça José de Alençar. There's usually a good deal going on at this time and the bars are busy with people fresh out of work. Later at night, however, these same bars tend to get rowdy, and are not ideal for a quiet drink. Women on their own may prefer the bar on the fifth floor of Hotel Lord (open until 9pm).

Eat seafood at one of the countless places along the seafront, which range from simple barracas to full-blown restaurants offering high-quality meals. The main concentration begins about half way along Avenida Kennedy. It takes about 45 minutes to walk the length of it and, as a rule, the further east you head the better the food. While the smart restaurants such as El Trapiche (3956; tel 244-4400) and Peixada do Meio (4632; tel 224-2719), serve excellent food, more fun and lively are the restaurants under the trees. You can also feast on the snacks sold in the street, such as the hot tapioca cakes. Wherever you decide to hang out in this area, take plenty of small change to give the street children, beggars and artists who scour the beachside restaurants.

A more unusual restaurant in this area is the one in the Clube Nautico, a huge peppermint-green building with a colonial feel. It is on the corner of Avenida Des. Moreira and Tabosa, and you need not be a member of the swimming club to eat there.

EXPLORING

Fortaleza's modest sights will not keep you long. The first place to visit is the Centro de Turismo, housed in the 19th-century jail a couple of blocks from the waterfront: it covers an entire block between Ruas Senador Pompeu and General Sampaio. The complex is worth visiting primarily for the tourist office and the Museu de Arte e Cultura Populares, which includes good examples of local crafts.

A couple of blocks southeast of the tourist centre is Praça dos Mártires, a shady but rather forlorn square known more commonly as the Passeio Público. Beyond is Praça da Sé, which is dominated by the hideous modern cathedral. Steering well clear of it and heading up Rua Conde D'Eu, you reach the Mercado Central, which is the best place in the city to buy local crafts — primarily embroidery, textiles, lace and clothes. Rua General Bezerril is also a good street in which to buy hammocks. The main covered market is rather spiritless, and more interesting are the stalls scattered about the surrounding streets, particularly those selling roots, plant extracts and other mysterious potions. In addition to the central market, craft fairs take place on most days of the week in various parts of the city; ask at the tourist office for details. There is a daily craft market in the evenings opposite Hotel Praiana, on Avenida Kennedy.

Near the Mercado Central is the Museu do Ceará, which is housed in the old provincial assembly building on the corner of Ruas Floriano Peixoto and São Paulo. The anthropological and historical museum previously housed on Avenida Barão de Studart was, at the time of going to press, being transferred here.

The only city beach good for swimming is Praia do Futuro, around the headland beyond the port. It is fairly built-up and busy at weekends. You can watch the fishermen bring in their *jangadas* (boats), and eat wonderful fresh fish at the barracas.

ENTERTAINMENT

Fortaleza is famous for the dance and music style known as forró. The city's *danceterias* are the best places in which to watch or take part. These function on most Fridays and Saturdays, but don't usually get going until midnight. The most famous venue is the Clube do Vaqueiro, on the BR-116 east of the city; ask at the tourist office for information to check that there is something on.

HELP AND INFORMATION

Tourist Information: Emcetur has its office in the Centro de Turismo described above (tel 231-3566). The staff are helpful and give out maps and information on tours in the area. The Tourist Police (PM-TUR) has kiosks on several street corners in the centre and along the seafront.

Communications: there is a Teleceará office at Rua Floriano Peixoto 99, on the corner of Rua João Moreira. The main post office is between Ruas Floriano Peixoto and General Bezerril, at the southern end of Rua Senador Alençar. Another small office (for stamps) is on the corner of Rua Dr Moreira and Senador Pompeu.

Money: the best place to change money is in the casas de câmbio by the beach: Tropical, a kiosk by the beach near the bottom of Rua D. Moreira changes cheques and cash at reasonable rates.

Ceará — The Coast

EAST OF FORTALEZA

The beaches dotted along the coast up to the Jaguaribe river and the famous Canoa Quebrada, are fairly developed; beyond this point, however, there is plenty of scope for those with a hammock or tent to explore some of the state's most unspoilt beaches. Prainha, Iguape and Morro Blanco are the most popular beaches within easy access of Fortaleza. While impressive enough and feasible day trips, development means that they are crowded in the high season and rather forlorn at other times of year.

Morro Blanco. If you're heading east, stop off at Morro Blanco for a couple of hours. The village is named after a large dune which provides wonderful views of the red sand cliffs to the east — it is a hot but not difficult climb, and once you are out of sight of the village the atmosphere becomes suddenly ethereal.

Morro Blanco lies a few miles north of Beberibe, which is 50 miles/80km from Fortaleza. There are a couple of direct buses a day from the city bus station; but most go only as far as Beberibe (2 hours), from where you can take a taxi for about $3.

Canoa Quebrada. During the 80s the dunes and sculpted cliffs of this fishing village turned it into one of the most popular destinations among travellers to Ceará. Attention has moved increasingly to Jericoacoara west of Fortaleza (see below), but Canoa Quebrada still attracts travellers and a fairly large number of Brazilians. In summer it is one of the liveliest beaches in Ceará: you can hire horses, go sandskiing, etc. and there are even discos at weekends. Despite the amount of visitors, there is still no electricity or running water. Accommodation remains scant and always basic.

There are no direct buses to Canoa Quebrada from Fortaleza, so get a bus to Aracati (6 miles/10km south) and change. São Benedito operates nine daily services, leaving between 5am and 7pm. The journey takes about three hours, longer if the bus stops a lot. Buses also run to Aracati from Natal.

If there are too many people for your liking in Canoa Quebrada, go to Majorlândia, which is only a couple of miles southeast of Aracati. It is much quieter than Canoa Quebrada despite being more accessible: the Aracati bus company has a direct service from Fortaleza to Majorlândia at 7am daily, which takes three hours and costs around $2.50.

To reach the remotest spots further east, take a bus to the small fishing village of Icapuí (about four hours from Fortaleza) and walk from there.

WEST OF FORTALEZA

Beaches are better along the coast west of Fortaleza. Icaraí, Pecém and Paracuru are all recommended, but being the nearest to the capital they are busy at weekends and during the holidays. Nevertheless, there are few people around during the week and the swimming is good.

As you head further northwest, the beaches become steadily less accessible and also less crowded. Trairi, three hours by a direct bus from Fortaleza, is a lovely place in which to base yourself for a few days; a dirt road leads a few miles along the coast to the fine, unspoilt beach of Mundaú: you may be able to arrange a lift from Trairi, otherwise walk. Another stunning beach is Almofala, also accessible by bus in about seven hours.

Jericoacoara. This remote fishing village has become the firm favourite among travellers and young Brazilians; it can get fairly crowded from January to March. As at Canoa Quebrada, people while away the hours climbing the dunes, riding horses, and going on trips with the local fishermen. You can rent houses, hammocks or hammock space, and there are a couple of pousadas. There is no electricity or water; all facilities are basic.

To get to Jericoacoara, take a Redentora bus from Fortaleza to Gijoca (7-8 hours; $5.50), which leaves at 8am and 8pm. Gijoca is also accessible from Sobral (see *Ubajara*). From Gijoca trucks run a shuttle service (of sorts) the 15 miles/24km to Jericoacoara — a journey of some 90 minutes. During the rains you may have to get there by boat.

UBAJARA

When you've had your fill of the sea, don't fail to head inland to visit the Parque Nacional de Ubajara. The landscapes in this part of Ceará are beautiful, culminating in the cloud forest and hills which rise like a mirage out of the dry scrubland near the border of Piauí. The village of Ubajara is the best place to sample life in the highlands, and it is also the jumping-off point for the national park, which is about half an hour's walk east of town. The forest is an oasis of green in the sertão, and has waterfalls and spectacular views. The main attraction used to be the cable car ride down to some caves, but the car has been out of action for several years. The only option now is to walk down: the park office should have maps, otherwise you would be wise to hire a guide since the path is not easy to follow.

Ipu Brasilia runs buses from Fortaleza to Ubajara at 6.30am, 10am, 1pm and 9pm, which take about six hours; the fare is $5.50. Brasileiro also runs two daily services. Alternatively, get a bus to Sobral or Tianguá (regular services with Brasileiro or Ipu Brasilia) and change. The best place to stay in Ubajara is the Pousada de Neblina, a mile or so out of town towards the park entrance.

If planning to head due south from Ceará, the best route is via Juazeiro do Norte, in the heart of the sertão near the border with Pernambuco. This is a pilgrimage town and therefore is full of hotels and has buses running to all parts of the Northeast. Juazeiro do Norte was the home of Padre Cícero, one of the Northeast's unofficial saints, who died in 1934. There is a pilgrim trail up the hill to the park where a statue of him stands.

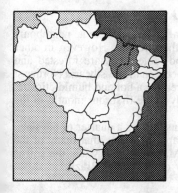

PIAUI and MARANHAO

Piauí is Brazil's poorest state, with the lowest population density in the Northeast. The sertão is at its most arid and harsh in Piauí and natural resources are extremely limited. Nor does it have the beaches to attract tourists: Piauí's coastline is just 18 miles/30km long. Teresina, the capital, is nothing more than a stopping-off place, and there is little else to detain you — except for one national park and, possibly, the appeal of one of Brazil's most untouristed regions.

TERESINA

This city is ugly and unbearably hot. The single outstanding fact about Teresina is that it is the only Northeastern capital not to lie on the coast. Only the more determined among those travelling west from Ceará will be able to avoid it. If you aren't keen on long bus journeys, Teresina is the logical place to stay overnight between buses. If you have time to kill, wander by the Parnaíba river or visit the Museu do Piauí (primarily folklore) and the market in Praça Marechal Deodoro; nearby, overlooking the river, is the Mercado Troca-Troca or bartering market, which is active at weekends.

Arrival and Departure. There are regular bus services to and from Fortaleza, Juazeiro do Norte, Sobral, São Luís and Imperatriz (as well as the other main

Northeastern cities) and from Belém; most journeys west from Teresina are hard-going and often crowded. Those headed for São Luís who have time on their hands, can travel north to Parnaíba and then head west along a seldom travelled route west into Maranhão.

There are services south to Brasília along a bad road, and to Recife along a better surface. The bus station is east of the centre.

Accommodation. For cheap lodgings look around Praça Saraiva, southeast of the main square — try the Fortaleza (tel 222-2984) — or along Ruas São Pedro and Alvaro Mendes. For a more comfortable room go to the Sambaíba at Rua G. Ferreira 230-N.

PARQUE NACIONAL DE SETE CIDADES

This park is famous for the unusual rock formations created by wind and rain erosion. The network of paths gives plenty of scope for walking, but the park is in the high sertão and therefore extremely hot.

The park lies just off the Teresina-Fortaleza road, so needs no great diversion. It is 16 miles/26km north of Piripiri, about three hours from Teresina and nine from Fortaleza. There is a free IBDF (forestry department) bus into the park, which leaves from the main square in Piripiri between 6 and 7am; otherwise hitch or take a taxi. Piracuruca, north of the park, is an alternative jumping-off point, though there is no forestry bus. It is possible to camp, but there is also a IBDF hostel. The hotel near the park entrance is less convenient for exploring the park.

MARANHAO

This is the second largest state in the Northeast after Bahia. Like its neighbours it is largely flat, with some highlands in the southern region. However, in other ways Maranhão is very different: it is wet, and large areas are forested and extremely fertile — indeed it marks the transition between the mostly arid Northeast and the tropical forest of the Amazon. Be prepared for a hot and humid climate, in which rain can fall at any time, but particularly in the first four months of the year.

The *babaçu* palm, which is used for oil and nuts, covers a quarter of the state, and rice is also grown in abundance. It is perhaps surprising that many of the gold miners working in Amazonia come from Maranhão: but while the soil is fertile, land distribution is as unequal as in any other part of Brazil.

SAO LUIS

The state capital lies on an island enclosed by two bays, and is linked to the mainland by a bridge. It is crowded (population 625,000), dirty, run-down and overwhelmingly poor, and yet it is the most interesting of the smaller Northeastern capitals. Founded in 1612, São Luís is the only city in Brazil to have been settled by the French. It was conquered three years later by the Portuguese, who were themselves pushed out by the Dutch for a few years. São Luís was an important port at one stage. There is still a sizeable historic centre, though many of the old buildings are literally crumbling away.

São Luís holds a certain fascination, and it has a rich folkloric tradition: the local festival of Bumba-meu-boi in June is famous nationally. In addition, there are unspoilt beaches. For air travellers, the city is an easy stop while hopping around the northeast coast. But for overland travellers São Luís is not a place you can simply pass through en route elsewhere: it requires a positive diversion north from the BR-316 that links Teresina and Belém.

Arrival and Departure. The airport (tel 225-0044) is 8 miles/13km south of the centre; buses to town — marked São Cristóvão — run every hour until late. Airline offices are as follows: Varig at Avenida Dom Pedro II 268 (tel 222-5066), Vasp at Rua do Sol 43 (tel 222-4655) and Transbrasil in Praça João Lisboa (tel 232-1414).

There are direct buses to and from Teresina (7 hours), Fortaleza (17-18 hours), Belém (12-13 hours) and Recife (25 hours), as well as Rio and other far-off destinations. The bus station (tel 223-0253) is a few miles from the centre, in Santo Antônio district towards the airport. Buses run to and from Praça João Lisboa in the centre; these are marked Alemanha, and take 10-15 minutes. There is no city bus station, but many routes have a stop in or around Praça Deodoro, or Praça João Lisboa itself.

Accommodation. Most hotels are in the old city. Cheap ones are primarily around Praça Benedito Leite, particularly on the streets running southwest of it; you should be fairly vigilant in this area at night. One of the better cheap places is the Estrela (Rua da Estrela 370; tel 222-1083); also recommended is Hotel São Marcos at Rua de Saúde 178 (tel 232-3763). Good value in the middle-range is Hotel Lord at Rua de Nazaré 258 (tel 222-5544), near Praça Benedito Leite.

If you want to stay by the beach in the smart suburb of São Francisco across the Ponte Sarney bridge from the centre, expect to pay around $20. This area is full of restaurants, and is lively at night. There is a campsite near Calhau beach.

Eating and Drinking. In the old city try the Base da Lenoca (Avenida Dom Pedro II 187) or the Solar do Ribeirão (Rua do Ribeirão 141). Xique-Xique (Avenida Castelo Blanco 807), on the street running north from the Sarney bridge, in São Francisco, serves good regional food.

Exploring. The historic centre, known as the Zona, is on a hill on the west side of the island. From the waterfront, busy with fishing boats and ferries, you can walk along the broad Avenida Dom Pedro II. This street gives some idea of the fine building work done in the 17th and 18th centuries. On the left as you head away from the waterfront is the handsome Palácio dos Leoes, which is open 3-6pm on weekdays (except Tuesday). It has a charming, run-down interior, and provides wonderful views over the bay. Nearby is Praça Benedito Leite, an attractive square with a disappointing cathedral. Southwest of here is the heart of the Zona, with its ancient cobbled streets, and rundown mansions. One of the finest sights in the city is Praça de Portugal, which boasts a number of superb tiled facades. Towards the bay is the Mercado da Praia Grande, the old round market where you can buy wonderful and cheap food.

The best museum in this area is the Museu do Negro, at the southwestern end of Rua da Estrela. Housed in the old slave market (Cafuá das Mercés), at Rua Jacinto Maia 43, it illustrates the history of the slave trade, and also gives an insight into black culture in Brazil; it opens 1.30-5pm Tuesday to Friday. Also good is the folklore museum in the Centro de Cultura Popular at Rua 28 de Julho 221 (open Monday to Friday).

Praça João Lisboa is another lovely square, as is the nearby Largo do Riberão, with its ancient fountain. A couple of blocks south, at Rua do Sol 302, is the Museu Histórico e Artístico: the 19th-century mansion and museum inside are both worth exploring. Opening hours are 2-6pm Tuesday to Friday, 3-6pm at weekends.

Bumba-meu-boi: the official day of this festival is 24 June, but the carnival-style celebrations begin a few days ahead, and can continue into September. Festivities are centred around a dance featuring a bull (*boi*), a slave, his lover and his master.

Help and Information. The tourist office (Maratur), at Travessa Almeida 137, is of limited use, but has maps. Banks, including Banespa at Rua do Sol 404, change cash and cheques, but the rate is poor. The post office is on Praça João Lisboa, and the telephone office in Praça Benedito Leite.

Around São Luís

Beaches. There are several fine beaches on the island north of the city, including Calhau and Olho d'Agua. The best is Aracají, 12 miles/19km away, which is quiet and has only a couple of pousadas. Buses run from Rua da Paz, west of Praça João Lisboa. Be warned that the sea can be rough, tides come in fast and, in good weather, you can expect the usual crowds.

The paucity of roads means that to explore the coast further afield from São Luís, you must rely on the boats that ply erratically between the coastal villages. Enquire at the port (Estação Marítima) near the end of Avenida Dom Pedro II. São José do Ribamar, on the east side of the island and accessible by bus, is also a good place to pick up boats.

Alcântara. This small town (population 20,000) lies across the bay west of São Luís, and is a delightful place to visit. Founded in 1648, Alcântara was state capital before the rise of São Luís, and its old centre is even more decayed than that of its neighbour — many buildings are in ruins. The finest architecture is in Praça Gomes de Castro and along Rua Grande.

Alcântara is most easily accessible by ferry: boats leave the Estação Marítima at 8am and return at 1pm and 3pm, depending on the tide; the journey takes about 80 minutes. There are several pousadas, including the Pelourinho in Praça Gomes de Castro.

The most important town in the interior is Imperatriz, set in cattle country off the main road to Brasília. It is a fast-growing and unsavoury place, with a serious crime scene that reflects the problems caused by the fight for land within the state. Stopping overnight is barely recommendable: if you must, stay at the Presidente (Rua Manoel Bandeira 1774; tel 721-0433).

THE AMAZON

The Amazon conjures up more images and arouses stronger emotions than any other part of Brazil, and perhaps even of South America as a whole. The attention, sadly, is a result of the destruction of the rainforest and the indigenous peoples. The devastating exploitation of the region has been going on for decades, but was suddenly brought to the world's notice during the 1980s.

Amazonia, the area watered by the great Amazon river and its tributaries, is three times the size of the European Community. While sparsely populated, new towns spring up constantly. The region's 200,000 Indians are heavily outnumbered by immigrants from other parts of Brazil. Colonization — during the days of the empire as well as in modern times — has forced them away from the principal waterways and deeper and deeper into the forest. The most serious flood of immigrants came in the 1970s and 80s when successive governments encouraged land-hungry labourers, principally from the Northeast, to migrate to Amazonia — thus conveniently avoiding the thorny issue of land reform. Symbolic of this policy was the construction of the controversial Transamazonian Highway or Transamazônica, built to facilitate the settlement of migrants and to integrate the Amazon into the national economy.

Amazonia contains just under a third of the world's tropical forests. Yet uncontrolled exploitation in the last 20 years has destroyed around 10% of it. Each year an area about the size of Belgium is affected. Recently the most serious threat has been from timber extraction, rather than the clearing of trees to provide farming and cattle-grazing land. The unsuitability of the weak soil for agriculture means that every year thousands of farmers end up in the shanty towns that surround the Amazonian cities. Meanwhile, deforestation renders one of the world's great recycling systems virtually useless: when the soil has no canopy to protect it, the nutrients are quickly washed away. In addition, intense rain causes serious flooding and erosion.

Some of the most devastating deforestation has been caused by mining, both by multinational projects and by the so-called *garimpeiros*, or freelance gold-diggers. The most serious damage done by the garimpeiros, however, is to the Amazon Indians — above all to the Yanomami tribe of the northern state of Roraima, who have come to symbolize more than any other group the struggle of the indigenous peoples. While the garimpeiros are themselves victims — in so far as they have been forced away from their home states by iniquitous land distribution — the Indians are under more immediate threat owing to their small number. They have been forced off their traditional lands (some have joined the failed farmers in the shanty towns), the women have been raped, and the pollution caused by the toxic mercury used to separate the gold from other minerals has been a serious health risk. And thousands have already died from diseases such as malaria and tuberculosis, to which the Indians have no immunity.

The assassination in 1988 of Chico Mendes, president of the rubber tappers' union in Acre state, was one of the most important events in the recent history of the Amazon. His murder was condemned internationally, and the growing awareness of the plight of the Amazonian peoples forced the Brazilian government to act. Until now the environmental policy of Collor has been all but ridiculed: the campaigns of blowing up airstrips used by the garimpeiros are seen largely as publicity stunts; the setting aside of land as reserves is woefully slow, and boundaries are ignored by miners anyway; and little has been done to transform FUNAI into an effective protection agency for the Indians. The spotlight falls on the Amazon in 1992 at the UN-sponsored Earth Summit in Rio. It can only be hoped that international pressure will produce important resolutions to promote conservation in the region.

Amazonia is made up of six states. The largest and most important are Amazonas and Pará, with their respective capitals of Manaus and Belém. They are also the states most visited by travellers. Trips up the Amazon river and into the jungle are the main attractions. The mining areas of the interior may be fascinating, but violence is commonplace in these Wild West-style camps. For a less troublesome taste of life in the interior, head for the capitals of the smaller states in western and northern Amazonia, such as Porto Velho and Boa Vista. Both present possible routes out of the country.

Manaus and Belém are close to the equator, and the climate is always hot and muggy. Rain falls all year round, most frequently from January to June, and most heavily in the upper Amazon and along the coast north of Belém.

TRAVELLING UP THE AMAZON

The Tranamazônica has driven a spear into the heart of Amazonia, but it is the least reliable route through the region: like the other roads in this part of Brazil, it is unpaved and a total wash-out during the rains. Transport along it is scant at any time. When dry the roads are hard and tough on the buses, let alone the passengers. Belém is the Amazonian city most easily reached by road, but while journeys from the Northeast are just bearable, those to and from the west are an endurance test. Nevertheless, travelling by road is an eye-opening experience since it enables you to see at close hand the damage wrought by colonization. The regional airline, TABA (Transporte Aéreo de Bacia Amazônica), serves the main centres, but few people visit Amazonia without travelling by boat.

The main waterways are so broad and the forest often so dense that you see little in terms of wildlife or people. However, there is a fair amount of river traffic to look at, including children who paddle out to ask for gifts. In addition, you will have plenty of time to get to know your travelling companions and catch up on a few letters.

The Amazon river, with its 1,100 tributaries, carries 20% of the world's fresh water. It is 150 miles wide at its mouth, and is broad and deep enough to be navigable by ocean steamers as far as Iquitos in Peru, 2,300 miles/3,700km upstream. Note that 'the Amazon' is a generic name for the river. The Rio Amazonas actually splits into the Negro and Solimoes near Manaus.

The most usual boat routes are between Belém and Manaus, and between Manaus and Porto Velho. ENASA, a government company, runs passenger boats along the Belém-Santarém-Manaus route, but not to Porto Velho. The best option in both cases, however, is to take a privately-owned cargo boat, which has hammock space on deck, and perhaps a few cabins. The quality of the boats varies enormously; the better ones offer surprisingly good facilities, with clean toilets and showers, and fairly decent meals.

ENASA boats run along a number of river routes, have one class only, and are renowned for their crowded and unpleasant conditions: overflowing loos, terrible food, etc. The fare from Belém to Manaus is $50, half that to Santarém. This is $5-10 cheaper than with the private vessels, but the journey is slower. ENASA also runs a monthly tourist boat, with a swimming pool and air-conditioning, for which you must pay at least $240 per person.

Whichever boat you opt for, expect it to be overloaded. To avoid being thrown down below with the cargo, arrive in good time to claim your hammock space — be prepared to fight for it and then stand your ground. Buy your ticket a couple of days in advance if possible.

PARA

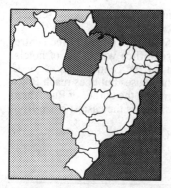

The state of Pará includes about a third of Amazonia. The most many travellers see of it is the colourful city of Belém. Inland, Pará is the site of the most notorious mining projects in the region. In the 1990s the most serious threat is posed by the Grande Carajás Project, the largest open-mining operation in Amazonia: the hills of the Serra do Carajás in southern Pará are said to contain billions of tonnes of high-grade iron ore. The main problem, however, is the accompanying development and settlement — a city of 400,000 is planned — rather than the mine itself. The World Bank is just one of the multinationals involved in the controversial project.

Belém

Belém and Manaus vie for the position of the largest Amazon city. There isn't much in it, both having a population of around one million. But Belém certainly feels much more of a city than its rival. Away from the bustling waterfronts, the two cities are totally different, with Belém's old district retaining an air of elegance that Manaus has long lost. Yet the capital of Pará is not simply a relic of faded colonial chic. Beyond the centre shanties spill out along the riverfront.

Belém lies on the southern bank of the Amazon delta, near the mouth of the Tocantins river and about 75 miles/120km from the Atlantic. It was founded by the Portuguese in 1616 and its earliest prosperity came with the spice trade. Thousands of Indians were forced into a life of slavery, but the supply was limited and the lack of labour helped bring about Belém's eventual decline during the 19th century. Astoundingly, the city's days of economic success were not over. Its resurgence came with the rubber boom, and by the beginning of the twentieth century it was a flourishing city, and responsible for half of the country's rubber exports. The heady days of the rubber boom have long since gone, but Belém remains the largest and most important port on the Amazon, and the economic centre of the North.

Belém is in many ways the most appealing of the Amazonian cities. Many travellers come here simply to catch a boat into the interior, but most people end up staying longer than they had planned.

CITY LAYOUT

The city centre is easy to get around. Avenida Vargas is the main commercial street, linking the large Praça da República to the docks. The main riverside road is Rua Castilho Franca, which runs west from Vargas towards the main port and Ver-o-Pêso market; the heart of the old city is south of here. There is little to take you out of the city centre.

The map produced by Paratur is the best one available. If the tourist office is closed, you should be able to pick up a copy from news stands for about $1; those on Vargas are most likely to stock it.

ARRIVAL AND DEPARTURE

Air. Belém is served by a few international flights, including from Miami,

Paramaribo (Surinam) and Cayenne (French Guiana). The main daily services within Brazil are from Manaus, Santarém and Rio.

Val de Cans airport (tel 223-4122/231-6022) is 5 miles/8km east of the centre. There is a branch of Banco do Brasil, and a tourist office with a list of hotels, and maps. Buses, marked P. Socorro and bound for the centre, pass every 15 minutes or so. This route takes you right around the houses but does reach Praça da República eventually; the stop nearest the square is at the corner of Rua Abreu and Avenida Correia, at the top of Avenida Vargas; this is the easiest place from which to get the bus back to the airport too.

A fixed-rate taxi to the centre costs around $8.

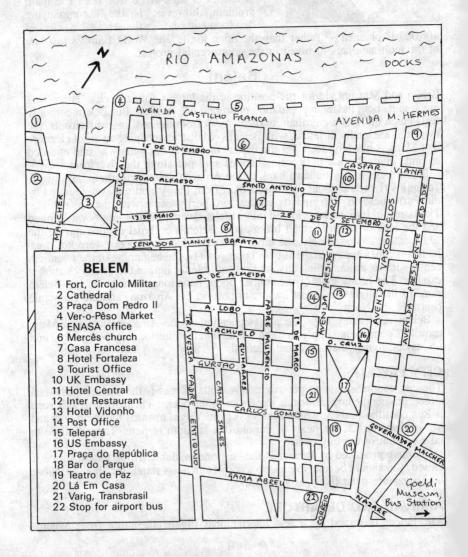

BELEM

1 Fort, Circulo Militar
2 Cathedral
3 Praça Dom Pedro II
4 Ver-o-Pêso Market
5 ENASA office
6 Mercês church
7 Casa Francesa
8 Hotel Fortaleza
9 Tourist Office
10 UK Embassy
11 Hotel Central
12 Inter Restaurant
13 Hotel Vidonho
14 Post Office
15 Telepará
16 US Embassy
17 Praça do República
18 Bar do Parque
19 Teatro de Paz
20 Lá Em Casa
21 Varig, Transbrasil
22 Stop for airport bus

Airline offices: Varig — Avenida Vargas 768 and 363 (tel 225-4222).
Transbrasil — Avenida Vargas 780 (tel 224-6977).
Vasp — Avenida Vargas 620 (tel 222-9611, 224-5588).
TABA — Avenida José Malcher 883 (tel 223-6300).
Surinam Airways — Rua Santo Antônio 432 (tel 224-7144).

Bus. The bus station (tel 228-0500) is a couple of miles southeast of the centre, at the junction of Avenidas Malcher and Barroso. Most buses passing the terminal (on the other side of the road) are headed for the centre, usually along Avenidas Barata and Nazaré. To get to the station from downtown, catch any bus marked Aeroclube from Avenida Vargas, Praça da República or Avenida Bittencourt; allow about 15 minutes.

In addition to the long-distance services listed below, there are daily buses to Recife and other destinations in the Northeast. And for masochists there are direct daily services to Rio, São Paulo and Belo Horizonte.

> *Brasília:* 36 hours, $44; daily overnight with Transbrasiliana (and one leito), usually via Imperatriz (11 hours, $14).
> *Santarém:* 34 hours, $34; direct buses (often delayed) about once a week. It is better to change at Marabá (16 hours south by regular bus); this is an unsavoury place, so don't hang around.
> *São Luís:* 12 hours, $16; daily overnight with Transbrasiliana and São João.
> *Teresina and Fortaleza:* five daily to Teresina with Boa Esperança and Transbrasiliero (12 hours, $19); two buses a day with Itapemirim and Timbira buses to Fortaleza (24 hours, $34), via Teresina.

Boat. Passenger boats, both private and ENASA, serve Santarém and Manaus; the journey to Santarém takes three days, to Manaus five.

The weekly ENASA service to Manaus is scheduled to leave on Wednesday, but delays are common. For information and tickets go to the ticket office in the large hangar-like building at the eastern end of Avenida Castilho Franca (tel 223-3011); the customs house is virtually opposite.

Unlike in Manaus, it is not immediately clear where the private boats congregate. Belém's harbour area is extensive, and a certain amount of leg work is necessary to find boats heading up the Amazon. Some leave from the docks along Avenida Marechal Hermes, where the riverside is lined with warehouses. Most boats gather around Armazem (Warehouse) 10, at the eastern end, although there never seems to be more than one or two boats moored here at any one time. Representatives of particular boats sometimes hang around near the ENASA office, and may well offer to take you to their vessels. The 20-minute walk from the centre is not a particularly pleasant one, and the area is best avoided after dark.

Boats also leave from the so-called Estrada Nova, which lies south of the centre. The unpaved streets and ramshackle houses are in total contrast to the scene in central Belém and it's good to have an excuse to visit it. To get there take any bus marked Cremação or Tamoios from Castilhos Franca; ask to be dropped at the bottom of Avenida José Bonifacio, towards the southern end of Avenida Bernardo Saião, which runs right along the waterfront. From here you must simply walk southeast along the river, and approach any likely looking vessel. Note that this waterfront area is best explored in company and should be avoided after dark. A taxi should not cost more than about $6 for the round trip.

ACCOMMODATION

The cheapest hotels are in the old city, mostly on or off Rua Castilhos Franca, near the market. While lively during the day, this is not a safe area at night, and you are advised to head a couple of blocks inland. The best place actually on the waterfront is the Ver-o-Pêso, at Avenida Castilhos Franca 208 (tel 224-2267), which has rooms for around $10. Cheaper and quieter hotels are on Travessa Guimarães: nearest the harbour is the Vitória Rêgia (number 260; tel 224-2833/241-3475), with Hotel Fortaleza nearby at 276. The latter, in a wonderful building, is the cheaper of the two with rooms for about $5 per person.

One of the most popular places in town is the huge Hotel Central (Avenida Vargas 290; tel 222-3011/3823), on the corner of 28 de Setembro. It is a fine, art deco building and has rooms without bath for $8/$12-15. Slightly upmarket is the Hotel Vidonho (Rua O. de Alameida 476; tel 225-1444) nearby, which charges $12/$18.

EATING AND DRINKING

The cheapest place to eat during the day is in the market by the waterfront. Anyone with a weak stomach should probably head instead for one of the simple restaurants off Presidente Vargas, such as the Inter (28 de Setembro) and Na Brasa (Nazaré 125), just off Praça da República.

It would be a shame not to treat yourself to a meal at Lá Em Casa, at Avenida José Malcher 247 (tel 225-0320/223-1212), just a couple of blocks east of the main square. The restaurant itself is splendid, with its terrace sheltered under the branches of a huge tree. The food is exquisite. Most dishes are typical of Pará, including the famous *pato no tucupí*, duck cooked in the juice of the manioc root. Feijoadas are available at weekends. Best of all is the Menu Paraense, which is a set meal giving a taste of many different regional specialities, and is one of the greatest gastronomic experiences on offer in Brazil. It costs about $8, but could easily feed two people.

Another place with a good reputation and in a similar price range is the restaurant in the Circulo Militar on the waterfront: see *Exploring*. The food, particularly the fish, is excellent, and dining is enhanced by the views over the bay (but occasionally marred by the piano playing).

The most famous watering-hole in town is the Bar do Parque, a raised open-air terrace in Praça da República. Drinks aren't cheap, and there is a mad rush for shelter when the heavens open, but otherwise this is a fun place to have a beer. On the other side of the street near the Hilton, at Vargas 794, is the Casa do Suco, which makes delicious juices from all manner of Amazonian fruits.

EXPLORING

Praça da República, scattered with fountains and mango trees, is Belém at its most elegant. It is divided into two halves, the main part being shady and peaceful, the other busy with stalls, people and traffic. Overlooking the square is the late 19th-century Teatro de Paz, a fine building which symbolizes the wealth brought by the rubber boom. It is smaller than its counterpart in Manaus (built some time later), but with shocking-pink walls it is in many respects more appealing. The theatre is open 8am-noon and 2-6pm Monday to Friday (as well as for the odd performance).

Avenida Vargas is handsome in its way, but many of the old buildings have been replaced by modern high-rises. More interesting are the narrow streets that run west through an area with some fine colonial architecture; you can still see the remains of azulejo decoration. The liveliest streets are Avenida Santo Antônio and its continuation Rua João Alfredo, a pedestrian zone where shops spill out onto the road. Half way along is the lovely Praça Mercês — a surprisingly peaceful spot in the midst of so much bustle. Igreja das Mercês dates from the mid-17th century, and is Belém's oldest church.

You eventually reach Praça Dom Pedro II, a big, ugly square inhabited primarily by shoeshines and people sleeping rough. Ignoring for the moment the harbour and the Ver-o-Pêso market to your right, walk west up the hill to the rundown and ghostly Praça Frei Brandão. The cathedral contains some interesting paintings, but is usually shut. The church on your right is a charmingly decrepit building that is increasingly overgrown with weeds — at the time of going to press it was under restoration.

Enclosed within thick white walls on the opposite side of the square is the Forte de Castelo, built by the Portuguese soon after they arrived. It is now a club called the Circulo Militar with a high-class restaurant. Fortunately, you don't have to splash out on a meal to enjoy the views. You must pay $0.20 to get in, but once inside you can sit among the old cannon free of charge, or just have a drink at the bar.

Retracing your steps, head for the waterfront. Small fishing boats are moored in the docks, some of them piled with ceramics and baskets — the Amazonian equivalent of a car boot sale. Picking your way through piles of fish, people and vultures, you come to the Mercado Ver-o-Pêso, which stretches the length of Avenida Castilhos Franca. Like the harbour, the market is at its busiest and most colourful in the morning, when the boats are being unloaded. The market is primarily for fresh Amazonian produce, and it is a fascinating place to wander. A few stalls sell crafts and many dispense religious charms and medicinal herbs.

Museu Emílio Goeldi. This is the best museum in town and should not be missed. It is part of a complex which also contains a zoo and lovely botanical gardens — a pleasant oasis of calm. The museum's collection is primarily anthropological and archaeological. A visit is a wonderful educational experience, and is particularly profitable if you have just arrived to the Amazon region. The text is more important than the objects on display in some respects, which is reflected in the translation of the entire Portuguese text into English and other languages.

Museu Emílio Goeldi is at Avenida M. Barata 376, near Calle Alcindo Cacela. It is open 9am-noon and 2-6pm Tuesday to Saturday and until noon on Sundays. The museum is nine long blocks southeast of Praça da República, and can be reached by buses marked Nazaré or Aeroclube; get off on Avenida Bittencourt. About the only advantage of going on foot is that you can stop off at the Basilica da Nazaré, on Avenida Nazaré. This is an impressive modern church containing a statue of the Virgin, which is said to have been carved in Nazareth and brought to Brazil by the Jesuits. The Cirio de Nazaré festival, which takes place in October, is one of the biggest religious celebrations in the country and is attended by hundreds of thousands of people. The main procession is on the second Sunday of October, though celebrations continue for the next couple of weeks.

SHOPPING

The most interesting shopping area is at the Ver-o-Pêso market. You can buy crafts here made by Marajó and Tapajós Indians, although the selection is fairly small. There are several craft shops on Avenida Vargas, including a FUNAI shop in the arcade at Avenida Vargas 762, on Praça da República. Crafts are also on sale in the Paratur complex in Praça Kennedy.

Stalls in the centre sell leather goods and T-shirts, mainly in Praça da Mercês (Monday to Saturday) and in Praça da República (daily). On Sunday mornings stalls in the main square sell deliciously gooey cakes.

HELP AND INFORMATION

Tourist Information: the tourist office is in the Feira de Artesanato in Praça Kennedy, near the waterfront (tel 224-9633). Pick up a free map and the *Guia Belém*, which has useful listings. To contact the Tourist Police phone 224-9460.

Communications: the central post office is at Avenida Vargas 498 (tel 224-0444) and the main telephone office (Telepará) in Praça da República, at the corner of Vargas and Riachuelo.

Money: there are several casas de câmbio, including the Carajás in the arcade at Avenida Vargas 762 and the Casa Francesa at Padre Prudêncio 40. Travellers cheques can be a problem, and to change these you may have to rely on the banks; these are found mainly on Avenida Vargas, although there are several on Rua 15 de Novembro, including Lloyds at 275.

Consulates. All South American consulates are east of the main square.
Bolivia: Avenida M. Barata 661, (tel 229-6829), beyond the Goeldi Museum.
Colombia: Travessa Benjamin Constant 1903, apt 203 (tel 222-7756).
Peru: Travessa 14 de Abril 1769 (tel 229-4100).
UK: Rua Gaspar Viana 490, above Expresso Mercantil Turismo, near the top of Avenida Vargas (tel 223-4353, 224-4822).
USA: Avenida Oswaldo Cruz 165 (tel 223-0800), north side of Praça da República.

Around Belém

Beaches. The most popular beaches are those on Ilha do Mosqueiro, connected to the mainland by a bridge, about 47 miles/75km due north. There are a few hotels, and buses run to Mosqueiro town every 30 minutes from 6am-7pm; the journey takes about 1½ hours and costs $1.

The best beaches, however, are further afield. Among them is Algodoal, an isolated fishing village on the Atlantic coast northeast of Belém. The sea can be rough but it is a beautiful spot and visited by only a few local people and travellers. Get a bus to Marudá (about three hours from Belém) and then a boat. There are a few simple hotels in both Algodoal and Marudá.

Icoraçí. This village lies 12 miles/20km east of Belém and is an important crafts centre, famous for its cermaics. Buses leave from Avenida Vargas and from outside the Rodoviária.

Ilha do Marajó. This large island lies in the Amazon delta. While its west side is mainly jungle, the eastern half consists of savannah which is grazed by thousands of buffalo and submerged under water during the January to June wet season. Its Indian inhabitants have long been famous for their ceramics, examples of which are in Belém's Goeldi museum.

The port of Souré is the island's main town, lying across the bay due north of Belém. There are some good beaches nearby, the best of which are Praias Araruna and do Pesqueiro, 5 miles/8km and 8 miles/13km away respectively; the latter has the best transport services and a few simple pousadas. If you base yourself in town, stay in the Marajó or the cheaper and more central Souré hotel. The island is rich in wildlife (including venomous snakes and blood-thirsty insects), but the best way to see this is to go on an organized tour from Belém.

ENASA has three boats a week to Souré, which take four hours and cost $4 economy, $12 especial and $30 cabin. There are also private boats.

A trip can also be made to Belterra, 37 miles/60km south, or Fordlândia, beyond. Both towns grew up around rubber plantations created by Henry Ford in the 1920s and 30s. The boom never materialized, but the plantations are still operational and are now in the hands of the Brazilian government. The attraction lies not in the rubber trees (or lack of them), but in the incongruity of seeing an all-American town in the heart of the Amazon.

AMAPA

The small state of Amapá is a poor, malarial region bordered to the south by the Amazon river and to the north by French Guiana. Its capital is Macapá which lies virtually on the equator. The vast majority of Amapans, 180,000 of them, live in the capital.

The travellers most likely to go to Macapá are those intending to go overland into French Guiana. Since the border crossing at Oiapoque is not always open, check before embarking on what is an interesting but hard journey: the road is poor and bus services equally so.

Belém is the best place from which to approach Macapá. Twice-weekly ferries are operated by the Representação do Governo do Território de Macapá (RGTM), at Avenida Castillo Franca 234 (tel 222-8710). Boats take around 27 hours and dock at Porto Santana; travelling the 17 miles/28km north to Macapá gives you the chance to cross the equator.

AMAZONAS

This is Brazil's largest state. With a surface area of 1.6 million square kilometres, Amazonas is almost as big as Mexico, but has only a tiny fraction of the population.

Manaus

The state capital is hot, steamy, shabby and chaotic. It is also curiously engaging. Manaus tries hard to be a modern city, but doesn't quite succeed: the regular torrential downpours flood the drains and bring life to a complete standstill. Finding such a large city, complete with opera house, in the middle of the jungle is a bizarre experience. Yet once there it is easy to forget the location — in many ways Manaus is a city like any other, with more than its fair share of apartment blocks, shopping centres, pollution, cars, poverty and crime. However, the waterfront, where vessels and people vie for space in near-anarchy, is a world away from the commercial district a couple of blocks inland. Arriving by boat throws you straight into the heart of this human theatre.

Manaus lies on the northern bank of the Rio Negro, and is the hub of Amazonia. From its port boats set off to all corners of the region and even into the jungles of Peru; it is a distribution centre for produce from a vast area. Manaus was only a minor trading post until the rubber boom of the late 19th century, when it became one of the Americas' most flourishing towns. The city's opera house embodies the prosperity of this period. Most of modern Manaus illustrates rather more clearly the decline that followed the demise of the rubber trade in the 1920s, and the tragedy now facing the Amazon region. What colonial buildings remain are gradually disintegrating, unable to cope with the intense tropical rain and years of neglect. Shanties spill out onto creeks which are little more than rubbish dumps and a breeding ground for disease.

In 1967, in an attempt to revitalize the local economy, Manaus was declared a tax free zone. Multinational industries set up factories, and Brazilians soon flooded in to take advantage of the tax concessions. They continue to do so, but rumours suggest that the future of the Zona Franca is in doubt. This bodes ill for the economic status of a city whose central area is one large shopping precinct, but is good for the surrounding forest, threatened by development.

CITY LAYOUT

The shop signs reduce the streets in the centre into one homogenous mass. This is particularly true of the tax-free shopping area — between Avenida 7 de Setembro and the river — much of which is pedestrian. In this central zone do not confuse Rua Guillerme Moreira with Rua Dr Moreira.

Praça 15 de Novembro, not far from the Porto Flutante (Floating Port), is site of the local bus station and the cathedral; the latter dominates the centre but is nothing special to look at. Avenida Eduardo Ribeiro is the main commercial street.

Maps. The map given out by the tourist office is the best of the free maps available. If you can't be bothered to trek to the tourist office, make do with the maps you can pick up in the smart hotels (e.g. Hotel Amazonas) and travel agencies. For a more detailed city plan go to Mundo dos Mapas at Rua Saldanha Marinho 773, one block west of Avenida Vargas. A laminated map of Manaus costs about $13, and they also stock maps of the Amazon, Brazil, etc.

ARRIVAL AND DEPARTURE

Air. As well as frequent connections with Brazilian cities on the main airlines, and flights into the interior with TABA, there are regular flights to and from South American capitals, Mexico and Miami. Varig has several flights a week to and from Iquitos (Peru), though the fare is cheaper if you make a connection at Tabatinga at the border.

The Eduardo Gomes international airport (tel 212-1210/1431) is on Avenida Santos Dumont, 8 miles/13km from the centre. It has no exchange facilities. Buses run every half hour or so to Praça 15 de Novembro, near the waterfront. Fixed-rate taxis charge around $12 to go to the town centre. Returning to the airport, you can pick buses up along Avenida Vargas; they are marked Aeropuerto or Eduardo Gomes.

Airline offices: Varig — Rua Marcílio Dias 284 (tel 234-1116).
Vasp — Rua G. Moreira 179 (tel 234-1266).
Transbrasil — Rua G. Moreira 150 (tel 233-2288).
TABA — Avenida Eduardo Ribeiro 664 (tel 232-0806/0676).

Bus. Roads connect Manaus with Porto Velho to the south and Boa Vista to the north. During the rains you will probably be laughed at if you ask at the station about buses. Weather permitting, however, there should be daily buses to Porto Velho along the BR-319 highway, which take 22-24 hours and cost about $40. The

BR-174 to Boa Vista is unpaved, and the trip takes a whole day ($45). União Cascavel is the main company operating out of Manaus; it also has services to Cuiabá and Campo Grande. Owing to the small number of bus services, buy your ticket several days in advance.

The Rodoviária (tel 236-2732) is on Rua Recife, a couple of miles from the centre towards the airport. City buses run downtown from across the road. The taxi fare to the centre is about $6. To return to the station, you can catch several buses from Praça 15 de Novembro; bus number 5 (marked Cidade Nova), which runs along Avenida Vargas, also passes the terminal.

Boat. The larger boats that travel the longer distances congregate at the Porto Flutante. The operation here is remarkably well-organized, and there is even a hut selling souvenirs. Boats are moored all around the jetty, with signs advertising their destination and the day and time of the next departure. It is always wise to shop around: prices don't vary much, but the quality and the speed capacity of the vessels does. The smaller boats that gather near the Mercado Municipal (the so-called Escadaria dos Remédios) are generally headed for the interior, although you may find the odd one going longer distances.

The Port Captain's office is in a big white building near the floating harbour at Rua Marquês de Santa Cruz 264 (tel 234-9662). Someone at the counter marked Informaçoes should be able to give you a list of boats heading for any particular destination, and can usually recommend the best ones too. People going to or from Peru or Colombia must have their passports stamped at the Customs House, which is near the gates of the Floating Harbour; it is open 8am-5pm.

Santarém and Belém: there is at least one departure a day for Santarém, and the fare is $25 (first class), a few dollars less for second. The journey takes 26-30 hours, depending on the boat and conditions. The most recommended boat is O Globo do Mar which claims to be the fastest and is undoubtedly the most comfortable; at the time of going to press O Globo departed at 5pm on Fridays. Also recommended, in descending order of preference, are the Cisne Branco (Sunday), Rio Nilo (Thursday) and Onze de Maio (Tuesday). Few boats go straight through to Belém, but try asking around for the Navio Roraima or the Rondônia, which currently operate a direct service. The captains of boats to Santarém may sell onward tickets to Belém.

ENASA boats to Belém leave at 8pm every Thursday, in theory. You can book at the ENASA office at Rua Eduardo Ribeiro 58 (tel 232-4368).

Porto Velho: private boats to Porto Velho leave several times a week; these take about three days and charge $48 (first) and $42 (second).

Peru and Colombia: to reach Iquitos in Peru by boat you will almost certainly have to change at the border. Boats run to either Benjamin Constant or Tabatinga, both Brazilian towns lying across the Rio Solimoes from each other, at the point where Brazil, Peru and Colombia meet; the journey takes about six days from Manaus, and it is usually about a further four or five days to Iquitos from there. If leaving Brazil you must go to immigration in Tabatinga; Peruvian boats tend to leave from here anyway. From Tabatinga you can cross to Leticia in Colombia, which has domestic flights northwards — it costs around $60 to Bogotá.

ACCOMMODATION

Cheap hotels are concentrated along Avenida Joaquim Nabuco and two of its cross

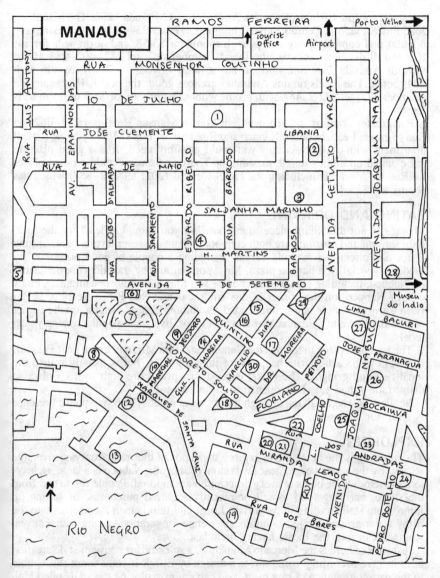

MANAUS

1 Teatro Amazonas
2 Colombian Embassy
3 Mundo dos Mapas
4 Manaus Shopping Centre
5 Praça Dom Pedro II
6 Cathedral
7 Praça 15 de Novembro
8 Local buses
9 Post Office
10 São Cristovão Tours

11 Port Captain's Office
12 Customs
13 Porto Flutante
14 Vasp
15 Telephone Office
16 Bemge
17 Amazon Explorers
18 Hotel Amazonas
19 Mercado Municipal
20 Canoas Bar

21 Hotel San Martín Manaus
22 Amazonas Indian Turismo
23 Hotel Jangada
24 Bar Galo Carijo
25 Pensão Sulista
26 Max's 24-hour restaurant
27 Hotel Doral
28 Museu do Homem do Norte
29 Praça da Polícia
30 Varig

streets nearer the harbour, Ruas dos Andradas and Miranda Leão. The best along Joaquim Nabuco is Pensão Sulista (number 347; tel 234-5814). It is extremely popular and comparatively cheap, with rooms for $5/$8, and dorm beds for $4. If it is full the best option is the Doral (number 687; tel 232-4102, 233-4631), towards Avenida 7 de Setembro. It has a range of rooms ($8-18), mostly with bathrooms. The hotels on dos Andradas are less good: the best is Hotel Jangada (number 473; tel 232-2248), with rooms without bathroom for $5/8 or dorm beds for $4.

For greater comfort, try the new San Martín Manaus Hotel (tel 234-3162) on Rua Miranda Leão, between Nabuco and Rua Pessoa. For $24/$35 you get a small apartment with all the facilities you could possibly need. It is a good place to get cleaned up after a jungle expedition. There are several middle range places on Rua G. Moreira, including the Hotel Central (202; tel 232-7887) which has rooms for $35-45.

EATING AND DRINKING

Manaus is not a brilliant place to eat out, but you should at least try the local fish: *jaraquí* and *pirarucú* are both common. There are several restaurants around Praça da Polícia, off Avenida Vargas, including a couple of good pizzerias; try the local speciality, a banana pizza. Most popular among travellers are the places on Nabuco, including Quara's Lanchonete and Max's 24-hour restaurant. A block east of Nabuco, on the corner of dos Andradas and Rua Pedro Botelho, is Bar Galo Carijo, a simple but recommended restaurant. Central Natalia, on the corner of Rua Barroso and Saldanha Marinho is outdoor, lively and popular among young locals.

The trendiest place in town is the Canoas Bar (Rua Miranda Leão, near Pessoa). It is said to be a favourite hang-out of jungle guides, but is usually full of the local rich and gringos. The music is good, but prices are high so it's a place to drink rather than eat. It is open from 8pm onwards.

Be vigilant when walking through the streets at night. The heavy police presence is there for a reason.

EXPLORING

The morning is the best time to explore the chaos of the waterfront and riverside streets. By the water's edge, near the bottom of Joaquim Nabuco is a large, rickety-looking jetty where boats of every description are moored. People run to and from the shore, carrying food to sell or recently-acquired purchases, or setting up impromptu stalls trading in fresh fish. Local children launch themselves into the filthy water around the jetty. Vultures scavenge for scraps. Anyone with a strong stomach can join the locals having breakfast.

Just west of here is the Mercado Municipal, a splendid art nouveau-style creation built in 1896 according, some say, to a design by Eiffel. If you are not susceptible to the nauseous stench of raw meat, you can enjoy exploring the stalls piled high with jungle produce. There are even a few crafts, but the best buys are the dried tongues of pirarucú fish — about $1 each and a good substitute for a pumice stone. The local council has plans to give the market a facelift: this may reduce the health risk, but will dampen the atmosphere too.

Continuing west along Marquês de Santa Cruz you reach the Porto Flutante. This floating harbour was built without fixed piers to cope with the fluctuations of the river level, which can be as much as 46ft/14m. It was the work of British engineers, constructed at the beginning of this century.

Teatro Amazonas. The most stunning landmark in Manaus is the opera house, known as the Teatro Amazonas, which rises up elegantly and incongrously near the northern end of Avenida Eduardo Ribeiro. It features briefly in the film *Fitzcarraldo*. The gold dome punctures the city's skyline, adding the only touch of brightness to the often cloud-heavy skies. When the opera house was built in 1898, it was one of the largest of its kind in the world. The floor of the building was constructed from logs floated up from the mouth of the Amazon. It is made up of several halls. The finest is the theatre itself, sumptuously upholstered in velvet, plus the ballroom, where paintings depict jungle scenes. The building is open to the public from 9-6pm, daily except Monday. Visitors must pay about $6 for a tour.

Museums. Manaus has two good museums. Nearest the centre is the Museu do Homem do Norte, at Avenida 7 de Setembro 1385, near the corner of Joaquim Nabuco. This small museum is particularly interesting for its explanations regarding the cultivation of jungle crops; there are also fascinating photographs and old documents. It opens 9am-noon and 2-5pm Tuesday to Friday, mornings only on Monday.

Several blocks east across the bridge and to the left up Duque de Caxias, is the Museu do Indio. Created by Salesian nuns, the museum is excellent, though the patronizing attitude of the missionaries can be aggravating. The exhibits illustrate the lives and customs of the upper Rio Negro Indians, particularly the Tukano tribe, and include marvellous feather head-dresses. There is a FUNAI shop downstairs. The museum opens 8am-noon and 2-5pm, Monday to Friday, 8am-noon on Saturday.

Anyone wanting to research the Amazon and its people should visit the Instituto Geográfico e Histórico do Amazonas at Rua Bernardo Ramos 117, which has a huge library covering the Amazon through history. It opens 8am-noon on weekdays. The institute is near the western end of Avenida 7 de Setembro, just beyond Praça Dom Pedro II, a shady, peaceful square.

Parque Zoológico. Eight miles/13km west of town is the Parque Zoológico CIGS, an exhibition of mostly wretched animals collected by the army while on manoeuvres in the jungle. It is open 8am-5pm. To get there take any bus marked Ponte Negra from the local bus station; ask for 'CIGS'.

Ponte Negra is three miles beyond the zoo, and is the site of the luxury Tropical Hotel and the city's main river beach. Swimming is not recommended due to the pollution.

HELP AND INFORMATION

Tourist Information: Emamtur is at Avenida Tarumá 379 (tel 234-5503/5983), and opens 7am-6pm on weekdays. It is a fair trek from the centre, ten blocks north of Avenida 7de Setembro.

Money: several banks in the pedestrian zone exchange cash and travellers cheques, including Bemge at Rua G. Moreira 296, which also does credit card withdrawals. Lloyds has a branch at Rua G. Moreira 147. Hotels and travel agencies will usually change money out of banking hours.

Communications: the main post office is at Rua Marechal Deodoro 117, near the corner of Rua Teodoro Souto. It opens 8.30am-5.30pm.

The TeleAmazonas telephone office is at Rua G. Moreira 320, near the corner of Avenida 7 de Setembro. It is open 6am-11.30pm. Manaus time is one hour behind that in eastern Brazil.

Consulates. *Bolivia:* Avenida Eduardo Ribeiro 520 (Manaus Shopping Centre), room 1410 (tel 234-6661/237-8686).
Colombia: Rua Dona Libânia 62 (tel 234-6777), a couple of blocks east of the opera house, on the corner of Rua Marcal.
Peru: Rua Tapajós 536 (tel 234-7900/236-3666).
Venezuela: Rua Recife 1620 (tel 236-0406), north of the centre.
UK: Avenida Eduardo Ribeiro 520 (Manaus Shopping Centre), 12th floor (tel 234-1018). The consul shares the office of Wilson Sons Agencia de Navegação, but he is often absent.
USA: Rua Recife 1010 (tel 234-4807/4546), north of the centre in Adriánopolis district, near the cemetery; take any bus bound for the bus station or airport.

JUNGLE TOURS

The best trips take you away from the main waterways and along the narrow channels, known as *igarapés*. This is where you're likely to see the most wildlife. But while the lucky ones encounter monkeys, alligators, parrots and perhaps even an elusive toucan, others come away having seen nothing but the odd exotic-looking sparrow. Obviously, the longer the trip the more likely you are to get into the 'real' jungle. However an imaginative or well-organized trip even of just a couple of days can be exciting. The best tours combine a boat trip with a jungle trek, although trekking is usually out of the question during the rainy season. Most recommended are the trips that simply enable you to experience life in the jungle, but many agencies gear trips around one or more of a number of specific destinations, such as the Anavilhanas archipelago, 62 miles/100km up the Rio Negro.

Choosing a Tour. Organizing a river or jungle tour involves a certain amount of shopping around. You are advised to choose an agency that has been recommended to you or one of those listed in this book. For the longer tours you can expect to pay in the region of $60-80 for the first day, $30 for subsequent days. You either sleep in hammocks in the forest, or perhaps on the boat; some agencies have their own jungle lodges.

There are plenty of agencies and independent guides to choose from, and you should be able to find something to suit your requirements regarding the duration, degree of comfort, etc. Discuss every aspect of the tour, from whether lifejackets are provided to whether the price includes all food. Check the itinerary carefully and ascertain whether or not your guide can speak good English or any other language. Most tours require a minimum number of people, but there is some leeway according to the season and the level of trade; the price may be open to negotiation for the same reasons. Finally, remember to take plenty of repellent, sunblock, plastic bags, and extra food and water.

Agencies: the most recommended agency is Amazonas Indian Turismo (Rua dos Andradas 335). It offers imaginative and environmentally-sensitive tours that bring you into close contact with the jungle. Their best trips involve building your own shelter in the jungle and staying there for a couple or more nights. Expect to pay around $120 for three days, and $25 for each extra day — one of the cheapest deals in town.

The other most reliable agencies are: Amazon Explorers (Rua Bocaiúva 189 first floor; tel 232-3052, 233-9339), São Cristóvão (Rua Marechal Deodoro 89, first floor; tel 233-3231); and Selvatur (Praça Adalberto Vale; tel 234-8639/8984), next to Hotel Amazonas — one of the most expensive.

Independent Guides: if you go with an independent guide, make sure he or she is registered with Embratur; note that independent guides are not necessarily much cheaper than the agencies. Boatmen and prospective guides hang out near the harbour by the Mercado Municipal, although you are likely to be approached anywhere along the waterfront. Most boatmen try to charge about $80 for a five-hour trip in the igarapés, but this is for the hire of the entire boat, so can work out fairly cheaply if you are in a group; if there are just a couple of you, you should be able to get a discount.

The Meeting of the Rivers. The confluence of the Rios Negro and Solimoes is about 10 miles/16km east of Manaus. The meeting of the two rivers is an impressive sight since the black waters of the Negro and yellow, muddy waters of Solimoes flow parallel for about 11 miles/18km without mixing. During the high season, the confluence can become a chaotic mass of camera-clicking tourists.

Amazon Explorers and Selvatur each run a tour, to which hotels and other agencies subscribe; but the boats carry around 150 people and the level of enjoyment is debatable. It is combined with a visit to Lago de Janauri, a small reserve about 10 miles/16km from Manaus; the main attraction offered on this last stretch are the famous Vitoria Regia lilies, which are up to three metres in diameter and strong enough to stand on; they disappear between October and March. The entire trip costs around $30. It is as well to book in advance, but otherwise turn up at the agency around 8am, or ask at your hotel.

One alternative is to arrange a trip to the confluence with a local boatman at the harbour; allow about three hours. But the simplest, most entertaining and cheapest way is to get the bus to the village of Vila Buriti, from where there is a regular free ferry across to Careiro on the south bank. Buses south to Porto Velho take this route. Here you can have a beer or a snack in the café before taking the boat back. There are buses to Vila Buriti from the local bus station.

RORAIMA

The gold rush of the 1980s had devastating consequences on the state of Roraima, particularly on the mountainous area in the northwest. This is the home of the Yanomami Indians, currently numbering around 9,000 in Brazil (they also live in Venezuela). Since 1987 they have seen their territory shrink as more than 45,000 garimpeiros invaded their land. Their survival depends on the projected dwindling of alluvial gold deposits, and on Collor's promises to legalize a vast protected homeland; an area almost the size of Suriname has been earmarked as a reserve, but the military and mining companies are making its establishment difficult.

Bordered by Venezuela and Guyana, Roraima is real frontier country. It is in this capacity that the state and its capital, Boa Vista, is a destination for travellers en route north.

BOA VISTA

The capital of Roraima (population 75,000) is also the gold-miners' capital. A planned city, Boa Vista is an ugly, concrete creation that is utterly out of place and unpleasantly hot to boot. It's not a particularly friendly city either, and the local police (who maintain a high profile) seem to dislike most foreigners. In *Ninety-Two Days* (the account of a trip from Guyana to Brazil in 1934) Evelyn Waugh doesn't have a good word to say about the place.

There is nothing much to do except walk along the Rio Branco, browse around the shops full of mining equipment, and watch gold merchants doing deals with the garimpeiros.

Arrival and Departure. *Air:* Boa Vista is well served by domestic flights, in addition to services with Varig (Rua Dr Filho 91; tel 242-2226) to and from Georgetown in Guyana, and Puerto Ordaz in Venezuela. The airport (tel 224-3680) is a couple of miles from the centre, most easily reached by taxi.

Bus: buses to and from Boa Vista fill quickly, so book in advance. Eucatur runs buses between Boa Vista and Manaus, 490 miles/785km south. The journey takes anything over 16 hours — the road is rough, breakdowns are common, and there are often delays at the ferry crossing over the Rio Branco. The bus station (tel 224-0606) is on Avenida das Guianas, just a mile or so from town; local buses run along Benjamin Constant and the main square, or else it's a 30-minute walk.

A bus leaves every morning for Santa Elena, on the Venezuelan border, taking at least six hours. Buses wait for passengers to go through immigration, and then take them into Santa Elena itself. You will probably need to stay in town since you are unlikely to get onward transport northwards the same day.

Travelling overland isn't the easiest way into Guyana, though it is certainly an adventure. Buses leave, unreliably, once or twice a day for Bonfim, and take $3\frac{1}{2}$-4 hours. Brazilian immigration is in Bonfim, but from there you must walk the three miles to the Rio Tacutu, which marks the border. Local people take you across to Lethem in their boats. The nearest Guyanan consulates are in Brasília or São Paulo; even with a visa you may be turned away — Guyanan officialdom seems paranoid about visitors.

Accommodation. Hotels are expensive and often full. Some of the cheapest places are on Rua Benjamin Constant, including the Roraima (number 321; tel 224-3721). For more comfort stay at Eusébio's (Rua Cecília Brasil 1107; tel 224-0300), a couple of blocks northwest of the Palácio do Governo.

Help and Information. Banco do Brasil, behind the Palácio do Governo, changes money. There are also a few unofficial moneychangers, including garimpeiros, on Rua Dr A. Filho (west of the main square), who deal in cash and cheques, and offer fairly good rates.

The Venezuelan Consulate is at Rua Benjamin Constant 525E (tel 224-2182), east of the square. Visa processing normally takes one day.

RONDONIA

The state of Rondônia was created out of chunks of Amazonas and Mato Grosso in 1981. It has been one of the areas hardest hit by the land rush, and World Bank-funded road building and colonization projects have been responsible for the destruction of around 20% of its rainforest. The state's population increased a hundredfold in the first ten years of its existence — which is only too well illustrated by the number of towns that have already sprung up along the BR-364 highway, constructed in the 1980s.

PORTO VELHO

The capital of Rondônia, like Boa Vista, is treated simply as a pitstop by most travellers. And yet it has a great deal more to offer than the capital of Roraima. Porto Velho is an arresting sight, lying atop the high banks of the Rio Madeira, and a busy and lively place. The town is full of brash garimpeiros, and you feel like an extra in some Wild West movie.

Arrival and Departure. *Air:* between them, Varig (Avenida Campos Sales 2666; tel 221-8555), Vasp (corner of Ruas Afonso Pena and Ten. Aranha; tel 223-3755) and TABA (Rua Prudente de Morais 39; tel 221-5493) connect Porto Velho to all of Brazil's major cities and various Amazonian towns. There are daily flights to Manaus, Cuiabá, Brasília, Rio Branco and Corumbá.

The airport (tel 221-3935) is 4 miles/7km north of town; local buses run into the centre.

Boat: the journey by boat along the Rio Madeira from Manaus is an interesting trip, past colourful houseboats and goldpanners. It should take three days, longer when the river is low. Boats heading back to Manaus tend to leave at the end of the week, but ask around at the port in the centre. Services to Manicoré, a fairly pleasant town midway between Manaus and Porto Velho, are more frequent, so you may decide to do the journey in two stages.

Bus: services run daily between Manaus and Porto Velho during the dry season, along the mostly paved but poor BR-319; the journey takes about 24 hours in good conditions. There are buses to Rio Branco and Cuiabá, as well as an astonishing range of services all over the country. The bus station is on Avenida Presidente Kennedy, at the southern end of Avenida 7 de Setembro, the main commercial street, about 13 blocks from the main square.

Accommodation and Food. Try Hotel Yara (Avenida Osório 255), just west of the main square, or the Nunes (7 de Setembro 1195), a few blocks further south; the Cuiabano opposite is also reasonable. There are several good places to eat by the river, including a couple near the northern end of Rua Dom Pedro II. The best place to splash out on good fish is Caravela do Madeira (Rua Ariquemes 104), north of the centre.

Exploring. Porto Velho's main attraction is the Railway Museum on the waterfront. It is full of memorabilia dating from the days of the Madeira-Mamoré railway, which used to run between Porto Velho and Guajará-Mirim on the Rio Mamoré and the Bolivian border. It was completed in the second decade of this century, in order to provide Bolivia with an outlet to the Atlantic — via the Madeira and Amazon rivers. This was a concession Brazil made after its annexation of the Bolivian territory of Acre during the rubber boom. Trains haven't run the length of the old railway line for years; indeed most of it has been turned into the main southbound road. One section still functions and at weekends — usually just Sundays — during the dry season, you can take an old steam train to Santo Antônio, just 4 miles/7km south of Porto Velho: a short, but entertaining ride.

Help and Information. Change money in the hotels or at Banco do Brasil (corner of Avenidas Alençar and Dom Pedro II). The post office is near the corner of Avenidas Pres. Dutra and 7 de Setembro. The phone office is on Rogeiro Weber, near the corner of Dom Pedro II.

GUAJARA-MIRIM and THE BOLIVIAN BORDER

About 200 miles/320km southwest of Porto Velho is Guajará-Mirim. Across the Mamoré river is the Bolivian town of Guayaramerin. One bus a day runs from Porto Velho, taking at least seven hours; TABA flies three times a week.

Guajará-Mirim is a bustling little place with a population of 30,000. The main street is 15 de Novembro, where you'll find some of the best hotels (the Mini-Estrela at number 460 and the Fenix Palace opposite) and the bus station. You can change money at Banco do Brasil, and there is a Bolivian consulate in Hotel Alfa at Avenida Leopoldo de Matos 239. Before leaving town, get your passport stamped at the Polícia Federal (Avenida Antônio Correia da Costa 842). Ferries cross to Guayaramerín, from where there is transport to Riberalta: see page 356.

Most people wouldn't bother coming to Guajará-Mirim unless they were headed for Bolivia. However, it is possible to go on a most interesting trip along the Rio Mamoré to the Forte Principe da Beira, a ruined 18th-century fort. Boats leave infrequently (ask at the harbour or in the Port Captain's office at Avenida 15 de Novembro 418) and take about three days. The nearest town to the fort is Costa Marquês, 15 miles/24km south, with a couple of hotels. Since it is connected by road to the BR-364, you can go by bus either back to Porto Velho or south to Mato Grosso; you will almost certainly need to change at Presidente Medici, on the highway.

ACRE

This remote corner of Amazonia is one of the least developed parts of Brazil. Since the 1970s, however, even Acre (pronounced *a-cray*) has witnessed developments similar to those devastating other parts of the Amazon. It was in Acre that Chico Mendes fought to preserve the livelihood of the rubber tappers, in direct opposition to the interests of the muscle-flexing *fazendeiros* — for which he paid with his life. His simple home in Xapurí, southwest of Rio Branco, is now a museum, containing a few sad mementoes.

The capital, Rio Branco, is a lively market town with a population of 160,000.

It is 306 miles/490km southwest of Porto Velho, about 15 hours by bus along a partially paved road. There is also an airport. Unless you are heading into Bolivia or enjoy remote Amazonian towns, there's not much point in a visit. The BR-364 extends west to Cruzeiro do Sul. Do not attempt to penetrate further west, to Pucallpa in Peru, since this is Sendero Luminoso territory. An easier though little used border crossing is from Brasiléia to the Bolivian town of Cobija, from where you can fly to La Paz (see page 356).

Acre is one hour behind other states in Amazonia, and some say it is years behind the rest of Brazil.

THE CENTRE WEST

The area of Brazil commonly described as the Centre West is made up of the two Mato Grosso states, Goiás, Tocantins and the so-called Distrito Federal. It is an intriguing area of modern, planned cities, primeval swamps rich in wildlife, and remote frontier country. Territorial divisions within the region have changed dramatically over the last few decades, a sign of bureaucratic concerns and economic development: the Distrito Federal was inaugurated at the time of the creation of Brasília in 1960, and Tocantins was created as recently as 1989.

To the east of the region are the dusty, rolling hills and scrub of the central plateau. Further west the terrain flattens to form the low-lying plain and swamp of the Pantanal, which covers significant areas of the Mato Grosso states. To the north the dense tropical forest is home to some of Brazil's last-surviving Indians.

It is not surprising that such terrain did not attract early Portuguese explorers. The first real settlements appeared in the early 18th century, following the discovery of gold, but large-scale development only began this century. As if making up for lost time, the central states are now the country's fastest growing region. New roads have turned the Centre West into the principal gateway to the Amazon.

There is very little tourism in the area. The Pantanal, with its magnificent wildlife, is undoubtedly one of the highlights of Brazil. But even here the level of tourism is comparatively small, due to the terrain and the lack of infrastructure. Brasília's staggering modernist architecture pulls a few visitors, and Tocantins' wild and remote Ilha do Bananal appeals to adventurous types. But most of the region is ignored.

The best time to travel in the area is during the comparatively cool and dry period from July to September. During the rains the Pantanal floods and is virtually inaccessible.

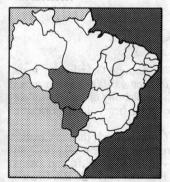

THE MATO GROSSO STATES

CUIABA

The capital of Mato Grosso is probably the most appealing city in central Brazil. Cuiabá is modern, rather expensive and at times oppressively hot, but also bustling and entertaining. The city has thrived on the opening up to development of the Mato Grosso and southern Amazonia: its population — currently 350,000 — grows steadily. There is a constant flow of settlers passing through the city, many of them headed along the BR-364 northwest into Rondônia. For travellers

Cuiabá is primarily a base from which to visit the Pantanal or a pitstop en route to or from the Amazon, but it is worth taking the time to explore.

The heart of Cuiabá is the busy Praça da República, which is where you'll find the city's best museums. These form part of the Fundação Cultural de Mato Grosso, and include good anthropological and historical displays. Also worth a visit is the Museu Rondon (do Indio) at the university, which is on Avenida Fernando da Costa. For a scene more characteristic of life in the city, visit the buzzing fresh produce market by the bridge; there are several good bars and cafés nearby.

Arrival and Departure. As well as daily flights from Brazil's main cities, FAB has irregular flights from Porto Velho. The airport (tel 381-2211) is in Várzea Grande, on the other side of the Cuiabá river.

There are frequent buses every day from Campo Grande (10 hours), and several daily services from Goiânia (14 hours), Brasília (22 hours) and Porto Velho (24 hours). The BR-163 north to Santarém is dreadful, and even in the dry season bus services are extremely unreliable. The station (tel 321-4703) is on Avenida Marechal Rondon, a couple of miles north of the centre. Buses run to Praça da República, where there is a tourist office.

Accommodation. The best hotels are the Mato Grosso (Rua Comandante Costa 2522; tel 321-9121), with a good restaurant, and the Real Palace in Praça Ipiranga (tel 321-7703). Expect to pay at least $10. For a cheaper and rougher night stay near the old bus station, around the junction of Ruas Gen. Vale and Baltazar Navarros, south of the centre.

For a few beers, check out the bars along Avenida C.P.A., which runs east of Avenida Tenente Duarte.

Around Cuiabá
Chapada dos Guimarães. The best trip out of town, apart from to the Pantanal, is to Chapada dos Guimarães, a small town in the mountains about 42 miles/68km northeast of Cuiabá. It boasts the state's oldest church, a spring-fed swimming pool and, above all, beautiful scenery. The scope for walks is limited for anyone dependent on public transport. Nevertheless, the Véu de Noiva waterfall, which is one of the highlights of the area, is not difficult to reach; simply get off the Cuiabá-Chapada bus near Buruti, and follow the track. Buses between Cuiabá and Chapada run several times a day, and take about $2\frac{1}{2}$ hours. There are a couple of hotels in Chapada.

MATO GROSSO DO SUL
CAMPO GRANDE
The capital of Mato Grosso do Sul only since the 70s, Campo Grande was a late developer. However, it already has a population of over 430,000 and no mean collection of high-rises. A few ranchers' shops and the availability of some excellent steak are some of the few reminders that the city lies at the heart of a major cattle region.

Although there is less temptation to spend time in Campo Grande than in Cuiabá, it is a relaxed and manageable city. Don't fail to visit the excellent Museu Dom Bosco, which is packed full of fascinating exhibits — from Indian crafts and fossils to vast collections of insects and stuffed animals. It is at Rua Barão do Rio Branco 1843, and opens daily.

Arrival and Departure. Campo Grande is accessible by air, bus and train. The airport (tel 763-2444) is 4 miles/7km west of town.

There are regular bus services to and from Cuiabá (10 hours), Corumbá (7 hours) and São Paulo (14 hours). If going to Foz do Iguaçu take a bus to Cascavel and change. The bus station is near the corner of Rua Nabuco and Avenida Afonso Pena (tel 383-1678), an easy walk west of the centre.

Campo Grande lies on the Corumbá-Bauru/São Paulo railway, and there are services three times a week in both directions, though the schedule is notoriously unreliable. The journey to Corumbá takes about 12 hours, to Bauru 19 hours. The station is on Avenida Calógeras (tel 383-2762), five blocks north of Avenida Barão do Rio Branco.

Crossing into Paraguay: the pleasant Brazilian border town of Ponta Porã is contiguous with Pedro Juan Caballero in Paraguay. It is served by several buses a day from Campo Grande (6 hours) and a daily train (9 hours). The Francia (Rua Guia Lopes) and the Internacional (Avenida Internacional 2604; tel 431-1243) are reasonable hotels. Get your Brazilian exit stamp from the Polícia Federal at Rua Marechal Floriano 1483.

Accommodation. The cheapest hotels are found near the railway station. Among the better ones are the Gaspar (Avenida Mato Grosso 2; tel 383-5121) and the União (Avenida Calógeras 2828). A couple of blocks nearer the centre is the Anache at Rua M. Rondon 1396 (tel 383-2841).

Help and Information. The city tourist office is on Avenida Barão do Rio Branco, in Praça Coelho. For more general information go to the state office at Avenida Afonso Pena 3149. Also on Afonso Pena, the main street, is Banco do Brasil (number 2202) where you can change money at poor rates. The post and telephone offices are both in Rua Dom Aquino, on the corners of Calógeras and Rui Barbosa respectively.

The Bolivian Consulate is at Rua Abraão Júlio Rahe 1539, Paraguay's at Rua Coelho 1198, apt 201.

CORUMBA

The border town of Corumbá lies in a splendid situation overlooking the Rio Paraguai; across the river is Bolivia. Despite being a major drug-trafficking and gun-running centre, and unremittingly hot, Corumbá is a relaxed place. Situated right on the edge of the swamp, it is the southern gateway to the Pantanal. The steady flow of visitors is also due to the town's position on the main border crossing into Bolivia.

The main place of interest in Corumbá is the Museu do Pantanal, in Praça do República; the collection includes stuffed animals and Indian weaponry. It opens daily except Sunday.

Arrival and Departure. *Air:* only Vasp (Rua 15 de Novembro 392) has connections with Corumbá, with daily flights to Campo Grande, Cuiabá, Brasília and Goiânia, as well as cities further afield including Belém and Belo Horizonte. If headed for Bolivia take an internal flight from Puerto Suárez, across the border near Quijarro. The airport (tel 231-5842) is 20-30 minutes walk southwest of the centre.

Bus: there are buses to Cuiabá (18 hours), Ponta Porã (12 hours) and other towns in the region, but it is usually easier to change at Campo Grande, which is six hours away and served by frequent buses. The bus station (tel 231-37830) is just east of the train station.

Train: trains to Campo Grande and Bauru currently run thrice-weekly, though services seem likely to be reduced; Corumbá to Bauru takes 30 hours.

Trains to Santa Cruz in Bolivia leave from across the border in Quijarro, which is where you must buy your ticket. There are services most days, but the only recommended train to take is the ferrobus, which currently leaves at 9am on Tuesday, Thursday and Saturday, and takes 12 hours. The journey is slow and somewhat notorious (see page 358), but it is the only sensible overland route to Santa Cruz. The train station (tel 231-2876) is seven blocks south of Praça Independência, the main square.

If leaving the country, get your passport stamped at the Polícia Federal office in the railway station. Buses to the border, some 5 miles/8km away, leave hourly from Praça da República. Once across the bridge and through immigration, buses run into Quijarro.

The Bolivian Consulate is at Rua Coelho 852.

Accommodation. Good-value hotels include the Grande Hotel Corumbá at Rua Frei Mariano 468 (tel 231-1021), and Hotel Beira Rio (Rua M. Cavassa 109; tel 231-2554) overlooking the river. The cheapest places are near the railway station, such as Hotel Schabib at Rua Frei Mariano 1153.

The Pantanal

The remains of an ancient inland sea the size of England, this unique swamp is one of the best places in which to see wildlife on the continent. The Pantanal supports an incredible range of fauna and flora, which can be observed far more easily than in the Amazon. The abundant birdlife is best seen during the dry season, since this is when vast colonies gather in the trees along the edge of the savannah to breed. Among the 600 species it is possible to spot, parakeets are among the most common. Lucky people will also see emus and rheas (though not in the trees). As far as larger animals are concerned, you would be extremely unlucky not to see *jacaré* (alligators), and you stand a good chance of seeing at least one or two of the following: capybaras (a large rodent), monkeys, otters, anteaters, deer, wild boar and snakes. You cannot miss the cows, millions of which graze the swamps.

Access is only really feasible in the dry season. During the rains (October to March) much of the swamp is covered in three metres of water. While hot during the day in the dry season, temperatures drop at night.

EXPLORING THE SWAMP
The Pantanal is bound to the north by the BR-070 highway, to the east by the BR-163 and to the south by the BR-262, with the cities of Cuiabá, Campo Grande and Corumbá as the main points of reference. While transport around the edge of the swamp is fairly easy, penetrating it is more difficult.

Independent travel often requires a certain amount of hitching, and some people decide to go on an organized tour. Most operators use a lodge (*fazenda*), or occasionally a houseboat, as a base from which to go on excursions. The best way to experience the Pantanal, however, is to travel independently to one of the lodges in the swamp, and organize your own guided trips from there. Most of

least a week. But you would do better to get a lift on one of the boats that actually go into the swamp doing the rounds of the fazendas to pick up cattle — a great way to spend a few days.

From Campo Grande. A few bases are most easily reached from Campo Grande, including Aquidauana and Miranda off the BR-262, and Coxim off the Cuiabá road, but none is actually within the swamp.

GOIAS and BRASILIA

GOIANIA

The capital city of Goiás state was created in the 1930s as part of President Vargas' campaign to open up the west. It wasn't designed to house its current population of one million, but Goiânia is surprisingly clean and spacious. Being cheaper than Brasília it may be a better overnight stop for anyone travelling to or from the Mato Grosso. Goiânia is well served by air and road transport. The airport (tel 207-1288) is in Setor Santa Genoveva, two miles northeast of the centre. The bus station is at Rua 44 (Setor Norte Ferroviário; tel 224-8466), north of the centre. Goiânia is four hours by bus from Brasília, 14 hours from Cuiabá and São Paulo, and 17 from Campo Grande.

Many of the city's hotels are on Avenida Anhangüera: best are the Lord (3195; tel 224-0666) and the Samambaia (1157; tel 261-1444).

GOIAS VELHO

This small town 90 miles/144km northwest of Goiânia, is the most interesting place to visit in Goiás. Founded by bandeirantes in 1727 following the discovery of gold, Goiás Velho enjoyed a brief boom and was the state capital at one time. Its narrow winding streets are a pleasant antidote to the modern thoroughfares of Goiânia, and there are a number of handsome baroque churches. The Museu das Bandeiras, in the old town hall on Praça Brasil Caiado, illustrates the history of the early pioneers.

Goiás Velho is served by frequent buses from Goiânia (3 hours) and is an easy day trip. If you want to stay over, there are a couple of reasonable hotels on Avenida Dr Deusdete Ferreira de Moura.

Brasília

Described by the journalist Isabel Hilton as 'the illegitimate offspring of an intellectual love affair between an architect and a dictator', Brasília is one of the world's great white elephants. A monument to modernism, the city sits incongruously in the middle of the hot plains of Goiás state. It lies within the so-called Distrito Federal.

Commissioned by President Juscelino Kubitschek, and built in just three years, Brasília is a designer city par excellence. However, it has in many ways been a failure. The most immediate result of its creation was rampant inflation, since money to finance the project was borrowed from abroad. It has done little to encourage sustainable economic development in the region — the construction of new roads have turned the Centre West primarily into a gateway to the Amazon.

Brasília's population — currently at around 1.5 million — rises gradually, but many of the new arrivals merely swell the already sizeable favelas. The bureaucrats tempted to Brasília by big salaries and swimming pools, escape whenever possible.

Brasília was the fruit of the collaboration of three men — an urban planner (Lúcio Costa), an architect (Oscar Niemeyer) and a landscape designer (Burle Marx). The futuristic architecture of Niemeyer has always been the city's most potent symbol and is undeniably breathtaking. Yet once new and sparkling, Brasília is now rather shabby. There is next to no street life and the place is completely dead at weekends. It feels more like a film set taken over by squatters than a real city.

A visit to Brasília is a must for anyone interested in 1950s architecture. But the capital's appeal is, first and foremost, as a curiosity. It is the ideal place to stop off at if you have a sector of your air pass to use up.

City Layout. The shape of Brasília, which lies on the shores of an artificial lake, is normally likened to an aeroplane. But while the layout is impressive in theory, coping with it in real life can be a headache. The use of numbers rather than names to differentiate the streets is just part of the conspiracy to make the life of the visitor a nightmare.

Running the length of the five-mile long 'fuselage' is a superhighway, the Eixo Monumental. The 'wings', on either side, are made up primarily of apartment blocks, divided up into Super-Quadras. They lie either side of the Eixo Rodoviário, which runs at right angles to the main highway. The city's central bus station is situated where the Eixos Monumental and Rodoviário cross, and is a useful reference point; it is also one of the liveliest parts of the city. Nearby, to the west, are the main commercial areas — the Setor Comercial Sul and Norte; Avenida W3 is the main commercial street. The Sul shopping complex looks as if it was built as a training ground for urban muggers. The newer Norte centre is much better.

At the eastern end is the Praça dos Tres Poderes and the Setores Embaixadas. The majority of embassies are in the Setor Embaixadas Sul (SES) — on Avenida das Naçoes, which runs along the lake.

Arrival and Departure. Many domestic flights stop over in the capital, and there is a shuttle connection with Rio (tel 248-4411). There are connections also with North American cities and some European capitals. The airport (tel 248-5131/5588) is 7 miles/12km south of the centre. Buses from here to the central rodoviária run every 15 minutes.

Frequent buses run to and from Rio (19 hours), São Paulo (16 hours) and Belo Horizonte (12 hours), and also the cities within the Centre West. Less regular daily buses serve Belém (38 hours), Salvador (24 hours), etc. The huge rodoferroviária (tel 233-7200) is west of the centre in the Setor Noroeste; bus 131 runs to the central city bus station.

Trains use the rodoferroviária too. There is a weekly train service between Brasília and Campinas, with connections to São Paulo.

Accommodation and Food. One reason travellers shun Brasília is the lack of low-budget accommodation. Staying in the two main hotel districts — Setor Hoteleiro Norte and Sul or SHN and SHS — will set you back at least $40 per night. The most moderately-priced hotels are in the northern zone, and include El Pilar (Quadra 3, bloco E; tel 223-1570) and Hotel Mirage (Quadra 2, Lote N; tel 225-7160). You can sometimes get a discount at weekends.

The only concentration of cheap hotels is in Taguatinga district, several miles west of the rodoferroviária. They include Pousada Brasília (Projeção L; tel 562-5055) and the Globo (CNB4, Lote 1; tel 561-1716). Buses run there from both the central bus station and rodoferroviária.

There are some cheap restaurants along Avenida W3 Sul, around the central bus station and in the south hotel sector. There is a food court in the Norte shopping centre. If you want to overdose on meat in pleasant lakeside surroundings, go to the Churrascaria do Lago where all the flesh you can eat costs around $15. It is next to the Brasília Palace Hotel — a short walk north along the shore from Palácio da Alvorada.

Exploring. A good place to start an exploration of Brasília is on the observation deck of the TV tower (Torre de TV), which lies in the centre of the Eixo Monumental near the western edge of the wings; there is a craft fair at its base most weekends. The central rodoviária is another good vantage point. East of here is one of Niemeyer's greatest creations and Brasília's most striking landmark — the cathedral. It has proved much more successful than the one in Rio. The main body of the cathedral is below ground — what you see is the roof. It overlooks the Esplanada dos Ministérios, which runs east to Praça dos Tres Poderes and is lined with government ministries: extensions have been built to most of these, but at the back so as not to destroy the original layout.

The 'Square of the Three Powers' is the heart of Brazilian government. On the right is the Palácio do Itamarati, which houses the Ministry of Foreign Affairs. It is one of the city's most impressive buildings, and contains beautiful gardens. It is open for tours at 4pm (Monday to Friday), but permission in advance is required: call 211-6640. Dominating the square is the twin-towered Palácio do Congresso — nicknamed 'air sandwich' by the locals. The unusual semispherical buildings are the assembly halls of the Congress and Senate, and are open for visits 2.30-5pm on weekdays. Behind Congress is the less remarkable Palácio do Planalto, where the president works. If you're lucky, you may see him on a walkabout, most probably on a Friday. The president's official residence, the Palácio do Alvorada, is by the lakeside some way behind.

If the idea of traipsing through the streets doesn't appeal, go on a bus tour. Brasília is the one place where this is a good plan. You can do this either by taking a bus that follows a circular route (e.g. 106 from the central bus station), or by going on an organized tour. There are many agencies in the shopping arcade of Hotel Nacional in SHS (Lote 1), most of which offer trips of three or four hours; some also have representatives at the airport. Alternatively, arrange a trip with one of the independent guides that accost you on the street; they often hang around the cathedral. Carlos Romeo Feldkirchner is a trustworthy guide who charges $15 for two to three hours; you can contact him on 371-1248.

Help and Information. Staff at the tourist desks in the airport and bus station, can give advice on accommodation and tours. Money is best changed at hotels and travel agencies, where rates are surprisingly good.

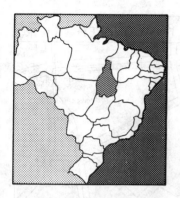

TOCANTINS

Unless taking the overland route along the Brasília-Belém highway, you are unlikely to come into contact with the state of Tocantins, a bureaucratic whim that lacks not only an identity but also a capital. Tocantins' one claim to touristic fame, the Ilha do Bananal, must in fact be approached via Mato Grosso.

ILHA DO BANANAL

Formed by a split in the Rio Araguaia and measuring 200 miles/320km in length, Ilha do Bananal is the world's largest river island. It is a beautiful and wild place, whose remoteness has left it firmly off the beaten track. But although few travellers venture into the area, Ilha do Bananal has seen an invasion of settlers who have devastated both the forest and the lives of the Carajás Indians, only a few hundred of whom survive. The wildlife, although also affected by the changes, is spectacular — the marshes support a range of fauna and flora not dissimilar to that found in the Pantanal. The island is flooded during the wet season, so is best visited between June and October.

To visit Ilha do Bananal you must apply for a permit in advance from the Park Director in Goiânia (IBDF, Rua 229, No 95, Setor Universitário, 74000). Having done this, take a bus to Barra do Garças, in Mato Grosso. From here, buses run north to the town of São Felix, (17 hours), which is a possible starting-point for boat trips. The most popular base, however, is further north at Santa Teresinha, where you can organize trips through the Hotel Bananal, or independently.

SAO PAULO

In his book *Brazilian Adventure*, written in 1932, Peter Fleming describes São Paulo as 'like Reading, only much farther away'. Fortunately for the British, Reading did not become what is possibly the largest city in the world. The population of São Paulo is inestimable. The figure is often put at a rather non-committal 'over ten million', but it is almost certainly between 15 and 20 million. São Paulo is urban sprawl *par excellence*.

The city's vast size reflects its economic dominance of Brazil. Even in Peter Fleming's day there were skyscrapers and the other trappings of a solidly 20th-century city. The picture now is less optimistic. São Paulo is afflicted with large areas of concrete jungle and the same malaises as its counterparts elsewhere: boundless wealth alongside wretched poverty. Its reputation for crime is second to none.

São Paulo may be the businessman's capital of Brazil, but in vain does it vie with Rio in the long-standing battle for supremacy in terms of international recognition. It is not surprising that travellers with a choice usually opt to avoid the city altogether. But São Paulo should be visited, if only to experience what has been described as hell on earth. And São Paulo is not all bad: the city has an inexplicable but undeniable appeal. Its vibrant atmosphere is due in part to the astounding racial mix — São Paulo has the largest immigrant communities in Brazil.

717

The city is drenched in a sickly yellow-brown smog. Pollution and high humidity mean that there are often periods of constant drizzle. Sudden changes in temperature are common and sunny skies are rare. Some visitors relish the relatively cool climate.

CITY LAYOUT

It is hard to get your head around a city that is about 40 miles/64km long and 20 miles/32km wide. The centre is not user-friendly either. The traditional heart of the centre takes up the area roughly between Praça da República and Praça da Sé. However, the focus has to some extent spread southwards, towards the newer areas around Avenida Paulista, particularly the smart districts of Cerqueira César and the Jardims, southeast of this street. Characterized by luxury apartment blocks and fortress-like villas, the main reason to come here is to eat or to go to a consulate.

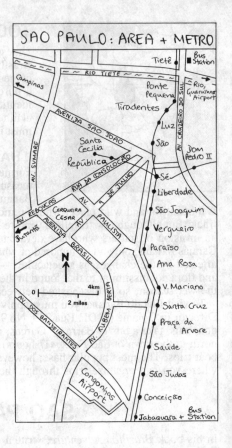

The two other areas you are most likely to spend time in are Liberdade and Bixiga (also known as Bela Vista), the Japanese and Italian quarters respectively; both are south of but not far from the centre.

Maps. You can get good city maps from the tourist office, but if you are planning to stay for some time, you should invest in the *Quatro Rodas* guide to São Paulo, which contains a detailed breakdown of streets.

ARRIVAL AND DEPARTURE

Air. São Paulo has three airports. All international flights land at Guarulhos International (GRU) at Cumbica, 21 miles/35km northeast of the city. It also serves many domestic destinations. Phone 945-2111/2107 for information. You can exchange money at the Banespa bank. There is a regular bus service into the city to Praça da República ($3). To take a cab direct from the airport will set you back at least $20. Buses back to the airport from Praça da República run from 5am-midnight.

The shuttle services from Rio, Belo Horizonte and Curitiba use Congonhas airport (CGH), 8 miles/14km south of the centre but firmly within the urban sprawl. The flights from Rio are most efficient, leaving every 30 minutes and taking an hour; the fare is around $60. Buses connect the airport and Praça da República every 30 minutes from 6am to 9.30pm. Phone 531-7444 or 240-1100 for information. Banespa has a foreign exchange desk.

Viracopos (VCP) is 60 miles/96km southwest of São Paulo, 6 miles/10km from Campinas, and is anything but convenient. VCP handles some international flights and others from Rio, Cuiabá and Vitória.

Airline offices: most airlines have their offices within easy reach of Praça da República. Many South American airlines, including Avianca, Ladeco, LanChile, LAP and LAB are based on Avenida São Luís.
Varig-Cruzeiro — Rua da Consolação 362 (tel 231-9244).
Transbrasil — Avenida São Luis 250 (tel 259-7066).
VASP — Rua Libero Badaró 106, Centro (tel 220-3622).

Bus. São Paulo has two bus terminals. Tietê is connected to the centre by Metro. It has services to all parts of the country (and abroad). There is a shuttle service to Rio (6 hours), and frequent buses to virtually anywhere you can think of, including Campo Grande (16 hours), Curitiba (6 hours), Porto Alegre (18 hours), Belo Horizonte (10 hours) and Brasília (15 hours).
   The second station is in Jabaquara, at the southern end of the Metro line. Buses to nearby destinations on the coast leave from here.

Train. At the time of going to press, trains between São Paulo and Rio had been suspended. Trains run inland to Bauru (for connections to Campo Grande and Corumbá) and to Campinas (for Brasília). The Luz terminal, in Praça da Luz north of the centre, is accessible by Metro.

CITY TRANSPORT
Walking around is feasible in some downtown areas, but in most parts it is not practical. City transport above ground is hampered by streets jammed with the city's estimated 4.5 million vehicles, said to represent 25% of the total in Brazil. Take the metro whenever possible. Avoid travelling at peak hours since neither the bus nor underground systems can cope with the demand. *São Paulo — This Month* has information on buses and the metro; transport maps are also available at some stations and news stands.

Metro. The underground trains are fast, cheap, easy to use and generally safe, though they are best avoided at night. There is a north-south and an east-west line, intersecting at Praça da Sé; new lines are under construction. Since the bus and train stations, the two main squares in the centre and the Liberdade district are all served by metro, you may not need to use the buses much. Trains run from 5am to midnight.

Bus. São Paulo's buses are ancient and impossibly crowded: statistics have revealed that there are eleven passengers per square metre in the average bus. In addition, routes are often circuitous and confusing. Fortunately, buses to many destinations pass through Praça da República.

Taxi. Travelling by taxi is cheap, and is strongly advised at night. If you don't hail a taxi, you can order one by calling 229-7688 or 941-2555.

ACCOMMODATION
Although many hotels are geared for the business traveller, there is a vast choice of cheaper options. There is a surfeit of beds and getting a discount should be

no problem — if you go for a businessman's hotel, you may be able to negotiate a 50% discount at weekends.

There are many cheap hotels around the Luz train terminal, particularly on or near Ruas das Andradas and Santa Ifigênia, to the west. Since this area takes in a red-light district, be wary of hotels doubling up as brothels. Safe bets are Hotel Ofir (Rua das Andradas 258; tel 223-8822), Hotel Pauliceía (Rua Timbiras 216; tel 220-9433), off Santa Ifigênia, and the Istria (Rua Aurora 519; tel 220-7522).

Better hotels can be found in the streets around the Praça da República, which is also a more pleasant area in the evenings; expect to pay $15-20. Recommended are the Las Vegas at Rua Vitória 390, the São Sebastião (Rua 7 de Abril 364), the Plaza Marabá (Avenida Ipiranga 757) and the Amazonas (Avenida Carvalho 32; tel 220-4111), off Praça da República.

The third best area for accommodation is around the Liberdade metro station, where there is a mixture of budget and medium-range hotels. Several are on Ruas dos Estudantes and da Glória, including the Isei at Rua da Glória 290 (tel 278-6677). More expensive but good value is the Banri at Rua Galvão Bueno 209 (tel 270-8877).

EATING AND DRINKING

With its ethnic variety, it is not surprising that São Paulo has a huge choice of restaurants. Many are geared for foreign businessmen with large expense accounts, but there are plenty of cheaper alternatives. São Paulo is the fast food capital of Brazil, and is the home of the *bauru*, or roast beef sandwich. Around Praça da República you'll find mainly lanchonetes and churrascarias. It is usually worth heading further afield for more interesting restaurants.

Italian restaurants are scattered all over the city. The greatest concentration is in Bixiga, the Italian quarter and one of the few old areas left in the centre. It is an entertainingly sleazy part of town, and it's worth taking time to explore the district. Having worked up an appetite you can take advantage of the bars, cafés and the mass of pizzerias and pasta joints. Many are on or off Rua 13 de Maio. Recommended are Gigetto (Avanhandava 63) and Speranza (Rua 13 de Maio 1004).

There is a more varied selection of restaurants in the exclusive Cerqueira César district, but prices are generally high. There are several places on Rua Oscar Freire 523, including David's at number 913, which serves excellent French food. The bars at the southern end of Rua Augusta and in the surrounding streets are popular among students.

Anyone frustrated by the high prices and small number of Japanese restaurants in Europe will relish the chance to eat in the district of Liberdade. There are several places on Rua Thomas Gonzaga, including the Yamanga at 66. Simpler alternatives are the Tanji at Rua dos Estudantes 166 and the Deigo in Praça Almeida Jr.

EXPLORING

Most of the city's colonial heritage has long since been demolished. The Pátio do Colégio, a replica of the original 16th-century Jesuit mission, just north of Praça da Sé, and the nearby cathedral, completed in the 1950s, rather sum up what the city has to offer in the way of architecture. Nevertheless, there are a few oases of interest, and several good museums and fairs. If you can't face the traffic-choked streets, go on one of the bus tours which operate from Praça da República on Sundays (9am-3pm).

The huge Praça da República is hard to avoid. One of the best things about it is the Edificio Italia in the southern corner. This is the city's tallest building and gives a good view from the top. Three blocks southeast of the square in Praça Ramos de Azevado is the Teatro Municipal, one of the finest structures in São Paulo and the city's main classical music venue.

South of Praça da República, along the daunting, six-lane Avenida Consolação, is the main downtown area, with its high-rise office blocks and shopping centres. Along Avenida Paulista are some of the city's few surviving colonial mansions — mostly built by São Paulo's coffee barons — one of which now houses a branch of McDonalds. There are also several fine art nouveau and art deco houses, scattered amongst the black and mirrored glass that make up the mass of skyscrapers. At number 1578, near the corner of Rua Peixoto Gomide, is one of the highlights of the city, the Museu de Arte de São Paulo. It contains an impressive collection of European art, including the works of Italian Renaissance and French Impressionist artists, with a rather token display of Brazilian works. It is within walking distance of the Paraíso metro station, and is open 1-5pm Tuesday to Friday, 2-6pm at weekends.

Southwest of the centre is Instituto Butantã (Avenida Dr Vital Brasil 1500), a scientific and medical research centre famous for its study of venomous snakes. Its collection of serpents is said to be the largest in the world and can be seen 9am-5pm daily except Monday. Buses run from Praça da República. If São Paulo's greatest tourist attraction leaves you cold, go to the Casa do Bandeirante in Praça Lobato, also in Butantã district. This is an 18th-century ranch house which is one of the few vestiges of São Paulo's pioneer days. It opens 9am-5pm, Tuesday to Sunday.

São Paulo's main fairs take place at the weekends. On Sundays there is a so-called 'hippy' craft fair in Praça da República: the best thing about it is the Bahian food. Also good for food is the excellent Japanese market on Sunday afternoons in Praça da Liberdade. The flea market in Praça Orione and Rua Rui Barbosa in Bixiga is fun, though you may not want to buy much.

ENTERTAINMENT

Not much can beat an evening spent in the vibrant Bixiga district — whether in a bar or in one of its seedy clubs. On a Saturday, in the early evening, don't miss a show at the Vai Vai samba school at Rua São Vicente 276. For a more sedate atmosphere go to Cerqueira César, which is a safer district to be in late at night. Bars and clubs along Oscar Freire and Rua Haddock Lobo are open into the small hours. Further south, at Rua Mata 70, Clyde's is a popular bar/restaurant with live music. Downtown, one of the best samba shows is put on at Plataforma 1 (Avenida Paulista 424; tel 287-1234).

For more formal entertainment, see the monthly *Este Mes Em São Paulo*, mentioned above, which has an English section, and *Veja* magazine; both have listings of forthcoming events.

CRIME AND SAFETY

São Paulo is a city of frightening statistics, particularly those dealing with crime: on average, seven people are assaulted every hour, and one murder takes place every 90 minutes. The problem affects primarily the favelas around the city, but you must be extremely vigilant against street robbers. The main roads in the centre are busy and comparatively safe during the day. At night mugging is a potential danger wherever you are, so avoid deserted, ill-lit streets.

HELP AND INFORMATION

Tourist Information: the main Paulistur kiosk is on Avenida Ipiranga in Praça da República. The two other most convenient desks are at the Liberdade and Sé metro stations and the Teatro Municipal. They are generally open 9am-6pm, Monday to Friday, and on Saturday afternoons.

Communications: the three most central Telesp (telephone) offices are at Rua 7 de Abril 295 (open 24 hours), near Praça da República, nearby in Praça Dom José Gaspar, and in the Luz terminal.

The main post office is in Praça do Correio on Avenida São João, open 8am-9pm Monday to Saturday; another is at Praça da República 390.

Money: the main concentration of casas de câmbio is around Praça da Republica and on Avenida São Luís. The Amex office is at Kontik-Franstur, 2nd floor, Rua Marconi 71 (tel 255-0043), south of Praça da República.

Polícia Federal: Avenida Prestes Maia 700 (tel 223-7177), downtown.

Embassies and Consulates. *Argentina:* Rua Araújo 216, 8th floor, Centro (tel 256-8555).
Bolivia: Rua Quirino de Andrade 219, 3rd floor, Centro (tel 255-3555).
Chile: Avenida Paulista 1009, 10th floor, Cerqueira César (tel 284-2044).
Colombia: Rua Marconi 53, 10th floor, Centro (tel 255-6863).
Ecuador: Avenida Paulista 807, 2nd floor, Paraíso (tel 289-9708).
Guyana: Avenida Paulista 807, 22nd floor, Paraíso (tel 251-1310).
Paraguay: Avenida São Luís 112, 10th floor, Centro (tel 259-3579).
Peru: Rua Suécia 114, Jardim Europa (tel 853-9372).
UK: Avenida Paulista 1938, 17th floor, Cerqueira César (tel 287-7722).
Uruguay: Al. Campinas 433, 7th floor, Cerqueira César (tel 284-5998).
USA: Rua Presidente João Manuel 933, Jardim America (tel 881-6511).
Venezuela: Rua Italia 539, Jardim Europa (tel 883-3000).

SAO PAULO STATE

The state of São Paulo is the size of Great Britain. It is the most developed and the richest part of the country. The identity of the state as a whole is in many respects eclipsed by the sprawling capital. Few people take much time to explore this part of Brazil, often put off by the thought of negotiating São Paulo city. Although the coastal communities lack the character they do elsewhere in the country, there are still a few fine beaches, particularly to the northeast of Santos, Brazil's main port. The industrial plants and factories feeding Santos dominate the interior of the state, where the countryside is full of sprawling, grim-looking towns.

PARANAPIACABA

This small town, 30 miles/48km southeast of São Paulo, is the best place to visit from the city. This is mainly because of the journey there: along a 19th-century railway line which runs dramatically across the Serra do Mar and down to Santos on the coast. Trains currently run only as far as Paranapiacaba, near the top of the escarpment, though there is a project under way to restore the rest of the line. The tourist train runs every Sunday at 9.30am from the Luz terminal in São Paulo, returning mid-afternoon. The journey takes a couple of hours, so you have several hours to explore the charming old town of Paranapiacaba, with its railway buildings and other 19th-century relics.

The Paulista Coast

ILHA DE SAO SEBASTIAO

Also known as Ilhabela, this is the largest island along the Brazilian coast. With its dramatic volcanic peaks, thick jungle and some fine beaches, it is one of the highlights of the coast between São Paulo and Rio. During the summer you must contend with hordes of holidaymakers and inflated prices. Even at other times of year you should avoid the weekends. Otherwise, head away from the developed west coast, but be prepared for few accommodation facilities — you will either have to camp, or negotiate shelter from one of the local fishermen.

A reasonable road runs along the west coast, and it is served by buses, taxis, and horses and carts; you can also hire motorbikes. The most sheltered beaches are on the north coast, one to two hours walk from Vila Ilhabela, the island's only town. Greater seclusion is to be had on the Atlantic, about two hours walk along a rough road from the west side. The track ends up by Praia dos Castelhanos, which has good surf and is the most popular beach. Praias da Fome and do Poço are quieter; they are both accessible by boat in less than an hour from dos Castelhanos. There is good hiking through the jungle, which is peppered with some beautiful waterfalls; hire a guide to tackle the more isolated parts.

Arrival and Departure. Frequent ferries sail to the island from the town of São Sebastião, which is accessible by bus from São Paulo. Boats run from early morning until late, and take just 15 minutes. While these dock some distance south of Vila Ilhabela (buses take passengers into town), there are other ferries which run every couple of hours direct to the town, taking 45 minutes.

Accommodation. You'll be lucky to get a room for less than $20, so if you are on a strict budget head for one of the campsites; there are several along the western coast. One of the cheapest hotels in town is the São Paulo near the dock, at Rua Dr Carvalho 46 (tel 72-1158).

A cheaper option is to stay in São Sebastião, the bustling and surprisingly unspoilt colonial town on the mainland; but to visit the island just for a day means seeing only the most crowded areas.

UBATUBA

The town of Ubatuba, which lies 144 miles/230km northeast of the state capital, is a smart resort area for Paulistas. However, there are some lovely secluded coves to the north: simply get any local bus going up the coast and ask to be dropped off. Among the best beaches are Itamambuca and Promirim, 7 miles/12km and 14 miles/22km north of Ubatuba respectively. Accommodation can be found on the most popular beaches and campsites all along the coast. Otherwise use Ubatuba as a base; there are cheap hotels along Rua Conceição.

Ubatuba is served by direct buses from São Paulo ($3\frac{1}{2}$ hours) and also from nearby Rio de Janeiro state.

IGUAPE

The coast southwest of Santos has little to recommend it. The only area worth exploring is around the island town of Iguape, 130 miles/208km and 3½ hours by bus from São Paulo. Iguape is a charming place, with a small collection of decaying colonial relics. A five-minute ferry ride away is Ilha Comprida, an extraordinarily long and thin island running parallel to the coast. The Atlantic shore is one long beach, and if you are willing to walk some distance south, you can find some quiet spots. There are several campsites on the coast, but hotels are cheaper in Iguape — try those on Avenida Ademar de Barros.

SOUTHERN BRAZIL

The three states of southern Brazil are Paraná, Santa Catarina and Rio Grande do Sul. They take up an area characterized by wooded mountains and grassy plains, where much of the land is given over to agriculture. This is the most developed part of Brazil, and the per capita income is higher than anywhere else in the country. The character of much of the region is so different to that of most of Brazil, that at times it is hard to believe you are in the same country.

The major factor behind this difference is the European influence — the result of a wave of immigration, mainly from Italy, Germany and Eastern Europe — which began in the 19th century. The towns and cities in the south give off an air of efficiency and orderliness not found elsewhere in Brazil; even the slums — of which the large cities have their fair share — are almost neat.

Travellers devote comparatively little time to southern Brazil, and those who bother to venture into the region usually visit the Iguaçu falls and then move on elsewhere. Yet although the south clearly lacks the verve and character indicative of the more northerly states of Brazil, it doesn't deserve to be completely ignored. Paraná state boasts the most spectacular train ride in the country and Santa Catarina has beaches to be proud of. Interesting trips can be done inland too, where the ethnic mix is more clearly visible: while the European communities in the cities have become largely integrated, the smaller settlements in the interior show fewer signs of the passage of time. Some of the inhabitants still speak their native language.

Rio Grande do Sul, Brazil's southernmost state, is dominated by prairies where millions of cows, pigs and sheep dot the landscape. This is the traditional homeland of the *gaúchos*, cattle-herders famous for their ponchos and baggy trousers known as *bombachas*. While the stereotypical gaúcho may be a dying breed, the people of Rio Grande do Sul retain a strong regional identity.

The south has a temperate climate. Pleasant, warm weather is the norm, the breeze from the Atlantic preventing the chance of unbearable temperatures. Rainfall is comparatively high: the dry season simply denotes a period when it rains less than during the summer.

PARANA
Curitiba

The capital of Paraná is held up by some as a symbol of the prosperity and efficiency to which the country as a whole should aspire. Others regard it as an aberration of a Brazilian city: even finding a bar serving caipirinha, that most traditional of Brazilian cocktails, is a challenge.

Curitiba, with a population of approaching 1.5 million, is a modern commercial centre. Although founded by gold-miners in the 17th century, there is little left of the old town. It is a clean and orderly city whose rubbish recycling programmes have won praise from the UN. But while Curitiba lacks great excitement, the Italian immigrant community and the large student population livens up what would otherwise be an unremittingly dull city.

Curitiba is the transport hub of the state and is the natural stopping-off place for anyone exploring the South. It is one of the most convenient Brazilian cities to merely pass through: it is easy to get around, and comparatively unpolluted and hassle-free. Furthermore, Curitiba is the starting-point for the spectacular train ride to Paranaguá.

City Layout. The most useful reference points in the heart of the city are Praça Tiradentes and Largo do Ordem, both in the old part of town. Rua 15 de Novembro, the most central part of which is pedestrian, is Curitiba's main thoroughfare. The Rodoferroviária (combined bus and train station) and the cheapest hotels are about 20 minutes walk southeast of the centre. The broad streets in this area are busy with traffic and do not make for a particularly pleasant walk.

Maps: the information kiosk in the bus station usually has plans of the town centre. Otherwise get hold of the monthly *Veiga* magazine, which includes a basic map; this can be picked up free from some hotels, or at the tourist office. If you're hanging around for some time, you could buy the map and guidebook available for $5 from news stands.

Arrival and Departure. *Air:* the Afonso Pena airport (tel 282-1143) is 10 miles/16km southeast of the centre. Banco do Brasil changes travellers cheques, and is open 10am-4pm on weekdays. Several bus routes run from the airport to the city centre, taking about half an hour. Most pass the Rodoferroviária, but check before boarding. Taxis charge $6. To return to the airport, catch the bus from the east side of Praça Rui Barbosa.

Transbrasil is at Alameda Cabral 39 (north of Praça Osório), Varig at Rua 15 de Novembro 614 (tel 222-2522), just west of the post office, and Vasp at number 537, opposite (tel 221-7422).

Bus: the Rodoferroviária is on Avenida Afonso Camargo (tel 225-6622). You can catch buses to the centre from across the road, though cheap hotels are nearby. To return to the station from the centre, take buses marked Oficinas or Centenário from Praça Rui Barbosa.

Buses to the principal long-distance destinations are as follows:

Asunción (Paraguay) — daily overnight buses with Pluma and La Paraguaya de Transporte (LPT), via Foz; the fare is $20.

Brasília - 22 hours, $30; daily morning and evening bus with Real Expreso.

Buenos Aires — 30 hours, $58; 2am daily with Pluma, including leito bus on Friday. Gral Urquiza runs a bus daily except Wednesday and Saturday.

Florianópolis — 6 hours, $7; hourly with Catarinense (5am-11pm), either non-stop or via Joinville.

Foz do Iguaçu — 10 hours, $9; most buses (plus three leito) are run by Sulamericana, mainly overnight; Pluma and LPT have overnight buses too.

Joinville — 2½ hours, $3; several daily with Itapemirim and Penha.

Porto Alegre — 11 hours, $16; three daily (and one leito) with Pluma; buses may follow either the coastal or inland route.

Santiago (Chile) — 55 hours, $88; thrice-weekly with Pluma.

São Paulo — 6 hours, $10; hourly with Cometa and Itapemirim (6am-midnight) plus one leito.

CURITIBA   0 |——————| 1km

½ mile

1 Rodoferroviária
2 Hotels Império and Maia
3 Hotel Nova Lisboa
4 City Hotel
5 Post Office
6 University of Paraná
7 Praça Santos Andrade
8 Varig
9 Vasp
10 Confeitaria Schaffer
11 Jade Turismo
12 Museu Paranaense
13 Praça Tiradentes
14 Hotel Amazônia
15 Cathedral
16 São Francisco
17 Praça Garibaldi
18 Fundação Cultural
19 African Bar
20 Praça Osório
21 Praça Rui Barbosa

Train: the train you are most likely to take from Curitiba is to Paranaguá; for further details see page 729.

Car Rental: if you don't pass through the airport, the most central agents are Budget (Rua João Negrão 1762; tel 225-5266) and Localiza (Avenida Cândido de Abreu 336; tel 253-0330).

Getting Around. Many city bus routes pass through Praças Rui Barbosa and Tiradentes; buses from the latter tend to serve the northern districts.

In addition to the buses, there is the so-called Linha Direita, a fledgling public transport system which is basically an overground metro line that uses buses and streets rather than trains and railway tracks. The stops are bizarre-looking tubes at the side of the road, which have a turnstile at the entrance where you pay. Buses align their doors with those of the tube and you board, as if getting onto an underground train. There is just one line, which doesn't serve any areas particularly useful to the visitor, but others are planned; pick up a map from the tourist office.

There are taxi ranks in all the main squares, or phone 264-6464.

Accommodation. There are many hotels close to the bus station. Most of them are fairly expensive — the real cheapies often double up as brothels — but it is hard to find cheaper deals in the centre.

There are several on Avenida Afonso Camargo, opposite the station. The Império (Afonso Camargo 367; tel 264-3373) and the Maia next door, are fairly typical of the area, charging $10-13/$14-17. The alternative is to stay in the rather grotty Boa Viagem nearby, which charges a mere $2.50/$4. Better are the hotels on Avenida 7 de Setembro, a marginally quieter street one block north of Camargo. At number 1948 is the Nova Lisboa (tel 264-1944), with rooms for $12/$16. The function of the nearby City Hotel (Rua Francisco Torres 806; tel 264-3366) is open to question — payment in advance is required and only your first name is written in the book — but it is clean and charges just $4/$6.

If your heart is set on staying centrally, try the Amazônia (Alameda Dr Murici 861; tel 222-8859), a couple of blocks west of Praça Tiradentes.

Eating and Drinking. Most people spend their evenings in the historic quarter, particularly around Largo do Ordem, where there is a clutch of restaurants which spill out onto the pavements, their piped music vying for supremacy. Among them are the Jenneffer, which serves a fairly good pizza (slowly), and the Hummel Hummel, which has a predominantly German menu. Green Land is a vegetarian restaurant further west in Praça Garibaldi. Just off this square, at the northern end of Alameda Dr Murici, is the African Bar, which has reggae and videos, and is a popular watering-hole among the trendier locals. A number of the restaurants in the old centre put on live music at weekends.

Another concentration of restaurants is on and around Ruas Cruz Machado and Saldanha Marinho, southwest of Largo do Ordem. For the best value eat at the small Restaurante Fornir, on Cruz Machado near the corner of Alameda Cabral, where you can eat a filling meal for just $2. The clientele is predominantly young and the atmosphere is friendly and unpretentious. The Old Friend's Music House at Rua Saldanha Marinho 688 is fairly expensive, but has free jazz. A few blocks south is the large Praça Osorio, where you can join the locals for an early evening drink beneath the lights of the wonderful Art Deco Edifício Garcez.

For the best pizzas head northwest of the centre to the Italian district of Santa

Felicidade. Many restaurants are on Avenida Manoel Ribas, though it's worth exploring the side streets too. To get there catch a bus marked Santa Felicidade or São Braz from Praça Tiradentes.

Anyone not wishing to stray too far from the bus station can get a bite to eat in one of the simple restaurants around the junction of Ruas Francisco Torres and Nilo Cairo, though they close early.

Exploring. Rua 15 de Novembro, or the southern half of it at least, is Curitiba at its liveliest; the transition comes beyond Praça Santos Andrade, a large square dominated by the imposing University of Paraná building. The pedestrian zone of Rua 15 de Novembro, known as Rua das Flores, stretches southwest of here as far as Praça Osório. It is lined with some well-restored early 20th-century buildings, and there are several old-style tea rooms. Though disappointing when compared to the fine confeitarias in Rio, they are a change from your common or garden café; the Schaffer (number 424) is the best.

A couple of blocks southwest of Praça Santos Andrade is the bustling Praça Generoso Marquês. Overlooking the square is a grand Art Nouveau building, formerly the Prefeitura and now the Museu Paranaense. The exhibits contend with the building for your attention, and for the most part lose out. The numerous paintings of local dignitaries are of no immediate interest to the foreign visitor, and other objects on display vary from weaponry to chamber pots. However, the top floor is devoted to the Indians of Paraná, and houses some wonderful sculptures and an inspired exhibition of pencil drawings done by Guaraní children. The museum is open 10am-6pm, Tuesday to Friday, and 1-6pm on Mondays and at weekends.

Behind the Museu Paraense is Praça Tiradentes, a square busy with buses and people on the move. Walking alongside the ugly cathedral you reach the heart of the old city, or Largo do Ordem. Facing you is the 18th-century church of São Francisco, which is the oldest building in Curitiba. It looks unpromising from the outside, but the interior is refreshingly simple. West up the hill is Praça Garibaldi, the historic centre's most pleasant square. There is a good craft fair here from 10am to 2pm on Sundays. Among the most notable buildings is a 19th-century palace which houses the Fundação Cultural, and the grand Sociedade Garibaldi, founded in 1883 as a centre for Italian immigrants.

If you are interested in other immigrant groups, visit the Memorial da Imigração Polonesa in the Bosque de João Paulo II; it is at the end of Avenida Dr Cândido de Abreu, north of the centre. There are reconstructions of houses built by the Polish pioneers at the end of last century, and displays of photographs, tools, etc. The museum is behind the Centro Civico and is open 9am-5pm daily except Tuesday. To get there catch bus 104 from Praça Tiradentes, or any bus marked Abranches or Vila Suiça. On Sundays buses go from the Passeio Público, the park north of Praça Santos Andrade.

Help and Information. *Tourist Information:* the tourist office is in an unlikely-looking house at Rua Senador Xavier de Silva 147 (tel 225-2972, 223-3535), near Rua Duque de Caxias — in a residential area six blocks north of Praça Garibaldi. The staff are unhelpful, but they have a few hand-outs, including *Veiga*, a monthly magazine with a moderately useful listings section. The office is open 8am-noon and 2-6pm Monday to Friday.

Money: change money at travel agencies, of which there are several along Rua

Buses using the Graciosa route between Paranaguá and Curitiba stop in Morretes, and there are frequent services from both towns along the BR-277; the journey from either place takes an hour. The train also stops here.

As a side trip from Morretes visit Antonina, a decaying colonial town with even greater charm, on the Bay of Paranaguá 9 miles/14km east. Buses run every hour from Morretes, and there is one hotel and a campsite.

Marumbi National Park. Catch any bus along the Graciosa road, and ask to be dropped near the village of São João de Graciosa, about 25 minutes north of Morretes. From here you can walk to the park entrance, where you can usually pick up a map of the trails. It is possible to visit Marumbi as a day trip, but anyone with a tent should take advantage of the campsite.

Paranaguá. This is the main port of Paraná and one of the country's biggest channels for exports. At first sight Paranaguá doesn't seem a promising destination. What colonial buildings remain are in a sorry state, and the climate is hot and stuffy. However, the main docks are out of the town, and the atmosphere in Paranaguá proper is surprisingly intimate. Few people choose to hang around longer than they have to, but the waterfront is lively at weekends.

There is not a lot to occupy you while you wait for the bus or train out of town, but it's worth having a wander round before gravitating towards the purveyors of seafood and other goodies along the bay. The most interesting part of Paranaguá is the band of streets nearest the waterfront. There are a series of markets in this area: the uncannily clean Mercado Municipal near the bus station and, nearer the centre, a small craft fair and the fish market; the food hall opposite is a good place to eat. The highlight, however, is the early 18th-century Jesuit college, that faces the bay not far from the bus station. The beautiful stone building houses the excellent Museu de Arqueologia e Artes Popular. Most exhibits relate to the Tupi-Guarani Indians, and include a fascinating array of wooden tools. The museum opens 10am-5pm Tuesday to Friday, noon-5pm on other days.

There is a tourist information kiosk outside the railway station on Avenida Arthur de Abreu, where you can pick up a map of the town.

Accommodation: there are a couple of cheap hotels on Rua Correia de Freitas, including the Hotel Litoral (number 45; tel 422-0491), with rooms at $5-10, and the Auana Palace opposite (tel 422-0948), which is slightly more expensive. Nearer the waterfront, on Rua 15 de Novembro, are the Tropical (number 234), with doubles for $12; but the real bargain in town is the Luz next door, which has doubles for $5.

ILHA DO MEL

This unusually shaped island, lying at the mouth of the Bay of Paranaguá, is the only place along the Paraná coast that is really worth exploring. It boasts some fine beaches and there is good scope for walking, particularly in the hilly southern half. Ilha do Mel gets busy in the summer, but the island is a protected area, so development is under strict control. The number of visitors is monitored closely.

Arrival and Departure: boats to the island leave from Pontal do Sul, 30 miles/48km and one hour by bus south of Paranaguá. Graciosa buses direct from Curitiba leave hourly between 6am and 11pm. The actual dock is a couple of miles from Pontal do Sul, and minibuses and taxis ferry people to and fro; otherwise walk. Boats leave roughly every hour from 8am to 5pm, and serve both Nova Brasília and Praia dos Encantadas, the island's two villages; the journey takes 30-40 minutes. Out of the main holiday season boat services are less frequent; if plans to build a bridge come off, this will not be a problem.

Boats run between Nova Brasília and Praia dos Encantadas; otherwise return to the mainland and take the ferry.

Beaches: most accommodation is around Nova Brasília, the bigger of the two settlements. Most people camp or rent lodgings or hammock space from the local people. Indeed this may be the only option at weekends, when the small number of hotels fill quickly. The latter are found mainly near Praia da Fortaleza, the most popular beach, and Farol das Conchas further south.

The best beaches, on the southeastern coast, can be reached on foot from Praia dos Encantadas, on the island's southwestern tip. Praia de Fora is the most accessible, being just a stone's throw across the island, while Praia do Miguel and Praia Grande are about two hours walk further north. Be warned that the walking is fairly tough going if you have a heavy pack. Praia dos Encantados itself is a less appealing village than Nova Brasília, which has several lively bars and restaurants.

The only destination that generally succeeds in tempting people inland is the Iguaçu falls. However, if you are travelling by bus along the BR-277 west of Curitiba, you could break off for a few hours to visit the Vila Velha national park, where sandstone rocks have been moulded by natural erosion. Buses bound for Ponta Grossa pass near the park, 60 miles/96km northwest of Curitiba, leaving almost hourly from 6am and 10.30pm; the journey takes 90 minutes, and it is a further 30-minute walk north from the road to the park. Buses on to Ponta Grossa, 12 miles/20km away, continue until 5 or 6pm. There are several hotels in Ponta Grossa, and buses on to Foz. Otherwise, continue 64 miles/100km to Prudentópolis, an interesting town the majority of whose inhabitants are of Ukrainian origin; stay at Hotel Lopes, at Avenida São José 2595 near the main square.

The Iguaçu Falls

FOZ DO IGUACU

The border town of Foz do Iguaçu has nothing going for it in terms of appeal. This is perhaps surprising considering its position as the jumping-off point for one of the world's greatest tourist attractions. There is no aura of prosperity, despite the number of visitors that flood in to visit the falls and to profit from the duty-free shops in Ciudad del Este, across the border in Paraguay. One of the few consolations is that Ciudad del Este is an even worse place; another is that the Iguaçu falls are only a short bus ride away. If you take an instant disliking to Foz, base yourself in Puerto Iguazú in Argentina, which is a more pleasant town.

Arrival and Departure. There are daily flights from Rio, São Paulo and Curitiba. The airport (tel 74-1744) is 10 miles/18km from town, roughly mid-way between Foz and the falls. Buses run from the airport to the local bus terminal every 30 minutes between 6am and 7pm, then hourly until 11pm.

The bus station is on Avenida Brasil (tel 73-2255/1525), in the centre. Book in advance when possible. The main long-distance services from Foz (daily unless otherwise stated) are as follows:

Asunción: 5 hours, $8; two with Pluma and Nuestra Señora de la Asunción.
Buenos Aires: $40; two daily except Thursday and Sunday.
Curitiba: 10 hours, $15; twelve with Sulamericana, mostly overnight.
Florianópolis: 16 hours, $24; several overnight, with Catarinense and Pluma; some
call in at Joinville.
Porto Alegre: 14 hours, $21; four with Unesul.
Rio: 22 hours, $30; three (and one leito) with José dos Campos or Pluma.
São Paulo: 16 hours, $22; eight (and two leito) with Pluma, noon-9.30pm.

Getting Around/Crossing Borders. Avenida Brasil is the main commercial street,
but all the buses you are likely to use (except those to Ciudad del Este) run along

FOZ DO IGUACU

1 Bus Station
2 Local bus station
3 Hotel Tarobá
4 Tia Ana restaurant
5 Pousada Paquetá
6 Paraguayan Consulate
7 O Astro Hotel
8 Varig, Vasp
9 City Hotel
10 Dick Turismo
11 Transbrasil
12 Telephone Office
13 Câmbio Iguaçu
14 Post Office
15 Praça Getúlio Vargas
16 Bus stop for falls
17 Argentinian Consulate

Avenida Juscelino Kubitschek, known as Avenida JK. The local bus station —
Terminal Transportes Urbanos (TTU) — is near the eastern end of Avenida JK.

There is an efficient system of local buses between Brazil, Argentina and
Paraguay. Buses run between the TTU in Foz and the bus station in Puerto Iguazú
every 15-30 minutes from 7am to 8pm. They operate on a similar schedule between
Foz and Ciudad del Este; buses to Paraguay can be picked up along Almirante
Barroso.

If crossing either border just for the day there is no need to get your passport
stamped; and if you normally need a visa, this is not required for a day trip. At
the frontier an official may board the bus to examine passports and enquire whether
you're returning the same day; but they don't always bother. If you are leaving
Brazil permanently and need to go through immigration, you can walk across the
border and pick up another bus from the other side.

Accommodation. You can expect to be greeted at the bus station by touts competing
for your custom. The hotels in the immediate vicinity of the bus station are either
two or three star or fairly grotty. The standard levels out as you head west, but
you probably won't find a room for less than $14; the cheapest deals are offered
by O Astro (number 660) and City Hotel (number 938). You don't have to look
far, however, to find more salubrious surroundings and greater peace and quiet.
The best choice is Pousada Paquetá (Rua Naipi 679; tel 74-5946). This is a quiet
and extremely friendly hotel where a pleasant, clean room with bathroom, and
an excellent breakfast, costs $8. Furthermore, Tia Ana's restaurant, where you
can eat one of the tastiest meals in Brazil for less than $3, is a block away on
Xavier da Silva. For more creature comforts stay in the Tarobá (Rua Tarobá 878;
tel 74-3890), a couple of blocks southwest of the Paquetá. Rates are $17/$25.
Wherever you stay, be vigilant when out on the streets after dark.

There is a Camping Clube do Brasil site (tel 74-1310) down the road that runs
off to the left by the park entrance, 10 miles/16km from Foz.

Help and Information. *Tourist Information:* Foztur has a kiosk in Praça Vargas,
at the west end of Avenida JK, which is open around the clock. The free map
is mediocre but the staff are helpful.

Communications: the post office is in Praça Vargas, and the telephone office on
the corner of Rua Edmundo de Barros and Floriano Peixoto; it is open 7am-
midnight daily.

Money: the best rates for cash are from casa de câmbio Iguaçu (Rio Branco 664)
and Dick Turismo (Brasil 40), which opens 8am-6pm, at weekends too.

Consulates: Argentina — Rua Dom Pedro II 26 (tel 74-2877), northwest of Praça
Vargas. Paraguay — Rua Bartolomeu de Gusmão 480 (tel 72-1162/9).

THE FALLS

Just a lot of water if you ask me' is how the Iguaçu Falls are remembered in
Graham Greene's *Travels with my Aunt*. They are, however, both higher than
Niagara and broader than Victoria — a breathtaking sight in the most literal sense.
The magnificence lies not only in the falls themselves, but also in the surrounding
jungle where exotic butterflies and birds are as common as mud. Keep an eye
out for the coatimundi, cuddly creatures that look like a cross between an anteater
and a racoon, and are extraordinarily tame: they are often seen squabbling over
food thrown to them by tourists.

To see the greatest volume of water and the jungle at its most lush, visit between April and July. This is also a good time in terms of crowds. The greatest number of tourists visit in January, February and July. However, the chance that you'll be disappointed, whatever time of year you go, is slight. Unlucky were those who visited in the winter of 1977, when the falls dried up completely.

The classic view of Iguaçu is from the Brazilian side, but the bulk of the falls are in Argentina; this is also the best side to explore the jungle. To see the falls on both sides in a single day is possible if you make an early start, but it involves a lot of toing and froing. Try to visit the falls during the week, and not just to avoid the crowds: at weekends only the biggest cataracts make enough noise to drown out the aggravating sound of the helicopters circling overhead. (A 15-minute ride will set you back $40 if you are tempted to join in.) Take a plastic bag for your camera since certain falls give a real showering.

The Brazilian Side. The falls are 20 miles/32km and 40 minutes by bus southeast of Foz. Buses run on the hour every hour at weekends, every two hours during the week — going out on the even hour and returning on the odd. The first bus leaves Foz at 8am, and the last one back from the park is at 7pm; the fare is $0.70. Buses leave from the city bus terminal and are marked Cataratas. Those marked Parque Nacional go only as far as the park entrance, which is several miles from the actual falls; buses pause here for visitors to pay the $1 entrance fee. The park opens 6am-7pm.

Buses drop passengers outside the luxury, marshmallow-pink Hotel das Cataratas. A walkway runs down through the trees along the side of the cliff, and provides progressively spectacular views of the falls. Having had your fill of magnificence you can either take the lift to the top of the cliff and follow the road back to the hotel, or return up the path.

The Argentinian Side. Buses for the falls leave on the hour 8am-6pm from Puerto Iguazú bus station. The fare is $1.50, though the usual deal is that you buy a series of tickets for the various trips within the park — a $12 package that even provides you with a supply of pesos with which to pay the entrance fee; since cruzeiros are accepted around Puerto Iguazú (at a poor rate), there is no need to obtain any other pesos at all.

The first stop is the visitors' centre, where you can pick up a map and visit the small museum. From here you can walk to the main area of the park, which you should allow at least three or four hours to explore. There are two paths, the so-called upper and lower circuits, which take you above and below the falls. The latter is the more extensive and of greater interest; it also gives access to the departure point for boats across to Ilha San Martín. Boats in theory leave every five minutes, but in reality it's more according to demand. The small, jungle-covered island has several interconnecting paths running around it. These trails, above all the Sendero del Balcón, provide some of the best views of this part of the falls and also along the Iguaçu river.

From the visitors' centre, you can continue by bus to the Garganta del Diablo, or Devil's Throat. The bus from Puerto Iguazú passes the visitors' centre at half past the hour and takes about 20 minutes to cover this last stretch. A short distance from the bus stop is the walkway which leads you across the river and eventually immerses you in the spray and deafening sound of Iguaçu's most impressive gathering of falls.

PART 3

Normandy, 2004

for Ross

i Fishing at Port en Bessin

Close by, the boy's father
stacks oblong white cartons,

orderly as rows of carrara crosses.
His son reels your arcing pirouette in air,

slaps you on stone near my paralysed toes. Chipped, red
sunsets convulsing in your eye,

and nothing between us but fear of a boy,
the sudden, over-shoulder snap of his neck,

like a hook in the throat, should my foot start
to push you back over the edge.

ii American cemetery, Saint-Laurent

Thousands of gull feathers, upright, stone-still,
as if behind a mother's back

boys fled to pillow-fight in a room
transformed as cliff top for the day,

and the sound of water at boil point downstairs
was ocean spray flittering like cloth,

beyond mending when she scoops
feathers that fall

on a carpet of dust,
each finding its place in the weave.

FOREWORD

This book will give you the flavor of an Englishman, with the spice of a new adventure.

You will feel the inside thoughts and struggles of a travelling minister, as well as the divine direction for the next step on the foreign roads of new adventure.

You will find the reality of a miracle is found in the risk of a prayer. When pain is removed then the struggles to go to difficult new places is also removed.

You will discover the importance of a miracle in your Christian adventure and you will be touched by the reality of so many people who have never heard the good news. The light shines brightest when you're in the darkest of places.

In this book you will not only feel the experience of travel in unknown territory but the difficult challenge of continued ministry despite the failure of friends. The race is a long one but we must run to finish it with a 'well done' at the end.

Kevin McNulty
Daytona Beach, Florida
October 2018

Drs Kevin and Leslie McNulty of Christian Adventures International are based in Daytona Beach, USA. They have travelled throughout the world encouraging those involved in outreach and facilitating conferences for evangelists to share ideas, resources and fellowship. In 1998 they founded the Tent 100 Ministry, based in Moscow, which this year celebrates the faithfulness of God as they commission their one hundredth tent.

www.mcnultyministries.com

growing quickly. By now we were employing around twenty-five people between the two companies. I was so ambitious for bigger and better things: a Mercedes car, developing a four-bedroom house. My life was all about lifestyle and providing material things for me and my family. This meant I was working very long hours. I was a workaholic from Monday to Friday. At the weekends I would be involved with our children's activities such as swimming, Brownies and Cubs and, of course, football.

Eileen and I had always wanted to go to Canada. I wanted to see the place where my father was born and we both had relatives to meet. We went as a family. We thoroughly enjoyed visiting people and seeing the sights such as Niagara Falls. It was amazing.

Back at home I was invited to become a Freemason and I joined the golf club. I thought I had 'made it'. I would be out on stag nights, out with the boys down the pub – I was becoming 'a bit of a drinker'.

When I reflect on what I am writing I can see that, like many non-believers, prayer was an instinct to a crisis: 'Please, God'. I wouldn't say that at this stage in my life I considered myself religious, nor would anyone who knew me then. Personal crisis or tragedy is the common reason for praying, to gain comfort and to feel less isolated. If I'm brutally honest maybe it's an insurance policy in some cases.

I would silently recite the Lord's Prayer and then ask for my loved ones to be kept safe and well. Many people are driven to pray at some point in their lives. I have learnt praying spontaneously is about us reaching out. God hears everyone's prayers. He is waiting for us all to come to Him and have our own relationship. According to Romans 12:3, 'God hath dealt to every man the measure of faith.' God didn't give us different measures of faith; we all received *the* measure of faith. I was to find this out in the days ahead.

A while later we celebrated our silver wedding anniversary. I asked Eileen if she would like to go away somewhere. Her reply: 'No, I don't want to go away. I want to share what we have with friends and family.'

This was the way she wanted to witness to our faith. We decided to renew our marriage vows and invite not only our family and old friends but also the whole church to join us. We had become a part of the body of Christ together. We wanted to witness to everyone that our hope and love was built on Jesus Christ and His righteousness and that He had changed our lives. It was a wonderful time of celebration and thanksgiving for God's sustaining presence in our lives.

Now Eileen was faced with another complication of the diabetes: gangrene in her foot, which needed to be partly amputated. She faced this latest difficulty with her usual courageous attitude. She was determined to walk into the church afterwards and had a smile for all the folk. God was giving her strength to face tomorrow. Maybe she wasn't so mobile now but Eileen could still pray for the many people God placed on her heart. She quietly prayed, adding herself at the end.

Reflection:

'Yea, thou I walk through the valley of the shadow of death, I will fear no evil: for thou art with me; thy rod and thy staff they comfort me.' (Psalm 23:4)

41

Chapter 9

WILL NEVER FORGET

In June 1997 we were privileged when the world-famous evangelist Dr T.L. Osborn visited our church. Over the course of two sermons he encouraged his listeners to realise that what God will do for *one* person He will do for every person. *'Everyone means you're the one'* was one of his favourite sayings. Then in his seventies, Dr Osborn, with his late wife Daisy, had for the previous half-century demonstrated not only the irresistible nature of the gospel message, but also the power of God in being able to heal broken lives, both spiritually and physically. He was the author of a number of Christian bestsellers including *Healing the Sick, The Message that Works* and *Soulwinning.* This last book I just couldn't put down. When Dr T.L. Osborn spoke there was so much passion, love and grace in his words. The seed that had been previously sown in me to go out and proclaim the gospel became deeply rooted.

He also introduced us to the song 'You're the Only Jesus Some Will Ever See' and, as we were sitting singing it in one service, I experienced another one of those moments when I knew God was speaking to me directly, calling me again. I will never forget that moment. I stood alone in the service, with my arms raised, physically feeling on fire as God re-affirmed to my spirit that this was the way He wanted me to go. This experience has become part of my testimony which I have shared wherever God has taken me in the world. I have played that song so many times; the words are so inspirational, underlining the teaching of Jesus, how HE cares about the ONE.

Another of Dr T.L. Osborn's sayings was: 'Let's minister love to a hurting world. It begins with you and me.' Our responsibility for sharing the good

'See, I have inscribed you on the palms of My hands. Your walls are continually before Me.' (Isaiah 49:16 NKJV)

'For as we have many members in one body, but all the members do not have the same function, so we, being many, are one body in Christ, and individually members of one another. Having then gifts differing according to the grace that is given to us, let us use them: if prophecy, let us prophesy in proportion to our faith; or ministry, let us use it in our ministering; he who teaches, in teaching; he who exhorts, in exhortation; he who gives, with liberality; he who leads, with diligence; he who shows mercy, with cheerfulness.' (Romans 12:4–8 NKJV)

Tracts are a great way of communicating the gospel. We have handed out thousands of these hands all over the world. Everyone loves them. Recently someone sent me a picture from Washington DC where the hand tract has been stuck to the front door of a house.

I took some of these tracts on a mission trip to Cambodia – they made such an impact. I decided we needed to print them in the Khmer language, which we organised and included the local pastor's details. We gave the PDF file to someone who wanted to produce the tracts in Russian. It's amazing how new digital technology allows us to share the means of sharing the gospel with fellow evangelists around the world.

In addition to producing tracts, I have also used the MacBook to develop a package of training material called 'Ignite'. This includes a seminar presentation series called 'Caring and Sharing' which I have used here in England and in mission schools in Belarus, Bulgaria, Cambodia and Russia.

The Bible says:

'And he gave some, apostles; and some, prophets; and some, evangelists; and some, pastors and teachers; for the perfecting of the saints, for the work of the ministry, for the edifying of the body of Christ: till we all come in the unity of the faith, and of the knowledge of the Son of God, unto a perfect man, unto the measure of the stature of the fulness of Christ.' (Ephesians 4:11–13

room with many sewing machines, a carpentry workshop, laundries and an amazing craft department. I could see real dedication in the carers and teachers.

In accordance with Yauheni's plan, we took the orphans to a theme park for the day. It was a wonderful opportunity to bless these children, as the orphanage's funds did not generally extend to such treats. And yes, of course, there was a visit to the ice cream shop. It was great to have Olga with us to interpret for me again.

Of all the young people at the orphanage one particularly made an impression on me. When we arrived, a youth around sixteen or seventeen years old was sitting outside next to some amazing pieces of woodwork. Sasha had produced windmills and garden furniture of a very high standard. I was told that at the end of the year he would have to leave and fend for himself. I will never forget Sasha waving as we left. For sometime after the visit I found he was often on my mind and I would pray for him. We met again several years later when I was teaching at a mission school training week. God had faithfully had His hand on him.

Yauheni had arranged for me to speak every night and Olga went with me to each of the preaching engagements. I was truly blessed everywhere I went. The pastors would invite us back to their homes after the service. Olga had certainly put the word around that I like the famous 'borscht' – cold beetroot soup with sour cream.

At the weekend we did a children's ministry outreach. A lot of parents came with their children so that we were able to share the gospel with them too. The two young ladies who had responded to the message at the beginning of the week were back again. On Sunday morning I was privileged to share in Yauheni's home church. The building was like a town house and none of the rooms were large enough to accommodate the entire congregation. I spoke in the main room and hoped that my voice, and my translator's, would carry to the people sitting in the corridor and adjoining rooms. Happily, the church now has a very large building where the congregation can meet all together in one room.

On the day I was leaving, Yauheni received a phone call: the Bishop of Belarus had heard about some of the services and wanted to meet Yauheni

Chapter 20

MISSION TO ZAMBIA

John from Avanti Ministries was arranging another trip to Africa, this time to Zambia, and I was invited to be part of it. We were a team of four evangelists with the primary aim of ministering in the prisons. It was truly an amazing time.

The Holy Spirit was so evident in the mission right from the planning stage. Firstly, we had to raise the finance for the four of us – John, Shaun, George and myself – to be able to travel. John and I were invited to share our testimonies at a church men's breakfast. After we had given our testimonies John explained our plans for the trip and showed the group a few pictures from the trip to Uganda to illustrate the need and the size of the task in front of us. He said that we still needed to raise £2,000 in order to be able to fund the outreach. We had an amazing response and many people gave us pledges of financial support. Then one man stood up and pledged £1,000 which gave us exactly the amount that we needed.

We hear reports that conditions in UK prisons are poor; in Zambia they were dire. We were ministering in men's and women's prisons in the Copper Belt region. In the men's prisons we saw boys as young as twelve incarcerated with adults. In the women's prisons there were mothers with young children. There were two young women nursing tiny babies – 'Blessing' and 'Gift' – both just one month old. How could one ever forget them or their names? Many of the inmates were on remand. Some had been in jail for over a year and were still waiting to find out with what crime they were going to be charged. Each day we followed the Holy Spirit's leading and we saw literally

Chapter 23

NEVER SEEN THIS BEFORE

I was being asked why I grew a beard. Well I can reveal it came about as a result of an accident at home just before I was about to leave for a trip to Macedonia. A candle burning near the TV flared up and I foolishly panicked and poured water on it to extinguish the flame. The hot wax splashed up and badly burnt my face. Shaving was out of the question.

On the same day as I burnt my face I received a telephone call from one of my old drinking pals. I hadn't heard from Jack for a long time. He had never really accepted me becoming a Christian and was never happy for me to talk about my faith. He had called to tell me he was very unwell; he had been diagnosed with cirrhosis of the liver. I was devastated by this news but at the same time it made me realise that this might have been me had God not delivered me from the level of alcohol consumption associated with my past social drinking habits. I told him that I was leaving on a mission trip the next day and asked if we could say the Lord's Prayer together. He said OK and so I prayed, Jack adding his 'Amen' at the end.

Sadly, Jack's condition worsened and he eventually passed away. I look back and realise that 'there but for the grace of God go I'. Sometimes I look at myself in the mirror and think of how I was saved, healed and delivered. I thank God for the grace and mercy He has shown to me

Tent Mission in Macedonia

This time Tim and I were meeting up with Yauheni, Sofi and Johannes and going to Macedonia to minister in a big tent in Stip. Each day one of

Chapter 26

TENT MISSIONS IN BULGARIA AND THE WAY 2

Tim invited me to be part of his Spearhead team for a tent mission to Yambol in Bulgaria. We would be working with our friend Sofi and other Bulgarians from her Tent 100 team and the local Romany people. We all felt God had something good planned for this mission and there was an air of expectation.

We arrived in Yambol late one evening and the next morning we were up early to help finish setting up the tent and preparing for the children's ministry. Bulgarian and English team members gelled together brilliantly. On the first day we had about thirty-five children turn up and I introduced everyone to my evangelist friend Joe Crow, a hand puppet which became a firm favourite with the team and the children alike.

The first evening outreach service and the tent was almost full. Everyone was so excited and with each Bulgarian church leader wanting to share his or her testimony, or minister, or sing a song, it ran well over time. I began to wonder if Tim would ever get to speak. When he was eventually given the microphone, the Holy Spirit put a real burden on his heart for the gypsy men. They are very much like English men: reserved, quite proud and normally unwilling to respond in meetings. When Tim made an appeal at the end of his message sixteen people came forward to receive Jesus as their Lord and Saviour, thirteen of them being men. Praise God! What a wonderful start! After this we spent another hour and a half praying with over a hundred people who needed a physical touch from Jesus. A dear lady walked over to meaning of being sent by Jesus. The needs are so enormous, and the conditions so difficult, that every power of the mind falters and fails. We tend to forget that the one great reason underneath all missionary work is not primarily the elevation of the people, their education, nor their needs, but is first and foremost the command of Jesus Christ – *'Go therefore and make disciples of all the nations . . .'* (Matthew 28:19).

I then shared on the importance of church and how I love the church, that the church should be inwardly secure but should be outwardly focused, looking to develop disciples. It was a message to encourage them to take church, REAL CHURCH, outside the walls of the building. I also shared from 2 Corinthians 5:20–21, highlighting verse 20: *'We are therefore Christ's ambassadors, as though God were making his appeal through us. We implore you on Christ's behalf: be reconciled to God'* (NIV).

It was time for Joe Crow to come out of the bag and share the Lord's Prayer with everyone and invite everyone to pray. I explained how Joe and I had worked together all over the world and how Joe was a great help when I took him into the jungle with the Orang Asli people. I shared my testimony of how I came to Christ through my first wife's illness, and how a scripture had changed my life: *'For the wages of sin is death, but the gift of God is eternal life in Christ Jesus our Lord'* (Romans 6:23 NIV). I had realised I was a sinner and needed to turn from my sin. I held my wallet up for all to see and explained how, in responding to God's offer of salvation, I had swapped my self-reliance on what I could earn, for the confidence that I had in God's Word (and here I held up my Bible) to direct my path in life. A merciful God, a God of second chances in so many ways: He had turned my life around; He had saved Eileen and eventually taken her home to be with Him; He had brought Judy Choo-Ean and me together. I used my testimony to challenge the congregation for their own salvation. This spoke to a number of people who raised their hands and joined in the prayer of repentance. Then God started to give me words of knowledge for healing and I invited people to come forward. Immediately God was touching people with the power of the Holy Spirit and they were testifying to being healed.

We had run over time and still people were coming up to me telling how God had healed them. One lady gave a short testimony of how she had

Chapter 29

HOW GREAT THOU ART
A TESTIMONY OF GOD'S AMAZING GRACE

We, Judy and I, want to share our story, an amazing chapter in both of our lives in the last year or so, giving God the Glory. The song 'How Great Thou Art' gets deep down inside us. We chose this hymn twenty-one years ago when we got married. 'Then sings my soul, my Saviour God, to Thee, how great Thou art, how great Thou art!' I knew this would be a chapter in this book.

I arrived at Gatwick Airport from a blessed time ministering in Bulgaria and came down to earth with a bump. I headed straight for a local hospital where my wife Judy had an appointment with a consultant heart specialist. She was suffering from breathlessness and was undergoing tests for potential heart failure. I had been praying and felt in my spirit that she did not have heart failure.

Everyone was surprised when a mass was found attached to her pancreas. Man, I was praying. She had a biopsy, which was inconclusive. I felt in my spirit again that this 'mass' was a cyst. The panel of consultants met and it was suggested that Judy should go to a Harley Street clinic for a PET scan.

GALLERY

Mission School

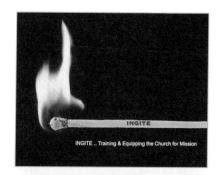

X   x marks the spot, that you can employ, to remove your,

Y   yoke and let your yearning secure your joy; your,

Z   zest to reach your zenith, of spiritual cosmic energy
and all of this resulting and culminating in Victory
of your very own making achieving and approaching,
your Personal Performance Coaching.

From my private collection written for me...

Choosing and Visualising a Goal

So the first experience I had of the coaching process was to embrace my sad emotional state and take care of myself emotionally. I was still attending a bereavement counsellor at this time. Gradually the process emerged of visualising a goal in great detail and then breaking it down into manageable steps and planning the *what, why, when, where, how,* and *with whom* I would accomplish these. It all seemed like common sense. The goal began because I had wanted a new carpet in my bedroom. I chose a pink carpet, but a darker shade of pink that would not get stained easily. Next I chose which furniture to keep in the bedroom, and which to remove. I donated a dark mahogany chest of drawers to my son; these had been my husband's, and I replaced them with my lovely rose coloured desk where I use my laptop computer.

Clearing the room was quite emotional – deciding which of my husband's possessions to keep and which to let go. I let most things go but kept a few special items which I could still visualise him wearing. PaTrisha emphasised the importance of daily reviewing and working towards the goal.

At this point I enrolled two of my sons in the project. Between us we emptied the room, and then we painted it. I kept the same basic colour scheme because I travelled far. In reality I was on a hamster wheel which, after some years, did little more than squeak a lot. I couldn't have stopped that manic turning if I tried.

What happened was that I got fired. The pin fell out of the wheel. Disaster. End of the world. Darkness. Yet it was also the best thing that could have happened. I had wanted to do something completely different for some years and now I had no excuse. So of course what it really meant was: Survival. New Beginning. Light.

Looking back with the little wisdoms of hindsight and personal insight, I realise that there were unconscious processes within me which had probably engineered the dismissal, because a few months before I had felt compelled to start a series of 'Self Mastery' programmes. These were (are) programmes which involve a deeply transformational journey, enabling the individual to make a fresh start while seeing life with a new and purer insight. It was so potent and illuminative that I knew that this was what I wanted to do. All my values and principles were represented in what I was being taught. I liked who I was becoming. The mirror was no longer quite so distorted, the glass a lot cleaner than it had ever been. I felt that I was becoming – at long last – who I am, and who I am supposed to be. It wasn't an easy transformation, for it required great courage, honesty and willingness to change, and I have never seen myself as having a natural abundance of these qualities. But somewhere along the line, after much hard work, I managed it.

The change within me was so powerful that the process was almost a personal form of alchemy: transforming the dark, battered heavy and bent lead of my old personality into something that I felt was golden, and certainly valuable to me at least. It was a natural next step for me to become a trainer and coach in what I was being taught. It might sound altruistic but I really did feel that I wanted to make a contribution, to help people change their lives as mine had been changed. And having been on that side of the auditorium, looking up at a succession of speakers, I knew exactly what they felt like, and what they wanted, and what they were afraid of.

A contribution by

Anthony Matthews

A graduate LCSi - LifeCoach School international
student from Holland/Australia.

One of the many deadly diseases that hit hard especially in the third world countries, is "Poverty." People unable to live in civilized conditions dying of hunger, and illnesses, surrounding children and adults alike. We never think such a tragedy may perhaps one day become our own reality. Why would we, after all, we are fortunate living in a Western world where most of the society have privileges that other parts of the world do not - Right? Wrong!

Until it happens to us and we experience these traumatic experiences ourselves, we know not how much humankind suffers in their losses of materialism, emotionally, mentally, physically, even spiritually, other than what we hear or watch from the Media and TV.

Poverty can strike anyone anywhere in the world as it did me, and I live in a Western world, leaving me bankrupt, homeless, unemployed, having no social benefits, with three children to support, being a single parent.

As a business woman, I lost my business, home, whole livelihood over four ill-fated, painful devastating years.

Temporarily housed by the council, in a wooden type shed, in a middle of the field, with two similar units, we had to sleep on the cold floors with only a few blankets to share for warmth. When my home was reprocessed I had to leave all possessions there, taking only a few clothes each.

Within four days of being in temporary accommodation, we were burgled twice, loosing the small things we did have for food, shelter and survival.

Welcome on board.

The journals of history are full of men and women who have done extraordinary feats, folk who lived extraordinary lives. They have developed themselves to be extra-ordinary. They are the ones who have carried on, kept their motivation up and kept on going. They have developed their own success system; they have followed the strategies of other successful people and kept true to their own integrity.

Here are a few names of those men and women who have executed their right to believe 100% and more in themselves.

They are just a few of those extra-ordinary members of the human race   –

> Helen Keller
> Martin Luther King
> Albert Einstein
> Mahatma Gandhi
> Leonardo da Vinci.

ACTION

Turn to a fresh page in your PPCA-Z journal and write a list of any extra-ordinary folk you have heard about or know personally.

Do you know why you listed those people?

What is it that you recognise about those people that stirs your motivation?

D

Delegate [A good idea]

Deliver [Make it realistic]

Direction [Plot your route]

Discipline [✓]

U   Un-limited [Visualise your future and go beyond...]

V   Victory   vs.   W   Weakness

X   [Marks the spot]

Y   [Yes You]

Z [Zenith]

INTRODUCTION

This book is the end product of years of dinner parties at my French home that involved guests who were well-informed and opinionated, and with whom the exchanges set about sorting out the problems of the world. What I have written is intended both as a summary of what has frustrated me and them and, in response, presents an historical perspective that hopefully provides an insight into many of the complex issues that were raised.

However, please do not view this work as having academic pretension. Rather it is offered as a pocket-sized source of reference material that might inspire argument, and counter argument, at your own *soirees*...... from the welcoming *aperitifs* until well into the night.

My RANT has been carefully researched, but if omissions and errors have been incorporated inadvertently I apologise.

Cheers then, to your next [good-humoured] dinner-table debate!

A soiree in Northern France

In fact the prayers of the world help little with any form of disaster whether made by 'man or God'. What always does help in situations of extreme tragedy is the comfort of fellow human beings. Friends, families and often total strangers rally round and help. Requests for aid go out and are always subscribed to and here we have another anachronism. Religions in general, but particularly Christianity, eschew the very idea of wealth – the parable of the rich man and the eye of the needle instantly comes to mind - yet the minute they need help they always call upon the general public, rich and poor, to give generously. What would they do without money? All the prayers in the world do not actually help - it is only money and physical aid that help. This is often put down to God's good influence but in reality it has to do with photographs, publicity, journalists, spin and the generosity and compassion of people, whether religious or not. When all these factors move into top gear things happen. Many may think this is down to God and believe that their cries for help have been met by Him, but rather it is down to people, and if there was not a single prayer ever said then people would still help, and help generously.

Two classic examples of this were Russia in the 20s and 30s, and Ethiopia in the 70s. In the 1920s after Stalin came to power he decided to get rid of the Kulaks. These were peasants who owned their own small farms and did not fit in with the communist ideal of state ownership, and actively opposed it. Furthermore, they were a thorn in his side as they resisted collectivisation because their property was sacred to them. However, they were the main producers of food. As Stalin went ahead with his five-year collective plans the Kulaks were rounded up and either shot on the spot if they resisted, or sent to Siberia to die in gulags which were just a Russian form of concentration camp and source of slave labour. As a direct result of this policy millions of people, mainly children, died of hunger as food shortages became apparent. The problem was, you need is in the Koran and for the rest, Allah will provide. It is a telling point that probably the most successful and civilized principality in Europe for nearly 400 years was that of Cordoba on the Iberian peninsular where, from about 750 AD, it was independent from the central control of Baghdad. There, the emirs practiced religious tolerance both of Christians and Jews, and the three religions lived peacefully side by side. The city flourished in every way; via commerce, learning, and the arts. This tolerance led to a thriving and prosperous community where trade burgeoned and knowledge was valued. Under the Umayyads there were at least 70 libraries open to the public where not only scholars but anyone could go and study. These institutions were almost unknown in the rest of Europe at that time. Regrettably, as soon as the Christians regained the city, the church instantly put an end to toleration and learning, the libraries disappeared and the Muslims and Jews were persecuted and forced to flee or convert.

One of the greatest problems of our age is the suicide terrorist. The very word is, of course, another dichotomy. In the West we call them terrorists, but to many Muslims, including some born and bred in the West, they are *mujahedeen*, soldiers, and martyrs. What makes 'normal' terrorists defeatable is the fear of being caught, the possibility of their own death or, of course, the achievement of their goals. Even if this is a compromise, as, for example, in Northern Ireland, a settlement can bring terrorism to an end. There, in very simple terms, the opposing terrorist factions and both the Catholic and Protestant communities got tired of the battle and came to a negotiated settlement which really suited neither side, but with which both could get along. This cannot happen with fundamentalist Islam. There can be no compromise because this would involve some sort of recognition that other religions could be right and this would go against the letter of the Koran which, in turn, is blasphemy. If the fear of death does not exist, and the been lessened. Today we have a government with a sizeable majority so it can and does do exactly as it pleases. Britain is supposedly still one of the freest countries in which to live but there are definite signs that the pendulum is swinging in the opposite direction.

It should be said at this point that society does not go out of its way to help itself. Overall we are far more selfish than used to be the case. This inevitably leads to an increase in yobbishness and even lawlessness which in turn is used as a justification for a government's endless quest for more power and control. There does seem to be an inverse relationship between a caring society and crime. The more caring a society, the less crime there is. The more selfish we become, the less we care for others and the more crime goes up. We then blame the government which has to do something about it and this plays right into its eternal search for more information on, and control over, people. Governments the world over seem to have the need to dominate their subjects. Meanwhile the public really want to keep their cake and eat it. It seems that everything that goes wrong is the government's fault and the government should do something about it. What has happened to the idea of people doing things for themselves? Britain is well on the way to becoming a totally controlled nanny state. The will to do something to help yourself is rapidly disappearing. All manner of pressure groups, for every conceivable cause, spring up to lobby for their point of view. This also plays into government's hands because they then use this as an excuse to do something and it's called 'listening to the people'. Invariably this means taking on more power with a concomitant loss of individual freedom. Britain has far too many inspectors who seem to be appointed in order to cover just about every aspect of an individual's life. Supposedly they are there to look after us and on this basis we seem to go along with them, but in actual fact for every one appointed there is a diminution of personal freedom. A quick look through the manifestos of any of therefore the technology exists. The proliferation of CCTV cameras has been achieved without any consultation whatsoever, so why should not any further form of spying - in fact, it is inevitable! It will always be described as being for the general good and an aid to the fight against crime. Whilst it may help in the detection of criminals although even this is doubtful, it definitely does nothing to deter crime as the figures demonstrate.

Mention is now made of having similar technology in every car so that all journeys can be monitored. The justification never changes; if you have nothing to hide then you have nothing to fear, or alternatively it is wrapped up in 'greenery' so that it is presented as being good for the environment. However, no mention is made of the fact that you can then be monitored wherever you go. This will no doubt be a great help to private investigators keeping an eye on errant husbands and wives, for no matter how secure we are assured that the information is, it always seems to get into the wrong hands. It is easy to foresee a time in the not too distant future when every house will be required to have a camera installed. The government may insist initially that cameras are put only into criminal's homes but this will merely be the first step. They will then ask for volunteers from the general public to have them installed in their houses for 'their own security'. There are always well-meaning souls who want to help the government tackle crime, and so they volunteer. This will then be hailed as a great success and every home will have to have one. This may seem a fanciful scenario today but if you went back 40 or 50 years and told people that there would eventually be thousands of cameras in every town and city in Britain, with control rooms manned by people 24 hours a day watching the movements of every person going by, they would have said you were 'nuts', or at least had been reading too much Orwell. Yet this has happened and without public consultation as to whether or not it is desirable. Even those upholders of freedom of speech and the invading participants, or at least their political masters, that there is no instant solution to the Iraqi question now that the infrastructure has been demolished. When a working government that has been running a country for years is destroyed overnight it can hardly be replaced instantly, which is what the US thought would happen once the celebrations were over and Saddam gone. It was anticipated, mistakenly, that the population would just get back to work and elect a new government. Nor was allowance made for the demarcation of the country by the British during imperial times. This, in turn, led to little notice being taken of the diversity of religious, tribal and nationalist sentiments that existed then, and still do. It is impossible to quash the insurgency in Iraq and given that it took over six months for the elected government to actually form an administration. The occupying forces should learn something from that, notably, that it will not work. The elected politicians forming the government do not get along with each other, nor will they ever, so effective government is highly unlikely. The occupying forces will stay there until, eventually, they are compelled to make an undignified retreat as did the United States from Vietnam, Britain from Aden, and Russia from Afghanistan. Unfortunately the religious and national diversity that exists in Iraq is such that a peaceful solution to their problems is as far away as is the case in the Israeli-Palestinian debacle, and both these difficulties still have years to run.

In 1956 Colonel Nasser of Egypt nationalised the Suez Canal which was mainly owned by the British. This was seen as a direct threat to British interests and the government of the day decided upon armed intervention with the aid of France which was a minor shareholder. Israel was persuaded to join in as she, too, saw her interests threatened. The invasion was successful and the canal was soon back in British [and French] hands. However, this did not fit with US aims. They were courting Nasser's friendship. They voted atmosphere of friendship and co-operation, it would have a far better chance of survival, for there are extremists on both sides who do not want to see this work. Opening the borders to free trade, as in Europe, for example, would bring peace faster than wasting millions on building a wall. The Berlin version did not work and nor will the Israeli one. All that a wall does is to form a barrier to dialogue and becomes a very visible sign of division. This only creates more frustration, unhappiness and ill-will and gives the hotheads more ammunition. One way or another peace will happen eventually, but the bloodier the conflict that brings it about, the less is the likelihood that it will survive. It will no doubt take statesmen of great stature on both sides to make the concessions necessary for a peaceful birth of Palestine and at present it is difficult to see such people even on the horizon. Added to this is the fact that when such visionaries do appear there is usually also a fanatic ready to assassinate him or her. But should one emerge then the two states could become the leaders of the Middle East because their joint potential in trade and agriculture is way above that of the surrounding countries. The exception, perhaps, is Lebanon which was the jewel of the Middle East until they engaged in a civil war and were occupied by their neighbour Syria in the name of peace. This caused years of resentment which finally broke out into demonstrations that forced the Syrians to leave. This alone should be proof of how countries can tear themselves apart and decline from immense wealth to relative poverty. War and religious conflict are a sure way to undermine a country, and a people, and all the prayers in the world do not, never have done, and never will, help. It is always down to people to sort things out and the depressing thing is that it is always the ordinary man, or more correctly the woman and child, in the street who most suffer. These are the ones who bear the brunt of the pain, both mental and physical, and neither politicians nor religious leaders really give a damn when their principles are involved. The rallying cry is always on behalf of the grow and sell a potato that is not on the official list? Such nonsensical and arbitrary rules only serve to niggle people. Enterprises all over Britain have been put out of business because of idiotic EU rules. The laws on abattoirs provide an example. Here the Commission introduced a new set of rules which meant the closure of about 80% of British abattoirs because they were considered too small and unable to afford the new changes demanded by the legislation. These new rules were supposed to be of benefit to the animals but they actually did the opposite for animal welfare and a great deal for the 'jobs for the boys' brigade. The British government, instead of pointing out that small abattoirs were perfectly good and should be allowed to carry on, just caved in and closed them down. This actually does much more harm to the animals which now have to be conveyed sometimes hundreds of miles. The fact that many viable businesses were destroyed and people put out of work did not seem to matter. The government just shrugged and pointed a finger at the Commission. That the government was not interested in fighting for these small businesses probably had more to do with the lobbying power and party donations of big business. Even should the home government disagree with the rulings, they nevertheless have to implement them or engage in an arduous procedure to opt-out. You would have thought that no matter how arduous the opt-out, the government would fight for its own businesses, and of course, when it suits it does opt-out. However, the government does like to play it both ways and if it wants to push through unpopular legislation then it can direct the blame at the Commission.

Venerable media pundits pose the question every day on how we can reduce our personal emissions, and leading politicians just never stop harping on about it, and yet the actual evidence that CO_2 emissions cause global warming just does not stack up. When they have extracted the maximum taxes that they can, and when and if they actually get carbon emissions down and yet the temperature keeps going up, what then? Levels will eventually come down again as always they have throughout history, but the pirates who have taxed people unnecessarily will not be around to take the blame, or to answer for their thievery.

As a postscript to the above, on March, 8, 2007 Channel 4 featured a first class programme called the *Great Global Warming Swindle*. This was a well-researched analysis and incorporated the views of a number of eminent scientists who were of the opinion that carbon dioxide has little to do with global warming. Their thesis is that solar activity is the main influence on the temperature of the earth, and an hour's worth of extremely plausible evidence was presented to back up such theories. They produced evidence from ice cores, from periods of high CO_2 emissions when temperatures actually fell, and much more. Unlike their global warming colleagues who are only 80% to 90% sure, they seemed to be 100% sure that they were right. Under the circumstances you would expect such a programme to cause a stir in the media and it did. During the following weeks it was mentioned in a number of publications mainly to its detriment. An article in *The Guardian* actually said that it was misleading and a misrepresentation of the facts and that the DVD of the documentary should not be put on the market. However, the producers of the film stood by every word of it and accused the complaining scientists of trying to gag them because they were angry. Looked at dispassionately, if it were such a farrago of lies why not treat it with contempt rather than try to get it banned? Needless to say the DVD went on sale but the world carried on as usual on councils have even started charging people to park in front of their own houses. Then there is road tax. In France this was abolished a few years ago and instead the tax was placed on fuel which, although it did increase prices, is nevertheless a much fairer way of taxing motorists. However, fuel is still cheaper in France than it is in Britain where both it and road taxes seem to go up on a regular basis.

France is a far less consumerist society. The French are much happier with their lot and would not dream of going out of their way to make a fast buck. In the aftermath of the 1999 storms in which a great many roofs were damaged, the roofers could have made a killing but they did not. Their quotes for repairs were no higher than they would have been for the same job under normal conditions. Quotes normally stand for about three months before they are reviewed in Britain. However, in France you find that builders, roofers, plumbers and electricians will usually honour a quote a year later without any additions. Workers are expected to work their full hours. They may take between one and two hours for lunch but there are no further breaks for tea or coffee at any other time.

Customer satisfaction comes high on the French agenda. At one end, having a meal in a restaurant will usually be accompanied by the waiter asking if everything is alright and if you are enjoying it. At the other end, buying a car or some other expensive object from a trader rather than a supermarket will always be followed up by a letter or at least a 'phone call to check whether everything is functioning properly. Whilst supermarkets may be cheaper, especially on items like fridges, freezers, washing machines and the like, any after sales service is hard to get and often almost nonexistent. In contrast, from a small trader it is usually excellent.

Patriotism plays an important part in French life. It seems as though British politicians are trying to instil a bit of this into the British

Angela

Remember Richard
— New Year when
was it ?!

Liz

0131·226·3766

so at their own peril. The first and fundamental hazard is that the sources of the power the Treasury exercises – which forms such crucial element in the image that it projects – may not be as easy to locate as the abiding myth of the Treasury as the unsleeping watchdog ruthlessly imposing its rules throughout government (without fear or favour) would suggest. When the curtain is lifted, events taking place both on stage and behind the scenes show that power is exercised conditionally, not absolutely and by negotiation, not fiat. The processes by which this achieved – the negotiations and relationships, both political and official – have been charted before, most famously by Heclo and Wildavsky (1974) in the early 1970s: but the abiding lesson is that, whatever its apparent strength, Treasury power is less than absolute.

There is a paradox here, too. The Treasury may prevail, but not necessarily through the institutional Treasury. A former senior Treasury official has commented that a 'strong Treasury' is 'shorthand for many attitudes, arrangements and approaches that go beyond the official Treasury' (Monck, 1997: 279). However, the task of charting the processes by which these attitudes, arrangements and approaches affect the outcomes of policy-making is a complex one, not to be lightly undertaken. All the elements that appear from the outside to guarantee that the policies the Treasury has espoused will be implemented: central location, the shining abilities of the civil servants, even the political authority of the Chancellor are not in themselves sufficient to ensure that the outcomes will meet Treasury objectives.

Students of British government now often refer to the emergence of what they call a 'hollow state' in the United Kingdom (Weller, Bakvis and Rhodes, 1997). Power, to put the argument crudely, has fled from the central institutions of the nation-state, in Whitehall and Westminster. It has departed upwards (to Brussels and the global financial markets), outwards, to other centres of authority, both in the private sector and the twilight zone where state and market meet (quangos) and downwards to new public institutions being created in other parts of the United Kingdom. At the same time, there has been a substantial reduction in the number of functions performed by the state itself, brought about on the basis that government 'should specialise in the activities which it can uniquely provide' and leave the rest to be purchased in the market or provided by third-sector organizations operating outside the state bureaucracy (Foster and Plowden, 1996: 58). This in turn has led to changes both in the size of public bodies and the nature of the tasks that those working in them are expected to perform.

Certain aspects of this argument remain controversial. In 1995, Simon Jenkins wrote an impassioned account of the way that, in his view, arrogant centralizing tendencies came to dominate government during the Conservative years, with the Treasury playing an especially infamous role. However, there is no doubt that both the role of the state and its architecture have been fundamentally altered over the past twenty years. There are those who would go so far as to describe the results of this process as 'fragmentation' of the machinery of government. This must necessarily have consequences for a department like the Treasury, located as it is at the centre of a system that has been subjected to this hollowing process. Tracing the consequences of these changes and their implications for the exercise of power is another complex and difficult task.

Treasury people

If they succeed in securing entry to this universe in flux, researchers will then run another sort of risk – of what could be crudely called 'co-option'. For the image is in one respect at least not misleading: the Treasury does indeed contain a remarkable number of exceptionally able people. This makes the task of conducting interviews there challenging and the resulting dialogue, if the job has been properly done, rewarding. It is easy, in such company, to be flattered into believing that what you hear presented with such beguiling fluency is the whole story.

However, this aspect of life in the Treasury has not always been presented positively. In the introduction to their collection of interviews, conducted in the Treasury in 1982, Hugo Young and Anne Sloman summarize the mythology that surrounds this small group: 'Treasury mandarins are powerful, yet silky smooth; influential, but strangely unknown; clever, devious, inscrutable and not a little self-satisfied' (1984: 21).

Nor is this a reputation only current among outsiders; something of the same flavour can be detected, in a more discreet form, in comments from elsewhere in government. The Treasury's unique combination of intellectual excellence and small size do lift it above the common ruck of Whitehall. Not for nothing is the habitual shorthand comparison of the working environment there as like the common room of an Oxford college – though the phrase departments supply the detail and so the interactions are not factual seminars but manoeuvres over control. The Treasury style is that of 'demurral' – requesting more information (Chapman, 1997: 25–6, after Wright) – putting it in the position of seeming to be pronouncing upon the merits of a policy. From early on this attitude caused resentment, summed up in Lord Salisbury's notorious parliamentary attack of 30 January 1900. Salisbury as Conservative Prime Minister chose the anniversary of Charles I's beheading to suggest that

> the Treasury has obtained a position in regard to the rest of the departments of the Government that the House of Commons obtained in the time of the Stuart dynasty. It has the power of the purse, and by exercising the power of the purse it claims a voice in all decisions of administrative authority and policy. (Roseveare, 1969: 183, also quoted by Chapman, 1997)

Even a century later, we are yet to resolve the two questions Salisbury posed: does the Treasury improperly extend its control over money to control over policy? And to do its job does it need to participate in decisions where the financial content in the policy considerations promoted by the spending department may be low?

The power of parliamentary accountability has long been an adjunct to the authority of the Treasury over spending departments. An important source of Treasury strength was the right from 1861 to present the estimates of all department to parliament (Chapman, 1997: 18). The growth of parliamentary audit in the 1860s (through the Public Accounts Committee and Comptroller and Auditor-General) provided the Treasury with convenient allies as the spending department has to defend decisions and practices whether or not the Treasury had a hand in them. On the other hand, Chapman, in his generally benign presentation of Treasury powers, sees the Treasury as being issue-based and fully involved in the parliamentary and political environment (ibid.: 103) – the 'most political of departments' from the perspective of open and closed politics (ibid.: 104).

The key relationship at the political level, as we have already indicated, is that between the Prime Minister and the Chancellor. But the ever-increasing attention devoted to this relationship has obscured a longer-running theme: the Treasury's concern that in social policy the Prime Minister would ultimately side with the big spenders. Paradoxically, this has been a Conservative rather than Labour theme, at least before 1979. Harold Macmillan was the prime example, seeking to subvert Treasury-driven norms in the early 1960s with his talk of 'modernisation' (Lowe, 1997b). A succession of weak Chancellors and bad relationships with Prime Ministers in the 1960s and 1970s (documented by Dell, 1996) suggests that the concept of a strong axis only started with James Callaghan and Denis Healey in 1976 and has subsequently been evident only intermittently. A more important theme has been the developing presumption that every public expenditure round would be more difficult than the last. Here, the collective Cabinet weight of spending ministers has diminished relative to the strategic economic judgment of Prime Minister and Chancellor. Lending institutional weight to this theme has been the role of Chief Secretary as the minister for public expenditure from 1961, acting as something more than the Chancellor's junior minister.

Reactions to the 'overmighty Treasury'

The Treasury has often faced the threat of shearing-off, designed to make it institutionally weaker by distributing the finance, economics and public expenditure functions in different ways. The Treasury set itself up for this by dividing at Permanent Secretary level (in 1956) and right down the organization (in 1962) into two sides – 'pay and management' and 'finance and economy' (including the public-sector group). The first split was within this latter side through the creation of the Department of Economic Affairs (1964–9) initially under Labour's Deputy Leader, George Brown, but this did not long survive Brown's loss of reputation within the Labour government. The Civil Service Department (1968) took away the management side and grew very strong under William Armstrong, taking on computing, procurement and training for the civil service, with its head, as Head of the Civil Service, on a promotion track from the Treasury (Armstrong and then Douglas Allen). A further rivalry was with the Department of Trade and Industry (formerly the Board of Trade and the Ministry of Technology), a pro-growth department seeking a monopoly of contacts with industry. Over the years the Treasury has won these battles, and the really threatening fission – of public expenditure control – has not been pursued. Sometimes for accidental reasons of the personalities of ministers and officials, the rival ministries have been seen off and the

'the rest of the Committee considered that the income guarantee in its present form was not of high priority, and thought it premature to lay down long-term policy' (ibid.).

In this sub-committee's work the spending departments made the pitch that they had to go well beyond the Conservatives' previously planned increases they had long criticized as inadequate, but the Treasury held the macroeconomic ring and were able to deploy two variables no longer available in the 1990s: physical capacity constraints (in housebuilding and social services) and the balance of payments (in defence and overseas aid). Given the crisis mentality of the time, the wish to conform spending decisions to the National Plan, and the fact that the debate was about the moderation of rates of increase rather than 'cuts', the Treasury was able to outgun the spending departments, leaving Anthony Crosland making the rather plaintive point he was to make during the IMF crisis in 1976:

> We are in danger of getting the public expenditure problem out of perspective. Certainly we must be ruthless and stringent in the immediate period of economic difficulty. But to sacrifice basic socialist principles for a few million pounds which cannot fall due for at least 4 years would suggest a certain lack of faith in our economic policies. We are, after all, a rich country on a long-run view; and taxation takes an unusually low proportion of GDP. . . . (C(65)99 9.7.65 in CAB/129/121)

Getting ministers to perceive public expenditure as a problem had been a long-term Treasury objective. Against their earlier fears, the PESC process was offering a location for the eventual defeat of the combined forces of the social spending departments. Social expenditure was deployed as a matter of economic impact and not as a political and social tool under both Labour and Conservative governments. As Heclo and Wildavsky traced, relations between Treasury officials and their opposite numbers came to be focused on the PESC plan and were much less a fragmented series of bids for more spending promoted by appeals to the Prime Minister and to public demand. The Treasury's victory was sealed by the post-devaluation squeeze of 1967–9. But it was only temporary. Once the economy was in better shape the dynamics of the PESC system, now fully in place, reverted to the pro-spending bias the Treasury had always feared.

The high noon and decline of PESC

It took a while for the full PESC system to take shape. Although the first PESC report had been published in 1961 and a system of comprehensive five-year 'forward looks' started in the mid-1960s, it was not until 1969 that the annual white paper 'The Government's Expenditure Plans' started to be published. Many parts of the system that are often attributed wholly to the Plowden report were elaborated at this time. Plans were by programme (not department) and were related to usually optimistic forecasts of the capacity of the economy to absorb government expenditure, but not to the tax-raising process. They were expressed in what came to be called 'funny money' – figures that were not the same as the amounts actually expended. They were expressed in 'survey prices' (as prevailing in the autumn before the year of the survey), and in 'volume terms' which stripped out both general and relative inflation; at the time it was thought that the prices of public social services would rise faster than private because there was less room for productivity improvement (the 'relative price effect'). What now seems like the fallacy of this presumed effect defines the difference between the 1960s, where the generation of inputs was the object of social policy, and the 1990s, where the inputs are perceived as a cost burden and there is great hope of 'efficiency gains' in the delivery of services.

By the mid-1970s PESC was breaking down as a synoptic control mechanism, in ways already explored very fully in Heclo and Wildavsky, Heald, and Thain and Wright. The main problem was the use of volume terms planning in a period of high inflation. The conversion factors from volume terms to cash, and the delay in notifying them, caused an injection of resources late in financial years. The application of the relative price effect, which was designed to protect services from the impact of relative inflation, could be very destabilizing if the price indices by service surged – as they easily could if services relied on the purchase of labour or land. Nearly all social services in kind had severe cost pressures in the early 1970s which politicians and managers could not resist. The result was the notorious 'missing £5 billion' by which actual expenditure in 1974–5 could not be related back to 1971 plans (Thain and Wright, 1995: 43; Heclo and Wildavsky, 1981 edn: xxi–xxii).

The public expenditure crisis of late 1976, in which cuts were imposed in order to win backing and credits from the International renounced, and it was a liberation from a century of preoccupation and often mutual resentment.

Running costs control brought out the worst in Treasury–department arguments, and were a constant feature of our interviews in 1996. Because of the palpable impact of decisions, and sometimes because of their trivial size, they provided constant opportunities for ministerial intervention. One vignette is of the way that the size of the regional offices of the NHS executive was fixed. As described by a Health Department participant:

> the Treasury line, which I think did have something to do with Ken Clarke, was a purist line on the separation of purchasers and providers, and taking the hands off. The great Treasury phrase was 'light touch', which was to some extent synonymous with small numbers and therefore low cost, but one felt there was more to it than that. But on the other hand, I never was absolutely certain how far Ken Clarke was driving that, because we had a plan for regional offices which involved them being around 125–135 staff numbers, and the Treasury were pressing for them to be 25, and we did get the impression that this was Ken Clarke driven. I mean, they said it was Ken Clarke driven, and we got to the point where we needed a decision, we had to break through, so a great meeting was set up with Ken Clarke and Virginia [Bottomley]. . . . Alan Langlands [NHS Chief Executive] made his pitch, and there were other issues being discussed, specifically the size of the Department of Health . . . on the regional offices we won almost before we started, and Treasury officials were gobsmacked, and slightly embarrassed, because it just collapsed in the face of the arguments. Now I think what happened was that a deal had been done before the meeting, which we didn't know about and they didn't know about, between Virginia and Ken, and that's why it just seemed like pushing on an open door. In return for that we had rather a bad time on [running costs] – it was the price for being successful.

In departments with a small ratio of running costs expenditure to programme expenditure, Treasury 'punishment' can be a potent weapon. The clearest recent example of this is the decision in 1995 to attack the Department of Social Security by clawing back from running costs an overspending (through underestimation of demand) on benefits expenditure, which is by far the largest element of social policy spending that is not cash-limited. The Treasury pursued this tactic with a potent combination of regret and relish. In the words of one of their officials:

> there have been occasions where if the DSS has declined to deliver previously agreed policy savings with us, we have said to them that 'OK, you're telling us that it is politically impossible or operationally impossible. However, we have agreed with you certain figures for Social Security spending and we have incorporated them into the Budget, and the Budget arithmetic is based on them, and you can't just walk away from them and say that because you had a problem on this or that, it's not going to be done' and the matter is then left, because if the matter is then left, we blow a hole in the budget strategy, so what we've said to them is that in that situation we need an alternative policy saving, that is the best thing to do, for which they say 'Well, that's impossible for the following fifty-eight political reasons. There's no way that we could find any new policy saving'. Now again my position on that is we can't just leave it at that. Our responsibility is to deliver certain public expenditure numbers that have been agreed in the Budget. The DSS do have one or two cash-limited budgets, of which the main one is the administrative expenditure, and so our tactic has been to take it out of that and say 'Well, in that case the shortfall comes off your administrative expenditure but we will restore that if you come up with an agreed policy saving'. Now that is probably the biggest single cause of tension and annoyance between the DSS and the Treasury at working level, that we do that. My defence is that, I can see it causes them difficulties but, one, I have to do it in order to deliver my prime objective, and secondly, it does seem to have worked, because it has produced ... it has led them to somehow find a number of policy savings that I am absolutely certain would never have been volunteered if that pressure hadn't been put upon them.

The outcome in 1995 was a defeat for DSS, with a 25 per cent cut in running costs over three years imposed on them. DSS particularly regretted the loss of year-end flexibility on running costs that this implied.

introduced and the decision taken to apply it to all departments, which of course meant that we had to do the same exercise in the Treasury, it was an opportunity in a way of sweeping up all the other thing that we had been doing over the previous two or three years' (Treasury and Civil Service Committee, 1995: Q5).

Here the motives of the Treasury bear examination. Were they trying to be accommodating to other departments and remedy the history of poor relations? Were they trying to set a good example? Or were they seeking to catch the tide of synoptic and fundamental review of government business to entrench their position still further? Our interviews found that opinion in the Treasury and the social spending departments divided along different lines. A central position – the thoughtful line from the Treasury – is to see the process as an inevitable response to modernizing trends and of our understanding of organizational psychology and sociology. Examination of the conduct and implementation of the FER can throw light on these questions.

The conduct and implementation of the review

The model for the review was the scrutiny mode, as developed by Margaret Thatcher's Efficiency Unit under Derek Rayner. The essence of this format is speed (a fixed and ambitious timetable) and 'juniority' (setting a mid-level but rising official to challenge the prejudices of seniors). Both these variables have characteristics of 'bouncing' – securing action against better judgment. In the Treasury FER the reviewing officer was balanced against an outsider steering the exercise, and the choice of each was a combination of aptitude and availability. Jeremy Heywood, effectively the author of the review, had been Norman Lamont's private secretary, a post which marked him out as a rising star of his generation. The timing of the review was in part related to Heywood's availability. His talents have subsequently been displayed to advantage in Number 10 since 1997 first as the Prime Minister's private secretary for economic matters and then as Principal Private Secretary – a position diminished in influence since Tony Blair brought in Jonathan Powell as his chief of staff, but still a key one in Whitehall.

Sir Colin Southgate of EMI was seen as having the right combination of skills – not a grandee, working in a 'modern' industry, and available. His appointment came after a search for an outside consultant in which Howard Davies also featured. Southgate had been on a course at Chevening at which a group of six permanent secretaries including Burns met a group of six senior industrialists. Southgate's role was to provide a 'looking over the shoulder' role to contrast with Heywood's rather earnest intellectual cogency. Southgate was useful in protecting the Treasury from criticism, and seems to have been a personally a success: as Heywood told MPs, 'Sir Colin Southgate no doubt talked to a lot of his industrial colleagues. He was overseeing the whole exercise and I think we got a lot of value from that' (Q22). Southgate contributed a lively preface to the Heywood report ('I have been amazed by the number of "grades" of staff the Treasury has' (HM Treasury, 1994: 21)) which shows a sympathetic personal engagement with his task.

The review team's approach was to deduce its preferred organizational form from an examination of the work done by the Treasury and the opinions of organizations relating to it. In the case of the social spending departments, this was done by a written questionnaire; Principal Finance Officers were not interviewed. In principle this was a sound approach, but it ran the risk of homing in on an over-categorical answer. One of us, in an article written with Christopher Hood and Oliver James, saw it as standing in the tradition of a recurring theme in economic thinking about institutional design – a largely cerebral set of regulators set and monitor targets but are not involved in detailed interventions; the working style may change but the capacity for ultimate control does not (Parry, Hood and James, 1997: 404–5). By basing the approach on a relatively static set of 'grumbles' by the Treasury's customers, and construct institutional responses to then, the review ran the risk of misunderstanding the dynamic and random nature of political negotiation within government (ibid.: 407–9).

Before Heywood began the review he was sent to the Harvard Business School for three months – not to follow any formal programme of study but to absorb ideas. Relevant business school ideas in currency there included delayering, building long-term relationships, stripping out non-core businesses, pleasing the customer, and empowerment. The area which seems to have had most impact on the FER was that of flexible hierarchies in which work was done well at the point of delivery – rather than the civil service approach of multiple processing of work up a grade-defined hierarchy, as both a refinement and an insurance. The civil service tradition of checks and balances is very strong, and particularly in the form of a system of stratified hierarchies in which an upward channel of

Heywood did not at the time when he wrote the report have any direct experience of the expenditure teams' work. His approach through empowering the Grade 5 team leaders had radical implications for both the Treasury itself and more generally. The civil service tradition is of matching hierarchies and grade consciousness. Work moves up and down hierarchies, with the possibility on either side of pushing issues to higher levels if there is dissatisfaction with outcomes. As it is the spending department that is generally on the defensive, the right of appeal and de-emphasis of the role of any single individual is of particular value to it. The FER prescription of the strong team leader with ultimate responsibility for outcomes runs counter to previous civil service practice. A key element in our research has been our attempt to analyse its effects.

In the new Treasury structure, team leaders operate in relatively greater isolation: senior colleagues are there for advice but not necessarily for support in the sense of blurring of responsibilities. Team leaders deal direct with the Chief Secretary, and holders of the latter post that we interviewed emphasized their liking for this arrangement. The officials responsible for the work, usually young, energetic and politically astute, become well-known personalities to the Chief Secretary, who can run the relationship as an extended private officer or seminar rather than by an engagement conducted through mandarins. As one former Chief Secretary put it to us, 'to do the business properly it is essential to deal directly with "the youngsters at the end of the table"'. The FER makes explicit what has been steadily emerging through successive reforms in the civil service: that the lead official on a defined area of work has a more influential role than a nominally senior official with a co-ordinating or supervisory role.

This new structure could be readily assimilated to the existing culture of the 'democratic republic of the Treasury' in which meetings are large and inclusive, junior officials are present in order to contribute rather than spectate, and there is no departmental position agreed in advance – it is accepted that differences can be argued out in front of Ministers.

It has always been the culture in the Treasury that this is a democratic organization where different views are not only discussed but are also exposed at a high level, including to Ministers, so we are much more comfortable about giving the Chief Secretary and the Chancellor a choice saying that 'there are two or three ways you could go on this', and giving them a balanced submission and saying very clearly and candidly and honestly what the advantages and disadvantages are of each, and just because you might hold to proposition A, it is certainly your duty to fully discuss the disadvantages of A and the advantages of the others, but it is also quite in order to say 'I personally favour A, but some of my colleagues don't agree and they favour B, so let's have a meeting and let's thrash it out'. Now that is much more common in the Treasury than it is anywhere else.

What we observe now is a 'reverse grade drift' in which responsibilities are pushed down as low as possible. In a way new to the civil service, competence leads to trust and responsibility within the present post rather than to rapid promotion out of it. This applies particularly to the Grade 7 (former Principal) level, where the fast-stream training grades merge into the main administrative structure.

However, the Treasury's push to identify and sustain individual responsibilities poses new challenges to those who have to make the relationship between the Treasury and other departments work. Since the nineteenth century spending departments have been used to trading down in their dealings with the Treasury, accepting that a lower-grade official would carry the responsibility for the initial processing of business with them. One Treasury official reminisced to the visiting BBC interviewers in 1982 about past times with 'a very young man telling a responsible finance officer that he's got it all wrong and shouldn't be building a bypass round Stevenage or whatever' (Hancock in Young and Sloman, 1984: 52). The crucial difference is now that there is no effective 'court of appeal' above the Treasury's nominated negotiator. The days when a discreet telephone conversation with the Under Secretary could sort things out, with the option of going to the Treasury's Second Permanent Secretary in charge of public expenditure if that failed, have effectively gone. This further tilts the balance of influence in the Treasury's favour and demands a behavioural shift from its partners.

Of course, the new structures introduced in the FER have not been presented as a yet further grab for Treasury aggrandisement. Rather the opposite. The chief architect of the changes, Terry Burns, referred repeatedly to the need for the Treasury to adopt a more positive and responsive approach to its 'customers' in the spending departments. More stable relationships, based on better mutual from your point of view'; our own perspective is that an analysis based on personalities is far from useless if they are indeed the main motivator of behaviour and that officials are seeking the kind of gratifying collegial behaviour which is seen as part of the civil service mentality. In this, we would supply some correction to the emphasis in the core executive literature on structural rather than behavioural factors in our understanding of the centre of government.

But at the same time it was also clear that the new framework and the mantras about concentrating on strategic issues and settling on agreed principles as a basis for discussions (whether as a formal concordat or in the shape of strategy papers on individual issues) was beginning to have an effect. Although our first round of interviews took place near the beginning of the period when the new system had become operational, there were signs of increased willingness to accept the legitimacy of the Treasury's interest in policy questions. In some cases the value of having a second opinion on some of the issues that were causing difficulties within the spending departments was explicitly recognized, though it was difficult to escape the impression that there was something rather patronising about the comments that PFOs made on Treasury documents.

In sum, the attitudes of PFOs (in 1996) seemed to be wary but on balance accepting of the intentions, if not always the execution, of the post-Heywood approach. But the nature of the response varied from department to department. Although PFOs kept in close touch with each other, meeting informally on occasion to concert tactics, the nature of the relationship with the Treasury differs so greatly between departments that there could never be any question of a uniform 'line'. Partly this is a question of Treasury stereotypes of departmental reliability (already discussed in Chapter 2). Partly it is a matter of scale. The DSS, as by far the biggest spender, is always bound to attract disproportionately close Treasury attention. The story, as it was told to us, of the steady increase in the Treasury's level of confidence in the DSS's capacity to manage its vast budget is outlined in the next chapter. But it is important to register here that the relationships with departments have developed differently for reasons that are not directly determined by questions of personality, important those these can sometimes be, and will never be precisely similar, though they may converge over time.

Where there were still disagreements between spending departments collectively and the Treasury they were around questions like the Treasury's tendency to overstress the applicability of lessons of good practice in an individual programme area ('benchmarking') as a means of making a case for immediate improvements across the board. This linked with a perennial complaint that the Treasury officials had no real understanding of the difficulty of implementing policy changes and would learn lessons the hard way if they were to move to a spending department post.

The Treasury's enthusiasm for imposing incremental savings in departmental running costs was another issue that raised some hackles all round. But it was the response of one interviewee with recent Treasury experience that best summed up the general flavour of the PFO's contribution. Essentially (he said) what he looked for was an *adult* relationship which would survive changes in personalities.

Developing the new style

The Treasury was, of course, well aware that the initial response of the spending departments to the new Treasury approach to the relationship would be cautious. One of the Deputy Directors (Alice Perkins, the administrator in the grade with the strongest non-Treasury background) was given the specific responsibility of ensuring that the message that the Treasury was seriously committed to improving relations with its 'customers' was successfully got across.

In a subsequent review of this operation, a scoreboard of performance was produced. Ratings by customers were built in as part of this exercise and showed a substantial improvement from a rather sceptical atmosphere at the start, in 1996. Some PFOs had been happy to adopt a co-operative approach, but according to the Treasury's own account 'others were suspicious and in one or two cases downright hostile'. When PFOs were asked in February 1996 to rate the Treasury's performance they gave it 6 out of 10 – equivalent to satisfactory. But when asked about changes since the FER changes had been introduced almost half (45 per cent) thought that relationships had deteriorated.

As a result, a whole range of activities were introduced: visits to departments, regular scheduled meetings with opposite numbers, feedback sessions on survey decisions, the development of joint approaches to key strategic decisions and awaydays between Treasury teams and departments. Delegations were generally increased and in several instances concordats were in draft. This activity had been supplemented and reinforced by the experience of working

Lilley's priority after 1993 was to repair the damage done by what was in many ways an untypical example of a 'big bang' policy that had detonated destructively. As we saw in the discussion of Frank Field's role, the Treasury sought to gain a consensus on a stable policy. Lilley and his civil servants were not able to prevent the agency from lurching from crisis to crisis, shedding chief executives and repeatedly failing to deliver on forecast savings. Understanding the Treasury's role in all this is helped by an appreciation of the fact that they value the resilience of policies. One that causes political controversy and fails to meet its targets is of little attraction, making us suspect that in this case the official line of shared responsibility (as presented, for instance, by DSS Permanent Secretary Sir Michael Partridge to the House of Commons Public Accounts Committee, 1995) is nearer the truth than social policy analysts have credited.

2 Disability benefits

This was also seen by ministers in 1993 as a key area of policy failure. The problem here was not the concept of benefits for the disabled, which has well-established precedents, but the exponential growth in costs, heavily influenced by changes on the labour market. By 1994, the annual cost of these benefits had risen to £8 billion as large numbers of the long-term sick and those suffering from chronic disability were encouraged to leave the labour market. Lilley's response was to attempt to contain expenditure by changing the rules on eligibility through imposing an 'objective medical test'. Under its amended title of 'Incapacity Benefit' it was estimated that the main benefit in this area would cost £2 billion less by 2000. However, the change left the Treasury less than wholly satisfied: as one official told us in 1996:

> on Invalidity Benefit our view was that DSS were relying far too much for the savings on the great new medical test. We agreed that there needed to be a new medical test. We agreed that it should be taken out of the hands of GPs, but we had our doubts as to whether the new medical test was going to generate the level of savings that the DDSs were expecting. A new medical test is the sort of change to the benefit system that the DSS like because it can be presented terribly rationally as meaning the benefits will continue to go toward deserving cases, and it's only the undeserving who get kicked off benefit, whilst our focus was

we want that, but as well we want the actual levels of the benefit restricted so that for sure we will know that for every million people or every 100 000 people on the benefit we're going to spend less on it because we've actually chopped some element out of it, so that the age additions are less generous, that there is no additional pension element in invalidity benefit any more . . . things like that. So we will always want to rely on things that will deliver savings in a more certain manner, and the DSS will tend to want to rely on things that deliver savings from behavioural change or from clearly withdrawing the benefit or taking out of eligibility for the benefit certain classes of previous claimants who they can present as undeserving.

The Treasury were sceptical about the 'all-work' test – on the surface a check against giving benefit to those who were not 'really disabled' but in practice a kind way of denominating the unemployability of many who were marginal to the labour market. The was similar dissatisfaction in the Treasury with the Disability Living Allowance, introduced in 1992 to meet the additional needs of the severely disabled and of a nature least likely to commend it to Treasury officials because of its unclear definitional boundaries. This agenda continued into the Labour government, with the Treasury by no means lacking sophistication and realism in their understanding of the issues.

3 Housing benefit

This was another area of very rapid growth in expenditure (11 per cent per annum in the course of the earlier 1990s) and as such a prime target for action. There is also some overlap with the previous issue: long-term sick and disabled are the fastest growing group of those claiming Housing Benefit. But mainly the growth represents the outcome of an important policy shift, away from subsidizing bricks and mortar towards supporting individuals. It also reflects the ideological bias of Conservative governments in moving from rent control towards market level rents. Action on this front has been easier in some respects, in that the tapers of withdrawal from benefit can be altered for those in work but harder on that action involves co-operation with local authorities, who have not generally been sympathetic to the government's overall objectives.

Treasury officials have a realistic sense of the issues involved here and a grasp of the details of policy:

because he did not trust officials there to do the kind of job that he had in mind. Although the NHS review of 1988–9 was undertaken at No. 10 rather than the Treasury, the first thinking on the education reforms the year before was the responsibility of a Treasury official (Lawson, 1992: 619). This approach reflects the type of lingering suspicion revealed in the internal discussions within the Treasury reported in Chapter 2 and Lawson's personal views (Chapter 3).

Complex service delivery mechanisms

The mechanisms for delivering services in these three fields (and hence for spending public money) that have evolved over the decade since these reforms are extremely complex. A variety of different bodies share responsibility. Some are independent agencies – NDPBs (Non-Departmental Public Bodies), managed by Chief Executives according to the terms of a framework document. Some (Health Trusts) are of intermediate status, governed by directors with responsibilities for budget holding but responsible to the Secretary of State. Some (Training and Enterprise Councils and housing associations) are either commercial bodies or sometimes charities, as universities definitely are. Grant Maintained Schools have a distinct legal identity and separate responsibilities for employing and paying staff but a dependent status; other state schools are responsible to local authorities but have their own budget covering most items in their expenditure.

The patterns of resource flows and subsequent dispersal of accountability are consequently also immensely complex. Many critics identified this consequence of the reforms of the late 1980s as being likely to cause particular difficulty for the Treasury, as the numbers and varieties of 'local public spending bodies' (as defined by the Nolan Committee with a breadth unwelcome to government) proliferated (Weir and Beetham, 1999). The Treasury, like most civil servants, had been alert to the different legal statuses of these different entities, but has now been drawn into the common sense approach of the 1990s of following public money wherever it goes.

In addition, the central responsibility for managing the health service has since 1996 been located outside Whitehall altogether with the NHS Executive, based in Leeds. This is staffed by top-level civil servants but absorbed the functions of the former regional health authorities and so has many staff with health service backgrounds. The executive has to work with the senior officials in

London; the whole structure is held together by a Steering Group in which the Chief Executive of the NHS Executive sits alongside the Permanent Secretary of the department.

Finally, in all cases there is a past history of mutual suspicion between the Treasury and the departments. Treasury stereotypes of the departments' competence run alongside departmental folklore about Treasury mistrust and interference. As seen from both sides, there was much scope for improvement at the time when the Treasury's internal reforms first came into operation.

This approach, as we saw in Chapter 5, has been sustained by a kind of 'ideology of mature relationships' which is particularly appropriate in areas like these where the arguments are not just about money. Under the Labour government, this behaviour has been reinforced by the fact that health (in particular) and education are especially important to Labour and are seen as deserving of trust in a way not found in social security.

In the first phase (1995–7) of the Treasury's reform process, a number of the key issues emerged that were common to all of the policy areas. Some were broad: the question of whether to produce a concordat or strategy documents covering the whole range of the departments' activities. Others were operational issues. These included the way in which capital programmes were addressed and the level at which the Treasury was prepared to authorize delegation of responsibility. Linked to this was the extent of use of the Private Finance Initiative (PFI), the origins and implications of which are explored in Chapter 3. The Treasury's attempt to introduce a regime in which a regular substantive reduction in departmental running costs could be achieved by efficiency savings – a *quid pro quo* for greater local exercise of responsibility – is another example of a general approach with specific local applications.

However, many of the issues pursued by the spending teams were particular to the policy area concerned and to some degree shaped by the personalities of those involved (as in the social security case). An important part of our research was to examine this interaction between policy and personality in the three areas, which we now explore in turn.

The health case

The Treasury's internal view of the Health department has been substantially modified from the profoundly suspicious approach delivery – both for practical reasons and as a matter of principle. At its most threatening, this approach was presented to us as an illegitimate intrusion on the role of Ministers in spending departments; unconstitutional, even. In 1963, W.J.M. Mackenzie's celebrated 'translation' of the Plowden report put it that 'the Departments are in effect operating companies, and the job of their managers is to manage; not to try to act as directors of the holding company' (quoted by Lowe, 1997a: 489). One PFO expressed a similar thought in seeing the Treasury as holding

> a view which I think the rest of British government should stand firmly against, that they see themselves as getting out of the detail and operating at a strategic level across every strategic issue that government faces. They see themselves actually as a holding company for the British government, with a lot of operating companies, being controlled by the 'Hanson head office' who will check them mostly on numbers, but will also have an overall sort of company strategy which will be capable of affecting every aspect of life, and they think they're capable of doing that, and they could not be more wrong, in my view. And a lot of this is covered. If they came out and said, in just exactly the terms I've used now, that that was what they were about, loudly, they would have met with a sort of fierce response, but I do think that is actually what they think they're about, and as I say, it would be disastrous if they were allowed to get away with it. They've got enough power as it is, in my view.

Tendencies in this direction have been obscured, but not checked, by the important priority given to health and education by Labour governments. Real expenditure increases have been accompanied by the mechanisms and rhetoric of Treasury-enforced strategic control.

On the other side, the Treasury would argue that Ministers are perfectly well able to look after themselves. The use by Health Department Ministers of their access to Downing Street to argue the seasonal case for increase in the health budget is a case in point. And the introduction of the EDX procedure meant that departmental ministers had an even better chance to put their case. This did seem to be Labour's experience in 1997–8 when, despite the stronger than ever Treasury steer on the process, education and health ministers were able to advance their case, gain additional resources for their departments and survive or prosper individually in the 1998 reshuffle.

In general, the Treasury was pleased with the improvements in relationships with health, education and housing after the FER. Team leaders were put in place with the ability and sensitivity to understand what had gone wrong in previous years. Although not all the boxes in the 'Perkins grid' (see Chapter 5) of mechanisms and procedures for promoting better relations were filled in – or were likely to be – the general tenor of improved interaction had in many cases obviated the need for them. There is also the perennial concern of the Treasury side with the quality and accessibility of information. Given that this is one of the keystones of the Burns edifice, any failure to secure access in the form that the Treasury believes it needs (and that it is entitled to have) is potentially a serious omission.

After the ideological experiments of the Conservative years – which some in the Treasury bought into and promoted with excessive enthusiasm – relations between them and service deliverers have reverted to a more benign pattern in a way that has not been evident in social security. This is partly the effect of a Labour government, but partly a realistic sense on the Treasury's part that there is no longer-term gain to be secured from starving such important services to death. Provided that additional expenditure can be applied in a non-inflationary way – especially on the pay bill – the case for spending for investment and to avert long-term harm is conceded. Treasury relations with agencies and quangos, and in the health case with the complex structure of an NHS now once again undergoing reform, are causing less concern. It seems that the anxieties of those who felt that the greater complexity of the service delivery map coupled with political pressure to build up the services would make it impossible for the Treasury to deal efficiently with the outputs of the new system have so far proved unfounded.

to reduce the gaps but not eliminate them entirely. There seems to be a structural element of spending advantage, favouring Scotland and Northern Ireland more than Wales, that makes the Treasury combative and the territorial departments defensive.

The past two decades have seen a growth in these Treasury reservations about the position of Scotland, bound up with Scotland's transformation from an economically weak part of the United Kingdom into a nation with at least average income and wealth. The attraction to several Whitehall officials of transfer to the new Scottish administration when it was taking on new staff in 1999 was a testament to this. As put to us in a striking passage by one senior Treasury official:

> Personally, I think that Scotland in particular is massively over-provided in terms of any possible objective assessment of its relative needs, but that's just a personal point of view, and it wasn't really desperately relevant in terms of the formula because there was no predisposition to look at the formula. Personally I feel that at some point it may be that it ought to be addressed, at least in relation to Scotland. Expenditure per head is 35 per cent higher than England. That's extraordinary when you think about it. Scotland's GDP per head is higher than the UK average. Its unemployment rate is lower and yet its public spending is 35 per cent higher – I'm talking about the programmes that the Secretary of State controls – leave aside social security where you'd expect it to be mainly the same. Now I think you have to ask yourself 'why?' That may have been entirely understandable when Scotland was a basket case, you know, the beginning of the seventies, relatively high unemployment, declining industry in Scotland. It's not like that now, so why do we go on giving them all this extra money?

The point to emphasize here is that policy remains driven by ministers, and that the Treasury would acknowledge that the present intellectually unsatisfactory relativities might be a necessary price of the stability of the United Kingdom. For different reasons, Conservative and Labour ministers have chosen to preserve the formula, which does not exclude eventual equalization on the basis of need but ensures that it would be achieved only slowly. The decision in 1997 to preserve it after devolution means that changing it would involve a political negotiation between levels of government. Should change become possible, the official Treasury can be expected to lead the assault with a fair degree of gusto.

The impact of devolution

The formula system was conceived with devolution in mind, but the prospect of the policy being carried through by the Labour Party in the 1990s if anything undermined the formula. This was because its lack of dynamism seemed to threaten the entrenchment of privilege, and the transformation of what started as a flexible civil service arrangement into a legal right. Hence there were attempts to sharpen the impact of the formula: the 1992 adjustment, greater Treasury scrutiny of non-block items, and evidence that convergence was beginning to bite. An associated theme was the 'English backlash' as Labour MPs showed the fragility of party solidarity by drawing an association between Scottish 'overspending' and any lack of money for projects in their areas: this prompted the Treasury Select Committee investigation of 1997.

Labour's devolution policy had to be put together very rapidly in order to have sufficient detail in the White Papers to allow the policy to be put to a referendum. The Scottish White Paper was further constrained by a manifesto declaration that it would be 'firmly based' on the report of the Scottish Constitutional Convention, a multi-party but imperfectly drafted document. The White Papers embodied a victory for the Scottish and Welsh Offices by generally opting for a maximalist approach to devolution. They preserved and endorsed the Barnett formula; and more importantly built in some uncontrollability to the expenditure of the devolved administrations by not putting an explicit cap on local authority self-financed expenditure. This will be outside the assigned budget (the new name of the Block, and bigger as it is to include non-EU funded (domestic) agriculture, forestry and nationalized industries), but not outside the planning total. Therefore the resources available to the Parliament could in principle be increased by cutting local authority grants and forcing up council tax (most neatly by increasing the ratio between higher and lower valuation bands). The control problems this poses were addressed in some exquisite phrasing in the Scottish White Paper:

> Should self-financed expenditure start to rise steeply, from council tax payers in Scotland to exercise its [capping] powers. If growth

bank fixes interest rates and reassures the markets, leaving the finance ministry politicians less exposed. For spending on social policy, the implications of this style were worrying, as it united a traditional approach of the Treasury to the style of the Brown team to use the authority of the office and the confidence of the Prime Minister (signalled by his allowing Brown to chair the Cabinet's Economic Affairs Committee as well as the Public Expenditure Committee) to drive through policy.

The government was fortified by its attempt to demonstrate greater 'transparency' in economic policy making. One example was the reference of the assumptions behind their predecessors' spending plans to the National Audit Office. Their report issued on 19 June (National Audit Office, 1997) gave only limited support to any assertion that the Conservative spending plans were based on unsound economic assumptions. The NAO had not previously been equipped for this role and it did not confirm suggestions of a 'fiscal black hole'. It is now to 'have a continuing role in auditing the public finances in future Budgets' (HM Treasury, 1997b: para. 1.28). This role was confirmed in the 'Code of Fiscal Stability' entrenched in legislation in 1998.

Internally, the process of adaptation to the incoming regime and a new team of ministers was presented to the outside world by the Treasury's permanent secretary as an exceptionally smooth one. As expressed by Terry Burns in his 1997 lecture,

> clearly . . . the speed with which the agenda has been advanced owes much to careful planning by the Labour Party in preparation for government. The new government took office not just with an agenda but with detailed proposals for the timetable and the policies. In turn, we were able to play our part because of our own detailed contingency planning and improvements in our organisation on which we had been working: a more managerial, flexible, consultative and task-oriented culture. (Burns, 1997)

Burns presented the interest rate transfer as a necessarily secretive operation for which the Treasury had done some hypothetical advance thinking, but here and especially in his interview during the Scottish Television documentary of October 1997 he seemed to display some discomfort at the Brown style. It was no surprise when Burns retired in June 1998, to a life peerage and praise from Brown so effusive as to hint at insincerity.

The heavily-trailed intention was said to be to use the first

Table 9.3 'Welfare-to-work' measures

£m July 97 (March 98) estimates	Peak annual expend.	Total expend. 1997–2002
£60 per week to employers for 6 months for taking on a 16–25-year-old out of work for more than six months + £750 for training	830 (650)	3150 (2620)
£75 per week employer subsidy for 6 months for those out of work for more than two years	100 (160)	350 (450)
Advice, training, day and after school care for lone parents; childcare cost relief for lone parents on in-work benefits increased from £60 to £100 per week and age limit from 11 to 12	60	200
Help for disabled and those on incapacity benefit		200

Sources: HM Treasury (1997c: table 2.1) and HM Treasury (1998a: table 3.1).

Labour Budget to launch the process of overhauling the entire welfare state. In practice, the 'modernisation of welfare' (to use the Treasury's own description) turned out to consist principally of the promised 'welfare-to-work' strategy, the attempt to provide jobs or training places for the young and long-term unemployed through income hypothecated from a 'windfall tax' on privatized utilities. For a Labour policy this did bear the impact of the workfare tendencies of the Conservatives. For those unemployed for six months, the age of majority for a right to income maintenance was in effect raised from 18 to 25. 25 corresponds to nothing; it is way above the age at which education will normally have been completed and family and housing responsibilities may have been taken on. Hardship cases were defined narrowly, and receive only 60 per cent of the benefit level.

While the benefit restrictions are under the government's control, the provision of jobs or training places relies on the private and voluntary sectors – especially through the diversion of public money to employers to take on the young or long-term unemployed. While the intentions have won wide support, the instruments (summarized in Table 9.3) are less secure. The dangers that this approach

Table 10.1   Labour social expenditure plans in real terms

£ billion (1997–8 prices)	Conservative overhang			Labour's own plans		
	1997–8	1998–9	1999–2000	2000–01	2001–02	Change
Education and employment	14.7	13.8	14.7	16.0	16.8	+14.2
Health	35.3	36.1	38.1	39.9	41.5	+17.6
Social security	94.4	95.6	98.4	98.4	101.2	+5.9
Education (total)	36.2	37.1	39.0	41.3	43.1	+19.1
DEPARTMENTAL EXPENDITURE LIMITS	162.7	164.0	169.7	175.6	180.5	+10.9
ANNUALLY MANAGED EXPENDITURE	157.1	160.2	163.3	166.3	170.8	+8.7
TOTAL MANAGED EXPENDITURE	319.8	324.2	333.0	341.9	351.3	+9.8
as % GDP	40.1	40.0	40.3	40.5	40.7	

Note: Social security (benefits) not published in real terms, estimated from deflator for total managed expenditure

Source: calculated from HM Treasury (1998g: tables 2 and A3).

security was the main contributor, offering a £1.5 billion underspend in 1998–9 (just four months after the previous estimate). This enabled Brown to offer another winter sweetener of £250 million to the NHS as part of an unsystematic ragbag of a speech that announced further refinement of tax and contribution thresholds. The Treasury's own social policy was moving forward.

As far as the Treasury itself was concerned, the CSR report had nothing to say on its future organizational shape or whether the cuts associated with the FER had finally been superseded by a tooling-up for new responsibilities. There was talk of continued efficiency improvements (HM Treasury, 1998g: para. 25.9) but staffing had started to move up again – from 954 in 1996–7 to 964 in 1997–8 and a planned 985 in 1998–9 (HM Treasury, 1998d: table 1B). Total Treasury expenditure (of which only about one-third are running costs) for 1998–9 was planned at £164 million in April but had risen to £170 million (HM Treasury, 1998g: table 25.1). These data are difficult to interpret consistently because of transfers of functions (for instance, the Treasury is taking on the insurance responsibilities from the Department of Trade and Industry), but they do suggest that the hair-shirt years are over. One sign of this was that the Deputy Director position in Spending that became vacant in early 1998 and seemed ripe for abolition was filled. Another is that the planned PFI-financed refurbishment of the Treasury building in Great George Street, which would have involved a temporary relocation away from Whitehall, was put on the back-burner, to re-emerge in autumn 1998 as a more modest project that would be completed while shuffling staff around the building.

Emerging from the welfare reform exercise

Social security remained under review after the CSR report, partly to accommodate the period of consultation promised in the field Green Paper. The new Secretary of State, Alistair Darling, brought over from the Treasury his sure touch and sense of focus. After various leaks that disability and widows' pensions were being targeted, the announcement on 28 October 1998 (Department of Social Security, 1998b) was of mainly medium-term significance. The means-testing of widows' pensions for those of working age was another sign that Beveridgean contributory principles were now of very little salience. The main innovation was of a compulsory 'single work-focused gateway' interview for all new benefit claimants of working age. Consultation was launched on new tests of employability to replace the 'all-work' disability test. Incapacity Benefit was to require a recent national insurance contribution record, and to become means-tested for those in receipt of occupational pension benefits.

Much more significant in expenditure terms was the Government's announcement of its policy direction for pensions in a Green Paper on 15 December 1998 (Department of Social Security, 1998c). Press reports over the summer and autumn suggested that the Treasury had 'seized control' of the review and ruled out compulsory coverage of stakeholder pensions for the same reasons as in 1985 (the alleged burdens on business and the taxpayer). The outcome was a victory for Treasury-friendly themes. SERPS was to be replaced by a flat-rate State Second Pension, also pay-as-you-go but confined to low earners (under £9000 a year), with credit for carers. A new brand of stakeholder pensions was to be given fairly modest fiscal encouragement but only for the next bracket up to around average earnings, and a structure more in line with savings vehicles than traditional pension funds. No one was to be compelled to take out a personal pension. The notion that a significant minority of the workforce might enter old age without earnings-related provision was entrenched into social security policy.

the downsizing of the Treasury – its own decision, matching the similar downsizing it was forcing on other departments – can also be seen as the last stage of a rebellion among other ministers to cut its influence, non-financial as well as financial ... it might be thought that politicians considering their 'political' and other short-term interests might welcome this development, but as well as the difficulties for financial control predicted in Chapter 10, a serious risk is that a consequence will be a further declined in policy co-ordination and in the efficiency and economy with which business is conducted. (Foster and Plowden, 1996: 237)

Our evidence is that the post-FER Treasury quite consciously withdrew from detailed control of the new self-regulating networks and did not become a victim of them. Far from downsizing itself psychologically, it remained ready to take on the new policy challenges set it by a Chancellor with an explicit social policy agenda and a strong sense of turf; it had won the contest for control of welfare strategy. The Treasury could still be arrogant and bounce departments around, but it had developed a better sense of collegial behaviour; its 'village' was more open to outside influence. It had convinced itself that it had ironed out past snags in its relations with departments and was exercising the proactive role in which the Chancellor was casting it in constructive ways – a belief generally supported by anecdotal evidence from spending departments. By 1999 the Treasury was no longer starving itself in terms of running costs, and was adapting the management prescriptions of the FER rather more sensibly. In sum, the assumption that it would be dangerous to feed its power could be in need of questioning.

Over the years, attempts to constrain the Treasury and promote countervailing forces have never quite worked, because the financial nexus of government that has the capacity to drive everything else can only be in one place. The alternative with which we are left is the strengthening of the Treasury as the only centre of power where social policies can be effectively related to the overriding economic strategy of the government. Our research, and the experience of Labour's first two years, leads us to think that there is a good argument for fitting-out the Treasury to exercise in a more systematic and informed way the hegemony that it is in any case in the process of grasping.

Bibliography

Bailey, A. (1997) 'The Spending Department Perspective', in D. Corry (ed.), *Public Expenditure: Effective Management and Control*. London: The Dryden Press.

Barnett, C. (1986) *The Audit of War*. London: Macmillan.

Barnett, J. (1982) *Inside the Treasury*. London: Andre Deutsch.

Beer, S. (1956) *Treasury Control*. Oxford: Clarendon Press.

Bridges, Lord (1964) *The Treasury*. London: George Allen and Unwin.

Brittan, S. (1971) *Steering the Economy*. London: Penguin.

Brittan, S. (1996) *Capitalism with a Human Face*. London: Fontana Press.

Brown, G. and Cook, R. (1983) *Scotland: the Real Divide*. Edinburgh: Mainstream.

Brown, G. (1996) *The Treasury's Mission under Labour*, speech at the Manchester Business School, 29 April.

Brown, G. (1997) *Responsibility and Public Finance*, speech, 20 January.

Bruce-Gardyne, J. (1986) *Ministers and Mandarins*. London: Sidgwick & Jackson.

Burns, Sir T. (1994a) 'Change and the Treasury' (Lecture at Durham University, 27 April).

Burns, Sir T. (1994b) 'Some Reflections on the Treasury', in S. Holly (ed.), *Money, Inflation and Employment: Essays in Honour of James Ball*. Cheltenham: Edward Elgar.

Burns, Sir T. (1995) 'The Management of Economic Policy' (Eleanor Rathbone Memorial Lecture, University of Manchester, 28 March).

Burns, Sir T. (1997) *Preparing the Treasury for the Election* (Frank Stacy Memorial Lecture, Civil Service College, 1 September).

Cabinet Office (1996) *Competing for Quality Policy Review*. London: The Stationery Office.

Cabinet Office (1999) *Modernising Government*, Cm 4310. London: The Stationery Office.

Cairncross, A. and Watts, N. (1989) *The Economic Section 1939–1961*. London: Routledge.

Cairncross, A. (ed.) (1989) *The Robert Hall Diaries 1947–1953*. London: Unwin Hyman.

Cairncross, A. (1997) *The Wilson Years: A Treasury Diary 1964–69*. London: The Historians' Press.

Castle, B. (1980) *The Castle Diaries 1974–76*. London: Weidenfeld & Nicolson.

Caulcott, T. (1996) *Management and the Politics of Power: Central and Local Government Compared*. London: LGC Communications.

Chapman, R. (1997) *The Treasury in Public Policymaking*. London: Routledge.

Clarke, Sir R. (1971) *New Directions in Government*. London: HMSO.

Clarke, Sir R. (1978) *Public Expenditure: Management and Control*. London: Macmillan.

Corry, D. (ed.) (1997) *Public Expenditure: Effective Management and Control*. London: The Dryden Press.

of political support, labour, land, equipment and finance. The *initiation* of policy-making commences with the receipt of these demands, and the generation of alternative policy proposals to deal with them. The *formulation* of policy involves a choice of between these policy alternatives and the condensing of the policy into a set of specific proposals for action. The *implementation* of the chosen policy involves the carrying out of those proposals.[2]

Such a simple model of the policy process inevitably omits a great deal that is important. To begin with, government is active, not passive; in many ways it can act to develop the resources with which it works (e.g. by investment in productive enterprises), and through access to the media and party organizations it can also create demands for action. Second, policy is not a simple process but a complex one, in which problems, dealt with by different agencies, are 'factored'; that is, divided up for the convenience of the organization. We shall return to this question in a moment. Third, a policy does not, or at least should not, end when a choice of policy has been made. There is no certainty that it will actually be carried out unless the policy-maker to seek information on the consequences and evaluates them with a view to guiding future policy decisions. The people who carry out decisions are seldom those who make policy. Some of the desired consequences may not have been achieved and some of the actual consequences may be quite unintended. The *evaluation* of policy outcomes, therefore, is an integral part of what essentially is a public learning process. We, in turn, have to evaluate the evaluators, and we do this by examining three themes; who decides, what gets done and who benefits.[3]

Primarily we are concerned with who decides. Ideally, as Plato was the first to observe, decision-makers should be omniscient. Yet decisions have to be made by human beings, and human beings are the product of their personal environment. Though, as we shall see, decisions and actions in foreign policy are not always based on a full and accurate perception of the situation, they must inevitably be based on at least a superficial understanding of their state and its position in the world. Every child is brought up with an idea of its position in the world, and the mature citizen derives from this

People's Republic of China was accorded, Taiwan ceased to be regarded as a valid international entity.

In the according of recognition, as in all other matters, the international system recognizes that some states are practically if not in legal theory, more powerful and more influential than others. The old European state system explicitly recognized a hierarchy of great powers, middle powers and minor powers; something of this has been formally embedded in the structure of the United Nations, where a veto was given to the five permanent members of the Security Council (China, France, the USSR, the United Kingdom and the United States), but no one seriously doubts that, formal equality notwithstanding, the world of today is dominated by the superpowers, while even the United Nations has been unable to stretch the principle of equality to accept the 'microstates' as full and equal members. The states of today continue to use a regular system of communications and decide disputes from time to time in accordance with a system of international law which originated in the same European state system. Lastly, they recognize that in the anarchical world of the international system, security is of prime importance, and that this traditionally has been assured by maintaining the 'balance of power' so that no one state can become too powerful and so achieve hegemony over all the others. Though the balance of power concept cannot work properly for the whole world system in the circumstances of a bipolar world dominated by only two superpowers, it does continue to work at a regional level, and it still therefore forms part of the mental furniture of the diplomat from a new state when he begins to take part in the wider sphere of international politics, for which neither the history of his country nor his own personal experience is likely to have adequately prepared him.

To understand what he is then likely to do, we must seek first of all to understand the nature of the politics of new states. The politics of the nation-state is in all respects but one comparable with politics on any other level on which politics may be observed: the family the organization, the tribe. The processes that go on are very similar, and these smaller organizations may well be regarded as sub-sets of the state as a whole, or, to use the terminology now commonly employed, they may be following the Second World War by the framers of the charter of the United Nations. To the extent to which the United Nations charter has received the agreement of member states, it constitutes the foundation of modern international law, but only insofar as it specifically supersedes the existing complex structure of bilateral and multilateral agreements, and it is by no means certain, given the many ambiguities in the charter—some of them deliberate—that decisions of the United Nations General Assembly or Security Council form legislation in the traditional sense that that word is understood in a domestic political context.[24]

Before the move that led to the creation of first the League and then the United Nations, many scholars and statesmen had argued that the solution to the problems of international order were to be sought less in the strengthening of the structure of international law than in the provision of a judiciary capable of interpreting it. This legalistic view found enthusiastic advocates in the United States, and the establishment of the Central American Court in 1907 was a landmark in the move towards the establishment of international courts capable of settling disputes.[25] The principle that international law should be supplemented not only with legislature but also a judiciary was carried forward into the structures both of the League and of the United Nations, and signing the charter of the United Nations obliges a country to become a party to the statute of the International Court of Justice at The Hague, commonly known as the World Court, founded in 1945 to replace the League's Permanent Court of International Justice (1921).[26]

The problem with the judicial approach to international law remains a fundamental one, namely the assumption of the sovereignty of states. This implies that states cannot be called to account except with their own agreement, and, not surprisingly, they therefore do not agree to be called to account. In consequence, not only have many important and obviously justiciable cases not been taken to the World Court, for example Argentina's claim to South Georgia and the South Sandwich Islands (1948), which Britain offered to adjudicate, but the decisions of those that have (e.g. Argentina's claim to the Beagle Channel Islands held by Chile), have not always been accepted. When this occurs the failure of the process calls degree of continuity may well be given from the fact that the bureaucratic structure tends to stay very similar despite such transitions. Whether a government is military or civilian, the civil service remains in office dealing with the day-to-day routine. This, of course, includes that specialized part of it which is concerned with the administration of diplomacy, with which I shall deal separately in Chapter 4.

GOVERNMENTAL STRUCTURES

Governments generally have more freedom in the making of foreign policy than in most areas, but this is not to say that they do not have important differences between them, the most obvious and most important difference being due to the role of the head of state. In most modern states the head of state is termed a 'president', and the government over which he presides is republican; that is to say, it is a government in which at least in theory every citizen may take part. But the term 'president' is somewhat deceptive. There are two types of presidents. In Europe presidents are characteristically individuals who serve the functions formerly assumed by limited monarchs; they play a purely ceremonial role and act as heads of state not not as head of government, this latter function being devolved to a prime minister. In most of the rest of the world the head of state and head of government are combined in one person, who is an executive president, with power to appoint and to dismiss officials, to operate the administration, to take command of the armed forces, and so on. Though presidential government in this sense does not always bear a very close relationship to its type example, that of the United States, it has many of the powers which we attribute to that system, and its peculiar nature is immediately evident when we consider three aspects that are of major significance for the making of foreign policy.[5]

Where the offices of head of state and head of government are combined, ambassadors, who are invariably accredited to a head of state, enjoy direct access to the individual who is the key policy-maker.[6] Conversely, the making of foreign policy is a constitutional as well as an actual responsibility of that same either the secular authority or the religious one. But certainly in the new states of the twentieth century, and particularly those that have become independent since 1945, the press, radio and television seldom if ever, function as neutral transmitters or information. This is hardly surprising, since it is now well recognized by social scientists that they do not perform this role in the sense always assumed by pluralist thinkers. By virtue of the way in which they transmit information, the media put their own particular interpretation upon it, and it is the information plus the interpretation which reaches the hearer.[40] Moreover, in the majority of the new states, the low level of tolerance that governments demonstrate towards criticism, as manifested in most of the southern African states, including such diverse countries as Malawi, Tanzania and Zimbabwe, have led them to introduce, or to seek to introduce, a one-party state, in which the media form part of the apparatus of social control. By working on behalf of the government to transmit only that view which the government wishes its subjects to receive, the media therefore perform a role in creating the public opinion which is totally dependent upon that of the ruling authorities, and in no way forms separate independent force. Nor, given the ready accessibility in particular of radio and television, is it any more necessary to have a specialist intellectual background to interpret the information, so that no role is left open for independent thought within the system as it exists.

Despite this, the very fact that governments have to rely on others to man and operate the media system means that they must to some extent depend upon technicians who are capable of diverging from their own point of view. And the ability of members of the élite closest to the government to form their own impressions of what is going on, through personal or family channels, means that they too may well form impressions which diverge from those that the government would wish to propagate. It is this rather specialised form of public opinion which can, and in certain circumstances does, act to convey its views to those actually holding political power. While it is not public opinion in the sense in which the term has been generally accepted, élite public opinion does form, to some extent a corrective to the views of the

the reaction of the United States, and here there is detailed evidence that the failure was due to a lack of systematic information and understanding about the American political process and not simply due to failure to accept unwelcome ideas. As Moneta puts it:

On the other hand, the 'surprise' of the military government at what it considered to be a 'betrayal' on the part of the U.S. government appears to be the result of: (1) Assumptions as to implicit commitments contracted by the United States vis à vis the regime, in exchange for the collaboration provided by the latter in Central America and on obligations stemming from the Tratado Interamericano de Asistencia Reciproca (TIAR); and (2) Contacts and conversations that might have referred to these matters indirectly and that took place with eminent high-ranking military and civilian personages in the Reagan Administration (among others Ambassador Jeane Kirkpatrick and the under secretary for Latin American affairs, Thomas Enders). It is a fact, for example, that with the exception of a limited group of members of Congress, practically no feelers were put out or approaches made to the legislature. On the other hand, a large number of the contacts made by the Argentine military diplomats in Washington were with persons belonging to the so-called South African lobby.[25]

Moneta ascribes the ultimate mistake in going ahead with the Malvinas campaign in Argentina less to the Foreign Ministry's failure to supply information than the military government's tendency to disregard it, but there is clearly here enough evidence to suggest that this in itself was the product of a lack of systematic reporting. If such a serious mistake can be made in a matter of such transcendental importance, it can be assumed that a lack of systematic reporting is very widespread in Third World countries.

Defective, or at least deficient records systems are a natural concomitant of irregular reporting. As anyone who has done first-hand research in Third World archives will be aware, the conditions can be very difficult indeed. Records are frequently inadequately catalogued, and in the worse cases they may in fact be simply rolled up in bundles and consigned to a storeroom, the access to which is known only to an aged retainer who has worked there all his life.

I have said that, in new states, by definition, there are no diplomatic records dating from before independence. The sole exception to this will be those informal records maintained by an insurgent movement fighting for the liberation of the state helped hasten the collapse of the Ghanaian economy and create the conditions for the military coup which overthrew Nkrumah in 1966.[26] His successors, seeking to renew the process of development, have not enjoyed his advantages, either of a high price for cocoa or of the enthusiasm of the early years of independence.

Moreover, the pattern of communications has been totally transformed since 1945 by the perfection of air transport. Today for the first time, for example, there is quick direct communication between the Amazonian provinces of Peru, centred on the town of Iquitos built at the highest point to which seagoing vessels could attain, and the national capital Lima, on the foothills of the Andes. This has important political consequences. It guarantees that the Peruvian government (like the Bolivian, Brazilian, Colombian and Venezuelan governments) can exercise control in the Amazonian provinces which in the past were dangerously remote and a prey to other powers. In the high Andes, as in the disputed areas of the Himalayas and Kashmir, the construction of roads has come relatively late, and some areas have until the 1960s been effectively beyond the reach of the central government. This no longer is the case. Secondly, this network of control, the air transport of the region, is kept firmly in the hands of the military, which is therefore crucial to the administration of large areas of national territory even under a nominally civilian government. Last but not least, this development of military technology has to some extent leapt ahead of the economically valuable networks of communication and formed its own system of control. The need to create economically rather than militarily valuable communications is correspondingly downgraded. The tendency in fact in general for Third World élites to undervalue economically useful but technologically unspectacular transportation systems is accentuated by the fact that the political élites of the Third World tend themselves to be urbanized, and to view transport as a matter of carrying passengers rather than freight. Though air transport can undoubtedly be of great value in rushing vegetables and fruit to market over long distances—daffodils from the Channel Islands, tomatoes from Spain, avocados from Israel and even high value industrial products of light

territory occupied by non-European populations was accompanied by the belief that these populations were unable to
govern themselves, and followed by the spread, on a systematic
basis, of the Crown Colony system. The effect of this, as in the
West Indies, was actually to reduce the amount of participa-
tion open even to settlers, though for the other part it did
represent an improvement on direct naval command, as in the
case of the islands of the South Atlantic.[8] Not surprisingly, a
tradition of resentment was established; sometimes there were
revolts and those revolts were suppressed. Despite the spread
of democracy at home, the colonies were administered in an
increasingly authoritarian manner by civil servants operating
under the general oversight of a minister who was certainly not
responsible to the colonists.

In order to obtain independence, then, a powerful social
movement had to be generated among the inhabitants of the
colonies. Sometimes, as in the case of Kenya where it was
regarded as a reversion to barbarism instead of an advance to
self-determination, the independence movement was not
successful. There independence came in the end as part of the
general move towards self-government in the world through
the United Nations.[9] In other cases, it was resisted to a greater
or lesser degree. The extent and duration of this resistance
varied according to external rather than internal factors; the
intrinsic strength of the metropolitan state, the extent of its
colonial commitments, pressure from allies and tactical
considerations all playing a part. Thus France and Britain were
better able to resist pressures for independence than the
Netherlands and Belgium, but France conceded independence
to Tunisia to concentrate on retaining Algeria, while Britain,
having conceded independence to many other states, lingered
too long in Aden because of its historical importance as a way-
station to colonies that had long since gone their own way.
Hence it was forced in the end into an almost humiliating
retreat from a state (South Yemen) which immediately
proclaimed its Marxist affinities. And Belgium sought to make
a rapid handover of power in Zaire, while Portugal with little
more military power at its disposal fought tenaciously for
eleven years to retain its entire empire.[10]

The course of independence is the main factor determining
the nature of the immediate post-colonial leadership, since the

neighbours in 1948–49, mounted attacks in return on Egypt in 1956 and on Egypt and Syria in 1967. Apparently surprised by the Yom Kippur War of 1973, now a classic instance of the sort of 'intelligence failure' which for most new states would be unavoidable, it was able to hold its gains of 1967 against the combined pressures of the majority of members of the United Nations, not least because it was apparent that in the last resort no one but the superpowers had the capacity to force it to do otherwise. On the other hand, deployment of the Israeli army in an offensive role in the occupation of Southern Lebanon in 1982 proved a political disaster, destroying the last vestiges of central authority in Lebanon and bringing the Syrians in as the dominant external influence. The strength of the Israeli army, its deep attachment to its own territory, turned to a liability when fighting on foreign soil, and as so often in history, it proved impossible to impose a political settlement by military force.[45]

Other research has suggested that there is a tendency for richer countries to more belligerent than poorer ones.[46] The tendency, if it exists, is however a weak one, and some of the world's poorest states have plunged into war: Ethiopia and Somalia in the Horn of Africa over the disputed territory of the Ogaden; Tanzania in Uganda to overthrow the regime of General Amin; Mauritania in the Western Sahara; Honduras in 1969 against El Salvador (the 'Football War') and, more recently, in conjunction with the United States against Nicaragua.[47] The form of government of the states concerned does not appear to be very significant either, especially given that it is sometimes a very subjective judgement into which category a state falls. It is perhaps merely an impression that whereas democratic states find it harder to go to war than dictatorships, they also find it harder to make peace. But the longer experience of the Latin American states offers serious grounds to doubt that military governments are more likely to go to war than civilian ones; indeed, the rhetoric and heedless belligerence of civilian governments in Bolivia were mainly responsible for Latin America's biggest foreign war of the twentieth century, the Chaco War between Paraguay and Bolivia (1932–37).[48] As we have already seen in Chapter 2, moreover, small states may be more belligerent if they believe

This is ironic, since it implies it has little alternative to reacting to events rather than guiding them. Most writing on international relations assumes that a country will, in the manner of the great powers, seek to make use of its power positively, to achieve desired changes in the international environment. Among those who see international politics as being primarily about use of power, two specialized uses have attracted particular attention. For some, the principal purpose of the use of state power is to create a secure environment by a balance-of-power strategy.[12] This strategy assumes that there are a number of states of roughly comparable capacity, and that the formation of rival alliances between them, roughly equal in strength, will maintain this stable relationship, as long as states have the freedom to cross from one alliance to the other. In a bipolar world dominated by two superpowers, the lesser states are locked into a position in which there is no freedom for them to move in this way, and it is doubtful indeed if their weight would be sufficient to make any appreciable difference. Traditional balance-of-power strategy, therefore, no longer operates even among the medium-sized powers. In the case of Third World states, it may operate, but only on a narrow regional basis. Again, the case of South America is the most striking example in which traditional balance-of-power politics can still operate, though it has to be said that in the age of the Cold War it can only do so in a somewhat modified fashion.

This, however, does not mean that states will not continue to strive to attain, or, in the case of ex-colonies formerly part of powerful empires, return to a situation in which they can influence events by shifting their allegiances. Nor, unfortunately, does it follow that the superpowers will not act to preclude them. Afghanistan is an obvious example, given that the Soviet Union has defended its intervention there by claiming that it was at risk from Western subversion. But Afghanistan, it seems, also demonstrates that even in the ranks of the superpower policy-makers there are also still to be found adherents of the rival, geopolitical school of interpretation.[13] If so, this is bad news for the Third World states most likely to attract their continued interest and attention.

It is the contention here that the importance of these views of

12. Mark A. Thompson, *The Secretaries of State, 1681–1782* (Oxford: Clarendon Press, 1932), esp. pp. 1–5.
13. These residual functions of the United States secretary of state include custody of the Great Seal of the United States, countersigning certain official papers, keeping records including those of foreign relations, serving as a channel of communication between the federal and state governments in overseas extradition proceedings, and receiving the resignation of the president and vice-president. Many other functions were transferred to other departments at various dates between 1812 and 1950, after which the secretary of state has been essentially a minister of foreign affairs. See Plischke, pp. 170–1.
14. DeConde, p. 157.
15. Barros, 'Formulation of Brazilian Foreign Policy'; Alvaro Lins, *Rio-Branco (O Barão do Rio-Branco)* (São Paulo: Companhia Editorial Nacional, 1965); Frank D. McCann, Jr, *The Brazilian-American Alliance, 1937–1945* (Princeton, NJ: Princeton University Press, 1974).
16. Joseph S. Tulchin, 'Authoritarian Regimes and Foreign Policy: The Case of Argentina', in Muñoz and Tulchin (eds.), p. 191.
17. Edward S. Milenky, *Argentina's Foreign Policies* (Boulder, Col.: Westview Press, 1978), pp. 81–3.
18. Satow, pp. 119–21.
19. Carolyn McMaster, *Malawi—Foreign Policy and Development* (Devizes, Wilts.: Davison, 1974), pp. 27–8.
20. *Ibid.*, pp. 44–5.
21. Joseph Wayas, *Nigeria's Leadership Role in Africa* (London: Macmillan, 1979), pp. 28 ff.; Mazrui, *Africa's International Relations*, pp. 41 ff.
22. John Kenneth Galbraith, *A Life in Our Times: Memoirs* (London: André Deutsch, 1981), p. 391.
23. India was a member of the League of Nations and from 1945 to 1947 it was a member of the United Nations before independence was formally accorded.
24. Carlos J. Moneta, 'The Malvinas Conflict: Analysing the Argentine Military Regime's Decision-Making Process', in Muñoz and Tulchin (eds.), pp. 119–32.
25. *Ibid.*
26. Peter Calvert, *The Mexican Revolution, 1910–1914: The Diplomacy of Anglo-American Conflict* (Cambridge: Cambridge University Press, 1968), e.g. at pp. 182–5.
27. The tangled history of early Guiana is outlined in James Rodway, *Guiana: British, Dutch and French* (London: T. Fisher Unwin, 1902). On Belize, see, *inter alia*, D.A.G. Waddell, *British Honduras: A Historical and Contemporary Summary* (London: Oxford University Press for Royal Institute of International Affairs, 1961); C.H. Grant, *The Making of Modern Belize* (Cambridge: Cambridge University Press, 1976); O. Nigel Bolland, *The Formation of a Colonial Society* (Baltimore, Md.: Johns Hopkins Press, 1977); R.A. Humphreys, *The Diplomatic History of British Honduras, 1638–1901* (London: Oxford University Press for Royal Institute of International Affairs, 1961), p. 79.

Guardian, The

Guelke, Adrian, 'International legitimacy, self-determination and Northern Ireland', *Review of International Studies*, 11, No. 1, January 1985, pp. 37–52

Gutteridge, William, *Military Institutions and Power in the New States,* New York: Praeger, 1965

Haas, Ernst B., *Beyond the Nation State: Functionalism and International Organization*, Stanford, Cal.: Stanford University Press, 1965

Haas, Michael, 'Societal approaches to the study of war', *Journal of Peace Research*, 4, 1965, pp. 307–23

Haig, Alexander M., Jr., *Caveat: Realism, Reagan, and Foreign Policy*, London: Weidenfeld & Nicholson, 1984

Hall, D.G.E., *A History of South East Asia*, New York: St. Martin's Press, 3rd edn., 168

Halliday, Fred, *The Making of the Second Cold War*, London: Verso, 1984

Halliday, Fred, *Iran: Dictatorship and Development*, Harmondsworth: Penguin Books, 1979

Hanson, J.L., *Monetary Theory and Practice*, London: Macdonald and Evans, 5th edn., 1974

Hargreaves, John D., *West Africa Partitioned: Volume I, The Loaded Pause, 1885–1889*, London: Macmillan, 1974

Harr, John Ensor, *The Professional Diplomat*, Princeton: Princeton University Press, 1969

Hatch, John, *Two African Statesmen: Kaunda of Zambia and Nyerere of Tanzania*, London: Secker & Warburg, 1976

Hayden, Ralston, *The Senate and Treaties, 1789, 1817; The Development of the Treaty-making Functions of the United States Senate during their Formative Period*, New York: The Macmillan Co., 1920

Hayter, Teresa, *The Creation of World Poverty*, London: Pluto Press

Heale, M.J., *The Making of American Politics,* London: Longman, 1977

Herman, Valentine, and Lodge, Juliet, *The European Parliament and the European Community*, London: Macmillan, 1978

Herz, John H., *International Politics in the Nuclear Age*, New York: Columbia University Press, 1959

Herzog, Arthur, *The War-Peace Establishment*, New York: Harper & Row, 1963

Hirsch, Fred, *The Social Limits of Growth,* London: Routledge, 1977

Holsti, K.J., *International Politics: a framework for analysis,*

Winter Wood

Coldest night this year, I walk the wood
At midnight in the warmth of singing blood,
Having drawn the curtains of my window
And seen the moon on violet-tinted snow.

No one else is out in all this land
Where silver birches doubly silvered stand
And oaks grown rowan-delicate unfurl
A winter blossoming of lace and pearl.

Puddles wheeze and blanch beneath my tread
But do not break; the branches overhead
Let crystal dust drift downward as I go
Through bracken fleece and brambles tyred with snow.

Stars burn greenly in the slate-black air.
Fox and badger do not leave their lair.
Cold is this kingdom, marvellous its light.
Nothing else will cross my track tonight.

Blooding

Coming back in late September twilight
After a good day out, the children singing,
A full moon yellow in the east and sunset
Dulling in the west above the cornfields,
We came on something in the quiet road:
A hare, run over, left to die, back legs
Smashed quite flat: a stuck moth, fluttering,
And yet not dead, but panicking wild-eyed,
Arching in the dazzle, pushing up
On boxer's shoulders, falling, pushing up.
No one spoke. My children looked and waited.
Me? What competence had I in death?
I started off to let the car roll forward,
All set to do it in the modern way,
A filthy casual obliteration,
And could not: took a spanner and knelt down
Saying words. The great eyes rolled, went quiet.
I lifted it, the body cold as dew
Before I even laid it in the bracken.
No more singing. At the door my wife
Met us: "What on earth . . ." My little one:
"Daddy couldn't help it", ran upstairs.

The Beechwoods, Autumn

Stillness, like a trance of time. We look
Down avenues of silver, listening.
There come these days, more beautiful than spring,
Calm as a reflection. Nothing's far.
Perspectives flatten: look, love, here we are
Safe in an illuminated book,
Gold leaf and shafted light, with one green spray
Patterned on the blue ground of the sky,
Or see us quaint as in a tapestry
Walking under trees' brocaded silence.
So autumn has renewed our innocence.
How can this end? No word is said; a ray
Travels back and forth, a rainbow dancer
Between two trunks on threads of gossamer.

An unbeneficed priest might be put in at a modest income for the 'cure of souls'. It is possible that the vacancy resulted from the power struggle between the English Crown and the Papal Court in Rome. The climax of that disharmony came early in the 13th century when Pope Innocent III used against England and the Church in the land his ultimate sanction: the Papal Interdict. All religious services were suspended, churches closed, Masses forbidden. Marriage, Holy Baptism and Christian Burial all ceased.   English Bishops supported the Pope against the English Crown, and English clergy followed suit. King John took financial revenge upon the Church, but finally capitulated. Through the 13th century, synods were attempting to ensure that churches were served by resident and if possible beneficed clergy.

It is not perhaps chance that the next priest in charge of the parish of Godshill known to us was installed in 1275, three years after the accession to the throne of England of Edward I: a strong king.   Edward originated in Winchester, then regarded as capital city of England, and cathedral city of the Diocese which included the Isle of Wight. The new priest was Thomas of Winchester (de Wyntonia). He had a substantial task before him, for there is evidence of relapse from Christian faith during the preceding decades and the resurgence of pagan rituals on the Island.

The Incumbents from 1275 were :
> Thomas of Winchester 1275 - 1284
> Adam de Hales   1284 - 1294
> Peter de Avebury   1294 - 1302
> John de Kirkby   1302-1308

In 1308 there was a dispute over the presentation. The right of patronage was also vested in the Abbot of Lyra, who put forward Roger Hankyn.   Bishop Woodlock of Winchester made the appointment, but the Pope ordered an enquiry into the procedure, and the Papal Commission overturned the appointment. The Bishop then appointed his own relative, Richard Woodlock. When he arrived at Godshill Church, he found a defiant group from local Monastic Houses had barricaded themselves in Godshill church, and he was confronted by armed men who barred his way. They were affronted both by the substance of the situation and one suspects the authority of the English Crown. The Bishop appealed, not to the Pope but to the King, who gave judgment in his favour.

Sequestration followed, and the outcome was the disciplining of the Benedictine leaders on the Island by the Pope, with the full rigours of excommunication.

However, Richard Woodlock was Rector only into the following year (1309), before being succeeded by Richard de Hale or Hall, but he too only for a short time, since it was still 1309 or 1310 when Richard de Tickhill or Tekhill became Rector. In 1312, Roger Hankyn was appointed for a second term, but before the end of that year Harry de Wellford received the benefice, which by contrast he held for 22 years, and with him came the restoration of some element of stability. Thus in the 4 years from mid-1308 to 1312 (inclusive) appear six separate terms of office, before stability was restored.

sinking of the "Mary Rose" off Southsea within sight of the elderly King Henry VIII. On land, the invading forces were repelled by the Islanders under their Captain, Richard Worsley of Appuldurcombe, but not before villages were burnt and pillaged. The inferior English fleet which lay at anchor off St Helens declined or was powerless to intervene. The shortcomings of both land-based forces and naval power had been exposed, despite the success of the local Militia. The English nation was in a state of shock. The response of the Crown was to order the strengthening of both the resources of the English Navy (not our present concern) and the defences of the Island. It is then that the forts were built.

The accession to the throne in 1553 of Mary, meant a reversal of policies. Despite the honourable part played by Sir Richard Worsley, she replaced him as Captain of the Island on account of his Reformed sympathies. She confiscated from Reformist George Mill, signatory to the sale of the Church plate, the patronage of the Godshill living, which she bestowed on the Bishop of Winchester. In her reign there was perhaps no need for defence, but upon her death in 1558, Sir Richard was restored to office, and (with the Governor of Portsmouth) was commissioned to survey and repair Military fortifications on both sides of the Solent. The forts at Yarmouth and Sandown were restored.

Sir Richard was issued with Articles of Instruction in strong terms for the defence of the Island against foreign incursions, and was given correspondingly strong executive powers. He was to supervise the training of picked men in the use of the latest portable defensive weapon, the harquebus, fired from a tripod with the use of newly introduced gunpowder. All who owned land to the annual value of 10 marks were to recruit and pay a Harquebutior, under the command of the Captain of the Island. Musters for military training of the able-bodied were introduced. Each community was obliged to provide armour and equipment for the Militia, and this included the obligation to maintain a cannon. In Godshill, the hut to house it was part of the property erected in Elizabethan times, much later known as 'The Batswing'. There the Vestry had accommodation for the Parish Constable and Lock-up. Over 200 years later there still survived 18 of these cannon on the Island, of between 1 and 6 lbs.

The economic resources of the Island were to be protected: timber, imported coal, and peat extracted as fuel from the marshy bogs at Munsley (Godshill) and Blackwater. The Captain's authority extended to the harvesting and sale of crops, and the sale of the fish catch. There is a real sense of placing the Island on a war-ready footing and keeping it in that state. Attacks had in the past come with little or no warning, and constant preparedness was thus essential, not least because Elizabethan policy was favouring intervention in France in support of the Protestant Huguenots. Though the village of Godshill was not on the coast, the preparations were ordered for all communities.

These precautions did deter the French from launching invasion, but after 1570 the might of Catholic Spain was equally feared. Funds for defence and defensive strategy came from the Exchequer. The Armourers and Harquebus makers worked within Carisbrooke Castle, but others across the Island in administrative posts were singled out for aid. A sum of 24 shillings and 10 pence was allotted

It seems that there were high expectations that the local school could provide a sound and helpful education for sons of both rich and poor. In practice however, it was only a very few of the poor families who felt able to afford to lose the earnings of a son for several years. Moreover, there was a tendency for practical folk living at subsistence level by exercising their practical skills to take the short-term view and regard book-learning as an irrelevant luxury suitable only for the rich.

Also in 1615, an Indenture was completed (following the Will of Lady Anne Worsley long before) between Sir Richard Worsley (her descendant) and Sir William Mewys of Bridge Court & 12 other trustees, confirming her annual charitable endowment.

In the same year, 1615, Richard Gard (Guard) of Princelet Manor Farm and Blackpan, gave £5 yearly in perpetuity out of his rents 'to the use and maintenance of an Usher to teach the children in the Free School of Godshill, if the said school should be used and maintained as a Free Grammar School of learning.'

The judgment of the diarist Oglander was that Richard Gard was 'a crafty knave as any' and 'a most penurious base fellow and of little religion'. Contrast a tablet in Godshill Church, which in paraphrase of the Latin inscribed opposite it, reads:

'Here lies the mortal part of Richard Gard
While his freed spirit meets with heaven's reward,
His gifts endowed the schools, the needy raised,
And by the latest memory will be praised.
And may our Isle be filled with such a name
And be like him whom virtue clothed with fame
Blest with the poor, the scholars, too, were blest
Through such a donor that is gone to rest.'

(Oglander's verdict on this man's father - also Richard Gard -was that he too was 'a notable slie fellow, dishoneste and given to filchinge')

In 1617 a difficulty arose over a collection. In 1614 another Grammar School had been founded in Newport, some 5 miles to the north-west, with larger gifts supplemented by Public Subscription across the Island. £100 was collected in Godshill, but it became clear that many donors thought the cause to which they were donating was the School in their own village. Eventually Lord Hunsford (as Sir George Carey former Captain of the Island) adjudicated, reaching a compromise of £50 to each cause.

Much later, the Vestry Minutes of 1806 confirm that the gift of Gard was being duly paid at Midsummer and St Thomas' Day (21st December). The receipt from John White Esquire of £2 for a half-year stipend was referred to 'issuing out of Blackpan Farm and given to the Usher of the Free Grammar School of learning at Godshill'. There was also £5 a year 'out of Bathingbourne' (the Rice gift or the Dale gift) for the Usher, paid at Michaelmas.

***

21st November 1785 "Elizabeth Spearing, a travelling woman, aged 79 years was buried by the House of Industry". "By" here would refer to the instructions and expense, one presumes, rather than geographical location. (Larger Workhouses did have their own burial-grounds.)

8th April 1786 "Natural son of Frances Matthew, an infant, was buried by the House of Industry".

Sometimes a trade was mentioned, such as shoemaker (Jacobs) or carpenter (March Snudden).

20th September 1791 John Swan, Clerk and Schoolmaster aged 72 years was buried in the Churchyard". He may have been clerk to the Vestry, but 'Clerk' here probably means Cleric, Clerk in Holy Orders.

18th November 1791 the Revd Daniel Walsh, Curate under the Revd John Barwis, also aged 72 when buried in the Churchyard. (It was he who wrote the vivid account of the damage by lightning to All Saints Church in January 1778 despatched to Sir Richard Worsley Bt.)

26th April 1792 "David Jerome, a Pauper, was buried, at Godshill at the expense of the Parish".

In 1793 two boys died aged 14, both described as 'a pauper', and a third aged 16 ('natural son').

In 1795, "John Newman, Labourer, 68 years, hanged himself".

In 1797, "Mary, daughter of William and Ann Rogers, aged 22 years, hanged herself".

***

Some long-settled families:

Urry/Urrey

This surname is recorded on the Island continuously over the centuries, starting as early as 1160/1175 relating to land of the newly founded Abbey at Quarr. The surname is met with again about 1283, 1363, 1507 and in Queen Elizabeths' reign. In 1606, a complete list of the 105 Freeholders living on the Island included five men with the surname Urry. Further records from 1625 & 1638 relate that the Hearth Tax records for the whole Island name no fewer than 15 householders with the surname Urry. In 1683, among the gentlemen signing a petition were three Urrys. In 1780, five manors were owned by different members of the family.

In Godshill parish, Thomas Urry was poor enough to be exempt from Hearth Tax, but Mr William Urry lived in Rookley with 4 hearths. Although the family were never centred on Godshill, there were several of the surname living within the parish boundary. For example, James Urry was a Churchwarden at Godshill in 1835.

It is no surprise therefore to find that in the Godshill Registers of Marriages, Baptisms and Burials there are in the years 1669 to 1788 a total of 26 entries with the surname Urry, from several households. Again, not all were materially successful: in one case there is reference to the House of Industry (colloquially the Workhouse). Later, in 1915, the Register of Electors gives an address for one

The Old Chantry House stood a short distance on the Shanklin side of the Chine which descended the hill south of the Church down to the Square. By 1820/21 the house had through age and lack of maintenance fallen into a dilapidated state. The Revd Henry Worsley took a step that was to arouse a sharp reaction. He pulled down part of the Old Chantry School House in order to rebuild it as a residence for himself and his family. This action frustrated any enlarging of the school on that site as had originally been envisaged by Lady Anne Worsley and generations of Trustees since her time.

There was a bitter disagreement when the position was known. Head of the Appuldurcombe Worsleys at this time (by marriage) was Baron Yarborough, and he was both a School Trustee and a member of the Vestry. Lord Yarborough offered a way forward: the gift of both a new site and a new building for the school(s), opposite the foot of the Chine which ran down on the west side of the Church. An entry in the Vestry Minute book records the gift of the site of the school, the new building and the grounds, with the donors stipulation that the property should not be used as a residence by any schoolmaster or mistress. This stipulation was prudent, but was perhaps an implied rebuke to Lord Yarborough's relative by marriage.

In 1824, this new School cost £300 to build and comprised one room for boys and one for girls. Local children were taught the 3 Rs and practical skills. The Ushers under Mr Worsley were Finnemore and William Read. Mrs Read, his wife, was now engaged to instruct 20 poor girls of the parish. As his part of the new arrangement, Henry Worsley agreed to forego the Master's salary, thus providing funds to pay the Woman Usher, and moreover to supervise the Ushers without salary. The Reads and Finnemore lived elsewhere in the village. The 1827 schoolroom at the Old Chantry House was pulled down when the new school was built. The work of the new school was maintained by the Trustees out of past endowments supplemented by voluntary charitable payments. Not until 1833 was there any grant from central funds.

The picture was further confused, since Mr Worsley also taught private pupils at his home 'in his own time'. This was in effect the ghost of the Tudor foundation of the Free Grammar School for classical education. At some time in the 1820s, Mr Worsley resigned as Curate (but not as Master.) He became Vicar of Old St Lawrence (4 miles to the south), but continued to live at the newly reconstructed Chantry House.

Until December 1821 Vestry Meetings were held regularly once or twice a year. From then until June 1829, there is no record of any such meeting. In June 1829 the meeting in the Parish Church 'was holden as a means of regularising and disciplining such Vestry Meeting summonses'. It is not unreasonable to make connection between that irregularity, and the situation created by the Rev Henry Worsley in taking over the Chantry House. By the time of the 1829 meeting Mr Worsley had left the post as curate at Godshill.

At the foot of the hill, the Village Square was busy by the standards of the day, but the only wheeled traffic was a variety of horse-drawn conveyance. There was a small grocery and general store to the north-west, in the thatched cottage now known as 'The Bats-wing', the sixth of the 16th century cottages. On the north was a Bakehouse ('Welcomes'). On the west side were a thatched cottage and a house known as 'Syringa'. It was in the Square that those going to Church or about other business would tether their horses, and later their bicycles. Worshippers would ascend the steep way and then up the steps, at the top of which was for years a narrow wicket-gate. Enterprising choirboys would 'obligingly' open this for those climbing up, with a touch of the cap and a courteous greeting and out-stretched palm. This would yield quite an income, and the privilege was passed down to the next generation, until in more sensitive times the Vicar removed the gate. It was not thrown away, but was re-used in the Tower Room at the ascent to the Bell chamber. (Note JVJ was told this piece of history by someone who used to have an out-stretched palm and five or six decades later became Captain of the Tower.)

It is also told how customers of the Bell Inn would noisily descend Church Shute Hollow, with the occasional brawl in the Square, and other offensive ways of evidencing their over-generous consumption. The residents at 'Syringa' suffered particularly from the customers from the Bell sitting on the low front window-sill. There is a suggestion that Essex Cottage, the next cottage, was named after Thomas Cromwell, Earl of Essex under Henry VIII, or possibly a later Earl.

The next house was The Vicarage, where Mr Ratcliffe himself lived. The earlier history is told in Section 13. It stood on the site of the Chantry House which had housed the little Grammar School until converted by the Rev Henry Worsley.

Next was Willow Tree Cottage, and then a stone and thatched 17th century cottage named 'The Homestead'. Further south, lying back up a long path was an old thatched cottage where the village boot & shoemaker/repairer lived, and finally before reaching the overgrown 'Hollow Glade' was the 17th century Poplar Cottage. On the Shanklin side of 'Hollow Glade' was built, on the initiative of Lord Yarborough, 'the Griffin' as a new Public House intended to replace the small and seedy Bell Inn, which was moreover not geographically well-suited to serve the needs of visitors to the village.

Further south was Lodwell Farm, a small dairy farm, with rich meadowland behind.

At the foot of Shanklin Chine was a large gateway at the entrance to Park Farm. Almost opposite there, stood a lovely 18th thatched cottage called 'Tyne Cottage'. Village rumour had it that this dwelling was built for occupation by a mistress of one of the Worsleys.

On the east side opposite the Griffin was a thatched cottage and then a tile-roofed house before the Methodist Chapel. Lord Yarborough gave the land for the present Chapel, replacement for the small weatherboarded structure of John Bull's time that the congregation had out -grown.

The Home I Left Behind
25th April 1959

Tonight my thoughts fly back the years
through sunshine and through rain
Through storms and clouds to the happy hours
of my childhood days again
To that dear spot there in Glasha and the house where I was born
Just forty years ago today on a dewy April's morn'.
My father was a labourer and worked the humble spade
We could afford no luxuries from the wages he was paid
But still we were so happy and the peace of God did find
In that little earthly paradise - the home I left behind.

I can still see my father's loving face as he, stories to us, told
There gathered 'round the big turf fire that defied all frost and cold
And we listened so attentively as in minute detail
He told of giants and leprechauns and many a fairy tale.
We were only children then and he held us on his knees
As my mother with her needle worked, our torn clothes to piece
Memories of those happy days keep coming to my mind
And my thoughts are back in Glasha in the home I left behind.

Oh! How I loved you Glasha and your gentle mountain rills
That flowed down to greet the river at the foot of 'Gragra hills
How we paddled in your waters and played among the heather
And grew up so united in our happy home together.
But our family now is scattered, some are on a foreign strand
While some are here and happy in their own dear native land
And though we might have different views
we're all of the same mind
When we come to talk of Glasha and the home we left behind.

with the very same ingredients, kneaded and baked in the same manner would taste differently according to the hand that made it. Even if two sisters in the same house made bread it would taste differently. Indeed I can still remember being the recipient of a cut of bread and it tasted nicer to me than all the sweet luxuries of today.

Every housewife in the rural areas baked her own bread in ovens and on the griddle. The oven was an enclosed round container with a cover on top on which red coals were placed whilst the oven was hanging high over the fire or else placed on the hearth beside the fire with red hot coals placed underneath. The cover would be lifted occasionally to inspect the progress of the cake whilst baking. When baked you had a fine fat round cake with the cross impressed on it as the baker cut into the dough with the tip of the knife before placing it in the oven. What I remember mostly as a child is getting a little bit of the dough when my mother had it kneaded and then shaping it into the image of a pig or a horse or other form and then baking it on the griddle beside the big cake. In the same manner when my mother baked a big currant loaf we would ask for some of the mixture to shape and bake our own scones.

But the meal and flour was not always presented in a loaf. It was often cooked in a skillet pot by boiling the meal, constantly stirring it, adding a little flour to blend it together until a fine pot of "gruel" was ready. Holding a mug of thick milk we would sit around the pot and take spoonfuls of the hot gruel and dip it into the milk to cool before swallowing it down. The crusted bit clinging to the side of the pot was the tastiest of all!

Washing clothes was a more vigorous job than it is now. A washboard was a closely corrugated board placed in a tub of hot water, which had been boiled in a pot over the open fire. The clothes were vigorously rubbed up and down after applying them with a generous smearing of "Best Pale" soap. This job would tax the muscles as well as skinning the knuckles and required lots of elbow grease.

24

To lead them o'er difficult years
We miss the sweet ring of your laughter
From your heart ever gay and so light
With grief my poor fingers are trembling
As this sad lamentation I write.

Cruel death threw me back the gold ring from your finger
Which united us ten years ago
Little I thought on that happy morn
So soon I'd be parting with you
Little reminders of our love
I find among souvenirs
They once brought a joy to my bosom
Now they bring nothing but tears.

For the one that I loved so dearly
How you helped me and soothed my brow
You were all a man every wished for
Oh, who can I turn to now?
To you Blessed Mother in Heaven
Who has felt more sorrow and loss
As you gazed on your Son crucified
Standing at the foot of the cross.

How can I then a wretched poor sinner
Ask to be freed of sickness or pain
When Thy heart O Immaculate Mother
Was pierced again and again?
Mary take my motherless children
Under your Sacred Wing
And guard them from the snares of Vile Satan
'Till they'll meet their fond mother again
I know she was fitted for Heaven
Lord I do not grudge her to Thee
With your Mother her sweet lips are pleading
For her five darling children and me.

I remember too at lunch-time in the hot summer's sun

To a pool down in the river across Schollard's we would run

I remember Liam Mullane then tall and

strong in his birthday suit attired

Diving from the bank into the pool a feat we all admired.

There with our tops and thaws we passed the happy time away

I doubt if any children play those innocent games today

Another thing my memory holds oft there in the cold morning

We played a game of '41' in Ned Sheehy's chimney corner.

Where are our comrades now some scattered o'er many lands

Some gone across the great divide to join the angels' bands

Be they near or far away my memory sees them still

As when we went in days gone by to that schoolhouse on the hill.

There is a story told of a farmer who, when hiring a strong looking man in Newcastle West, asked him for a reference from his previous employer. The servant went to his last employer who, knowing he wasn't able to read, gave him a note which read: "Feed him well and take him aisy, mighty strong but woeful lazy". Be that as it may, there were very few lazy at the time for all were willing and able to work and had to keep up their quin for there were so many others ready to step into their place.

Some of those servant boys and girls were welcomed at night into labourers houses in the locality where they worked and it was something like home to them where they could enjoy the cheery atmosphere in the comfort of a warm house and sit around the fire and, in some cases, the labourer's wife would look after their laundry and mending with sheer compassion for them. Some of those servants were befriended and fell in love and married and settled down in East Limerick.

As well as hiring fairs in Newcastle West, there was also a huge market for all farm produce. This market was held weekly, on a Thursday. Here you would find huge consignments of oats, barley and potatoes, generally wrapped in the twenty-stone bags in which the Treble-X bags of meal were delivered to the shops. Here too on market day the talismen or "hand me downs" had their stalls of second-hand clothes - and what gifted men they were with words and wit.

Emigration in West Limerick was another course open to those who could not find employment. Hard as it was to find employment, it was much harder to find the fare for the boat to America where many of our emigrants were wont to travel at the time. Sometimes a rich aunt or uncle in the U.S.A. would present a nephew or niece with the cost of travelling and they, in their turn, would finance other sisters and brothers to travel from the savings from their hard won earnings in America. Not alone did they help their sisters and brothers to travel, they also helped those left at home for they never seemed to forget those less fortunate living here.

Confessions were being held in the church and there were several waiting to be heard. The priest was going towards the box to start hearing but he was in a hurry to get his duty fulfilled as he had an important appointment later to attend. As he was passing by a man he knew well, he said to him, "any chance Jack you'd wait over for another night, sure you didn't kill anyone since your last Confessions". Jack agreed and as he was coming down from the church he met his neighbour Paddy. "Is the Priest hearing, Jack?" said Paddy. "He is hearing alright Paddy" said Jack "but I'm afraid you don't need to go in to him. It's only murder cases he's hearing tonight".

One day a Priest found a dead ass at his gateway, so he rang the Gardai requesting them to see to his removal. The Garda replied "I thought it was the Priest's duty to look after the dead". "I'm aware of that" said the Priest, "but 'twas only right that I should inform the next of kin".

Turraree

Dear Turraree, that verdant plain hemmed by the sheltering hills
I long to see your face again and hear your rippling rills
Go babbling to the river to join the mighty sea
In dreams I am forever with you Dear Turraree.

In childhood days I roamed along your meadows soft and green
And listened to the wild birds song and see the bright flowers lean
To greet the morning's rising sun as it gaily did appear
Dancing as its red beams shone to the lark's sweet notes so clear.

Though far from you I had to roam, in my heart you do abide
With longing thoughts of my dear home at morning noon and night
My memory steals along the road to the sweet old Kerryline
Where with a girl I often strolled in summer evenings fine.
Where the Irish air was fresh and sweet and love did play its part
Where we caressed with kisses sweet that filled our youthful hearts.

But now from far across the sea in dreams those days I view
And I pray that when the Lord calls me he'll send me home to you
No matter where my legs may roam, at home my heart will be
I pray Thee then to guide me home to my own dear Turraree

The Banks of the Gale

Sweet river flowing through the valley along by the town of Athea
There in the days of my childhood with my comrades I gaily did play.
My mind is now back by its waters with a memory that cannot grow stale
For no matter how far I may wander my heart lies in the breast of the Gale.

In fancy I see my old playmates all together as in days gone by
In Colbert's green inch by the river, their skill with the football to try.
The cheers through the valley re-echoed as the ball o'er the crossbar did sail
As they kept up the fame of their fathers, the veterans from the banks of the Gale.

With rod and with line there we sported and many happy hours passed away
As white and brown trout we landed as we listened to the lark's merry lay.
There in the hot summer evenings in our birthday suit we'd hit the trail
To take a dive into the "Pouleen" then jump across the banks of the Gale.

The law there seldom was broken in this haven of happiness and peace

Except for a drink at the local ignoring "Time Gentlemen, please".
Or in winter our menu to vary and have a change from fat bacon and kale
In spite of the bailiff's close vigil a salmon we'd poach from the Gale.

Minding the House
(Written in 1960)

Thank God it is all over, 'tis a relief to my brain
My wife she is now better and is on her feet again
One day last week she got the flu and in bed she had to stay
She said to me "Paddy, I can't get up. Could you manage anyway?"

"Yerra, Nell", " says I , "Why not I. What is there to be done
Only get the children out to school. To me twill be just fun".
But, now I know what fun it was and you'll know just as well
When you hear the muddle I got into - those days were just like hell.

I always thought that women had the finest time on earth
Just gossiping with the neighbours while sitting by the hearth
But now for them I've pity - they're wonderful no doubt
How they find time for gossip, I'll never figure out.

On the day I was housekeeping my wife said from the bed
"Is there any chance now Paddy you'd throw down a cake of bread"
"I will" said I "just tell me the ingredients I want
I'll blend them together and I bet you 'twill be grand".

Before I had it finished I'd a path made to the bed
Asking where I'd find this and that to put in the cake of bread
And when I had it finished and ready for to bake
There was as much flour on my hands and clothes as there was
inside the cake!

I put it in the oven over a fire of black ciaráns
And I said now while 'tis baking I'll run for butter to Mullanes
I happened to be delayed there and alas when I returned
And looked into the oven my cake was black and burned.

The Old Fair of Athea

Thank God it has come round again, the 14th of November,
And whilst there's life and breath in me that day I will remember,
So I'll bid farewell to Birmingham for here I cannot stay,
I must be there to meet my friends at the Old Fair of Athea.

Never once in all my years that fair I ever missed,
If my employers say that I can't go, Oh how I will insist,
I'd risk my very life itself not alone my pay,
For while I'm alive I will attend the Old Fair of Athea.

'Tis there you'll see hard bargains struck and tempers seem to rise,
Before the final deal is clinched and luck exchanged in the price,
But many of the bargains are finished in the bar,
In one of the many pubs after letting back a jar.

And after a few pints from Arthur Guinness,
And a few small ones from J. J.,
You wouldn't go back from Muhammad Ali,
At the Old Fair of Athea.

You'll meet old friends and new ones and comrades by the score,
Some of whom you hadn't met for twelve long months before,
They'll shake your hand in parting and this you'll hear them say,
Please God we'll meet again next year at the Old Fair of Athea.

Now the cattle are thinning out and the street is free once more,
The barricades are coming down from the windows and the doors,
The "hand me downs" are shouting they have clothes to throw away,
For just one pound you'd get well dressed at the Old Fair of Athea.

The dance then in the village that night would crown it all,
When all the laughing boys and girls would fill Tim Kelly's hall,
And to Frank Lohan's lively music they'd tip-toe light and gay,
Who could miss such an occasion at the Old Fair of Athea?

Trip Through Limerick.

We'll drive through Limerick County where there's pleasures all the
way
From the Dock Road near the city to the hillsides of Athea,
Through the rich lands of the Golden Vale to Mountcollins far off
height
By Newcastle West, Strand and Tour, oh what a pleasant sight

Of castles, lakes and rivers where the angler can rest
And chat with the pleasant people sublimely or in jest
And listen to the grand old songs, joyful songs and sad
Of racing, football, hurling, of the good times and the bad.

Thrown in for good measure you'll hear of the Banshee's wail
Of pishogues and ghosts and giants
and the leprechaun's busy trail
No road is without historic landmark in this
County of poets and song
And the scenery is enthralling as we glide along.

By old Shanagolden where
Shanid Castle and Old Abbey stand
And the famed hill of Knockpatrick
where St. Patrick blessed the land
We can view the Desmond Castle overlooking Shannon's tide
Where the Knight at the Valley in splendour doth reside.

SECTION ONE
Roads and Shops

The north side of the Carfax, 1855. Although this is a very early photograph, it was not actually used for a postcard until the beginning of the next century, when Mr Honeywood published his series of 'Old Horsham', proving that there is nothing new about nostalgia. William Holden, wholesale wine and spirit merchants, whose rather grand premises adorn this picture, was succeeded by the brewers King & Son, who later became King & Barnes. On either side are private houses, which would certainly have constituted most of the buildings around the Carfax at that period.

The Queen's Head Hotel, Queen Street, photographed in the late nineteenth century, before it was rebuilt as a larger, three-storey structure. It was in the stables of this hotel, a year after the event, that the body of John Lawrence was exhibited, the last man to be publicly executed in Horsham. A dubious distinction, but still hundreds of people were willing to pay tuppence to view the gruesome sight. The inscription 'King & Son's' referred to the Horsham brewers of that name. James King came to Horsham in 1850 and traded as a brewer in the Bishopric. In 1870 he amalgamated his business with Satchell's, the North Parade brewery, and it was then that the business became known as King & Son's.

The Queen Street hostelry The Sussex was one of four public houses in this short street in 1850. Now only the Queen's Head survives, yet Horsham once shared the national record for the town with the highest number of pubs relative to its population – there were once over fifty. The Sussex was another house selling James King's beer. Having established himself by the late 1800s, he co-existed with another Horsham brewery, which traded as G.H. Barnes & Co. at the East Street brewery. The two breweries united in 1906 and were known thereafter as King & Barnes Ltd. In 1912, with the closure of Michell's West Street brewery, the business took the name which it still uses today, Horsham Brewery.

The King's Arms on the north side of the Bishopric, around the turn of the century. This is a timber-framed building with a brick front, and it must have been particularly busy when the market was held in the Bishopric. This was also known as Lower West Street and Oxford Road, but more often it was called The Rookery, either because of the rooks which nested in the trees there, or more likely because of the fights and squabbles in the area – its residents were likened to a bunch of quarrelsome rooks. The Bishopric once had open sewers running down the south side, with rough stone bridges for pedestrians. It was said that on market days almost every cottage functioned as a beer house.

Another photograph of the Horsham Recreation Silver Band, this time taken out of doors, with the band sporting very smart boaters. The date of this picture was around 1907. Included in the line up are a host of well-known Horsham names, such as Jupp, Tulett, Dewdney and Dench. Seated in the second row (third from left) is the band leader William Albery, who later wrote such books as *The Parliamentary History of Horsham*.

Horsham Camera Club visiting Christ's Hospital School, *c.* 1920. The Prince of Wales laid the foundation stone of the school when it moved from London to its present site in 1897. Boys first occupied the houses built beside the stately avenue, but they are now joined by girls. The school caters for a wide variety of interests so no doubt there was a camera club here to welcome this group. The interest taken by the townsfolk in the famous school on their doorstep has always been generously reciprocated.

Mr Samuel Gardener, the Southwater blacksmith standing at the door of his forge, horseshoe at the ready, *c.* 1903. His granddaughter recalled the sound of the clanging of the hammers from the forge as she lay in bed in the early mornings, and also the (perhaps more welcome) sound of Aubrey Charman delivering the milk from his churns.

This advertising handbill probably from the early 1920s vividly illustrates the start of the technological age in a country village such as Southwater. Samuel Gardener's blacksmith's business had existed for over a century, but had now become a motor and cycle engineer's with a garage taking the place of the forge on the main Horsham to Worthing road. The list of items supplied reflects the progression of technology in the twentieth century.

Established over 100 years.

Lady's and Gent.'s New Cycles from £5 5s. Any make supplied Cycle Accessories.	ACETYLENE WELDING done on the Premises.	New & second-hand MOTOR CYCLES. Petrols Oils Carbide.
Prams re-tyred.	Electric Bells re-charged.	

Agent for Motor Insurance.

S. GARDENER,

Motor and Cycle Engineer,

The Garage, Southwater

TUBES from 1/4.		LOOSE CARBIDE, 4d. lb.	
Tyres, Tubes, Lamps, Chains, Enamels, Pumps, Bells. Gold Size. Flash Lamp Batteries, etc., etc.	Perfection Stoves and Cookers supplied. Spare parts in Stock. Chimneys, Wicks, etc., etc.	Builders' Ironwork. Pumps and Locks Fitted or Repaired. Hot and Cold Water Installations.	

UNDER PERSONAL SUPERVISION.

PROMPT ATTENTION.   SATISFACTION GUARANTEED.

Fred Holmes, The Printer, 17, North Street, Horsham.

73

An idyllic view of Billingshurst, *c.* 1907. I particularly like the driver of the cart who appears to be relaxing on top of his load, and presumably leaving the horse to make any decisions, such as circumventing the sixpenny bazaar cart. The latter is apparently carrying a selection of chinawear, which must have been good value at *6d* a time. As seen here, Billingshurst was perhaps little changed from the village of William Cobbett's day. He wrote in 1830: 'A very pretty village, and a very nice breakfast, in a very neat little parlour of a very decent public house.' Praise indeed.

Christ's Hospital School near Horsham, with visiting dignitaries. The occasion is almost certainly the opening of the new Science School by the Prince of Wales (president of the school) on 14 October 1930. With the Prince are the Headmaster, Mr H.L.O. Flecker and the Bishop of Worcester, the Rt Revd E.H. Pearce.

Champion's Mill, Wisborough Green, *c.* 1900. This was an attractive white smock mill with a domed cap. Several dates have been suggested for its erection, possibly around 1820. It was described in 1860 as 'a freehold mill in good working condition'. In 1910 Mr Champion, together with a number of enthusiastic helpers, tried to adjust the cap. After several attempts, they were hurled into the air and gave up. The cap and sweeps were taken down six months later, and the mill was roofed in 1915. It then became dangerous, so it was pulled down, leaving only the base. After 1960 this was converted into part of a private residence.

Wisborough Green, *c.* 1907. The village was often referred to simply as Green, and this is a very pleasant view with the old mill still intact in the background. There is a tradition that no one can be considered a true resident of the village until he or she has fallen in the pond at least once. There were several local industries; the Huguenots brought their glass-making skills to this part of Sussex. There were limekilns, hence The Limeburners inn here. Yet another local occupation was copse cutting.

SECTION EIGHT

The Forest Villages

Roffey Camp was the home of the 22nd Battalion of the Royal Fusiliers for a time during the First World War. Here is a cartoon from their fortnightly gazette dated 26 June 1915, showing their dismay on being told they were to leave Roffey. The caption to the cartoon reads: 'Terrible effect of a notice in a hut at Roffey camp.'

Then they would go out into the street, posing as indigent old ladies, and beg coins from passers-by. One of my sisters, I forget which one, actually managed to wheedle a florin from our own mother, who failed to recognise her. We spent the florin on jamboree bags, sherbet fountains and those dangerous fireworks called 'jumping jacks'. We set them off all at once in a field of cows, and sat on the gate gleefully watching the ensuing stampede. It was only me who got spanked for it, however, since little girls in those days were not judged to be capable of such obviously boyish mischief.

As for me, I evolved through a series of pastimes, which began as a toddler. My first hobby was saying good morning. I had a little white floppy hat that I would raise to anyone at any time of day, in imitation of the good manners of my father, and I would solemnly intone 'good morning' in a lugubrious tone of voice that I had probably first admired in a vicar. After that I developed an interest in drains, and would squat before them, poking with a stick at the limp shreds of apple peel and cabbage that had failed to pass through the grate outside the kitchen. I noticed that in the autumn the leaves turned grey, and I discovered the miraculous binding quality of human hair when it is mixed with sludge. From this I progressed naturally to a brief fascination with dog manure, and am perplexed to this day as to why it was that occasionally one came across a little pile that was pure white. Nowadays one never sees such faecal albinism. My wife recalls that as a child she had assumed that such deposits were made by white poodles.

As infancy blossomed into childhood, so my interests multiplied. I made catapults, tormented the cat, pretended to be a cowboy, made boxes with air holes so that I could watch

'It means "Mercy, mercy. I'm innocent, I'm innocent",' said Dr Iannis coldly. 'Anyway, I don't know why you bother with communists. When the Italians sent for their help, they did nothing.'

'They sent about a dozen little boys with red armbands,' said Weber. 'We caught them straight away.'

'And then you shot them,' said the doctor. 'My point is that the communists are up in the hills, and there aren't any in the villages. Everyone you kill in the villages is innocent.'

Weber seemed not to have heard this. 'She was shrieking and clutching at her head, rolling about on the ground, and all my platoon were just watching me to see what I was going to do.'

'One day,' said the doctor, 'there will be a time when to have a political opinion is not a capital offence.'

'They shoot at us,' said Weber.

'Not very much,' retorted the doctor, 'and in any case, what else do you expect?'

Weber ignored the question. 'Doctor, I could smell the shit and urine. I could smell the panic. She was completely mad. And all that shrieking. It was going through my head, I could feel my brain beginning to explode, I just couldn't take it, it was the worst thing I've ever had to hear. And she was just rolling about, clutching on to my legs, "*Eleos, eleos. Eimai athoa, eimai athoa*", and then she began to foam at the mouth. It was horrible, so horrible.'

'So?' asked the doctor.

'My men were still looking at me, waiting for me to decide something. I could feel their eyes upon me, sort of half observing me, from the sides of their faces. And all the villagers were promenade. There he made him change into Turkish clothes, bundling the British ones into a carrier bag. In the meantime Susan went into the women's and put on a long flowery skirt that would cover her legs. She then donned one of her husband's long-sleeved shirts, buttoning it at the cuffs and collar, and tied on the headscarf. 'You look quite the Turkish, babe,' said Robert when they met again outside.

They found the car in the side street where they had left it, and drove out of town. Vinnie began to create a ruckus in the back. 'Where are we going?' he demanded. 'I want to know where we're going!'

'We're going to Oenoanda,' said Susan over her shoulder.

'Oh no,' he cried, 'I bet it's a hot stony place! I don't want to go to any more hot stony places! I hate hot stony places! I want to go home! Take me home!'

'It's an ancient ruined city,' said Robert, in a neutral tone of voice.

'It's a hot stony place,' whined Vinnie, adding, 'I've got a headache.' A little further on he complained, 'I've got a tummy-ache,' and his parents ignored him, as if he were a bad tune on the radio. 'Bumhole, bumhole, bumhole,' he chanted. 'Mummy is a bumhole, bumhole, bumhole.'

Oenoanda is a derelict city on the top of a high, steep mountain, and it is completely off the tourist route because there is no road up it, and the climb to the peak requires leg muscles of spring-steel. To reach it one has to drive some thirty kilometres past Kemer, through some remarkably majestic countryside, and then take a right turn on to a dirt track that leads ultimately to the tiny, ramshackle hamlet of Incealiler. The ruins boast some remarkable tombs and a very impressive wallet, and presented the wallet to Jean-Louis. '*Un regalito*,' he said, his eyes twinkling, '*un recuerdo de Colombia. Con mis mejores deseos.*'

Jean-Louis' confusion and horror were slowly beginning to subside, along with the insupportable thumping of blood behind his eyes and in his temples, and he took the wallet in his hands and gazed at it with childish wonder. He looked up at the man who had decided to give it to him so that he would not have to carry his cash insecurely in his socks, and he began to laugh, his shoulders heaving, and his breath coming in painful sobs. The Colombian was momentarily nonplussed, but then he smiled, leaned forward, and patted Jean-Louis on the cheek. It was a gesture both paternal and patronising, a gesture full of humour and sympathy and affection. He patted Jean-Louis' face again, and came up with the only appropriate English words he knew: 'Estupid gringo,' he said.

marvellous, because she had herself tried not looking up when somebody knocked at her door, but had always looked up none-theless, as if by reflex. Perhaps only those born to importance were capable of such coolness in the face of a knock.

Mamacita entered, and Don Agostin stood up to greet her. In his youth he had been a rakehell and an unmitigated dog, but at the age of forty-five he had become gallant and urbane, and so he seized her right hand and kissed it, not once but twice. 'Abuela,' he exclaimed, 'what a pleasure this is.' He waved her to a chair with an elegant sweep of his arm, and called out to the kitchen, 'Emma, a jug of guarapo for my guest.' He turned to Mamacita, and wiped his forehead with the tail of his shirt. 'Another infernal day,' he observed.

Mamacita pointed to the fan that was rotating slowly and half-heartedly above them. 'This is very nice,' she said drily, 'but it would be nicer if we could all have them. It is the heat that makes us behave badly.'

'We become ill-natured, do we not?' agreed Don Agostin. 'However, I have finally bullied and bribed the State Governor into electrifying the village, and soon we will have every sort of convenience, including refrigeration.'

'You are a good patron,' said Mamacita, 'everyone agrees.'

'Very kind, very kind,' replied Don Agostin, 'but all the same I am frequently reminded of my shortcomings.'

'At least you look after all your little bastards,' said Mamac-ita bluntly. 'There is many a patron who doesn't.'

Don Agostin flushed, but remained dignified. 'Now what can I do for you? As you know, Abuela, nothing is too trivial or too great when matters concern she who delivered me into this world.'

extra curve to the formation of her cheekbones. Manolito told me that in reality her cheeks are quite full and that you cannot discern the line of the cheekbones at all, but in her tomb it gave her the appearance of noble blood and gentle education.

Perhaps it was her mouth that made a prisoner of my brother. It was the mouth of an innocent, and yet of one who knew all the carnality of a sensual woman in the prime of desire. The lips were closed, and yet they seemed to be at the point of opening, as though tempting one to a kiss. There was amusement playing about those lips, betrayed by the two tiny laughter lines at either end. It was the kind of amusement of one who knows a harmless secret; it made one want to say, 'OK, what's up? What are you hiding behind your back? Is it a present, or are you going to put a spider down my shirt when you think I am not looking?' It was a very sweet smile.

Because of that ineffable face I can remember next to nothing about the rest of the corpse. The face had a way of fixing your gaze in the expectation of being able to discern some subtle change of mood or the passing of a thought. I think that she had a ring with a large lilac stone on one hand, and I remember that the line of her body seemed as graceful and liquid as the flow of her hair upon her shoulders. All I can say is that she was so lovable that not only I, but also everyone in the village, thought of Manolito's passion as understandable.

But if you want to see her now you will be disappointed. She lives only in the memory of those who are now old, such as myself, because the fact is that the mountain swallowed her up.

We all believed that the mountain was dead, and in fact it was during the generation of my great-great-grandfather that the people stopped giving gifts to the mountain in order with my woman's beauty and the taste of the Earthmother in my mouth; and no one knows who amongst these cabocos will take the longing from my tongue.'

Amadea watched the *bufeo* break through the reflection of the moon upon the waters, and cried, 'Ay, good dolphin, who takes half the fish ungrudged from our nets before our very eyes. Ay, *bufeo*, who saves the drowning fishermen and carries him ashore between two of you. Ay, *bufeo*, whom we never kill and never eat because you love each other so much and so publicly that our hearts are moved inside us. Ay, *bufeo*, when will I give up my solitudes of a perpetual virgin?'

She rested her head in her arms, and her capuchin monkey clambered upon her shoulders and inspected her tangled hair. She reached up and stroked it, and then there was a soft footstep on the sandbar beside her. She looked up through her tears and the alcoholic haze of chicha, and saw that the *bufeo* had become a man. She saw that he was tall and golden-skinned, that his eyes were of different colours, and that he was completely naked. He was holding out his hand with something in it, and all at once she was glad that she had painted herself freshly with annatto, that she had scoured her parasites with fishes' teeth, that she had withheld herself so long. She reached out for the earth knowing in advance that it was the quintessence of soil.

The *bufeo* watched as her expressions changed with the delight of the rainbow of flavours. It tasted first of piraruca, then of spit-roast tapir, then of capybara, then of piranha except without the annoying little bones, then of granadillas, then of guava, then of sweet grapefruit, and then of two tastes unknown to her experience, because they were the tastes of apples and

On the package he wrote, 'To the Gringo Presedent.' Tucking it under his arm, he went to find Paulo, who was going into town. He gave the heavy bundle to Paulo, along with some money for the stamp, and asked him to post it in the town when he got there. Paulo accepted the parcel with a smile, and agreed.

Paulo was not the best choice for this mission. Like so many others in that place he had grown up with a casual dishonesty that never meant any harm, but which has effectively paralysed progress for hundreds of years. He was also as curious as a monkey. In short, he spent the money as part of the payment for a prostitute, and he opened the parcel. He gave one of the fish to a woman he was trying to butter up in one of the villages, and the other one he ate himself, sitting on the riverbank whilst he watched a cacique making a nest.

It served Paulo right that he caught erysipelas from the prostitute, but Joao was never the wiser. It gave him great confidence that he had played a vital part in the affairs of the world, and this was reflected in his ever greater progress at school and the consequent admiration of the young teacher. All the same, it is doubtful whether Joao had given Paulo enough money to send the parcel, it is doubtful that it ever would have got through US Customs, and infinitely doubtful that the president would ever have received the package. If he had done so, it is certain that he would not have understood the connection between two dead fish and the fall of two tyrants.

In any case, he had known about that by other means almost as soon as it had happened.

Andouillette has to be told that they are going at half past five. He sits calmly in the driver's seat, drumming his fingers on the steering wheel whilst she flutters in and out trying to remember where she has left her handbag, her keys, the tissues, the dogfood, and (most difficult of all) trying to remember whether or not she has forgotten anything that she hasn't recalled. For the fifth time René gets out of his car and inspects the caravan to check that all is well. He prods the linkage of the towing apparatus, he kicks the tyres with the toecaps of his shoes, he tugs at the electrical connections, and he scrutinises imperfections in the paintwork, lifting his chin so he can take proper advantage of the lower half of his bifocals. Andouillette thinks complacently that when he does this he looks just exactly like a professor.

René Andouil observes dispassionately as from outside the house he discerns the random passage of his wife from one room to another. He remembers how her permanent level of mild panic had once struck him as peculiarly lovable and appealing, how it had eventually become exasperating, and how he has finally learned to witness it with the same puzzled detachment with which one might, for example, watch a group of outlandish foreigners playing cricket.

'It's going to be a lovely day,' he says to himself. The dawn is pleasantly chilly, an even mist is lifting off the sea, and the rich iodine smell of seaweed is drifting in off the beach. Luc-sur-Mer is a lovely place in which to live, and it seems almost silly to leave it in order to go on holiday somewhere else. The trouble is that every August the town fills up with Parisians who also think it is a lovely place. They bring with them their impatience and arrogance, their jostle and noise, they bring those pop bands that glances. 'The back's locked,' says Andouil desperately. 'It might take me some time to find the key.'

'We think the door might be open already,' says the sergeant. 'We're a bit psychic, you see. Isn't that strange?'

Andouil is dumbfounded, and he sits tight in the car as the two gendarmes open the caravan door. Andouil knows that he is doomed. He has visions of heavy fines, and years in prison with Algerian Islamic terrorists, paedophiles from Dieppe and sodomitic heroin-addicted rapists from Marseilles. Andouil allows his head to slump forward on to the wheel, and his mind goes numb. He discovers the true meaning of resignation.

The sergeant returns and says, 'That's all right, then, sir. Of course there's no one in the back. We should have trusted you. We looked everywhere.'

'No one in the back?' repeats Andouil. 'No one in the back?'

'Just as you said, sir. We wish you a very good day.'

Andouil is still for a moment, but then he leaps out of the car and opens the door of the caravan. He stumbles in and looks around. His eyes seem unable to focus. Outside he hears the clattering sound of the motorbikes starting up, and the collective roar of the vehicles moving off. He calls out, 'Sausage? Sausage?'

There is no reply. He lifts the mattress to see if Andouillette has hidden underneath. He opens the cupboard and peers into the tiny space under the sink. He lifts the mattress again, and bobs down to look under the table. He stands up, exclaims, 'My God, my God,' and runs out into the sunshine. It occurs to him in a flash that Andouillette must have gone into the woods when he had done so himself, and he realises that he will have to take the caravan back in the direction of Alençon. He only

The foreigner had cut the cheese-toast in half, and had eaten it reluctantly, out of politeness rather than because he wanted it. In deference to Mehmet's obvious hunger, he had left the second half, and now it was going cold on the table. He was annoyed because he had wanted Mehmet to enjoy it at its best.

The stranger paid the bill, and was just thinking that he would never see Mehmet again, when the latter reappeared, all triumphant smiles. 'Thirty-two,' he exclaimed.

'*Otuziki*,' repeated the foreigner, impressed. Mehmet was about to sit down, when he noticed that his hands had become very grubby indeed. He looked at them, showed them to the foreigner with a disgusted expression on his face, tutted, and disappeared into the men's room. He washed first his hands, and then his face. He sprinkled water on to his hair, and stood in front of the mirror to comb it carefully into place. When he reappeared he was neat and respectable, and his shoulders were squared.

Mehmet sat down at the table, and the foreigner indicated the cheese-toast, pointed at him, and said, '*Yemek*.'

'I'm not hungry,' said Mehmet, 'I bought it for you. You eat it.'

The stranger saw the longing in Mehmet's eyes, and under-stood the delicacy of the situation. He linked the fingers of his hands, and made a rotund gesture above his stomach, indicating that he was completely full. He wrapped the cheese-toast in a paper napkin, and pointed at Mehmet, and then at his own watch, showing a later hour. Mehmet was initially puzzled, and then realised that the stranger was telling him to eat it later. It was an excellent compromise. With every show of reluctance and indifference, Mehmet accepted the cheese-toast. He put it

'We've had a great evening,' said Prudente. 'You'll find that Luis is good company.'

The thief eyed the four men and grew suspicious. They all had neatly brushed hair, broad shoulders, bulky jackets, freshly shaved faces and very shiny shoes. It did not seem quite right.

'This is him, is it?' asked one of the men, and Prudente nodded.

The thief howled and protested as he was dragged towards the Military Police car, forced up against it, disarmed, searched and handcuffed. One of the men briefly inspected the thief's Browning automatic and handed it to Prudente. The thief was pushed into the vehicle, and Prudente leaned in through the window. The thief was shaking with fear, whimpering, almost unable to speak.

'Don't take it too badly,' said Prudente soothingly. 'You've had the traditional meal, the traditional smoke, even a chance to repent. We've had a great time. I would shake your hand and wish you well, but I can't because of the handcuffs. It's a pity.' He reached out his hand, and patted the thief comfortingly upon the shoulder. '*Adeus.*' To the four men he said, 'Good night, boys, go carefully.'

'Good night, Sergeant,' they chorused in reply, and Prudente de Moraes watched the car pull away from the kerb and head towards the Túnel Rebouças. A twinge of regret tugged at his heart, and he set off back towards Ipanema beach, where he bought a can of Guarana, sat on the steps, looked up at the Southern Cross, and listened to the sea.

and his staff of beavers applauded as he moved through the hallway. Once outside he came under the protection of a team of falcons, who took off in arrow formation with Edgar at the centre.

Half an hour later their destination came into view, and the waiting crowd pointed excitedly at the sky as they began their descent. An impressive structure of red sandstone, the House of Eagles had been constructed beside a giant waterfall, its cascading waters a feature of the view from inside. At the entrance, a hallway led to a spiral staircase, along which hung framed portraits of eagles, all former leaders of the Great Wood. On the first floor a set of golden double doors opened into the great hall, where rows of pews led to a stage of black marble, whose centrepiece was a statue of a giant eagle. Suspended from the ceiling, and dominating everything, the eagle's wings stretched almost the width of the hall.

Edgar's arrival sent a buzz of excitement through the hall, with only the front row of eagles – themselves former leaders of the Great Wood – maintaining a stony silence. Behind them, ducks were boasting about their wares and some squirrels were swapping places, trying to get a better view of the stage. Further back, a goat security guard was doing his best to find seats as a group of badgers flashed their tickets angrily. At the rear of the hall were two rows of beavers who had squeezed in close to separate themselves from a pew of skunks to their right.

There was a hush as a senior goat moved onto the stage and invited Edgar to step forward. At that moment all differences were set aside, and even the gap between the beavers and the skunks narrowed, as animals united under the flag of the Great Wood. Taking his glasses from an inside pocket, the goat began to read from a scroll, which an assistant was holding in front of him at eye level.

'In the name of the Great Eagle, do you, Edgar, swear to uphold the constitution of this wood and, using the powers vested in the office of leader, do you promise to protect all creatures great and small?'

'I do.'

'Do you swear that from this day onward you will place the interests of the Great Wood before all others?'

'I do.'

'Do you promise to cherish and maintain the memory of the Great Eagle?'

'I do.'

'I hereby declare Edgar the Eagle to be leader of the Great Wood.'

There was a huge cheer as the ram handed over the seal of office and left the stage. Edgar stood on the rostrum, head bowed, waiting for the applause to subside. Eventually he began to speak in a voice that trembled at first but gradually grew more confident and resolute.

'Many years ago the Great Eagle descended from the sun, and spotting this land from afar, he decided to make it his own. Carrying creatures from other woods on his great wings, he populated this wood and built the House of Eagles in which we now stand. Drawing strength from the sun, from whence he had come, he created rivers and lakes and the most exquisite varieties of plants and shrubs. In all of this, the Great Eagle had a dream – not of riches or power, nor of sloth or indulgent gratification.'

only to be restored in the stillness of the night. Gradually the sleighs went quiet as energy and heat became burning issues for the animals of Great Eagle Wood. January passed, doing nothing to reduce the white visitor's stranglehold, and it was February before his grip loosened, the sun rising from the shadows to bid him a tearful farewell.

Emerging from hibernation, animals yawned and stretched, and there was a clank of metal as shop shutters were pulled open and ducks once again began to ply their wares throughout the wood.

'Spring Pillow Sale – Buy One Get One Free' promised a sign in Bill's shop window, where eager bargain hunters were purchasing on the double. Grocery shops were busy too, as families queued to stock up on supplies after the long winter. For some, however, the thaw had come too late, and the old-timers, whose numbers had dwindled, were the hardest hit of all.

As the Great Wood struggled to make the transition from winter to spring, in Chestnut Hill one animal was faced with a battle all of his own. Bob, a foreman with the local construction firm, was an ordinary, hard-working beaver who believed in getting things done. He was a family beaver too, and at weekends he could often be seen with Beryl and their growing kits as they played beside one of the wood's many streams. Lately, however, Bob had been behaving strangely, and Beryl was concerned.

'What's the matter, love?' she asked when they had a quiet moment to themselves.

'Huh?'

'You don't seem to be yourself these days, Bob.'

'Don't I?'

'You're… I don't know. Just different. Like you're here but you're not really here.'

'I don't know what you mean, Beryl.'

'If you've got something on your mind, Bob, you should tell me. Maybe we can talk about it.'

'It's nothing, Beryl, honestly. I'm just a bit tired.'

Beryl was worried. Bob wasn't just a hard-working beaver, he was also a very good-looking beaver, and there was no shortage of envious females willing to take her place. But that wasn't it. There was something clsc, something about Bob's behaviour that had her worried.

'Bob has changed,' she confided to her friends.

'What? Bob?' they all responded disbelievingly.

But Beryl was right. Bob *had* changed. Gone was the cautious beaver who saved and scrimped to pay their bills, the father who fretted about everything from food supplies to the weather forecast. In his place was a beaver who spoke of dead certs and sure things, of being between opportunities and of how long it would take to become a millionaire.

Afterwards, everyone claimed that they'd known all along, but it was Beryl who said it first: 'Bob wants to be like a duck.'

'Bob wants to be like a duck! Imagine that!' said Beryl's friends.

Soon, Bob was the only topic of conversation on Chestnut Hill, as everyone discussed the state of his health and wondered if anything like this had ever happened before. They had all heard of the beaver who woke up screaming, having dreamt that he was a frog. Someone had a cousin who had received a blow to the head and started to climb trees

Chapter Four

*T*he failure of Bob's businesses meant that he had to return to work, but with the construction industry experiencing a slowdown jobs were scarce or non-existent. Worse still, trying to be like a duck had left him hopelessly in debt. Beryl did what she could to make things stretch, but there was neither food nor comfort for their growing kits.

'I'm cold, Mum,' complained the youngest, wrapping herself in a blanket to generate whatever heat she could.

'I'm hungry,' cried another, gnawing at the legs of the table. 'When is dinner, Mum?'

Beryl did another trawl of the cupboards and the spaces behind the drawers, but even the safe places had given up what they had. Meanwhile, Bob kept out of the house and trudged slowly along the pathways of the wood, foraging for firewood.

'It's hopeless,' said Beryl, when he returned. 'What's to become of us?'

Bob shrugged his shoulders and, putting a handful of

twigs in the fire, he produced a pretentious waft of smoke, which drifted sideways instead of up. Leaning against the dresser, he poured some water from a tumbler and wondered how things had come to this. At least when he was trying to be like a duck he had been able to look on the bright side. That's what ducks did, even if things weren't working out. The big sale would come tomorrow, and if it didn't there was always the next opportunity. The truth was that business was in a duck's blood, making success just a matter of time.

Beavers were different, thought Bob. Renowned for the thoroughness of their work, they were always in demand, especially by ducks. Lacking their employers' ambition and drive, however, beavers were mainly concerned with getting by from day to day.

Bob was disturbed from his reverie by a knock on the door. He opened it and was handed a scrolled parchment by a young fox who disappeared without a word. Bob studied the curious lettering on its outside section.

The beaver called Robert,
12 Chestnut Hill,
Beavers' Grove.

Scratching his head, Bob wondered what it could be. The Beaver Construction Team had sent him a certificate for his attendance record the previous year, but as he was no longer working for them it could hardly be another one. It could, of course, be the licence for his flying school, which wouldn't be of much use now. Rolling the parchment open, Bob began to read slowly.

4th April
Dear Sir,
I wish to inform you that you are in breach of clause

'To stop him being thrown out of his house,' added another.

The rat nodded and began to return along the oak, smiling to himself. It was typical of ones so young, he thought. Older beavers, who knew the value of money, wouldn't entertain such nonsense. Back in the vault, the rat filled the six withdrawals from the bottom row of silver, creating a gap that was visible but only barely so. On the River Bank a total of twelve beavers awaited his return, the six in front taking their silver from the carriage, while those behind placed fresh withdrawal orders. By ten o'clock a hundred beavers had come and gone and half the stock of silver had been whittled away. That left one and a half rows remaining, as well as the two rows of gold at the top. The next hour saw more of the same, the relentlessness of the withdrawals raising fears that the bank might run short. With the ducks due to lodge their day's takings at four, however, the rat remained confident that he would survive.

By twelve o'clock, only a half-row of silver remained in the vault's bottom tiers. The rat was beginning to feel uneasy, and as he scuttled along the pole towards the River Bank, he noticed something that gave him even more cause for concern. The fresh-faced young beavers had come and gone, and fathers, grandfathers and uncles had arrived instead. Even worse were the large demands from the wealthier older beavers, their withdrawals dwarfing anything that had gone before. By lunchtime the vault's bottom rows were empty and, with his stock of gold disappearing fast, it was clear that the rat was in trouble.

Wasting none of his lunch break, the rat hurriedly locked the door of the bank. Scuttling across the oak, he headed up the hill towards the clearing, where he disturbed a dozing rabbit, before being spotted by a branch of squirrel youngsters.

'Where are you going?'

'Mind your own business,' snapped the rat.

'That is our business,' chorused the squirrels.

'What?'

'It's our job to find out where everyone's going.'

The rat mumbled something under his breath and continued on his way, as the squirrels climbed higher in the tree to follow his movements. Soon he arrived at government buildings where, after a slight delay, he was received by Edgar the Eagle.

'Sit down, rat. It's nice of you to call. We see so little of you. Cup of tea?'

'I'm here on business.'

'Business? I see.'

'The beavers are making withdrawals. They're putting it in some kind of Savings and Loan place.'

'That's nice. You're always saying they don't make enough use of their money.'

'You don't understand, Edgar. The beavers are withdrawing *all* their money.'

'Well, isn't that what banks are for? Giving folk back their money when they need it.'

'Yes, but not everyone's money, all at once.'

Edgar paused for a moment and poured himself a cup of tea.

'Are you sure you won't have some?'

'Quite sure, thank you,' replied the rat impatiently.

'It's a side effect of the potion,' said the mallard, his green head bobbing from side to side.

'What is?'

'The spot – the potion seems to bring it on.'

Bill nodded blankly and started the next game with a pawn to king four. He was getting tired and he soon found his game suffering against the re-energised mallard.

'Checkmate!' That's one back for me. Seven one,' said the mallard triumphantly.

Bill won the next game, but then lost five on the trot, bringing the score to eight six. By the next day the mallard had his measure, but Bill was too tired to care. At midnight he watched through his open eye as the mallard, following his usual routine, disappeared to another room and returned looking even zippier than before.

'So what do ya think?' asked the mallard, nudging Bill to a state of semi-consciousness.

'Huh?'

'Pillows are history, buddy. Everyone's goin' to be workin' night an' day from now on. There'll be no time for sleepin'.'

Bill lay slumped across the table, half opening an eye as the mallard whispered in his ear. Pay him off, he said, and he'd keep his invention under wraps. That way, animals would still buy pillows, and everyone could sleep peacefully, especially the duck called Bill.

The next day, a worried duck tried to clear his head so he could decide what to do. One option was to do nothing and hope the problem would go away. Paying off the mallard was another possibility, but could he be trusted not to put the potion on sale? He could take up Edgar's offer, of course, and sell off part of his business. The last option had two advantages − selling would protect him if pillows *did* go out of fashion, and if they didn't he could use the extra money to expand his business. Opting to sell, Bill informed Edgar, saying that he wanted to finalise the sale as soon as possible.

Edgar immediately began the search for investors to buy into the pillow business. He propositioned some goat police, who said they'd sleep on it, which they did before saying no. A family of squirrels thought about it too, but their stock answer was no. It was a question of confidence, thought Edgar. What was needed was a good news story, someone who would talk pillows up. Frogs could do it, of course, but nobody would believe them. A cheerful thrush called Thomas was a potential sort too, but he was considered by some to be a bit of a lightweight.

The farm bull was another possibility. Having spent his youth imprisoned on a farm in another wood, the bull, a born optimist, had waited for his chance and made good his escape. In all of Great Eagle Wood, nobody could talk things up quite like the farm bull. Wherever he stood the grass was greener, and some animals even believed that he could see the sun shine at night. Mention of pillows sent him into a frenzy of excitement.

'Pillows? Now there's a business. Why, that duck's pillows are the talk o' the wood. You're askin' me should you buy into pillows? Is the moon white? Are ducks smart? Is tomorrow comin'? Pillows? Take it from me, buddy, if ya

'Oh, I see! How silly of me. The Top Line is up there. There's the Middle Line. So this has to be…'

'The Bottom Line,' said the fox matter-of-factly, his interjection making Abby's ears turn red with embarrassment.

'What's the Bottom Line?'

Ignoring the question, the counting fox continued to stack the coins, the cash mountain now obscuring all but his head from view. Another basket arrived from pillow sales in the shop, sending the cash mountain even higher.

'Excuse me,' Abby repeated, 'what is the Bottom Line?'

'Why, it's *profit*, of course,' replied the fox.

'Profit?'

'Can you see the cash from the sale of pillows?' said the fox, pointing at the coin mountain on his desk.

'Yes.'

'Out of that we must pay the beavers, and the duck who supplies the cloth for the pillow bags.'

'And the rest is profit?'

'No,' snapped the fox. 'We also have to pay the moulting farm for their feathers.'

'And the rest is profit,' said Abby again.

'No, not until we pay our overheads.'

'Overheads?'

'Those ladies,' replied the fox with a sigh, raising his eyes towards the overhead hens.

'So, once everybody's been paid, what's left over is called profit?'

'Exactly, and to survive, every business must make a profit.'

'Of course! That's why profit is the Bottom Line,' said Abby, as the counting fox turned away and began to ignore her once again.

'There's just *one* more thing.'

'What?' said the fox impatiently, the incessant list of questions producing a frown that stretched across his forehead.

'Who gets the profit?'

'Not me!' snapped the fox, gesturing towards the coin mountain.

'Is it the beavers? Do they get the profit?'

'Of course not. They get paid by the hour.'

'So is it the overhead hens?' asked Abby, wondering if that might explain their impatience with the beavers.

The fox sighed and shook his head, and suddenly Abby had the answer.

'It's Bill, isn't it? *He* gets the profit.'

'At last!' sighed the fox. 'The stockholders always get the profit.'

'Aren't ducks smart?' said Abby. 'Everyone else does the work, and they get the profit. No wonder they don't need hands!'

Hearing of Edgar's return, Abby waved goodbye, and the counting fox threw his eyes towards the ceiling. She walked quickly through the Middle Line, a glance upward confirming that she was being watched by the overhead hens. Returning to the shop, Abby thanked the duck called Bill for his hospitality. Then it was time to leave, and to tell her grandfather about all she had learned.

before her good wing responded, allowing her to regain the height she had lost. Battling on its own to keep her up, her good wing then began to tire, and Abby closed her eyes as she plummeted towards the ground. Knowing that her already weakened body stood no chance of surviving a second fall, the little eagle cried out as she braced herself for the impact.

'Help! Please help!'

Below her, a host of leafy branches veered from side to side, offering what chance there was of a soft landing. Suddenly, caught in an upward draught, they leaned skywards, as though reaching out to the flailing eagle. Higher up, Abby too felt the rising current, and she was held almost suspended in mid-air.

'It's you. Isn't it? It's the wind. Thank you, oh, thank you!'

A second later there was a loud clatter and Abby was dragged sideways as her injured wing began to thrash about noisily. Then her good wing joined in and she began to climb into the sky.

'It's Abby! It's Abby! Abby is flying!' shouted some squirrel youngsters, climbing skywards on branches for a better view. The single-voice swans saw her too as she passed the River Bank, with her injured wing flapping loudly and the good one struggling to bring a semblance of order. Doubling back, she circled over the Freedom Tower, where Bob was yelling with excitement.

'You did it, Abby! You did it! I knew you would. I just knew you would.'

'It wasn't just me, Bob. Only for the wind…'

Later, in the night sky, a strange-looking twosome was seen heading for the Freedom Tower. One, slowed by his passing years, laboured to stay with the pace, while the other led the way, her wings stronger but lacking the harmony of the elder. On arriving at the top of the Tower, Edgar gasped as his eyes measured the drop to the ground.

'You shouldn't have taken such a risk, Abby. You could have ...' His words trailed off as his chest swelled with pride at the enormity of what she had done. Building up her wing had been important, he felt, as was her choice of a beaver to help her reach the top. The Freedom Tower had been pivotal too, its height allowing the most time possible for her wings to do their job. Then there was the wind – perhaps the most crucial element of all.

'There's rain on the way, Granddad.'

'Rain?'

'The trees have been asking for days. Now, at last, the sky has agreed.'

Looking up at the blue sky, Edgar was about to question her strange observation when he felt a drop on his head. It was followed by a second, then several more, and soon the branches beneath the Tower were devouring the sky's liquid offering.

'How did you know?'

'What?'

'About the rain.'

'I just did.'

Edgar shook his head in wonder at the strange things his granddaughter spoke of. How did she know of the trees' thirst, or of the sky's delay in gifting them the water they craved? Wasn't it the wind that had cushioned her fall as she plunged from the Freedom Tower? They had always been

'Which one?' asked Bob, his voice trembling with excitement.

'A–B,' said the spider. 'Yes, I remember distinctly. It's in A–B.'

Aiming to the left, the spider propelled his chair in the direction of the cabinet nearest the door. Opening a drawer, he bypassed several Annette files, and skipped through ants, badgers and bats. Taking a file marked 'Beaver called Bob' from the cabinet, he began to read aloud:

Full name: Robert
Family: Partner's name Beryl, and four kits, names unknown
Address: 12 Chestnut Hill, Beaver's Grove
Occupation: Construction worker
Ambition: Wants to become like a duck
History: Several failed business ventures

'Is that all it says? Is there anything about becoming like a duck?' asked Bob.

'There doesn't seem to be. Wait, I remember now. It's filed under D.'

Veering to the right, the spider opened the C–D cabinet, and began to scan the files.

'Dogfish, dormouse, the duck called Bill, ducking taxes…'

'Is there anything about becoming like a duck?'

'Here's one about *things becoming to a duck.*'

'That could be it! Read it out.'

'The following are things becoming to a duck: a long bill, controlled swagger, closely webbed feet, creamy white skin…'

'Does it say anything about beavers?'

'Let's see… no, I don't think so.'

'There must be something. Try the other cabinets!'

Annette's big brother did a trawl of the E–F cabinet, which contained files mainly about eagles and foxes. There was nothing under G–H about becoming like a duck, or in any other section for that matter. Something under W–Z caught one of the spider's eyes.

'Here's one about web design. It says...'

'Who cares what it says?' replied Bob impatiently.

'Well if that's your attitude!' said the spider, banging the drawer shut with one of his legs.

'I'm sorry. It's just that I want so much to be like a duck, and I really thought this was my chance.'

'Maybe you should see a shrink. Or have an operation.'

'An operation?'

'Yeah, they could fit you with a bill, cut off your arms and maybe muck up your feet a bit.'

'You don't understand. You see, I don't want to *be* a duck.'

'You don't?'

'No, I want to be *like* a duck.'

'Oh!'

'I just want to have my own business. If only I knew how!'

A raucous cheer from the message centre made the floor beneath them shake. It signalled the end of Annette's address to the spiders, who would start to return to their work stations any second now.

'You'd better go.'

'Yeah, I guess so.'

'I hope you find what you're looking for.'

'Thanks.'

Bob waved goodbye and closed the door behind him.

promising that a second invention, which he was keeping under his cowboy hat, would soon turn things around. A month later, his glow-in-the-dark sunglasses caused quite a stir, and the Great Wood came to life at night as luminous eyes darted about in the darkness. Unfortunately, one week on, interest had waned, with all except the glow-worms opting for a return to anonymity.

Ronen was unrepentant. Progress wasn't easy, he said, but he had seen the future, and it didn't have trees. The wood was moving towards a new age of enlightenment, and he would need more scientists, and even better inventions if he was to stay ahead. Making light of his problems, the cowboy duck used his holdings of web stock to secure an even larger loan, which he kept safe and secret in his SPV.

Meanwhile, with her big brother continuing to gather vast amounts of intelligence, the black widow Annette seemed on track to take over the wood. Even as her influence grew, however, some animals began to question whether she actually possessed magical powers. The reality, as many had begun to realise, was that most things bought on the web still had to be manufactured and delivered. Also, there had been complaints from customers about receiving either the wrong goods or wrong sizes. Most worrying of all were the allegations of fraud, with some animals claiming that web swindlers had misused their Wood Express credit card. Ultimately, the consensus was that although Annette did have powers, they were not *magical* powers.

As the allure of the black widow faded, an animal who had been in poor health made a miraculous recovery. The brown bear had suffered from a blood disorder, his doctors said. Now, infused with a fresh supply of B-negative, he was once again his old self.

'Don't say you weren't warned!' he raged, growling so loudly that the entire wood knew of his return. 'Why, that Annette is just an ordinary spider,' he fumed, giving what was arguably an unfair assessment of the black widow's abilities.

This time, however, the Great Wood listened carefully to the brown bear's words, and Annette's price plummeted as animals dumped her stock.

The suddenness of the black widow's collapse left many animals at a loss, and worst hit of all was Ronen, the cowboy duck.

'What am I goin' to do, Bob?' he asked his beaver friend.

'Do about what?'

'The web stock was the collateral for my secret loans. Now it's almost worthless!'

'So?'

'So the rat will want his money back.'

'Can't you just give it to him?'

'I don't have it!'

'You don't have it?'

'How could I, when the beaver scientists have blown everything on wind power. It's all their fault!'

Bob shook his head, as the cowboy duck answered the telephone. It was typical of Ronen, he thought, blaming black robe. Taking his place on the bench, he opened a file and began to speak, slowly and deliberately.

'In the case of Great Eagle Wood versus the farm bull, the defendant is accused of irrational optimism. How do you plead?'

'Innocent, your honour.'

'You are conducting your own defence, I understand. Is that correct?'

'I sure am, your honour,' replied the farm bull.

'Very well. The prosecution may call its first witness.'

A senior legal fox rose from his chair, and bowed as he addressed the judge.

'The prosecution calls the farm bull, your honour.'

Smiling confidently, the defendant strode towards the witness box, and took the oath.

'Can you begin by telling the court something about yourself?' asked the legal fox, holding the lapels of his jacket with both hands.

The farm bull thought for a moment, wondering how best to describe himself. Handsome was a word he had heard used, and he knew that some regarded the ring on his nose to be quite a distinctive feature. Of late, his right ear had become discoloured, something he decided not to mention. Socially, he was unattached, his mother having been his first and only significant udder.

'Well, I'm about seven feet tall, with green eyes. I have a brown coat an'…'

The courtroom erupted in laughter, and the owl judge banged his gavel on the bench, shouting, 'Order in court!'

'We are well aware of your physical features, thank you,' remarked the legal fox caustically. 'Now perhaps you would be kind enough to tell the court about your outlook on life.'

'Why, I'd say I was born with an optimistic nature. Once, I was held prisoner on a farm, but I knew that one day I'd escape, 'cause I believe that everyone gets a chance in life to improve himself.'

'What you're saying is that you believe your glass is always half full?'

'No, sir, I do not. The way I see things in this wood, every glass is full right up to the brim.'

'You are optimistic about other things besides glasses, aren't you?'

'Yes sir, I am. Take stock prices. Why, there's no limit to how high they can go in this wood.'

'So stock prices will just keep going up. Is that how you see it?'

'That's right, sir. With the quality o' ducks in this wood, the sky's the limit for stock prices.'

'Now, you look like a bull of above average intelligence....'

'Why, thank you, sir. If I wasn't under oath I'd be inclined to say the same about you.'

The farm bull's quip sparked off spontaneous laughter in the courtroom, and even the owl judge struggled to keep a straight face as he banged his gavel and shouted 'Order in court!' for a second time. In the witness box the farm bull seemed satisfied that the early exchanges were going his way. He was not to know that things were about to change.

'So stock prices will keep going up, is that your view?'

'Yes, sir, stock prices are on the move, and that move is up.'

'Do you know...' asked the legal fox, stopping in mid-sentence and giving a sly sort of smile, '... of anything else that always goes up?'

'Yes it does!'

'It has a funny way of showing it.'

'What do you mean?'

'You know the duck called Bill, don't you?'

'Everyone knows Bill. His pillows are famous.'

'Well, his factories keep blowing up smoke.'

'Bill's factories? But he has beavers doing the work.'

'Not any more. It's all machines now.'

'Maybe he doesn't realise.'

'Realise what?'

'That the smoke is hurting you.'

'He doesn't care. Nobody cares about the sky anymore.'

'I care!'

'Ha! Who's going to listen to an eagle like you?'

'One day I'll be the leader of Great Eagle Wood. Then I'll *make* them care!'

'You will?'

'I promise I will.'

The sky's steely blue began to soften as it warmed to the gutsy little eagle. Someone in the Great Wood cared after all, and that made a difference. Looking down, Abby saw the fire from the east continue its push towards the Freedom Tower.

'It's killing the trees,' she said sadly. 'Soon there will be nowhere for the birds to make their nests.'

The sky remembered how much it too had loved the trees.

'And the flowers,' said Abby, 'they're choking in the fire.'

A tear began to form in the little eagle's eye as she watched the suffering of her beloved wood. Growing heavier, it hung like a tiny raindrop, before breaking loose and floating away in the wind. Moved by the little eagle's love of the Great Wood, the sky became heavy with sadness.

Soon a teardrop fell, and then several more, as it too began to weep for the Great Wood. Seeing the sky's tears, the wind lifted them onto its back and carried them eastwards, then dipping lower it unloaded them onto the great fire.

The fire from the east screamed with shock as it absorbed the sky's watery contents. Its fringes, unable to withstand the deluge, flickered and died. At its centre, however, it dug deep and, pushing itself higher, once again refused to be put out.

Descending from the sky, Abby saw Bob still trapped beside the Freedom Tower and she began to despair. She had cajoled the wind into battle, and even reined in a reluctant sky, yet it seemed nothing could halt the advance of the fire from the east. Then, as flames licked the horizon, Abby recalled the advice she had received from her grandfather when she was a young eagle.

'If there's no other way, you must fight fire with fire.'

Abby studied the high grass to the east of the Freedom Tower. It would catch fire, she was pretty sure about that, and with the help of the wind from the west it would burn away from the Tower. Flying downwind towards the inferno, she turned her head from the intense heat as she drew close. Swooping down, she plucked a burning branch from the ground, and then she was airborne again, heading west towards the Freedom Tower. There she released her fiery load onto the undergrowth to the east of the Tower, before flying back for a second branch. The operation was repeated until the undergrowth to the east of the Tower was alive with orange.

seemed to make badgers happy. If the therapy didn't work, so what? He would become like a duck too, which was what he'd always wanted. That meant he could buy Beryl a bigger house. Bob was on the point of saying yes, when his cautious beaver side began to wonder about downsides.

'Don't worry about the law,' said the duck, as though he was reading his mind. 'Sox is an ass! Cowboy ducks are too smart for the likes of him.'

'What about Abby?' screamed a voice inside his head. 'She believes in you, Bob! What's *she* going to think?'

'All you've gotta do is a bit of snippin',' said the duck, leering at him from across the table.

'And Ronen. Don't say you've forgotten about him!' It was the voice again, and when reminded of the suffering caused by the cowboy duck, Bob felt his head start to pound.

'You're gonna be rich,' said the duck. 'Just like me.'

'Stop! Stop!' screamed Bob, covering his ears and jumping up from the chair, which went flying as he fled from the room. In the shop, the queue of she-badgers moved quickly to one side as he barged his way past and disappeared through the door.

Outside, he stumbled about in a daze, as the voice and the urgings of the re-tail therapy duck continued to thrash about in his head.

'Hey, watch where you're going, buddy,' shouted a traffic cop, shaking his head when Bob knocked against a lamp-post and almost fell onto the road. Passers-by stared as he wandered about in a daze before collapsing in a heap outside the duck called Bill's shop. He lay there until word reached Abby, who rushed to his side.

'Are you okay, Bob? Come on, let's get you up.'

'It's over, Abby.'

'What's over? Something has happened, hasn't it?'

'I'm no good at anything.'

'Yes you are!'

'No, I'm not. I'm never going to be like a duck.'

'You will be if you believe, Bob.'

'A beaver is all I'm ever going to be. I might as well just face it.'

'Don't give up hope, Bob. Anything is possible in Great Eagle Wood.'

Abby comforted her friend, and the sky grew darker and the wind fell silent as the beaver covered his head and wept.

'Is he okay, Miss Abby?' asked the duck called Bill, his enormous stomach preceding him as he appeared from inside the shop.

'I don't know. I just found him like this.'

'What happened, Bob? Ya don't look so good.'

'I was in this re-tail therapy place, and…'

'Re-tail therapy? Why, that joint is run by a cowboy duck. Come on inside, Bob. Pick out a pillow for Beryl. Have one on me!'

Bob mumbled some words of thanks as he was helped into the shop, where Bill began to show off his pillows.

'This one here is called 'the sleek'. It's all the rage with the females. I prefer the plain ones myself, not very fashionable, but more room for yer head. Still, it's your choice, Bob. The customer is king, that's what I always say!'

'What about those?'

'Ya like the red ones, Bob? Why, those pillows just weren't movin'. Well, look at 'em! They sure ain't pretty. But they're the meanest pillows on the market. Ya wanna know how we shifted 'em?'

'Did you sell them as punch bags?'

"Are you able to give me an idea of what this is about?"

"I am afraid not - and certainly not on the phone. It will have to be face to face. Unfortunately, we cannot trust anything to letters or emails either. It has to be in person. Where are you living at the moment?"

"I divide my time between an apartment I rent in Manchester and my mother's home in Scotland. Right now however, I am in the Gloucester area. But before I say any more, I think I should tell you that something very strange is happening at the moment. I am afraid I am being followed."

"That does not surprise me at all," interrupted Poska.

"Why would you say that?" inquired Jack.

"Well this is all linked into the reason we have to meet. Where did you say you were?"

"Gloucester," responded Jack.

"OK, just hold on a moment."

There was no sound on the line for a minute or so and Jack wondered if they had been disconnected until Poska came back on the line.

"Sorry about that Mr Troughton, I was just asking my secretary to check something for me, but before I get onto that, can you make yourself free the day after tomorrow?"

"It's not going to be easy, but if this is as important as you infer it is, then I will make it happen."

"That's good, then one more thing. How long did you say you have known you were under surveillance?"

"Just a day or two," answered Jack.

"Well, you should not assume that it has been for just as short a time as that. I believe it could have been going on for several days, perhaps even as much as a week. I should also warn you that if you have conducted any conversations in public places, like coffee shops or restaurants for example, it may well be that those meetings will have been recorded."

"Why would anyone want to record such innocuous conversations?" asked Jack incredulously.

"Well, by recorded I mean at least 'listened to' by a third party using a small directional microphone. They may not have wanted to physically record your conversations for posterity - just to listen in on what you have been saying. Perhaps most of what you said was innocuous but they would not know that until they had heard what you were saying of course. Once again, we must not talk about this any more on the phone please. We will talk when we meet. My secretary has just checked and the best London station from Cheltenham will be to Paddington. There is a train shortly after six a.m. apparently."

"Why so early?" asked Jack.

"It means that you will arrive at rush hour and the platforms will be crowded. It is likely that someone will again try and follow you. And by the way, be sure to book First Class."

"That won't be necessary," Jack responded.

"It most certainly will. Please do as I suggest. Now listen carefully. When you get off the train make your way to WH Smiths at the front of the station. Outside and to the left and beside the incline that takes people from the station to the main road, you will see a free-standing stall selling Paddington Bear memorabilia - soft toys, mugs and that sort of thing. When you approach the stall, linger for just a minute or so. One of my people will be in the vicinity to identify you. They will then signal to me that you have arrived and you are then to make your way to the First Class lounge which is situated on platform one. It is the platform on the far left of the station. Press the button to the left of the door and it will open electronically. Show your ticket to the person at the desk and they will direct you to the lounges. Pass the one on the left and proceed to the one furthest on, which is furnished with green chesterfield sofas and chairs. You will see me in the left hand corner of the room. There will be people sitting on the sofa across the room but don't be concerned about them over-hearing us, as they will be with me. Incidentally, when you board at platform two in Cheltenham, do so into Standard Class and walk through to First Class later. If they have signalled to anyone that you are on the London train they will not be

"Do you want me to go on Jack or is this too much for you?" asked Poska.

"No, you better continue. But all you are saying is throwing up more questions in my mind than answers - but I am going to wait until you are through, so please go on?"

"OK, well, Escobar's story is that they pulled over to a pay phone and the police officer phoned a contact number for the organisation. He was told to wait by the phone. In the meantime, the medic was checking your wife's vital signs and had confirmed that, though breathing was shallow and she was not responding to speech, she was very much alive - at least for the moment. The medic watched as the phone rang in the cubicle and saw the officer lift the receiver.

After a few minutes the man returned to the vehicle and issued the orders he had been given. They had been commanded to proceed to an address about fifteen minutes away.

The story is, and frankly we all find this very hard indeed to believe, that a woman had died violently at the hands of the traffickers just a few hours earlier and the injuries were not inconsistent with those that could have been sustained in a traffic accident."

"Aw come on - that's too big a stretch of the imagination," argued Damian. "Escobar is just spinning you a yarn to get you to comply with his wishes. It's just too much of a coincidence - frankly it's ridiculous. With respect Mr Poska I am surprised that a man like you would be taken in by it. It just could not have happened."

Poska did not respond defensively. He just looked over to Jack who was now sitting back on his sofa, his arms folded and staring into space, clearly not knowing what or whom to believe.

"We of course put this to Escobar. The thing is that preposterous stories, even alibis, often turn out to be true. You have to realise that no one concocting an account would usually think of offering such unreasonable evidence. Nevertheless, we still do not know the veracity of what Escobar told us."

"So you are implying," interrupted Jack, "that the body of the other woman, the one who was actually dead and was a similar age and build to my wife, was swapped with Celia's? In other words, it was the second woman that was eventually booked in to the mortuary."

And then as if light had just dawned - not to reveal a new day but a frighteningly fresh horror, Jack continued. "But this was four years ago. If this is remotely true and Celia is still alive, what has my wife being going through in all those years? Please don't tell me that she has been at the mercy of those monsters. She is a strong woman but she could never live through an ordeal like that."

"First of all," continued Poska calmly, "I am not implying anything at all. This is all Escobar's story, as you know. He is saying that it solved an immediate problem of disposing of a body. If your wife was alive, and survived, they at least had some space to work out what to do with her."

"But I can't see how the medic would be willing to go along with this. It would be more than his job was worth," said Damian.

"You have to understand how things work," continued Poska. "The police and medics work together all the time. They are known to one another. It is possible that the corrupt officer would have known, or even threatened, the medic's family. Also, if Celia had died as a result of the medic's negligence - and taken her to a morgue instead of Emergency, he could at best be facing a severe disciplinary charge."

"But there's still the issue of what they would be able to do with someone who had been injured to the degree that Celia would have been."

"Now that is a very fair point," agreed Poska. "However, these gangs have tentacles everywhere. There is often in-fighting among them - or between them and rival competitive groups. This may involve gun shot injuries or knife wounds and such like. You can be sure they have people on call who, for the right fee, will address such issues with no questions asked. It is just a short step from that to private clinics. It is only when major surgery is necessary that things primarily to check on me. There is a small kitchen where I can make meals for Wesley and me and leading from that, is a utility room that houses a washing machine, tumble drier and an ironing board.

I sometimes wonder why I take the trouble to commit all these thoughts to writing. It is perhaps because, deep down somewhere, lurks a fear that I will again lose the memories that I am currently accumulating. I don't keep these papers on open view but if they really wanted to check what I was writing, they could easily do so. The room is so small there is nowhere to hide anything. They obviously know there is no risk that I would try and escape and are understandably confident that there is nothing I would do to put my baby in jeopardy. The very thought that they would take him from me, let alone harm him, fills me with absolute dread. He is my lifeline and my only source of hope. I sense that I need him every bit as much as he needs me.

I can't say that, apart from the obvious emotional pain of my confinement, anyone has gone out of their way to be cruel to me. I have been neither physically nor even verbally abused. The best word I can use to describe the emotional atmosphere here is sterile - as sterile as the surfaces of the clinic I first woke up in.

What I really can't get my head around, is why they are keeping me here at all? Why would they have even saved my life in the first place? It makes no sense.

Each week, usually on a Thursday, a man visits me. Sometimes he brings someone with him and sometimes he doesn't. They ask me about my past, even though I have told them that everything is lost to me. I sometimes get the feeling that they are trying to trick me. Perhaps they believe that I am holding something back - well that's the impression I get anyway. It's strange that after all this time I still do not know anyone's name. They never introduce themselves to me. The two who come I think of as 'moustache' and 'brown shoes'. Sometimes they ask me to do tests - to assess my skills I would imagine. Once they brought in a computer and watched as I typed. On another occasion 'brown shoes' gave me a set of questions and

43

puzzles. I imagine that was to get an idea of what IQ I might have. Who knows? It seems that I impressed them with my typing skills, as since then I have had a steady stream of copy typing to do and translation work. They obviously know more about my background than I do and have worked out that I can speak both languages fluently. At first I thought that this was an expensive and complicated way to retain a secretary. But the more I ran this through my mind, the more I realised that there could be no better way to keep highly sensitive business completely confidential. However, surely it would be impracticable to use this as a long term strategy.

Last week, 'moustache' hinted at a 'fresh development in the New Year' but didn't elucidate. I will have to wait and see I suppose.

I was hoping that by now I would get flashbacks that would give me a clue to my life before all this happened but I am as much in the dark as ever I was. One thing however is unusual and is happening with increased regularity. It started in the middle of the night when I was having a disturbing dream. None of my dreams ever make sense and I rarely can remember what I have dreamt once I wake up. Anyway, this particular night I woke up and to my astonishment, found myself praying. I came to the conclusion the next morning, that this was something to do with the disturbed state I was in. However, this is now occurring with increased regularity. Does this indicate that some kind of religious belief played a part, perhaps even a significant part, in my background? Why else would I find myself 'calling on Jesus' for help? It's very odd but all I know is that when I pray, I feel more at peace afterwards. I shall give this some more thought and may even begin to pray intentionally, rather than just in the middle of the night.

her personal fate in her hand? And was this not entirely unfair? All she had had to worry about to this point was Wesley's future and her own. Now all this was being thrust upon her. It was just too much.

"I know about your story," Olga continued, without waiting for any assurances from the woman she knew as Tania. "Everything has been explained to me. I know about your amnesia. I know that you are being held here against your will. I know that they have said that they will harm both you and your son if you do not cooperate with them."

"Why have your eyes been sweeping the room ever since you came into my apartment?" asked Celia - not addressing what the woman had just said but seeking to have her earlier concerns addressed.

I was looking for surveillance equipment - cameras, microphones, things like that. I wanted to know if anyone could be listening in. But unless it is extremely minute and exceptionally sophisticated, I can't see anything."

"I wouldn't imagine there would be anything like that in here," answered Celia. "Why would there be? I don't have visitors, and the ones I do, are with 'them' anyway. You are English aren't you? I did not expect that. Olga's not a very English name - more Baltic wouldn't you say?"

Olga noticed how the woman was bouncing from one subject to another and she realised why. Not only had she lost her memory, she had probably lost some basic social skills. Her only conversational interaction to this point, was in the context of an interrogation. She was clearly struggling with conversation and she probably could not remember ever engaging in 'small talk'.

"I was born in Russia to Russian parents but I went over to the UK to study. After that, I worked for a marketing and branding company and they had some high-end clients and wanted a more refined accent for some reason. They even paid for me to have elocution lessons would you believe? Anyway it seems to have worked and most people are not aware of any accent at all."

"I see you have brought a parcel with you," said Celia, once again not addressing herself to what she had just heard but reflecting a thought she had had in her mind as the visitor had come in."

"Oh yes, I nearly forgot. These are for you. You said you wanted some books to read and they asked me to bring these for you," said Olga, passing the package over.

Olga watched, as instead of leaving the parcel to one side until she had gone, the woman busied her fingers in an attempt to undo the package in front of her. She obviously had not only been bereft of company, she also had been starved of anything to read.

"They want me to befriend you as a means of spying on you." Olga said coming immediately to the point.

Celia's head shot up abruptly and her fingers released the string she had been trying to untie. Was this woman for real? Was she really trying to tell her she was 'on her side'? There would surely be no way that she would say a thing like that, unless it was true. Why should there be?"

"I am going to tell you my story Tania. I am calling you 'Tania' because that is the name they gave me and they obviously gave you. But I would not be too sure that that is really your name. In fact, I would not take on trust anything that they have told you."

"Do you really think that that is possible?" asked Celia. "I mean the account of the accident is true because I know the physical state I was in when I regained consciousness. They couldn't be lying about that."

"No, I think you are right there," agreed Olga. "But that's about all you can know for sure."

Olga spent the next few minutes outlining her story including the fact that she, like Tania, was also being controlled and in very much the same way. Celia believed everything she was hearing. She drank in every word and Olga realised how, if she really had wanted to, she could have so manipulated this woman's complete emotional vulnerability. But she had no intention of doing that. On the contrary, beyond her ultimate goal of freeing herself and her family from the clutches of the organisation with which she was embroiled, she was

Celia 2009 December

It's nearly Christmas and I have broken my ankle. This is the first time I have put pen to paper like this in over two years. I have to admit that I have missed doing it. But I remembered how therapeutic I used to find it, so I have started again. I have in mind to do it regularly but I need to be very careful what I include in these 'ruminations'. I always feel an added tension around when the 'visitors' are due to come. It's not only 'moustache' and 'brown shoes' that turn up these days to give me my instructions, other people come too but all are just as incommunicative. I am just given my instructions and expected to get on with it.

The woman who looks after Wesley when I am working has changed too. I never liked her and neither did Wesley. The new one is very different and she has a couple of children herself - a boy about the same age as Wesley and a girl two years older. My handlers allow her to bring them with her when she comes. It's more for her benefit than mine. She does not seem to be warm towards those that bring her in the same way that the other woman was. Perhaps they have a similar kind of hold over her as they do over me. I don't know. She doesn't talk much but when she does, at least she is pleasant. Bringing her little ones probably saves her having to have a child minder of her own and of course it's brilliant for Wesley. The three of them get on well - although Wesley says that the older girl is 'too bossy' and always has to be in charge. Anyway, it's a huge answer to prayer and brings a modicum of normality into his little world. The language barrier was a problem to begin with. I speak to Wesley in English and she and the children only understand Estonian.

But I am surprised how much he is able to pick up now. Kids are so adaptable. The woman, her name is Angelika, speaks a little English and likes to practice it on me in those few moments we get together - usually as she arrives and just before she goes.

She is always anxious to get home as soon as possible after I return from my duties and naturally I understand that. Who would want to stay in a confined space like this any longer than they had to?

I only see Olga about every six weeks now. They see no reason for her to come here as often as she had been doing. They remain under the impression that she is monitoring me and apparently she feeds them bits of information that somehow seems to keep them happy. The one good thing is that when she does come, they sometimes let her stay for a couple of days. Wesley has missed her as much as I have and always gets excited when he learns that she is scheduled to be here. When that happens I hear nothing but "How many more days until auntie Olga gets here Mummy?" He never lets up. She is the only 'family' that he has apart from me of course.

She tells me that the people in St. Petersburg are happy with my work and that means that they are similarly satisfied with her performance in matters relating to me. She does not talk much about the other work that she is involved in. I am sure her motive is more about not compromising me, than wanting to keep me in the dark. Her parents struggle but at least she still has them.

My duties consist largely of monitoring the other members of the organisation. There is an innate culture of suspicion that assumes that only the people in the top echelon can be entirely trusted. The rest it is assumed are syphoning off profits, making alliances with competitors and things like that. Needless to say, I would rather not be doing anything like this at all but at least what I am being forced to do is not putting any innocent people in danger.

Since I last added to my journal, several remarkable things have happened. I feel a shiver going down my spine even as I write. I

There was total silence in the room. No one spoke and her mother and father, seeing that she had failed to argue with the statement, took it as an indication that they were right.

"You know the kind of life that I was drawn into Olga and I am ashamed of many things that I did. I am not going to make excuses. Certainly I won't. In my mind I was trying to put food on the table for my family - but lots of people have been just as needy as us, without having to resort to crime or being involved with the sort of people I eventually became entangled with."

He paused briefly to catch his breath and to rest a moment.

Olga wanted to speak but was well aware that it was only going to prolong the conversation longer and make him increasingly tired. She had to let him go on without further interruption, however hard it was for her.

"I am concerned," he went on, "that you have been drawn into the same web. You know the reason why I stopped. It was because I had come to faith. I don't know how your mother and I would have survived the ordeal of these past few years without our trust in God. I really don't. However, I recently have come to learn all that has been happening while I have been confined to my bed and while your mother has had the burden of caring for me."

This time it was Olga's mother who began to interrupt, but before she could break in, her husband raised a bony arm towards her and so she drew back.

"It breaks my heart to think that by pulling myself away from their net, it has only served to drag you into their clutches. I can see from your face that you are wondering how I found out. The fact is, that when I was working for them I made some friends. They were not high up in the organisation. They were people like me, who because of circumstances, had got themselves into the same mess as I had.

Some of them dropped by to see me from time to time. There would be those, I have no doubt who were really only here to monitor me but there were others who I knew were genuine in their concern. It was on one of those occasions something was inadvertently 'let slip' by them, during our conversation about you being mixed up with what they were doing. The person concerned, as soon as he had said it, tried to cover up what he had said, but it was like trying to un-spill milk. It was out and I insisted that he must explain himself. As you can imagine, I was heartbroken when I then began to understand the truth. I became only slightly more at ease when he told me the level to which you had been enmeshed. It has been some kind of surveillance work has it?"

Olga lowered her eyes and momentarily removed the gaze that had been locked on her father from the first moment she had drawn her chair alongside his bed. That said enough.

"I am relieved about that," her father continued. "I would have been horrified beyond words if it had been anything more. But this conversation that your mother and I had planned to have with you, is about far more than relaying the information you have heard so far. Olga, I may be weak and frail but you really have to listen to me now."

Olga's eyes moved back to her father and locked on to his eyes like a limpet on a rock.

"There is to be no argument and not the slightest compromise about what I am going to require of you. Your mother and I are one in this. Listen to me. We absolutely insist."

Olga was aware that she was holding her breath.

"When the most recent supply of medication was brought, I was informed that I had only weeks, rather than months to live. In fact, my end may come even quicker than that. I have no fear of dying, as I know that death is not the end. I know, that whatever happens, your mother and I will meet again one day. And I hope that I will be reunited with you too Olga. And here we come to it. When my time comes and the funeral takes place, you must not, and I definitely mean must not, attend."

Olga instinctively began to rise to her feet. Her mother's hand had been still resting on her shoulder in affection and support but now it applied itself gently in restraint. She resumed her sitting position and looked enquiringly towards her father.

implications began to cascade into her mind. She became aware of her hands moving up to the sides of her head as if by steadying herself in that way she could control all the thoughts - all the opportunities, dangers, risks and rewards from escaping from her brain.

Eventually, she drew her hands back to her knees and stared directly across to her friend, locking her eyes on her. She addressed Olga quietly and firmly as if she was weighing every word as she spoke and was assessing their potential impact.

"There are some things that I need to tell you Olga. They are things, when you hear them you will wonder why I have not shared them earlier - a lot earlier in fact. You may assume that the reason why I previously had not done this was because I did not trust you. You may even begin to doubt the level of the friendship that you thought we had.

It's true that in the early days I did not feel I could trust anyone. This was probably because I was not even entirely sure who I was. I think there were times when I even went as far as doubting my own sanity if I am honest. Later on I kept these things to myself, because I thought that if I shared with you everything I knew, it would put you in danger should ever these people try to interrogate you or if they became suspicious. Anyway, I did what I did for what I considered were the best reasons at the time. Whether I was right or wrong remains to be seen.

First of all you need to know that my name is not Tania. It is Celia. I don't know what my actual surname is but I am quite sure it will not be 'Edwards'. If they gave me a false Christian name, I have no doubt that the surname is fictitious as well.

I also know that my husband's name is not Tom but Jack, and that he and I once visited a church building in Tallinn and also frequented a cafe nearby. I won't go into, at this stage, how I know all these things - we can unpack all that at a later point if you want."

Olga looked across at Celia with an expression that mixed incredulity and a whole smorgasbord of other emotions. She looked as though she wanted to say something but though her mouth was open, nothing seemed to be able to come out.

Celia anticipated an interruption but wanted to continue with all she had yet to say, and so held her hand up in front of Olga as if she was a policewoman attempting to halt traffic in a busy street.

"I also know," Celia continued, "that one of my husband's best friends is a man called Damian Clarke and I know that he is married to a woman called Sue."

At the mention of Damian's name, Olga blurted out in amazement, "How on earth would you know that name Tania, or Celia, whatever you are called? There is no way that you could have heard that name within these four walls or even outside for that matter. It's impossible!"

"I did not 'hear' the name at all Olga," continued Celia. "Once when you were here in this room, you left to go to the bathroom and while you were out, Wesley went over to your briefcase and started playing with it. By the time I had noticed what he was doing, files were all over the floor. I pulled him away and told him off but as I was inserting them back into your case, I saw the name 'Damian Clarke' on one of them and felt I knew the name from somewhere. When I saw the appended photograph, I was absolutely certain that I did. I could hear you returning, and obviously did not want you to think that I was rummaging through your stuff, so I was not in a position to see anything more. I clearly could not question you, as to why someone I thought I knew had any connection with you or why you should have his file in your possession."

"Wow, wow, wow!" exclaimed Olga, as pieces of a jigsaw were being assembled in her consciousness and the connections that were being made began to take on an entirely fresh significance.

Olga's head seemed to her as if it was about to burst. It was as if a war was taking place between an army of 'exclamation marks' and a regiment of 'question marks'. And right now, the battle seemed to be at a stalemate with neither side in total control. Olga knew that her visit tonight would convey data that her friend might find hard to it towards her, she realised that it didn't feel like the torch as it was oblong and not curved and plastic rather than metal. In some way it reminded her of a miniature TV remote. She would not know it then, but this was the device that earlier that morning, Kuznetsov had jettisoned in temper from his car window in the belief that the gates were not opening because it's battery had failed or that it was broken. As she moved it around in her hand she pressed the button instinctively - simply because the button was there. The gates did not operate because the gates were not there and had been carried off for replacement or repair. But as she pressed she felt that there was a reaction. She heard a whirring sound behind her and as she turned to see where the sound was coming from, she saw one of the three garage doors behind her, rise.

Olga continued to feel around on the ground until she had located the torch she had originally been looking for. She then ran into the garage, pressed an adjacent button on the fob to close the door behind her and that done, she felt confident enough to put on the garage light.

She looked around and to her absolute delight, saw a door that linked the garage to the main house. She made for the door and turned off the garage light behind her. She pressed the switch on her torch, headed swiftly to the entrance hall where the she knew the keypad was located, pressed in 34561 and successfully disarmed the alarm.

She stood motionless for a few moments in order to catch her breath and gather her thoughts. She now had to think where Kuznetsov's office was. She believed it to be on the second floor - the first room on the left at the top of the stairs. Olga set off in that direction, found it, and entered the room. There at one end was the large desk with the green leather inlay that she remembered - the one she had first seen in St. Petersburg before he moved to Tallinn. Olga moved to the left hand drawer where she believed the papers to be. She had never actually seen them and even if they had been there, she realised he could have moved them somewhere else - even perhaps to a safe. If that were the case, it would certainly be 'game over'. She tugged on the drawer, never for a moment believing that it would be open. It didn't. Olga looked at her watch and realised the Kuznetsov's would be ordering the cheese board by now or even be on their coffee. She had to move fast.

Olga reached into another pocket of her anorak to retrieve the sharp tool that she had brought with her. In an ideal world it would have been wonderful to leave the premises without any trace that she had been there, but she knew that that was not going to happen. When Kuznetsov came into the room, either late that night or sometime tomorrow, he would immediately realise that an intruder had been in his study but she could not do anything about that. Then, when he examined the desk and saw what had been taken, he would very quickly realise that he had been set up and why. Very soon after that he would be off at speed in the direction of Celia's apartment.

When she inserted the tool, the desk lock quickly gave way, and to her undiluted relief, Olga saw the passports and papers laying there in front of her. She snatched them up quickly, checking that nothing was missing.

She was just about to head for the door to leave when her training kicked in again. She re-examined the drawer and saw that its length was only about two thirds the depth of the desk. This might just be the design of the furniture. She tried the right hand draw which turned out not to be locked, and immediately saw that this one stretched back the full length of the desk. She had been right in her assumption, there must be a concealed panel! Olga pulled out the drawer and when it did not come out the entire way, smashed with her fist at the back panel.

The thin softwood quickly gave way to reveal a hidden compartment that held two things: a thick brown paper packet bound with masking tape and a revolver. She took out the cutting tool, she had used to force open the drawer and slashed the side of the packet to reveal a stack of high denomination euro currency. She put the packet under her arm, left the gun, and fled the scene - but not before she had re-armed the alarm. If the couple returned, and it would not be long before they did, and they found the alarm off they would be

Jack 2010 May

Jack was at his mother's home in central Scotland and was seated in his favourite chair. Even though he still shared his time between West Lothian and his rented place in Manchester, no one ever sat in, what his mother and her sister Elizabeth, who lived with her, referred to as 'Jack's chair'. Even when a visitor called and was asked to take a seat, they would be directed to some other chair in the room rather than that one. Of course, it was silly, but he knew that they did it as yet another way of trying to making him feel special. And he loved the chair too.

As he laid the paper he had been reading on the coffee table in front of him, he noticed that today was the first of May. His mother was in the kitchen baking but he knew she was still within ear shot.

"Did you hear the news on the TV earlier?" he called out, only raising his voice slightly. She may have been getting on in years but she possessed amazing hearing for her age.

"Apparently someone placed a bomb in Times Square, New York but fortunately for everyone nearby, it failed to detonate."

Jack had no idea of the bombshell that would hit him before that day would end.

Olga was sitting in the hotel bedroom. It was only a matter of minutes since Celia had left and so she was not expecting her for at least an hour or so. Wesley was sitting cross-legged on the bed glued to some cartoon on the wide screen TV on the wall. He was entirely engrossed.

Olga was seated in an arm chair next to her bed. She was holding the ivory coloured receiver of the hotel phone in her hand. She was examining it as if she had never seen one before but what she was really doing was mulling something over and over in her mind. *Will I make the call or not and if I do, is this the right time?*

Damian was sitting in his home office examining a spreadsheet. He had just reconciled some 'end of the month' figures.

Olga was still looking at the receiver in her hand but had reached a decision. She got through to reception and asked if, should she want to make an international call, did she need to do it via reception or could she dial the number direct. She was told that she could dial direct; though the woman on the desk warned her that the hotel charged an extra premium and there were less expensive ways of making international calls than from her room.

For Olga, expense was not now her major concern.

She thanked the person on reception and then enquired if she and her friend wished to stay a couple of days longer, would the room still be available and would cash be accepted. There had been a pause as the woman behind the desk addressed her monitor and having assured herself that a credit card was registered against the room, confirmed that the room would be available and cash would be entirely suitable.

Olga dialled the number and on the third ring a man's voice answered.

Damian looked away from the screen when the phone chirped, lifted the receiver and said, "Damian Clarke."

"Hello, Mr Clarke."

It was a woman's voice at the other end. He did not recognise it, although there was something about it that was vaguely familiar. The line sounded a little more distant than usual. He could hardly make the caller out and so assumed that the person the other end may not have heard him.

"So what is the problem may I ask?"

"In short," said Kuznetsov, "I need to know their name."

"Oh I am afraid that is out of the question sir, the person left very strict instructions."

"I am sure they did," continued Kuznetsov, "but I still need to know their name."

As he said this he opened his jacket a fraction to reveal a black leather wallet. The Maitre D' took in not just the wallet but the small black stud with a white crown in the centre and concluded that anyone who owned a Mont Blanc wallet, probably would not miss the cash it contained if ever it came to a gratuity.

Kuznetsov would not have noticed then but the man glanced down at his shoes. People could fake designer wallets and watches, but the cut and condition of a person's footwear was what really spoke volumes. Kuznetsov could see that the man was hesitating and he concluded rightly, that he would already have been given something for retaining his discretion. Kuznetsov removed the wallet and then retrieved a note, which he retained in his fingers.

"I am assuming this person paid by credit card rather than cash, am I right?"

The man moved his hand towards the note and Kuznetsov withdrew it only slightly but added a second note of the same denomination to it.

"And I assume it was a woman and not a man. Am I right there too?"

Again the hand came forward and again the note was withdrawn and shortly accompanied by a third note.

A couple walking past towards their table witnessed the last move. There was nothing in the least bit strange with someone in a restaurant of this standard offering money to a Maitre D' but when they saw the amount involved, they came very quickly to the conclusion that the establishment may be well out of their league if this was the type of gratuity that was expected of its guests.

Kuznetsov could see that he had won the trial of strength - and by a large margin.

"This money will be yours on one condition."

"It's more than my job's worth sir if I pass on anything."

"Your job will be safe and there will be no repercussions. I will promise you that," continued Kuznetsov. "In fact you won't need to 'tell' me anything at all."

"Then how?"

"I am going to hand you this money and I am going to leave. Before close of business tonight, someone will approach you. You will hand him an envelope. In that envelope will be a photostat of the credit card details that were used. Do you understand?"

"I understand, perfectly," said the Maitre D'.

The following day Kuznetsov sat behind his damaged desk and picked up the phone. The vast majority of police forces throughout Europe employ officers of integrity and Estonia is no exception. However, it is also true, that every police force contains a minority that do not operate at the highest level of morality, hence the need to employ departments that police the police.

Kuznetsov had a number on his payroll and the one he was about to ring, on his private number, he knew to be someone who specialised in IT.

"But if I do as you ask, the computer request will be traced," said the voice at the other end of the line, once Kuznetsov had explained what he needed to be done.

"If you do not do as I ask," responded Kuznetsov threateningly, then there will be consequences for you and for your family." And then applying more carrot than stick, added in a gentler tone, "Remember all the 'privileges' we have already put your way and which we will continue to offer?"

"Yes, I know but."

"But nothing, my friend, all I am asking you to do, is to look at the card details that I am about to forward to you and then check where it has been used after a transaction at the Maison D'Or and right up to the present time - that's all. Can you do it or can you not?"

"Do they, auntie Olga? I didn't know that. I only cry when I am sad."

Moving quickly on from that thought he said, "I asked Mummy why my daddy was appearing now when I was three - almost three and a half - and she did not know what to say. Then she said it was because my daddy had lost me and did not know where I was and even didn't know where Mummy was. That's very strange auntie Olga isn't it? I lose toys sometimes but not often. Yesterday I thought I had lost this TV control," he said picking it up from the bed cover. "But it seems that Daddies lose people. Don't you think that's strange too, auntie Olga?" He paused thoughtfully for another moment and then said, "But never mind, he has found me now." And bouncing up and down again in excitement, he came over to Olga and gave her a massive hug.

Celia also opened the door at the word 'Come', took Poska's hand and settled herself on the seat opposite him that she assumed was the one that Olga had recently vacated.

"Celia, I can't say how delighted I am to meet you at last after all I have heard about you," Poska began. "I'm reticent to say 'How are you?' Those seem such totally inadequate words to apply to the nightmare that I know you must have endured. And then on top of that, you have just had to go through all that has transpired in the past twenty-four hours."

"I know," Celia responded. "Some things can't be put into words can they? I suppose 'it is what it is,' as they say. Olga has been a life-saver, figuratively and literally over these past years. And then of course, there has been my faith in God."

"Oh really?" interjected Poska. "How can that be? You have hardly been out of your apartment since your accident, so you would hardly have had the opportunity to attend church."

"No indeed," agreed Celia. "But faith isn't entirely about church is it? Though I have to say, I am very much looking forward to connecting with one as soon as I am able to do so. The rekindling of my memories seem to have paralleled with my sense of faith.

Obviously, it must have been entrenched in me before the accident and will have been something I would have shared with Jack."

"Ah, Jack," said Poska, "You certainly did and of course you were instrumental in him becoming a Christian in the first place."

"How on earth would you know that?" said Celia, both surprised and startled.

"Of course, you wouldn't know this, but your husband and I have become firm friends over the years. He was a major catalyst in me becoming a Christian myself. So if you think of it Celia, I may not have become a Christian had it not been for you. However, if I read my Bible correctly, it is a work of the Holy Spirit isn't it that draws us to God? So perhaps, if it had not been you, it may have been someone else. But enough of that, we must march on. Time is of the essence. Celia, what I want you to do is to walk me through everything from when you woke up in hospital after the accident, right through to today. You obviously won't be able to cover everything, we are talking about years - but at least try and cover the salient points."

Celia did so and Poska was amazed how much detail she was able to include in spite of everything, and the degree to which her story corroborated the account that Olga had given. It was clear too that there had been absolutely no collusion between the two of them.

"Look Celia, I do not want to detain you any longer. In a few hours Jack will be here won't he? So before you go, do you have any questions for me?"

Celia paused for a moment before speaking. "It's not so much a question, Mr Poska," she said, "it's more about the parcel containing the money. I assume Olga told you about that."

"Yes she did" said Poska, wondering where the conversation was now going to lead. "I believe that it is a very large sum indeed - around a quarter of a million euros or something of that level."

"Yes, that's right, but did she, by any chance, mention someone called Angelika?"

"She did," answered Poska. "But not in relation to the money. My understanding," and here he glanced down to his notes and then with my own experience. Although not completely aware of what it meant at the time, I felt there was a hint of stereotyping in some of his ideas and deductions.

This has resulted in my having a rather questioning attitude towards historians, especially those who more recently have dealt with Australian Catholic beginnings. In their treatment of Therry, they have left no stone unturned in an effort to be honest and impartial, which is commendable indeed and makes for interesting reading. However, if this public airing of all the dirty linen one could possibly unearth were applied to everyone, then even the canonised saints would be in danger of losing their haloes. When the negative perceptions are canvassed from all possible sources and featured as prominently as the positives, a distorted picture can emerge. Human nature being what it is, it's the negatives that make the headlines; it's the negatives that make the greatest impression; it's the negatives that tend to be remembered. Finding that elusive fine line between the two is not easy.

Father Terry Southerwood writes:

> It is sad and possibly lacking in charity to put this material on record more than 160 years after it was penned, but the alleged darker side of character and temperament need to be balanced with the obvious virtues. (p 16)

The fact is however, that very often, instead of a balance, a grave imbalance occurs. The "obvious virtues" become less obvious, and even well-nigh invisible, while the "alleged darker side" becomes very obvious, even lighting up in technicolour in the memory of the reader.

Although he may have been overly sympathetic towards Therry, I believe Dr Eris O'Brien did a commendable job. I have basically followed in his shoes, while also availing myself of more recent works.

I do not claim any historical expertise or literary scholarship, nor have I visited the original documents in the various archives.

My many years of experience in the art of pastoring and searching for a pastoral spirituality constitute my only claim to have anything unique to offer. I believe, for example, that Therry's way of approaching the pastoral scene he encountered in the 1820s was spot-on. Apart from St Mary's Chapel, he didn't undertake any major time-consuming projects. Like the Good Shepherd, he concentrated on getting to know his flock and their needs. He could have assumed, for example, that as chaplain he knew what was best for them and set about creating the corresponding infrastructure. This is what many of the Therry writers would have wanted him to do. Indeed, some who succeeded him as pastors have gone about things in that way, ending up rather surprised and disappointed that the people didn't quite buy what they had set up.

Although quite impetuous by nature, Therry sensibly bided his time. He allowed himself the luxury of settling into his strange new environment. He gradually got acquainted with the convict scene by taking the time and the trouble to talk to the convicts, to listen, and to discern things for himself. What he heard and saw convinced him that the best pastoral practice for him in those early years was to respond with a sense of passion and urgency to so many who "were walking in the valley of darkness" and great suffering. The weightier matters, the infrastructure for the bigger Church, would have to wait. In the 1820s the call he heard was the call Jesus heard, the call of the Suffering Servant:

> to bring good news to the poor,
> to proclaim liberty to captives,
> and release the prisoners,
> to heal the broken-hearted. (Isaiah 61:1, 2)

The fact that he was mystically inclined, drew deeply from the well of the Eucharist and other Sacraments, was a dedicated and avid student of the Bible and was even a poet of sorts, meant that spirituality was a major driving force in his life. It was a force that sustained him day after

Although he did modify the rules later and also made them less than mandatory, they certainly posed a problem for Therry. Conolly had by now gone to Van Diemen's Land as chaplain there, leaving Therry all on his own in New Holland. Would he be pliant and accommodating and fall in completely with the wishes of the bureaucracy, thereby becoming a persona grata to the powers-that-be? Or, when the urgent need of people clashed with the letter of the law, would he put people first, going on the Gospel dictum that "the Sabbath was made for people", not vice versa?

Predictably, he chose the latter, aware of the storms it could cause from time to time with the authorities. As one would expect, the wisdom emanating from his superior in Madagascar, Bishop Slater, and indeed his own common sense, advised compliance where at all possible. This was Therry's normal practice; he didn't set out to be difficult, as some writers suggest. Even the moral principle of *epikeia* allows the setting aside of the law in exceptional circumstances and, of course, given the politico-religious tension, New Holland in the 1820s was hardly free of all anti-Catholic/Irish prejudice and discrimination. The surprising fact is that Therry and Macquarie got on reasonably well. (It was later on, towards the mid 1820s, that relations between the chaplain and the then Governor began to boil over.)

The challenge which these regulations posed paled in comparison to the challenge of the new convict world that had now become Therry's scene. When they arrived in Port Jackson, some convicts were assigned to prisons, from which hundreds were marched out daily in regimental file and distributed among the public works in and about Sydney Town. Watching them parade along, Therry noticed, to his dismay, the chains clanking at their heels and the downcast pained looks on their faces. During the day he noticed gangs of them pulling wagons through the streets, laden with gravel and stones — performing functions usually discharged by horses or bullocks. The streets dirty and unplanned, lit at night by a few flickering oil lamps, were thick with mud in winter and dust in summer. Pools of stagnant filth lay festering in their surface drains ... Many of the inhabitants were as dirty as the streets. Water shortages were frequent in the summer and daytime bathing, in beacher or in the harbour, was forbidden. (Martin p 2). Some convicts were assigned to settlers who needed labourers for leases they had taken up, often in remote inaccessible places as far as 300 km from Sydney Town.

"The assignees", as they were called, were made to toe the line under threat of the lash. Gangs could be procured for special work like dairying, planting and harvesting. During the 1820s, convicts played a major role in opening up the frontiers, undertaking hazardous explorations, building bridges and roads and clearing scrub for grazing and cultivating. Dame Mary Gilmore summed it up:

I was the convict
Sent to hell
To make in the desert
The living well:
I split rock
I felled the tree —
The nation was
Because of me.

The Singing Tree 1971

If the convicts kept out of trouble, after three years of hard labour (for some, six years), they could win limited freedom, called "a ticket of leave". This allowed them to work on their own behalf under supervision.

Not only was the convict scene unique and daunting, but the whole topography of NSW was so different. Almost untouched by the hand of man, it was as nature had fashioned it and earthquakes moulded it. In summer it was a landscape of hard white glaring sunshine. In the shimmering heat, the trees threw little shade and rivers brought no water. The trees were often so close together and the undergrowth in the low scrub was so thick that even horses had great difficulty getting through. The little

"This man", the pharisees complained, "associates with sinners and eats with them". Therry saw this as a practical precedent for himself but with this difference: he was happy that he, too, was one of the sinners whom Jesus loved, maybe more of a sinner than the convicts ... but loved and cherished none the less. Therry did give precious time and attention to them but he also received from them; it was a two-way exchange. Their stories and their woundedness contributed to his growth.

As he passed along the corridors, stopping to say a word of encouragement at each cell, looking in on the factory floor or the exercise yard or the road gangs, he gave them a sense of hope and they gave him a sense of having touched the hem of His garment like the woman in Luke's Gospel. (8:43–48) Apprised of a miscarriage of justice or unnecessarily harsh treatment or inhuman conditions or discrimination because of nationality or religion, Therry left no stone unturned, and even went all the way to Government House. His advocacy was sometimes graciously acted on by the Governor, but much more frequently he became an irritation to the authorities — a meddling priest!

He felt he had to stand up and fight to rekindle confidence and hope in his downtrodden flock. While this was approved of by most people, it was misunderstood and treated with deep suspicion by the powers-that-be. They did not make their attitude to him a local matter. Their reports overseas painted him in very negative terms indeed. As a result, officials at the Colonial Office in London who had never seen him looked on him as their *bête noire*. This even surprised Dr Ullathorne, a Benedictine priest who was to become very prominent in the colony and who was not at all a great admirer of Therry: "That considerable trouble had been taken to impress the Colonial Office unfavourably in his [Therry's] regard appears evident, ... there exists strange and erroneous notions in that department with respect to his character and conduct." These strange and erroneous notions were not confined to the people in the Colonial

Office. They found ready acceptance even among some of his own colleagues and, indeed, they have managed to infiltrate the Australian Church of our day, thus contributing to the diminishing and in some cases the demonising of Therry.

gruffly, "I'm not going to trouble the church if I can help it. When I was in the Iron Gang down the country we had a full-belly of Church, I can tell you. Old Sam Marsden used to preach at us a hurricane one day and the next used to get us fifty lashes for sneezing or coughing while he was talking." (*Old Pioneering Days in the Sunny South*)

For Catholics, especially, compulsory Church attendance posed a big problem. At that time, going to a Protestant Church service was tantamount to a denial of their own religion. It was a sort of betrayal.

As the *Australian* so rightly pointed out (29/1/1825) "...it is repulsive to a religious mind to adopt ... those rites it has been taught to consider heretical". Yet, whatever their scruples, they had to go to Church. If a man humbly asked to stay behind because he was a Presbyterian or a Catholic, he was exposing himself to a flogging. "To Church or be flogged" was the rule, 25 lashes for the first refusal, 50 for the second, and so on. The practice, continuing long after Therry's arrival, was the subject of many letters of complaint. To cite just one, a man was put in the stocks for refusing to go to Church. Two days later a magistrate sentenced him to 14 days on the treadmill. When that was completed, he was so weak he had to go to hospital, and an order was given that, if he were not suffering from dysentery, he was to be given 100 lashes!

Fortunately for Catholics and other conscientious objectors, Governor Brisbane, who succeeded Macquarie, acknowledged the right of convicts (and military personnel) to liberty of conscience. Thus, compulsory Church attendance was overruled. However, in chain gangs and in properties where convicts were assigned, this enlightened legislation met with serious opposition. Whether such convicts could enjoy the only privilege granted to them depended on the bigotry or otherwise of overseers, private masters and magistrates.

Letters from convicts to Therry telling of unmerciful punishments for refusing to go to Church continued to come. Therry lost no time in reprimanding the offenders. If this didn't work, which it usually didn't, he himself approached the Governor to point out strongly that many convicts were still menaced, put to death, imprisoned, or flogged for disobeying a law that His Excellency had long since abrogated.

Flogging was the punishment meted out for a host of other misdemeanours, in addition to refusal to go to Church. Often it was administered by the magistrates themselves, some of whom were also clergymen. (In the 1830s even the mild-mannered Englishman, Dr Ullathorne, referred to the aforementioned Samuel Marsden as "the flogging parson".) Sometimes when making social visits, a magistrate would administer the lash to an unruly servant on behalf of the host.

Although humiliating and demeaning, this flogging was probably a variation of the lash that didn't always leave permanent scars. But when the flogging was ordered by the Court and carried out by the NSW Corps, it was quite a different matter.

In 1830 Fr Therry got an urgent call to Bathurst, 200 km over the Blue Mountains west of Sydney, to attend the execution of a convict whose undoing had begun with such a flogging. For over 25 years of white settlement, the Blue Mountains in Sydney's west were an impenetrable barrier which no-one had ever succeeded in getting through. Many a frustrated restless convict looked at the dense blue tree-clad wall that cradled the setting sun and wondered what was on the other side. Was it true that it was a Shangri-la where a colony of white people lived in luxury and freedom, or did it hide the shores of the great land of China?

Some in their dire longing decided to find out for themselves, only to succumb to the inevitable in the jungle of high cliffs and dense bush. Eventually, three intrepid explorers equipped for the task, Blaxland, Lawson and young WC Wentworth (whose names are perpetuated in Blue Mountains' towns today), managed to do the impossible by keeping to the ridges, whereas the other prudence, commonsense and patience, he might have made it easier for Therry to work at a rapprochement.

Power, unfortunately, was egged on by their nominal superior, Fr Conolly, in Van Diemen's Land. Foolishly he advised Power to consider himself "exempt from any preconceived authority of him over you. You are not responsible to Therry in the least degree for any act of yours". For a man like Power, already "plagued by ill-health, with a bad temper and even (according to Darling) addicted to drinking to excess" (O'Farrell, p 22), this was the worst advice he could get. It was a dangerous prescription for division and confrontation. Priests can sometimes, for whatever reason — maybe jealousy or rivalry — be unjustly critical of one another. With friends like that, who needs enemies!

Seeing that any possibility of teamwork seemed out of the question, the two priests did a wise thing: they separated, Power going to Parramatta, Therry staying in Sydney Town. Later on Darling reversed those placings. He wanted to give Therry as wide a berth as possible. But even while based at Parramatta, Therry's presence was still sought after in Sydney, as well as in all the other places that had or were being opened up. In October 1827, when Newcastle and Maitland (200 km to the north of Sydney) were not yet towns but important penal settlements, the *Australian* reports that Therry celebrated Mass in Newcastle on two consecutive Sundays and, in the interval, made a tour of the Hunter district, visiting and ministering to the convicts who were digging and recovering coal from the pits. Therry himself described the first of these incursions to a Maitland priest in the early 1860s. His account gives a glimpse of the grit and determination and commitment of the man:

It is now many years ago since I celebrated the first Mass in Maitland under very painful and peculiar circumstances. I heard that a number of convicts were to be executed there at the end of the week. The overland route was almost impassable. There was only one small Government steamer going to the

Hunter River district, in which Maitland is situated, each week. I was refused a passage in the steamer by the Government authorities. I started on horseback with a trusted friend. After travelling uninterruptedly for a day and a night we reached Maitland at five in the morning of the day fixed for the execution. I at once set about preparing the men for death. I then celebrated Mass, administered Holy Communion to them and, a few hours afterwards, attended at their execution ... (Comerford, Vol 1)

In November 1830 Therry laid the foundation of the first Catholic Church in the Hunter district on Stockade Hill, Maitland, just opposite the gallows. On returning from his country trips, he usually applied to Government House for reimbursement by way of travel allowance, which was made available to Power whenever he applied. For the unsalaried Therry, the one who did nearly all the travelling far and near, the answer was either blank silence or a blunt refusal.

James Meehan, the Surveyor General, was giving the nod to fellow rebels who, in turn, spread the word to their friends and neighbours. Some proceeded from Campbelltown through Bargo Brush, on to Bungonia and Goulburn, and thence to areas in the far south-west. Others went to Appin and on towards the south coast, where they found some very desirable grazing land. In this extensive southern parish, as well as emancipist and ticket-of-leave people, there was a growing proportion of native-born and free immigrants, and some were reporting ownership of sizeable quantities of stock.

Therry felt strongly called to the almost impossible task of keeping in touch with all of them.

And so began a new series of missionary journeys that would mean endless hours in the saddle or the gig, sometimes in the extreme heat but, more often, in the icy conditions of southern NSW. These pioneer settlers were embarking on a new and exciting venture of pushing the frontiers of European-style cultivation into the virgin scrub and forests. Although they were confidently taking up leases, they probably had little or no experience of land clearance and cultivation in the dry arid conditions that were normal in the new colony.

Therry, a sort of veteran by now, and an extensive landowner, probably knew more about the needs of the land and the conditions conducive to running cattle and sheep than most of them. He followed them, even into the most remote and inaccessible places, places which as yet had no names, or had names like Bong Bong, Norwood, Ryansvale, etc. Some of these names have since been discarded.

Today, travelling south-west from Campbelltown, it is very easy to journey to Berrima (about 50 km from Campbelltown), Goulburn (153 km), Gunning (201 km), Yass (236 km), or south to Bungonia (143 km), Lake George (217 km), Gundaroo (210 km), Braidwood (240 km), or towards the ACT and Queanbeyan (245 km), Michelago (290 km), Bredbo (310 km), and the Monaro district. Modern transport and good roads make it a delight to tour around these areas today — so much so that it's almost impossible to imagine what it would have been like in the 1830s.

When Therry visited the newly leased properties or stations all over this district, most of the above towns/cities weren't even in the pipeline. A "station" was generally an area of many thousands of acres with no boundaries or, as they say, with the skyline as a boundary. In this huge slice of undeveloped bushland, there may have been two or three scattered huts. With no roads or fences to act as guide, Therry had to rely on what bushmen called the sixth sense, the sense of direction. One either had it naturally or acquired it. Without it, a bushman would be perpetually "bushed"; even with it, finding the leaseholder's hut was a time-consuming and frustrating job.

For Therry, however, exploring the bush had many compensations. The Aborigines had taught him about the great variety of kangaroos and how to recognise other animals, like the wombat, the bandicoot, the mole, the anteater, the platypus, and the wily dingo.

Government for a grant of land nearer the centre of the planned township, which he (Polding) deemed would be much more suitable.

This had all the ingredients for a stand-off between the two determined clerics, each of whom were convinced that his was the right spot. The stand-off didn't eventuate because a much bigger stand-off was simmering in far-away Van Diemen's Land, which was demanding urgent action from the Bishop. The Polding site in a street named after the Surveyor General James Meehan was the one chosen, the foundation stone being blessed on August 27th 1838, when Yass became a separate parish with Port Phillip (Melbourne) as an outchurch.

The pastor of Hobart Town and its people were at loggerheads; the pastor being none other than Therry's travelling companion of the early days, Fr Philip Conolly. They had worked together in 1820 in Sydney. The more prosaic and enigmatic Conolly, being the older and senior by ordination, had automatically been nominated Vicar-General, with Therry playing second fiddle as his assistant. This was the first of those impossible parish priest/curate duos. Many more were to follow.

Knowing that it wasn't going to work, Conolly and Therry had sensibly decided to part company. Therry boarded a ship to Van Diemen's Land, but a providential storm forced the craft back to Sydney Cove. The next thing we know, Conolly is the one on board! Maybe he had come to realise that the demanding Sydney scene needed the more outgoing robust Therry. However, amazingly, even in distant Hobart, Conolly continued to be Vicar-General of New Holland and therefore, in theory at least, Therry's superior.

Although Therry was far too preoccupied to pay attention to ecclesiastical niceties like this, it did annoy Conolly that his office was not being deferred to. As a result, in correspondence with Bishop Slater and some years later with Frs Power and Dowling, Conolly was exceedingly critical of Therry, and quite unfraternal, in fact almost un-Christian. Fellow Tasmanian writer

TA Southerwood, expresses some indignation also at Therry's failure to bow to his "Superior" (as he called him) in Hobart. Quoting Conolly, he assures us that Therry is "imprudent", "lacking in tact and diplomacy", full of "conceit and affection", "blatantly disobeys official instructions", "collects money for his own use", "should never put pen to paper because he has neither the ability nor learning to qualify him to write"! "In fact he should return to Ireland forthwith . . .".

That a peeved and hurt Conolly at a low ebb in far away Van Diemen's Land, should pen these lines about his high-profile colleague in the rapidly developing New Holland is understandable. The using of them, in the late 20th century, as a serious commentary on Therry's character is another matter. Father Southerwood is surprised that Sydney people do not fully subscribe to his profile of the insubordinate Therry. In fact they are quite pleased that the old pioneer followed his own unique wisdom as he dealt with the very unusual situation prevailing in New Holland at the time.

Things had come to crisis point in Hobart between the people and their pastor, who was not only unwell but was under Censure of Suspension which had been imposed by the Bishop when he visited Hobart with Ullathorne in March 1836. Polding had to send someone who would succeed Conolly as Vicar-General of Van Diemen's Land and work towards some kind of reconciliation. It wasn't an easy task. He had already sent one of the new arrivals, Fr Cotham, to assist Conolly. Finding the situation impossible, Cotham had informed Polding that it would take a senior man like Therry.

Thus the mantle fell on the pastor of Campbelltown. He had the most experience and sway with ordinary people. In March 1838, when the intense summer heat was giving way to the soothing nor-easterlies of autumn, just as he was getting the parish of Campbelltown into some shape after three exhausting years, Therry faced his gig towards Yass once more and thence the long 800 km track south to Port Phillip Bay, where he would embark

In a subsequent letter to a friend, Polding made it clear that even though the bookkeeping was very messy, with Therry's personal money and Church money hopelessly intertwined, Willson should, from the start, have faced the fact that, ultimately, the buck stops with the Bishop. For the sake of peace, if not for justice, he did accept that progressively, as the sorry drama developed. Had he cut his losses and done so earlier, what a difference it would have made!

Polding also pointed out that even though his presence was now becoming counter-productive, Therry's ministry in Hobart, the land he purchased, the buildings he erected and the salaries he secured from the Government had benefited the Church, and thereby benefited Willson, perhaps more than he was prepared to admit. "Therry has made himself a good name with the Government, he has raised a zeal among the people and even as here, so there, he has pioneered ... effectually ... During the 20 years and upwards he has laboured in these missions, not a shadow of suspicion has passed over his moral character."

Having put the positive side, he goes on to the negative: "he is eccentric, fond of notoriety ... a bad manager of money matters, though he prides himself on this head". (O'Brien, p 230) Perhaps this last phrase sheds a little light on Therry's propensity to be in debt — as does a little clerical snippet of wisdom that Polding and Willson happen on together, namely, "an Irishman is never comfortable out of debt!".

As the saga continued, many solutions were proposed. In 1845, when Willson and Therry agreed that Therry's indebtedness would be reduced to £1,000, things looked good, but there was a tail attached: Therry was forbidden to meet that amount by raising funds directly or indirectly anywhere in Tasmania. The next proposal was to appeal to the Governor to let St Mary's land be mortgaged to pay off the debt on St Joseph's. This was agreed to by both sides, but the Governor gave a thumbs-down response because St Mary's land was a government grant. This was followed by another proposal involving mortgaging Church land, which seemed very satisfactory but, again, it was refused by the Governor.

Proposal followed proposal. Accountants, solicitors and private arbiters were engaged, but to no avail. Even the Colonial Secretary, JE Bicheno, the Solicitor General, V Fleming, Judge Montague, bank manager Charles Swanston, solicitor Robert Pitcairn and the Caveat Commissioners tried hard and often to work out an acceptable solution. Dr Gregory OSB, Polding's Vicar-General in Sydney, tried his hand. Later newly ordained Bishops Davis OSB (Maitland), Murphy (Adelaide) and Goold (Melbourne) came to help, the last two being the ones who eventually made the breakthrough that led to resolution. To the great relief of the harassed Bishop and priest and the whole community, Christmas 1857 brought the long-awaited peace.

While this marathon dispute was continuing, the Bishop and the priest were busy doing the Lord's work. The Bishop's work as reformer of the penal system took him to various places in Tasmania and the mainland and to the infamous penal settlement on Norfolk Island. He was responsible for effecting much-needed changes in the treatment of convicts and the eventual discontinuing of convict transportation. He did everything he felt it was possible for him to do to bring the dispute with Therry to resolution. Understandably enough, his frustration and antagonism deepened as the years wore on. His logical mind saw the unpredictable and erratic priest as a dangerous enemy and a crazy one at that ("... as mad as ever").

At times he was at loggerheads with the Archbishop and the Sydney clergy and, even to an extent, Propaganda's Cardinal Franzoni, because he felt they were more or less siding with the enemy. For a while it looked as if both he and Therry were at breaking point. In his utter frustration, the Bishop felt that his bête noire, even though a teetotaller, was doing the rounds of the Hobart pubs and other such places telling some terrible tales chaplain. Being a secular priest he hadn't taken a vow of poverty as Religious do. He could have money and possessions as his own personal property, like any other citizen. This opened up a range of options, but it also made it necessary to keep proper books and accounts so that there was a clear separation between what belonged to the Church and what belonged personally to Therry.

Unfortunately, notwithstanding his entrepreneurial skills, his "lack of management in temporal affairs" led to that separation becoming very blurred. No-one, least of all Therry himself, seemed to know what was what. To his mind it was irrelevant. It wasn't an issue. Being a completely dedicated churchman, what belonged to him personally, by that very fact, belonged to the Church also. A teetotaller all his life, his was a very spartan lifestyle; he never spent anything on any of the refinements and luxuries that could have made life more comfortable for him. (In all the Therry correspondence and documentation, there is only one allusion, and that the result of hearsay, to his having indulged in anything approaching luxury. It is in a John O'Sullivan letter to Hobart in 1840. It could even be a bit of mild O'Sullivan irony!)

His failure to keep proper records and to keep his own personal and Church transactions separate was anathema to clerics trained in accounting correctness, especially the young Dr Ullathorne, who took over from him in the early 1830s in Sydney, and Bishop Willson, who did likewise in Hobart in 1844. (While not condoning his neglect in this, it should be noted that among Therry's successors there have been some notable clerical mavericks like himself, who paid scant attention to bookkeeping and separating the different accounts but who, with minimum cost to the Church, managed to leave behind parish plants and properties that would have cost the more orthodox a small fortune!)

(It could be noted too that if the Church is seen to be interested in a property, the price, for one reason or another, can increase considerably. This might necessitate buying in some other name; this, too, can lead to complications!)

Therry's involvement in land acquisition began very simply and without any effort from him. When James Nestor of Bark Huts (now South Strathfield) was dying, he left a will addressed to Fr Therry, to be delivered immediately after death. He asked him to be his executor, to give him a decent burial, pay some small debts and, in gratitude for Therry's many kindnesses to him, to accept ownership of his holding and a small herd of cattle! Nestor was one of many ex-convicts who had become quite successful in developing a small parcel of land. So often they were all alone in NSW, with no relatives or special friends to leave their property to. The stigma of penal servitude had left them pariahs. They trusted Therry and, in leaving their property to him, felt they could chalk up a little credit with the Lord for themselves.

The Government, too, having such enormous tracts of land to lease out, was not averse to including Therry in its disposal. Although they were not a fraction of the land grants to the Anglican Church (under Archdeacon Scott's Church and School Corporation), several fairly large tracts were registered under Therry's name. Governors Brisbane and Darling were very niggardly towards him, yet they did set aside several land grants, the deeds of which were eventually transferred to Therry by Governor Bourke in the 1830s.

In the mid 1830s the fact that the church he had started in Campbelltown ten years before was still unfinished was a great worry to Therry. His name was associated with tracts of land here and there throughout the colony but, unfortunately, that didn't translate into ready cash to buy the scarce materials and pay the tradesmen. He secured a donated site in Appin by putting in the footings for a small church in 1837 but, strapped for cash, couldn't proceed any further. He saw that he needed more than just land. He needed land that could produce something readily saleable, maybe a good cattle run, where animals could be prepared for the market. The

Polding didn't agree. He felt that charity, especially in matters relating to Gregory and himself, was frequently missing. He was sorely disappointed with McEncroe for refusing to censor Heydon and his Journal. McEncroe, like his friend in Balmain, was very loyal to Polding, constantly defending him at very heated meetings and, many a time, saving him from the consequences of the mistakes of his unfortunate Vicar-General Gregory. However, he felt that freedom of the press was a matter of principle and, therefore, didn't lend itself to compromise.

Thus it was that in 1861 McEncroe left St Mary's presbytery, which had become the Benedictine monastery, after just on 30 years and took up residence as pastor at St Patrick's Church Hill. Polding just couldn't live in the same house as his most loyal confrère any more.

In the Good Shepherd Seminary in Sydney, a painting of Archdeacon John McEncroe hangs next to the one of Therry mentioned in the Prologue. The McEncroe caption reads: "An Irish priest, prominent in Sydney administration, who worked successfully against Polding's plan for the Catholic Church in Australia". Besides its obvious negative and disparaging connotations, it seems to be at variance with the truth. Although McEncroe probably didn't believe in Polding's plan, the indications are that he didn't actually work against it. "Benedictinisation", unfortunately, had within it and within its most ardent advocates, like Gregory, the seeds of its own demise.

The *Freemans Journal* continued to be unfettered by ecclesiastical authority. It was a popular adult expression of Catholic news and stimulated Catholic thinking on matters of faith and morals. Often its freedom was obviously a thorn in the side of the Archbishop, but he valiantly put up with it. He must have concluded that freedom is like that. It costs. That seems par for the course. Not everyone is willing to pay that price.

By the mid '40s of this century, Polding's fourth successor, Cardinal Norman Thomas Gilroy, had the

Catholic Weekly, the *Freemans Journal's* successor, well under his ecclesiastical thumb. It lost its catholic character and became the official organ of orthodoxy, as interpreted by the Archbishop and the Vatican. If it dared to enter into controversy and express contrary viewpoints, it could be in serious trouble.

"Controversy" has become a bad word in Church circles. The art of debating and discussing the many and varied facets of Christian life and teaching have been all but lost. The conservative and radical wings of the Church could have spoken with and challenged each other (in all charity of course). They could have stimulated deep and fruitful thought and reflection by presenting their different viewpoints without the fear of being hauled over the coals. Australian Catholics have now to look elsewhere for the meatier, more interesting bits of contemporary Catholic thinking ... perhaps in some overseas Catholic magazines or in the secular press which, however, often gets it wrong. Instead of being an organ of religious correctness, the *Catholic Weekly* could have been a real voice for many people who are feeling increasingly alienated and ill at ease in a Church that is gradually veering towards the right.

McEncroe and Therry believed in a free religious press in spite of its many inherent dangers. They saw that it promoted Catholic adult education, whetted people's spiritual tastebuds and set them talking and thinking and looking for more. It also sold papers.

The funeral cortege, extending from St Mary's to the Devonshire Cemetery (now Central Railway), was the largest ever seen in Sydney. Crowds of people lined the streets for almost the entire distance, assembling in depth at different points. Nearly every house and place of business showed some sign of mourning. Many business premises were closed entirely.

The hundreds of letters he left behind are testimony to the amazing role he played in the lives of so many people in early NSW. Many of the convicts brought with them letters to Therry from their parish priests in Ireland, asking for his watchful care of them. When a convict was seeking a ticket of leave or applying to bring out his wife and family from the Old Country, he went to Therry to have the long official document drawn up in correct English.

Letters from abroad to convicts as well as free settlers were often addressed c/o Rev Father Therry. His address was frequently used as a mail-sorting office for people who were moving around or could be classed as having no fixed abode. Letters came from public servants in country districts asking Therry's help to get them employment in Sydney Town, where there would be the opportunity to confess and "hear" Mass again. Letters from convicts in dreaded Norfolk Island and elsewhere, who weren't given a fair trial or perhaps no trial at all, looking to Therry to get them justice ... letters from desperate people in danger of being thrown out on the streets with their kids, unless Therry intervenes .... And so the list goes on. It's little wonder that so many in Sydney paused to pay their respects on the occasion of his funeral.

He was buried close to his co-worker and, to some extent, his erstwhile sparring partner, Fr Power. Subsequently, his great friend Archdeacon McEncroe joined him in the same grave, with Archbishop Polding being buried close by. At the turn of the century, when the old Devonshire Cemetery was resumed as the Central Railway Station, the bodies of all four were removed to

St Mary's Cathedral to be interred under the altar dedicated to the Irish Saints. When the crypt was redecorated in 1948 all four were reinterred side by side at the head of the eastern transept. The subsequent addition of artistic embellishments, including a colourful mosaic floor, has made the crypt an appropriately special and sacred ambience.

Perhaps the special charism Therry bequeathed to the Church in Australia is the one encapsulated in this little pericope:

> Father Therry, another saint of the convict world, saw that all conversion must begin with an acknowledgment of human frailty, that when persons carry that moral weakness into the Church, they should be greeted with the welcome: "join the club". Then a truly mutual exchange occurs. There must always be this mutuality and reciprocal exchange for life and growth to occur in the whole Church. Therry's was a long way from the Constantinian image of conversion — of a Church that draws on power and strength, a no-give Church. Too often conversion to Catholicism is portrayed as a total capitulation, an unconditional surrender — hands up — to the See of Rome, with nothing happening in the Church itself except numerical growth. It's only when we think of the Church being, by definition, a Church of sinners that we can conceive of its structures being formed to reflect that truth, where weak attracts weak. (Kennedy, p 10)

On April 9th 1839, Therry penned some lines in the *Hobart Times* that beautifully express this — the compassionate and flexible approach of the Good Shepherd:

> I trust I should with divine assistance, be prepared cheerfully to sacrifice property, liberty, life, everything but the strict integrity of the faith and essential purity of morals. Even the discipline of our Church, sacred and salutary as it has proved to be, might be materially altered in favour of those of her

▶ Luscombe, TR, 1967. *Builders and Crusaders*. Lansdowne Press, Melbourne.

▶ McGovern, JJ, 1934. *John Bede Polding*. ACR.

▶ Maher, Brian, 1997. *Planting the Celtic Cross*. Brian Maher, Canberra.

▶ Martin, EA, 1884. *Daniel Henry Deniehy Life & Speeches*. George Robertson & Co, Melbourne, Sydney.

▶ Meredith, J and Whalan, Rex, 1979. *Frank the Poet*. Red Rooster, Melbourne.

▶ Murtagh, James, 1946. *Australia The Catholic Chapter*. Sheed & Ward, Melbourne.

▶ O'Brien, Rev Eris, 1922. *The Life of Archpriest JJ Therry*. Angus & Robertson, Sydney.

▶ O'Brien, Rev Eris. *The Church in Australia 1788–1830*. Official Souvenir, Eucharistic Congress, 1953.

▶ O'Brien, John, 1975. *The Men of '38*. Lowden Publishing Co, Kilmore.

▶ O'Corrigan, Catherine RSC. 1 Rockwell Cres, Potts Point NSW. Researched but as yet unpublished works. Much of the information on Caroline Chisholm has come from this source, per Ted Kennedy.

▶ O'Farrell, Patrick, 1977. *The Catholic Church and Community in Australia*. Nelson, Melbourne.

▶ O'Riordan, John J, 1980. *Irish Catholics: Tradition & Transition*. Veritas Publications, Dublin.

▶ O'Sullivan, MMK, 1995. *A Cause of Trouble*. Crossing Press, Sydney.

▶ Petrement, S, 1976. *Simone Weil — A Life*. Pantheon Books, New York.

▶ Southerwood, Rev T, 1996. *Character Study of P Conolly and JJ Therry* (Talk). ACHS Vol 17.

▶ Therry Papers. Mitchell Library MS, 1810–1872.

▶ Turner, Naomi, 1992. *Social History of Catholics in Australia*. Collins Dove.

▶ Waldersee, James, 1974. *Catholic Society in NSW 1788–1860*. Sydney University Press.

▶ Walsh, KT, 1998. *Yesterday's Seminary*. Allen & Unwin.

▶ Watson, F, 1915. Editor Historical Records of Australia, HRA Library Committee, Commonwealth Parliament, Canberra.

▶ Yeats, William Butler, 1950. *Dancer at Cruachan and Cro-Patrick* in *Collected Poems*. Macmillan, Toronto.

SELECTED INDEX

Aborigines, ii, 14, 34, 44, 56, 75, 77, 81, 82, 85, 86, 87

Bark Huts, (St Anne's Sth Strathfield), 1, 18, 76, 109, 124, 129

Bathurst Town, 48, 49, 50, 138, 151

Blue Mountains, 19, 47, 49, 50, 69

Bourke, Governor (1831-37), 42, 57, 65, 67, 69, 70, 124

Brisbane, Governor (1821-25), 25, 33, 46, 99, 124

Campbelltown, 20, 22, 23, 72, 73, 74, 79, 80, 81, 84, 90, 91, 97, 119, 124, 127, 138, 142, 143, 152

Church Act (1836), 42, 43

Concord district, 129

Conolly, Philip Fr, 10, 11, 12, 52, 63, 89, 90, 91, 92, 93

Darling, Governor (1825-31), 33, 34, 38, 42, 54, 57, 60, 61, 63, 76, 124

Denison, Lieutenant-Governor of VDL, Governor of NSW, 114, 115, 146, 147

Divorce Legislation, 148

Dixon, James Fr, 4, 5, 6

Dowling, Christopher Vincent Fr, 57, 65, 66, 67, 89

Dwyer, Michael (Wicklow Chief), 119, 120

Dwyer, Mary (of the mountains), 120

England, John Bishop, 2, 3, 68, 138

Flogging, (cat o'nine tails), 2, 4, 5, 6, 24, 26, 27, 45, 46, 47

Franklin, Lieutenant-Governor of VDL (1837-43), 99

Freemans Journal, 135, 138, 139, 140, 141, 152

Goulburn Town, 79, 80, 81, 87, 119, 120, 126

Gregory, Rt Rev HG OSB, 107, 108, 134, 135, 137, 139, 140, 152

Harold, James Fr, 4, 6

Hobart Town, 91, 93, 97, 123, 128, 129

Jesuit Fathers, 113, 130, 131, 132

King, Governor of NSW (1800-06), 4, 5, 6, 26

McEncroe, John Fr, 25, 58, 68, 69, 77, 105, 135, 136, 138, 139, 140, 141, 153, 156, 157, 159, 166

Macquarie, Governor of NSW (1810-21), 3, 4, 11, 12, 32, 46, 48, 52, 53, 55, 93, 155

Maitland district, 63, 64, 151

Maoris, (NZ), 154

Martin, John, 115

Meagher, Thomas Francis, 113, 114, 117

Meehan, James, Deputy-Surveyor, 24, 52, 54, 80, 89

FOREWORD

WHEN Augusta Persse, to everyone's surprise, became Lady Gregory she moved some considerable distance up the social scale but, in the topographical scale, only seven miles to the south-west. Leaving Roxborough – perhaps in the phaeton that was her wedding present from her dashing step-brother, Dudley – she came to a house significantly different from the bustling mansion in which she had been brought up. Although Dudley's namesake, Dean of the diocese of Kilmacduagh, had built his house at Roxborough long before there were Gregorys at Coole, Sir William Gregory's twenty-eight-year-old bride found her own home, unlike her father's house, reverberant with echoes of a proud past. Her love and reverence for her husband's white, eighteenth-century house deepened during the long years of her widowhood to be distilled at last in *Coole,* that lyrical essay printed and published at the Cuala Press in 1931.[1]

This opens with an account of the library, evidently her favourite room, and her meditation on its other occupants throws as much light on her as on the lustrous shelves.

> Of the successive generations that have possessed them I think it was to one only they were dumb. Yet, not even one inheritor I believe, could have been so dull of eye as to fail to delight in the mere appearance of these walls of leather and vellum, mellowed by passing centuries, in the sudden illumination of golden ornament and lettering as the sun sinks towards the western hills.[2]

[1] A second edition (incorporating two chapters newly transcribed from the manuscript), edited by Colin Smythe and with a Foreword by Edward Malins, was published by the Dolmen Press in 1971.

[2] Compare with stanza 4 of Yeats's 'Coole Park and Ballylee, 1931'
> *Beloved books that famous hands have bound,*
> Old marble head, old pictures everywhere;
> Great rooms where travelled men and children found
> Content or joy; *a last inheritor . . .*
>
> (my italics)

This poem of course was written in the same year as Lady Gregory's *Coole* was published.

The riddle of that passage is explained on a later page:

> And as to William, the Under-Secretary, though he had been a good latin scholar at Harrow and Cambridge, I find little or nothing that he and Lady Anne added to the shelves, nor did they I fancy often disturb them, having their converse less with print than with people, living as they did chiefly in that still brilliant society of Dublin . . . the Viceroys and the Chief Secretary, Whitworth, Talbot, Wellesley, Anglesey, Peel, Goulburn, Lamb. He and Lady Anne, dining out, giving dinners, in the midst of history in the making, what printing on a page could compare with the weighty and the witty talk to which those ears were used?

Strangely, perhaps in part because of a certain resemblance to her husband, William the Under-Secretary and least literary of the Gregorys captured the imagination of his grandson's literary bride. He may have added nothing to the shelves of the Library, but he left another legacy – in a large, iron-clamped, leather-covered box bearing the inscription: "Correspondence of the Right Honourable William Gregory, 1813–1835".

Augusta and her husband talked of reading through its contents, but it was not until some years after his death in 1892 that, "being alone, with patience and long evenings on [her] side, [she] set to work, and came at last to the bottom of the box". Her decision to edit the correspondence, prompted perhaps by a wish to tighten her links with Coole, led her into a reading of history that turned her, she says in *Our Irish Theatre,* into a Home Ruler. "I defy anyone to study Irish history without getting a dislike and distrust of England." The letters themselves yielded no State secrets and *Mr. Gregory's Letter-Box,* for all its charm and interest as a period piece, sheds no new light on the course of history. It does, however, shed considerable light on its editor in the dawn of her development as a writer.

Reading the account books that record the expenditure of Secret Service money, her eye falls delightedly on "a regular payment of 100 1. per annum to a certain Dr. Parkinson 'for performance of two odes' on the birthdays of the King and Queen. That was the golden age for a Court poet". She comments on Mr. Gregory's personal account book: "I am glad that in spite of his usual economy of stops he affords a comma between the words 'Frank, washing, Betty, 4 *l.* 0 *s.* 7½ *d.*'" The same pretty wit turns to good account the most trivial aside in the letters, as when to those midnight Legislators. Old Sir George moves with a lock step, when we require double quick time, and General O'Loughlin considers that the danger is much exaggerated. No one dreams of those Rapparees taking the field against the King's troops; but the danger is not the less to the peaceable inhabitants who are attacked by them at night. Large bodies of Military are marching into the Country, there will be this day or to-morrow 2,000 Men in the County of Galway, and before the expiration of the ensuing week 800 more."

We used to hear traditions of this attack on Roxborough in my childhood. My father had been one of its defenders. It was attacked by moonlight, and the garrison could distinguish groups of men, one group surrounding an oak-tree on the lawn. My father took aim at the tree, thinking that in the uncertain light he would thus be sure of hitting one of the party. But his aim was surer than he thought, and next day it was seen that the bullet had gone to the heart of the oak. Other shots, however, were more successful, for trails of blood were to be seen in the morning, where the dead or wounded had been carried away.

The following extracts are from a letter written in 1813 by Baron Smith, in answer to an inquiry of Mr. Gregory's as to the state of religious parties in the North. The letter itself is, as Mr. Gregory says of another by the same writer, "of ponderous and elephantine proportions." Even in Court, the Baron's charges were usually on the same "elephantine" scale, and the vast MS. notes he was wont to arrive with were said to be "the terror of Grand Juries." But he seems to have been painstaking and for those days impartial, and one good deed of his deserves record, that of having learned Irish, that he might not be dependent on an interpreter in the examination of witnesses.

He writes:

"On state of Catholics and Protestants in the North of Ireland

Sept. 4, 1813.

'Perhaps the outline of my opinion will be this, that there does not appear to be a Party Spirit, or rather perhaps that *two* Party Spirits appear to be afloat, and very angrily and troublesomely busy in some of the Counties through which I have passed, that there are faults, animosities, ill-blood and aggression upon both sides, but that the Orange party have not infrequently given the original provocation, to minds ready I am afraid to take fire from a trifling spark, and by contumely and insult and a certain tone and indication easier to understand than to describe, of hostility, superiority, defiance and contempt, have exasperated feelings which a different conduct might assuage.——I am tempted to add that though I love and warmly share the loyalty of *Gentlemen,* there is a spurious and illiberal loyalty which grows up amongst the vulgar classes, and which is very turbulent, bigoted, riotous and affronting, very saucy, and overbearing, almost proud of transgression, necessarily producing exasperation, and often leading to the effusion of blood. It is a rebellious and insurrectionary propensity gone astray, and running contradictorily in the channel of Allegiance.

"A witness before me at Lifford, being asked why the Corps of Yeomanry to which he had belonged was disbanded, answered (on his oath) smiling and in an exulting way, 'Because it was too loyal.' I am afraid that, with it may be very pure intentions, some of our Country Gentlemen do not always find their fairness seconded by equal coolness, Intelligence or Judgment.

"I do not know, probably you do, whether those Bodies called Ribbon men are or are not of a decidedly political character, and a symptom of rebellious plans and organisation. I have heard the thing asserted and denied; but when I asked for proofs, I was put off with prejudice and empty noise. That they are a Religious Party is beyond question, and if it were not that the gross exaggerations which I have detected make me a little incredulous, I should say that they collect from distant quarters, are bound together by an obligation, appear suddenly in great numbers, act in concert, are very anti-Protestant, or at least violently anti-Orange, and if their present views and prospects are vague and immature and not unequivocally revolutionary, yet that a combination formed for one ill purpose may be equally applied to another equally or more mischievous one, and that objects at first undefined may with the aid that will be given soon settle into something very dangerously certain and precise."

The following, reported by Mr. Gregory to Mr. Peel, is an instance of religious intolerance in Dublin:

May 22, 1813. The Guinnesses "are very extensive porter brewers in Dublin, and a report having been invented that they had signed the petition against the Catholics, the houses of the publicans in which their Beer was sold became unfrequented, or large Parities going into the houses called for Beer, and asking the Landlord whether he bought from Guinness, on receiving an answer in the affirmative, threw the beer about the House, telling the owner if ever he bought any more from the same People, the next visit they paid him should be more expensive."

The Guinnesses, however, had been unjustly accused, as far

in consequence of which strong patrols were sent forward and every Precaution used as if the Story had been believed. . . . Tho' I attached no credit to the story, yet I remembered Emmett and the Castle caught napping."

In June of 1813 he had written: "If Buonaparte is successful, the standard of disunion between Ireland and England will soon be raised." In July Mr. Peel, announcing the "glorious and unexpected" news of the battle of Vittoria, orders a Gazette extraordinary to be published—"I am sure the expediency of giving all the publicity possible to good news in Ireland far outweighs every other consideration." And on Oct. 1 he writes: "I am glad to hear that O'Connell and the other itinerant demagogues made little impression in Galway, or if any an unfavourable one. I hear that at Mallow and in that neighbourhood the Gang was more successful. The reverses, however, of their good friend and ally in Germany will damp their efforts in the good old cause of riot and insurrection."

The Government informers were constantly kept at work. A memorandum is sent by Mr. Peel from the Irish Office in 1814.

"*Memorandum.*—June 11, 1814. Information has been for some time received by the Irish Government that a system of organization was forming among the lower orders in the County of Kildare and that frequent meetings of the disaffected took place. The person from whom this information principally came, and who is himself implicated in the proceedings of the disaffected, was desired to give notice of some specific meeting about to take place in order that measures might be taken for the apprehension of the persons and papers of the parties assembled. He stated that there would be a meeting in the town of Kildare on Sunday June 5, and a Magistrate was directed to be in readiness with a party of Military at the time appointed.

"It appears from the report of the Magistrate that on entering the House where it was reported that the meeting of the disaffected was to be held, he immediately went upstairs and found in an upper room several people who were in great confusion on hearing of the entrance of the soldiery, and destroyed several Papers which were on the Table. Seven of the persons present were arrested, and two papers seized, which are considered by the Attorney-General of Ireland to be decidedly of a treasonable nature, and to afford sufficient evidence with the testimony of the informer for the conviction of the persons apprehended, who are committed on a charge of High Treason.

"The papers are written by illiterate persons—they refer to orders given by the *executive Directory* that the Officers should

meet once a week until July 5—that no arms should be given
out until the Insurrection is to take place—as if they were sent
before some parts of the Country would be in a state of Rebellion
too soon. They state that the delegates from Dublin, Longford,
Louth, Meath, Westmeath, Kildare, Wicklow, Wexford, Carlow,
Kilkenny, demand clothing, arms and ammunition immediately.

"It appears from the magistrates of the Queen's County that
that County is in a disturbed state. That on Sunday night the
30th May eleven houses were robbed of arms and Money by a
party of the disaffected—nine on Monday night and three on
Tuesday."

A report docketed 1814, and signed only Q., says. "I went
yesterday according to promise to the County Kildare, and
remained there until yesterday. I spent the first day in Farrells-
town with a weaver named Donelly who works for me, and from
whom I received the following information. That there was a
system lately introduced in the neighbourhood which he understood to be somewhat similar to the Defenders of '96. That is
that none but Catholics were admissible, and that their object was
to protect themselves against the Orangemen or to retaliate in
case of necessity on either themselves or families, and that they
were bound to do this by an oath. Donelly told me that it was
a certainty a Mr. Richardson who now lives in Robertstown did
belong to a Regiment named the Foxhunters who killed some
Rebels in the Curragh in '98, the friends of whom are determined
to have revenge (these are his own words). He also mentioned to
me that Thos. Beaghan, a Farmer, who formerly lived on the
grounds Mr. Richardson lately purchased, with some others
similarly circumstanced, were determined to banish him out of
the country at the risk of their lives; however, that since the
soldiers went into the neighbourhood they were more cautious in
committing themselves. From Robertstown I went to Kildare, and
immediately repaired to the public house next the post office, as
directed. There I found six or seven persons drinking round a
kitchen fire, and from their appearance and manner of conversing
I immediately suspected them to be friends of the persons
arrested. One of them wished that instead of the horse race on
the Curragh to-morrow it might be the general Race, and the
last Race and big Race; at this kind of nonsense they continually
kept laughing. Rankin, the Bricklayer, stated that there was no
one concerned in it but the lowest order of Spalpeens whom the
sight of a Soldier would frighten to Death's door, and that since
their arrival one of them was afraid to raise their voice. He likewise mentioned to me that they took the name of Ribbonmen

vailed, are as favourable as the most sanguine can expect or desire.

"We are already very strong in Belgium. The Prussians and Austrians will have to the amount of at least 200,000 men in France in a very short time, and the Russian advanced Corps of 50,000 men will be up by the 15th of next month, and a regular succession constantly following."

Mr. Gregory to Lord Whitworth

Dublin Castle: April 10, 1815.

"I received your two letters of the 6th and 7th. . . .

"Nothing but the hearts of Jacobins could have refused obedience to the noble heroism of the Duchess of Angoulême at Bordeaux. The conduct of the troops was worse than treason. . . .

"I received this day a letter from Mr. Buxton, Chairman of the Sessions for the County of Meath, a very sensible discreet man, giving a melancholy account of that part of the County which borders on Cavan and Longford, from whence the Ribbon System has been introduced. They are in great want of troops and Magistrates, the first may with difficulty be supplied, but I do not know how the other can.

"Waterford has continued quiet since the severe Examples at the late assizes, the same Good would no doubt result from the same measures in other Counties, if the Parties injured were not afraid to prosecute. Yet whenever they do, Reward and Protection is always afforded."

Lord Whitworth to Mr. Gregory

Hertford St.: April 13, 1815.

"I have not written to you for some days, as I literally had nothing worth sending you. I mean as to common occurrences, for I am sure you and Lady Anne would have been kind enough to consider a favourable account of the Duchess' health as a matter of sufficient interest.

"I thank God she is as well as I can possibly expect, as are her daughters and grandsons. . . .

"I am happy to tell you that everything is going on well. The Regent told me last night that the Court of Vienna was as determined and as zealous in the Cause as he, or if possible anyone more anxious than himself, can wish or desire. I suppose in the course of the next week we shall hear what is to be done.

'Nothing can be a stronger proof of the zeal of the Court of Vienna than this determination to augment their armies on the Rhine at the expense of that of Italy; no stronger proof can be given of Austrian disinterestedness.

"I am sorry to find from all the letters which Peel receives and which I myself receive, that the bad spirit in Ireland does not improve. As long, however, as we can find employment for their friend Buonaparte at home, and I trust he will soon have much more than he will be able to meet, I do not apprehend anything serious.

"There was an angry discussion last night in the House of Lords on what should have been done to keep Buonaparte in Elba. It put one in mind of the old saying, 'It is too late to shut the stable door when the steed is stolen.' The French call it preparing a *bouillon pour un mort*, and so it is. In fact the Opposition knew well that Government dared not avow the real cause of mischief, which was the stupid magnanimity of Alexander, lest they should indispose him now when it is so important to conciliate him. Such is the liberality and candour of politicians!"

Mr. Gregory to Mr. Peel

Dublin Castle: April 19, 1815.

"The official Letter from the Lords Justices will declare their apprehensions of withdrawing 5,000 troops from Ireland at this critical Period. . . .

"Although it was my Duty to word my official Letter in such manner as the Lord Justices directed, yet I should ill repay the Confidence placed in me by Lord Whitworth and you, if I allowed it to pass as my own opinion. I perfectly agree that the Lower Orders are most dreadfully bent on Mischief, that in many places the Catholic population are united by the most horrible oaths of Association, that there are great numbers of concealed Arms in their possession, and that no Man can foresee when this Madness may break out into open Insurrection. Yet I can never believe there is any formidable State of Organization. The most timid and the most zealous have never been able to discover any Leader beyond the lowest description of Persons—no Depôt of Ammunition or Arms, no Committees, nothing resembling the systematic plans of the Rebellion of 1798, but the Evil Spirit which pervades the Country. If an Insurrection should break out under these

LORD TALBOT

Dublin Castle: October 9, 1817.

"The Earl Talbot, who embarked at Holyhead at five o'clock on Wednesday, the 8th inst., on board his Majesty's yacht the *William and Mary*, arrived in this harbour at one o'clock this day. . . . His lordship, attended by a squadron of dragoons, proceeded to the Castle, and the Council having attended at four o'clock, was introduced in form to his Excellency Earl Whitworth, who received him sitting under the canopy of state in the Presence Chamber, from whence a procession was made in the usual state to the Council Chamber. The Council sitting, his lordship's commission was read, and the oaths being administered to him, his lordship was invested with the collar of the most illustrious order of St. Patrick, and received the Sword of State from the Earl Whitworth."—*Ann. Register.*

I have read through a great mass of letters from Lord Talbot to Mr. Gregory. Some are too trivial and some too personal for publication, but all radiate kindliness and a sense of duty.

Though he set his face from first to last against the claims of the Catholics, O'Connell gives him the credit of impartiality, and Lord Cloncurry speaks of him as "an honest, high-minded gentleman." The King's visit and the famine of 1821 are the chief landmarks of his administration. His wife's death, and his sudden and ungracious dismissal saddened and, for a time, embittered his memories of the viceroyalty. Had Mr. Peel continued Chief Secretary, Lord Talbot's four years in Ireland would probably have been one long "Amen" to his clear, prompt decisions. But in May, 1818, Mr. Peel resigned.

With the appointment of "the amiable, clever and irresolute Charles Grant," began what I may call the sandwich system of government in Ireland, of which Lord Grenville writes: "What can exceed the ridicule of thus systematically coupling together a friend and an enemy to toleration, like fat and lean rabbits, or the man and his wife in a Dutch toy, or like fifty other

73

absurdities made to be laughed at, but certainly never before introduced into politics as fixed and fundamental systems for the conduct of the most difficult and dangerous crisis of a country."

It was natural that the Orange party should feel aggrieved at his appointment, but he seems also by his unpunctuality, carelessness and neglect of answering letters to have offended his own supporters. Some resolutions against him were even carried at a Catholic meeting at Athenry, "but," writes Mr. Gregory, "though aimed at Grant, they, according to our national Blunders hit the Lords Justices."

Ministers called out that he did not keep them informed of the state of affairs, and complained of his indecision, now blowing hot, now cold, at one moment declaring no troops were wanted, the next, clamouring for them. It must in any case have been uphill work for him. He came over primed with theories of popular government, but found small obstacles in his way at every turn. To understand his position one may imagine how Mr. Morley would have felt when holding office in Ireland, had he been flanked with Lord Londonderry as a Viceroy, and Colonel Saunderson as an Under Secretary.

Groans for "Popish Grant" were given at the decoration of King William's statue, and the correspondence of Lord Talbot and Mr. Gregory shows how little they welcomed this advanced "Catholic" thrust between them. Dublin Castle cannot have been for him a bed of roses.

Mr. Grant was all for turning his theories to practice without loss of time, while Mr. Gregory, fulfilling the usual role of the permanent official, acted as a practical, restraining Sancho Panza to the new Quixote. Mr. Grant, anxious to seize the first opportunity of showing confidence in the Catholics, proposes to make Lord Gormanstown a Commissioner of Fisheries. Mr. Gregory replies that no one could be more respectable, "but I doubt whether he would be gratified by being named as a Commissioner. His habits are very retired, and he has never accustomed himself to publick business. You have already two Commissioners for that immediate neighbourhood."

He proposes what he believes to be a benevolent reform, of sending female convicts to Cork by ship instead of by road. But Mr. Gregory convinces him that the present mode of conveyance "in covered him cars, on springs," is much more comfortable, and much preferred by them.

He had at Cambridge written a prize poem on the restoration of learning in the East, and was anxious to repeat his triumph by apply for the Police; this was always left to the unbiassed decision of the Magistracy, but that when the measure *was* decided upon, and the request *was* made, that the Govt. would be disposed to examine into the state of the Case, with every wish to be indulgent, etc. etc. He agreed, but I think expected more.

"I congratulate you and the Country on Peel's brilliant speech. It ranks amongst the best of the day.

"Considering the Wood is in my view, and is, I hear, full of Cocks, I have written at length. Whether you will be able to read it is another thing."

December 12.

"You will *not* have requisition for the peelers here.

"Clonbrock begins to flinch, and the more so as Mr.——, who was strenuous in his wish to have them, has now changed his opinion. Locally speaking he is right, and if all your Galway friends were as stout in heart and body as he seems to be, certainly there would be no necessity for them. He has established a chain of signals by Bonfires, and patroles at the head of forty well-armed followers every other night at least, and on the least symptom of the approach of these rascals a fire is lighted and 300 or 400 fellows are, and have been, in less than an hour, at some specified rendezvous."

He had good shooting at Garbally, Marble Hill, and other Galway places, and seems fully to have enjoyed his days there, the last happy ones he was to know for a long time.

Lady Talbot, whose health had for some time given cause for anxiety, died December 30, 1819. She had given birth to a son in October. There is an entry almost two years later in Mr. Gregory's note-book, "Gerald Talbot christened at the Lodge in the Park. Duke and Duchess of Leinster and the Chancellor sponsors."

A month after her death Lord Talbot writes from Hatfield : —

January 23, 1820.

"It is now very long since I either wrote to or heard from you. I am much as usual, calm at times, wretched at others—such must be my Lot for a long long time. But a truce to my misfortunes, for which no one more sincerely feels than you do. I will proceed to tell you that I went to Town yesterday, where I saw Lords Liverpool and Sidmouth, from both of whom I experienced the kindest reception, and heard that I had had the good fortune to give satisfaction during my stay in Ireland, and

I ascertained what *you* will not dislike to hear, that as far as our friends are concerned, *no* change of opinion has taken place respecting the Catholic Question. Indeed, Lord Sidmouth distinctly said, 'He would not stay in any administration that would concede that vital point.'

"So much for that. This was obtained by my asking distinctly if we were to apprehend a charge of opinion on it, as from Grant's speech we really were a good deal alarmed."

And from Ingestre on February 1 : —

"So our poor dear old King is gone. If this event should make any difference as to my return, *i.e.*, if I ought on account of it to come back directly, *pray* say so.

"I write by this post to Lord Sidmouth, to say I am ready to go if Government wish me to do so."

Ingestre: February 4.

"Well, my dear Gregory, here we are living under the auspices of a new King, who I am sorry to say has been (I believe very) ill at the commencement of His reign.

"By a letter from Bloomfield yesterday, I learn that H. M. is better than even the bulletins report him to be. I called twice at Carlton House, but owing to the Duke of Kent's death I did not ask to see the then Regent.

"I trust our good King will emulate the virtues of his good and moral Father. I hear that he was very much affected on reading His address to the Privy Council.

'. . . Pray also be active about Dr. Lloyd. He, I imagine, would expect to be the provost in the event of Ebrington's moving to the Bench, to which I see less objection than to anybody in our list, and to which our Masters here are inclined. Be careful in ascertaining Lloyd's tenets as to Catholic matters, for Plunkett will be zealous, you know, on that point, and he is in high favor with Government. But I do not think anything is in immediate contemplation for him *here*. Lord Sidmouth distinctly told me *He would not*, were he in my situation, consent to any person being made Provost who was not a *staunch protestant*. Depend upon it we are well backed in that Quarter, as also at Carlton House—at least so said Lord S——.

"I am so much out of the way of hearing news, I can find you none, but from what Lord Harrowby said before the late King's death had occurred I should not wonder if parliament were to and immortal memory," at the Lord Mayor's dinner. But the toast was proposed by the Lord Mayor himself, and though Lord Cloncurry and other decided "Catholics" turned down their glasses, the King's representative may not have felt free to refuse the toast to one of the King's predecessors.

His letters show what a warm spot there was in his heart for Ireland, and how sore he is for a time after his recall, but he "goes to look at flowers," at the wonderful scarlets and crimsons flaming over the grey mud of Holland. Then he takes up the threads of country life aagin, attends the Magistrate's meetings, looks after his property, establishes a sheep show, and does his duty.

The following letters were written in the first soreness of dismissal. He may have found comfort in the fact that Mr. Grant was also recalled, and succeeded by Mr. Goulburn, but he does not allude to it.

Lord Talbot to Mr. Gregory

Ingestre: January 2, 1822.
"I enclose a letter which I have found here, from our dear friend Lord Whitworth. What comfort does it not bring to me. It almost reconciles me to my fate.

"You will be glad also to hear that persons of all parties in this County are indignant at the treatment I have experienced, and I have heard it whispered that a public dinner is in contemplation to me expressive of their regard, and to assure me I hold the same place in their Esteem I ever did. This (if true) is most gratifying. You shall of course hear more when I do. I long to hear the arrangements in all your departments. If Phillimore is right as to the sensation felt in England about our good Attorney, I fear others will soon follow me and him.

"Lord W. told me he meant to lose no time about Saurin's business. I thought Goulburn particularly *cordial* at taking leave. He'll soon go."

[Enclosure]   Knole: December 2, 1821.
"I will tell you candidly why I have not written to you. I was so hurt and disgusted at what had occurred, that I could not trust myself to mention it to you until I heard from yourself how you felt about it. I am not surprised at your feelings, and I partake them most sincerely. In all the course of my political life I never knew anything more unjust, more unmerited, more

illiberal, or more absurd. I ask of everybody what Lord Wellesley can do, or will do, that Lord Talbot has not done, or would do, if you gave him power to act. If they mean to give him powers which you have been asking for in vain, they will add still to their injustice, for why should not you carry these powers into effect as well as he.

"It is cruel and barbarous usage, but such only as those who engage in politics must expect, and particularly with such people as those with whom we have now to do—whose principle it is to give up everything and everybody rather than give up their places.

"But, my dear Talbot, I will not add to your spleen by venting my own. Come and see us as soon as you can.

"W."

Lord Talbot to Mr. Gregory

Boodles: Jan. 10, 1822.

"Here I am after a semi-conversation with Lord Sidmouth— which was interrupted by the Duke of York's coming into the room. The meeting was most distant on my part, Lord S. saying 'Little did I think, Lord T., that you and I should meet with painful feelings.' 'Most painful indeed, my Lord,' returned I.

" 'Have you heard of the King's gracious intentions towards you?' 'No, my Lord.' 'I wrote to you at Ingestre.' 'I had left home before your Lordship's communication arrived, I suppose.' 'Well,' said Lord S., 'the purport of the letter was to express H.M.'s commands to you to go to Brighton to be *His* Guest at the Pavilion.'

"To which I answered, 'I can set out this moment or to-morrow, whichever day your Lordship may instruct me to go. Am I' (said I coldly) 'to go in Uniform or in frac.' This hit. But after a little Lord S. said, 'We must talk over the matter unreservedly.' 'My Lord, the matter is soon discussed. I have been turned out of office in less time than I should deem it right to turn a servant away, without having been told *Why*— in other words I have been condemned unheard. Had Lord Grey come into power he could not have treated me more unceremoniously. It is for your Lordship to tell me *How* I have deserved this treatment. I thank God I do not feel conscious of meriting it.' I then added that I had been taken out of my County with an unspotted Character, that whatever might be the opinion of the public respecting me,

Like so many great lawyers, his mind failed at the last, but he never lost the authoritative character that had belonged to him. Once a curate who had incautiously included him in a petition for sinners was obliged to make a precipitate retreat through the window.

An old member of the Irish Bar, to whom I was talking of him, said, "I would not say he had a disagreeable manner, but I saw him very much out of temper twice: once when he gave his farewell charge to the Bench, and was raging against the Government for having turned him out in favour of Campbell—not that he had anything to complain of, for he had feathered his nest well; and once when we dined at Judge ——'s, and after dinner came family prayers. When we knelt down, his chair was next mine—oh, he was very angry indeed!"

The chief feat accomplished by Lord Wellesley in Ireland was the dethroning of Plunket's rival, Saurin, the Attorney-General.

His removal was decided on in 1821, but not carried out until the following year. No one, it is said, had courage to say the word of dismissal until Lord Wellesley arrived. The secret kept itself, and no one, friend or enemy, ventured to hint to him that it was in the air. The following letters show how even the loyal and official mind of Mr. Gregory is moved when Saurin is first threatened, to try and stir up the Viceroy to mutiny on his behalf.

He writes to Lord Talbot June 6, 1821 : —

"Your letter of the 4th has filled me with great alarm, as the Conduct intended to be pursued towards the Attorney-General satisfies me that a new system of Government is to be adopted in Ireland, and that the old and faithful supporters of the Crown must make way for recent Converts."

And on July 7 he writes : —

"I cannot say how much your letter from Sherborne has distressed me, as it discloses an unfeeling Perseverance on the part of Ministers to remove a faithful and invaluable servant of the Crown, from no other than the selfish motive of gaining the parliamentary support of a powerful Advocate, who has for so many years been a powerful Antagonist. In my mind *you* can at once put an end to this disgraceful transaction by declining to be the Channel of Communication, whether official or not, and by declaring that it cannot be made so long as you remain Viceroy of Ireland. I do not think after such a Declaration the measure would be persevered in, nor do I think they would venture on your Removal for the sole Purpose of carrying it into effect. I am aware that this is bold and hazardous Counsel, but you will, I am sure, give me the Credit of its being disinterested."

Lord Talbot writes on November 21 : —

"Saurin's fate is sealed. We (the Chancellor and I) have received a Communication on the subject. But as yet we are only to proceed and obtain Donner's resignation of the C. Justiceship, which is then to be offered to Saurin (in pretty decided language tho'). Bushe is either to have Norbury's situation if he will resign it, or be promised the succession to it. I have written to the Chancellor requesting his assistance. I am very happy in the reflection that I made a stand for Saurin last year."

But Mr. Gregory refuses to be comforted : —

November 22.
". . . Yet when these two very important objects (resignation of the Chief Justice and the Attorney-General) are surmounted, if they can be, what is to be done with Bushe? I shall be surprised if he agree to abide the Disgrace of being superseded by Plunkett, and be satisfied with a promise of dead Norbury's shoes. It is a vile transaction, and will overwhelm the administration with Reproach and shame."

Lord Talbot writes with evident relief on November 24, 1821 : —

"I am *not* to be the Channel of communication with poor Saurin. The Chancellor, who is so much better qualified, has undertaken it. So far I disagree with you, that I do not think Saurin is the first to whom the Business should be communicated. The Chief Justice, in my opinion, and in that of Lord Manners (to whom I read parts of your Letter), is the person with whom he will begin. If the Chief resigns, to whom the *whole* case is to be made known, then there is a something to offer to the Attorney. If the Chief will not resign then the whole thing stops, for a while at least.

"I do *not* think the Attorney will be Chief Justice. What do you say? Then what a business. I enclose to you Lord L.'s Letter to me, by which you will perceive it is a measure of Government.

"However much I deprecate this transaction, and believe me I do so as sincerely as you do yourself, I still think that a Govern-

the Government and allowing an experiment to be made by those
who thought they could conduct it as to Catholic emancipation
with adequate securities. If the Country was inert on the subject,
it was fair to calculate that they desired such an experiment, and
under those circumstances I should undoubtedly have counselled
the resignation of Peel, Lord Liverpool and Lord Eldon. But the
propriety of such a course appears to me to be now much altered.
I believe that a Government could not make an arrangement
of the Question in the face of the decision of the House of Lords
and of the growing feeling all over this country against it. The
effect, therefore, of any Govt. undertaking it would be to over-
turn them and to leave the King in the situation of having no
materials out of which to form a Govt. to succeed them. Under
these circumstances I think it may be a public duty to continue
the Government as it is, and although many circumstances which
have occurred make it extremely unpleasant personally to those
whom I have mentioned to continue in the Government, yet
upon the whole I think it may be their duty to do so. What their
deciison will be I do not at present know. Peel's situation as the
Irish Minister is the most awkward and the more embarrassing
as being the *only* Protestant Minister in the House of Commons.
But he will not do anything rash, though his feeling is undoubtedly
for retirement. Should Lord Liverpool and Peel retire, it is most
probable that I shall accompany them. Should Peel alone withdraw I shall be in a most disagreeable difficulty, as his withdrawal
would rest upon purely a personal feeling. Should they decide
upon continuing in office things will for the present remain as
they are, and all these disagreeable contests and divisions will
have to be renewed in the ensuing session of Parliament. You
shall be the first to know what step is likely to be taken. I have
given you very hastily an outline of what is under deliberation.
You will of course consider it quite confidential, and say nothing
yet to any one whatever."

Irish Office: February 17, 1827.
"I called this morning upon Peel, with a view to the discussion
of the course proper to be pursued on the Roman Catholic
question, when in the middle of our discussion a message was
brought to us that Lord Liverpool had been attacked by
Apoplexy. He had as usual received his letters at breakfast, and
not having rung his bell as usual afterwards, was found by his
Servant senseless on the Floor.[1] Remedies were immediately

---

[1] The letter found in his hand was one from Stapleton, giving an unfavourable account of Canning's health.

applied, and he is partially restored to his senses, but his right side is disabled, and the hopes of his further recovery very slight. As a public man he may be reckoned as dead. He has long been advised by his physicians to give up public business, as likely to produce a seizure of this kind, and whatever reasons he may before have had to neglect their injunction will of course cease to operate now.

"I have lost in him a kind and amiable friend, whose sound principle and practical piety entitled him to every confidence and respect, and the Country has lost an able and successful Minister, whose integrity never was questioned, and whose motives of action were always pure and just.

"It is useless to conceal from you (though, of course, it is to you alone that I make the disclosure) my opinion that this will break up the Government. The embarrassments of the King in making a new Government will be extreme. He cannot find Protestants enough to make a Protestant Government, he will not like a Catholic one, and I think that a mixed one can go on no longer, deprived as it must be of the Lord Chancellor and Lord Liverpool. At the present moment all are too much stunned by the blow to be able to form any rational calculation as to the probable march of events. I will, therefore, hazard no opinion. You may depend upon hearing from me the moment I see even a ray of daylight.

"As far as regards the R. Cath. question, the death or retirement of Lord L. will be a serious blow. It would appear as if God had determined to punish us by depriving us of those best calculated to defend the Church in the danger with which it is threatened. But it is vain to attempt to scrutinise his purpose. Before this event I had reason to believe that we had a majority in the House of Commons. I cannot say what may be the result now.

"Canning still continues ill, but they say he is better. How wonderfully the removal of Lord Londonderry and Lord Liverpool has opened the path to his ambition, and how fearfully it will show the vanity of human objects, if at the moment when everything appears within his Grasp his health should prevent his availing himself of the opening!"

Irish Office: March 9, 1827.

"I write to you for information on a subject on which your knowledge of Ireland may enable you to give me an answer, and on which I think from something which I have heard to-day, that it may be necessary to form an opinion. I have heard it surmised

against the preposterous over-taxation of Ireland since the Union.
But both then and later, when he spent three years at the Swedish
Court trying to recover the money advanced to Bernadotte for
the war with Napoleon, he experienced the truth of the homely
proverb, "It is hard to get butter out of a dog's mouth." He was
a Christ Church man and a trustee of the British Museum. Not
only did O'Connell, though disqualified for taking his seat in
the House, head the poll, but the vivid glimpse given on the
day of the election of his power and the unity of the people on
the Emancipation question startled all those in England who had
eyes to discern the signs of the times. Lord Palmerston says in
his journal, "The Clare election began a new era, and *was an
epoch in the history of Ireland.* . . . There were 30,000 Irish
peasants in and about Ennis in sultry July, and not a drunken
man among them save O'Connell's own coachman, and not a
blackthorn." And again he writes: — "I speak of the election for
Clare which led to Catholic Emancipation, which led by a new
defection in the Tory party to the Reform Bill, which led to a
complete social and political revolution in our country." The
fire had indeed begun to burn the stick, and the stick to beat
the dog, and the dog to bite the pig, if we may so term the
long-obstructed bill for Catholic Emancipation.

O'Connell had done his share of the work, but he was not
without helpers. A petition in favour of the Bill was now
presented by the Protestant landowners of Ireland, representing
more than three fourths of its landed property. Peel's own
brother-in-law, Dawson, speaking at Londonderry, avowed himself a convert to Emancipation. The stars in their courses fought
for it. Of the Archbishops, Magee was too old and Beresford too
gentle to direct the canons of the Church against the enemy.
Rank, talent, property, all had come round to the Liberal side.

Those who still held out, the members of the Brunswick clubs
in Ireland, held a meeting, to raise their voices for the last time
against relief, but their thinned ranks proclaimed that the hour
of dissolution was near.

Moore, who had been singing down anti-Catholic feeling in
London drawing-rooms, sharply satirised the gathering in his
Letter from Beelzebub—

> "Who the devil, he humbly begs to know,
> Are Lord Glendine and Lord Dunlo?
> Or who with a grain of sense would go
> To sit and be bored by Lord Mayo?
> What living creature—except his nurse—

> For Lord Mountcashel cares a curse?
> Or thinks 'twould matter if Lord Muskerry
> Were t'other side of the Stygian ferry?"

Not names, one must confess, that have had "buoyancy to float down the stream of time."

In England the Bill had been brought forward again and again with varying fortunes. Grattan had for the last time introduced it in 1819. In March of that year Vesey Fitzgerald writes to Mr. Gregory: —

"Grattan has just given his Catholic notice for the 22nd of April. They rumour here that they are to make the greatest division that they have ever made. I believe it not. Nor do I portend anything but angry exasperating discussions. I do not envy you your situation in Dublin, or in truth just now your responsibility."

And Mr. Gregory writes to him in May: —

"After all the vaunted Expectations of a great Majority against the Catholic Claims I cannot by any means attribute to accident or trick that they were rejected only by two. I much fear the apathy of the Protestants, and that the present House of Commons is more Popish than the last. Here all is quiet, though the Protestants are much dismayed, they have no democratic Leaders to inflame the Minds of the People as their adversaries practice."

At Grattan's death, Plunket succeeded him as the Irish advocate of the measure in the House of Commons. The Catholic leaders, however, became dissatisfied with him after a time, and chose Sir Francis Burdett as their representative.

In 1821 it was lost on the second reading by a majority of 39, giving rise to a fashionable toast of "the thirty-nine who saved the thirty-nine articles."

In 1825 it passed the Commons, but was rejected in the Lords through the effect of the Duke of York's violent speech against it, concluding with the words: "These are the principles to which I will adhere and which I will maintain and act up to, to the latest moment of my existence, *whatever may be my situation in life*. So help me God!"

This was the speech that was printed in gold and distributed widely by the Protestant party. Canning, pointing to a copy of it, said "This is a sign of the times which augurs ill for future

Sligo. I send his letter . . . but surely he has no sort of claim, and how can we refuse the local member?"

Mr. Gregory to Mr. Grant

July 30, 1819.

"The Bishop of Clogher dead, the Lord Lieutenant writes by this Post to Lord Liverpool and you. How fortunate you are being absent from Dublin during the First hungry Importunities for the division of the Spoils. . . ."

Lord Talbot to Mr. Gregory

August 31, 1819.

"Henry D——'s Letter, I must freely confess, disgusted and annoyed me. I am really not aware what his Brother's *Claims* are, but as far as I am a competent judge of them, they have not been ill attended to, as they have procured 1,100*l.* a year in the Church for his Brother. . . .

"Did Grant tell you that Lord Liverpool still wished 600*l.* pension to be given to Lord Brandon. I answered this by saying it was impossible without Lord L. would allow me to give away 1,500*l.* this year instead of the customary 1,200*l.* Lord L. should not make positive promises without communicating with us. . . ."

November 15, 1819.

"Lord Glerawly presents his compts. to Mr. Grant. . . .

"Lord G. has for a long time been soliciting a living for his Brother-in-law, the Revd. Mr. Johnston, contiguous to Lord Annesley's estates . . . but the Irish Government have not hitherto paid that attention to his request which Lord Glerawly would naturally have expected, especially as Lord G. (tho' not having the honour of being personally acquainted with Mr. Grant) begs leave to inform him that he has for a length of time supported the present administration and had to contest his seat in two successive Parliaments at a most enormous expense and trouble."

(Answer. Government will not interfere with the patronage of a Bishop.)

From Col. C. to Mr. Gregory

"Dear Sir,—I had the honour of your last letter, and cannot but observe that I am the only member for a County in Ireland that would have been refused such a request as my last. I have always understood that every one of those small situations that become vacant in the County was and is given to the member who supports Government even without applying for them. I did apply the moment it became vacant and I have been refused. I have experienced similar refusals before.

"I wrote to Mr. Peel some time back relative to a conversation that took place between you and me on the subject of Clerk of the Crown for this County, having in consequence of that conversation promised it to Mr. John Hurley should it become vacant. He has now brought me the resignation of the present clerk, which I enclose, and I hope there will be no difficulty in naming this gentleman to the situation. He is in every respect fully qualified to fill it."

From Mr. Gregory to Col. C.

"Dear Sir,—In answer to your Letter expressing your surprise that you should have been refused the nomination to a small revenue place in the Co. of Kerry, as you considered when such situations became vacant they were always granted to the Member for the county in which they are situated who supported the Government, I am directed by the Lord Lieutenant to refer you to your letter of the 3rd of February last, to Mr. Peel, in which you declared the conditions on which you had given your support to the Government, and as his Excellency has no prospect of being able to gratify your Expectations he concluded it was not your Intention to continue your support."

Mr. Gregory to Mr. Peel

March 30, 1816.

"Nothing will drive the Irish members to Parliament unless convenient to themselves, and yet if they declare themselves for the Government, they think they are entitled to every branch of Patronage as much as though they gave a useful support."

Mr. Peel thus notes some of the letters he returns to Mr. Gregory.

"But eno' of this d——m subject. I saw Lord Manners, who appears quite well."

Ingestre: Feb. 28, 1829.

". . . I feel acutely the blow that is about to be inflicted on the Country.

"As at *present* informed, my vote will be as it ever has been; but if in a conscientious examination into the Arguments to be adduced and facts which we *Hear* are to be brought forward, I see reason to alter that opinion, I shall do so. If you ask me what I think, I think you will find me the uncompromising defender of those principles in which I have been brought up and have ever professed. I am not one who will give up deep and firmly rooted principles because a Duke of Wellington may be driven from his post . . . fiat justitia ruat Coelum. I can safely say I have never felt a political Question so deeply—it has positively made me ill—deprived me of all comfort and peace of mind.

"Depressed in spirits, deprived of hope, I wandered about London like one possessed with an Evil Spirit. Yet the Question will be carried at all risks and at all events. I shall be at my post tho' I cannot summon up resolution to speak (tho' I will not say to what I may be goaded). I intend to watch every clause, every word of the intended Acts of Parliament. I cannot but think Peel conscientious—he has lost everything to gain nothing. I have not seen him, but I hear he says he is *conscientious* in adopting ·he Line which he has painfully taken.

"Hoping your Daughter is restored to you in health, with Cecil's Love to you all, believe me, unalterably yours."

London: March 25, 1829.

". . . I have not seen Peel, nor do I know that I quite wish to seen him—for although I give him every credit for *honest conviction* on his part of the *expediency* (that is our new and fashionable phrase), if not absolute necessity for a change, I cannot forget he is no longer the bold assertor of those principles in which I have been brought up, and which notwithstanding all his oratory I still conceive to be necessary to the well-being of the Country. But I will call when he is more at leisure to see individuals who have no demands upon his time.

"I saw W. Peel yesterday, and I told him I was not yet arrived at that pitch of political proficiency when I could reconcile it to myself to sacrifice *principle to expediency*, neither would I do so. If you recollect the W. Peel at Grenden you would scarcely recognise him in London. I mean the expression, not the person of the man.

"I am told we shall be beaten by a majority of fifty-eight in
H. of Lords. I fear the *Reaction,* for certainly the feelings of the
public are against the measure. W. Peel having stated some
difficulties which in his opinion justified the bill, said to me,
'What would you do?' I replied, 'Upon my word I do not know,
but allow me to ask you, what do you expect to do now?' I got
as little satisfaction from him. I hear six Irish Bishops are come
or coming over to see the King on this business. This is all very
well—but they might as well have staid at home. The present
Premier will not consent to retrograde, and the doors of the
Constitution are to be set wide open to all persons wishing to
enter them. Some people doubt of Lord Manners. Surely he
cannot after his Uniform opposition to R. C. Emancipation turn
round and vote for it. But you will say, 'Look at Peel!' I can
only shake my head and say, very true!

"Yet I think 'Tom' staunch. I have heard the magnificence of
your present L.L.[1] is unbounded, quite princely. Yet a more
unassuming person cannot exist. I hope you will like them both!
They are amiable in private life...."

London: April 1, 1829.

"The bill for R. C. Emancipation was yesterday brought to the
Lords, by Peel in person. Little did I ever expect to have seen
our friend at the bar of our House upon such an occasion. Had
I been told of such a circumstance two years, nay one year ago,
I should have scouted it as impossible.

"As I have a perfect conviction of Peel's honesty, morality
and religious principles, I cannot entertain a doubt of his *motives,*
but perhaps I should say *fears* which have induced him to sacrifice
his Character for consistency and firmness. But having so far
given him credit, I hope I shall not be reproached with a wish to
derogate from his character if I say that in future I *cannot confide*
in his stability. *Expediency* is a sorry word. I say give me *principle*
as my watchword.

"No one in future can be fairly reproached with abandoning
principles, friends or party—all, all, must yield to expediency!
Be it so; when we know whereof politicians are made we can
measure the proportion of faith to be reposed in them by that
Scale. I am glad you approve of my line of conduct. I wish so to
vote that I can say to myself, 'You have acted conscientiously
and done your Duty.' ...

"I hardly know what to think of Lord Manners. He is

[1] Duke of Northumberland.

he has in hand. I hope, indeed I expect, that Lord Stanley will join him. My Idea is that the Duke will go to the Horse Guards, that Aberdeen will succeed him at the F.O., and Lord Stanley, Aberdeen. This may be visionary, but I suspect it will sooner or later be the case. If I could see Peel and Stanley cordially acting together I should then consider the thing safe.

"I wonder how Lady Haddington will be liked. She is a highly principled virtuous woman, but I fear that neither her appearance or her manners will suit your vivacious people. When known she will be liked and esteemed."

Ingestre: April 10, 1835.

"I cannot find words to express the state of despondency in which the resignation of Peel has cast me.[1] The Game is up as far as mortals are concerned.

"But thank GOD I have a firm reliance in the Almighty's Mercy, and if we are to suffer here, it will, I doubt not, turn all to our ultimate happiness, if we conduct ourselves in heavy hour of Trial and Adversity with propriety and resignation.

"So courage, mon Ami.

"We have addressed our Sovereign and Peel on the occasion.

"We have also formed a Conservative Association, from which I hope we shall derive some strength, and not suffer ourselves to be *be-Whigged*, as this formerly loyal County is now.

"I conclude Haddington has resigned."

Ingestre: May 7, 1835.

". . . By a letter from Haddington, to whom I wrote to congratulate him on not serving under these O'Connell be-ridden Whigs, and on his having gained the good opinion of all that was good and honourable in Ireland, I find he is, like me, warmly attached to your Country. By the by he thanks me for having obtained for him your acquaintance, and, he adds, 'I hope his friendship.'

"What work these O'Connells are making! I am not without hope that it will all work to a good end, although much dirt must be thrown aside before we are safely through our dangers!

"Alvanly has behaved *well*. Mr. O'Connell had a shot more than he ought to have had at him."

---

[1] On the defeat of his Government on the Tithe Bill.

From Lord Haddington to Mr. Gregory

London: May 30, 1835.

"My dear Sir,—Your very kind answer to the very hurried lines
I wrote to you on the morning of my departure reached me soon
after my arrival here. I wrote in haste, and in a state of mind
not very likely to produce an adequate impression of the feelings
I wished to convey to you. You will, however, believe that I
entertained them very sincerely, that I truly value your friendship
and good opinion, and am duly sensible of the advantage I
derived from the kindness and frankness with which on several
occasions you answered my call on you for your opinion and
advice.

"I will not dwell on the feelings with which we left Ireland,
and continue to think of the day of our departure. You understand them, I am quite sure, and will believe me when I say
that Ireland is never out of our anxious and painful thoughts,
tho' there is much to dwell upon that is deeply gratifying to us.
The kindness we met with during our stay and on our coming
away was too remarkable ever to be forgotten, or to be
remembered during life without gratitude and delight. But these
very feelings aggravate the painful necessity with which we think
of the present position and future prospects of a country doomed,
it would seem, never to be at peace, and yet requiring but Peace
to make it one of the happiest and most flourishing regions in the
world.

"I will leave that subject, however, as I think it will be more
agreeable to you to hear about the state of things in this part of
the world than to read reflections and lamentations about your
own Country, from one whose knowledge is so imperfect as compared with your own as to her real state.

"If speculations on politics have ever been doubtful, true it is
that under the reform régime they are more uncertain than ever.
My speculation, however, is, that the present Government will
outlive the Session. In the first place I think they are determined
to do so, and that is no small help to a party not overburdened
with high feelings of honour, nor embarrassed by much political
principle of a very squeamish character. In the second place it is
obviously not in Peel's intention to press them with a view of
turning them out. He will deal with their measures, but they are
determined to afford him very few measures to deal withal. They
have unblushingly thrown everything overboard, and the radicals
and dissenters are too wise in their generation not to play into
their hands and wait their time, by which they diminish the

FLINT, Sir Charles William (proxy to Rt. Hon. Sir Henry Wellesley at installation of the Bath, 1812, cr. Kt. 1812), 42, 55

FLYN, Mr. (Daniel O'Connell's brother-in-law), 63

FOSTER, John Leslie (c. 1781–1842, M.P. for Dublin University 1807–12, Yarmouth (Hants) 1816–18, Armagh City 1818–20, Louth County 1824–30), 75

FOWLER, Rev., 87

FOX, Charles James (1749–1806, M.P. for Midhurst 1768–74, Malmesbury 1774–80, Westminster 1780–1806), 27, 34

FREMANTLE, Sir William Henry (1766–1850)

FRENCH, Arthur (c. 1764–1820, M.P. for Roscommon 1785–1820, his son John, rector of Grange Silvae, Co. Kilkenny, became 2nd Baron De Freyne), 168

FRENCH, Martin, 168

GAS Light Company, 15

GEORGE III, King (b. 1738, reg. 1760–1820, George William Frederick), 27, 91

GEORGE IV, King (b. 1762, reg. 1820–1830, George Augustus Frederick), 27, 28, 47, 55, 56, 91, 92–6, 97, 98, 108, 112, 114, 117, 141, 153, 154, 160, 161, 163, 190

GIFFORD, Sir Robert Gifford, 1st Baron (1779–1826, Attorney General 1819, Lord Chief Justice of the Court of Common Pleas, and the Master of the Rolls in 1824), 139

GILLRAY, James (1757–1815, caricaturist), 154

GINDERS, Mr., 182, 196

GLADSTONE, William Ewart (1809–98, Prime Minister 1868–74, 1880–85, 1886, 1892–94), 32

GLANDINE, Lord, see Norbury, 1st Earl of (Lady Gregory misspelled the title as Glendine)

GLENGALL, Richard Butler, 2nd Earl of (1794–1858), 98

GLENGALL, Countess of (c. 1777–1836, née Emily Jefferys, widow of 1st Earl), 15, 173

GLERAWLY, Lord, see Annesley, 3rd Earl

GLOUCESTER AND EDINBURGH, William Frederick, Duke of (1776–1860), 99

GODERICH, Frederick John Robinson, 1st Viscount (1782–1859, 1st Lord of the Treasury 1827–28, cr. Viscount in 1828, and Earl of Ripon in 1833), 144, 147, 162, 186

GORMANSTON, Jenico Preston, 12th Viscount (1775–1860), 74

GORT, Charles Verecker, 2nd Viscount (1782–1859, beat French forces at Killala Bay in 1798), 171

GOULBURN, Henry (1784–1856, M.P. for Horsham 1808–12, St. Germains 1812–18, West Looe 1818–26, Armagh 1826–31, Cambridge University 1831–56, Secretary for Ireland 1821–28, Chancellor of the Exchequer 1828–30, 1841–46), 6, 14, 17, 37, 107, 111, 118, 119, 121, 126, 131, 133, 136, 137, 139, 151, 155, 163, 172–3

GRANARD, George Forbes, 6th Earl of (1760–1837, General in the

Army, Clerk of the Crown and Hanaper in Ireland), 111

GRANT, Charles (1778–1866, M.P. for Inverness burghs 1811–14, 1814–18, Inverness-shire 1818–35, Chief Secretary for Ireland 1819–23, Vice-President of the Board of Trade 1823–27, President of the Board 1827–28, President of the Board of Control 1830–34, cr. Baron Glenelg in 1835), 14, 16, 73, 74, 75, 76, 77–8, 79, 82, 83, 85, 96, 102, 103, 105, 120, 131, 132, 137, 170, 175, 187, 191

GRANT, Sir Robert (1779–1838, M.P. for Elgin burghs 1818–26, Inverness burghs 1826–30, Norwich 1830–32, Finsbury 1832–34, when he became Governor of Bombay. He was a champion of the Jews, and in the 1830s unsucessfully tried to repeal their civil disabilities), 76

GRANVILLE, Granville Leveson-Gower, 1st Earl (1773–1846, y.s. of 1st Marquess of Stafford, cr. Viscount Granville in 1815, Ambassador Extraordinary and Plenipotentiary to Russia in 1804 and later Ambassador to France), 55, 144

GRATTAN, Henry (1746–1820, M.P. for Charlemont in the Irish Parliament 1775–1800, one of its leaders until he was accused of being a member of the United Irishmen, and dropped from the Irish Privy Council. The accusation was groundless. In the U.K. House of Commons he sat for Malton 1805–06, Dublin 1806–20), 27, 28, 81, 122, 131, 159

GRATTAN, James (1783–1854, served in the Peninsula and at Waterloo), 59

GREGORY, Lady Anne (c. 1767–1833, née Trench), 6, 12, 16, 42, 45, 56, 87, 119, 165, 181, 185

GREGORY, Anne (1793–1868, married Lt. Col. R. Johnston Walsh), 212

GREGORY, Lady (1852–1932, née Isabella Augusta Persse), 5, 7, 215

GREGORY, Sir William Henry (1816–92, M.P. for Dublin 1842–47, for Galway County 1857–72, when appointed Governor of Ceylon 1872–77), 12, 13, 35, 148, 185, 189, 204, 213, 214; *Autobiography*, 118

GREGORY, Major (William) Robert (1881–1918), 8, 214

GREVILLE, Charles (father of the following), 197

GREVILLE, Charles Cavendish Fulke (1794–1865), *Memoirs (1817–60)*, 76, 153, 164, 165, 204

GREVILLE, Henry William (1801–72, brother of the above), 190

GREY, Charles Grey, 2nd Earl (1764–1845, M.P. for Northumberland 1786–1807, when he succeeded to the earldom, Prime Minister in 1830), 55, 96, 107, 202

GRIMSTON, James Grimston, Viscount (1809–95, became 2nd Earl Verulam in 1845), 205

GUILLAMORE, Standish O'Grady, 1st Viscount (1766–1840, Chief Baron of the Exchequer of Ireland 1805–31, when cr. Viscount), 129

GUINNESS, Rev. Mr., 86

GUINNESS family, 23–4

GUNS, the Miss, 45

ERRATA AND ADDENDA

p. 51	8 lines up	for Castsle, read Castle
p. 74	4 lines up	correct as 1898 edition, but probably should be covered-in for covered him
p. 91	14 lines up	correct as 1898 edition, but Ebrington should read Elrington
p. 101	line 27	for liberities read liberties
p. 107	line 10	for aagin read again
p. 117	line 13	close quotation marks after *lux*
p. 127	line 17	correct as 1898 edition, but Townsand should read Townsend
p. 177	line 14	for Gergory, read Gregory
p. 204	3 lines up	for tic doulourteux, read tic douloureux

INDEX

p. 221 BOND, V.Rev. Dr. Wensley, delete first 1772-1813
for BROOKES'S read BROOKS'S
second line of BURKE entry, dates should read 1774-80, and 1780-94

p. 222 insert before 'CARDERS' entry, 'CARAVATS', 65
CHARLES X, King of France (1757-1836, reg. 1824-30), 140
CHRIST Church, Oxford entry, for 58 read 158
CONSTABLE Act. This is the Constabulary Act of 1822 (3 Geo. IV, c. 103)

p. 223 COERCION Act, for (1833), read (1822)

p. 224 top line. for DAY read DALY
DAVIS, Mr. delete reference to William Davis
DECIES, Most Rev. William Beresford, for Ossory 1782-94, read 1782-95
for DRYDEN John, read DRYDEN, John

p. 225 ELLIS, Master, correctly Thomas Ellis (c. 1774-1832, M.P. for Dublin City 1820-26)
ELRINGTON, Thomas, delete c. before birthdate
insert before next entry EMMET, Robert (1778-1803, United Irishman, brother of the following), 39
for FARNELL, read FARRELL
FITZGERALD, Lord Edward, 2nd line of entry, read, leader of the United Irishmen

p. 226 FLYN, Mr. in text, but must be FINN, William Francis (1789-1862, M.P. for Co. Kilkenny 1832-37, married O'Connell's sister Alicia in 1812)

FREMANTLE, Sir William Henry, insert after dates, resident secretary for Ireland 1789-1800, M.P. for Enniskillen 1806-06, Harwich 1806-07, Saltash 1807-08, Tain burghs 1808-12, Buckingham borough 1812-27, supporter of Catholic Emancipation, Kt. 1827), 120

GORT, for Verecker, read Vereker. The exact place of his engagement with the French was at Collooney, Co. Sligo, not Killala

p. 227 GOULBURN, Henry, for Secretary for Ireland, read Chief Secretary for Ireland

GREY, Charles Grey, for Charles Grey, 2nd Earl, read Charles, 2nd Earl, and for 107 read 108

p. 228 HOBHOUSE, for Secretary for Ireland 1832-33, read Chief Secretary for Ireland 1833

p. 229 INSURRECTION Acts, insert (54 Geo. III, c. 180, and 3 Geo. IV, c. 1)

IRISH Church Temporalities Act, insert (3 & 4 Will. IV, c. 37)

p. 231 LITTLEHALES, Sir Edward, was military under-secretary for Ireland. Delete query entry about Joseph Littledale

LLOYD, Dr. insert Bartholemew (1772-1837, Professor of Mathematics, Natural and Experimental Philosophy, and Greek at T.C.D., Provost 1831-37)

LOUIS XVIII delete entry

MAHON, Nicholas, insert (c. 1746-1841, Dublin woollen merchant, active in Catholic Emancipation movement, and a delegate to the Catholic Convention of 1792)

MAHON, Charles James Patrick, read, The O'Gorman Mahon

p. 232 read MANNERS-Sutton, Charles

MANSELL, Dr. for 165, read 168

MANDERS, Alderman, insert (probably Richard Manders, Lord Mayor of Dublin 1801-02)

MORGAN, Lady, read *O'Donnell,* 8

MORLEY, Mr., insert John (1838-1923, Chief Secretary for Ireland 1886, 1892-95, cr. Viscount Morley of Blackburn 1908)

for MOUNT CASHEL, read MOUNTCASHELL

for MOUNT EARL, read MOUNT-EARL

p. 233 O'CONNOR, Arthur, insert after date, a prominent United Irishman, and after Philipstown 1791-95, imprisoned in 1798, freed and went to France 1802, in 1804 appointed General of Division in French Army, strongly opposed to O'Connell and his policies.

O'CONNOR, Mrs. A. for Condorset, read Condorcet

p. 234 PEACE Preservation Act, correctly, Peel's police measure of 1814 (54 Geo. III, c. 131), and add page refs. 41, 89-90

p. 235 PIGOTT, correctly Richard Pigott (?1828-89, journalist and

Preface

Eva Perón, Pelé and Paddington Bear are perhaps South America's most celebrated characters. That a politician's wife, a footballer and a fictional animal from darkest Peru can attain such status says much about the continent's eccentric image in the eyes of the rest of the world. The fourteen countries making up South America can also boast brilliant novelists, spectacular dancers, and millions of charming, welcoming and generous ordinary people.

Researching this book has been a succession of surprises: fresh strawberries in the Andes, a salt cathedral inside a hill in Colombia, the vibrance of Lima's nightlife, the arduousness of life for Indian tin miners on the Bolivian altiplano, finding piped water in the middle of the world's driest desert in Chile, the Welsh community in Argentinian Patagonia and the seemingly unending beach which caresses Brazil. The drama of South America is played out against stunning backdrops, ranging from the truly wild life of the Amazon to majestic mountains teetering on the Caribbean coast.

Mixed with fascinating Indian cultures and an exuberant music scene, plus an undeniably colourful political life and an obsession with soccer, South America has everything you could possibly want plus much that you can do without. The *Travellers Survival Kit: South America* helps you to avoid crooks, cholera and cockroaches. It points instead towards clean and cheerful board and lodging, good museums and great hikes.

As the world marks Columbus' voyages of discovery 500 years ago, increasingly many visitors are discovering that South America has much more to offer than dictators and drugs.

Emily Hatchwell
Simon Calder

Oxford
March 1992

free of charge, or for only a nominal fee. Some airlines, such as Avianca or LanChile, give cut-price fares for internal flights if you book them while purchasing your international ticket, so this is another factor in choosing a carrier.

The main airlines, their routes and sample round-trip fares are given below:

Aeroflot: the Russian carrier flies once a week or so between Moscow and Lima, calling at Shannon in Ireland, and from Moscow to Buenos Aires via Dakar in Senegal (West Africa). Fares are around £600 from London including the connecting flight, available from JLA or SAX. With the former Soviet Union in economic and political turmoil, the future of the airline must be in doubt.

Aerolíneas Argentinas: flies between London and Buenos Aires twice weekly via Rio. Discounted tickets are most readily available to Buenos Aires and Santiago.

Air France: has connections in Paris for most big South American cities. At the start of 1992 Air France had the cheapest fares from London to Bogotá, Caracas and Rio, but just a limited number were available on each flight. It is the only carrier to serve French Guiana from Europe.

American Airlines: serves every South American country except the Guianas from Miami, with connections from London. Unfortunately, most outward journeys require an overnight stop in Miami; AA is predominantly a business traveller's airline and sells few discount tickets — the best agency to try is JLA.

Avianca: the Colombian national carrier has a 'bus stop' service from Paris and Frankfurt via Madrid and Caracas to Bogotá, with some services to Cartagena. As well as some good open-jaw arrangements, Avianca sells a 'Condor Air Pass' which is exceptionally good value for anyone travelling extensively in Latin America by air; see below.

British Airways: the South American network is thin, consisting only of Rio, São Paulo, Buenos Aires, Caracas and Bogotá. All are served from London Heathrow, and recently BA has been selling heavily discounted tickets through agents.

Delta: this US carrier links Europe with the north of South America via Miami.

Iberia: Spain's national airline has good services via Madrid to most South American capitals. It runs a small fleet within the region which provides connections to and from its intercontinental flights.

salida	departure
taquilla	ticket office
terminal	bus station; railway station
	may be *terminal de tren*
norte	north
sur	south
este	east
oeste	west
izquierda (a la)	left (on the)
derecha	right
derecho, (di)recto	straight on

Never underestimate the size of South America nor the difficulty in travelling around it. Road quality varies from adequate to abysmal. Travel is severely restricted during wet weather since most minor roads are unpaved and difficult to negotiate. South America has only a small and dwindling railway network, and trains are generally slower than the buses. Air travel is the only quick way to get around. Within individual countries it is cheap, but international journeys can be horribly expensive.

Public transport is in general much more efficient (or at least more frequent) than in the West, since the vast majority of the population relies upon it. Services operate strictly according to demand, however, so in some areas you will have no choice but to hitch. Travelling in Brazil or Argentina can be as fast and reliable as in the West. In rural parts of other countries getting around is usually fun, but not for those in a hurry, nor if you try to impose Western notions of comfort and predictability.

Maps. The best series is published by International Travel Map Productions, PO Box 2290, Vancouver, BC V6B 3W5, Canada. South America is divided into three — Northwest, Northeast and South — to a scale of 1:4,000,000. These excellent maps are distributed in the UK by Bradt Publications, 41 Nortoft Road, Chalfont St Peter, Bucks SL9 0LA (tel 02407-3478), and cost £6 each. You can obtain a limited range of maps in the country itself: these are usually issued by the tourist office or by the equivalent of the AA. Topographical maps, of use to hikers, are produced in many nations by the Instituto Geográfico Militar (or Nacional). They are not widely available in the way that Ordnance Survey maps are in the UK; you normally have to buy them from the IGM/IGN office in the capital, and must show your passport. Since some governments regard the maps as a potential threat to security, you may have to apply through the Defence Ministry, and even obtain a permit.

It makes sense, in many cases, to obtain whatever maps you can in advance. The best stockists in the UK are:

Stanfords: 12-14 Long Acre, London WC2E 9LP; tel 071-836 1321; some of its maps are impossible to find anywhere else, not even in South America.

The Map Shop: 15 High Street, Upton-on-Severn, Worcestershire WR8 0HJ; tel 0684-593146; most of its business is mail order — ask for a catalogue. It also produces sheets listing maps available on specific countries.

AIR

South America has a wacky selection of airlines. Some, like the Brazilian carriers and Aerolíneas Argentinas, are as good as any in the world. Others overbook, and quick-drying boots are the best — heavy footwear is a hindrance if you are tipped out of a boat. Avoid boots which have a Gore-tex lining since these will not last in jungle conditions. An experienced supplier of gear for tropical conditions is New Frontiers, 45-51 Church Street, Croydon CR9 1QQ (tel: 081-688 1830).

Bradt Publications (41 Nortoft Road, Chalfont St Peter, Bucks SL9 0LA; tel: 02407-3478) imports and publishes its own guides, many of which are aimed at trekkers. It has a number of books in its *Backpacking* series, on Peru and Bolivia, Chile and Argentina, and Ecuador. The one which covers Mexico and Central America is essential reading for those attempting the trek through the Darién Gap between Panama and Colombia. Another specialist book is *South America's National Parks: A Visitor's Guide* by William C. Leitch (Moorland, 1990), which is a reasonable introduction to the main reserves. The author concentrates on Argentina, Chile and Brazil, but also covers other countries. It includes maps, information on facilities, etc.

Beaches. Except for land-locked Bolivia and Paraguay, all South American countries would like to think that they have the continent's best beach. Most of them can boast sandy, palm-fringed shores along at least part of their coast. Realistically, however, Brazil comes top: fortunately, its coastline is long enough for even the unadventurous traveller to find a secluded spot.

Brazil holds many other attractions besides, but Venezuela and Uruguay depend upon their beaches for tourism. While impressive enough, beaches in these countries are best avoided in high season — particularly those in Uruguay, which are swamped by thousands of Argentinian holidaymakers every year. Argentina has its own beaches but, like those in Peru and Ecuador, they are incidental rather than a positive attraction. For a more exotic beach holiday fly to the San Andrés islands of Colombia; and for the best fresh-water swimming go to the Lake District of southern Chile.

If you are planning a spell by the sea, note that beaches are often dirty during the rainy season: the rise in river levels brings rubbish into the sea and back onto the sand.

Safety: certain beaches are infamous for the height or power of the waves, or for their strong currents. While this may attract surfers or strong swimmers, it can also be dangerous. Lifeguards and red warning flags are rare. Rip tides occur in certain areas and cause a number of deaths every year. The theory of a rip tide is simple: water being washed onto a beach must escape somewhere. If a beach is concave, the most natural route for the escaping water is in a strong, narrow channel down the middle. This is known as the neck, and can be spotted by the trained eye — it is usually discoloured. Swimmers caught in a rip should never try to fight it; swim with it, until you reach the area where it dissipates; then head to the shore at a 45° angle. Some experienced and perhaps foolhardy swimmers go in search of rip tides as a sport.

the main symptoms are severe headache, high fever and anaemia. Malaria can occur in most South American countries, though Chile and all but the far north of Argentina are unaffected. In addition, mosquitoes cannot survive above 8,200ft/2,500m.

People are often reluctant to take anti-malaria tablets because of worries about side effects. While these are rare, usually involving only the odd spell of mild nausea, ask your consultant to give you a run-down of other possible effects. You must begin the course one week before your departure and continue for four to six weeks when you get back. The biggest mistake is to stop taking the tablets after your return, since the parasite left by the mosquito can spend 28 days incubating in the liver. Experiments for a vaccine are presently in progress, but this is unlikely to be developed for another decade.

Your doctor will advise you on what to take. Chloroquine and proguanil (brand name: Paludrine) are usually recommended; they can be bought over the counter at any pharmacy. Enquire also about a new and more effective drug, mefloquine, which has recently come on the market; it is currently available only by prescription. If you want to bypass your doctor phone the Malaria Reference Laboratory in London. It has a 24-hour recorded message with the latest information on specific malaria zones and the recommended dosage; call 071-636 7921.

Prophylactic medications do not give complete protection since certain strains of mosquito have developed resistance to anti-malarial drugs. It is vital to minimize the risk of being bitten: see *Mosquitoes*, above.

Rabies. An exceedingly dangerous viral infection, rabies is transmitted by mammals: notably dogs, monkeys or bats. Although the disease is rare among travellers, anyone who plans to spend extended periods in rural areas is strongly advised to get inoculated. If you are bitten, scratched or licked by an animal, wash the area with soap and water, encourage limited bleeding and cleanse with alcohol.

The vaccine gives good protection, but does not make you immune; it means that any treatment you receive if you are bitten is likely to work more effectively than it would otherwise. The rabies vaccine is expensive. It is administered in two or three doses, usually one month apart.

Yellow Fever. Monkeys are the chief carriers of this disease, which is usually transmitted to humans by mosquitoes. Most cases are only mild: typical symptoms are fever, headaches, abdominal pain and vomiting. About one in twenty sufferers dies, usually of kidney or liver failure. No drug exists to combat the disease but the vaccination is highly effective and lasts for ten years. You will be issued with an International Certificate of Vaccination, which becomes valid ten days after you have had the injection. Some countries will ask to see it if you are coming from a yellow fever zone (or if you have been to one in the previous ten days), so hang on to it.

In South America there are yellow fever areas, and areas without yellow fever but with mosquitoes capable of spreading the disease; the latter are known as receptive zones. The entire northern part of South America — i.e. north of a line drawn from the Brazilian coast, along the southern border of Paraguay, through the Bolivian Altiplano, and to the Peruvian coast — is a yellow fever area. The area south of here — excluding the extreme south of Argentina and Chile, which is unaffected — is a receptive zone.

is *pabellón*, a blend of beans, rice, plantains and shredded beef. Other treats are the high-altitude fruits, such as strawberries, grown along the north of the country. Strong Caribbean influences are felt on the coast, and in some places you may think it's plantain with everything.

DRINKING

The two leading beers are Polar ('tipo Pilsen') and Cardenal ('tipo Munich'). Both are perfectly palatable but uninspiring, 5% alcohol by volume. If you want to convince yourself you're behaving like a local, order a bottle *vestida de novia* — dressed like a bride, i.e. covered in frost. More interesting is Stout La Negra, a dark and characterful brew. Avoid Maltín sin alcohol, which is sweet, fizzy and tastes like beer before it is brewed — which is exactly what it is; disgusting. Whiskies, the like of which have never been seen in Scotland — Old Rarity and Chequers — are widely available, as are White Horse and Ballantine's. Typically a beer costs under $1, a rum $2, a *nacional* whisky $3 and an imported Scotch $4. Venezuelan wine is truly disgusting and dangerous. It should be avoided at all costs. Do not upset your friends by taking any home as presents.

Eighty years ago, Venezuela was regarded by the rest of South America as a land of ignorant peasants. Today it has an artistic life unrivalled elsewhere on the continent. Although oil revenues have dried up, the opera, ballet and theatre on offer in the main cities compare with the best in the world. It is strongly recommended that you see a performance or two, particularly in Caracas, where oil money has paid for some excellent venues. Fine arts are well represented in the capital and elsewhere.

SPORT

In contrast to the sublimity of the arts in Venezuela, sporting life is rough. Bullfighting and cockfighting are immensely popular, and all the big cities have venues for each. The Nuevo Circo bullring in Caracas, adjacent to the bus station, is one of the finest in South America.

Neither sport, however, is as closely followed as soccer and baseball. The local soccer teams are thoroughly second division, but are nonetheless popular. The season runs from October to May. US baseball is shown frequently on television, and newspapers give an immense amount of coverage to it.

Horseracing, and the consequent betting, also has a strong following. Racing has suffered remarkably little from the ban on the import of thoroughbreds which was introduced in 1975. The oldest classic race is the Presidente de La República, which takes place each April 19. It is followed in May by the Triple Crown, consisting of races named for José Antonio Páez, the Ministry of Agriculture and the Republic of Venezuela. The country's longest race, the two-mile (3.2km) Fuerzas Armada, is run in July. Most important in the Venezuelan racing calendar is the Simón Bolívar which takes place in Caracas on the last Sunday in October. The three main courses are at La Rinconada in Caracas, Valencia and Santa Rita. Most bets are long-odds combinations, and are placed off-track. The most popular wager is the *cinco y seis*, the 5 & 6 — it is based on a forecast of the winners of six races, though it pays out for five correct. Odds can be as high as 10,000-1.

Eating and Drinking. Venezuelan food in the Guayanese style is served at Rancho Doña Carmen; try *takari*, a curry-type dish, or just one of the many local cooling drinks. If you want to eat on the riverside, you can sit in the open at the plain Restaurant Mirador, opposite the Correo del Orinoco Museum; meat dominates the menu. Some way out of town towards Puerto Ordaz you will come across a cluster of shelters. This is Carne Asada Said Morales, a Creole-style barbecue, the idea being to buy as much meat as you want and then have it cooked over a fire and eat it with cornmeal *bollitos*.

CIUDAD GUAYANA/PUERTO ORDAZ

The confluence of the Orinoco and Caroni rivers is the site for the new city of Ciudad Guayana, a.k.a. Puerto Ordaz. In the 1980s it was reputed to be the fastest growing urban centre in the world, which gives an indication of how thoroughly unpleasant it is. Furthermore, the two names are confusing; neither seems to have official ascendancy.

The city itself has one modest attraction — the Cachamy Park, close to the city centre, which is the site of the 70ft/21m-high Cachamy Falls. The countryside around Ciudad Guayana is more interesting than the city itself; indeed it captivated Sir Walter Raleigh when he came here in the 17th century. About 90 minutes east of the Ciudad Guayana are two Spanish colonial forts, San Francisco and San Diego de Alcala.

If tempted to stick around, the best place to stay is Hotel la Guayana (Avenida Las Américas; tel 27-379). For the best pizzas in town go to El Churrasco (Edificio Marimar, on the east side of Carrera Upata). The Restaurant San Salvador (Calle Tumeremo, between Las Américas and Calle Caicara) is always full and the food comes to the tables in earthenware pots.

Beyond here the road leads through El Dorado to the Brazilian border at Santa Elena de Uairén. This region supplies hydroelectric power, providing half Venezuela's electricity and freeing oil for export. The highway to Brazil is in fairly good condition. It crosses La Gran Sabana, a plateau built of ancient rock formations.

ANGEL FALLS

The most stunning sight in the Guayana highlands is the Angel Falls, a 3,300ft/1,000m drop. The origin of the name is the stuff of legend. In 1923 Jimmie Angel, a daredevil pilot, got talking to an old prospector in a Panama City hotel. The gold hunter talked of a stream full of gold in the Guayana Highlands. Angel was quickly persuaded to fly him there in return for $5,000. The story goes that they landed on a remote plateau, the prospector found a stream and panned numerous nuggets of gold. The pair flew back, the prospector sold his haul for $27,000 and suddenly died.

Angel, predictably, returned to Venezuela to seek out the source of the gold. He eventually found the mountain, Auyán Tepuy, but was unable to locate the stream filled with gold. Instead, he found the 1,000 metre-high falls which bear his name.

The mountain rises a mile or more. The top has been described as a gigantic saucer, collecting rainwater during the wet season and cascading down. Angel discovered one of the few places on the mountain where the water flows year-round, much to the delight of the Venezuelan tourist authorities. To put the Angel Falls in perspective, it is twenty times the height of Niagara Falls, yet the volume

Communications

Colombia is five hours behind GMT throughout the year.

Telephone To call Colombia from abroad, the country code is 57.

Colombia has an excellent telecommunications network, called simply Telecom. Individual areas have their own local networks, such as Tele Cartagena, which connect with Telecom. Like other utilities, the telephone system is prone to attack by guerrillas. Links to abroad are efficient, and cheaper than those from the neighbouring countries of Ecuador and Venezuela. You can even pay for calls (or buy phonecards) with credit cards. The 'Home Country Direct' service to the UK is 980 44 0057, to Canada 980 19 0057, and to an AT&T operator in the USA 980 11 0010 — collect calls can be made from any payphone.

Telecom is moving towards cardphones as the standard public telephone. You buy a *targeta pre-pago* for around $5 or $10; the former allows a call of about four minutes to the USA, three minutes to the UK. The international code from Colombia is 90, followed by the country code, etc.

Area codes for long-distance calls within Colombia are all prefixed with 9, as follows:

Armenia 967	Bucaramanga 976	Cúcuta 975
Barranquilla 958	Cali 923	Manizales 968
Bogotá 91	Cartagena 953	Medellín 94

Rates are lowest 7pm-7am and at weekends, with a smaller reduction over lunchtime (noon-2pm). Dial 00 for long distance assistance. Free calls are prefixed 9800. Emergency numbers are also free; dial 05 for the fire brigade, 04 for the police.

Telecom has plenty of telephone offices, open long hours, which can put through international calls for you. The staff are especially helpful to foreign visitors with a shaky grasp of telecommunications systems.

Telegram and Fax. International cables can be sent from all Telecom offices. The cost of a 12-word telegram to North America is around $3, to Europe $5. Within Colombia you can send a 60-word one for $1. Most offices can also handle faxes, for around twice the call charge.

Mail. One of the oddest features of Colombian infrastructure is that it has two postal services, both state-owned. The one called Adpostal is the slower of the two and should be avoided (unless you want to send postcards at cut-price rates, and don't mind them taking several weeks). Adpostal has blue and white cylindrical mail boxes (made in Scotland).

The more efficient mail operation is run by the national airline Avianca and uses its aircraft to provide a quick service both inside Colombia and abroad. Post offices are always part of, or adjacent to, Avianca airline offices. You must take your mail to the office or look for the special Avianca post boxes.

Avianca also runs the poste restante service — anything addressed to *Lista de Correos, town, province, Colombia* will turn up at the Avianca office. To retrieve it you need to consult a prepared list of mail for each of the last 30 days (this can be a tedious process in Bogotá or Cartagena). If it is there, you show your passport and pay a modest fee for each piece.

THE MEDIA

Newspapers. The life of a journalist in Colombia is a harrowing one. The cocaine

Cinema. The two leading art cinemas are Cinemateca Teatro Popular de Bogotá (Carrera 5a, number 14-71) and the Los Acevedo auditorium of the Museo de Arte Moderno (Calle 24 number 6-55).

Theatre. The Teatro Colón in Candelaria (on Calle 10 between Carreras 5 and 6) is a delightful theatre with a varied repertoire.

CRIME AND SAFETY

The dangers in Bogotá are often exaggerated by people who have not been there. Most visitors are unscathed, but nowhere is truly safe. Some long-term residents reckon that the most dangerous quarter is close to the centre of town, at Carrera 9 and Calle 22. Around this junction is pure sleaze, with lots of drug-trading and prostitution. Snatch thieves are common. You may be warned by locals not to go west of Carrera 10, and certainly no further than Avenida Caracas; in fact it should be safe in numbers, in daylight.

Others believe that the dangers are greater in the south of the city, the poorest quarter. Anywhere south of Calle 7 during daylight, or south of Calle 10 after dark, should be regarded as unsafe. At night whole areas of the city are out-of-bounds, mostly places away from the main avenues.

HELP AND INFORMATION

The tourist office (tel 281 4341) is fearsomely difficult to find. It is at *local* (office) 3 on the ground floor of the Centro de Comercio Internacional, the skyscraper emblazoned Banco Cafetero on Calle 27 just west of the Tequendama complex. You must show your passport to gain access to the building. The tourist office opens 9am-1pm and 2-5pm from Monday to Friday.

American Express: the agent in Bogotá is Tierra Mar y Aire, a travel agent on the second level of the Tequendama complex. It opens 8am-6pm from Monday to Friday, 9am to noon on Saturday. TMA cannot cash travellers cheques; if you need to acquire US dollars, go to Imex on the 15th floor of Carrera 7 number 32-29.

Telecom: the main Telecom office is on Calle 23 just south of Carrera 13. More convenient is the office in the Hotel Tequendama complex; it opens 8am-9.30pm daily except Sunday (9am-7.30pm).

Post Office: the main one shares premises with the Avianca office at Carrera 7 and Calle 16, i.e. just north of the Parque de Santander. Its hours are 8am-7.30pm from Monday to Friday, 9am-1pm on Saturdays. The Poste Restante office is in the basement. It is open much shorter hours, 9am-1pm and 2-4pm, Monday to Friday only.

DAS: the head office of the security service, for visa extensions, is at Carrera 27 number 17-85.

British Embassy: 4th floor, Torre Propaganda Sancho, Calle 98 number 9-03, Bogotá; tel 218 5111; fax 218 2460. Open 9am-noon from Monday to Friday, plus 1.30-4pm on Tuesdays and Thursdays.

US Embassy: Calle 38, number 8-61; the entrance is on the northwest side of the compound. Out of hours, US citizens can call 285 1300 for assistance.

to perfume and lingerie, all jumbled together in no apparent order. Also lining Calle Ayos and many of the surrounding streets enterprising Colombians have set up temporary table stalls selling the most extraordinary selection of goods, with one seeming to specialize in identical pieces of unrecognisable metal, another in ratchets, the next in tiny plastic Madonnas. No matter how nonchalantly you try to pass by these vendors, nothing will convince them that a 12lb sledgehammer was not exactly what you had been looking for in order to continue your journey around South America.

Continuing along Calle Ayos and crossing Avenidas Carlos Escallon and Venezuela you eventually reach a small park — Parque del Centenario. In the middle, street performers give anything from a solo rendition on pan pipes to complete dramas. Along the southern side of the park runs Calle de la Media Luna. Turn left; at the far end is the bronze sculpture of two old shoes, the tribute to the poet who likened his birthplace to used footwear.

La Popa Monastery, which dominates Cartagena, was built in 1607. The stones for its columns were dragged up the hill. Its commanding position made it the scene of many battles, and for a time Vernon used it as his headquarters when besieging the old city. It fell into disrepair at the start of the 20th century, but was restored by Augustine monks in 1961. Today it is home to two priests, and the place of business for numerous traders.

Get a taxi to the top — visitors have been attacked while walking along the winding road up to it. The views from the summit, with Cartagena glinting beneath you, are reward enough, but a tour of the monastery itself is well worthwhile. The chapel on the left as you go in is devoted to the Virgen de la Candelaria, and her image wears a dress glittering with silver thread. From 24 January to 2 February each year festivities are held in her honour. A display case full of gold and silver representations of parts of the body shows tributes to the saint from Catholics. These are reminiscent of pre-Columbian artifacts.

Crime and Safety. Other cities in Colombia have the reputation that Cartagena deserves. As the country's premier tourism destination, it attracts the greatest number of villains who prey upon visitors. Bocagrande — where most of the rich tourists stay — is the most dangerous area.

Help and Information. *Telecom:* offices in Bocagrande on Calle 6 between Avenida 2 and 3. Open 9am-9.45pm daily, except Sunday and holidays when it closes an hour earlier. *Tourist office:* Casa del Marques de Valdehoyos, Carrera Factoria; open 8.30am-12.30pm and 2-4pm. Singularly unhelpful.

FURTHER AFIELD

La Boquilla. This is the beach due north of the city. Buses from Cartagena run north every 15 minutes to this beachside settlement, which is one of the strangest resorts in Colombia. The road disappears at the top end of Cartagena airport runway, and vehicles start driving along the sand. The houses are mostly breezeblock shacks (though many have colonnades), and pigs trot around town at leisure.

You can stay in La Boquilla's biggest building, the Hotel Los Morros, an extraordinary blue and yellow edifice. On Sundays, La Boquilla is full of people from Barranquilla. Although it is two hours away, this is their nearest beach, and the buses are parked in ranks on the sand. For the rest of the week, pigs outnumber people.

Bus: the terminal is a huge edifice at Calle 30 number 2A-29, across the river and some way northeast of the city centre. A taxi to the central district costs about $1. Cali has good links with the Pacific coast at Buenaventura, with Bogotá and to Medellín. For Popayán and points south, a highly efficient collective taxi system runs from the terminal.

Accommodation. The Hotel Americana, at the corner of Carrera 4 and Calle 9 (tel 824379), is a prime place to stay — $25 for a comfortable double room. Slightly cheaper, but still elegant, is the Menéndez at Calle 10 and Avenida Colombia (tel 803156) — overlooking the river. A room here is around $15. The Astoria is half a block from the main square on Calle 11 between Carreras 5 and 6. Downtown and downmarket, the Hotel Colonial — *su casa en Cali* — on Calle 15 between Carreras 4 and 5 is cheap and quite nasty. The Savoy, around the corner on Carrera 4 near the corner of Calle 14, is about the same price — $8 double — and standard.

Eating and Drinking. In the commercial centre, on the south side of the street, El Mirador is the place at which to be seen. It has a balcony overlooking Carrera 4, good food, excellent beer and jolly waiters. If you get an attack of the munchies at 4am, La Estancia is a 24-hour restaurant on Carrera 3 betwen Calles 9 and 10.

Cuisine is classier north of the river along Avenida 6. One of Colombia's best pizzerias, Pizza 19, is just at the start of it. A little further along is a 24-hour branch of Dunkin' Donuts, followed by the good and basic Restaurant Balocco. Beyond here style and prices pick up.

Exploring. The single most rewarding and refreshing place in Cali is the delightful La Merced archaeological museum. Its location is the convent house of La Merced. It is a beautifully cool haven, and has some fascinating pre-Columbian relics. The city's most interesting church is San Francisco, on the corner of Carrera 6 and Calle 10. Inside, the stout pillars offset the delicate decor. It is especially moving during Mass.

Help and Information. *Tourist information:* the main CNT tourist office is just north of the river at Calle 12 number 3N-28 (tel 686972).

Telecom: Calle 10 number 6-25 (tel 812971).

British Consulate: Office 407, Edificio Garcés, Calle 1 number 1-07 (tel 832752).

POPAYAN

This historic place, population 40,000, is the delight of southern Colombia. It lies in the gently rolling plains south of Cali. Unfortunately the gently rolling plains took the description literally, and a dreadful earthquake on Holy Thursday 1983 wrought disaster upon the town. Over 100 citizens died, and the beautiful architecture was badly affected. A rebuilding programme has resulted in much of the charm of Popayán being restored, and it feels like a proud, civilized and relaxing place — with no sign of the natural catastrophe. The best time to visit is Easter Week, when the town stages the best celebrations in Colombia.

Town Layout. The centre of Popayán is a neat grid. Bridges lead across towards the Pan-American Highway: the route between Cali and the Ecuadorean border at Ipiales passes Popayán, arcing around the west side of town.

travel, you will begin or end the trip in the dark, unsalubrious streets of Guayaquil. Most people advocate starting in Alausí, a pleasant village where it is easier both to ascertain the correct schedule and to buy tickets.

The line from Alausí is served by steam engines as far as Bucay, where the Andes and the coastal lowlands meet — roughly midway between Alausí and Guayaquil. Seating on this train ranges from wooden carriages with semi-padded seats through cattle wagons with hard benches to open platforms with no seats at all. For the best views (and the dirtiest clothes) join the people on the roof. Ask a trustworthy person inside to look after your bags (and don't forget to duck when you go through tunnels). Each train is accompanied by a surprisingly large crew, whose principal job in the mountain section is to adjust the tension between carriages to ensure that they stay on the tracks. Derailments, however, are common.

On leaving Riobamba the line runs close to Volcán Chimborazo, with fine views on a clear day, and then skirts the beautiful Lake Colta. The journey to Alausí takes about two hours. A short distance southwest of Alausí, at Sibambe, the Guayaquil and Cuenca lines meet. Nearby is the famous *nariz del diablo* (devil's nose) double switchback. This terrifying track takes the line around a vertical mountainside, forcing the train through a complicated zigzag manoeuvre. Below, the line twists and turns as it snakes its way down the narrow valley, crossing from side to side. The vegetation becomes semi-tropical and vast tree ferns tower over the train.

Bucay is reached in four or five hours from Alausí. Since this stretch is the best bit of the journey, many people use Bucay (two hours by bus from Guayaquil) as an alternative boarding and disembarking point. It is easy to get off and flag down passing buses. At Bucay a diesel engine takes over for the last five to seven hours to Guayaquil. On the approach to the city, plantations and ranchlands are replaced by rice paddies — a fascinating but depressing sight. Whole families inhabit corrugated-iron shacks raised on stilts above the saturated fields, with their animals crowded onto the small piece of land beneath. The train finally trundles into Duran, across the Guayas river from central Guayaquil.

BUS

Ecuador has a good road system, with a fairly comprehensive and efficient network of buses. Furthermore, by South American standards journey times are pleasantly short. Most services are frequent, and only at the height of the Ecuadorean holiday periods, or during festivals, need you buy a ticket in advance. Buses to the remoter parts of the west coast or southern Oriente are the least frequent; and these are also the regions where you are likely to experience the greatest delays, primarily in the wet season.

Three levels of service exist. Companies such as Patria, Imbabura and Sucre operate nationally, between the largest towns and cities. Inter-provincial companies operate between the main towns of two or three provinces. Local companies serve one or two large towns and a few smaller ones, usually within a province. Many of these services overlap. For example, long-distance buses travelling along the Pan-American Highway and other main roads often call in at intermediate towns, thereby supplementing the more local services.

On shorter routes small buses called *micros* are used. These are meant to take about 30 people but often carry at least 40. On remoter routes, where the road is poor, expect to travel on a *ranchero* — a bus body on a truck chassis with open sides and bench seating, and with a lot of people sitting on the roof.

IBARRA

This quiet colonial town (population 60,000) is the capital of Imbabura Province. While treated by travellers primarily as a stopover for the train connection to San Lorenzo (or rather for the bus connection to the station from where the train currently leaves), Ibarra is worth exploring. It has many cobbled streets lined with colonial buildings, and the town centre is based around two big and shady squares, Plaza Pedro Moncayo and Plaza La Merced. There are several churches with ornately carved façades.

Arrival and Departure. *Bus:* several bus companies offer regular connections to Otavalo and Quito to the south, and Tulcán for Colombia to the north. The Pan-American Highway bypasses the town, and the bus station is ten minutes walk from the centre. Local buses run regularly along the main road past the terminal heading to the city centre. If you decide to walk, look out for bogus policemen, since several travellers have been accosted along this stretch. Buses for Otavalo can also be picked up where the main road running south from the town centre crosses the railway line.

Train: the station is in the centre of town, four blocks southeast of Plaza La Merced. The journey by train from Otavalo is more attractive than by road, but the line is often closed.

The daily railbus to San Lorenzo currently departs from Lita, a village near the start of the coastal strip midway between Ibarra and San Lorenzo. If the line is in a healthy state, the service may begin from Carchí, a much shorter distance northwest of Ibarra. You need to start queueing for tickets at the station at dawn, or earlier, with no guarantee that the railbus will actually run. Notification that it did not make it up the day before or that repairs are being done will probably only be given at the moment that tickets were due to go on sale. The train is always crowded.

Accommodation. Residencial Colón (Narváez 5257), on the opposite side of the roundabout to the railway station, is clean and friendly with good facilities. Residencial Vaca, on Bolívar two blocks east of Plaza Pedro Moncayo, is also recommended. A step above both these is the Majestic, a modern place on Olmedo, half a block east of Plaza La Merced. Hotel Imbabura (Oviedo 933 at Narváez), is an old house with a large central courtyard and makes up in character for what it lacks in facilities. All the hotels are relatively cheap during the week, but the better ones fill up with Colombians at weekends and raise their rates accordingly.

Eating and Drinking. Olmedo and Oviedo are both good streets to look for food. A pleasant place for breakfast or tea is Café Pushkin, next door to the Majestic hotel. For good seafood try La Gaviota in Plaza La Merced, which often has *sancocho de bagre* — a spicy catfish soup. The best restaurant in the city is La Estancia, in the same square: an added attraction is the small private archaeology museum.

Almost immediately after leaving Ibarra the highway begins a long descent into the hot, dry Chota valley with its sugar plantations and a large number of black inhabitants. The highway splits, with the main route to Tulcán running east through San Gabriel, and an alternative route going through Mira and El Angel. (Another road heads northwest to Lita.) The first road climbs steeply out of the Chota valley

One of the most interesting buildings in Riobamba is the Convento de la Concepción. The religious art museum inside is of less appeal.

Arrival and Departure. The railway station is in the centre of town. The daily railbus from Quito (138 miles/223km north) arrives at about 8pm and returns to the capital at 7am the next day. The line to Guayaquil was due to re-open in 1992, and the steam train service is projected to leave at 6am.

Riobamba is an important crossroads, where roads from the southern Sierra, the coastal lowlands, Quito and the Oriente, all meet. The main bus station is half a mile northeast of the town centre, though buses to Baños leave from the Oriente bus terminal, a couple of miles away at Avenida Espejo and Luz Elisa Borja.

Accommodation. Two good hotels are the Los Shiris (10 de Agosto and Rocafuerte), one block east of the railway station, and Segovia, at Constituyente 2228 just off Parque Maldonado. However, Hotel Metro, at the entrance to the railway station yard, is hard to resist. It was a majestic hotel in the golden age of the train and still hints at its former status, with wood panelling, substantial bannisters and solid furniture in all the rooms. It is well equipped, clean and friendly and charges just $2. Another pleasant hotel, but a touch seedy, is the Imperial (Rocafuerte 22-15 at 10 de Agosto), a block from the rail station.

Eating and Drinking. La Biblia (Francia and Constituyente) and La Cabaña Montecarlo (Moreno 2041) are both good restaurants. La Delicia, in the former home of Simón Bolívar, is even better; it is on Constituyente, a block from the station. All three offer varied menus and on certain nights of the week lay on live music. Los Alamos, close to Hotel Metro, is also recommended. For the best-value breakfast go to Café Paola in Pichincha, two blocks east of the station.

Around Riobamba

Chimborazo. At 20,700ft/6,310m, this is the highest peak in Ecuador. Its summit is the furthest from the centre of the earth, beating Mount Everest easily because of the 'bulge' around the Equator. To climb it an experienced guide is essential; this can be organized in Riobamba or Quito. The Hotel Imperial in Riobamba is a good source of information.

Guano. This small village doesn't appear to have suffered from the fact that it is called 'sea-bird excrement'. The local people weave carpets, which hang in doorways and shop fronts all over the village. Guano is half an hour north of Riobamba, and buses shuttle constantly between the two.

ALAUSI

This is a delightful little place set in fine countryside 100 miles/160km south of Riobamba. It consists of little more than a few attractive pastel-coloured buildings gathered around a railway station. The main reason to make a special trip to Alausí is to begin the train ride down to Guayaquil (described on page 184). When the railway line running north to Riobamba is reopened, the importance of Alausí will be greatly reduced. For the time being, however, it is a much more manageable place to start the trip. The daily train bound for Guayaquil currently leaves at 9am and takes 9-11 hours. Tickets go on sale at 8am. The Guayaquil and Cuenca lines meet at Sibambe, which is 9 miles/15km west of Alausí. There is no accommodation similar at the nearby Hotel Gloria — basic rooms and showers, with a pleasant garden to sit in. Even by mainland standards rooms (usually shared) are reasonably priced at $1.50-2.

If you prefer to stay in the harbour area, two of the best choices are the Palmeras and Salinas, a couple of blocks inland from Avenida Darwin; they charge about $10. Los Amigos, next to the TAME office on Darwin, is a better deal, as are the Flamingo and the Elizabeth, also in the centre.

Eating and Drinking: the best value restaurant is Las Ninfas, beside the creek at the southern end of the harbour; tables outside offer a good view of the sealions and pelicans at play on the jetty. The Four Lanterns, just north of the Sol y Mar, and the Intrepida, beside the Sol y Mar, are good too. Their menus are not extensive, so get there early for the best choice.

Few places, other than the more expensive hotels, are open for breakfast. You may have to rely on the excellent yoghurt shop on Darwin, the supermarket beside the harbour jetty, or the bakery four blocks up the inland road to the airport.

THE OUTER ISLANDS

San Cristóbal (Chatham). Puerto Moreno, the main village on the island, is the capital of Galapagos Province and the location of the islands' second airport. Many tour groups start here, but it is not nearly as good as Puerto Ayora for organizing independent trips. The town and rest of the island do not warrant a visit in their own right.

Santa Fé. This small dry rocky island, also known as Barrington, has a cactus forest and some large lava lizards. Boats moor in a lovely sandy bay, which is good for snorkelling.

Bartolomé. This is a small but particularly interesting island. The volcano at the east end offers a wonderful view over the island and the black lava flows on the adjoining Santiago Island. In the centre of the island is a huge rock pinnacle, the base of which is a favourite haunt of penguins. Nearby is North Beach, where you can swim.

Santiago (San Salvador or James). At Sullivan's Bay, close to Bartolomé, is an extensive, accessible lava flow whose surface is contorted and fractured in unimaginable waves and ripples. The nearby sandy bays are good for snorkelling. On the western side of the island, at Puerto Egas, there are small sand dunes and superb rock pools where marine iguanas feed. Sealions and fur seals gather in nearby lava tunnel inlets and blowholes.

Isabela (Albemarle). This island is by far the largest in the group. It has the highest volcanoes in the Galapagos, some of which are still quite active. At the southern end is Puerto Villamil, the only settlement of any size on Isabela, with nearly 1,000 people and a hotel. It is also possible to camp.

You can climb up a steep path to the top of Alcedo Volcano, in the centre of the island, which takes about four hours. From the edge of the crater you may be able to see a few of the giant tortoises that live inside it. If you want to enter the crater or visit the geyser further around the crater rim, you need to camp there overnight. All water and food must be carried and sun cream is essential.

tastes like a cross between lamb and rabbit — is not of universal appeal either. Nevertheless, it has to be tried. On organized treks *pachamanca*, a whole lamb cooked underground by hot stones, is often served as a final supper and is absolutely delicious.

Heart and beef kebabs (*anticuchos*) are a common sight on sizzling grills in the street; and in most markets there is at least one vendor selling portions from a complete roast pig or lamb. *Ají, arequipeño* and *picante* are all terms for a fearsome red-hot chilli sauce that is a common accompaniment with all manner of foods, both in the street and at restaurants.

Fish is a great speciality along the coast. *Ceviche* — raw fish marinated in lime — is a national dish, often eaten for breakfast. However, this delight has been in gastronomic Coventry since the cholera outbreak. *Chilcano* is a thick fish stew, and *chupe* is a fish soup, often with an egg in it. Ensure that fish is well cooked.

The 180 varieties of potatoes indigenous to Peru cover an extraordinary range. Some are tiny, inedible-looking black things that have been freeze-dried for storage, called *chuño*. Others are red, squiggly and hairy, known as *ochra*. Unfortunately, potatoes are rarely served in restaurants — except as chips. Instead, you will have to make do with rice. If you're lucky you may come across *papa relleno*, a deep-fried mashed potato ball filled with olives, vegetables and sometimes meat. This is a good snack, as are *salteñas*, small savoury pasties a little similar to those eaten by the ton in Bolivia. *Empanadas*, vaguely cheesey buns often with sugar on top are found everywhere and are sometimes pleasant, though always strange.

The tropical lowlands provide Peru with a wonderful selection of weird and wonderful fruit and vegetables. Though bananas are not used in cooking as much as in Ecuador, *chifles*, delicious fried banana slices, are often sold at the roadside.

Peruvians have a sweet tooth, but their preference for dry cakes is a mystery. Most edible are those stuffed with *manjar blanca*, a fudgey confectioner's filling; *churros*, deep-fried pancakes filled with manjar are a speciality of Lima. In the late afternoon people set up stalls in the street and start frying *picarones*, which are batter rings served with sugar and sometimes honey. *Espumilla*, whisked egg white served in ice-cream cornets, has to be one of the most bizarre street foods.

A set lunch (*almuerzo*) or dinner (*merienda/cena*) is good value at $1.50 or so. Chinese restaurants, common on the coast, are usually good, but their menus generally vary little from those of the ordinary Peruvian restaurant. One of the most popular Chinese dishes is *arroz chaufa*, a cheap special fried rice.

DRINKING

Peru's best known brew is a sickly yellow soft drink called Inka Kola, which is even more popular than Coca Cola or Pepsi. It is reputedly made from camomile, but has a taste somewhere between banana and chewing gum. The country's most famous alcoholic drink is a clear brandy called *pisco*. While not especially drinkable on its own, it can be made into the delicious *pisco sour* cocktail by whisking it up with ice, sugar, egg-white and lemon juice.

Peru produces some perfectly palatable wines, mainly produced along the south coast. The best are Tacama and Ocucaje from Ica, and Tabernero from Chincha. Rum is locally produced amongst the vast sugar plantations of the northern coast and is very cheap. Ron Cartavio is the main brand.

All the main cities, and even Pucallpa in the jungle, have breweries. Between them they produce a fairly good range of beers, the best being Cristal (from Lima), Arequipeña and Cusqueña; in most places you can only buy the local brew. There is also a dark beer known as Malta, produced by Cusqueña.

with supporting diagrams and objects, are used to recreate the everyday life of people living in the desert over a thousand years ago. It opens 9am-9pm, Tuesday to Friday and 10am-7pm on Saturdays and Sundays. To get there take a bus or colectivo along Arequipa, and then change to another running eastwards along Prado.

Museo Amano: if you are even slightly interested in textiles the collection at the Amano Museum (Retiro 160; tel 41-2909), off Angamos in Miraflores, should not be missed. It is the private collection of a Japanese family and viewing is by appointment only, Monday to Friday, 2-5pm. A large room contains cabinets of carefully protected textiles from all the pre-Inca coastal cultures. Those from Paracas steal the show with the fineness of the weave, their elaborate motifs and incredibly bright colours.

SPORT

There is a good race course in the suburb of Monterrico, beside the Pan-American Highway; meetings are held most weekends in the summer. The cricket club is off Avenida Camino Real in central San Isidro. For a more authentic Peruvian experience go to a match at the main football stadium, which is beside the Paseo de la República, beyond Avenida 28 de Julio. Alternatively, brave the country's national bull-fighting stadium, in Plaza Acho north of the river across Puente Palma, or the cock-fighting ring on Sandia, a couple of blocks from the Parque Universitario.

ENTERTAINMENT

If you're keen to stay out late, you are advised to do this in Miraflores or in San Isidro, rather than in the centre, which is quiet and dangerous.

For classical entertainment go to the theatre on Huancavelica, two blocks west of Unión, which stages plays, opera, etc., often performed by overseas touring groups. Listings for cinemas are given in the yellow section of *La República* and in the *Crónicas* section of *El Comercio*. For something other than the usual gore, there are several cinema clubs showing foreign (but not necessarily recent) films. They include the Cine Club Euroidiomas, Juan Fanning 520 (Miraflores) and El Cinematógrafo at Pérez Roca 196 in Barranco. El Pacífico in Miraflores, on the roundabout at the end of Arequipa, shows the better new American releases. The best cinema in the centre is on the east side of Plaza San Martín, which usually shows reasonable movies. Most foreign films are shown in their original language, with Spanish subtitles.

In Miraflores there is a video bar in Pasaje San Ramón, and several other bars stay open into the early hours. Satchmo's (La Paz 538), two blocks east of Larco, is a popular jazz bar, but its elegant New Orleans ambience doesn't come cheap — expect to pay upwards of $15 for an evening out. The New Wave Disco, in Miraflores' central square, is also very popular at weekends.

If you are keen on dancing, head for a salsadromo. The biggest and best is La Máquina del Sabor, in a huge warehouse on the beachfront at La Herradura, beyond Barranco and Chorrillos. It has a big dance floor in front of a massive stage, on which a huge band plays into the night. The range of food and drink is limited but the prices are reasonable: admission (and a free drink) is about $5. Transport back to your hotel can be a problem, so arrange a taxi in advance. There are other salsadromos and discos in central Miraflores, Monterrico and San Isidro.

For traditional creole music listen out for information about forthcoming peñas;

Arrival and Departure. The train to Huancayo leaves Lima at 8am, Monday to Saturday, and takes 10 hours to reach Huancayo. Tickets ($4) can be bought only on the day of departure; take your own food. Though earth tremors and terrorist actions close the line every so often, it is always repaired promptly. If you do not feel like returning to Lima by train, Sudamericano runs regular buses during the day; the journey takes eight hours.

Accommodation. The best places to stay are Hostal El Mesón de Don Jesús (Giráldez 634; tel 226826) and Hostal Huanca (Pasaje San Antonio 113; tel 223956). Both are family-run, secure and reasonably comfortable, and they send someone to meet arriving trains. The best place to eat is Pizzería La Cabaña (Giráldez 724) and there is a wide selection of other restaurants along Avenida Real, the main street.

THE COAST SOUTH OF LIMA

This section covers the coastal strip from Lima south to Tacna, near the Chilean border, and including Arequipa. A growing proportion of travellers heading to or from Chile zoom down the Pan-American Highway, stopping only to visit the Nazca Lines. To do so means missing out on a number of wonderful sights.

Immediately south of Lima fertile valleys and desert alternate; much of the latter is taken up with chicken houses.

PISCO

The days when Pisco was a major whaling port are long gone, though you can still find whalebones on the beach. Nowadays, Pisco is renowned throughout South America for the local brandy named after the town. The place itself is uninteresting, and the vast majority of people who stop off do so solely to visit the nearby Ballestas Islands and the Paracas Peninsula.

Arrival and Departure. Pisco is situated a couple of miles west of the Pan-American Highway and through buses don't generally detour into the town centre. Ormeño and San Martín run buses between Pisco and Ica and Lima, and Paracas Express to the capital only. Between them they offer regular services throughout the day. All bus company offices are within a block of the main square.

Accommodation. Two of the best places to stay are a fair distance from the town centre. Most popular is the Youth Hostel (Balta 639, Pisco Playa; tel 2492), southwest of the centre near the Paracas road. A few blocks away, close to the jetty and overlooking the sea, is the Hotel Portofino; this was once one of the port's finest hotels, but its quality has declined with the price, now just $2-3. It is a 20-minute walk to either from the centre: while the main road to the seafront (San Martín) is safe, do not venture off into the side streets.

In the town centre Hotel Pisco, in an old, characterful building in Plaza de Armas, is popular and cheap at $2. Of the more comfortable hotels the best is the Belén (a block southwest of the main square).

Eating and Drinking. Roberto's restaurant, on Mancerá a block south of the square, deserves its good reputation, particularly for the seafood; the back dining-room resembles a warehouse. In and around the square are lots of snack bars.

journey costs about $15; tickets can be bought from 6am on the day of departure. The Arequipa train leaves at 9.15pm and takes about ten hours, costing $18. The railway station occupies the eastern side of the main square. Moneychangers hang around outside.

Bus: there is a constant flow of combis to Puno, an hour away; they leave from in front of Hostal Perú in Juliaca's main square. Buses are infrequent and slower, but also cheaper. The road to Qosqo is so poor that many people try to avoid it. Nevertheless, Cruz del Sur, Sur Peruano and Ormeño each offer at least two departures per day, mostly at night.

The same bus companies run several services a day to Arequipa, but the road is as poor as that to Qosqo, and they are best avoided. To enjoy the spectacular landscapes in reasonable comfort, take a colectivo. Juliaca Express, which has a small office on Chávez, a block from the railway station, offers daily departures in large American cars. The trip takes seven hours and costs about $20; book a day or two in advance.

Accommodation. Hostal Perú, on the main square, is the best place to stay, with rooms arranged around a courtyard, a plentiful supply of blankets and hot showers. It is clean, secure and reasonable value at $4. The main alternative is the slightly cheaper Hostal Yasur, four blocks north along Calle Nuñez from the train station, close to the market. Most of the other cheap hotels are worse than basic.

Eating and Drinking. Hotel Turistas (two blocks south from the station and three west along Piura) has the best restaurant in town. But although the food is good, the dining-room is gloomy and the waiters vague; it opens for dinner only, at 7pm. Virtually all the other restaurants call themselves chicken restaurants (*pollerías*), including Riko Riko in the square. It serves big platefuls of other things too, and the food isn't bad if you don't mind eating in a haze of smoke from the roasting chickens and to the sound of loud pop music.

QOSQO (Cusco)

For a city that was once the capital of one of the greatest empires the world has ever known, it is amazing that no one can agree on its name. However, Qosqo was acknowledged as the official title in 1991. Despite such confusion the city is the most important cultural centre in Peru, perhaps in the whole of South America. It has a population of over 200,000.

The Qosqo valley was inhabited by the Huari people some time before the Incas. There are extensive ruins from this period at the lower end of the Qosqo valley, notably at Pikillacta. Legend has it that the Inca city was founded around 1100AD by Manco Capac who, with his sister-consort Mama Ocllo, emerged mysteriously from the waters of Lake Titicaca. The story goes that Manco was in search of a fertile valley where, in good King Arthur style, his golden staff would sink deep into the ground. He found such a spot at an altitude of 11,665ft/3,500m. He named the site Qosqo, 'navel of the earth.'

The Incas laid out a great plaza at the heart of the city, the meeting point of the four quarters of the earth: Chinchaysuyo to the north, Condesuyo to the west, Collasuyo to the south and Antisuyo to the east. The city grew in size, in parallel with the gradual extension of the Inca empire. By the early 16th century it had 125,000 inhabitants, and was the administrative centre of a vast empire, and the principal seat of the Inca king. Even so, the Incas could not prevent the fall of the Great Exhibition of 1889 in Paris. The house was snapped up by a rubber baron and reassembled in Iquitos' main square. Constructed entirely of iron, it was highly innovative at the time. Nowadays it looks thoroughly neglected.

The houses of some of Iquitos' most impoverished inhabitants can be seen from the Malecón, but slums are more characteristic of Belén, a short distance upriver. Otherwise known, optimistically, as the 'Venice' of the Amazon', this floating suburb consists of wooden houses built on stilts. While in the dry season they sit high above the riverflats, during the rains they are accessible only by boat or precarious walkways. It is a potentially dangerous area, so only visit if there are several of you and do not go too far in. In the wet season canoe tours from the main dock or through a tour company give you a sobering glimpse of the appalling conditions in which the people live. Expect to pay about $15 a head.

At the northern end of town the river swings in towards the city and this is currently the principal dock area. It is a good place just to sit and watch the loading and off-loading of boats and the toing and froing of people. In the dry season most of the jungle produce is brought up from the dockside to be sold in street markets. In the wet season, when the river level is many metres higher, much of the produce remains on the boats at the water's edge; customers either board the boats or come alongside them in their canoes. On these occasions the dockside is a seething mass of people and boats. Whether at the dock or in the nearby streets the markets are highly colourful affairs with everything from enormous red paiche fish and tortoise meat to piles of exotic and fragrant tropical fruits.

Help and Information. *Tourist Information:* Foptur is at Arica 122, on Plaza de Armas.

Communications: the Entel office is at Arica 276, immediately behind the cathedral. The post office is at the corner of Arica and Morona.

Money: moneychangers hang around in the main square, which is also the location of Banco de Crédito, where you can change travellers cheques.

Immigration Office: Arica 477, open 9am-1pm, Monday to Friday.

Consulates: Brazil — Morona 283 (tel 232081). Columbia — Tarapacá 260 (tel 231461). They open Monday to Friday, 9am-noon and 3-5pm.

Jungle Trips

There are several well organized lodges near Iquitos, such as Explorama Lodge and Amazon Camp, but they are expensive, costing from $50 per person per day upwards. They are at least a day by boat from the city, and you need to travel this far to reach some reasonable wildlife-rich jungle. Even so, there are cayman, dolphins and manatees in the rivers, several species of primates, including the rare spider monkey, and plenty of birds, butterflies and insects.

Avoid companies, such as Las Cabañas de Santo Tomás and Expediciones Jungle Amazónica, which offer the hunting of rare animals as an option on their regular trips. A more reputable operator is Queen Adventures (Arica 297), which has several camps in the jungle just west of Iquitos. To see plenty of wildlife you will need to travel to one of their more distant camps, such as the one on the edge of the Pacaya-Samiri National Park (now under threat from oil exploration by Texas Crude). The average price for a trip lasting four or five days, for four people, is about $50 a day each, to include food, transport, a guide, sleeping gear and accommodation in jungle shelters.

AIR

Owing to the topography of Bolivia and the vagaries of land transport, you may well find it necessary to take internal flights. But although travelling by air is the most reliable way to get around, delays are not uncommon, cancellations in heavy rain are inevitable, and seats get booked up quickly during the holiday periods, particularly July and August. Be warned that the thinness of the atmosphere at high altitude can lead to bumpy landings.

Lloyd Aéreo Boliviano (LAB), known locally as Lloyd, has the widest network of internal flights. But while it operates services to all corners of the country, most flights originate in La Paz, with connections between other towns infrequent; there are only twice-weekly services between Cochabamba and Sucre, for example. The best-served route is that between La Paz and Santa Cruz, usually via Cochabamba. Fares are cheap, however, Cochabamba-Sucre costing $25, and Cochabamba-La Paz $35. Flights can be booked from abroad through LAB in London (071-930 1442) or Miami (1-800-327-7407). Most LAB offices in Bolivia should be able to give you a full timetable of their internal flights.

The main competition to LAB is TAM (Transportes Aéreos Militares), which is run by the armed forces. It offers less frequent services and to fewer destinations, but fares are often 20-30% cheaper, and it serves small towns in Amazonia not reached by LAB. TAM is expanding its number of offices around Bolivia, but in many towns you must go to the airport to make a booking. As a rule, you can only reserve a seat in the town from which you intend to fly.

Neither LAB or TAM serves Potosí which, at an altitude of over 13,000ft/3,965m, has only a small airstrip. The only airline to fly there is FAB (Fuerza Aérea Boliviana), run by the airforce; see page 373.

An airport tax of about $2.50 is payable on internal flights.

TRAIN

La rehabilitación y modernización de los ferrocarriles es una realidad, runs the slogan of Bolivian Railways. It is astonishingly wide of the mark, with no indication of any rehabilitating or modernizing taking place on the rusty old network. Nevertheless, you must try to travel on at least one Bolivian train: the views are almost invariably spectacular.

The railway system consists of two main lines which, with branches, can reach all the biggest towns in the country. The western line is the most extensive and more efficient. It links La Paz with Oruro, Potosí, Sucre and Cochabamba, as well as with Peru, Chile and Argentina. The eastern network, which runs eastwards to Brazil and south to Argentina is notoriously chaotic and bumpy. The main drawback, with either line, is that services are not that frequent and are notoriously erratic. Nor do the railways escape the effects of the rains either. Lines may be washed out, and even if services are not cancelled altogether, long delays are likely.

Fares on the ordinary trains are less than for the equivalent bus journey, reflecting fairly accurately the degree of comfort (or lack of it) in which you can hope to travel. For long journeys you are strongly recommended to take the passenger-only *ferrobus*; this is, essentially, a bus adapted to run on tracks. The ferrobus has one *pullman* and one *especial* carriage, the former being about 20% more expensive. Since most long train journeys run overnight, you are should go pullman class and make the most of the padded, reclining seats, blankets and breakfast service. Note that if you go to the railway station and ask about trains (*trenes*), you are unlikely to be given details about the ferrobus, which is considered a completely different thing.

The atmosphere is good, its restaurant serves excellent food, and there is a healthy balance of tourists and locals. Marko Tambo (Calle Jaén 710; tel 340416) has a good reputation and is probably the next best place, with shows Thursday-Saturday. Peña Naira (Sagárnaga 161; tel 325736) is one of the most famous, with daily shows, but it is pure gringo territory; the restaurant is separate.

The Teatro Municipal (Calle Sanjínes; tel 375245) has opera, ballet and orchestral performances. The Casa de la Cultura (Avenida Santa Cruz at Potosí; tel 374688/9) puts on films, as well as art exhibitions, and it is also a good place to find out about other events around the city. The Cinemateca Boliviana (tel 325346), at Pichincha and Indaburo, shows good international, non-mainstream films.

Festivals. The greatest festival in La Paz is the Fiesta del Señor del Gran Poder, patron of the Gran Poder district in the Indian quarter. It takes place at the beginning of June, and there are colourful processions, with lots of singing, dancing and drinking.

HELP AND INFORMATION

Tourist Information: IBT has its HQ and information centre on the 18th floor, Edificio Ballivián, Calle Mercado (between Loayza and Colón). It is open 8.30am-12.15pm and 2.30-6.30pm Monday to Friday, and 9am-1pm on Saturday. The staff are helpful and give out city plans and maps of the Yungas trails. The tourist police (tel 367441) has an office on the same floor.

Club Andino (Calle México 1638, corner of Otero de la Vega; tel 324682) is a mine of information on hiking, particularly in the Cordillera Real. It opens 9.30am-12.30pm and 3-6pm Monday to Friday, and 8-9am on Saturdays. Outside the office is a noticeboard advertising equipment and expeditions.

Post Office: corner of Santa Cruz and Oruro. It opens 8am-8pm Monday to Saturday, and until noon on Sunday. A passport is required to withdraw letters from poste restante, but you can collect mail for a friend.

Telephone Office: the central Entel office, which opens 8-10.30am daily, is at Calle Ayacucho 267 (between Camacho and Mercado). A smaller and more peaceful Entel office is in Edificio Libertad, behind the Casa de la Cultura on Calle Potosí, or on the ground floor of the Sheraton.

Money: the best area for casas de cambio is along Ayacucho, Camacho, Mercado and Colón; most change both cheques and cash. Street moneychangers operate in the same area, particularly outside the Café de La Paz. The most famous cambio among travellers is the place known as the shampoo shop at Yanacocha 319. It is worth visiting just for the experience of its improbability. The shopfront has a motley display of mundane items such as shampoo, cheap brandy and fake champagne. The enquiry 'cambio?' gets you ushered through to the back. Feeling like an extra in a spy movie, you find a carpeted, computerized, clandestine bank complete with besuited tellers. It gives excellent rates for both cash and travellers cheques.

American Express: Magri Turismo, Avenida 16 de Julio 1490, Edificio Avenida, 5th floor (tel 341201, 340762 or 323954). Useful as a poste restante, but does not change travellers cheques. It is open 9am-noon and 2-6pm Monday to Friday, 9am-noon on Saturdays.

Immigration Office: Avenida Landaeta 232, near Plaza Tamayo.

centre, although some say that it is one of the few permanent monuments of the indigenous Guaraní culture. It is an unusual site, consisting of high-relief sculptures actually carved into the mountain: niches, steps, channels and terraces have been cut into the huge sandstone rock, and include some animal figures. At the foot of the rock are the remains of a few buildings.

Ask to be dropped off about 3 miles/5km east of Samaipata, from where it is a fairly strenuous one-hour uphill hike. If you are short of time or are lacking the energy, you can take a taxi from town most of the way. There is a small archaeological museum in Samaipata.

Buses from Santa Cruz to Samaipata leave from the bus station and take about three hours. If you are planning to continue to Cochabamba, you should be able to piece together truck rides west from Samaipata. There are a couple of hotels in town if you need to stay overnight.

COCHABAMBA

Bolivia's second largest city is predominantly modern, bearing few vestiges of its early colonial origins. Furthermore, few of the one million inhabitants are of indigenous descent. It is easy to conclude that Cochabamba is therefore just another big, characterless and gloomy South American city. Yet it is an excellent base for a stay of a few days. The attractions of the city itself are few, but the surrounding countryside is one of the most rewarding areas to explore in the country: it has beautiful scenery, crumbling colonial villages, seldom-visited Inca ruins and some excellent markets.

Cochabamba lies in a broad, fertile valley surrounded by sweeping hills and in the shadow of the Cordillera Central. As you walk through the hectic and polluted streets of the city, the glimpses of snow-capped peaks are a constant reminder that greater joys await you beyond the suburbs; and that at an altitude of a meagre 8,430ft/2,570m, the temperatures in Cochabamba are pleasantly warm compared to those on the Altiplano.

Economically, Cochabamba has seen better days, and there are a lot of people sleeping rough on the streets. But despite this, and the fact that the city has a growing reputation as a drug centre, Cochabamba is an unthreatening place.

City Layout. The centre of Cochabamba lies in a fold of the Río Rocha. The two principal commercial streets are Heroínas and Ayacucho. Plaza 14 de Septiembre, the main square, is just southeast of where the two meet. Good maps are sold by street traders just south of the junction. The southern end of the city centre is marked by the railway station and the San Sebastían hill; beyond it, a couple of miles from the centre, is the airport.

Street numbers in addresses increase by 100 for each block from the two main avenidas, and always consist of four digits — even if the first one is zero, e.g 0123.

Arrival and Departure. *Air:* Cochabamba is served by international flights, but none are non-stop; all these services, as well as most internal ones, are stopovers between La Paz and Santa Cruz, a route served every day by LAB (on Ayacucho just south of Heroínas). Links with other centres are much less frequent, e.g. just three times a week to Sucre. TAM (Hamiraya 0122, near the corner of Heroínas; tel 28101) serves smaller centres.

The descent into Cochabamba is alarming, with a tight turn unnervingly close to the ground giving the impression that you are about to land in the main square:

chemicals abound. Take a torch if you have one, though you will be given a miner's helmet and lamp.

The pick-up truck will pause for you to buy gifts for the miners from women selling coca leaves, dynamite and cigarettes. Having been whisked up Cerro Rico, from where there are breathtaking views back over Potosí, most guides take you on a brief tour above ground before taking you inside the mountain itself. You will be given coca to prepare you for the difficult conditions underground — the guide encourages everyone to chew the leaves, as the miners do, in order to numb the senses against the pain and fear involved. Most tours include a staged explosion, where a piece of rock is dynamited — normal manners disappear as the fuse burns. By the end of 1991, no tourist had died in Cerro Rico, though around 15 miners are killed each year. It is known as 'the mountain that eats men alive'. Poisoning from silicosis is widepread, and the life expectancy of a miner is 38 years.

To visit the mines independently, take micro 4 to the end of its route, and walk up the trail to the mountain. Do not venture into the mines without an experienced guide.

Laguna de Tarapaya. This lake is about 15 miles/24km northwest of Potosí, off the La Paz road. The water is warm but swimming can be dangerous because of the strong currents. The scenery is stunning, however, and it's a good place for a picnic. Trucks that pass the lake leave from Plaza Chuquiumina, near the main bus station; otherwise go on a tour.

ORURO

No traveller need spend long in this dusty and rather ugly city. Oruro is buffeted by cold winds blowing across the Altiplano, and any architecture of beauty has almost crumbled out of existence; out in the suburbs the adobe houses that blend into the hillside seem to be similarly doomed. The only part of Oruro that has any colour is around the market which, in true Bolivian style, spills over a whole series of streets.

Oruro is a hundred miles (160km) south of La Paz. The town was founded in 1601 following the discovery of silver deposits in the area. Mining remains an important source of income, though tin is the only metal mined in any quantity now. Unemployment in Oruro, which has a population of about 180,000, has been a serious problem since the 1985 tin crash.

Oruro would seem to have little going for it, and it is traditionally relegated to the list of places to pass through as rapidly as possible. However, there are a few things worth seeing in the town itself, and some interesting trips in the surrounding area, including to the remote salt deserts. The one time of year when no one should miss a visit to Oruro is during its carnival — the so-called Diablada — which is one of the most spectacular cultural events in South America.

Arrival and Departure. *Bus:* the terminal is on Buenos Aires, one block east of the railway line — a long walk or five minutes on micro 5 or 8 northeast of the main square. The main long-distance services are as follows:

Cochabamba — 5 hours, $4; frequent services all day.
La Paz — 3 hours, $3; every half hour throughout the day.
Potosí — 8-9 hours, $5; a rough journey served by only a few daily buses, all leaving at around 7pm. Some buses continue to Sucre, but you would do better to change at Cochabamba.

company. These are rather like the *Michelin* series, and are issued in three volumes covering the North, Centre and South. Geared to the Chilean family on a motoring holiday, they include detailed regional maps, plans of even the most obscure places, distances between towns, as well as hotel listings and background information. Even if you don't speak Spanish, they are well worth the $8 (per volume); and there are plans to bring out an English edition in 1993. You can buy them in most bookshops and some CTC offices.

The *Gran Mapa Caminero de Chile* and the *Atlas Caminero de Chile* are detailed road maps that are widely available. Excellent maps and information are also available from the Automóvil Club de Chile (Vitacura 8620, tel 212-5702/3/4). The Departamento de Estudios Vialidad Nacional (Morandé 59, Oficina 344, Santiago), has a set of 14 maps to the entire country.

AIR

Due to the enormous length of the country, air travel is a popular way of getting around. LanChile, Ladeco and Saba all operate internal flights, and services are in general frequent and regular. It is possible to pay for domestic flights abroad, in conjunction with your international ticket. Fares work out cheaper this way. LanChile offers a series of internal air passes, which must also be purchased before arrival. One covering all the main towns and valid for 21 days costs $450. If you are not in a hurry you would do better to combine the north and south passes, giving six weeks travel for $500. In London, call 071-233 7288 for more details.

Saba is the newest airline on the scene, running just two aeroplanes: one daily on the Santiago — Antofagasta — Iquique — Arica route and the other daily from Santiago to Punta Arenas via Puerto Montt. Saba's one-way fares from Santiago are currently: Arica $120, Iquique $114, Antofagasta $100, Puerto Montt $80, and Punta Arenas $153; return flights are double this. At present this means that Saba is undercutting the other lines by around 40%, so expect price reductions in the future from LanChile and Ladeco.

All domestic flights leaving Santiago are subject to a $5 departure tax per passenger. Other airports normally charge around $2.50.

TRAIN

Chile has some 5,000 miles/8,000km of railway line, but most of it is used only for freight. Apart from a few stretches in the north (Arica and Calama to Bolivia and Arica to Peru), passenger services are concentrated in southern Chile. The main line runs south from Santiago to Puerto Montt, with branch lines fanning off, for example to Concepción and Valdivia. The network is seasonal, with a reduced service in winter. For example the daily service south from Santiago to Puerto Montt stops at Temuco, from where you must cover the last stretch by bus.

There are two classes of train. *Expresos* are the slowest and most basic; all tickets are sold on the day of departure, so it is worth arriving early to grab a seat. *Rápidos* are of a higher standard, but are often booked up well in advance. These sometimes have sleeper carriages, which are a bonus on long journeys and come in two types: the simple *dormitorio* or the more modern *gran dormitorio*. The former are mostly German-built, dating from the 20s and 30s. They are made up of bunks arranged end to end, like those in the film *Some Like It Hot*. Travelling this way is comfortable and fun, particularly in the cheaper, top bunk.

First class train travel works out more expensive than the bus, but second class is cheaper. Bring your own food, as meals are expensive. There is an efficient,

To convert dollar cheques into dollars cash, go to American Express (Agustinas 1360, 4th floor; tel 699-0782), which doesn't charge commission.

Visa and MasterCard holders can get money from Fincard (Morandé 315; tel 698-4260, 699-2632) which offers a 24-hour service.

Immigration Office: Moneda 1342. Extensions cost $3 from the Extranjero section of the Departamento de Pasaportes. Join the queue to the left; the long one on the right is for one-year visas and work permits.

Embassies and Consulates. *Argentina:* Vicuña MacKenna 41 (tel 222-8977/6853).
Australia: Gertrudis Echeñique 420, Las Condes (tel 228-5065).
Bolivia: Avenida de Santa María 2796, Las Condes (tel 232-8180/4997).
Brazil: MacIver 255, 15th floor (tel 398867, 336657).
Canada: Ahumada 11, 10th floor (tel 696-2256/9).
Colombia: La Gioconda 4317, Las Condes (tel 206-1919/1314).
Ecuador: Providencia 1979, 5th floor (tel 231-5073/2015).
New Zealand: Isidora Goyenechea 3516, Las Condes (tel 231-4204/6).
Paraguay: Huérfanos 886, 5th floor (tel 394640, 395112).
Peru: Providencia 2653, office 808 (tel 232-6275/0869).
UK: Avenida El Bosque Norte 0125 (3rd floor), in Providencia, near metro Tobalala (tel 231-3737; fax 231-9771). It is open 9am-noon.
USA: Agustinas 1343, Suite 529; the Consulate is at Merced 230 (tel 6710133).

AROUND SANTIAGO

Pomaire. Situated above the Maipo valley 60 miles/96km southwest of the capital, Pomaire is a small town famous for its potters. It is also renowned for its cider, which you can sample at the excellent Restaurante San Antonio. Pomaire is served by frequent buses from behind the Estación Central metro station. On the way out of Santiago on Route 78 is Maipú, the site of O'Higgins' decisive battle of independence in 1817.

Callejón del Maipo. The countryside in the Maipo valley southeast of Santiago is magnificent. There are plenty of places that make good stops. The village of El Volcán, 50 miles/80km from the capital, was destroyed by a landslide, but boasts a marvellous setting. In the mountains 8 miles/12km northeast is the Refugio Alemán Lo Valdés, which rents out chalets for $12 per person (including food). This is an excellent place in which to recover from the stresses of life in the capital. There is plenty of scope for walking, including in the nearby El Morado National Park.

El Volcán is served by several daily buses from Parque O'Higgins; these go via Puente Alto and San José del Maipo, where you should also be able to pick up local services. The journey alone makes the trip worthwhile. In summer you should be able to get to the lodge by colectivo from El Volcán, and hitching is easy.

Farellones. Thirty miles/48km east of Santiago, Farellones is one of Chile's best ski centres. In summer it is also a popular among walkers, and the views are spectacular. The most affordable place to stay is Club Andino, which has dorm beds for around $10. At weekends buses run to Farellones from Plaza Baquedano. On weekdays take a bus to Las Condes from Calle Merced, from where you must hitch the last few miles to the resort. Ski rental costs around $12 and a one-day pass $15; charges often rise at weekends and during the mid-July to mid-August peak season.

The best of a poor choice of hotels are the Rancagua (San Martín 85 and Cáceres; tel 232663), or the cheaper Hotel España (San Martín 367; tel 223963). There is a tourist office at Germán Riesco 277.

CURICO

This town retains an air of colonial elegance, and is charmingly provincial despite having a population of 75,000. It is set in a scenic landscape of hills scattered with vineyards. Some fine old architecture has survived the earthquakes, including the church of San Francisco on the Plaza de Armas. For a good view of the city and the surrounding countryside, walk up Cerro Condell, four blocks northwest of the square. The market, between Rodríguez and Peña, has artesanía from the surrounding villages, and good food. To arrange a visit to a local winery, contact Javier García-Berro Montilla of Miguel Torres (tel 75-310455).

All services are within easy reach of Plaza de Armas, the main square. The railway station is four blocks west, the bus terminal is three blocks north, and the best hotels are nearby, along Peña; they include Residencial Prat (433) and the Rahue (410). Plaza de Armas is the best area for restaurants and bars too: on the north side is the popular Club de la Unión. The tourist office is also in the square, in the Municipalidad.

TALCA

This is a substantial industrial city (population 300,000 people), and the capital of Maule (VII) Region. It was founded in the 17th century, but little dates from before 1928, the year of the last big earthquake to hit the town. Talca's claim to fame is that Chile's independence was declared here in 1818. This incident is commemorated in the Museo O'Higginiano at 1 Norte 875. The museum building was originally the Liberator's childhood home and later the scene of the signing of the independence charter. It opens daily except Monday.

Stay at the Alcázar (Calle 2 Sur 1359) or the Cordillera (Calle 2 Sur 1360, tel 233078). Most hotels are along and between Calles 1 Sur and 2 Sur, which is also a good area for cafés and restaurants. The tourist office is in the main square.

The railway station, at 11 Oriente and 2 Sur, is the first stop for express trains from Santiago to Puerto Montt. The bus station, one block away at 12 Oriente and 2 Sur has frequent departures for Santiago, Chillán, Vilches and Constitución, and other important towns.

Around Talca

Vilches. Forty miles/64km east of Talca, Vilches is a good base from which to explore the surrounding mountains and lakes. The Parque Gil de Vilches, about a mile northeast of town, has many lovely walks and contains the Piedras Tacitas, huge stones erected long ago by Indians. To the southeast rises the the 12,630ft/3,850m Descabezado (beheaded) volcano.

Stay at the Hostería Rancho Los Canales, which has beds in log cabins for $12. The owners have ample local knowledge, and can advise about walks in the area. One such is to the waterfalls in Parque Nacional Siete Tazas, 13 miles/20km towards Curicó.

Laguna del Maule. This lake is high in the mountains near the Argentinian border, 100 miles/166km southeast of Talca. A paved road runs by it, continuing on over the Pehuenche Pass to San Rafael in Argentina. This is a popular destination in summer, when you should be able to hitch. There are no buses.

park. Traucomontt in Puerto Montt can help you arrange an independent trip there, and also runs tours.

CHILOE ISLAND

On a bad day this is a wet, foggy and windswept island. In summer, on the other hand, the abundant sun allows you to take advantage of some wonderful beaches. Chiloé's temperate, humid climate is ideal for the impenetrable rainforest that still covers much of its interior. But this is disappearing fast thanks to the depradations of the pulp and paper industry. The most developed parts of Chiloé are in the north and east, where most of the 115,000 inhabitants live.

The island was originally inhabited by the semi-nomadic Chonos. Then conquistadores arrived in the mid-16th century, and were followed by Mapuche Indians, pirates, and later Jesuit missionaries. Following the expulsion of the Jesuits from South America in 1767, the Franciscans continued the missionary work, building scores of beautiful wooden churches. After its defeat in the battle for independence in 1817, the defeated Spanish army retreated to Chiloé — which fell to Chile nine years later.

Whether due to the place itself or from its turbulent history, Chiloé has acquired a mythology rivalling that of ancient Greece. The main figures are the Pincoya, a sea nymph of such beauty that whoever sees her is struck dumb, and the Trauco, a lecherous creature who seduces women with spells. There are numerous good and evil spirits, and gods that reside in volcanoes and on the sea bed. Many Chilotes remain in awe of the Brujería, an order of witches with a mafia-like organization, and endowed with extraordinary powers and unparalleled wickedness — as described in Bruce Chatwin's *In Patagonia*. Certainly you will not find a baby in Chiloé without a red cord around its neck, to ward off the evil eye.

Witches and evil spirits apart, Chiloé should not be missed: the island has a special atmosphere that makes it completely different from anywhere else in the country. It has lovely beaches, beautiful scenery, delightful fishing villages, and extremely friendly people. Furthermore, many of Chiloé's unique missionary churches have survived, often without the help of a single nail.

Arrival and Departure. Chiloé is 155 miles/250km long and 30 miles/50km wide. It is separated from the mainland by a narrow strait. Two ferries run a shuttle service between Pargua on the mainland, and Chacao on the far north of the island. The easiest way to make the journey is on a through bus from Puerto Montt to Ancud or the island capital, Castro; some buses continue south to the ports of Chonchi and Quellón on the east coast. There are also direct buses to Chiloé from more distant towns.

During the summer there are boat services between the island's east coast ports and Chaitén and Puerto Chacabuco, near Coihaique; in winter the mainland ports offer more frequent sailings to the south.

Ancud. Although not the capital Ancud, on the north coast, is the island's main centre of population. Within walking distance north of the town is the 18th-century Fuerte San Antonio, which was the last Spanish outpost in South America. It has been restored to something resembling its former glory. The fort-like building in the main square is an interesting museum of local history. There is a tourist office in the Plaza too.

Among the best places to stay for around $5, are the Miranda (Mocopulli 753) and the Residencial (Aníbal Pinto 515). The Hospedaje Montenegro (Blanco 541, as a mission, Ushuaia is now a bustling tourist centre with over 35,000 permanent residents, duty-free status, and a sprawl of concrete buildings climbing the surrounding hills. For all the tackiness, Ushuaia is not an unpleasant place. But go prepared for abundant rain (even in summer) and bitingly cold winds. Few visitors are brave or masochistic enough to come here in winter, though the skiing is great.

Ushuaia has an excellent museum, the Museo Territorial, with photographs of the early days of colonization and the Indian tribes. But the real attraction lies outside the town, in the magnificent scenery of high mountains and glaciers interspersed with alpine meadows and beech forest, that characterizes the Tierra del Fuego National Park.

Arrival and Departure. There are two or more buses a day between Ushuaia and Río Grande, operated by Transporte Los Carlos (Triunvirato 57). This four-hour journey is terrific, skirting the shores of the beautiful Lago Fagnano for part of the way. Access has been improved by the building of a new road.

The ferry service across to Puerto Williams has been discontinued. Private yachts occasionally do the journey, but be prepared to pay through the nose. Try asking at Onas Tours (25 de Mayo 50), which operates a boat called *Barracuda*, or at one of the other agencies.

The easiest way to Puerto Williams is by air: the fare is over $50, an astonishingly high price considering the distance covered. There is at least one flight daily between Ushuaia and Río Grande, Río Gallegos, El Calafate, Perito Moreno and Buenos Aires, and several flights a week to other destinations in southern Argentina. The main carriers are Aerolíneas Argentinas (Maipú and Lasserre; tel 91218) and Lade (San Martín 542). Austral has a half-price night flight to Buenos Aires, but this is often booked a week in advance. Local buses to the airport run along Maipú. Note that flights are often cancelled due to bad weather conditions; take off is impossible in high winds.

Accommodation. Hotels fill quickly in summer; try the Kau Pen (Piedrabuena 118 and San Martín) and the Casa Sánchez (Deloqui 395), both travellers' favourites at about $8. The latter is particularly good: cheap, friendly and with good vegetarian food. The nearby Hospedaje Turístico (Deloqui 271) and the seafront Hospedaje Ona (9 de Julio 27) charge $12-15.

Eating and Drinking. Cafetería Ideal (San Martín and Roca) is cheap and has good pizzas. La Pasiva (San Martín 1275) is also good value. Los Cañelos, which overlooks the sea at Maipú and 9 de Julio, is recommended for seafood, though isn't particularly cheap. For typical Argentinian parrilla, try Tío Carlos (Colón 756). Cafetín Volver is a museum-cum-bar, and serves good pisco sour.

Help and Information. Most services are on or just off San Martín. The tourist office is at San Martín 524, the post office is near the corner of Godoy, and Entel near the junction with Roca. Banco del Sud (Roca 30) or Banco de la Nación (San Martín and Rivadavia) change cash or cheques. Duty-free shops will also change cash. Banco del Sud allows you to withdraw up to $50 on a Visa or Access credit card.

The Chilean Consulate is at Malvinas Argentinas 236 and Jainen (tel 21279).

All are operated with tokens, known as *fichas* or *cospeles*, which are available from phone offices and street kiosks, and cost $0.20. There are no warning pips before you are cut off, so put in more tokens than you need — you will get back those you don't use. At peak hours one token lasts two minutes, at other times six.

Codes: the main provincial codes are: Buenos Aires — 1; Córdoba — 51; Corrientes — 783; Formosa — 717; Jujuy — 882; Mendoza — 61; Neuquén — 943; Posadas — 752; Resistencia — 722; Salta — 87; San Luís — 652; Tucumán — 81; and Santa Fé — 42.

Fax. As yet there are few public fax facilities, though many businesses have their own machines. The main post office in Buenos Aires tries to charge an exorbitant $20 to send a one-page fax. The cheapest place to send and receive faxes in the capital is the ASATEJ student travel bureau (Florida 833, 1st floor; tel 312-8476, fax 334-2793), which makes an initial charge of $5, then $4 per minute. Reception costs $1 per sheet.

Telex. The larger telephone offices have an efficient public telex system, though this is usually available just 8am-8pm — which means that you cannot take advantage of the reduced rates. However, the telex office in Buenos Aires, in the basement of the main phone office, is open 24 hours. The minimum charge is for one minute ($4 to Europe), and if you run just slightly over, you will be charged for a whole extra minute.

THE MEDIA

Newspapers. Argentina's newspapers are of a generally high standard, with good coverage of national and world news. The two major ones are *La Nación* and *Clarín*, both published in Buenos Aires. The former is the better and more independent of the two, though *Clarín* is the most widely available nationally. *La Prensa*, another serious paper, is right of centre. While these papers have a broad readership, in the provinces people still prefer to read their own regional papers.

Gossip and scandal of the kind which dominates the tabloids in Britain is confined to specific publications, such as *Seminario*, which have no pretensions to being newspapers. Numerous papers and magazines cater for the sports fan, of which the most famous is *El Gráfico*.

Argentina's one English-language paper is the *Buenos Aires Herald*, which began as a maritime gazette about 100 years ago. It still covers maritime affairs, but also includes all kinds of other news for a varied readership, with the usual listings, schedule of World Service programmes, news of bridge club meetings, etc. British newspapers are not widely available, though in Buenos Aires you can find the usual selection from the USA.

Radio. National radio operates on AM throughout the country, though radio broadcasting in Argentina is largely locally based. In most places on FM you can pick up only one or two stations, which usually offer a mixture of news, commercials and music. In Buenos Aires, on the other hand, you can pick up several dozen, including jazz and classical stations.

Television. Argentinian television seems to be dominated by high-tension soap operas such as *Amigos son los Amigos* (with theme music by Queen) or serializations of bodice-ripping pulp novels. The best thing you can hope for is has an aggressively Italian and even 19th-century feel. La Boca's atmosphere is best appreciated by walking down Necochea, a swinging street where the loud music and outrageously kitschy bars assault you from all sides. La Boca is the Montmartre of Buenos Aires; its main attraction is the thoroughfare and street market known as El Caminito.

The Museo de Bellas Artes de la Boca at Pedro de Mendoza 1835 is worth a visit. It contains paintings by many of the district's artists (past and present), often depicting local scenes. It is open daily, though opening times vary. You can walk to La Boca by following Paseo Colón south from the centre, but it's quite a trek. Otherwise, catch bus 29 from Plaza de Mayo.

La Recoleta. Lying just north of the centre, La Recoleta is traditionally Buenos Aires' most exclusive suburb. The small Plaza Pellegrini, at the northern end of Avenida 9 de Julio, is the best place to begin an exploration of the area. Head northwest along Avenida Alvear or Quintana, where cafés are busy during the day and late into the night. On the 1800 block of Alvear are most of the expensive couture shops, together with exclusive apartment buildings and professional dog-walkers, exercising some of their pampered canine residents.

Both streets lead to a string of squares, with pleasant cafés and tango musicians. At the top end of Quintana, by Plaza Intendente Alvear, is the Basílica del Pilar, a fine early 18th-century church. Next to it is the Cementerio de la Recoleta, where Eva Perón and many other luminaries are buried. The ostentatious mausoleums of distinguished families, jostling with each other along the tiled pathways, are the equal of anything in the cemeteries of Montparnasse or Highgate. Finding Evita's mausoleum is quite an achievement, though anyone you meet can point you in the right direction. The door is always adorned with fresh flowers — a sign that she is still very much in the people's hearts.

Also in Plaza Alvear is the Buenos Aires Cultural Centre, where exhibitions, films and shows are put on, and where you can pick up information about other events in the city. Around lunchtime on Saturdays there is a market in the square. Its 'hippy' tag is hardly deserved, though there is often a band playing Beatles covers on the lawn, and the usual joss-sticks and jewellery are on sale.

Palermo. In 1836 the dictator Rosas struck out into the marshland east of La Recoleta, and began to build his private landscaped residence in what is now the wealthy suburb of Palermo. Some time after his overthrow the vast parkland, including the magnificent Parque Tres de Febrero, was given to the people. It now contains Buenos Aires' main polo fields, racecourse, Botanical Gardens and Zoo. The latter has some interesting Patagonian species in generously-scaled recreations of their natural habitat. To get there, take subte line D to Plaza Italia, just near the botanical gardens. On arrival, horse-drawn carriages (*mateos*) will offer to take you round.

If you are in Buenos Aires at the end of July and beginning of August, don't miss the agricultural show, which is held at the Sociedad Rural showground, just opposite the botanical gardens. There are rodeo competitions and wonderful barbecues.

La Chacrita Cemetery. This is the city's biggest and most impressive cemetery, where Perón himself and Carlos Gardel (of tango fame) are buried. It is at Guzmán 780, west of the centre; to get there take B-line to Federico Lucroze station.

For a more scenic route, cross the border at Bernardo de Irigoyen, 197 miles/317km northeast of Posadas. It is $2\frac{1}{2}$ hours by bus from Eldorado, midway between Puerto Iguazú and San Ignacio on the RN12. Dionisio Cerqueira, in Brazil, is a short walk across the border. There are simple lodgings in Bernardo de Irigoyen.

NORTHERN ARGENTINA
— THE CHACO

The Chaco was explored early on by the Spanish, but potential settlers were beaten back by the fierce Indians. It was not until the late 1800s that the area was opened up through genocidal tactics. It remains a wild region, Argentina's 'back of beyond'.

A look at any map will show that there is very little going on in the western half of the Chaco. This part of the vast northern plain is very hot and humid in summer, and afflicted by flash floods which wash out roads and make agriculture difficult. The uncultivated areas are covered with quebracho ('axe-breaker tree') forests or thornscrub. In total contrast is the eastern Chaco, which is more lush and tropical.

SANTIAGO DEL ESTERO

Known simply as Santiago, the provincial capital is a historic city dating back to 1553. But few old buildings survive, and while Plaza Libertad is attractive, the same cannot be said of the rest of the city. Furthermore, the weather is typical of the Chaco, and summer brings both temperatures above 113°F/45°C and suffocating humidity — during the afternoon the whole city goes to bed. Visit Santiago either in winter for the festival of folk music beginning on July 24, or for the carnival, which is famously raucous.

Arrival and Departure. Santiago's two railway stations have been closed, and trains between Tucumán (3 hours) and Buenos Aires (17 hours) stop at La Banda station, 4 miles/7km north. Buses run daily from the terminal at Pedro El Gallo and Saavedra to various provincial capitals of the north.

Accommodation and Food. Hotel Iovino (Moreno 602 S; tel 213331) is good, and is one of the cheapest in Santiago, at a staggering $18. Residencial Petit Colonial (La Plata 165; tel 211261) and the Santa Fé (Santa Fé 255, near the bus station) are only marginally cheaper.

RESISTENCIA

The capital of Chaco province is surprisingly bustling considering the heat that often afflicts the city. To escape from the melting-hot temperatures in the streets, visit the Museo Histórico (Donovan 425) or, even better, the Fogón de los Arrieros at Brown 350. This is a kind of writers' community centre founded in the 1930s and filled with a motley collection of objets d'art. It has a bar where you can go and drink in the evenings.

Arrival and Departure. There are flights to Resistencia from most nearby provincial capitals once or twice a week. A bus runs to the airport, 5 miles/8km south, and there is also a direct bus to Corrientes airport across the river. Trains serve Buenos Aires (28 hours), Rosario (22 hours) and Santa Fé (16 hours). And there are buses to all the major cities nearby from the bus station on Santiago to visit the park is on a tour; this may well take in Valle de la Luna, 48 miles/78km south in San Juan province.

THE CUYO

In the early days of colonization Chile exercised great influence on the Cuyo region, until 1776 when the towns of Mendoza, San Juan and San Luís became part of Argentina proper. Huge mountains dominate the Cuyo; these are best explored from San Juan and the surrounding villages. Away from the mountains the Cuyo region is extremely arid, particularly in San Luís province.

San Juan Province

San Juan is one of the richest of the Andean provinces. This is thanks partly to its grapes, which produce most excellent wines, but also to the lakes, which attract thousands of angling and sailing visitors every year. The rugged mountains are of wider appeal; during the summer you can arrange mule treks into the Andes from a number of small villages.

SAN JUAN

This city's colonial life began in 1562, but in pre-Columbian times there were numerous Indian settlements on this site. It witnessed the development of several distinct cultures, including the sophisticated Angualasto culture, which was thriving at the time of the Spanish Conquest. History is harder to trace in modern San Juan, which was severely damaged by an earthquake in 1944. But the centre was rebuilt sympathetically, and although few of the original buildings remain, the city has a pleasant atmosphere.

The best thing to see is the museum at La Laja, an hour out of town. It has a superb pre-Hispanic archaeological collection, including artefacts and mummies from numerous indigenous cultures; the star of the exhibition is the remarkably well preserved frozen corpse of a sacrificial victim. To get to La Laja, take colectivo 20 from Bay 1 of the bus terminal. There is one direct service a day to the museum, leaving at 11.45am, and half a dozen buses on Sundays.

City Layout. San Juan is divided north-south by Avenida San Martín, and east-west by Avenida Mendoza. Street numbers start again at zero once a street crosses over Mendoza or San Martín, which is shown by the suffix N (Norte), S (Sur), O (Oeste) or E (Este) — a vital part of any address.

Arrival and Departure. There are flights daily to Córdoba and Buenos Aires and weekly to a number of other provincial capitals; the airport is 9 miles/14km southwest of town. San Juan lies on the railway connecting Buenos Aires and Mendoza, which are 19 hours and 3 hours away respectively. The railway station is on España block 200 S. The bus terminal is at Estados Unidos and General Paz, with good services everywhere in the region and beyond.

Accommodation and Food. The Central (Mitré 131 E; tel 223174) costs $10, and is friendly and scrupulously clean. Of the cheaper options the Austria (Sarmiento 272 N; tel 210274) is by far the best. For a private room ($5-8) try Señor Jorge Malaisi (San Martín 685 O; tel 226018).

The Comedor Central (Ignacio de la Rosa 171 E) serves good typical food

Crossing into Chile: a most enjoyable route into Chile begins in Puerto Blest, from where you can pick up local transport to Puerto Alegre on Laguna Frías. You must take a boat across to Puerto Frías, near the Chilean border, where it should not be difficult to arrange a lift over the pass. From the small Chilean town of Peulla ferries run a regular service across Lago Todos los Santos to Petrohué — a lovely journey taking three hours.

EL BOLSON

This is an attractive Patagonian town 77 miles/124km south of Bariloche. During the 1960s people came to El Bolsón to escape the rat-race, but many have now abandoned their log cabins and returned to the cities; only a few remain. The surrounding hills and forests provide wonderful terrain for walking, and the town is busy in summer. The best trip is to Lago Puelo, a beautiful and tranquil lake spanning the Chilean border, 10 miles/15km southwest of town; it is accessible by bus (also from Esquel). Club Andino Piltriquitron at Sarmiento and Roca is a good source of information about hiking and about trips, including to the local ski slope.

There are four buses a day to Bariloche (4 hours), and buses daily except Sunday to Esquel. One of the cheapest places to stay is Residencial El Bolsón (Angel del Agua 364; tel 0944-92594). Private accommodation is available at Roca 641 or from Roberto Bobadilla at San Martín 1119. For the best parrillas and pizzas in town go to the restaurants along San Martín.

THE COAST

Viedma. In a brave — most people would say demented — move to devolve power from Buenos Aires, the capital of Río Negro was nominated in 1987 as the next federal capital of Argentina. Yet Viedma can't even boast a full complement of paved streets, and the edict looks unlikely ever to be translated into reality. The small town is a deeply unlively and unappealing place. You may well sympathize with the town's first governor, Victor Molina, who in 1920 decamped to Carmen de Patagonés, a picturesque little town across the Río Negro estuary.

Viedma is accessible by train from San Antonio Oeste, (5 hours) and Bahía Blanca (6 hours), with which it is also connected by bus. Buses also run to Comodoro Rivadavia and other southerly destinations. One of the few cheap hotels is the Roma (25 de Mayo 147), though it's still poor value at $12.

Follow the Governor's example and stay in Carmen de Patagonés, with its meandering streets and charming buildings. Try the Residencial Reggiani (Bynon 420; tel 61389). Colectivos and an occasional ferry connect Carmen de Patagonés and Viedma.

If travelling across to the Lake District or heading southwards you may need to change at San Antonio Oeste, a small nondescript town 112 miles/180km west of Viedma. It marks the point where the roads from Patagonia and Bariloche meet. Buses pass through San Antonio several times a day between Viedma and various Patagonian towns, as well as services west to Bariloche. San Antonio also lies on the railway, 22 hours from Buenos Aires. The street opposite the bus station, Sarmiento, has several hotels.

Chubut Province

For many people, Patagonia only really begins with the province of Chubut, where

Most roads are paved, and there is little traffic away from Montevideo and the coastal road. Even so, driving can be a hazardous business — not only because of the number of ancient cars, but also because the Uruguayans are notoriously bad drivers, even by South American standards. It seems that many of them are also likely to be drunk: recent statistics have shown both that about one in four of the workforce is an alcoholic, and that two out of three traffic accidents are a result of drunken driving.

All the big car hire firms have agents in Montevideo, including Avis and Hertz which also have offices in Punta del Este. Car hire costs a minimum of $15 a day, to which must be added insurance (around $10), $0.20 per km and 16% tax. Petrol is expensive at around $1 a litre. Although an IDP is in theory necessary, most companies accept a national licence.

ACCOMMODATION

You'll be hard pushed to find a bed in a hotel for less than $5, and $10 is the average price for a double room. During the peak season most places in the resorts charge at least $30.

Uruguay has an excellent youth hostel network, however, where you generally pay about $3. For a full list of hostels contact the Asociación de Alberguistas de Uruguay at Pablo de María 1583 in Montevideo. This is the only place where you can buy a membership card, which costs $14 and is valid for a year. But you can also buy six 'coupons', which works out cheaper for a short stay; and in practice you can often get away with a few nights on a standard IYHF card. Some hostels are closed in winter.

EATING AND DRINKING

Uruguayan cuisine is similar to that of Argentina, though the beef is often better. And since the quality is almost universally good, you don't gain much by eating in an expensive restaurant. Steaks are a daunting size, and asking for one on the bone is a good way to reduce the amount of flesh you are expected to eat. Order a mixed grill only if you haven't eaten for several days.

Specialities include *puchero*, a delicious mess of mixed meats, beans and vegetables, and *chivito*, a steakburger. There are many different kinds of spicy sausage; *morcilla dulce* is a sweet black sausage made with dried fruit and nuts. *Medialuna* ham and cheese sandwiches, found in Argentina, are also common.

Drinking. The local spirits are *grappa* (made from wine sediment) and *caña* (made from sugar cane), which are both strong and often rough. You would do better to stick to beer, though the local wine can be surprisingly palatable too. One interesting mixture is *clérico*, which is a cocktail of wine and fruit juice and tastes rather like sangria. As in Argentina, *maté* is a popular hot drink, especially among the gauchos in the northern regions. A *cortado* is a strong white coffee.

SPORT

Soccer is the only sport to have had a great impact on Uruguay, and the Centenario stadium in Montevideo remains one of the great shrines of South American football. The country's victory in the 1950 World Cup was astonishing considering the size of its population. But since then, with the exception of a poor 0-0 draw in the opening match of the 1966 World Cup finals at Wembley, the national team has not excelled. Paraguay is better, though don't mention this to Uruguayans.

Peru: from Lima via La Paz on LAP and American Airlines.

From the USA. The only direct flights are on LAP and American Airlines from Miami. Each has three services a week, scheduled so that there is a flight daily except Sunday. At the time of going to press, the cheapest way to reach Asunción from Miami is on Lloyd Air Boliviano (LAB) via Santa Cruz, where an overnight stay is required. However, the best value for travellers intending to travel more widely in South America is the LAP airpass from Miami. It covers travel across the modest LAP network within South America, but be warned that services are infrequent and that you'll spend a great deal of time at the airport in Asunción. Call 1-800-327-3551 for details.

From Europe. If you are determined to enter Paraguay by air from Europe, the fastest option is a connecting flight via Brazil, e.g. with Varig. Alternatively, Iberia has flights once a week to Asunción from Madrid, via Rio and São Paulo. LAP runs a service twice a week from Frankfurt.

SURFACE
From Brazil. *Foz do Iguaçu/Ciudad del Este:* the most straightforward border crossing into Paraguay from Brazil is the one across the Río Paraná from Foz do Iguaçu. The only drawback is that Ciudad del Este is an abominable place, and that both Brazilian and Paraguayan sides of the border are chaotic. Local buses from Foz across the bridge are frequent but usually crowded. Make sure you have worked your way to the front by the time you reach the bridge; otherwise it may be impossible to get off.

There is no obvious immigration office on the Brazilian side. You can usually just approach the Federal Police cabin in the middle of the road, where someone will take your tourist card and wave you through. Paraguayan immigration is just the other side of the bridge, a short but not particularly pleasant walk along a road choked with traffic. Immigration procedures should be over in just a matter of minutes. The moneychangers outside are safe to deal with; ask at the tourist desk for the current rate. Pick up another bus coming from Foz on its way to the bus station, from where frequent buses leave for Asunción and Encarnación, taking 4-5 hours to either city. Alternatively take one of the through buses from Foz direct to Asunción (see page 732).

Ponta Porã/Pedro Juan Caballero: the Brazilian town of Ponta Porã is accessible by bus or train from Campo Grande. Once across the frontier — simply a road dividing the two towns — buses run direct to Asunción. This border is used by few people except the locals who come and go all day; access by road is likely to be affected by rain; see page 711.

There are a number of other crossing points from Brazil, but they are off the beaten track and require time and effort to reach. For example, boats run every couple of weeks from Corumbá along the river Paraguay to Asunción. If you suspect that the novelty may pall after a while, get off at Bahía Negra, from where you can fly to the capital, or at Concepción, from where you can continue by bus or air.

From Argentina. *Clorinda/Asunción:* for the most direct road access to Asunción from Argentina, cross the border at Puente Loyola/Puerto Falcón near Clorinda,

AROUND ASUNCION

Asunción is ideally placed for circular trips, one of which takes in Luque, Areguá, Ypacaraí, Itauguá and Capiatá. While these aren't outstanding destinations in themselves, taken as a whole they make a good day's excursion. The circuit can be done clockwise or anti-clockwise. Anyone who hasn't as yet had a whirl on the steam train should go clockwise. Note, however, that this cuts the day short since the train doesn't leave Asunción until 12.15pm. Taking the train in the other direction is less practical since it leaves Ypacaraí at 4.30am. Trains run daily Monday to Saturday.

Local buses serve all the towns, and once on the Ciudad del Este highway, virtually any passing bus will do.

Luque and Areguá. After giving you a close-up view of Asunción's slum areas, the train reaches Luque at about 1pm, and Areguá at 1.40pm. Both towns are old colonial settlements, with many white-washed, single-storey buildings. While Luque has bustling streets, a market, and a few pleasant cafés, Areguá is positively soporific. There's nothing to be lost by wandering around either place, if only to marvel at the contrast between them.

Areguá lies on the southern shores of Lago Ypacaraí, and in summer fills up with holidaymakers. The lake is of no great beauty and is increasingly polluted, but going on boat trips is a popular pastime. Boats sometimes ply between Areguá and San Bernardino, a more popular and unusually lively resort on the eastern shores of the lake. There is a hospedaje in Areguá on the main street near the lake, but for greater choice go to San Bernardino, which is accessible by bus along the road that branches north between Ypacaraí and Caacupé.

There is a constant stream of buses between Asunción and Areguá, which go via Capiatá or Luque; buses 28 and 30 run between Luque and the centre of Asunción. To continue around the circuit, take the hourly bus to Ypacaraí, about 10 miles/16km southeast of Areguá on the main Ciudad del Este road; the journey takes about 40 minutes. The Asunción train also terminates in Ypacaraí.

Itauguá. This dusty roadside town lies a short distance west of Ypacaraí. The local women are famous for their lace-making, an art taught to them by Spanish nuns in the 18th century, though the so-called ñandutí is certainly not to everyone's taste. Scouring the lace and souvenir shops that are scattered along the busy highway is only mildly rewarding, but you can sometimes see the women at work. For a more pleasant stroll, seek out the main part of Itauguá south of the highway. There is a small, low-key market and several attractive colonial streets lined with orange trees.

Capiatá. Lying about ten minutes west of Itauguá and 12 miles/19km east of the capital, Capiatá is another small town riven in two by the highway. The reason to stop off here is to visit the cathedral, a couple of blocks north of the highway. The church was founded in 1640, and the interior is a rundown version of the one in Yaguarón (see below). It is not nearly as beautiful, but there is some interesting carving and fine paintwork. Bus 27 links Capiatá and central Asunción.

A more extended trip takes in Caacupé, Pirebuy and Yaguarón. This first town lies in hilly country some 35 miles/56km east of Asunción. It is the site of a modern but beautiful basilica which is Paraguay's holiest shrine. The Virgen de los Milagros attracts pilgrims all year round, but the main day of celebration is December 8.

wave of immigration from Europe during the 19th and 20th centuries. Immigrants came by the million, and settled mainly in the southern states and along the coast. Large numbers of Asians also made their home in the country, and Brazil has the largest Japanese colony in the world. There has been much intermarriage, but pure-blooded foreign communities also survive, where their native language is still spoken.

The Indians living in Brazil at the time of the Conquest lived mainly in the south and in Amazonia. Of the estimated 220,000 Indians in the country today, 80% live in the Amazon; there are also isolated pockets in Mato Grosso. The Guaraní in the south, originated in Paraguay, but have migrated north and east over the centuries. The tribe was once one of the biggest in Brazil, but today numbers only about 2,500. The early Portuguese settlers tried to force the Indians to work on the plantations, but they did not adjust well to agricultural work. Instead, during the 17th and 18th centuries, the colonizers brought in African slaves to work on the plantations and in the gold mines. At the end of the 19th century there were an estimated five million blacks in Brazil. The ancestors of these slaves live primarily in the Northeast, although there is also a fair amount of black blood in Rio and Minas Gerais.

Power and money in Brazil are concentrated in the hands of the white middle-class European descendants in the south. Both the blacks and Indians must fight to make themselves heard: the blacks have suffered a long history of discrimination, and the Indians in Amazonia struggle to hold on to their rights in the face of uncontrollable colonization. The Fundação Nacional de Indio, or FUNAI, was set up by the government to protect the indigenous people and their territory, but the organization is paralysed by a lack of funds, and has proved to be both inept and corrupt.

Religion. On paper, 80-90% of Brazilians are Catholic, making Brazil the largest Catholic country in the world. However there is an increasing number of new evangelicals and Afro-Brazilian spiritualist sects also have a big following. The latter have their origins in the Northeast, particularly in Bahia, although they are practised in other parts of the country too. The main sects are Candomblé, Macumba and Umbanda. They are derived from the assimilation of African and Catholic religious beliefs, a process which developed among slaves during the colonial period. Candomblé was banned until 1970.

Meeting the People. The traditionally hedonistic image of the Brazilian people is something of a caricature, although if you confined yourself to the beaches and clubs of Rio you might begin to believe in it. The uninhibited and overtly sensual atmosphere generated is not confined to the inhabitants of Rio — there are numerous places where women can feel positively prudish if wearing long trousers — but it is usually toned down elsewhere. Hand in hand with a lack of self-consciousness is an appealing tolerance and lack of pretentiousness. Homosexuality and bisexuality, as well as heterosexuality, are all openly displayed. In what other country would you expect a transvestite to win a national women's beauty competition?

Nevertheless, the life and attitudes of those living along the coast are poles away from those inland. Brazilians of the interior are generally more conservative in their outlook, particularly among the altogether meeker Indians, and the independent-minded and rather diffident inhabitants of the sertão.

Crime and Safety

Stationing a lion or tiger outsi[de] is the latest trend in home se[curity] — a sign of the desperate [measures] taken by the rich to protect [against] burglary.

Crime and violence has escalated in tandem with the worsening e[conomic] situation and the concomitant social tension. The maintenance of law and orde[r] is virtually impossible, not least because of rampant corruption: a police station was recently shut down in Bahia when it was discovered to be running one of the country's biggest car robbery gangs.

Violence affects primarily the shanty towns (*favelas*) that surround Brazil's cities, particularly Rio, São Paulo, Salvador and Recife. The murder of street children — of which there are an estimated seven million in Brazil — is a particularly alarming trend, and one that is at last receiving growing international attention. Travellers are unlikely to be aware of, let alone come into contact with, any such crime scene — apart from through gory photographs seen in *O Povo* or other sensationalist papers. But while the violence is confined almost completely to the slums, it inevitably spills out into the city centres — usually in the form of thieves after rich pickings.

To protect yourself and your belongings, reread the tips given on page 63 in the general introduction. Be extra vigilant but not paranoid: common sense should be sufficient. Mugging and street theft is rare in small towns, so it is in the cities that you should be most careful. Downtown areas are often empty at night; in the coastal cities the beach district is usually the safest place to be after dark.

Wear as few clothes as possible — no one wears many clothes in Rio — so that thieves can see that you've got nothing to hide; and carry your watch in your pocket. Avoid carrying a daypack if possible: to do so is yet another sign that you are a gringo tourist, and cutting the straps is an established ruse, particularly on crowded buses. The best solution is to have a supply of sturdy plastic bags, which are likely to attract little attention. If you feel uneasy, leave your camera behind, and keep a spare stash of money in your shoe.

Emergency Numbers. Police: 190; Fire Brigade: 193. A tourist police force exists, but its representatives are few and far between.

Drugs. It is in the Amazon, where an international drug-trafficking scene is fast developing, that you are most likely to come into contact with drugs. Cocaine, for example, is sold openly in the streets of Porto Velho, capital of Rondônia. If you are caught with drugs you may be able to bribe your way out of it, but you would be mad to count on it. The planting of drugs on foreigners is rare, except at the Bolivian border near Corumbá.

Health and Hygiene

In addition to the standard inoculations listed in the general introduction, further protection is advisable, particularly if you are venturing into the Amazon and the Northeast, which present the worst health risks. Water contamination, which kills thousands of Brazilians every year, is particularly rife in these regions. Chagas' disease (see page 70) is also endemic in northern areas though it is difficult to catch.

Yellow fever is endemic in Brazil. You may be asked to show a vaccination

To get the 8.30am ferry you must leave Rio by 6am; alternatively go the day before and stay overnight. Buses to Angra dos Reis are more frequent than those to Mangaratiba, but if you get any bus along the BR-101, you can simply get off at the turn-off. The journey to Angra dos Reis takes about $2\frac{1}{2}$ hours.

Accommodation: the island's lack of hotels is one reason why the beaches remain so quiet. The existing hotels are expensive, and during the high season you must book a room in advance. The Mar da Tranquilidade (tel 021-780-1861) and the Alpino (tel 011-220-7633) are in Abraão, while the Paraíso do Sol (tel 021-263-6126) is at Praia Grande, some $2\frac{1}{2}$ hours walk from the port. Many travellers end up staying with local fishermen or using one of the campsites, most of which are around Abraão. It is forbidden to camp away from the sites.

Parati. This town is set in the most stunning stretch of coast along the Costa Verde — backed by dramatic jungle-covered mountains, and overlooking the calm Baia da Ilha Grande. Parati was an important centre of the slave trade and its heyday came, like Rio's, during the 18th-century gold rush in Minas Gerais. Many of the existing fine buildings were constructed during this period. Parati's most recent boom is a result of the building of the BR-101 highway. Along it travels a flood of tourists, who come to admire this most unique colonial relic and lie on the stunning beaches.

While the beaches succeed in absorbing the tourists with surprising ease, the town itself, with a resident population of just 25,000, has inevitably suffered. The central area is pedestrianized. You can stroll along the cobbled streets undisturbed by traffic, but at the height of the season you can spend most of your time dodging people. At other times of year, however, the town feels less like a museum and the native tranquillity is more obvious.

Arrival and Departure: Parati lies midway between Rio and São Paulo. There are about six buses a day from Rio ($4\frac{1}{2}$ hours), and four a day from São Paulo (4 hours); buses from Angra dos Reis leave every couple of hours. The Rodoviária is on Rua Roberto Silveira, a short walk from the old town. The tourist office is on the same street, near Praça Macedo Soares.

Accommodation: budget rooms are hard to find, particularly during the peak season. The cheapest places are Pousada Fortaleza at Rua Abel de Oliveria 31 (tel 71-1338), with doubles from $12 and Hotel Estalagem (tel 71-1626) at Rua Mal Santos Dias 9, which costs a little less. You can camp at most beaches, and there are several sites near the town: including at Praia do Pontal, across the river about 10 minutes north of Parati. If you don't have a tent, most beaches have private rooms for rent and even the odd pousada.

Beaches: the beaches on the mainland are the most accessible, and are often better than those on the islands in the bay. While some are accessible by bus or foot others can only be reached by boat. The latter obviously tend to be the quietest, but arranging transport can be expensive: to hire a boat costs about $10 per hour. The best option is to get dropped off and arrange to be picked up later, or in a few days time. Talk to the fishermen at Praia do Pontal or at the quay in town. You could also take the risk of not arranging transport back, and hope to get a lift back with another boat. A beach easily accessible by boat is Praia das Lulas, which is about an hour around the headland east of Parati.

square and the bus station. The town's bars and restaurants are simple affairs, but lively and friendly.

Pássaro Verde runs six buses a day from Belo Horizonte, leaving roughly every three hours between 5.30am and 9pm; the journey is terrific and takes 5-6 hours.

Serro. A good day trip from Diamantina is to Serro, 57 miles/92km east, in the valley of the Rio Jequitinonha. You can take the 6am bus out and the 3.30pm one back, although there are a couple of hotels. The journey is wonderful, and the reward is a beautiful hillside town, with lovely squares and quiet streets.

THE SPA TOWNS

The area southwest of Belo Horizonte is famous for its spa towns, sometimes referred to as the *Circuito das Aguas*. Even if you don't wish to take the waters, these resorts are the best places to stay if you want to explore what is one of the most beautiful parts of the state. Many people seem content to admire the view from the bus as they head south to São Paulo, but it's worth considering a stop-off en route. Be prepared for a dearth of cheap accommodation and for lots of tourists in the high season.

The best spas to head for are Caxambú and São Lourenço. Each has a Parque dos Aguas, where the springs are collected, with a fine array of pavilions and bath-houses. Both towns can be reached by bus from Belo Horizonte: Sul de Minas and Ensa buses leave several times daily for São Lourenço (5 hours), with less frequent services to Caxambú ($6\frac{1}{2}$ hours). Buses also run from Rio and São Paulo. If you stay in São Lourenço, try to visit the charming town of Cristina, about 30 minutes' bus ride away.

Those who prefer a livelier atmosphere should head for the large town of Poços de Caldas, which lies in an extinct crater west of the São Paulo road. Ensa runs buses several times a day from Belo Horizonte.

THE NORTHEAST

This region is arguably the most fascinating part of Brazil. While being the poorest economically, it is the richest culturally and historically. The atmosphere is livelier than anywhere else in the country, and new arrivals from Curitiba or Belo Horizonte will find life has a new edge.

The large black population has inherited a strong African influence, which touches every aspect of life, particularly in the coastal areas. However, it is the religious cults that are perhaps the most characteristic and intriguing symbol of the fusion of African and Brazilian cultures. Furthermore, although the blacks living in Rio have made that city's carnival world famous, carnival really belongs to the blacks of the Northeast. So does Brazilian music.

The nine states of the Northeast take up a million square miles, roughly the size of Argentina. While the coast is fertile — and proved ideal for the cultivation of sugar, cotton and cocoa by Brazil's earliest colonizers — the land becomes steadily drier as you head inland. The interior is taken up by the sertão, a forbidding landscape of arid scrubland and impoverished communities. The sparsely populated region has a very different character from the exuberant coast and attracts few travellers. But for a glimpse of a different world, it is well worth a visit.

You are likely to spend most of your time in the states of Bahia and Pernambuco. While both share the Northeast's finest evidence of the Portuguese occupation,

Rua Jangadeiros Alagoanos. There is a campsite both here and at Praia do Francês, just south of town.

Around Maceió

Beaches. Those north of town are the more impressive and quieter than the city beaches, though this entire stretch of coast can get busy at weekends. Garça Torta, 9 miles/14km from Maceió, and Pratagí, a mile or so further north, are both recommended. There are also good beaches around Barra de Santo Antônio, 28 miles/45km north of the capital.

Marechal Deodoro. Alagoas is the home state of President Collor. And 13 miles/21km southwest of Maceió is the birthplace of the first President of the Republic — Marechal Deodoro. There is a museum dedicated to him. However, this small town, once state capital, is more rightly famous for its remarkable colonial architecture. The highlights are the convent of São Francisco (1684) and its excellent Museu de Arte Sacra, and the church of Matriz da Conceição (1755).

Penedo. The town of Penedo, lies 108 miles/173km southwest of Maceió, on the northern shores of Rio São Francisco, which forms the border with Sergipe. This is a wonderful little place that sees remarkably few tourists. It has some attractive colonial buildings, among them the 18th-century convent of São Francisco and adjacent church, and the Igreja da Corrente (1764). Penedo also has a colourful market (best on Saturdays), and you can arrange boat tours up the river: ask around at the port.

Penedo is a couple of hours by bus from Maceió. It has little accommodation; try Pousada Colonial in Praça 12 de Abril.

PERNAMBUCO

The state of Pernambuco is, like Bahia, a region steeped in history. It was once the battleground of clashes between the Dutch and Portuguese, and evidence of both sets of colonizers survive — including one of Brazil's finest architectural complexes in Olinda. Recife boasts its own colonial buildings but, like Salvador, it also reflects its position at the head of an impoverished state. The sertão, already sparsely populated, becomes gradually emptier, as farmers whose crops have failed are forced to move into the city; others seek work in the São Francisco valley, which is said to be the largest marijuana-growing area in the world.

No one should miss out on Recife or Olinda, but since Pernambuco's beaches are not the best in the Northeast, after that a trip inland is recommended.

Recife

A first impression of Recife as a polluted, modern urban sprawl is not far wrong. Much of the city is ugly and smelly, and not somewhere anyone would wish to spend a lot of time. But don't write off Recife completely. Life here is never dull; and in amongst the office blocks are some fine buildings and entertaining streets.

information desk is open all hours, helpful and well-stocked with maps. The bank doesn't change foreign currency, but if you're desperate you can change small amounts of cash — at an appalling rate — in the magazine/book shop.

Buses into the centre leave from the other side of the car park, and take just 20 minutes. The bus terminates in Rua Pedro Pereira, one block southwest of Praça José de Alencar; catch it from here to return to the airport. A fixed-rate taxi into town costs about $5.

All the main airlines have branches on Barão do Rio Branco in the centre. Varig/Cruzeiro at 1179 (tel 231-5114), VASP at 959 (tel 244-6222) and Transbrasil at 1251 (tel 231-3500).

Bus. The Rodoviária (tel 272-1566) is west of the centre in Fátima district, not far from the airport. Bus 13/Aguanambi heads downtown, stopping in Rua 24 de Maio. To return to the station catch it from Praça Carreira; other buses (e.g. 503) stop on Rua Sampaio, by Praça Alençar.

Phone 186 for bus information. The main long-distance services from Fortaleza are as follows: Belém (22 hours, $32) three daily with Timbira and Itapemirim, and a leito on Wednesdays; Brasília (24 hours, $50) five a week at 9pm with Vipu; João Pessoa (10 hours, $15) daily at 8pm with Viação Nordeste; Natal (7 hours, $12) seven buses a day with Viação Nordeste, including a leito service; Recife (12 hours, $18) several evening departures with Expresso de Luxo and one leito bus at 8pm ($34); Salvador (21 hours, $28) daily with Itapemirim and Penha, with a leito service; São Luís (17 hours, $22) three buses daily with Expresso de Luxo; and Teresina (10 hours, $14) four overnight services with Expresso de Luxo.

Car Rental. Hiring a car is most easily done at the airport unless you want a beach buggy, in which case try the agencies on Avenida da Abolição, such as Junna's Buggy at number 2310 (tel 244-7872/261-3004).

ACCOMMODATION

The streets in the centre quieten dramatically out of working hours, some of them doubling up as the red-light district after dark. Being out late at night is not recommended, although there are usually plenty of people around Praça José de Alençar until 11pm. Staying by the seafront is a more expensive option, but the advantage is that the beach area is not only safer but also much livelier than the centre: at weekends there are discos, concerts, volleyball matches, etc., and you can watch the local cool guys do their stuff in the skateboard pit.

Centre. The low-budget hotels are found mainly between Praça José de Alençar and the Mercado Central. On the square itself is the huge and decrepit Hotel Lord (tel 231-6188/6212). There are good views from the top floors, but be prepared for a lot of noise from the bars in the square and the buses in the adjacent streets. Rooms with bath cost $8/$12, including a good breakfast on the roof terrace.

Cheaper are the hotels on Rua Senador Pompeu. The best options on this street are Hotel Moreira (562; tel 252-4665), which has rooms without bath for $7/$10, and the Savoy on the next block (number 492; tel 252-2582), which has rooms with shower at similar rates. For a few more creature comforts, go to the Hotel Passeio (Rua Dr Moreira 221; tel 252-2104) in Praça dos Mártires, which charges $10-18 and has triple rooms. Around the corner and slightly more expensive is

SANTAREM

One of the oldest settlements in the region, Santarém is a fairly unremarkable river port. It is sleepy and unsophisticated in a charming kind of way — a pleasant place to delay your progress up the Amazon. Contact with the local Tapuiçu Indians was first made around 1630. Some thirty years later the Jesuits set up a mission, around which Santarém grew. It is now the third largest town in the region and a busy port. Its population of 250,000 includes a fluctuating medley of Indians, gold prospectors and rubber gatherers. In amongst them are a few descendants of Confederate refugees who came from the USA after their defeat in the American Civil War.

Arrival and Departure. *Air:* flights between Belém amd Manaus stop over in Santarém and TABA (Rua Floriano Peixoto 607; tel 522-1939) connects the town to smaller centres in the interior. The airport (tel 522-4328) is 10 miles/15km from the centre, but there are no buses. Either take a taxi or try to get a ride on a bus run by the Hotel Tropical (Avenida Furtado 4120) for its residents.

Bus: the Transamazônica and the so-called Ruta Transgarimpeira, which runs north from Cuiabá in Mato Grosso, meet near Rurópolis, 119 miles/190km south of Santarém. Travelling along the latter is an endurance test. The principal destinations accessible by bus during the dry season are Belém (via Imperatriz), Cuiabá, Marabá and São Luís. Santarém's bus station (tel 522-1342) is on Avenida Cuiabá, 3 miles/5km from the centre. Buses marked Rodagem run to the station from near the market.

Boat: boats sail daily between Manaus and Santarém, but less frequently from Belém; both journeys take 2-3 days. Ask about private boats along the waterfront downtown or at the Cais do Porto, a couple of miles west of the centre. ENASA is at Rua Senador Lameira Bittencourt 459 (tel 522-1138).

Accommodation. What cheap hotels there are in Santarém can be found in the vicinity of the Mercado Modelo, near the banks of Rio Tapajós. Among the better options are Hotel São Luis on Rua Senador Lemos (tel 522-5940) and Hotel Equatorial (Avenida Rui Barbosa), a couple of blocks further south. The latter is the best of the cheaper ones, charging $10 for a double. If you are looking for comfort, the Santarém Palace at Avenida Rui Barbosa 726 (tel 522-5285) is good value.

As far as restaurants are concerned, there are a number of places in Praça do Pescador, off Rua Lameira Bittencourt. None of them serve *haute cuisine*, but O Mascote is one of the most popular and is at least lively.

Exploring. The best thing to do in Santarém is to walk along the waterfront. Avenida Tapajós runs alongside the river from the Docas do Pará, where large boats dock, to Mercado Modelo and the commercial district. En route you may be able to arrange a trip by boat to the nearby confluence of the murky Amazonas and clear Tapajós rivers. This is often combined with a tour up the Tapajós to Alter do Chão, about three hours from Santarém. This village lies on a lovely lagoon called Lago Verde, and there are sandy beaches which are excellent for swimming in the dry season. Alter do Chão is also accessible by a rough road: buses leave from near the market three times a day and take about 90 minutes. The two forms of transport — bus and boat — can be combined for a modest jungle expedition.

the lodges are expensive: the cheapest cost around $30 per night, which may include half or full board. You must usually book and pay through a travel agent, but try to deal direct if possible. The cheapest option is to camp, and this is possible in some places. Don't sleep in the open air without a mosquito net.

When arranging your own trips, decide whether you want to go by horse or canoe. Expect to pay around $20 per day, compared to the $60 per day an agency is likely to charge. Taking into account the cost of your room and board, the price difference is not that great; but if your fazenda is in a good location, you should be able to see a fair amount of wildlife without going on a full-blown tour. If you can't afford to go into the Pantanal proper, at least spend a couple of days in one of the swamp towns.

The best cities from which to approach the Pantanal are Cuiabá and Corumbá. The latter is generally acknowledged to be the better base since it lies nearer the swamp and the largest number of fazendas. But Cuiabá is better for anyone travelling independently because it gives access to the Transpantaneira Highway, the only decent road to penetrate the swamp.

From Cuiabá. The Transpantaneira runs as far as Porto Jofre, some 150 miles/240km south of Cuiabá. Public transport runs only as far as Poconé, 64 miles/102km south of the city; buses leave every couple of hours and take $2\frac{1}{2}$ hours. There are several hotels in town, of which the most central is the Skala in Praça Rondon (tel 721-1407). Beyond Poconé you must drive, take a taxi or hitch. There is only a limited supply of rentable cars in Poconé, and you may decide to take advantage of the greater choice in Cuiabá. Check about the state of the roads in advance: they worsen beyond Poconé, the numerous rickety bridges being the main cause for concern. Taking a taxi to Porto Jofre costs about $60. The alternative is to hitch, which can be done most successfully at weekends.

The journey south to Porto Jofre is wonderful, with animals and birds gathering at either side of the road. There are a few lodges along the way; the cheapest is the Pousada Pixaim, about 42 miles/68km from Poconé.

Porto Jofre, on the Cuiabá river, is the end of the line. It is a good base for guided trips, and you can also explore on your own, since simply by walking along the Transpantaneira you are guaranteed to see a whole range of animals and birds. The Santa Rosa Pantanal is the only hotel, and takes advantage of its monopoly by charging $35 for mediocre accommodation. Reserve a room by phoning 322-0077 in Cuiabá, or book through an agent. Anyone with a tent or hammock should camp.

From Corumbá. There are many lodges within reach of the BR-262 between Corumbá and Campo Grande. Recommended are Fazenda Leque (Rua América 262, Corumbá; tel 231-1598), east of Porto Manga, and Rancho no Paraíso, 110 miles/176km from Corumbá in Necolândia, one of the most interesting parts of the Pantanal.

For a low-budget, independent trip visit the swamp town of Porto Manga, a popular fishing centre on the Paraguai river 40 miles/64km southeast of Corumbá, and accessible by bus. A more interesting but longer excursion is to Porto Esperança, further down the Rio Paraguai. Near the town is Fazenda Santa Blanca, a recommended lodge; reserve a room at Rua 15 de Novembro 659 in Corumbá (tel 231-1460).

One of the most rewarding ways to explore the swamp is to take a boat from Corumbá. A cattle boat runs north to Cáceres once or twice a month, taking at

15 de Novembro. Jade Turismo is a tried and tested place, at the corner fo Rua Riachuelo; you may have to queue.

Telephone Office: the main Telepar office is at Rua Visconde de Nácar 1415, just south of Praça Osório.

Post Office: the main office is at Rua 15 de Novembro 700, on the corner of Rua João Negrão. It opens 9am-6pm on weekdays, 8am-noon on Saturday. To send a telegram you must go to the Agencia Postal Telegráfica at Marechal Deodoro 298 (near Barão do Rio Branco). It is open 9am-6pm on weekdays and 8am-noon on Saturdays for stamps, 6am-midnight daily for telegrams.

Bookshop: Livraria Osório (Rua Cruz Machado 463; tel 224-3904) buys, sells and exchanges English and other foreign-language books.

Consulates. *Chile:* Edif. Arnaldo Thá, Marechal Deodoro 235, 1st floor (tel 232-0436), southeast of Praça Osório.
Paraguay: Edif. Wawel, Rua Voluntários da Pátria 400, 5th floor (tel 222-9226).

CURITIBA TO PARANAGUA

The most popular excursion from Curitiba is to Paranaguá, a town on the coast some 62 miles/100km east. The appeal stems primarily from the train journey there. The railway crosses the Serra do Mar providing magnificent views of gorges, waterfalls and out to sea, as the train rattles over vertiginous bridges and around terrifying ridges.

Train: trains to Paranaguá from Curitiba run only at weekends. The *litorina* is a modern Japanese-built diesel train, with reassuringly large brakes. It has a recorded commentary and makes a couple of extra stops to take pictures. However, unless you are a late riser or in a hurry there is little reason not to opt for the ordinary train (*comum*), which takes around four hours — about an hour longer than the other. The litorina leaves at 8.30am, returns at 3.30pm, and costs $6.50; the normal train leaves at 7am, returns at 4.30pm and costs $1.75. Out of the peak season the schedule may vary, so check (tel 234-8441). Try to book a seat the day before, for either train, particularly during the holiday period. For the best views sit on the left-hand side for the journey there.

Bus: many people go to Paranaguá by train and return by bus. The buses follow one of two routes: the straightforward BR-277 highway, or the so-called Estrada da Graciosa. The latter takes you on a spectacular ride through the lush hills and waterfalls of the Marumbi National Park (see below). The only bus taking the Graciosa road leaves Curitiba at 7.45am; from Paranaguá it leaves at 3pm. Buses along the BR-277 leave almost hourly between 6.30am and 10pm; these take about 90 minutes as compared to $2\frac{1}{2}$ hours along the Graciosa road. Buses fill up early at weekends, so arrive at the station in good time.

Morretes. If you wish to break the journey to Paranaguá, get off at Morretes, a charming riverside town lying at the foot of the Serra Madre. Not a great deal goes on here, but there are a few colonial remnants and at weekends it is busy with people having lunch at restaurants by the river. You can eat excellent fish, but the local speciality is *barreado*, a type of beef stew. The Nhundiaquara (Rua General Carneiro; tel 462-1228) is the only hotel worth staying at, with double rooms for $14.

requires some planning and much patience. You need to board a Rosignol bus from Georgetown any day except Sunday at 5am, which should get you to the west bank of the Berbice River by 8am. If it all works, a ferry will be waiting to take you across the river to New Amsterdam, a ramshackle but not unpleasant town that's worth a wander around. From here a connecting bus continues to the twin towns of Springlands and Skeldon, known collectively as Corriverton. This is on the west bank of the Corentijne River, which forms the boundary with Surinam. Although the boat leaves at noon, it is essential to start the check-in process early; no booking system seems to operate. The voyage takes just over an hour to reach Nieuw Nickerie on the Surinam side. From here buses take passengers on to Paramaribo, with luck by nightfall.

In the reverse direction it is necessary to make an even earlier start, or to stay overnight at Nieuw Nickerie.

At the time of going to press it appeared that a coastal ferry service was operating weekly between Georgetown and Albina, on the Surinam/French Guiana border, calling at New Amsterdam.

Between Surinam and French Guiana: the land border between Albina in Surinam and St Laurent in French Guiana was reopened in 1991: boats across the Maroni river take about 45 minutes.

GETTING AROUND

The road network is limited almost entirely to the coastal areas, with little that is paved. Journeys often involve crossing rivers by ferry — providing much scope for delays. The rains severely disrupt both surface and air travel. Flights are often heavily booked, and last minute changes can be impossible; if heading into the interior, arrange the return flight before setting off, and check the schedule from the other end on arrival.

In the interior (at any time of year), you must rely primarily on river transport; motorized canoes operate on all navigable rivers. Boats connect some coastal communities, but these are more erratic. Other options are horse or jeep. Permits may be needed to go into the interior and to visit Amerindian settlements. Going on a tour is the best option if time is short.

EXPLORING

The Guianas have no irresistable Caribbean beaches because the number of rivers flowing into the coastal waters make the sea murky and uninviting. The best trips are to be made into the interior, for which an adventurous nature is a great asset. There is little infrastructure for tourism, the terrain makes travel difficult, and accommodation is limited outside the capital cities and a few coastal towns. Venturing inland needs good preparation, suitable clothing and, more often than not, a guide. A hammock and mosquito net are essential if getting around independently.

HEALTH

The Guianas have all the health problems associated with poor, low-lying tropical countries, particularly malaria which is a high risk inland; mosquitoes along the coast are not malarial. A more serious worry is the spread of Aids. French Guiana has the highest incidence of HIV infection in the world, and the other two Guianas are not far behind; Guyana has 200 confirmed cases of Aids. Given the extent of prostitution, the figures are likely to worsen. See page 74 for advice on what precautions to take.

Buses back to the visitors' centre (and Puerto Iguazú) leave the bridge at ten or five minutes to the hour. The last bus back to Puerto Iguazú leaves at 7pm.

ITAIPU

This is the site of the world's largest hydroelectric power station, a joint Brazilian and Paraguayan project begun in 1984. The construction of the plant destroyed the world's largest waterfall and has damaged the local environment irreversibly. However, since it lies above the junction of the Iguaçu and Paraná rivers, the dam has not affected the Iguaçu falls, which are just 12 miles/19km south. The plant has a capacity to supply one third of Brazil's and all of Paraguay's energy requirements, though as yet it has not done so: the 18th and final turbine was opened only in 1991.

Itaipú is open 8-11am and 2-5pm Monday to Saturday, 8am-noon on Sunday. Visitors are taken on guided tours, which begin on the hour. Buses to Itaipú are marked Canteira da Obra, and leave Foz city bus station every 30 minutes between 5.30am and 7pm.

SANTA CATARINA

Florianópolis

The romantic-sounding state capital is a rather disappointing city. It was founded in the 18th century, but despite the survival of cobbled streets and a few attractive buildings, the old city struggles to hold its own. That Florianópolis sees such a flood of visitors is due solely to the beauty of Santa Catarina island, on which the city lies.

The city is a little lack-lustre, though the centre is quiet and inoffensive. This is because modern high-rises have been built mainly along the northern shore of the headland, and since industry has stayed put on the mainland. It's worth strolling around in between trips to the beach. The most interesting building is probably the 18th-century Palácio Cruz e Souza, on the west side of Praça 15 de Novembro, the main square: it houses an unremarkable history museum (closed Mondays).

To see Florianópolis positively come to life, visit during the carnival celebrations, or which the city is famous.

Arrival and Departure. There are daily flights from Rio, São Paulo and Porto Alegre as well as from Foz do Iguaçu. The airport (tel 33-0879) is 7 miles/11km outh of town. Buses run frequently to the centre.

There are regular bus services to and from Curitiba (6 hours), São Paulo (12 ours) and Porto Alegre (8 hours), as well as daily services from Foz do Iguaçu (6 hours), Campo Grande (28 hours), Rio (18 hours) and Buenos Aires (27 hours). 'he bus station is just north of Avenida Gustavo Richard, which runs east from onte Colombo Sales, the southernmost of the two bridges that connect lorianópolis to the mainland.

ccommodation. Most hotels are central and within easy walking distance of e rodoviária and Praça 15 de Novembro. Rooms are fairly expensive, especially iring the peak season, when vacancies are also in short supply.

The cheapest deals are primarily west of the main square, and include several fairly grotty places near the bus station. Better are the Sumare, at Rua Felipe Schmidt 53, on the road heading northwest from the main square; Hotel Colonial at Rua Conselheiro Mafra 45, nearby; and the Felipe on Rua João Pinto, a couple of blocks southeast of the square.

There are cheap lanchonetes in the centre, but for more choice and good seafood, go to Beira Mar Norte, which runs along the northern shore.

Help and Information. There are tourist offices at the bus station and in the main square; the HQ is near the mainland end of Colombo Sales bridge.

The post office is in Praça 15 de Novembro, and the telephone office is near the corner of Ruas Paiva and Guilherme, a couple of blocks north of the square. The best rates for changing money are offered by agents in the Ceisa Center shopping arcade (Rua Vidal Ramos).

ILHA DE SANTA CATARINA

The island of Santa Catarina is stunningly beautiful, boasting lush green hills, sand dunes, lagoons, fine beaches, and untainted fishing villages. Domestic and Argentinian tourists flock there between December and February. But since they tend to stick to a small number of beaches, there are many spots that remain remarkably unspoilt. The most frequented beaches have hotels; elsewhere you should be able to rent beach houses, and there are plenty of campsites. Since many of the beaches are within easy reach of Florianópolis, day trips are perfectly feasible.

Beaches. The island's most developed beaches — Canasvieiras, Jurerê and dos Ingleses — are on the north side of the island, where the calm waters are good for swimming. The best beaches, however, are those washed by the Atlantic. Praia Moçambique (or Grande) stretches for 9 miles/14km, and is the longest on the island. There are few facilities on the beach itself, but at the southern end is Barra da Lagoa, a lovely fishing village which has hotels and beach houses. Behind it is pine forest and a salt-water lagoon called Lagoa da Conceição. The lake is best explored from Lagoa, on the western shores; this town has several hotels and is a good base from which to go on some excellent walks.

South of Barra da Lagoa are the best surfing beaches, which are popular among the young and lively in season. The most famous is Praia Joaquina, where the Brazilian surfing championships are held every January. For greater tranquillity head for Campeche and Armação, further south; beware of the strong currents.

Getting Around. There is a simple road network around virtually the entire island. Buses from Florianópolis run a moderately frequent service, although these serve the coastal towns rather than the beaches themselves. During the peak season, minibuses serve the beaches directly.

Since the most used roads around the island are good, many people decide to rent a car; there are several agents along Avenida Rio Branco, north of the centre in Florianópolis. Hitching is also easy.

North of Florianópolis

JOINVILLE

This is the first major town in Santa Catarina state as you approach from Paraná

It lies not far from the coast just 77 miles/123km south of Curitiba. Joinville is the state's most important industrial centre, with a population of over 340,000. Progress has meant that the influence of the town's 19th-century German founders is not as tangible as it is elsewhere. Nevertheless, you can see some of the brick and timber-framed — so-called *enxaimel* — houses that are characterisitic of the region.

There isn't much to do in Joinville, but it is a relaxed town, and a reasonable stopping-off place. The best examples of enxaimel architecture are along the cobbled Rua 15 de Novembro. This street and Rua Princesa Isabel, which runs parallel, are the city's main thoroughfares. For an insight into the history of Joinville, visit the Museu Nacional de Imigração e Colonização (Rua Rio Branco 229), just south of Praça da Bandeira, the main square; the photographic collection is particularly interesting. The museum is open 9am-6pm daily except Mondays.

The best hotels are the Principe (tel 22-8555) at Rua Jerónimo Coelho 27 and the nearby Ideal (number 98), south of Praça Bandeira.

Arrival and Departure. Buses from Curitiba use the good BR-101 and run regularly between 5.30am and 8.30pm; the journey takes $2\frac{1}{2}$ hours. Buses to and from Florianópolis take three hours, and run from 6.30am to 11pm. There are also direct services from Porto Alegre (9 hours), Foz do Iguaçu (10 hours), São Paulo (9 hours) and Rio (15 hours). The rodoviária (tel 22-2291) is just off the BR-101, about 30 minutes walk west of the centre; buses also leave frequently for Praça de Bandeira.

The tourist office, where you can pick up a map and change money, is in Praça Nereu Ramos.

BLUMENAU and POMERODE

Both these towns were founded by German immigrants. Unlike Joinville, Blumenau is self-consciously and excruciatingly Germanized. However, if you can bear the general theme-park atmosphere, it is worth wandering around the centre. Some of the most interesting brick and timber-frame houses are now museums, including the Museo da Família Colonial at Alameda Duque de Caxias 78 (closed Sundays). To get there walk east along the main Rua 15 de Novembro, and over the bridge across a tributary of the Rio Itajaí.

The Rodoviária is a few miles north of the centre. It is served by hourly buses from Joinville and Florianópolis, taking two and three hours respectively. There are a couple of decent hotels along Rua 7 de Setembro, south of the river.

In contrast to Blumenau's rather spurious claims to be the most German of Brazilian towns, the small town of Pomerode is a more legitimate candidate. Indeed 90% of the inhabitants are of German descent, and the majority still speak their native language. Pomerode also boasts some fine architecture. The only hotel to speak of is the Schroeder at Rua 15 de Novembro 514 (tel 87-0933). The tourist office is on the same street. Pomerode lies 20 miles/32km north of Blumenau, and there is a frequent bus service; it is also accessible direct from Joinville and Florianópolis.

PORTO BELO

There are numerous beaches along the coast between Joinville and Florianópolis, but the only place worth going out of your way to visit, is Porto Belo. This village lies on a peninsula south of the port of Itajaí. The best and most popular beaches are the lovely Praias Bombas and Bombinhas, which are close to each other overlooking the bay a few miles east of Porto Belo. The surf is good and there are barracas and cabins for rent, in addition to a couple of hotels, a youth hostel and campsites.

Santa Catarina — Inland

The scenery in the interior of Santa Catarina state is stunning, and it is well worth taking this overland route to Iguaçu or Mato Grosso. Or else simply treat it as a roundabout way south into Rio Grande do Sul.

The most spectacular route takes you inland from Criciúma (accessible by bus from Florianópolis) across the Serra Geral. The city of Lages is the place to aim for initially, though a more pleasant place to stay overnight is São Joaquim, 47 miles/76km southeast. Situated at 4,460 ft/1,360m above sea level, São Joaquim is the highest town in Brazil, and temperatures drop well below freezing in winter. Accommodation is limited, but there are a couple of decent hotels on Rua Joaquim Pinto.

About 131 miles/208km northwest of Lages is the town of Joaçaba. This is not a particularly appealing place either, but it lies in the beautiful valley of the Rio do Peixe and is another possible overnight stop. Stay at Hotel Comércio (Rua 7 de Setembro 183; tel 22-1779). From Joaçaba buses run north to Foz, as well as south to Passo Fundo in Rio Grande do Sul.

RIO GRANDE DO SUL

Porto Alegre

The capital of Rio Grande do Sul was founded in 1772, but the overriding atmosphere is solidly 20th-century. Nevertheless, some older structures have weathered the changes brought by the city's success as a port and commercial centre. Porto Alegre is not worth making a huge diversion to see, but it is lively, and also hard to avoid if you are travelling around the state. The city has a population of approaching 1.4 million.

Porto Alegre lies on the hilly banks of the broad Rio Guaíba, near where it empties into the huge Lagoa dos Patos. Ships sail up through the lake from the Atlantic, via Rio Grande on its southern shores.

Arrival and Departure. Porto Alegre can be reached by air from all over the country, as well as Montevideo, Buenos Aires and Santiago. The airport (tel 43-5638) is 6 miles/10km north of the city and is linked to the centre by a one-line Metro, which also serves the rodoviária; get off at the Mercado Público. The ride takes about ten minutes.

The rodoviária (tel 21-2599) is near the banks of the river northeast of the centre; it's not a particularly pleasant walk into town, and you would do better to take the metro to the Mercado Público. Long-distance buses serve Florianópolis (8 hours), Curitiba (11 hours) and São Paulo (18 hours) several times a day. In addition, there are services direct to Foz (17 hours) and Rio (26-27 hours); and also to Montevideo (13 hours) and Buenos Aires (24 hours). There are a couple of buses a day to Chuí (7 hours), on the frontier with Uruguay. Services to Uruguaiana, across the river from Paso de los Libres, in Argentina, are more frequent.

Accommodation. It isn't hard to find a cheap hotel near the centre. Try the Henrique (Rua General Vitorino 182) or the Palácio (Avenida Vigário José Inácio 644). The best place if you want to be near the rodoviária, is the São Luís (Avenida Farrapos 45; tel 28-1722), though the noise can be troublesome. The local mosquitoes are voracious.

Eating and Drinking. Porto Alegre is a city for serious meat-eaters. There are churrascarias everywhere and the steak is usually excellent. Restaurants are surprisingly scarce in the centre, and you must head into the suburbs to find the best places. Two of the most easily-reached districts are Floresta and São Geraldo, northeast of the centre and both accessible along Avenida Farrapos. In town, the Pulperia (Travessa do Carmo 76) is popular; it is in the Cidade Baixa, south of the centre. There are several good bars along Avenida Osvaldo Aranha, which runs along the northeastern edge of Parque Farroupilha.

Exploring. The old city is centred around the characterless Praça Deodoro, up the hill south of the commercial district near the river. A short distance east of the cathedral is the Museu Julho de Castelhos, at Rua Duque de Caxias 1231. This history museum is the only one worth visiting in town; it is closed on Mondays.

Southeast of Praça Deodoro is Parque Farroupilha. It is busy in the early evening and on Sunday mornings, when there is a market, known as the Brique da Redençao. Stalls sell crafts, antiques and junk. Porto Alegre's permanent market, the Mercado Público, is housed in an interesting 19th-century building in Praça 15 de Novembro, near the docks. Rua 7 de Setembro, the major thoroughfare through the city's commercial district, runs west from the market. Parallel to it is Rua dos Andradas, part of which is pedestrian and known as Rua da Praia; this is an important shopping area and is busy in the early evening.

The best place to hear traditional gaúcho music is at one of the various Centros de Tradição Gaúcha. Ask for details at the tourist office, refer to the local paper, or contact the Movimento Tradicionalista Gaúcho at Rua Guilherme Schell 60 in Santo Antônio district (tel 23-5194).

Help and Information. *Tourist Information:* there are information kiosks in Praça 15 de Novembro and at Travessa do Carmo 84 (Cidade Baixa); free maps are available.

Money: there are several casas de câmbio, including Exprinter at Avenida Salgado Filho 247. Others can be found on Rua dos Andradas.

Communications: the main post office is at Rua Siqueira Campos 1100, a couple of blocks north of Praça Florência. The telephone office is near the corner of Avenida Borges de Medeiros and Avenida Salgado Filho.

Consulates: Argentina — Rua Annes Dias 112, 1st floor (tel 24-6799).
Paraguay — Rua Quintino Bocaiúva 655, 801 (tel 46-1314).
Uruguay — Rua Siqueira Campos 1171, 6th floor (tel 24-3499).

LITORAL GAUCHO
The so-called Litoral Gaúcho is disappointing for anyone familiar with the coast

of Santa Catarina, and fierce winds sweep in from the Atlantic in winter. Even if you are heading south of Porto Alegre into Uruguay, there is little reason to stop off along the way. The two main centres in the southern reaches of the state are Pelotas and Rio Grande. If you want to make an overnight stop, it makes most sense to stay in Pelotas, which is a large but not unpleasant town just off the BR-116; the best hotel is the Rex in Praça Pedro Osório, the main square. Rio Grande, although hardly worth a visit in its own right, is in an impressive spot at the mouth of Lagoa dos Patos, and the harbour is fun to explore. Stay in the Paris Hotel at Rua Floriano Peixoto 112 (tel 32-8944) in the old centre.

SERRA GAUCHA

The interior of Rio Grande do Sul makes for the most rewarding trips. The Serra Gaúcha is an attractive region of hills and mountains north of Porto Alegre; it is excellent walking country. The area was settled primarily by German and Italian immigrants in the 19th century, and in some communities their influence is very much apparent.

Gramado and Canela. These resorts lie several miles apart 80 miles/128km north of the capital. The Alpine flavour has been manufactured and is a little painful, but it cannot detract from the stunning scenery — with abundant flowers in spring, and often snow in winter. Both towns are busy during the summer. Buses run from Porto Alegre and Caxias do Sul (see below).

While Gramado is the prettier of the two towns, Canela makes a better base since it is just 5 miles/8km south of the Parque Estadual do Caracol, which is the most accessible area for walking. Paths lead to a number of waterfalls, the most spectacular of which is the 130-metre Caracol itself. Buses run three or four times a day from Canela.

Some of the cheapest hotels in Canela are on Rua Oswaldo Aranha, including the Jubileu and the Bela Vista. There is also a campsite in the park. Hotels are more expensive in Gramado. The best hotels are the Planalto (Avenida Vorges de Medeiros 2001; tel 286-1210) and the Luiz (Rua Salgado Filho 432; tel 286-1026).

Parque Nacional de Aparados da Serra. This beautiful, forested park is near the Santa Catarina border, 45 miles/72km north of São Francisco de Paula. Access is not easy, but it is seriously worth making the effort to see the the magnificent Itaimbezinho canyon, which contains two 350-metre waterfalls. The simplest way to visit is to go on a tour from São Francisco de Paula. The alternative is to take a bus bound for Cambara do Sul and walk the 10 miles/16km from the turn-off. Note that the road to the park is likely to be impassable after rain.

Bento Gonçalves. The region around Caxias do Sul and Bento Gonçalves is the heart of Brazil's wine industry. Many of its inhabitants are of Italian descent. Caxias is a big city and the main transport hub of the region. There are a few cheap hotels on Rua Sinimbu if you need to stay overnight, but you would do better to head straight for Bento Gonçalves, further west. The town is surrounded by vineyards, and you can go on tours around the wineries (*adegas*). But one of the best outings is on the steam train through beautiful country to Jaboticaba. It runs on Sundays and takes three hours. Reserve a ticket in advance, at the tourist office at Rua Marechal Deodoro 70.

Although many of the settlements further inland are seldom memorable, travelling into the interior of Rio Grande do Sul at least provides a glimpse of the gaúcho heartland. Wherever you stop, ask about rodeos and livestock shows, which are the real highlight of visits to this area.

The biggest settlement is Santa Maria, which is a useful stopping-place if you are heading overland into Uruguay or Argentina. The best hotel is the Glória at Avenida Rio Branco 369 (tel 221-l690). From Santa Maria buses and trains run to both the Argentinian and Uruguayan borders. Uruguaiana is the state's most used border crossing into Argentina, and is also an important cattle centre. Santana do Livramento, on the Uruguayan frontier, is an unpreprossessing place; a more interesting route is via Bagé, a pleasant town with buses to the frontier at Aceguá.

SAO MIGUEL

The ruins of São Miguel are about all Brazil has left to recall the period during the 17th and 18th centuries when there were more than 30 Jesuit missions in an area that spread from Argentina and Paraguay into what is now Rio Grande do Sul. The so-called *reduçãos* were a law unto themselves until the Spanish and Portuguese rulers expelled the Jesuits in 1767. Many Guaraní Indians were killed, and those missions which weren't destroyed were simply abandoned and left to crumble. The best ruins are in Argentina and Paraguay, but São Miguel is a good example of the intriguing combination of European baroque and native Guaraní art. The ruined church is impressive, and the site attracts a fair number of tourists.

São Miguel is accessible by bus from Santo Angelo, which is served by bus from the main towns in the region. There are buses west across into Argentina too. Santo Angelo has a few hotels if you don't stay in São Miguel itself.

The Guianas

**Guyana
Surinam
Guyane
(French
Guiana)**

Georgetown, Guyana

The Guianas were dubbed by Evelyn Waugh 'those three little gobs of empire'. Colonized by neither the Spanish nor Portuguese, the Guianas are the odd ones out in South America, culturally distinct and geographically isolated from their Hispanic neighbours. A recent traveller complained that 'Guyana is Norfolk with palm trees, Surinam is Holland with palm trees, and French Guiana is Flanders with palm trees and a Club Mediterranée'. But, despite a certain uniformity, each is unique and fascinating.

The Spanish made first contact with the area at the end of the 16th century, but rejected it as being uninhabitable and poor in natural resources. This decision left the coast clear, literally, for the Dutch, French and British. All three were eager to get a foothold on a continent hitherto carved up between the Spanish and Portuguese. They squabbled endlessly over territory, however, a quarrel finally resolved only in the early 19th century.

Two treaties were important: firstly the Treaty of Breda in 1667, in which the Dutch ceded Manhattan Island to the British in return for what is now Surinam, and the French gained what was to become French Guiana. Power struggles in Europe resulted in further disagreements, and the borders were finalized only under the Treaty of Vienna, signed after the Napoleonic Wars. There are still territorial disputes: Venezuela and Surinam between them claim most of Guyana, and French Guiana wants part of Surinam.

Pronouncing the names of the countries is a hazardous business. The three countries are collectively known as the Guianas — ghee-*ar*-nas. British Guiana became Guyana — guy-*arn*a. The French colony, Guyane, is spoken gwee-*ann*. And the old Dutch colony is known as Surinam — soo-ree-*nam*.

The word *guiana* is thought to be an indigenous word meaning 'land of water'.

742

It was well chosen. The Guianas are waterlogged, riddled with rivers, and covered almost entirely by dense jungle. They share similar topography: swampy coastal plain, savannah further inland and then the forest-covered hills of the Guiana Highlands. The highest mountains are in the Serra Tumucumaque, a remote region along the southern borders of Surinam and French Guiana. These highlands, together with the tentacles of rivers stretching inland, have provided a natural boundary between the Guianas and the rest of South America.

Most people live in the coastal strip, the only area that is really cultivable: rice and sugar are the principal crops. Gold and diamonds are mined in more remote areas of the interior; this is carried out mostly by independent panners, many of whom come over the border from Brazil. More economically important is mining for bauxite (the raw material of aluminium). It has wrought environmental havoc and threatened tribal settlements, events which have been exacerbated more recently by a fast-developing timber industry.

Each country has strong cultural and financial links with its colonial power. A different source of foreign-currency earnings is growing. The relative emptiness of the region makes it an ideal trans-shipment point for drugs between the Andean countries and markets in Europe.

Climate. Rainfall and humidity are high, with little variation in temperature around the year — it is either hot or very hot. The northeast tradewinds, however, bring some relief by the coast. The wet seasons are November to February and April to August. The heaviest rain occurs during the latter period, when torrential and electrical storms are common.

The best time to visit is between January and April; September to November is the main dry season, but the heat is at its worst during this period. French Guiana

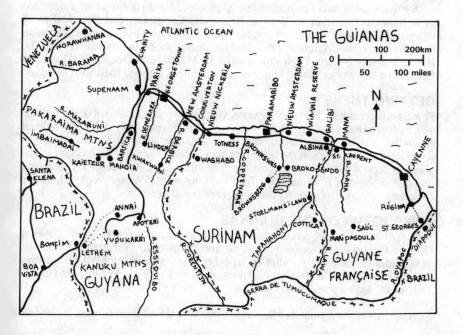

is the wettest of the three — rain is possible at any time of year, being heaviest from December to July.

Time. All three Guianas are three hours behind GMT.

PEOPLE

The Guianas have the most unusual racial mix to be found in South America. The largest group are Creoles, which make up about half of the population in French Guiana. In Surinam and Guyana, however, Asians are far more numerous. East Indians (also referred to as Hindustanis, to avoid confusion with Amerindians) form the largest ethnic group in both countries. Surinam has a large number of Indonesians too.

During the early days of colonization, Africans were brought to work on the region's newly established plantations. The descendants of these slaves still live in the area. In Guyana, they make up about 30% of the population. In Surinam and French Guiana most blacks are the so-called bushnegroes or bush blacks. Their ancestors are slaves who escaped from plantations in Surinam during the period of confusion that followed the Manhattan-Dutch Guiana swap in 1667. They settled in remote parts of the jungle, and their descendants live mostly along the Marowijne river, which marks part of the border between Surinam and French Guiana. The Asians were brought into the area following the abolition of slavery in the mid-19th century. After the completion of their indenture, they went into agriculture or commerce. Most Asians live in the country, while blacks are concentrated in the towns.

The original American Indian inhabitants live semi-nomadic lives in the jungle and savannah of the interior. Their culture, like that of the bushnegroes, has suffered from contact with the Europeanized coast. Many have also moved into the towns.

Due to the large Asian communities, Islamic and Hindu holidays are celebrated as well as the Christian holidays at Easter and Christmas, and the usual array of national holidays. The most notable are the Muslim observance of Ramadan (late February-late March in 1993, 11 days earlier each year thereafter) and the Hindu festivals of Holi Paghwah, usually in March, and Deepavali (Divali) in October or November. Small Chinese communities celebrate their own holidays.

GETTING THERE

Few travel agents have heard of Cayenne, Georgetown and Paramaribo, the capitals and international gateways of the Guianas. It is advisable to enlist the help of specialist agencies mentioned on page 24, particularly South American Experience, and to consult the information in *Getting There* for each country. The cheapest deals are from Paris to Cayenne. The following section deals with reaching one of the Guianas from another. *Travel arrangements change frequently in the Guianas, so it is essential to check current schedules.*

LINKS BETWEEN THE GUIANAS

Air. Surinam Airways has services several days each week between Cayenne (French Guiana), Georgetown (Guyana) and Paramaribo (Surinam). A one-way ticket from Paramaribo to either of the other cities costs about $150, with a one-week return fare at $200. Other airlines, such as Cruzeiro do Sul, Air Guyana and ALM, have sporadic services.

Surface. *Between Guyana and Surinam:* to travel overland from Guyana to Surinam

GUYANA

Population: 800,000   **Capital: Georgetown (190,000)**

'One people, one nation, one destiny' is the motto of Guyana. 'One hell of a mess' is how its present social and political problems might be described. One consequence is that Guyana, in particular the capital Georgetown, is the most dangerous place in South America. Travellers are constantly warned against walking around, and the brutally effective 'choke and rob' is used on those who fail to heed the warnings. Visitors to Rio, Lima, and other cities with a reputation for crime may be relieved to learn that these places are much safer than Georgetown.

Guyana has no significant tourism. Judging from the hassle obtaining a visa can involve, the government wants to keep it that way. But despite the third-degree questioning necessary to get into the country, and the first-degree hassle you face in the capital, Guyana is a fascinating and rewarding destination. A country where the Ford Capri and the Morris Oxford are the most popular makes of car, and cricket is the national sport, is bound to have a great deal of charm. Furthermore, a country in which most people have their roots in India or Africa, is a complete contrast to the rest of South America.

Guyana itself is rooted firmly in the English-speaking Caribbean. It has players in the West Indian cricket team, and is a member of Caricom (the Caribbean common market). Guyana is roughly the size of the UK. If its neighbours had their way, it would hardly exist at all: Venezuela has a long-standing claim to everything west of the Demerara River, on which Georgetown stands, a demand which covers over 70% of the Guyanan territory. Surinam has its eyes on a slice in the southeast.

The majority of Guyanans live in the coastal belt — a strip of largely reclaimed land that lies beneath sea level, and is under constant threat of flooding; a complex system of canals, dykes and dams prevents disaster. The largest area of savannah is the Rupunini, in the southwest, but most of the interior consists of hilly jungle, the latter occupying over 80% of the country's area. The Pakaraima range near the border of Venezuela, is the main mountainous area. Spanning the border with Venezuela and Brazil is Mount Roraima, the inspiration for *The Lost World* by Sir Arthur Conan Doyle. It is difficult to climb from Guyana, and is best approached from Venezuela.

East Indians and Africans make up 50% and 30% of the population respectively. Both groups retain their distinct cultural identity, and many people speak Urdu and Hindi. English is the dominant language, though it is strongly Caribbean, spoken with a heavy accent, and with surprising turns of phrase, e.g. 'good night' meaning 'good evening'. A standard form of address may surprise you; in line with its socialist leanings, the term 'comrade' is used. In print, it is abbreviated to Cde.

The local people are overwhelmingly friendly and helpful. The negligigible number of visitors and the extent of abject poverty mean, however, that you may feel much more of a 'target' than in other parts of South America. This may manifest itself as gratuitous verbal abuse, being blatantly overcharged by traders, or by being robbed. Take great care, and the advice of well-meaning locals, to avoid the latter.

HISTORY

The Dutch were the first to settle in Guyana, around 1620. The British and French soon joined in the establishment of settlements: it was the French who developed Georgetown, the capital, in 1782. The Dutch regained control, but problems in Europe soon diverted their attention, and Britain occupied parts of the region at the turn of the 19th century. In 1815 the Dutch ceded the colonies of Essequibo, Demerara and Berbice, which became British Guiana some years later.

British Guiana was a splash of Imperial red on the South American canvas for almost a century and a half. The bond began to loosen, however, in 1952, when it was granted a new constitution and internal self-government. The People's Progressive Party (PPP), an alliance of Africans and Indians, had formed under the leadership of Cheddi B. Jagan. A Marxist, he won an overwhelming victory in the 1953 elections. The British authorities disapproved of the new prime minister, and deposed him after three months. One immediate result was a split in the PPP, with the African faction becoming the People's National Congress (PNC). Politics have been based on the two main racial groupings ever since, although both parties originally followed Marxist-Leninist ideology. Guyana has never achieved real stability, with turbulent periods characterized by racial disturbances and economic crises. After the deposition of Jagan, a black called Forbes Burnham became prime minister. He was leader of the PNC, which has been the dominant force in Guyanan politics ever since. More moderately socialist than Jagan, Burnham and the PNC were preferred by both the UK and the USA.

British Guiana became independent in 1966, and in 1970 proclaimed itself the Cooperative Republic of Guyana. It remains part of the British Commonwealth. The 1970s saw much nationalization and close relations with Eastern bloc countries. Elections of dubious quality kept the PNC in power, and in 1980 Burnham announced a new socialist constitution and was elected President. In 1985, having ruled Guyana for 21 years, Forbes Burnham died; a mausoleum was erected for him in Georgetown's Botanical Gardens, but the embalming failed. So, rather than being displayed intact Lenin-style, his remains are interred in a casket in the mausoleum.

Burnham was succeeded by the then Prime Minister, Desmond Hoyte. The new President won a resounding victory in elections held that December. His presidency signalled a reversal of the Marxist-African 'cooperative' principles of the 70s, in favour of a more liberal, market-orientated approach, actively encouraging foreign investment. Relations with the USA improved. These measures were an attempt to deal with Guyana's appalling economic mess: the country faced total collapse in 1982, and was saved only by large amounts of foreign aid. Political interference in everyday life by the ruling party is rife. Even the telephone directory is rigged; the PNC is listed under 'Government Departments', as is its offshoot, the Women's Revolutionary Socialist Movement. (If, however, you wish to discuss politics with a minister, all their home phone numbers are listed on a special page in the directory.)

In 1992 Desmond Hoyte was facing growing dissatisfaction, with the economy in shambles, allegations of irregularities in the electoral register, and uncertainty about the future of democracy. Jagan, the old Marxist, is still alive and fighting for the PPP, now part of the Patriotic Coalition for Democracy. Opposition leaders and independent newspapers have called for an interim government to tackle the economy and organize fair elections. The Carter Foundation and the Organization of American States are actively involved in monitoring political events.

The Jonestown Massacre. The event for which Guyana is best known was the mass suicide in 1978 of nearly 1,000 members of a religious sect. The Reverend Jim Jones started the cult — the People's Temple — in California. He later moved it into the jungle of northwest Guyana, to a camp he called Jonestown. After complaints of coercion by the families of cult members, a US Congressman and three journalists investigated the site. As they were about to leave from Port Kaituma airstrip, they were shot dead. Realizing that US retribution was inevitable, Jones ordered the mass suicide of the sect. Those who chose to die drank cyanide from a huge drum; children and unwilling adults had the poison injected or were shot. The grisly episode reflected badly upon Guyana, since the president at the time allegedly received bribes from Jones. No official enquiry into the episode has ever been held, and there have been allegations that the cult forced local Amerindians into slavery. The resulting poor publicity may be one reason why foreign visitors find it so difficult to enter Guyana.

GETTING THERE

Air. There are no direct flights from Europe to Georgetown; instead you must go via Port of Spain in Trinidad or Bridgetown in Barbados. While the agencies mentioned on page 24 can offer good deals, it is also worth trying some which specialize in Caribbean destinations. In Britain, try Nedac Travel Services, 80 Portland Road, London SE25 (tel 081-655 1695) or Kimaja Travel, Bon Marché Buildings, 444 Brixton Road, London SW9 (tel 071-733 1118). These agencies tend to use British Airways flights connecting with Liat in Barbados, or BWIA via Trinidad, with a typical round-trip flight costing £600. The other option, on Cubana via Havana, has erratic schedules.

From North America, Guyana Airways Corporation (GAC) has three services a week from New York, three from Miami and one from Toronto. BWIA has fast connections in Trinidad with New York and Miami.

The only direct flights from Venezuela are twice-weekly (Thursday and Sunday) from Caracas on Aeropostal. From Brazil, Cruzeiro do Sul has services from Manaus via Boa Vista.

A tax of 10% is applied to international tickets bought in Guyana. In addition, departure tax of $10 — payable in US, UK or Guyanan currency — is levied upon departure.

Surface. See page 744 for details of links between the Guianas. It is possible to enter Guyana overland from Brazil, usually by bus from Boa Vista to Bonfim, across the river from Lethem in southwest Guyana. Unfortunately links beyond here are slow and unreliable, with the GAC flights not operating regularly at the start of 1992.

RED TAPE

Citizens of Caricom countries need no visa for Guyana. Everyone else does, and it is fearsomely difficult to obtain one. Personal application is strongly recommended, since postal applicants may be called for interview anyway. Apply six weeks in advance if possible. The following advice applies to the UK; applying in Surinam or Paramaribo may be easier, but from anywhere else it is likely to be harder.

The first stage is to obtain the application form from the Visa Section of the Guyana High Commission: 3 Palace Court, Bayswater Road, W2 4LP (tel 071-229 7684/8; fax 071-727 9809). The office, east of Notting Hill Gate tube station, opens 9.30am-2.30pm daily. The completed form must be submitted in duplicate with a passport (valid for at least six months), two photographs and 'supporting evidence'. For those with relations or a business contact in Guyana, this can be a letter of invitation. Independent travellers must supply evidence of funds of at least £1,000. This can be a bank statement or a receipt for travellers cheques. Ideally you should have an onward or return air ticket, but understandably you may prefer not to get one until you have a visa.

The second stage is the interview, a tough grilling where your motives and plans are closely examined. Anyone suspected of being a photographer or journalist can expect a bad time. Successful applicants have stressed their desire to explore the great outdoors of Guyana, or shown interest in the colonial architecture of its towns. You may spend an hour or two in the waiting room while your case is discussed. If you persuade the officials that you are a suitable candidate, you pay the fee of £20.

Visas are valid for three months from the date of issue. The length of stay permitted is decided upon arrival. You must have a ticket out of Guyana, plus at least $50 for each day of your intended stay. To extend your visa, go to the Immigration Office in Georgetown; it is in the old railway station on Lamaha St, between Carmichael and Waterloo Streets.

The Embassy of Guyana in the USA is at 2490 Tracy Place NW, Washington, DC 20008 (tel 202-265-6900), with a consulate in New York at 866 UN Plaza, NY 10017 (tel 212-527 3215).

MONEY

The Guyana Dollar has depreciated rapidly in recent years, to the extent that coins are almost worthless. Changing money is relatively easy, and pounds sterling are as welcome as US dollars. The best rates are from licensed exchange houses or 'cambios' (one of very few Spanish words to have been imported into the Guyanan vocabulary); but many ordinary shops outside the capital will change money too. Travellers cheques are less popular than cash, and can be changed only in banks or cambios at rates slightly worse than for cash.

The black market is conducted mostly by villains, and should be avoided. Credit cards are accepted in some big hotels and restaurants, but are of only limited use. It is impossible to withdraw cash on them, but at the time of writing British visitors could cash a cheque at 'he Bank of Guyana in central Georgetown. You simply turn up with your cheque book and guarantee card, and write a cheque which is paid in sterling, US dollars or local currency.

Banks are open 8am-12.30pm from Monday to Thursday, on Fridays additionally from 3-5pm.

COMMUNICATIONS

Mail. The world's rarest postage stamp is a flawed 1c stamp printed in Georgetown in 1856. It is now worth around $3 million, and the press which made it is in the capital's museum. The stamps for postcards home are much less valuable, but more attractive. Postage is among the cheapest in South America, running at around $0.05 for a postcard to Europe. Guyana is an excellent place from which to send back unwanted belongings. The staff at the warehouse-like central post office in Georgetown will help you through the bureaucracy, but be sure to take your passport. A 5kg air mail parcel might cost as little as $10, and takes about three weeks to Europe. Religious homilies above the counter in the post office bear repetition: 'Trust in the Lord ... and he shall direct thy paths' — and, hopefully, those of your parcel.

Telephone. The international country code for Guyana is 592.

Calls abroad are much cheaper from Guyana than from elsewhere on the continent. A three-minute call from Guyana Telephone & Telegraph (GT&T) offices to the UK costs just $5. Local people realise the extremely good value this represents, so queues at offices are often long. Guyana has some cardphones which accept prepaid cards; these are the only public payphones — all the coin-operated payphones have been stolen.

Area codes in Guyana are as follows: Georgetown — 2; Bartica — 5; Linden — 4; New Amsterdam — 3. Be careful how you handle the telephone: the directory warns solemnly 'do not jiggle the receiver or interfere with the dial'. Unfortunately, thieves interfere with the cables. It is estimated that only 70% of the country's 21,000 telephones work, the remainder being out-of-order due to the theft of cables.

Telegram. If the queue for international calls is too long, and you just want to tell your mother you've arrived safely, then a telegram is cheap and effective. Twelve words to the UK costs no more than a dollar.

Media. Guyana has a lively selection of newspapers. The best is the *Stabroek News*, a truly independent paper with incisive journalism. It began as a weekly, initially printed in Trinidad because the government would not allow a critical newspaper to be published in Guyana. So popular was the *Stabroek News* that the government had to relent, and it is now published in Georgetown, daily except Monday.

The *Guyana Chronicle* is a government-run daily; its coverage is limited and sometimes laughable — full of pictures of the President dispensing largesse to his subjects. The weekly *Mirror* is rabidly pro-PPP.

The main radio station, the Voice of Guyana, transmits mainly reggae music, diluted with bursts of speech: 'Deaths and Messages' at 6.05am, BBC News at 8am and BBC Sports Round-Up at several times through the day. The limited television service — GTV — transmits on one channel for a few hours each day.

GETTING AROUND

The only detailed map of the country is the *Administrative Map*, last published in 1981. It is sold, for $3, at a few bookshops in Georgetown, though supplies are dwindling with no evidence of refurbishment. Buy it, if only because the nomeclature of Guyana is a delight. Between Georgetown and the Surinam border you pass through Success, Paradise, Profit and Whim. Searching for the right district in the Guyana telephone directory you leaf through Friendship, Industry and Ogle before reaching Triumph, Vigilance and Vryheid's Lust.

Air. Easily the best way to get around Guyana's inhospitable terrain is by air. But unfortunately domestic services on the state airline — Guyana Airways Corporation — are almost moribund; and fares are by no means cheap, often $80-100. Enquire about the prospect of domestic services at the small hut around the back of GAC's headquarters at 32 Main St, Georgetown. Other places, including the Kaieteur Falls, can be reached only if you charter an aircraft.

Boat. The main navigable rivers are the Mazaruni, Essequibo, Potaro, Demerara and Berbice. Government steamers ply the Essequibo and Berbice, but services are unreliable due to flooding and rapids. There is also a government-run service between several ports on the coast. Smaller boats, mostly high-speed launches, operate locally. Be sure to ascertain the correct fare from locals before boarding (or you will be mercilessly overcharged) and check the times of return boats if you are on a day-trip.

Bauxite tugs travel regularly along the Berbice River, between New Amsterdam and the mines at Kwakani; you can ask the captain for a lift.

Road. Traffic travels on the left. Driving standards are appalling, with 150 road deaths each year. Although traffic signals have been erected in Georgetown, none of them work. The only decent all-weather roads are in the coastal area east of the Essequibo river: along the coast to the border with Surinam and inland as far as Linden. Plans exist to extend this road as far as the Brazilian border, but there is a long way to go. Many of the roads inland are those linking the mines.

Privately operated minibuses scurry along most of the surfaced roads, with routes radiating from Georgetown. Services are frequent during daylight, though crowded. Reggae music is played at high volume on most of them. Nothing much runs after dark. On the important routes along the coast, ferries theoretically operate in conjunction with the buses. When heading inland, the only option may be to take the buses run by the mining companies.

Rail. Traces of the excellent rail network survive as disused track, but sadly passenger services no longer operate.

Travel in the Interior. The authorities are sensitive about foreigners heading into the interior, and some areas are positively off-limits. Most boats and aircraft heading inland are met by police, and your documents are likely to be checked. For some places, a permit is required; tour operators will advise. One of the best is Torong Guyana, based at 56 Coralita Avenue, Bel Air Park East, Georgetown (tel 65298). Another is Rainbow River Safari (54 Lamaha Gardens, Georgetown; tel 52169); it also has a UK office at 29 Halsmere Road, London SE5 9JQ (tel 081-671 1414). Expect to pay $250-300 for an average three day trip involving flights.

ACCOMMODATION

The only positively comfortable hotels are in the capital, and these are expensive — $60 double is typical. Even at this price there is no guarantee that power cuts will be avoided; They are frequent and often long-lasting.

Georgetown has plenty of budget rooms, though mosquitoes and noise are problems. Coastal towns also have a fair supply of basic rooms. Accommodation in the Interior is surprisingly expensive — $20-30 for even fairly simple lodgings — which explains the seemingly high cost of tours.

EATING AND DRINKING

You can eat extremely well at the best restaurants in Georgetown, and enjoy Caribbean ingredients such as yams and okra. Elsewhere, the standard fare is chicken, beef or pork with rice and beans. Guyana has a surprisingly high number of Chinese restaurants, which dish up Cantonese dishes as well as local cuisine.

The term 'liquor restaurant' indicates a place which sells alcohol, but don't rely upon food being served. Stick to beer when choosing your drink. Banks is the dominant brew, and is entirely palatable; the company also makes a sweet, dark beer. Both are made at the company's brewery, Thirst Park, in the south of Georgetown. 'Wine' and 'sherry' sold in Guyana have nothing in common with Western concepts of these drinks. Sherry, for example, contains yeast, sugar, rice and 'port flavour'. You might, however, want to try a favourite local cocktail, the Brown Cow — nine parts Tia Maria, one part milk.

Soft drinks are sweet and fizzy — such as Banko Shandy (actually ginger beer) and Malta, like drinking weak, fizzy treacle.

SPORT

Despite its location, Guyana forms part of the West Indies cricket team. The first Test match to be played at the cricket ground at Bourda, Georgetown, was the first in which the West Indies beat England. The ground is several feet below sea level — the only one in the world. The low-level produces unusual atmospheric conditions which causes the ball to deviate through the air more violently than elsewhere. Tensions in the ground often run high: a riot occurred after a disputed run-out in England's tour of 1953-54; and in 1979, the crowd indicated its displeasure at a stoppage of play by causing $100,000-worth of damage.

England's last three visits there have not yielded a single ball bowled in anger. Twice, the tests were completely rained off, and the third time the Test was called off because the government refused to countenance a visit by the South African-linked Robin Jackman. The Sports Minister is the former West Indian test opener Roy Fredericks, and the legendary batsman Clive Lloyd is a local luminary.

Cricket is played on the most unlikely patches of ground, and other sports — soccer and baseball — are minority interests. Anyone tempted to join a knockabout game of cricket in the park is warned that the locals enjoy testing visitors with dangerously fast bowling.

The other great sporting interest is horseracing. The busiest premises in Georgetown are the betting shops, where huge sums are staked upon British races. The press gives as much space to racing form as it does to politics. Translated to local time in Guyana, the 4.15 at Newmarket becomes the 1.15, so place your bets early in the day. The only local equivalent is goat racing, which rather lacks the glamour of the Turf.

CRIME AND SAFETY

Many of the meagre number of visitors to Guyana are attacked. Little subtlety is employed; a robber grabs you by the neck from behind, choking you while he or an accomplice steals your wallet or bag. You may also be chopped up — not quite as bad as it sounds, this being local slang for being beaten up. Observe all the warnings you are given about areas to avoid. In particular, poorer areas of Georgetown are dangerous at any time of day, and you should not walk anywhere in the capital after dark. Though you may feel ridiculous taking a taxi a few hundred yards, it is likely to be a good investment.

To stay on the right side of the law, don't take photographs of any government building — including any post office.

HELP AND INFORMATION

Guyana has no tourist board; such information as is available can be gleaned from travel agents. High Commissions and embassies abroad are unable to supply much information.

Public Holidays. February 23 — Republic Day; May 1 — Labour Day; May 5 — Indian Heritage Day; first Monday in July — Caricom/Caribbean Day; and first Monday in August — Freedom Day

GEORGETOWN

The capital of Guyana lies at the mouth of the Demerara River. It began life in 1748 as a Dutch *brandwagt* (guard post) called Stabroek — which survives as the name of one of the central districts of Georgetown. The original capital of the colony of Demerara was Borssalen, on an island in the river. In 1781, however, the British captured the colony and selected Stabroek as administrative centre. The following January, French forces invaded and began the first proper development of a town, which they called Nouvelle Ville. They laid out streets and dug the canals which are often attributed to the Dutch, who regained control after three years.

Back under British sovereignty, the name changed to Georgetown in 1815. The capital has an unmistakable Caribbean-cum-British colonial feel, yet with a definitely local influence: alongside the faded Victorian elegance bequeathed by the British, are the features more characteristic of a rather provincial South American town: fine, 19th-century mansions alongside rickety houses raised on stilts and ramshackle tin-roofed shacks. It is laid out on broad streets, cut through with a canal in the centre, with plenty of trees providing elegance and shade. Just wandering the streets, soaking in the atmosphere, and watching a game of cricket is most rewarding.

City Layout. Georgetown occupies the east bank of the Demerera River where it meets the Atlantic. In the north end of the city is the Pegasus Hotel; the main thoroughfare, High St, begins here and threads south, changing first into Main St, wiggling past the Bank of Guyana building and continuing as the Avenue of the Republic. Most official buildings are on or close to this road. Notable landmarks are the large Stabroek Market (pronounced Star-brook) and the vast St George's Cathedral. The main east-west thoroughfare is Regent St. Some streets are so wide that they have different names for the northern and southern halves, e.g. Church St/North Road and South Road/Croal St.

Arrival and Departure. *Air:* the international Timehri Airport is 25 miles/40km south of the city by the Demerara River. It has a branch of the National Co-operative Bank, open long hours and giving reasonable rates, and a post office. Minibus number 42 runs from the airport car park to the Georgetown terminal at Stabroek Market. The fare is under $1, though foreign visitors are often asked for five times as much. A taxi to the centre of Georgetown should cost $15.

Internal services operate from Ogle airfield, a few miles east of Georgetown, reached by any Rosignol bus.

Airlines: GAC — 32 Main St (tel 57337, 64011 or 64012); also represents Cubana and Aeropostal. Domestic flight information is dispensed from the shed around the back.

BWIA — 4 Robb St (corner of Savage St); open 8am-3pm from Monday to Friday, 8-11am on Saturdays.

Surinam Airways — Middle St, between Main and Carmichael Streets; this office can make reservations but does not sell tickets, which must be obtained through agents.

Varig/ALM — Camp St, between Charlotte St and South Road.

Liat — Main St, opposite Hotel Tower.

Bus: as well as bus 42 to and from the airport, Stabroek Market is also the starting point for services to Parika and Linden. Buses to Rosignol (for New Amsterdam) leave from next to the City Hall on Avenue of the Republic.

City Transport. The inter-urban buses pick up passengers for local journeys within

Georgetown. The one proper local service is route 40, which runs between Kitty (south of Stabroek Market) and Campbellville, via the city centre; the fare is $0.10.

Some taxi drivers try to overcharge heavily. In fact, a flat fare for inner city journeys applies, roughly $1 by day and 50% more at night. Try to find out what the going rate should be and stick to it. Either agree the fare in advance or thrust the correct amount into the driver's hand and get out before he has a chance to object. To summon a taxi by phone, call the cab rank outside the Hotel Tower on 63866.

Accommodation. The ritziest place in town is the Pegasus Hotel, a circular Forte Crest monstrosity (tel 52856). A double room costs $85. Better value, are a couple of places further south on Main St. The elegant Park Hotel at number 37 (tel 54911) costs $70. The Hotel Tower at number (tel 72011) is big and charmless, but it has a good swimming pool and excellent restaurants — an advantage if you are concerned about your safety at night. It charges $60 double. All three of these hotels may insist upon being paid in hard currency, a hangover from the days when the value of the the Guyana dollar was sustained at an artificially high level.

Guest houses are hotter, more prone to insects, and much cheaper. The Promenade *(sic)* Guest House, on Carmichael St just south of the old railway station, charges just $6 double. The Rima (upstairs at 92 Middle Street; tel 57401) is comfortable and costs $10 per night for a double. Demico House (tel 56372) is a big pub/hotel by Stabroek Market, right in the middle of the action. As such it is extremely noisy, so the $8 for a double with bathroom does not seem such a bargain.

Eating and Drinking. You may also want to avoid Demico House because of the 'No Women Allowed' sign on the entrance to its main bar. A much more civilized place to enjoy an aperitif is the front garden of the Palm Court restaurant at 35 Main St. Sadly, the food fails to live up to the ambience.

The best restaurant is the Caribbean Rose, at 175 Middle St near Bank St (tel 51687). It is an attractive place on the top floor, with pleasant views, an excellent menu and good service. Expect to pay up to $10 per person, including a couple of beers. A similar price buys the eat-all-you-can buffet served at the Hotel Tower on Main St, which has a different speciality every night. The Caribbean evening is particularly recommended, as is the Sunday brunch.

On Robb St at King St, two first-floor restaurants face each other. Country Pride (tel 57699) is plain, while the Rice Bowl (66706) has some interesting Chinese and East Indian dishes. Other local curiosities include the Silly Mid On restaurant on Regent Road near the cricket ground, which describes itself as Guyana's Number One Black Pudding Centre.

Exploring. Begin a walking tour at the sea wall close to the Pegasus Hotel, where the murky Atlantic is kept separate from the muddy town. High Street and its continuation to the south, Main Street, are full of Victorian colonial houses. One blot on the landscape is the European Community building at the corner of Barrack St — a breezeblock monstrosity.

The old railway station is a block east, a corrugated iron shed which now houses the immigration office. Continuing down Main St you pass the British High Commission to the right. Go on past the Hotel Tower, and turn left to reach St George's Anglican Cathedral. Built in 1892, its impressive 142-foot tower makes it the highest wooden building in the world. It is a cool, shady and airy oasis. On the opposite side of Avenue of the Republic (as Main Street has now become)

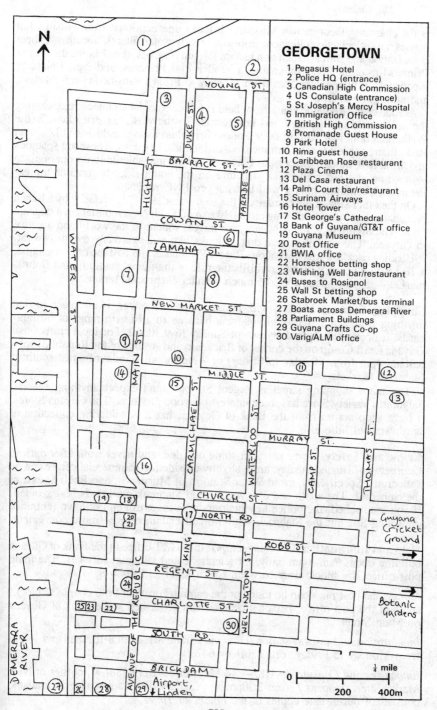

GEORGETOWN

1 Pegasus Hotel
2 Police HQ (entrance)
3 Canadian High Commission
4 US Consulate (entrance)
5 St Joseph's Mercy Hospital
6 Immigration Office
7 British High Commission
8 Promanade Guest House
9 Park Hotel
10 Rima guest house
11 Caribbean Rose restaurant
12 Plaza Cinema
13 Del Casa restaurant
14 Palm Court bar/restaurant
15 Surinam Airways
16 Hotel Tower
17 St George's Cathedral
18 Bank of Guyana/GT&T office
19 Guyana Museum
20 Post Office
21 BWIA office
22 Horseshoe betting shop
23 Wishing Well bar/restaurant
24 Buses to Rosignol
25 Wall St betting shop
26 Stabroek Market/bus terminal
27 Boats across Demerara River
28 Parliament Buildings
29 Guyana Crafts Co-op
30 Varig/ALM office

is the charming Georgetown Museum. It looks unexceptional from outside, but houses a most eclectic collection: dripstones (early water filters), documents about colonization and slavery (such as a receipt for Ten Negroes, dated 1801), the former Prime Minsterial 1960's limonsine, a Vanden Plas Princess, and even a piece of moonrock. It opens 9am-5pm from Monday to Friday, 9am-noon on Saturdays, and admission is free.

Avenue of the Republic south from here is full of colonial architecture, including the police station, city hall and law courts. To the west, on Brickdam, is the Parliament building, built in 1839. Follow Brickdam to its conclusion at D'Urban Park, then bear left for the entrance to the Botanical Gardens. These are spacious and attractive, though the curious Forbes Burnham mausoleum looks out of place — a white and red spider-like structure on the south side. It contains the ex-President's remains, plus a wall bearing pro-PNC reliefs.

On the other side of the Gardens is the zoo, a modest affair prefaced by a bunch of manatee (sea cows) flolloping around like small Loch Ness monsters in a stagnant pool. The highlight is the capybara, the largest rodent in the world and a native to Guyana. The size of a large dog, it looks like a dangerously overgrown rat.

Heading back towards town along Regent Road takes you past the cricket ground, a Test match venue which also fulfils the role of municipal stadium, and Bourda market — a pale shadow of the much grander Stabroek Market.

Shopping. Stabroek Market, with its landmark of a tower, is the place to find anything from a hundredweight of fresh bananas to a bizarre range of birthday cards. It opens 7am-4pm daily except Sunday (6-9.30am). For local crafts, visit Guyana Craft Co-op on the corner of Brickdam and Avenue of the Republic (open 8.30am-4pm from Monday to Friday) or Amerindian Handicrafts just south of Stabroek Market.

The main shopping street is Regent St, but don't expect anything special. Jaigobin's Variety Store has some interesting wood products. The Guyana Stores, a huge shop across from the Bank of Guyana, has a bewildering collection of hardware but little else.

Crime and Safety. Never carry anything of value, and never walk after dark in Georgetown. During the day, areas slightly outside the commercial centre can be dangerous. Specifically, avoid Water St north of Murray St, and Robb St east of the cathedral. The south end of town, beyond Stabroek market, is best avoided. If you are robbed, the police headquarters is at the north end of town (entrance on Young St), but the Stabroek station on Brickdam may be more convenient.

Help and Information. *Communications:* the GT&T office in the Bank of Guyana building opens 7am-10pm daily, for telephone and telegram services. The main post office is a block away between North Road and Robb St.

Money: the best rates can be found at the cambios on Wall St, a couple of blocks south of the post office. Personal cheques can be cashed at the Bank of Guyana on Main Street.

Immigration: old railway station (enter via Parade St), open 8-11.30am and 1-4pm from Monday to Friday; call 63011 or 64700.

Embassies and Consulates: UK — 44 Main Street (tel 65881-4), corner of New Market Street. It opens 7.30am-2.30pm on weekdays. The reading material available consists of out-of-date copies of the *Financial Times*.

USA — Duke St, between Young and Barrack Streets; open 8am-1pm.
Canada — corner of High and Young Streets, opposite Pegasus Hotel.
Argentina — 91 Middle St (tel 59288).
Brazil — 308 Church St (tel 57970).
Colombia — 306 Church St (tel 71410).
Surinam — 304 Church St (tel 67844), open 8-11am on Mondays, Wednesdays and Fridays.

FURTHER AFIELD

The best view of Georgetown is the one from Best, the settlement across the river from the capital (also known as Vreed en Hoop). Take a launch from the quay at the south end of Stabroek Market. The journey takes three minutes and costs $1. Walk for five minutes to the main road junction. On your right is the old railway station (now the Terminal Co-operative Store). Follow the track past Vreed en Hoop school until you reach a fork. Bear right along a track which becomes a solid stone wall; follow it until you break out of the undergrowth. Head over the grassland onto a concrete jetty, which juts out to mark the confluence of the Demerara River and the Atlantic Ocean. Look across to Georgetown in its modest, muddy glory, with half-submerged ships filling the foreground.

On the west bank life is much quieter. You can cross back to Georgetown by bus 32, over a long, clanking causeway, or continue west by the same bus to Parika. In under an hour, all told, you reach this minimalist town with not much to it other than a market and a quay.

Bartica. Twenty-five years ago, in *Journey to Guyana*, Margaret Bacon observed Bartica's 'half-built look of a town that has never quite fulfilled the role it was planning to play, and at the same time the dilapidated look of a town that has declined from what it once was'. A quarter of a century has not enhanced this river port. Bartica is a mess, but an attractive one. It is also the main gateway to the interior, situated at the confluence of the Essequibo and Mazaruni rivers.

The *Lady Northcote* vehicle ferry sails from Parika on alternate days at 10am, arriving at Bartica at 5pm. The next day it sails back. Fast launches operate from next to the market at Parika, taking only two hours and costing $5. Note that the last boat back from Bartica each day is at about 2pm, so if you go on a day trip make an early start.

If you miss the last boat back, or intend to stay overnight, the only accommodation is Mike's Guest House at Lot 29, a basic place which costs $4 for a double room. Eating out is best at Pam's Hide Out Restaurant, upstairs opposite the Metropolitan cinema, where you get chicken with everything. You can change money at Balran's Variety Shop.

West of the Essequibo. Boats leave Parika for Adventure, on the far bank of the Essequibo, at 5pm and 1am, taking four hours and costing $1.50. From here a road runs north as far as the charming town of Charity.

Linden. On the Demerara river 65 miles/104km south of Georgetown, Linden is the second-largest town in Guyana. It's not much of a place, but you can visit the mines from where bauxite has been extracted since the early 20th century. Buses to Linden leave from Georgetown's Stabroek Market and take two hours. There is only limited accommodation in town, but a big resort complex has been built on the road from Georgetown.

Kaieteur Falls. Remote and unspoilt, deep in the forest along the Potaro River, these are among the world's great falls. At a height of some 740ft/225m, the drop at Kaieteur is almost five times the height of Niagara. No visitor to Guyana should miss Kaieteur. While at their best during the rains, they are spectacular at any time — not only because of the falls themselves, but also thanks to the jungle setting and the birds. The water is brown because of the decaying vegetation.

Kaieteur is 150 miles/240km southwest of Georgetown. The easiest access is by air. If you are in a group, you may consider chartering a 17-seater, which costs $100 per person: call 52002. The other option is to see what tours might be running. These are often frustratingly short, allowing less than an hour at the falls, which are ten minutes through the jungle from the airstrip.

To travel to Kaieteur independently overland, you must aim first for Bartica. From here it is possible to travel overland in a day to Kangaruma (government rest house), by boat to Tukeit (ditto), from where it is 2-3 hours walk to the falls; you may wish to take a guide for the last stretch. Take full camping and jungle gear.

Imbaimadai. This is a small mining settlement on the Mazaruni River, 100 miles/160km southwest of Georgetown. Most of its inhabitants are gold panners and diamond-hunters, who live in shacks along the river. You may be able to get one of the locals to take you to the 80-foot Maipuri falls and the 14th-century Temehri cliff paintings, which are accessible only by boat; this is a wonderful trip into the jungle. You can also arrange to visit Amerindian villages. The only sensible way to go to Imbaimadai is to fly. There is a rundown guest house.

Lethem and the Rupunini Savannah. The grasslands of southwestern Guyana are one of the most rewarding areas to explore. For anyone travelling between Guyana and Brazil, they are a gift. Lethem, the gateway to the savannah, lies on the Brazilian border, just a few hours away from Boa Vista in Roraima.

Lethem is a friendly place, and it's easy to find people to take you exploring. The forested Kanuku mountains are a short distance east, and you may be able to arrange to visit the Wai Wai tribe, which is one of Guyana's oldest Indian settlements. Other possible excursions are to the Moco Moco waterfall and up nearby mountains. Around Easter rodeos take place at some of the cattle ranches in the area.

There are a few places to stay in Lethem, the best of which are the Cacique Guest House and the Government Rest House. A better place for organized tours is the Manari Ranch, 7 miles/11km from Lethem.

Lethem is served by occasional flights from Georgetown which take about one hour; expect to pay around $75 single. Avoid the wet season if possible, when there is serious flooding. Transport at any time isn't easy, and many people get around on horseback.

If crossing into Brazil, emigration procedures are carried out at the police station in town. You cross the river by boat to reach Bomfim, about four hours by bus from Boa Vista.

SURINAM

Population: 380,000   **Capital: Paramaribo (150,000)**

The worst land deal in history was struck by the Dutch in 1667. They exchanged Manhattan, now the richest real estate in the world, for this sweaty slab of South

America. It hit the headlines briefly at the end of 1990, following a military coup. Since then the country has slipped back into the anonymity that characterized its previous existence. Surinam has never had any illusions of being a prime destination for travellers, and during the late 80s it was virtually off-limits owing to a civil war: travellers were allowed to visit only the capital, Paramaribo, and a couple of other places considered to be safe. In 1991, peace accords between the government and guerrillas were signed, leaving one of the least-visited countries in Latin America open again to exploration.

The country is almost five times the size of the Netherlands, but has only one-fortieth of the inhabitants. Yet the comparatively small population is diverse, being particularly interesting for its large numbers of Indonesians. In some rural villages Indonesian women wear a sarong, but national costumes only normally appear during festivals; this is when you are most likely to see Javanese music and dancing performed.

Surinam has a surprisingly extensive system of nature reserves, including turtle-nesting sites. Unfortunately the parks were neglected during the civil war, and they have minimal facilities for visitors. Some of the most interesting trips can be made into the interior along the rivers in eastern Surinam, where scattered communities of Amerindians and bushnegroes live.

HISTORY

The British were the first Europeans to establish a settlement in what is now Surinam. In 1651 Willoughby, the governor of Barbados, sent an expedition of planters and African slaves to set up plantations in the region. After the 1667 Treaty of Breda, in which the UK acquired Manhattan, the new Dutch colony almost fell apart. The British planters left and their slaves escaped into the jungle. Meanwhile, disputes continued across the Atlantic, and in 1799 the UK reoccupied the colony. The issue was not finally settled until the Treaty of Vienna in 1815. Even then, the Netherlands showed little interest in the colony, their attention being monopolized by their territorial possessions in the East Indies.

In 1950, Dutch Guiana was granted a measure of home rule. There followed a turbulent period, with race riots, civil tension and high unemployment. The Netherlands granted full independence in 1975, and Surinam adopted parliamentary democracy. The newly-elected coalition government was led by Prime Minister Henck Arron. He was overthrown by army officers in 1980, and the next seven years were dominated by Lieutenant Colonel Desi Bouterse, leader of the armed forces. He vowed to make Surinam a non-aligned socialist state, and ties were forged with Nicaragua, Cuba and Grenada. Independent news organizations were closed and all political parties were banned. In December 1982, 15 opposition leaders were executed while in custody, accused of plotting against the government.

In 1985 Bouterse began his flirt with democracy, lifting the ban on political parties. Opposition against the dictatorship did not die, however, and in 1986 an ex-army officer, Ronny Brunswijk, launched an insurgency. The so-called Jungle Commando rebels were mainly bushnegroes. The heaviest fighting was concentrated in the east, and many villagers fled to French Guiana. The guerrillas are said to have controlled about 95% of the country, and by 1987 the civil war had brought aluminium industry to a virtual standstill. A crisis seemed imminent.

As a result of this pressure, Boutese changed the constitution in 1987, providing for the election of a National Assembly who would in turn elect an executive president. In the November 1987 elections the Front for Democracy and Development, a coalition of the three main opposition parties, won a landslide victory. Their leader, Ramsewak Shankar, became president and Henck Arron vice-president.

Bouterse remained chief of staff, but relations with Shankar were strained. The situation culminated in a bloodless coup on Christmas Eve 1990. The army officers ostensibly responsible for the coup denied Bouterse's involvement. However, he returned to his post as chief of staff (having stood down briefly) and remains the grey eminence of Surinam affairs.

The coup leaders installed an interim government and promised to hold elections within 100 days. Elections were eventually held in May 1991. The New Front (a coalition of four parties) won 30 seats, the army-backed National Democratic Party 12, and the Democratic Alternative nine. The situation remains fluid, and the Netherlands has not yet resumed aid.

One positive achievement in 1991 was the signing in March of a peace agreement between Bouterse and the rebels, which in theory puts an end to four years of fighting during which about 500 people have been killed, and some 10,000 refugees have fled.

GETTING THERE

From Europe, the only direct sevices are from Amsterdam, with KLM and Surinam Airways. The local airline also flies on Tuesdays and Thursdays from Miami. The only direct flight from Brazil is the Monday service with Cruzeiro do Sul from Belém via Cayenne.

RED TAPE

Most nationalities require a visa, though British citizens are exempt. For information and application forms contact Surinam's Embassy in the Netherlands, at Alexandra Gogelweg 2, 2517 JH Amsterdam (tel 31 20-64 26 137; fax 20-64 65 311). They will fax visa requirements to you and also send what tourist brochures they have. Apply at least three or four weeks in advance if possible. The Surinamse Embassy in the USA is at 4301 Connecticut Avenue NW, Suite 108, Washington, DC 20008 (tel 202-244-7488), with a consulate in Miami. For anyone already in South America not planning to pass through Cayenne or Georgetown, the nearest embassies are in Caracas and Brasília.

The length of stay permitted is decided on arrival, but is usually two months. Those not needing visas will be issued with a tourist card. Extensions are available from the Immigration Office on Van't Hogerhuysstraat in Paramaribo.

MONEY

The local currency is the Surinam guilder (Sf), divided into 100 cents. It is officially tied to the US dollar, currently fixed at around $1.80. Banks and some hotels can change money, though the latter are unlikely to accept travellers cheques. On the black market, however, you can change money at over five times the official rate. Since this is illegal, dealing on it should be done with discretion: your main opportunity will be at the borders, where moneychangers hang around the ferry docks. American Express is the most widely accepted credit card in Surinam.

Banks open 8am-2pm Monday to Friday and 8-11am on Saturday.

GETTING AROUND

The coastal road linking Nieuw Nickerie and Albina via Paramaribo is paved and comparatively good. The rest of the network is patchy, as are the buses. Surinam Airways' flights (including charters) into the interior were heavily restricted during the civil war. Services have been stepped up, but boat will often be your only means of transport.

HELP AND INFORMATION

Language. Dutch is the official language. A Creole language known as Sranang Tongo is a lingua franca understood by most groups. English is also widely spoken, and Hindi and Javanese are used in some communities. The main daily papers are all in Dutch.

Public Holidays. The main holidays are February 25 (Revolution Day), July 1 (National Union Day) and November 25 (Independence Day).

PARAMARIBO

The capital is situated on the Surinam River some miles inland from the sea. It has some lovely colonial-style wooden buildings, both grand mansions and simpler dwellings. More recent additions in the suburbs are the flash palaces built by drug barons.

The population of Paramaribo is predominantly Creole. But the Hindu temples, mosques and other religious temples that are scattered around the city, symbolize the diversity more prevalent elsewhere in Surinam.

Arrival and Departure. Zanderij airport is 28 miles/45km south of Paramaribo. Airlines usually organize a minibus or shared taxi service into town: this costs about $5. Taxis charge more than ten times that; they aren't metered, so agree a price beforehand. There is a bank in the terminal building, where you can also arrange car rental. An airport tax of $15 is payable upon departure.

Domestic flights leave from Zorg-en-Hoop airfield, in a residential suburb a mile or so southwest of the centre.

Airlines: Surinam Airways is at 6 Waterkant. Varig has an agent on the first floor of the Krasnapolsky hotel on Domineestraat (tel 475022, 475050). KLM is at Mr. Dr. de Mirandastraat 9 (tel 472421, 471863).

Accommodation and Food. There isn't a great choice of affordable lodgings, though rates improve markedly if you change money on the black market. Try Fanna Guest House (31 Prinsessestraat; tel 476789), which is welcoming and charges $10 for a double room. If staying for a longer period stay at the YWCA Guesthouse at Heerenstraat 14-16 (tel 476981). Both men and women can stay there, with double rooms for $12 ($20 with shower).

If you can't find a particularly pleasant place to sleep, you should at least be able to console yourself by having a good meal. The thing to eat is *rijsttafel*, an Indonesian speciality consisting of numerous different dishes, often including other traditional dishes such as *gado gado* (vegetable salad with peanut sauce) and *nasi goreng* (fried rice). Peanut butter soup is a speciality of more local origin. Try Deli on Watermolenstraat (off Keizerstraat) or La Bastille on Kleine Waterstraat, northeast of the centre. The foodstalls on Waterkant by the river serve cheap, wholesome food both during the day and in the evening.

Paramaribo is well off for cafés. A particularly popular one is Orlando's Coffee Shop on Grote Hofstraat, west off Watermolenstraat; opposite is an excellent Chinese restaurant called Iwan's.

Exploring. Overlooking the river is the old Fort Zeelandia. It began as a garrison, was later turned into a prison, then into a museum, but is now occupied once more by the military. You can stroll around the grounds, but be wary of taking photographs.

A short distance inland from the fort is Eenheidsplein, a grassy square watched over by the Presidential (People's) Palace. Formerly the Governor's residence, this is a fine wooden mansion, dating originally from 1730. The other buildings in the square, including the Court of Justice and a couple of government ministries, are all rather imposing. A more impressive structure is the nearby Parliament Building, at the bottom of Gravenstraat, on the corner of Combeweg. Just to the north, is the Palmentuin, a pleasant park named after its mass of palm trees.

More fine architecture can be seen along Gravenstraat. Near the corner of Mgr. Wulfinghstraat is the Roman Catholic cathedral, built in 1885. It is claimed by some to be the largest wooden building in South America. Whether it is or not, the cathedral is one of the city's most memorable sights, with its twin towers and simple, unpainted interior. On the other side of Gravenstraat, on Kerkplein, is the 19th-century Reformed Church, where independence was declared. If you make a diversion north to Koningstraat, you will find several Hindu temples.

Domineestraat, which runs southwest off Keizerstraat, is the main shopping street. It's not a bad place to have a drink, and there are a couple of moderately good bookshops. A more entertaining place to watch shoppers at work is in the market along Waterkant. East Indians and Indonesians from the country come into the city to trade, giving the area a special atmosphere.

Help and Information. *Tourist Information:* Waterkant 8 (tel 471163, 478421) not far from Eenheidsplein. Staff try to be helpful, though their knowledge about the interior is limited. City maps are usually available.

Money: Algemene Bank Nederland at Kerkplein 1 (tel 471555) changes money; otherwise try one of the smart hotels, such as the Krasnapolsky (Domineestraat 39). Black marketeers hang around along Waterkant.

Communications: the post office is near the corner of Dr N. Wagenweg and Korte Kerkstraat, one block north of Keizerstraat. Telegrams and telex can be sent from Telesur, on Heiligenweg (off Waterkant). Phone calls, from the same office, cost $12 for three minutes to the UK.

Embassies and Consulates: Guyana — 82 Gravenstraat. UK — VSH United Buildings, Van't Hogerhuysstraat (tel 472870). USA — Dr Sophie Redmondstraat 129 (tel 472900), opposite the Ambassador Hotel.

FURTHER AFIELD

The best organization to help you explore further afield is Stinasu (Foundation for Nature Preservation in Surinam), which runs the country's protected areas. Its head office is at Jongbawstraat 14 (tel 475845, 471856) in Paramaribo. Stinasu can provide information and maps, and also organizes a small number of trips. The main parks have accommodation of some sort, but you will normally need to take food.

Brownsberg National Park. This is an area of protected tropical rainforest about $2\frac{1}{2}$ hours south of Paramaribo. It is home to a variety of wildlife, including monkeys, deer, macaws and toucans. There are limited trails, maps of which should be available from the park office. You can also explore by canoe.

The park is near Brownsweg, 60 miles/96km from the capital. There used to be a railway line from the coast, but the village is now only accessible by bus, which runs every morning. From there you must arrange a lift for the 10 miles/16km southwest to Brownsberg itself. Central Lodge has self-catering bungalows in the park; otherwise camp.

Wia-Wia Reserve. This is one of the most accessible parks in Surinam. It is a nesting ground for various species of turtle (including the leatherback), and is also home to a variety of birds, including flamingoes, scarlet ibis, storks and thousands of migratory birds. To see the turtles visit between February and July.

Wia-Wia, which lies east of Paramaribo, must be approached by boat: firstly up Commewijne River to the village of Alliance, and then by a boat to Matapica beach (1½-2 hours), which is within reach of the nesting sites. Both the boat from Alliance and accommodation (there are two lodges) must be arranged in advance through Stinasu.

You may be able to get a boat direct to Alliance from Paramaribo. Otherwise go first to Nieuw Amsterdam and ask around at the port there.

West to Nieuw Nickerie. The journey from Paramaribo west to the Guyanan border is interesting: across the Coppename estuary, past swamps rich in birdlife, coconut groves and, nearer the Guyanan border, the country's main concentration of rice fields. Nieuw Nickerie itself is prosperous without being particularly memorable. It is 150 miles/240km from Paramaribo, lying close to the confluence of the Nickerie and Corantijn rivers.

Buses running west along the coast from Paramaribo leave from Waaldijkstraat, off Dr Sophie Redmondstraat. The trip to Nieuw Nickerie takes about five hours. The best of a poor bunch of guest houses are the Dorien (central) and Ameer Ali's, near the ferry dock. See page 744 for information on crossing the border.

East to Albina. Catch the ferry across the Surinam river from Leonsberg, a suburb of Paramaribo accessible by bus from the centre. From Meerzorg, on the other side of the river, it is about 90 miles/144km to the eastern border at Albina. En route you pass through several Hindustani villages, the large Indonesian village of Tamanredjo and, on the Cottica river, Moengo. This is a bauxite-mining town, with a bizarre North American feel.

Albina is a sleepy place, with just a few guest houses. Its status as a popular holiday spot was disrupted by the civil war, though things have looked brighter since the signing of the peace accord.

Albina is the traditional base for trips by boat into the interior to visit Amerindian and bushnegro villages. The main attraction downriver is the Galibi reserve where, between February and July, giant turtles lay their eggs. It is 2½ hours by canoe north of Albina, past several Amerindian settlements; arrange transport by the waterfront. There are lodges at Galibi and nearby Babuensanti.

Inland, the place to head for is Stoelmansiland, at the confluence of the Lawa and Tapanahony rivers. There is a guest house, and spending a few days here satisfies some travellers' desire for adventure. You may also be able to arrange to travel by boat up the Tapanahony river to the Gran Holo Falls, or to bushnegro villages on the Marowijne. You can get to Stoelmansiland by boat from Albina along the Maroni river in about two days, or by air.

FRENCH GUIANA (Guyane)

Population: 90,000   **Capital: Cayenne (40,000)**

French Guiana is the only European colony remaining in the New World. Furthermore, it has the same status as any other French *Departement*: therefore, it is officially — and extraordinarily — not only part of France, but also of the European Community.

French Guiana, the size of Portugal, is the most sparsely populated and the least penetrable of the three jungle-covered Guianas. There is astonishingly little infrastructure, with only one road to speak of, running along the coast. Even so, it has more foreign visitors than its Guianan neighbours. The one industry which makes the country more than a colonial backwater is space: the European Space Agency has its launch pad west of Cayenne, the capital. About once a month a satellite is sent into space aboard an Ariane rocket. Indians have been dispossessed of land to allow the site to be developed, and the immediate environment has been wrecked.

Land and people's rights are under threat in the interior too. The jungle is extremely rich biologically, yet none of it is protected against development. Hunting is a lucrative business — endangered species are eaten and their skins exported — and the authorities do nothing to stop the trade. The desire for economic independence from France is encouraging rapid exploitation of the timber and mineral resources in the jungle. New roads are penetrating deeper and deeper into the bush. Fortunately, most of the 5,000 surviving Amerindians have so far remained comparatively unaffected by developments; most of them live along the upper reaches of the Lawa and Oyapoc rivers.

Tourism is being developed with charter flights from France bringing in visitors to a couple of beach resorts and to Devil's Island, the former penal colony described by Henri Charriére in his book *Papillon*. Venturing away from the coast is difficult, partly because there are no national parks.

HISTORY

The French first settled along this stretch of the coast in 1604, but without much success, partly because of the hostile response from the indigenous Indians. As elsewhere in the region, the colony was the object of numerous stormy disputes between the European powers with interests in the region: both the Dutch and British held it at various stages, and even the Portuguese had a go. The Dutch ceded the territory in 1667, which was finally confirmed as French in 1817.

The history of French Guiana has not been characterized by great successes. The country saw a brief boom in the 1850s following the discovery of gold, but this was a mere flash in the pan. The gold brought more trouble than good since it led to border disputes with Brazil and Surinam: these lasted much longer than the gold did.

The same period marked the country's increasing use as a penal colony. The dispatch of convicts to this far off corner of the French empire was part of an ill-judged plan to colonize and to encourage the development of the territory. Having completed their sentence, prisoners would remain in French Guiana as exiles for an equal period. Tropical diseases killed off 90% of them, and the last penal colony was closed only in the 1950s.

In 1946 Guyane Française was given Overseas Department status by France. Because of heavy economic support from the mother country, few Guyanais support independence, although many would prefer greater autonomy. In the 1970s a number of demonstrations showed growing discontent concerning the economic situation and French neglect; a period of repression was followed by reforms in the early 80s, which brought some decentralization. The country is represented in France by one member of the Senate and one member of the National Assembly. Locally, there are General and Regional Councils.

In 1983 the left-wing parties won a majority of votes but not of seats; the balance of power is held by the separatist Union des Travailleurs Guyanais (UTG). In March 1985 the Parti Socialiste Guyanais (PSG) and left-wing independents increased their representation.

GETTING THERE

Air France has flights from Paris on Wednesday and Friday, requiring an overnight stopover in France if starting from London. Since these services count as internal flights discounted fares are difficult to obtain. The standard Economy fare costs over £800 return. Air France also flies to Cayenne from Miami on Sunday. Cruzeiro do Sul has flights twice a week from Belém, one via Macapá and the other via Paramaribo.

The eastern border crossing, from Oiapoque in Brazil to St Georges, is not always open to foreigners. Furthermore, the trek overland or by boat north from Macapá is extremely rough, though it is also possible to fly to Oiapoque. If the border post is open, boats take just 15 minutes to cross the Oyapoc river. See page 768 for transport from St Georges, or page 744 for getting to French Guiana from Surinam.

RED TAPE

Few nationalities require visas for visits of up to three months, so long as they can show a return or onward ticket. European Community, North American and Australasian citizens are all exempt. French citizens don't even need a passport.

Diplomatic representation abroad is provided by France, but trying to get information about French Guiana is virtually impossible. The French Consulate General, which processes visas in the UK, is at 6a Cromwell Place, London SW7. For information you can try phoning 071-581 5292 but they usually just tell you to phone 0898-200289, which is a long-winded taped message regarding general visa requirements for France. Also try the Embassy at 58 Knightsbridge, SW1X 7JT (tel 071-235 8080), preferably in person. The French Embassy in the USA is at 4101 Reservoir Road NW, Washington, DC 20007 (tel 202-944 6000).

MONEY

The local currency is the French Franc (FFr), and prices are similar to those in France — making French Guiana more expensive than its neighbours.

Changing travellers cheques is difficult outside Cayenne and Kourou, where you'll find the main concentration of banks: even here cheques can cause problems. The most reliable exchange house is the Banque Nacionale de Guyane, which usually allows you to withdraw cash on Visa too.

GETTING AROUND

Public transport in French Guiana is almost non-existent, as is the road network: the paved road along the coast west from Cayenne to St Laurent, on the border with Surinam, is virtually the extent of it. The route is served usually by just one bus a day, supplemented by the odd collective taxi; neither is wont to run on

Sundays. You may well be tempted to join the locals in a little impromptu hitching. Car hire is available at the airport and in Cayenne, which can ease movement west along the coast road.

Air Guyane (GAT) serves the main towns — including flights daily to St Georges, Maripasoula and Saül — but seats are heavily booked.

Travelling any distance inland — in search of wildlife or Amerindian and bushnegro villages, or simply to experience the jungle — usually requires local guides. You may need a permit to visit Indian villages along the upper reaches of the Maroni and Oyapoc rivers. This is virtually impossible to obtain on the spot, so you should write in advance to the Préfecture in the capital (Place de Grenoble, Cayenne).

HELP AND INFORMATION

It is virtually impossible to obtain tourist information about French Guiana. The French Tourist Office (178 Piccadilly, London W1V 0AL; tel 071-491 7622) is of no use at all, and you would do better to call the office in Paris dealing solely with French Overseas Departments. Write to Rue Auber 12, or call 010 33 1-42 68 11 07.

Language. The official language is French, but most people speak a Creole patois. English is also widely spoken. The main newspapers are in French.

CAYENNE

The capital was named after the hot red pepper, which has been exported from French Guiana since the 17th century. Cayenne, the city, has an undeniably French flavour, seen in some handsome architecture and in the pavement cafés. The city lies at the mouth of the Cayenne river and is the home of one half of French Guiana's population. Yet it is a quiet place, livening up only in the early evening.

Arrival and Departure. Rochambeau airport is 11 miles/17km southwest of the city. There are no exchange facilities at the airport. A taxi into town (there are no buses) will cost Fr40-50. The addresses of airlines downtown are as follows: Air France — Place des Palmistes (tel 302740); Air Guyane — Rue Lalouette 2 (tel 317200, 356555); Surinam Airways — Place Schoelcher (tel 317298); Varig — Rue René Jadfart 90 (tel 303967/70), a block south of the canal.

Buses west along the coast are run by Ruffinel from Avenue Galmot, a few blocks south of Canal Laussat; book in advance if possible. Collective taxis, also headed along the coast, leave from Avenue de la Liberté, usually in the morning.

Accommodation and Food. Budget rooms are hard to find. The best deal, though by no means cheap, is Hotel Neptima (Rue F. Eboué 21; tel 311115), four blocks east of Place des Palmistes.

Seafood is the thing to eat, shrimps being the most plentiful and cheap. Creole restaurants serve all manner of meats, but avoid the flesh of endangered species such as cayman. Avenue de Gaulle and Rue Christophe Colombe have a reasonable supply of restaurants and cafés.

Exploring. The city's two main and finest squares — Place de Grenoble and the nearby Place des Palmistes — have the pick of the city's architecture. The main commercial thoroughfare, Rue de Remiré, leads off this large second square, and leads into Avenue Géneral de Gaulle. Seven blocks east is the cemetery, where the tombstones make interesting reading.

The old city is known as La Crique, named after the creek (actually the Canal Laussat) which runs through it. This is the liveliest and most interesting part of town, particularly at weekends. The market, one block north of the creek, is fascinating though also alarming: as well as fresh produce and a few crafts, you can also buy birds and animal skins; many of the people trading are from the interior. There are good snack bars along the canal. The harbour, a short walk northwest, is also fun; ask here about boat trips upriver. Neither of these areas are particularly safe after hours.

Help and Information. *Tourist Information:* the city information office is in the Pavillon du Tourisme in the Botanical Garden (tel 312919). The state office (ARDTLG) is at Rue Lalouette 12 (tel 309000). City maps are available from most bookshops.

Money: the best bank to deal with is Banque de la Guyane in Place Victor Schoelcher, due south of Place de Grenoble.

Post office: Place de Grenoble, opposite the Préfecture.

Consulates: Brazil — Rue Helder 12, on Place des Palmistes (tel 300467).
Surinam — 38 Rue Christophe Colombe. Visa processing time is unpredictable, taking anything from a few days to a month.
USA — Rue Blenac 14, Fort de France (tel 631303).
UK — Honorary Consul at 16 Avenue Monnerville (tel 311034, 304242), near the market.

KOUROU

Lying 40 miles/64km west of Cayenne, Kourou is an oasis of technology in this jungle-covered country. Before the dramatic decade of the 1960s, when the development of the rocket launching site began, Kourou was just a tiny fishing village. It is now a town of around 10,000 people, with shops, banks and other amenities found nowhere else in the country except in Cayenne. In addition, the local environment has been polluted by the indiscriminate dumping of harmful waste products and the release of toxic fumes.

Though the Ariane rocket programme has been cutback since the 70s, Kourou remains an important space centre: the Centre Spatial Guyanais (CSG) stretches for several miles west of the town. To arrange a visit call 334919, preferably several days in advance; tours are not possible every day. In the town itself you can still enjoy the riverside setting, marred though it is by modern dvelopments. You can also rent canoes to explore the mangrove swamps.

Hotels in Kourou cater primarily for those involved with the space programme and are therefore expensive. The cheapest of the smart hotels is the Diamant (Rue Simarouba; tel 321090). For a more down to earth night stay at the Studio Sodexho, in Place Newton. There are lots of restaurants on Avenue de Gaulle and Avenue des Roches.

ILES DE SALUT

This trio of islands, off the coast near Kourou, were the site of one of the world's most notorious penal colonies. Their name was not somebody's idea of a bad joke. The Islands of Salvation were actually christened during the 17th century, in the days when settlers fled there from the disease-ridden jungle on the mainland.

Despite their history as a prison for France's worst criminals, the Iles de Salut are stunning. Ile Royale is the largest island, though it takes less than an hour to walk right around it. Several old buildings survive, including the former warders' mess, which is now the Auberge des Iles du Salut — at $40 a night hardly a bargain but a wonderful place to stay. The most beautiful island of all is St Joseph, just a five-minute ride from Royale; boats leave several times a day. On it are the remains of the huge solitary confinement compound, described so vividly in *Papillon*.

Devil's Island is virtually impossible to reach from the sea, its isolation making it an ideal place for punishing political prisoners. The most famous inmate was Alfred Dreyfus, a Jewish French army officer who was found guilty of spying in 1894. His conviction was seen by many as unsound and it sparked off a fierce debate about anti-Semitism throughout Europe. The publicity brought to his case by the so-called 'Dreyfus Affair' resulted in the eventual pardon of the officer. Sadly, few boatmen are willing to run the risk of taking people there.

There is a boat service to Ile Royale from near Hotel des Roches (Avenue des Roches; tel 320066) in Kourou. It leaves at 8am and returns at 4pm; the journey takes about an hour. You can buy tickets in travel agencies, either in Kourou or Cayenne. The round trip to Royale costs about $25.

ST LAURENT DU MARONI

The second largest town in French Guiana is situated on the broad Maroni river which marks the border with Surinam. Ask around by the quay to arrange short trips upriver in a canoe (*pirogue*). Away from the busy scene along the waterfront, St Laurent is a sleepy town — very different and much smaller than during the days of the penal colonies, when it was the receiving station for convicts. You can wander around what's left of the prison, or Camp de Transportation, but ask at the gendarmerie if you want to see the cells.

The best place to stay in town is the Star Hotel (Rue Thiers; tel 341084). The tourist office is at rue du Colonel Chandon 16 (tel 341086).

Mana. This is a delightful little place 25 miles/40km north of St Laurent. Ten miles/16km northwest is an Amerindian village called Les Hattes, from where you can walk to a beach where leatherback turtles lay their eggs between April and July. There are a couple of hotels in Mana, or else camp or stay with the local villagers in Les Hattes.

Maripasoula. This is a good trip, some three or four days up the Maroni from St Laurent. The small town of Maripasoula is the gateway to Wayana Indian country, which stretches southwards into Brazil. Since the Maroni river is a supply route for Amerindian and bushnegro villages, you should not have too much difficulty arranging transport into the interior; you may need to do it in several stages. Maripasoula is also served by air. There is a simple guest house in Maripasoula.

St Georges. The eastern frontier town of St Georges is a base from which to go on trips up the Oyapoc river. You can visit the Maripa falls in a couple of days, but to go much further up you will need a permit. The road west to St Georges is unpaved and is badly affected by heavy rain. There is no public transport. If there's no hitchable traffic, you may be able to piece together a few boats along the coast and then upriver; otherwise, go by air: flights run daily from Cayenne. The best place to stay is Hotel Modestina. As you settle down, reflect on the fact that you are in one of the remotest places in all of South America.